THE BOOK COLLECTOR'S HANDBOOK OF VALUES
1982–1983

The Book Collector's
HANDBOOK OF VALUES

by

VAN ALLEN BRADLEY

1982–1983 EDITION

G.P. Putnam's Sons
New York

FOURTH REVISED, ENLARGED EDITION

Copyright © 1972, 1975, 1978, 1982 by Van Allen Bradley
All rights reserved. This book, or parts thereof,
must not be reproduced in any form without permission.
Published simultaneously in Canada by General
Publishing Co. Limited, Toronto.

Library of Congress Cataloging in Publication Data

Bradley, Van Allen, date.
  The book collector's handbook of values.

1. Rare books—Handbooks, manuals, etc.
2. Rare books—Bibliography. 3. Great Britain—
  Imprints—Bibliography. 4. United States—Imprints—Bibliography.
5. Rare books—Prices. I. Title.
Z1029.B7 1982   011'.44   81-10610
ISBN 0-399-12629-5   AACR2

Printed in the United States of America

INTRODUCTION
to the Fourth Edition

If the trends of the recent inflationary past continue, the 1982 auction season is likely, as usual, to turn up occasional record prices for rare books. Sensational sales of collectible books get the headlines, as do those of art and antiques. But there is a vast difference between a painting by Picasso or an Old Master and a first edition by Edgar Allan Poe. That difference is primarily a matter of dollars: many millions for art as against a few thousand for books.

Every book collector with a degree of experience in his field is sophisticated enough to know that although properly chosen books can be a sound investment, they are rarely regarded as objects for speculative adventure.

Multimillion dollar paintings are not uncommon today, but it was a singularly rare event in the history of rare books when on April 7, 1978, the General Theological Seminary's Gutenberg Bible was sold at auction at the New York gallery of Christie, Manson & Woods for a world record price for a printed book—$2,200,000. This particular Bible was one of a very small number of existing copies of the first book printed from movable type. The buyer was Bernard Breslauer, a bookseller acting for the Stuttgart Museum. At the same auction house in 1977, elephant folio copies of John James Audubon's *The Birds of America* came up at two separate sales. The first copy was sold for $352,000 and the second for $396,000. Each sale set a world record for a book by an American.

As each year passes, new sales records at both the auction and retail levels continue to lend glamour and excitement to the book collecting field. Early in 1981, for example, a first edition of Edgar Allan Poe's *The Raven and Other Poems*, which for years had been a $3,000–$4,000 book at retail, brought a record $24,000 at auction.

Another 1981 auction sensation was a first edition of Nathaniel Hawthorne's anonymous *Fanshawe*, which brought $12,000. Its previous high mark at auction had been $4,000 in 1975. Thomas Hardy's famous *Tess of the D'Urbervilles*, with a 1975 auction record of $550, fetched an astonishing $4,500 when offered in 1981.

Even sharper increases continue to be registered at retail in various specialized fields. Just a few years ago one could find a fine copy of the limited, signed edition of John Steinbeck's *In Dubious Battle* (99 copies, signed) for around $1,500. In 1980 the price at retail was $2,000–$2,250. By mid-1981, as this is written, it is a $2,750 book. And so it goes.

These present trends are merely part of the continuing pattern of feverish excitement that dominated the world of rare books throughout the 1970s and that seems certain to make the 1980s one of the great decades of book collecting. When the first edition of *The Book Collector's Handbook of Values* appeared in 1972, we had just come through the stimulating period of the late 1960s and the 1970s in which the interest in scarce and rare Americana had surged to previously undreamed-of heights with the dispersal at auction of the library of the late Thomas W. Streeter. Throughout the 1970s a continuing rise in values in all book fields—especially in Americana, literary first editions, and color-plate books—made it imperative for me to revise and update this *Handbook* for a second edition in 1975 and for a third edition in 1978. Modern first editions soared to new all-time records in the fall of 1977 and the spring of 1978 with the sale of the library of Jonathan Goodwin at the New York galleries of Sotheby Parke Bernet.

Inflation obviously has had a considerable impact on rare books as in all other areas of value. It is not altogether responsible, however, for the continuing rise in prices across the entire spectrum of book collecting. In any season good and important books can be depended upon to rise in value at the rate of about 15 to 20 percent a year, which compares favorably with the best money market funds. Even *bad* books, or totally unimportant but for one reason or other collectible books, also rise in value, especially in an inflationary period. Hence the necessity for a continuing updating of *The Book Collector's Handbook of Values,* which has now been brought abreast, as best we could, of the current price trends.

The specific prices and price ranges in this edition are based primarily on the catalogue entries of leading American and English book dealers and the auction records of leading American and English galleries for the period 1978–1981. They are *not* to be construed as "Bradley's prices." They are a reflection of the rare book trade as it exhibits itself today. As in past editions of this *Handbook,* I have in the case of a very few very rare books made estimates or projections of possible future higher prices. Since I am by nature conservative, I will not be surprised if these estimates are exceeded.

This *Handbook* had its origins in several predecessors—*Gold in Your Attic* (1958), *More Gold in Your Attic* (1961), and *The New Gold in Your Attic* (1968)—which grew out of a syndicated column on rare books that I wrote for *The Chicago Daily News* and other newspapers from 1957 to 1971. In developing the first *Handbook* over an eight-year period beginning in 1964, I found it necessary to totally update the original price ranges twice before first publication of the book in 1972. These ranges were largely restructured in 1975 for the second edition and again in 1978 for the third edition.

In this fourth edition, which has been revised almost line by line, it has again been necessary to adjust the price ranges. In most cases the price trend has been upward, although there are also a number of downward revisions, especially among literary works of dimming popularity. Readers familiar with the earlier *Handbook* versions will be pleased to note, I am sure, that this revision also incorporates many hundreds of books and authors not previously included. At the same time, we have endeavored to eliminate some of the less useful material and to make further corrections and revisions of erroneous or confused entries.

WHAT THIS BOOK IS ALL ABOUT: Readers approaching this *Handbook* for the first time will quickly discover that in several aspects it differs in arrangement from most listings of rare books and pamphlets. The method used from the start in 1964 was based on what appeared to me to be the needs of the general reader as reflected in the response to my syndicated column "Gold in

Your Attic," which was referred to earlier. As far as I know, the only comparable books of the kind I was aware of when I began the "Gold in Your Attic" books and the *Handbook* series were Seymour de Ricci's 1921 *The Book Collector's Guide* (Rosenbach) and William Targ's 1936 manual *10,000 Rare Books and Their Prices* (Black Archer Press).

My aim was to prepare a comprehensive work that would be of use not only to the general reader, but also to the serious and sophisticated collector and to libraries, scholars, and booksellers as well.

THE SCOPE AND METHOD OF THE BOOK: My first decision was to limit the entries and thus provide a single-volume reference as opposed to a multivolume work. The book is thus devoted primarily to nineteenth- and twentieth-century books, using the year 1800 as a starting point. Since a compilation of this kind is not a bibliography in the true sense, I decided to discard orthodox bibliographical form and list books alphabetically as an expedient method of making the book useful to the largest number of readers. In other words, if a book has an author named on the title page, it will be found, if included here, under the author's name as published, even though that may be a pseudonym. Thus, while most bibliographical works list Mark Twain's books under his real name, Samuel Langhorne Clemens, you will find him here under Twain. Another example: Mary Baker Eddy is widely known, but *Science and Health* is listed here under Mary Baker Glover, the name she used on the title page of that famous book. If an author's book is anonymous, it will be found listed here under its title, even though its authorship may be generally well known. An example is T. S. Eliot's anonymous *Ezra Pound His Metric and Poetry,* which is listed here under the title rather than under Eliot's name. In most cases in which this unorthodox method has been used, I have provided cross-references for the quick use of anyone who may be trying to locate a book.

A third ground rule I established was to exclude, with some exceptions, books with a retail value in the current market of less than $25, because to have included lower-priced books would have made necessary an index running into hundreds of thousands of entries—an obviously impossible work without the cooperation of a large research staff and one that no commercial publishing house could possibly price within the means of the readers I wanted to reach.

A fourth ground rule was to limit the inclusions wherever possible to books *in fine condition and in their original binding* and to describe both the bindings and the editions (including bibliographical points of identification). Thus, with the exception of limited or signed editions issued as a regular part of publishing procedure, I have eliminated in most cases signed copies, unique or presentation copies, books annotated in the author's hand, etc. The reasons for these decisions are, first, that *in most cases rebound copies are worth less* than copies in original binding and, second, that an author's signature or other writing by the author may greatly enhance the value of the book. In other words, my chief aim was to include only books in their original condition—i.e., as issued by the publisher and unaffected by anything that may have been done to them after publication.

Finally, by examining the catalogues (and often the stocks) of leading booksellers in both England and America, as well as the book auction records of the major galleries, I have attempted to provide as accurately as possible an up-to-date range of prices within which a scarce or rare book might be expected to be available at retail. [The auction prices are indicated with a capital A, followed by the auction season concerned; example: "$150 (A, 1981)."] The auction records were intended as both a support and a background for the use of experienced collectors, librarians, and booksellers, as well as an aid to the general reader in understanding and interpreting the book market. In many cases—especially with rare and very expensive books—the only price information available to layman or professional is in the auction records. Parenthetically, I should add that auction prices in the range of up to $750–$1,000 are in most cases at what should be considered the "wholesale" level—prices paid by dealers—since it is the dealers who make up most of the audience at rare book auctions. Thus, a book that brings $50 or $150 at auction will generally wind up in some dealer's catalogue at half again or twice that price, and often more. In the price ranges above $1,000, however, the field is somewhat trickier, and quite frequently the auction prices are close to retail values. The reason for this is that collectors, libraries, and institutions commonly authorize major booksellers to bid for them at auctions on a 10 percent fee arrangement. In other words, a library may authorize a dealer to pay $1,000 for a book for which, if obtained, it will pay the dealer $1,100 (plus travel or other allowances), the extra $100 representing the dealer's 10-percent commission for acting as representative. A further aspect of auction bidding that has emerged in recent years is the application by the galleries of a 10-percent surcharge beyond the auction price. In other words, a $1,000 price at auction means $1,100. (We have not accounted for these surcharges in most of the records shown in this edition.)

One other point to be made about the auction records is that they often present problems confusing even to the most experienced bookman, such as wide variations in the prices on the same book in the same year—for example, $15 to $85. In general, there are reasons for these variations (usually a matter of condition), which one can solve only by consulting the auction catalogue (or through the happenstance of having attended the sale). From these comments then, it should be obvious that the book auction records, as accurate as their compilers try to make them, are not an absolute guide to values and must be used with caution and interpreted with a fairly sophisticated knowledge of the book trade in general.

CONDITION IS THE KEY: Let me underscore the fact that the price ranges indicated herein are for books *in original binding and in fine condition.* The price spreads are included because the book market is a free market in which each dealer is at liberty to price a book as he personally values it in relation to his own knowledge of scarcity and demand and basic value. Thus, a New York dealer may have a book priced at $75, a London dealer at $110, and a San Francisco dealer at $65. From this, it should be obvious that shopping around may sometimes be advisable. In general, however, the international rare book trade is a vast, loose network of independent dealers in which there is, with certain limits, a general unanimity of opinion concerning the values of books.

By and large it is *condition* that determines the price asked for a scarce or rare book. In recent years there has been a strong trend among collectors (and sometimes libraries) to accept only the finest copies available—regardless of price.

In considering the prices included in this compilation, it should always be kept in mind that inferior copies—poor, average, or even good to very good copies—may be worth less than the prices I have noted, as are rebound copies. Obviously, books with defects—lacking dust jackets (if originally included, as with most books published since 1900) or having torn pages, soiled covers, or pages written on or underlined—are going to be worth less than the prices I have shown. Additionally, it should be kept in mind that the book market is steadily changing and that quite often the value of a book will rise sharply within a short space of time; so that even before this book is in your hands, the prices listed for some items may be considered low.

POINTS: Bibliography is not an exact science, and no library, least of all my own, could possibly contain a complete bibliographical guide to the more than 20,000 separate items I have listed in this book. Wherever possible, I have included the most reliable data I could find in order to assist the reader in identifying the first editions, as well as first issues, first states, etc. More detailed information on many of the major works listed may be consulted in bibliographies.

HOW DOES ONE TELL A FIRST EDITION? This is the question asked most frequently, and it is one of the most difficult questions to answer. There is, in fact, no single statement that will serve as an adequate answer. In general, it can be said that if the date on the title page of a book agrees with the date on the verso, or back, of the title page, the book may be assumed to be a first edition, provided there are no indications to the contrary. The question is, however, much more complicated than that; this is one of the reasons why it was necessary to include in many of the entries herein the bibliographical points of identification.

There is unfortunately no unanimity of method among either English or American publishers of identifying their first editions. Henry S. Boutell's *First Editions of Today and How to Tell Them* (Peacock Press), in its 1965 fourth edition, revised, contains a relatively up-to-date list of statements by modern American and English publishers concerning their various methods of identifying their books. A useful adjunct to this work is a little book published in 1977 by the Spoon River Press, Box 3635, Peoria, Illinois, 61614, entitled *A First Edition?*, compiled by Edward N. Zempel and Linda A. Virkler. It updates the information in Boutell and covers American and English publishers not included in that work.

In the case of nineteenth-century books, the practices of publishers were equally various, so that, in summary, I must say that aside from the rule of thumb about title page and copyright page agreement, every book must be considered as an individual problem. Unless the book itself is somehow identifiable as a first edition, it may be necessary to consult author bibliographies (and other library or bookseller resources, including catalogues) for exact information (unless I have included it herein).

ABOUT SELLING YOUR BOOKS: The rare book trade, like most antiquarian businesses, is a relatively small market operated by dealers of varying degrees of competence, style, and temperament. The prices given in this handbook are prices at the retail level and are *not* prices that a dealer can be expected to pay. Whether you sell at retail to collectors or at wholesale to dealers is your own choice. In my experience, most dealers are willing to pay about 50 percent of retail value (and sometimes more) for books for which they have immediate customers or a relatively steady demand. In general, they incline to pay less—20 percent to, say, 35 percent—for books for stock. This, I think, is what must be expected when one considers that dealers must often sit with books for years before finding a customer for them. Meanwhile, rent and salaries and all the other items of overhead, including the frightfully high present cost of printing catalogues, goes on and on. The net profit in the rare book trade is not noticeably large.

One final word: *Never be guilty of asking a dealer to price your books for you* (asking for a free appraisal). Most dealers will make appraisals—but probably they will expect to be paid a fee. One dealer I know charges $500 a day for appraising large collections. Another has a flat fee of $25 for appraising a single book. The best thing to do is to prepare your own list of books, identifying them as best you can, and decide what you want for them. Do not take a large lot of books to a dealer and ask him to look at them. He simply does not have the time. It is far better to list them first and show him the list, asking if he has a possible interest in them. Your list should include the following information: author's name; title of book (from the title page); place and date of publication (from the title page); copyright date (from the back of the title page); a statement of the edition (if shown or known); a description of the binding (leather, cloth, paper, etc); a description of the condition, noting all defects such as binding wear, torn pages, writing in the book, etc. If your books are right for the dealer, he will be glad to examine and buy them. In the event, finally, that you cannot price your own books, you may wish him to make an offer, but ask this only if you have confidence in the dealer and are willing to accept his judgment. Do not put him in a competitive position by taking a list around to his competitors to angle for the best price you can find.

BOOKS AS TREASURES: I have prepared this book mainly for readers who are interested in scarce and rare books as items to buy and treasure rather than to sell, although selling for profit is certainly an honorable practice. Whatever emphasis I have placed on price in all my writing about books has been with the hope of helping readers to identify scarce and rare items and of encouraging the collector to use caution in his buying and to obtain the finest possible copy within his means. I think it is wholly right for the booklover to cherish his prizes while at the same time conducting his search for fine books in such manner that they will always be worth at least as much as he pays for them. In fact, the whole history of book collecting shows that the really good books always increase in value as the years pass. There is a certain comfort, I think, in knowing that one has bought wisely and well.

VAN ALLEN BRADLEY
Scottsdale, Arizona
December 20, 1981

ACKNOWLEDGMENTS

The list of those to whom I am indebted for help, either directly or indirectly, in the compilation of this *Handbook* lengthens steadily with each edition. Librarians, collectors, and booksellers have been most generous in sharing their knowledge. To all these I wish again to acknowledge my gratitude. From others whom I may have omitted unintentionally from the list that follows I beg indulgence and express my thanks.

The list begins with Sharon Bradley, still my severest critic and most able assistant. I must also add my thanks to my editor, Elisabeth Jakab, and her assistant, Nancy Perlman. Others to whom I am indebted are: the late Ben Abramson; Robert J. Adelsperger; the late Ramon F. Adams; George Allen; Jack Bartfield; the late Jacob S. Blanck; Nelson Bond; James M. W. Borg; William Boozer; the late Frances Brewer; Andreas Brown; Matthew J. Bruccoli; the late Roger Butterfield; J. Bryan III; Richard H. Cady; Joseph Camardo; the late John Carter; Leland Case; George Chamberlain; George Charney; Jacob L. Chernofsky; C. E. Frazer Clark, Jr.; Aaron Cohen; Mrs. Louis Henry Cohn; Nathaniel Cowen; James Cummins; Lloyd W. Currey; Peter Decker; the late Philip C. Duschnes; Bruce Duncan; Jeff Dykes; J. M. Edelstein; Charles Feinberg; the late Lew D. Feldman; Arthur Freeman; Doris Frohnsdorff; Ralph D. Gardner; Franklin Gilliam; Michael Ginsberg; the late Adrian H. Goldstone; the late Everett D. Graff; Harold E. Graves; Lawrence Gutter; William Hanzel; Richard Harwell; W. R. Hasbrouck; Robert G. Hayman; Michael Heaston; Melissa and Mark Hime; David Holmes; Irwin T. Holtzman; Peter B. Howard; Warren R. Howell; the late Wright Howes; John H. Jenkins; Mary Johnsen; Richard Colles Johnson; Thomas J. Joyce; Nick Karanovich; Kenneth Karmiole; Lyle H. Kendall, Jr.; the late John S. Van E. Kohn; Dean Krakel; Lawrence Kunetka; Donald La Chance; the late Richard Leekley; Barry R. Levin; Harry A. Levinson; Jennifer Hamilton; Robert and Christine Liska; George and Judith Lowry; T. N. Luther; Mary Ann and Sol Malkin; Lawrence McGilvery; Larry McMurtry; Pauline Millen; Richard and Martha Mohr; Matthew Monahan; the late Harry T. Moore; Lawrence Moskowitz; Donald and Howard S. Mott; Kenneth Nebenzahl; Maurice F. Neville; Ralph G. Newman; Thomas Orlando; John Payne; Carl Petersen; the late William Pieper; Maurice F. Powers; the late David Randall; Ronald R. Randall; Randy Rau; Milton Reissman; Kenneth W. Rendell; William S. Reese; Jack Rittenhouse; the late Jim Roman; Leon and Barbara Rootenberg; Fred Rosenstock; Justin G. Schiller; John Scopazzi; Barry Scott; Arthur and Florence Shay; Daniel G. Siegel; Col. Henry A. Siegel; Ralph B. Sipper; James E. Sisson III; Harold Byron Smith, Sr.; John Stark; the late Vincent Starrett; Harry L. Stern; Peter L. Stern; Harry Strange; John Swingle; Drury Sylvester-Craig; Terence Tanner; William Targ; W. Thomas Taylor; Lawrence W. Towner; Nigel Traylen; Harvey and Linda Tucker; C. E. Valverde; C. E. Van Norman, Sr.; Donald and Geneva Vento; Ray S. Walton; Ben and Lou Weinstein; Stephen Weissman; the late Ernest J. Wessen; James M. Wells; Fred J. White, Jr.; Barry A. Wiedenkeller; Robert A. Wilson; Clarence Wolf; J. Howard Woolmer; William P. Wreden; and Jake Zeitlin.

A Note on References

Besides the innumerable bookseller catalogues consulted in revising this book, I have frequently referred to the catalogues of the major book auction houses, Christie, Manson & Woods, Sotheby Parke Bernet, and Swann Galleries, all of New York City, as well as the London catalogues of Christie's and Sotheby's. For quick reference, of course, the indispensable guides to the auction market remain the annual and cumulative index volumes of *American Book-Prices Current* and the English series *Book Auction Records*.

The individual author bibliographies consulted are far too numerous to be listed here. Basic bibliographical works consulted range upwards into the thousands of books, but perhaps the two most valuable series have been the first six volumes of Jacob Blanck's *Bibliography of American Literature* (Yale University Press) and the eight-volume catalogue of *The Celebrated Collection of Americana Formed by the Late Thomas Winthrop Streeter* (Parke-Bernet). A few of the individual works that have served me well include Whitman Bennett's *A Practical Guide to American Book Collecting* (Bennett Book Studios); William Targ's books *Modern English First Editions and Their Prices, 10,000 Rare Books and Their Prices*, and *American First Editions and Their Prices* (all published by the Black Archer Press); Percy H. Muir's *Points, 1874–1930* (Constable); Robert W. Henderson's *Early American Sport* (Barnes); John C. Eckel's *The First Editions of the Writings of Charles Dickens* (Inman); T. W. Field's *An Essay Towards an Indian Bibliography* (Scribner, Armstrong); Ramon F. Adams' fine compilations, *The Rampaging Herd* and *Six-Guns and Saddle Leather* (Oklahoma); Percy Muir's *English Children's Books, 1600–1900* (Praeger); Jacob S. Blanck's *Peter Parley to Penrod* (Bowker); Henry S. Boutell's *First Editions of Today and How to Tell Them* (Peacock Press); Merle Johnson's *American First Editions* (Mark Press); Wright Howes' *U.S.-iana* (Bowker); Henry R. Wagner's *The Plains and the Rockies*, revised by Charles L. Camp (Grabhorn Press); Lyle H. Wright's three volumes, *American Fiction,1774–1850, American Fiction, 1851–1875*, and *American Fiction, 1876–1900* (Huntington Library); the Lilly Library exhibition catalogue *Three Centuries of American Poetry* (Indiana); Solon J. Buck's *Travel and Description, 1765–1865* (Illinois State Historical Society); Cecil J. Byrd's *A Bibliography of Illinois Imprints, 1814–58* (Chicago); Colton J. Storm's *A Catalogue of the Everett D. Graff Collection of Western Americana* (Chicago); Peter Decker's catalogue of the library of George W. Soliday (Antiquarian Press); the fourth edition of *The Oxford Companion to English Literature*, edited by Sir Paul Harvey, and its counterpart, *The Oxford Companion to American Literature*, edited by James D. Hart (both published by Oxford); Gary M. Lepper's *A Bibliographical Introduction to 75 Modern American Authors* (Serendipity); Gale Research's two helpful series, the annual *Bookman's Price Index* and the four volumes of *First Printings of American Authors;* William S. Reese's *Six-Score: The 120 Best Books on the Range Cattle Industry* (Jenkins); B. D. Cutler's and Villa Stiles' *Modern British Authors: Their First Editions* (Greenberg); I. R. Brussel's *Anglo-American First Editions, 1826–1900, East to West* (Constable); Jay Monaghan's *Lincoln Biography*, 2 volumes (Illinois State Historical Society); Jacob Schwartz's *1100 Obscure Points* (Ulysses Bookshop); Howard Haycraft's *Murder for Pleasure* (Appleton-Century-Crofts); Jack D. Rittenhouse's *The Santa Fe Trail: A Historical Bibliography* (New Mexico); the catalogue of the Thomas Wayne Norris collection of books on California and the Far West (Holmes); Chris Steinbrunner's and Otto Penzler's *Encyclopedia of Mystery and Detection* (McGraw-Hill); Everett F.Bleiler's *Checklist of Fantastic Literature* (Shasta); Sidney Kramer's *A History of Stone & Kimball and Herbert S. Stone & Company* (Forgue); the Lilly Library exhibition catalogue *The First Hundred Years of Detective Fiction, 1841–1941* (Indiana); Robert Ernest Cowan's *A Bibliography of the History of California and the Far West* (Long's); E. I. Edwards' *Desert Voices: A Descriptive Bibliography* (Westernlore); Eric Quayle's *The Collector's Book of Books* (Potter) and *The Collector's Book of Detective Fiction* (Studio Vista); George Robert Minkoff's *A Bibliography of the Black Sun Press* (Minkoff); and Lawrence Lande's *A Bibliography of Canadiana* (McGill).

This random listing could go on indefinitely. Many other references in my own library and from other sources were consulted in the effort to make this compilation as broadly useful as possible. It is not, however, intended to be a bibliographical substitute for the more detailed original sources. New and more definitive bibliographical works are appearing year after year, and the serious dealer, librarian, and collector should be on the alert for them. The best single guide to such literature is the book review section of the journal of the antiquarian book trade, *AB Bookman's Weekly,* Box AB, Clifton, New Jersey 07015.

A

A. *Empedocles on Etna and Other Poems.* By A. Green cloth. London, 1852. (By Matthew Arnold.) First edition. $400–$500. London, 1896. Ballantyne Press. One of 210. $150–$200.

A. *Strayed Reveller (The), and Other Poems.* By A. Dark green cloth London, 1849. (By Matthew Arnold.) First edition. $400–$500.

A., T.B. *The Bells: A Collection of Chimes.* By T.B.A. Brown cloth. New York, 1855. (By Thomas Bailey Aldrich.) First edition. $200–$300.

ABBEY, Edward. *Desert Solitaire.* Brown cloth. New York, (1968). First edition. In dust jacket. $35–$50.

ABBEY, James. *California. A Trip Across the Plains in the Spring of 1850.* 64 pp., printed wrappers. New Albany, Ind., 1850. First edition. $3,000–$4,000.

ABBEY, John Roland. *Scenery of Great Britain and Ireland in Aquatint and Lithography, 1770–1860.* Frontispiece in color, numerous other illustrations. Buckram. London, 1952. First edition. One of 500. In dust jacket. $1,000–$1,500.

ABBOT (The). 3 vols., boards. Edinburgh, 1820. (By Sir Walter Scott.) First edition. $600–$800. Also, worn and stained, $325 (A, 1974). Philadelphia, 1820. 2 vols., boards. First American edition. $150–$250.

ABBOTSFORD, and Newstead Abbey. By the Author of "The Sketch-Book." Boards. London, 1835. (By Washington Irving.) First edition. $400–$800. Philadelphia, 1835. Blue or green cloth, paper labels. First edition, first printing, with copyright notices on both pages 2 and 4. $500–$600.

ABBOTT, Berenice. *The World of Atget.* Illustrated. Black cloth. New York, 1964. First edition. $75–$100.

ABBOTT, E. C. (Teddy Blue), and Smith, Helena Huntington. *We Pointed Them North.* Illustrated. Cloth. New York, (1939). First edition. In dust jacket. $85–$100.

ABBOTT, Jacob. See *Rollo Learning to Talk.*

A'BECKETT, Gilbert Abbott. *The Comic History of England.* Illustrated in color by John Leech. 20 parts in 19, blue wrappers. London, 1846–48. First edition. $400–$500. London, 1847–48. 2 vols., cloth. First edition in book form. $200–$250.

AB-SA-RA-KA, Home of the Crows. Folding map. Cloth. Philadelphia, 1868. (By Mrs. Henry B. Carrington.) First edition. $200–$250. Philadelphia, 1869. Cloth. Second edition. $75–$100. Philadelphia, 1878. Cloth. Third edition. $40–$80. Philadelphia, 1879. Fifth edition. $40–$60. Philadelphia, 1890. $75–$100.

ACELDAMA, a Place to Bury Strangers In. By a Gentleman of the University of Cambridge. Wrappers. London, 1898. (By Aleister Crowley.) First edition. $400–$600. Author's first book.

ACKERLEY, J.R. *My Dog Tulip.* Cloth. London, 1956. First edition. In dust jacket. $50.

ACKERMANN, Rudolph (publisher). *A History of the University of Cambridge* [and] *A History of the University of Oxford.* Illustrated with color plates. 4 vols., red morocco. London, 1815–14. First editions. Together, $6,000–$8,000. Separately: *Cam-*

bridge, $4,000–$4,500. Defective copy, $1,500 (A, 1980). *Oxford*, $2,000–$3,000. Defective copy, $1,200 (A, 1980).

ACKERMANN, Rudolph. *The Microcosm of London*. 104 colored aquatint plates by Pugin and Rowlandson. 3 vols., half morocco. London, (1808-10). First edition. $8,000 and up. London, 1904. 3 vols., parchment and boards. $200–$300.

ACKLEY, Mary E. *Crossing the Plains and Early Days in California*. Illustrated. Boards, printed label on spine. San Francisco, 1928. First edition. $150–$175.

ACTIVE Anthology (The). See Pound, Ezra.

ACTON, Harold. *The Last of the Medici*. Introduction by Norman Douglas. Portrait. Boards. Florence, Italy, 1930. First edition. One of 365 signed. In dust jacket. $75–$125.

ACTS, Resolutions and Memorials, Adopted by the Second Legislative Assembly of the Territory of Arizona. Boards. Prescott, Ariz., 1866. $400–$600. Prescott, 1867. *Acts*, etc., for 3d Assembly. Boards. $300–$400.

ADAMS, Andy. *The Log of a Cowboy*. Map, 6 plates. Brown pictorial cloth. Boston, 1903. First edition, first issue, with map and dated title page. In dust jacket. $150–$250. Lacking jacket, $65–$125.

ADAMS, Ansel (photographer). *Images: 1923–1974*. Illustrated. Folio, cloth. New York, 1974. First edition. In dust jacket. $150–$250. Another issue: One of 1,000, with original signed print. $800–$1,000. Also, $475 (A, 1978).

ADAMS, Ansel (photographer). *Making a Photograph*. Cloth. London, (1939). First edition. In dust jacket. $150–$200. London, (1948). Cloth. In dust jacket. $100–$150.

ADAMS, Ansel (photographer). *My Camera in Yosemite Valley*. Illustrated. Folio, wrappers. Yosemite and Boston, 1949. First edition. $400–$500.

ADAMS, Ansel (photographer). *Portfolio Two: The National Parks and Monuments*. San Francisco, 1950. Grabhorn printing. One of 100. $8,000–$10,000. Also, $8,500 (A, 1978).

ADAMS, Charles F., Jr., and Adams, Henry. *Chapters of Erie, and Other Essays*. Terracotta or green cloth. Boston, 1871. First edition. $50–$60.

ADAMS, Henry. See Adams, Charles F., Jr. Also see *Democracy; Mont Saint Michel and Chartres*.

ADAMS, Henry. *The Education of Henry Adams*. Blue cloth, leather spine label. Washington, 1907. First edition. One of 100. $2,000–$2,500. Boston, 1918. Revised and edited by Henry Cabot Lodge. Blue cloth. First trade edition. In dust jacket. $85–$100. New York, 1942. Limited Editions Club. Etchings by Samuel Chamberlain. Cloth. Boxed. $60–$75.

ADAMS, Henry. *A Letter to American Teachers of History*. Green or blue cloth. Washington, 1910. First edition. Signed by the author. (Blanck suggests that most copies were signed). $150–$200.

ADAMS, J.C. *Life of J.C. Adams*. (Cover title.) 29 pp., printed wrappers. (New York, 1860.) First edition. $1,500–$2,000. Lacking covers, and with caption title only: *The Hair-Breadth Escapes and Adventures of "Grizzly Adams."* $1,000—$1,500.

ADAMS, John Quincy. *Oration on the Life and Character of Gilbert Motier de Lafayette*. Wrappers. Washington, 1835. First edition. $75–$100. Another issue: One of a few on thick paper, specially bound in morocco. $200–$250. (Note: Inscribed copies bring more, of course, as with all Presidential items.)

ADAMS, Léonie. *High Falcon and Other Poems*. Cloth. New York, (1929). First edition. In dust jacket. $100.

ADAMS, Léonie. *Those Not Elect.* Boards. New York, 1925. First edition. In dust jacket. $50–$75. Author's first book.

ADAMS, Ramon. *The Rampaging Herd.* Illustrated. Green cloth. Norman, Okla., 1959. First edition. In dust jacket. $200–$250.

ADAMS, Richard. *Watership Down.* Cloth. London, 1972. First edition. In dust jacket. $150–$250. New York, 1974. Cloth. First American edition. In dust jacket. $75–$100.

ADAMS, Will. *Errata: or, The Works of Will. Adams.* 2 vols., boards. New York, 1823. (By John Neal.) First edition. $100–$150.

ADAMS, William Taylor. See Ashton, Warren T.; Optic, Oliver.

ADE, George. *Artie.* Cloth. Chicago, 1896. First edition. $35–$50. Author's first book.

ADE, George. *Fables in Slang.* Tan decorated cloth. Chicago, 1900. First edition. $30–$50.

ADE, George. *One Afternoon with Mark Twain.* Stiff wrappers. (Chicago), 1939. First edition. One of 350. $75–$100.

ADE, George. *Revived Remarks on Mark Twain.* 36 pp., wrappers. Chicago, 1936. First edition. One of 500 signed. $50–$75. Also, 500 copies unsigned. $15–$20.

ADE, George. *Stories of the Streets and of the Town.* Edited by Franklin J. Meine. Cloth. Chicago, 1941. Caxton Club. One of 500. $40–$60.

ADE, George. *The Sultan of Sulu.* Illustrated. Pictorial cream wrappers. New York, 1903. First edition, with "Published May, 1903," on copyright page. $50–$75.

ADELER, Max. *Out of the Hurly-Burly.* Illustrated by A.B. Frost and others. Decorated cloth. Philadelphia, 1874. (By Charles Heber Clark.) First edition. $75–$100. Author's first book and first book illustrated by Frost.

ADVENTURES of a Brownie (The), as Told to My Child. By the Author of "John Halifax, Gentleman." Cloth. London, 1872. (By Dinah M. Craik.) First edition. $250–$350.

ADVENTURES of a Post Captain (The). By a Naval Officer. 25 colored plates. Boards. London, (1817). (By Alfred Thornton.) First edition. $350–$500.

ADVENTURES of Robin Day (The). 2 vols., purple cloth, paper label on spine. Philadelphia, 1839. (By Robert Montgomery Bird.) First edition. $250–$350.

ADVENTURES of Timothy Peacock, Esquire (The). By a Member of the Vermont Bar. Cloth. Middlebury, Vt., 1835. (By Daniel Pierce Thompson.) First edition. $600. Also, $240 (A, 1979). Author's first novel.

ADVENTURES of Ulysses (The). Frontispiece, engraved title page. Boards, paper label. London, 1808. (By Charles Lamb.) First edition. $750–$1,000. Also, $450 (A, 1978).

ADVENTURES of a Yankee (The), or The Singular Life of John Ledyard. By a Yankee. Woodcuts. Boards and morocco. Boston, 1831. (By John Ledyard.) First edition. $300–$400.

ADVENTURES of a Younger Son (The). 3 vols., boards. London, 1831. (By Edward John Trelawny.) First edition. $400–$500. Author's first book.

AESCHYLUS. *Agamemnon: A Tragedy.* Translated by Edward FitzGerald. Wrappers. (London, 1865). First edition. $150–$250. London, 1876. Half leather. One of 250. $75–$125.

AESOP. *Fables.* Sir Roger L'Estrange translation. Illustrated by Stephen Gooden. Vellum. London, 1936. One of 500 signed by Gooden. Boxed. $850–$1,000. New York, 1933. Limited Editions Club. Samuel Croxall translation. Illustrated by Bruce Rogers. Boards and vellum. Boxed. $125–$150.

AGAPIDA. Fray Antonio. *A Chronicle of the Conquest of Granada.* 2 vols., boards and cloth, paper labels. Philadelphia, 1829. (By Washington Irving.) First edition. $400–$500. Large paper issue: $600–$800. London, 1829. 2 vols., boards. First English edition. $300–$400.

AGASSIZ, Louis. *Lake Superior.* 16 plates. Cloth. Boston, 1850. First edition. $200–$250.

AGATE, James. *Ego: The Autobiography of James Agate.* Illustrated. Cloth. London, (1935). First edition. In dust jacket. $40–$60.

AGATE, James. *A Shorter Ego: The Autobiography of James Agate.* 2 vols., half morocco. London, (1945). One of 100 signed. $100–$125

AGE of Bronze (The). Plain drab wrappers. London, 1823. (By George Gordon Noel, Lord Byron.) First edition. $400–$600. Rebound in modern wrappers, lacking half title, $60.

AGEE, G.W. *Rube Burrows, King of Outlaws.* 194 pp., wrappers. (Cincinnati, 1890.) First edition. $50–$75. Chicago, (1890). $35–$45.

AGEE, James. See *Brooks-Bryce Anglo American Prize Essays—1927.*

AGEE, James. *A Death in the Family.* Blue cloth. New York, (1957). First edition, first issue, with title page printed in blue, "walking" for "waking" on page 80. In dust jacket. $75–$125. Advance issue: Blue wrappers. $150–$200.

AGEE, James. *Four Early Stories.* Illustrated. Boards. West Branch, Iowa, 1964. One of 285. In tissue dust jacket. $100–$175.

AGEE, James. *Let Us Now Praise Famous Men.* Walker Evans photographs. Black cloth. Boston, 1941. First edition. In dust jacket. $200–$300. Boston, 1960. Black cloth. In dust jacket. $25–$35.

AGEE, James. *The Letters of James Agee to Father Flye.* Black cloth. New York, 1962. First edition. In dust jacket. $25–$35.

AGEE, James. *The Morning Watch.* Wrappers. Rome, 1950. First edition. $275–$375. (Offprint from Botteghe Oscure.) Boston, 1951. Boards. First American edition. In dust jacket. $75–$100.

AGEE, James. *Permit Me Voyage.* Cloth. New Haven, 1934. First edition. In dust jacket. $400–$500. Author's first book.

AGRICOLA, Georgius. See Hoover, Herbert C. and Lou Henry.

AIKEN, Conrad. *Blue Voyage.* Cloth. New York, 1927. First edition. In dust jacket. $100–$125. New printing: One of 125 signed. $200–$250.

AIKEN, Conrad. *Bring! Bring!* Cloth. New York, 1925. First edition. In dust jacket. $85.

AIKEN, Conrad. *The Coming Forth by Day of Osiris Jones.* Green cloth. New York, 1931. First edition, first issue, with Scribner "A" on copyright page and "The Music" in capital letters on page 37. In dust jacket. $75–$100.

AIKEN, Conrad. *Costumes by Eros.* Cloth. New York, 1928. First edition. In dust jacket. $125.

AIKEN, Conrad. *Earth Triumphant and Other Tales in Verse.* Cloth. New York, 1914. First edition. $150–$200. Author's first book.

AIKEN, Conrad. *Great Circle.* Cloth. New York, 1933. First edition. In dust jacket. $150–$200.

AIKEN, Conrad. *The Jig of Forslin: A Symphony.* Cloth. Boston, 1916. First edition. In dust jacket. $75–$125.

AIKEN, Conrad. *King Coffin.* Blue cloth. New York, 1935. First American edition. In dust jacket. $50–$60.

AIKEN, Conrad. *Preludes for Memnon.* Cloth. New York, 1931. First edition. In dust jacket. $75–$100.

AIKEN, Conrad. *Priapus and the Pool.* Boards. Cambridge, Mass., 1922. First edition. Printed by Bruce Rogers. One of 425. $125. One of 50 (of the same edition) on hand-made paper and signed. $100–$150. New York, 1925. New edition, with added poems. $50.

AIKEN, Conrad. *Punch: The Immortal Liar.* Cloth. New York, 1921. First edition. In dust jacket. $100–$125.

AIKEN, Conrad. *Scepticisms.* Green cloth, lettered in red. New York, 1919. First edition, first binding. In dust jacket. $75–$100.

AIKEN, Conrad. *Selected Poems.* Cloth. New York, 1929. First edition. One of 210 on large paper, signed. Boxed. $250–$300. Trade edition: In dust jacket. $50.

AIKEN, Conrad. *Thee.* Illustrated by Leonard Baskin. Boards. New York, (1967). First edition. One of 100 signed by author and artist. Boxed. $200.

AIKEN, Conrad. *Time in the Rock.* Cloth. New York, 1936. First edition. In dust jacket. $75–$85.

AIKEN, Conrad. *Turns and Movies and Other Tales in Verse.* Printed wrappers over boards. Boston, 1916. First edition. $100–$110.

AINSWORTH, Ed. *The Cowboy in Art.* Illustrated, including color. Cloth. New York, (1968). First trade edition. In dust jacket. $50–$75.

AINSWORTH, W. Harrison. *Cardinal Pole.* 3 vols., cloth. London, 1863. First edition. $300–$400.

AINSWORTH, W. Harrison. *Jack Sheppard.* Portrait and illustrations by George Cruikshank. 3 vols., green cloth. London, 1839. First edition. $300–$500. London, 1839–40. Illustrated. 15 parts, wrappers. $1,000–$1,250.

AINSWORTH, W. Harrison. *The Leaguer of Lathom.* 3 vols., cloth. London, 1876. First edition. $400–$500.

AINSWORTH, W. Harrison. *Merry England: or Nobles and Serfs.* 3 vols., green cloth. London, 1874. First edition $250–$300.

AINSWORTH, W. Harrison, *The Miser's Daughter.* Illustrated by George Cruikshank. 3 vols., black cloth. London, 1842. First edition. $250–$400.

AINSWORTH, W. Harrison. *Old Saint Paul's.* Illustrated by John Franklin and Phiz. 3 vols., cloth. London, 1841. First edition. $250–$350 (Also issued in 12 paperbound parts.) London, 1847. Red cloth. First octavo edition. $150–$200.

AINSWORTH, W. Harrison. *The Tower of London.* Illustrated by George Cruikshank. 13 parts in 12, wrappers. London, 1840. First edition. $800–$1,000. London, 1840. Purple cloth. First book edition. $600 and up.

AKEN, David. *Pioneers of the Black Hills.* Pictorial wrappers. (Milwaukee, 1920?) First edition. $75–$125. Worn, $50.

AKERLY, Lewis F. *The Geology of the Hudson River.* Colored map. Boards. New York, 1820. First edition. $250–$275.

ALARIC at Rome: A Prize Poem. Recited in Rugby School. June XII, MDCCCXL. 12 pp., pink pictorial and printed wrappers. Rugby, England, 1840. (By Matthew Arnold.) First edition. $7,480 (A, 1978). Author's first book of verse.

ALBEE, Edward. *The American Dream.* Cloth. New York, (1961). First edition. In dust jacket. $50–$65.

ALBEE, Edward. *Tiny Alice.* Cloth. New York, 1965. First edition. In dust jacket. $75–$85. London, (1966). Cloth. First English edition. In dust jacket. $50–$75.

ALBEE, Edward. *Who's Afraid of Virginia Woolf?* Cloth. New York, 1962. First edition. In dust jacket. $100–$125.

ALBEE, Edward. *The Zoo Story. The Death of Bessie Smith. The Sandbox: Three Plays.* Blue cloth. New York, (1960). First edition. In dust jacket. $100–$135. Author's first book.

ALCOTT, A. Bronson. *Sonnets and Canzonets.* Illustrated with photographs. Cloth. Boston, 1882. First edition. One of 50 signed. $200–$300. (Note: The trade edition, lacking photographs, not especially valuable—about $50 in fine condition.)

ALCOTT, Louisa May. *Flower Fables.* Frontispiece and 5 plates. Cloth. Boston, 1855. First edition. $100–$200.

ALCOTT, Louisa May. *Hospital Sketches.* Printed green boards or cloth. Boston, 1863. First edition, first printing, in boards, with ad on back announcing Wendell Phillips' *Speeches* at $2.50 (not $2.25). $100–$150.

ALCOTT, Louisa May. *Kitty's Class Day.* 12 pp., printed buff wrappers. Boston, (1868). First edition. $300–$350. (Note: Issue points on this pamphlet are debatable; see Blanck's *Bibliography of American Literature.*)

ALCOTT, Louisa May. *Little Men.* Frontispiece. Blue cloth. London, 1871. First edition. $125–$150. Boston, 1871. Green cloth. First American edition, first issue, with ads at front listing *Pink and White Tyranny* as nearly ready. $250–$300.

ALCOTT, Louisa May. *Little Women.* Frontispiece and 3 plates, 2 vols., cloth. Boston, 1868-69. First edition, without "Part One" on spine of Vol. 1 and with Vol. 2 having no notice of *Little Women, Part First,* on page iv. $1,500–$2,000. London, 1869. Blue cloth. First English edition. $400–$500. New York, 1967. Limited Editions Club. Illustrated. Brocade cloth. Boxed. $40–$50.

ALCOTT, Louisa May. *Morning-Glories, and Other Stories.* Frontispiece and 3 plates. Cloth. Boston, 1868. First edition. $75–$125.

ALCOTT, Louisa May. *An Old-Fashioned Girl.* Double frontispiece and 2 plates. Cloth. Boston, 1870. First edition, first issue, no ads on copyright page. $75–$125. Second issue, with ads on copyright page. $50.

ALCOTT, Louisa May. *The Rose Family.* 47 pp., printed wrappers, or cloth. Boston, 1864. First edition. Wrappers: $200–$300. Cloth: $150.

ALDINGTON, Richard. *A.E. Housman and W.B. Yeats, Two Lectures.* Boards. (Hurst, England), 1955. Peacocks Press. One of 350. In glassine dust jacket. $75–$100.

ALDINGTON, Richard. *All Men Are Enemies.* Boards and buckram. London, 1933. One of 110 signed. $100–$125.

ALDINGTON, Richard. *At All Costs.* Boards and buckram. London, 1930. First edition. One of 275 signed. $50–$75. Trade edition: Wrappers. $35.

ALDINGTON, Richard. *Balls and Another Book for Suppression.* Wrappers. London, 1930. Blue Moon Booklets No. 7. First edition. $75–$100. Also privately issued: (Westport), 1932. (Title: *Balls.*) Sewed, self-wrappers. One of "99 & a few others." $100–$150.

ALDINGTON, Richard. *The Colonel's Daughter: A Novel.* Green cloth. London, 1931. First edition. One of 210 signed. $75–$100.

ALDINGTON, Richard. *D.H. Lawrence.* Wrappers. Seattle, 1927. First edition. $35. London, 1930. Boards. First English edition. One of 260 signed. In tissue dust jacket. $75. Another issue: Orange wrappers. $35–$50.

ALDINGTON, Richard. *Death of a Hero.* Cloth. London, 1929. First edition. In dust jacket. $50–$100. Paris, 1930. 2 vols., printed wrappers. Unexpurgated text. One of 300. $200–$250.

ALDINGTON, Richard. *Ezra Pound and T.S. Eliot: A Lecture.* Boards. London, 1954. Peacocks Press. First edition. One of 350. $75–$100. Another issue: Full morocco. One of 10 trial copies on Azure paper, signed. $200–$300.

ALDINGTON, Richard. *Fifty Romance Lyric Poems.* Black cloth. New York, 1928. First edition. One of 9 on green paper, signed. $300–$475. Another issue: One of 900 signed. $75–$100.

ALDINGTON, Richard. *A Fool i' the Forest.* Cloth. London, 1925. First edition, limited, signed. In dust jacket. $75–$100.

ALDINGTON, Richard. *Images (1910-1915).* (Cover title.) Pictorial wrappers. (London, 1915). First edition. $250. Author's first book.

ALDINGTON, Richard. *Images of War.* Illustrated. Boards and cloth. London, 1919. First edition. One of 120 on paper. $75–$85. Another issue: One of 50 with hand-colored illustrations. $100–$150. Another issue: One of 30 on vellum, signed. $200–$250.

ALDINGTON, Richard. *Images—Old and New.* Stiff boards. Boston,1916. First edition. In dust jacket. $75–$85.

ALDINGTON, Richard. *Last Straws.* Green suede. Paris, 1930. Hours Press. First edition. One of 200 signed. $125–$150.

ALDINGTON, Richard. *Love and the Luxembourg.* Red buckram. New York, 1930. First edition. One of 475 signed. Boxed. $50–$75.

ALDINGTON, Richard. *The Love of Myrrhine and Konallis.* Cloth. Chicago, 1926. First edition. One of 150 signed. $100–$125.

ALDINGTON, Richard. *Stepping Heavenward.* Boards and cloth. Florence, Italy, 1931. One of 808 signed. In dust jacket. Boxed. $100–$150. London, 1931. Boards. $25–$35.

ALDISS, Brian W. *The Brightfount Diaries.* Cloth. London, (1955). First edition. In dust jacket. $75. Author's first book.

ALDRICH, Thomas Bailey. See A., T.B.

ALDRICH, Thomas Bailey. *The Ballad of Babie Bell and Other Poems.* Brown cloth. New York, 1859. First edition, first issue, with Broadway address for publisher. $75–$125.

ALDRICH, Thomas Bailey. *Friar Jerome's Beautiful Book.* Red vellum, linen ties. (Boston, 1836.) One of 250 on large paper. $125–$150.

ALDRICH, Thomas Bailey. *Judith and Holofernes.* Cloth. Boston, 1896. First edition. One of 50 with paper labels. $125–$175. Trade edition: $35.

ALDRICH, Thomas Bailey. *Judith of Bethulia.* Cloth. Boston, 1904. First edition. In dust jacket. $75.

ALDRICH, Thomas Bailey. *The Poems of Thomas Bailey Aldrich.* Illustrated. Illuminated wrappers. Boston, 1882. First edition. One of 6 on vellum. $400–$500.

8

ALDRICH, Thomas Bailey. *Prudence Palfrey*. Cloth. Boston, 1874. First edition. $75–$100.

ALDRICH, Thomas Bailey. *A Sea Turn and Other Matters*. Pictorial cloth. Boston, 1902. First edition, first printing. In dust jacket. $100.

ALDRICH, Thomas Bailey. *The Story of a Bad Boy*. Cloth. Boston, 1870. First edition, first issue, with line 20 on page 14 reading "scattered" and line 10 on page 197 reading "abroad." $400–$500. Boston, 1895. Illustrated by A.B. Frost. Decorated cloth. $35–$50.

ALDRIDGE, Reginald. *Life on a Ranch*. Frontispiece and 3 plates. Stiff wrappers. New York, 1884. First edition. $225–$500.

ALDRIDGE, Reginald. *Ranch Notes in Kansas*. 4 plates. Pictorial cloth. London, 1884. First English edition (of *Life on a Ranch*; see above). $150–$200.

ALEXANDER, E.P. *Military Memoirs of a Confederate*. Maps, 3 plates. Cloth. New York, 1907. First edition. $125–$150.

ALEXANDER, Hartley B. (editor). *Sioux Indian Painting*. 50 color plates. 2 vols., large folio, loose in pictorial cloth portfolios, with ties. Nice, France, (1938). First edition. One of 400. $500–$800. Also, $450 (A, 1977).

ALEXANDER, John H. *Mosby's Men*. Illustrated. Cloth. New York, 1907. First edition. In dust jacket. $100–$125.

ALEXANDER, William. *Picturesque Representations of the Dress and Manners of the Austrians*. 50 color plates. Full contemporary morocco. London, (about 1813). $600–$750. Also, similar volumes, about 1814, covering the Chinese (50 color plates), Russians (64 plates), Turks (61), English (50), similar values.

ALEXANDRE, Arsène. *The Decorative Art of Leon Bakst*. Notes on the Ballets by Jean Cocteau. Translated by Harry Melvill. Portrait. 77 plates, 50 in color. Folio, half vellum. London, 1913. First edition. $1,250–$1,500. Another issue: One of 80 with an original watercolor. $1,500–$2,000.

ALGER, Horatio, Jr. See Starr, Julian. Also see *Timothy Crump's Ward*.

ALGER, Horatio, Jr. *Abraham Lincoln, The Backwoods Boy*. Illustrated. Pictorial cloth. New York, 1883. First edition, first issue, with ads listing this book as No. 2 in "Boyhood and Manhood" series. $75–$100.

ALGER, Horatio, Jr. *Bertha's Christmas Vision: An Autumn Sheaf*. Blind-stamped cloth. Boston, 1856. First edition. $350–$425. Author's first book.

ALGER, Horatio, Jr. *Dan, the Detective*. Illustrated. Cloth. New York, 1884. First edition. $300–$400.

ALGER, Horatio, Jr. *Dean Dunham*. Stiff tan pictorial wrappers. New York, 1890. First edition. (No. 32 in weekly series of "Leather-Clad Tales of Adventure and Romance.") $100–$125.

ALGER, Horatio, Jr. *The Five Hundred Dollar Check*. Pictorial tan cloth. New York, (1891). First book edition, first issue, with United States Book Co. imprint on title page and "Porter & Coates" on spine. $400–$450. Later issue, with "Lovell" on spine, $100–$150.

ALGER, Horatio, Jr. *From Canal Boy to President*. Illustrated. Green cloth. New York, 1881. First edition, first issue, with pages 266 and 268 transposed and with erratum slip tipped to page 267. $40–$60. Later printings, about $20.

ALGER, Horatio, Jr. *Grand'ther Baldwin's Thanksgiving*. Purple cloth. Boston, (1875). First edition, published by Loring. $100–$125.

ALGER, Horatio, Jr. *Luke Walton, or The Chicago Newsboy*. Cloth. Philadelphia, (1889). First edition. $50–$75.

ALGER, Horatio, Jr. *Mark Stanton.* Wrappers. New York, 1890. (Leather-clad paperback.) First edition. $100–$125.

ALGER, Horatio, Jr. *Ragged Dick; or Street Life in New York with the Boot-Blacks.* Pictorial title page, 3 illustrations. Cloth. Boston, (1868). First edition, first issue, with *Fame and Fortune* listed in ads for publication in December. $750–$1,000.

ALGER, Horatio, Jr. *Ralph Raymond's Heir.* Printed brown wrappers. New York, (1892). (Idle Hour Series paperback.) First edition. $50–$60.

ALGER, Horatio, Jr. *Robert Coverdale's Struggle.* Pictorial colored cover. New York, (1910). New Medal Library No. 555. First edition. $500 and up.

ALGER, Horatio, Jr. *The Western Boy.* Pictorial title. Cloth. (New York, 1878). First edition, with G.W. Carleton ad at front of book. $325–$450.

ALGER, Horatio, Jr. *The Young Miner; or Tom Nelson in California.* Boards and cloth. San Francisco, 1965. Book Club of California. One of 450. $75–$85.

ALGER, Horatio, Jr., and Cheney, O. Augusta. *Seeking His Fortune and Other Dialogues.* Pictorial cloth. Boston, (1875). First edition. $500–$750. New York, 1882. Boards. Reprint by Ward & Drummond. $50–$60.

ALGREN, Nelson. *The Man with the Golden Arm.* Cloth. Garden City, 1949. First edition. In dust jacket. $50–$75.

ALGREN, Nelson. *The Neon Wilderness.* Green cloth. Garden City, 1947. First edition. In first state dust jacket without publisher's blurbs. $50–$75.

ALGREN, Nelson. *Never Come Morning.* Introduction by Richard Wright. Blue cloth. New York, (1942). First edition. In dust jacket. $150–$175.

ALGREN, Nelson. *Somebody in Boots.* Brown cloth. New York, (1935). First edition. In dust jacket. $350–$400. Author's first book.

ALGREN, Nelson. *A Walk on the Wild Side.* Boards. New York, (1956). First edition. In dust jacket. $35–$50.

ALHAMBRA (The). See Crayon, Geoffrey.

ALKEN, Henry. *The National Sports of Great Britain.* 50 colored plates. Folio, boards (?) or morocco. London, 1820 (–21). First edition, first issue, with engraved 1820 title page and with watermarks dated 1816 and 1818. $12,000 and up. London, 1821. Second issue, without 1820 title page. $10,000 and up. Also, $8,800 (A, 1979). London, 1823. Second edition. $8,000 and up. Also, $4,000 (A, 1975). London, 1824. Morocco. $750–$1,000. London, 1825. Boards. First octavo edition. $600–$750. Large paper issue: $2,600 (A, 1980). London, 1903. Boards and cloth. $1,000 and up. Another edition: (New York), 1904. Half morocco. $1,000 and up.

ALKEN, Henry. *Scraps from the Sketch-Books of Henry Alken.* 42 colored plates. Boards. London, 1821. First edition. $1,500–$2,500. London, 1822. Contemporary half morocco. $800–$1,000. London, 1825. Morocco. $800–$1,000.

ALKEN, Henry. *Shooting, or One Day's Sport of Three Real Good Ones, However Ignorant of Sporting Rules.* 6 color plates. Buff printed wrappers (dated 1824). London, 1823. First edition. $1,500–$2,000.

ALLAHAKBARRIE Book of Broadway Cricket for 1899. Illustrated. Parchment wrappers. (London, 1899). (By Sir James M. Barrie.) First edition, signed and limited. $400–$500. Also, $350 (A, 1981).

ALLAN, J.T. (compiler). *Central and Western Nebraska, and the Experiences of Its Stock Growers.* (Cover title.) 16 pp., pictorial wrappers. Omaha, 1883. $200–$250. (Note: A Union Pacific land department pamphlet.)

ALLAN, J.T. (compiler). *Western Nebraska and the Experiences of Its Actual Settlers.* 16 pp., wrappers. Omaha, 1882. $200–$250.

ALLEN, Miss A.J. (compiler). *Ten Years in Oregon.* Portrait. Calf. Ithaca, N.Y., 1848. First edition. $150–$250. Second issue, same date, portrait omitted, pages added. Sheep, $150–$250. Ithaca, 1850. Pictorial cloth. $40–$50.

ALLEN, Hervey. See Allen, William Hervey.

ALLEN, Hervey, *Anthony Adverse.* Blue cloth. New York, 1933. First trade edition, first printing, with publisher's monogram on copyright page and with numerous typographical errors, among them "Xaxier" for "Xavier" in line 6 of page 352, "ship" for "shop" in line 18 of page 1086, and the word "found" repeated in line 22 of page 397. In dust jacket. $50–$75. De luxe issue: 3 vols., suede boards. One of 105 signed. $200–$300. New York, 1937. Limited Editions Club. 3 vols., orange cloth. One of 1,500. Boxed. $50–$75.

ALLEN, Hervey. *The Bride of Huitzil.* Boards and cloth. New York, 1922. First edition. One of 350 signed. $50–$75.

ALLEN, Hervey. *Israfel: The Life and Times of Edgar Allan Poe.* 2 vols., cloth. New York, 1926. First edition, first state, with wineglass on table in Longfellow portrait facing page 529. In dust jackets. $75–$100. De luxe issue: Three-quarters leather. One of 250. $100–$125.

ALLEN, Hervey. *Wampum and Old Gold.* Boards. New Haven, 1921. First edition. One of 500. $50–$75.

ALLEN, Hervey, and Mabbott, Thomas O. (editors). *Poe's Brother.* Boards. New York, (1926.) First edition. One of 1,000. Boxed. $75–$100.

ALLEN, Ira. *A Concise Summary of the Second Volume of the Olive Branch.* 24 pp., wrappers. Philadelphia, 1807. $100–$125.

ALLEN, J.A. *Notes on the Natural History of Portions of Montana and Dakota.* 61 pp., wrappers. Boston, 1874. $100–$125.

ALLEN, James Lane. *Flute and Violin.* Cloth. New York, 1891. First edition. $45–$65. Author's first book.

ALLEN, W.A. *The Sheep Eaters.* 6 plates. Cloth. New York, 1913. First edition. $100–$125.

ALLEN, William A. *Adventures with Indians and Game.* 25 plates. Cloth, or half leather. Chicago, 1903. First edition. $150–$200.

ALLEN, William Hervey. *Ballads of the Border.* Printed wrappers. (El Paso), 1916. (By Hervey Allen.) First edition, probable first state, with author's name misspelled "Hervy" on copyright page. $400–$600. There were many later printings. Author's first book.

ALLIES' Fairy Book (The). 12 colored plates, other illustrations by Arthur Rackham. Buckram. London, (1916). One of 525 signed by the artist. $500–$900. Trade edition: Blue cloth. First issue, with pictorial end papers. In dust jacket. $150–$200.

ALLINGHAM, William. *Sixteen Poems.* Selected by William Butler Yeats. Boards and linen. Dundrum, Ireland, 1905. Dun Emer Press. One of 200. $125–$150.

ALLISON, William. *The British Thoroughbred Horse.* Cloth. London, 1901. First edition. $100–$150. London, 1907. Second edition. $75–$125.

ALMONTE, Juan Nepomuceno. *Noticia Estadistica sobre Tejas.* 3 folding tables. Boards or wrappers. Mexico, 1835. First edition. $2,500–$3,000.

ALNWICK Castle, with Other Poems. Printed tan wrappers. New York, 1827. (By Fitz-Greene Halleck.) First edition. $200–$300.

ALONZO and Melissa. Contemporary leather and boards. Brattleboro, Vt., 1824. (By Isaac Mitchell.) $25–$35. (Note: See author entry for first edition.)

ALTA California. By a Captain of Volunteers. 64 pp., cloth. Philadelphia, 1847. First edition. $450–$600.

ALTER, J. Cecil. *James Bridger: Trapper, Frontiersman, Scout, and Guide.* 18 plates. Cloth. Salt Lake City, (1925). First edition. One of 1,000 signed. $150. Columbus, Ohio, 1951. Cloth. In dust jacket. $25–$35.

ALTISONANT, Lorenzo. *Letters to Esq. Pedant, in the East.* Boards, Cambridge City, Ind., 1844. (By Samuel Klinefelter Hoshour.) First edition. $150–$200. Cincinnati, 1850. Boards. $75.

ALTOWAN; Or Incidents of Life and Adventure in the Rocky Mountains. By an Amateur Traveller. Edited by J. Watson Webb. 2 vols., cloth. New York, 1846. (By Sir William Drummond Stewart.) First edition. $350–$500. Also, $300 (A, 1978). (Note: Howes says this was "probably actually written by Webb.")

ALVAREZ, A. *Lost.* Cloth. (London), 1968. First edition. One of 250 signed. $75–$100.

AMBLER, Eric. *A Coffin for Dimitrios.* Cloth. New York, 1939. First edition. In dust jacket. $150–$200.

AMERICAN Arguments for British Rights. Wrappers. London, 1806. (by William Loughton Smith.) $150–$200.

AMERICAN Caravan (The). Cloth. New York, 1927. First edition. In dust jacket. $150.

AMERICAN Caravan (The Second). Cloth. New York, 1928. First edition. In dust jacket. $145.

AMERICAN Caravan IV: A Yearbook of American Literature. Cloth. New York, 1931. First edition. In dust jacket. $150–$200.

AMERICAN Church Silver of the 17th and 18th Centuries. Boards. Boston, 1911. Boston Museum of Fine Arts. $50–$75.

AMERICAN Cruiser (The). Cloth. Boston, 1846. (By Capt. George Little.) First edition. $100–$125.

AMERICAN Shooter's Manual (The). By a Gentleman of Philadelphia County. Frontispiece, 2 plates, errata. Contemporary calf. Philadelphia, 1827. (By Dr. Jesse Y. Kester?) First edition. $2,000–$2,500. Philadelphia, (1827). Second edition. $1,000–$1,500.

AMERICANA—Beginnings: A Selection from the Library of Thomas W. Streeter. 97 pp., wrappers. Morristown, N.J., 1952. One of 325. $100–$200.

AMES, John Henry. *Lincoln, the Capital of Nebraska.* Wrappers. Lincoln, 1870. First edition. $150.

AMIS, Kingsley. *Bright November.* 32 pp., leatherette. London, (1947). First edition. $100–$150. Author's first book.

AMIS, Kingsley. *Lucky Jim.* Cloth. Garden City, 1954. First American edition. In dust jacket. $75–$100.

AMMONS, A.R. *Expressions of Sea Level.* Blue cloth. (Columbus, 1963.) First edition. In dust jacket. $50–$75.

AMMONS, A.R. *Ommateum: With Doxology.* Cloth. Philadelphia, (1955—actually 1954). First edition. $800–$1,000. The poet's first book.

AMSDEN, Charles A. *Navaho Weaving.* 122 plates, many in color. Cloth. Santa Ana, 1934. First edition. $150–$200. Albuquerque, 1948 (actually 1949). Cloth. $100. Chicago, (1964). Cloth. $35–$50.

AMUNDSEN, Roald. *"The Northwest Passage."* Illustrated, 2 folding maps in pocket. 2 vols., cloth. London, 1908. First edition in English. $150.

ANALYSIS of the Hunting Field (The). 7 colored plates by Henry Alken, 43 woodcuts. Green or red cloth. London, 1846. (By Robert Smith Surtees.) First edition, first issue, green cloth (some copies with preface dated 1846, some dated 1847). $750–$1,000. Second issue, red cloth: $500–$600.

ANCIENT and Modern Michilimackinac. (Cover title.) 48 pp., wrappers. (St. James, Mich.), MDCCCLIV (1854). (By James Jesse Strang.) First edition, first issue. $1,000 and up. Another, dated 1854, but "obviously" (according to Howes) on later paper, of undetermined value.

ANDERSEN, Hans Christian. *The Complete Andersen.* Translated by Jean Hersholt. Handcolored illustrations by Fritz Kredel. 6 vols., buckram and boards. New York, 1949. Limited Editions Club. Boxed. $125–$150.

ANDERSEN, Hans Christian. *Fairy Tales.* 12 colored plates and numerous black-and-white illustrations by Arthur Rackham. Vellum. London, (1932). De luxe edition. One of 525 signed by the artist. $750–$1,000. Another edition: London, (1924). 12 color plates by Kay Nielsen. Full vellum or morocco. One of 500 signed by Nielsen. $1,250–$2,000.

ANDERSEN, Hans Christian. *Stories from Hans Andersen.* 28 color plates by Edmund Dulac. Vellum, silk ties. London, (1911). One of 750 signed by Dulac. $600–$700. Another issue: Pigskin. One of 100 on Japan paper. $800–$1,200.

ANDERSON, David. *The Enchanted Galleon.* Signed frontispiece photo by Ansel Adams. (San Francisco, 1930.) First edition. One of 60. Boxed. $200–$300.

ANDERSON, Maxwell. *You Who Have Dreams.* Blue boards. New York, 1925. First edition. One of 1,000. In dust jacket. $50–$75. Signed issue (25): $150–$175. Author's first book.

ANDERSON, Poul. *The Broken Sword.* Cloth. New York, (1954). First edition. In dust jacket. $75–$100.

ANDERSON, Poul. *Vault of the Ages.* Cloth. Philadelphia, (1952). First edition. In dust jacket. $75. Author's first book.

ANDERSON, Robert L. *Thwarted Ambitions.* Introduction by Sherwood Anderson. Wrappers. Marion, Va., (about 1935). First edition. $150–$200. Marion, (1935). Second edition. $50–$60.

ANDERSON, Sherwood, *Alice and the Lost Novel.* Boards. London, 1929. First edition. One of 530 signed. In dust jacket. $50–$75.

ANDERSON, Sherwood. *Beyond Desire.* Tan cloth. New York, (1932). First edition. One of 165 signed. $125–$150. Trade edition: Cloth. In dust jacket. $75–$85.

ANDERSON, Sherwood. *Dark Laughter.* Half vellum and boards. New York, 1925. First edition. One of 350 signed. Boxed. $100–$125. (There were also 20 copies lettered and signed by the author.) Trade edition: Black cloth. In dust jacket. $35.

ANDERSON, Sherwood. *Death in the Woods and Other Stories.* Boards. New York, (1933). First edition. In dust jacket. $60–$80.

ANDERSON, Sherwood. *Dreiser.* Wrappers. No place, no date. Harvest Press. (50 copies.) $150–$200.

ANDERSON, Sherwood. *Horses and Men.* Orange cloth. New York, 1923. First edition, first issue, with top edges stained orange. In dust jacket. $100–$150.

ANDERSON, Sherwood. *Many Marriages.* Black cloth. New York, 1923. First edition, first issue, with top edges stained orange. In dust jacket. $100–$125.

ANDERSON, Sherwood. *Marching Men.* Crimson cloth. New York, 1917. First edition. In dust jacket. $200–$300.

ANDERSON, Sherwood. *Mid-American Chants.* Yellow cloth. New York, 1918. First edition. In dust jacket. $125–$175.

ANDERSON, Sherwood. *The Modern Writer.* Boards. San Francisco, 1925. First edition. One of 950. Boxed $75–$100. Another issue: One of 50 on vellum, signed. $250–$300.

ANDERSON, Sherwood. *Nearer the Grass Roots.* Half cloth. San Francisco, 1929. Grabhorn printing. First edition. One of 500 signed. $125–$150.

ANDERSON, Sherwood. *A New Testament.* Half vellum and boards. New York, 1927. First edition. One of 265 large paper copies, signed. In slipcase. $125–$175. Trade edition: Cloth. In dust jacket. $35.

ANDERSON, Sherwood. *Puzzled America.* Cloth. New York, 1935. First edition. In dust jacket. $150–$175.

ANDERSON, Sherwood. *No Swank.* Cream-colored cloth. Philadelphia, 1934. First edition. One of 50 signed. $200–$300. Also, 950 unsigned. $75–$100.

ANDERSON, Sherwood. *Poor White.* Blue cloth. New York, 1920. First edition, first issue, with top edges stained blue. In dust jacket. $100–$175. London, (1921). First English edition. In dust jacket. $100–$125.

ANDERSON, Sherwood. *Sherwood Anderson's Notebook.* Boards and cloth. New York, 1926. One of 225 signed. In slipcase. $100–$125.

ANDERSON, Sherwood. *Tar: A Midwest Childhood.* Cloth. New York, 1926. First edition. In dust jacket. $40–$60. Another printing: New York, (1926). Boards. One of 350 signed. In glassine jacket and slipcase. $100–$150.

ANDERSON, Sherwood. *The Triumph of the Egg.* Plates. Green cloth. New York, 1921. First edition, first issue, with top edges stained yellow. In dust jacket. $50–$75.

ANDERSON, Sherwood. *Windy McPherson's Son.* Decorated brown cloth. New York, 1916. First edition. In dust jacket. $750–$1,000. Also, $600 (A, 1977). Author's first book.

ANDERSON, Sherwood. *Winesburg, Ohio.* Yellow cloth, paper label on spine. New York, 1919. First edition, first issue, with top stained yellow, end paper map at front, line 5 of page 86 reading "lay," and with broken type in the word "the" in line 3 of page 251. In dust jacket. $450–$600. Lacking jacket. $200–$250. Second issue, top unstained. In dust jacket. $250–$400. New York, 1978. Limited Editions Club. $40.

ANDRÉ, John. *Major André's Journal.* Edited by Henry Cabot Lodge. Facsimile maps, plans, and other illustrations. 2 vols., full vellum. Boston, 1903. First edition. One of 467. Boxed. $500–$600. Another issue: One of 10 on Japan vellum. $750–$1,000.

ANDREAS, A.T. *Atlas Map of Peoria County, Illinois.* 25 maps in color. Boards. Chicago, 1873. First edition. $300–$400.

ANDREAS, A.T. *History of Chicago.* Illustrated. 3 vols., morocco and cloth. Chicago, 1884–86. First edition. $300–$350. Another issue: Full morocco. $350–$450.

ANDREAS, A.T. *History of the State of Kansas.* Morocco or pictorial boards. Folding map. Chicago, 1883. First edition. $400–$500.

ANDREAS, A.T. *Illustrated Historical Atlas of the State of Iowa.* Colored maps and views. Three-quarters morocco. Chicago. 1875. $400–$600.

ANDREWS, Eliza Frances. *The War-Time Journal of a Georgia Girl, 1864–65.* 16 plates. Cloth. New York, 1908. First edition. $75–$100.

ANDREWS, Jane. *Ten Boys Who Lived on the Road from Long Ago to Now.* Illustrated by Charles Copeland. Pictorial cloth. Boston, 1886. First edition. $100–$125.

ANDREWS, William Loring. *Among My Books.* Vellum. New York, 1894. First edition. One of 2 printed on vellum. $5,000 (A, 1979).

ANDREWS, William Loring. *A Choice Collection of Books from the Aldine Presses.* Wrappers. New York, 1885. First edition. One of 50. $200–$300. Author's first book.

ANDREWS, William Loring. *An Essay on the Portraiture of the American Revolutionary War.* Green morocco. New York, 1896. First edition. One of 185. $100–$125. Another issue: One of 15 on Japan paper. $300–$400.

ANGEL in the House (The). Cloth, paper label. London, 1854. (By Coventry Patmore.) First edition. $100–$150. London, 1863. 2 vols., cloth. $75–$100.

ANNE of Geierstein; or, The Maiden of the Mist. 3 vols., boards, paper labels. Edinburgh, 1829. (By Sir Walter Scott.) First edition. $250–$450. Also, $100 (A, 1973).

ANNUAL Anthology (The). 2 vols., old mottled calf. Bristol, England, 1799 and 1800. First editions. With leaf C3 (page 37) of Vol. 2 uncanceled, printing the uncorrected version of line 3, stanza X, of Robert Southey's "Battle of Blenheim." $150–$200.

ANNUAL Review: History of St. Louis, etc. Folding map. 47 pp., wrappers. St. Louis, 1854. $200–$250.

ANTHOLOGY of Younger Poets (An). Edited by Oliver Wells. Boards. Philadelphia, 1932. First edition. One of 500. In dust jacket. $50–$60. (Contains five poems by William Faulkner.)

ANTIQUARY (The). 3 vols., boards. Edinburgh, 1816. (By Sir Walter Scott.) First edition, with pages 27–30 of Vol. 1 uncanceled. $350–$450.

ANTI-TEXASS Legion (The): Protest of Some Free Men, States, and Presses Against the Texass Rebellion. 72 pp., wrappers. New York, 1844. $200–$350.

ANTONINUS, Brother. *A Canticle to the Waterbirds.* Illustrated. Cloth. Berkeley, 1968. (By William Everson.) First edition. One of 200 signed. (Issued without dust jacket.) $75–$100. Trade issue: Wrappers (2,000 copies). $15–$20.

ANTONINUS, Brother. *The Last Crusade.* Half vellum and cloth. (Berkeley, 1969.) (By William Everson.) One of 165 signed. In acetate dust jacket. $125–$150.

ANTONINUS, Brother. *Novum Psalterium PII XII.* Folio, blue morocco. Los Angeles, 1955. (By William Everson.) One of 48. $350–$450.

ANTONINUS, Brother. *The Poet Is Dead: A Memorial for Robinson Jeffers.* Boards and leather. San Francisco, 1964. Auerhahn Press. (By William Everson.) First edition. One of 205 signed. In plain white dust jacket. $125–$150. (Five copies were issued in a slipcase. Value: about $200.)

ANTONINUS, Brother. *Who Is She That Looketh Forth as the Morning.* Boards. Santa Barbara, 1972. (By William Everson.) First edition. One of 250 signed. In acetate dust jacket. $75–$100.

APOCRYPHA (The). Authorized version. Full-page woodcuts by Stephen Gooden, Eric Jones, etc. Folio, black vellum. London, 1929. Cresset Press. One of 30 on handmade paper with an extra set of illustrations signed by the artists. Boxed. $600–$800. Another issue: Boards. One of 450. Boxed. $250–$275.

APOLLINAIRE, Guillaume. *The Poet Assassinated.* Translated by Matthew Josephson. Boards. New York, 1923. First American edition. $50.

APPEAL by the Convention of Michigan . . . in Relation to the Boundary Question Between Michigan and Ohio. 176 pp., stitched. Detroit, 1835. $375. (A, 1967).

APPEAL to the American People (An): Being an Account of the Persecutions of the Church of Latter Day Saints. 60 pp., wrappers. Cincinnati, 1840. Second edition. $500–$600.

APPEAL (An) to the Clergy of the Church of Scotland. 12 pp., stitched, without wrappers. Edinburgh, 1875. (By Robert Louis Stevenson.) First edition. $5,000 and up. Also, $3,200 (A, 1925). (About 3 copies known.)

APPERLEY, C.J. See Nimrod. Also see *Memoirs of the Life of the Late John Mytton, Esq.*

APPLEGATE, Jesse. *A Day with the Cow Column in 1843.* Pictorial cloth. Chicago, 1934. Caxton Club. One of 300. $75–$100. Another edition: (Portland), 1952. One of 225. $75–$100.

APPLEGATE, Jesse. *Recollections of My Boyhood.* 99 pp., pictorial wrappers. Roseburg, Ore., 1914. First edition. $750.

APULEIUS, Lucius. *The XI Bookes of the Golden Asse.* Translated by William Adlington. Printed on handmade paper in an Italian semi-gothic type, initial letters in red and blue. Folio, decorated green boards, linen spine. Chelsea (London), 1924. Ashendene Press. One of 165. Boxed. $1,000–$1,250. Also, $750 (A, 1979). Another issue: One of 13 on vellum. Full morocco. $4,000–$6,000. Also, $3,600 (A, 1977).

ARAGON, Louis. *The Red Front.* Translated by E. E. Cummings. Wrappers. Chapel Hill, (1933). First American edition. $250.

ARISTOPHANES. *Lysistrata.* 8 plates by Aubrey Beardsley. Boards. London, 1896. One of 100. $500–$750. London, (1926). Translated by Jack Lindsay. Illustrated by Norman Lindsay. Half morocco. One of 725 signed by the artist. $200–$300. New York, 1934. Limited Editions Club. Translated by Gilbert Seldes. Illustrated by Pablo Picasso. Boards. Boxed. $1,250–$1,500. (Note: There is sometimes offered with this book a set of 6 proofs of the original Picasso etchings for the edition, each signed by Picasso. There were 150 issued in cloth portfolios. $2,500–$3,000, or more.)

ARISTOTLE. *Politics and Poetics.* Illustrated by Leonard Baskin. Buckram. (New York), 1964. Limited Editions Club. Boxed. $80–$125.

ARKWRIGHT, William. *The Pointer & His Predecessors.* Illustrated. Half or full morocco. London, 1906. First edition, deluxe issue. One of 750. $400–$500. Trade issue: cloth. $200–$250.

ARLEN, Michael. *The Green Hat.* Cloth. London, (1924). First edition. In dust jacket. $75–$100. New York, 1925. (Acting version.) Boards. One of 175 signed. $75–$100.

ARLEN, Michael. *The London Venture.* Illustrated. Pictorial cloth. London, 1919. First edition. In dust jacket. $75–$100. Author's first book.

ARLEN, Michael. *May Fair.* Cloth. London, (1925). First edition. In dust jacket. $50.

ARMAGEDDON: A Fragment: Avalon. Wrappers. Charleston, S.C., 1923. First edition. Contains poems by John Crowe Ransom and others. $200 and up.

ARMES, George A. *Ups and Downs of an Army Officer.* Illustrated. Pictorial cloth. Washington, 1900. First edition. $200–$250.

ARMITAGE, John. *The History of Brazil.* 2 portraits. 2 vols., boards. London, 1836. First edition. $600–$800.

ARMOUR, John P. *Edenindia; A Tale of Adventure.* Pictorial cloth. New York, 1907. First edition. $40–$50.

ARMOUR, Samuel. *History of Orange County, California.* Illustrated. Cloth. Los Angeles, 1921. $100–$125.

ARMSMEAR: The Home, the Arm and the Armory of Col. Samuel Colt: A Memorial.

Plates, map. Cloth. New York, 1866. First edition. Inscribed by Mrs. Colt. $400–$500. Also, $275 (A, 1978). Another issue: Full morocco. Presentation copy from Mrs. Colt. $1,000.

ARMSTRONG, A. N. *Oregon: A Brief History and Description of Oregon and Washington.* Cloth. Chicago, 1857. First edition. $350–$500.

ARMSTRONG, Moses K. *History and Resources of Dakota, Montana and Idaho.* Map. Printed wrappers. Yanktown, Dakota Territory, 1866. First edition. $3,500–$4,000.

ARNO, PETER. *Oops, Dearie!* Red cloth. New York, 1927. First edition. In dust jacket. $100–$125. Author's first book.

ARNOLD, Henry V. *The Early History of the Devil's Lake Country,* 105 pp., printed wrappers. Larimore, N. D., 1920. First edition. $100–$125.

ARNOLD, Henry V. *The History of Old Pembina, 1780–1872.* Wrappers. Larimore, N. D., 1917. First edition. $100–$150.

ARNOLD, Matthew. See: A. (pseudonym—first entry in list). Also see *Alaric at Rome.*

ARNOLD, Matthew. *Cromwell: A Prize Poem.* Wrappers. Oxford, 1843. First edition. $400–$600.

ARNOLD, Matthew. *Culture and Anarchy.* Cloth. London, 1869. First edition. $150–$200.

ARNOLD, Matthew. *Discourses in America.* Cloth. London, 1885. First edition. $75–$125.

ARNOLD, Matthew, *Essays in Criticism.* Cloth. London, 1865. First edition, with one ad leaf. $150–$200. Second series: Cloth. London, 1888. First edition. $150–$200.

ARNOLD, Matthew. *God and the Bible.* Cloth. London, 1875. First edition. $75–$150.

ARNOLD, Matthew. *Last Essays on Church and Religion.* Cloth. London, 1877. First edition. $125–$150.

ARNOLD, Matthew. *Merope: A Tragedy.* Cloth. London, 1858. First edition. $125–$150.

ARNOLD, Matthew. *Mixed Essays.* Cloth. London, 1879. First edition. $100–$125.

ARNOLD, Matthew. *New Poems.* Green cloth. London, 1867. First edition. $150–$250.

ARNOLD, Matthew. *Poems.* Cloth. London, 1853. First edition. $125–$150. London, 1855. (Second Series.) Cloth. First edition. $125–$150. Boston, 1856. Cloth. $75.

AROUND the Horn in '49. See *Journal of the Hartford Union Mining and Trading Company.*

ARRANGEMENT of Places. Will Each Gentleman Kindly Take in to Dinner the Lady Seated on His Right. 12 pp., wrappers. (Program of 70th birthday dinner for Mark Twain at Delmonico's.) (New York), 1905. $75–$125.

ARRIGHI, Ludovico. *The Calligraphic Models of Ludovico degli Arrighi.* 64 pp., facsimile. Marbled boards and vellum. Paris, 1926. One of 300. $600–$800. Also, $400 (A, 1979).

ARRINGTON, Alfred W. See Summerfield, Charles.

ARTHUR Mervyn; or Memoirs of the Year 1793. By the Author of Wieland. 2 vols., calf. Philadelphia, 1799–1800. (By Charles Brockden Brown.) First edition. $400–$600, or more. (Note: The 1799 volume and the Second Part are usually listed separately in catalogues and bibliographies; relative values: $200 and up for the first, $150 and up for the second. For first English edition, see author entry.)

ARTHUR, T. S. *Ten Nights in a Bar-Room, and What I Saw There.* Cloth. Philadelphia, 1854. First edition, first issue, with both Lippincott and Bradley named in imprint and woodcut frontispiece by Van Ingen. $150–$200.

ARTHUR, T. S. *True Riches.* Cloth. Boston, 1852. First edition. $35–$50.

ARTHUR, T. S. *Words for the Wise.* Cloth. Philadelphia, 1851. First edition. $40–$50.

ASHBEE, Henry Spencer. *An Iconography of Don Quixote, 1605–1895.* Half cloth. London, 1895. First edition. $200–$300.

ASHBERY, John. *The New Spirit.* Pictorial wrappers. New York, (1970). First edition. One of 65 signed. $75–$125. Also, 100 unsigned. $25–$30.

ASHBERY, John. *Some Trees.* Foreword by W. H. Auden. Cloth. New Haven, 1956. First edition. In dust jacket. $100–$150.

ASHBERY, John. *Sunrise in Suburbia.* Wrappers. New York, 1968. First edition. One of 100 signed. $75. Also, 26 copies lettered A to Z. $150.

ASHBERY, John. *Turandot and Other Poems.* Illustrated. Wrappers. New York, 1953. First edition. One of 300. $400–$600. Author's first book.

ASHDOWN, Clifford. *The Adventures of Romney Pringle.* Cloth. London, 1902. (By R. Austin Freeman and J. J. Pitcairn.) First edition. $1,000–$1,500.

ASHE, Thomas. *Travels in America.* 3 vols., boards. London, 1808. First edition. $500–$600.

ASHENDENE Press. *See Descriptive Bibliography, etc.*

ASHLEY, Clifford W. *The Yankee Whaler.* Plates, some in color. Half cloth and boards. Boston, 1926. First edition. One of 156 signed, with original drawing. Boxed. $600–$800. Ordinary issue: $200–$300.

ASHLEY, William H. *The West of William H. Ashley.* Edited by Dale L. Morgan. Illustrated. Pictorial buckram. Denver, 1964. One of 750. $75–$100. De luxe issue: Half calf. One of 250 signed. Boxed. $250–$300.

ASHTON, John. *Real Sailor-Songs.* Boards, vellum spine. London, 1891. First edition. $100–$150.

ASHTON, Warren T. *Hatchie, the Guardian Slave.* Illustrated. Black cloth. Boston, 1853. (By William Taylor Adams.) First edition. $75–$100.

ASIMOV, Isaac. *The End of Eternity.* Cloth. Garden City, 1955. First edition. In dust jacket. $75–$100.

ASIMOV, Isaac. *Foundation.* Cloth. New York, (1951). First edition, first binding. In dust jacket. $150–$200.

ASIMOV, Isaac. *Foundation and Empire.* Red boards. New York, (1952). First edition, first binding, with spine imprint 2.2 cm across. In dust jacket. $125–$150.

ASIMOV, Isaac. *I, Robot.* Cloth. New York (1950). First edition, first binding. In dust jacket. $150–$200. Wrappers: $100–$150.

ASIMOV, Isaac. *Pebble in the Sky.* Tan cloth. Garden City, 1950. First edition. In dust jacket. $125–$150. Author's first book.

ASIMOV, Isaac. *Second Foundation.* Blue boards. (New York, 1953.) First edition, first binding. In dust jacket. $125–$150.

"ASK Mamma"; or, The Richest Commoner in England. 13 full-page color plates and 69 woodcuts by John Leech. 13 parts, red wrappers. London, (1857) and 1858. (By Robert Smith Surtees.) First edition. $600–$750, or more. London, 1858. Pictorial cloth. First book edition. $175–$250.

ASTON, James. *First Lesson.* Yellow cloth. London, (1932). (By T. H. White.) First edition. In dust jacket. $100–$125.

ASTON, James. *They Winter Abroad.* Yellow cloth. London, 1932. (By T. H. White.) First edition. In dust jacket. $100–$150. New York, 1932. Turquoise cloth. First American edition. In dust jacket. $75–$100.

ATALANTIS. Wrappers. New York, 1832. (By William Gilmore Simms.) First edition. $250–$350. Philadelphia, 1848. Cloth. $150–$200.

ATHELING, William. *The Issue at Hand.* Edited by James Blish. Cloth. Chicago, 1964. (By James Blish.) First edition. In dust jacket. $35–$50.

ATHERTON, Gertrude. See Lin, Frank.

ATHERTON, Gertrude. *Black Oxen.* Cloth. New York, (1923). First edition. One of 250 signed. In dust jacket. $75–$125.

ATHERTON, Gertrude. *The Conqueror.* Dark red cloth, gilt top. New York, 1902. First edition, first state, with page numerals on page 546 in upper left corner. $50.

ATHERTON, Gertrude. *What Dreams May Come.* Cloth. London, 1889. First English edition (of author's first book, which was issued in America under the pseudonym Frank Lin, which see). $150.

ATHERTON, William. *Narrative of the Suffering & Defeat of the North-Western Army, Under General Winchester.* Leather-backed boards, printed paper label. Frankfort, Ky., 1842. First edition. $150–$200.

ATKINSON, Eleanor. *Greyfriars Bobby.* Cloth. New York, 1912. First edition. In dust jacket. $75–$100.

ATTACHE (The); or, Sam Slick in England, (Second Series.) 2 vols., ribbed plum-colored cloth. London, 1844. (By Thomas Chandler Haliburton.) First edition, with 48 pages of ads at end of Vol. 2. $150–$200.

ATTERLEY, Joseph. *A Voyage to the Moon.* Boards. New York, 1827. (By George Tucker.) First edition. $400–$500.

ATWATER, Caleb. *A History of the State of Ohio.* Calf. Cincinnati, (1838). First edition. $150–$175.

ATWATER, Caleb. *Mysteries of Washington City.* Boards and leather. Washington, 1844. First edition. $125–$150.

ATWATER, Caleb. *Remarks Made on a Tour to Prairie du Chien; Thence to Washington City.* Boards. Columbus, Ohio, 1831. First edition. $150–$250.

AUBREY, Frank, *The Devil-Tree of El Dorado.* Illustrated. Cloth. London, 1896. (By Frank Atkins.) First edition. $250–$300.

AUBREY, Frank. *King of the Dead; A Weird Adventure.* Cloth. London, 1903. (By Frank Atkins.) First edition. $300–$350.

AUCHINCLOSS, Louis. See Lee, Andrew.

AUDEN, W. H. See Baudelaire, Charles; Rich, Adrienne Cecile.

AUDEN, W. H. *The Age of Anxiety.* Cloth. New York, (1947). First edition. In dust jacket. $75–$100. London, (1948). First English edition. In dust jacket. $50–$75.

AUDEN, W. H. *Another Time.* Cloth. New York, (1940). First edition. In dust jacket.

$100–$125. London, (1940). First English edition. (Issued as *Poems by W. H. Auden: Another Time.*) In dust jacket. $100–$125.

AUDEN, W. H. *The Collected Poetry.* Cloth. New York, (1945). First edition, first printing, with title page in green and black. In dust jacket. $100–$150.

AUDEN, W. H. *Collected Shorter Poems, 1930–1944.* Blue cloth. London, (1950). First edition. In dust jacket. $75–$125.

AUDEN, W. H. *Collected Shorter Poems, 1927–1957.* Cloth. London, (1966). First edition. In dust jacket. $50–$75.

AUDEN, W. H. *The Dance of Death.* Boards. London, (1933). First edition. In dust jacket. $75–$125.

AUDEN, W. H. *The Double Man.* Cloth. New York, (1941). First edition. In dust jacket. $75.

AUDEN, W. H. *The Enchafed Flood.* Cloth. New York, (1950). First edition. In dust jacket. $50.

AUDEN, W. H. *Epithalamion.* Unbound sheet, printed both sides, folded. Princeton, 1939. First edition. $300–$350. (About 100 printed.)

AUDEN, W. H. *For the Time Being.* Boards and cloth. New York, (1944). First edition. In dust jacket. $50–$75. London, (1945). Cloth. First English edition. In dust jacket. $50.

AUDEN, W. H. *Homage to Clio.* Printed wrappers. London, 1960. Advance uncorrected proof copy. $100–$125. London, 1960. Plum-colored cloth. First published English edition. In dust jacket. $35–$50.

AUDEN, W. H. *Look, Stranger!* Cloth. London, (1936). First edition. In dust jacket. $100–$150. (For first American edition, see Auden, *On This Island.*)

AUDEN, W. H. *Louis MacNeice: A Memorial Address.* Printed wrappers. London, 1963. First edition. $75–$100.

AUDEN, W. H. *Marginalia.* Engravings by Laurence Scott. Oblong, printed wrappers. (Cambridge, Mass., 1966). Ibex Press. First edition. One of 150 signed by author and artist. $125–$150. Another issue: One of 26 signed. $200–$250.

AUDEN, W. H. *New Year Letter.* Cloth. (London, 1941.) First edition. $75.

AUDEN, W. H. *On This Island.* Brown cloth. New York, (1937). First American edition. In dust jacket. $75–$100. (Note: The first edition of this was published in London, 1936, as *Look, Stranger!,* which see.)

AUDEN, W. H. *The Orators: An English Study.* Cloth. London, (1932). First edition. In dust jacket. $250–$300.

AUDEN, W. H. *Our Hunting Fathers.* Wrappers. (Cambridge), 1935. First edition. One of 22. $500–$1,000. Also, one of 5 (from the 22) on Incudine paper and lettered A to E. $1,000.

AUDEN, W. H. *Poem.* Wrappers. (Bryn Mawr), 1933. First edition. One of 5 on Fabriano paper (from an edition of 22). (Note: I can find no sales record for this except for the copy inscribed to T. S. Eliot and with a presentation autograph letter, signed, sold at Sotheby's in 1966 to a New York dealer for $624.) Another issue: One of 5 on Kelmscott paper. $315 (catalogue price).

AUDEN, W. H. *Poems.* Printed blue-green wrappers. London, (1930). First edition. In tissue dust jacket. $500–$750. Author's first published book. New York, (1934). Orange cloth. First American edition. In dust jacket. $50–$80. (Note: In 1928 Stephen Spender, the poet's friend, hand-printed "about 45" copies of a paperbound *Poems,* dated 1928 and printed at Frognal, Hampstead, England. A copy inscribed by Spender and later by Auden brought $8,500 at auction in 1973.)

AUDEN, W. H. *Selected Poems*. Cloth. London, (1938). First edition. In dust jacket. $100–$125. London, (1968). Boards. $20–$25.

AUDEN, W. H. *The Shield of Achilles*. Boards. New York, (1955). First edition. In dust jacket. $40–$50. London, (1955). First English edition. In dust jacket. $35.

AUDEN, W. H. *Some Poems*. Board. London, (1940). First edition. In dust jacket. $50–$75.

AUDEN, W. H. *Sonnet*. Wrappers. (Cambridge), 1935. First edition. One of 22. $500–$1,000.

AUDEN, W. H. *Spain*. Stiff covered wrappers. (London, 1937). First edition. $75–$100.

AUDEN, W. H. *Three Songs for St. Cecelia's Day*. Wrappers. (New York), 1941. First edition. One of 250. $200–$500.

AUDEN, W. H. *Two Songs*. Wrappers. New York, 1968. First edition. One of 100 signed. $100–$125.

AUDEN, W. H., and Isherwood, Christopher. *The Ascent of F6*. Cloth. London, (1936). First edition. In dust jacket. $100–$150.

AUDEN, W. H., and Isherwood, Christopher. *The Dog Beneath the Skin, or, Where Is Francis?* Cloth. London, (1935). First edition. In dust jacket. $100–$125. New York, 1935. Cloth. First American edition. In dust jacket. $40.

AUDEN, W. H., and Isherwood, Christopher. *On the Frontier*. Cloth. London, (1938). First edition. In dust jacket. $100–$150.

AUDEN, W. H., and MacNeice, Louis. *Letters from Iceland*. Plates, folding map. Green cloth. London, (1937). First edition. In dust jacket. $100–$150.

AUDSLEY, George Ashdown. *The Art of Organ-Building*. Illustrated. 2 vols., cloth. New York, 1905. $250–$300.

AUDSLEY, George Ashdown. *The Ornamental Arts of Japan*. 70 plates in gold and colors, 31 in monochrome, loose in 5 cloth portfolios. 2 vols., folio. New York, 1882–84. Artist's proofs edition. One of 50 signed. $600–$750. Another issue: 2 vols., morocco. (Not signed.) $500–$600. New York, 1883–84. Plates loose in 4 folders. One of 500 signed. $400–$500. New York, 1883–85. 2 vols. in 4 folders. One of 60. $400–$500.

AUDSLEY, George Ashdown, and Bowes, J. L. *The Keramic Art of Japan*. 63 plates, 42 in gold and colors; 4 plates of potters' marks, other illustrations. Morocco and cloth. Liverpool, 1875. First edition. $750–$1,000. London, 1881. Cloth. $100–$150.

AUDUBON, John James. *The Birds of America from Original Drawings*. 435 double elephant folio hand-colored plates without text. 87 parts in wrappers, or 4 leatherbound double elephant folio volumes. London, 1827–38. First edition. Excessively rare in the original parts. The last known sale (1974) was at world record price of $246,500. Two sets of the four leatherbound volumes were sold at auction in New York City in 1977—one at $320,000 and another at $360,000 (each with a 10 percent gallery surcharge). These sales successively set a world record price for a printed book at auction. New York, 1840–44. 500 colored plates. 100 parts in wrappers or 7 vols., full or half leather. First American and first octavo edition. $25,000 and up for fine copies. For various other 19th Century editions, many of which are imperfect when offered, consult the detailed records in the annual volumes of *American Book Prices Current*. New York, 1937. Edited by William Vogt. 500 plates in color. One-volume edition. Buckram. Limited issue on all-rag paper. Boxed. $200–$300. Trade edition: Buckram. In dust jacket. $100–$150. London, 1972–73. (*The Birds of America: A Selection of Plates*.) 2 vols., folio, half cloth. One of 250. $800–$1,000. Another issue: One of 1,000. $500–$600. Amsterdam, 1972–73. Facsimile edition. 435 color plates, 4 vols. in 6, folio, with a clothbound facsimile edition of Audubon's *Synopsis*. $4,180 (A, 1976).

AUDUBON, John James. *Delineations of American Scenery and Character*. Cloth. New

York, 1926. First edition. One of 42 large paper copies. $400–$500. Trade edition, same date. In dust jacket. $75–$100. (500 copies with London imprint.)

AUDUBON, John James. *Journal of John James Audubon, Made During His Trip to New Orleans in 1820–21*. Edited by Howard Corning. 2 plates. Boards and cloth. Boston, 1929. One of 250. $150–$200.

AUDUBON, John James. *Journal of John James Audubon, Made While Obtaining Subscriptions to His "Birds of America," 1840–1843*. Edited by Howard Corning. Plate. Boston, 1929. One of 250. $150–$200.

AUDUBON, John James. *The Original Water-Color Paintings by John James Audubon for the Birds of America*. Edited by Marshall B. Davidson. 2 vols., brown cloth. New York, 1966. First edition. Boxed. $150–$200.

AUDUBON, John James. *Ornithological Biography; or, An Account of the Habits of the Birds of the United States of America*. 5 vols., cloth. Edinburgh, 1831–49 (actually 1839). First edition of the text volume to accompany the double elephant folios of *The Birds of America*. $750–$1,000. Also, in half leather, $350 (A, 1977).

AUDUBON, John James. *The Quadrupeds of North America*. See Audubon and Bachman, *The Viviparous Quadrupeds, etc.*

AUDUBON, John James. *A Synopsis of the Birds of America*. Cloth, paper label. Edinburgh, 1839. First edition. $500–$750.

AUDUBON, John James, and Bachman, John. *The Viviparous Quadrupeds of North America*. 150 colored plates without text. 30 parts in wrappers, or 3 vols. (Vol. 1, 1845; Vol. 2, 1846; Vol. 3, 1848), folio, half morocco. New York, 1845–48. (Text issued, New York, 1846–53. 31 parts in wrappers or 3 vols., cloth, dated 1846, 1851, and 1853, the 3 vols. sometimes bound in 2. A 93-page supplement, with 6 colored plates was issued in 1854). First edition complete (consisting of the 3 plate volumes, the 3 text volumes, and the supplement). Rarely offered. The last complete set in the auction records brought $5,500 in 1970, but the recent sharp increases in color plate values make that price useless as a guide. Examples of mixed sets from recent auction records: 5 vols. (3 vols. in 2 of plates, 3 vols. of text, Vol. 1 and 2 being first editions), $22,000 (1977) and 5 vols. (3 vols. of text in second edition, 2 vols. of plates), $20,000 (1977). New York, 1849–54. Reissue under the title *The Quadrupeds of North America*. 155 colored plates (including all except one from the supplement to the original edition). 31 parts in wrappers, or 3 vols., morocco or half morocco, dated 1849, 1851, and 1854. First octavo edition. $12,000–$15,000. Numerous mixed sets and later editions widely available.

AUDUBON, John Woodhouse. *Audubon's Western Journal, 1849–50*. Edited by Maria R. Audubon. Folding map, 6 plates. Cloth. Cleveland, 1906. Reprint of Audubon's extremely rare and virtually unobtainable *Illustrated Notes of an Expedition Through Mexico and California*. $175–$200.

AUDUBON, John Woodhouse. *The Drawings of John Woodhouse Audubon, Illustrating His Adventures Through Mexico and California*. 34 full-page illustrations, including 2 in color. Folio, boards and cloth. San Francisco, 1957. Book Club of California. Grabhorn printing. One of 400. In plain dust jacket. $250–$300.

AUDUBON, Maria R. *Audubon and His Journals*. Edited by Elliot Coues. Plates. 2 vols. cloth. New York, 1897. First edition. $300–$400. New York, 1900. 2 vols., cloth. $200.

AUSCHER, Ernest Simon. *A History and Description of French Porcelain*. 24 plates in color. Morocco. London, 1905. First edition, limited. $200–$300.

AUSTEN, Jane. See *Elizabeth Bennet; Emma; Mansfield Park; Northanger Abbey; Pride and Prejudice; Sense and Sensibility*.

AUSTIN, Edward S. *The Housekeepers' Manual*. Wrappers. Chicago, 1869. First edition. $125–$175.

AUSTIN, Jane G. *Standish of Standish*. Tan cloth. Boston, 1889. First edition. $50–$75. (Note: Copies of the same date in gray-green cloth are of a later issue.)

AUSTIN, Mary. *The Flock*. Cloth. Boston, 1906. First edition. In dust jacket. $50–$60.

AUSTIN, Mary. *The Land of Little Rain*. Illustrated. Pictorial cloth. Boston, 1903. First edition. $75–$125. Author's first book. Boston, 1950. Illustrated by Ansel Adams. In dust jacket. $100–$150.

AUSTIN, Mary. *What the Mexican Conference Really Means*. 14 pp., wrappers. New York, (1915). First edition. $75–$100.

AUSTIN, Mary, and Adams, Ansel. *Taos Pueblo*. Photographs by Adams and text by Mrs. Austin. Folio, cloth, pigskin spine. San Francisco, 1930. Grabhorn printing. First edition. One of 107 (Johnson says 108) signed by author and illustrator. $4,000–$5,000.

AUSTIN, Mary, and Martin, Ann. *Suffrage and Government*. 14 pp., printed wrappers. New York, 1914. $75–$100.

AUSTIN, Stephen F. *Esposicion al Publico sobre los Asuntos de Tejas*. 32 pp., stitched. Mexico, 1835. First edition, with page 29 misnumbered 31. $7,500–$12,000. (A Texas dealer sold a copy to another dealer in 1977 for $8,000.) Presentation copy, $12,000 (sold by another Texas dealer in 1977).

AUTHENTIC Narrative of the Seminole War (An), and of the Miraculous Escape of Mrs. Mary Godfrey, and Her Four Female Children. Folding frontispiece in color, 24 pp., plain wrappers. Providence, R.I., 1836. $750–$1,000. New York, 1836. $750–$1,000.

AUTHORS Take Sides on the Spanish War. Wrappers. London, (1937). Left Review. $200–$300.

AUTHORSHIP: A Tale. Boards and cloth. Boston, 1930. (By John Neal.) First edition. $100–$150.

AUTOCRAT of the Breakfast Table (The). Illustrated. Cloth. Boston, 1858. (By Oliver Wendell Holmes.) First edition, first issue, with engraved half title, with period after word "Company" in imprint, and with left end paper at back headed "Poetry and the Drama" and right "School Books." $400–$600. (Fine copies increasingly rare. An unsolved controversy still exists over whether the first binding bore a five-ring or four-ring decoration on the spine. Jacob Blanck was uncertain, but some bookmen insist that the five-ring binding was the first. About six are known, according to Ronald Randall, a San Francisco bookseller.) Boston, 1859. Illustrated. Cloth. Large Paper edition. $250–$300. New York, 1955. Limited Editions Club. $50–$65.

AVEDON, Richard (photographer). See Baldwin, James; Capote, Truman.

AVIRETT, James B. *The Memoirs of Gen. Turner Ashby and His Compeers*. Portrait. Cloth. Baltimore, 1867. First edition. $125–$150.

AYESHA, The Maid of Kars. By the Author of "Zohrab," etc. 3 vols., boards. London, 1834. (By James Morier.) First edition. $300–$350.

B

B., A. *The Six Letters of A. B. on the Differences Between Great Britain and the United States of America.* Wrappers. London, 1807. First edition. $75–$100.

B., E. B. *Sonnets.* By E.B.B. 47 pp., without wrappers. Reading, England, 1847 (actually printed about 1883–90). (By Elizabeth Barrett Browning.) Thomas J. Wise's forgery—the fake first edition of "Sonnets from the Portuguese," which actually appeared first in the second edition of *Poems,* 1850, which see under author entry (Barrett and Browning); for later editions, see entry for *Sonnets from the Portuguese* under "Elizabeth Browning." The Wise forgery, bound in morocco, sold for a record (at the time) $1,250 at auction in 1930. Following its exposure as a fake in 1934, the value declined, but in 1967 at a sale in London featuring Wise forgeries a New York City dealer paid $1,680 at auction for a copy in morocco. This remarkable record continued in the 1976 auction season when a copy that had belonged to the late John Carter, who was chiefly instrumental in exposing Wise (see the entry under his name elsewhere in this book), came to auction in London and was sold to a book dealer for $3,096. This record continued into the 1979 season, when the Wise forgery brought $3,200 at auction in New York.

B., F. *The Kasidah of Haji Abdu El-Yezdi.* Translated and annotated by his friend and pupil, F. B. (Sir Richard Burton is translator). Yellow wrappers. London, (1880). First edition, first issue, without Quaritch imprint. $1,000 and up. Also, rebound in morocco, $600 (A,1979).

B., H. *The Bad Child's Book of Beasts.* Pictorial boards. Oxford, (1896). (By Hilaire Belloc.) First edition. $150–$200.

B., J. K. *The Lorgnette.* By J. K. B. Illustrated. Oblong, cloth. New York, (1886). (By John Kendrick Bangs.) First edition. $250. Author's first book.

BABB, James T. *A Bibliography of the Writings of William McFee.* Cloth. Garden City, 1931. First edition. One of 360 signed by McFee. Boxed. $125–$150.

BABBITT, E.D. *The Principles of Light and Color.* Illustrated. Cloth. New York, 1878. Second edition. $150–$175. East Orange, N.J., (1896). Cloth. $75–$100.

BABBITT, E.L. *The Allegheny Pilot.* 16 maps. 64 pp., wrappers. Freeport, Pa., 1855. First edition. $150–$250.

BACHELLER, Irving. *Eben Holden.* Cloth. Boston, (1900). First edition, first state, with line 13 on page 400 reading "go to fur," and with pine cones on spine with rounded top. $100–$150. (Later issue reads "go tew fur" and has flat-topped cones.)

BACON, Sir Francis. *The Essayes or Counsels Civill and Morall.* Folio, vellum. London, 1928. Cresset Press. Vellum. One of 250. $300–$400. Another issue: Pigskin. One of 8 on vellum. $8,080 (A, 1979). New York, 1944. Limited Editions Club. $100–$125.

BAHR, Jerome. *All Good Americans.* Preface by Ernest Hemingway. Blue cloth. New York, 1937. First edition. In dust jacket. $50–$75. Reissued in yellow cloth, 1939 (with "A" on copyright page—an exception to the Scribner method of marking only first editions with an "A"). $20.

BAILEY, Washington. *A Trip to California in 1853.* Portrait. Printed wrappers. (LeRoy, Ill.), 1915. First edition, with errata slip. $300–$350.

BAILY, Francis. *Journal of a Tour in Unsettled Parts of North America in 1796 & 1797.* Decorated cloth. London, 1856. First edition. $550–$750.

BAINBRIDGE, George C. *The Fly-Fisher's Guide*. Colored frontispiece and 7 colored plates. Half leather. Liverpool, 1816. First edition. $500–$600. Another issue: Morocco. One of 12. $800–$1,200.

BAIRD, Joseph A. *California's Pictorial Letter Sheets, 1849–1869*. San Francisco, 1967. Grabhorn printing. One of 475 signed. In plain dust jacket. $125–$250.

BAIRD, Spencer F.;Brewer, T.M.; and Ridgway, R. *The Water Birds of North America.* Hand-colored illustrations. 2 vols., cloth. Boston, 1884. First edition. $500–$600.

BAKER, Charles H. Collins. *Lely and the Stuart Portrait Painters*. 240 reproductions, some in color. 2 vols., buckram. London, 1912. One of 375. $400–$500. Another issue: Vellum. One of 30, with an extra set of plates. $800–$1,250.

BAKER, Charles H. Collins, and Constable, W.G. *English Painting of the Sixteenth and Seventeenth Centuries*. 82 collotype plates. Half leather. London, 1930. $200–$300.

BAKER, D.W.C. (compiler). *A Texas Scrap-Book*. Cloth. New York, (1875). First edition. $200–$300.

BAKER, George P. *The Pilgrim Spirit: A Pageant . . . Landing of the Pilgrims*. Cloth. Boston, 1921. First edition, first issue, with the name "Brewster" on page 74. (Some with errata slip.) $150–$200. (Note: Contains contributions by Robert Frost and Edwin Arlington Robinson.)

BAKER, Hozial H. *Overland Journey to Carson Valley, Utah*. Woodcut frontispiece and other illustrations. 38 pp., yellow printed wrappers. Seneca Falls, N.Y., 1861. First edition. $3,500–$5,000. San Francisco, 1973. Book Club of California. In plain dust jacket. $50.

BALDWIN, James. *Giovanni's Room*. Boards and cloth. New York, 1956. First edition. In dust jacket. $150–$200.

BALDWIN, James. *Go Tell It on the Mountain*. Cloth. New York, 1953. First edition. In dust jacket. $300–$400. Advance copy in jacket wrappers. $400. Author's first book.

BALDWIN, James. *If Beale Street Could Talk*. Leatherette. New York, 1974. First edition. One of 250 signed. Boxed. $50–$60.

BALDWIN, James. *Nothing Personal*. Illustrated by Richard Avedon. Boards. New York, 1964. First edition. Boxed. $175–$200.

BALDWIN, James. *A Story of the Golden Age*. Illustrated by Howard Pyle. Decorated brown cloth. New York, 1887. First edition. $150.

BALDWIN, James. *The Story of Siegfried*. Illustrated by Howard Pyle. Pictorial cloth. New York, 1882. First edition. $150.

BALDWIN, Joseph G. *The Flush Times of Alabama and Mississippi*. Blue cloth. New York, 1853. First edition. $200–$300. Author's first book.

BALLOU, Hosea. *A Candid Review of a Pamphlet Entitled "A Candid Reply."* Calf. Portsmouth, N.H., (1809). First edition. $50–$60.

BALLOU, Hosea. *Treatise on Atonement*. Calf. Randolph, Vt. 1805. First edition. $40–$50.

BALME, J.R. *American States, Churches and Slavery*. Cloth. London, 1863. First edition. $40–$50.

BALWHIDDER, The Rev. Micah. *Annals of the Parish; or The Chronicle of Dalmailing*. Boards, printed label. Edinburgh, 1821. (By John Galt.) First edition. $200–$300.

BALZAC, Honoré de. *The Hidden Treasure*. Illustrated. Boards. Kentfield, Calif., 1953. Allen Press. One of 160. $200–$250.

BANCROFT, George. *Poems*. Tan boards. Cambridge, Mass., 1823. First edition. $50–$75.

BANCROFT, Hubert Howe. *The Works of Hubert Howe Bancroft*. Illustrated. 39 vols., cloth. San Francisco, 1886–1890. First editions. $3,500–$3,750.

BANDELIER, Adolph F. A. *The Gilded Man*. Cloth. New York, 1893. First edition. $125–$150.

BANDINI, Joseph. *A Description of California in 1828*. Illustrated. Boards and cloth. Berkeley, Calif., 1951. One of 400. $75–$85.

BANGS, John Kendrick. See B., J.K.

BANGS, John Kendrick. *Bikey the Skicycle and Other Tales of Jimmie Boy*. Illustrated by Peter Newell. Decorated Cloth. New York, 1902. First edition. $75.

BANGS, John Kendrick. *A House-Boat on the Styx*. Illustrated. Cloth. New York, 1896. First edition. $50–$60.

BANGS, John Kendrick. *Mephistopheles: A Profanation*. Red wrappers. New York, 1889. First edition. $50–$75.

BANGS, John Kendrick. *Mr. Munchausen*. Cloth. Boston, 1901. First edition, first state, with Small, Maynard copyright. $50–$75.

BANGS, John Kendrick. *Mollie and the Unwisemen Abroad*. Illustrated. Cloth. Philadelphia, 1910. First edition. $65.

BANGS, John Kendrick. *Toppleton's Client*. Boards. London, 1893. First edition. $150. New York, 1893. Cloth. First American edition. $75–$100.

BANNERMAN, Helen. *The Story of Little Black Sambo*. Colored plates. Cloth. London, 1899. First edition. $800–$1,000. Also, stained and mended, $600 (A,1977).

BANTA, William, and Caldwell, J.W., Jr. *Twenty-Seven Years on the Frontier, or Fifty Years in Texas*. Frontispiece. Wrappers. Austin, 1893. First edition. $1,500 and up.

BARBE-MARBOIS, François. *The History of Louisiana, Particularly the Cession of That Colony to the U.S.A.* Boards. Philadelphia, 1830. First American edition and first in English. $350–$450.

BARHAM, Richard Harris. See Ingoldsby, Thomas.

BARING, Alexander. *An Inquiry into the Causes and Consequences of the Orders in Council; and An Examination of the Conduct of Great Britain Towards the Neutral Commerce of America*. Wrappers. London, 1808. First edition. $125–$150. New York, 1808. First American edition. $75–$100.

BARING, Maurice. *Algae: An Anthology of Phrases*. Wrappers, paper label. London, 1928. First edition. One of 100 signed. In dust jacket. Boxed. $100–$125.

BARKER, Eugene, C. *The Life of Stephen F. Austin*. 2 maps, plan, 6 portraits. Boards and vellum. Nashville, 1925. First edition. One of 250 signed. $250–$300. Trade edition: $75–$100.

BARKER, George. *Poems*. Cloth. London, (1935). First edition. In dust jacket. $50–$75.

BARKER, Matthew Henry. *The Old Sailor's Jolly Boat*. 24 full-page engravings by George and Robert Cruikshank. London, 1844. $200–$300.

BARLOW, Joel. *The Columbiad: A Poem*. Portrait and 11 plates. Contemporary or later morocco. Philadelphia, 1807. (New edition of *The Vision of Columbus*, which see in entry below.) $150.

BARLOW, Joel. *Joel Barlow to His Fellow Citizens of the United States*. (Caption title.) Wrappers. (Philadelphia, 1801.) First American edition. $100–$150.

BARLOW, Joel. *The Vision of Columbus: A Poem in Nine Books*. Sheep. Hartford, 1787. First edition. $200–$250. (Reprinted as *The Columbiad,* which see in entry above.)

BARNARD, George N. *Photographic View of Sherman's Campaign*. 61 gold-toned albumen prints, mounted, with lithographic captions. Oblong folio, morocco. New York, (1866). First edition. $10,000 and up. Also, $9,750 (A,1979).

BARNES, Charles Merritt. *Combats and Conquest of Immortal Heroes*. Full morocco. San Antonio, 1910. First edition. $75–$125.

BARNES, David M. *The Draft Riots in New York, July, 1863*. 117 pp., wrappers, or cloth. New York, 1863. First edition. $150–$200.

BARNES, Djuna. See *Ladies Almanack*.

BARNES, Djuna. *A Book*. 6 portraits, Black boards, paper label. New York, (1923). First edition. In dust jacket. $250–$300. Also, $130(A,1975).

BARNES, Djuna. *The Book of Repulsive Women*. Illustrated. Gold wrappers. (New York, 1915.) First edition. $350–$425. Author's first book. Yonkers, 1948. Stiff wrappers. One of 1,000. $75–$100.

BARNES, Djuna. *A Night Among the Horses*. Boards, cloth spine. New York, 1929. First edition. In dust jacket. $150–$200.

BARNES, Djuna. *Nightwood*. Cloth. London, (1936). First edition. In dust jacket. $125–$150. New York, (1937). First American edition. In dust jacket. $50–$75. Contains an introduction by T.S. Eliot.

BARNES, Djuna. *Ryder*. New York, 1928. Cloth. First edition. In dust jacket. $250–$350.

BARNES, Will C. *Apaches and Longhorns*. Edited by Frank C. Lockwood. Illustrated. Cloth. Los Angeles, 1941. First edition. In dust jacket. $125. Lacking jacket, $75.

BARNES, William C. *Tales from the X-Bar Horse Camp*. Illustrated. Boards. Chicago, 1920. First edition. $75–$100.

BARNEY, James M. *Tales of Apache Warfare*. 45 pp., wrappers. (Phoenix), 1933. $100–$125.

BARNEY, Natalie C. See *Tryphe*.

BARNEY, Natalie C. *Actes et Entr'actes*. Wrappers. Paris, 1910. First edition. $135–$150.

BARNEY, Natalie C. *Aventures de L'Esprit*. Wrappers. Paris, 1929. First edition. $175–$200.

BARNEY, Natalie C. *The One Who Is Legion*. Cloth. London, 1930. First edition. In dust jacket. $100–$125.

BARNEY, Natalie C. *Poems & Poemes*. Wrappers. Paris & New York, (1920). First edition. Limited edition. Copies on blue paper, $100–$150; white paper, $75–$125.

BARNFIELD, Richard. *Complete Poems*. Edited by Alexander B. Grosart, Frontispiece, 7 facsimiles of title pages. Half morocco. London, 1876. Roxburghe Club. $200–$300.

BARNUM, H.L. *The Spy Unmasked; or, Memoirs of Enoch Crosby*. Map, 5 plates. Boards. New York, 1828. First edition. $150–$250.

BARR, Robert. *The Triumph of Eugene Valmont*. Cloth. London, 1906. First edition. $200–$250.

BARREIRO, Antonio. *Ojeada sobre Nuevo-Mexico.* Illustrated, 3 tables. Marbled wrappers. Puebla, Mexico, 1832. First edition. $750–$1,000.

BARRETT, E.B. *The Battle of Marathon: A Poem.* Sewn, uncut. London, 1820. (By Elizabeth Barrett Browning.) First edition. (50 copies.) $8,000 and up. Also, with manuscript corrections by the author(?), $12,000 (A, 1981).

BARRETT, Elizabeth Barrett. *Poems.* 2 vols., dark green cloth, uncut. London, 1844. (By Elizabeth Barrett Browning.) First edition, with ads in Vol. 1 dated June 1. $1,500 and up. Later, 1844, no ads, $750–$1,000. Also, with ads dated January, 1845, $225 (A,1974). London, 1850. 2 vols. brown cloth. Second edition, first issue, with single address in imprint, called "New Edition." $500–$750. (First appearance of "Sonnets from the Portuguese" in a book.). London, 1856. 3 vols., cloth. $300–$400. London, 1873. 5 vols., cloth. $150–$250. (See Browning, Elizabeth Barrett entry.)

BARRETT, Elizabeth B. *The Seraphim and Other Poems.* Purple cloth. London, 1838. (By Elizabeth Barrett Browning.) First edition. $300–$400.

BARRETT, Elizabeth, and Browning, Robert. *Two Poems.* Printed wrappers. London, 1854. (By Elizabeth Barrett Browning, etc.) First edition. $125–$200.

BARRETT, Ellen C. *Baja California, 1535–1956: A Bibliography.* Blue cloth. Los Angeles, 1957. First edition. One of 500. $100–$150.

BARRETT, Francis. *The Magus, or Celestial Intelligencer.* Illustrated. Boards and leather. London, 1801. First edition. $300–$400.

BARRIE, Sir James M. See *The Allahakbarrie Book of Broadway Cricket for 1899.*

BARRIE, Sir James M. *The Admirable Crichton.* Illustrated by Hugh Thomson. Boards and cloth. London, (1914). $50–$75. Another issue: Vellum with ties. One of 500 signed by Thomson. $200–$300.

BARRIE, Sir James M. *Auld Licht Idylls.* Blue buckram. London, 1888. First edition, first issue, with black end papers. $100–$125. London, 1895. Illustrated by William Hole. Cloth. One of 550. $150–$250.

BARRIE, Sir James. M. *The Author.* White self-wrappers. Cincinnati, (1925). First edition. One of 20. $275.

BARRIE, Sir James M. *Better Dead.* Pictorial glazed yellow (or buff) wrappers. London, 1888 (actually 1887). First edition.$200–$300. Author's first book.

BARRIE, Sir James M. *Courage: The Rectorial Address Delivered at St. Andrews University, May 3rd, 1922.* Cream cloth, gilt top. London, (1922). First edition. Limited issue on large paper. $50–$75.

BARRIE, Sir James M. *An Edinburgh Eleven.* Wrappers. London, 1889. First edition, first issue, with "Gavin Ogilvy" on front cover and "J.M. Barrie" on title page. $125–$175. Later issue same date: Gray cloth. $75–$100.

BARRIE, Sir James M. *The Greenwood Hat: Being a Memoir of James Anon, 1885–1887.* 10 plates. Green leather, gilt top. London, 1930. First edition. One of 550. Boxed. $60–$80. (A number of inscribed copies have been noted.)

BARRIE, Sir James M. *"The Ladies' Shakespeare."* 7 pp., dark-red printed wrappers. London, 1925. First edition. One of 25. $60–$80.

BARRIE, Sir James M. *The Little Minister.* 3 vols., brown cloth. London, 1891. First edition, first issue, with 16 pages of ads in Vol. 1 dated "5G.9.91." $500–$750. New York, (1891). Lovell, Coryell & Co. Wrappers. First American edition. $100–$150.

BARRIE, Sir James M. *The Little White Bird.* Cloth. London, 1902. First edition. In dust jacket. $75–$100.

BARRIE, Sir James M. *My Lady Nicotine.* Blue buckram. London, 1890. First edition, first issue, with 6 pages of ads at back. $75–$125. New York, (1892). Wrappers. First American edition, with Walter Baker Co. ad on back. $75.

BARRIE, Sir James M. *Peter and Wendy*. Illustrated. Green cloth. London, 1911. First edition, $125–$150. New York, (1911). Cloth. First American edition, first issue, from English sheets. $50–$75. Later, printed in U.S., $35.

BARRIE, Sir James M. *Peter Pan in Kensington Gardens*. Illustrated in color and black and white by Arthur Rackham. Vellum. London, 1906. First edition. One of 500 signed by Rackham. $2,000–$3,500. Trade edition: Cloth. $250–$350. New York, 1906. First American trade edition. $250–$350. New York, 1907. Green cloth. $250–$350. London, 1907. Cloth, $250–$350. Note: There were several other clothbound editions (1909, 1910, 1912, 1920, etc) issued in New York and London, and these usually retail in the $200–$300 range if in fine condition.

BARRIE, Sir James M. *Quality Street*. Illustrated by Hugh Thomson. Vellum with silk ties. (London, 1913.) One of 1,000 signed by the artist. $300. Trade issue: Cloth. $100–$125.

BARRIE, Sir James M. *A Tillyloss Scandal*. Wrappers. New York, (1893). First edition, first issue, with publisher's address as "43, 45, 47 East 10th Street." $100–$150.

BARRIE, Sir James M. *Walker London*. Frontispiece. Green printed wrappers. New York, 1907. First edition. $100–$150.

BARRIE, Sir James M. *When a Man's Single: A Tale of Literary Life*. Blue buckram, gilt top. London, 1888. First edition, with ads at back. $125–$150.

BARRIE, Sir James M. *A Window in Thrums*. Cloth. London, 1889. First edition. With 6 pages of ads at back. $75–$100. London, 1892. Illustrated by William Hole. Blue cloth. One of 50. $250–$300. Another issue: One of 500. $75.

BARROW, John. *A Chronological History of Voyages into the Arctic Regions*. Illustrated, folding map. Boards and cloth. London, 1818. First edition. $350–$400.

BARROW, John. *A Voyage to Cochinchina, 1792–1793*. Folding map, 20 colored aquatint plates. Contemporary calf. London, 1806. First edition. $750–$1,000. Also, $770 (A,1979).

BARROWS, R.M. (compiler). *The Kitbook for Soldiers, Sailors, and Marines*. Pictorial boards. Chicago, (1943) First edition. In pictorial mailing box. $125–$150. (Contains J.D. Salinger's story "The Hang of It," his first book appearance.)

BARROWS, Willard. *Notes on Iowa Territory*. Folding map. 46 pp., cloth, printed front cover label. Cincinnati, 1845. First edition. $1,500–$2,000, or more.

BARRY, T.A., and Patten, B.A. *Men and Memories of San Francisco, in the "Spring of '50."* 2 plates. Flexible cloth. San Francisco, 1873. First edition. $125–$150.

BARTH, John. *Chimera*. New York, (1972). First edition. One of 300 signed. Boxed. $100–$125.

BARTH, John. *The End of the Road*. Cloth. Garden City, 1958. First edition. In dust jacket. $200–$250. London, 1962. First English edition. In dust jacket. $75.

BARTH, John. *The Floating Opera*. Cloth. New York, (1956). First edition, first issue, with "(1)" at foot of last page. In dust jacket. $250–$300. Author's first book. London, (1968). Cloth. First English edition. In dust jacket. $75–$100.

BARTH, John. *Giles Goat-Boy*. Cloth. Garden City, 1966. First edition. One of 250 signed. Boxed. $125–$150. Trade edition: Cloth. In dust jacket. $60–$75.

BARTH, John. *Lost in the Funhouse*. Cloth. Garden City, 1968. First edition. One of 250 signed. Boxed. $100–$125. Trade edition: Cloth. In dust jacket $35–$60.

BARTH, John. *The Sot-Weed Factor*. Cloth. Garden City, 1960. First edition. In dust jacket. $200–$300. London, 1961. Cloth. First English edition. In dust jacket. $100.

BARTHELME, Donald. *Come Back, Dr. Caligari*. Cloth. Boston, (1964). First edition. In dust jacket. $150–$175. London, 1966. Cloth. First English edition. In dust jacket. $50–$75. Author's first book.

BARTHELME, Donald. *Snow White*. Cloth. New York, 1967. First edition. In dust jacket. $50–$75. London, 1968. Cloth. First English edition. In dust jacket. $75.

BARTHELME, Donald. *Unspeakable Practices, Unnatural Acts*. Cloth. New York, (1968). First edition. In dust jacket. $75. London, 1969. Cloth. First English edition. In dust jacket. $50.

BARTLETT, J.S., M.D. *The Physician's Pocket Synopsis*. Leather. Boston, 1822. First edition. $75–$100.

BARTLETT, John. See *A Collection of Familiar Quotations*.

BARTLETT, John Russell. *Personal Narrative of Explorations and Incidents in Texas, New Mexico, California, etc.*. Folding map. 44 plates, 2 vols., pictorial cloth. New York, 1854. First edition. $500–$600. London, 1854. 2 vols., cloth. $400–$500.

BARTON, James L. *Commerce of the Lakes*. Folding table. 80 pp., wrappers. Buffalo, 1847. First edition. $100–$125.

BARTON, James L. *Lake Commerce*. 34 pp., wrappers. Buffalo, 1846. First edition. $75–$100.

BARTON, William P.C. *A Flora of North America*. 106 color plates. 3 vols., boards. Philadelphia, 1821, 1822, 1823. $3,500.

BASKIN, Leonard. *Figures of Dead Men*. Preface by Archibald MacLeish. Illustrated. Boards and cloth. (Boston), 1968. One of 100 signed by Baskin, with an original signed woodcut. $300–$450.

BASKIN, Leonard. *LB—Some Engravings*. 17 woodcuts. Stiff boards. Northampton, Mass., Gehenna Press, 1952. First edition, with each engraving signed and titled by Baskin. One of 10. In dust jacket. $2,000–$2,500.

BASKIN, Leonard. *The Wood Engravings of Leonard Baskin, 1948–1959*. 168 signed engravings. Folio, loose in half morocco case. Northampton, 1961. First edition. One of 24. $7,500.

BASS, W.W. (editor). *Adventures in the Canyons of the Colorado by Two of Its Earliest Explorers, James White and H.W. Hawkins*. Frontispiece, plate, facsimiles. 38 pp., wrappers. Grand Canyon, 1920. First edition. $150–$200.

BATES, Ed. F. *History . . . of Denton County Texas*. Plates. Cloth. Denton, Tex., (1918). First edition. $200–$400.

BATES, Finis L. *Escape and Suicide of John Wilkes Booth*. Illustrated. Pictorial cloth. Memphis, 1907. First edition. $75–$100.

BATES, H.E. *The Beauty of the Dead, and One Other Story*. Boards and cloth. London, 1941. Corvinus Press. One of 25. $250–$300.

BATES, H.E. *Flowers and Faces*. Engravings by John Nash. Boards. London, 1935. Golden Cockerel Press. One of 325. $150–$250. Another issue: Full morocco. One of 60 with an extra set of plates. $300–$400.

BATES, H.E. *A German Idyll*. Engravings. Morocco and cloth. Waltham Saint Lawrence, 1932, Golden Cockerel Press. One of 307. $150–$200.

BATES, H.E. *The Last Bread: A Play in One Act*. Wrappers. London, (1926). First edition. $75–$100. Author's first book.

BATES, H.E. *Sally Go Round the Moon*. Vellum. London, 1932. White Owl Press. One of 21 signed. Boxed. $300–$400.

BATES, H.E. *The Story Without an End*. Parchment. (London), 1932. White Owl Press. One of 25 signed, with a leaf of manuscript. $200–$250.

BATES, H.W. *The Naturalist on the River Amazons*. Illustrated, including folding map. 2 vols., cloth. London, 1863. First edition. $400–$500.

BATES, J.H. *Notes of a Tour in Mexico and California*. Cloth. New York, 1887. First edition. $75.

BAUDELAIRE, Charles. *Les Fleurs du Mal*. Illustrated by Auguste Rodin. Wrappers. New York, 1940. Limited Editions Club. Boxed. $100–$125. (Paris, 1947.) Illustrated by Matisse. Stiff illustrated wrappers. One of 320 copies, signed by Matisse. Boxed. $1,000–$1,250. Also, $800 (A, 1976).

BAUDELAIRE, Charles. *Flowers of Evil*. Edited by James Laver. Lithographs by Jacob Epstein. Buckram. New York, 1940. Limited Editions Club. Boxed. $100–$135.

BAUDELAIRE, Charles. *Intimate Journals*. Translated by Christopher Isherwood. Introduction by T.S. Eliot. Blue cloth, gilt top. London, 1930. First edition. One of 400. Boxed. $300. Another issue: One of 50 signed by Eliot. $450–$600. Hollywood, 1947. Cloth. Revised edition (with W.H. Auden introduction). Signed by Isherwood. In dust jacket. $150–$200.

BAUER, Max. *Precious Stones*. Translated from the German by L.J. Spencer. Plates. Half morocco. London, 1903. First edition. $250–$350. London, 1904. $200–$300.

BAUM, L. Frank. See Stanton, Schuyler. (Note: With the sale at auction in 1978 of the astonishingly rich Baum collection of Justin Schiller, a New York dealer in children's books, the immense complexity and scope of the Baum canon was revealed for the first time. It became obvious at once that existing Baum bibliographies require the Schiller catalogue as a supplement. Since this *Handbook* is *not* a bibliography, the selective listings that follow, based partly on the Schiller sale, should be used with caution.)

BAUM, L. Frank. *American Fairy Tales*. Illustrated. Pictorial cloth. Chicago, 1901. First edition. $150–$250.

BAUM, L. Frank. *The Army Alphabet*. Illustrated by Harry Kennedy. Pictorial boards. Chicago, 1900. First edition. In dust jacket. $750. Also, $550 (A, 1979).

BAUM, L. Frank. *The Cowardly Lion and the Hungry Tiger*. Color plates. Boards. Chicago, (1913). First edition. $200–$300.

BAUM, L. Frank. *Dorothy and the Wizard of Oz*. Illustrated by John R. Neill. Cloth. Chicago, (1908). First edition, first issue, with "Reilly & Britton Co." at bottom of spine. $300–$350. Also, $340 (A, 1978).

BAUM, L. Frank. *The Enchanted Island of Yew*. Illustrated by Fanny Y. Cory. Pictorial cloth. Indianapolis, (1903). First edition. In dust jacket. $250–$300.

BAUM, L. Frank. *Father Goose's Year Book*. Illustrated. Pictorial paper over cloth. Chicago, (1907). First edition. $150–$200.

BAUM, L. Frank. *The Life and Adventures of Santa Claus*. Illustrated in color. Cloth. Indianapolis, 1902. First edition, first state, without illustrations in the text. $300–$400.

BAUM, L. Frank. *The Marvelous Land of Oz*. Illustrated by John R. Neill. Cloth. Chicago, 1904. First edition, first issue, without "Published July, 1904" on copywright page. In dust jacket. $400–$500.

BAUM, L. Frank. *The Master Key*. Illustrated in color by Fanny Cory. Olive-green cloth. Indianapolis, (1901). First edition, first issue, with signatures of 8 pp. and with copyright line 1 21/32 inches wide. In dust jacket. $300–$400. Of lesser value: Second issue, signatures of 16 pp. Third issue, copyright line 1 25/32 inches wide.

BAUM, L. Frank. *Mother Goose in Prose*. Illustrated by Maxfield Parrish. Pictorial cloth. Chicago, (1897). Way & Williams. First edition. $750–$1,000. Chicago, (1901). Hill. 12 plates. Pictorial cloth. $200–$300.

BAUM, L. Frank. *A New Wonderland*. Illustrated by Frank Verbeck. Green cloth. New York, 1900. First edition. $400–$500.

BAUM, L. Frank. *Ozma of Oz*. Tan pictorial cloth. Chicago, (1907). First edition, first issue, with illustration in color on page 221. In dust jacket. $500–$750, possibly more.

BAUM, L. Frank. *The Patchwork Girl of Oz*. Illustrated. Light green pictorial cloth. Chicago, (1913). First edition, first state, with chapter heading on page 35 touching text. In dust jacket. $300–$400. (Later issue, tan cloth.)

BAUM, L. FRANK. *Queen Zixi of Ix*. Illustrated in color. Pictorial cloth. New York, 1905. First edition. $300–$400.

BAUM, L. Frank. *The Road to Oz*. Illustrated by John R. Neill. Pictorial green cloth. Chicago, (1909). Reilly & Britton. First edition $250–$300.

BAUM, L. Frank. *The Sea Fairies*. Illustrated. Light-green cloth. Chicago, (1911). First published edition, first issue, with three heads on cover label. $150–$200. (Second issue: cover label showing girl on a sea horse.)

BAUM, L. Frank. *The Songs of Father Goose*. Illustrated by W.W. Denslow. Colored pictorial boards. Chicago, 1900. First edition $200–$300.

BAUM, L. Frank. *The Wonderful Wizard of Oz*. Illustrated by W.W. Denslow. Green cloth. Chicago and New York, 1900. First edition, first issue, with 11-line colophon (not 13) on back end paper. $2,500–$3,500. (An extremely fine copy, the property of Melissa and Mark Hime of Idylwild, Calif., was sold for $5,400 in 1980—a record price. Justin Schiller's copy, inscribed, brought $2,400 at auction in 1978. Several binding states make this a difficult book to evaluate properly. If you find a copy with title page date of 1900, seek a specialist dealer's help.)

BAUM, L. Frank. *The Yellow Hen*. Illustrated. Pictorial boards. Chicago, (1916). First edition. $150–$250.

BAX, Clifford (editor). *Florence Farr, Bernard Shaw and W.B. Yeats*. Boards, linen spine, paper label. Dublin, 1941. Cuala Press. First edition. One of 500. In tissue dust jacket. $100–$150.

BAXTER, William. *Pea Ridge and Prairie Grove*. Cloth. Cincinnati, 1864. First edition. $80–$100.

BAY, J. Christian. *The Fortune of Books*. Illustrated. Blue cloth. Chicago, (1941). In dust jacket. $100–$125.

BAY, J. Christian. *A Handful of Western Books* **A Second Handful of Western Books** *A Third Handful of Western Books*. Illustrated. 3 vols., boards and cloth. Cedar Rapids, Iowa, 1935–36–37. First editions. Limited to 350, 400, and 400 copies, respectively. (Note: Most of these bear the Torch Press imprint. An unknown number bear the imprint of the Chicago bookseller Walter M. Hill. Matched sets are to be preferred.) Together, the three volumes, in tissue dust jackets. $150–$225 at retail. Odd volumes, in jackets, $50–$75, or more at retail. (See following item.)

BAY, J. Christian. *Three Handfuls of Western Books*. (Combined one-volume edition of preceding items.) Boards. (Cedar Rapids), 1941. One of 35. $150–$200.

BAYEUX Tapestry (The). Facsimile in color, by James Basire after C.A. Stothard. 17 double page plates in color. Folio, half calf. (London, 1823). $600–$750.

BAYLIES, Francis. *A Narrative of General Wool's Campaign in Mexico*. Frontispiece. 78 pp., printed yellow wrappers. Albany, 1851. First edition. $300–$400. Rebound in leather, $150.

BEAGLE, Peter S. *A Fine and Private Place*. Cloth. New York, 1960. First edition. In dust jacket. $75–$100. Author's first book.

BEAGLE, Peter S. *The Last Unicorn*. Cloth. New York, (1968). First edition. In dust jacket. $50–$60.

BEALE, Charles Willing. *The Secret of the Earth*. Yellow cloth. New York, (1899). First edition. $75.

BEALS, Carleton. *The Crime of Cuba*. 31 photographs by Walker Evans. Black cloth. Philadelphia, (1933). First edition. In dust jacket. $100–$150.

BEAN, Edwin F. (compiler). *Bean's History and Directory of Nevada County, California*. Half leather and boards. Nevada, Calif., 1867. First edition. $400–$750.

BEARD, Charles A. *An Economic Interpretation of the Constitution of the United States*. Cloth. New York, 1913. First edition, $200–$250.

BEARD, Charles R. *A Catalogue of the Collection of Martinware Formed by Frederick John Nettlefold*. 31 color plates, 46 in black and white. Half brown morocco. (London), 1936. $150–$200.

BEARD, Daniel C. *American Boy's Handy Book: What to Do and How to Do It*. Illustrated. Pictorial cloth. New York, 1882. First edition. $75–$125.

BEARDSLEY, Aubrey. *A Book of Fifty Drawings*. Scarlet cloth. London, 1897. First edition. $150–$250. Another issue: One of 50 on vellum. $400–$600.

BEARDSLEY, Aubrey. *Fifty Drawings*. Pictorial cloth. New York, 1920. First edition. One of 500. $200–$275. (Beardsley experts doubt that these are Beardsley's drawings.)

BEARDSLEY, Aubrey. *Last Letters*. Cloth. London, 1904. First edition. $75–$125.

BEARDSLEY, Aubrey. *A Second Book of Fifty Drawings*. Cloth. London, 1899. First edition. One of 1,000. $150–$250. Another issue: One of 50 on vellum. $400–$500.

BEARDSLEY, Aubrey. *Six Drawings Illustrating Théophile Gautier's Romance, "Mademoiselle de Maupin."* 6 plates, loose in half cloth portfolio, silk ties. London, 1898. One of 50. $200–$300.

BEARDSLEY, Aubrey. *Some Unknown Drawings of Aubrey Beardsley*. Edited by R.A. Walker. 32 plates and facsimiles. Buckram. London, 1923. First edition. One of 500 signed. In dust jacket. $125–$175.

BEARDSLEY, Aubrey. *Under the Hill and Other Essays in Prose and Verse*. 16 illustrations by the author. Buckram. London, 1904. First edition. One of 50 on Japan vellum. $400–$550. Trade edition: Pictorial cloth. $150–$200.

BEATON, Cecil. *The Book of Beauty*. 27 photographic plates, 90 text drawings. Buckram. London, 1930. One of 110 signed. $175–$250.

BEATTIE, George W. and Helen P. *Heritage of the Valley*. Cloth. Pasadena, 1939. First edition. In dust jacket. $60.

BEATTIE, William. *Switzerland Illustrated*. 107 plates by W.H. Bartlett, map. 2 vols., half calf. London, 1836. $750–$1,000.

BEAUCHAMPE; or, the Kentucky Tragedy. 2 vols., cloth. Philadelphia, 1842. (By William Gilmore Simms.) First edition. $200–$250.

BEAUMONT, Cyril W. *The History of Harlequin*. With a preface by Sacheverell Sitwell. 44 plates (5 colored), text decorations by Claudia Guercio. Decorated parchment boards, vellum spine. London, 1926. One of 325. In dust jacket. $250–$350.

BEAUMONT, Cyril W. *Puppets and the Puppet Stage*. 110 pp. of illustrations. Cloth. London, 1938. In dust jacket. $75–$125.

BEAUMONT, William. *Experiments and Observations on the Gastric Juice, and the Physiology of Digestion.* 3 engravings. Boards and cloth, paper spine label. Plattsburgh, N.Y., 1833. First edition. $2,000–$2,500. Also, boxed and rebacked, $1,540 (A, 1978). Boston, 1834. Boards and cloth, paper label. Second issue (first edition copy with Boston title page). $1,000–$1,200. Edinburgh, 1838. Boards and calf. First English edition. $500–$750.

BEAUMONT, William. *The Physiology of Digestion.* Edited by Samuel Beaumont. Cloth. Burlington, Vt., 1847. Second edition of *Experiments and Observations on the Gastric Juice.* $400–$500.

BEAUTY and the Beast. Boards, in printed paper case. London, (about 1810, 1811, or 1813?) (By Charles Lamb?) First edition. $1,000 and up. (Note: A copy with cover title only, issued in blue wrappers, brought $900 at a New York auction in 1981.)

BECK, Lewis C. *A Gazetteer of the States of Illinois and Missouri.* Folding map, 5 plates. Boards, paper label. Albany, 1823. First edition. $800–$1,000.

BECKER, Robert H. *Designs on the Land: Diseños of California Ranchos.* San Francisco, 1964. Grabhorn printing. One of 400. $150–$400.

BECKETT, Samuel. See Crowder, Henry.

BECKETT, Samuel. *All Strange Away.* Illustrated by Edward Gorey. New York, 1976. One of 200 signed. Boxed. $300–$350. One of 26 lettered and signed. $375–$450.

BECKETT, Samuel. *All That Fall: A Play.* Hardbound. New York, (1957). First American edition. One of 100 specially bound. $150–$200. Another issue: Wrappers (issued as a holiday greeting by the publisher). $100. London, 1957. Wrappers. First English edition. $50–$75.

BECKETT, Samuel. *Come and Go: Dramaticule.* Illustrated. Cloth. London, (1967). First edition. One of 100 signed. Boxed. $125–$150.

BECKETT, Samuel. *Echo's Bones and Other Precipitates.* 30 pp., printed wrappers. Paris, 1935. Europa Press. First edition. One of 25 on Normandy vellum, signed. $750–$1,000. Also, $600 (A, 1977). Another issue: One of 250 on Alfa paper, unsigned. $350–$450.

BECKETT, Samuel. *En Attendant Godot.* Wrappers. Paris, 1952. Editions de Minuit. First edition (of *Waiting for Godot*). One of 35 numbered copies. $5,000–$7,500. First trade edition: Wrappers. Paris, 1952. $200–$300.

BECKETT, Samuel. *Endgame.* Translated by the author. Dark red cloth. London, (1958). First English edition. In dust jacket. $50–$75. New York, (1958). Boards. First American edition. Limited issue: One of 100. Issued without dust jacket. $75–$100.

BECKETT, Samuel. *How It Is.* (Series A and Series B.) Translated from the French by the author. 2 vols., vellum and morocco. London, (1964). First editions. Each, 100 signed. In tissue dust jackets. Boxed. $500–$650.

BECKETT, Samuel. *The Lost Ones.* Half vellum (or half leather). London, 1972. First edition. One of 100 signed. Boxed. $150–$200.

BECKETT, Samuel. *Malone Dies.* Translated by the author. 120 pp., cream-colored canvas. New York, (1956). First American edition. One of 500. In transparent dust jacket. $125–$150. London, 1958. Black cloth. First English edition. In dust jac˙ $75–$100.

BECKETT, Samuel. *Malone Meurt.* Wrappers. (Paris, 1951.) First edition (of *Malone Dies*). In tissue dust jacket. $100–$150.

BECKETT, Samuel. *Molloy.* Printed wrappers. Paris, (1951). First edition (in French). One of 500 on Alfa paper. $200–$275. Paris, (1955). Olympia Press. Wrappers. First edition in English. $50–$75. New York, (1955). First American edition. In dust jacket, $75.

BECKETT, Samuel. *More Pricks Than Kicks*. Tan cloth. London, 1934. First edition. In dust jacket. $600–$750. Also, $375 (A, 1977). London, (1970). One of 100 signed. $200–$250.

BECKETT, Samuel. *Murphy*. Green Cloth. London, (1938). First edition, first binding. In dust jacket. $4,500 in a 1980 catalogue. Also, $2,420 (A, 1978). New York, (1957). Boards and cloth. First American edition. One of 100 signed. $300–$400.

BECKETT, Samuel. *No's Knife: Collected Shorter Prose, 1945–1966*. Either half calf or full buckram (bindings are not as recorded in bibliographies). London, (1967). First edition. One of 100 signed. (Series A.) Boxed. Another Issue: One of 100 signed. (Series B.) Boxed. Each $150–$250.

BECKETT, Samuel. *Poems in English*. Mottled tan leather-like cloth boards. London, (1961). One of 100 signed, "printed in advance of the first edition." $400–$500. Also, $225 (A, 1977). Also, a copy listed as "cloth, one of 100," inscribed to Nancy Cunard, $576 (A, 1969). Another issue: Cloth. One of 175 signed. In tissue dust jacket. $200.

BECKETT, Samuel. *Proust*. 72 pp., decorated boards. London, 1931. First edition. In dust jacket. $250–$350. Also, $150 (A, 1977). New York, (1957). Limited first American edition. One of 250 signed. Issued without dust jacket. $200–$300. London, 1965. One of 100 signed. $200.

BECKETT, Samuel. *The Unnamable*. Translated by the author. 179 pp., boards and cloth. New York, (1958). Grove Press. First American edition. One of 26 lettered copies, signed. $100–$150. One of 100 numbered copies. $75. Another issue: Printed wrappers. Review copy. $50.

BECKETT, Samuel. *Waiting for Godot*. Translated by the author. New York, 1954. First American edition. In dust jacket. $150–$250. London, (1956). Yellow cloth. First English edition. In dust jacket. $125–$175.

BECKETT, Samuel. *Watt*. Printed wrappers. Paris, (1953). Collection Merlin: Olympia Press. First edition. One of 25, lettered A to Y, on fine paper and signed by Beckett. $750–$1,000. First trade edition: Wrappers. $100–$125. New York, (1959). First American edition. $75–$100.

BECKETT, Samuel. *Whoroscope*. 6 pp., printed wrappers, with white (separate) band around the book. Paris, 1930. Hours Press. First edition. One of 100 signed and numbered (of a total edition of 300). $1,500–$1,750. Also, $800 (A, 1980). Another issue: One of 200 unsigned. $500–$750. Also, inscribed to Nancy Cunard, publisher of the book, with an autograph letter, signed, $2,280 (A, 1969). Author's first separately published work.

BECKETT, Samuel, and others. *Our Exagmination Round His Factification for Incamination of Work in Progress*. Printed wrappers. Paris, 1929. Shakespeare and Company. First edition. One of 96 (large paper) on verge d'Arches paper. $800–$1,000. Also, $600 (A, 1977). Ordinary issue: $200–$250.

BEDFORD, Hilory G. *Texas Indian Troubles*. Decorated cloth. Dallas, 1905. First edition. $300–$400.

BEEBE, Henry. *The History of Peru*. Leather. Peru, Ill., 1858. First edition. $150.

BEEBE, Lucius. *Aspects of the Poetry of Edwin Arlington Robinson*. Cloth. Cambridge, Mass., 1928. First edition. One of 200. In dust jacket. $75.

BEEBE, Lucius, and Clegg, Charles M. *Mixed Train Daily*. Illustrated. Cloth. New York, 1947. First edition. In dust jacket. $50.

BEEBE, William. *The Arcturus Adventure*. Boards and vellum. New York, 1926. Autograph (first) edition. One of 50 signed. $100–$150. First trade edition: Cloth. In dust jacket. $15–$20.

BEEBE, William. *Galapagos: World's End*. 9 color plates, 84 other illustrations. Buckram. New York, 1924. Autograph (first) edition. One of 100 signed. In dust jacket. $300–$400. First trade edition: Cloth. In dust jacket. $35.

BEEBE, William. *A Monograph of the Pheasants.* 90 color plates, 20 maps, other illustrations. 4 vols., folio, cloth. London, 1918–22. First edition. One of 600. $2,500–$3,000.

BEEBE, William. *Pheasants: Their Lives and Homes.* 64 plates (some in color). 2 vols., vellum. Garden City, 1926. First edition. One of 201 on large paper, signed. $500–$600. Trade edition: 2 vols., cloth. $250–$300. Garden City, 1931. 2 vols. $125–$150. Garden City, 1936. 2 vols. in one. $100–$125.

BEECHER, Edward. *Narrative of the Riots at Alton.* Cloth. Alton, Ill., 1838. First edition. $75–$100.

BEECHER, Harriet Elizabeth. *Prize-Tale: A New England Sketch.* Plain wrapppers, cloth spine. Lowell, Mass., 1834. First edition. $750. First book by Harriet Beecher Stowe.

BEECHER, Henry Ward. *Norwood, or Village Life in New England.* 3 vols., green cloth. London, 1867. First edition. $75–$300 (!). New York, 1868. Cloth. First American edition. $40–$50.

BEECHER, John. *"And I Will Be Heard."* Wrappers. New York, (1940). First edition. $50–$90. Author's first book.

BEECHER, John. *Here I Stand.* Wrappers. (New York, 1941.) First edition. One of 100 signed. $75–$100.

BEECHEY, F.W. *An Account of a Visit to California.* Map, color plates. Half vellum. (San Francisco, 1941). Grabhorn printing. One of 350. $150–$200.

BEECHEY, F.W. *Narrative of a Voyage to the Pacific and Beering's Strait.* 23 plates, 3 maps. 2 vols., brown cloth, or boards and cloth. London, 1831. First edition. $1,500–$2,000. London, 1831. 2 vols. Second edition. $500–$750. Philadelphia, 1832. Boards and cloth. First American edition. $400–$500.

BEECHEY, F.W. *A Voyage of Discovery Towards the North Pole.* Folding map, 6 plates. Cloth. London, 1843. First edition. $400–$600.

BEE-HUNTER (The); or, The Oak Openings. By the author of "The Pioneers," 3 vols., drab boards. London, 1848. (By James Fenimore Cooper.) First edition (of the novel published in America as *The Oak Openings*, which see as title entry). $200–$300.

BEER, Thomas. *The Mauve Decade.* Boards and cloth. New York, 1926. First edition. One of 165 signed. Boxed. $50–$75. Another issue: One of 15 signed. Boxed. $150–$200.

BEERBOHM, Max. *A Book of Caricatures.* Frontispiece in color, 48 drawings. Folio, boards and cloth, paper label, gilt top. London, (1907). First edition. In dust jacket. $250–$350.

BEERBOHM, Max. *Caricatures of Twenty-Five Gentlemen.* 25 plates. Cloth. London, (1896). First edition. $150–$250.

BEERBOHM, Max. *Cartoons: "The Second Childhood of John Bull."* 15 full-page tinted plates. Folio, half cloth. London, (1901). First edition. $100–$150. Another issue: Second issue. Plates in cloth folder. $75–$100. London, (1911). Folio, boards and linen. $75–$100.

BEERBOHM, Max. *A Christmas Garland.* Violet cloth, with gilt lettering and decorations. London, 1912. First edition. $100–$150.

BEERBOHM, Max. *Collected Works.* 10 vols., cloth. London, 1922–28. One of 780, first volume signed by the author. In dust jackets. $500–$600. (See *The Works of Max Beerbohm.*)

BEERBOHM, MAX. *Fifty Caricatures*. 50 plates. Pictorial green cloth. London, 1913. First edition. $150–$200.

BEERBOHM, Max. *The Happy Hypocrite: A Fairy Tale for Tired Men*. Printed green wrappers. New York, 1897. First edition. No. 1 of the Bodley Booklets. $200–$275. London, 1915. Illustrated by George Sheringham. Pictorial cloth. $25–$35. Another issue: Boards. One of 50 on Japan paper. $150–$200. London, (1918). 24 colored illustrations. Cloth. $100–$150.

BEERBOHM, Max. *More*. Green cloth, paper label (with extra label tipped in). London, 1899. First edition. $125–$150.

BEERBOHM, Max. *Observations*. Color frontispiece, 51 other illustrations. Cloth. London, 1925. First edition. In dust jacket. $100–$150. London, 1926. Buckram. One of 280 signed, and with an additional colored plate, signed. $200–$225.

BEERBOHM, Max. *The Poet's Corner*. Colored caricatures. Folio, pictorial boards. London, (1904). First edition, first issue. $150–$200. Second issue: Pictorial wrappers. $75–$125.

BEERBOHM, Max. *Rossetti and His Circle*. 23 colored caricatures. Blue cloth. London, (1922). First edition. One of 380 signed. In dust jacket. $150–$250. Trade edition: $75–$100.

BEERBOHM, Max. *Seven Men*. Blue cloth. London, 1919. First edition, first issue, in bright-blue cloth. In dust jacket. $125–$150. Second issue: Dark-blue cloth. In dust jacket. $50–$75.

BEERBOHM, Max. *A Survey*. 52 plates, including colored frontispiece. Purple cloth. London, 1921. First edition. One of 275 signed. In dust jacket. $250–$300. Trade edition: Cloth. In dust jacket. $150–$200. New York, 1921. Boards and cloth. First American edition. $100–$125.

BEERBOHM, Max. *Things New and Old*. Colored frontispiece, 49 other plates. White buckram. London, 1923. One of 380 signed and with extra signed plate. In dust jacket. $300–$350. Trade edition: Cloth. In dust jacket. $150–$175.

BEERBOHM, Max. *The Works of Max Beerbohm*. Cloth. New York, 1896. First edition. $200–$250. London, 1896. Cloth. First English edition. $150–$200. (Also see Beerbohm, *Collected Works*.)

BEERBOHM, Max. *Zuleika Dobson*. Smooth brown cloth, or rough cloth. London, 1911. First edition. In dust jacket. $350–$550. (Note: Percy H. Muir says there is no priority of issue for smooth brown cloth over rough cloth; they were issued simultaneously, but rough cloth is scarcer.) New York, 1960. Limited Editions Club. Cloth. Boxed. $50–$60.

BEERS, F.W., and Co. *Atlas of the Counties of Lamoille and Orleans, Vermont*. Maps in color. Half leather. New York, 1878. First edition. $175–$250.

BEETON, Mrs. Isabella. *The Book of Household Management*. Frontispiece and pictorial title in color, numerous other illustrations. 2 vols., cloth. London, 1861. First edition, first issue, with "18 Bouverie St." on title page. $500–$600. Also, $350 (A, 1978).

BEETON'S Christmas Annual. 28th Season. Illustrated. Wrappers. London, 1887. (Contains first appearance of A. Conan Doyle's *A Study in Scarlet*.) $7,500 and up? (A rebound copy was reported sold recently in England for $3,500.)

BEHAN, Brendan. *The Hostage*. Cloth. London, 1958. First edition. In dust jacket. $75–$100. New York, (1958). Boards. First American edition. One of 26 signed. Issued without dust jacket. $150. Trade edition: $35.

BEHAN, Brendan. *The Quare Fellow*. Black cloth. London, (1956). First edition. In dust jacket. $150. New York, (1956). First American edition. One of 100. In dust jacket. $100. Author's first book.

BEHN, Mrs. Aphra. *The Works of Mrs. Aphra Behn.* Edited by Montague Summers. Portrait. 6 vols., cloth-backed boards. London, 1915. One of 50 sets on handmade paper. $250–$300. Another issue: One of 760. $75–$100.

BELCHER, Sir Edward. *Narrative of a Voyage Round the World . . . 1836–1842.* 19 plates, 3 maps in pocket. 2 vols., cloth. London, 1843. First edition. $600–$800.

BELL, Acton. *Agnes Grey.* See Bell, Ellis and Acton. *Wuthering Heights.*

BELL, Acton. *The Tenant of Wildfell Hall.* 3 vols., dark claret-colored cloth. London, 1848. (By Anne Brontë.) First edition. $750–$1,000. Also, rebound in calf, $650 (A, 1974).

BELL, Clive. *Poems.* Wrappers. Richmond (London), 1921. Hogarth Press. First edition. One of 350. $250–$375

BELL, Currer (editor). *Jane Eyre: An Autobiography.* 3 vols., red, or claret, cloth. London, 1847. (By Charlotte Brontë.) First edition, first issue, with 36-page catalogue at back of first volume, dated June and October, with half titles, and with a leaf advertising the *Calcutta Review.* $5,000–$6,000. Also, imperfect, repaired copy, $4,000 (A, 1981). Another copy, rebound, $2,200 in a recent catalogue. London, 1847. Second edition. (Currer Bell as author instead of editor on title page.) $400–$600. London, 1848. Third edition. $200–$350. Paris, 1923. Illustrated by Ethel Gabain. Folio, wrappers. One of 460. $100–$150.

BELL, Currer. *The Professor.* 2 vols., plum-colored cloth. London, 1857. (By Charlotte Brontë.) First edition, with 2 pages of ads at end of Vol. 1 and 16 pages of ads at end of Vol. 2 dated June, 1857. $1,000 and up. One-volume issue: London, 1857 (actually 1858). In a remainder binding, with 1858 ads, $836 in a London catalogue, 1979. New York, 1857. Cloth. First American edition. $100.

BELL, Currer. *Shirley: A Tale.* 3 vols., deep claret-colored cloth. London, 1849. (By Charlotte Brontë.) First edition, with 16 pages of ads dated October, 1849, at end of Vol. 1. $1,000 and up. Also, worn, $484 (A, 1979).

BELL, Currer. *Villette.* 3 vols., olive-brown cloth. London, 1853. (By Charlotte Brontë.) First edition, with 12 pages of ads dated January, 1853, in Vol. 1. $1,500 and up. Also, $770 (A, 1979).

BELL, Currer, Ellis, and Acton. *Poems.* Dark-green cloth. London, 1846. (By Charlotte, Emily and Anne Brontë). First edition, first issue, published by Aylott and Jones. $2,000 and up. London, 1846 (actually 1848). Green cloth. Published by Smith, Elder & Co. Second issue, with 4-line errata slip. $500–$750. Philadelphia, 1848. Boards. First American edition. $400–$600.

BELL, Ellis (and Acton). *Wuthering Heights.* 3 vols., claret-colored cloth (third vol. titled *Agnes Grey,* by Acton Bell). London, 1847. (First two vols. by Emily Brontë, third by Anne Brontë.) First edition. (1,000 copies printed.) $15,000 and up. (A badly worn and defective set, with corrections in Charlotte Brontë's hand, was sold for $3,784 at a London auction house in June, 1975.) New York, 1931. Illustrated by Clare Leighton. Cloth. One of 450 signed by the artist. $150–$250.

BELL, Gertrude. *The Arab War.* Half linen. London, 1924. Golden Cockerel Press. One of 500. $250–$275.

BELL, Horace. *On the Old West Coast.* Edited by Lanier Bartlett. Plates and facsimiles. Half buckram and boards. New York, 1930. First edition. One of 20 signed by the editor. Boxed. $75–$100. Trade edition: Cloth. In dust jacket. $25–$30.

BELL, Horace. *Reminiscences of a Ranger.* Pictorial cloth. Los Angeles, 1881. First edition. $100–$150. Santa Barbara, 1927. Green cloth. In dust jacket. $40–$60.

BELL, John. *Discourses on the Nature and Cure of Wounds.* 2 plates. 2 vols. in one, leather. Walpole, N.H., 1807. First American edition. $150–$200.

BELL, Solomon. *Tales of Travel West of the Mississippi.* Map plates, Boards and cloth, leather label. Boston, 1830. (By William J. Snelling.) First edition. $300–$500. Also, $425 (A, 1979).

BELL, William A. *New Tracks in North America.* Plates and maps, some in color. 2 vols., cloth. London, 1869. First English edition. $150–$225.

BELLAMY, Edward. See *Six to One: A Nantucket Idyl.*

BELLAMY, Edward. *Equality.* Salmon-colored or blue cloth. New York, 1897. First edition. In dust jacket. $200–$250. Toronto, 1897. Wrappers. Copyright edition. $200.

BELLAMY, Edward. *Looking Backward, 2000–1887.* Pea-green, orange-brown, or gray cloth. Boston, 1888. First edition, first state, with printer's imprint of "J.J. Arakelyan" on copyright page. $350–$450. Another (second) issue: Gray wrappers. $200–$300, New York, 1941. Limited Editions Club. Cloth. Boxed. $30–$40.

BELLOC, Hilaire. See B.,H.

BELLOC, Hilaire. *The Book of the Bayeux Tapestry.* 76 colored facsimiles. Cloth. New York, 1914. $75–$125.

BELLOC, Hilaire. *Cautionary Tales for Children.* Pictorial boards. London, (1908). First edition. $85–$125.

BELLOC, Hilaire. *The Highway and Its Vehicles* Illustrated. Buckram. London, 1926. One of 1,250. $125–$200.

BELLOC, Hilaire. *New Cautionary Tales.* Illustrated. Half cloth. London, 1930. First edition. One of 110 signed. In dust jacket. $125–$150.

BELLOC, Hilaire. *The Praise of Wine.* Loose sheets in printed wrappers. (London, 1931). First edition. $100–$150.

BELLOC, Hilaire. *Verse.* Edited by W.H. Roughead. Buckram. London, 1954. Nonesuch Press. $75–$100.

BELLOC, Hilaire. *Verses and Sonnets.* Green cloth. London, 1896. First edition. $150–$200. Author's first book.

BELLOW, Saul. *The Adventures of Augie March.* Cloth. New York, 1953. First edition, first issue, with top edges orange. In first dust jacket without reviews. $125–$135.

BELLOW. Saul. *Dangling Man.* Cloth. New York, (1944). First edition. In dust jacket. $350–$450. London, 1946. Cloth. First English edition. In dust jacket. $150–$200. Author's first book.

BELLOW, Saul. *Henderson the Rain King.* Cloth. New York, 1959. First edition, first issue, top edges yellow. In dust jacket. $85–$100. London, (1959). First English edition. In dust jacket. $100.

BELLOW, Saul. *Herzog.* Stamped blue cloth. New York, (1964). First edition. In dust jacket. $50–$75. (Early copies lightly inked in printing. A debatable issue point, since all copies were bound.)

BELLOW, Saul. *Seize the Day.* Cloth. New York, 1956. First edition. In dust jacket. $75–$85.

BELLOW, Saul. *The Victim.* Cloth. New York, (1947). First edition. In dust jacket. $250–$275. London, (1948). First English edition. In dust jacket. $100.

BELTRAMI, G.C. *A Pilgrimage in Europe and America.* Portrait, folding map, other engravings. 2 vols., boards and linen. London, 1828. First English edition. $200–$250.

BEMELMANS, Ludwig. *Madeline.* Cloth. New York, 1930. First edition. In dust jacket. $75–$100.

BEMELMANS, Ludwig. *Now I Lay Me Down to Sleep.* Cloth, pictorial cloth label, leather spine label. New York, 1943. First edition. One of 500 signed. Boxed. $75–$100.

BEMELMANS, Ludwig. *Small Beer.* Cloth. New York, 1939. First edition. One of 75 with original colored illustrations. Boxed. $150–$200.

BENAVIDES, Alonso de. *The Memorial of Fray Alonso de Benavides, 1630.* Facsimile of Madrid edition of 1630. Boards. Chicago, 1916. One of 300. $300–$350.

BENCHLEY, Robert. *20,000 Leagues Under the Sea, or David Copperfield.* Cloth. New York, (1928). First edition. In dust jacket. $60–$75.

BENDIRE, Charles. *Life Histories of North American Birds.* 19 color plates. 2 vols., folio, cloth. Washington, 1892–95. First edition. $200–$300.

BENEDICT, Carl Peters. *A Tenderfoot Kid on Gyp Water.* Edited by J. Frank Dobie. Illustrated. Pictorial cloth. Austin, 1943. First edition. One of 550. $150–$175.

BENÉT, Rosemary, and Benét, Stephen Vincent. *A Book of Americans.* Illustrated. Cloth. New York, 1933. First edition. One of 125 signed. Boxed. $50–$75. Trade edition: Cloth. First issue, with publisher's monogram on copyright page. In dust jacket. $15–$20. Second issue: $7.50.

BENÉT, Stephen Vincent. See Rinehart, Mary Roberts, and Hopwood, Avery; Benét, Rosemary. Also see *The Yale Book of Student Verse, 1910–1919.*

BENÉT, Stephen Vincent. *Ballads and Poems: 1915–1930.* Pictorial boards. Garden City, 1931. First edition. One of 201 signed. Boxed. $100–$125. Trade edition: Cloth. In dust jacket. $15–$20.

BENÉT, Stephen Vincent. *Burning City.* Red fabrikoid. New York, (1936). First edition. One of 275 signed. In glassine dust jacket. Boxed. $75–$100. Trade edition: Cloth. In dust jacket. $25–$35.

BENÉT, Stephen Vincent. *The Devil and Daniel Webster.* Illustrated by Harold Denison. Buckram. Weston, Vt., (1937). First edition. One of 700 signed. In glassine dust jacket. Boxed. $100–$150. New York, (1937). Cloth. First trade edition. In dust jacket. $25.

BENÉT, Stephen Vincent. *The Drug Shop; or Endymion in Edmonstoun.* 24 pp., printed wrappers. (New Haven), 1917. First edition. 100 copies only. $250–$350. Also, signed, $280 (A, 1981).

BENÉT, Stephen Vincent. *Five Men and Pompey.* Wrappers over boards. Boston, 1915. First edition, first state, purple wrappers. $200–$250. Second state, brown wrappers. $100–$125. (Note: Johnson says there were "a few copies" on handmade paper.) Author's first book.

BENÉT, Stephen Vincent. *John Brown's Body.* Vellum boards. (Garden City, 1928.) First edition. One of 201 signed. Boxed. $350–$500. Trade edition: Cloth. In dust jacket. $25–$35. New York. 1948. Limited Editions Club. John Steuart Curry illustrations. Cloth. One of 1,500. Boxed. $35–$40.

BENÉT, Stephen Vincent. *Nightmare at Noon.* Printed wrappers. New York, (1940). First edition, first printing, with publisher's monogram on copyright page. $100–$150.

BENÉT, Stephen Vincent, and Benét, Laura. *A Portrait and a Poem.* Half morocco. Paris, 1934. First edition. One of 50. $275.

BENÉT, Stephen Vincent. *Tuesday, Nov. 5th, 1940.* 8 pp., wrappers. New York, 1941. First edition. One of 50. $100–$150.

BENÉT, William Rose. *Merchants from Cathay and Other Poems.* Green cloth. New York, 1913. First edition. $50–$60. Author's first book.

BENEZET, Anthony A. *The Family Physician.* Calf. Cincinnati, 1826. First edition. $275.

BENJAMIN, Asher, *The Practice of Architecture.* 60 full-page plates. Sheep. Boston, 1833. $400–$600. Also, $160 (A, 1979).

BENJAMIN, Asher. *The Rudiments of Architecture.* 36 plates, one folding. Calf. Boston, 1814. First edition. $800–$1,000. Boston, 1820. Second edition. $400–$600.

BENJAMIN, Asher, and Reynard, Daniel. *The American Builder's Companion.* 44 plates. Calf, or boards. Boston, (1806). First edition. $400–$500.

BENNETT, Arnold. See Bennett, E.A.; Wadsworth, Edward.

BENNETT, Arnold. *Anna of the Five Towns.* Cloth. London, 1902. First edition. $75.

BENNETT, Arnold. *The Bright Island.* Limp vellum. London, 1924. Golden Cockerel Press. One of 200 signed. $150–$200.

BENNETT, Arnold. *Clayhanger.* Cloth London, (1910). First edition. In dust jacket. $100–$125.

BENNETT, Arnold. *The Clayhanger Family.* Cloth. London, 1925. One of 200 signed. In dust jacket. $150–$200.

BENNETT, Arnold. *Don Juan de Marana.* Frontispiece. Vellum and boards. London, 1923. One of 100 signed. In dust jacket. $250–$300. Another issue: One of 1,000. $75–$100.

BENNETT, Arnold. *Elsie and the Child.* Color illustrations. Cloth. London, 1929. One of 100 signed. $150–$250. Another issue: One of 750. $100–$150.

BENNETT, Arnold. *From the Log of the Velsa.* Illustrated. White cloth. London, 1920. One of 110 signed. $150–$200.

BENNETT, Arnold. *Hilda Lessways.* Cloth. London, (1911). First edition. In dust jacket. $150–$250.

BENNETT, Arnold. *Imperial Palace.* 2 vols., vellum. London, (1930). First edition. One of 100 signed. $200–$300.

BENNETT, Arnold. *Journal 1929.* Boards. London, 1930. First edition. One of 75 signed. $125.

BENNETT, Arnold. *The Loot of Cities.* Wrappers. London, (1904). First edition. $400–$500. Another issue: Cloth. $300–$400.

BENNETT, Arnold. *Mr. Prohack.* Cloth. London, (1922). First edition. In dust jacket. $150.

BENNETT, Arnold. *The Old Wives' Tale.* Lavender, or pink, cloth, white lettering. London, 1908. First edition. $400–$600. London, 1927. 2 vols., parchment and cloth. Facsimile of the manuscript. One of 500 signed. $200–$250. New York, 1941. Limited Editions Club. Illustrated by John Austen. 2 vols., cloth. Boxed. $75–$125.

BENNETT, Arnold. *Things That Interested Me, Being Leaves from a Journal.* Cloth. Burslem, England, 1906. One of 100. $100–$125. London, 1921. Second Series. Cloth. In dust jacket. $75–$100. London, 1926. Third Series. Cloth. In dust jacket. $75–$100.

BENNETT, Arnold. *Things Which Have Interested Me.* Second Series. Parchment and boards. Burslem, 1907. One of 100 signed. $150–$200.

BENNETT, E.A. *A Man from the North.* Red cloth, stamped in white. London, (1898). First edition. $225–$250. Arnold Bennett's first book.

BENNETT, Emerson. *The Bandits of the Osage.* Printed wrappers (?). Cincinnati, 1847.

Published by Edwards & Goshorn. $400 and up. (Note: Blanck lists the first edition, same date, as published by Robinson & Jones. Estimated value at retail: $400–$600.)

BENNETT, Emerson. *Clara Moreland; or, Adventures in the Far South-West.* Printed wrappers or cloth. Philadelphia, (1863). First edition. $200–$300.

BENNETT, Emerson. *Leni-Leoti; or, Adventures in the Far West.* Printed orange wrappers. Cincinnati, 1849. First edition. $500–$600.

BENNETT, Emerson. *Mike Fink: A Legend of the Ohio.* Printed wrappers (?). Cincinnati, 1848. First edition. $500–$600. Cincinnati, (1852). Printed wrappers. Revised edition. $150–$200.

BENNETT, Emerson. *The Mysterious Marksman; or, The Outlaws of New York.* Wrappers. Cincinnati, (about 1855). First edition (?). $300 and up. (Note: This title not in Blanck.)

BENNETT, Emerson. *The Prairie Flower; or, Adventures in the Far West.* 128 pp., printed wrappers. Cincinnati, 1849. First edition. $400–$500. Later issue: Cloth. $250–$300. Cincinnati, 1850. Boards and cloth. New edition, revised. $200–$300.

BENNETT, Frederick D. *Narrative of a Whaling Voyage Around the World.* Frontispieces, folding map. 2 vols., cloth. London, 1840. First edition. $750.

BENNETT, George. *Gatherings of a Naturalist in Australasia.* 7 colored plates, one in sepia, numerous woodcuts. Cloth. London, 1860. $300–$400.

BENNETT, John. *Barnaby Lee.* Illustrated by Clyde O. De Land. Decorated cloth. New York, 1902. First edition. $75.

BENNETT, John. *Master Skylark: A Story of Shakespeare's Time.* Illustrated by Reginald Birch, Pictorial cloth. New York, 1897. First edition. $100–$125.

BENNETT, Melba Berry. *Robinson Jeffers and the Sea.* Decorated boards, morocco spine. San Francisco, 1936. Grabhorn printing. First edition. One of 300. In mustard-colored dust jacket. $100–$150.

BENSON, A.C. *Le Cahier Jaune.* Yellow wrappers. Eton, 1892. Limited edition. $100–$125. Author's first book.

BENSON, Frank W. (illustrator). *Etchings and Drypoints.* 285 reproductions. Text by Adam E.M. Paff. 4 vols., boards. Boston, 1917–29. One of 275, with frontispiece signed by Benson. In dust jackets. $500–$600.

BENSON, Henry C. *Life Among the Choctaw Indians.* Cloth. Cincinnati, 1860. First edition. $200–$250.

BENTLEY, E.C. *Trent's Last Case.* Blue cloth. London, (1913). First edition. In dust jacket. $250–$300. Lacking jacket, $50–$75.

BENTON, Frank. *Cowboy Life on the Sidetrack.* Illustrated. Pictorial cloth. Denver, (1903). First edition. $100–$125.

BENTON, J.A. *California As She Was, As She Is, As She is to Be.* 16 pp., pictorial wrappers, Sacramento, 1850. First edition. $2,250.

BEPPO, A Venetian Story. Drab wrappers. London, 1818. (By George Gordon Noel, Lord Byron.) First edition. $750–$1,000.

BERENSON, Bernard. *The Drawings of the Florentine Painters.* 180 full-page tinted plates. 2 vols., folio, half morocco. London, 1903. One of 355. $300–$400. New York, 1903. 2 vols. folio, boards and morocco. $150–$200. Chicago, 1938. 3 vols., small folio, boards, vellum spine. Amplified edition. $350–$450.

BERENSON, Bernard. *The Italian Painters of the Renaissance.* Illustrated. Cloth. London, (1952). Phaidon Press. $75–$100.

BERENSON, Bernard. *A Sienese Painter of the Franciscan Legend*. 26 color illustrations. Boards and cloth. London, 1909. First edition. $75.

BERENSON, Bernard. *Studies in Medieval Painting*. Illustrated. Cloth. New Haven, 1930. First edition. $75–$100.

BERENSON, Bernard. *Three Essays in Method*. Illustrated. Cloth. Oxford, 1927. First edition. $50–$75.

BERGER, Thomas, *Crazy in Berlin*. Cloth. New York, (1958). First edition. In dust jacket. $75–$85. Author's first book.

BERGER, Thomas. *Little Big Man*. Cloth. New York, 1964. First edition. In dust jacket. $65–$75.

BERGMAN, Ray. *Trout*. Flies in color. Full morocco. Philadelphia, 1938. First edition. One of 149 signed. $650–$750.

BERNARD, Auguste, *Geofroy Tory, Painter and Engraver*. Translated by George B. Ives. Boards. (Cambridge, Mass.), 1909. One of 370 designed by Bruce Rogers. $350–$400.

BERNERS, Dame Juliana. *A Treatyse of Fysshynge with an Angle*. Woodcuts. Full green morocco. London (Chelsea), 1903. Ashendene Press. One of 25 on vellum. $3,000–$3,500. Another issue: Vellum. One of 150 on paper. Boxed. $400–$600.

BERNSTEIN, Aline. *Three Blue Suits*. Frontispiece. Tan-blue cloth, paper labels. New York, 1933. First edition. One of 600 signed. Boxed. $75–$125. Author's first book.

BERQUIN-DUVALLON. See *Travels in Louisiana and the Floridas*.

BERRIGAN, Daniel. *Time Without Number*. Boards and cloth. New York, 1957. First edition. In dust jacket with wraparound band. $35–$50. Author's first book.

BERRY, Wendell. *November Twenty Six Nineteen Hundred Sixty Three*. Illustrated by Ben Shahn. Cloth. New York, (1964). First edition. Limited issue signed by Shahn and Berry. Boxed. $100–$125. Trade edition: $25.

BERRYMAN, John. See *Columbia Poetry, 1935*.

BERRYMAN, John. *The Dispossessed*. Boards. New York, (1948). First edition. In dust jacket. $250–$375.

BERRYMAN, John. *His Thought Made Pockets & the Plane Buckt*. Boards, leather spine. Pawlet, Vt., 1958. First edition. One of 26 lettered copies signed by the author. $400–$500. Another issue: Wrappers. One of 500. In printed envelope. $75–$100.

BERRYMAN, John. *Homage to Mistress Bradstreet*. Illustrated by Ben Shahn. Boards. New York, (1956). First edition. In dust jacket. $100–$150.

BERRYMAN, John. *Love and Fame*. Cloth. New York, 1970. First edition. One of 250 signed. Boxed. $100–$125. Also, presentation copies, lettered in various styles. $200. Trade edition: Cloth. In dust jacket. $20.

BERRYMAN, John. *Poems*. Printed blue wrappers. Norfolk, Conn., (1942). New Directions. First edition. Poet of the Month series. In dust jacket. $75–$100. Another issue: Boards. One of 500 hardbound copies. In dust jacket. $250–$300. Author's first book.

BERRYMAN, John. *Stephen Crane*. Cloth. (New York, 1950.) First edition. In dust jacket. $150–$200.

BERT, Edmund. *Treatise of Hawks and Hawking*. Illustrated. Boards, leather spine. London, 1891. One of 100. $150–$200.

BESANT, Walter. *The Art of Fiction*. Yellow cloth. Boston, 1885. First edition. $75–$100. (Note: Contains an essay on fiction by Henry James.)

BESSIE, Alvah C. *Dwell in the Wilderness.* Cloth. New York, (1935). First edition. In dust jacket. $100. Author's first book.

BETJEMAN, John. See O'Betjeman, Deirdre.

BETJEMAN, John. *Antiquarian Prejudice.* Wrappers. London, 1939. Hogarth Press. First edition. In slipcase. $75–$100.

BETJEMAN, John. *John Betjeman's Collected Poems.* Compiled by the Earl of Birkenhead. Scarlet leather. London, 1958. First edition. One of 100 signed. In slipcase. $150–$175. Trade edition: Cream-colored cloth. In dust jacket. $50–$60.

BETJEMAN, John. *Continual Dew.* Illustrated. Black cloth. London, (1937). First edition. In dust jacket. $75–$125.

BETJEMAN, John. *English Cities and Small Towns.* 8 color plates, 31 black and white illustrations. Brown boards. London, 1943. First edition. In dust jacket. $100–$125.

BETJEMAN, John. *A Few Late Chrysanthemums.* White buckram. London, 1954. First edition. One of 50 signed. $150–$200. Trade edition: Purple cloth. In dust jacket. $35–$50.

BETJEMAN, John. *First and Last Loves.* Illustrated. Cream-colored cloth. London, (1952). First edition. In dust jacket. $50–$60.

BETJEMAN, John. *Ghastly Good Taste.* Folding plate. Printed pink boards and cloth. London, 1933. First edition, first issue, with pages 119–120 not canceled. $75–$125. London, 1970. Half leather. One of 200 signed. Boxed. $100–$125.

BETJEMAN, John. *High and Low.* Buckram. London, (1966). First edition. One of 100 signed. $100–$125. Second printing: Yellow cloth. In dust jacket. $35.

BETJEMAN, John. *Mount Zion, or In Touch with the Infinite.* Illustrated. Red, white and blue striped boards, pictorial label on front cover. London, (1931). James Press. First edition. $500–$600. Author's first book.

BETJEMAN, John. *New Bats in Old Belfries.* Red cloth, paper label. London, 1945. One of a few signed copies on special paper with colored title page. In dust jacket. $150–$200. Unsigned, in dust jacket. $35–$40.

BETJEMAN, John. *Old Lights for New Chancels.* Portrait frontispiece. Wrappers. London, (1940). First edition. In dust jacket. $75–$85.

BETJEMAN, John. *An Oxford University Chest.* Photographs by Moholy-Nagy. Illustrations by Osbert Lancaster, etc. Marbled boards, cloth spine, gilt top. London, (1938). First edition. $150–$175.

BETJEMAN, John. *Poems in the Porch.* Illustrated. Pictorial wrappers. London, 1954. Talbot Press. First edition. $50–$75.

BETJEMAN, John. *Selected Poems.* Buckram. London, 1948. First edition. One of 18 signed. $300–$350. Trade edition: Red cloth. In dust jacket. $50–$60.

BETJEMAN, John. *Summoned by Bells.* Illustrated, Full green leather, gilt top. London, 1960. First edition. One of 125 signed. $125–$150. Trade edition: Green cloth. In dust jacket. $25.

BEVIER, Robert S. *History of the First and Second Missouri Confederate Brigades, 1861–1865.* 2 portraits. Cloth. St. Louis, 1879. First edition. $150–$200.

BEWICK, Thomas. (Note: The various works of this famous engraver exist in innumerable editions and issues. I have chosen only a few representative items here, omitting Bewick's *General History of Quadrupeds,* first published in 1790 and therefore not within the scope of this compilation.)

BEWICK Gleanings. Edited by Julia Boyd. 53 plates. Green morocco. Newcastle-on-Tyne, England, 1886. Large paper edition, signed, $400–$500.

BEWICK, Thomas. *A History of British Birds*. Woodcuts. 2 vols., contemporary leather. Newcastle, 1797–1804. First edition. $600–$800. Newcastle, 1821. 2 vols., green morocco. Each volume signed by Bewick. $400–$450.

BEWICK, Thomas. *Select Fables*. Portraits and woodcuts. Boards. Newcastle, 1820. First edition. $300–$400. Edinburgh, 1879. Vellum and white boards. Edition De Luxe on Whatman paper. One of 100. $250–$350.

BEWICK, Thomas. *The Water Colour Drawings of Thomas Bewick*. 40 illustrations in color. Half pigskin. London, 1930. Alcuin Press. $200–$300.

BEY, Pilaff. *Venus in the Kitchen*. Edited by Norman Douglas, with foreword by Graham Greene. Illustrated. Wrappers. London, (1952). "Proof Copy for Your Personal Reading" (so imprinted on front cover). $100–$125.

BEYER, Edward. *Album of Virginia*. 40 tinted lithograph views, plus decorated text. 2 vols., cloth, or half cloth (oblong folio plate volume and octavo text volume). Richmond, 1856. First edition. $6,000–$10,000, possibly more. (No copy of the first edition has appeared for public sale in modern times.) Richmond, 1857. $2,000 or more. Richmond, 1858. $1,820 (in dealer's catalogue).

BIANCO, Margery Williams. *Poor Cecco*. 7 mounted color plates by Arthur Rackham. Cloth. New York (or London), (1925). First edition, first issue, with pictorial end papers. In dust jacket. Boxed. $400–$550. Second issue, plain end papers. $350–$500. De Luxe signed issue: Half vellum and blue boards. One of 105 signed by the author. In dust jacket. Boxed. $5,000–$7,500.

BICKERSTAFF, Isaac. *The Rhode-Island Almanac for 1842*. Stitched. Providence, (1841). $200. (Note: Contains "Indian Barbarity," about Miss Fleming's captivity.)

BIDDLE, Owen. *The Young Carpenter's Assistant*. 46 plates. Morocco. Philadelphia, 1805. First edition. $500–$750.

BIDWELL, John. *Echoes of the Past About California*. 3 photographic views. Wrappers. Chico, Calif., (1914). First edition. $35–$50.

BIDWELL, John. *A Journey to California*. 48 pp., boards and cloth. San Francisco, 1937. $75–$100. (Note: One copy is known of the 1842 original of this narrative.)

BIERCE, Ambrose. See Grile, Dod; Herman, William; and Bowers, Mrs. Dr. J. Milton.

BIERCE, Ambrose. *Battle Sketches*. 8 wood engravings. Vellum. London, 1930. Shakespeare Head Press. One of 350. Boxed. $100–$150.

BIERCE, Ambrose. *Black Beetles in Amber*. Frontispiece. Light-gray or red cloth. San Francisco, 1892. First edition, first issue, with imprint of Western Authors Publishing Company. $150–$200. Second issue: Printed gray wrappers. Published by Johnson & Emigh. $200–$250.

BIERCE, Ambrose. *Can Such Things Be?* Golden brown cloth, or printed yellow wrappers. New York, (1893). First edition. Cloth: $50–$75. Wrappers: $100-$125. Washington, 1903. Maroon cloth. $10–$15.

BIERCE, Ambrose. *The Cynic's Word Book*. Olive-green cloth. New York, 1906. First edition, presumed first issue, without frontispiece. $150. Another (later?) issue: Frontispiece inserted. $100–$125. (Note: Blanck had seen no such copy, although Vincent Starrett had reported the existence of a frontispiece in some copies. Priority unknown.)

BIERCE, Ambrose. *Fantastic Fables*. Pictorial brownish yellow cloth. New York, 1899. First edition, first printing, with ads at back headed by "By Anna Fuller." $100–$125. Later, blue cloth, with ads headed "New Fiction." $50–$75.

BIERCE, Ambrose. *A Horseman in the Sky*. Boards and cloth. San Francisco, 1920. John Henry Nash printing. One of 400. $100–$125.

BIERCE, Ambrose. *In the Midst of Life*. Blue cloth. London, 1892. First English edition (of *Tales of Soldiers and Civilians*). $75–$100. (Second issue appeared in colored boards.) New York, 1898. Cloth. (Reprint of the *Tales* with three added stories.) $50–$60.

BIERCE, Ambrose. *The Letters of Ambrose Bierce*. Edited by Bertha C. Pope. Frontispiece portrait. Boards and cloth. San Francisco, 1922. Book Club of California. Printed by John Henry Nash. One of 415. $75–$100.

BIERCE, Ambrose. *My Favorite Murder*. Wrappers. (New York, 1916.) First separate edition. $125.

BIERCE, Ambrose. *The Shadow on the Dial and Other Essays*. Edited by S.O. Howes. Green buckram. San Francisco, 1909. First edition. In dust jacket. $75–$125.

BIERCE, Ambrose. *Shapes of Clay*. Portrait frontispiece. Blue or red cloth. San Francisco, 1903. First edition, first issue, with transposed lines on page 71. $300–$350. Second issue, corrected: $275.

BIERCE, Ambrose. *A Son of the Gods and a Horseman in the Sky*. Frontispiece. Vellum and boards. San Francisco, (1907). First separate edition. One of 1,000. In dust jacket. Boxed. $75–$100.

BIERCE, Ambrose. *Tales of Soldiers and Civilians*. Brown, green, or gray cloth. San Francisco, 1891. First edition. $250–$400. Some copies imprinted "Compliments of" on preliminary leaf and signed by Bierce—the so-called "limited" edition. $400–$500. New York, 1943. Limited Editions Club. Boards and leather. Boxed. $50–$60. (For first English edition see Bierce, *In the Midst of Life*.)

BIERCE, Ambrose. *Ten Tales*. Preface by A.J.A. Symons. Red cloth. London, 1925. First edition. In dust jacket. $50–$75.

BIERCE, Ambrose. *Write It Right: A Little Blacklist of Literary Faults*. Tan cloth. New York, 1909. First edition, first issue, 5¾ by 3 inches in size. In dust jacket. $150–$175. San Francisco, 1971. Grabhorn printing. One of 400. $50–$75.

BIERCE, Ambrose, and Danziger, Gustav Adolph. *The Monk and the Hangman's Daughter*. Illustrated by Theodore Hampe. Printed yellow wrappers, or gray cloth. Chicago, 1892. First edition. Wrappers. $150–$200. Cloth: $125–$150. (Note: Danziger was a pseudonym for Adolphe De Castro.) New York, 1907. Green cloth $50–$75. New York, 1967. Illustrated. Limited Editions Club. Boxed $50–$60.

BIGELOW, Jacob. *American Medical Botany*. 60 color plates. Vols. 1–3 in 6 vols., cloth, paper labels, or 6 parts, printed boards. Boston, 1817–1820. First edition. Cloth (6 vols.): $2,000–$2,500. Boards (6 parts): $2,500 and up.

BIGELOW, Jacob. *A Discourse of Self-Limited Diseases*. Wrappers. Boston, 1835. First edition. $400–$500.

BIGGERS, Don H. *From Cattle Range to Cotton Patch*. Illustrated. Stiff wrappers. Abilene, Tex., (about 1908). First edition. $400–$500. Bandera, Tex., 1944. Second edition. $65–$100.

BIGGERS, Earl Derr. *Behind That Curtain*. Cloth. Indianapolis, (1928). First edition. In dust jacket. $100–$125.

BIGGS, William. *Narrative of William Biggs, While He Was a Prisoner with the Kickepoo Indians*. 22pp., wrappers. (Edwardsville, Ill.?), June, 1826. First edition. $2,500–$3,000. (Howes, who located two copies, gives the date as 1825. Byrd located a privately held copy in Vermont and fixed the date at 1826. In March, 1978, a fourth copy, with back wrapper only, was located in California. Careful examination of the blurred printing date of this copy and of the copy held by the Newberry Library seems to indicate that 1826 is the correct date.)

BIGHAM, Clive. *The Roxburghe Club: Its History and Its Members, 1812–1927*. Half morocco. Oxford, 1928. First edition. $300–$500.

BIGMORE, E.C., and Wyman, C.W.H. *A Bibliography of Printing*. 3 vols., cloth, leather spine, London, 1880–86. First edition. One of 250 large paper copies. $300–$350. New York, 1945. 3 vols. in 2, buckram. Facsimile reprint, with type page enlarged. $150–$225.

BINGHAM, Caleb. *An Astronomical and Geographical Catechism for the Use of Children*. Wallpaper wrappers. Boston, 1802. Sixth edition. $75–$125.

BINGHAM, Helen M. *History of Green County, Wisconsin*. Frontispiece. Cloth. Milwaukee, 1877. First edition. $75–$100.

BINYON, Laurence. *The Art of Botticelli*. Muirhead Bone etching, 23 color plates. Folio, cloth, vellum spine, London, 1913. One of 275. $200–$300.

BINYON, Laurence. *A Catalogue of Japanese and Chinese Woodcuts*. 39 illustrations. Cloth. London, 1916. $150–$300.

BINYON, Laurence. *The Court Painters of the Grand Moguls*. 39 full-page plates, 9 colored. Cloth. Oxford, 1921. First edition. $150–$175.

BINYON, Laurence. *The Drawings and Engravings of William Blake*. Plates, some in color. Folio, vellum portfolio with ties. London, 1922. One of 200. $300–$400. Another issue: Vellum and boards. $150–$200.

BINYON, Laurence. *Dream-Come-True*. Woodcut frontispiece. Boards. London, 1905. Eragny Press. One of 175 on paper. $275–$450. Another issue: One of 10 on vellum. $750–$1,000.

BINYON, Laurence. *The Engraved Designs of William Blake*. Plates. Half cloth and boards. London, 1926. One of 100 with an extra set of plates. $600–$800. Without the extra plates. $200–$350.

BINYON, Laurence. *The Followers of William Blake*. 79 plates, 7 colored. Cloth. London, 1925. First edition. $150. Another issue: One of 100. $350–$400.

BINYON, Laurence. *The George Eumorfopolous Collection*. (Catalogue of the Chinese Frescoes.) 50 full-page color plates. Folio, gold and black cloth. London, 1927. One of 560. $350–$450.

BINYON, Laurence. *Little Poems from the Japanese Rendered into English Verse*. Wrappers. Leeds, England, 1925. Swan Press. First edition. One of 200. $150–$200.

BINYON, Laurence. *Painting in the Far East*. 30 plates. Cloth. London, 1908. First edition. $75–$100.

BINYON, Laurence, *Poems*. Wrappers. Oxford, 1895. Daniel Press. First edition. One of 200. $100–$150.

BINYON, Laurence, and Sexton, J.J. O'Brien. *Japanese Colour Prints*. 46 plates, some in color. Buckram. London, 1923. $100–$125. Another issue: Pigskin. One of 100 signed, with an extra set of plates. $400–$450.

BINYON, Laurence; Wilkinson, J.V.S.; and Gray, Basil. *Persian Miniature Painting*. Illustrated, including color plates. Folio, cloth. London, 1923. $600–$800.

BIOGRAPHICAL Dictionary (A) of the Living Authors of Great Britain and Ireland. Contemporary calf. London, 1816. (By John Watkins and Frederick Shoberl.) First edition. $200–$300.

BIOGRAPHICAL Note of Commodore Jesse D. Elliott (A). By a Citizen of New York. Printed boards. Philadelphia, 1835. (By Russell Jarvis.) First edition. $100–$125.

BIOGRAPHICAL Sketch, Words of the Songs, Ballads, etc., of the Composer and Vocalist, Stephen Massett. "*Jeems Pipes, of Pipesville*." Portrait. 52 pp., wrappers. New York, 1858. First edition. $75–$100.

BIOGRAPHICAL Souvenir of the State of Texas. Illustrated. Full leather. Chicago, 1889. $750–$1,000.

BIOGRAPHY of James Lawrence, Esq. Portrait. Printed paper boards. New-Brunswick, N.J., 1813. (By Washington Irving?) First edition. $150–$250.

BIOGRAPHY of Joseph Lane. By Western. Three-quarters morocco. Washington, 1852. $350.

BIRD, Robert Montgomery. See *The Adventures of Robin Day; Calavar; The Infidel; Nick-of-the-Woods; Peter Pilgrim; Sheppard Lee.*

BIRKBECK, Morris. See *An Impartial Appeal; Remarks Addressed to the Citizens of Illinois.*

BIRKBECK, Morris. *An Appeal to the People of Illinois, on the Question of a Convention.* 25pp., wrappers. Shawneetown, Ill., 1823. First edition. $500–$800. Also, $425 (A, 1967).

BIRKBECK, Morris. *Extracts from a Supplementary Letter from the Illinois.* 29 pp., half leather. New York, 1819. First edition $600–$800. Also, disbound and foxed, $400 (A, 1967).

BIRKBECK, Morris. *Letters from Illinois.* 2 folding maps. Boards and calf. Philadelphia, 1818. First edition. $100–$200.

BIRKBECK, Morris. *Notes on a Journey in America from the Coast of Virginia to the Territory of Illinois.* Boards. Philadelphia, 1817. First edition. $300–$400. Also, $140 (A, 1973). London, 1818. Map. Boards and calf. First English edition. $100–$200. Issued also without map, same date: $35–$50. (There were three other English editions in 1818; all are valued in the $75–$125 range.) Philadelphia, 1819. $35.

BISHOP, Elizabeth. *North & South.* Cloth. Boston, 1946. First edition. In dust jacket. $150–$250. Author's first book.

BISHOP, Elizabeth. *Poems.* Boards. London, 1956. First edition. In dust jacket. $75–$100.

BISHOP, Elizabeth, *Questions of Travel.* Cloth. New York, (1965). First edition. In dust jacket. $40–$50.

BISHOP, John Peale. *Act of Darkness.* Cloth. New York, 1935. First edition. In dust jacket. $50–$75. Author's first and only novel.

BISHOP, John Peale. *Green Fruit.* Boards and cloth. Boston, 1917. First edition. In dust jacket. $50–$75. Author's first book.

BISHOP, John Peale. *Minute Particulars.* Wrappers. New York, 1935. First edition. One of 165 signed. In glassine dust jacket. $150–$175.

BISHOP, John Peale, and Wilson, Edmund. *The Undertaker's Garland.* Cloth. New York, 1922. First edition. In dust jacket. $200–$250. Another issue: Boards. One of 50 for "bookseller friends." $350–$500. Bishop's second book.

BISHOP, Richard E. *Bishop's Birds: Etchings of Waterfowl and Upland Game Birds.* 73 reproductions. Pictorial cloth. Philadelphia, 1936. First edition. One of 1,050. $175–$250. Another issue: Parchment. One of 125 signed, with signed Bishop etching tipped in. Boxed. $300–$400.

BISHOP, Richard E. *Bishop's Wildfowl . . . Etchings and Oil Painting Reproductions.* Text by E. Prestrud and R. Williams. Color plates. Full calf. (St. Paul), 1948. First edition. $300–$400.

BISHOP, Zealia. *The Curse of Yig.* Black cloth. Sauk City, Wis., 1953. Arkham House. First edition. In dust jacket. $50–$60.

BISLAND, Elizabeth (editor). *The Life and Letters of Lafcadio Hearn.* Illustrated. 2

vols., cloth. Boston, 1906. First edition. One of 200 with a page of an original manuscript by Hearn. $400–$500. Trade edition: $25–$35.

BLACKBIRD, Andrew J. *History of the Ottawa and Chippewa Indians of Michigan.* Cloth. Ypsilanti, Mich., 1887. First edition. $150–$200.

BLACKBURN, Paul. *The Dissolving Fabric.* Wrappers. (Mallorca), 1955. Divers Press. $100–$125. Author's first book.

BLACKBURN, Paul. *Gin.* Half vellum. Mt. Horeb, Wis., (1970). First edition. One of 136. $125.

BLACKBURN, Paul (translator). *Guillem de Poitou.* Illustrated. Half morocco. Mt. Horeb, Wis., (1976). First edition, with pamphlet of notes in special envelope. First edition. One of 165. $225.

BLACKER, William. *Blacker's Art of Fly-Making.* Illustrated, including color plates. Cloth. London, 1855. $600–$800.

BLACKMORE, Richard D. *Lorna Doone: A Romance of Exmoor.* 3 vols., blue watered cloth. London, 1869. First edition. $750–$1,000. Also, worn and repaired, $350 (A, 1981).

BLACKMUR, R. P. *The Expense of Greatness.* Cloth. New York, 1940. First edition. In dust jacket. $50–$60.

BLACKMUR, R.P. *From Jordan's Delight.* New York, 1937. First edition. In dust jacket. $50–$60.

BLACKMUR, R.P. *The Good European & Other Poems.* Cloth, paper label. Cummington, Mass., 1947. First edition. One of 40 signed. $100–$150.

BLACKMUR, R.P. *The Second World.* Cloth. (Cummington), 1942. Cummington Press. First edition. One of 300. In dust jacket. $150–$200.

BLACKMUR, R.P. *T.S. Eliot.* Wrappers. (Cambridge, Mass.), 1928. First edition. $150–$200. Author's first book.

BLACKWATER Chronicle (The). By "The Clerke of Oxenforde." Illustrated. Cloth. New York, 1853. (By Pendleton Kennedy, or, as some suppose, by his brother John Pendleton Kennedy.) First edition. $300–$400.

BLACKWOOD, Algernon. *The Empty House and Other Ghost Stories.* Cloth. London, 1906. First edition. $125–$175. Author's first book.

BLACKWOOD, Algernon. *Incredible Adventures.* Cloth. London, 1914. First edition. In dust jacket. $150.

BLACKWOOD, Algernon. *The Lost Valley.* Illustrated. New York, 1914. First edition. One of 500. $150.

BLAIR, Robert. *The Grave: A Poem.* Portrait and 12 etchings by Schiavonetti after designs by Blake. Boards. London, 1808. $800–$1,000. (There was a large paper issue as well as an ordinary issue. Either is rare and valuable.)

BLAKE, W.O. *The History of Slavery and the Slave Trade.* Illustrated. Roan. Columbus, Ohio, 1857. First edition. $75–$100.

BLAKE, William. See Binyon, Laurence. (Note: There have been innumerable facsimile reproductions of the illuminated books of William Blake, poet, mystic, artist, and engraver [1757–1827], the originals of which are of the greatest rarity. A few of the more popular editions are listed here. For more complete listings, see *American Book-Prices Current* and the British publication *Book Auction Records*).

BLAKE, William. *America, a Prophecy.* Facsimile by William Muir of the rare 1793 first edition. Wrappers. Edmonton, Alberta, Canada, 1887. One of 50. $250–$400. (New

York), 1947. Cloth. $50–$60. London (Paris), 1963. Facsimile, with 18 plates. Boards and leather. One of 480. Boxed. $300–$400.

BLAKE, William. *The Book of Thel*. Facsimile, with hand-colored pages by William Muir. Folio, wrappers. London, 1920. One of 50. $400–$500. (Paris, 1956). Trianon Press. 8 plates in color with additional material showing progressive stages in the platework. Full morocco. One of 20 sets. $1,000 and up. Another issue: Half morocco. One of 380. Boxed. $250–$275.

BLAKE, William. *The Book of Urizen*. Facsimile of the 1794 first edition, with 27 plates reproduced by color-collotype and stencil. Half morocco. London (Paris), 1858. One of 480. In slipcase. $750 and up. Another issue: Full morocco. One of 20, with 27 plates and a set of progressive stages, guide sheet stencil proofs, and other material used in making one of the plates. In handmade case. $1,250–$1,500.

BLAKE, William. *Genesis*. Cummington, Mass., 1952. One of 170. $300 and up.

BLAKE, William. *Illustrations of the Book of Job*. Title page and 21 other plates engraved by Blake. Folio. London, 1825. First edition, with plate No. 1 misdated 1828. (In various bindings—cloth folders, wrappers, morocco, etc.) $8,000–$15,000. London, 1902. Facsimile. Wrappers. $200–$250. New York, 1935. 6 parts, folio, wrappers. One of 200. Boxed. $1,500–$1,800.

BLAKE, William. *Jerusalem*. Facsimile of the original illuminated book of 1804. 10 full-page and 45 half-page watercolors, 45pp. with colored designs. 5 parts, folio, wrappers. London (Paris), (1951). Trianon Press. One of 516. Boxed. $3,000–$4,000. In book form: Buckram. $1,750–$2,000.

BLAKE, William. *The Marriage of Heaven and Hell*. J.C. Hotten's facsimile of the 1790 original. 27 leaves hand-colored. Boards. (London, 1868.) $150–$250. Other editions: (Edmonton, 1885.) William Muir's facsimile. Wrappers. One of 50. $200–$250. London, 1960. Trianon Press facsimile. Folio, boards and morocco. One of 526. $600–$800. Another issue: One of 20 of the edition of 526 with a set of hand-colored plates (proofs, etc.). $1,500–$2,000.

BLAKE, William. *The Note-Book of William Blake Called the Rossetti Manuscript*. Edited by Geoffrey Keynes. 120pp. in facsimile. Buckram. London, 1935. Nonesuch Press. One of 650. In dust jacket. $200–$250.

BLAKE, William. *Pencil Drawings*. Edited by Geoffrey Keynes. 82 facsimile plates. Half buckram. London, 1927. Nonesuch Press. Limited edition. In dust jacket. $250–$350. Second Series: London, 1956. Cloth. Limited. In dust jacket. $200–$250.

BLAKE, William. *Songs of Innocence*. Frontispiece. Half cloth. San Francisco, 1924. Grabhorn printing. One of 100. $150–$200.

BLAKE, William. *Songs of Innocence and of Experience*. Facsimile reproduction in collotype of the 54 plates from the 1794 original. Full morocco. London, 1955. Trianon Press. One of 526. In slipcase. $750–$1,000.

BLAKE, William. *The Writings of William Blake*. Edited by Geoffrey Keynes. 3 vols., half vellum and marbled boards. London, 1925. Nonesuch Press. One of 1,500. Boxed. $300–$500. Thin paper issue: 3 vols. in one, morocco or limp vellum. One of 75. $750–$1,000.

BLANCHARD, Rufus (publisher). *Citizen's Guide for the City of Chicago: Companion to Blanchard's Map of Chicago*. Printed stiff wrappers, with the folding map bound in. Chicago, (1868). $600–$1,000.

BLANCHARD, Rufus. *Discovery and Conquests of the North West*. 7 maps and plates. 6 parts, wrappers, or bound together in morocco or cloth. Wheaton, Ill., 1879. First edition. In parts: $350–$400. Morocco or cloth: $75–$100. Wheaton (some copies say "Chicago"), 1880. (One 1880 copy noted with 1881 copyright.) Reprint edition. $75. Chicago (some copies say "Wheaton"), 1881. Enlarged edition, 11 maps and plates. $75. Wheaton, 1898–1900 (actually 1903). 2 vols. $75.

BLANCK, Jacob. *Peter Parley to Penrod.* Cloth. New York, 1938. One of 500. $75–$150. New York, 1956. Second edition. Cambridge, Mass., 1961. $35–$50.

BLAND, David. *A History of Book Illustration.* Illustrated. Cloth. Cleveland, (1958). First American edition. In dust jacket. $125–$150.

BLAND, Jane Cooper. *Currier & Ives: A Manual for Collectors.* 24 pages of color plates, other illustrations. Cloth. New York, (1931). $100–$125.

BLANDEN, Charles G., and Mathison, Minna (editors). *The Chicago Anthology.* Cloth. Chicago, 1916. First edition. $75–$100.

BLAVATSKY, H.P. *Isis Unveiled: A Master Key to the Mysteries of Ancient and Modern Theology.* 2 vols., cloth. New York, 1877. First edition. With inserted autograph slip of certification. $200–$250. New York, 1923. 2 vols., cloth. $50. New York, (1950). 2 vols., cloth. $50.

BLAVATSKY, H.P. *Nightmare Tales.* Black cloth. London, 1892. First edition. $150–$200.

BLAVATSKY, H.P. *The Secret Doctrine.* 2 vols., cloth. London, 1888. First edition. $100–$150. London, 1893–98. 4 vols. (3 vols. with index), cloth. $100. London, (1928). 3 vols., cloth. $50–$60.

BLEDSOE, A.J. *History of Del Norte County, California.* Printed wrappers. Eureka, Calif., 1881. First edition. $2,000 and up.

BLEDSOE, A.J. *Indian Wars of the Northwest.* Cloth or leather. San Francisco, 1885. First edition. $250–$300.

BLEW, William C.A. *A History of Steeple-Chasing.* 28 illustrations, 12 hand-colored plates. Cloth. London, 1901. $200–$250.

BLEW William C.A. *The Quorn Hunt and Its Masters.* Map, 12 hand-colored plates. Cloth. London, 1899. First edition. $125–$150.

BLIGH, William. *The Log of the Bounty.* Illustrated. 2 vols., buckram. London, (1937). Golden Cockerel Press. One of 300. $600–$750.

BLISS, Edward. *A Brief History of the New Gold Regions of Colorado Territory.* Map. 30pp., wrappers. New York, 1864. First edition. $1,250–$1,500. Rebound in leather and cloth, $950.

BLOCH, Robert. *The Eighth Stage of Fandom.* Cloth. Chicago, 1962. First edition. Limited and signed. In dust jacket. $125–$150.

BLOCH, Robert. *The Opener of the Way.* Cloth. Sauk City, Wis., 1945. Arkham House. First edition. In dust jacket. $100–$150. Author's first book.

BLOCH, Robert. *Psycho.* Boards. New York, 1959. First edition. In dust jacket. $75–$100.

BLODGETT, Henry W. *Autobiography,* Cloth. Waukegan, Ill., 1906. First edition. $125–$150.

BLOME, Richard. *Hawking or Faulconry.* London, 1929. Cresset Press. One of 650. $200–$250.

BLOSSOMS of Morality (The). 51 wood engravings. Half calf and boards. Philadelphia, 1810. (By Richard Johnson.) $45–$50.

BLOWE, Daniel. *A Geographical, Commercial, and Agricultural View of the United States of America.* Portrait, 2 maps, 4 plans. Calf. Liverpool, (1820). $200–$300.

BLUE Grotto (The) and Its Literature. 18pp., printed red wrappers. London, 1904. (By Norman Douglas.) First edition. $75–$100.

BLUNDEN, Edmund. *Dead Letters*. Decorated wrappers, paper label. London, 1923. Pelican Press. One of 50. $150–$175.

BLUNDEN, Edmund. *Japanese Garland*. 6 color plates. Boards and vellum. London, 1928. Beaumont Press. One of 80 signed. $200.

BLUNDEN, Edmund. *Masks of Time*. Illustrated by Randolph Schwabe. Boards and vellum. London, 1925. Beaumont Press. One of 80 on vellum, signed. $135–$150. Another issue: One of 310 on paper. In plain dust jacket. $88.

BLUNDEN, Edmund. *Near and Far*. Cloth. London, 1929. One of 160 signed. In dust jacket. $75–$100. Trade edition: In dust jacket. $20. New York, 1930. Boards. One of 105 signed. $75–$100.

BLUNDEN, Edmund. *Pastorals: A Book of Verses*. Wrappers. London, (1916). First edition. $125–$175. Author's first book.

BLUNDEN, Edmund. *Poems, 1914–1930*. Buckram. London, 1930. First edition. One of 200 signed. In dust jacket. $50–$60.

BLUNDEN, Edmund. *Retreat: New Sonnets and Poems*. Cloth. (London, 1928.) One of 112 signed. In dust jacket. $50–$75.

BLUNDEN, Edmund. *A Summer's Fancy*. Illustrated. Cloth, vellum spine. London, 1930. Beaumont Press. First edition. One of 80 on vellum, signed. $150–$200. Another issue: One of 325 on paper. $75. Soiled copy, $35.

BLUNDEN, Edmund. *To Nature*. Illustrated by Randolph Schwabe. Patterned boards, vellum spine. (London, 1923.) Beaumont Press. One of 80 on vellum, signed. $125–$150. Another issue: One of 310 on paper. $85–$100.

BLUNDEN, Edmund. *Undertones of War*. Cloth. London, 1928. First edition. In dust jacket. $125–$150.

BLUNDEN. Edmund. *Winter Nights*. Illustrated. Boards. London, 1928. First edition. One of 500 signed. $50–$60.

BLUNT, Edmund M. *Traveller's Guide to and Through the State of Ohio, with Sailing Directions for Lake Erie*. 16 pp., leather. New York, 1832. First edition. $500–$600. New York, 1833. Folding map in color. 28 pp., leather. $500–$600.

BLUNT, Wilfrid Scawen. See Proteus.

BLUNT, Wilfrid Scawen. *The Celebrated Romance of the Stealing of the Mare*. Translated from the Arabic by Lady Anne Blunt and done into verse by W.S.B. Boards and leather. Newtown, Wales, 1930. Gregynog Press. One of 275. $400–$750. One of 25 (of this edition) especially bound in morocco. $1,500–$2,000.

BLUNT, Wilfrid Scawen. *The Love-Lyrics and Songs of Proteus . . . with the Love-Sonnets*. Woodcut borders and initials. Stiff vellum with ties. London, 1892. Kelmscott Press. One of 300. $500–$750.

BLY, Robert. *The Light Around the Body*. Cloth. New York, 1967. First edition. In dust jacket. $40–$50.

BLY, Robert. *The Silence in the Snowy Fields*. Wrappers. Middletown, 1962. First edition. $35–$50. Author's first book.

BOCCACCIO, Giovanni. *The Decameron*. 1620 translation. Woodcuts by Fritz Kredel. 2 vols., boards and calf. New york, 1940. Limited Editions Club. One of 530. Boxed. $100–$125. Another Limited Editions Club edition: New York, 1930. Translated by Frances Winwar. 2 vols., cloth. Boxed. $50–$60. London, 1920. Ashendene Press. Folio, boards and linen. One of 105 on paper. $500–$750. Another issue: One of 6 on vellum. $1,250–$1,500.

BOCCACCIO, Giovanni. *Life of Dante*. Translated by Philip Henry Wicksteed. Woodcut title portrait. Boards and vellum. (Boston, 1904). One of 325 designed by Bruce Rogers. $75–$100.

BODE, Winston. *A Portrait of Pancho*. Illustrated,. Full leather. Austin, Tex., 1965. First edition. One of 150 signed. Boxed. $250–$350. Trade edition: Cloth. $35.

BODENHEIM, Maxwell. See Hecht, Ben, and Bodenheim, Maxwell.

BODENHEIM, Maxwell. *Crazy Man*. Cloth. New York, (1923). First edition. In dust jacket. $75.

BODENHEIM, Maxwell. *Duke Herring*. Cloth. New York, (1931). First edition. In dust jacket. $35–$50.

BODENHEIM, Maxwell. *Minna and Myself*. Red cloth. New York, 1918. First edition, first issue, with "Master-Posner" for "Master-Poisoner" on page 67. In dust jacket. $100–$150. Author's first book.

BODENHEIM, Maxwell. *The Sardonic Arm*. Illustrated. Black cloth. Chicago, 1923. First edition. One of 575. $50–$60.

BOEHME, Jacob. *Christosophia*. Leather. Ephrata, Pa., 1811–12. First American edition. $100–$150.

BOGAN, Louise. *Body of This Death: Poems*. Blue boards, linen spine, paper label. New York, 1923. First edition. In dust jacket. $250–$300. Author's first book.

BOGAN, Louise. *Dark Summer*. Cloth. New York, 1929. First edition. In dust jacket. $235–$250.

BOGAN, Louise. *Poems and New Poems*. Cloth. New York, 1941. First edition. In dust jacket. $50–$75.

BOGAN, Louise. *The Sleeping Fury*. Cloth. New York, 1937. First edition. In dust jacket. $35–$50.

BOGGS, Mae Helene Bacon (compiler). *My Playhouse Was a Concord Coach*. Maps, illustrations. Cloth. (Oakland, 1942.) First edition. $350–$450. (Most copies inscribed.)

BOKE of Noblesse (The). Addressed to King Edward IV on his Invasion of France in 1475. Half morocco. London, 1860. Roxburghe Club. $150–$200.

BOLDREWOOD [sic] Rolf (Bolderwood). *Robbery Under Arms: A Story of Life and Adventure in the Bush and in the Goldfields of Australia*. Decorated green cloth. London, 1888. (By Thomas A. Browne.) First edition. $400–$500.

BOLLER, Henry A. *Among the Indians*. Folding map, cloth, paper label. Philadelphia, 1868. First edition. $400–$500.

BOLTON, Herbert Eugene. *Anza's California Expeditions*. Folding map, illustrations. 5 vols., cloth. Berkeley, 1930. First edition. In dust jackets. $200–$275.

BOLTON, Herbert Eugene. *Athanase de Mezieres and the Louisiana-Texas Frontier*. Map, 2 facsimiles. 2 vols., cloth. Cleveland, 1914. First edition. $350–$400.

BOLTON, Herbert Eugene. *Coronado on the Turquoise Trail*. Illustrated. Cloth. Albuquerque, 1949. $45–$50.

BOLTON, Herbert Eugene. *Guide to Materials for the History of the United States in the Principal Archives of Mexico*. Printed wrappers. Washington, 1913. First edition. $150–$200.

BOLTON, Herbert Eugene. *The Rim of Christendom*. 12 plates, 3 facsimiles. Cloth. New York, 1936. First edition. In dust jacket. $100–$125.

BOLTON, Herbert Eugene (translator). *Font's Complete Diary of the Second Anza*

Expedition. Maps, plates, facsimiles. Cloth. Berkeley, 1931. First edition. $75–$100. Berkeley, 1933. Cloth. Second edition. $50–$60.

BOLTWOOD, Lucius M. *History and Genealogy of the Family of Thomas Noble.* Illustrated. Cloth. Hartford, 1878. First edition. $25–$30.

BOND, Henry. *Family Memorials.* Vol. 1. Buckram. Boston, 1855. (Watertown, Mass., genealogies, including Waltham and Weston.) $35–$50.

BOND, J. Wesley. *Minnesota and Its Resources.* Folding map, 6 plates, Cloth. Chicago, 1856. First edition. $100–$150.

BOND, Nelson. *Exiles of Time.* Cloth. Philadelphia, 1949. First edition. In dust jacket. $50. Another issue: One of 112 signed. Boxed. $75–$100.

BOND, Nelson. *Mr. Mergenthwirker's Lobblies and Other Fantastic Tales.* Cloth. New York, (1946). First edition. In dust jacket. $50. Author's first book.

BOND, Nelson. *Nightmares and Daydreams.* Cloth. Sauk City, (1968). First edition. In dust jacket. $25–$35.

BOND, Nelson. *The Thirty-first of February.* Cloth. New York, (1949). First edition. In dust jacket. $50. Another issue: One of 112 signed. Boxed. $75–$100.

BONFILS, Winifred B. *The Life and Personality of Phoebe Apperson Hearst.* Vellum, San Francisco, 1928. John Henry Nash printing. One of 1,000. In original tan flannel bag. $75–$100.

BONNELL, George W. *Topographical Description of Texas.* Boards. Austin, 1840. First edition. $2,000–$3,000.

BONNER, T.D. *The Life and Adventures of James P. Beckwourth, Mountaineer, Scout and Pioneer, etc.* Frontispiece and plates. Cloth. New York, 1856. First edition. $200–$250.

BONNEY, Edward. *Banditti of the Prairies; or, The Murderer's Doom!* Plates. Pictorial wrappers. Chicago, 1850. First edition, with imprint "Chicago, W.W. Dannenhauer 1850" on front cover. $4,000–$5,000. Philadelphia, (1855). $300–$400. Philadelphia, 1856. Third edition. $300–$400. Chicago, 1856. $400–$500. Chicago, 1858. 13 plates. Wrappers. $500.

BOOK of Commandments (A), for the Government of the Church of Christ. Boards. Zion (Independence, Mo.), 1833. (By Joseph Smith, Jr.) First edition. $10,000 and up.

BOOK of Common Prayer (The). Full red leather. New York (Boston), 1928 (actually 1930). Merrymount Press. One of 500. $1,000–$1,250.

BOOK of Job (The). Illustrated in color by Arthur Szyk. Boards. New York, 1946. Limited Editions Club. Boxed. $85–$125.

BOOK of Jonah (The) Illustrated by David Jones. Buckram. Waltham Saint Lawrence, 1926. Golden Cockerel Press. One of 175. In dust jacket. $1,000–$1,200.

BOOK of Kells (The). 48 color plates, 625 in black and white, 2 vols. facsimile, plus text volume, 3 vols. in all, vellum. Olten and Berne, Switzerland, 1950–51. One of 500. $5,000 and up. Also, $3,000 (A, 1979); $3,750 (A, 1974).

BOOK of the Law of the Lord (The). Saint James, A.R.I. (Beaver Island, Lake Michigan, 1851.) (By James Jesse Strang.) First edition. $5,000 and up (3 copies known). (Beaver Island, 1856.) Second edition, lacking title page (some supplied, and with preface, in modern type, circa 1920). $1,000. For a later edition, see James J. Strang entry.

BOOK of the Poets' Club (The). Orange wrappers. London, 1909. First edition. (Includes first printings of four Ezra Pound poems.) $475 (A, 1977).

BOOK of Princeton Verse 1916 (A). Edited by Alfred Noyes. Cloth. Princeton, 1916. First edition. In dust jacket. $100–$120. (Includes poems by Edmund Wilson, John Peale Bishop, and others.)

BOOK *of Princeton Verse II (A).* Cloth. Princeton, (1919). First edition. (First book appearance of three poems by F. Scott Fitzgerald.) In dust jacket. $300–$350. Also, $150 (A, 1977).

BOOK *of Psalms (The).* Illustrated by Valenti Angelo. Morocco. New York, 1961. Limited Editions Club. Boxed. $50–$60.

BOOK *of Ruth (The).* Boards. London, 1923. Nonesuch Press. One of 250. Boxed. $100–$125. New York, 1947. Limited Editions Club. Introduction by Mary Ellen Chase. Illustrated by Arthur Szyk. Boards. Boxed. $100–$110.

BOOK *of Tobit (The) and the History of Susanna.* Color plates by W. Russell Flint. Vellum, silk ties. London, 1929. One of 100 copies. With an extra set of plates. Boxed. $300–$400. One of 13 on vellum, signed by the artist. With duplicate plates in folder. $750–$1,000.

BOOK *of Vasser Verse (A).* Boards. (Poughkeepsie, 1916.) First edition. $100. (With 3 poems by Edna St. Vincent Millay.)

BOOK-LOVER'S *Almanac (The) for 1895.* Wrappers. New York, 1894. First edition. One of 100 on Japan paper. $100–$150.

BOOTH, Stephen. *The Book Called Holinshed's Chronicles.* Woodcut reproductions and original leaf from the 1587 edition. Decorated boards and cloth. San Francisco, 1968. One of 500. $150–$200.

BORDEN, Gail, Jr. *Letters of . . . to Dr. Ashbel Smith.* 9 pp., wrappers. Galveston, 1850. First edition. $1,000–$1,250.

BORDEN, Spencer. *The Arab Horse.* Cloth. New York, 1906. $150–$175.

BORDER *Beagles: A Tale of Mississippi.* 2 vols., boards and cloth, paper labels. Philadelphia, 1840. (By William Gilmore Simms.) First edition. $250–$350.

BORDERERS *(The): A Tale.* By the Author of "The Spy." 3 vols., drab tan boards, paper labels. London, 1829. (By James Fenimore Cooper.) First edition (of the novel published in America as *The Wept of Wish-Ton-Wish*). $600–$800.

BORGES, Jorge Luis. *The Congress.* Translated by Norman Thomas di Giovanni and Borges. Illustrated by Hugo Manning. Cloth. London, 1974. First edition. One of 50 signed. $175–$200.

BORGES, Jorge Luis. *Deathwatch on the Southside.* Wrappers. Cambridge, (1968). One of 150 signed. $50–$90.

BORNEMAN, Henry S. *Pennsylvania German Illuminated Manuscripts.* 38 colored reproductions. Oblong folio, cloth. Norristown, Pa., 1937. $200–$250.

BORROW, George. See Ewald, Johannes.

BORROW, George. *The Bible in Spain.* 3 vols., red cloth, paper labels. London, 1843. First edition. $300–$350.

BORROW, George. *Lavengro; the Scholar—the Gypsy—the Priest.* Portrait. 3 vols., blue cloth, paper labels. London, 1851. First edition. $400–$500. New York, 1936. Limited Editions Club. 2 vols., cloth. Boxed. $60–$80.

BORROW, George, *Proud Signild and Other Ballads.* Wrappers. London, 1913. First edition. One of 30. $150–$250.

BORROW, George. *The Romany Rye.* 2 vols., blue cloth. London, 1875. First edition. $200–$250.

BORROW, George. *Wild Wales: Its People, Language, and Scenery.* 3 vols., cloth, paper labels. London, 1862. First edition, with 32 pages of ads and without half titles in Vols. 2 and 3. $150–$250.

BORZOI 1920 (The). Half cloth. New York, 1920. (By Alfred A. Knopf.) First edition. One of 100 on San Marco paper. $35–$50. New York, 1925. Half cloth. One of 500 large paper copies. $35–$50.

BOSCANA, Father Geronimo. *Chinigchinich*. Translated by Alfred Robinson. Color plates, maps. Folio, boards and cloth. Santa Ana, 1933. $200–$250.

BOSQUI, Edward. *Memoirs*. Half cloth. (Oakland), 1952. Grabhorn Press. One of 350. $100–$125.

BOSSCHERE, Jean de. *12 Occupations*. Illustrated. Decorated wrappers. London, 1916. First edition. $300–$400. (Translated anonymously by Ezra Pound.)

BOSSERT, Helmuth T. *Peasant Art in Europe*. 130 full-color plates and 32 plates in black and white. Folio, cloth. London, 1927. First English edition. $100–$125. New York, 1927. First American edition. $100–$125.

BOSTON Prize Poems, and Other Specimens of Dramatic Poetry. Printed boards. Boston, 1824. First edition. $150–$200. Also, $100 (A, 1974). Longfellow's first appearance in a book.

BOSWELL, James. *Boswell for the Defence*. Edited by W.K. Wimsatt and Frederick A. Pottle. Illustrated, folding maps. Blue buckram, gilt, calf spine, leather label. London, 1960. Yale de luxe edition. One of 350. Boxed. $50–$75.

BOSWELL, James. *Boswell in Holland, 1763–1764*. Edited by Frederick A. Pottle. Illustrated, folding map. Blue buckram and calf. London, 1952. Yale de luxe edition. One of 1,050. Boxed. $35–$45.

BOSWELL, James. *Boswell in Search of a Wife*. Edited by F. Brady and Frederick A. Pottle. Blue buckram and calf. London, 1957. Yale de luxe edition. One of 400. Boxed. $75–$100.

BOSWELL, James. *Boswell on the Grand Tour: Germany and Switzerland*. Edited by Frederick A. Pottle. Illustrated, folding map. Blue buckram and calf. London, 1953. Yale de luxe edition. One of 1,000. Boxed. $50–$75.

BOSWELL, James. *Boswell on the Grand Tour: Italy, Corsica, and France*. Edited by F. Brady and Frederick A. Pottle. Illustrated, folding maps. Blue buckram and calf. London, 1955. Yale de luxe edition. One of 400. Boxed. $75–$100.

BOSWELL, James. *Boswell's Journal of a Tour to the Hebrides with Samuel Johnson, LL.D.* Boards, cloth spine, paper label. New York, 1936. First complete edition. One of 816. Boxed. $75–$100.

BOSWELL, James. *The Life of Samuel Johnson*. Portrait, 2 folding plates. Contemporary sheep. Boston, 1807. First American edition. $150. New York, 1938. Limited Editions Club. 3 vols., cloth. Boxed. $100–$150. New York, 1945. Illustrated by Gordon Ross. Cloth. One of 1,000 signed by Ross. $70–$80.

BOSWORTH, Newton. *Hochelaga Depicta: The Early History and Present State of the City and Island of Montreal*. Illustrated, including 2 folding maps. Cloth. Montreal, 1839. $200–$250.

BOUCHETTE, Joseph. *A Topographical Description of the Province of Lower Canada, with Remarks Upon Upper Canada*. Maps and illustrations. Boards and calf. London, 1815. First English edition. $300–$350. London, 1832. Boards. $100–$150.

BOUGARD, R. *The Little Sea Torch*. Colored plates and charts. Half leather and boards. London, 1801. First English edition. $1,500–$2,000. Also, $1,140 (A, 1978).

BOURDILLON, Francis W. *Among the Flowers, and Other Poems*. Decorated white cloth. London, 1878. First edition. $50–$75. Author's first book.

BOURJAILY, Vance. *The End of My Life*. Cloth. New York, 1947. First edition. In dust jacket. $50–$75. Author's first book.

BOURKE, John G. *An Apache Campaign in the Sierra Madre*. Illustrated. Printed wrappers, or pictorial cloth. New York, 1886. First edition. Wrappers: $225–$400. Cloth: $150–$175.

BOURKE, John G. *Mackenzie's Last Fight with the Cheyennes*. Portrait. 44 pp., printed wrappers. Governor's Island, N.Y., 1890. First edition. $600–$1,000.

BOURKE, John G. *On the Border with Crook*. Frontispiece portrait, other plates. Cloth. New York, 1891. First edition. $150–$175.

BOURKE, John G. *Scatologic Rites of All Nations*. Cloth. Washington, 1891. First edition. $100–$200.

BOURKE, John G. *The Snake-Dance of the Moquis of Arizona*. Plates, some in color. Pictorial cloth. New York, 1884. First edition. $150–$250. London, 1884. Half calf. First English edition. $150–$250. New York, 1891. Cloth. $100–$125.

BOURNE, Randolph. *The History of a Literary Radical*. Edited by Van Wyck Brooks. Cloth. New York, 1920. First edition. In dust jacket. $75.

BOWDITCH, Nathaniel. *The New American Practical Navigator*. Folding frontispiece map, 6 plates. Boards or full leather. Newburyport, Mass., 1802. First edition. $1,500–$2,000. Also, $1,450 (A, 1972).

BOWEN, Abel. *The Naval Monument*. 25 woodcuts. Calf. Boston, 1816. First edition. With errata slip. $225–$300.

BOWEN, Elizabeth. *Ann Lee's and Other Stories*. Cloth. London, 1926. First edition. $100–$125. New York, 1927. First American edition. In dust jacket. $75.

BOWEN, Elizabeth. *The Death of the Heart*. Cloth. London, 1938. First edition. In dust jacket. $150.

BOWEN, Elizabeth. *Seven Winters*. Boards and linen. Dublin, 1942. Cuala Press. One of 450. In tissue dust jacket. $100–$125.

BOWERS, Mrs. Dr. J. Milton. *The Dance of Life: An Answer to the "Dance of Death."* Red or green cloth. San Francisco, 1877. (By Ambrose Bierce?) First edition. $50–$97.

BOWLES, Jane. *Two Serious Ladies*. Cloth. New York, 1943. First edition. In dust jacket. $250–$325. Author's first book.

BOWLES, Paul. *The Delicate Prey and Other Stories*. Cloth. (New York, 1950.) First edition. In dust jacket. $75–$100.

BOWLES, Paul. *The Sheltering Sky*. Cloth. London, (1949). First edition. In dust jacket. $200–$300. New York, (1949). Cloth. First American edition. In dust jacket. $75–$100.

BOWLES, Paul. *Two Poems*. Wrappers. (New York, 1934.) First edition. $500–$750. Author's first book.

BOWLES, Paul. *Up Above the World*. Cloth. New York, (1966). First edition. In dust jacket. $40–$50.

BOWLES, Paul. *Yallah*. Illustrated with photos. Cloth. Zurich, 1956. First edition. $125–$150. New York, 1957. First American edition. In dust jacket. $100–$125.

BOX, Capt. Michael James. *Capt. James Box's Adventures and Explorations in New and Old Mexico*. Cloth. New York, 1861. First edition. $800–$1,500, possibly more. New York, 1869. Cloth. Second edition. $350–$600. (Both editions have become difficult to find.)

BOX, Edgar. *Death Before Bedtime*. Cloth. New York, 1953. (By Gore Vidal.) First edition. In dust jacket. $50–$60.

BOX, Edgar. *Death in the Fifth Position*. Cloth. New York, 1952. (By Gore Vidal.) In dust jacket. $75.

BOX, Edgar. *Death Likes It Hot*. Cloth. New York, 1954. (By Gore Vidal.) First edition. In dust jacket. $50–$60.

BOYD, Belle. *Belle Boyd in Camp and Prison, Written by Herself*. Cloth. New York, 1865. (By Belle B. Hardinge.) First American edition. $75. (There was a two-volume London first edition in 1865. No recent price data seen.) New York, 1866. Cloth. $50.

BOYD, James. *Drums*. Green cloth. New York-London, 1925. First edition. In dust jacket. $34–$50. Author's first book. New York, (1928). Illustrated by N.C. Wyeth. Cloth. One of 525 signed by author and artist. Boxed. $250.

BOYD, Nancy, *Distressing Dialogues*. Cloth. New York, (1924). (By Edna St. Vincent Millay.) First edition (so stated). In dust jacket. $50–$60.

BOYLE, Kay. *The Crazy Hunter*. Cloth. New York, (1940). First American edition. In dust jacket. $50.

BOYLE, Kay. *The First Lover and Other Stories*. Cloth. New York, (1933). First edition. In dust jacket. $50–$75.

BOYLE, Kay. *Gentlemen, I Address You Privately*. Cloth. New York, 1933. First edition. $50–$75.

BOYLE, Kay. *Monday Night*. Cloth. New York, (1938). First edition. In dust jacket. $75.

BOYLE, Kay. *Plagued by the Nightingale*. Cloth. New York, 1931. First edition. In dust jacket. $100–$125. London, 1931. Cloth. First English edition. In dust jacket. $125. Her first novel.

BOYLE, Kay. *A Statement*. Drawing by Max Weber. Wrappers. (New York, 1932.) First edition. One of 175 signed. $150.

BOYLE, Kay. *Short Stories*. Printed wrappers in gold or silver protective boards. Paris, 1929. Black Sun Press. First edition. One of 15 on Japan paper, signed. $600–$750. Also, $600 (A, 1977). Another issue: One of 150 on Van Gelder paper. In tissue dust jacket. Boxed. $100–$275. One of 20 on Arches paper, for France. $350–$475. Author's first book. (See following entry.)

BOYLE, Kay. *Wedding Day and Other Stories*. Decorated boards, cloth spine. New York, (1930). First American edition (of the author's first book, retitled). In dust jacket. $50–$75.

BOYLE, Kay. *The White Horses of Vienna*. Cloth. New York, (1936). First edition. In dust jacket. $50–$75.

"BOZ." See Dickens, Charles. Also see *Sketches by "Boz."*

"BOZ." *Master Humphrey's Clock*. 88 weekly parts, white wrappers. London, 1840–41. (By Charles Dickens.) First edition. $800–$1,200, or more. Second edition: 20 monthly parts in 19, green wrappers. $800–$1,000. Third edition: 3 vols., brown cloth. (First book edition, issued under Dickens' name, which see.)

"BOZ." *Memoirs of Joseph Grimaldi*. Edited by "Boz." Illustrated by George Cruikshank. 2 vols., pink cloth. London, 1838. (Edited and written in part by Charles Dickens.) First edition, first issue, with no border around last plate. $400–$600. Second issue, crude border around plate. $200–$300.

"BOZ." *Oliver Twist; or, The Parish Boy's Progress*. Illustrated by George Cruikshank. 3

vols., brown cloth. London, 1838. (By Charles Dickens.) First edition, first issue, with "Fireside" plate, Vol. 3. $1,500–$3,000. Second issue, with "Rose Maylie and Oliver" replacing "Fireside" plate. $1,100 (A, 1981). (For second edition, sometimes called third issue, 1839, with Dickens on title page, and for first octavo edition, in parts and in book form, see author entries under *Oliver Twist* and *The Adventures of Oliver Twist*.)

"BOZ." *The Strange Gentleman: A Comic Burletta*. Printed buff wrappers, London, 1837. (By Charles Dickens.) First edition. $250 and up. Facsimile edition: (London, 1871). $75.

BRACKENRIDGE, H.M. See *Strictures on a Voyage to South America, etc.*

BRACKENRIDGE, H.M. *A Eulogy, on the Lives and Characters of John Adams & Thomas Jefferson*. 18 pp., plain wrappers. Pensacola, Fla., 1826. First edition. $350.

BRACKENRIDGE, H.M. *Journal of a Voyage up the Missouri*. Printed boards. Baltimore, 1815. First edition (actually second appearance of the journal, which first appeared in author's *Views of Louisiana*, which see). $300–$500. Baltimore, 1816 (cover date 1815). Boards. Second edition. $150–$200.

BRACKENRIDGE, H.M. *Views of Louisiana; Together with a Journal of a Voyage up the Missouri River, in 1814*. Boards, or leather. Pittsburgh, 1814. First edition. $850–$1,250. Baltimore, 1817. Boards. (Containing only *Views* and not the *Journal*.) $200–$250.

BRACKENRIDGE, Hugh Henry. *Gazette Publications*. Leather. Carlisle, Pa., 1806. First edition. $200–$250.

BRADBURY, John. *Travels in the Interior of America*. Boards. Liverpool, 1817. First edition, with errata slip. $1,000–$1,500. London, 1819. Folding map. Boards. Second edition. $750–$1,000.

BRADBURY, Ray. *The Anthem Sprinters*. Cloth. New York, 1963. First edition. In dust jacket. $75–$100.

BRADBURY, Ray. *Dandelion Wine*. Yellow cloth. Garden City, 1957. First edition. In dust jacket. $85–$135.

BRADBURY, Ray. *Dark Carnival*. Black cloth. Sauk City, Wis., 1947. Arkham House. First edition. In dust jacket. $400–$450. London, (1948). Cloth. First English edition. In dust jacket. $200–$225. Author's first book.

BRADBURY, Ray. *Fahrenheit 451*. Boards. New York, (1953). First edition. In dust jacket. $150–$175. (About 50 author's copies were bound in cloth.) Another issue: Asbestos boards. One of 200 signed. Issued without dust jacket. $600–$800. (Note: Also issued in a Ballantine paperback. $40–$50.)

BRADBURY, Ray. *The Golden Apples of the Sun*. Cloth. Garden City, 1953. First edition. In dust jacket. $50–$75.

BRADBURY, Ray. *The Illustrated Man*. Tan cloth. Garden City, 1951. First edition. In dust jacket. $100–$150.

BRADBURY, Ray. *The Machineries of Joy*. Boards. New York, 1964. First edition. In dust jacket. $100.

BRADBURY, Ray. *The Martian Chronicles*. Cloth. Garden City, 1950. First edition. In dust jacket. $200–$250. New York, 1974. Limited Editions Club. $150–$200.

BRADBURY, Ray. *A Medicine for Melancholy*. Cloth. Garden City, 1959. First edition. In dust jacket. $50–$75.

BRADBURY, Ray. *The October Country*. Red cloth or boards. New York, (1955). First edition. In dust jacket. $125–$150.

BRADBURY, Ray. *The Silver Locusts*. Cloth. London, 1951. First English edition (of *The Martian Chronicles*). In dust jacket. $75–$100.

BRADBURY, Ray. *Switch on the Night*. Cloth. New York, 1955. First edition. In dust jacket. $50–$75.

BRADFORD, Gamaliel. *Daughters of Eve*. Illustrated. Cloth. Boston, (1930). First edition. One of 200 signed. In dust jacket. $50.

BRADFORD, Roark. *How Come Christmas*. Boards, paper label. New York, 1930. First edition. $75–$100.

BRADFORD, Roark. *Ol' King David an' the Philistines*. Illustrated. Boards. New York, 1930. First edition. In dust jacket. $50–$60.

BRADFORD, William. *The Arctic Regions*. 129 albumen prints. Folio, morocco. (London, 1873.) First edition. $5,000.

BRADLEY, James. *The Confederate Mail Carrier*. 15 plates. Cloth. Mexico, Mo., 1894. First edition. $150–$200.

BRADLEY, Joshua. *Accounts of Religious Revivals in Many Parts of the United States from 1815 to 1818*. Calf. Albany, N.Y., 1819. First edition. $50–$60.

BRADLEY, William Aspenwall. *The Etching of Figures*. Half vellum. Marlborough-on-Hudson, N.Y., 1915. Dard Hunter paper and printing. One of 250. $200–$300.

BRADY, William. *Glimpses of Texas*. Folding map in color. Stiff wrappers, or cloth. Houston, 1871. First edition. $1,000–$1,500.

BRAINE, John. *Room at the Top*. Cloth, London, 1957. First edition. In dust jacket with wraparound band. $125–$150. Author's first book.

BRAITHWAITE, William S. *Lyrics of Life and Love*. Cloth. Boston, 1904. First edition. $100–$125. Author's first book.

BRAITHWAITE, William S. (editor). *Anthology of Magazine Verse for 1913*. Wrappers or boards. Cambridge, Mass., (1913). First edition. $75–$100. Worn copy, $45. (First of the famous Braithwaite anthologies.)

BRAITHWAITE, William S. (editor). *Anthology of Magazine Verse for 1923*. Boards and cloth. Boston, 1923. First edition. One of 245 signed by Braithwaite. $100–$125.

BRAMAH, Ernest. *English Farming and Why I Turned it Up*. Cloth. London, 1894. First edition. Issued without dust jacket. $200–$250. Author's first book.

BRAMAH, Ernest. *The Eyes of Max Corrados*. Cloth. London, 1923. First edition. In dust jacket. $400–$450.

BRAMAH, Ernest. *Kai Lung's Golden Hours*. Cloth. London, 1924. One of 250 signed. $200.

BRAMAH, Ernest. *Max Carrados*. Cloth. London, 1914. First edition. $400–$500.

BRAMAH, Ernest. *The Transmutation of Ling*. Illustrated. Cloth. London, (1911). First edition. One of 500. $200–$300.

BRAMAH, Ernest. *The Wallet of Kai Lung*. Light-green cloth. London, (1900). First English edition, first issue, measuring 1½ inches thick. $50–$75. London, 1923. Boards. One of 200 signed. $125–$175.

BRAMAN, D.E.E. *Information About Texas*. Cloth. Philadelphia, 1857. First edition. $400–$600. Philadelphia, 1858. Cloth. Second edition. $250–$300.

BRAND BOOK of the Western South Dakota Stock Growers' Association. Illustrated. Cloth. Omaha, (1901). Worn copy, $250.

BRAND, Max. *Timbal Gulch Trail.* Cloth. New York, 1934. (By Frederick Faust.) First edition. In dust jacket. $100.

BRANDT, Herbert. *Arizona Bird Life.* Illustrated, including map and color plates. Green cloth. Cleveland, 1951. First edition. In dust jacket. $125–$150.

BRANGWYN, Frank. *The Etched Work of Frank Brangwyn.* Half cloth. London, 1908. Limited edition on large paper. $150–$175.

BRANGWYN, Frank. *The Historical Paintings in the Great Hall of the Worshipful Company of Skinners.* London, 1909. One of 525. $100–$135. Another issue: One of 25 on vellum $250–$300.

BRANGWYN, Frank, and Sparrow, Walter Shaw. *A Book of Bridges.* Half vellum. London, 1916. One of 75 on large paper, with an original lithograph signed by Brangwyn. $400–$500.

BRASHER, Rex. *Birds and Trees of North America.* 867 (sometimes fewer) hand-colored plates. 12 vols., oblong folio, half leather folders. (Kent, Conn., about 1929–32). One of 500 (actually only 100). $30,000 in a 1918 catalogue of Bernard Quaritch, Ltd., London.

BRATT, John. *Trails of Yesterday.* Portrait frontispiece and plates. Pictorial cloth. Lincoln, Neb., 1921. First edition. $100–$125.

BRAUTIGAN, Richard. *A Confederate General at Big Sur.* Cloth. New York, (1964). First edition. In dust jacket. $50.

BRAUTIGAN, Richard. *The Galilee Hitch-Hiker.* Wrappers. San Francisco, (1958). $50.

BRAUTIGAN, Richard. *In Watermelon Sugar.* Blue boards. San Francisco, (1968). First edition. One of 50 signed. $100–$125.

BRAUTIGAN, Richard. *Lay the Marble Tea.* Printed wrappers. San Francisco, (1959). First edition. $60.

BRAUTIGAN, Richard. *The Octopus Frontier.* Printed wrappers. San Francisco, (1960). First edition. $50–$60.

BRAUTIGAN, Richard. *The Pill Versus the Springhill Mine Disaster.* Tan boards, brown cloth spine. San Francisco, (1968). First edition. One of 50 signed. $100–$125.

BRAUTIGAN, Richard. *Please Plant This Book.* Wrappers, with eight seed packets enclosed. San Francisco, (1968). $75.

BRAUTIGAN, Richard *Four New Poets.* Wrappers. San Francisco, (1957). Inferno Press. First edition. $40–$60. Signed by Brautigan, $125. First book appearance of Brautigan, with three other poets.

BRAVO (The): A Venetian Story. 3 vols., boards, paper labels. London, 1831. (By James Fenimore Cooper.) First edition. $600–$800. Philadelphia, 1831. 2 vols., boards, paper labels. First American edition. $400–$600.

BRAYTON, Matthew. *The Indian Captive.* 68 pp., printed green wrappers, or boards. Cleveland. 1860. First edition. Wrappers: $450–$650. Boards: $250–$400. Fostoria, Ohio, 1896. Boards. Second edition. $75–$100.

BRENNER, Anita. *The Wind That Swept Mexico.* Illustrated with photographs. Cloth. New York, (1943). First edition. In dust jacket. $100–$150.

BRETON, Nicholas. *The Twelve Moneths and Christmas Day.* Cloth. London, 1927. Golden Cockerel Press. One of 500. In dust jacket. $250. New York, 1951. One of 100 signed by Bruce Rogers. $75.

BREWSTER, Sir David. *A Treatise on the Kaleidoscope.* 7 plates. Cloth. Edinburgh, 1819. First edition. $200–$250.

BRICE, Wallace. *A History of Fort Wayne.* 7 plates. Cloth. Fort Wayne, Ind., 1868. First edition. $100–$125.

BRIDGENS, Richard. *Furniture, with Candelabra and Interior Decoration.* 60 full-page color plates. Folio, boards. London, 1838. $350–$450.

BRIDGES, Robert. *Eros and Psyche, A Poem.* Woodcuts from drawings by Edward Burne-Jones. White pigskin. Newtown, Wales, 1935. Gregynog Press. One of 300. In buckram case. $750–$1,000. Another issue: One of 15 specially bound by George Fisher. $2,000–$2,500.

BRIDGES, Robert. *The Growth of Love.* Boards. Oxford, 1889. Daniel Press. First edition. One of 22. $300–$500. Oxford, 1890. One of 100. $150–$200. Portland, Me., 1894. Wrappers over boards. One of 40. $100–$125.

BRIDGES, Robert. *The Influence of the Audience.* Wrappers. Garden City, 1926. One of 100. Boxed. $100–$150.

BRIDGES, Robert, *Poems.* Cloth. London, 1873. First edition. $200–$300. Author's first book (suppressed by him in 1878).

BRIDGES, Robert. *Poems Written in the Year MCMXIII.* Blue printed boards and cloth. Chelsea (London), 1914. Ashendene Press. First edition. One of 85 with initials in red or blue. Boxed. $1,000–$1,250. Another issue: Vellum. One of 6 on vellum. $2,500–$3,500.

BRIDGES, Robert. *The Tapestry.* Boards. (London), 1925. First edition. One of 150. Boxed. $400–$650.

BRIDGES, Robert *The Testament of Beauty.* Buckram. Oxford, 1929. First published edition. One of 50 signed. In dust jacket. $200–$300. Another issue: One of 200, unsigned. $100–$125. Trade edition: Boards. $40. New York, 1929. One of 250. $75–$100.

BRIDWELL, J.W.(compiler). *The Life and Adventures of Robert McKimie.* 56 pp., pictorial wrappers. Hillsboro, Ohio, 1878. First edition, $750–$1,000.

BRIEF Description of Western Texas (A). Pictorial wrappers. San Antonio, 1873. (By W.G. Kingsbury.) First edition. $575–$750.

BRIEF History of Christ's Hospital (A). Boards, paper label. London, 1820. (By Charles Lamb.) First edition. $400–$500.

BRIFFAULT, Robert. *The Mothers.* 3 vols., cloth. New York, 1927. First edition $150–$175.

BRIGGS, L. Vernon. *Arizona and New Mexico, 1882; California, 1886; Mexico, 1891.* Portraits. Cloth. (Boston, 1932). First edition. $125–$150.

BRIGGS, L. Vernon. *History of Shipbuilding on North River, Plymouth County, Massachusetts.* 57 illustrations. Cloth. Boston, 1889. First edition. $150–$200.

BRIGHAM, Clarence S. *Paul Revere's Engravings.* 77 plates (some in color). Cloth. Worcester, Mass., 1954. First edition. In dust jacket. $150–$200.

BRILLAT-SAVARIN, J.A. *The Physiology of Taste.* Introduction by Arthur Machen. Portrait, other illustrations. Boards. London, 1925. One of 750. In dust jacket. $200–$225. New York, 1949. Limited Editions Club. Translated by M.F.K. Fisher. Half leather. Boxed. $75–$100.

BRINNIN, John Malcolm. *The Garden is Political.* Cloth. New York, 1942. First edition. In dust jacket. $50–$60. Author's first book.

BRISBIN, James S. *The Beef Bonanza*. 8 plates. Pictorial cloth. Philadelphia, 1881. First edition. $200–$250.

BRITISH Military Library (The). 47 maps, plans and plates, 29 color plates of military costume, 10 leaves of music. 2 vols., morocco. London, 1799–1801. $800–$1,200.

BRITTON, Wiley. *Memoirs of the Rebellion on the Border, 1863*. Cloth. Chicago, 1882. First edition. $75.

BRODIE, Walter. *Pitcairn's Island and The Islanders in 1850*. 4 plates. Cloth, paper label. London, 1851. First edition. $150. London, 1851. Second edition. $75–$100.

BROMFIELD, Louis. *Awake and Rehearse*. Boards. New York, (1929). First edition. One of 500 signed. In dust jacket. Boxed. $50–$75.

BROMFIELD, Louis. *The Green Bay Tree*. Cloth. New York, 1924. First edition. In dust jacket. $50–$75. Author's first book.

BRONK, William. *Light and Dark*. Wrappers. (Ashland, Mass.), 1956. First edition. $75–$100. Author's first book.

BRONTË, Anne. See Bell, Acton; Bell, Currer.

BRONTË, Anne. *Self-Communion*. 2 facsimiles. Boards. London, 1900. First edition. One of 30. $125.

BRONTË, Charlotte. See Bell, Currer.

BRONTË, Emily. See Bell, Ellis.

BRONTË, The Rev. Patrick. *Cottage Poems*. Blue boards. Halifax, 1811. First edition. $150–$200.

BRONTË, The Rev. P(atrick). *The Rural Minstrel*. Blue-gray boards. Halifax, 1813. First edition. $75–$100.

BROOKE, Arthur De Capell. *Travels Through Sweden, Norway, and Finmark, to the North Cape*. Map, 21 plates (2 colored). Calf, or boards and calf. London. First edition. $500–$750. London, 1831. Half calf. Second edition. $400–$500.

BROOKE, Arthur De Capell. *A Winter in Lapland and Sweden*. Calf, or boards and calf. London, 1826. First edition. $400–$500. London, 1827. Second edition. $200–$300.

BROOKE, H.K. *Annals of the Revolution*. Boards. Philadelphia, (1848). First edition. $125–$150.

BROOKE, Rupert. *Collected Poems*. Portrait. Cloth, paper labels. New York, 1915. First edition. $100–$150. (Of the first edition, 100 copies were especially bound for members of the Woodberry Society. Value: $500–$750.) London, 1919. Riccardi Press. One of 13 on vellum. $2,000–$2,750.

BROOKE, Rupert. *John Webster and the Elizabethan Drama*. Cloth. New York, 1916. First edition. In dust jacket. $125–$150.

BROOKE, Rupert. *Lithuania: A Drama in One Act*. Pictorial brown wrappers. Chicago, 1915. Chicago Little Theatre. First edition. $200–$250.

BROOKE, Rupert. *1914 and Other Poems*. Portrait frontispiece. Dark blue cloth, paper label. London, 1915. First edition. In dust jacket. $100–$200. New York, 1915. American copyright edition: 87 copies, folded sheets. $150–$200. (A few were specially bound in morocco. Value: $500–$600, possibly more.)

BROOKE, Rupert, *"1914": Five Sonnets*. Printed wrappers. London, 1915. First edition. In printed envelope. $100–$150.

BROOKE, Rupert. *The Old Vicarage, Grantchester*. Woodcut. Gray wrappers. London, 1916. First edition. $50–$75.

BROOKE, Rupert. *Poems*. Dark blue cloth, paper label. London, 1911. First edition. $150–$250. Author's first book of verse. (100 copies.)

BROOKS-Bryce Anglo American Prize Essays—1927. Illustrated. Boards, paper cover label. New York, (1927). First edition. $150–$200. (Contains James Agee's first book appearance.)

BROOKS, Bryant B. *Memoirs of Bryant B. Brooks*. Plates. Cloth. Glendale, Calif., 1939. First edition. One of 150. $100–$150.

BROOKS, Gwendolyn. *Annie Allen*. Cloth. New York, (1949). First edition. In dust jacket. $75–$100.

BROOKS, Gwendolyn. *The Bean Eaters*. Cloth. New York, (1960). First edition. In dust jacket. $75–$85.

BROOKS, Gwendolyn. *Bronzeville Boys and Girls*. New York, (1956). First edition. In dust jacket. $50–$75.

BROOKS, Gwendolyn. *Family Pictures*. Wrappers. Detroit, (1970). First edition. $30–$40.

BROOKS, Gwendolyn. *Maud Martha*. Cloth. New York, 1953. First edition. In dust jacket. $75–$100.

BROOKS, Gwendolyn. *Report from Part One*. Unbound advance copy. Detroit, (1972). (First page is publisher's blurb.) $50–$60.

BROOKS, Gwendolyn. *A Street in Bronzeville*. Cloth. New York, 1945. First edition. In dust jacket. $150–$175. Author's first book.

BROOKS, Van Wyck. *Letters and Leadership*. Cloth, paper label. New York, 1918. First edition. In dust jacket. $50.

BROTHER Jonathan. 3 vols., boards. Edinburgh, 1825. (By John Neal.) First edition. $750–$1,000.

BROTHERS (The): A Tale of the Fronde. 2 vols., cloth, paper labels. New York, 1835. (By Henry William Herbert.) First edition, first issue, in brown cloth. $200–$250. Author's first book.

BROUGHTON, William Robert. *A Voyage of Discovery to the North Pacific Ocean*. 9 plates and maps (7 folding). Half calf. London, 1804. First edition. $3,500–$5,000. Also, $3,000 (A, 1979).

BROUILLET, J.B.A. *Authentic Account of the Murder of Dr. Whitman and Other Missionaries*. 108 pp., wrappers. Portland, 1869. Second edition of *Protestantism in Oregon* (see item following). $1,000 and up.

BROUILLET, J.B.A. *Protestantism in Oregon: Account of the Murder of Dr. Whitman, and the Ungrateful Calumnies of H.H. Spalding, Protestant Missionary*. Wrappers. New York, 1853. First edition. $3,000 and up.

BROWER, Jacob V. *Memoirs of Explorations in the Basin of the Mississippi*. Maps. 8 vols., cloth. St. Paul, Minn., 1898–1904. One of 300. $400–$500.

BROWN, Bob. *Demonics*. Wrappers, Cagnes-sur-Mer, France, 1931. First edition. $300–$400.

BROWN, Bob. *Let There Be Beer*. Cloth. New York, 1932. First edition. In dust jacket. $45.

BROWN, Bob. *Readies for Bob Brown's Machine*. Wrappers. Cagnes-sur-Mer, France, 1931. First edition. $300–$400.

BROWN, Bob. *Words*. Boards. Paris, 1931. Hours Press. First edition. One of 150 signed. $265.

BROWN, Charles Brockden. See *Monroe's Embassy.*

BROWN, Charles Brockden. *Arthur Mervyn: A Tale.* 3 vols., boards. London, 1803. First English edition. $300–$400, (Note: The first edition was issued anonymously in America in 1799–1800. See entry under *Arthur Mervyn.*)

BROWN, Charles Brockden. *Carwin, the Biloquist, and Other American Tales and Pieces.* Boards. London, 1822. First English edition (of "Memoirs of Carwin, etc.," from William Dunlap's *The Life of Charles Brockden Brown,* which see). $350–$450.

BROWN, Fredric. *The Fabulous Clipjoint.* Blue cloth. New York, 1947. First edition. In dust jacket. $50–$75. Author's first book.

BROWN, Henry. *History of Illinois.* Map. Cloth. New York, 1844. First edition. $150–$200.

BROWN, J. Cabell. *Calabazas, or Amusing Recollections of an Arizona "City."* Illustrated. Printed wrappers. San Francisco, 1892. First edition. $250–$300.

BROWN, J. Willard. *The Signal Corps, U.S.A., in the War of the Rebellion.* Cloth. Boston, 1896. $100–$150.

BROWN, James S. *California Gold: An Authentic History of the First Find.* Portrait frontispiece. 20 pp., printed wrappers. Oakland, 1894. First edition. $175–$225. (55 copies printed.)

BROWN, James S. *Life of a Pioneer.* Portrait. 2 plates. Cloth. Salt Lake City, 1900. First edition. $100–$125.

BROWN, Jesse, and Willard, A.M. *The Black Hills Trails.* Numerous illustrations. Cloth. Rapid City, S.D., 1924. First edition. $100–$125.

BROWN, John. *Rab and His Friends.* Pictorial wrappers. Boston, 1859. First American edition. $50–$60.

BROWN, John Henry. *History of Dallas County from 1837 to 1887.* 114 pp., wrappers. Dallas, 1887. First edition. $150–$250.

BROWN, John Henry, *History of Texas, 1685–1892.* 25 plates. 2 vols., cloth. St. Louis, (1892–93). First edition. $200–$250.

BROWN, John Henry. *Indian Wars and Pioneers of Texas.* Plates. Cloth. Austin, Tex., (1896). First edition. $300–$400.

BROWN, John Henry. *Political History of Oregon.* Vol. 1 (All published.) Illustrated, folding map. Cloth. Portland, Ore., 1892. First edition. $300–$400.

BROWN, John H(enry). *Reminiscences and Incidents, of "The Early Days" of San Francisco.* Folding frontispiece plan. Cloth. San Francisco, (1886). First edition. $500–$600. San Francisco, (1933). Grabhorn printing. Half cloth. One of 500. $75–$100. Another issue: One of 25 in morocco, with additional reproductions, etc. $250–$350.

BROWN, John Henry, and Speer, W.S. *The Encyclopedia of the New West.* Calf. Marshall, Tex., 1881. First edition. $400–$500.

BROWN, John P. *Old Frontiers: The Story of the Cherokee Indians.* Cloth. Kingsport. Tenn., 1938. First edition. $75.

BROWN, Joseph M. *Astyanax: An Epic Romance of Llion, Atlantis, and Amaraca.* Illustrated. Cloth. New York, 1907. First edition. $75–$100.

BROWN, Paul. *Aintree.* Illustrated. Pictorial cloth. New York, 1930. Derrydale Press. First edition. One of 850. $200–$250. Another issue: One of 50 large paper copies with an initialed drawing by Brown. $750. Also $550 (A, 1977).

BROWN, Paul. *Spills and Thrills*. Illustrated. Cloth. New York, 1933. First edition. One of 750 signed. In dust jacket. $300.

BROWN, Samuel J. *In Captivity: The Experience, Privations and Dangers of Sam'l J. Brown, etc.* Text in 2 columns. Illustrated. Full leather. Mankato, Minn., (1896). First edition. $500–$600.

BROWN, Samuel R. *The Western Gazetteer, or Emigrant's Directory*. Sheep. Auburn, N.Y. 1817. First edition, first issue, with 3-line errata slip. $400–$600. Second issue, with 4-line errata. $200–$300. Third issue, with advertisements. $150–$250.

BROWN, Sterling. *Southern Road*. Illustrated. Cloth. New York, 1932. First edition. In dust jacket. $150.

BROWN, William C. *The Sheepeater Campaign in Idaho*. Folding map. 32 pp., wrappers. Boise, 1926. First edition. One of 50. $200–$300.

BROWN, William H. *The Early History of the State of Illinois*. 16 pp., printed wrappers. Chicago, 1840. First edition. $1,000–$1,250.

BROWN, William Robinson. *The Horse of the Desert*. Illustrated. Cloth. New York, 1929. Derrydale Press. One of 750. In dust jacket. $400–$500. Another issue: One of 75 signed. $2,500–$3,000.

BROWNE, Francis F. *Volunteer Grain*. Green cloth. Chicago: Way & Williams, 1895. First edition. One of 160. $300. (First book by the publisher.)

BROWNE, J. Ross. *Adventures in the Apache Country*. Illustrated by the author. Cloth. New York, 1869. First edition, $150–$200.

BROWNE, J. Ross. *Etchings of a Whaling Cruise*. 13 plates. Cloth. New York, 1846. First edition. $300–$400. New York, 1850. $200–$250.

BROWNE, J. Ross, *Report of the Debates in the Convention of California on the Formation of the State Constitution*. Cloth. Washington, 1850. First edition. $200–$250.

BROWNE, J. Ross. *Report . . . on the Late Indian War in Oregon and Washington Territory*. Half leather. Washington, 1858. First edition. $75–$100.

BROWNE, Thomas A. See Boldrewood, Rolf.

BROWNE, Sir Thomas. *Hydriotaphia: Urn Burial*. Waltham Saint Lawrence, 1923. Golden Cockerel Press. One of 115. $200–$300.

BROWNE, Sir Thomas. *Religio Medici*. Waltham Saint Lawrence, 1923. Golden Cockerel Press. One of 115 $300–$500. New York, 1939. Limited Editions Club. John Henry Nash printing. Boxed. $50–$75.

BROWNE, Sir Thomas. *Urn Burial and The Garden of Cyprus*. Edited by John Carter. 30 hand-colored drawings by Paul Nash. Folio, vellum and morocco. London, 1932. Curwen Press. One of 215. In slipcase. $1,500–$1,750.

BROWNING, Elizabeth Barrett. See B., E.B.; Barrett, E.B.; Barrett, Elizabeth B.; Barrett, Elizabeth Barrett. Also see *An Essay on Mind; Prometheus Bound*.

BROWNING, Elizabeth Barrett. *Aurora Leigh*. Cloth. London, 1857 (actually 1856). First edition. $100–$150.

BROWNING, Elizabeth Barrett. *Casa Guidi Windows: A Poem*. Green cloth. London, 1851. First edition. $150–$200.

BROWNING, Elizabeth Barrett. *The Enchantress and Other Poems*. Printed wrappers. London, 1913. First edition. One of 30. $250–$350.

BROWNING, Elizabeth Barrett. *Leila, A Tale*. Printed wrappers. London, 1913. First edition. One of 30. $250–$350.

BROWNING, Elizabeth Barrett, *Poems Before Congress*. Red cloth. London, 1860. First edition, with 32-page publisher's catalogue dated February, 1860. $150–$200.

BROWNING, Elizabeth Barrett. *Sonnets from the Portuguese*. (Note: For the first appearance of the sonnets, see *Poems* under "Elizabeth Barrett Barrett" entry; for the faked Thomas J. Wise first edition, see B., E.B., entry. The following entries are all reprinted versions of the original work.) (Boston), 1896. Copeland & Day. Hand-colored illustrations. Wrappers over boards. $150. London, 1887 (date 1889 on cover). Ballantyne Press. Morocco. One of 8 on vellum. $1,000. Chicago, (1899). One of 15. $150–$200. New Rochelle, 1900. Doves Press [*sic*]. One of 485. $50–$60. Another issue: One of 60 on vellum. $60–$80. (Boston), 1902. One of 250. $50–$75. London, 1906. Caradoc Press. Vellum. $75–$150. Another issue: One of a few printed in red and black on vellum. $500–$750. London, (1909). Buckram. One of 500. In dust jacket. $75–$100. San Francisco, (1910). Silk. $150–$200. London, 1914. Riccardi Press. Vellum. One of 12 on vellum. $1,200–$1,500. Montagnola, 1925. Morocco. One of 225. $150–$200. San Francisco, 1925–27. 2 vols., half vellum (including facsimile volume). One of 250. $50–$60. San Francisco, 1931. 2 vols. One of 250. $50–$60. New York, (1936). Illustrated by Willy Pogany. Cloth. In dust jacket. Boxed. $125–$150. New York, 1948. Limited Editions Club. Cloth. Boxed. $60–$75.

BROWNING, Robert. See Barrett, Elizabeth, and Browning, Robert. Also see *Pauline: A Fragment of a Confession.*

BROWNING, Robert. *Aristophanes' Apology*. Green cloth. London, 1875. First edition, with ad leaf at end. $100–$150.

BROWNING, Robert. *Asolando*. Red cloth. London, 1890. First edition. $150–$200.

BROWNING, Robert. *Balaustion's Adventure*. Beveled red-brown cloth. London, 1871. First edition. $100.

BROWNING, Robert. *Bells and Pomegranates*. 8 parts, printed wrappers. London, 1841–46. First edition, with half title for second part. $1,000 and up. (A set with three parts inscribed by Browning to an uncle brought $2,750 at auction in 1974. Another, with one number inscribed by the author, sold for $425 at auction in 1972.) First book edition (parts bound in one volume, cloth, with the half title to the second part). $350–$500.

BROWNING, Robert. *Christmas Eve and Easter Day: A Poem*. Cloth. London, 1850. First edition. $75–$125.

BROWNING, Robert. *Dramatic Romances and Lyrics*. Illustrated. Morocco. London, 1899. Ballantyne Press. One of 10 on vellum. $1,000–$1,250. Also, $481 (A, 1975). Another issue: Buckram. One of 210. $200.

BROWNING, Robert. *Dramatis Personae*. Red cloth. London, 1864. First edition. $125–$150. (London, 1910.) Doves Press. Vellum. One of 250 on paper. $600–$850. Another issue: One of 15 on vellum. $6,000 (A, 1978).

BROWNING, Robert. *An Essay on Percy Bysshe Shelley*. Edited by W.T. Harden. Sheets printed on vellum, unbound, in buckram folder and slipcase. (London), 1888. One of 4 (3?) printed on vellum. $750–$1,000.

BROWNING, Robert. *Fifine at the Fair*. Dark-brown cloth. London, 1872. First edition. $100.

BROWNING, Robert. *Men and Women*. 2 vols., green cloth. London, 1855. First edition, first binding. $300–$400. London, 1908. Doves Press. 2 vols., vellum. One of 262 printed in red and black. $1,250–$1,500. In a special Doves binding of morocco. $2,000 and up. Another issue: One of 12 on vellum. $14,000 (A, 1978).

BROWNING, Robert, *Pacchiarotto and How He Worked in Distemper: With Other Poems*. Beveled gray cloth. London, 1876. First edition, with ad leaf at end. $200–$300.

BROWNING, Robert. *Paracelsus*. Drab boards, paper label. London, 1835. First edition, first issue, with 8 pages of ads at front dated Dec. 1, 1842. $2,000 and up. Author's first acknowledged book.

BROWNING, Robert. *The Pied Piper of Hamelin*. 35 colored illustrations by Kate Greenaway. Pictorial boards. London, (1888). First edition. In dust jacket. $250–$350. London, 1934. Illustrated by Arthur Rackham. Limp vellum. One of 410. Boxed. $600–$800.

BROWNING, Robert. *The Ring and the Book*. 4 vols., green cloth. London, 1868–69. First edition, first binding, with spines of first 2 volumes in Arabic numerals and of next 2 in Roman numerals. $400–$600. New York, 1949. Limited Editions Club. 2 vols., boards and morocco. Boxed. $60–$80.

BROWNING, Robert. *Some Poems*. Frontispiece in color. Boards. London, 1904. Eragny Press. One of 215 on paper. $350–$450. Another issue: One of 11 on vellum. $1,250–$1,500.

BROWNING, Robert. *Sordello*. Boards, paper label. London, 1840. First edition, first issue, in boards (later issue being cloth). $400–$500.

BROWNING, Robert. *Strafford: An Historical Tragedy*. Stiff gray wrappers, paper label on front. London, 1837. First edition. $750–$1,000.

BROWNLOW, William. *A Political Register*. Boards. Jonesborough, Tenn., 1844. First edition. $150–$200.

BRUFF, J. Goldsborough. *Gold Rush: The Journals, Drawings and Other Papers of J. Goldsborough Bruff*. Edited by Georgia W. Read and Ruth Gaines. 21 plates, 2 vols., boards. New York, 1944. First edition. (1,158 printed.) $250–$300. New York, 1949. Illustrated. 2 vols. in one, cloth. (Abridged.) In dust jacket. $50.

BRUFFEY, George A. *Eighty-one Years in the West*. Portrait. 152 pp., wrappers. Butte, 1925. First edition. $75.

BRUNEFILLE, G.E. *Topo*. Illustrated by Kate Greenaway. Cloth. London, 1880. (By Gertrude Elizabeth Cambell.) First edition. $100–$125.

BRUNSON, Alfred. *A Western Pioneer*. 2 vols., cloth. Cincinnati, 1872 and 1879. First edition. $100–$125.

BRUNSON, Edward, *Profits in Sheep and Cattle in Central and Western Kansas*. 16 pp., wrappers. Kansas City, 1883. First edition. $200–$250.

BRUTUS. *The Crisis; or, Essays on the Usurpation of the Federal Government*. Half morocco. Charleston, 1827. (By Robert J. Turnbull.) First edition. $150–$200.

BRYAN, Daniel. *The Mountain Muse*. Leather. Harrisonburg, 1813. First edition. $150.

BRYANT, Edwin. *What I Saw in California*. Cloth. New York, 1848. First edition. $250–$350. New York, 1848. Cloth. Second edition. $150–$200. Santa Ana, Calif., 1936. Half morocco. $50–$75.

BRYANT, Gilbert Ernest. *The Chelsea Porcelain Toys*. 63 plates, 47 in color. Cloth. London, 1925. One of 650 signed. In dust jacket. $500–$600.

BRYANT, John Howard. *Poems*. Cloth. New York, 1855. First edition. $75–$100.

BRYANT, Wilbur F. *The Blood of Abel*. Cloth. Hastings, Neb., 1887. First edition. $200–$250.

BRYANT, William Cullen. *The Embargo; or, Sketches of the Times: A Satire*. (Cover title.) Self-wrappers (stitched); also plain slate blue or marbled paper wrappers. Boston, 1809. Second edition. Wrappers: $600 and up. Stitched: $500 and up. (For first edition, see title entry, *The Embargo*.)

BRYANT, William Cullen. *The Fountain and Other Poems*. Boards; or cloth, label on spine; or, cloth with gold stamping on front cover. New York, 1842. First edition. (No priority on bindings, according to Blanck.) $200–$300.

BRYANT, William Cullen. *Hymns.* Brown-orange or blue cloth. (New York, 1864). First edition, first state, with reading "Dwells on Thy works in deep delight" in second line of fourth stanza on page 9. $150–$200.

BRYANT, William Cullen. *Poems.* Brown or grayish printed boards (375 copies?—Blanck), or printed brown wrappers (200 copies?—Blanck). Cambridge, Mass., 1821. First edition. Boards: $1,250 and up. Wrappers: $1,500 and up. New York, 1832. Second edition. Boards and blue cloth. $300–$400. New York, 1836. Third edition. $150–$200. New York, 1947. Limited Editions Club. Illustrated by Thomas Nason. Leather. Boxed. $40–$60.

BRYANT, William Cullen. *Thirty Poems.* Brown cloth. New York, 1864. First edition, first state, wove paper, line 5 from bottom of page 213 reading "veielo." $100–$150. Second state, laid paper, reading "vuielo" on page 213. $75–$100.

BRYANT, William Cullen. *Unpublished Poems.* Illustrated. Boards. Boston, 1907. Bibliophile Society. One of 470 on vellum. Boxed. $75–$85.

BRYANT, W.N. *Bryant's Texas Almanac and Railway Guide, 1881–1882.* (Cover title.) Wrappers. Dallas, 1881. $375. Earlier: *Bryant's Texas Guide!* 2 folding maps. Wrappers. Austin, 1875. $650.

BRYCE, James. *The American Commonwealth.* 3 vols., cloth. London, 1888. First edition, first issue, with the chapter in Vol. 3 on the Tweed Ring, later suppressed. $100–$250. Second issue, with Tweed Ring matter omitted. $75–$125.

BRYHER, Winifred. *The Lament for Adonis.* Translated from the Greek. Wrappers. London, 1918. First edition. $300–$450. Author's first book.

BUCHAN, John. *The Marquis of Montrose.* Plates, maps, plans. Cloth. London, 1913. First edition. $100–$125.

BUCHAN, John. *The Pilgrim Fathers: The Newdigate Prize Poem, 1898.* Wrappers. Oxford, 1898. First edition. $100–$125.

BUCHAN, John. *Poems—Scots and English.* Blue cloth and boards. London, 1917. One of 50 signed. $150–$200.

BUCHAN, John. *Sir Quixote of the Moors.* Cloth. London, 1895. First edition, first issue, with full title on spine. $150–$200. New York, 1895. Cloth. First American edition. $75–$100. Author's first book.

BUCHAN, John. *The Thirty-Nine Steps.* Blue cloth. Edinburgh, 1915. First edition. In dust jacket. $200–$250.

BUCHANAN, Robert. *The Devil's Case.* Cloth. London, (1896). First edition. $75–$100.

BUCHANAN, Robert. *The Fleshly School of Poetry.* Pink or violet pictorial wrappers. London, 1872. First edition. $150–$175.

BUCHANAN, Robertson. *Practical and Descriptive Essays on the Economy of Fuel, and Management of Heat.* 2 plates. Boards. Glasgow, 1810. First edition $400–$600.

BUCHANAN, Robertson. *A Practical Treatise on Propelling Vessels by Steam.* 17 plates, one folding. Boards. Glasgow, 1816. First edition. $500–$750.

BUCK, Irving A. *Cleburne and His Command.* Plates. Cloth. New York, 1908. First edition. $75–$100.

BUCK, Pearl S. *East Wind: West Wind.* Cloth. New York, (1930). First edition. In dust jacket. $50–$60.

BUCK, Pearl S. *The Good Earth.* Tan cloth. New York, (1931). First edition, first issue, with "flees" for "fleas" in line 17 of page 100, with "John Day Publishing Company" on copyright page, and with top edges stained brown. In brown dust jacket. $200–$250. Later issue, green top edges, in dust jacket. $100–$150. Advance issue, for review: Printed wrappers. $200–$250.

BUCK, Pearl S. *Sons.* Cloth. New York, (1932). First edition. One of 371 de luxe copies, signed. In dust jacket. Boxed. $100–$125.

BUCK, Pearl S. (translator). *All Men Are Brothers.* Translated from the Chinese of Shui Hu Chuan, 2 vols. New York (1933). First edition. Boxed $50–$60. New York, 1948. Limited Editions Club. Edited by Lin Yutang. Illustrated by Miguel Covarrubias. 2 vols., stiff wrappers. Chinese silk paper, tied with thongs. Boxed. $125–$150.

BUCKINGHAM, Nash. *De Shootinest Gent'man and Other Tales.* Edited by Col. Harold P. Sheldon. Illustrated. Cloth. New York, (1934). Derrydale Press. First edition. One of 950. $450–$550.

BUCKINGHAM, Nash. *Mark Right!* Illustrated. Cloth. New York, (1936). Derrydale Press. One of 1,250. $350–$400.

BUCKINGHAM, Nash. *Ole Miss.* Edited by Paul A. Curtis. Illustrated. Leatherette. New York, (1937). Derrydale Press. One of 1,250. $400–$500.

BUCKLEY, Francis. *English Baluster Stemmed Glasses of the 17th and 18th Centuries.* 18 plates. Buckram. Edinburgh, 1912. $300–$350.

BUCKLEY, Francis. *Old London Drinking Glasses.* 14 plates. Buckram. Edinburgh, 1913. $150–$250.

BUCKLEY, Wilfred. *Diamond Engraved Glasses of the 16th Century.* 33 plates. Boards. London, 1929. One of 250. $300–$350.

BUCKLEY, William F., Jr. *God and Man at Yale.* Cloth. Chicago, 1951. First edition. In dust jacket. $50–$60.

BUDGE, Sir E. A. Wallis. *Amulets and Superstitions.* 22 plates, 300 other illustrations. Cloth. London, 1930. $150–$200.

BUDGE, Sir E. A. Wallis. *The Gods of the Egyptians, or Studies in Egyptian Mythology.* 98 color plates. 2 vols., pictorial cloth. London, 1904. $200–$250.

BUECHNER, Frederick. *A Long Day's Dying.* Cloth. New York, 1950. First edition. In dust jacket. $50–$75. Author's first book.

BUEL, J. W. *Life and Marvelous Adventures of Wild Bill, the Scout.* Frontispiece and plate. 93pp., pictorial wrappers. Chicago, 1880. First edition, presumed first issue, with cover dated 1880. $600–$800.

BUFFUM, E. Gould. *Six Months in the Gold Mines.* Printed wrappers, or cloth. Philadelphia, 1850. First edition. Wrappers: $400–$500. Cloth. $300–$350.

BUKOWSKI, Charles. *At Terror Street and Agony Way.* Cloth. Los Angeles, 1968. Black Sparrow Press. First edition. One of 75 signed by the author with an original illustration by the author. $150–$175.

BUKOWSKI, Charles. *Cold Dogs in the Courtyard.* Wrappers. (Chicago), 1965. First edition. One of 500. $40–$50.

BUKOWSKI, Charles. *Crucifix in a Deathhand.* Illustrated. Pictorial wrappers. New York: Loujón Press, (1965). First edition. Limited (to about 3,100) and signed. $50–$75. (Some copies, with special inscriptions, at higher prices.)

BUKOWSKI, Charles. *The Curtains are Waving, etc.* Printed wrappers. (Los Angeles), 1967. First edition. One of 125 signed. $125–$150.

BUKOWSKI, Charles. *The Days Run Away Like Wild Horses Over the Hills.* Boards. Los Angeles, 1969. First edition. One of 250 signed. In acetate dust jacket. $65–$75. Another issue: One of 50 with a drawing by the author. $125–$150.

BUKOWSKI, Charles. *Post Office.* Boards. Los Angeles, 1971. First edition. In acetate dust jacket. One of 250 signed. $50. Another issue: One of 50 signed, with an original drawing by the author. $150.

BUKOWSKI, Charles. *Run with the Hunted.* Pictorial wrappers. Chicago, (1962). First edition. $100–$150.

BULFINCH, Thomas. *The Age of Chivalry.* 6 illustrations. Brown cloth. Boston, 1859. First edition. $200–$250.

BULFINCH, Thomas. *The Age of Fable.* Brown cloth. Boston, 1855. First edition, first state, with names of both printer and stereotyper on copyright page. $200–$250. New York, 1956. Limited Editions Club. Illustrated by Joe Mugnaini. Cloth. Boxed. $50–$75.

BULLEN, A.H. *A Collection of Old English Plays.* 7 vols., boards, parchment spines. London, 1882–90. One of 150. $250–$350.

BULLEN, Frank T. *The Cruise of the "Cachalot."* Folding map and plates. Blue cloth. London, 1898. First edition. $250–$300. Author's first book.

BULLER, Sir Walter Lawry. *A History of the Birds of New Zealand.* 35 hand-colored plates. Cloth. London, 1873. First edition. $2,000–$2,500. London, 1887–88. 48 colored plates, 2 plain plates. 13 parts in 8, wrappers. $3,000 and up. London, 1888. 2 vols., half morocco. Second edition. $1,500–$2,000. With 1901 supplement of 2 vols., $4,500 in a 1981 catalogue.

BULLOCK, William. *Six Months Residence and Travels in Mexico.* 2 folding plans, folding view, 11 other views, 4 colored aquatint plates. Boards and cloth. London, 1824. First edition. $500–$600.

BULWER-LYTTON, Edward. See Caxton, Pisistratus. Also see *The Coming Race; Falkland; The Last Days of Pompeii; Pelham; Rienzi.*

BULWER-LYTTON, Edward. *Ismael; an Oriental Tale.* Boards. London, 1820. First edition. $400–$600. Author's first book.

BUNIN, I.A. *The Gentleman from San Francisco and Other Stories.* Translated by Leonard Woolf. Boards. (London), 1922. Hogarth Press. First edition. With errata slip. $150.

BUNNER, H.C. *A Woman of Honor.* Cloth. Boston, 1883. First edition. $50–60. Author's first book.

BUNTING, Basil. *Briggflatts.* Black cloth. London, (1966). One of 100 in cloth. In dust jacket. $100–$150. Another issue: Leather. One of 26. $300.

BUNTING, Basil. *Collected Poems.* Cloth. London (or New York), 1968. First edition. One of 150 signed, with accompanying numbered silk screen print. In dust jacket. $150–$175.

BUNTING, Basil. *First Book of Odes.* Boards. London, no date. One of 125. $100. Another issue: Cloth. One of 50. $75. Also, in boards: One of 26 lettered and signed. $150.

BUNTING, Basil. *Loquitur.* Full morocco. London, (1965). First edition. One of 26 signed. In dust jacket. $200–$225. Another issue: Cloth. One of 200. In dust jacket. $125.

BUNTING, Basil. *Redimiculum Matellarum.* Wrappers. Milan, 1930. First edition. $1,000–$1,250. Author's first book.

BUNTING, Basil. *Two Poems.* Wrappers. Santa Barbara, 1967. First edition. One of 30 signed (of an edition of 250). $150. Ordinary copies (not signed): $35–$50.

BUNTING, Basil, and Williams, Jonathan. *Descant on Rawthey's Madrigal: Conversations with Basil Bunting.* Boards. Lexington, Ky., (1968). One of 25 signed by Bunting and Williams. In dust jacket. $150–$175.

BUNYAN, John. *The Pilgrim's Progress.* Portrait frontispiece. Full brown morocco, gilt. London, 1849. Chiswick Press. $150–$200. London, 1928. Cresset Press. 10 wood engravings. 2 vols., folio, cloth. One of 195. $500–$750. Another issue: One of 10 on vellum with an extra suite of plates. $5,200 (A, 1979). New York, 1941. Limited Editions Club. 29 William Blake illustrations in color. One of 1,500. Boxed. $100–$150.

BURDETTE, Robert J. *The Rise and Fall of the Mustache.* Illustrated. Cloth. Burlington, Iowa, 1877. First edition. $35–$50. Author's first book.

BURGESS, Anthony. See Kell, Joseph.

BURGESS, Anthony. *Beds in the East.* Cloth. London, (1959). First edition. In dust jacket. $50.

BURGESS, Anthony. *A Clockwork Orange.* Cloth. London, (1962). First edition. In dust jacket. $400–$650. New York, (1963). First American edition. In dust jacket. $75–$100.

BURGESS, Anthony. *Devil of a State.* Cloth. London, (1961). First edition. In dust jacket. $50.

BURGESS, Anthony. *The Doctor Is Sick.* Cloth. London, (1960). First edition. In dust jacket. $100–$125. New York, (1960). Cloth. First American edition. In dust jacket. $35.

BURGESS, Anthony. *The Enemy in the Blanket.* Cloth. London, (1958). First edition. In dust jacket. $150–$200.

BURGESS, Anthony. *Honey for the Bears.* Cloth. London, (1963). First edition. In dust jacket. $50. New York, (1964). First American edition. In dust jacket. $35.

BURGESS, Anthony. *Nothing Like the Sun.* Cloth. London, (1964). First edition. In dust jacket. $75. New York, (1964). First American edition. In dust jacket. $30.

BURGESS, Anthony. *The Right to An Answer.* Cloth. London, (1960). First edition. In dust jacket. $50. New York, (1961). First American edition. In dust jacket. $35.

BURGESS, Anthony. *A Vision of Battlements.* Illustrated by Edward Pagram. Yellow cloth. London, (1964). First edition, first binding. In the first issue dust jacket with Pagram illustration. $50.

BURGESS, Gelett. *Are You a Bromide?* Boards, paper label on front cover. New York, 1906. First edition. In dust jacket. $100–$125.

BURGESS, Gelett. *Goops and How to Be Them.* 90 drawings by the author. Red cloth. New York, (1900). First edition. $250–$300. London, 1900. Illustrated by the author. Pictorial cloth. First English edition. $250–$300.

BURGESS, Gelett. *Le Petit Journal des Refusées: Number 1.* (All published.) Wrappers. San Francisco, 1896. First edition. (Printed on wallpaper.) $100 and up.

BURGESS, Gelett. *The Nonsense Almanack for 1900.* Wrappers. New York, (1899). First edition. $100–$150.

BURGESS, Gelett. *The Purple Cow!* Illustrated. 8 leaves. (San Francisco, 1895.) First edition, first state of first printing (printed on both sides of leaf) on rough China paper. $300–$400. Second state (printed on one side of leaf only). $150–$200. Author's first publication.

BURGESS, Gelett. *Vivette, or the Memoirs of the Romance Association.* Cloth. Boston, 1897. First edition. $50–$60. Author's first book, aside from *The Purple Cow* leaflet.

BURGESS, Thornton Waldo. *Old Mother West Wind.* Illustrated. Pictorial tan cloth. Boston, (1910). First edition. $150–$175. Author's first book for children.

BURKE, John. *Dreams and Derisions.* Illustrated by Rockwell Kent. Half morocco. (New York), 1927. (By Ralph Pulitzer.) First edition. One of 100 (of an edition of 300) signed by Kent. Boxed. $400–$500.

BURKE, Kenneth. *The White Oxen and Other Stories.* Cloth. New York, 1924. First edition. In dust jacket. $100–$125. Author's first book.

BURKE, Thomas, *Limehouse Nights.* Terra-cotta cloth. London, 1916. First edition. $50–$60. New York, 1926. Illustrated. Cloth. $50.

BURKE, W.S. (compiler). *Directory of the City of Council Bluffs and Emigrants' Guide to the Gold Regions of the West.* Folding map. 32pp., plus ads, patterned cloth. Council Bluffs, Iowa, 1866. First edition. $1,250–$1,500.

BURLEND, Rebecca. *A True Picture of Emigration.* Wrappers. London, (1848). First edition. $150.

BURNETT, Frances Hodgson. *The Drury Lane Boys' Club.* 78pp., blue wrappers. Washington, 1892. First edition. One of 800. $100–$150.

BURNETT, Frances Hodgson. *Editha's Burglar.* Illustrated by Henry Sandham. Pictorial brown cloth. Boston, 1888. First edition, first state, with "I thought I heard something" under frontispiece. $50–$75. Second state, with name only under frontispiece. $30–$40.

BURNETT, Frances Hodgson. *Little Lord Fauntleroy.* Illustrated by Reginald B. Birch. Pictorial gray-green (blue) or tan cloth. New York, 1886. First edition, first issue, with De Vinne Press imprint at end. $300–$400. London, 1886. Pictorial cloth. First English edition, with copyright page dated November 9, 1886. $100–$150.

BURNETT, Frances Hodgson. *The Secret Garden.* Illustrated. Cloth, pictorial label. New York, (1911). First edition. $100–$150. Another issue: with no illustrations. (Blanck knew of no priority.) $50–$75.

BURNETT, Frances Hodgson. *That Lass O'Lowrie's.* Illustrated. Cloth. New York, 1877. First edition, first state, with illustrator's name on title page. $100–$150. Author's first book.

BURNETT, Peter H. *Recollections and Opinions of an Old Pioneer.* Cloth. New York, 1880. First edition. $150–$250.

BURNETT, W.R. *Little Caesar.* Blue cloth. New York, 1929. First edition. In dust jacket. $100–$125. Author's first book.

BURNEY, Fanny (Frances). *Evelina.* 16 full-page illustrations by Arthur Rackham. Cloth. London, 1898. $75–$100.

BURNEY, Frances. See D'Arblay, Madame.

BURNEY, James. *A Chronological History of the Discoveries in the South Sea or Pacific Ocean.* Maps, charts, plates. 5 vols., contemporary boards and leather. London, 1803–17. First edition. Large paper issue: $5,000–$6,000. Ordinary issue: $4,000–$5,000.

BURNEY, James. *History of the Buccaneers of America.* 3 maps (2 folding). Contemporary three-quarters morocco. London, 1816. First separate edition. Large paper issue: $350–$450. Ordinary issue: $250–$300.

BURNHAM, Daniel H., and Bennett, Edward H. *Plan of Chicago.* Illustrated. Leather and/or cloth. Chicago, 1909. First edition. One of 1,650 copies. $300–$400. Another issue: Full vellum. $500–$600. (100 copies are said to have been issued thus. There was also an unknown number of copies bound in plain black linen wrappers. I once found five in a lot of architectural books.)

BURNS, John H. *Memoirs of a Cow Pony.* Illustrated. Pictorial cloth. Boston, (1906). First edition. $250.

BURNS, John Horne. *The Gallery.* Cloth. New York, (1947). First edition. In dust jacket. $50–$75. Author's first book.

BURNS, Robert, *Poems Ascribed to Robert Burns.* Boards. Glasgow, 1801. First edition. $400–$500.

BURNS, Robert, *Tam O'Shanter.* Illustrated, colored by hand. Stiff vellum. London, 1902. Essex House Press. One of 150 on vellum. $300–$375.

BURPEE, Lawrence J. *The Search for the Western Sea.* 6 maps, 51 plates. Cloth. London, 1908. First edition. $150–$200. New York, 1908. Cloth. First American edition $100–$150. Toronto, (1908). Cloth. First Canadian edition. $100–$150. New York, 1936. Maps and plates. 2 vols., cloth. In dust jackets. $50–$75.

BURR, Aaron. *The Private Journal of Aaron Burr.* Edited by W. K. Bixby. Portraits. 2 vols., half cloth. Rochester, 1903. One of 250 signed by Bixby. $150–$200.

BURROUGHS, Edgar Rice. *At the Earth's Core.* Illustrated. Cloth. Chicago, 1922. First edition. In dust jacket. $500–$600.

BURROUGHS, Edgar Rice. *Back to the Stone Age.* Cloth. Tarzana, Calif., (1937). First edition. In dust jacket. $300–$325.

BURROUGHS. Edgar Rice. *The Beasts of Tarzan.* Illustrated. Olive cloth. Chicago, 1916. First edition. In dust jacket. $750.

BURROUGHS, Edgar Rice. *The Chessmen of Mars.* Illustrated. Red cloth. Chicago, 1922. First edition. In dust jacket. $350–$450.

BURROUGHS, Edgar Rice. *The Eternal Lover.* Illustrated. Cloth. Chicago. 1925. First edition. In dust jacket. $600–$800. Without jacket, $200.

BURROUGHS, Edgar Rice. *A Fighting Man of Mars.* Frontispiece. Red cloth, New York, (1931). First edition, with Metropolitan Books imprint. In dust jacket. $100–$150.

BURROUGHS, Edgar Rice. *The Girl from Hollywood.* Red cloth. New York, (1923). First edition, first issue, with cloth lettered in green. In dust jacket. $250–$350.

BURROUGHS, Edgar Rice. *Jungle Tales of Tarzan.* Illustrated. Cloth. Chicago, 1919. First edition. In dust jacket. $750–$850. Without jacket, $200.

BURROUGHS, Edgar Rice. *The Master Mind of Mars.* Cloth. Chicago, 1928. First edition. In dust jacket. $150.

BURROUGHS, Edgar Rice. *The Mucker.* Cloth. Chicago. 1921. First edition. In dust jacket. $400–$500.

BURROUGHS, Edgar Rice. *The Outlaw of Torn.* Cloth. Chicago, 1927. First edition. In dust jacket. $300–$350.

BURROUGHS, Edgar Rice. *A Princess of Mars.* Illustrated. Cloth. Chicago, 1917. First edition. In dust jacket. $500–$600.

BURROUGHS, Edgar Rice. *The Return of Tarzan.* Cloth. Chicago, 1915. First edition. In dust jacket. $600–$800. Without jacket. $100–$150.

BURROUGHS, Edgar Rice. *The Son of Tarzan.* Illustrated. Cloth. Chicago, 1917. First edition. In dust jacket. $600–$800. Lacking jacket. $150–$200.

BURROUGHS, Edgar Rice. *Tarzan and the Ant Men*. Illustrated. Cloth. Chicago, 1924. First edition. In dust jacket. $500–$600.

BURROUGHS, Edgar Rice. *Tarzan and the Golden Lion*. Illustrated. Gold cloth. Chicago, 1933. First edition. $75–$100.

BURROUGHS, Edgar Rice. *Tarzan and the Jewels of Opar*. Illustrated. Dark-green cloth. Chicago, 1918. First edition. In dust jacket. $750–$1,000. Without jacket, $200.

BURROUGHS, Edgar Rice. *Tarzan and the Leopard Men*. Cloth. Tarzana, (1935). First edition. In dust jacket. $200–$250.

BURROUGHS, Edgar Rice. *Tarzan at the Earth's Core*. Cloth. New York, (1930). Metropolitan Books. First edition. In dust jacket. $250–$300. Without jacket, $75.

BURROUGHS, Edgar Rice. *Tarzan, Lord of the Jungle*. Illustrated. Cloth. Chicago, 1928. First edition. In dust jacket. $600–$750. Without jacket, $125–$150.

BURROUGHS, Edgar Rice. *Tarzan of the Apes*. Frontispiece. Red cloth. Chicago, 1914. First edition. In dust jacket. $3,000–$5,000. Without jacket, $1,000–$1,250. Author's first book. London, (1917). Orange-colored cloth. First English edition, with ads dated Autumn. In dust jacket. $250–$500.

BURROUGHS, Edgar Rice. *Tarzan the Untamed*. Illustrated. Cloth. Chicago, 1920. First edition. In dust jacket. $500–$750. Without jacket, $125.

BURROUGHS, Edgar Rice. *Tarzan Triumphant*. Illustrated by Stanley Burroughs. Cloth. Tarzana, (1932). First edition. In dust jacket. $100–$150. Without jacket, $35.

BURROUGHS, Edgar Rice. *Thuvia, Maid of Mars*. Illustrated. Cloth. Chicago, 1920. First edition. In dust jacket. $350–$500.

BURROUGHS, Edgar Rice. *The Warlord of Mars*. Frontispiece. Red cloth. Chicago, 1919. First edition, first issue, with "W.F. Hall" on copyright page. In dust jacket. $350–$500. Without jacket, $125.

BURROUGHS, John. *Bird and Bough*. Cloth. Boston, 1906. First edition. In dust jacket. $75–$100.

BURROUGHS, John. *Notes on Walt Whitman as Poet and Person*. Cloth, or blue wrappers. New York, 1867. First edition, first issue, leaves trimmed to 6 9/16 inches tall. Cloth: $100–$150. Wrappers: $75–$150. Later, 1867, clothbound, leaves 7 1/4 inches tall: $35–$40.

BURROUGHS, John. *Wake-Robin*. Green or terra-cotta cloth. New York, 1871. First edition. $75–$100.

BURROUGHS, John. *Winter Sunshine*. Cloth, New York, 1876. First edition. $40–$50.

BURROUGHS, William. See Lee, William.

BURROUGHS, William S. *Ali's Smile*. Oblong, boards and cloth. (Brighton), 1971. First edition. One of 99 signed. $150–$200. (Issued with a Burroughs LP record.)

BURROUGHS, William S. *The Last Words of Dutch Schultz*. Cloth. London, 1970. First edition. One of 100 signed. In tissue dust jacket. $125–$150.

BURROUGHS, William S. *The Naked Lunch*. Wrappers. Paris, (1959). Olympia Press. First edition. In dust jacket. $225. Second printing. Wrappers. Issued without jacket. $50–$75.

BURROUGHS, William S. *The Soft Machine*. Printed wrappers. Paris, (1961). Olympia Press. First edition. In dust jacket. $75–$100.

BURROUGHS, William S. *The Ticket That Exploded.* Wrappers. Paris, (1962). Olympia Press. First edition. In dust jacket. $50–$75

BURROUGHS, William S. *Time.* Illustrated by Brion Gysin. Wrappers. New York, 1965. First edition. One of 100 signed. $60–$90. Ordinary copies: $15–$20.

BURTON. Alfred. *The Adventures of Johnny Newcome in the Navy.* 16 colored plates by Rowlandson. Cloth. London, 1818. (By John Mitford.) First edition. $750–$1,000. (See John Mitford entry for second and third editions.)

BURTON, Harley True. *A History of the JA Ranch.* Portrait, map. Cloth. Austin, 1928. First edition. $400–$600.

BURTON, Sir Richard F. *The City of the Saints and Across the Rocky Mountains to California.* 7 plates. folding map, folding plan. Cloth. London, 1861. First edition. $400–$500.

BURTON, Sir Richard F. *Falconry in the Valley of the Indus.* Frontispiece, other plates. Cloth. London, 1852. First edition $750–$1,000.

BURTON, Sir Richard F. *First Footsteps in East Africa; or, an Exploration of Harar.* With 2 maps and 4 colored plates. Violet cloth. London, 1856. First edition, first issue, with 24pp. of ads dated March, 1856. $750–$1,000. Second issue: Red cloth. $650.

BURTON, Sir Richard F. *Goa, and the Blue Mountains.* Folding map, plates. Cloth. London, 1851. First edition. $600–$750.

BURTON, Sir Richard F. *The Gold-Mines of Midian and the Ruined Midianite Cities.* Folding map. Cloth. London, 1878. First edition $500–$750.

BURTON, Sir Richard F. *The Lake Regions of Central Africa.* Folding map. 12 colored plates. 2 vols., cloth. London, 1860. First edition. $600–$750.

BURTON, Sir Richard F. *The Land of Midian (Revisited).* Folding map. 16 plates, 6 colored. 2 vols., cloth. London, 1879. First edition, first issue, with ads dated "9.78" $500–$750.

BURTON, Sir Richard F. *Letters from the Battlefields of Paraguay.* Folding map, frontispiece. Cloth. London, 1870. First edition. $500–$600.

BURTON, Sir Richard F. *Personal Narrative of a Pilgrimage to El-Medinah and Meccah.* 16 plates (5 colored), 3 folding maps. 3 vols., cloth. London, 1855–56. First edition. $1,000–$1,250. Rebound in half leather, $800.

BURTON, Sir Richard F. *Vikram and the Vampire, or Tales of Hindu Devilry.* Illustrated, Pictorial cloth. London, 1870. First edition, first issue (black cloth). $150–$175.

BURTON, Sir Richard F. (translator). *The Book of the Thousand Nights and a Night.* (Arabian Nights). Illustrated by Valenti Angelo. 6 vols., boards, cowhide spines. New York, 1934. Limited Editions Club. Boxed. $150. Another Limited Editions Club edition: New York, 1954. Illustrated in color by Arthur Szyk. 4 vols. Boxed. $200–$250.

BURTON, Robert. *The Anatomy of Melancholy.* Illustrated by E. McKnight Kauffer. 2 vols., half vellum and boards. London, 1925–1926. Nonesuch Press. One of 750. $250–$400. Another issue: 2 vols. in one. One of 40 on vellum. $800–$1,000.

BURTON, W. *Josiah Wedgwood and His Pottery.* 32 color plates, 84 in black and white. Cloth. London. 1922. Limited Edition. In dust jacket. $200–$300.

BUTCHER, S.D. *S.D. Butcher's Pioneer History of Custer Country.* Illustrated. Cloth, or leather. Broken Bow, Neb., 1901. First edition. $100–$150.

BUTLER, Arthur G. *Beautiful Foreign Finches and Their Treatment in Captivity.* 60 colored plates by F. W. Frohawk. Cloth. London, 1904. $300–$400.

BUTLER, Arthur G. *Foreign Finches in Captivity.* 60 hand-colored plates. Cloth. London. 1894. First edition. $2,000–$3,000. London, 1899. Illustrated with chromolithographs. Cloth. Second edition. $300–$400.

BUTLER, Ellis Parker. See *Pigs Is Pigs.*

BUTLER, Ellis Parker. *Philo Gubb: Correspondence School Detective.* Yellow cloth. Boston, 1918. First edition. In dust jacket. $300–$350. Without jacket, $100.

BUTLER, Mann. *A History of the Commonwealth of Kentucky.* Portrait. Leather. Louisville, 1834. First edition. $300–$400.

BUTLER, Samuel. See *Erewhon.*

BUTLER, Samuel. *The Authoress of the Odyssey.* Maps and illustrations. Red cloth. London, 1897. First edition. $150–$200.

BUTLER, Samuel. *Erewhon Revisited Twenty Years Later.* Red cloth. London, 1901. First edition, with errata slip in preface. $150–$200.

BUTLER, Samuel. *A First Year in Canterbury Settlement.* Folding map. Red cloth. London, 1863. First edition, with 32 pages of ads and light-brown end papers. $250–$300. Author's first book.

BUTLER, Samuel. *Life and Habit.* Brown cloth. London, 1878. First edition, with brown end papers. $50–$75.

BUTLER, Samuel. *The Note-Books of Samuel Butler.* Edited by H.F. Jones. Cloth. London, 1912. First edition. $75–$100.

BUTLER, Samuel. *Seven Sonnets and A Psalm of Montreal.* Unbound, or printed wrappers. Cambridge, 1904. First edition. In wrappers: $300–$400. Value in unbound state:? (Note: Lord Esher's copy, in printed wrappers and with a specially made folding case with his bookplate, brought $420 at auction in 1967.)

BUTLER, Samuel. *The Way of All Flesh.* Red cloth, gilt, top edges gilt. London, 1903. First edition. $450–$600. New York, 1936. Limited Editions Club. 2 vols., leather. Boxed. $75–$100.

BUTTERFIELD, C.W. *An Historical Account of the Expedition Against Sandusky.* Portrait. Cloth. Cincinnati, 1873. First edition. $100–$150.

BUTTERFIELD, C.W. *History of the Discovery of the Northwest.* Cloth. Cincinnati, 1881. First edition. $150–$200.

BUTTERFIELD, C.W. *History of the Girtys.* Cloth. Cincinnati, 1890. First edition. $100–$150.

BUTTERFIELD, C.W. *History of Seneca County*, Ohio. Cloth. Sandusky, Ohio, 1848. First edition. $100–$150.

BUTTERWORTH, Benjamin J. *The Growth of Industrial Art.* 200 full-page plates. Folio, cloth. Washington, 1888. First edition. $250–$350. Washington, 1892. $200–$300.

BUTTERWORTH, Hezekiah. *Zig-Zag Journeys in Europe.* Boards. Boston, 1880. First edition. $50–$75.

BUTTS, Mary. *Armed with Madness.* Drawings by Jean Cocteau. Blue cloth. London, 1928. First edition. One of 100. $225–$275.

BUTTS, Mary. *Ashe of Rings.* Wrappers. (Paris, 1925.) First edition. Contact Editions. One of 100. Boxed. $200–$250. London, 1933. Cloth. First English edition. $75–$100.

BUTTS, Mary. *The Crystal Cabinet.* Cloth. London, (1937). First edition. $100–$150.

BUTTS, Mary. *Imaginary Letters*. Illustrated by Jean Cocteau. Cloth, paper label. Paris, 1928. First edition. One of 250. In glassine dust jacket. $150–$200.

BUTTS, Mary. *The Macedonian*. Boards. London, 1933. First edition. In dust jacket. $150.

BUTTS, Mary. *Scenes From the Life of Cleopatra*. Cloth. London, (1935). First edition. In dust jacket. $175–$200.

BUTTS, Mary. *Several Occasions*. Cloth. London, (1932). First edition. In dust jacket. $85–$125.

BUTTS, Mary. *Speed the Plow and Other Stories*. Yellow cloth. London, 1923. First edition. $85. Author's first book.

BYERS, William N., and Kellom, John H. *A Hand Book to the Gold Fields of Nebraska and Kansas*. Map. Blue pictorial printed wrappers. Chicago, 1859. First edition. $5,000–$6,000. Also, $3,700 (A, 1968).

BYNNER, Witter. See Morgan, Emanuel, and Knish, Anne.

BYNNER, Witter. *The New World*. Frontispiece. Decorated boards. San Francisco, 1919. One of 350. $50.

BYNNER, Witter. *An Ode to Harvard and Other Poems*. Cloth, or leather. Boston, 1907. First edition. Cloth. $50–$75. Author's first book.

BYNNER, Witter. *The Persistence of Poetry*. Full red buckram. San Francisco, 1929. Book Club of California. One of 325 signed. Boxed. $75–$100.

BYRD, Richard E. *Little America*. 74 maps and plates. Half vellum. New York, 1930. First edition. One of 1,000 signed. Boxed. $100–$125.

BYRD, Richard E. *Skyward*. 58 maps and plates. Boards. New York, 1928. First edition. One of 500 signed. In glassine dust jacket. Boxed. $100–$150.

BYRD, William (of Westover). *The Writings of "Colonel William Byrd of Westover in Virginia, Esqr."* Edited by John Spencer Bassett. Half vellum. New York, 1901. One of 500. $125–$150.

BYRNE, B. M. *Florida and Texas: A Series of Letters Comparing the Soil, Climate, and Productions of These States*. 40 pp., wrappers. Ocala, Fla., 1866. Third edition (of *Letters on the Climate, etc.;* see below). $250–$350.

BYRNE, B.M. *Letters on the Climate, Soils, and Productions of Florida*. 28 pp., wrappers. Jacksonville, 1851. Second edition. $300–$400. (Note: The first edition, for which I locate no reliable price data, was published in Ralston, Pa., according to Howes, who gives no date.)

BYRNE, Donn. *Brother Saul*. Brown batik boards, vellum spine. New York, (1927). First American edition. One of 500 signed. Boxed. $50–$60.

BYRNE, Donn. *Crusade*. Japan vellum and cloth. Boston, 1928. First American edition. One of 365 signed. Boxed. $50–$60.

BYRNE, Donn. *Destiny Bay*. Half vellum. Boston, 1928. First edition with "Published September, 1928" on copyright page. In dust jacket. $40–$60.

BYRNE, Donn. *Field of Honor*. Brown batik boards, vellum spine. New York, (1929). One of 500 large paper copies, signed by Dorothea Donn-Byrne (issued after the first trade edition). $50–$60.

BYRNE, Donn. *The Foolish Matrons*. Green cloth. New York, (1920). First edition, first issue with "I-U" on copyright page. In dust jacket. $75–$100.

BYRNE, Donn. *Hangman's House*. Illustrated. Half vellum. New York, (1926). First edition. One of 350 signed. Boxed. $50–$60.

BYRNE, Donn. *Messer Marco Polo*. Illustrated by C.B. Falls. Rust-colored cloth. New York, 1921. First edition, first printing, with conjugate of pages 145–146 used as terminal lining paper and with perfect type in the word "of" in the last line of page 10 and "forgettng" for "forgetting" in the third line of page 39. In dust jacket. $100–$125.

BYRNE, Donn. *Stories Without Women*. Frontispiece. Red ribbed cloth. New York, 1915. First edition. In dust jacket. $150–$200.

BYRNE, Donn. *The Strangers' Banquet*. Cloth. New York, (1919). First edition, with "M-T" on copyright page. In dust jacket. $50–$60.

BYRNE, William S. *Directory of Grass Valley Township for 1865*. 144pp., boards. San Francisco, 1865. $600–$750.

BYRON, George Gordon Noel, Lord. See Hobhouse, J.C.; Hornem, Horace. Also see *The Age of Bronze; Beppo; The Curse of Minerva; Don Juan; English Bards and Scotch Reviewers; Fugitive Pieces; Lara, a Tale; Monody on the Death of the Right Honorable R. B. Sheridan; Ode to Napoleon Buonaparte; Poems on Various Occasions; The Siege of Corinth.*

BYRON, George Gordon Noel, Lord. *The Bride of Abydos*. 72 pp., drab wrappers. London, 1813. First edition, first issue, with errata slip and with only 20 lines on page 47. $500 and up. Second issue, without errata slip and with 22 lines on page 47. $200 and up.

BYRON, George Gordon Noel, Lord. *Childe Harold's Pilgrimage: Canto the Third*. 79 pp., plain wrappers. London, 1816. First edition. (See entry for first two cantos, following.)

BYRON, George Gordon Noel, Lord. *Childe Harold's Pilgrimage: Canto the Fourth*. Drab boards, white label. London, 1818. First edition, first issue, with 6-line errata list on page 236 and with page 155 ending with "the impressions of," etc. (See following entry.)

BYRON, George Gordon Noel, Lord. *Childe Harold's Pilgrimage: A Romaunt*. (Containing Cantos I and II.) Drab boards, white spine label. London, 1812. First edition, first issue; with "Written beneath a Picture of J-V-D" on page 189 ("of J-V-D" omitted later). The most notable recent sale of the first two cantos was that of the Arthur A. Houghton copy, a repaired example but inscribed by Byron. It brought $4,400 at auction in New York in 1979. (Note: The three volumes of *Childe Harold's Pilgrimage* are almost always offered for sale as a set, although there are exceptions. They are listed separately here for bibliographical identification. Fine sets in boards and wrappers as issued are rare, and the last major offerings were in the 1940's. The retail value of a complete set in original bindings and in fine condition has not been tested in today's market, so far as I have determined. My own estimate: $10,000 and up. The listings of the three volumes, and their varying condition, in the auction records are too extensive to record here. Consult the annual volumes—not the 5-year indexes—of *American Book-Prices Current* for help with particular problems.)

BYRON, George Gordon Noel, Lord. *The Corsair: A Tale*. Plain drab wrappers. London, 1814. First edition, first issue, with 100 pages. $600–$800, possibly more. Second issue, 108 pages. $500 and up.

BYRON, George Gordon Noel, Lord. *The Deformed Transformed*. Drab wrappers. London, 1824. First edition. $300–$400.

BYRON, George Gordon Noel, Lord. *Fare Thee Well! A Poem*. (No regular title page.) 4 pp. No place, (1816). First edition. $6,000 at auction in London in 1972. (Only a few copies known. A copy bound with a first edition of *The Lament of Tasso* brought $5,060 at auction in 1979.)

BYRON, George Gordon Noel, Lord. *The Giaour: A Fragment of a Turkish Tale*. 41 pp., drab wrappers. London, 1813. First edition, on Whatman paper watermarked 1809–10. $500 and up.

BYRON, George Gordon Noel, Lord. *Hebrew Melodies*. Wrappers. London, 1815. First edition, first issue, with ad for *Jacqueline* on reverse of signature E4. $500 and up. Also, $225 (A, 1970). Second issue, without *Jacqueline* ad. $200 and up.

BYRON, George Gordon Noel, Lord. *Hours of Idleness*. Drab boards. Newark, England, 1807. First edition, first issue, with line 2 of page 22 reading "Those tissues of fancy, etc." Second issue, with line 2 of page 22 reading "Those tissues of falsehood, etc." Either issue $1,000 and up, possibly more. Also, a worn copy in half calf, $375 (A, 1974).

BYRON, George Gordon Noel, Lord. *The Island, or Christian and His Comrades*. Plain drab wrappers. London, 1823. First edition, with paper watermarked 1822. $1,000 and up. Also, $700 (A. 1974).

BYRON, George Gordon Noel, Lord. *The Lament of Tasso*. 19 pp., stitched, without wrappers. London, 1817. First edition. $500 and up.

BYRON, George Gordon Noel, Lord. *Letter to [John Murray] on the Rev. W.L. Bowles' Strictures on the Life of Pope*. 55 pp., drab wrappers. London, 1821. First edition, first issue, without 1819 watermark on 4 leaves before ads. $750 and up. Second issue, with the watermark. $300.

BYRON, George Gordon Noel, Lord. *Manfred, a Dramatic Poem*. 80 pp., drab wrappers, without lettering or labels. London, 1817. First edition, first issue, without quotation on title page and with printer's imprint in 2 lines on back of title page. $500 and up. Second issue, with printer's imprint in one line. $200–$300. Third issue, with Hamlet quotation on title page. $150–$200. London, 1929. Fanfrolico Press. Full vellum. One of 30 on vellum. $600–$800. Another issue: Half parchment. One of 550. $75–$125.

BYRON, George Gordon Noel, Lord. *Marino Faliero, Doge of Venice*. Drab boards. London, 1821. First edition, first issue, with speech on page 151 beginning "What crimes?" $500 and up. Second issue, with speech on page 151 beginning "His crimes!" $100–$300.

BYRON, George Gordon Noel, Lord. *Mazeppa: A Poem*. Plain drab wrappers. London, 1819. First edition, first issue, with imprint on page 70. $200–$350. Second issue, with imprint on back of page 71. $200–$300.

BYRON, George Gordon Noel, Lord. *The Parliamentary Speeches of Lord Byron*. Drab wrappers. London, 1824. First edition. $750 and up.

BYRON, George Gordon Noel, Lord, *Poems*. Boards, or wrappers (?). London, 1816. First edition, first issue, with leaf of "Notes" and 2 ad leaves. $400–$600.

BYRON, George Gordon Noel, Lord. *The Prisoner of Chillon, and Other Poems*. Drab wrappers, London, 1816. First edition, first issue, with recto of signature E8 blank. $300–$500. Rebound in modern wrappers, $100 and up.(London, 1865.) Day & Son. 20 plates. $300–$400.

BYRON George Gordon Noel, Lord. *Sardanapalus, The Two Foscari, Cain*. Boards, paper label on spine. London, 1821. First edition, $300–$500, or more. Worn, hinges cracked, $350; another, $225.

BYRON, George Gordon Noel, Lord. *Werner: A Tragedy*. Plain drab wrappers. London, 1823. First edition, first issue, with ad for this book on page 188. $600–$800. Second issue, without ad for this book. $300 and up.

C

C., C. *Poems for Harry Crosby.* Frontispiece. Boards. Paris, 1931. Black Sun Press. (By Caresse Crosby.) First edition. One of 22 on Van Gelder paper. $150–$200. Another issue: One of 500 on Lafuma paper. $50.

C.3.3. *The Ballad of Reading Gaol.* Cinnamon-colored cloth, vellum spine. London, (1898). (By Oscar Wilde.) First edition. One of 30 on Japanese vellum. $5,000 and up. Also inscribed, $4,800 (A, 1981). Another issue: Two toned cloth. One of 800. In dust jacket. $1,000–$1,500. Also, dust jacket chipped, $700 (A, 1977). Lacking jacket, $500 and up. (Worn copies for less.) London, 1898. Cloth, Second edition. $300–$400. London, 1898. Cloth. Third edition (bearing Wilde's name). One of 99 signed. $400–$500. London, 1924. Woodcuts by Hans Masereel. Half cloth. One of 450. $200–$300. New York, 1937. Limited Editions Club. $60–$100.

CABALLERIA Y COLLELL, Juan. *History of the City of Santa Barbara from Its Discovery to Our Own Days.* Translated by Edmund Burke. Plate, facsimile. 111 pp., wrappers. Santa Barbara, 1892. First edition. $150–$200.

CABELL, James Branch, *Ballades from the Hidden Way.* Boards. New York, 1928. First edition. One of 839 signed. In tissue dust jacket. $40–$60. Another issue: One of 8 on gray paper. $500–$1,000. (Only 5 copies known.)

CABELL, James Branch. *Beyond Life.* Dark brown cloth. New York, 1919. First edition, first binding. $75–$100.

CABELL, James Branch. *Branchiana.* Green cloth. Richmond, Va., (1907). First edition. $400–$500. (147 copies issued). According to Nelson Bond, a Cabell bibliographer, there were 10 copies in red, not green, cloth. His last sale: $1,500 for an inscribed copy.

CABELL, James Branch, *Chivalry.* Illustrated by Howard Pyle and others. Red cloth. New York, 1909. First edition. In printed glassine dust jacket. Boxed. $100–$125.

CABELL, James Branch. *The Cords of Vanity.* Cloth. New York, 1909. First edition, first state, with *The* omitted on spine and cover. $75–$100. New York, 1920. Cloth. In dust jacket. $25.

CABELL, James Branch. *The Eagle's Shadow.* Red cloth. New York, 1904. First edition, first state, with dedication "M.L.P.B." and frontispiece of seated figure, $150–$200. Author's first book.

CABELL, James Branch. *Gallantry.* Illustrated in color by Howard Pyle. Decorated cloth, gilt top. New York, 1907. First edition, first binding, silver-gray cloth, stamped with white, silver, and gold lettering. In printed glassine dust jacket. Boxed. $75–$100.

CABELL, James Branch. *Hamlet Had an Uncle.* Black leather. New York, (1940). First edition. One of 125. In slipcase. $200.

CABELL, (James) Branch, *Jurgen.* Reddish-brown cloth. New York, 1919. First edition, first state, with line rules on page 144 intact. In dust jacket. $300 and up. Lacking jacket, $150 and up. London, 1921. Illustrated by Frank C. Pape. Cloth. First English edition. In jacket, $100. London, 1949. Golden Cockerel Press. Half morocco. One of 500. $150. Another issue: Full leather. With an extra engraving. Boxed. $600.

CABELL, James Branch. *Ladies and Gentlemen.* Cloth. New York, 1934. First edition.

In dust jacket. $35–$45. Another issue: Silver cloth. One of 153 signed. In slipcase. $150.

CABELL, James Branch, *The Line of Love*. Illustrated in color by Howard Pyle. Decorated green cloth, pictorial label. New York, 1905. First edition, first state, binding stamped with white and gold lettering. In glassine dust jacket. $100–$150.

CABELL, James Branch. *The Majors and Their Marriages*. Wrappers or cloth. Richmond. (1915). First edition. Either issue: $500 and up.

CABELL, James Branch. *The Music from Behind the Moon*. 8 engravings. Boards. New York. 1926. First edition. In glassine dust jacket and slipcase. $50–$75.

CABELL, James Branch. *The Nightmare Has Triplets*. 16 pp., wrappers. (Garden City, 1937.) First edition, with Doubleday promotional letter laid in. $100–$150.

CABELL, (James) Branch. *The Rivet in Grandfather's Neck*. Cloth. New York, 1915. First edition. In dust jacket. $50.

CABELL, James Branch, *Smirt*. Cloth. New York, 1934. First edition. In dust jacket. $35. Another issue: One of 153 signed. In slipcase. $150.

CABELL, James Branch. *Smith*. Cloth. New York, 1935. First edition. In dust jacket. $35. Another issue: One of 153 signed. In slipcase. $150.

CABELL, (James) Branch, *Sonnets from Antan*. Half cloth. New York, 1929. Grabhorn printing. First edition. One of 718 signed. $75–$85.

CABELL, James Branch. *The Soul of Melicent*. Color illustrations by Howard Pyle. Dark blue cloth. New York, (1913). First edition, first binding. In dust jacket. $300. Without jacket, $100. Second binding, blue cloth. $65.

CABELL, James Branch. *Special Delivery*. Silver boards and vellum. New York, 1933. First edition. One of 207 large paper copies, signed. In slipcase. $100.

CABELL, James Branch. *Taboo*. Cloth. New York, 1921. First edition. One of 100 signed. In dust jacket, $250. Also, 820 copies unsigned. $20–$25.

CABELL, James Branch, *The Way of Ecben*. Boards. New York, 1929. First edition. One of 850 signed. In glassine dust jacket. Boxed. $50–$75.

CABEZA DE VACA, Álvar Núñez. *The Narrative of Alvar Núñez Cabeza de Vaca*. Translated by Buckingham Smith. 8 maps. Cloth. Washington, 1851. One of 110. $500-$850. New York 1871. Three-quarters morocco. One of 100. $250–$350. (For another issue, under another title, see following entry.)

CABEZA DE VACA, Álvar Núñez. *Relation . . . of What Befel the Armament in the Indias Whither Pamphilo de Narvaez Went for Governor, etc.* Hand decorations in color by Valenti Angelo. Boards. San Francisco, 1929. Grabhorn printing. One of 300. Boxed. $400–$500.

CABINET of Natural History and American Rural Sports (The). 3 vols., half calf. Philadelphia, 1830–32-33. First book edition. (Published by J. and T. Doughty; includes 29 monthly parts [dated 1830 to 1834]. 57 plates, 54 colored.) $15,000–$20,000.

CABLE, George W. *The Creoles of Louisiana*. Illustrated. Maroon pictorial cloth. New York, 1884. First edition. $75–$100.

CABLE, George W. *Gideon's Band: A Tale of the Mississippi*. Illustrated. Cloth. New York, 1914. First edition. In dust jacket. $100–$125.

CABLE, George W. *The Grandissimes*. Cloth. New York, 1880. First edition. $150–$200. New York, 1899. Illustrated. Vellum. One of 204. $50.

CABLE, George W. *Old Creole Days*. Decorated red, brown, or blue cloth. New York, 1879. First edition, first state, with no ads at back. $200–$250. Second state with ads.

$100 and up. Author's first book. New York, 1897. Vellum. One of 204. $50–$75. New York, 1943. Limited Editions Club. Boxed. $50–$60.

CABLE, George W. *The Southern Struggle for Pure Government.* Wrappers. Boston, 1890. First edition. $75–$100.

CABLE, George W. *Strange True Stories of Louisiana.* Illustrated. Pictorial cloth, paper label. New York, 1889. First edition. $35–$50. London, 1890. Cloth. First English edition. $50.

CAESAR, Julius. *Commentaries.* Translated by Somerset de Chair. Woodcuts by Clifford Webb. Buckram. London, 1951. Golden Cockerel Press. One of 250. $300. Another issue: One of 70 specially bound. $800–$1,000.

CAIN, James M. *The Postman Always Rings Twice.* Cloth. New York, 1934. First edition. In dust jacket. $500 and up.

CAIN, James M. *Our Government.* Cloth. New York, 1930. First edition. In dust jacket. $40–$50. Author's first book.

CAIN, James M. *Serenade.* Black cloth. New York, 1937. First edition. In dust jacket. $75–$125.

CAIN, James M. *Three of a Kind.* Cloth. New York, 1943. First edition. In dust jacket. $100–$225.

CAINE, Hall. *The Eternal City.* Cloth. London, 1901. First edition. $40–$50.

CALAVAR: or, The Knight of the Conquest. 2 vols., purple cloth, printed paper labels, Philadelphia, 1834. (By Robert Montgomery Bird.) First edition. $300–$400. Author's first book. Philadelphia, 1847. 2 vols., printed wrappers. Revised edition. $200–$250.

CALDWELL, Erskine. *American Earth.* Brown cloth. New York, 1931. First edition, with code letter "A" on copyright page. In dust jacket. $40–$60.

CALDWELL, Erskine. *The Bastard.* Illustrated. Cloth. New York, (1929). First edition. One of 200 signed. In glassine dust jacket. $200–$300. Unsigned, $50–$75. Author's first book.

CALDWELL, Erskine. *God's Little Acre.* Black cloth. New York, 1933. First edition. In dust jacket. $150–$200. In chipped jacket, $100. Without jacket, $35–$50.

CALDWELL, Erskine. *Journeyman,* Red buckram, paper band. (New York, 1935.) First edition. One of 1,475. In glassine dust jacket. Boxed. $40–$50.

CALDWELL, Erskine. *Kneel to the Rising Sun and Other Stories.* Reddish-brown buckram, labels, top edges gilt. New York, 1935. First edition. One of 300 signed. Boxed. $100–$125. Trade edition: Cloth. In dust jacket. $25–$30.

CALDWELL, Erskine. *Mama's Little Girl.* 2 drawings by Alfred Morang. Printed wrappers. Mount Vernon, Me., 1932. One of 75. $150–$250.

CALDWELL, Erskine. *A Message for Genevieve.* Drawing by Alfred Morang. Printed wrappers. Mount Vernon, 1933. First edition. One of 100. $125–$150.

CALDWELL, Erskine. *North of the Danube.* Photographs by Bourke-White. Linen. New York, (1939). First edition. $75–$100.

CALDWELL, Erskine, *Poor Fool.* Illustrated. Blue buckram. New York, 1930. First edition. One of 1,000. $125–$150.

CALDWELL, Erskine. *Southways.* Gray-blue cloth. New York, 1938. First edition. In dust jacket. $50–$75.

CALDWELL, Erskine. *Tenant Farmer.* Green wrappers. New York, (1935). First edition. $75–$85.

CALDWELL, Erskine. *Tobacco Road*. Cloth. New York, 1932. First edition, with code letter "A" on copyright page. In dust jacket. $200–$250.

CALDWELL. Erskine. *We Are the Living*. Cloth. New York, 1933. One of 250 signed. In glassine dust jacket. Boxed. $50–$75. Trade edition: In dust jacket. $30.

CALDWELL, Erskine, and Bourke-White, Margaret. *Say, Is This the U.S.A.* Illustrated. Pictorial boards. New York, (1941). First edition. In dust jacket. $75–$100.

CALDWELL, J. A. *History of Belmont and Jefferson Counties. Ohio,* Half leather. Wheeling, Ohio, 1880. $100–$200.

CALDWELL, J.F.J. *History of a Brigade of South Carolinians*. Cloth. Philadelphia, 1866. First edition. $200–$250.

CALDWELL, Taylor. *Dynasty of Death*. Cloth. New York, 1938. First edition. In dust jacket. $40-$65. Author's first book.

CALHOUN, James S. *Official Correspondence of James S. Calhoun While Indian Agent at Santa Fe*. Illustrated, 4 maps. Cloth. Washington, 1915. First edition. $100–$125.

CALIFORNIA Illustrated. By a Returned Californian. 48 plates. Cloth, New York. 1852. (By J.M. Letts.) First edition, first issue, anonymous. $300–$450. Later issue, same year, author named, $200–$350.

CALIFORNIA Sketches, with Recollections of the Gold Mines. Half leather. Albany, 1850. (By Leonard Kip.) First edition. $750–$1,000.

CALISHER, Hortense. *In the Absence of Angels*. Cloth. Boston, 1951. First edition. In dust jacket. $100–$125. Author's first book.

CALL, Richard Ellsworth. *The Life and Writings of Rafinesque*. 2 plates, 3 facsimiles. 227 pp., wrappers. Louisville, 1895. First edition. $100–$150.

CALLAGHAN, Morley. *A Native Argosy*. Cloth. New York, 1929. First edition. In dust jacket. $125–$150.

CALLAGHAN, Morley. *No Man's Meat*. Boards and cloth, paper label. Paris, 1931. First edition. One of 525 signed. In tissue dust jacket. Boxed. $300–$325.

CALLAGHAN, Morley. *Strange Fugitive*. Cloth. New York, 1928. First Edition. In dust jacket. $200–$275. Author's first book.

CALVERT, Frederick. *The Isle of Wight Illustrated*. Sepia lithograph frontispiece, colored map. 20 colored acquatint plates. Cloth. London, 1846. $600–$900.

CALVERT, George C. *A Defence of the Dilettante*. San Francisco, 1919. Grabhorn printing. One of 200. $600–$750.

CALVIN, Ross. *Sky Determines*. Cloth. New York, 1934. First edition. In dust jacket. $50–$60.

CAMERON, Julia M. *Victorian Photographs of Famous Men and Fair Women*. Boards and vellum. London, 1926. First edition. One of 450. $300–$450. New York, 1926. Boards and cloth. First American edition. One of 250. $300–$400. (Contains an introduction by Virginia Woolf.)

CAMPBELL, Alexander, and Owen, Robert. *Debate on the Evidence of Christianity*. 2 vols. in one, calf. Bethany, Va., 1829. First edition. $150–$175.

CAMPBELL, Alexander, and Rice, N.L. *A Debate . . . on the Action, Subject, Design and Administration of Christian Baptism*. Boards. Lexington, Ky., 1844. First edition. $125–$150.

CAMPBELL, Archibald. *A Voyage Round the World*. Folding frontispiece map. Boards. Edinburgh, 1816. First edition. $1,000–$1,250.

CAMPBELL, J.L. *Idaho and Montana Gold Regions.* Map. Half morocco. Chicago, 1865. Second edition. $1,500–$2,000.

CAMPBELL, J.L. *The Great Agricultural & Mineral West.* Folding ad leaf and map. Printed wrappers. Chicago, 1866. "Third Annual Edition." $1,500–$2,000.

CAMPBELL, John W., Jr. *Invaders from the Infinite.* Boards. Hicksville, N. Y., (1961). First trade edition, first binding (later cloth). $75. Reading, Pa., (1961). Boards. First edition, limited. One of 112 with signed plate. $175.

CAMPBELL, John W., Jr. *The Mightiest Machine.* Cloth. Providence, (1947). First edition. $75.

CAMPBELL, Patrick. *Travels in the Interior Inhabited Parts of North America.* 3 plates. Cloth. Toronto, 1937. First American edition. One of 550. $125–$150.

CAMPBELL, Roy. *Adamastor: Poems.* Cloth. London, (1930). First edition. One of 90 signed. $125–$150. Trade edition: Cloth. In first issue dust jacket with author's name twice on spine. $75. Second issue jacket, corrected: $35. Cape Town, 1950. Half calf. Illustrated edition. $100–$110.

CAMPBELL, Roy. *Broken Record.* Cloth. London, 1934. First edition. In dust jacket. $50–$60. Another issue: Vellum. One of 50 signed. $200–$300. Another issue: One of 8 signed. $400–$500.

CAMPBELL, Roy. *Choosing a Mast.* Illustrated by Barnett Freedman. Boards. London, 1931. First edition. One of 300 signed. $125–$175.

CAMPBELL, Roy. *The Flaming Terrapin.* Boards, cloth spine, paper label. London, 1924. First edition. $150–$175. Author's first book.

CAMPBELL, Roy. *Flowering Reeds: Poems.* Cloth. London, 1933. First edition. One of 69 signed. $150–$200. Another issue: Cloth. One of 8 signed. $400–$500. Trade edition: Cloth. In dust jacket. $75.

CAMPBELL, Roy. *The Georgiad.* Boards and cloth. London, 1931. One of 150 signed. $150. Another issue: Vellum. One of 20 on goatskin parchment paper, signed. $350–$400. (Some copies include bullfight drawings by the poet on end papers.)

CAMPBELL, Roy. *The Gum Trees.* Illustrated by David Jones. Boards. London, 1930. First edition. One of 400 signed. $100-$150.

CAMPBELL, Roy. *Mithraic Emblems.* Cloth. London, 1936. First edition. One of 30 signed. $300–$400. Another issue: One of 8 signed. $400–$500.

CAMPBELL, Roy. *Poems.* Decorated boards and morocco. Paris. 1930. Hours Press. First edition. One of 200 signed. $250–$350.

CAMPBELL, Roy. *Pomegranates.* Illustrated by James Boswell. Cloth. London, 1932. First edition. One of 99 signed. In glassine dust jacket. $150–$200.

CAMPBELL, Roy. *The Wayzgoose: A South African Satire.* Brown cloth. London, 1928. First edition. $75–$100.

CAMUS, Albert. *The Fall.* Folio, boards. (Kentfield, Calif., 1966.) Allen Press. One of 140. $350–$450.

CAMUS, Albert. *September 15th, 1937.* Wrappers. Bronxville, 1963. First edition. One of 50 for presentation, privately printed by Valenti Angelo. $200.

CANFIELD, Chauncey L. (editor). *The Diary of a Forty-Niner.* Colored map. Pictorial boards. San Francisco, 1906. First edition. $75.

CANNON, George Q. *Writings from the "Western Standard." Published in San Francisco.* Full morocco. Liverpool, 1864. First edition. $100–$150.

CANNON, J.P. *Inside of Rebeldom: The Daily Life of a Private in the Confederate Army.* Cloth. Washington, 1900. $125.

CANOVA, Andrew P. *Life and Adventures in South Florida.* 4 plates. Printed light-green wrappers, Palatka, Fla., 1885. First edition. $200–$250.

CAPA, Robert. *Slightly Out of Focus.* Illustrated. Cloth. New York, 1947. First edition. In dust jacket. $50–$75.

ČAPEK, Karel. *Krakatit.* Cloth. New York, 1925. First edition. In dust jacket. $100–$125.

ČAPEK, Karel. *Tales from Two Pockets.* Cloth. London, (1932). First edition in English. In dust jacket. $50–$75.

CAPOTE, Truman. *Breakfast at Tiffany's.* Yellow cloth. New York, (1958). First edition. In dust jacket. $75–$100.

CAPOTE, Truman. *A Christmas Memory.* Cloth. New York, (1966). First edition. One of 600 signed. Boxed. $125–$175.

CAPOTE, Truman. *In Cold Blood.* Black cloth. New York, (1965). First edition, first printing. One of 500 signed. In glassine dust jacket. Boxed. $100–$125. Trade edition: Cloth. In dust jacket. $25–$35. Advance copy, in wrappers: $100–$150.

CAPOTE, Truman. *The Grass Harp.* Rough linen. (New York, 1951.) First edition, first binding. In dust jacket. $75–$100. Second binding, smooth cloth. In dust jacket. $40–$60.

CAPOTE, Truman. *The Grass Harp: A Play.* Boards. New York, (1952). First edition. In dust jacket. $100–$150.

CAPOTE, Truman. *Local Color.* Illustrated. Boards and cloth. New York, (1950). First edition. In dust jacket. $100–$150. London, (1950). Red leather. First English edition. One of 200. $100–$150.

CAPOTE, Truman. *Observations.* Photographs by Richard Avedon. Folio, boards. New York, (1959). First edition. Boxed. $175–$200.

CAPOTE, Truman. *Other Voices, Other Rooms.* Cloth. New York, (1948). First edition. In dust jacket. $100–$150. Author's first book.

CAPOTE, Truman. *The Thanksgiving Visitor.* Cloth. New York, (1968). First edition. One of 300 signed. Boxed. $175–$200.

CAPOTE, Truman. *A Tree of Night and Other Stories.* Cloth. New York, (1949). First edition. In dust jacket. $100–$125.

CAPRON, Elisha S. *History of California.* Colored map. Cloth. Boston, 1854. First edition. $75–$100.

CAPT. SMITH and Princess Pocahontas: An Indian Tale. Boards. Philadelphia, 1805. (By John Davis.) First edition, first issue, with undated copyright notice. $2,000.

CARELESS, John. *The Old English 'Squire: A Poem in Ten Cantos.* 24 colored plates. Cloth. London, 1821. (By William A. Chatto.) First edition. $300–$450. Another issue: Large paper. $400–$600.

CAREY, C.H. *History of Oregon.* Maps. Cloth. Chicago, 1922. Author's edition. $50–$75.

CAREY, David. *Life in Paris.* Illustrated by George Cruikshank. Full leather. London, 1822. First edition. $1,000–$1,200. Another issue: Large paper. $1,300 (A, 1980).

CARL Werner, An Imaginative Story. 2 vols., cloth. New York, 1838. (By William Gilmore Simms.) First edition. $300–$400.

CARLETON, William M. *Fax: A Campaign Poem.* Illustrated. Printed wrappers. Chicago, 1868. First edition. $500. Author's first book.

CARLSON, Anton J. *The Control of Hunger in Health and Disease.* Cloth. Chicago, (1916). First edition. $100–$150.

CARLTON, Robert. *The New Purchase: or, Seven and a Half Years in the Far West.* 2 vols., boards. New York, 1843. (By Baynard R. Hall.) First edition. $150–$200.

CARLYLE, Thomas. See *Sartor Resartus.*

CARLYLE, Thomas. *The French Revolution.* 3 vols., boards and cloth. London, 1837. First edition, first issue, with 2 pages of ads at end of Vol. 2. $750–$1,000. London, 1839. 3 vols., cloth. Second edition. $200. London, 1910. Illustrated. 2 vols., half vellum. One of 150 on large paper. $200. New York, 1956. Limited Editions Club. Boxed. $50–$75.

CARLYLE, Thomas. *Occasional Discourse on the Nigger Question.* Wrappers. London, 1853. First edition. $300–$400.

CARLYLE, Thomas, *On Heroes, Hero-Worship, & the Heroic in History: Six Lectures.* Purple cloth. London, 1841. First edition. $350–$450.

CARLYLE, Thomas. *Past and Present.* Cloth. London, 1843. First edition. $200–$300.

CARLYLE, Thomas. *Shooting Niagara: and After?* Printed green wrappers. London, 1867. First edition. $150–$200.

CARMAN, Bliss. See Carmen [sic], Bliss; Lighthall, William D.

CARMAN, Bliss. *The Gate of Peace: A Poem.* Boards and cloth. New York, 1907. One of 112 signed. $200. (Note: All except 24 destroyed by fire, says Johnson.)

CARMAN, Bliss. *Poems.* 2 vols., half leather. New York, 1904. First edition. One of 500 signed. $150–$175. Boston, 1905. 2 vols., boards. One of 500 signed. $150–$175.

CARMAN, Bliss. *The Princess of the Tower.* Boards. New York, 1906. First edition. One of 62 signed. $225–$350.

CARMAN, Bliss. *The Vengeance of Noel Brassard.* Boards and cloth. Cambridge, 1919 (actually 1899). First edition, with misdated title page reading "MDCCCCXIX." $150.

CARMAN, Bliss, and Hovey, Richard. *Songs from Vagabondia.* Boards. Boston, 1894. First edition. Limited Edition. $75–$100.

CARMEN, Bliss. *Low Tide on Grand Pre.* 13 pp., wrappers. Toronto, (1889? 1890?). (By Bliss Carman.) First edition (pirated). $200–$250. Author's first book, with his name misspelled. New York, 1893. Lavender cloth. First United States edition. $50–$100.

CARNEVALI, Emanuel. *A Hurried Man.* Wrappers. Paris, (1925). Contact Editions. First edition. $175–$225.

CAROLINE Tracy: *The Spring Street Milliner's Apprentice.* Illustrated. Half leather. New York, 1849. First edition. $50–$75.

CARR, Mrs. Comyns (Alice). *North Italian Folk: Sketches of Town and Country Life.* Hand-colored illustrations by Randolph Caldecott. Boards. London, 1878. First edition. One of 400. $200. (New York), 1878. First American edition. (250 copies). $200.

CARR, John. *Early Times in Middle Tennessee.* Cloth. Nashville, 1857. First edition. $150–$200.

CARR, John. *Pioneer Days in California.* Portrait. Cloth. Eureka, Calif., 1891. First edition. $100–$125.

CARR, John Dickson. *Death Turns the Tables.* Cloth. New York, 1941. First edition. In dust jacket. $50–$75.

CARR, Spencer. *A Brief Sketch of La Crosse, Wisconsin.* 28 pp., sewed. La Crosse, 1854. First edition. $250–$300.

CARRINGTON, Mrs. Henry B. See *Ab-Sa-Ra-Ka, Home of the Crows.*

CARRINGTON, John Bodman, and Hughes, George Ravensworth. *The Plate of the Worshipful Company of Goldsmiths.* Illustrated. Red cloth. Oxford, 1926. $125–$175.

CARROLL, H. Bailey. *The Texan Santa Fe Trail.* Illustrated. Cloth. Canyon, Tex., 1951. Boxed. $75–$100.

CARROLL, H. Bailey, and Haggard, J.V. (translators). *Three New Mexico Chronicles.* Cloth. Albuquerque, 1942. $50–$75.

CARROLL, Lewis. See Dodgson, Charles L.; Spavery.

CARROLL, Lewis. *Alice's Adventures in Wonderland.* 42 illustrations by John Tenniel. Red cloth. London, 1865. (By Charles L. Dodgson.) First edition (suppressed by the author). $10,000 and up? Very rare in original binding. Modern sales records range from $2,464 for a copy "badly worn, leaves stained, etc.," (A, 1961) and $2,375 (A, 1971), for a worn and repaired copy, to $11,760 (A, 1965) and $16,000 (A, 1962) for presentation copies inscribed by the author. The rebound Jerome Kern copy brought $10,000 in 1929. (Because of the extreme rarity of the original edition, the collecting fraternity in general has come to accept the New York edition of 1866—the first American edition—as the "first edition," which it, in fact, is, since it consists of the sheets of the suppressed London first edition with a new title page displaying the New York imprint of its publisher, Appleton.) New York, 1866. Red cloth. First American edition (and *second issue* of the first edition). $2,500 and up. Also, worn and shaken $700 (A, 1980). A rebound copy in full red leather was catalogued in 1980 by the Victoria Book Shop in New York at $2,200. London, 1866. Red cloth. Second edition (and first published English edition). $1,500–$2,000 and up. Also, worn copies, $600 (A, 1981); $748 (A, 1979). Boston, 1869. Green cloth. First edition printed in America. $300–$400. London, 1907. Illustrated by Arthur Rackham. Cloth. One of 1,130 signed by Rackham. $750–$850. Also, with an original Rackham watercolor, $1,300 (A, 1974), New York, (1907). Half cloth. One of 550. $300–$400. London, 1914. Tenniel illustrations. Vellum. One of 12 copies on vellum. $1,250–$1,500. Ordinary issue: One of 1,000. $100–$150. New York, (1929). Illustrated by Willy Pogany. Pictorial cloth. $150–$200. Paris, 1930. Black Sun Press, Illustrated by Marie Laurencin. Wrappers. In folder, tissue jacket, and slipcase. $1,000–$1,200. New York, 1932. Limited Editions Club. Signed by Alice Hargreaves, the original "Alice." $600–$850. Ordinary issue: $450. New York, 1969. Salvador Dali illustrations. Folio, loose signatures in folder and leather-backed case. Limited edition, signed by Dali. $1,250–$1,500.

CARROLL, Lewis. *Alice's Adventures Under Ground.* 37 illustrations by the author. Red cloth, gilt edges. London, 1886. (By Charles L. Dodgson.) First edition. $150–$200. (Note: This is a facsimile of the original manuscript from which *Alice's Adventures in Wonderland* was developed.)

CARROLL, Lewis. *Feeding the Mind.* Gray boards and cloth. London, 1907. (By Charles L. Dodgson.) First edition. $75–$125.

CARROLL, Lewis. *The Game of Logic.* With envelope containing 9 counters and board diagram. Cloth. London, 1886. (By Charles L. Dodgson.) First (private) edition. $750–$1,000. Only a few copies known. London, 1887. Second edition. $200–$300. (Listed incorrectly in many auction records as the first edition.)

CARROLL, Lewis. *The Hunting of the Snark.* Illustrated by Henry Holiday. Pictorial cloth, gilt edges. London, 1876. (By Charles L. Dodgson.) First edition. In dust jacket. $250–$350. Lacking jacket. $100–$150. Presentation copy: Red and gold cloth. With leaflet "An Easter Greeting to Every Child who Loves 'Alice.'" $572 (A, 1979). New York, 1903. Illustrated by Peter Newell. Cloth. In dust jacket. $75–$125.

CARROLL, Lewis. *Jabberwocky and Other Poems*. Illustrated. Boards. Los Angeles, 1933. (By Charles L. Dodgson.) First edition. One of 50. $100.

CARROLL, Lewis. *Phantasmagoria and Other Poems*. Blue cloth. London, 1869. (By Charles L. Dodgson.) First edition, $200–$300.

CARROLL, Lewis. *Rhyme? and Reason?* Illustrated by A.B. Frost and Henry Holiday. Green cloth. London. 1883. (By Charles L. Dodgson.) First edition. $150–$200.

CARROLL, Lewis. *Sylvie and Bruno*. Illustrated by Harry Furniss. Cloth. London, 1889. (By Charles L. Dodgson.) First edition. In dust jacket. $125–$150. Lacking jacket, $65–$85.

CARROLL, Lewis. *Sylvie and Bruno Concluded*. Illustrated by Harry Furniss. Cloth. London, 1893. (By Charles L. Dodgson.) First edition, first issue, with error in table of contents. $100–$125.

CARROLL, Lewis. *A Tangled Tale*. Illustrated by A.B. Frost. Pictorial cloth. London, 1885. (By Charles L. Dodgson.) First edition. $150–$175.

CARROLL, Lewis. *Three Sunsets and Other Poems*. Frontispiece and other illustrations. Cloth. London, 1898. First edition. $150–$200.

CARROLL, Lewis. *Through the Looking Glass, and What Alice Found There*. 50 illustrations by John Tenniel. Red cloth. London, 1872. (By Charles L. Dodgson.) First edition, first issue, with "wade" on page 21. $750–$1,000. Also, $550 (A, 1981). Boston, 1872. First American edition. $60–$80. New York, 1931. Cheshire House. Cloth. $50. New York, 1935. Limited Editions Club. Signed by Alice Hargreaves. Boxed. $300–$400. Mount Vernon, N.Y., 1935. Illustrated. Leather. $50–$75.

CARROLL, Lewis. *The Walrus and the Carpenter*. Boards. Los Angeles, 1932. (By Charles L. Dodgson.) First edition. One of 60. $100.

CARRUTH, (Fred) Hayden. *The Voyage of the Rattletrap*. Illustrated by H.M. Wilder. Pictorial cloth. New York, 1897. First edition. $35–$50.

CARRUTH, Hayden. *Journey to a Known Place*. Cloth. Norfolk, 1961. First edition. In tissue dust jacket. $75–$100.

CARRYL, Charles E. *Davy and the Goblin*. Illustrated. Pictorial brown cloth. Boston, 1886. First edition, first issue, with "Korea" misspelled in terminal ad. $150–$200. Second issue, error corrected. $100.

CARSON, Christopher. See Grant, Blanche C.

CARSON, James H. *Early Recollections of the Mines, and a Description of the Great Tulare Valley*. Folding map. 64 pp. printed wrappers (with cover title reading "Second Edition. Life in California, etc."). Stockton, Calif., 1852. First edition (in book form; earlier appearance was in the San Joaquin *Republican*). $2,000 and up. Also, spine repaired, $1,500 (A, 1968); lacking maps, $475 (A, 1973 and 1954). Oakland, 1950. 2 maps. One of 750. Reprint edition. $50 (See next entry.)

CARSON, James H. *Life in California*. Map. Cloth. Tarrytown, N.Y., 1931. (Reprint of *Early Recollections of the Mines*.) $50.

CARSTARPHEN, J.E. *My Trip to California in '49*. 8 pp., wrappers. (Louisiana, Mo., 1914.) Limited edition. $75–$150.

CARTER, Frederick. *D.H. Lawrence and the Body Mystical*. Frontispiece. Half vellum. London, 1932. First edition. One of 250 on vellum. In glassine dust jacket. $150.

CARTER, John, and Muir, Percy H. *Printing and The Mind of Man*. Cloth. (London), 1967. First edition. In dust jacket. $275–$350.

CARTER, John, and Pollard, Graham. *An Enquiry into the Nature of Certain 19th Century Pamphlets*. 4 plates. Cloth. London, 1934. First edition. In dust jacket. $150–$200.

CARTER, Robert G. *Four Brothers in Blue.* Frontispiece. Cloth. Washington, 1913. First edition. $650. Washington, 1913. Second edition (so-called "Imperfect Edition" made up of magazine installments bound with first edition text). $1,250.

CARTER, Robert G. *Massacre of Salt Creek Prairie and the Cow-boy's Verdict.* 48 pp., wrappers. Washington, 1919. First edition. $300.

CARTER, Robert G. *The Old Sergeant's Story: Winning the West from the Indians and Badmen in 1870 to 1876.* Portrait, plates. Cloth. New York, 1926. First edition. $150–$200.

CARTER, Robert G. *On the Border with Mackenzie.* 3 portraits. Cloth. Washington, (1935). First edition. $400–$500.

CARTER, Robert G. *On the Trail of Deserters.* Printed wrappers. Washington, 1920. One of 250. $150–$200.

CARTER, Robert G. *Pursuit of Kicking Bird: A Campaign in the Texas "Bad Lands."* 44 pp., wrappers. Washington, 1920. First edition. (100 copies printed.) $250–$325.

CARTER, Susannah. *The Frugal Housewife: or, Complete Woman Cook.* Illustrated. Boards. Philadelphia, 1802. $150–$200.

CARTER, W.A. *History of Fannin County, Texas.* Cloth. Bonham, Tex., 1885. First edition. $850–$1,000.

CARTIER-BRESSON, Henri. *The Decisive Moment.* Illustrated. Boards. New York, (1955). First edition. In dust jacket. With pamphlet of captions laid in. $400–$500.

CARTIER-BRESSON, Henri. *The Europeans.* Boards. New York, (1955). First edition. $350–$450.

CARTIER-BRESSON, Henri. *The People of Moscow.* Cloth. New York, 1955. First edition. In dust jacket. $150–$225.

CARUTHERS, W.A. See *The Kentuckian in New-York.*

CARY, Joyce. *An American Visitor.* Cloth. London, 1933. First edition. In dust jacket. $125–$150.

CARY, Joyce. *The Horse's Mouth.* Cloth. London, (1944). First edition. In dust jacket. $50–$100. New York, (1944, actually 1950). Cloth. First American edition. In dust jacket. $35. (London), 1957. Marbled boards, vellum spine, leather label. One of 1,500 containing a discarded chapter from the novel. $100–$150.

CASEMENT, Roger. *Some Poems of Roger Casement.* Portrait. Gray printed wrappers. Dublin, 1918. First edition. $150.

CASENDER, Don Pedro. *The Lost Virgin of the South.* Cloth. Tallahassee, 1831. (By Michael Smith.) First edition. $750–$1,000. Courtland, Ala., 1833. Cloth. Second edition. $400–$600.

CASKODEN, Edwin. *When Knighthood Was in Flower.* Pictorial cloth. Indianapolis, 1898. (By Charles Major.) First edition, first issue, with 1897 copyright and no notice of reprints on copyright page. $60–$75.

CASLER, John. *Four Years in the Stonewall Brigade.* Folding facsimile. Cloth. Guthrie, Okla., 1893. First edition. $100–$125.

CASS, Lewis. *Substance of a Speech Delivered by Hon. Lewis Cass, of Michigan . . . on the Ratification of the Oregon Treaty.* 16 pp., sewed. Detroit, 1846. $75-$100.

CASTANEDA, Carlos. *The Teachings of Don Juan/A Yaqui Way of Knowledge.* Cloth. Berkeley, 1968. First edition. In dust jacket. $50–$75. Author's first book.

CASTENADA, Carlos E. *Our Catholic Heritage in Texas, 1519–1810.* 5 vols., cloth. Austin, 1936–42. First edition. $750–$1,000.

CASTLE Dismal; or, the Bachelor's Christmas. Boards. New York, 1844. (By William Gilmore Simms.) First edition. $200–$300.

CASTLE Rackrent; An Hibernian Tale. Boards. London, 1800. (By Maria Edgeworth.) First edition. $500–$600.

CASTLEMAN, Alfred L. *Army of the Potomac: Behind the Scenes.* Cloth. Milwaukee, 1863. First edition. $75–$100.

CASTLEMAN, John B. *Active Service.* Plates. Cloth. Louisville, 1917. $75.

CASTLEMON, H.C. (Harry). *Frank on the Lower Mississippi.* Illustrated. Cloth. Cincinnati, 1867. (By Charles Austin Fosdick.) First edition. $50–$60.

CASTLEMON, Harry. *Guy Harris, the Runaway.* Printed wrappers, New York, 1887. (By Charles Austin Fosdick.) First edition, first issue. $75.

CASTLEMON, Harry. *The Sportsman's Club Among the Trappers.* Plates. Cloth. Philadelphia, 1874. (By Charles Austin Fosdick.) First edition. $50–$60.

CAT Morgan's Apology. Broadside. New Haven, 1953. (By T.S. Eliot.) First edition. One of 30 printed by Eliot's bibliographer, Donald Gallup. $750 and up. Also, $550 (A, 1978).

CATES, Cliff D. *Pioneer History of Wise County, Texas.* Illustrated. Stiff wrappers. Decatur, Tex., 1907. First edition. $200–$300.

CATHER, Willa. See McClure, S.S.; Milmine, Georgine. Also see *The Sombrero.*

CATHER, Willa. *Alexander's Bridge.* Blue, purple, and other colors of cloth. Boston, 1912. First edition, first issue, with "Willa S. Cather" on spine (later "Willa Cather") and with title and author's name in box on front cover and half title before title page. $300–$400. Another issue (?): "Willa S. Cather" on spine but title only in box on cover. $200–$225. Later issue, with half title after title page: $150. London, 1912. Brown cloth. First English edition (erroneously titled *Alexander's Bridges*). In dust jacket. $125–$175.

CATHER, Willa. *April Twilights.* Brown boards, paper labels. Boston, 1903. First edition. Issued without dust jacket. $800–$1,000. London, 1924. Cloth. First English edition. $100. Author's first book. New York, 1923. Boards and parchment. First revised edition. One of 450 signed. Boxed. $200–$250.

CATHER, Willa. *Death Comes for the Archbishop.* Green cloth. New York, 1927. First edition. In dust jacket. $50–$60. Another issue: Boards and cloth. One of 175 signed. Boxed. $300–$350. One of 50 on vellum, signed. Boxed. $800–$1,000. London, 1927. Black cloth. First English edition. In dust jacket. $50–$75. New York, 1929. Illustrated by Harold von Schmidt. Vellum. One of 170 signed. Boxed. $450–$600.

CATHER, Willa. *A Lost Lady.* Cloth. New York, 1923. First edition, first issue, in green cloth (later tan). In dust jacket. $50–$60. Another issue: Boards and cloth. One of 20 lettered A to T, signed. In glassine dust jacket. Boxed $400–$500. One of 200 numbered copies (same issue). $250–$300. Advance issue: Printed wrappers. $400.

CATHER, Willa. *Lucy Gayheart.* Cloth. New York, 1935. First edition, first printing (so stated). In dust jacket. $35. Another issue: Buckram. One of 749 signed. In dust jacket. Boxed. $150–$200.

CATHER, Willa. *My Antonia.* Illustrated by W.T. Benda. Brown cloth. Boston, 1918. First edition, first issue, with illustrations on glazed paper inserted. In dust jacket. $400–$600. Lacking jacket, $200–$250. London, 1919. Cloth. First English edition. In dust jacket. $200. Lacking jacket, $50.

CATHER, Willa. *My Mortal Enemy.* Boards and cloth. New York, 1926. First edition. In dust jacket. Boxed. $35. Another issue: Boards and cloth. One of 220 signed. Boxed. $250–$300.

CATHER, Willa. *Not Under Forty*. Cloth. New York, 1936. First edition, first printing (so stated). In dust jacket. $25–$30. Another issue: One of 333 large paper copies on vellum, signed. Boxed. $200–$300.

CATHER, Willa. *The Novels and Stories of Willa Cather*. 13 vols., two-toned cloth. Boston. 1937–41. Autograph edition. One of 970 signed. In dust jackets. $750–$850.

CATHER, Willa. *O Pioneers!* Colored frontispiece by Clarence Underwood. Cloth. Boston. 1913. First edition, first issue, either tan or cream ribbed cloth (later, brown) and with last page of text on tipped-in leaf. In dust jacket. $250–$300. Lacking jacket, $100–$150. Second issue (brown cloth). In dust jacket. $150–$200.

CATHER, Willa. *Obscure Destinies*. Green cloth. New York, 1932. First edition. In dust jacket. $30–$40. Another issue: Vellum and boards. One of 260 on vellum, signed. $200–$300.

CATHER, Willa. *One of Ours*. Cloth. New York, 1932. First edition. In dust jacket. $50–$75. Another issue: Boards. One of 35 on vellum, signed. Boxed. $400–$500. Another issue: One of 310 on handmade paper, signed. Boxed. $250–$400. Second printing (of trade edition): Boards ("For bookseller friends"). $35–$50.

CATHER, Willa. *The Professor's House*. Orange and blue cloth. New York, 1925. First edition. In dust jacket. $75. Another issue: Buckram and boards. One of 40 on vellum (of an issue of 225), signed. $575. One of 185 (of this issue), signed. $250–$350.

CATHER, Willa. *Sapphira and the Slave Girl*. Cloth. New York, 1940. First edition (so stated). In dust jacket. $25. (Note: Trade binding of this is often faded under the dust jacket. The faded copies are worth less—$7.50–$10.00.) Another issue: Half buckram. One of 520 signed. In dust jacket. $200–$250.

CATHER, Willa. *Shadows on the Rock*. Green cloth. New York, 1931. First edition, advance issue, mislabeled "Second edition" on copyright page. In dust jacket. $50–$100. Regular trade edition ("First edition" on copyright page): In dust jacket. $30–$40. Another issue: Marbled boards. Leather label. One of 619 signed. In dust jacket. Boxed. $200–$250. Another issue: Full orange vellum. One of 199 on vellum, signed. In dust jacket. Boxed. $350–$400.

CATHER, Willa. *The Song of the Lark*. Blue cloth. Boston, 1915. First edition, first issue, with boxed ads on copyright page. In dust jacket. $200–$300. Lacking jacket, $75 and up.

CATHER, Willa. *The Troll Garden*. Crimson cloth. New York, 1905. First edition, first issue, with "McClure Phillips & Co." at foot of spine. $300–$350. (If with dust jacket, much more.)

CATHER, Willa. *Youth and the Bright Medusa*. Cloth. New York, 1920. First edition. In dust jacket. $35–$50.. Another issue: One of 25 signed. $500–$600.

CATHER, Willa, and Canfield, Dorothy. *The Fear That Walks by Noonday*. Boards, paper label. New York, 1931. First edition. One of 30. $750–$1,000. Also, $650 (A, 1977). (Note: This first appeared in *The Sombrero*, which see under title entry.)

CATHERWOOD, Frederick. *Views of Ancient Monuments in Central America, Chiapas, and Yucatan*. Colored title page, engraved map, 25 lithographs. Folio, half morocco. London, 1844. First edition. $10,000 and up. Also, $18,700 and $8,960 (A, 1978). New York, 1844. First American edition. Equally valuable. Barre, Mass., 1965. One of 500 facsimile copies. $300–$400.

CATHERWOOD, Mrs. Mary Hartwell. *Spanish Peggy*. Red cloth. Chicago, 1899. First edition. $35–$50.

CATHOLIC Anthology. 1914–1915 (The). Edited by Ezra Pound. Gray boards. London,

1915. First edition, $400–$500. Also, $300 (A, 1977). (Note: Includes T.S. Eliot's "The Love Song of J. Alfred Prufrock" and four other poems.)

CATLIN, George. *Letters and Notes on the Manners, Customs, and Conditions of the North American Indians.* 2 maps (one folding), one chart, 309 illustrations. 2 vols., cloth, paper labels. London, 1841. First edition, first issue, with "Frederick" for "Zacharias" on page 104, $1,000–$1,250. Also, $340 (A, 1978); $505 (A, 1977). Second issue. $600–$750. London, 1841. 2 vols., cloth. Second edition. $750–$1,000. New York. 1841. 2 vols., cloth. First American edition. $600–$800. (Note: Many other later editions, some with plates colored by hand, titles altered, etc. See American and British auction records.)

CATLIN, George. *O-Kee-Pa, a Religious Ceremony.* 13 colored lithographs. Cloth. London, 1867. First edition, $1,500–$2,000. Also, $900 (A, 1972). Philadelphia, 1867. Cloth. $750–$1,000. Also, $650 (A, 1979).

CATLIN, George, *North American Indian Portfolio.* 25 colored plates mounted on cardboard: text in cloth-backed wrappers. Large folio, morocco-backed cloth portfolio. London, 1844. First edition. $15,000 and up. (Copies with plates missing bring less, of course. See auction records.) London, (1845?). Second edition. 31 colored plates. $12,500. (Chicago, 1970.) Facsimile of 1844 edition. One of 1,000. $100. One of 26 (of this edition). $250 and up.

CATO. *Cato's Moral Distichs.* Facsimile of 1735 Philadelphia edition printed by Benjamin Franklin; with an original leaf bound in. Cloth. San Francisco, 1939. One of 250. $100–$150.

CATON, John Dean. *The Last of the Illinois, and a Sketch of the Pottawatomies.* 36 pp., wrappers. Chicago, 1870. First edition. $150–$200.

CATTLE Raising in South Dakota. 32 pp., wrappers. (Forest City, 1904.) $100–$125.

CAVALCANTI, Guido. *Rime.* (In English and Italian.) Edited by Ezra Pound. 40 plates. Stiff red printed wrappers. Genova, Italy, (1932). First edition. $100–$150.

CAVE, Roderick. *The Private Press.* Illustrated. Cloth. London, (1971). First edition. In dust jacket. $150–$200.

CAVENDISH, George. *Life of Thomas Wolsey, Cardinal Archbishop of York.* Edited by F. S. Ellis. Limp vellum with ties. London, 1893. Kelmscott Press. One of 250. $500–$750. Another issue: One of 6 on vellum. $3,000–$4,000.

CAWEIN, Madison J. *Blooms of the Berry.* Cloth. Louisville, 1887. First edition. $75–$125. Author's first book.

CAWEIN, Madison J. *The Pact, the Fool, and the Faeries.* Decorated cloth. Boston, (1912). First edition. In dust jacket. $75–$100.

CAWEIN, Madison J. *The Triumph of Music and Other Lyrics.* Wrappers. (Louisville), 1888. First edition. $50–$75.

CAXTON, Pisistratus. *What Will He Do with It?* 4 vols., cloth. Edinburgh. (1859). (By Edward Bulwer-Lytton.) First edition. $300–$400.

CAXTON, William. *The History of Reynard the Foxe.* Vellum. London, 1892. Kelmscott Press. One of 300. $1,250–$1,500. Another issue: One of 10 on vellum. $3,000–$4,000.

CELEBRATION of the 73rd Anniversary of the Declaration of Independence . . . on Board the Barque "Hannah Sprague," etc. 16 pp., wrappers. New York, 1849. First edition. $75–$150.

CELIZ, Fray Francisco, *Diary of the Alarcon Expedition into Texas, 1718–1719.* Translated by Fritz L. Hoffman. 10 plates. Boards. Los Angeles, 1935. One of 600. $125–$175.

CELLINI, Benvenuto. *The Autobiography of Benvenuto Cellini.* Translated by John

Addington Symonds. Illustrated by Salvador Dali. Blue cloth, gilt top. Garden City, 1946. One of 1,000 signed by Dali. Boxed. $150–$200.

CENDRARS, Blaise. *Panama or the Adventures of My Seven Uncles.* Translated from the French and illustrated by John Dos Passos. Pictorial wrappers. New York, 1931. First edition. One of 300 signed by Cendrars and Dos Passos. Boxed. $150–$175.

CERVANTES, Miguel de. *Don Quixote.* (Note: Because this seventeenth-century classic has gone into innumerable editions, the folllowing listings are limited to a few representative selections. See the British and American auction records for more extensive listings.)

CERVANTES, Miguel de. *The History of Don Quixote of the Mancha.* P.A. Motteux's translation revised anew (1743). 21 illustrations by E. McKnight Kauffer. 2 vols., morocco. London, 1930. Nonesuch Press. $300–$400.

CERVANTES, Miquel de. *The History of the Valorous and Wittie Knight-Errant, Don Quixote of the Mancha.* Thomas Shelton translation. Woodcut initials and borders by Louise Powell. 2 vols., pigskin. London, 1927–28. Ashendene Press. One of 225 on paper. $2,000–$2,750. Another issue: One of 22 on vellum. $6,000–$7,000.

CERVANTES, Miguel de. *The History of the Valorous and Witty Knight-Errant, Don Quixote of the Mancha.* Thomas Shelton translation. Daniel Vierge illustrations. 4 vols., boards. New York, 1906–07. One of 140. $350–$400.

CERWIN, Herbert (compiler). *Famous Recipes by Famous People.* Illustrated. Wrappers. Del Monte, Calif., (1936). First edition. (Issued by Hotel Del Monte.) $100–$125. (Includes contributions by Gertrude Stein, John Steinbeck, and others.) Later: San Francisco, 1940. In dust jacket. $50–$75.

CHABOT, Frederick Charles. *Pictorial Sketch of Mission San Jose de San Miguel de Aguayo on the San Antonio River.* Illustrated, including color plates and photographs. Full leatherette. San Antonio, 1935. First edition. One of 12. $1,250.

CHABOT, Frederick Charles. *With the Makers of San Antonio.* Illustrated. Cloth. San Antonio, 1937. First edition. One of 25 copies (India proof issue) for presentation. $750.

CHADWICK, Henry. *The Game of Base Ball; How to Learn It, How to Play It, and How to Teach It.* Cloth. New York, (1868). First edition, with rules for 1868. $75–$100.

CHADWICK, Hector M. and N.K. *The Growth of Literature.* 3 vols., cloth. Cambridge, 1932–40. $95.

CHAGALL, Marc (illustrator). *Drawings for the Bible.* (French issue: *Dessins pour la Bible.*) Text by Gaston Bachelard. Boards. New York (and Paris). 1960. (Constituting *Verve, No. 37/38.)* $2,000–$2,500. Also, $1,500 (A, 1979).

CHAGALL, Marc (illustrator). *Illustrations for the Bible.* Edited by Jean Wahl. Translated by Samuel Beckett from the Paris title of the same year (*Eaux-fortes pour la Bible*). 29 lithographs (17 in color), 105 plates. Pictorial boards in color. New York (or Paris), 1956. First edition. $2,000–$2,500. (This is *Verve, No. 33/34,* issued in French and in English.)

CHAGALL, Marc (illustrator). *The Jerusalem Windows.* (French: *Vitraux pour Jerusalem.*) Text by Jean Leymarie. Cloth. New York (or Monte Carlo), 1962. In dust jacket. $250–$300.

CHAGALL, Marc (illustrator). *The Lithographs of Chagall.* Text by Fernand Mourlot. 27 original lithographs. 4 vols., quarto, cloth. Monte Carlo and New York or Boston, 1960–74. In dust jackets. $5,000–$6,000 or more. Single volumes in a wide retail range of $1,000 to $1,500 each. Some recent representative auction prices: Vols. I–IV, $1,650; Vols. I–III, $1,700 (twice) and $1,200; Vols. I and II only, $1,600; Vol. I only, $1,200; Vol. II only, $600; Vol. III only, $85.

CHAGALL, Marc (illustrator). *The Story of the Exodus.* 24 colored lithographs, Bible text. Folio, stiff white wrappers. Paris-New York, 1966. First edition. One of 285. $8,750 (A, 1978).

CHAHTA-IMA. *La Nouvelle Atala ou La Fille de L'Esprit.* Printed wrappers. Nouvelle-Orleans (New Orleans), 1879. First edition. $300–$325. (Note: Contains a contribution by Lafcadio Hearn—his first book appearance.)

CHAINBEARER (The), or, The Littlepage Manuscripts. 3 vols., tan boards. London, 1845. (By James Fenimore Cooper.) First edition. $300–$350. New York, 1845. 2 vols., wrappers. $600–$800. (Note: Name is misspelled "Fennimore" on front cover.)

CHAMBERS, Andrew Jackson. *Recollections.* 40 pp., stapled. No place, (1947). First edition. $75–$100.

CHAMBERS, Robert W. *The King in Yellow.* Chicago, 1895. First edition. Green cloth with lizard design (preferred binding, perhaps earliest). $125–$150. Second binding, $75–$100.

CHAMBERS, Robert W. *The Red Republic: A Romance of the Commune.* Pictorial cloth. New York, 1895. First edition. $75.

CHAMISSO, Adelbert von. *A Sojourn at San Francisco Bay 1816.* 8 plates. Half cloth. San Francisco, 1936. Grabhorn printing. One of 250. $125–$150.

CHAMISSO, Adelbert von. *The Wonderful History of Peter Schlemihl.* 6 illustrations. Printed wrappers. London, 1843. First edition. $300–$400.

CHANDLER, Raymond. *The Big Sleep.* Cloth. New York, 1939. First edition. In dust jacket. $750–$1,250. (Reasonably near-fine copies for less.) Author's first book.

CHANDLER, Raymond, *Farewell, My Lovely.* Brown cloth. New York, 1940. First edition. In dust jacket. $2,000. Also, in soiled jacket, $1,600 (A, 1981).

CHANDLER, Raymond. *The Lady in the Lake.* Cloth. New York, 1943. First edition. In dust jacket. $500 and up.

CHANDLER, Raymond. *The Little Sister.* Cloth. London (1949). First edition. In dust jacket. $150–$200. Boston, 1949. Cloth. First American edition. In dust jacket. $200–$250.

CHANDLER, Raymond. *The Long Good-Bye.* Boards. London, (1953). First edition. In dust jacket. $250–$300.

CHANDLER, Raymond. *Playback.* Cloth. London, (1958). First edition. In dust jacket. $125–$200.

CHANDLER, Raymond. *The Smell of Fear.* Cloth. London, (1965). First edition. In dust jacket. $100–$150.

CHANNING, William Ellery (1780–1842). *The Duties of Children.* Wrappers. Boston, 1807. First edition. $100–$150. Author's first publication.

CHANNING, William Ellery (1780–1842). *A Sermon Delivered at the Ordination of the Rev. Jared Sparks, etc.* Stitched. Baltimore, 1819. First edition. $75–$150.

CHANNING, William Ellery (1818–1901). *John Brown, and the Heroes of Harper's Ferry: A Poem.* Green cloth. Boston, 1886. First edition. $75–$150.

CHANTICLEER: A Bibliography of The Golden Cockerel Press. Waltham Saint Lawrence, 1936. One of 300. $200–$250.

CHANUTE, Octave. *Progress in Flying Machines.* 85 illustrations. Cloth. New York, (1894). First edition. $200–$250.

CHAPELLE, Howard I. *The Baltimore Clipper.* Illustrated. Cloth (leatherette). Salem,

Mass., 1930. In dust jacket, $125. Another issue: Marbled boards. One of 97. $200–$250.

CHARLEVOIX, Pierre F. X. *Journal of a Voyage to North America.* Folding map. 2 vols., boards and cloth. Chicago, 1923. Caxton Club. First American edition. $150–$200.

CHARTERED Surveyor (The), His Training and His Work. Foreword by the Rt. Hon. Winston Churchill. Boards and cloth. London, (1932). First edition. $100.

CHASE, Charles M. *The Editor's Run in New Mexico and Colorado.* Illustrated. Pictorial wrappers. Lyndon, Vt., 1882. First edition. $200–$300.

CHASE, Owen (and others). *Narratives of the Wreck of the Whale Ship "Essex."* 12 wood engravings by Robert Gibbings. Cloth. London, 1935. Golden Cockerel Press. One of 275. $400–$450.

CHATTERTON, E. Keble. *Ship-Models.* Edited by Geoffrey Holme. 142 plates, many in color. Buckram. London, 1923. One of 1,000. $200–$250.

CHATTERTON, E. Keble. *Steamship Models.* 128 plates, some in color. Buckram. London, 1924. One of 1,000 signed. $250–$300.

CHATTO, William A. See Careless, John.

CHAUCER, Geoffrey. (Note: The editions of Chaucer, like those of the Bible, Shakespeare, and other classic universal works are too numerous to permit a complete listing here. Following are a few outstanding representative items.)

CHAUCER, Geoffrey. *The Canterbury Tales.* Colored plates by W. Russell Flint. 3 vols., limp vellum, silk ties. London, 1913. Riccardi Press. One of 500. $500–$800. Also, one of 12 on vellum, and with extra plates in cloth portfolio. $3,000 or more. New York, 1930. Illustrated by Rockwell Kent. 2 vols., pigskin. One of 75 signed. $1,250 and up. Another issue; Cloth. One of 924 signed. $350–$450. Waltham Saint Lawrence, 1929–31. Golden Cockerel Press. Eric Gill engravings. 4 vols., folio, boards, morocco spine. One of 485. $3,000–$4,500. Another issue: One of 15 on vellum. Boxed. $8,000–$10,000, or more. New York. 1946. Limited Editions Club. Illustrated by Arthur Szyk. Half pigskin. Boxed. $250–$300.

CHAUCER, Geoffrey. *The Ellesmere Chaucer. (The Canterbury Tales.)* Facsimile, including 71 pages illuminated in gold and colors. 2 vols., folio, half morocco. Manchester, England, 1911. $750–$1,000.

CHAUCER, Geoffrey. *Troilus and Criseyde.* Edited by Arundell del Re. 5 full-page illustrations, 5 half-page decorations, and engraved title page by Eric Gill. Folio, boards and morocco. Waltham Saint Lawrence, 1927. Golden Cockerel Press. One of 225. $4,000–$5,000.

CHAUCER, Geoffrey. *Works.* Woodcut illustrations, borders, and initials. Folio, boards. London, 1896. Kelmscott Press. One of 425. $10,000 and up. Also, $8,250 (A, 1980); $7,500 (A, 1977). Another issue: White blind-stamped pigskin, in wooden box with brass hinges and clasps, by the Doves Bindery. One of 2 on vellum and 46 on paper. $10,000–$15,000.

CHAYEVSKY, Paddy. *Television Plays.* Cloth. New York, 1955. First edition. In dust jacket. $50–$60.

CHEEVER, Henry T. *The Island World of the Pacific.* Frontispiece. Calf. Glasgow, (1850). First edition. $150.

CHEEVER, John. *The Enormous Radio and Other Stories.* Cloth. New York, 1953. First edition, with "1" on copyright page. $100–$125.

CHEEVER, John. *Homage to Shakespeare.* 15 pp., blue buckram. Stevenson, Conn., (1968). First edition. One of 150 signed. In dust jacket. $125–$150.

CHEEVER, John. *The Housebreaker of Shady Hill and Other Stories.* Cloth. New York, 1958. First edition. In dust jacket. $75–$100. London, 1958. Boards. First English edition. In dust jacket. $65–$90.

CHEEVER, John. *Some People, Places and Things That Will Not Appear in My Next Novel.* Cloth. New York, (1961). First edition. In dust jacket. $100–$150.

CHEEVER, John. *The Wapshot Chronicle.* Cloth. New York, (1957). First edition. In dust jacket. $50–$60. London, 1957. First English edition. In dust jacket. $50.

CHEEVER, John. *The Way Some People Live.* Cloth. New York, (1943). First edition. In dust jacket. $250–$325. Author's first book.

CHERRY-GARRARD, Apsley. *The Worst Journey in the World: Antarctic, 1910–1913.* Maps and panoramas, color plates. 2 vols., boards, paper labels. London, 1922. First edition. $250–$300.

CHESNUTT, Charles W. *The Conjure Woman.* Pictorial cloth. Boston, 1899. First edition. $125–$150. Author's first book.

CHESNUTT, Charles W. *Frederick Douglass.* Limp leather. Boston, 1899. First edition. $75–$100.

CHESNUTT, Charles W. *The House Behind the Cedars.* Pictorial cloth. Boston, 1900. First edition. $200-$250.

CHESNUTT, Charles W. *The Wife of His Youth and Other Stories.* Cloth. Boston, 1899. First edition. $100–$150.

CHESTERTON, G.K. *The Ballad of the White Horse.* Cloth. London, 1911. First edition. In dust jacket. $50–$75. London, (1928). First illustrated edition. One of 100. In dust jacket. $100–$150.

CHESTERTON, G.K. *Charles Dickens Fifty Years After.* Wrappers. No place, 1920. One of 25. $200.

CHESTERTON, G.K. *Chaucer.* Cloth. London, 1932. First edition. In dust jacket. $35.

CHESTERTON, G.K. *Collected Poems.* Boards and parchment. London, 1927. One of 350 signed. $150.

CHESTERTON, G.K. *The Coloured Lands.* Illustrated by the author. Boards. London, 1938. First edition. In dust jacket. $75–$100.

CHESTERTON, G.K. *Four Faultless Felons.* Cloth. London, (1930). First edition. In dust jacket. $125–$150.

CHESTERTON, G.K. *Greybeards at Play: Rhymes and Sketches.* Boards and buckram. London, 1900. First edition. $300–$500. Author's first book.

CHESTERTON, G.K. *The Innocence of Father Brown.* Illustrated by S. S. Lucas. Red cloth. London, 1911. First edition. In dust jacket. $300–$500.

CHESTERTON, G.K. *London.* 10 tipped-in photogravure plates by Alvin Langdon Coburn. Half cloth. London, 1914. First edition. $350–$450.

CHESTERTON, G.K. *The Man Who Was Thursday.* Cloth. London, 1908. First edition. $250–$350.

CHESTERTON, G.K. *Manalive.* Color frontispiece. Cloth. London, (1912). First edition. In dust jacket. $200–$250.

CHESTERTON, G.K. *The Poet and the Lunatics.* Cloth. London, 1929. First edition. In dust jacket. $100–$125.

CHESTERTON, G.K. *The Scandal of Father Brown*. Cloth. New York, 1935. First American edition. In dust jacket. $50–$75.

CHESTERTON, G.K. *The Secret of Father Brown*. Cloth. London, (1927). First edition. In dust jacket. $300–$350. Without jacket, $50–$60.

CHESTERTON, G.K. *The Sword of Wood*. Boards. London, 1928. First edition. One of 530 signed. In dust jacket. $100–$125.

CHESTERTON, G.K. *The Wild Knight and Other Poems*. Half vellum. London, 1900. First edition. $75-$100.

CHESTERTON, G.K. *The Wisdom of Father Brown*. Cloth. London, 1914. First edition. In dust jacket. $300–$400.

CHICAGO: A Strangers' and Tourists' Guide to the City of Chicago. Illustrated, including 4 folding plates and a folding map. Cloth. Chicago, 1866. First edition. $125–$150.

CHICAGO Illustrated. (Cover title.) 52 tinted lithograph views. Text by James W. Sheahan. Oblong folio, morocco. (Chicago, 1866–67.) Jevne and Almini, publishers. First edition, second issue $4,000–$5,000. (The original issue was in 13 parts and is now very rare. Probable value: $10,000 and up—if one should be offered for sale.) New York, 1952. 12 plates. Portfolio. Reprint edition. $150–$250.

CHILD, Andrew. *Overland Route to California*. Full leather. Milwaukee, 1852. First edition. $5,000–$7,500.

CHILD, Lydia Maria. See *Emily Parker; Evenings in New England; The First Settlers in New England; The Frugal Housewife; Hobomok*.

CHILD'S Book About Whales (The). Woodcuts. 16 pp., printed wrappers. Concord, N.H., 1843. $150.

CHILD'S Botany (The). Boards. Boston, 1828. (By Samuel Griswold Goodrich.) First edition. $75–$100.

CHILDS, C.G. (engraver). *Views in Philadelphia and Its Vicinity*. Engraved title page, plan, 24 engraved views. Cloth or boards. Philadelphia, 1827–(30). First edition. $2,000–$2,500.

CHITTENDEN, Hiram M. *The American Fur Trade of the Far West*. Folding map, plan, 3 facsimiles, 6 plates. 3 vols., green cloth. New York, 1902. First edition, $350–$400. New York, 1936. Plates. 2 vols., cloth. Boxed. $150–$175.

CHITTENDEN, Hiram M. *History of Early Steamboat Navigation on the Missouri River*. 16 plates. 2 vols., cloth. New York, 1903. One of 950. $150–$200.

CHIVERS, Thomas Holley. *Conrad and Eudora*. Cloth. Philadelphia, 1834. First edition. $150–$250.

CHIVERS, Thomas Holley. *Eonchs of Ruby: A Gift of Love*. Printed white boards. New York, 1851. First edition. $150–$250.

CHIVERS, Thomas Holley. *The Lost Pleiad and Other Poems*. Printed tan wrappers. New York, 1845. First edition. $200.

CHIVERS, Thomas Holley. *Memoralia*. Boards. Philadelphia, 1853. First edition. $100–$125.

CHIVERS, Thomas Holley. *Nacoochee: or, The Beautiful Star*. Cloth. New York, 1837. First edition. $300–$350.

CHIVERS, Thomas Holley. *The Path of Sorrow*. Blue boards, purple cloth, paper label. Franklin, T(enn.), 1832. First edition. $400–$500. Author's first book.

CHIVERS, Thomas Holley. *Search After Truth*. Printed tan wrappers. New York, 1848. First edition. $150–$200.

CHRISTIANISM: Or Belief and Unbelief Reconciled. 59 pp., cloth, paper label. (London, 1832.) (By Leigh Hunt.) First edition. (75 printed.) $500–$750. Also, $425 (A, 1978).

CHRISTIE, Agatha. *Hercule Poirot's Christmas*. Orange cloth. London, (1939). First edition. In dust jacket. $150–$200.

CHRISTIE, Agatha. *The Hound of Death and Other Stories*. Cloth. London, 1933. First edition. In dust jacket. $250. Without jacket, $100.

CHRISTIE, Agatha. *The Man in the Brown Suit*. Cloth. London, 1924. First edition. In dust jacket. $250–$300. Without jacket, $150.

CHRISTIE, Agatha. *Murder in Mesopotamia*. Orange cloth. London, (1936). First edition. In dust jacket. $300–$350.

CHRISTIE, Agatha. *The Mysterious Affair at Styles*. Cloth. London, 1920. First edition. In dust jacket. $2,000 and up. Also, without jacket, $1,100 (A, 1981).

CHRISTIE, Agatha. *Sad Cypress*. Red cloth. London, (1940). First edition. In dust jacket. $250–$300.

CHRISTMAS Gift from Fairy-Land (A). Cloth. New York, (1838). (By James Kirke Paulding.) First edition, second (?) issue. $150–$200. (Note: This was also published under the title *A Gift from Fairy-Land*.)

CHRONICLES of the City of Gotham. Half cloth. New York, 1830. (By James Kirke Paulding.) First edition. $200–$250.

CHURCHILL, Winston (American novelist). *The Celebrity*. Cloth. New York, 1898. First edition. $25–$30. Author's first book.

CHURCHILL, Sir Winston S. See *The Chartered Surveyor*.

CHURCHILL, Sir Winston S. *Addresses Delivered in the Year 1940, etc*. Cloth. San Francisco, 1940. Grabhorn Press. One of 250. $200–$225.

CHURCHILL, Sir Winston S. *Arms and the Covenant: Speeches*. Compiled by Randolph S. Churchill. Frontispiece. Buckram. London, 1938. First edition. In dust jacket. $150–$200.

CHURCHILL. Sir Winston S. *Beating the Invader*. 2 pp., unbound (as issued). (London, 1941.) $200–$300.

CHURCHILL, Sir Winston S. *Great Contemporaries*. Illustrated. Cloth. London, 1937. First edition. In dust jacket. $100–$125.

CHURCHILL, Sir Winston S. *Ian Hamilton's March*. Portrait, maps, plans. Red cloth. London, 1900. First edition. $250–$300. New York, 1900. First American edition. $150.

CHURCHILL, Sir Winston S. *India: Speeches*. Orange wrappers. London, (1931). First edition. In dust jacket. $150–$300. Second impression: Green wrappers. $75–$125.

CHURCHILL, Sir Winston S. *Liberalism and the Social Problem*. Cloth. London, 1909. First edition. $150–$250.

CHURCHILL, Sir Winston S. *London to Ladysmith via Pretoria*. Maps and plans. Fawn-colored cloth. London, 1900. First edition. $200–$225. New York, 1900. Buckram. First American edition. $100–$125.

CHURCHILL, Sir Winston S. *Lord Randolph Churchill*. Frontispieces, plates. 2 vols., cloth. London, 1906. First edition $100–$125.

CHURCHILL, Sir Winston S. *Marlborough: His Life and Times*. Plates, facsimiles, maps, plans. 4 vols. morocco, gilt tops. London (1933–38). First edition. One of 155 signed. $1,000–$1,400. Also $616 (A, 1979). Trade edition: 4 vols., cloth. In dust jackets. $125–$150.

CHURCHILL, Sir Winston S. *My African Journey*. Maps and plates. Pictorial red cloth. London, 1908. First edition. $150–$200.

CHURCHILL, Sir Winston S. *My Early Life*. Portraits, maps, plates. Cloth. London, 1930. First edition. $150–$175. New York, 1930. Illustrated. Cloth. First American edition. $75–$100.

CHURCHILL, Sir Winston S. *The People's Rights*. Pictorial wrappers, or cloth. London, (1909). First edition, first issue, with index. Either binding: $300–$400. Second issue. $100–$150.

CHURCHILL, Sir Winston S. *The River War*. Portraits, colored maps, folding illustrations. 2 vols., pictorial cloth. London, 1899. First edition. $500–$600.

CHURCHILL, Sir Winston S. *Savrola: A Tale of the Revolution in Aurania*. Blue cloth. New York, 1900. First edition. $600–$750. London, 1900. Cloth. First English edition. $300–$350.

CHURCHILL, Sir Winston S. *Secret Session Speeches*. Cloth. London, (1946). First edition. In dust jacket. $50–$75. (Some copies especially bound in leather and inscribed: $300–$400.)

CHURCHILL, Sir Winston S. *Step by Step, 1936–1939*. Green cloth. London, 1939. First edition. $125–$150.

CHURCHILL, Sir Winston S. *The Story of the Malakand Field Force*. Portrait and 5 maps and plans. Cloth. London, 1898. First edition, first issue, with errata slip preceding first map. $600–$800.

CHURCHILL,Sir Winston S. *Thoughts and Adventures*. Cloth. London, (1932). First edition. $125–$150.

CHURCHILL, Sir Winston S. *The World Crisis*. Maps, plans, other illustrations. 6 vols., cloth. London, 1923–31. First edition. $200–$250.

CHURCHILL, Sir Winston S., and Martindale, C.C., S.J. *Charles IXth, Duke of Marlborough, K.G.* Wrappers. London, 1934. First edition. $125–$150.

CHURCHWARD, James. *The Children of Mu*. Illustrated. Cloth. New York, 1931. First edition. In dust jacket. $75–$100.

CHURCHWARD, James. *The Lost Continent of Mu*. Cloth. New York, 1931. First edition. In dust jacket. $75–$100.

CHURCHWARD, James. *The Sacred Symbols of Mu*. Cloth. New York, 1933. First edition. In dust jacket. $75–$100.

CINCINNATUS. *Travels on the Western Slope of the Mexican Cordillera*. Engraved title page. Cloth. San Francisco, 1857. (By Marvin T. Wheat.) First edition. $200–$300.

CINDERELLA. Retold by C.S. Evans. Frontispiece in color and numerous silhouette illustrations by Arthur Rackham. Half cloth. London, 1919. One of 525 signed by the artist. In dust jacket. $500–$600. Another issue: Half vellum: One of 325 on vellum, signed by Rackham, with an extra plate. $750–$1,000.

CLAIBORNE, John Herbert. *Seventy-five Years in Old Virginia*. Cloth. New York, 1905. $50–$75.

CLAPPE, Louise A.K.S. *California in 1851 (in 1852): The Dame Shirley Letters*. 2 vols. San Francisco, 1933. Grabhorn printing. One of 500. $75–$150.

CLARK, Charles E. *Prince and Boatswain: Sea Tales from the Recollection of Rear-Admiral Charles E. Clark.* Blue cloth. Greenfield, Mass., (about 1915). (Edited by John P. Marquand and James M. Morgan.) First edition. $50. Marquand's first book appearance.

CLARK, Charles M. *A Trip to Pike's Peak and Notes by the Way.* Frontispiece, 18 woodcuts. Cloth. Chicago, 1861. First edition. $600–$850.

CLARK, Daniel. *Proofs of the Corruption of Gen. James Wilkinson, and of His Connexion with Aaron Burr.* Boards. Philadelphia, 1809. First edition. $750–$1,000.

CLARK, Daniel M. *The Southern Calculator, or Compendious Arithmetic.* Boards. Lagrange, Ga., 1844. $100–$125.

CLARK, John A. *Gleanings by the Way.* Cloth. Philadelphia, 1842. First edition. $200–$300.

CLARK, Roland. *Gunner's Dawn.* Illustrated, including signed frontispiece. Leatherette. New York, 1937. Derrydale Press. First edition. One of 950. Boxed. $500–$750. Another issue: One of 50 signed with 8 signed engravings. $2,000–$2,500.

CLARK, Roland. *Pot Luck.* Illustrated, including signed frontispiece etching. Half leather. West Hartford, Vt., (1945). First edition. One of 150. $800–$1,000. Another issue: Cloth. One of 460 signed. Boxed. $300–$400. Trade edition: $30–$40.

CLARK, Roland. *Roland Clark's Etchings.* Illustrated, with a signed frontispiece etching. Folio, cloth. New York, (1938). Derrydale Press. First edition. One of 800. Boxed. $750–$1,000. Another issue: Half morocco. One of 50 (presentation) with 2 signed etchings. $3,500 (A, 1977).

CLARK, Stanley. *The Life and Adventures of the American Cowboy.* Illustrated. Pictorial wrappers. (Providence), 1897. First edition. $150. Another edition, title changed: *True Life in the Far West by the American Cowboy.* Wrappers with author's photo. (Providence, about 1898?) $150.

CLARK, Walter (editor). *Histories of the Several Regiments and Battalions from North Carolina in the Great War, 1861–1865.* Plates. 5 vols., cloth. Raleigh, 1901. $225.

CLARK, Walter Van Tilburg, *Christmas Comes to Hjalsen.* Pictorial wrappers. Reno, 1930. First edition. In original mailing envelope. $300–$400. Author's first book.

CLARK, Walter Van Tilburg. *The Ox-Bow Incident.* Cloth. New York, (1940). First edition. In dust jacket. $50–$75.

CLARKE, A.B. *Travels in Mexico and California.* Printed wrappers. Boston, 1852. First edition. $750–$1,000. Waterstained, $500. Later issue: Cloth. $650.

CLARKE, Arthur C. *Childhood's End.* Cloth. New York, (1953). First edition. In dust jacket. $75–$125.

CLARKE, Arthur C. *Earthlight.* Cloth. New York, (1955). First edition. In dust jacket. $75–$100.

CLARKE, Arthur C. *Interplanetary Flight.* Cloth. London, (1950). First edition. In dust jacket. $75–$100. Author's first book.

CLARKE, Austin. *The Vengeance of Fiona.* Cloth. Dublin, 1917. First edition. In dust jacket. $200. Author's first book.

CLARKE, Lewis. *Narrative of the Sufferings of Lewis Clarke During a Captivity of More Than Twenty-five Years.* Portrait. Wrappers. Boston, 1845. First edition. $100–$150.

CLARKE, Rebecca S. See May, Sophie.

CLASS Poem. Printed wrappers. (Cambridge, Mass.), 1938. (By James Russell Lowell.) First edition. $200–$300. Author's first published work.

CLASS Poem. 1915. 4pp. (New Haven), 1915. (By Archibald MacLeish.) $2,500 (A, 1977). Author's first separately published work.

CLAVELL, James. *King Rat.* Cloth. Boston, (1962). First edition. In dust jacket. $40–$50. Author's first book.

CLAY, John. *My Life on the Range.* Illustrated. Cloth. Chicago, (1924). First edition. $175–$200.

CLAYTON, W(illiam). *The Latter-Day Saints' Emigrants' Guide.* 24 pp., plain wrappers. St. Louis, 1848. First edition. $3,000–$5,000.

CLEMENS, Samuel Langhorne, See Twain, Mark. Also see *Date 1601; What Is Man?*

CLEVELAND, Richard J. *A Narrative of Voyages and Commercial Enterprises.* 2 vols., cloth. Cambridge, Mass., 1842. First edition. $600–$750.

CLOCKMAKER (The); or the Sayings and Doings of Samuel Slick of Slickville. Cloth, paper label. Halifax, 1836. (By Thomas Chandler Haliburton.) First edition. $200–$250. Philadelphia, 1836. Boards. First United States edition. $150. Boston, 1838. $75–$100.

CLUM, Woodworth. *Apache Agent: The Story of John P. Clum.* Illustrated, including frontispiece in color of Geronimo. Cloth. Boston, 1936. First edition. In dust jacket. $50–$75.

CLUTTERBUCK, Captain, *The Monastery.* 3 vols. boards, paper labels. Edinburgh, 1820. (By Sir Walter Scott). First edition. $300–$400.

COATES, Robert M. *The Eater of Darkness.* Wrappers, paper labels. (Paris, 1926.) Contact Editions. First edition. $400–$450. New York, 1929. Cloth. First American edition. $250–$300.

COATES, Robert M. *Yesterday's Burdens.* Cloth. New York, (1933). First edition. In dust jacket. $150.

COATSWORTH, Elizabeth. *The Cat Who Went to Heaven.* Illustrated by Lynd Ward. Cloth. New York, 1930. First edition. In dust jacket. $50–$75.

COBB, Humphrey. *Paths of Glory.* Cloth. New York, 1935. First edition. In dust jacket. $50–$60.

COBB, Irvin S. *Back Home.* Illustrated. Cloth. New York, (1912). First edition, first printing with "Plimpton Press" slug on copyright page, and first binding, with publisher's name in 3 lines on spine. $75–$100. Author's first book.

COBB, Irvin S. *Old Judge Priest.* Cloth. New York, (1916). First edition, first issue, with square-diamond insignia on title page. In dust jacket. $100–$125.

COBB, Irvin S. *Piano Jim and the Impotent Pumpkin Vine. "Charley Russell's Best Story—to My Way of Thinking."* 24 pp., wrappers. No place, 1947. One of 100. $150.

COBBETT, Thomas B. *Colorado Mining Directory.* Cloth. Denver, 1879. First edition. $400–$500.

COBBETT, William. *Rural Rides.* Woodcut map. Boards and cloth. London, 1830. First edition. $600–$800. London, 1930. Edited by G. D. H. and Margaret Cole. Illustrated. 3 vols., boards. $300–$400.

COBDEN-SANDERSON, T.J. *Amantium Irae: Letters to Two Friends, 1864–1867.* Frontispiece portrait. Limp vellum. Hammersmith (London), 1914. Doves Press. One of 150. $300–$400. In a Doves binding of morocco. $1,500.

COBDEN-SANDERSON, T.J. *The City Metropolitan.* London. 1911. Doves Press. Limited edition. $200-$250. (About 300 copies.)

COBDEN-SANDERSON, T.J. *The City Planned*. London, 1912. Doves Press. Limited edition. $200-$250. (About 300 copies.)

COBDEN-SANDERSON,T.J. *Credo*. London, 1908. Doves Press. One of 250. $200–$250.

COBDEN-SANDERSON, T.J. *The Ideal Book or Book Beautiful*. Vellum. London, 1900. Doves Press. One of 300. $200–$250. Another issue: One of 12 on vellum. $1,500–$2,000.

COBDEN-SANDERSON, T.J. *The Journals of T.J. Cobden-Sanderson, 1879–1922*. Illustrated. 2 vols., cloth. London, 1926. First edition. One of 1,050. $175–$200.

COBURN, Alvin Langdon. *London*. Introduction by Hilaire Belloc. 20 tipped-in Coburn photogravures. Folio, boards. New York, (1909). $3,000. With new leather spine, $2,400.

COBURN, Alvin Langdon. *More Men of Mark*. Boards. New York, 1922. First edition. Boxed. $400–$500.

COBURN, Wallace D. *Rhymes from the Round-up Camp*. 8 Charles M. Russell drawings. Limp pictorial morocco. (Great Falls, Mont.), 1899. First edition, first issue, with "the" instead of "a" in title. $400–$500. Later, with "a." $300–$350. Second edition: $150–$250.

COCKERELL, S.C. (editor). *Laudes Beatae Mariae Virginis*. Printed in red, black, and blue. Boards and linen. London, 1896. Kelmscott Press. One of 250. $1,000–$1,250. Another issue: One of 10 on vellum. $3,000–$4,000.

COCKERELL, S.C. (editor). *Some German Woodcuts of the 15th Century*. 35 reproductions. Boards and linen. London, 1897. Kelmscott Press. One of 225. $400–$500. Another issue: One of 8 on vellum. $2,000–$3,000.

COCTEAU, Jean. *Orphee*. Translated by Carl Wildman. Frontispiece by Pablo Picasso. Boards. London, 1933. First edition in English. One of 100 signed by Cocteau and Picasso. $650 and up.

COFFIN, Charles C. *The Boys of '76*. Illustrated. Pictorial cloth. New York, 1887. First edition. $75–$100.

COFFIN, Joshua. *A Sketch of the History of Newbury, Newburyport, and West Newbury*. Map, tables. Cloth. Boston, 1845. $100–$150.

COFFINBERRY, Andrew. *The Forest Rangers*. Boards. Columbus, 1842. First edition. $200.

COHN, Albert M. *George Cruikshank: A Catalogue Raisonné*. Illustrated. Brown cloth. London, 1924. First edition. One of 500. $300–$400.

COHN, David L. *New Orleans and Its Living Past*. Illustrated. Cloth. Boston, 1941. Limited, signed edition. $75–$100.

COHN, Louis Henry. *A Bibliography of the Works of Ernest Hemingway*. Illustrated. Cloth. New York, 1931. First edition. One of 500. $85–$125. (Colophon calls for 5 lettered copies; there were none.)

COKE, Henry J. *A Ride Over the Rocky Mountains to Oregon and California*. Portrait. Cloth. London, 1852. First edition. $150–$250.

COLBERT, E. *Chicago: Historical and Statistical Sketch of the Garden City*. 120 pp., wrappers. Chicago, 1868. First edition. $100–$150.

COLERIDGE, Samuel T. See *Lyrical Ballads*.

COLERIDGE, Samuel T. *Aids to Reflection*. Drab boards, paper label. London, 1825. First edition. $150–$175.

COLERIDGE, Samuel T. *Biographia Literaria.* 2 vols., green or blue boards, paper labels. London, 1817. First edition. $300–$400.

COLERIDGE, Samuel T. *Christabel: Kubla Khan, A Vision: The Pains of Sleep.* Plain drab wrappers, or boards. London, 1816. First edition, first issue, with 4 pages of February ads at back, and with a half title. $2,000–$2,500. Also, $1,980 (A, 1979); with March ads, $600 (A, 1981). London, 1904. Eragny Press. Colored frontispiece. Boards. One of 226 on paper. In dust jacket. $350–$500. Another issue: One of 10 on vellum. $1,200–$1,500.

COLERIDGE, Samuel T. *Confessions of an Inquiring Spirit.* Cloth. paper label. London, 1840. First edition, $75–$100. Boston, 1841. Cloth, paper label. $40.

COLERIDGE, Samuel T. *Hints Towards the Formation of a More Comprehensive Theory of Life.* Boards. London, 1817. First edition. $750 and up.

COLERIDGE, Samuel T. *A Lay Sermon Addressed to the Higher and Middle Classes.* Printed wrappers. London, 1817. First edition. $750 and up.

COLERIDGE, Samuel T. *Notes, Theological, Political, and Miscellaneous.* Cloth. London, 1853. First edition. $400–$500.

COLERIDGE, Samuel T. *Osorio: A Tragedy.* Boards, paper label. London, 1873. First edition. Limited issue on large paper. $400–$485.

COLERIDGE, Samuel T. *Poems Chosen Out of the Works of Samuel Taylor Coleridge.* Woodcut borders and initial letters. Vellum. London, 1896. Kelmscott Press. One of 300. $500–$750. Another issue: One of 8 on vellum. $2,500–$3,500.

COLERIDGE, Samuel Taylor. *Remorse: A Tragedy in Five Acts.* Stitched. London, 1813. First edition. $1,000 and up. Also, with defects, $400 (A, 1978).

COLERIDGE, Samuel T. *The Rime of the Ancient Mariner.* Illustrated by Gustave Doré. Cloth. New York, 1877. $125–$150. Boston, 1893. Cloth. Illustrated by J.N. Paton. $75. London, 1899. Vale Press. Illustrated by Charles Ricketts. Boards. One of 210. $200–$250. London, 1903. Essex House, Frontispiece. Vellum. One of 150 on vellum. $350–$450. London, 1910. Illustrated by Willy Pogany. Stiff vellum. One of 25 on vellum, signed by Pogany. In cloth wrapper and slipcase. $750–$1,000. Another issue: Calf. One of 525 signed by Pogany. $500–$600. Clothbound: $200–$350. Bristol, England, 1929. 10 engravings by David Jones. Canvas. One of 60 with extra set of engravings, signed by the artist. $1,500 and up. Another issue: Boards and cloth. One of 470 signed by Jones. $500–$600. Oxford, 1930. Boards and cloth, designed by Bruce Rogers. One of 750. $150–$200. London, 1944. Corvinus Press. Half buckram. $500–$750. (21 copies.) Los Angeles, (1964). Tamarind Workshop. Colored lithographs. Printed wrappers. One of 45. $1,000 and up.

COLERIDGE, Samuel T. *Selected Poems.* Vellum. London, 1935. Nonesuch Press. One of 500. $200–$250.

COLERIDGE, Samuel T. *Sibylline Leaves: A Collection of Poems.* Drab boards, paper label. London, 1817. First edition, with errata leaf. $750–$1,000. Also, defective, $320 (A, 1981).

COLERIDGE, Samuel T. *Specimens of the Table Talk of the Late Samuel Taylor Coleridge.* Frontispiece. 2 vols., boards with labels. London, 1835. First edition. $750–$1,000.

COLERIDGE, Samuel T. *The Statesman's Manual; or the Bible the Best Guide to Political Skill and Foresight.* Blue-green printed wrappers. London, 1816. First edition. $750–$1,000.

COLERIDGE, Samuel T. *Zapolya.* Wrappers. London, 1817. First edition. $650–$750.

COLLECTION of Familiar Quotations (A). Brown cloth. Cambridge, Mass., 1855. (By John Bartlett.) First edition. $250–$350.

COLLEGE Musings, or Twigs from Parnassus. 112 pages, boards. Tuscaloosa, Ala., 1833. (By William Russell Smith.) First edition of the first Alabama book of poetry. $750.

COLLIER, John. *Green Thoughts.* Linen. London, 1932. First edition. One of 550 signed. With errata slip. $50–$75.

COLLIER, John. *His Monkey Wife.* Cloth. London, 1930. First edition. In dust jacket. $125–$175. New York, 1935. First American edition. In dust jacket. $50–$75. Author's first book.

COLLIER, John. *Pictures in the Fire.* Cloth. London, 1958. First edition. In dust jacket. $50–$75.

COLLIER, John. *Tom's A-Cold.* Cloth. London, 1933. First edition. In dust jacket. $200–$225.

COLLIER, John. *Witch's Money.* Cloth. New York, 1948. First edition. One of 350 signed. In glassine dust jacket. $150–$200.

COLLIER, John Payne. *A Bibliographical and Critical Account of the Rarest Books in the English Language.* 2 vols., half cloth. London, 1865. First edition. $200–$300. New York, 1866. 4 vols., cloth. First American edition. One of 75 on large paper. $250–$300.

COLLIER, John Payne. *Memoirs of Edward Alleyn.* Cloth. London, 1841. First edition. $100–$125.

COLLINS, Charles. *Collins' History and Directory of the Black Hills.* 91 pp., printed yellow wrappers. Central City, Dakota Territory, 1878. First edition. $2,000–$2,500. Also, $1,200 (A,1968).

COLLINS, Charles (compiler). *Collins' Omaha Directory.* Printed boards. (Omaha, 1866). First edition. $750 and up.

COLLINS, David. *An Account of the English Colony in New South Wales.* 2 maps. 23 plates. Leather or boards. London, 1804. Second edition. $750–$1,000.

COLLINS, Dennis. *The Indians' Last Fight; or, the Dull Knife Raid.* 8 plates. Cloth. (Girard, Kan., about 1915.) First edition. $150–$200.

COLLINS, John S. *Across the Plains in '64.* Pictorial cloth. Omaha, 1904. First edition. $100–$125.

COLLINS, Mrs. Nat. *The Cattle Queen of Montana.* Compiled by Charles Wallace. Illustrated. Stiff wrappers. St. James, Minn., 1894. First edition. $1,000 and up. Spokane, (about 1898–1902). Plates. Pictorial wrappers. $150–$200.

COLLINS, Lieut. R.M. *Chapters from the Unwritten History of the War Between the States.* Cloth. St. Louis, 1893. First edition. $200–$300.

COLLINS, Wilkie. *After Dark.* 2 vols., cloth. London, 1856. First edition. $300–$400.

COLLINS, Wilkie. *Antonina.* 3 vols., cloth. London, 1850. First edition. $250–$350. Author's first novel.

COLLINS. Wilkie. *Armadale.* Illustrated. Cloth. New York, 1866. First edition. $200–$300. London, 1866. Illustrated. 2 vols., cloth. First English edition. $200–$300.

COLLINS, Wilkie. *The Dead Secret.* 2 vols., cloth. London, 1857. First edition. $250–$350.

COLLINS, Wilkie. *The Evil Genius.* 3 vols., cloth. London, 1886. First English edition. $300–$400. New York, 1886. Cloth. First American edition. $200. New York, 1886. Wrappers. Second American edition. $100–$125.

COLLINS, Wilkie. *The Frozen Deep: A Drama.* Printed wrappers. No place, 1966. First printing. One of a few copies privately printed. $1,000 and up. London, 1874. 2 vols., cloth. First published edition (*The Frozen Deep and Other Tales*). $250–$350.

COLLINS, Wilkie. *The Law and the Lady.* 3 vols., cloth. London, 1875. First edition. $300–$400. New York, 1875. Illustrated. Wrappers. First American edition. $200–$250.

COLLINS, Wilkie. *The Legacy of Cain.* 3 vols., cloth. London, 1889. First edition. $250–$350.

COLLINS, Wilkie. *Memoirs of the Life of William Collins, R.A.* 2 vols., cloth. London, 1848. First edition. $300–$350. Author's first book.

COLLINS, Wilkie. *Miss Gwilt, A Drama in Five Acts.* Wrappers. No place, 1875. First edition. $250–$350. (Altered from the novel *Armadale.*)

COLLINS, Wilkie. *Mr. Wray's Cash-Box.* Frontispiece. Cloth. London, 1852. First edition. $200–$300.

COLLINS, Wilkie. *The Moonstone: A Romance.* 3 vols., purple cloth. London, 1868. First edition, first issue, with half titles, with misprint "treachesrouly" on page 129 of Vol. 2, and with ads in Vols. 2 and 3. $1,500–$2,000 (Presentation copies have been sold in recent years for $2,500 to $3,500). Play version: Privately printed, 1877. Unbound as issued. $1,000 and up. New York, 1959. Limited Editions Club. Cloth. Boxed. $50–$60.

COLLINS, Wilkie. *No Name.* 3 vols., red cloth. London, 1862. First edition. $300–$400. New York, 1863. Cloth. First American edition. $200.

COLLINS, Wilkie. *The Queen of Hearts.* 3 vols., cloth. London, 1859. First edition. $2,500–$3,500.

COLLINS, Wilkie. *The Woman in White.* Illustrated by John McLenan. Brown cloth. New York, 1860. First edition, first issue, with the woman on spine in white. $300–$500. London, 1860. 3 vols., cloth. First English edition (published a month after the first American edition), first issue, with ads at end of Vol. 3 dated August 1, 1860. $1,000–$1,500. Also, $950 (A, 1978). New York, 1964. Limited Editions Club. Boards. Boxed. $40–$45.

COLMAN, George, the Younger. See Mathers, John.

COLMAN, Sir Jeremiah. *The Noble Game of Cricket.* 105 plates, 33 colored. Buckram. London, 1941. One of 150. In dust jacket. $600–$750.

COLOPHON (The): A Book Collector's Quarterly. 48 vols. boards, including clothbound indexes and *The Annual of Bookmaking.* New York, 1930–50. Complete set. $800–$1,000.

COLT, Miriam Davis. *Went to Kansas.* Cloth. Watertown, N.Y., 1862. First edition. $350–$500.

COLTON, Calvin. *Tour of the American Lakes.* 2 vols., boards. London, 1853. First edition. $150–$200.

COLTON, J.H. (publisher). See *The State of Indiana Delineated.*

COLTON, J.H. (publisher). *Particulars of Routes, Distances, Fares, etc.* 12 pp. (11 of text). (Caption title.) Accompanying Colton's Map of the United States . . . and a Plan of the Gold Region. Map folded into brown cloth covers, with printed paper label; text attached to inside of front cover. New York, 1849. First edition, first issue, with "longitude West from Greenwich" at top of map. $1,000 and up.

COLTON, Walter. *Three Years in California.* Map, 6 portraits, 6 plates, folding facsimile. Black cloth. New York, 1850. First edition. $150–$200.

COLUM, Padraic. *Creatures.* Illustrated. Boards. New York, 1937. First edition. One of 300. In dust jacket. $50–$75.

COLUMBIA Poetry, 1935. Cloth or wrappers. New York, 1935. First edition. One of 500. $100–$150. (Includes 4 poems by John Berryman, his first book appearance.)

COLUMBIA Verse: 1897–1924. Boards and cloth. New York, 1924. First edition. $100–$125. (Note: Poems by Louis Zukofsky and others.)

COLUMBUS, Christopher. *The Voyages of Christopher Columbus; Being the Journals, etc.* Translated by Cecil Jane. 5 maps. Half vellum. London, 1930. One of 1,050 on vellum. $100–$125.

COMBE, William. See: Doctor Syntax; Quiz. Also see *The English Dance of Death; The Dance of Life; The Tour of Doctor Prosody; A History of Madeira; Journal of Sentimental Travels, etc.; The History of Johnny Quae Genus.*

COMBS, Leslie. *Narrative of the Life of Gen. Leslie Combs.* (Cover title.) 23 pp., plus errata leaf, wrappers. (New York, 1852.) First edition. $250. Another issue: (Washington), 1852. 20 pp., printed wrappers. Rebound in cloth, $130 (A, 1967—the Streeter copy, with no mention of first edition).

COMING Race (The). Scarlet-orange cloth, blocked in black and gold, Edinburgh, (1871). (By Edward Bulwer-Lytton.) First edition. $400–$500.

COMMERCIAL Tourist (The); or, Gentleman Traveller; A Satirical Poem. 5 colored plates by I.R. Cruikshank. Boards with label. London, 1822. (By Charles William Hempel.) First edition. $200–$250.

CAMPTON-BURNETT, Ivy. *Dolores.* Cloth. Edinburgh, 1911. First edition. $750–$1,000. Author's first book (suppressed by her).

COMPTON-BURNETT, Ivy. *Pastors and Masters.* Cloth. London, 1925. First edition. In dust jacket. $75–$100.

CONARD, Howard Louis. *"Uncle Dick" Wootton, the Pioneer Frontiersman of the Rocky Mountain Region.* Portrait, 31 plates. Decorated cloth, or leather and cloth. Chicago, 1890. First edition. $150–$200.

CONCLIN, George. *Conclin's New River Guide, or a Gazeteer of All the Towns on the Western Waters.* 44 full-page route maps. 128 pp., wrappers. Cincinnati, 1850. $100–$150. Cincinnati, 1853. $100–$150.

CONFEDERATE Receipt Book. Wrappers. Richmond, 1863. First edition. $300–$500.

CONFESSIONS of an English Opium-Eater. Boards, paper label. London, 1822. (By Thomas De Quincey.) First edition, first issue, with ad leaf at end. $1,000–$1,500. Second issue, lacking ad leaf: Boards, $750–$1,000. Rebacked copy, issue not stated, $600. Philadelphia, 1823. Boards, paper label. First American edition. $400–$450. London, 1885. Morocco. One of 50 large paper copies. $200. New York, 1930. Limited Editions Club. Boards. Boxed. $75–$100.

CONFESSIONS of Harry Lorrequer (The). Illustrated by Phiz. 11 parts, pictorial pink wrappers. Dublin, 1839. (By Charles Lever.) First edition. $400–$600. Another issue: Cloth. First edition in book form. $300–$400. Author's first book.

CONGREVE, William. *The Complete Works of William Congreve,* Edited by Montague Summers. 4 vols., boards and cloth. London, 1923, Nonesuch Press. One of 825. $150–$200. Another issue: Boards and vellum. One of 75 on handmade paper. $300–$400.

CONKLIN, E. *Picturesque Arizona.* Illustrated. Green cloth. New York, 1878. First edition. $175.

CONNELLEY, William E. *Quantrill and the Border Wars.* Illustrated. Red buckram. Cedar Rapids, Iowa, 1910. First edition. $75–$125.

CONNELLEY, William E. *The War with Mexico, 1846–47; Doniphan's Expedition.* 2 maps, illustrations. Cloth. Topeka, 1907. First edition. $125–$150.

CONNELLEY, William E. *Wild Bill and His Era*. 12 plates. Cloth. New York, 1933. First edition. In dust jacket. $75–$85.

CONNELLEY, Marc. *The Green Pastures*. Illustrated in color by Robert Edmond Jones. Green boards. New York, 1930. One of 550 signed. Boxed. $100–$150. Some signed copies issued in morocco: $150–$200. Trade edition: Green cloth. In dust jacket. $65.

CONNETT, Eugene V. *Magic Hours*. 2 mounted plates by the author. 20 pp., gray boards, paper label. New York, 1927. Derrydale Press. First edition. One of 100. $7,400 (A, 1980). (First Derrydale Press book.)

CONNETT, Eugene V. (editor). *American Big Game Fishing*. Illustrated, including color plates. New York, (1935). Derrydale Press. First edition. One of 4,850. In dust jacket. Boxed. $400.

CONNETT, Eugene V. (editor). *Upland Game Bird Shooting in America*. Illustrated, including color plates. Pictorial cloth. New York, 1930. Derrydale Press. First edition. One of 850. $600–$1,000. Another issue: Brown morocco. One of 75 with 6 original signed etchings. $3,000–$3,500.

CONNICK, Charles J. *Adventures in Light and Color*. Color plates and collotype plates. Buckram. New York, (1937). First edition. De luxe issue, with 42 plates in color, 48 in collotype. $250–$400. Trade issue: 36 colored plates. Cloth. $200. London, 1937. 36 color plates, 48 in collotype. Cloth. First English edition. $100–$150. (Note: Contains the first printing of Robert Frost's poem "Unless I Call It a Pewter Tray.")

CONNOLLY, A.P. *A Thrilling Narrative of the Minnesota Massacre and the Sioux War of 1862–1863*. Illustrated. Cloth. Chicago, (1896). First edition. $150–$200.

CONNOLLY, Cyril. See Palinurus.

CONNOLLY. Cyril. *The Rock Pool*. Wrappers. Paris, (1936). Obelisk Press. First edition. $250–$350. Author's first book.

CONOVER, George W. *Sixty Years in Southwest Oklahoma*. Illustated. Cloth. Andarko, 1927. First edition. $75–$100.

CONRAD, Joseph. See anonymous entry *The Nigger of the "Narcissus," Preface*. (Under N.)

CONRAD, Joseph. *"Admiralty Paper."* Facsimile plate. Blue wrappers. (New York, 1925.) First edition. One of 93. $200–$300.

CONRAD, Joseph. *Almayer's Folly: A Story of an Eastern River*. Dark-green cloth. London, 1895. First edition, first issue, with first "e" missing in "generosity" in the second line from last on page 110. $500–$600. "Colonial" edition, same place and date, $300–$400. New York, 1895. Cloth. First American edition. $350–$450. Author's first book.

CONRAD, Joseph. *The Arrow of Gold: A Story Between Two Notes*. Dark-blue cloth. Garden City, 1919. First edition, first issue, with the reading "credentials and apparently" in line 16 of page 5. In dust jacket. $350–$400. Second issue ("credentials and who"): In dust jacket. $200–$250. London, (1919). Dark-green cloth. First English edition, first issue, with running head intact on page 67. In dust jacket. $150–$200. Second issue, with "A" missing in "Arrow" in headline on page 67. In dust jacket. $75–$125.

CONRAD, Joseph. *The Black Mate*. Green cloth. (Edinburgh), 1922. First edition. One of 50. $400–$600.

CONRAD, Joseph, *Chance: A Tale in Two Parts*. Sage-green cloth. London, (1913). First edition, first issue, with "First published in 1913" on verso of integral title page. In dust jacket, $1,500–$2,000. Also $1,300 (A, 1976) and, with a letter from Thomas J. Wise laid in, $1,700 (A, 1977). Second impression and/or third impression, with tipped-in "1913" title page. $250. Later issue, with tipped in title page bearing 1914 date on verso: $150–$200. Garden City, 1913. Dark blue cloth. First American edition.

One of 150 issued for copyright purposes. $750 and up. Also, $572 (A, 1979). New York, 1914. Cloth. First published American edition. In dust jacket. $75–$125.

CONRAD, Joseph. *The Children of the Sea.* Mottled blue-gray cloth. New York, 1897. First edition (of the book published in England as *The Nigger of the "Narcissus").* $300–$400.

CONRAD, Joseph. *The Dover Patrol.* Light-blue wrappers. Canterbury, 1922. First edition, first issue, without title page. One of 75. $200–$275.

CONRAD, Joseph. *Joseph Conrad's Letters to His Wife.* Limp imitation leather. London, 1927. First edition. One of 220 signed by Jessie Conrad. $150–$200.

CONRAD, Joseph. *Last Essays.* Green cloth. London, 1926. First edition. In dust jacket. $100–$125.

CONRAD, Joseph. *Laughing Anne: A Play.* Full vellum, gilt top, uncut. London, 1923. First edition. One of 200 signed. Boxed. $250–$300.

CONRAD, Joseph. *Letters from Joseph Conrad to Richard Curle.* Boards and cloth. New York, 1928. First edition. One of 850. $100–$150. Another issue: Black cloth. One of 9 on green paper, $300–$350.

CONRAD, Joseph. *Life and Letters.* 2 vols., dark blue cloth. London, 1927. First edition. $100–$125. Garden City, 1927. Illustrated. First American edition. In dust jacket. $75–$100.

CONRAD, Joseph. *Lord Jim.* Gray-green cloth. Edinburgh, 1900. First edition. $200–$300.

CONRAD, Joseph. *The Mirror of the Sea; Memories and Impressions.* Light green cloth. London, (1906). First edition, with 40 pages of ads dated August, 1906. $175–$225. New York, 1906. Blue cloth. First American edition. In dust jacket. $100.

CONRAD, Joseph. *The Nigger of the "Narcissus."* Gray cloth. London, 1898. First published English edition (of *The Children of the Sea*). $300–$400. (A copyright issue of about 7 copies was published in London, 1897, in wrappers. An inscribed copy of this book sold for $4,900 in 1928). New York, 1965. Limited Editions Club. Boxed. $50–$65. (Also, see title entry, anonymous.)

CONRAD, Joseph. *Nostromo: A Tale of the Seaboard.* Bright blue cloth. London, 1904. First edition, first issue, with 7 preliminary leaves and 478 pages of text. $225–$250. Second issue, with 8 preliminary leaves and 480 pages of text: $150–$175. New York, 1904. Green cloth. First American edition. $75–$100. New York, 1961. Limited Editions Club. Boxed. $50.

CONRAD, Joseph. *Notes by Joseph Conrad in a Set of His First Editions in the Possession of Richard Curle.* Buckram, paper label. London, 1925. First edition. One of 100 signed by Curle. $100–$125.

CONRAD, Joseph, *Notes on Life and Letters.* Green cloth. London, 1921. First edition, first issue, with "S" and "A" missing from the word "Sea" in "Tales of the Sea" in table of contents. One of 33 privately printed. In dust jacket. $500–$600. Also, presentation copy, $280 (A, 1968). First trade edition, with same errors in contents page: In dust jacket. $100–$125. Second issue, with "S" and "A" put in by hand press: In dust jacket. $75. Third issue, page reprinted: In dust jacket. $50.

CONRAD, Joseph, *Notes on My Books.* Boards, parchment spine, paper labels. London, 1921. First English edition. One of 250 signed. In dust jacket. $250–$300.

CONRAD, Joseph. *One Day More: A Play in One Act.* Blue wrappers. London, 1917. First edition. One of 25 signed by Clement Shorter, who had it printed privately. $750. Another copy, signed by Conrad, $1,000. London, (1919). Beaumont Press. Boards. First published edition. One of 24 on vellum. $750, or more. Another issue: One of 250. $200–$250. Garden City, 1910. Boards. First American edition. One of 250 signed. In dust jacket. $200–$250.

CONRAD, Joseph. *An Outcast of the Islands.* Dark-green cloth, top edges gilt. London, 1896. First edition, first issue, with "this" for "there" in fourth line from last on page 26 and "absolution" for "ablution" in line 12 of page 110. $275–$350. New York, 1896. Wrappers and cloth. First American edition. Wrappers: $450. Cloth: $200–$250.

CONRAD, Joseph. *The Point of Honor: A Military Tale.* Illustrated by Dan Sayre Groesbeck. Decorated cloth. New York, 1908. First edition, first state, with "McClure" at base of spine. $150–$250.

CONRAD, Joseph. *The Rescue: A Romance of the Shallows.* Dark-blue cloth. Garden City, 1920. First edition. In dust jacket. $150–$200. London, 1920. Flexible red cloth (text differing from other editions). First English edition, first issue. One of 40 privately printed advance copies. $400–$500. London, 1920. Green cloth. First published English edition. In dust jacket. $150–$200.

CONRAD, Joseph. *The Rover.* Green cloth. London, (1923). First edition. In dust jacket. $150–$175. Garden City, 1923. Boards. First American edition. One of 377 signed. In dust jacket. Boxed. $400–$500. Trade edition: Cloth. In dust jacket. $100–$175. Toronto, 1923. Cloth. First Canadian edition. $150–$175.

CONRAD, Joseph. *The Secret Agent: A Drama in Three Acts.* Portrait frontispiece. Boards and parchment. London, 1923. First edition. One of 1,000 signed. In dust jacket. $300–$400. Trade edition: Cloth. First issue, with misprint on page 117 and with 40 pages of ads at end. In dust jacket. $125–$175.

CONRAD, Joseph. *The Secret Agent: A Simple Tale.* Red cloth. London, (1907). First edition, with September ads at end. $200–$250.

CONRAD, Joseph. *A Set of Six.* Blue cloth. London, (1908). First edition, first issue, with ads dated February, 1908. $200–$250. Second issue, with ads dated June, 1908: $150–$200.

CONRAD, Joseph. *The Shadow-Line: A Confession.* Pale-green cloth. London, (1917). First edition, first issue, with 18 pages of ads at end. In dust jacket. $200–$250.

CONRAD, Joseph. *Some Reminiscences.* Yellow wrappers. New York, 1908. First edition (advance issue for copyright purposes). One of about 6 copies. $2,000 or more. London, 1912. Dark-blue cloth. First published edition. In dust jacket. $125–$175.

CONRAD, Joseph. *Suspense.* Boards. Garden City, 1925. First edition. One of 377. In tissue and paper dust jacket. $150–$225. Trade edition: Cloth. In dust jacket. $150–$275. London, 1925. Dark-red cloth. First English edition. In dust jacket. $150–$275.

CONRAD, Joseph. *Tales of Hearsay.* Dark-green cloth. London, (1925). First edition. In dust jacket. $125–$175. Garden City, 1925. Dark-blue cloth. First American edition. In dust jacket. $150–$175.

CONRAD, Joseph. *Tales of the Sea.* Pale green wrappers. London, 1919. First edition. One of 25. $1,000–$1,250.

CONRAD, Joseph. *Tales of Unrest.* Brown cloth. New York, 1898. First edition. $250–$300. London, 1898. Dark green cloth. First English edition, first issue, with all edges untrimmed. $200–$250.

CONRAD, Joseph. *'Twixt Land and Sea Tales.* Olive-green cloth. London, 1912. First edition, first issue, with misprint "Secret" instead of "Seven" on front cover. In dust jacket. $750 and up. Second issue, with "Seven" stamped over erased word "Secret": In dust jacket. $200–$250.

CONRAD, Joseph. *Typhoon.* Illustrated. Dark-green cloth. New York, 1902. First edition, first issue, with 4 pages of ads. In dust jacket. $200–$250. Without jackets, $75–$100. London, 1903. Dark-gray cloth. First English edition, first issue, with windmill device and without "Reserved for the Colonies only" on verso of half title. In dust jacket. $200–$250. Without jacket, $85–$125.

CONRAD, Joseph. *Under Western Eyes.* Red cloth. London, (1911). First edition, first issue, with ads dated September, 1911. In dust jacket. $200–$250.

CONRAD, Joseph. *Victory: An Island Tale.* Dark blue cloth. Garden City, 1915. First edition. In dust jacket. $200–$250. London, (1915). Red cloth, with 35 pages of ads at back and "Author's Note," which is not in the American edition. First English edition. In dust jacket. $150–$175.

CONRAD, Joseph. *Within the Tides: Tales.* Sage-green cloth. London, 1915. First edition. In dust jacket. $300–$400.

CONRAD Joseph. *Youth: A Narrative and Two Other Stories.* Light-green cloth. Edinburgh, 1902. First edition, first issue, with ads dated "10/02" at end. In dust jacket. $300–$400. Without jacket, $100–$125. Kentfield, Calif., (1959). Allen Press. Illustrated. Boards. One of 140. Boxed. $600–$750.

CONRAD, Joseph, and Hueffer, Ford M. *The Inheritors: An Extravagant Story.* Pictorial yellow cloth. New York, 1901. First edition, first issue, with the dedication leaf reading "To Boys and Christina." Only a few copies known. $1,000 and up. First published edition, with a corrected dedication, on a stub: "To Borys and Christina": $150–$200. London, 1901. Yellow cloth. First English edition, first issue, without dedication leaf. $150–$200.

CONRAD, Joseph, and Hueffer, Ford M. *Romance: A Novel.* Bright-blue cloth. London, 1903. First edition, with 8 pages of ads at end. In dust jacket. $250–$350. New York, 1904. Cloth. First American edition. In dust jacket. $100–$150.

CONRAD, Capt. Thomas Nelson. *The Rebel Scout.* Cloth. Washington, 1904. First edition. $75–$100.

CONROY, Jack. *The Disinherited.* Cloth. (New York, 1933.) First edition. In dust jacket. $125–$150. Author's first book.

CONSIDERANT, Victor. *European Colonization in Texas.* 38 pp., wrappers. New York, 1855. First edition. $350–$750.

CONSTABLE, Henry. *Poems and Sonnets.* Woodcut border, ornamental woodcut initials. White pigskin. London, 1897. One of 210. $100–$150.

CONSTITUTION and Laws of the Cherokee Nation. Leather. St. Louis, 1875. $350–$400.

CONSTITUTION and Laws of the Muskogee Nation. Sheep. St. Louis, 1880. $200–$250.

CONSTITUTION and Playing Rules of the International Baseball Association . . . and Championship Record for 1877. 77 pp., wrappers, Jamaica Plain, Mass., 1878. $100–$150.

CONSTITUTION and Rules of Business of the Essex Western Emigration Co. 8 pp., wrappers. Lawrence, 1856. $125–$150.

CONSTITUTION of the Confederate States of America. Leather. Montgomery, 1861. Rebacked copy, $650 (A, 1977).

CONSTITUTION of the Republic of Mexico and the State of Coahuila and Texas (The). Half calf. New York, 1832. $1,000–$1,500.

CONSTITUTION of the State of Sequoyah. Folding map in color. 67 pp., self-wrappers. (Muscogee, Indian Territory, 1905.) First edition, with last page numbered. $3,500–$4,000. Second edition, same date, no page number on last page. $3,000.

CONSTITUTION of the State of West Texas. (Cover title.) 35 pp., wrappers. Austin, (1868). First edition. $600.

CONSTITUTION of the U.S.A. . . . Also, an Act to Establish a Territorial Government for Utah. 48 pp., sewed. Salt Lake City, 1852. $750–$1,000.

CONTACT Collection of Contemporary Writers. Edited by Robert McAlmon. Wrappers. (Paris, 1925.) Contact Editions. One of 300. $500–$600. (Contains work by Ernest Hemingway, James Joyce, Ezra Pound, Gertrude Stein, William Carlos Williams, and others.)

CONWAY, Moncure D. *Barons of the Potomack and Rappahannock.* Illustrated. Boards. New York, 1892. Grolier Club. First edition. One of 360. $50–$100.

CONWAY, Moncure D. *The Life of Thomas Paine.* Frontispiece. 2 vols., cloth. New York, 1892. First edition. $50–$75.

COOK, D.J. *Hands Up, or 20 Years of Detective Life in the Mountains and on the Plains.* 32 plates. Wrappers. Denver, 1882. First edition. $250–$300. Cloth, same date, later issue: $200–$250. Denver, 1897. Second edition, enlarged, with *20 Years* changed to *35 Years* in title. $50–$60.

COOK, Frederick A. *My Attainment of the Pole.* Illustrated. Cloth. New York, 1911. First edition. $75–$100.

COOK, James H. *Fifty Years on the Old Frontier.* Plates. Cloth. New Haven, 1923. First edition. In dust jacket. $50–$75. Lacking jacket, $35.

COOK, John R. *The Border and the Buffalo.* Plates. Pictorial cloth. Topeka, 1907. First edition. $40–$60.

COOKE, John (editor). *The Dublin Book of Irish Verse.* Dark-green limp leather. Dublin, 1909. First edition. $100. Another issue: Cloth. $50–$60. (Note: Contains three poems by James Joyce.)

COOKE, John Esten. See Effingham, C. Also see *Leather Stocking and Silk; The Life of Stonewall Jackson.*

COOKE, John Esten. *A Life of General Robert E. Lee.* Cloth. New York, 1871. First edition. $75–$100.

COOKE, John Esten. *Surry of Eagle's Nest.* Illustrated by Winslow Homer. Cloth. New York, 1866. First edition, with Bunce and Huntington imprint. $100–$125.

COOKE, Philip St. George. *The Conquest of New Mexico and California.* Folding map. Cloth. New York, 1878. First edition. $150–$250.

COOKE, Philip St. George. *Scenes and Adventures in the Army.* Cloth. Philadelphia, 1857. First edition. $350–$400.

COON, James Churchill. *Log of the Cruise of 1889 D.T.S.C., New Smyrna to Lake Worth, East Coast of Florida.* 119 pp., printed wrappers. Lake Helen, Fla., 1889. First edition. $100–$150.

COOPER, J. W. *Game Fowls, Their Origin and History.* Colored lithographs. Pictorial green cloth, gilt, West Chester, Pa., (1869). $150–$200.

COOPER, James Fenimore. See *The Bee-Hunter; The Borderers; The Bravo; The Chainbearer; The Deerslayer; The Headsman; The Heidenmauer; Home as Found; The Last of the Mohicans; Lionel Lincoln; The Monikins; The Pathfinder; The Pilot; The Pioneers; The Prairie; Precaution; Ravensnest; The Red Rover; The Redskins; Satanstoe; The Spy; The Two Admirals; The Water Witch; The Wept of Wish Ton-Wish; The Wing-and-Wing; Wyandotte.*

COOPER, James Fenimore. *The American Democrat.* Green cloth. Cooperstown, 1839. First edition. $375.

COOPER, James Fenimore. *The Battle of Lake Erie.* Printed wrappers. Cooperstown, N.Y., 1843. First edition. $400–$600.

COOPER, James Fenimore. *The History of the Navy of the United States of America.* Maps. 2 vols., cloth. Philadelphia, 1839. First edition. $150–$250. London, 1839. 2

vols., cloth. First English edition. $200–$250. Paris, 1839. 2 vols. in one, half leather. $100–$150.

COOPER, James Fenimore. *The Jack O'Lantern.* 3 vols., drab brown boards, purple cloth, paper spine labels. London, 1842. First edition (of the novel issued anonymously in America as *The Wing-and-Wing*, which see as title entry). $600–$800.

COOPER, James Fenimore. *Lives of Distinguished American Naval Officers.* 2 vols., cloth, or 2 vols., printed blue wrappers. Philadelphia, 1846. First edition. Cloth: $400–$450. Wrappers: $500–$600.

COOPER, James Fenimore. *Notions of the Americans.* 2 vols., boards, paper labels. London, 1828. First edition. $400–$500. Philadelphia, 1828. 2 vols., boards, paper labels. First American edition. $350–$450.

COOPER, Thomas. *On Irritation and Insanity.* 2 portraits. Boards. London, 1833. $150.

COOVER, Robert. *The Origin of the Brunists.* Wrappers. New York, (1966). First edition, advance copy. $250–$350. Regular edition: Boards. In dust jacket. $100–$150. London, 1967. First English edition. In dust jacket. $75. Author's first book.

COOVER, Robert. *A Theological Position.* Cloth. New York, 1972. First edition. In dust jacket. $40–$60.

COOVER, Robert. *The Universal Baseball Association, J. Henry Waugh, Proprietor.* Boards. New York, (1968). First edition. In dust jacket. $75–$85. London, (1970). First English edition. $30.

COPLAND, Robert (translator). *The History of Helyas Knight of the Swan.* Illustrated. Pigskin. New York, 1901. Grolier Club. One of 325. $150–$200.

COPPARD, A.E. *Adam and Eve and Pinch Me.* White buckram. Waltham Saint Lawrence, 1921. Golden Cockerel Press. First edition. One of 160 (from an edition of 500). $100–$125. Another issue: Orange boards. One of 340. $150. New York, 1922. Boards and cloth. First American edition. $35–$50.

COPPARD, A.E. *The Black Dog.* Boards and cloth. London, 1923. First edition. $50–$75.

COPPARD, A.E. *Cherry Ripe: Poems.* Illustrated. Full purple and green morocco. (Monmouthshire, England), 1935. Tintern Press. One of 10 signed. $200–$250. Another issue: One of 150. $75–$125.

COPPARD, A. E. *Pink Furniture.* Illustrated. Vellum. London, 1930. First edition. One of 260 signed. In dust jacket. $75–$100.

COPPARD, A.E. *Silver Circus.* Full vellum. (London, 1928.) First edition. One of 125 signed. $75–$100.

COPPARD, A.E. *Yokohama Garland and Other Poems.* Illustrated. Boards and buckram. Philadelphia, (1926). Centaur Press. First edition. One of 500 signed. Boxed. $75–$100.

CORELLI, Marie. *Barabbas.* 3 vols., cloth. London, (1893). First edition. $150–$175.

CORELLI, Marie. *The Mighty Atom.* Cloth. London, 1896. First edition. $150–$175.

CORELLI, Marie. *Ziska: The Problem of a Wicked Soul.* Cloth. Bristol, England, 1897. First edition. $75–$125.

CORNER, William. *San Antonio de Bexar.* Map, 16 plates. Cloth. San Antonio, 1890. First edition. $75–$100.

CORNFORD, Frances. *Autumn Midnight.* Woodcuts by Eric Gill. Wrappers. London, 1923. First edition. $125–$150.

CORNWALL, Bruce. *Life Sketch of Pierre Barlow Cornwall.* 6 portraits. Boards. San Francisco, 1906. First edition. $200–$250.

CORRILL, John. *A Brief History of the Church of Christ of Latter Day Saints.* 50 pp., sewed. St. Louis, 1839. First edition. $5,000 and up.

CORSO, Gregory. *Ankh.* Oblong, magenta wrappers. New York, 1971. First edition. One of 100 signed. $50–$75.

CORSO, Gregory. *Gasoline.* Wrappers. San Francisco, (1958). City Lights Books. First edition. $50–$60.

CORSO, Gregory. *10 Times a Poem.* Flexible pictorial boards. No place, 1971. First edition. One of 20 signed, with holograph poem on colophon page. $125–$150.

CORSO, Gregory. *The Vestal Lady on Brattle and Other Poems.* Printed wrappers. Cambridge, Mass., 1955. First edition. $150–$200. Author's first book. (250 copies.)

CORVO, Baron (Frederick William Rolfe). See Rolfe, Fr. Also see *Tarcissus.*

CORVO, Baron. *Chronicles of the House of Borgia.* 10 plates. Pictorial red buckram. London, 1901. (By Frederick William Rolfe.) First edition. $250–$300. New York, 1901. Dark red or black cloth. First American edition. $150–$200.

CORVO, Baron. *The Desire and Pursuit of the Whole.* Veridian (dark green) cloth. London, (1934). (By Frederick William Rolfe.) First edition, first binding. In dust jacket. $125–$150. London, (1953). Cloth. In dust jacket. $25.

CORVO, Baron. *In His Own Image.* Blue-gray cloth. London, 1901. (By Frederick William Rolfe.) First edition, with ad leaf. $225–$300. Variant issue: Red cloth, with "Bodley Head" imprint on spine, instead of "John Lane." $237 in a 1975 catalogue.

CORVO, Baron. *Letters to Grant Richards.* Boards. (Hurst, England, 1952.) (By Frederick William Rolfe.) Peacocks Press. First edition. One of 200. $150–$200.

CORVO, Baron. *Stories Toto Told Me.* Printed green wrappers. London, 1898. (By Frederick William Rolfe.) First edition. No. 6 of the Bodley Booklets. $300–$400.

COSSLEY-BATT, Jill L. *The Last of the California Rangers.* Illustrated. Three-quarters green morocco. New York, 1928. First edition. One of 200 signed. $75–$100. Trade edition: Cloth. In dust jacket. $30.

COSTAIN, Thomas B. *The Silver Chalice.* Cloth. Garden City, 1952. First edition. One of 750 signed. Boxed. $40–$50. Trade edition: In dust jacket. $10–15.

COSTAIN, Thomas B. *The White and the Gold.* Cloth. Garden City, 1954. First edition. One of 250 signed, with a page of the manuscript tipped in. Boxed. $50–$60. Trade edition: In dust jacket. $10–$15.

COSTANSO, Miguel. *The Spanish Occupation of California.* Portraits, folding maps. Boards. San Francisco, 1934. One of 550. In slipcase. $150.

COTTEN, Bruce. *Housed on the Third Floor, Being a Collection of North Caroliniana.* 100 facsimiles of title pages. Cloth. Baltimore, 1941. First edition. $325.

COUES, Elliott (editor). *New Light on the Early History of the Greater Northwest.* Frontispiece, facsimile, 3 maps in pocket of Vol. 3. 3 vols., cloth. New York, 1897. One of 1,000. $200–$250. Another issue: Half vellum. One of 100 on large paper. $300–$400.

COULTER, E. Merton. *Travels in the Confederate States: A Bibliography.* Cloth. Norman, Okla., 1948. First edition. In dust jacket. $75.

COUNT Julian; or, the Last Days of the Goth. Cloth. Baltimore, 1845. (By William Gilmore Simms.) First edition. $200–$250.

COUNT Julian: A Tragedy. Boards, printed label. London, 1812. (By Walter Savage Landor.) First edition. $300–$400.

COURSEY, O.W. *"Wild Bill" (James Butler Hickok).* Illustrated. Cloth. Mitchell, S.D., (1924). First edition. $50–$60.

COURTAULD, George. *Address to Those Who May Be Disposed to Remove to the United States of America.* 40 pp., wrappers. Sudbury, 1820. First edition. $1,250.

COUTS, Cave J. *From San Diego to the Colorado in 1849.* 3 maps on 2 sheets. Boards. Los Angeles, 1932. First edition. $100–$125.

COUTS, Joseph. *A Practical Guide for the Tailor's Cutting Room.* 13 colored plates, 14 uncolored. Half morocco. London, (1848). $300–$400.

COWAN, Robert E. *A Bibliography of the History of California and the Pacific West, 1510–1906.* Boards and linen. San Francisco, 1914. First edition. One of 250. Boxed. $300–$400. San Francisco, 1933. 3 vols., boards and cloth. $300–$400.

COWARD, Noel. *"I'll Leave It to You."* Wrappers, London, 1920. First edition. $100. Author's first book(?).

COWLEY, Malcolm. *Blue Juniata: Poems.* Cloth. New York, (1929). First edition. $100–$150.

COWLEY, Malcolm. *Racine.* Wrappers. Paris, 1923. First edition. $100–$150. Author's first book.

COX, Isaac. *The Annals of Trinity County.* Half cloth. San Francisco, 1940. John Henry Nash printing. One of 350. Boxed. $50–$75.

COX, James. *Historical and Biographical Record of the Cattle Industry and the Cattlemen of Texas and Adjacent Territory.* Colored frontispiece, other illustrations. Decorated leather. St. Louis, 1895. First edition. $3,000–$4,000, possibly more. New York, 1959. 2 vols., half leather, Boxed. One of 500. $100–$150.

COX, Nicholas. *The Gentleman's Recreation.* London, 1928. Cresset Press. One of 600. $150–$175. Another issue: One of 50. $300–$350.

COX, Palmer. *The Brownies Around the World.* Illustrated. Cloth. New York, (1894). First edition. $125–$175. (Worn copies much less, of course, as with all much-read juvenile books.)

COX, Palmer. *The Brownies at Home.* Pictorial boards. New York, (1893). First edition. In dust jacket. $125–$150. Worn and rubbed, $75.

COX, Palmer. *The Brownies: Their Book.* Green glazed pictorial boards. New York, (1887). First edition, first issue, with DeVinne Press seal immediately below copyright notice. In dust jacket. $500–$750. Second issue, with seal about 2½ inches from bottom of page. In dust jacket. $400–$500. (Worn copies less.)

COX, Palmer. *Queer People with Wings and Stings and Their Kweer Kapers.* Pictorial boards. Philadelphia, (1888). First edition. $75–$125. Worn and rubbed, $35.

COX, Palmer. *Queerie Queers with Hands, Wings and Claws.* Pictorial boards. Buffalo, ("about 1887"). First edition. $75–$150. Worn, $40.

COX, Ross. *Adventures on the Columbia River.* 2 vols., boards. London, 1831. First edition. $750–$1,000. New York, 1832. Cloth or boards. First American edition. $350–$500.

COX, Sandford C. *Recollections of the Early Settlement of the Wabash Valley.* Cloth. Lafayette, Ind., 1860. First edition. $100–$125.

COXE, Louis O. *The Sea Faring and Other Poems.* Cloth. New York, (1947). First edition. In dust jacket. $50–$60. Author's first book.

COY, Owen C. *Pictorial History of California*. 261 photographs. Cloth. Berkeley, 1925. $100.

COYNER, David H. *The Lost Trappers*. Cloth. Cincinnati, 1847. First edition. $300–$400. Cincinnati, 1850. Cloth. Second edition. $150–$200.

COZZENS, Frederick S. *Acadia*. 2 plates. Cloth. New York, 1859. First edition. $75–$85.

COZZENS, James Gould. *By Love Possessed*. Cloth. New York, (1957). First edition. In dust jacket. $35–$50.

COZZENS, James Gould. *Cock Pit*. Cloth. New York, 1928. First edition. In dust jacket. $100–$125.

COZZENS, James Gould. *Confusion*. Cloth. Boston, 1924. First edition. In dust jacket. $125–$150. Author's first book.

CRABBE, George. *The Borough: A Poem*. Boards, printed label. London, 1810. First edition. $150–$250.

CRABBE, George. *Tales of the Hall*. 2 vols., boards. London, 1819. First edition. $200–$300.

CRAIG, Edward Gordon. *Ellen Terry and Her Secret Self*. White cloth. London, 1931. First edition. One of 256 signed. Boxed. $300–$400.

CRAIG, John R. *Ranching with Lords and Commons*. 17 plates. Pictorial cloth. Toronto, (1903). First edition. $200–$300.

CRAIK, Dinah M. See *The Adventures of a Brownie; The Fairy Book; John Halifax, Gentleman*.

CRAKES, Sylvester. *Five Years a Captive Among the Black-Feet Indians*. 6 plates. Cloth. Columbus, Ohio, 1858. First edition. $300–$350.

CRAM, Ralph Adams. *Ruined Abbeys of Great Britain*. Full calf. Boston, 1927. One of 350 signed. $200.

CRANCH, Christopher Pearse. *Giant Hunting: or, Little Jacket's Adventures*. Illustrated. Pictorial cloth. Boston, 1860. $100–$125.

CRANCH, Christopher Pearse. *Kobboltozo*. Illustrated by the author. Cloth. Boston, 1857. First edition. $100–$125.

CRANCH, Christopher Pearse. *The Last of the Huggermuggers*. Illustrated. Cloth. Boston, 1856. First edition. $125–$150.

CRANE, Hart. See *The Pagan Anthology*.

CRANE, Hart. *The Bridge*. 3 photographs by Walker Evans. Stiff printed wrappers. Paris, 1930. Black Sun Press. First edition. One of 200, (weighing 19¼ ounces each). In glassine dust jacket. Boxed. $1,000–$1,250. Also, $750 (A, 1977). Also, 20 (or 25?) advance copies not for sale, on thin paper and weighing 15¼ ounces each. $1,500–$2,000. Another issue: One of 50 on Japan vellum; signed. In glassine dust jacket and slipcase. $2,000–$2,500. Also, $1,800 (A, 1977). Also, 8 lettered copies on vellum, signed by the poet. $3,500–$5,000. New York, (1930). Cloth. First American edition. In dust jacket. $150–$200.

CRANE, Hart. *The Collected Poems of Hart Crane*. Edited by Waldo Frank. Portrait frontispiece. Red cloth. New York, (1933). First edition, first issue, with flat spine and imprint of "Liveright Inc., Publishers." In dust jacket. $100–$150. Second issue, with rounded spine and imprint of "Liveright Publishing Corporation": In dust jacket. $50–$75. Another issue: Brown cloth. One of 50 "for friends." $350–$500.

CRANE, Hart. *Two Letters*. Leaflet, 4 pp. Brooklyn Heights, 1934. First edition. One of 50. $350–$450.

CRANE, Hart. *Voyages.* Illustrated by Leonard Baskin. Oblong, wrappers in board folder. New York, 1957. First edition. One of 975. $300–$400.

CRANE, Hart. *White Buildings.* Foreword by Allen Tate. Boards, cloth spine. (New York), 1926. First edition, first issue, with Tate's first name misspelled "Allan." In dust jacket. $1,000–$1,250. Second issue, with tipped-in title page, Tate's name spelled correctly: In dust jacket. $275–$375. Lacking jacket, $100–$150. Author's first book.

CRANE, Stephen. See Smith, Johnston. Also see *The Lanthorn Book; Pike County Puzzle.*

CRANE, Stephen. *Active Service.* Light-green cloth. New York, (1899). First edition. In dust jacket. $150–$200. London, 1899. Cloth. First English edition. $75–$100.

CRANE, Stephen. *The Black Riders and Other Lines.* Yellow cloth or gray decorated boards. Boston, 1895. First edition. (500 copies.) $350–$400. Another issue: Plain boards, paper label. One of 50 printed in green ink on vellum. No copies noted for sale in recent years. Estimated value: $1,000 and up. (Note: Johnson reports three copies of this issue were said to have been bound in full vellum.)

CRANE, Stephen. *The Collected Poems of Stephen Crane.* Edited by Wilson Follett. Cloth. New York, (1930). First edition. In dust jacket. $50–$60.

CRANE, Stephen. *George's Mother.* Tan cloth. New York, 1896. First edition. $50–$75. London, 1896. Cloth. $40–$60.

CRANE, Stephen. *Great Battles of the World.* Illustrated by John Sloan. Red cloth. Philadelphia, 1901. First edition. $85–$125. London, 1901. Cloth. $50–$75.

CRANE, Stephen. *Last Words.* Red cloth. London, 1902. First edition. $150–$200.

CRANE, Stephen. *Legends.* 4 pp., printed buff wrappers. Ysleta, Tex., 1942. First edition. One of 45. $150–$200.

CRANE, Stephen. *The Little Regiment and Other Episodes of the American Civil War.* Cream-yellow buckram. New York, 1896. First edition, first state, with 6 pages of ads at the back, the first page headed "Gilbert Parker's Best Books." In dust jacket. $300–$400. Without jacket, $75–$125. London, 1897. Cloth. First English edition. $50–$75.

CRANE, Stephen. *A Lost Poem.* Wrappers. New York, (1932). First edition. One of 100. $50–$60.

CRANE, Stephen. *Maggie: A Girl of the Streets.* Cream-yellow buckram. New York, 1896. Second (revised) edition, first state, with title page printed in capital and lower case Roman type, according to Jacob Blanck. $250–$350. Second state, capital letters only. $100–$150. London, 1896. First English (revised) edition. $200. (For first edition, see Johnston Smith, *Maggie: A Girl of the Streets.*)

CRANE, Stephen. *The Monster and Other Stories.* Illustrated. Red cloth. New York, 1899. First edition. $200–$250. London, 1901. Revised edition, with four stories added. $100–$150. (No American edition of this revision recorded.)

CRANE, Stephen. *The Open Boat and Other Tales of Adventure.* Dark-green pictorial cloth. New York, 1898. First American edition. In dust jacket. $300–$350. Also, $170 (A, 1976). Without jacket, $100. London, 1898. First English edition, with nine added stories. $100–$125.

CRANE, Stephen. *The Red Badge of Courage.* Cream-yellow buckram. New York, 1895. First edition, first state, with perfect type in the last line on page 225. In dust jacket. $1,000 and up. Lacking jacket, $500–$750. New York, 1896. Cloth. $75–$100. New York, (1931). Grabhorn printing. Illustrated by Valenti Angelo. Boards. One of 980. $75–$150. New York, 1944. Limited Editions Club. Illustrated. Embossed morocco. Boxed. $85–$125.

CRANE, Stephen. *The Third Violet*. Cream-yellow buckram. New York, 1897. First edition. $150–$200. London, 1897. Cloth. First English edition. $100.

CRANE, Stephen. *War Is Kind*. Illustrated by Will Bradley. Pictorial gray boards. New York, 1899. First edition. $500–$600. Also, $300 (A, 1977).

CRANE, Stephen. *Whilomville Stories*. Illustrated by Peter Newell. Light-green cloth. New York, 1900. First edition. $75–$125. London, 1900. Blue cloth. First English edition. $75–$85.

CRANE, Stephen. *Wounds in the Rain*. Cloth. London, 1900. First edition. $150–$200. New York, (1900). Cloth. First American edition. $100–$125.

CRANE, Stephen, and Barr, Robert. *The O'Ruddy*. Cloth. New York, (1903). First edition. In dust jacket. $350–$550.

CRANE, Walter. *The Bases of Design*. Blue-gray cloth. London, 1898. First edition. $75–$100. Signed copy, $125.

CRANE, Walter. *Flora's Feast*. Illustrated by the author. Boards. London, 1889. First edition. $150.

CRANE, Walter. *Of the Decorative Illustration of Books Old and New*. Illustrated. Cloth. London, 1896. First edition. One of 130. $150–$175. London, (1921). In dust jacket. $50–$60.

CRANE, Walter. *Renascence: A Book of Verse*. 39 designs by Crane. Boards, vellum spine. London, 1891. Chiswick Press. One of 100 large paper copies. $175–$200. Another issue: One of 44 on vellum, signed. $300–$350. Trade edition: $50–$60.

CRANE, Walter. *Slate and Pencil-Vania*. Illustrated. Pictorial half cloth. London, 1885. First edition. $125–$150.

CRANE, Walter. *Triplets*. Designs in color by Crane. Half vellum. London, 1899. First edition. One of 750. $400.

CRANE, Walter. *Valentine and Orson*. 8 color illustrations. Printed wrappers. (London, about 1870–73.) Sixpence Toy Book. $150.

CRANFORD. By the author of "Mary Barton," "Ruth," etc. Green cloth. London, 1853. (By Elizabeth C. Gaskell.) First edition. $800–$1,000.

CRAPSEY, Adelaide. *Verse*. Cloth. Rochester, 1915. First edition. $125–$150. Worn, $95.

CRARY, Mary. *The Daughters of the Stars*. Illustrated by Edmund Dulac. Half vellum. London, 1939. One of 500 signed by the author and the artist. In dust jacket. $400–$550.

CRAWFORD, F. Marion. *An American Politician*. 2 vols., cloth. London, 1884. First English edition. $175–$200. The true first edition dated Boston, 1885, actually preceded this edition by a few days.

CRAWFORD, F. Marion. *A Cigarette Maker's Romance*. 2 vols., cloth. London, 1890. First English edition. $75–$100.

CRAWFORD, F. Marion. *Katharine Lauderdale*. 3 vols., cloth. London, 1894. First edition. $150–$200.

CRAWFORD, F. Marion. *Man Overboard*. Cloth. New York, 1903. First edition. $125–$150.

CRAWFORD, F. Marion. *Uncanny Tales*. Cloth. London, 1911. First edition, first issue, without comma after "T" in address on title page. $150–$200.

CRAWFORD, Lewis F. *Rekindling Camp Fires*. Illustrated. Half leather. Bismarck,

N.D., 1926. First edition. One of 100 signed. Boxed. $150–$200. Trade edition: Cloth. In dust jacket. $75–$100.

CRAWFORD, Lucy. *The History of the White Mountains.* Cloth. Portland, Me., 1846. First edition. $100–$125.

CRAWSHAY, Richard. *The Birds of Tierra del Fuego.* 21 color plates by J.G. Keulemans, 23 photographic views, map. Half morocco. London, 1907. One of 300. $400–$600.

CRAYON, Geoffrey. *The Alhambra.* 2 vols., drab boards, printed spine label. London, 1832. (By Washington Irving.) First edition. $300–$400. Philadelphia, 1832. Anonymously published ("By the Author of 'The Sketch-Book' "). 2 vols., boards and cloth, paper spine label. First American edition. $200–$300.

CRAYON, Geoffrey. *Bracebridge Hall, or The Humourists.* 2 vols., drab brown boards, paper label. New York, 1822. (By Washington Irving.) First edition. $750–$1,000. London, 1822. Boards, paper label. First English edition (simultaneous with the American?), text ending on page 403, Vol. 2. $500–$600. New York, 1896. Surrey Edition. Arthur Rackham illustrations. 2 vols., pictorial cloth. $150–$250.

CRAYON, Geoffrey. *The Sketch Book of Geoffrey Crayon, Gent.* 7 parts, wrappers. New York, 1819–20. (By Washington Irving.) First edition. Parts 1 through 5 dated 1819, parts 6 and 8 dated 1820. $5,000–$10,000. Rebound in book form, $1,000–$1,500. (Note: Second editions so identified on wrappers. Like *Salmagundi*, this is a complicated work to identify, and it exists in many variations. See Blanck, *A Bibliography of American Literature.*)

CRAYON, Geoffrey. *Tales of a Traveller.* 2 vols., boards and cloth, paper label. London, 1824. (By Washington Irving.) First edition, first state, with page 395 of Vol. 2 blank. $800–$1,000, or more. Philadelphia, 1824. 4 parts, wrappers. First American edition, first issue, with "H.C. Cary" (instead of Carey) on title page. $1,000 and up.

CREELEY, Robert. Note: Mr. Creeley has been (at least among his contemporaries) a prolific and popular poet, a few of whose better known books are listed here. Much of his work has appeared in elaborately designed and illustrated books, portfolios and broadsides produced in Germany, England, and elsewhere in a bewildering variety of issues and bindings. We have made no effort to list these complicated items because they are difficult to trace through auction records and catalogues.

CREELEY, Robert, *All That Is Lovely in Men.* Drawings by Dan Rice. Pictorial wrappers. Asheville, 1955. Jargon No. 10. First edition. One of 200 signed by Creeley and Rice. In dust jacket. $150–$200.

CREELEY, Robert. *The Charm.* Leather-backed cloth. (Mt. Horeb, Wis.), 1967. Perishable Press. First edition. One of 250 signed. Issued without dust jacket. $75–$150. San Francisco, 1969. Wrappers. One of 100 signed. $100.

CREELEY, Robert. *Divisions and Other Early Poems.* Wrappers. (Mt. Horeb), 1968. First edition. One of 110. $125–$150.

CREELEY, Robert. *5 Numbers.* Wrappers. (New York, 1968.) First edition. One of 170 signed. $75–$100. (Republished in Germany as *Numbers.*)

CREELEY, Robert. *For Love, Poems 1950–1960.* Cloth. New York. (1962). First edition, with "A" on copyright page. In dust jacket. $50–$75. (Issued also in wrappers.)

CREELEY, Robert. *The Gold Diggers.* Wrappers. (Mallorca), 1954. Divers Press. First edition. $100–$150. New York, (1965). Cloth, or wrappers. First American edition. $50–$60.

CREELEY, Robert. *The Immoral Proposition.* Wrappers. (Baden, Germany, 1953.) First edition. (200 copies.) $150–$200.

CREELEY, Robert. *The Kind of Act Of.* Wrappers. (Mallorca), 1953. Divers Press. First edition. $150–$250.

CREELEY, Robert. *Le Fou*. Frontispiece. Decorated wrappers. Columbus, Ohio, 1952. First edition. In tissue jacket. $150–$200. Author's first book.

CREELEY, Robert. *Poems, 1950–1965*. Vellum and boards. London, (1966). First edition. One of 100 signed. In slipcase. $200–$250.

CREELEY, Robert. *A Sight*. Drawings by R.B. Large portfolio, silk-screened facsimiles of handwritten poems. London, 1967. First edition. One of 50 signed. $300–$325. Also, 50 unsigned. $100–$150.

CREELEY, Robert. *The Whip*. Cloth. (Worcester, England), 1957. First edition. One of 100. $150–$200. Another issue: Wrappers. One of 500. $85–$100.

CREMONY, John C. *Life Among the Apaches*. Cloth. San Francisco, 1868. First edition. $200–$250. Second issue: 6 engravings added. $200–$250.

CREUZBAUR, Robert (compiler). *Route from the Gulf of Mexico and the Lower Mississippi Valley to California and the Pacific Ocean*. 5 maps in pocket. 40 pp., cloth. New York, 1849. First edition. $4,000–$5,000.

CREVEL, René. *Mr. Knife, Miss Fork*. Translated by Kay Boyle. Illustrated by Max Ernst. Cloth. Paris, 1931. Black Sun Press. One of 200. $2,000–$2,300. Another issue: One of 50 specially bound, signed by Crevel and Ernst. $3,500–$4,000.

CREWS, Harry. *The Gospel Singer*. Cloth. New York, 1968. First edition. In dust jacket. $100–$125. Author's first book.

CREYTON, Paul. *Martin Merivale; His X Mark*. Cloth. Boston, 1854. (By John Townsend Trowbridge.) First edition, first state, with Creyton, not Trowbridge, on spine and stereotyper's slug on copyright page. $75–$125. (Second state has Trowbridge on spine.)

CREYTON, Paul. *Paul Creyton's Great Romance!! Kate the Accomplice; or, the Preacher and the Burglar*. Pictorial pink wrappers. Boston, (1849). (By John Townsend Trowbridge.) First edition, with 1849 cover date. $1,000 and up. Author's first book.

CRITERION (The); A Quarterly Review. Vol. I, No. 1. Wrappers. London, October, 1922. First edition. This magazine contains the first appearance in print of T.S. Eliot's poem "The Waste Land." $400 (A, 1977).

CROAKER, Croaker & Co., and Croaker, Jun. *Poems*. 36 pp., printed tan wrappers. New York, 1819. (By Joseph Rodman Drake and Fitz-Greene Halleck.) First edition. $500 and up. First book by each author. (Note: Reissued: *The Croakers*. Green cloth. New York, 1860. One of 250. $100–$150.)

CROCKET, George L. *Two Centuries in East Texas*. Dallas, (about 1932). First edition. $150–$200.

CROCKETT, David. See *Davy Crockett*.

CROCKETT, David. *An Account Of Col. Crockett's Tour to the North and Down East*. Cloth. Philadelphia, 1835. (By Augustin S. Clayton?) First edition. $150–$200.

CROCKETT, David. *A Narrative of the Life of Col. David Crockett*. Written by Himself. Cloth. Philadelphia, 1834. First edition, with 22 pages of ads at end. $200–$250.

CROFTS, Freeman Wills. *The Cask*. Cloth. London, 1920. First edition. In dust jacket. $600–$800.

CROFTS, Freeman Wills. *The Groote Park Murder*. Blue cloth. London, (1923). First edition. In dust jacket. $175–$200.

CROFTS, Freeman Wills. *The Pit-Prop Syndicate*. Blue cloth. London, (1922). First edition. In dust jacket. $200–$225.

CROMWELL: An Historical Novel. 2 vols., brown cloth, paper labels, New York, 1838. (By Henry William Herbert.) First edition, first issue, with 12 pages of ads. $150–$200.

CRONIN, A.J. *Hatter's Castle.* Cloth. London, 1931. First edition. In dust jacket. $100–$125. Author's first book.

CROSBY, Caresse. See. C.,C.

CROSBY, Caresse. *Crosses of Gold: A Book of Verse.* Hand-colored illustrations. Green parchment. Paris, 1925. First edition. One of 100. $300–$350. Revised edition, same date: Boards. $50. Author's first book.

CROSBY, Caresse. *Painted Shores.* Illustrated with 3 watercolors. Wrappers. Paris, 1927. First edition. One of 222 on Arches paper. In tissue dust jacket. $225.

CROSBY, Harry. *Chariot of the Sun.* Introduction by D.H. Lawrence. Wrappers. Paris, 1931. Black Sun Press. One of 500. $150–$200.

CROSBY, Harry. *Mad Queen: Tirades.* Drawing by Caresse Crosby. Stiff wrappers. Paris, 1929. Black Sun Press. One of 20 signed. $400–$500.

CROSBY, Harry. *Shadows of the Sun.* Printed wrappers. Paris, 1929. Black Sun Press. First edition. One of 44. In glassine jacket. $300–$400.

CROSBY, Harry. *Sleeping Together: A Book of Dreams.* Wrappers. Paris, 1931. Black Sun Press. One of 500. $100–$150.

CROSBY, Harry. *Torchbearer.* Notes by Ezra Pound. Wrappers. Paris, 1931. Black Sun Press. One of 500. $100–$150.

CROSBY, Harry. *Transit of Venus.* Printed wrappers. Paris, 1928. Black Sun Press. First edition. One of 44. $300–$400. Paris, 1929. Wrappers. Second edition. One of 200. In glassine dust jacket. Boxed. $75–$100. Paris, 1931. Preface by T.S. Eliot. One of 500. In glassine jacket. $100–$150.

CROSBY, Sylvester S. *The Early Coins of America.* 12 parts in 11, wrappers. Boston, 1873–75. $500–$600. Boston, 1878. 10 plates. Morocco. $300.

CROSBY, Thelma, and Ball, Eve. *Bob Crosby, World Champion Cowboy.* Illustrated. Pictorial cloth. Clarendon, Tex., (1966). First edition. $40–$50.

CROTCHET Castle. By the Author of *Headlong Hall.* Boards, paper label, London, 1831. (By Thomas Love Peacock.) First edition. $350–$400.

CROTHERS, Samuel McCord. *Miss Muffet's Christmas Party.* Pictorial vellum wrappers. St. Paul, (1892). First edition. $50–$60. Author's first book.

CROTTY, D.G. *Four Years Campaigning in the Army of the Potomac.* Half morocco. Grand Rapids, 1894. First edition. $75–$85.

CROWDER, Henry; Beckett, Samuel; Aldington, Richard; and others. *Henry-Music.* Pictorial boards. Paris, 1930. Hours Press. First edition. One of 100 signed by Crowder. (Includes poems by the authors set to music by Crowder, a black musician.) $2,500–$3,000.

CROWLEY, Aleister. See Therion, The Master. Also see *Aceldama.*

CROWLEY, Aleister. *Ahab and Other Poems.* Wrappers. London, 1903. $100–$150. Another issue: Vellum. Printed on vellum. $200–$300.

CROWLEY, Aleister. *Magic in Theory and Practice.* Cloth. London, 1929. First edition. In dust jacket. $150–$175.

CROWLEY, Aleister. *Magick.* 4 vols., red wrappers. Paris, 1929. $100–$150.

CROWLEY, Aleister. *Moonchild: A Prologue*. Green cloth. London, 1929. First edition. In dust jacket. $250.

CROWLEY, Aleister. *Olla: An Anthology of Sixty Years of Song*. Frontispiece. Cloth. London, (1946). First edition. One of 500. In dust jacket. $150–$175.

CROWLEY, Aleister. *Songs of the Spirit*. Cloth. London, 1898. First edition. One of 50. $250–$300.

CROWLEY, Aleister. *The Soul of Osiris*. Boards, cloth spine, paper label. London, 1901. First edition. $125–$175.

CROWLEY, Aleister. *The Stratagem and Other Stories*. Boards. London, (1929). Mandrake Press. First edition. In dust jacket. $100–$125.

CRUIKSHANK, George. See *The Humourist; More Hints on Etiquette.*

CRUIKSHANK, George. *George's Table Book*. Illustrated. Cloth. London, 1845. First edition. $125–$225.

CRUIKSHANK, George. *Illustrations of Time*. 6 leaves of illustrations. Oblong, wrappers. London, 1827. First edition. $400.

CRUIKSHANK, Percy. *Hints to Emigrants, or, Incidents in the Emigration of John Smith*. 9 full-page etchings. Pictorial wrappers. London, (about 1830). $400–$500.

CRYSTAL Age (A). Black or red cloth. London, 1887. (By W.H. Hudson.) First edition, with 32 pages of ads at end. $350–$450.

CUFFE, Paul. *Narrative of the Life and Adventures of Paul Cuffe, a Pequot Indian*. Wrappers. New York, 1839. $175–$225.

CUISINE Creole (La). Pictorial cloth. New York, (1885). (Compiled by Lafcadio Hearn.) First edition. $1,000 and up. Also, stained and worn, $850 (A, 1978). New Orleans, 1922. Cloth. Second edition. $75–$100.

CULLEN, Countee. *The Ballad of the Brown Girl*. Cloth and boards, paper label. New York, 1927. First edition. One of 500. Boxed. $125–$150.

CULLEN, Countee. *The Black Christ and Other Poems*. Decorations by Charles Cullen. Boards. New York, 1929. First edition. One of 128 signed. Boxed. $150–$175. Trade edition. In dust jacket. $75–$100.

CULLEN, Countee. *Color*. Drawings by Charles Cullen. Boards and cloth. New York, 1925. First edition. In dust jacket. $75–$100. Author's first book.

CULLEN, Countee (editor). *Caroling Dusk*. Cloth. New York, 1927. First edition. In dust jacket. $100–$125.

CUMING, F. *Sketches of a Tour to the Western Country*. Leather. Pittsburgh, 1810. First edition. $300–$400.

CUMINGS, Samuel. *The Western Pilot*. Printed boards. Cincinnati, 1825. $600–$1,000. Cincinnati, 1829. $400. Cincinnati, 1832. $325.

CUMMINGS, E.E. See *Eight Harvard Poets*. Also see Aragon, Louis.

CUMMINGS, E.E. (No title.) Illustrated by the author. Folio, cloth. New York, 1930. First edition. One of 491 signed. $250–$300.

CUMMINGS, E.E. &. Green gold-flecked boards. New York, 1925. First edition. One of 111 on Vidalon paper, signed. Boxed. $200–$250. Another issue: One of 222 on rag paper, signed. Boxed. $100–$125.

CUMMINGS, E.E. *Anthropos: The Future of Art*. Half cloth. (New York, 1944.) First edition. One of 222. In cloth dust jacket. Boxed. $150–$300.

CUMMINGS, E.E. *Christmas Tree*. Green decorated boards. New York, 1928. First edition. In glassine dust jacket. $400–$450. Also, $275 (A, 1977).

CUMMINGS, E.E. *Ciopw*. Cloth. New York, 1931. First edition. One of 391 signed. $400–$500. Also, $300 (A, 1975).

CUMMINGS, E.E. *Complete Poems*. 2 vols., cloth. (London), 1968. One of 150. In glassine dust jacket. Boxed. $200.

CUMMINGS, E.E. *Eimi*. Yellow cloth. (New York, 1933.) First edition. One of 1,381 signed. In dust jacket. $250–$275. New York, (1958). Boards and cloth. Third edition. One of 26 lettered and signed. In glassine jacket. $350–$500.

CUMMINGS, E.E. *The Enormous Room*. Tan buckram. New York, (1922). First edition. With or without fifth word ("shit") of last line on page 219 inked out. In dust jacket. $300–$400. London, 1928. Cloth. First English edition. In dust jacket. $125–$175. Author's first book.

CUMMINGS, E.E. *Fairy Tales*. Illustrated. Cloth. New York, 1950. First edition. In dust jacket. $40–$50.

CUMMINGS, E.E. *50 Poems*. Cloth. New York, (1940). First edition. One of 150 signed. In glassine dust jacket. Boxed. $200–$300.

CUMMINGS, E.E. *Him*. Decorated boards, vellum spine and corners. New York, 1927. First edition. One of 160 signed. Boxed. $200–$250. First trade edition: Cloth. In dust jacket. $60–$75.

CUMMINGS, E.E. *I: Six Nonlectures*. Cloth. Cambridge, Mass., 1953. First edition. One of 350 signed. In dust jacket. $150–$200. Trade edition: Cloth. In dust jacket. $40–$60.

CUMMINGS, E.E. *is 5*. Gold-flecked orange boards, cloth spine. New York, 1926. First edition. In dust jacket. $75–$100. Another issue: Black boards. One of 77 signed. Boxed. $350–$450. Also, $275 (A, 1977).

CUMMINGS, E.E. *95 Poems*. Cloth. New York, (1958). First edition. One of 300 signed. In glassine dust jacket. Boxed. $200–$250.

CUMMINGS, E.E. *No Thanks*. Oblong, dark-blue cloth. (New York, 1935.) First edition. One of 90 on handmade paper, signed. In dust jacket. Boxed. $250–$350. Another issue: Morocco. One of 9 on Japan vellum, signed. With a manuscript page. $1,500–$2,000. Also, $1,300 (A, 1977). Another issue: First trade edition. One of 900 on Riccardi Japan paper. $50–$75.

CUMMINGS, E.E. *Poems 1905–1962*. Edited by George J. Firmage. Half calf. London, 1963. First edition. One of 225. With errata slip. In acetate dust jacket. $200–$250.

CUMMINGS, E.E. *Santa Claus*. Frontispiece. Cloth. New York, (1946). First edition. One of 250 signed. In glassine jacket. $150–$175. Trade edition: $20–$30.

CUMMINGS, E.E. *Tulips and Chimneys*. Boards and cloth. New York, 1923. First edition. In dust jacket. $200–$300. Mount Vernon, N.Y., 1937. Boards, vellum spine. One of 481. In dust jacket. $200–$300. (Of this edition, there were supposed to be 148 signed by the author, but the sheets were lost between printer and binder.)

CUMMINGS, E.E. *W* [*Viva: Seventy New Poems*]. Folio, buckram and boards. New York, 1931. First edition. One of 95 signed. In glassine dust jacket. $375–$475. Trade edition. In silver dust jacket. $125–$175.

CUMMINGS, E.E. *XLI Poems*. Cloth, gilt label. New York, 1925. First edition. In dust jacket. $150.

CUMMINGS, Ray. *The Girl in the Golden Atom*. Gold cloth. New York, 1923. First edition. In dust jacket. $75–$125.

CUMMINS, Ebenezer H. *A Summary Geography of Alabama.* Wrappers. Philadelphia, 1819. First edition. $1,000 (A, 1980).

CUMMINS, Ella Sterling. *The Story of the Files: A Review of California Writers and Literature.* Illustrated. Decorated boards or cloth. (San Francisco), 1893. $100–$125.

CUMMINS, Jim. *Jim Cummins' Book.* Illustrated. Cloth. Denver, 1903. First edition. $300–$350.

CUMMINS, Mrs. Sarah J.W. *Autobiography and Reminiscences.* Portrait. Printed wrappers. (La Grande, Ore., 1914.) First edition. $75–$150. Reprint edition: (Walla Walla, Wash., 1914.) $25–$30.

CUNARD, Nancy. *Black Man and White Ladyship: An Anniversary.* 10 pp., red wrappers. (Toulon), 1931. First edition. $200–$250.

CUNARD, Nancy. *Outlaws.* Cloth. London, 1921. First edition. $200. Author's first book.

CUNARD, Nancy (editor). *Negro: Anthology.* Illustrated, including colored folding map. Brown buckram. London, 1934. First edition. $1,000–$1,500.

CUNARD, Nancy. *Parallax.* Pictorial boards. London, 1925. Hogarth Press. First edition. $350–$400.

CUNDALL, Joseph. See Percy, Stephen.

CUNNINGHAM, Eugene. *Famous in the West.* Illustrated. Printed wrappers. El Paso, 1926. First edition. $200.

CUNNINGHAM, Eugene. *Triggernometry: A Gallery of Gunfighters.* 21 plates. Pictorial cloth. New York, 1934. First edition. In dust jacket. $125–$150. Without jacket, $75.

CUNNINGHAME GRAHAM, R.B. See Graham.

CURIE, Marie. *Pierre Curie.* Boards. New York, 1923. First American edition. One of 100 signed. Boxed. $750.

CURLEY, Edwin A. *Nebraska: Its Advantages, Resources and Drawbacks.* Illustrated. Cloth. London, 1875. First edition. $75–$150.

CURSE of Minerva (The). 25 pp., dark-brown glazed wrappers. London, 1812. (By George Gordon Noel, Lord Byron.) First edition. $2,500 and up.

CURTIS, Edward S. *The North American Indian.* Prefaced by Theodore Roosevelt. More than 1,500 plates. 20 quarto vols., half morocco, and 20 half morocco portfolios of plates. Cambridge, Mass., 1907-30. First edition. One of 500 sets (about half this number actually issued). Signed by Curtis and Roosevelt (some by Curtis only). At auction: $60,500 and $60,000 at separate sales in 1977; $60,000 in 1976; $32,000 in 1975; $31,000 in 1974.

CURTIS, George William. See *Nile Notes of a Howadji; The Potiphar Papers.*

CURTISS, Daniel S. *Western Portraiture, and Emigrants' Guide.* Illustrated, folding map. Cloth. New York, 1852. First edition. $200–$250.

CUSHING, Frank Hamilton. *My Adventures in Zuni.* Illustrated. Cloth. Santa Fe, (1941). First edition. One of 400. In dust jacket. $250.

CUSHING, Luther S. *Manual of Parliamentary Practice.* Leather. Boston, 1845. First edition. $175.

CUSHMAN, H.B. *A History of the Choctaw, Chickasaw and Natchez Indians.* Cloth. Greenville, Tex., 1899. First edition. $250–$300.

CUSTER, Elizabeth B. *"Boots and Saddles,"* or *Life in Dakota with General Custer.* Portrait and map. Pictorial cloth. New York, 1885. First edition $40–$60.

CUSTER, Elizabeth B. *Tenting on the Plains.* Frontispiece. Gray cloth. New York, 1887. First edition. $50.

CUSTER, George A. *My Life on the Plains.* 8 illustrations. Cloth. New York, 1874. First edition. $150–$175.

CUTBUSH, James. *The American Artist's Manual.* 39 plates. 2 vols., cloth. Philadelphia, 1814. $175–$200.

CUTTS, James M. *The Conquest of California and New Mexico.* Map, 3 plans. Cloth. Philadelphia, 1847. First edition. $150–$200.

CYNWAL, Wiliam (*sic*). *In Defence of Woman.* 10 colored engravings. Full blue morocco. London, (1956). Golden Cockerel Press. One of 100 with an extra engraving. $200. Another issue: Buckram. One of 500. $50–$75.

D

D.,B., and M.,W.G. *Rumpel Stiltskin*. By B.D. and W.G.M. Edited by Michael Sadleir. Boards. London, 1952. (By Benjamin Disraeli and [William] George Meredith.) Roxburghe Club. One of 66. $350–$400.

D.,H. *Collected Poems*. Cloth. New York, 1925. (By Hilda Doolittle.) First edition. $300–$400.

D.,H. *Hedylus*. Decorated boards and cloth. Stratford-on-Avon (Oxford), 1928. (By Hilda Doolittle.) First edition. One of 775. In dust jacket. $150–$200.

D.,H. *Hippolytus Temporizes*. Decorated boards and cloth. Boston, 1927. (By Hilda Doolittle.) First edition. One of 550. Boxed. $250–$275.

D.,H. *Hymen*. Pale green wrappers. New York, 1921. (By Hilda Doolittle.) First American edition. $150–$200. London, 1921. Boards. $150–$200.

D.,H. *Kora and Ka*. Printed wrappers. (Dijon, 1934.) (By Hilda Doolittle.) One of 100. $400–$500.

D.,H. *Palimpsest*. Wrappers. (Paris), 1926. Contact Editions. (By Hilda Doolittle.) First edition. $200–$250. Boston, 1926. Decorated boards and cloth. First American edition. One of 700. In dust jacket. $75–$200.

D.,H. *Red Roses for Bronze*. Printed wrappers. New York, 1929. (By Hilda Doolittle.) First edition. $65–$85.

D.,H. *Sea Garden: Imagist Poems*. Printed wrappers over boards. London, 1916. (By Hilda Doolittle.) $200–$275. Also, $150 (A, 1977). Boston, 1917. Green wrappers. First American edition. $100–$150. Author's first book, except for a translation.

D.,H. *Selected Poems*. Boards. New York, (1957). First edition. One of 50 signed. $250. (Issued without dust jacket.)

D.,H. *The Tribute and Circe—Two Poems*. Cloth. Cleveland, 1917. (By Hilda Doolittle.) First edition. One of 50. $150–$200.

D.,H. *The Usual Star*. Wrappers. London, 1928 (actually Dijon, France, 1934). (By Hilda Doolittle.) First edition. One of 100. $400–$500.

D.,H. *The Walls Do Not Fall*. Cloth. New York, 1944. (By Hilda Doolittle.) First edition. In dust jacket. $50–$75. London, 1944. Stiff wrappers. $50–$75.

D.,H. (translator). *Choruses from Iphigeneia in Aulis*. Translated from the Greek of Euripides, Wrappers. Cleveland, 1916. (By Hilda Doolittle.) First edition. $1,000 or more. Also, $675 (A, 1977). (40 copies printed.) London, 1919. Stiff wrappers. $250–$350.

DACUS, J.A. *Life and Adventures of Frank and Jesse James*. Cloth. St. Louis, 1880. First edition. $300–$350.

DAHL, Roald. *Kiss Kiss*. Cloth. New York, 1960. First edition. In dust jacket. $50.

DAHL, Roald. *Some Time Never*. Cloth. New York, 1948. First edition. $35–$50.

DAHL, Roald. *Someone Like You*. Cloth. New York, 1953. First edition. In dust jacket. $40–$60.

DAHLBERG, Edward. *Bottom Dogs*. Introduction by D.H. Lawrence. Cloth. London, (1929). First edition. One of 520. In dust jacket. $200–$400. Trade edition: In dust jacket. $40–$60. New York, 1930. Boards. First American edition. In dust jacket. $100–$150. Author's first book.

DAHLBERG, Edward. *The Confessions of Edward Dahlberg*. Illustrated. Cloth. New York. (1971). First edition. One of 200 signed. Boxed. $50–$75.

DAHLBERG, Edward. *Do These Bones Live?* Red cloth. New York, (1941). First edition. In dust jacket. $50–$75.

DAHLBERG, Edward. *The Flea of Sodom*. Cloth. London, (1950). First edition. In dust jacket. $75.

DAHLBERG, Edward. *From Flushing to Calvary*. New York, (1932). First edition. In dust jacket. $50–$75.

DAHLBERG, Edward. *Kentucky Blue Grass Henry Smith*. Drawings by Augustus Peck. Orange boards, blue cloth spine. Cleveland, 1932. First edition. One of 10 signed. In dust jacket. $600–$750. One of 85 numbered copies (not signed). In dust jacket. $200–$400.

DAHLBERG, Edward. *The Sorrows of Priapus*. Illustrated by Ben Shahn. Printed white boards. (New York, 1957.) Thistle Press. First edition. One of 150 signed by author and artist. Extra signed lithograph laid in. In glassine dust jacket. Boxed. $150–$225.

DALE, Edward Everett. *The Range Cattle Industry*. Plates. Cloth. Norman, Okla., 1930. First edition. $150–$200.

DALE, Harrison Clifford (editor). *The Ashley-Smith Explorations*. 2 maps, 3 plates. Cloth. Cleveland, 1918. First edition. One of 750. $125–$175. Glendale, Calif., 1941. Cloth. Revised edition. One of 750. $75–$100.

DALI, Salvador. *Hidden Faces*. Cloth. New York, 1944. First edition. In dust jacket. $35–$60. London, 1973. Half vellum. One of 100 signed by Dali. With limited pamphlet *Postface to Hidden Faces*. Boxed. $200–$250.

DALI, Salvador. *The Secret Life of Salvador Dali*. Illustrated. Cloth, pictorial labels. New York, 1942. First American edition. One of 119 copies with an original Dali drawing. In dust jacket. Boxed. $600–$800. Trade edition: Cloth. In dust jacket. $125–$150.

DALTON Brothers and Their Astounding Career of Crime (The). By an Eye Witness. Pictorial wrappers. Chicago. 1892. First edition. $150.

DALTON, Emmett. *When the Daltons Rode*. Portrait and plates. Pictorial cloth. Garden City, 1931. First edition (so stated). In dust jacket. $50–$$60.

DAMON, S. Foster. *William Blake: His Philosophy and Symbols*. Boards. Boston, 1924. First American edition. $50.

DAMON, Samuel C. *A Journey to Lower Oregon and Upper California, 1848–49*. Half cloth. San Francisco, 1927. Grabhorn printing. One of 250. $125–$150.

DAMPIER, William. *A New Voyage Round the World*. 4 maps, portrait. Half vellum. London, 1927. One of 975 on vellum. $150–$200.

DAMSEL of Darien (The). 2 vols., boards or wrappers, paper spine labels. Philadelphia, 1839. (By William Gilmore Simms.) First edition, first issue, with errata slip before the first page of text in first volume. $300–$500.

DANA, Edmund. *Geographical Sketches on the Western Country; Designed for Emigrants and Settlers*. Boards. Cincinnati, 1819. First edition. $400–$600.

DANA, J.G., and Thomas, R.S. *A Report of the Trial of Jereboam O. Beauchamp*. 153 pp., wrappers. Frankfort, Ky., (1826). First edition. $500.

DANA, Richard Henry, Jr. See *Two Years Before the Mast.*

DANA, Richard Henry, Jr. *To Cuba and Back: A Vacation Voyage.* Brown cloth. Boston, 1859. First edition. $100–$125.

DANCE of Life (The). Frontispiece. Engraved title, 26 plates by Thomas Rowlandson. Boards, or cloth. London, 1817. (By William Combe.) First edition. $1,000 or more.

DANIEL, John W. *Character of Stonewall Jackson.* Cloth. Lynchburg, Va., 1868. First edition. $75–$85.

DANIELS, Jonathan. *Thomas Wolfe: October Recollections.* Cloth. Columbia, S.C., (1961). First edition. One of 750 signed. In dust jacket. $50–$60.

DANIELS, William M. *A Correct Account of the Murder of Generals Joseph and Hyrum Smith, at Carthage, on the 27th Day of June, 1844.* 24 pp., wrappers. Nauvoo, Ill., 1845. First edition, first issue, without plates. $2,500–$3,500. Second issue, with two woodcut engravings added. $2,000 or more. Rebound in morocco, paper covers bound in, $1,100 (A, 1966).

DANTE ALIGHIERI. *La Divina Commedia,* or *The Divine Vision of Dante Alighieri.* In Italian and English. Illustrated. Orange vellum. London, 1928. Nonesuch Press. One of 1,475. $400–$500. (As *The Comedy of Dante Alighieri:*) San Francisco, 1929. 4 vols., vellum. John Henry Nash printing. One of 250. $850–$1,000. New York, 1932. Limited Editions Club. Boxed. $200–$250. San Francisco, 1958. 3 vols. Grabhorn printing. One of 300. $200–$300.

DA PONTE, Lorenzo. See *The Memoirs of Lorenzo Da Ponte.*

D'ARBLAY, Madame. *Memoirs of Doctor Burney.* (Arranged by his daughter, Madame D'Arblay.) 3 vols., boards. London, 1832. (By Frances Burney.) First edition. $250–$350.

DARBY, William. *The Emigrant's Guide to the Western and Southwestern States and Territories.* 3 maps, 2 tables. Leather. New York, 1818. First edition. $300–$400.

DARBY, William. *A Geographical Description of the State of Louisana.* Map. Leather. Philadelphia, 1816. First edition. $300–$350. New York, 1817. Second edition, with 2 maps and large folding map. $300–$400.

DARBY, William. *A Tour from the City of New York, to Detroit, in the Michigan Territory.* 3 folding maps (one in some copies). Boards and calf. New York, 1819. First edition. $150–$300.

DARLINGTON, Mary Carson (editor). *Fort Pitt and Letters from the Frontier.* 3 maps, 3 plates. Cloth. Pittsburgh, 1892. First edition. One of 100 large paper copies. $150–$200. Ordinary issue: One of 200. $100–$125.

DARTMOUTH Verse, 1925. (Portland, Me.), 1925. Mosher Press. One of 500. (Note: Contains an introduction by Robert Frost.) $100.

DARWIN, Charles. *The Descent of Man.* Illustrated. 2 vols., green cloth. London, 1871. First edition, first issue, with errata on back of title page in Vol. 2 and with ads in each volume dated January. $500–$875. Second issue: $450. New York, 1871. 2 vols., cloth. First American edition. $200–$300.

DARWIN, Charles. *The Expression of the Emotions in Man and Animals.* Plates. Cloth. London, 1872. First edition. $500–$750. London, 1890. Cloth. Second edition. $150–$200.

DARWIN, Charles. *On the Origin of Species by Means of Natural Selection.* Green cloth. London, 1859. First edition, with ads at end dated June. $5,000–$6,000. Worn copies, $3,500 and $3,250. Also, $3,700 (A, 1980). London, 1860 Folding diagram. Cloth. Second edition. $450–$500. New York, 1860. Folding diagram. Cloth. First American edition. $750–$1,000. New York, 1963. Limited Editions Club. Illustrated. Leather. Boxed. $150–$200.

DARWIN, Charles. *The Voyage of H.M.S. Beagle.* Illustrated by Robert Gibbings. Folio, decorated sailcloth. New York, 1956. Limited Editions Club. One of 1,500 signed by Gibbings. Boxed. $125–$175.

DASHIELL, Alfred (editor). *Editor's Choice.* Cloth. New York, (1935). First edition. In dust jacket. $50–$75. (Includes first book appearances of stories by Faulkner, Hemingway, and Wolfe.)

DATE 1601. Conversation as It Was by the Social Fireside, in the Times of the Tudors. 7 single leaves, with title on front of first leaf, unbound. (West Point, N.Y., 1882.) (By Samuel Langhorne Clemens.) First authorized edition. $500–$750. Also, $380 (A, 1968). Another edition: (Bangor, Me., 1894.) Calf. $150–$200. Also, $70 (A, 1968). San Francisco, 1925. Grabhorn printing. One of 100. $150–$200. (Note: There have been numerous pirated printings of this *sub rosa* item, including at least two unauthorized 1880 printings. See BAL.)

DAUBENY, Charles. *Journal of a Tour Through the United States and Canada . . . 1837–1838.* Folding map. Cloth. Oxford. 1843. First edition. One of 100. $300.

DAVENPORT, Cyril. *English Embroidered Bookbindings.* Cloth. London, 1899. First edition. $150–$200. Another issue: One of 50. $400–$450.

DAVENPORT, Cyril. *Roger Payne: English Bookbinder of the Eighteenth Century.* Chicago, 1929. Caxton Club. One of 250. $450–$600.

DAVENPORT, Cyril. *Royal English Bookbindings.* Frontispiece, 7 other color plates, 27 other illustrations. Cloth. London, 1896. $150.

DAVENPORT, Cyril. *Samuel Mearne, Binder to King Charles II.* Chicago, 1929. Caxton Club. First edition. One of 250. $450–$500.

DAVENPORT, Homer. *My Quest of the Arab Horse* Cloth. New York, 1909. First edition. $125–$150.

DAVIDSON, Donald. *Lee In the Mountains and Other Poems.* Cloth. Boston, 1938. First edition. In dust jacket. $100–$125.

DAVIDSON, Donald. *An Outland Piper.* Boards. Boston, 1924. First edition. In dust jacket. $200–$250. Author's first book.

DAVIDSON, Donald. *The Tall Men.* Boards, cloth spine, label. Boston, 1927. First edition. $75.

DAVIDSON, Donald. *The Tennessee.* Illustrated. 2 vols., cloth. New York, 1946–1948. First edition. In dust jackets. $100.

DAVIDSON, Gordon Charles. *The North West Company.* 5 folding maps. Cloth. Berkeley, 1918. First edition. $100–$125.

DAVIDSON, James Wood. *The Living Writers of the South.* Cloth. New York, 1869. First edition. $75–$100. (Note: Contains two poems constituting first book appearance of Joel Chandler Harris.)

DAVIDSON, John. *Plays.* Aubrey Beardsley frontispiece. Pictorial cloth. London, 1894. First edition. One of 500. $150–$200. Another issue: Buckram. $300.

DAVIDSON, John. *Testaments.* 3 vols., wrappers. London, 1901–02–03. First editions. $200–$225.

DAVIES, Rhys. *The Song of Songs and Other Stories.* Wrappers. London, (1927). First edition. One of 100 signed. $100.

DAVIES, W.H. *The Autobiography of a Super-Tramp.* Preface by Bernard Shaw. Buckram. London, 1908. First edition. $75–$125.

DAVIES, W.H. *The Lover's Song Book.* Marbled boards and cloth. Newtown, 1933.

Gregynog Press. First edition. One of 250 signed. $200–$250. Another issue: Morocco. One of 18 bound by George Fisher. $1,000–$1,250.

DAVIES, W.H. *Selected Poems.* Portrait. Green morocco. Newtown, 1928. Gregynog Press. One of a few (from an edition of 310) specially bound by the Gregynog Bindery. $1,000–$1,250. Ordinary issue: Marbled boards and buckram. $150–$200.

DAVIES, W.H. *The Soul's Destroyer, and Other Poems.* Buff printed wrappers. (London, 1905.) First edition. $200–$300. Author's first book.

DAVIS, Duke. *Flashlights from Mountain and Plain.* Illustrated by Charles M. Russell. Cloth. Bound Brook, N.J., 1911. First edition. $100–$125.

DAVIS, Edmund. W. *Salmon-Fishing on the Grand Cascapedia.* Half vellum. (New York), 1904. First edition. One of 100. $750–$1,000. Also, $700 (A, 1980).

DAVID, Ellis A. *Commercial Encyclopedia of the Pacific Southwest.* Cloth. Oakland, 1915. $100–$150.

DAVIS, Hubert. *The Symbolic Drawings . . . for "An American Tragedy."* Foreword by Theodore Dreiser. 20 drawings. Folio, gold and silver boards, cloth spine. (New York, 1930.) One of 525 signed by Dreiser and Davis. $150–$200. (Some copies were never signed.)

DAVIS, John. See *Walter Kennedy: An American Tale.*

DAVIS, Paris M. *An Authentick History of the Late War Between the United States and Great Britain.* Calf. Ithaca, 1829. First edition. $100–$125.

DAVIS, Rebecca Harding. *Kent Hampden.* Cloth. New York, 1892. First edition. $35.

DAVIS, Rebecca Harding. *Margaret Howth: A Story of To-Day.* Cloth. Boston, 1862. First edition. $75–$100. Author's first book.

DAVIS, Richard Harding. *The Adventures of My Freshman.* Wrappers. (Bethlehem, Pa., 1883.) First edition. $500–$1,000. (About 10 copies known to exist.)

DAVIS, Richard Harding. *Cuba in War Time.* Illustrated by Frederic Remington. Boards. New York, 1897. First edition. $100–$125.

DAVIS, Richard Harding. *Dr. Jameson's Raiders vs. the Johannesburg Reformers.* Wrappers. New York, 1897. First edition. $300. Also, chipped, $150 (A, 1978).

DAVIS, Richard Harding. *Gallegher and Other Stories.* Yellow wrappers. New York, 1891. First edition, first issue. $200. Later, cloth. $35–$40.

DAVIS, Richard Harding. *The West From a Car-Window.* Illustrated by Frederic Remington. Cloth. New York, 1894. First edition. $50–$75.

DAVIS, William Heath. *Sixty Years in California.* Cloth. San Francisco, 1889. First edition. $200–$250. San Francisco, 1929. 44 maps and plates. Half morocco. Second edition. One of 2,000 (with title changed to *Seventy-five Years in California*). $100–$125. Another issue: Argonaut Edition. One of 100, with added plates and a page of the author's manuscript. $300–$350. San Francisco, 1967. Illustrated. Cloth. In dust jacket. $100–$125.

DAVIS, William J. (editor.) *The Partisan Rangers of the Confederate States Army.* 65 plates. Cloth. Louisville, 1904. (By Adam R. Johnson.) First edition. $150.

DAVIS, William W.H. *El Gringo; or New Mexico and Her People.* Frontispiece. Cloth. New York, 1857. First edition. $75–$225.

DAVIS, William W.H. *The Fries Rebellion.* 10 plates. Cloth. Doylestown, Pa., 1899. First edition. $100–$125.

DAVIS, William W.H. *The Spanish Conquest of New Mexico: 1527–1703.* Folding map, plate. Cloth. Doylestown, 1869. First edition. $150.

DAVISON, Lawrence H. *Movements in European History.* Brown cloth. London, 1921. (By D.H. Lawrence.) First edition, first binding. $300. Also, $160 (A, 1979). Second binding, light blue cloth. $150–$200.

DAVY, Sir Humphrey. *On the Safety Lamp for Coal Miners.* Folding plate. Boards. London, 1818. First edition. $400–$600. Also, $375 (A, 1977).

DAVY Crockett; or, *The Lion-Hearted Hunter.* 96 pp., wrappers. New York, (about 1875). $100–$125.

DAVY Crockett's Almanac, of Wild Sports in the West. Pictorial wrappers. Nashville, (1834 to 1841). Depending on condition, the Nashville almanacs for these years are worth individually from $500 to $1,000 each, possibly more. Howard S. Mott, Inc., of Sheffield, Mass., catalogued the 1834 issue, Vol. 1, No. 1, at $850 in 1981. Other Crockett Almanacs with Boston and Philadelphia imprints through the 1830's and into the 1850's bring $100 to $500 at retail.

DAWSON, Lionel. *Sport in War.* Illustrated by Lionel Edwards. Half leather. London, 1936. First edition. One of 75 signed. $150–$200.

DAWSON, Moses. *A Historical Narrative of the Civil and Military Services of Maj.-Gen. William Henry Harrison.* Boards. Cincinnati, 1824. First edition, first issue, with 15-line errata slip. $400–$600. Later issue, with 24-line errata slip: $300–$400.

DAWSON, Nicholas. *California in '41. Texas in '51. Memoirs.* Frontispiece. Cloth. (Austin, Tex., about 1910.) First edition. $500–$800. Inscribed copies, up to $1,000.

DAWSON, Nicholas. *Narrative of Nicholas "Cheyenne" Dawson.* Colored illustrations. Half cloth. San Francisco, 1933. Grabhorn Press. One of 500. In dust jacket. $75–$100. (Second edition of the preceding item.)

DAWSON, Simon J. *Report on the Exploration of the Country Between Lake Superior and the Red River Settlement and the Assiniboine and Saskatchewan.* Illustrated, folding maps, 45 pp., half leather and cloth. Toronto, 1859. First edition. $200–$300.

DAWSON, Thomas F., and Skiff., F.J.V. *The Ute War: A History of the White River Massacre, etc.* 184 pp., printed wrappers with ads. Denver, 1879. First edition. $2,000 and up. Later issue, without ads, $1,000–$1,500.

DAWSON, William Leon. *The Birds of California.* Illustrated. 4 vols., folio cloth. San Diego, 1923. $400–$500. Another issue: Half leather. One of 350. $400–$500. Another issue: One of 100 signed. $500–$600. Later, a "Student's Edition," 3 vols., cloth. $200 and up.

DAWSON, William Leon. *The Birds of Ohio.* Illustrated. 2 vols., cloth. Columbus, Ohio, 1903. $100–$150.

DAWSON, William Leon, and Bowles, John H. *The Birds of Washington.* 2 vols., boards. Seattle, 1909. First edition. One of 200 signed. $200–$300. Another issue: "Edition De Luxe." One of 85. $300–$400.

DAY, Sherman. *Report of the Committee on Internal Improvements, on the Use of the Camels on the Plains, May 30, 1885.* 11 pp., unbound. (Sacramento), 1885. $50–$60.

DAY-LEWIS, Cecil. *Beechen Vigil & Other Poems.* Green wrappers. London, (1925). First edition. $250–$300. Author's first book.

DAY-LEWIS, Cecil. *Country Comets.* Boards. London, 1928. First edition. Boxed. $60–$80.

DAY-LEWIS, Cecil. *The Magnetic Mountain.* Boards. London, 1933. Hogarth Press. First edition. One of 100 signed. In dust jacket. $150. Trade edition: In dust jacket. $35.

DAY-LEWIS, Cecil. *Noah and the Waters.* Cloth. London, 1936. Hogarth Press. First edition. One of 100 signed. In dust jacket. $150. Trade edition: In dust jacket. $35–$50.

DAY-LEWIS, Cecil. *A Time to Dance.* Cloth. London, 1935. Hogarth Press. First edition. In dust jacket. $50–$75.

DAY-LEWIS, Cecil (translator). *The Graveyard by the Sea.* (With title page for Paul Valéry's *Le Cimetière Marin* as right-hand page beside the title page for Day-Lewis's translation.) Marbled wrappers. London, (1945—actually 1947). First edition. One of 500. In fawn envelope. $250–$300.

DEAN, Bashford. *Catalogue of European Daggers.* 85 plates. Half cloth. New York, 1929. One of 900. $85–$100.

DEARBORN, Henry. *The Revolutionary War Journals of Henry Dearborn, 1775–1783.* 6 plates. Cloth. Chicago, 1939. Caxton Club. One of 350. Boxed. $125–$150.

DEARDEN, Robert R., Jr., and Watson, Douglas S. *An Original Leaf from the Bible of the Revolution and an Essay Concerning It.* San Francisco, 1930. Grabhorn printing. One of 515 with leaf from 1782 Bible. $300. Another issue: One of 50 with 2 leaves. $500–$600. Another issue: One of 15 with 2 leaves plus a leaf from the Benjamin Franklin printing of the "Confession of Faith." $800–$1,000.

DEBAR, J.H. *The West Virginia Handbook and Immigrant's Guide.* Folding map. Cloth. Parkersburg, W.Va., 1870. First edition. $100–$150.

DE BARTHE, Joe. *The Life and Adventures of Frank Grouard, Chief of Scouts.* Frontispiece, 67 plates. Pictorial cloth. St. Joseph., Mo., (1894). First edition. $250–$300.

DEBOUCHEL, Victor. *Histoire de la Louisiane.* Boards. Nouvelle-Orléans, 1841. First edition. $350–$400.

DECALVES, Don Alonso (pseudonym). *New Travels to the Westward.* 48 pp., sewed. Greenwich, Mass., 1805. $75–$85.

DE CAMP, L. Sprague. *Demons and Dinosaurs.* Cloth. Sauk City, Wis., 1970. First edition. In dust jacket. $50–$75.

DE CAMP, L. Sprague, and Pratt, Fletcher. *Land of Unreason.* Cloth. New York, (1942). First edition. In dust jacket. $100–$125.

DE CHAIR, Somerset. *The Golden Carpet.* Frontispiece. Half morocco. London, 1943. Golden Cockerel Press. One of 470. $100–$125. Another issue: One of 30 specially bound and inscribed. $300–$400.

DE CHAIR, Somerset. *The Silver Crescent.* Photographs. Half morocco. London, 1943. Golden Cockerel Press. One of 470. $100–$125. Another issue: Full morocco. One of 30 specially bound and inscribed. $300–$400.

DE CHAIR, Somerset. *The Story of a Lifetime.* Engravings by Clifford Webb. Full sheep. Waltham Saint Lawrence, 1954. Golden Cockerel Press. One of 100 signed. Boxed. $150–$250. Another issue: One of 10 signed. $400–$600.

DECLARATION of the Immediate Cause Which Induce and Justify the Secession of South Carolina from the Federal Union, and the Ordinance of Secession. Wrappers. Charleston, 1860. First edition, first issue, with misprinted "Cause" for "Causes." $400–$500.

DE CORDOVA, J. *Texas: Her Resources and Her Public Men.* Tables. Cloth. Philadelphia, 1858. First edition, first issue, without index. $350–$500.

DE CORDOVA, J. *The Texas Immigrant and Traveller's Guide Book.* Cloth. Austin, 1856. First edition. $350–$600, possibly more.

DEERSLAYER (The); or, *The First War-Path.* By the Author of "The Last of the Mohicans." 2 vols., purple cloth, paper labels on spine. Philadelphia, 1841. (By James Fenimore Cooper.) First edition. $2,000–$2,500. London, 1841. First English edition. 3 vols., cloth. $1,000–$1,500. Rebound in half calf, a little worn, $250.

DEFOE, Daniel. *The Life and Strange Surprising Adventures of Robinson Crusoe.* New York, 1930. Limited Editions Club. Boxed. $150–$175. (Also see, *The Life, and Most Surprising Adventures* title entry.)

DEFOE, Daniel. *The Life and Surprising Adventures of Robinson Crusoe.* 54 pp., wrappers. New York, (1864). First Beadle Dime Classic edition, first issue, with publisher's address as 118 William Street. $50–$75.

DE FOREST, John W. *Miss Ravenel's Conversion from Secession to Loyalty.* Cloth. New York, 1867. First edition. $75–$100.

DE FOREST, John. W. *Playing the Mischief.* 185 pp., wrappers. New York, 1875. First edition. $75. New York, 1876. Second printing. $25.

DE GIVRY, G. *Witchcraft, Magic and Alchemy.* Translated by J.C. Locke. 366 illustrations, 10 color plates. Cloth. London, (1931). In dust jacket. $150–$200.

DE GOURMONT, Remy. *The Natural Philosophy of Love.* Translated by Ezra Pound. Boards. New York, (1922). First edition. In dust jacket. $125–$150. London, 1926. Boards and cloth. First English edition. One of 1,500. In dust jacket. $100–$125.

DE GOUY, L.P. *The Derrydale Cook Book of Fish and Game.* 2 vols., buckram. New York, (1937). Limited edition. Boxed. $250–$350. Also, $175 (A, 1980).

DE HASS, Wills. *History of the Early Settlement and Indian Wars of Western Virginia.* 4 plates, folding facsimile. Decorated cloth. Wheeling, W. Va., 1851. First edition. $200-$250.

DELAFIELD, John, Jr. *An Inquiry into the Origin of the Antiquities of America.* 11 plates, including 18-foot-long folding tissue-paper plate. Cloth. New York, 1839. First edition. $150–$250.

DE LA MARE, Walter. See Ramal, Walter.

DE LA MARE, Walter. *Behold, This Dreamer.* Colored frontispiece. Parchment. London, 1939. First edition. One of 50 signed. $125-$150.

DE LA MARE, Walter. *Broomsticks and Other Tales.* Wood engravings. Half cloth, leather label on spine. London, 1925. First edition. One of 278 signed. In dust jacket. $75–$100.

DE LA MARE, Walter. *Crossings: A Fairy Play.* Decorated boards. (London, 1921.) Beaumont Press. First edition. One of 264. Boxed. $75–$100. Another issue: Vellum. One of 56 signed. Boxed. $150–$175. Also, there were apparently 13 copies on vellum especially for presentation. One of 3 such, signed by C. W. Beaumont, was sold at auction in the 1975 season for $150.

DE LA MARE, Walter. *Desert Islands and Robinson Crusoe.* Engravings by Rex Whistler. Cloth. London, 1930. One of 650 signed. In dust jacket. $75–$100. First trade edition: Cloth. In dust jacket. $20.

DE LA MARE, Walter. *Ding Dong Bell.* Boards. London, 1924. First edition. One of 300 signed. In dust jacket. $50–$75. Trade issue: Cloth. In dust jacket. $25.

DE LA MARE, Walter. *Down-Adown-Derry.* Illustrated by Dorothy P. Lathrop. Blue cloth. London, 1922. First edition. In dust jacket. $75–$100.

DE LA MARE, Walter. *Henry Brocken.* Cloth. London, 1904. First edition, first issue, without gilt on top edges. In dust jacket. $150–$200.

DE LA MARE, Walter. *Lispet, Lispett and Vaine.* Woodcut decorations. Limp vellum. London, 1923. One of 200 signed. Boxed. $75–$125.

DE LA MARE, Walter. *The Lord Fish*. Illustrated by Rex Whistler. Parchment. London, (1933). First edition. One of 60 signed. In dust jacket. Boxed. $125–$150.

DE LA MARE, Walter. *Memories of a Midget*. Boards. London, (1921). First edition, first issue, with "Copyright 1921" on verso of title page. One of 210 signed. Boxed. $100–$150. Trade edition: Cloth. In dust jacket. $25.

DE LA MARE, Walter. *On the Edge: Short Stories*. Illustrated. Pink cloth. London, 1930. First edition. One of 300 signed. In dust jacket. $100–$150. Trade edition: In dust jacket. $30.

DE LA MARE, Walter. *Peacock Pie: A Book of Rhymes*. Illustrated in color by Claud Lovat Fraser. Boards and cloth. London, 1924. One of 250 signed. In dust jacket. $100–$125.

DE LA MARE, Walter. *Poems, 1901 to 1918*. 2 vols., boards and linen, leather labels. London, 1920. First edition. One of 210 signed. $100–$125.

DE LA MARE, Walter. *The Riddle and Other Stories*. Cream cloth. London, (1923). First edition. One of 310. In dust jacket. $50–$75. Another issue: "Author's edition." One of 25 for presentation. $150–$175.

DE LA MARE, Walter. *Seven Short Stories*. Colored illustrations. Boards. London, 1931. First edition. One of 170 signed. Boxed. $100–$125.

DE LA MARE, Walter. *Songs of Childhood*. Colored plates. Vellum and boards. London, 1923. One of 310 signed. In dust jacket. $125–$150. (Published earlier under his pen name, Walter Ramal, which see.)

DE LA MARE, Walter. *The Sunken Garden*. Boards and linen. (London), 1917. Beaumont Press. First edition. One of 230 signed. Boxed. $50–$60. Another issue: Vellum. One of 20 on Japan paper, signed. Boxed. $125–$150.

DE LA MARE, Walter. *This Year: Next Year*. 8 mounted color plates. Decorated cloth. London, (1937). First edition. One of 100 signed. In dust jacket. $150–$200.

DE LA MARE, Walter. *Two Tales*. Vellum and boards. London, 1925. First edition. One of 250 signed. Boxed. $100–$125.

DE LA MARE, Walter. *The Three Mulla-Mulgars*. Green cloth. London, 1910. First edition, first issue, with errata slip. In dust jacket. $200-$250. London, (1925). Illustrated by J.B. Shepherd. Boards. One of 250 signed. $125–$150.

DELAND, Margaret. *Florida Days*. Illustrated. Pictorial tan cloth. Boston 1889. First edition. In dust jacket. $150. Without jacket, $40–$50.

DELAND, Margaret. *Old Chester Tales*. Illustrated by Howard Pyle. Cloth. New York, 1889. First edition, first issue, with "Chelsea" for "Chester" on page 5. $60–$75.

DELAND, Margaret. *The Old Garden and Other Verses*. White cloth and flowered cloth. Boston, 1886. First edition. $50–$75. Author's first book. Boston, 1894. Illustrated by Walter Crane. Cloth. $150–$200.

DELANO, Alonzo. See *Pen-Knife Sketches*.

DELANO, Alonzo. *Life on the Plains and Among the Diggings.* Frontispiece and 3 plates. Cloth. Auburn, N.Y., 1854. First edition, first issue, with page 219 misnumbered 119 and with no mention of number of thousands printed. $350–$600.

DELANO, Alonzo. *Pen-Knife Sketches, or Chips of the Old Block*. Colored illustrations. Decorated boards. San Francisco, 1934. Grabhorn Press. One of 550. $50–$75. (For anonymous edition, see title entry.)

DELANO, Amasa. *A Narrative of Voyages and Travels, in the Northern and Southern Hemispheres*. 2 portraits, folding map, errata leaf. Boards, paper label. Boston, 1817. First edition. $400–$600.

DELANO, Judah. *Washington (D.C.) Directory.* Calf. Washington, 1822. First edition. $500 and up.

DELANO, Reuben. *Wanderings and Adventures of Reuben Delano.* 3 plates. 102 pp., wrappers. Worcester, Mass., 1846. First edition. $150.

DE LA SALLE, Nicolas. See La Salle, Nicolas de.

DELAVAN, James. See *Notes on California and the Placers.*

DELAY, Peter J. *History of Yuba and Sutter Counties, California.* Illustrated. Three quarters leather. Los Angeles, 1924. $100–$150.

DELL, Floyd. *The Briary-Bush.* Cloth. New York, 1921. First edition. In dust jacket. $35.

DELL, Floyd. *Moon-Calf.* Cloth. New York, 1920. First edition. In dust jacket. $30–$50.

DELL, Floyd. *Runaway.* Boards. New York, (1925). First edition. One of 250 signed. Boxed. $50.

DELL, Floyd *Women as World Builders.* Cloth. Chicago, 1913. First edition. In dust jacket. $75–$100. Author's first book.

DEMIJOHN, Thom. *Black-Alice.* Cloth. Garden City, 1968. (By Thomas K. Disch and John T. Sladek.) First edition. In dust jacket. $50–$75.

DEMOCRACY: An American Novel. White cloth, printed red end papers. New York, 1880. (By Henry Adams.) First edition. No. 112 in "Leisure Hour Series." Probable first issue with March 31, 1880, in last line on front pasted-down end paper. $200–$400. Also, $120 (A, 1975). Probable second issue, dated April 15, $100–$150.

DE MORGAN, William. *It Never Can Happen Again.* Portrait. 2 vols., cloth. London, 1909. First edition. In dust jackets. $75–$100. With jackets torn, $30.

DE MORGAN, William. *Joseph Vance.* Light green cloth. London, 1906. First edition. $40–$60. Author's first book.

DEMOS: A Story of English Socialism. 3 vols., brown cloth. London, 1886. (By George Gissing.) First edition. $600–$750.

DENBY, Edwin. *In Public, In Private: Poems.* Illustrated. Gray cloth. Prairie City, Ill., (1948). First edition. In dust jacket. $150–$200.

DENNY, Arthur A. *Pioneer Days on Puget Sound.* Cloth. Seattle, 1888. First edition, with errata slip. Seattle, 1908. One of 850. $50–$75.

DENTON, Sherman F. *As Nature Shows Them: Moths and Butterflies of the United States East of the Rocky Mountains.* 56 colored plates. 2 vols., half leather. Boston, (1900). One of 500. $500–$750. Also, $500 (A, 1979).

DEPONS, François. *Travels in Parts of South America, During the Years 1801–1804.* Folding map and plan. Contemporary boards. London, 1806. $300–$400.

DEPONS, François. *A Voyage to the Eastern Part of Terra Firma.* Translated by an American Gentleman. Map. 3 vols., boards (none located) or contemporary leather. New York, 1806. (Translated by Washington Irving, Peter Irving, and George Caines.) First American edition (and first in English). In leather: $300–400. Washington Irving's first book.

DEPREDATIONS and Massacre by the Snake River Indians. 16 pp., sewed. (Washington), 1861. $100–$125.

DE QUILLE, Dan. *History of the Big Bonanza.* Illustrated. Decorated cloth. Hartford, 1876. (By William Wright.) First edition, first issue, without plate No. 44. $100–$125.

DE QUILLE, Dan. *A History of the Comstock Silver Lode and Mines*. Printed wrappers. Virginia City, Nev., (1889). (By William Wright.) First edition. $150–$200.

DE QUINCEY, Thomas. See *Confessions of an English Opium Eater; Klosterhiem, or, The Masque.*

DE QUINCEY, Thomas. *The Logic of Political Economy*. Cloth, paper label. Edinburgh, 1844. First edition. $150–$250.

DE RICCI, Seymour. *The Book Collector's Guide*. Green cloth. Philadelphia, 1921. First edition. $75–$125.

DERLETH, August. *Dark of the Moon*. Cloth. Sauk City, Wis., 1947. First edition. In dust jacket. $60–$75.

DERLETH, August. *Habitant of Dusk*. Illustrated. Pictorial boards. Boston, 1946. First edition. One of 300 signed. In dust jacket. $50.

DERLETH, August. *In Re: Sherlock Holmes*. Cloth. Sauk City, 1945. First edition. In dust jacket. $75–$125.

DERLETH, August. *Last Night*. Half vellum. Mt. Horeb, Wis., 1978. First edition. One of 150. $155.

DERLETH, August. *The Memoirs of Solar Pons*. Foreword by Ellery Queen. Cloth. Sauk City, 1951. First edition. One of 2,038. In dust jacket. $75–$85.

DERLETH, August. *Not Long for This World*. Black cloth. Sauk City, 1978. First edition. In dust jacket. $85–$100.

DERLETH, August. *Place of Hawks*. Illustrated. Cloth. New York, (1935). First edition, In dust jacket. $75–$100.

DERLETH, August. *The Reminiscences of Solar Pons*. Cloth. Sauk City, 1961. First edition. In dust jacket. $75–$100.

DERLETH, August. *The Return of Solar Pons*. Cloth. Sauk City, 1958. First edition. In dust jacket. $75–$100.

DERLETH, August. *Someone in the Dark*. Cloth. (Sauk City), 1941. Arkham House. First edition, first issue, 17.6 cm. tall. In dust jacket. $250–$300. Later: Falsely issued "first edition," a facsimile, bound with a headband (not on the first binding) and 18.35 cm. tall. (Some say Derleth issued it, but I have seen a note from Derleth blaming a "sly friend.") In jacket. $125–$150.

DERLETH, August. *Something Near*. Cloth. Sauk City, 1945. First edition. In dust jacket. $125–$150.

DERLETH, August, and Lovecraft, H.P. *The Lurker at the Threshold*. Cloth. Sauk City, 1945. First edition. In dust jacket. $100–$125.

DE ROOS, Fred F. *Personal Narrative of Travels in the United States and Canada in 1826*. 14 plates and plans. Boards. London, 1827. First edition. $300–$400. Second edition, same date. 14 lithographs, 2 maps. Boards. $200–$300.

DERRY, Derry down. *A Book of Nonsense*. Illustrated. Oblong, printed wrappers. London, (1846). (By Edward Lear.) First edition. One of 175. $2,000 and up. Author's first book for children. (For second edition, see Lear listing.)

DESCENDANT (The). Decorated cloth. New York, 1897. (By Ellen Glasgow.) First edition, first printing, with single imprint on title page, and first binding, with author's name omitted from spine. $75–$100. Author's first book.

DESCRIPTION of Central Iowa (A), with Especial Reference to Polk County and Des Moines, the State Capital. 32 pp., stitched. Des Moines, 1858. $400–$500.

DESCRIPTION of Tremont House (A), with Architectural Illustrations. Boards. Boston 1830. (By William G. Eliot.) First edition. $50–$75.

DESCRIPTIVE Account of the City of Peoria (A). 32 pp., wrappers. Peoria, 1859. $125–$150.

DESCRIPTIVE and Priced Catalogue of Books, Pamphlets, and Maps (A), etc. (Thomas Wayne Norris catalogue.) Patterned boards and red cloth. Oakland, 1948. Holmes Book Co.—Grabhorn. One of 500. $100–$150.

DESCRIPTIVE Bibliography of the Books Printed at the Ashendene Press, 1895-1935. 15 collotype plates, 10 of bindings; 2 photogravures, and numerous specimen pages, initial letters, woodcuts, etc. Cowhide. Chelsea, 1935. One of 390. Boxed. $2,000–$2500.

DESCRIPTIVE Catalogue of the Marine Collection to Be Found at India House (A). 35 plates, 11 hand-colored. Half leather. New York, 1935. (By Carl C. Cutler.) One of 1,000. $200–$250.

DESCRIPTIVE, Historical, Commercial, Agricultural, and Other Important Information Relative to the City of San Diego, California. 22 photographs. 51 pp., wrappers. (San Diego), 1874. $1,000.

DE SHIELDS, J. T. *Border Wars of Texas.* Cloth. Tioga, Tex., 1912. First edition. $150–$200.

DE SHIELDS, J. T. *Cynthia Ann Parker.* Frontispiece, 3 portraits. Pictorial cloth. St. Louis, 1886. First edition. $150–$175.

DES IMAGISTES: An Anthology. Cloth. New York, 1914. (Edited by Ezra Pound.) First edition. $150–$200. London, 1914. Boards. First English edition. $75–$100. (Note: Includes poems by Pound and James Joyce.)

DE SMET, Pierre-Jean. *Letters and Sketches.* Illustrations, folding leaf, "The Catholic Ladder." Cloth. Philadelphia, 1843. First edition, first issue, with 352 (not 344) pages. $750–$1,000.

DE SMET, Pierre-Jean. *Life, Letters and Travels of Father Jean-Pierre de Smet.* Edited by Hiram M. Chittenden. Map, 3 plates, 3 facsimiles. 4 vols., cloth. New York, 1905. First edition. $400–$500.

DE SMET, Pierre-Jean. *Oregon Missions and Travels over the Rocky Mountains.* Folding map, 12 plates. Cloth. New York, 1847. First edition. $300–$400.

DE SMET, Pierre-Jean. *Western Missions and Missionaries.* Cloth. New York, 1863. First edition. $150–$250.

DE TONTY, Henri. *Relation of Henri de Tonty Concerning the Explorations of La Salle.* Text in French and English. Half vellum. Chicago, 1898. Caxton Club. One of 194. $200–$250.

DESPERATE Remedies: A Novel. 3 vols., red cloth. London, 1871. (By Thomas Hardy.) First edition. $2,500–$3,000. Author's first book (500 printed). New York, 1874. Yellow cloth. First American edition, with "Author's Edition" on copyright page. $150–$200.

DESTINY; or The Chief's Daughter. 3 vols., boards. Edinburgh, 1831. (By Susan Edmonstone Ferrier.) First edition. $300–$400. Worn, $200. Rebacked, $180.

DEUTSCH, Babette. *Banners.* Boards, paper label. New York, (1919). First edition. In dust jacket. $100–$150. Author's first book.

DEUTSCH, Babette. *A Brittle Heaven.* Blue cloth. New York, (1926). First edition. In dust jacket. $50–$75.

DEUTSCH, Babette. *Fire for the Light.* Cloth. New York, (1930). First edition. In dust jacket. $50–$75.

DE VINNE, Theodore L. *Aldus Pius Manutius*. Boards and cloth. With original leaf from *Hypnerotomachia Poliphili*. Printed by Aldus in 1499. San Francisco, 1924. Grabhorn printing. One of 250. $500–$600.

DE VINNE, Theodore L. *The Invention of Printing*. Half morocco. New York, 1876. First edition. $100–$125. New York, 1878. Cloth. Second edition. $75–$100.

DE VINNE, Theodore L. *Title Pages as Seen by a Printer*. Illustrated. Half calf. New York, 1901. Grolier Club. One of 340. $125–$150.

DE VOTO, Bernard. *Across the Wide Missouri*. 81 plates, some in color. Cloth. Boston, 1947. First edition. One of 265. Boxed. $100–$125. Trade edition: Cloth. In dust jacket. $25–$35. New York, no date. Book Collectors Society edition. One of 100. $100–$125.

DE VOTO, Bernard. *The Crooked Mile*. Cloth. New York, 1924. First edition. In dust jacket. $50–$75. Author's first book.

DE VRIES, David. *Voyages from Holland to America, 1632–1644*. Cloth. New York, 1853. One of 125. $150–$175.

DE VRIES, Hugo. *The Mutation Theory*. 12 color plates, text illustrations. 2 vols., cloth. Chicago, 1909–10. First edition. $250.

DE VRIES, Peter. *The Blood of the Lamb*. Blue boards. Boston, (1961). First edition. In dust jacket. $35–$50.

DE VRIES, Peter. *But Who Wakes the Bugler*. Illustrated by Charles Addams. Cloth. Boston, 1940. First edition. In dust jacket. $75–$100. Author's first book.

DE WITT, David Miller. *The Judicial Murder of Mary E. Surratt*. Cloth. Baltimore, 1895. First edition. $75–$85.

DE WOLFF, J.H. *Pawnee Bill (Maj. Gordon W. Lillie): His Experience and Adventures on the Western Plains*. Illustrated. Pictorial boards. No place, 1902. First edition. $125–$150.

DEXTER, A. Hersey. *Early Days in California*. Pictorial cloth. (Denver), 1886. First edition. $200–$250.

DEXTER, F. Theodore. *Forty-Two Years' Scrapbook of Rare Ancient Firearms*. Cloth. Los Angeles, (1954). Limited edition. $75–$150.

DIAZ DEL CASTILLO, Bernal. *The Discovery and Conquest of Mexico, 1517–1521*. Translated by A. P. Maudslay. Illustrated by Miguel Covarrubias. Leather. New York, 1942. Limited Editions Club. Boxed. $150–$175.

DIAZ DEL CASTILLO, Bernal. *The True History of the Conquest of Mexico*. Translated by Maurice Keatinge. Map, errata leaf. Contemporary half leather. London, 1800. First edition in English. $250–$350.

DIBDIN, Thomas Frognall. Note: The following listings of this famous bibliographer's work record mainly rebound copies of such volumes that have appeared recently in the auction records and in catalogues of book dealers. They are intended only to indicate price ranges within which these books may likely be obtained.

DIBDIN, Thomas Frognall. *Aedes Althorpianae*. Illustrated. 2 vols., boards. London, 1822. First edition. $250–$300. (Note: This work consists of the fifth and sixth volumes of a 7-volume set usually listed as *Bibliotheca Spenceriana*, which see in entry following.) Another issue: Large paper, bound in full leather. One of 55. $500 and up.

DIBDIN, Thomas Frognall. *The Bibliographical Decameron*. Illustrated. 3 vols., morocco, London, 1817. First edition. Large paper issue: One of 50 copies. $1,000 and up. Ordinary issue: Boards. $500–$750, or more.

DIBDIN, Thomas Frognall. *The Bibliomania; or Book Madness*. Drab boards, paper label. London, 1809. First edition. $750–$1,000. London, 1811. 2 vols., morocco. Second edition. $300–$400. Large paper issue: One of 18. $750–$1,000. Other issues in 2 vols.-in-one-format, half leather: $100–$200. London, 1842. Calf. Third edition. $300–$400. London, 1876. Half morocco. Large paper edition, limited. $200. Boston, 1903. Bibliophile Society. 4 vols., boards. One of 483. $150–$250.

DIBDIN, Thomas Frognall. *Bibliotheca Spenceriana*. 7 vols., contemporary leather. London, 1814–15, 1822 and 1823. (4 vols., 1814–15, *Books Printed in the XV Century;* 2 vols., 1822, *Aedes Althorpianae*; one vol., 1823, *Catalogue of Books . . . Formerly in the Library of the Duke de Cassano Serra*.) First editions. $1,000–$1,500.

DICK, Philip K. *The Man in the High Castle*. Cloth. New York, (1962). First edition. In dust jacket. $150–$200.

DICKENS, Charles. Note: It is only necessary to examine the major book auction records of the last few years to understand the price advances in the Dickens market. Almost every set of Dickens parts and virtually all the book editions to come to market are defective and/or rebound. Gather ye Dickens while ye may.

DICKENS, Charles. See "Boz." Also see *Sketches by "Boz"; The Loving Ballad of Lord Bateman; More Hints on Etiquette*.

DICKENS, Charles. *The Adventures of Oliver Twist*. 24 illustrations by George Cruikshank. 10 monthly parts, green wrappers. London, 1846. "New edition." (Actually third edition, as stated in preliminary pages, and sometimes called first octavo edition; for earlier editions see *Oliver Twist* under "Boz" and Dickens.) Recent price range at retail: $2,500–$3,000. London, 1846. Slate-colored cloth. Third edition (in book form). $500–$600.

DICKENS, Charles. *American Notes for General Circulation*. 2 vols., brown cloth. London, 1842. First edition, first issue, with second page of "Contents to Volume I" numbered XVI. $500–$750. New York, 1842. Yellow wrappers. First American edition. $200–$300.

DICKENS, Charles. *The Battle of Life: A Love Story*. Engraved title page and frontispiece by Maclise. Cloth. London, 1846. First edition, first issue, imprint on engraved title page in 3 lines, with "A Love Story" printed. $350–$400. Second issue, with imprint in 3 lines and " A Love Story" engraved on a scroll. $200–$300.

DICKENS, Charles. *Bleak House*. Illustrated by H.K. Browne. 20 parts in 19, blue pictorial wrappers. London, 1852–53. First edition. $800–$1,200. Defective copies for less. Example: $300 (A, 1981); $370 (A, 1980). London, 1853. Green cloth. First book edition. $400–$500. Rebound in half leather, $150.

DICKENS, Charles. *A Child's History of England*. Frontispiece. 3 vols., reddish cloth. London, 1852–53–54. First edition, with title pages dated. $400–$600. Second edition: $200.

DICKENS, Charles. *The Chimes*. 13 illustrations. Engraved title page. Red cloth. London, 1845. First edition, first issue, with imprint as part of engraved title. $200–$400. Second issue, publisher's name below engraving: $85–$100. New York, 1931. Limited Editions Club. Illustrated by Arthur Rackham. Cloth. Boxed. $300–$450. Soiled copy, $195.

DICKENS, Charles. *A Christmas Carol*. 4 colored plates and 4 woodcuts by John Leech. Brown cloth. London, 1843. First published edition, first issue, with "Stave I" (not "Stave One") on first text page, and with red and blue title page and green end papers. $1,500 and up. Worn sets and sets in mixed states (bibliographically) retail for much less—usually in the range of $300–$500 and up. Also available at these prices, or less: Second issue, with "Stave I," red and blue title page, and yellow end papers. Third issue, with "Stave One," red and blue title page, and yellow end papers. Trial issue: London, 1844. (Richard Gimbel's "first state.") Title page in red and green, with green or yellow end papers. $1,000 and up. Philadelphia, 1844. Yellow cloth. First American edition. $400 and up. London, (1915). Illustrated in color by Arthur Rackham. Pictorial vellum. Large paper edition. One of 525. $1,250–$1,500. Also, $1,100 (A, 1981). Boston, 1934. Limited Editions Club. Boards and cloth. Boxed. $50–$100. San Francisco, 1950. Grabhorn printing. Boards. One of 250. $200–$250.

DICKENS, Charles. *The Complete Works of Charles Dickens*. Edited by Arthur Waugh, Hugh Walpole, Walter Dexter, and Thomas Halton. Illustrated. 23 vols., buckram (each vol. a different color), leather labels, gilt, with an original engraved steel plate. London, 1937–38. Nonesuch Press. One of 877 sets. $3,000–$4,000

DICKENS, Charles. *The Cricket on the Hearth*. Illustrated. Crimson cloth. London, 1846. First edition. $125–$150. New York, 1846. Wrappers. First American edition. $100–$125. New York, 1933. Limited Editions Club. Cloth. Boxed. $50–$75.

DICKENS, Charles. *Dombey and Son*. Illustrated by H.K. Browne. 20 parts in 19, green pictorial wrappers. London, 1846–47-48. First edition, with 12-line errata slip in Part V. $750–$1,000. Also, $750 (A, 1981).New York, 1846–48. 20 parts in 19, wrappers. First American edition, $300 and up. London, 1848. Dark-green cloth. First book edition. $200–$250. New York, 1948. 2 vols., cloth. First American book edition. $75–$100. New York, 1957. Limited Editions Club. 2 vols., buckram. Boxed. $100–$110.

DICKENS, Charles. *Great Expectations*. 3 vols., purple cloth. London, 1861. First edition, first issue, with ads dated May, 1861. $5,500 (A, 1974)—the famous Jerome Kern-Barton Currie copy, which sold in 1929 for $3,500, a price unsurpassed until the William E. Stockhausen sale in New York City on November 19, 1974. Also, defective, $3,200 (A, 1981). New York, 1937. Limited Editions Club. Cloth. Boxed. $40–$60.

DICKENS, Charles. *Hard Times, for These Times*. Green cloth. London, 1854. First edition. $300–$400. New York, 1966. Limited Editions Club. Boxed. $80–$100.

DICKENS, Charles. *The Life and Adventures of Martin Chuzzlewit*. Illustrated by Phiz, 20 parts in 19, green wrappers. London, 1844. First edition, first issue, with "£" sign after "100" in reward notice on engraved title page. $1,250–$1,750. Imperfect copies, $475, $650, and various other prices noted. London, 1844. Prussian blue cloth (later, brown cloth). First book edition, first issue. $600-$800. Rebound in morocco, $125.

DICKENS, Charles. *The Life and Adventures of Nicholas Nickleby*. Frontispiece portrait by Maclise, illustrations by Phiz. 20 parts in 19, green pictorial wrappers. London, 1838-39. First edition, first issue, with "vister" for "sister" in line 17, page 123, part IV. $1,000–$1,250. London, 1839. Cloth. First book edition. $400-$500.

DICKENS, Charles. *Little Dorrit*. Illustrated by H.K. Browne. 20 parts in 19, blue wrappers. London, 1855-57. First edition, first issue, with errata slip in Part XVI and uncorrected errors in Part XV. $1,000–$1,250. Imperfect copies, $450, $425, etc., etc. London, 1857. Green cloth. First book edition, first issue. $400-$500.

DICKENS, Charles. *Master Humphrey's Clock*. Illustrated by George Cattermole and H.K. Browne, 3 vols., brown cloth. London, 1840–41. First book edition. $500–$600. (See entry under "Boz" for editions in parts.)

DICKENS, Charles. *Mr. Nightingale's Diary*. Green or brown cloth, gilt. Boston, 1877. First American edition. $250. (Note: This book was published originally as an anonymous pamphlet in London in 1851. The Dickens bibliographer John C. Eckel reports only "three known copies traceable." Estimated value: $1,000 and up.)

DICKENS, Charles. *The Mystery of Edwin Drood*. 12 illustrations by S.L. Fildes. 6 parts, green pictorial wrappers. London, 1870. First edition. $500–$750. Also, $400 (A, 1980). London, 1870. Green cloth. First book edition. $175–$200. Boston, 1870. Wrappers. First American edition, $150–$200. Brattleboro, Vt., 1873. Cloth. "Completed by the Spirit-Pen of Dickens, Through a Medium." (By Thomas P. James.) First edition in this form. $27.50–$50.

DICKENS, Charles. *Oliver Twist*. 3 vols., brown cloth, London, 1839. Second edition (or third issue of the 1838 original, which see under "Boz" entry). With Dickens on title page instead of "Boz." $200–$300. (For third, or first octavo, edition, see Dickens, *The Adventures of Oliver Twist*.)

DICKENS, Charles. *Our Mutual Friend*. Illustrations by Marcus Stone. 20 parts in 19, green pictorial wrappers. London, 1864–65. First edition. $1,250–$1,500. Worn set,

$300 (A, 1980). London, 1865. 2 vols., brown cloth. First book edition. $400–$500. New York, 1865. Green cloth. First American edition. $150–$200.

DICKENS, Charles. *The Personal History of David Copperfield*. Illustrated by H.K. Browne. 20 parts in 19, green pictorial wrappers. London, 1949–50. First edition. $2,000–$3,000. London, 1850. Dark-green cloth. First book edition, first state, with engraved title page dated 1850. $300–$600. Rebound in morroco, $200.

DICKENS, Charles. *Pictures from Italy*. Illustrations on wood by Samuel Palmer. Dark blue cloth. London, 1846. First edition, first issue, with pages 5 and 270 unnumbered and with 2 pages of ads. $300–$400.

DICKENS, Charles. *The Posthumous Papers of the Pickwick Club*. Illustrated by R. Seymour and Phiz. 20 parts in 19, green wrappers. London, 1836–37. First edition. The most difficult of all of Dickens' works to obtain in collector's condition and therefore impossible to evaluate without close examination. Literally hundreds of "points" must be met for a "perfect Pickwick," as is evidenced in John C. Eckel's bibliographical notes covering 42 pages in *The First Editions of Charrles Dickens*. The Jerome Kern copy (once owned by Dr. R.T. Jupp) brought $28,000 at auction in 1929. Among the high auction prices in recent times have been $3,700 in 1980 and $4,250, achieved in New York in 1974 and twice on separate sets at the same sale in London in 1971. In 1965 the Louis Silver copy sold for $2,800. London, 1837. Green cloth. First book edition, first issue, with the name "Tony Veller" on the signboard on the engraved title page. $600–$800, or more. Philadelphia, 1836–37. 5 vols., boards. First American edition. $300 and up. New York. 1933. Limited Editions Club. 2 vols., cloth. Boxed. $50–$60.

DICKENS, Charles. *A Tale of Two Cities*. Illustrated by H.K. Browne, 8 parts in 7, blue wrappers, London, 1859. First edition, first issue, with page 213 misnumbered "113." $3,500–$5,000. A very fine set was offered in a 1981 catalogue at $4,500. London, 1859. Red or green (scarcer) cloth. First book edition, first state, with dated engraved title page. $1,500–$2,000. Also, $1,800 (A, 1978). Second issue, page 213 correctly numbered: $450–$750.

DICKENS, Charles. *The Uncommercial Traveller*. Lilac cloth. London, 1861. First edition, with ads dated December, 1860, at end. $300–$500.

DICKENS, Charles. *The Village Coquettes: A Comic Opera*. Gray boards, or unstitched, unopened sheets. London, 1836. First edition. Very rare in original boards. In sheets: $400 and up.

DICKENSON, Jonathan. See Dickinson, Jonathan.

DICKENSON, Luella. *Reminiscences of a Trip Across the Plains in 1846*. Pictorial cloth. San Francisco, 1904. First edition, $400–$500.

DICKERSON, Philip J. *History of the Osage Nation*. (Cover title.) Illustrations and map. 144 pp., wrappers. (Pawhuska, Oklahoma Indian Territory, 1906.) First edition. $150–$250.

DICKEY, James. *Buckdancer's Choice*. Cloth. Middletown, (1965). First edition. In dust jacket. $65–$75.

DICKEY, James, *The Eye-Beaters, Blood, Victory, Madness, Buckhead and Mercy*. Cloth. Garden City, 1970. First edition. One of 250 signed. Boxed. $75–$85. Trade edition: In dust jacket. $25.

DICKEY, James. *The Suspect in Poetry*. Boards or wrappers. (Madison, Minn.), 1964. First edition. In dust jacket. $35–$45.

DICKEY, James. *Two Poems of the Air*. Calligraphic text. Decorated boards. Portland, (1964). Oblong, decorated boards. First edition. One of 300 signed by the poet and the calligrapher, Monica Moseley Pincus. In slipcase. $125–$150.

DICKINS, James. *1861 to 1865, by an Old Johnnie: Personal Recollections and Experiences of the Confederate Army*. Cloth. Cincinnati, 1897. First edition. $100–$150.

DICKINSON, Emily. See *A Masque of Poets.*

DICKINSON, Emily. *Further Poems of Emily Dickinson.* Edited by Martha Dickinson Bianchi and Alfred Leete Hampson. Green cloth. Boston, 1929. First edition. One of 465 on large paper. In dust jacket. Boxed. $150–$175. Trade edition: Cloth. In dust jacket. $50–$75.

DICKINSON, Emily. *Letters of Emily Dickinson.* Edited by Mabel Loomis Todd, 2 vols., green cloth. Boston, 1894. First edition, first binding, with Roberts Brothers imprint on spine. In dust jacket. $400–$450. Second printing: 2 vols., brown cloth. $100–$150.

DICKINSON, Emily. *Poems.* Edited by Mabel Loomis Todd and T.W. Higginson. White and gray cloth. Boston, 1890. First edition. $750–$1,000. Also, $550 (A, 1977). Author's first book. London, 1891. Cloth. First English edition. $350–$400. New York, 1952. Limited Editions Club. Morocco. Boxed. $60–$80.

DICKINSON, Emily. *Poems: Second Series.* Edited by T.W. Higginson and Mabel Loomis Todd. Gray or gray-green cloth, or white cloth with green spine. Boston, 1891. First edition with white silk ribbon page marker. $200–$300. Some special copies issued in decorated boards, calf spine: $350–$450.

DICKINSON, Emily. *Poems: Third Series.* Edited by Mabel Loomis Todd. Gray, green, or white and green cloth. Boston, 1896. First edition, first binding, with Roberts Brothers imprint on spine. $300–$350.

DICKINSON, Emily. *Riddle Poems.* Decorations by Leonard Baskin. Half morocco, (Northampton, Mass.), 1957. Gehenna Press. One of 25 signed by Leonard and Esther Baskin. $1,000. Ordinary issue (225 copies): $300–$400.

DICKINSON, Emily. *The Single Hound: Poems of a Lifetime.* Boards and cloth. Boston, 1914. First edition, with "Published, September, 1914," on copyright page. In dust jacket. $350–$450. Lacking jacket, $200. Boston, 1915. Boards and cloth. Second edition. In dust jacket. $125–$150.

DICKINSON, Emily. *Unpublished Poems.* Edited by Martha Dickinson Biachi and Alfred Leete Hampson. Green cloth, pink label on spine. Boston, 1935. First edition. One of 525 de luxe copies. Boxed. $150–$200. Boston, 1936. Green cloth. First trade edition. In dust jacket. $50–$75.

DICKINSON, Henry C. *Diary of Henry C. Dickinson.* Plates. Cloth. Denver, (about 1889). First edition. One of 225. $75–$125.

DICKINSON, Jonathan. *Narrative of a Shipwreck in the Gulf of Florida.* Leather, Stanford. N.Y., 1803. (By Jonathan Dickenson.) $400–$500. Burlington, N.J., 1811. Leather, $150–$200. Salem, Ohio, 1826. (*The Shipwreck and Dreadful Sufferings of Robert Barrow*). Half calf. $150–$200. (Note: These are variant titles of reprintings of Dickenson's *God's Protecting Providence,* first published in Philadelphia in 1699, of which only 4 perfect copies are known.)

DIDIMUS, H. *New Orleans as I Found It.* Double columns, 125 pp., wrappers, New York, 1845. (By Edward H. Durrell.) First edition. $200–$350.

DIDION, Joan. *Run River.* Cloth. New York, (1963). First edition. In dust jacket. $100–$110. Author's first book.

DIDION, Joan. *Slouching Towards Bethlehem.* Boards. New York, (1968). First edition. In dust jacket. $50–$75.

DI DONATO, Pietro. *Christ in Concrete.* Boards. Chicago, 1937. First edition. In glassine jacket. $50–$60. Author's first book.

DIEHL, Edith. *Bookbinding: Its Background and Technique.* Illustrated. 2 vols., cloth, New York, 1946. First edition. $300–$350. Also, $200 (A, 1979).

DIENST, Alex. *The Navy of the Republic of Texas, 1835–1845.* Blue leather (presentation binding). Temple, Tex., (1909). First edition. $500–$750. Also in cloth: $250–$300.

DIETZ, August. *The Postal Service of the Confederate States of America*. 2 color plates. Half leather. Richmond, 1929. First edition. $100–$150.

DIGBY, Sir Kenelm. *Poems from Sir Kenelm Digby's Papers in the Possession of Henry A. Bright*, 2 portraits, facsimile. Half morocco. London, 1877. Roxburghe Club. One of 80. $150–$250.

DILLON, George. *The Flowering Stone*. Cloth. New York, 1931. First edition. In dust jacket. $50–$60.

DIMSDALE, Thomas J. *The Vigilantes of Montana*. 228 pp., printed wrappers. Virginia City, Mont., 1866. First edition. $1,500–$2,000. Rebound in half calf, $1,250 in a 1981 catalogue. Virginia City, 1882. 241 pp., printed wrappers. Second edition. $200–$215. Cloth, $150. Helena, Mont., (1915). 26 plates and 4 facsimiles. Third edition. $30–$40. Helena, 1915. Fourth edition, $27.50.

DINESEN, Isak. *Out of Africa*. Cloth. New York, (1938). First edition. In dust jacket. $75.

DINESEN, Isak. *Seven Gothic Tales*. Cloth. New York, 1934. First edition. In dust jacket. $100–$125.

DINSMOOR, Robert. *Incidental Poems*. Boards and cloth, paper label. Haverhill, Mass., 1828. First edition. $250–$300. Worn and soiled, $150. (Note: Contains first appearance of John G. Whittier's poems in a book.)

DIOMEDI, Alexander. *Sketches of Modern Indian Life*. 79 pp., wrappers. (Woodstock, Md. 1894?) First edition. $125–$150.

DI PRIMA, Diane. *New Mexico Poems*. Wrappers. (New York, 1968.) First edition. One of 50 signed. $75.

DI PRIMA, Diane. *This Kind of Bird Flies Backward*. Introduction by Lawrence Ferlinghetti. Illustrated. Wrappers. (New York, 1958). First edition. $50–$75. Author's first book.

DIRECTORY of the City of Mineral Point for the Year 1859. Map. 64 pp., sewed. Mineral Point, Wis., 1859. $200–$250.

DIRECTORY of Newark for 1835–6. Half leather. Newark, N.J., 1835. First edition. $500 and up.

DISCARDS (The). By Old Wolf. 22 pp., wrappers. (Yakima, Wash.?), 1920. (By Lucullus V. McWhorter.) $150.

DISCOURSE on the Aborigines of the Valley of the Ohio (A). Folding map, 51 pp., sewed. Cincinnati, 1838. (By William Henry Harrison.) First edition. $150–$200.

DISIECTA Membra. 54 pp., red wrappers. London, 1915. (By Norman Douglas.) First edition. One of 100. $200.

DISNEY, Walt (or Disney Studios). *The Adventures of Mickey Mouse: Book I*. Illustrated. Pictorial boards. Philadelphia, (1931). First edition. In dust jacket. $350. London, 1931. Boards. First English edition. In dust jacket. $275.

DISNEY, Walt. *The Golden Touch*. Cloth. London, 1935. First edition. $200.

DISNEY, Walt. *Honest John and Giddy*. Cloth. New York, (1940). First edition. In dust jacket. $100–$150.

DISNEY, Walt. *Little Red Riding Hood and the Big Bad Wolf*. Illustrated. Boards. Philadelphia, (1934). First edition. $150.

DISNEY, Walt. *Mickey Mouse*. Illustrated. Pictorial wrappers. Racine, Wis., (1933). $150–$200.

DISNEY, Walt. *Mickey Mouse in King Arthur's Court*. Pictorial boards. London, (about 1932). $300–$350.

DISNEY, Walt. *Mickey Mouse Story Book*. Illustrated. Pictorial boards or cloth. Philadelphia, (1931). First edition. Boards: $150–$200. Cloth: $250–$300.

DISNEY, Walt. *The Pop-Up Minnie Mouse*. Illustrated with 3 double page pop-up cutouts. Pictorial boards. New York, (1933). $200–$250.

DISNEY, Walt. *Stories from Walt Disney's Fantasia*. Illustrated. Boards. New York, (1940). First edition. In dust jacket. $200.

DISRAELI, Benjamin. See D.,B., and M.,W.G. Also see *Henrietta Temple; The Letters of Runnymede; The Tragedy of Count Alarcos; Vivian Grey; The Young Duke.*

DISRAELI, Benjamin. *Coningsby; or, The New Generation*. Boards. London, (1844). First edition. $350–$450. Rebound, $240.

DISRAELI, Benjamin. *Sybil, or The Two Nations*, 3 vols., half cloth. London, (1845). First edition. $400–$500.

DISRAELI, Benjamin. *The Voyage of Capt. Popanilla*. Boards, printed label. London, 1828. First edition. $250–$300.

DISTURNELL, John. *The Influence of Climate in North and South America*. Cloth. New York, 1867. First edition. $100–$125.

DISTURNELL, John (publisher). *Disturnell's Guide Through the Middle, Northern, and Eastern States*. Map of New York City, folding map. Cloth. New York, June, 1847. First edition. $75.

DISTURNELL, John (publisher). *The Emigrant's Guide to New Mexico, California, and Oregon*. Folding map, 46 pp., brown cloth. New York, 1849. First edition, first issue, with map published by Disturnell and dated 1849. $750–$1,000. Second edition, same date: Wrappers. With 1849 Disturnell map including "Col. Hays' Route." $1,000 and up. New York, 1850. Cloth. $500–$600. (Note: Howes cites an 1849 edition with "map published by Colton," Colton Storm's catalogue of the Graff collection calls the Disturnell map "preferable.")

DISTURNELL, John (publisher). *The Great Lakes or Inland Seas of America*. Cloth. New York, 1868. $150–$200.

DISTURNELL, John (publisher). *The Upper Lakes of North America: A Guide*. Cloth. New York, 1857. First edition. $100–$150.

DIX Ans sur la Côte du Pacifique par un Missionaire Canadien. 100 pp., wrappers. Quebec, 1873. (By François X. Blanchet.) First edition. $150–$200.

DIX, John Ross. See Jones, J. Wesley.

DIXON, Richard W. *Odes and Eclogues*. Wrappers. Oxford, 1884. Daniel Press. One of 100. $200–$250.

DIXON, Sam Houston. *The Heroes of San Jacinto*. Illustrated. Cloth. Houston, 1932. $75–$125.

DIXON, Sam Houston. *The Poets and Poetry of Texas*. Illustrated. Cloth. Austin, 1885. First edition. $250.

DIXON, Thomas, Jr. *The Clansman*. Cloth. New York, 1905. First edition. $40–$50.

DOBIE, J. Frank. *Apache Gold and Yaqui Silver*, Illustrated by Tom Lea. Buckram. Boston, 1939. First (Sierra Madre) edition. One of 265 signed by author and artist. Boxed. $600–$1,000. Trade edition: Cloth. In dust jacket. $40–$50.

DOBIE, J. Frank. *Bigfoot Wallace and the Hickory Nuts*. 7 pp., wrappers. Austin, 1936. First edition. One of 300 signed. $350.

DOBIE, J. Frank. *Carl Sandburg and Saint Peter at the Gate*. Illustrated. Boards. Austin, 1966. One of 750. Boxed. $85–$125.

DOBIE, J. Frank. *Coronado's Children*, Maps, illustrated. Cloth. Dallas, (1930). First edition, first issue, without the word "clean" in dedication. In dust jacket. $200–$225.

DOBIE, J. Frank. *Cow People*. Full leather, including variant binding with hair on it. Boston, (1964). First edition. One of 75 de luxe copies. $500–$1,000. Trade edition: Cloth. In dust jacket. $20–$25.

DOBIE, J. Frank. *The First Cattle in Texas and the Southwest*. Stapled. Austin, 1939. First edition. $75–$125.

DOBIE, J. Frank. *The Flavor of Texas*. Illustrated. Cloth. Dallas, 1936. First edition. $100–$125.

DOBIE, J. Frank. *Folklore of the Southwest*. 16pp., wrappers. No place, 1924. First edition. $100-$150.

DOBIE, J. Frank. *Guide to Life and Literature of the Southwest*. Illustrated. Wrappers. Austin, 1943. First edition. $35–$50.

DOBIE, J. Frank. *John C. Duval, First Texas Man of Letters*. Illustrated. Cloth. Dallas, 1939. First edition. One of 1,000. In dust jacket. $150.

DOBIE, J. Frank. *The Longhorns*. 16 plates by Tom Lea. Rawhide. Boston, 1941. First edition. One of 265 signed. Boxed. $1,000–$1,750. Trade edition: Pictorial cloth. In dust jacket. $35.

DOBIE, J. Frank. *The Mustangs*. Illustrated. Leather. Boston, (1952). First edition. One of 100 with original drawing. Boxed. $2,500–$3,000. Trade edition: Cloth. In dust jacket. $50–$75.

DOBIE, J. Frank. *On the Open Range*. Illustrated. Pictorial cloth. Dallas, (1931). First edition. One of 750. $300–$375.

DOBIE, J. Frank. *Tales of the Mustang*. Boards. Dallas, 1936. First edition. One of 300 for the Book Club of Texas. Boxed. $750–$1,000.

DOBIE, J. Frank. *A Vaquero of the Brush Country*. Boards and cloth. Dallas, 1929. First edition, first issue, with "Rio Grande River" (in error) on end-sheet maps. In dust jacket. $100–$125. Author's first commercially published (trade) book. London, 1948. Cloth. First English edition. In dust jacket. $100–$125.

DOBIE, J. Frank. *The Voice of the Coyote*. Illustrated. Cloth. Boston, 1949. First edition. In dust jacket. $50–$60. Another issue: Limited edition, with an inserted slip signed by Dobie. $300–$450.

DOBIE, J. Frank, and others (editors). *Mustangs and Cow Horses*. Illustrated. Cloth. Austin, 1940. First edition. $150–$175. Without jacket, $100.

DOBIE, J. Frank (editor). *Legends of Texas*. Cloth. Austin, 1924. First edition. $100–$125.

DOBSON, Austin. *Horace Walpole, A Memoir*. Illustrated by Percy and Leon Moran. Boards. New York, 1890. One of 50 on Japan paper. $150–$200.

DOBSON, Austin. *Three Unpublished Poems*. 6 leaves, brown wrappers. Winchester, England, 1930. First edition. $75–$100.

DOBSON, Austin. *Vignettes in Rhyme*. Cloth. London, 1873. First edition. $100–$150. Author's first book.

DOCTOROW, E.L. *Big as Life*. Cloth. New York, (1966). First edition. In dust jacket. $50–$75.

DOCTOROW, E.L. *Ragtime*. Cloth. New York, (1975). First edition. One of 150 signed. Boxed. $150–$175. Trade edition: In dust jacket. $25–$35.

DOCTOROW, E.L. *Welcome to Hard Times*. Cloth. New York, 1960. First edition. In dust jacket. $75–$125. Author's first book.

DOCUMENTOS Relativos al Piadoso Fondo de Misiones para Conversión y Civilización de las Numerosas Tribus Barabaras de la Antiua y Neuva California. 60pp. bound with 8 pp. *Esposición a la Comisión, etc.* Mexico, 1845. $300–$500.

DODDRIDGE, Joseph. *Notes, on the Settlement and Indian Wars, of the Western Parts of Virginia and Pennsylvania, etc.* Calf. Wellsburgh, Va., 1924. First edition. $400–$600.

DODGE, Grenville M. *Biographical Sketch of James Bridger, Mountaineer, Trapper and Guide*. 2 plates. 10 leaves, wrappers. Kansas City, (1905). First edition, without preface. $100–$150. New York, 1905. 3 plates, one folding. 27 pp. wrappers. $100.

DODGE, Grenville M. *How We Built the Union Pacific Railway*. 30 plates. Printed wrappers. Council Bluffs, Iowa. (1908?). First edition, first issue, without printer's name on page before title page. $100–$150.. Second issue, $50–$100. Another edition: (New York, 1910 or 1908?) $50–$75.

DODGE, Grenville M. *Union Pacific Railroad, Report of G.M. Dodge, Chief Engineer, to the Board of Directors on a Branch Line from the Union Pacific Railroad to Idaho, Montana, Oregon, and Puget's Sound*. Large folding map. 13 pp., wrappers. Washington, 1868. First edition. $300. Second edition, same date: $225.

DODGE, J.R. *Red Men of the Ohio Valley*. Illustrated. Cloth. Springfield, Ohio, 1859. First edition. $75–$100. Springfield, 1860. Second edition. $50–$75.

DODGE, M.E. *Hans Brinker; or, The Silver Skates*. Frontispiece, 3 plates by Thomas Nast. Cloth. New York, 1866. (By Mary Mapes Dodge.) First edition. $350–$400. New York, 1876. Cloth. With a new postscript by the author. $50.

DODGE, M.E. *The Irvington Stories*. Frontispiece, 4 plates. Cloth. New York, 1865. (By Mary Mapes Dodge.) First edition. $75–$100. Author's first book.

DODGE, Mary Mapes. See Dodge, M.E.

DODGE, Mary Mapes. *Donald and Dorothy*. Illustrated. Cloth. Boston, 1883. First American edition. $50–$75.

DODGE, Orvil. *Pioneer History of Coos and Curry Counties, Oregon*. Illustrated. Cloth. Salem, Ore., 1898. First edition. $100–$125.

DODGE, Richard Irving. See *A Living Issue*.

DODGE, Richard Irving. *The Black Hills*. 14 tinted plates, folding map. Cloth. New York, 1876. First edition. $100–$125.

DODGE, Richard Irving. *Our Wild Indians*. Illustrated. Cloth. Hartford, 1882. First edition. $75–$100.

DODGE, Richard Irving. *The Plains of the Great West and Their Inhabitants*. Illustrated, folding map. Cloth. New York, 1877. First edition. $75–$100.

DODGE, Theodore A. *Riders of Many Lands*. 19 illustrations by Frederic Remington. Cloth. New York, 1894. First edition. $100–$125.

DODGE, William Sumner. *Oration: "Liberty, Her Struggles, Perils and Triumphs."* 30 pp., wrappers. San Francisco, 1868. First edition. $50–$125.

DODGE, William Sumner. *A Waif of the War; or, The History of the 75th Illinois Infantry*. Cloth. Chicago, 1866. $150–$175.

DODGSON, Campbell (editor). *An Iconography of the Engravings of Stephen Gooden*. Illustrated. Buckram. London, 1944. One of 500. $150–$175. Another issue: Buckram, vellum spine, with original proof frontispiece (etching) signed by Gooden. One of 160. Boxed. $375.

DODGSON, Charles L. See Carroll, Lewis; Spavery. Also see *An Index to "In Memoriam."*

DODGSON, Charles L. *Lawn Tennis Tournaments*. 10 pp., sewed, without wrappers. London, 1883. First edition. $200–$300. Also, $165 (A, 1979).

DODGSON, Charles L. *Euclid and His Modern Rivals*. Charts and diagrams. Red cloth. London, 1879. First edition. $100–$125.

DODSON, W.C. (editor). *Campaigns of Wheeler and His Cavalry, 1862–1865*. Cloth. Atlanta, 1899. First edition. $150.

DOLBEN, Digby Mackworth. *The Poems of Digby Mackworth Dolben*. Edited by Robert Bridges, Portrait, plates. Boards, cloth spine, paper label. London, 1911. First edition. $100–$125.

DOMENECH, Emmanuel. *Seven Years' Residence in the Great Deserts of North America*. Folding map, 5 tinted plates. 2 vols., cloth. London, 1860. First edition. $300–$400.

DOMESTIC Cookery: The Experienced American Housekeeper. Calf. New York, 1823. $150.

DOMESTIC Manners of the Americans. 24 plates, 2 vols., cloth, paper labels, London, 1832. (By Frances Trollope.) First edition. $400–$500. Rebound copy, $275. New York, 1832. Cloth. First American edition, $100–$150.

DONAN, P. *Gold Fields of Baker County, Eastern Oregon*. Folding map, 36 pp., wrappers. Portland, (1898). First edition. $150–$200.

DON Juan. 6 vols., boards, paper labels (*Don Juan*, 1819, followed by books of same title containing Cantos III, IV, and V; VI, VII, and VIII; IX, X, and XI; XII, XIII, and XIV; XV and XVI). London, 1819–21–23–23–23–24. (By George Gordon Noel, Lord Byron.) First editions. $1,000 and up. (Note: A complete set of the first editions, accompanied by the second edition of Cantos I–II, brought $700 at a New York auction in 1974.)

DONLEAVY, J.P. *The Ginger Man*. Green wrappers. Paris, (1955). Olympia Press. First edition. $400–$600. New York, (1958). Cloth. First American edition (revised). In dust jacket. $50–$125. Author's first book.

DONNE, John. *Complete Poetry and Selected Prose*. Edited by John Hayward. Blue morocco. London, 1929. Nonesuch Press. One of 675. Boxed. $200–$250. Another issue: Thin paper edition. $300–$350.

DONNE, John. *Love Poems*. Portrait. Boards. London, 1923. Nonesuch Press. One of 1,250. $100–$150.

DONNE, John. *Poems*. 2 vols., cloth. New York, 1895. Grolier Club. One of 380. $100.

DONOHO, M.H. *Circle-dot, a True Story of Cowboy Life 40 Years Ago*. Frontispiece. Cloth. Topeka, 1907. First edition. $75–$85.

DOOLITTLE, Hilda. See D.,H.; Helforth, John.

DOOMED City (The). Folding map. 54 pp., wrappers. Detroit, 1871. (By Charles H. Mackintosh.) $35–$50.

DORING, Ernest N. *The Guadagnini Family of Violin Makers.* Illustrated. Cloth. Chicago, 1949. First edition. $400–$600. De Luxe edition: $750 and up.

DORING, Ernest N. *How Many Strads?* Illustrated. Red cloth. Chicago, 1945. First edition, first printing. One of 1,400. Boxed. $200–$300.

DORMAN, Caroline. *Wild Flowers of Louisiana.* Illustrated. Cloth. New York, 1934. $75–$85.

DORN, Edward. *Gunslinger: Books I and II.* 2 vols., suede. Los Angeles, 1968–69. Black Sparrow Press. One of 26 signed. $250–$300. (Also in wrappers and other signed issues.)

DORN, Edward. *The Shoshoneans.* Photographs. Oblong, cloth. New York, 1966. First edition. In dust jacket. $100–$125.

DORN, Edward. *What I See in the Maximus Poems.* Wrappers. (Ventura, Calif.), 1960. First edition. $75–$100. Author's first book.

DOS PASSOS, John. See Cendrars, Blaise.

DOS PASSOS, John. *Airways, Inc.* Blue boards and cloth. New York, (1928). First edition. In dust jacket. $50–$60.

DOS PASSOS, John. *The Bitter Drink.* Boards. San Francisco, (1939). Grabhorn Press. First edition. One of 35. $400–$450. Also, $240 (A, 1979).

DOS PASSOS, John. *Facing the Chair: Story of the Americanization of Two Foreign-born Workmen.* Wrappers. Boston, 1927. First edition. $75–$100.

DOS PASSOS, John. *Ford and Hearst.* San Francisco, 1940. Grabhorn Press. One of 35. $200–$250.

DOS PASSOS, John. *The 42nd Parallel.* Decorated orange boards and cloth. New York. 1930. First edition. In dust jacket. $100–$125.

DOS PASSOS, John. *Most Likely to Succeed.* Cloth. New York, (1954). First edition. One of 1,000 signed. In dust jacket. $50–$75.

DOS PASSOS, John. *1919.* Orange-red cloth. New York, (1932). First edition (so stated). In dust jacket. $125–$150.

DOS PASSOS, John. *Number One.* Gray and pink cloth. Boston, 1943. First edition. In dust jacket. $35–$50.

DOS PASSOS, John. *One Man's Initiation—1917.* Pale-blue cloth. London, (1920). First edition, first issue, with broken type on page 35. In dust jacket. $250–$300. Second state: $200–$250. Author's first book. New York, 1922. Red cloth, paper label. First American edition. One of 500 from English sheets. In dust jacket. $150.

DOS PASSOS, John. *Orient Express.* Illustrated in color by the author. Cloth. New York, 1927. First edition. In dust jacket, with "M-A" on copyright page. $75–$100.

DOS PASSOS, John. *A Pushcart at the Curb.* Pictorial boards and cloth, paper label. New York, (1922). First edition, first state, with "GHD" insignia on copyright page. In dust jacket. $75.

DOS PASSOS, John. *Rosinante to the Road Again.* Yellow boards and cloth, paper labels. New York, (1922). First edition, first state, with "GHD" on copyright page. In dust jacket. $125–$150.

DOS PASSOS, John. *Three Soldiers.* Black cloth. New York, (1921). First edition, first state, with "signing" for "singing" on page 213. In first state dust jacket, with publisher's blurbs on all sides. $400–$450. Lacking jacket. $75–$85. Advance copy: Tan wrappers. $275 (A, 1977).

DOS PASSOS, John. *U.S.A. (The 42nd Parallel, 1919, The Big Money).* Illustrated by Reginald Marsh, 3 vols., buckram. Boston, 1946. First illustrated edition. One of 365 signed. Boxed. $100–$125. Trade edition: 3 vols., cloth. $50–$60.

DOS PASSOS, John. *The Villages Are the Heart of Spain.* Cloth. Chicago, (1937). First edition. One of 1,200. $75–$100.

DOSTOEVSKY, F.M. *The Grand Inquisitor.* Translated by S.S. Koteliansky. Introduction by D.H. Lawrence. Vellum. (London), 1930. First edition. One of 300. Boxed. $150–$275(!).

DOUGHTY, Charles M. *Travels in Arabia Deserta.* Illustrated, folding map in pocket. 2 vols., cloth. Cambridge, 1888. First edition. $750–$1,000. New York, 1923. Introduction by T.E. Lawrence. 2 vols. $100–$175. New York, 1953. Limited Editions Club. Boxed. $40–$50.

DOUGHTY, William. *The Physical Geography of the North Pacific Ocean and Peculiarities of its Circulation.* 27 pp., wrappers. Augusta, Ga., 1867. First edition. $200.

DOUGLAS, Lord Alfred. *The City of the Soul.* Vellum boards. London, 1899. First edition. $100–$125.

DOUGLAS, Lord Alfred. *In Excelsis.* Cloth. London, 1924. First edition. One of 100 signed. In dust jacket. $75–$100.

DOUGLAS, Lord Alfred. *Lyrics.* Cloth. London, 1935. First edition. One of 50 signed. $100–$125.

DOUGLAS, Lord Alfred. *My Friendship with Oscar Wilde.* Boards and cloth. New York, 1932. $75–$100.

DOUGLAS, Lord Alfred. *Oscar Wilde and Myself.* Cloth. London, 1914. First edition. In dust jacket. $100–$125.

DOUGLAS, Lord Alfred. *Poèmes.* Text in English and French. Portrait frontispiece. Wrappers. Paris, 1896. First edition. One of 20 on Hollande paper. (Usually inscribed.) $400–$500. Ordinary issue: $40–$50. Author's first book.

DOUGLAS, C.L. *Cattle Kings of Texas.* Illustrated. Cloth. Dallas, (1939). First edition. $75–$150. Second edition, same date: Rawhide. Limited. $300–$400.

DOUGLAS, C.L. *Famous Texas Feuds.* Illustrated. Decorated cloth and leather. Dallas, (1936). First edition. In dust jacket. $100–$125.

DOUGLAS, C.L. *The Gentlemen in White Hats.* Illustrated. Cloth. Dallas, (1934). First edition. In dust jacket. $100–$125.

DOUGLAS, David. *Journal Kept by David Douglas During His Travels in North America 1823–27.* Portrait. Cloth. London, 1914. First edition. One of 500. $150–$200.

DOUGLAS, George. *The House with Green Shutters.* Cloth. London, 1901. (By George Douglas Brown.) First edition. $50–$60.

DOUGLAS, James. *The Gold Fields of Canada.* 18 pp., wrappers. Quebec, 1863. $150.

DOUGLAS, Norman. See Bey, Pilaff; Douglass, G. Norman; McDonald, Edward D.; Normyx. Also see *The Blue Grotto and Its Literature; Disiecta Membra; Index; Some Antiquarian Notes; Three Monographs.*

DOUGLAS, Norman. *Alone.* Red cloth. London, 1921. First edition, first issue, with Postscript on page 140 and erratum slip facing page 156. In dust jacket. $50.

DOUGLAS, Norman. *The Angel of Manfredonia.* Boards and cloth. San Francisco, 1929. One of 225 signed. $100–$150.

DOUGLAS, Norman. *Birds and Beasts of the Greek Anthology.* Frontispiece. Blue boards, paper label. (Florence, Italy), 1927. First edition. One of 500 signed. In dust jacket. $100–$150.

DOUGLAS, Norman. *Capri: Materials for a Description of the Island.* Illustrated. Boards and cloth, leather label. Florence, 1930. First edition. One of 500 signed. $150–$200. Another issue: Blue cloth. De Luxe issue. One of 103 signed. $400–$500.

DOUGLAS, Norman. *D.H. Lawrence and Maurice Magnus.* Portrait frontispiece. Tan wrappers. (Florence), 1924 (actually, 1925). First edition, with pink printed price slip tipped in. $75–$100.

DOUGLAS, Norman. *Experiments.* Boards, paper label. (Florence), 1925. First edition. One of 300 signed. In dust jacket. $75–$100. London, 1925. One of 300 signed. $50–$75.

DOUGLAS, Norman. *Fountains in the Sand.* Illustrated. Blue cloth, blocked in white. London, (1912). First edition, first state of binding; first issue, with 16 plates. $75–$100.

DOUGLAS, Norman. *How About Europe?* Decorated boards. (Florence), 1929. First edition. One of 550 signed. In dust jacket. $50–$75. London, 1930. Orange cloth. In dust jacket. $50.

DOUGLAS, Norman. *In the Beginning.* Printed boards, leather label. (Florence), 1927. First edition. One of 700 signed. In dust jacket. $125–$150. New York, (1928). Boards. First American edition. In dust jacket. $50–$75. London, 1928. Cloth. In dust jacket. $100.

DOUGLAS, Norman. *London Street Games.* Buckram. London, (1916). St. Catherine Press. First edition. One of 500. $75–$125. London, (1931). Boards and cloth. Second edition. One of 110 signed. $100–$150. Trade issue: $25–$30.

DOUGLAS, Norman. *Looking Back: An Autobiographical Excursion.* Illustrated. 2 vols., boards and buckram. London, 1933. First edition. One of 535 signed. In dust jacket. $125–$135. New York, 1933. Brown cloth. First American edition. In dust jacket. $35–$40.

DOUGLAS, Norman. *Nerinda (1901).* Orange boards. Florence, 1929. First edition. One of 475 signed. In dust jacket. Boxed. $85–$125.

DOUGLAS, Norman. *Old Calabria.* Brown buckram. London, (1915). First edition, first issue, with white end papers. In dust jacket. $75–$85. Boston, 1915. Light-green cloth. First American edition. In dust jacket. $40–$60.

DOUGLAS, Norman. *One Day.* Portraits. Full scarlet leather. Chapelle-Reanville, France, 1929. Hours Press. First edition. One of 200 on Rives paper, signed. $200–$250. Another issue: Boards. One of 300. $75–$100.

DOUGLAS, Norman. *Paneros.* Gold cloth and boards, leather label. Florence, (1930). First edition. One of 250 signed. In dust jacket. Boxed. $100–$150. London, 1931. Boards and cloth. First English edition. One of 650. $75–$100. New York, 1932. Illustrated. Vellum. First American edition. One of 750. Boxed. $50–$75.

DOUGLAS, Norman. *Siren Land.* Frontispiece portrait, plates and map. Cloth. London, 1911. First edition. $100–$150. New York, (1923). "New and revised edition." In dust jacket. $50.

DOUGLAS, Norman. *Some Limericks.* Gold-colored linen. (Florence), 1928. First edition. One of 110 signed. $150. (New York), 1928. Cloth. First American edition. $100–$125. (Florence), 1929. Wrappers. $75–$100. Another issue: Buckram. $75–$100. (Chicago, about 1928–30?) Buckram. $75. Second impression. $50. Boston, 1942. Boards and leather. "4th Continental Edition." Boxed. $50.

DOUGLAS, Norman. *South Wind.* Brown cloth. London, (1917). First edition. $150–$200. London, 1922. Cloth. One of 150 on blue paper, signed. $200–$250. New York,

1928. Illustrated by Valenti Angelo. One of 250 signed by Douglas. Boxed. $100–$135. Chicago, 1929. Illustrated by John Austen. 2 vols., buckram. In dust jacket. Boxed. $65–$85. Another issue: 2 vols. in one, half morocco. One of 40 signed. $150–$200. New York, 1932. Limited Editions Club. Boxed. $40–$50.

DOUGLAS, Norman. *Summer Islands: Ischia and Ponza.* Blue cloth. London, (1931). First edition. One of 500. In dust jacket. $50–$65. (New York), 1931. The Colophon. Illustrated. Cloth. First American edition. One of 500 signed. Boxed. $50–$75.

DOUGLASS, G. Norman. *Contribution to an Avifauna of Baden.* 12 pp., without covers. (London?, 1894.) (By Norman Douglas.) First edition. $125–$150.

DOUGLASS, G. Norman. *On the Darwinian Hypothesis of Sexual Selection.* 16 pp., wrappers. London, 1895. (By Norman Douglas.) First edition. One of 25. $250–$350.

DOUGLASS, G. Norman. *On the Herpetology of the Grand Duchy of Baden.* 64 pp., pale gray-blue wrappers. London, 1894. (By Norman Douglas.) First edition. $125–$200.

DOUGLASS, G. Norman. *Report on the Pumice Stone Industry of the Lipari Islands.* 8 pp. London, 1895. (By Norman Douglas.) First edition. One of 125. $200–$300. (France), 1928. Hours Press. Second edition. One of 80. Inscribed, $132 (A, 1979).

DOVES PRESS BIBLE. (A general term.) See *The English Bible.*

DOW, George Francis. *The Arts and Crafts in New England.* Illustrated. Half cloth. Topsfield, Mass., 1927. First edition. In dust jacket. $150–$200.

DOW, George Francis. *The Sailing Ships of New England: Series Three.* Illustrated. Cloth. Salem, 1928. First edition. In dust jacket. $75–$100.

DOW, George Francis. *Slave Ships and Slaving.* Illustrated. Buckram. Salem, 1923. $100–$125. Another issue: Half cloth. Large paper. One of 97. $200–$250. Salem, 1927. Buckram. In dust jacket. $100–$125.

DOW, George Francis. *Whale Ships and Whaling.* Illustrated. Buckram. Salem, 1925. First edition. One of 950. $125–$150. Another issue: Half cloth. Large paper. One of 97. $275–$350.

DOW, George Francis, and Edmonds, John H. *The Pirates of the New England Coast.* 29 plates. Cloth. Salem, 1923. First edition. In dust jacket. $75–$100. Another issue: Large paper. One of 84. $150. New York, 1968. New edition. $30.

DOW, Lorenzo. *The Life and Travels of Lorenzo Dow.* Half calf. Hartford, 1804. First edition. $300–$400.

DOWDEN, Edward. *A Woman's Reliquary.* Boards, cloth spine. Dundrum, Ireland, 1913. Cuala Press. One of 300. $50–$60.

DOWNEY, Fairfax. *Indian-Fighting Army.* Ilustrated. Cloth. New York, 1941. First edition. In dust jacket. $50–$75. New York, 1944. Cloth. In dust jacket. $25.

DOWNFALL and Death of King Oedipus (The). 2 parts, blue wrappers, or (later) bound together in blue wrappers. (Guildford, England, 1880-81.) (By Edward FitzGerald.) First edition. Bound together. $400–$500.

DOWNIE, William. *Hunting for Gold: Personal Experiences in the Early Days on the Pacific Coast.* Frontispiece. Half morocco or cloth. San Francisco, 1893. First edition. $150–$200.

DOWNING, Andrew Jackson. *The Architecture of Country Houses.* Illustrated. Pictorial cloth. New York, 1850. First edition. $150–$200.

DOWNING, Andrew Jackson. *The Fruits and Fruit Trees of America.* 69 hand-colored plates. Half morocco. New York, 1850. $750–$1,250.

DOWSON, Ernest. *Decorations: In Verse and Prose.* Vellum. London, 1899. First edition. $75–$100.

DOWSON, Ernest. *The Pierrot of the Minute.* Illustrated by Aubrey Beardsley. Cloth. London, 1897. First edition. One of 300 on handmade paper. $250–$350. Another issue: One of 30 on Japan paper. $600–$800. New York, 1923. Grolier Club. One of 300 designed by Bruce Rogers. $125–$150.

DOWSON, Ernest. *The Poems of Ernest Dowson.* Illustrated by Aubrey Beardsley. Cloth. London, 1905. First edition. In dust jacket. $150–$200.

DOWSON, Ernest. *Verses.* Cover decorations by Aubrey Beardsley. Vellum. London, 1896. First edition. One of 30 on Japan paper. $400–$500. Another issue: One of 300 on handmade paper. $200–$300.

DOYLE, A. Conan. See *Beeton's Christmas Annual; Dreamland and Ghostland.*

DOYLE, A. Conan. *The Adventures of Sherlock Holmes.* Illustrated by Sidney Paget. Light-blue cloth. London, 1892. First edition, first binding, lacking lettering on street sign. $500–$600. (Note: A notorious book for cracked hinges. If so defective, value drops to $200–$275, or even less.) Later binding, $200–$275.

DOYLE, A. Conan. *The Case-Book of Sherlock Holmes.* Red cloth. London, (1927). First edition. In dust jacket. $500–$650. New York, 1927. First American edition, with "GD" on copyright page. In dust jacket. $500–$750 (!).

DOYLE, A. Conan. *The Doings of Raffles Haw.* Cloth. London, 1892. First edition, first binding, smooth blue cloth. $250. New York, (1892). Cloth. First American edition. $75–$150. Also, $70 (A, 1980).

DOYLE, A. Conan. *The Firm of Girdlestone.* Dark red-brown cloth, black lettering. London, 1890. First edition. $50–$75.

DOYLE, A. Conan. *The Great Shadow.* Pictorial wrappers. Bristol, England, 1892. First edition. $150–$200. Also, in cloth. $125–$150.

DOYLE, A. Conan. *The Great Shadow and Beyond the City.* Illustrated. Tan cloth. Bristol, England, (1893). First edition. $75–$100.

DOYLE, A. Conan. *His Last Bow.* Red cloth. London, 1917. First edition. $150–$200. New York, 1917. Cloth. First American edition. $40–$60.

DOYLE, A. Conan. *The History of Spiritualism.* 2 vols., cloth. London, (1926). First edition. $150–$200.

DOYLE, A. Conan. *The Hound of the Baskervilles.* Illustrated by Sidney Paget. Decorated red cloth. London, 1902. First edition. $400–$600. Worn, $185. Garden City, (1902). First American edition, first issue, without the "Published 1902" line on copyright page. $400–$500. Toronto, 1902. First Canadian edition. $250.

DOYLE, A. Conan. *The Land of Mist.* Cloth. London, (1926). First edition. In dust jacket. $125–$150.

DOYLE, A. Conan. *The Maracot Deep and Other Stories.* Cloth. London, (1929). First edition. In dust jacket. $100–$125.

DOYLE, A. Conan. *The Memoirs of Sherlock Holmes.* Illustrated by Sidney Paget. Blue cloth, gold letters. London, 1894. First edition. $500–$600. New York, 1894. Blue cloth. First American edition. $250–$300. (Suppressed by Doyle.)

DOYLE, A. Conan. *Micah Clarke.* Blue cloth. London, 1889. First edition. $125–$150. New York, 1894. Cloth. First American edition. $50–$75.

DOYLE, A. Conan. *My Friend the Murderer.* Blue cloth. New York, (1893). First edition. (A piracy suppressed by Doyle and never published in England.) $200–$250. Later: Wrappers. $200–$250.

DOYLE, A. Conan. *The Refugees: A Tale of Two Continents.* 3 vols., green cloth. London, 1893. First edition. $400–$500. New York, 1893. Illustrated. Cloth. First American edition. $50–$200(!).

DOYLE, A. Conan. *The Return of Sherlock Holmes.* Cloth. London, 1905. First edition. $300–$500. New York, 1905. Cloth. First American edition. $75–$100.

DOYLE, A. Conan. *Round the Red Lamp.* Red cloth. London, 1894. First edition, with October ads. $100–$125.

DOYLE, A. Conan. *The Sign of Four.* Frontispiece. Dark-red cloth. London, 1890. First edition, first issue, with "Spencer Blackett's Standard Library" on spine. $1,500–$2,000. Also, $1,400 (A, 1981).

DOYLE, A. Conan. *The Speckled Band.* Stage diagrams. Printed brown wrappers. London, 1912. First edition. $300–$400.

DOYLE, A. Conan. *The Stark Munro Letters.* Frontispiece and vignette title page. Dark-green or blue cloth. London, 1895. First edition. $100–$125. New York, 1895. Red cloth. First American edition. $50.

DOYLE, A. Conan. *A Study in Scarlet.* Illustrated. White wrappers. London, 1888. First edition in book form, first issue, with "younger" correctly spelled in preface. $15,000 (A, 1981). Rebound copies, $5,000 and up. (For actual first edition, see *Beeton's Christmas Annual.*)

DOYLE, A. Conan. *Through the Magic Door.* Cloth. London, 1907. First edition. $75–$100.

DOYLE, A. Conan. *Uncle Bernac.* Red cloth. London, 1897. First published edition. $50–$60. New York, 1897. Red cloth. First American edition. $25.

DOYLE, A. Conan. *The Valley of Fear.* Illustrated by Arthur I. Keller. Red cloth. New York, (1914). First edition. $125–$150. London, 1915. Red cloth. First English edition. $150–$200.

DOYLE, A. Conan. *The White Company.* 3 vols., dark-red cloth. London, 1891. First edition. $400–$600. New York, 1895. Illustrated. Cloth. First English edition. $125–$135.

DOYLE, A. Conan, and Barrie, James M. *Jane Annie: Or the Good Conduct Prize.* Wrappers. London, 1893. First edition. $200–$250.

DOYLE, John T. *In the International Arbitral Court of The Hague: The Case of the Pious Fund of California.* 106 pp., unbound. San Francisco, 1906. $100–$150.

DOYLE, John T. *On Behalf of the Roman Catholic Church of Upper California. Points in Reply Submitted by Messrs. Doyle and Doyle of Counsel for the Prelates.* 8 pp., self-wrappers. No place, (1902). $50–$100. Another edition: (Menlo Park, Calif., 1902.) 11 pp., wrappers. $50–$100.

DOYLE, John T. *The Pious Fund Case.* 67 pp., unbound. San Francisco, 1904(?). $100–$150.

DRABBLE, Margaret. *Virginia Woolf: A Personal Debt.* Wrappers. New York, 1973. First edition. One of 110 signed. $100–$125.

DRAFT of a Constitution Published Under the Direction of a Committee of Citizens of Colorado. Denver, 1875. $150–$300.

DRAGO, Harry Sinclair. *Outlaws on Horseback.* Illustrated, map. Cloth. New York, 1964. First edition. One of 150 signed. Boxed. $60–$100.

DRAGO, Harry Sinclair. *Wild, Woolly & Wicked.* Illustrated by Nick Eggenhofer. Cloth. New York, 1960. First edition. One of 250 signed. $50–$75. Trade edition: In dust jacket. $20.

DRAGOON Campaigns to the Rocky Mountains. By a Dragoon. Blue cloth. New York, 1836. (By James Hildreth.) First edition. $300–$400.

DRAKE, Benjamin. *The Great Indian Chief of the West.* Illustrated. Cloth. Cincinnati, 1856. Reprint edition of *The Life and Adventures of Black Hawk.* $50–$60.

DRAKE, Benjamin. *The Life and Adventures of Black Hawk.* Portrait and plates. Cloth. Cincinnati, 1838. First edition. $150–$175.

DRAKE, Benjamin. *Life of Tecumseh, and His Brother the Prophet.* Cloth. Cincinnati, 1841. First edition. $75–$100. Cincinnati, 1852. $40.

DRAKE, Benjamin. *Tales and Sketches of the Queen City.* Cloth. Cincinnati, 1838. First edition. $75–$100.

DRAKE, Benjamin, and Mansfield, E.D. *Cincinnati in 1826.* 2 plates. Leather. Cincinnati, 1827. First edition. $100–$150.

DRAKE, Daniel. *An Account of Epidemic Cholera, as It Appeared in Cincinnati.* 46 pp., wrappers. Cincinnati, 1832. First edition. $200–$300.

DRAKE, Daniel. *Natural and Statistical View, or Picture of Cincinnati and the Miami Country.* 2 folding maps. Printed boards. Cincinnati, 1815. First edition. $300–$600.

DRAKE, Daniel. *Pioneer Life in Kentucky: A Series of Reminiscential Letters from Daniel Drake, M.D., of Cincinnati to His Children.* Portrait. Cloth. Cincinnati, 1870. First edition. $150–$200.

DRAKE, Daniel. *A Practical Treatise on the History, Prevention, and Treatment of Epidemic Cholera.* Cloth, paper spine label. Cincinnati, 1832. First edition. $400–$500.

DRAKE, Daniel. *A Systematic Treatise, Historical, Etiological, and Practical, on the Principal Diseases of the Interior Valley of North America.* (First series.) Maps and plates. Full leather. Cincinnati, 1850. First edition. $600–$800. Philadelphia, 1854. (Second series.) First edition. $300–$400.

DRAKE, Daniel, and Wright, Guy W. (editors). *The Western Medical and Physical Journal, Original and Eclectic.* Vol. 1. Leather. Cincinnati, 1827–28. $150–$200.

DRAKE, Joseph Rodman. See Croaker.

DRAKE, Joseph Rodman. *The Culprit Fay and Other Poems.* Frontispiece, vignette title page. Blue or purple cloth. New York, 1835. First edition. $100–$150. (Also bound in full morocco.) New York, 1923. Grolier Club. One of 300. $75–$100.

DRAKE, Joseph Rodman, and Halleck, Fitz-Greene. *The Croakers.* Green cloth. New York, 1860. One of 250. $100–$150. (See Croaker for first edition.)

DRAKE, Leah Bodine. *A Hornbook for Witches.* Cloth. Sauk City, Wis. 1950. First edition. In dust jacket. $600–$800.

DRAKE, Morgan. *Lake Superior Railroad: Letter to the Hon. Lewis Cass.* 24 pp., wrappers. Pontiac, 1853. $200–$300.

DRANNAN, Capt. William F. *Thirty-one Years on the Plains and in the Mountains.* Illustrated. Cloth. Chicago, 1899. First edition. $150–$175.

DRAPER, John William. *Human Physiology.* Illustrated. Cloth. New York, 1856. First edition. $125–$150.

DRAPER, John William. *A Treatise on the Forces Which Produce the Organization of Plants.* 4 plates. Cloth. New York, 1844. First edition. $125–$150.

DRAYSON, Capt. Alfred W. *Sporting Scenes Amongst the Kaffirs of South Africa.* 8 colored plates by Harrison Weir. Cloth. London, 1858. First edition. $150–$200.

DRAYTON, John. *Memoirs of the American Revolution.* Portrait, 2 maps. 2 vols., cloth. Charleston, 1821. First edition. $500–$750. Also, $700 (A, 1977).

DRAYTON, John. A *View of South-Carolina.* 2 maps, 2 tables, 3 plates. Boards. Charleston, 1802. First edition. $800–$1,000.

DRAYTON, Michael. *Poems.* Edited by J. Payne Collier. Half morocco. London, 1856. Roxburghe Club. $100–$150.

DREAM Drops, or Stories from Fairy Land. By a Dreamer. Wrappers, or cloth. Boston, (1887). (By Amy Lowell.) First edition. Wrappers (151 copies): $1,000 and up. Also, soiled, $700 (A, 1981). Cloth (99 copies): $1,700. Also, $900 (A, 1977). Author's first book.

DREAM of Gerontius (The). Wrappers. London, 1866. (By John Henry, Cardinal Newman.) First edition, printed dedication "J. H. N." $1,000 and up.

DREAMLAND and Ghostland: An Original Collection of Tales and Warnings. 3 vols., pictorial red cloth. London, (1887). First edition, first binding (red cloth). $750 and up. Also, $325 (A, 1970). (Note: Contains 6 stories by A. Conan Doyle.)

DREISER, Theodore. See Davis, Hubert.

DREISER, Theodore. *An American Tragedy.* 2 vols., black cloth, white end papers. New York, 1925. First edition, first issue, with Boni & Liveright imprint. In dust jackets. Boxed $100–$150. Another (later) issue: 2 vols., blue boards and cloth. First limited edition. One of 795 signed. In dust jackets. Boxed. $200–$300. London, 1926. Cloth. In dust jacket. $100. New York, 1954. Limited Editions Club. Boxed. $60–$80.

DREISER, Theodore. *A Book About Myself.* Ribbed red cloth, white end papers. New York, (1922). First edition. In dust jacket. $40–$50.

DREISER, Theodore. *The Carnegie Works at Pittsburgh.* Decorations by Martha Colley. Boards, paper label. Chelsea, N.Y., (1927). First edition. One of 150. In dust jacket. $100–$125. Another issue: Cloth. One of 27 on Marlowe Antique paper with a manuscript sheet in a special pocket at back of the book. In dust jacket. $200–$300.

DREISER, Theodore. *Chains: Lesser Novels and Stories.* Decorated boards and cloth. New York, 1927. First edition. One of 440 signed. Boxed. $150–$250. Trade edition: Dark-blue cloth. In dust jacket. $35–$50.

DREISER, Theodore. *The Color of a Great City.* Illustrated. Black cloth, white end papers. New York, (1923). First edition. In dust jacket. $75–$100.

DREISER, Theodore. *Dawn: A History of Myself.* Boards and cloth. New York, (1931). First edition. One of 275 signed. Boxed. $125–$150. Trade edition: Red and black cloth. In dust jacket. $40–$50.

DREISER, Theodore. *Dreiser Looks at Russia.* Cloth. New York, 1928. First edition. In dust jacket. $85.

DREISER, Theodore. *Epitaph: A Poem.* Illustrated by Robert Fawcett. Full leather. New York, (1929). Heron Press. First edition. One of 200 on Van Gelder paper, signed. Boxed $200–$275. Another issue: Silk. One of 200 on Keijyo Kami paper, signed. $200–$275. Another: Cloth. One of 700 signed. Boxed. $50–$60.

DREISER, Theodore. *The Financier.* Mottled light-blue cloth. New York, 1912. First edition, first issse, with "Published October, 1912" and code letter "K-M" on copyright page. In dust jacket. $75–$125.

DREISER, Theodore. *Free, and Other Stories.* Slate-blue cloth. New York, 1918. First edition. In dust jacket. $50–$75.

DREISER, Theodore. *A Gallery of Women.* 2 vols., boards and vellum. New York, 1929. First edition. One of 560 signed. In dust jackets. Boxed. $200–$300. Trade edition: 2 vols., brown cloth. In dust jackets. Boxed. $100–$150. (Precedes limited.)

DREISER, Theodore. *The "Genius."* Ribbed red cloth, white end papers. New York, 1915. First edition, first issue, 1¾ inches thick, and with page 497 so numbered. In dust jacket. $200–$275. Second issue, 1½ inches thick, no number on page 497. In dust jacket. $125–$150.

DREISER, Theodore. *The Hand of the Potter.* Light-green boards and cloth, paper label. New York, 1918. First edition, first issue, with natural linen spine (second issue is blue). In dust jacket. $100–$125. Second issue: $50–$75.

DREISER, Theodore. *Hey, Rub-A-Dub-Dub!* Dark-blue cloth. New York, 1920. First edition. In dust jacket. $50–$75.

DREISER, Theodore. *A Hoosier Holiday.* Illustrated. Light-green boards and dark-green cloth. New York, 1916. First edition, first issue, with page 173 as an integral leaf. In dust jacket. $250–$300.

DREISER, Theodore. *Jennie Gerhardt.* Frontispiece. Mottled light-blue cloth. New York, 1911. First edition, first issue, with "is" for "it" in line 30 of page 22. In dust jacket. $200–$250. Second issue, text corrected. $100–$150.

DREISER, Theodore. *Moods, Cadenced and Declaimed.* Marbled boards and cloth, white end papers. New York, 1926. First edition. One of 550 signed. Boxed. $125–$150. New York, 1928. Cloth. First trade edition (with new material). In dust jacket. $75–$100.

DREISER, Theodore. *My City.* Colored etchings by Max Pollak. Folio, boards and cloth. New York, (1929). First edition. One of 275. $150–$250.

DREISER, Theodore. *Plays of the Natural and the Supernatural.* Light-green boards, linen spine, green end papers. New York, 1916. First edition. In dust jacket. $125–$150. (Second issue has 4-page essay, "The Anaesthetic Revelation," tipped in at back.)

DREISER, Theodore. *The Seven Arts: Life, Art and America.* 28 pp., cream wrappers. New York, 1917. First edition. $75–$100.

DREISER, Theodore. *Sister Carrie.* Dark-red cloth, white end papers. New York, 1900. First edition. $1,000 and up. Also, $800 (A, 1977). (I have never seen this in dust jacket. If such a copy exists, the value should be $1,500 and up.) Author's first book. New York, 1907. Colored frontispiece. Cloth. First illustrated edition. $100. New York, 1939. Limited Editions Club. Cloth. Boxed. $85–$100.

DREISER, Theodore. *The Titan.* Mottled light-blue cloth. New York, 1914. First edition. In dust jacket. $75–$100.

DREISER, Theodore. *Tragic America.* Gray cloth. New York, (1931). First published edition. In dust jacket. $75–$100. (Note: There also exist a few copies—6 or 12?—of a suppressed prepublication issue bound for the author's private use. Value: $500 and up?)

DREISER, Theodore. *A Traveler at Forty.* Illustrated by W. Glackens. Red cloth. New York, 1913. First edition. In dust jacket. $50–$60.

DREISER, Theodore. *Twelve Men.* Blue cloth. New York, 1919. First edition. In dust jacket. $50–$75.

DREW, C.S. *Communication . . . of the Origin and Early Prosecution of the Indian War in Oregon.* 48 pp., sewed. Washington, 1860. First edition. $100–$125.

DRIFTWOOD Flames. Boards, Nashville, Tenn., (1923). First edition. In dust jacket. $500. (Includes 5 poems by Robert Penn Warren, his first book appearance.)

DRIGGS, George W. *Opening of the Mississippi; or Two Years' Campaigning in the Southwest.* Cloth. Madison, Wis., 1864. First edition. $150–$200.

DRINKWATER, John. *Abraham Lincoln.* Scarlet or purple wrappers, printed label on spine. London, 1918. First edition, with pen-and-ink correction of misprint on page (5). In dust jacket. $50–$75. Another issue: Red boards. In dust jacket. $25–$35.

DRINKWATER, John. *A Book for Bookmen.* Buckram. London, 1926. First edition. One of 50 signed. $75–$100.

DRINKWATER, John. *Loyalties.* Illustrated. Vellum and boards. (London), 1918. Beaumont Press. First edition. One of 30 on Japan vellum, signed. $300–$350. Another issue: Boards and cloth. One of 120. $100–$125. Another issue: One of 50 with hand-colored illustrations. $150–$200.

DRINKWATER, John. *Persephone.* Cloth. (New York, 1926.) First edition. One of 550 signed. $100–$125.

DRINKWATER, John. *Persuasion: Twelve Sonnets.* Wrappers. London, 1921. First edition. One of 50 signed. $75–$100.

DRINKWATER, John. *Poems.* Cloth. Birmingham, England, 1903. First edition. $150. Author's first book.

DRINKWATER, John. *Rupert Brooke: An Essay.* Boards. London, 1916. First edition. One of 115. $100–$125.

DRINKWATER, John. *Tides: A Book of Poems.* Boards. (London), 1917. Beaumont Press. First edition. One of 250. $125–$150. Another issue: Full vellum. One of 20 on vellum, signed. $300–$400.

DRINKWATER, John, and Rutherston, Albert. *Claud Lovat Fraser: A Story of His Life.* Portrait frontispiece by Rutherston, 39 Fraser illustrations, 20 in color. Cloth. London, 1923. One of 450 signed. $200–$300.

DRIPS, Joseph H. *Three Years Among the Indians in Dakota.* 139 pp., wrappers. Kimball, S.D., 1894. First edition. $750–$1,000.

DRUMHELLER, "Uncle Dan." *"Uncle Dan" Drumheller Tells Thrills of Western Trails in 1854.* Portraits. Cloth. Spokane, 1925. First edition. $100–$125.

DRURY, Dru. *Illustrations of Exotic Entomology.* Edited by J.O. Westwood. 150 hand-colored plates. 3 vols., half leather. London, 1837. $500–$600.

DRURY, The Rev. P. Sheldon (editor). *The Startling and Thrilling Narrative of the Dark and Terrible Deeds of Henry Madison, and His Associate and Accomplice Miss Ellen Stevens, Who Was Executed by the Vigilance Committee of San Francisco, on the 20th September Last.* Illustrated. 36 pp., pictorial wrappers. Cincinnati, (1857). First edition. $200–$300. Philadelphia, 1865. $100–$150.

DRYDEN, John. *Alexander's Feast.* Vellum. London, 1904. Essex House. One of 140 on vellum. $300–$375.

DRYDEN, John. *All for Love.* 2 vols., folio, half vellum. San Francisco, 1929. John Henry Nash printing. One of 250. $100–$150.

DRYDEN, John. *Dramatic Works.* Edited by Montague Summers. 6 vols., buckram and marbled boards. London, 1931–32. Nonesuch Press. $400–$500. Another issue: One of 50 sets on Van Gelder paper. $500–$600.

DRYDEN, John. *Of Dramatick Poesie. An Essay, 1668. Preceded by a Dialogue on Poetic Drama by T.S. Eliot.* Marbled boards, cloth spine. London, 1928. First edition. One of 580. In dust jacket. Boxed. $100–$125. Another issue: Boards and vellum. One of 55 signed by Eliot. In dust jacket. Boxed. $625.

DRYDEN, John. *Songs and Poems.* Illustrated. Half cloth. Waltham Saint Lawrence, England, 1957. Golden Cockerel Press. One of 400 (of an edition of 500). $225–$300. Another issue: Specially bound in morocco. One of 100, with a duplicate set of plates. $800–$1,000.

DRYSDALE, Isabel. *Scenes in Georgia.* Frontispiece. 83 pp., boards and cloth, paper label. Philadelphia, (1827). First edition. $80–$100.

DUBLIN Book of Irish Verse (The). See Cooke, John (editor).

DU BOIS, John. *Campaigns in the West, 1856–61: The Journal and Letters of Col. John Du Bois with Pencil Sketches by Joseph Heger.* Plates, folding map. Boards and leather. Tucson, 1949. Grabhorn Printing. First edition. One of 300 signed by George P. Hammond as editor. $150–$200.

DU BOIS, John Witherspoon. *Life and Times of William Lowndes Yancey.* 9 plates. Cloth. Birmingham, Ala., 1892. First edition. $100–$150.

DU BOIS, W.E. Burghardt. *The Gift of Black Folk in the Making of America.* Cloth. Boston, 1924. First edition. In dust jacket. $125–$150.

DU BOIS, W.E. Burghardt. *The Souls of Black Folk.* Cloth. Chicago, 1903. First edition. In dust jacket. $400–$500.

DU CHAILLU, Paul. *Stories of the Gorilla Country.* Woodcuts. Pictorial cloth. New York, 1868. First edition. $150–$175.

DUER, John K. (editor). *The Nautilus: A Collection of Select Nautical Tales and Sea Stories.* 48 pp., plain wrappers. New York, 1843. First edition. $50–$75.

DUERER, Albrecht. *Of the Just Shaping of Letters.* Decorations by Bruce Rogers. Marbled boards. New York, 1917. Grolier Club. One of 195. $400–$500.

DUFF, E. Gordon. *Early English Printing.* Illustrated. Folio, half morocco. London, 1896. One of 300. $125–$150.

DUFF, E. Gordon. *Fifteenth Century English Books.* Facsimile plates. Boards and cloth. Oxford, 1917. $125–$150.

DUFF, E. Gordon. *William Caxton.* Boards and cloth. Chicago, 1905. Caxton Club. One of 145 with an original leaf from Chaucer's *Canterbury Tales* of 1478. $1,000–$1,250. Also, $700 (A, 1974). Another issue: One of 107 without the leaf. $200–$300.

DUFLOT DE MOFRAS, Eugene. *Exploration du Territoire de l'Oregon.* Illustrated. 2 vols., leather; plus atlas, folio, cloth. Paris, 1844. First edition. $3,500–$7,500.

DUFLOT DE MOFRAS, Eugene. *Travels on the Pacific Coast.* Translated by Marguerite E. Wilbur. 2 folding maps, 8 plates. 2 vols., half leather. Santa Ana, 1937. $150–$175.

DUFY, Raoul. *Madrigaux.* 25 hand-colored illustrations. Loose sheets in paper folder and slipcase. Paris, (1960). One of 200. $150–$200.

DU HAYS, Charles. *The Percheron Horse.* Full-page plates. Vellum. No place (Gillis Press), 1886. $150–$200.

DUKE, Basil W. *History of Morgan's Cavalry.* Portrait. Cloth. Cincinnati, 1867. First edition. $75–$125. New York, 1906. 9 maps, 4 portraits. Cloth. Revised edition. $50.

DUKE, Basil W. *Reminiscences.* Cloth. Garden City, 1911. First edition. $75–$125.

DULAC, Edmund. *Edmund Dulac's Fairy Book.* 15 color plates. Ivory cloth. New York or London, (1916). One of 350 signed. $500–$650.

DULAC, Edmund. *Sinbad the Sailor and Other Stories from the Arabian Nights.* Illustrated by Dulac. Vellum. London, (1911). One of 500 signed. $750–$1,000.

DU MAURIER, Daphne. *Rebecca.* Cloth. London, 1938. First edition. In dust jacket. $250–$350.

DU MAURIER, George. *The Martian*. Illustrated by the author. Cloth. London, 1908. First edition. In dust jacket. $250–$300.

DU MAURIER, George. *Peter Ibbetson*. Edited and illustrated by George Du Maurier. 2 vols., gray cloth. London, 1892. First English edition, probable first issue, with brown lettering. $150–$200. Second issue, lettered in black. $125–$150. (Mixed sets sometimes occur and were probably so issued at the time.) New York, 1963. Limited Editions Club. Boards. Boxed. $35–$50.

DU MAURIER, George. *Trilby*. 3 vols., gray cloth. London, 1894. First edition. $500–$750. Also, $700 (A, 1976); stained and soiled, $140 (A, 1981). New York, 1894. Tan pictorial cloth. First American edition. $50–$75. London, 1895. Illustrated. Half vellum. One of 250 signed. $100–$150. New York, 1895. Vellum. One of 250 signed. $100–$150.

DUN COW (The): An Hyper-Satyrical Dialogue in Verse. 12 leaves, blue wrappers. London, 1808. (By Walter Savage Landor.) First edition. $1,000 and up? Also, half calf, $648 (A, 1969).

DUNBAR, Paul (Laurence). *Oak and Ivy*. Blue cloth. Dayton, Ohio, 1893. (By Paul Laurence Dunbar.) First edition. $250–$350. Author's first book.

DUNBAR, Paul Lawrence. *Howdy, Honey, Howdy*. Illustrated. Cloth. New York, 1905. (By Paul Laurence Dunbar.) First edition. $200.

DUNBAR, Paul Lawrence. *Joggin' Erlong*. Illustrated. Cloth. New York, 1906. (By Paul Laurence Dunbar.) First edition. $150.

DUNBAR, Paul Lawrence. *L'il Gal*. Photographs by Leigh Richmond Miner. Pictorial green cloth. New York, 1904. (By Paul Laurence Dunbar.) First edition. In dust jacket. $100–$125.

DUNBAR, Paul Lawrence. *Lyrics of Lowly Life*. Cloth. New York, 1908. (By Paul Laurence Dunbar.) First edition. In dust jacket. $100–$125.

DUNBAR, Paul Lawrence. *Majors and Minors: Poems*. Frontispiece portrait. Cloth. (Toledo, 1895.) (By Paul Laurence Dunbar.) First edition, probable first binding, with beveled edges. $100–$150.

DUNBAR, Paul Lawrence. *Poems of Cabin and Field*. Illustrated. Pictorial cloth. New York, 1899. (By Paul Laurence Dunbar.) First edition. $75–$100.

DUNBAR, Paul Lawrence. *The Strength of Gideon and Other Stories*. Illustrated by E.W. Kemble. Cloth. New York, 1900. (By Paul Laurence Dunbar.) First edition. $100–$125.

DUNBAR, Paul Lawrence. *The Uncalled*. Cloth. New York, 1898. (By Paul Laurence Dunbar.) First edition. $75–$100.

DUNCAN, Andrew (editor). *The Edinburgh New Dispensatory*. 6 plates. Contemporary calf. Edinburgh, 1803. First edition edited by Duncan. $75–$100.

DUNCAN, Isadora. *Art of the Dance*. Illustrated. Half cloth. New York, 1928. Limited edition. $200–$225.

DUNCAN, Isadora. *My Life*. Illustrated. Cloth, leather label. New York, 1927. One of 650. $125–$150.

DUNCAN, John M. *Travels Through Part of the United States and Canada in 1818 and 1819*. 14 maps and plates. 2 vols., calf. Glasgow, 1823. First edition. $300–$600. New York, 1823. 2 vols., half calf. First American edition. $100–$175.

DUNCAN, L. Wallace. *History of Montgomery County, Kansas*. Half leather. Iola, Kan., 1903. First edition. $100–$150.

DUNCAN, L. Wallace. *History of Wilson and Neosho Counties, Kansas*. Half leather. Fort Scott, Kan., 1902. First edition $100–$150.

DUNCAN, Robert. See *Epilogos*.

DUNCAN, Robert. *A Book of Resemblances*. Illustrated by Jess (Collins). Cloth. New Haven, 1966. First edition. One of 203 signed. In tissue dust jacket. $100–$125.

DUNCAN, Robert. *Caesar's Gate: Poems, 1949–1950*. Illustrated by Jess (Collins). Wrappers. (Mallorca), 1955. Divers Press. First edition. One of 200. $100–$125. Another issue: One of 13 signed. $250–$350.

DUNCAN, Robert. *Derivations*. Cloth. London, (1968). Fulcrum Press. First edition. One of 162 signed. In dust jacket. $75–$100. Trade edition: $15–$20.

DUNCAN, Robert. *Faust Foutu*. Wrappers. (Stinson Beach, Calif., 1959.) First complete edition. One of 50 signed and including a special color drawing by the author. $125–$200. Also, 700 unsigned. $25.

DUNCAN, Robert. *The First Decade*. Cloth. (London, 1968.) Fulcrum Press. First edition. One of 150 signed. In dust jacket. $50–$60. Trade edition: $15.

DUNCAN, Robert. *Heavenly City, Earthly City*. Illustrated by Mary Fabilli. White boards. (Berkeley), 1947. First edition. In dust jacket. $200–$300. (There were also 100 specially signed green cloth presentation copies. Value: $400–$500.) Author's first book.

DUNCAN, Robert. *Letters*. Illustrated. Decorated wrappers. (Highlands, N.C. 1958.) First edition. One of 450. $50. Another issue: Boards and calf. One of 60 signed, with an original drawing by Duncan on end papers. $150–$200.

DUNCAN, Robert. *Medieval Scenes*. Wrappers. San Francisco, (1950). First edition. One of 250 signed. $150–$250.

DUNCAN, Robert. *Six Prose Pieces*. Boards. (Mt. Horeb, Wis.), 1966. First edition. One of 70. In dust jacket. $225–$250. (Some copies signed by the poet.)

DUNCAN, Robert. *A Selection of 65 Drawings*. Cloth portfolio. Los Angeles, 1970. First edition. One of 300 signed. Boxed. $50–$75. Another issue: One of 26 lettered copies, signed, with an original drawing. $200–$245.

DUNDASS, Samuel. *Journal of Samuel Rutherford Dundass*. 60pp., wrappers. Steubenville, Ohio, 1857. First edition. $1,500–$2,000, possibly more.

DUNIWAY, Mrs. Abigail J. *Captain Gray's Company; or, Crossing the Plains and Living in Oregon*. Cloth. Portland, 1859. First edition. $1,500–$3,000. Also, worn, repaired, waterstained, $800 (A, 1979).

DUNLAP, William. *Diary: Memoirs of a Dramatist*. 3 vols., buckram. New York, 1931. One of 100. $150–$200.

DUNLAP, William. *The Life of Charles Brockden Brown*. Frontispiece. 2 vols., blue-gray boards, gray-green spine. Philadelphia, 1815. First edition. $300–$400. (Note: Contains first printing of "Memoirs of Carwin" and other Brown items; see Brown entry.)

DUNLAP, William. *A History of the American Theatre*. Purple muslin, paper spine label. New York, 1832. First edition. $100–$150. London, 1833. 2 vols., half calf. First English edition. $50–$75.

DUNLAP, William. *A History of the New Netherlands*. Illustrated, including 2 folding maps. 2 vols., boards and cloth, or cloth. New York, 1839 (and 1840). First edition, with errata leaf. $200–$250.

DUNLAP, William. *History of the Rise and Progress of the Arts of Design in the United States*. 2 vols., green boards and cloth. New York, 1834. First edition. $200–$250. Boston, 1918. Plates. 3 vols., cloth. $150–$200.

DUNLAP, William. *Memoirs of the Life of George Frederick Cooke*. Frontispieces. 2 vols., boards. New York, 1813. First edition. $150–$200.

DUNLAP, William. *A Narrative of the Events Which Followed Bonaparte's Campaign, etc.* Frontispiece. 5 plates. Leather. Hartford, 1814. First edition. $150–$200.

DUNN, Jacob Piatt. *Massacres of the Mountains.* Folding map and illustrations. Pictorial cloth. New York, 1886. First edition. $200–$225.

DUNN, John. *History of the Oregon Territory and British North-American Fur Trade.* Folding map. Cloth. London, 1844. First edition. $450–$800.

DUNN, John. *The Oregon Territory and the British North American Fur Trade.* Wrappers. Philadelphia, 1845. First American edition (of *History of the Oregon Territory, etc.*). $300–$400.

DUNNE, Finley Peter. See *Mr. Dooley in Peace and in War.*

DUNNE, Finley Peter. *Mr. Dooley at His Best.* Half cloth. New York, 1938. One of 520, with a page of the original manuscript. $100–$125.

DUNNE, John Gregory. *Delano: The Story of the California Grape Strike.* Cloth. New York, 1967. First edition. In dust jacket. $50–$75. Author's first book.

DUNSANY, Lord. *The Book of Wonder.* Illustrated by Sidney H. Sime. Cloth. London, 1912. In dust jacket. $100–$150.

DUNSANY, Lord. *The Chronicles of Rodriguez.* Frontispiece. Light-brown cloth, vellum spine, leather label. London, 1922. Limited and signed. In dust jacket. $200–$250.

DUNSANY, Lord. *The Compromise of the King of the Golden Isles.* Illustrated by T.M. Cleland. Gold boards and cloth. New York, 1924. Grolier Club. One of 300. $125–$150

DUNSANY, Lord. *Five Plays.* Illustrated. Cloth. London, 1914. First edition. $50–$75.

DUNSANY, Lord. *The Gods of Pegana.* Illustrated. Boards and cloth. London, 1905. First edition. In dust jacket. $100–$125. London, 1911. Pegana Press. Boards. Second edition. One of 50. $50.

DUNSANY, Lord. *A Journey.* Dark-blue boards. London, (1944). First edition. One of 250 initialed by the author. Boxed. $100–$110.

DUNSANY, Lord. *The King of Elfland's Daughter.* Frontispiece. Orange cloth, vellum spine, leather label. London, (1924). One of 250 signed. In dust jacket. $350–$450.

DUNSANY, Lord. *The Old Folks of the Centuries: A Play.* Boards. London, 1930. First edition. One of 100 signed. In dust jacket. $150–$200.

DUNSANY, Lord. *Selections from the Writings of Lord Dunsany.* Edited and with introduction by William Butler Yeats. Boards and linen. Churchtown, Dundrum, Ireland, 1912. Cuala Press. One of 250. $125–$150.

DUNSANY, Lord. *The Sword of Welleran and Other Stories.* Illustrated by Sidney Sime. London, 1908. First edition. In dust jacket. $150.

DUNSANY, Lord. *Time and the Gods.* Illustrated by Sidney Sime. Cloth. London, 1906. First edition. $100–$135. London, (1922). Illustrated. Orange cloth, vellum spine, leather label. One of 250 signed. In dust jacket. $200–$300.

DUNSANY, Lord. *Tales of War.* Boards. Dublin, (1918). First edition. In dust jacket. $100–$125. Boston, 1918. First American edition. In dust jacket. $50–$60.

DUNTHORNE, Gordon. *Flower and Fruit Prints of the 18th and Early 19th Centuries.* Illustrated. Folio, cloth. Washington, 1938. One of 750, with folding plate listing subscribers. Boxed. $500–$750. Lacking the subscriber plate. $450–$500.

DUNTON, John. *Letters Written from New-England*. Half morocco. Boston, 1867. Prince Society. One of 150. $100–$150.

DU PONCEAU, M. *Mémoire au Sujet des Prétentions du Gouvernement des États Unis sur l'Alluvion du Fleuve Mississippi, etc.* Nouvelle-Orléans, 1808. Half calf. First edition. $500–$750.

DU PONT, S.F. *Extracts from Private Journal-Letters of Capt. S.F. Du Pont . . . During the War with Mexico*. Boards. Wilmington, 1885. First edition. $2,000.

DU PONT, Samuel F. *Official Dispatches and Letters of Rear Admiral DuPont, 1846–48; and 1861–63*. Half leather. Wilmington, 1883. First edition. $300–$350.

DURRELL, Lawrence. See Norden, Charles; Peeslake, Gaffer; Royidis, Emmanuel. Also see *The Fifth Antiquarian Book Fair*.

DURRELL, Lawrence. *The Alexandria Quartet*. Buckram. London, (1962). First collected edition of *Justine, Balthazar, Mountolive*, and *Clea*. One of 500 signed. Boxed. $300–$350. New York, (1962). Marbled boards. First American edition. One of 199 signed. Boxed. $350–$400.

DURRELL, Lawrence. *Balthazar*. Cloth. London, 1958. First edition. In dust jacket. $75–$85.

DURRELL, Lawrence. *Beccafico*. Translated and edited by F.-J. Temple. Wrappers. LaLicorne, 1963. First edition. One of 150 signed. $150.

DURRELL, Lawrence. *Bitter Lemons*. Illustrated. Cloth. London, 1957. First edition. In dust jacket. $100–$125.

DURRELL, Lawrence. *The Black Book: An Agon*. Wrappers. Paris, (1938). Obelisk Press. First edition. $500–$850. Paris, (1959). Wrappers. In dust jacket. $35–$50. New York, 1960. First American edition. In dust jacket. $35.

DURRELL, Lawrence. *Clea*. Cloth. London, (1960). First edition. In dust jacket. $75–$85.

DURRELL, Lawrence. *Deus Loci*. Printed blue-gray wrappers. Ischia, Italy, 1950. First edition. One of 200 signed. $200–$250.

DURRELL, Lawrence. *In Arcadia*. Music by Wallace Southam. Wrappers. London, 1968. Turret Books. First edition. One of 100 signed. $150–$175.

DURRELL, Lawrence. *Justine*. Cloth. London, 1957. First edition. In dust jacket. $75–$100.

DURRELL, Lawrence. *La Descente du Styx*. Translated by F.-J. Temple. Wrappers. (Paris, 1964.) First edition. One of 250 signed. $75–$125.

DURRELL, Lawrence. *Mountolive*. Cloth. London, (1958). First edition. In dust jacket. $75–$85.

DURRELL, Lawrence. *Nothing Is Lost, Sweet Self*. Music by Wallace Southam. Pictorial wrappers. (London, 1967.) Turret Books. First edition. One of 100 signed. $150.

DURRELL, Lawrence. *On the Suchness of the Old Boy*. Illustrated by Sappho Durrell. Pictorial wrappers. London, 1972. One of 226 signed. $100–$125.

DURRELL, Lawrence. *The Parthenon*. Wrappers. (Rhodes, 1945 or 1946.) First edition. One of 25. $150–$200. Also, inscribed, $675.

DURRELL, Lawrence. *Pied Piper of Lovers*. Cloth. London, 1935. First edition. $1,100 in a 1978 catalogue. Author's first novel; exceedingly scarce.

DURRELL, Lawrence. *A Private Country: Poems*. Gray cloth. London, (1943). First edition. $75–$100.

162 LAWRENCE DURRELL

DURRELL, Lawrence. *Private Drafts*. Illustrated. Very small, pictorial wrappers (Nicosia, Cyprus), 1955. Proodos Press. One of 100 signed. $350–$400.

DURRELL, Lawrence. *Prospero's Cell*. Illustrated. Cloth. London, (1945). First edition. In dust jacket. $75–$100.

DURRELL, Lawrence. *Quaint Fragment*. Portrait. Blue wrappers, or rose-red boards and cloth. (London), 1931. Cecil Press. First edition. $5,000 and up. Of two known copies, one in rose-red boards, spine worn, was catalogued by a New York bookseller (about 1963) at $750. This copy was sold at the Jonathan Goodwin auction in October, 1977, for $3,500. According to the Goodwin sale catalogue, there is an unbound copy at the University of California in Los Angeles. Author's first book.

DURRELL, Lawrence. *Six Poems, from the Greek of Sekillianos and Seferis*. Pictorial wrappers. Rhodes, 1946. First edition. Limited (50?). $300–$350. Also, a presentation copy, signed, $650 (A, 1977).

DURRELL, Lawrence. *Ten Poems*. Cloth. London, 1932. Caduceus Press. First edition. One of 12. $500 and up.

DURRELL, Lawrence. *Transition: Poems*. London, 1934. First edition. $3,000.

DURRELL, Lawrence. *Two Excursions into Reality*. White boards. Berkeley, 1947. First American edition (of *Zero and Asylum in the Snow*.). In dust jacket. $50–$75.

DURRELL, Lawrence. *Zero and Asylum in the Snow*. Wrappers. Rhodes, 1946. First edition. $100–$150.

DUSTIN, Fred. *The Custer Tragedy*. 3 folding maps in pocket. Blue cloth. Ann Arbor, 1939. First edition. One of 200. $300–$400.

DUTCHMAN'S Fireside (The). 2 vols., cloth. New York, 1831. (By James Kirke Paulding.) First edition, first issue, with date of May, 1831, in ad on back cover of Vol. 1. $150–$200.

DUVAL, John C. *The Adventures of Big-Foot Wallace*. 8 plates. Green cloth. Philadelphia, 1871. First edition. $500–$600.

DUVAL, John C. *Early Times in Texas*. Cloth. Austin, 1892. First edition. $150–$200.

DUVAL, K.D., and Smith, Sydney Goodsir (editors). *Hugh MacDiarmid: a Festschrift*. Cloth. Edinburgh, (1962). First edition. One of 50 with holograph poem signed by MacDiarmid tipped in. In dust jacket. $100–$125.

DWIGGINS, W.A. *Towards a Reform of the Paper Currency*. Boards. New York, 1932. Limited Editions Club. One of 452 signed. In dust jacket. Boxed. $400–$450.

DWIGHT, Timothy. *A Discourse on Some Events of the Last Century*. Printed gray-blue wrappers. New Haven, 1801. First edition. $150–$200.

DWIGHT, Timothy. *The Psalms of David, Imitated in the Language of the New Testament*. Leather. Hartford, 1801. First edition. $150–$200.

DWIGHT, Timothy. *Travels in New-England and New York*. 3 maps. 4 vols., boards. New Haven, 1821–22. First edition, with errata slip in last volume. $200–$300.

DWINELLE, John W. *The Colonial History of the City of San Francisco*. Map. Printed wrappers. San Francisco, 1863. First edition. $600. Also, $300 (A, 1968). San Francisco, 1866. Map, 3 plates. Third edition, second issue, with inserted slip "No. CLXXI-Bis" and 7 pages of addenda. $600–$850.

DYER, Mrs. D.B. *"Fort Reno,"* or *Picturesque "Cheyenne and Arrapahoe Army Life,"* *Before the Opening of Oklahoma*. 10 plates. Cloth. New York, 1896. First edition. $150–$200.

EASTLAKE, William. *Go In Beauty*. Cloth. New York, (1956). First edition. In dust jacket. $100–$125. Author's first book.

EASTMAN, Mary H. *The American Aboriginal Portfolio*. Engraved title page; 26 plates. Cloth. Philadelphia, (1853). First edition. $500–$600.

EASTON, John. *A Narrative of the Causes Which Led to Phillip's Indian War*. Map. Cloth. Albany, 1858. First edition. $60–$75.

EATON, Daniel Cady. *The Ferns of North America*. 2 vols., cloth. Salem, Mass., and Boston, 1880. First edition. $300–$400.

EATON, Rachel Caroline. *John Ross and the Cherokee Indians*. Cloth. Menasha, Wis., 1914. First edition. $150–$250.

EBERHART, Richard. *A Bravery of Earth*. Cloth. London, (1930). First edition. In dust jacket. $200–$250. Author's first book.

EBERHART, Richard. *Brotherhood of Men*. Wrappers. (Pawlet, Vt., 1949.) Banyan Press. First edition. One of 200 signed. $100–$150. Another issue: One of 26 signed. $200–$250.

EBERHART, Richard. *Collected Verse Plays*. Boards and cloth. Chapel Hill, (1962). First edition. One of 100 signed. In glassine dust jacket. $100–$125.

EBERHART, Richard. *An Herb Basket*. Illustrated. Wrappers. (Cummington, Mass.), 1950. First edition. One of 155. $150–$200.

EBERHART, Richard. *Reading the Spirit*. Cloth. London, 1936. First edition. In dust jacket. $150–$175. New York, 1937. Cloth. First American edition. $125–$150.

EBERHART, Richard. *Thirty-one Sonnets*. Cloth. New York, (1967). First edition. One of 99 signed. Boxed. $100–$150.

ECCLESIASTICUS. See *The Wisdom of Jesus, Son of Sirach*.

ECHO, The. Marbled boards and leather. (New York, 1807.) (By Richard Alsop, Lemuel Hopkins, Theodore Dwight, etc.) First edition. $75–$100.

ECHOES. By Two Writers. Printed wrappers. Light brown wrappers (Lahore, India, 1884.) (By Rudyard Kipling, with eight poems credited to his sister Beatrice.) First edition, printed at the Civil and Military Gazette Press. $600–$800. Also, inscribed by Kipling, lacking backstrip, $1,800 (A, 1975); $400 (A, 1972); inscribed by Kipling, $2,300 (A, 1971).

ECKENRODE, Hamilton J. *The Revolution in Virginia*. Cloth. Boston, 1916. First edition. $50–$60.

EDDINGTON, Arthur Stanley. *Stellar Movements and the Structure of the Universe*. Illustrated. Cloth. London, 1914. First edition. $150–$250. Author's first book.

EDDINGTON, Arthur Stanley. *The Internal Constitution of the Stars*. Cloth. Cambridge, 1926. First edition. $150–$200.

EDDISON, E.R. *The Worm Ouroboros*. Illustrated by Keith Henderson. Cloth. London, (1922). First edition. In dust jacket. $100–$150. Author's first book. New York, 1926. Illustrated. Cloth. First American edition. In dust jacket. $50–$75.

EDDY, Mary Baker. See Glover, Mary Baker.

EDE, Charles (editor). *The Art of the Book*. Illustrated. Cloth. London, (1951). First edition. Boxed. $75–$100.

EDE, Harold Stanley. *A Life of Gaudier-Brzeska*. Numerous plates (some colored), other illustrations. Cloth. London, 1930. One of 350. In dust jacket. Boxed. $350–$450.

EDELMAN, George W. *Guide to the Value of California Gold.* Disbound. Philadelphia, 1850. First edition. $1,000–$2,000.

EDGAR, Patrick Nisbett. *The American Race-Turf Register.* Vol. 1. (All published.) New York, 1833. First edition. $150.

EDGEWORTH, Maria. See *Castle Rackrent; The Modern Griselda*

EDMONDS, Walter D. *Drums Along the Mohawk.* Cloth. Boston, 1936. First edition. In dust jacket. $100.

EDMONDS, Walter D. *Rome Haul.* Cloth. Boston, 1929. First (presentation) edition, with "Published February, 1929" on copyright page. One of 1,001. In dust jacket. $150–$200. Trade edition: In dust jacket. $40–$50. Author's first book.

EDWARD, David B. *The History of Texas.* Folding map in color. Cloth. Cincinnati, 1836. First edition. $400–$650.

EDWARD VIII. *Farewell Speech of King Edward the Eighth Broadcast from Windsor Castle, December MCMXXXVI.* Large, decorated linen, white leather spine. San Francisco, 1938. Grabhorn Press. One of 200. $250.

EDWARDS, Billy. *Gladiators of the Prize Ring, or Pugilists of America.* Illustrated. Folio, red cloth. Chicago, (1895). $100–$200.

EDWARDS Chicago Directory (The). 40 pp., boards. Chicago, 1871. "Fire edition." $150–$250.

EDWARDS, E.I. *Desert Voices: A Descriptive Bibliography.* Illustrated. Tan buckram. Los Angeles, 1958. First edition. One of 500. In dust jacket. $100–$150.

EDWARDS, E.I. *The Valley Whose Name is Death.* Map. Cloth. Pasadena, 1940. First edition. $100–$125.

EDWARDS, Frank S. *A Campaign in New Mexico with Col. Doniphan.* Folding map. 184 pp., wrappers (cover date 1848), and cloth. Philadelphia, 1847. First edition. Wrappers: $500–$600. Cloth: $300–$400.

EDWARDS, J.C. *Speech in Relation to the Territory in Dispute Between the State of Missouri and the United States, etc.* 20 pp., sewed. Washington, 1843. $100–$175.

EDWARDS, John N. *Noted Guerrillas.* Frontispiece, 15 plates. Cloth. St. Louis, 1877. First edition. $100–$125.

EDWARDS, John N. *Shelby and His Men, or The War in the West.* Portrait, folding map. Cloth. Cincinnati, 1867. First edition. $50–$75.

EDWARDS, John N. *Shelby's Expedition to Mexico.* Cloth. Kansas City, 1872. First edition. $75–$125.

EDWARDS, Jonathan. *Marcus Whitman.* Portraits. 48 pp. Spokane, 1892. First edition. $50–$75.

EDWARDS, Jonathan (1703–58). *Some Thoughts Concerning the Present Revival of Religion in New-England.* Calf. Lexington, Ky., 1803. $100–$150.

EDWARDS, Philip Leget. *California in 1837.* Wrappers. Sacramento, 1890. First edition. $150–$200.

EDWARDS, Philip Leget. *The Diary of Philip Leget Edwards: The Great Cattle Drive from California to Oregon in 1837.* Boards. San Francisco, 1932. Grabhorn Press. One of 500. In dust jacket. $75–$100. (This reprints *California in 1837.)*

EDWARDS, Philip Leget. *Sketch of the Oregon Territory; or, Emigrant's Guide.* 20 pp. Liberty, Mo., 1842. First edition. $5,000 and up. (Only one copy known.)

EDWARDS, Samuel E. *T e Ohio Hunter.* Portrait. Cloth. Battle Creek, 1866. First edition. $500–$750.

EDWARDS, W.F. (publi: her). *W. F. Edwards' Tourists' Guide and Directory of the Truckee Basin.* Illustr; ted. Cloth. Truckee, Calif., 1883. First edition. $450–$600.

EDWARDS, Weldon. *M moir of Nathaniel Macon, of North Carolina.* 22 pp., wrappers. Raleigh, 1862. $150–$200.

EFFINGHAM, C. *The Virginia Comedians.* 2 vols., wrappers, or cloth. New York, 1854. (By John Esten Co ,ke.) First edition, first issue, with "earsed" for "erased" in line 3, page 249, Vol. 2. ' Vrappers (cover date 1855): $200–$250. Cloth: $150–$200.

EGAN, Pierce. See *Real Life in London.*

EGAN, Pierce. *S[,rting Anecdotes.* 16 engraved plates, advertisement leaf at end. Morocco. London, 1804. First edition. $250–$350. London, 1825. Plates, including 3 in color. Moroc/ ,. $250–$350.

EGE, Ralph. *ioneers of Old Hopewell.* Portrait. Cloth. Hopewell, N.J., 1908. $75–$100.

EGGLESTC N, Edward. *Among the Elgin Watch-Makers.* (Cover title.) Illustrated. 8 pp., wra, pers. Chicago, (1873?). First edition. $100 or more.

EGGLES' ON, Edward. *The Book of Queer Stories, and Stories Told on a Cellar Door.* Green :loth. Chicago, 1871. First edition. $200–$250.

EGGLF ,TON, Edward. *The Circuit Rider.* Decorated cloth. New York, 1874. First edition first state, without the word "illustrated" on title page. $50–$60.

EGG' ESTON, Edward. *The Hoosier School-Boy.* Illustrated by George D. Bush. Pictori /cloth. New York, 1883. First edition, first issue, with "Cousin Sukey" frontispiece ; d first chapter ending on page 16. $100–$125.

E(,LESTON, Edward. *The Hoosier Schoolmaster.* Illustrated by Frank Beard. Brown ,r terra-cotta cloth. New York, (1871). First edition, first state, with line 3 of page 71 reading "was out" (not "is out"). $200–$250.

EGGLESTON, Edward. *The Manual: A Practical Guide to the Sunday-School Work.* Cloth. Chicago, 1869. First edition, first issue, with A. Zeese imprint. $100–$150. Author's first book.

EGGLESTON, Edward. *Mr. Blake's Walking-Stick.* Frontispiece and one plate. Light-gray wrappers. Chicago, 1870. First edition. $300–$350.

EGGLESTON, George Cary. *How to Educate Yourself: With or Without Masters.* Cloth. New York, 1872. First edition, first issue, with "ready in September" over ads at back. $75. Author's first book.

EGLE, William H. *History of Dauphine and Lebanon Counties (Pennsylvania).* Cloth. Philadelphia, 1883. $75–$100.

EGLE, William H. *An Illustrated History of the Commonwealth of Pennsylvania.* Cloth. Harrisburg, 1876. First edition. $75–$100.

EGLINTON, John. *Irish Literary Portraits.* Boards and cloth. London, 1935. (By William C. Magee). First edition. $50–$75.

EGLINTON, John. *Some Essays and Passages.* Selected by William Butler Yeats. Boards, linen spine. Dundrum, Ireland, 1905. (By William C. Magee.) Dun Emer Press. One of 200. $135–$175.

EIGHT Harvard Poets. Boards. New York, 1917. First edition. In glassine dust jacket. $150–$175. (Contains poems by E.E. Cummings, John Dos Passos, and others.)

1862 Trip to the West (An). 10 plates. Full limp leather. Pawtucket, R.I., (1926). (By Lyman B. Goff.) First edition. $600–$1,000.

EISENHOWER, Dwight D. *The White House Years: Mandate for Change, 1953–1956*. Cloth. Garden City, 1963. First edition. One of 1,434 signed. Boxed $200–$275.

EISENHOWER, Dwight D. *The White House Years: Waging Peace, 1956–1961*. Cloth. Garden City, 1965. First edition. One of 1,434 signed. Boxed. $200–$275.

EL GABILAN. Pictorial cloth. Salinas, Calif., 1919. Salinas High School Year Book, with 3 contributions by John Steinbeck, his first appearance in print. $1,000 and up. Also, ends of spine frayed. $1,000 (A, 1977).

ELIA; *Essays Which Have Appeared Under That Signature in the London Magazine*. Boards. London, 1823. (By Charles Lamb.) First edition, first issue, without Waterloo Place address in title page imprint. $750 and up. London, 1823. Boards. Second issue. $300–$500. (See Lamb entries.)

ELIA . . . *Second Series*. Boards, paper label. Philadelphia, 1828. First edition. (By Charles Lamb.) $200–$300. (See Lamb entry.)

ELIOT, George. See Strauss, Dr. David Friedrich.

ELIOT, George. *Adam Bede*. 3 vols., brown or salmon-colored (orange) cloth. Edinburgh, 1859. (By Mary Ann Evans.) First edition. $1,500–$2,000.

ELIOT, George. *Daniel Deronda*. 8 parts, wrappers. Edinburgh, 1876. (By Mary Ann Evans.) First edition, with erratum slip in Part 3. $1,500 and up. Book edition: 4 vols., cloth. $600–$800.

ELIOT, George. *Felix Holt, the Radical*. 3 vols., rust-colored cloth. Edinburgh, 1866. (By Mary Ann Evans.) First edition. $400–$750. (Note: A copy in a "very rare" blue cloth binding was catalogued by a London dealer at $1,320 in 1981.)

ELIOT, George. *Middlemarch: A Study of Provincial Life*. 8 parts, pictorial wrappers. Edinburgh, 1871. (By Mary Ann Evans.) First edition. $1,500 and up. Also, $1,200 (A, 1978). Edinburgh, 1871–72. 4 vols., cloth. First book edition. $1,500–$2,000. Also, $1,200 (A, 1978).

ELIOT, George. *The Mill on the Floss*. 3 vols., salmon-colored cloth. Edinburgh, 1860. (By Mary Ann Evans.) First edition. $750–$1,000. Also, $475 (A, 1978).

ELIOT, George. *Romola*. 3 vols., green cloth. London, 1863. (By Mary Ann Evans.) First edition, first issue, with 2 pages of ads at end of Vol. 2. $750–$1,000. Also, $650 (A, 1978).

ELIOT, George. *Scenes of Clerical Life*. 2 vols., maroon cloth. Edinburgh, 1858. (By Mary Ann Evans.) First edition. $1,000–$1,500. Also, $1,700 (A, 1977)—a "superb" copy. Author's first book.

ELIOT, George. *Silas Marner: The Weaver of Raveloe*. Orange-brown cloth. Edinburgh, 1861. (By Mary Ann Evans.) First edition. $450–$600.

ELIOT, T. S. See Ridler, Anne; Perse. St. John; Dryden, John. Also see *Cat Morgan's Apology; The Catholic Anthology; The Criterion; Ezra Pound: His Metric and Poetry; Harvard Class Day 1910*.

ELIOT, T. S. *After Strange Gods: A Primer of Modern Heresy*. Black cloth. London, (1934). First edition. In dust jacket. $110–$150. New York, (1934). Red cloth. First American edition. In dust jacket. $50–$75.

ELIOT, T. S. *Animula*. Illustrated. Yellow wrappers. (London, 1929.) Ariel Poems, No. 23. First edition. $35–$50. London, 1929. Yellow boards. Large paper issue. One of 400 signed. $100–$150.

ELIOT, T. S. *Ara Vus Prec* (with spine reading *Ara Vos Prec*). Black boards and cloth, paper label. (London, 1920.) Ovid Press. First edition. One of 30 signed. $1,000–

$1,250. Also, $900 (A, 1977). Another issue: One of 220 numbered (but not signed) copies. $400–$600. (Note: There were also 4 presentation copies printed on Japan vellum. The correct title is *Ara Vos Prec*. Gallup has a note on binding variants, but I find it confusing.)

ELIOT, T. S. *Ash-Wednesday*. Blue cloth. New York and London, 1930. Fountain Press. First edition. One of 600 signed (200 for England, 400 for the United States). In cellophane dust jacket. Boxed. $300–$500. Also, $306 (A, 1978). London, 1930. Brown cloth. First English trade edition. In green dust jacket. $75–$125. New York, 1930. Black cloth. First American trade edition. In glassine dust jacket. $50–$75.

ELIOT, T. S. *Charles Whibley: A Memoir*. Gray wrappers. (London), 1931. English Association Pamphlet No. 80. First edition. $100. (Note: Of the edition of "probably" 4,000, says Donald Gallup in *T. S. Eliot: A Bibliography*, about 2,055 were issued without wrappers by the English Association and were reissued with other pamphlets for members.)

ELIOT, T. S. *The Classics and the Man of Letters*. Blue wrappers. London, 1942. First edition, first state, with "t" of the "the" on title page correctly printed. $50–$60.

ELIOT, T. S. *The Cocktail Party*. Green cloth. London, (1950). First edition, with or without misprint "here" for "her" in first line of page 29. (Gallup gives no priority to copies with the misprint.) In dust jacket. $35–$50. New York, (1950). First American edition, first issue, with pages 35–36 as an uncanceled leaf and without the words "First American edition" on copyright page. In dust jacket. $550 in a 1978 catalogue. (Only about 10 copies known.) Second issue, pages 35–36 tipped in: In dust jacket. $50.

ELIOT, T. S. *Collected Poems, 1909–1935*. Advance proof in printed paper covers. London, (1936). First edition. $250–$400. (Note: Text and typography differ from first published edition.) London, (1936). Blue cloth. First published edition. In dust jacket. $150–$200. New York, (1936). Blue cloth. First American edition. In dust jacket. $100.

ELIOT, T. S. *Dante*. Gray boards. London, (1929). First edition. In dust jacket. $75–$100. Another issue: Blue-green boards. One of 125 signed. $500–$600.

ELIOT, T. S. *The Dry Salvages*. Blue wrappers. London, (1941). First edition. $40–$50.

ELIOT, T. S. *East Coker: A Poem*. 8 pp., wire-stitched, unbound. (London), 1940. Reprint from the Easter number of *The New English Weekly*. 500 copies printed. "Second" edition. $75. London, (1940). Yellow wrappers. First Faber & Faber edition. $60. (Note: The first appearance of this poem was in a 4-page supplement to *The New English Weekly*, Easter, 1940. A copy of this supplement brought $50 at auction in 1969.)

ELIOT, T. S. *El Canto de Amor de J. Alfred Prufrock*. Wrappers (with sheets laid in). Mexico, 1938. One of 50. $150–$200.

ELIOT, T. S. *Elizabethan Essays*. Gray cloth. London, (1934). First edition, first issue, with misprint in series note on half title, "No. 21" (later copies have series note correctly printed "No. 24"). $125.

ELIOT, T. S. *The Family Reunion*. Wrappers. London, (1939). "Proof copy," so imprinted on front cover. Signed on cover by Eliot. In dust jacket. $400–$500. London, (1939). Gray cloth. First edition. In dust jacket. $75–$100. New York, (1939). Black cloth. First American edition. In dust jacket. $50–$60.

ELIOT, T. S. *For Lancelot Andrewes*. Blue cloth, paper label. London, (1928). First edition. In dust jacket. $100–$150. Garden City, 1929. Purple-brown cloth. First American edition. In dust jacket. $75–$100.

ELIOT, T. S. *Four Quartets*. Black cloth. New York, (1943). First edition, first impression, with "First American edition" on copyright page. One of only 788 copies of an original impression of 4,165, 3,377 of which were destroyed because of incorrect margins. In dust jacket. $500–$650. Second impression, without the edition note on copyright page and without code designations in brackets used in subsequent impressions. In dust jacket. $150–$200. London, (1944). Tan cloth. First English edition. $75–$125. London, (1960). Marbled boards and white parchment spine. One of 290 signed. Boxed. $1,000–$1,600.

ELIOT, T. S. *From Poe to Valéry*. Dark-blue boards. New York, (1948). First edition. One of 1,500. In original green paper mailing envelope. $100. Without envelope, $60–$80. Washington, 1949. White wrappers with cover title. One of 1,000. $30–$50.

ELIOT, T. S. *The Frontiers of Criticism*. 20 pp., wrappers. (Minneapolis, 1956.) First edition. $60–$80.

ELIOT, T. S. *Homage to John Dryden*. Stiff off-white wrappers. London, 1924. Hogarth Press. First edition. $100–$125.

ELIOT, T. S. *Journey of the Magi*. Wrappers. New York, 1927. First American edition. One of 27 printed to obtain American copyright. $1,000–$1,250. Also, $1,000 (A, 1977). (Only 12 were released for sale.) London, 1927. Wrappers. First edition. $125–$150.

ELIOT, T. S. *John Dryden: The Poet, the Dramatist, the Critic*. Frontispiece in color. Marbled boards and cloth. New York, 1932. First edition. One of 110 signed. In cellophane dust jacket. $400. Trade edition: Mulberry boards. In white dust jacket. $50–$60.

ELIOT, T. S. *Marina*. Illustrated. Blue wrappers. (London, 1930.) Ariel Poems No. 29. First edition. $35–$50. London, 1930. Blue boards. Large paper issue. One of 400 signed. $125–$175.

ELIOT, T. S. *Murder in the Cathedral*. Gray wrappers. Canterbury, 1935. First (acting) edition. One of 750. $250.

ELIOT, T. S. *Notes Towards the Definition of Culture*. Cloth. London, (1948). First edition. In dust jacket. $50–$60. (Note: There were also 18 copies bound with "a" for "the" in the title on the spine, but none was placed on sale, according to Eliot's bibliographer, Donald Gallup. A copy was sold at auction in October, 1977, for $425.) New York, (1949). Black cloth. First American edition. In dust jacket. $25–$35.

ELIOT, T. S. *Old Possum's Book of Practical Cats*. Yellow cloth. London, (1939). First edition. In dust jacket. $150–$175. New York, (1939). Gray cloth. First American edition. In dust jacket. $35.

ELIOT, T. S. *Poems*. Decorated wrappers, white paper label. Richmond, England, 1919. Hogarth Press. First edition, first issue, with "capitaux" for "chapitaux" in line 11, page (13). $800–$1,000. Also, $800 (A, 1977). New York, 1920. Tan boards. First American edition (of *Ara Vos Prec*). (Note: this also includes the contents of the 1919 first edition of *Poems*.) In yellow dust jacket. $200–$250. Later: Brown dust jacket. $125 (A, 1977).

ELIOT, T. S. *Poems, 1909–1925*. Blue cloth, white paper spine label. London, 1925. First edition. In cream-colored dust jacket. $100–$150. Another issue: White linen, gilt. One of 85 signed (actually issued in 1926). In glassine dust jacket. $850. New York, (1932). Blue cloth, gilt. First American edition. In cream-colored dust jacket. $50–$75.

ELIOT, T. S. *A Practical Possum*. Wrappers. Cambridge, Mass., 1947. First edition. One of 80. $500 and up. Also, $500 (A, 1977).

ELIOT, T. S. *Prufrock and Other Observations*. 40 pp., buff printed wrappers. London, 1917. First edition. $1,600–$2,000. Also, a review copy with printed slip and one word in Eliot's hand. $2,500 (A, 1977). Author's first book.

ELIOT, T. S. *Religious Drama: Medieval and Modern*. Red cloth. New York, 1954. First edition. One of 300 signed. In glassine dust jacket. $200–$400. (Note: There were also 26 lettered copies issued for presentation.)

ELIOT, T. S. *The Rock*. Heavy gray wrappers. London, (1934). First edition. (The paperbound issue was sold at the theatre in advance of the book's hardbound publication.) $125–$175. Hardbound issue: Boards. In dust jacket. $150.

ELIOT, T. S. *The Sacred Wood*. Blue cloth. London, (1920). First edition, first issue, with publisher's name at foot of spine measuring 3 mm. and without ads. In first issue dust jacket, without the sub-title on front. $225–$250.

ELIOT, T. S. *Selected Essays, 1917–1932*. Blue vellum. London, (1932). First edition (English issue). One of 115 signed. In cellophane dust jacket. $500–$600. Also, $450 (A, 1978). First trade edition: Red cloth. In dust jacket. $75–$100. Advance proof copy in wrappers: $500–$600. New York, (1932). First trade edition (American issue). In dust jacket. $100–$150.

ELIOT, T. S. *Shakespeare and the Stoicism of Seneca*. (Cover title.) Gray wrappers. London, 1927. First edition. $100–$150.

ELIOT, T. S. *A Song for Simeon*. Illustrated. White boards, gilt. London, 1928. Large paper signed edition. One of 500 signed. $200–$250.

ELIOT, T.S. *Sweeney Agonistes*. Blue boards. London, (1932). First edition. In dust jacket. $125–$150.

ELIOT, T.S. *Thoughts After Lambeth*. Brown wrappers. London, (1931). First edition. $100–$125. Another (simultaneous) issue: Gray cloth. In glassine dust jacket. (300 published.) $150–$250.

ELIOT, T.S. *T.S. Eliot: The Complete Poems and Plays*. Blue-green cloth. New York, (1952). First edition. In dust jacket. $50–$60.

ELIOT, T.S. *Triumphal March*. Illustrated by E. McKnight Kauffer. Boards. London, 1931. First edition. One of 300 signed. $150–$200.

ELIOT, T.S. *Two Poems*. Wrappers, paper label. (Cambridge), 1935. First edition. One of 22. $400–$500. Another issue: One of 5 on vellum, signed. $1,000.

ELIOT, T.S. *The Undergraduate Poems of T.S. Eliot*. Printed gray wrappers. Cambridge, Mass., (1949). First edition. One of about 1,000. $100–$125.

ELIOT, T.S. *The Use of Poetry and the Use of Criticism*. Red cloth. London, (1933). First edition. In dust jacket. $50–$75.

ELIOT, T.S. *The Waste Land*. Flexible black cloth, gilt. New York, 1922. First edition, first issue, with the flexible binding, the word "mountain" correctly spelled in line 339 of page 41, and the limitation numbers stamped in type 5 mm. high. One of 1,000 (of which about 500 were issued thus, according to Donald Gallup, Eliot's bibliographer). In salmon-colored dust jacket. $1,250–$1,500. Second state, flexible black cloth, with dropped "a" in "mountain." (The remaining copies of the first impression—about 500 being in this state.) In dust jacket. $750–$1,000. New York, (1923?). Black cloth. Second edition (so identified in colophon, but actually a second impression from the first edition type). In dust jacket. $200–$300. Richmond, 1923. Hogarth Press. Blue marbled boards, paper label. First English edition, first issue, with border of asterisks on the label. $500–$750. Also, $350 (A, 1977). Later, no asterisks, $200–$250. London, (1961). Marbled boards, white parchment spine. One of 300 signed. Boxed. $1,000–$1,700.

ELIOT, T.S. *What Is a Classic?* Green wrappers. London, (1945). First edition. One of 500. $150–$175. First trade edition: Blue cloth. In dust jacket. $20–$30.

ELIOT, T.S. *Words for Music*. 4 pp., wrappers. (Bryn Mawr), 1934 (actually 1935). First edition. One of 20 (so stated, but actually more, according to Donald Gallup). $750.

ELIZABETH Bennet; or, Pride and Prejudice: A Novel. 2 vols, boards and linen, paper label. Philadelphia, 1832. (By Jane Austen.) First American edition of *Pride and Prejudice*. $400–$500. Also, loose in binding, $130 (A, 1975).

ELKIN, Stanley. *Boswell*. Cloth. New York, (1964). First edition. In dust jacket. $75–$85. Author's first book.

ELKIN, Stanley. *The Making of Ashenden.* Wrappers. Lonodn, 1972. First edition. One of 100 signed. $75–$100. Ordinary copies (500): $25–$30.

ELKUS, Richard J. *Alamos.* Foreword by Barnaby Conrad. Half suede and cloth. San Francisco, 1965. Grabhorn Press. One of 487. $100–$150.

ELLICOTT, Andrew. *The Journal of Andrew Ellicott.* 14 maps and plates. Morocco. Philadelphia, 1803. First edition, with errata leaf. $1,500–$1,750. Also, $1,056 (A, 1979). Philadelphia, 1814. Half leather. Second edition. $300–$400.

ELLIN, Stanley. *Mystery Stories.* Cloth. New York, 1956. First edition. In dust jacket. $75–$100.

ELLIOTT, D.G. *A Monograph of the Felidae, or Family of Cats.* 43 hand-colored lithographs. Folio, full morocco. London, 1883. $15,000.

ELLIOTT, D.G. *A Monograph of the Pittidae, or Family of Anti-Thrushes.* 31 hand-colored plates. Half leather. New York, 1863. First edition. $22,000.

ELLIOT, D.G. *A Monograph of the Tetraoninae, or Family of the Grouse.* 27 color plates. 5 parts in 4, boards. New York, (1864)–65. First edition. $12,000–$15,000. Also, in a folio half morocco binding. $12,000. (See the British and American auction records for several other Elliot monographs on birds, all of which are extremely valuable for their color plates.)

ELLIOT, D.G. *The New and Heretofore Unfigured Species of the Birds of North America.* 72 hand-colored plates. 2 vols., half morocco. New York, (1866–69). First edition. $19,000.

ELLIOT, W.J. *The Spurs.* Plates and map. Cloth. (Spur, Tex., 1939.) First edition. $100–$150.

ELLIOTT, The Rev. Charles. *Indian Missionary Reminiscences.* Boards. New York, 1835. First edition. $75.

ELLIOTT, David Stewart. *Last Raid of the Daltons.* Illustrated. 72 pp., wrappers. Coffeyville, Kan., 1892. First edition. $350–$500. Coffeyville, 1892 (actually 1954). 60 pp. Second edition. (Facsimile, abridged.) $25–$50.

ELLIOTT, John, and Johnson, Samuel, Jr. *A Selected Pronouncing and Accented Dictionary.* Oblong, boards. Hartford, 1800. $75–$100.

ELLIOTT, W.W. *History of Arizona Territory.* Map and plates. Half cloth. San Francisco, 1884. First edition. $750–$1,000.

ELLIS, Edward S. See *On the Plains.*

ELLIS, Edward S. *The Life and Adventures of Col. David Crockett.* Half leather. New York, 1861. First edition. $75–$125.

ELLIS, Edward S. *The Life and Times of Christopher Carson.* Wrappers. New York, (1861). First edition. $80–$125.

ELLIS, Frederick S. *A Lexical Concordance to the Poetical Works of Percy Bysshe Shelley.* Half morocco. London, 1892. First edition. $125–$150.

ELLIS, Frederick S. (editor). *Psalmi Penitentiales.* Woodcut designs and initials. Boards and linen. London, 1894. Kelmscott Press. One of 300. $400–$500. Another issue: One of 12 on vellum. $2,000–$3,000.

ELLIS, Frederick S. (editor). *The Romance of Syr Ysambrace.* Printed in black and red. Woodcut borders and designs by E. Burne-Jones. Boards and linen. London, 1897. Kelmscott Press. One of 350. $350–$450. Another issue: One of 8 on vellum. $3,000–$4,000.

ELLIS, Frederick S. (editor), and Caxton, William, and Morris, William (translators). *The Book of the Order of Chivalry (L'Ordre de Chevalerie).* Printed in black and red.

Woodcut by E. Burne-Jones. Vellum with ties. London, 1893. Kelmscott Press. One of 225. $750–$1,000. Another issue: One of 10 on vellum. $3,000–$4,000.

ELLIS, George F. *Bell Ranch As I Knew It.* Illustrated. Half cloth and fabrikoid. Kansas City, (1973). First edition. One of 250 with a signed print. Boxed. $75. Trade edition: In dust jacket. $15.

ELLIS, Havelock. *Kanga Creek: An Australian Idyll.* Blue boards. Waltham Saint Lawrence, 1922. Golden Cockerel Press. One of 25 on handmade paper, signed. $300–$350.

ELLIS, Havelock. *Marriage Today and To-Morrow.* San Francisco, 1929. Grabhorn printing. One of 500 signed. $50–$75.

ELLIS, John B. *Free Love and Its Votaries; or, American Socialism Unmasked.* Illustrated. New York, (1870). First edition. $200–$250.

ELLIS, William. *The American Mission in the Sandwich Islands.* Boards. Honolulu, 1866. First edition. $200–$250.

ELLIS, William. *Polynesian Researches, During a Residence of Nearly Six Years in the South Sea Islands.* 10 plates and maps, 16 woodcuts, 2 vols., half calf and marbled boards. London, 1829. First edition. $400–$600.

ELLIS, William Turner. *Memories: My 72 Years in the Romantic County of Yuba, California.* Boards and cloth. Eugene, Ore., 1939. John Henry Nash printing. In dust jacket. $75–$100.

ELLISON, Harlan. *Rumble.* Pictorial wrappers. New York, (1958). First edition. $50–$60. Author's first book.

ELLISON, Harlan (editor). *Dangerous Visions.* Cloth. Garden City, 1967. First edition. In dust jacket. $75–$100.

ELLISON, Ralph. *Invisible Man.* Cloth. New York, (1952). First edition. In dust jacket. $75–$125. Author's first book.

ELLSWORTH, Henry W. *Valley of the Upper Wabash, Indiana.* Folding map, 3 folding lithographs. Stiff wrappers. New York, 1838. First edition. $200–$250.

ELLSWORTH, Lincoln. *The Last Wild Buffalo Hunt.* 32 pp., cloth. New York, 1916. First edition. $50–$75.

ELMER, Jonathan. *An Eulogium on the Character of Gen. George Washington.* 25 pp., half leather. Trenton, N.J., 1800. $400–$600.

ELMORE, James B. *Love Among the Mistletoe, and Poems.* Cloth. Alamo, Ind., 1899. First edition. $35–$50.

ELMSLIE, Kenward. *Pavilions.* Wrappers. New York, 1961. First edition. One of 300. $40–$60.

ELTON, R.H. *Jackson Almanac, 1836.* 36 pp., wrappers. (New York, 1835.) $150.

ELWOOD, Louie B. *Queen Calafia's Land.* San Francisco, 1940. Grabhorn Press. One of 325. $75–$100.

EMBARGO (The), or Sketches of the Times; A Satire. By a Youth of Thirteen. (Cover title.) 12 pp., self-wrappers (stitched). Boston, 1808. (By William Cullen Bryant.) First edition. $1,000 and up. (For second edition, see author and title.)

EMERSON, Charles L. *Rise and Progress of Minnesota Territory.* 64 pp., pictorial printed wrappers. St. Paul, 1855. First edition. $350–$400.

EMERSON, Joseph. *Female Education.* 40 pp., plain wrappers. Boston, 1822. First edition. $75–$100.

EMERSON, Lucy. *The New-England Cookery*. Boards. Montpelier, Vt., 1808. First edition. $300–$400. Also, $170 (A, 1978).

EMERSON, Peter Henry. *Marsh Leaves*. 16 photogravures. Cloth. (London, 1895.) First edition. One of 300. $3,000–$3,500.

EMERSON, Ralph Waldo. See *Nature*.

EMERSON, Ralph Waldo. *An Address Delivered Before the Senior Class in Divinity College, Cambridge . . . 15 July, 1838*. 31 pp., blue wrappers. Boston, 1838. First edition. $150–$200. Also, foxed, $80 (A, 1974).

EMERSON, Ralph Waldo. *An Address Delivered in the Court-House in Concord, Massachusetts, on 1st August, 1844, on the Anniversary of the Emancipation of the Negroes in the British West Indies*. 34 pp., tan wrappers. Boston, 1844. First edition. $150. (Also issued stitched, without wrappers.)

EMERSON, Ralph Waldo. *The American Scholar*. ("An Oration Delivered Before the Phi Beta Kappa Society.") 26 pp., wrappers or unlettered cloth. Boston, 1837. First edition. Wrappers: $500–$750. (Very rare.) Cloth: $250–$350.

EMERSON, Ralph Waldo. *The Conduct of Life*. Cloth. Boston, 1860. First edition, first issue, without signature mark "1" and with ads dated December, 1860. $150–$200.

EMERSON, Ralph Waldo. *English Traits*. Cloth. Boston, 1856. First edition. $100–$150.

EMERSON, Ralph Waldo. *Essays*. Cloth. Boston, 1841. First edition, first binding, without "First Series" on spine. $300–$400. London, 1906. Vellum. Doves Press. One of 300 on paper. $600–$700. Another issue: One of 25 printed on vellum. $3,500–$4,000. Also, $2,000 (A, 1978); $2,600 (A, 1974). New York, 1934. Limited Editions Club. Boards. Boxed. $50–$60.

EMERSON, Ralph Waldo. *Essays: Second Series*. Cloth. Boston, 1844. First edition, probable first binding, with "2D Series" on spine. $250–$300.

EMERSON, Ralph Waldo. *A Historical Discourse, Delivered Before the Citizens of Concord, 12th, September, 1835*. 52 pp., blue wrappers. Concord, 1835. First edition. $150–$250.

EMERSON, Ralph Waldo. *The Journals of Ralph Waldo Emerson*. 10 vols., green cloth. Boston, 1909–14. First edition. $100. Another issue: Tan linen. One of 600 on large paper. $300–$400.

EMERSON, Ralph Waldo. *Lectures and Biographical Sketches*. Cloth. Boston, 1884. First edition. $75–$85.

EMERSON, Ralph Waldo. *Letters and Social Aims*. Cloth. Boston, 1876. First edition. $100–$150.

EMERSON, Ralph Waldo. *May-Day and Other Pieces*. White cloth. Boston, 1867. First edition, first issue, with "flowers" for "hours" on page 184. $75–$100. (Also issued in other colors of cloth.) London, 1867. Cloth. First English edition. $50–$75.

EMERSON, Ralph Waldo. *The Method of Nature*. 30 pp., printed tan wrappers. Boston, 1841. First edition. $150–$200.

EMERSON, Ralph Waldo. *An Oration Delivered Before the Literary Societies of Dartmouth College, July 24, 1838*. Wrappers. Boston, 1838. First edition. $100–$125.

EMERSON, Ralph Waldo. *Poems*. Green cloth. London, 1847. First edition, first issue, with "Chapman Brothers" on foot of spine and ads dated Nov. 16, 1846. $250–$350. Boston, 1847. Yellow boards, paper label. First American edition, first issue, with 4 pages of ads dated Jan. 1, 1847. $500–$750. New York, 1945. Limited Editions Club. Full leather. Boxed. $35–$50.

EMERSON, Ralph Waldo. *Representative Men*. Black or brown cloth. Boston, 1850.

First edition, first issue, with hourglass design on front and back covers. $150–$250. London, 1850. Brown or green cloth. First English edition (possibly issued simultaneously with the American edition, according to Blanck). $150–$250.

EMERSON, Ralph Waldo. *Society and Solitude.* Green cloth. Boston, 1870. First edition. $75–$100.

EMILY Parker, or Impulse, Not Principle. Frontispiece. Buff boards. Boston, 1827. (By Lydia Maria Child.) First edition. $150–$175.

EMMA. By the author of "Pride and Prejudice," etc. 3 vols., blue or brown paper boards, drab paper spine, paper labels. London, 1816. (By Jane Austen.) First edition. $4,000 and up. Also, rebacked, repaired, $1,600 (A, 1978); another, $2,090 (A, 1979); rubbed, one hinge cracked, $2,750 (A, 1974). New York, 1964. Limited Editions Club. Illustrated in color by Fritz Kredel. Buckram. Boxed. $75–$85.

EMMART, Emily Walcott (translator). *The Badianus Manuscript.* By Martinus de la Cruz. 118 colored plates. Cloth. Baltimore, 1940. $150–$175.

EMMETT, Chris. *Shanghai Pierce, a Fair Likeness.* Illustrated, map. Cloth. Norman, (1953). First edition. In dust jacket. $50–$60.

EMMONS, George T. *The Emmons Journal.* 11 pp., wrappers. Eugene, Ore., (1925). $75–$100.

EMMONS, Dr. (Richard). *Tecumseh: Or, The Battle of the Thames.* 36 pp., wrappers. New York, 1836. $60–$80.

EMMONS, Samuel Franklin. *Geology and Mining Industry of Leadville, Colorado.* 2 vols., half leather, including atlas with colored maps. Washington, 1883. $300–$400.

EMORY, William H. *Notes of a Military Reconnaissance.* 68 plates, 6 maps and plans. Cloth. Washington, 1848. House version. First edition. $150–$250. Another issue: Same place and date. Senate version. $150–$250.

ENGELS, Frederick. *Socialism, Utopian, and Scientific.* Red cloth. London, 1892. First edition in English. $150–$200.

ENGLE, Paul. *Worn Earth.* Boards. New Haven, 1932. First edition. In dust jacket. $75. Author's first book.

ENGLEHARDT, Zephyrin. *The Franciscans in Arizona.* Map, plates. 236 pp., wrappers. Harbor Springs, Mich., 1899. First edition. $200.

ENGELHARDT, Zephyrin. *The Franciscans in California.* Illustrated. Wrappers. Harbor Springs, 1897. First edition. $200.

ENGLISH Bards and Scotch Reviewers. 54 pp., drab printed boards. London, (1809). (By George Gordon Noel, Lord Byron.) First edition, first issue, without preface. $2,000 and up. Also, $900 (A, 1977). Later issue, with preface: $500 and up.

ENGLISH Bible (The). 5 vols., folio, vellum. London, 1903–05. Doves Press. One of 500. $3,000–$5,000. In special bindings by the Doves Bindery, $7,500–$10,000. Auction example: $7,500 (1979). Also, one of 2 on vellum. $124,000 (A, 1978). (One other copy on rejected, "retrie" or "retree" stock, is said to exist.)

ENGLISH Dance of Death (The). Frontispiece, engraved title and 74 color plates by Thomas Rowlandson. 24 parts, wrappers. London, 1814–16. (By William Combe.) First edition. $1,000 and up. London, 1814 (or 1815)–16. 2 vols., cloth. First book edition. $1,750–$2,000.

ENGLISH, William B. *Rosina Meadows, the Village Maid.* Wrappers. Boston, 1843. First edition. $100–$125.

ENSIGN and Thayer's Traveller's Guide Through the States of Ohio, Michigan, Indiana, Illinois, Missouri, Iowa and Wisconsin. (Variant titles.) Folding colored map.

Leather. New York, 1850. $150–$200. Buffalo, 1853. $100–$150. New York, 1853. $100–$125. New York, 1854. $100–$125.

EPILOGOS. (Cover title.) Printed red wrappers. (Los Angeles, 1967.) (By Robert Duncan.) First edition. One of 100 signed, and with an original Duncan drawing (from an edition of 115). $150–$200.

EPIPSYCHIDION: Verses, etc. Drab wrappers. London, 1821. (By Percy Bysshe Shelley.) First edition. $3,000 and up. Auction record: spine missing, "only known copy in wrappers," $1,400 (1945). In half morocco. $2,800 (A, 1978). Montagnola, Italy, 1923. Vellum. One of 222. $750.

EPITOME of Electricity and Galvanism (An). By Two Gentlemen of Philadelphia. Boards. Philadelphia, 1809. (By Jacob Green and Ebenezer Hazard.) First edition. $150–$200.

EPSTEIN, Jacob. *Epstein: An Autobiography*. Illustrated. Leatherette. London, 1955. One of 195 signed. In dust jacket. $250–$350.

EPSTEIN, Jacob. *Let There Be Sculpture*. Frontispiece, 47 illustrations. Vellum. (London, 1940.) One of 100 signed. Boxed. $500–$600.

EPSTEIN, Jacob. *Seventy-Five Drawings*. Oblong, vellum. London, 1929. One of 220 signed. $150–$250.

EREWHON, or Over the Range. Brown cloth. London, 1872. First edition. (By Samuel Butler.) $150–$300. Newtown, Wales, 1932. Gregynog Press. Illustrated. Sheep. One of 275 on Japan vellum. $250–$300. Another issue: One of 25 specially bound in morocco by George Fisher. $850–$1,000. New York, 1934. Limited Editions Club. Introduction by Aldous Huxley. Illustrated by Rockwell Kent. Cloth. Boxed. $25–$50.

ERWIN, Milo. *The History of Williamson County, Illinois*. Cloth. Marion, Ill., 1876. First edition. $100–$150.

ESPEJO, Antonio de. *New Mexico: Otherwise the Voiage of Anthony Espeio, Who in the Yeare 1583, With His Company, Discovered a Lande of 15 Provinces, etc.* Boards. (Lancaster, 1928.) First edition. One of 200. $200–$300.

ESSAY on Mind (An), with Other Poems. Blue-gray boards, white label on spine. London, 1826. (By Elizabeth Barrett Browning.) First edition, first issue, with the reading "found" in line 15, page 75. $825–$1,000. Also, $475 (A, 1978).

ESSAYS from Poor Robert the Scribe. Boards, leather spine. Doylestown, Pa., 1815. (By Charles Miner.) First edition. $150–$200.

ESSAYS of Howard on Domestic Economy. Contemporary calf. New York, 1820. (By Mordecai Manuel Noah.) First edition. $80–$125.

ESSE, James. *Hunger: A Dublin Story*. Printed wrappers. Dublin, 1918. (By James Stephens.) First edition. $75–$100.

ESSHOM, Frank. *Pioneers and Prominent Men of Utah*. Cloth. Salt Lake City, 1913. $100–$125.

ESTAVA, José María. *La Campana de la Mision*. Boards and cloth. Xalapa-Enriquez, Mexico, 1894. First edition. $150–$200.

ESTIENNE, Henri. *The Frankfort Book Fair*. Chicago, 1911. Caxton Club. One of 300. $150–$250.

ETHELL, Henry C. *The Rise and Progress of Civilization in the Hairy Nation and the History of Davis County*. Cloth. Bloomfield, Iowa, 1883. First edition. $150.

ETHNOLOGIC Dictionary of the Navajo Language (An). By the Franciscan Fathers. 536 pp., wrappers. St. Michaels, Ariz., 1910. One of 200 on Japan vellum. $500–$600.

ETZENHOUSER, R. *From Palmyra, New York, 1830, to Independence, Missouri, 1894.* 444 pp., wrappers. Independence, 1894. First edition. $100–$150.

EUGENE Aram: A Tale. 3 vols., boards, paper labels. London, 1832. (By Edward Bulwer-Lytton.) First edition. $125–$200.

EULOGY on the Life of Gen. George Washington (An). Wrappers. Newburyport, Mass., 1800. (By Robert Treat Paine, Jr.) First edition. $100–$125.

EUPHRANOR: A Dialogue on Youth. Green cloth. London, 1851. (By Edward FitzGerald.) $200–$250. London, 1885. Green cloth, or stitched, without ads at end. Second edition. $75–$100. (Note: A few copies were bound for presentation, appendix canceled, corrections made in FitzGerald's hand.) Another edition: (Guildford, 1882.) (With subtitle *A May-Day Conversation at Cambridge* instead of *A Dialogue on Youth.*) Half leather and green boards. Third edition. One of 50 (not so stated). $50–$75.

EURIPIDES. *The Plays of Euripides.* Translated by Gilbert Murray. Illustrated. 2 vols., folio, red buckram. Newtown, Wales, 1931. Gregynog Press. One of 500. $350–$450. Another issue: Folio, 2 vols. in one, morocco. One of 25 specially bound by George Fisher. $2,000–$2,250.

EVANGELICAL Hymns. 24 pp., stitched. Greenwich, Mass., 1807. First edition. $75–$100.

EVANS, Augusta Jane. *St. Elmo.* Cloth. New York, 1867. (By Augusta Jane Evans Wilson.) First edition. $150–$200.

EVANS, Elwood. *Puget Sound: Its Past, Present and Future.* 16 pp., wrappers. Olympia, Wash., 1869. First edition. $200–$300.

EVANS, Elwood. *Washington Territory.* 51 pp., wrappers. Olympia, 1877. First edition. $250–$300.

EVANS, Estwick. *A Pedestrious Tour, of 4,000 Miles, Through the Western States and Territories.* Portrait. Boards. Concord, N.H., 1819. First edition. $600–$750.

EVELYN, John. *Memoirs, Illustrative of the Life and Writings of John Evelyn, Esq., F.R.S.* Edited by William Bray. Folding pedigree, 8 plates. 2 vols., calf. London (Bath), 1818. First edition. $600–$800. Also, $400 (A, 1978).

EVENINGS in New England. By an American Lady. Brown boards. Boston, 1824. (By Lydia Maria Child.) First edition. $150–$200.

EVENTS in Indian History, Beginning with an Account of the Origin of the American Indians, etc. 8 plates. Sheepskin. Lancaster, Pa., 1841. (By James Wimer.) First edition. $150–$200. Lancaster, 1843. Second edition. $100–$125.

EVERETT, Edward. *A Defence of Christianity.* Boards, paper label. Boston, 1814. First edition. $100–$125. Author's first book.

EVERETT, Edward. *An Oration Delivered on the Battlefield of Gettysburg, etc.* 48 pp., cloth wrappers. New York, 1863. $1,000–$1,500. Includes one of the early book appearances of Abraham Lincoln's Gettysburg Address. See: Lincoln, Abraham.

EVERETT, Horace. *Regulating the Indian Department.* Folding map. Cloth. (Washington, 1834.) $200–$250.

EVERSON, William. See Antoninus, Brother.

EVERSON, Bill (William). *These Are the Ravens.* (Cover title.) 11 pp., stapled self-wrappers. San Leandro, Calif., 1935. First edition. $250–$350. Author's first book.

EVERSON, William. *Blame It on the Jet Stream.* Illustrated. Oblong, boards. Santa Cruz, 1978. First edition. One of 150 signed. Without dust jacket. $100–$125.

EVERSON, William. *The Blowing of the Seed*. Green or brown flowered boards, leather spine. New Haven, 1966. First edition. One of 218 signed. $100–$125.

EVERSON, William. *In the Fictive Wish*. Cloth. (Berkeley, 1967.) Oyez Press. One of 200 signed. In plain dust jacket. $75–$125.

EVERSON, William. *The Masculine Dead: Poems, 1938–1940*. Green cloth. Prairie City, Ill., (1942). First edition, with tipped-in errata sheet. $900.

EVERSON, William. *Poems: MCMXLII*. Self-wrappers. (Waldport, Ore., 1945.) One of 500. $50–$75.

EVERSON, William. *A Privacy of Speech*. Illustrated. Boards. Berkeley, 1949. First edition. One of 100 (actually fewer than 50). $800–$1,000.

EVERSON, William. *The Residual Years*. Illustrated by the author. Wrappers. (Waldport, 1944.) First edition. One of 330 signed. $100. (New York, 1948.) Boards. One of 1,000. In dust jacket. $50–$65. (This edition, published by New Directions, is a collection of four prior works. It was reissued in hardback and in wrappers in 1968.)

EVERSON, William. *San Joaquin*. Boards. Los Angeles, 1939. First edition. One of 100. $300–$400.

EVERSON, William. *The Springing of the Blade*. Decorated cloth. (Reno, 1968.) First edition. One of 180 signed. (Issued without dust jacket.) $75–$100.

EVERSON, William. *Tendril in the Mesh*. Boards. (San Francisco), 1973. First edition. One of 250 signed. $65–$100.

EVERSON, William. *Triptych for the Living*. Illustrated. Limp vellum. (Oakland, 1951.) First edition. One of 200 (actually fewer than 100). $600–$850.

EVERSON, William. *The Veritable Years: 1949–1966*. Boards. Santa Barbara, 1978. First edition. One of 50 signed, with a holograph poem. In dust jacket. $75–$100.

EVERSON, William. *X War Elegies*. Illustrated. Wrappers. Waldport, 1943. First edition, first state, wrappers lettered in black and yellow. $100–$135. Waldport, 1944. Expanded edition (retitled *War Elegies*). One of 975. $125. One of 30 in full calf, signed. $250–$300.

EVERSON, William. *The Year's Declension*. Boards. Berkeley, 1961. First edition. One of 100 signed. $125–$175.

EVERTS, Truman C. *Thirty-Seven Days of Peril*. San Francisco, 1923. Grabhorn printing. One of 375. $50.

EVERTS and Kirk. *The Official State Atlas of Nebraska*. Plates, 207 colored maps. Half calf. Philadelphia, 1885. $300–$600.

EVIDENCE Concerning Projected Railways Across the Sierra Nevada Mountains. Calf. Carson City, Nev., 1865. $750–$1,000, possibly more.

EVIL of Intoxicating Liquor(The) and the Remedy. 24 pp., sewed. Park Hill, Okla., 1844. $150–$250.

EVJEN, John O. *Scandinavian Immigrants in New York, 1630–1674*. Illustrated. Cloth. Minneapolis, 1916. First edition. $75–$125.

EWALD, Johannes. *The Death of Balder*. Translated by George Borrow. Cloth, paper label. London, 1899 (actually 1892). One of 250. $100–$150.

EWELL, Thomas T. *A History of Hood County, Texas*. Cloth. Granbury, Tex., 1895. First edition. $500–$800.

EXAMINATION of the President's Reply to the New Haven Remonstrance (An). 69 pp., wrappers. New York, 1801. (By William Coleman.) First edition. $75–$100.

EXETER Book of Old English Poetry (The). Folio, buckram. London, 1933. $75–$80.

EXLEY, Frederick. *A Fan's Notes*. Cloth. New York, (1968). First edition. In dust jacket. $40–$50. Author's first book.

EXPLOSICIÓN del Ministro de Hacienda. (Cover title.) 11 pp., wrappers. Mexico, 1836. $200–$300.

EXTRACTS from the Autobiography of Calvin Coolidge. Miniature book. Blue calf. Kingsport, Tenn., 1930. $35–$50.

EYE WITNESS (An). *Satan in Search of a Wife*. 4 full-page woodcuts and 2 vignettes by George Cruikshank. Pink wrappers. London, 1831. (By Charles Lamb.) First edition. $500–$750. Rebound, $200 (A, 1979).

EZRA Pound: His Metric and Poetry. Portrait frontispiece by Gaudier-Brzeska. Rose paper boards, lettered in gold on front cover. New York, 1917 (actually 1918). (By T.S. Eliot.) First edition. In plain buff dust jacket. $400–$500. Lacking jacket, $250–$350.

F

F., M. T. *My Chinese Marriage*. By M.T.F. Green boards and cloth. New York, 1921. (By Mai Taim Fran king, although long attributed to Katherine Anne Porter as ghost-writer.) First edition. $100–$125. (Note: The late John S. Van E. Kohn, New York bookseller, once told me he had seen a letter in which Miss Porter denied authorship of the book and said that she only typed it.)

FABLE for Critics (A). Cloth, or boards. New York, (18)48. (By James Russell Lowell.) First edition, first state, without "A Vocal and Musical Medley" on title page and with pages 63 and 64 misnumbered. $200–$225. Rebound in leather, $115.

FABLES of Esope (The). Translated out of the Frensshe into Englysshe by William Caxton. 37 engravings on wood by Agnes Miller Parker. Sheepskin. Newtown, Wales, 1931. Gregynog Press. One of 250. $600–$800.

FACSIMILES of Royal, Historical, Literary, and Other Autographs in the Department of MSS., British Museum. Edited by George F. Warner, 150 plates. 5 parts, folio, sewed. London, 1899. $200–$300.

FACTS Concerning the City of San Diego, the Great Southwestern Sea-port of the United States, with a Map Showing the City and Its Surroundings. 14 pp., wrappers. San Diego, (1888). $200–$300.

FACTS Respecting Indian Administration in the Northwest (The). 74 pp., wrappers. (Victoria?, 1886.) $150–$200.

FAHEY, Herbert. *Early Printing in California*. Illustrated. Cloth. San Francisco, 1956. Grabhorn Press. One of 400. $250–$300.

FAIRBANKS, George R. *Early History of Florida*. 82 pp., sewed. St. Augustine, 1857. First edition. $200–$350.

FAIRBANKS, George R. *The Spaniards in Florida*. 120 pp., wrappers, Jacksonville, 1868. First edition. $150–$300.

FAIRCHILD, T.B. *A History of the Town of Cuyahoga Falls, Summit County*. 39 pp., cloth. Cleveland, 1876. $100–$200.

FAIRFIELD, Asa Merrill. *Fairfield's Pioneer History of Lassen County, California*. 4 plates, folding map. Pictorial cloth. San Francisco, (1916). First edition. $150–$200.

FAIRY Book (The). Frontispiece and 81 woodcuts by Joseph A. Adams. Brown cloth. New York, 1837. (By Dinah M. Craik.) First edition. $125–$200.

FAIRY Garland (A). 12 colored illustrations by Edmund Dulac. Half vellum. London, (1928). First edition. One of 1,000 signed by the artist. $400–$550.

FAITH Gartney's Girlhood. Cloth. Boston, 1863. (By Mrs. A.D.T. Whitney.) First edition. $75–$100.

FAITHFUL Picture (A), of the Political Situation in New Orleans. 38 pp. (New Orleans), 1807. (By Edward James Workman.) (Also attributed to Edward Livingston.) $400–$500. Boston, 1808, 48 pp. $300.

FALCONER, Thomas. *Letters and Notes on the Texan Santa Fe Expedition, 1841–42*. Edited by F.W. Hodge. Portrait. Half cloth. New York, 1930. $150–$200.

FALCONER, Thomas. *On the Discovery of the Mississippi, and On the South-Western, Oregon, and North-Western Boundary of the United States.* Folding map, errata leaf. Cloth. London, 1844. First edition, first issue, with the map (later absent). $500–$750.

FALCONER, William. *A New Universal Dictionary of the Marine.* 35 full-page and folding plates. Half calf, leather label. London, 1815. $300–$400.

FALKLAND. Boards. London, 1827. (By Edward Bulwer-Lytton.) First edition. $750–$1,000. Author's first novel.

FALKNER: A Novel. 3 vols., cloth, paper labels. London, 1837. (By Mary Wollstonecraft Shelley.) First edition. $400–$600.

FALKNER, J. Meade. *The Lost Stradivarius.* Cloth. London, 1895. First edition. $100–$150.

FAMILY Robinson Crusoe (The). Translated from the German of M. Wiss (Johann David Wyss). 2 vols., boards. London, 1814. First edition in English. $4,000 (A, 1981). Also, see *The Swiss Family Robinson.*

FANNIE, Cousin (translator). *Red Beard's Stories for Children.* Silhouette illustrations. Boards, yellow label. Boston, 1856. $75–$100.

FANNY. 49 pp., printed gray wrappers. New York, 1819. (By Fitz-Greene Halleck.) First edition. $300–$400. Author's first separate book. (Note: There also exists a pirated 1819 edition, 67 pp.)

FANSHAWE; A Tale. Brown or buff boards, purple cloth spine, paper labels. Boston, 1828. (By Nathaniel Hawthorne.) First edition. $12,000 (A, 1981). Author's first book.

FANTE, John. *Ask the Dust.* Cloth. New York, 1939. First edition. In dust jacket. $25–$35.

FANTE, John. *Wait Until Spring, Bandini.* Cloth. New York, (1938). First edition. In dust jacket. $75–$100. Author's first book.

FARM Yard Story. 12 pp., with pull-out color illustrations. Glazed printed green boards. Boston, 1865. L. Prang & Co. $150–$200.

FARMER, Philip Jose. *The Green Odyssey.* Cloth. New York, 1957. First edition. In dust jacket. $500–$750(!).

FARNHAM, S.B. *The New York and Idaho Gold Mining Co.* Folding map. 23 pp., wrappers. New York, 1864. $200–$300.

FARNHAM, Thomas J. *History of Oregon Territory.* Frontispiece map. Wrappers. New York, 1844. First edition. $200–$300.

FARNHAM, Thomas J. *Travels in the Californias.* Map and plates. Cloth. New York, 1844. First edition, second (or clothbound) issue. $1,500 and up. Also, worn, with map mounted, $1,100 (A, 1979). (Note: The first edition was issued first in 4 paperbound parts, which are rare in fine condition.)

FARNHAM, Thomas J. *Travels in the Great Western Prairies.* Cloth, leather label. Poughkeepsie, 1841. First edition. $500–$600. Ploughkeepsie (sic), 1843. Tan boards, lavender cloth. $1,000 and up. London, 1843. First English edition. $300–$500.

FARQUHARSON, Martha. *Elsie Dinsmore.* Red cloth. New York, 1867. (By Martha Finley.) First edition, with publisher's address misprinted "605" for 506 Broadway on title page. $2,500 (A, 1977). (Reasonably nice copies available for much less.)

FARRELL, James T. *Calico Shoes and Other Stories.* Blue cloth. New York, (1934). First edition. In dust jacket. $150–$200.

FARRELL, James T. *Gas-House McGinty*. Cloth. New York, 1933. First edition. In dust jacket. $100–$150.

FARRELL, James T. *Guillotine Party*. Green cloth. New York, (1935). First edition. In dust jacket. $75–$150.

FARRELL, James T. *Judgment Day*. Cloth. New York, 1935. First edition, with "thay" for "they" in third line of page 218. In dust jacket. $75–$150.

FARRELL, James T. *A Misunderstanding*. Cloth. New York, 1949. One of 300 signed. In tissue jacket, $50–$75.

FARRELL, James T. *$1,000 a Week and Other Stories*. Cloth. New York, (1942). First edition. In dust jacket. $75–$100.

FARRELL, James T. *Young Lonigan: A Boyhood in Chicago Streets*. Cloth, New York. 1932. First edition. In dust jacket. $175–$275. Without jacket, $75–$100. Author's first book.

FARRELL, James T. *The Young Manhood of Studs Lonigan*. Brown cloth. New York, (1934). First edition, with errata slip listing eight typographical errors, among them "Connolly" for "Connell" in line 18 of page 88. In dust jacket. $150–$250.

FAST, Edward G. *Catalogue of Antiquities and Curiosities Collected in the Territory of Alaska*. 32 pp., wrappers. (New York), 1869. $45–$50.

FAULKNER, J.P. *Eighteen Months on a Greenland Whaler*. Portrait. Cloth. New York, 1878. $175–$200.

FAULKNER, William. See Dashiell, Alfred; Petersen, Carl; Wells, Oliver.

FAULKNER, William, *Absalom, Absalom!* Folding map at end. Printed paper boards, cloth spine. New York, 1936. First edition. One of 300 signed. $1,250. Also, $500 (A, 1979); $650 (A, 1975). First trade edition: Cloth. In dust jacket. $250–$300. London, (1936). Buff cloth. First English edition. In dust jacket. $200–$250.

FAULKNER, William. *As I Lay Dying*. Beige cloth. New York. (1930). First edition, first issue, with dropped "I" on page 11 and top edges stained brown. In dust jacket. $750–$850. (Note: In this book the preferred binding state has all the lettering complete and undamaged.) Second issue, with "I" correctly positioned. In dust jacket. $500–$600.

FAULKNER, William. *Big Woods*. Green cloth. New York, (1955). First edition, first printing. In dust jacket. $80–$100.

FAULKNER, William. *Collected Stories of William Faulkner*. Gray cloth. New York, (1950). First edition. In dust jacket. $75–$85.

FAULKNER, William. *Doctor Martino and Other Stories*. Red and black cloth. New York, 1934. First edition. One of 360 signed. In acetate jacket. Boxed. $850–$1,000. Trade edition: Blue cloth. In dust jacket. $400–$550. London, 1934. Brick-red cloth. First English edition. In dust jacket. $200–$300.

FAULKNER, William. *A Fable*. Blue buckram. (New York, 1954.) First edition, first printing. One of 1,000 signed. In tissue dust jacket. Boxed. $350–$450. Trade edition: Maroon cloth. In dust jacket. $85–$100.

FAULKNER, William. *Go Down, Moses and Other Stories*. Salmon-colored boards, red cloth spine. New York, (1942). First edition, first printing. One of 100 signed. $3,500–$4,000. Also, $3,750 (A, 1977); $3,000 (A, 1975). Trade edition: Cloth (in various colors). In dust jacket. $350–$400. London, 1942. Cloth. First English edition. In dust jacket. $150–$200.

FAULKNER, William. *A Green Bough*. Wood engravings by Lynd Ward. Tan cloth, paper labels. New York, 1933. First edition. One of 360 signed. Issued without dust jacket. $500–$750. Also, $375 (A, 1977). Trade edition: Green cloth. In dust jacket. $250–$450.

FAULKNER, William. *The Hamlet*. Green cloth and boards. New york, 1940. First edition, first printing. One of 250 signed. In cellophane dust jacket. Boxed. $1,000–$1,250. Also, $750 (A, 1977); $850 (A, 1975); $750 (A, 1974). Trade edition: Black cloth. In dust jacket. $300–$350.

FAULKNER, William. *Idyll in the Desert*. Red marbled boards, paper label. New York, 1931. First edition. One of 400 signed. In glassine dust jacket. $750–$850. Also, lacking jacket, $400 (A, 1977).

FAULKNER, William, *Intruder in the Dust*. Black cloth. New York, (1948). First edition, first printing. In dust jacket. $150–$300. London, 1949. Blue cloth. First English edition. In dust jacket. $150–$200.

FAULKNER, William. *Jealousy and Episode*. Cloth. Minneapolis, 1955. First edition. One of 500. (Issued without dust jacket.) $200.

FAULKNER, William. *Knight's Gambit*. Red cloth. New York, (1949). First edition. In dust jacket. $150–$225.

FAULKNER, William. *Light in August*. Beige buckram. (New York, 1932.) First edition, first printing. In dust jacket and glassine wrapper. $500–$750.

FAULKNER, William. *The Mansion*. Black cloth. New York, (1959). First edition. One of 500 signed. In acetate dust jacket. $400–$500. First trade edition: Blue cloth. In dust jacket. $125–$175. Also, a set of advance galley proofs, $550 (A, 1977). London, 1961. Cloth. First English edition. In dust jacket. $75–$100.

FAULKNER, William. *The Marble Faun*. Mottled green boards, printed labels. Boston, (1924). First edition. (About 500 copies issued.) In dust jacket. $5,000–$7,000. Also, inscribed twice by Faulkner, $6,250 (A, 1977).

FAULKNER, William. *The Marionettes*. Unopened sheets. (Charlottesville, 1975.) First edition. One of 100. Boxed $250–$300. Another issue: One of 26 lettered copies. $400–$500.

FAULKNER, William. *Mayday*. Illustrated. Notre Dame, (1977). First edition. One of 150. With a pamphlet about the book by Carvel Collins. Boxed. $250.

FAULKNER, William. *Mirrors of Chartres Street*. Illustrated. Tan cloth. (Minneapolis, 1953.) First edition. One of 1,000. In dust jacket. $150–$200.

FAULKNER, William. *Miss Zilphia Gant*. Brownish red cloth. (Dallas), 1932. Book Club of Texas. First edition. One of 300. In glassine dust jacket. $1,000–$1,250. Also, $650 (A, 1977): $550 (A, 1974).

FAULKNER, William. *Mosquitoes*. Blue cloth. New York, 1927. First edition. In first-issue dust jacket, with mosquito design. $1,000–$1,250. Also, $1,000 (A, 1975).

FAULKNER, William. *New Orleans Sketches*. Edited by Carvel Collins. Brown boards. New Brunswick, N.J., 1958. First American edition, first printing. In dust jacket. $100–$150.

FAULKNER, William. *Notes on a Horsethief*. Decorations by Elizabeth Calvert. Decorated in green cloth. Greenville, Miss., 1950. First edition. One of 950 (of 975) signed. (Issued without dust jacket.) $400–$450. One of 25 copies marked "for presentation" and signed. $600–$750.

FAULKNER, William. *The Portable Faulkner*, Edited by Malcolm Cowley. Cloth. New York, 1946. First edition. In dust jacket. $75–$125.

FAULKNER, William. *Pylon*. Folding facsimile. Half blue cloth and silver boards. New York, 1935. First edition. One of 310 signed. Boxed. $600–$750. Also, $425 (A, 1977); $450 (A, 1975). Trade edition: Blue cloth, with black band. In dust jacket. $250–$325.

FAULKNER, William. *The Reivers: A Reminiscence*. Maroon cloth. New York, (1962).

First edition, first printing. One of 500 signed. In acetate dust jacket. $500–$650. Also, $300 (A, 1975). Trade edition: Red cloth. In dust jacket. $40–$50.

FAULKNER, William. *Requiem for a Nun.* Half black cloth, marbled boards. New York, (1951). First edition. One of 750 signed. In acetate dust jacket. $500–$600. Trade edition: Green and black cloth. In dust jacket. $150–$200. London, 1953. Boards. In dust jacket. $75–$100. Play version: New York, (1959). Adapted by Ruth Ford. Gray boards. First edition, first printing. In dust jacket. $50–$60.

FAULKNER, William. *A Rose for Emily and Other Stories.* Edited by Saxe Commins. Pictorial wrappers. New York, (1945). First separate edition. $75.

FAULKNER, William. *Salmagundi.* Tan wrappers. Milwaukee, 1932. Casanova Press. First edition, first state, with bottom edges untrimmed. One of the first 26 copies of a total edition of 525. Boxed. $800–$1,000. Also, $750 (A, 1977). Other copies from the 525-copy run, boxed. $600–$700. (Note: Includes a poem by Ernest Hemingway, listed on title page.)

FAULKNER, William. *Sanctuary.* Magenta boards and gray cloth. New York, (1931). First edition, first printing, with "First Published, 1931" on copyright page. In dust jacket. $850–$1,250. London, 1931. Red cloth. First English edition. In dust jacket. $150–$200.

FAULKNER, William. *Sartoris.* Black cloth. New York, (1929). First edition. In dust jacket. $750–$1,000.

FAULKNER, William. *Soldiers' Pay.* Blue cloth. New York, 1926. First edition. In dust jacket. $1,750–$2,000. Also, in jacket and signed by Faulkner, $4,250 (A, 1977). Lacking jacket, $300 and up. London, 1930. Green cloth. First English edition. In dust jacket. $300–$350. Author's first novel.

FAULKNER, William. *The Sound and the Fury.* Black, white, and gray patterned boards, white cloth spine. New York, (1929). First edition, first printing, with "First Published 1929" on copyright page. In dust jacket. $1,000–$1,250. Also, $850 (A, 1977); $425 (A, 1975); $325 (A, 1974). London, 1931. Black cloth. First English edition. In dust jacket. $200–$300.

FAULKNER, William. *These 13.* Tan and red cloth. New York, (1931). First edition. One of 299 signed. In tissue dust jacket. $650–$950. Trade edition: Blue and gray cloth. In dust jacket. $300–$400. London, 1933. Blue cloth. First English edition. In dust jacket. $150–$200.

FAULKNER, William. *This Earth.* Illustrated by Albert Heckman. 8 pp., stiff tan wrappers. New York, 1932. First edition. (1,000 copies.) In plain white envelope. $135–$200.

FAULKNER, William. *The Town.* Tan cloth, top edges red. New York, (1957). First edition, first printing. One of 450 signed. In acetate dust jacket. $450–$650. Trade edition: Red cloth. In dust jacket. $100–$150. London, 1958. Red boards. First English edition. In dust jacket. $75–$100.

FAULKNER, William. *The Unvanquished.* Illustrated by Edward Shenton. Boards and red cloth. New York, (1938). First edition, first printing. One of 250 signed. $600–$750. Also, $350 (A, 1977). Trade edition: Gray cloth. In dust jacket. $150–$250.

FAULKNER, William. *The Wild Palms.* Red cloth and boards. New York, (1939). First edition, first printing. One of 250 signed. In glassine dust jacket. $500–$650. Also, $425 (A, 1977). Trade edition: Tan cloth. In dust jacket. $75–$100. Advance issue: Green wrappers. $675. London, (1939). Cloth. First English edition. In dust jacket. $100–$150.

FAULKNER, William. *William Faulkner's Speech of Acceptance Upon the Award of the Nobel Prize for Literature.* Beige wrappers. (New York, 1951.) First separate edition, first printing. One of 1,500 by the Spiral Press. $35. Second printing. One of 2,500. $25. Third printing. One of 3,500. $15.

FAULKNER, William (editor). *Sherwood Anderson & Other Famous Creoles.* Drawings by William Spratling. Green boards, paper label. New Orleans, 1926. First edition. One of about 50 hand-tinted copies (of an issue of 250 numbered copies, from a 400-copy edition). With "W. Spratling" on front end paper. $1,000 and up. Other copies, $600–$800. Also, worn. $550 (A, 1977). Unnumbered copies. $300–$400 at retail.

FAUST, Frederick. *Dionysus in Hades.* Boards. Oxford, 1931. First edition. One of 500. $75–$100. (Faust wrote Western fiction under the pen name Max Brand.)

FAUX, William. *Memorable Days in America.* Half leather. London, 1823. First edition. $200–$250.

FEARING, Kenneth. *Angel Arms.* Boards. New York, 1929. First edition. In dust jacket. $100–$125. Author's first book.

FEARING, Kenneth. *The Big Clock.* Cloth. New York, (1946). First edition. In dust jacket. $50–$65.

FEAST of the Poets (The). By the Editor of the Examiner. Boards, paper label. London, 1814. (By Leigh Hunt.) First edition. $250–$350.

FEATHERSTONHAUGH, George W. *A Canoe Voyage Up the Minnay Sotor.* 2 folding maps, 2 plates, 2 vols., cloth. London 1847. First edition. $350.

FEIBLEMAN, James K. *Death of the God in Mexico.* Cloth. New York, (1931). First edition. In dust jacket. $100–$150. Author's first book.

FEININGER, Andreas. *Feininger on Photography.* Illustrated. Cloth. New York, (1949). First edition. In dust jacket. $75–$100.

FELLOWS-JOHNSTON, Annie. *The Little Colonel.* Green cloth. Boston, 1896. First edition. $75–$100.

FENOLLOSA, Ernest F. *Certain Noble Plays of Japan.* From manuscripts of Fenollosa, chosen and finished by Ezra Pound. Introduction by W.B. Yeats. Boards, linen spine. Churchtown, Dundrum, Ireland, 1916. Cuala Press. One of 350. $250.

FENOLLOSA, Ernest F. *The Chinese Written Character as a Medium for Poetry.* Foreword by Ezra Pound. Black cloth, parchment spine. London, (1936). First edition. In dust jacket. $175–$225. New York, (1936). Green boards. First American edition. In dust jacket. $100–$125.

FERBER, Edna. *American Beauty.* Cloth. Garden City, 1931. First edition. Limited and signed. In dust jacket. $50–$75.

FERBER, Edna. *Dawn O'Hara: The Girl Who Laughed.* Colored frontispiece. Cloth. New York, (1911). First edition. In dust jacket. $100–$150. Author's first book.

FERBER, Edna. *Giant.* Cloth. Garden City, 1952. First edition. In dust jacket. $50–$60.

FERBER, Edna. *A Peculiar Treasure.* Boards and cloth. New York, 1939. First edition. One of 351 signed. In dust jacket. Boxed. $50–$75.

FERBER, Edna. *Sarotoga Trunk.* Blue buckram. New York, 1941. First edition. One of 526 signed. In dust jacket. Boxed. $150–$175. Trade edition: Cloth. In dust jacket. $35–$40.

FERBER, Edna. *Show Boat.* Green boards, white vellum spine. Garden City, 1926. First edition. One of 201 signed. Boxed $150–$200. Another issue: Decorated boards (presentation copies, not signed). One of 1,000. $40–$50. Trade edition: Yellow cloth. In dust jacket. $25.

FERBER, Edna. *So Big.* Cloth. Garden City, 1924. First edition. In dust jacket. $50.

FERLINGHETTI, Lawrence. *Pictures of the Gone World.* Stiff black printed wrappers, and boards. San Francisco, (1955). Wrappers, with wraparound label (500 copies):

$150–$225. Another issue: Hard covers. One of 25 signed. $300–$350. Author's first book.

FERLINGHETTI, Lawrence. *The Secret Meaning of Things.* Cloth. (New York, 1968.) First edition. One of 150 signed. Boxed. $50. Trade edition: In dust jacket. $15. Also issued later in wrappers.

FERNÁNDEZ DE SAN SALVADOR, Augustin. *Los Jesuitas Quitados y Restituidos al Mundo. Historia de la Antigua California.* Cloth or leather. Mexico, 1861. First edition. $300–$400.

FERRIER, Susan Edmonstone. See *Destiny, or, The Chief's Daughter; Marriage.*

FERRINI, Vincent. *No Smoke.* Red cloth, cover and spine lables. Portland, Me., 1941. First edition. $25. Author's first book.

FEUCHTWANGER, Dr. Lewis. *A Treatise on Gems.* Cloth. New York, 1838. First edition. $100–$125.

FICKE, Arthur Davison. See Morgan, Emanuel, and Knish, Anne.

FIDFADDY, Frederick Augustus. *The Adventures of Uncle Sam in Search After His Lost Honor.* Boards. Middletown, Conn., 1816. First edition. $100–$150.

FIELD, Eugene. *Culture's Garland.* Cloth, or printed gray wrappers. Boston, 1887. First edition. Wrappers: $35–$50. Another issue: Wrappers, leaves untrimmed. One of 6 (or 12?). Inscribed, $250. Blue cloth: $50.

FIELD, Eugene. *Florence Bardsley's Story.* Green cloth. Chicago, 1897. First edition. One of 25 on Japan vellum. $100–$150. Another issue: One of 150 on paper. $75–$100. Trade edition: Cloth. $15.

FIELD, Eugene. *The Holy Cross and Other Tales.* Vellum. Cambridge, (Mass.), and Chicago, 1893. First edition. One of 20 on vellum, signed by the publisher. $100–$150. Another issue: Blue cloth. One of 110 on paper, signed by the publisher. $100–$125. Trade edition: Cloth, $40–$50.

FIELD, Eugene. *The House.* Boards. New York, 1896. First edition. One of 150 large paper copies. $100–$150.

FIELD, Eugene. *How One Friar Met the Devil and Two Pursued Him.* Boards. Chicago, (1900). First edition. One of 300. $75–$85.

FIELD, Eugene. *A Little Book of Tribune Verse.* Cloth. Denver, 1901. First edition. One of 750. $75–$85.

FIELD, Eugene. *A Little Book of Western Verse.* Blue-gray boards and cloth. Chicago, 1889. First edition. One of 250 large paper copies. $100–$150. New York, 1890. Cloth. First trade edition. $25. (Note: The first appearance of "Little Boy Blue.")

FIELD, Eugene. *The Love Affairs of a Bibliomaniac.* Frontispiece. Blue cloth. New York, 1896. First edition, first issue, with 8 titles listed. $75–$100. Another issue: Half vellum. One of 150 on Holland paper. $125–$175.

FIELD, Eugene. *Love-Songs of Childhood.* Vellum. New York, 1894. First edition. One of 106 on Van Gelder paper. $100–$150. Another issue: One of 15 on Japan vellum. $250–$300. Trade edition: Blue cloth. $25.

FIELD, Eugene. *Poems of Childhood.* 9 color plates by Maxfield Parrish. Cloth. New York, 1904. First edition. $125–$135.

FIELD, Eugene. *Second Book of Tales.* Half vellum. Chicago, 1896. First edition. One of 150. $75–$100.

FIELD, Eugene. *Second Book of Verse.* Boards, leather label. Chicago, 1892. First edition. One of 300. In dust jacket. $100–$125. Another issue: One of 12 with manuscript poems. $400–$450.

FIELD, Eugene. *Sharps and Flats*. 2 vols., blue cloth. New York, 1900. First edition. $50–$75. New York, 1901. 2 vols., half vellum. One of 150. $100–$125.

FIELD, Eugene. *The Stars: A Slumber Story*. Boards. New York, 1901. First edition. $50–$75.

FIELD, Eugene. *The Symbol and the Saint*. Wrappers. (Chicago), 1886. First edition. $300–$400.

FIELD, Eugene. *The Temptation of Friar Gonsol*. Illustrated. Vellum. Washington, 1900. One of 300 on paper. $75–$125. Another issue: One of 10 on vellum. $200–$225. (Note: This is another edition of *How One Friar Met the Devil and Two Pursued Him.*)

FIELD, Eugene. *Tribune Primer*. Gray-blue wrappers. (Denver, 1881.) First edition. $2,000 (1970 catalogue). Author's first book.

FIELD, Eugene. *With Trumpet and Drum*. Boards. New York, 1892. First edition. One of 250. $100–$150. Another issue: One of 12 on vellum. $250–$300. Trade edition: Cloth. $20.

FIELD, Joseph E. *Three Years in Texas*. Wrappers. Greenfield, Mass., 1836. First edition. $3,500.

FIELD, Rachel. *Hitty: Her First Hundred Years*. Illustrated by Dorothy P. Lathrop. Decorated cloth, paper label. New York, 1929. First edition. In dust jacket. $100–$125.

FIELD, Rachel. *Rise Up, Jennie Smith*. Wrappers. New York, (1918). First edition. $75. Author's first book.

FIELD, Stephen J. *Personal Reminiscences of Early Days in California*. Red cloth. (San Francisco, 1880?) First edition. $150–$250. Second edition: (Washington, 1893.) Half morocco. $100–$150.

FIELDING, Henry. *A Journey from This World to the Next*. Illustrated. Buckram. London, 1930. Golden Cockerel Press. One of 500. $150.

FIELDING, T.H. *A Picturesque Description of the River Wye*. 12 colored aquatint plates. Boards. London, 1841. $600–$800, or more.

FIELDING, T.H., and Walton, J. *A Picturesque Tour of the English Lakes*. Color vignette and 48 colored aquatint plates. Cloth. London, 1821. $1,250–$1,500. Large paper issue: $1,500–$2,000.

FIFTH Antiquarian Book Fair (The): A Handlist of Exhibitors Introduced by Lawrence Durrell. 12 pp. stapled, wrappers. London, 1962. One of 10 on green paper, signed. $250. Also, $125 (A, 1978).

FIGUEROA, José. *The Manifesto*. (Translated from the original as published in Monterey in 1835.) Printed wrappers. San Francisco, 1855. First edition in English. $500–$750. Also, $375 (A, 1977).

FILISOLA, Gen. Vicente. *Evacuation of Texas*. 68 pp., half leather. Columbia, Tex., 1837. First edition in English (of item following). $2,500–$4,000, possibly more. (Sometimes called "the first real book published in Texas.")

FILISOLA, Gen. Vicente. *Representación dirigida al Supremo Gobierno por el General Vicente Filisola, en Defensa de Su Honor y Aclaración de Sus Operaciones como General en Gefe del Ejarcito sobre Tejas*. 82 pp., wrappers. Mexico, 1836. First edition. $1,250.

FILLEY, William. *Life and Adventures of William Filley*. 7 plates and half-page cut, 96pp., wrappers. Chicago, 1867. Printed by Fergus. First edition, $1,000–$1,500, possibly more. Another edition, same place and date: 112 pp., wrappers. Printed by Filley & Ballard. Second edition. $400–$600.

FINLAY, John. *Journal Kept by Hugh Finlay, Surveyor of Post Roads.* Leather and cloth. Brooklyn, 1867. One of 150. $100–$150.

FINLEY, Ernest L. (editor). *History of Sonoma County.* (California.) Morocco. Santa Rosa, 1937. First edition. $75–$100.

FINLEY, James B. *History of the Wyandott Mission at Upper Sandusky, Ohio.* Calf. Cincinnati, 1840. First edition. $200–$250.

FINLEY, Martha. See Farquharson, Martha.

FINN, Huck. See Twain, Mark, *Tom Sawyer Abroad.*

FINNEY, Charles G. *The Circus of Doctor Lao.* Illustrated. Cloth. New York, 1935. First edition, with July on copyright page. In dust jacket. $100–$150. Author's first book.

FINNEY & Davis (publishers). *Biographical and Statistical History of the City of Oshkosh.* 76 pp., half leather. Oshkosh, 1867. First edition. $75–$100.

FIRBANK, Arthur Ronald. *Odette D'Antrevernes.* Pink or blue-gray wrappers. London, 1905. First edition. $250–$350. Also, about 10 sets of unbound signatures were made for presentation. A signed copy sold at auction for $650 in October, 1977. Author's first book.

FIRBANK, Ronald. *Concerning the Eccentricities of Cardinal Pirelli.* Cloth. London, 1926. First edition. In dust jacket. $100–$150.

FIRBANK, Ronald. *The Flower Beneath the Foot.* Cloth. London, 1923. First edition. In dust jacket. $75–$100. New York, 1924. First American edition. In dust jacket. $75.

FIRBANK, Ronald. *Inclinations.* Illustrated. Cloth. London, 1916. First edition. One of 500. In dust jacket. $100.

FIRBANK, Ronald. *Odette: A Fairy Tale for Weary People.* Illustrated. Wrappers. London, 1916. First separate edition. $75.

FIRBANK, Ronald. *Prancing Nigger.* Introduction by Carl Van Vechten. New York, (1924). First edition. In dust jacket. $75–$100.

FIRBANK, Ronald. *The Princess Zoubaroff.* Cloth. London, 1920. First edition. In dust jacket. $100–$150. (513 copies.)

FIRBANK, Ronald. *Santal.* Wrappers. London, 1921. First edition. In glassine dust jacket. $135.

FIRBANK, Ronald. *Sorrow in Sunlight.* Cloth. London, 1925. First English edition (of *Prancing Nigger*). One of 1,000. In dust jacket. $50.

FIRST Annual Report of the Directors of the Central Mining Co. 13 pp., wrappers. Detroit, 1855. $75–$100.

FIRST Annual Review of Pierce County. (Wisconsin.) 48 pp., wrappers. Prescott, Wis., 1855. $100–$125.

FIRST Catalogues and Circulars of the Botanical Garden of Transylvania University at Lexington in Kentucky, for the Year 1824. 24 pp., sewed. Lexington, 1824. (By C.S. Rafinesque.) $150–$250.

FIRST Published Life of Abraham Lincoln (The). (Reprint of John Locke Scripps biography.) Half vellum. (Detroit, 1970.) Cranbrook Press. One of 245. $75.

FIRST Settlement and Early History of Palmyra, Wayne County; New York (The). 10 pp., printed wrappers. Palmyra, 1858. $150.

FIRST Settlers of New England (The), or, Conquest of the Pequods, Narragansets and

Pokanokets. By a Lady of Massachusetts. Boards. Boston, (1829). (By Lydia Maria Child.) First edition, first issue, with undated title page. $75–$100.

FISH, Daniel. *Lincoln Bibliography.* Red cloth. New York, (1906). One of 75 signed. Boxed. $100–$150.

FISH, H.C. *The Voice of Our Brother's Blood: Its Source and Its Summons.* 16 pp., sewed. Newark, 1856. First edition. $100–$150.

FISHER, George. *Memorials of George Fisher, etc.* Cloth. Houston, 1840. First edition. $500–$1,000, possibly more.

FISHER, Harry C. *The Mutt and Jeff Cartoons.* Oblong folio, pictorial boards and cloth. Boston, 1910. First edition, $75–$150. First Mutt and Jeff book.

FISHER, John, Bishop of Rochester. *A Mornynge Remembraunce.* Frontispiece by C.R. Ashbee. Vellum. London, 1906. Essex House Press. One of 125. $75–$100. Another issue: One of 7 on vellum. $400–$500.

FISHER, O.C. *It Occurred in Kimble.* Illustrated. Pictorial cloth. Houston, 1937. First edition. One of 500. $100–$200.

FISHER, Richard S. *Indiana: Its Geography, Statistics, County Topography.* Large folding map in color. Cloth. New York, 1852. First edition. $150–$175.

FISHER, Vardis. See *Idaho: A Guide in Word and Picture.*

FISHER, Vardis. *April: A Fable of Love.* Morocco. Caldwell, Idaho, and Garden City, 1937. First edition. One of 50 signed. $150–$175. Trade edition: Cloth. In dust jacket. $50–$75.

FISHER, Vardis. *Children of God, an American Epic.* Leather. Caldwell, 1939. First edition. One of 100 signed. $150. New York, 1939. Cloth. First trade edition. In dust jacket. $40–$50.

FISHER, Vardis. *City of Illusion.* Cloth. New York, (1941). First edition. In dust jacket. $50. Caldwell, 1941. One of 1,000. In dust jacket. $50–$60. Another issue: Morocco. One of 100 signed. $150.

FISHER, Vardis. *Dark Bridwell.* Cloth. Boston, 1931. First edition. In dust jacket. $50–$75.

FISHER, Vardis. *Forgive Us our Virtues.* Morocco. Caldwell, 1938. First edition. One of 75 signed. $125–$150. Trade edition: Cloth. In dust jacket. $50.

FISHER, Vardis. *In Tragic Life.* Cloth. Caldwell, 1932. First edition. In dust jacket. $50–$75. Another issue: Leather. One of 25 signed. $150. Garden City, 1932. Cloth. In dust jacket. $50.

FISHER, Vardis. *The Neurotic Nightingale.* Cloth. (Milwaukee, 1935.) First edition. One of 300 signed. In dust jacket. $125–$150. One of 25 unsigned (for review). In dust jacket. $100.

FISHER, Vardis. *No Villain Need Be.* Cloth. Caldwell, 1936. First edition. In dust jacket. $50. Another issue: One of 75 in full leather, signed. $150. Garden City, 1936. In dust jacket. $50.

FISHER, Vardis. *Odyssey of a Hero.* Half cloth. Philadelphia, 1937. First edition. One of 50 signed. $150. Trade edition: Cloth. In dust jacket. $50.

FISHER, Vardis. *Passions Spin the Plot.* Cloth. Caldwell, 1933. First edition, first state, with 1933 date (suppressed). In dust jacket. $100–$125. Caldwell, 1934. Second state (dated 1934). In dust jacket. $50. Another issue: Morocco. One of 75 signed. $125–$150.

FISHER, Vardis. *Sonnets to an Imaginary Madonna.* Boards, pink paper labels. New York, 1927. First edition. In dust jacket. $75–$125. Author's first book.

FISHER, Vardis. *We Are Betrayed*. Cloth. Caldwell, (1935). First edition (so stated). In dust jacket. $50–$75. Another issue: Morocco. One of 75 signed. $150. Garden City, 1935. Cloth. In dust jacket. $35–$50.

FISHER, William (compiler). *An Interesting Account of the Voyages and Travels of Captains Lewis and Clark*. 2 portraits. Calf. Baltimore, 1812. First edition. $200–$350. Baltimore, 1813. 2 portraits, 4 (sometimes 3) plates. Calf. $100–$250.

FITCH, Clyde. *The Knighting of the Twins and Ten Other Tales*. Illustrated. Decorated cloth. Boston, (1891). First edition. $150.

FITE, Emerson D. and Freeman, Archibald (editors). *A Book of Old Maps Delineating American History*. 74 maps in facsimile, colored frontispiece. Folio, cloth. Cambridge, Mass., 1926. First edition. In dust jacket. $200–$250.

FITHIAN, Philip Vickers. *Journal and Letters, 1767–1774*. 8 plates. Cloth. Princeton, 1900. First edition, $50–$75.

FITTS, Dudley. *Two Poems*. Wrappers. No place, (1932). First edition. One of 100 signed. $75–$100.

FITZ GERALD, Edward. See Aeschylus. Also see *The Downfall and Death of King Oedipus; Euphranor; The Mighty Magician; Polonius; Readings in Crabbe's "Tales of the Hall"; Rubaiyat of Omar Khayyam; Salaman and Absal; The Two Generals*.

FITZ GERALD, Edward. *Letters and Literary Remains of Edward FitzGerald*. Edited by William Aldis Wright. Frontispiece plates. 3 vols., cloth. London, 1889. First edition. $150–$250. London, 1902–03. 7 vols., cloth. One of 775. $300–$350.

FITZ GERALD, Edward. *Letters of Edward FitzGerald*. Frontispiece. 2 vols., cloth. London, 1894. First edition. $75–$85.

FITZ GERALD, Edward. *Letters of Edward FitzGerald to Fanny Kemble, 1871–1883*. Edited by William Aldis Wright. Frontispiece portrait. Cloth. London, 1895. First edition. $75–$100.

FITZ GERALD, Edward (translator). *Six Dramas of Calderon*. Watered crimson cloth. London, 1853. First edition. $75–$100.

FITZGERALD, F. Scott. See *A Book of Princeton Verse II*.

FITZGERALD, F. Scott. *All the Sad Young Men*. Dark-green cloth. New York, 1926. First edition, first printing, with Scribner seal on copyright page and perfect type on page 248. In dust jacket. $750–$1,100. Also, $600 (A, 1979). Without jacket, $100–$150.

FITZGERALD, F. Scott. *The Beautiful and Damned*. Dark-green cloth. New York, 1922. First edition, first issue, with no ads at back and with "Published March, 1922" on copyright page. In first-issue dust jacket with title in solid black. $1,250–$1,500. Signed copy, $2,500 in a 1980 catalogue. In second-issue jacket, title in outline lettering. $600–$850. Also, $600 (A, 1977). Without jacket, $100–$125. Toronto, 1922. Cloth. First Canadian edition. In dust jacket. $100–$200. Without jacket, $50.

FITZGERALD, F. Scott. *The Crack-Up*. Edited by Edmund Wilson. Patterned boards and cloth, paper label. (New York, 1945.) New Directions. First edition, first printing, with title page in red and black. In dust jacket. $100–$125.

FITZGERALD, F. Scott. *Flappers and Philosophers*. Cloth. New York, 1920. First edition, first printing, with "Published September, 1920" and publisher's seal on copyright page. In dust jacket. $500–$600. Also, in frayed jacket, $375 (A, 1977). Without jacket, $150.

FITZGERALD, F. Scott. *The Great Gatsby*. Dark-green cloth. New York, 1925. First edition, first issue, with "sick in tired" in line 9 of page 205. In first issue dust jacket, with lower-case "J" on back panel and with flaps listing books by Fitzgerald and Lardner. $3,000–$4,000. In second issue dust jacket, with "Perilously Near a Masterpiece" on back of jacket. $750–$1,000. Without jacket, $100–$150. Washington, 1973. Facsimile of the manuscript. Buckram. Limited edition. Boxed. $75–$100.

FITZGERALD, F. Scott. *The Mystery of the Raymond Mortgage.* 12 pp., wrappers. New York, 1960. First edition. One of 750. $200–$225.

FITZGERALD, F. Scott. *Tales of the Jazz Age.* Dark-green cloth. New York, 1922. First edition, first issue, with "Published September, 1922" and Scribner seal on copyright page. In dust jacket. $500–$600. Also, in frayed dust jacket. $280 (A, 1979). Without jacket, $85–$100. Glasgow, (1923). Cloth. First English edition. $75–$100.

FITZGERALD, F. Scott. *Taps at Reveille.* Green cloth. New York, 1935. First edition, first state, with "and was" in line 15, page 351. In dust jacket. $800–$1,000. Without jacket, $100–$125.

FITZGERALD, F. Scott. *Tender Is the Night.* Dark-green cloth. New York, 1934. First edition, first issue, with Scribner "A" and seal on copyright page. In dust jacket. $600–$800. Without jacket, $75–$100.

FITZGERALD, F. Scott. *This Side of Paradise.* Dark-green cloth. New York, 1920. First edition, first printing, with "Published April, 1920" and publisher's seal on copyright page. In dust jacket. $1,500–$1,750. Without jacket, $200–$300. Third issue: with the author's "apology" leaf, signed, $750. Author's first novel.

FITZGERALD, F. Scott. *Thoughtbook of Francis Scott Key Fitzgerald.* Introduction by John R. Kuehl. White boards. Princteon, 1965. First edition. One of 300 copies. In glassine dust jacket. $100–$125.

FITZGERALD, F. Scott. *The Vegetable.* Dark-green cloth. New York, 1923. First edition, first printing, with "Published April, 1923" and publisher's seal on copyright page. In dust jacket. $600–$800. Lacking jacket, $150.

FITZGERALD, F. Scott, and others. *The Evil Eye: A Musical Comedy in Two Acts.* Boards and cloth. (Cincinnati, New York, & London, 1915.) First edition. $1,500–$2,000.

FITZGERALD, F. Scott. *Fie! Fie! Fie! Fi-Fi! A Musical Comedy in Two Acts.* Boards and cloth. (Cincinnati, New York & London, 1914.) First edition. $1,000–$1,250. Also, $650. (A, 1977).

FITZGERALD, F. Scott, and others. *Safety First: A Musical Comedy in Two Acts.* Boards and cloth. Cincinnati, New York & London, (1916). First edition. $1,500–$2,000. Also, $1,000 (A, 1977).

FITZGERALD, Robert. *Poems.* Orange cloth. New York, 1935. $75–$100. Author's first book.

FITZGERALD, Zelda. *Save Me the Waltz.* Green cloth. New York, 1932. First edition. In dust jacket. $450–$500. Also, $300 (A, 1977).

FITZHUGH, George. *Cannibals All! Or, Slaves Without Masters.* Cloth. Richmond, Va., 1857. First edition. $150–$250.

FIVE Cummington Poems. Wrappers. Cummington, Mass., 1939. First edition. One of 300. $300–$550.

FIVE Young American Poets. 3 vols, cloth. Norfolk, Conn., 1940, 1941, and 1944. New Directions. First editions. In dust jackets. $75–$100 each.

FLANNER, Janet. *The Cubical City.* Cloth. New York, 1926. First edition. In dust jacket. $50–$75. Author's first book.

FLAPDOODLE, Phineas. *Letter to the Park Commissioner* .Self-wrappers. Paris, (1937). (By Henry Miller.) First edition. $125.

FLAUBERT, Gustave. *Herodias.* Half cloth. London, (1901). Eragny Press. One of 226. $400–$500.

FLAUBERT, Gustave. *Salambo*. Boards. London, 1931. Golden Cockerel Press. One of 500. $150–$185.

FLAUBERT, Gustave. *A Sentimental Education*. Illustrated. 2 vols., blue cloth. London 1898. First English edition. $225

FLECKER, James Elroy. *God Save the King*. Wrappers. (London, 1915.) First edition. One of 20. $175.

FLECKER, James Elroy. *The Golden Journey to Samarkand*. Dark-blue cloth. London, 1913. First edition. In dust jacket. $50. Another issue: Boards. One of 50 signed. $150.

FLECKER, James Elroy. *The Last Generation*. Pictorial wrappers. London, 1908. First edition. $100.

FLEMING, Alexander. *Penicillin*. Cloth. London, 1946. First edition. $125–$150.

FLEMING, E.B. *Early History of Hopkins County, Texas*. Cloth. No place, 1902. $350–$450.

FLEMING, Ian. *Casino Royale*. Cloth. London, (1953). First edition. In dust jacket. $1,500–$1,750. Also, $1,300 (A, 1981). Author's first book.

FLEMING, Ian. *Dr. No*. Black cloth (with girl's silhouette on front cover). London, (1958). First edition, first binding. In dust jacket. $100–$150.

FLEMING, Ian. *Live and Let Die*. Cloth. London, (1954). First edition. $500–$850(!).

FLEMING, Ian. *On Her Majesty's Secret Service*. Boards. London, (1963). First edition. One of 220 signed. $500–$600. Trade edition: In dust jacket. $50–$75.

FLEMING, Sandford. *Memorial of the People of Red River to the British and Canadian Governments*. 7 pp., printed front paper cover. Quebec, 1863. $500–$600.

FLEMING, Walter L. *Documentary History of Reconstruction*. 9 facsimiles. 2 vols., half calf. Cleveland, 1906–07. First edition. $85–$150. (Occasionally available more cheaply; John H. Jenkins thinks "there is a remainder lot floating around out there.")

FLETCHER, Charles H. *Jefferson County, Iowa, Centennial History*. 35 pp., printed wrappers. Fairfield, Iowa, 1876. $75–$100.

FLETCHER, John Gould. *Fire and Wine*. Cloth. London, (May, 1913.) First edition. In glassine dust jacket. $200–$225. Author's first book.

FLETCHER, John Gould. *Irradiations: Sand and Spray*. Green wrappers. Boston, 1915. First edition. $75–$100.

FLETCHER, John Gould. *Japanese Prints*. Illustrated. Cloth. Boston, 1918. Four Seas Press. First edition. $100–$150. Another issue: Full leather. One of 25 on vellum with a signed manuscript poem by Fletcher. $500.

FLETCHER, John Gould. *Preludes and Symphonies*. Cloth, paper label, New York, 1930. First edition. In dust jacket. $75–$100.

FLETCHER, John Gould. *XXIV Elegies*. Cloth. Santa Fe, (1935). First edition. One of 400 signed. In dust jacket. $50–$75.

FLETCHER, W.A. *A Rebel Private, Front and Rear*. Portrait. Cloth. Beaumont, Tex., 1908. First edition. $500–$850.

FLEURY, Claude. *A Short Catechism, Containing a Summary of Sacred History, and Christian Doctrine*. Calf. Detroit, 1812. $1,250–$1,500.

FLICKINGER, Robert E. *Pioneer History of Pocahontas County, Iowa*. Cloth. Fonda, Iowa, 1904. First edition. $75–$85.

FLINDERS, Matthew. *Narrative of His Voyage in the Schooner Francis.* Engravings by John Buckland Wright. Cloth. Waltham Saint Lawrence, 1946. Golden Cockerel Press. One of 750. $300–$400. Another issue: One of 100. $750–$1,000.

FLINT, Micah P. *The Hunter and Other Poems.* Boards. Boston, 1826. First edition. $80–$100.

FLINT, Timothy. *A Condensed Geography and History of the Western States, or the Mississippi Valley.* 2 vols., tan boards, paper labels. Cincinnati, 1828. First edition. $300–$400. Soiled copy, $175.

FLINT, Timothy. *Indian Wars of the West.* Calf, or half leather. Cincinnati, 1833. $200–$300.

FLINT, Timothy. *Lectures Upon Natural History.* Cloth. Boston, 1833. First edition. $125–$250.

FLINT, Timothy. *Recollections of the Last Ten Years.* Tan boards, paper label. Boston, 1826. First edition. $400–$500.

FLINT, W. Russell. *Breakfast in Perigord.* Illustrated. Half morocco. London, 1968. One of 525 signed by Flint. Boxed. $300–$350.

FLINT, W. Russell. *Drawings.* 134 plates. Half morocco. London, 1950. One of 125 signed by Flint, with an original drawing in folder at end. Boxed. $600–$1,000. Another issue: One of 500. $300–$500. Trade issue: Cloth. In dust jacket. $100–$150.

FLINT, W. Russell. *Minxes Admonished or Beauty Reproved.* Illustrated, including color. Morocco and boards. (London), 1955. Golden Cockerel Press. Boxed. $200–$225. Another issue: One of 150 specially bound. $600–$800.

FLOURE (The) and The Leafe, & the Boke of Cupide, God of Love, or the Cuckow and the Nightingale. 2 large woodcut initial words from the Kelmscott Chaucer. Printed in black and red. Boards and linen. (Hammersmith, London, 1896.) Kelmscott Press. One of 300. $400–$600. Another issue: One of 10 on vellum. $1,500–$2,000.

FLOWER, Richard. *Letters from Illinois, 1820–1821.* 76 pp., wrappers. London, 1822. First edition. $600–$850.

FLOWER, Robin (translator). *Love's Bitter-Sweet.* Boards and linen. Dublin, 1925. Cuala Press. One of 500. In dust jacket. $125–$175.

FOOL'S Erand (A). By One of the Fools. Cloth. New York, 1879. (By Albion W. Tourgee.) First edition. $75–$85.

FOOTE, Henry Stuart. *Texas and the Texans,* 2 vols., cloth. Philadelphia, 1841. First edition. $450–$600.

FORBES, Alexander. *California: A History.* 10 lithographs, map colored in outline. Cloth. London, 1839. First edition, with errata slip. $500–$600. San Francisco, 1919. Map, 10 plates. One of 250 signed by the publisher. $250–$350. San Francisco, 1937. John Henry Nash printing. Marbled boards. One of 650. In dust jacket. $75–$100. San Francisco, 1939. $50–$60.

FORBES, Edwin. *Life Studies of the Great Army.* 40 plates. Half morocco. (New York), 1876. First edition. $350–$400.

FORBES, Edwin. *Thirty Years After: An Artist's Story of the Great War.* 80 full-page plates, 20 portraits. 4 vols., folio, cloth. New York, (1890). First edition. $150–$250. Another issue; 2 vols., cloth. $75–$150.

FORBES, Sir James. *Oriental Memoirs.* 21 colored plates, other illustrations, 4 vols., contemporary full red morocco. London, 1813. First edition. $1,250–$1,500. London, 1834–35. 3 vols. (including atlas), half morocco. $650–$750.

FORBES, James Grant. *Sketches, Historical and Topographical, of the Floridas.* Map (not in all copies). Boards, paper label. New York, 1821. First edition. With the map. $500–$600. Without map, $250–$350.

FORBUSH, Edward Howe. *Birds of Massachusetts and other New England States.* Color illustrations by L.A. Fuertes. 3 vols., cloth. (Boston), 1925–27–29. First edition. $300–$350.

FORD, Charles Henri. *A B C's.* Cloth. Prairie City, Ill., (1940). First edition. $300–$400.

FORD, Charles Henri. *The Garden of Disorder and Other Poems.* Boards and cloth. London, (1938). First edition. One of 30 signed. (Issued without dust jacket.) $150–$175.

FORD, Charles Henri. *A Pamphlet of Sonnets.* Drawing by Pavel Tchelitchew. Printed wrappers. Majorca, 1936. First edition. One of 40 signed by Ford and Tchelitchew. $75–$125.

FORD, Charles Henri, and Tyler, Parker. *The Young and Evil.* Wrappers. Paris, (1933). First edition. $300–$400.

FORD, Ford Madox. See Conrad, Joseph, and Hueffer, Ford Madox. (Note: Ford changed his name from Hueffer to Ford in 1919.) Also see *The Imagist Anthology.*

FORD, Ford Madox. *The Great Trade Route.* Illustrated. New York, 1937. First edition, first issue, without illustrator's name on title page or dust jacket. $75–$100.

FORD, Ford Madox. *It Was the Nightingale.* Cloth. London, (1934). First edition. In dust jacket. $55–$65.

FORD, Ford Madox. *Joseph Conrad: A Personal Remembrance.* Frontispiece, 2 other plates. Green cloth. London, 1924. First edition. In dust jacket. $100–$150.

FORD, Ford Madox. *Last Post.* Cloth. London, (1928). First English edition. In dust jacket. $100–$125.

FORD, Ford Madox. *Mister Bosphorus and the Muses.* Illustrated by Paul Nash. Half cloth. London, (1923). First edition. One of 70. In dust jacket. $300–$400. Ordinary issue: In dust jacket. $150–$200.

FORD, Ford Madox. *New Poems.* Cloth. New York, 1927. One of 325 signed. In glassine dust jacket. $200–$250.

FORD, Ford Madox. *New York Is Not America.* Cloth. London, 1927. First edition. In dust jacket. $100–$125. (New York, 1927.) First American edition. In dust jacket. $75–$100.

FORD, Ford Madox. *No Enemy.* Cloth. New York, 1929. First edition. In dust jacket. $200–$250.

FORD, Ford Madox, *No More Parades.* Cloth. London, (1925). First edition. In dust jacket. $200–$225. Without jacket, $75.

FORD, Ford Madox. *Vive le Roy.* Cloth. Philadelphia, 1936. First edition. In dust jacket. $200–$250. London, 1937. Cloth. First English edition. In dust jacket. $150–$200.

FORD, Ford Madox. *The Wicked Man.* Cloth. New York, (1931). First edition. $75.

FORD, Ford Madox Hueffer. *Women & Men.* Wrappers. Paris, 1923. Three Mountains Press. First edition. One of 300. $250–$350.

FORD, Henry Chapman. *Etchings of the Franciscan Missions of California.* 24 matted plates, unbound, 28 pp. of text, stitched, in half morocco portfolio. New York, 1883. Imperial edition. One of 50 signed by the artist. $2,000 and up.

FORD, Paul Leicester. *Franklin Bibliography.* Half leather. Brooklyn, 1889. First edition. One of 500. $150–$200.

FORD, Paul Leicester. *The Great K & A Robbery*. Pictorial cloth. New York, 1897. First edition, first issue, without "Train" before "Robbery" on title page. $75–$100.

FORD, Paul Leicester. *The Honorable Peter Stirling and What People Thought of Him*. Red cloth. New York, 1894. First edition, first state, with "Sterling" for "Stirling" on front cover. $125–$150. London, 1898. Cloth. First English edition. $50–$60.

FORD, Paul Leicester (editor). *Webster Genealogy* . . . . By Noah Webster. 16 pp., wrappers. Brooklyn, 1876. First edition. (250 copies.) $100. Ford's first book, printed by him on his own press at age 11.

FORD, Thomas. *A History of Illinois*. Cloth. Chicago, 1854. First edition, first issue, with "1814" (instead of "1818") in the extended title. $75–$100.

FORD, Thomas. *Message of the Governor* . . . *the Disturbances in Hancock County*. 21 pp., disbound. Springfield, Ill., 1844. $600. (On the Mormon disorders in Illinois.)

FORD, Webster. *Songs & Sonnets*. Cloth. Chicago, 1910. (By Edgar Lee Masters.) First edition, $125–$150.

FORE and Aft: or, Leaves from the Life of an Old Sailor. By "Webfoot," Illustrated. Cloth. Boston, 1871. (By W.D. Phelps.) First edition. $200–$250.

FOREMAN, Grant. *Advancing the Frontier*. Maps. Cloth. Norman, Okla., 1933. First edition. In dust jacket. $75–$100.

FOREMAN, Grant. *Indian Removal*. Cloth. Norman, 1932. First edition. In dust jacket. $100–$150.

FOREMAN, Grant. *Indians and Pioneers*. Map, 8 plates. Cloth. New Haven, 1930. First edition. In dust jacket. $100–$150.

FOREMAN, Grant. *Pioneer Days in the Early Southwest*. Illustrated. Folding map. Cloth. Cleveland, 1926. First edition. $100–$150.

FOREST and Stream Fables. Sewed. New York, (1886). (By Rowland Evans Robinson.) First edition. $150. Author's first published work.

FORESTER, C.S. *The African Queen*. Cloth. Boston, 1935. First American edition. In dust jacket. $250.

FORESTER, C.S. *Brown on Resolution*. Cloth. London, (1929). First edition. In dust jacket. $400–$450. (American first edition: *Single-Handed*, New York, 1929. In dust jacket. $50–$60.)

FORESTER, C.S. *Hornblower and the Hotspur*. Cloth. Boston, 1962. First edition. In dust jacket. $40.

FORESTER, C.S. *Lieutenant Hornblower*. Cloth. Boston, 1952. First edition. In dust jacket. $40.

FORESTER, C.S. *Lord Hornblower*. Cloth. London, (1946). First edition. In dust jacket. $50–$60. Boston, 1946. Cloth. First American edition. In dust jacket. $40–$50.

FORESTER, C.S. *Lord Nelson*. Illustrated. Cloth. Indianapolis, (1929). First American edition. In dust jacket. $50–$75.

FORESTER, C.S. *Loves Lies Dreaming*. Green cloth. Indianapolis, (1927). First American edition, first issue, with middle initial "E" instead of "S" on binding. In dust jacket. $75–$125. Lacking dust jacket, $60–$75.

FORESTER, C.S. *Mr. Midshipman Hornblower*. Cloth. London, (1950). First edition. In dust jacket. $50–$60. Advance proof in wrappers: $200.

FORESTER, C.S. *Napoleon and His Court*. Illustrated. Cloth. London, (1924). First edition. In dust jacket. $100.

FORESTER, C.S. *A Pawn Among Kings*. Cloth. London, (1924). First edition. In dust jacket. $500–$600. Author's first book.

FORESTER, C.S. *Plain Murder*. Cloth. London, (1930). First edition. In dust jacket. $150–$200. Advance uncorrected proof, plain wrappers: $300 in a 1980 catalogue.

FORESTER, C.S. *The Ship*. Cloth. London, (1943). First edition. In dust jacket. $50–$60.

FORESTER, C.S. *The Sky and the Forest*. London, (1948). First edition. In dust jacket. $50–$60.

FORESTER, Frank. See Forrester, Frank; Herbert, Henry William; Herbert, W.H.

FORESTER, Frank. *American Game in Its Seasons*. Illustrated by the author. Cloth. New York, 1853. (By Henry William Herbert.) First edition. $150–$200.

FORESTER, Frank. *The Complete Manual for Young Sportsmen*. Illustrated by the author. Cloth. New York, 1856. (By Henry William Herbert.) First edition. $200–$250.

FORESTER, Frank. *The Deerstalkers*. Printed wrappers. Philadelphia, 1849. (By Henry William Herbert.) First edition. $500–$600. New York, 1930. Derrydale Press. $50–$75.

FORESTER, Frank. *Field Sports in the United States, and the British Provinces of America*. 2 vols., green cloth. London, 1848. (By Henry William Herbert.) First edition, first issue, with "Provinces of America" on title page (changed later to "Provinces of North America"). $250–$300. New York, 1849. 2 vols., green cloth. First American edition, first issue, with "Ruffed Grouse" frontispiece. (Issued as *Frank Forester's Field Sports of the United States, etc.*) $150–$200.

FORESTER, Frank. *Frank Forester and His Friends*. 3 vols., salmon cloth. London, 1849. (By Henry William Herbert.) First edition. $150–$250.

FORESTER, Frank. *Frank Forester's Fish and Fishing of the United States and British Provinces of North America*. Illustrated by the author. Blue cloth. London, 1849. (By Henry William Herbert.) First English edition. (Note: Possibly issued simultaneously with the American first edition, according to Blanck.) $150–$250. New York, 1850 (actually 1849). Blue cloth. First American edition. $100–$150. New York, 1850. Second American edition, with bound sheets of the *Supplement* of 1850 bound in. (See Forester, *Supplement*.) $100–$150.

FORESTER, Frank. *Frank Forester's Fugitive Sporting Sketches*. Edited by Will Wildwood (Fred E. Pond). Cloth or wrappers. Westfield, Wis., 1879. (By Henry William Herbert.) First edition. Wrappers: $250. Cloth: $150.

FORESTER, Frank. *Frank Forester's Horse and Horsemanship of the United States and British Provinces of North America*. Plates, pedigree tables. 2 vols., purple cloth. New York, 1857. (By Henry William Herbert.) First edition. $150–$250 .

FORESTER, Frank. *Hints to Horse-Keepers*. Frontispiece, 23 plates. Cloth. New York, 1859. (By Henry William Herbert.) First edition. $125-$150.

FORESTER, Frank. *The Hitchcock Edition of Frank Forester*. 4 vols., cloth. New York, 1930. (By Henry William Herbert.) Derrydale Press. First edition. One of 750. $350–$400. Also, $225 (A, 1980).

FORESTER, Frank. *My Shooting Box*. Frontispiece, 2 plates. Cloth. Philadelphia, 1846. (By Henry William Herbert.) First edition, first state, with ads dated May, 1845, on page 180 and "mattter" for "matter" in last line of page 35. $500–$750. New York, 1941. Derrydale Press. Illustrated. Leatherette. One of 250. $400.

FORESTER, Frank. *Supplement to Frank Forester's Fish and Fishing*. Frontispiece. Cloth. New York, 1850. (By Henry William Herbert.) First edition. $100–$150.

FORESTER, Frank. *Trouting Along the Catasauqua*. Boards. New York, 1927. Derrydale Press. (By Henry William Herbert.) First edition. One of 423. In dust jacket. $350–$400.

FORESTER, Frank. *The Warwick Woodlands*. Printed tan-yellow wrappers. Philadelphia, 1845. (By Henry William Herbert.) First edition. $1,000 and up. Rebound, $500 and up. New York, 1851. Illustrated. Cloth, or printed wrappers. Second edition. Wrappers: $500. Cloth: $200–$300. New York, 1934. Derrydale Press. Leatherette. $300–$400.

FORESTER, Harry. *Ocean Jottings from England to British Columbia*. Cloth. Vancouver, 1891. $75–$100.

FORNEY, Col. John W. *What I Saw in Texas*. (Cover title.) Map and plates. 92 pp., pictorial wrappers. Philadelphia, (1872). First edition. $250–$350. Second edition. $200–$300.

FORREST, Lieut. Col. Charles R. *A Picturesque Tour Along the Rivers Ganges and Jumna, in India*. 24 colored plates, colored vignettes. Cloth, or leather. London, 1824. First edition. $2,000–$2,500.

FORREST, Earle R. *Missions and Pueblos of the Old Southwest*. Illustrated. Cloth. Cleveland, 1929. First edition. In dust jacket. $150–$175.

FORRESTER, Frank. *Fishing with Hook and Line*. Printed wrappers. New York, (1858). (By Henry William Herbert.) First edition, with Brother Jonathan imprint. $1,000 and up. Also, $900 (A, 1962)—"one of two known copies."

FORSTER, E.M. *Abinger Harvest*. Plain brown printed wrappers. London, (1936). First edition. Advance proof copy, including "A Flood in the Office," later eliminated. $300–$400. First published edition, first issue, with "A Flood in the Office" included: Cloth. In dust jacket and cellophane wrappers. $200–$225.

FORSTER, E.M. *Alexandria: A History and a Guide*. Folding map in pocket at rear. Boards. Alexandria, Egypt, 1922. First edition. $150–$225. Alexandria, 1938. Boards. Second edition. One of 250 signed. $150–$200.

FORSTER, E.M. *Anonymity: An Enquiry*. Illustrated boards. London, 1925. Hogarth Press. First edition. $150–$175.

FORSTER, E.M. *Aspects of the Novel*. Dark-red cloth. London, 1927. First edition. In dust jacket. $100–$150. Without jacket, $75.

FORSTER, E.M. *The Celestial Omnibus and Other Stories*. Brown cloth. London, 1911. First edition. $100–$125.

FORSTER, E.M. *Desmond McCarthy*. Gray wrappers. No place, 1952. Millhouse Press. First edition. One of 72. $150–$200.

FORSTER, E.M. *The Eternal Moment and Other Stories*. Red cloth with gold stamping. London, 1928. First edition, first binding. In dust jacket. $100–$275(!).

FORSTER, E.M. *Goldsworthy Lowes Dickinson*. Plain wrappers. London, 1934. First edition. $125. First published edition: Cloth. In dust jacket. $85–$100.

FORSTER, E.M. *The Government of Egypt*. Wrappers, paper label. London, (1920). (Official recommendations of a Labour committee, 1919.) First edition. $100–$150.

FORSTER, E.M. *Howard's End*. Cloth. London, 1910. First edition. In dust jacket. $200–$250.

FORSTER, E.M. *The Longest Journey*. Cloth. London, 1907. First edition. In dust jacket. $250–$300.

FORSTER, E.M. *A Passage to India*. Red cloth. London, 1924. First edition. In dust jacket. $350–$450. Without jacket, $100–$200, possibly more. Another issue: Boards and cloth. One of 200 signed. In slipcase. $600–$750.

FORSTER, E.M. *Pharos and Pharillon.* Boards. Richmond, 1923. Hogarth Press. First edition. $200–$250. New York, 1923. Orange cloth. First American edition. In dust jacket. $100–$125.

FORSTER, E.M. *A Room with a View.* Cloth. London, 1908. First edition. In dust jacket. $225–$275. Without jacket, $150.

FORSTER, E.M. *Sinclair Lewis Interprets America.* (Cover title.) 10 pp. stapled, self-wrappers. (Cambridge, Mass., 1932.) First edition. One of 100. $75–$100.

FORSTER, E.M. *The Story of the Siren.* Wrappers. Richmond, 1920. Hogarth Press. First edition. (500 copies printed.) $200–$250.

FORSTER, E.M. *Where Angels Fear to Tread.* Cloth. Edinburgh, 1905. First edition, first issue, with this title not mentioned in ads at back. In dust jacket. $500–$750. Without jacket, $500. Author's first book. New York, 1920. Black cloth. First American edition. In dust jacket. $75–$85.

FORSYTH, James W., and Grant, F.D. *Report of an Expedition up the Yellowstone River, Made in 1875.* Folding map. 17 pp., wrappers. Washington, 1875. $150–$200.

FORT Braddock Letters. Boards and calf. Worcester, Mass., 1827. (By John G.C. Brainard.) $75.

FORT, Charles. *The Book of the Damned.* Cloth. New York, 1919. First edition. In dust jacket. $200–$225. Without jacket, $75 and $100.

FORT, Charles. *Lo!* Illustrated by Alexander King. Cloth. New York, (1931). First edition. In dust jacket. $75.

FORT, Charles. *The Outcast Manufacturers.* Cloth. New York, 1909. First edition. In dust jacket. $300–$350. Without jacket, $75–$100. Author's first book.

FORTUNES of Colonel Torlogh O'Brien (The). 10 monthly parts, wrappers. Dublin, 1847. (By Joseph Sheridan Le Fanu.) First edition. $400–$500. First book edition: Illustrated. Clothbound. $300–$350.

FORTUNES of Nigel (The). 3 vols., boards, paper labels. Edinburgh, 1822. (By Sir Walter Scott.) First edition. $400–$500.

FORTUNES of Perkin Warbeck (The). 3 vols., boards, cloth spine, printed labels. London, 1830. (By Mary Wollstonecraft Shelley.) First edition. $500–$600.

FOSS, Sam Walter. *The Song of the Library Staff.* Illustrated by Merle Johnson. Stapled. New York, 1906. First edition. $40–$50.

FOSTER, Charles. *The Gold Placers of California.* Map. Printed wrappers. Akron, Ohio, 1849. First edition. $3,000 and up. Also, $1,750 (A, 1968).

FOSTER, The Rev. G.L. *The Past of Ypsilanti.* 48 pp., printed wrappers. Detroit, 1857. First edition. $150.

FOSTER, George G. (editor). *The Gold Regions of California.* Frontispiece map. Printed wrappers. New York, 1848. $300–$500. London, (1849). $100–$150.

FOSTER, George G. *New-York by Gas-Light.* Wrappers. New York, 1850. First edition. $150–$175.

FOSTER, Isaac. *The Foster Family, California Pioneers.* Illustrated. Cloth. (Santa Barbara, 1925.) $100–$150.

FOSTER, James S. *Advantages of Dakota Territory.* 51 pp., wrappers. Yankton, 1873. First edition. $1,000–$1,500.

FOSTER, James S. *Outlines of History of the Territory of Dakota and Emigrant's Guide to the Free Lands of the Northwest.* Folding map. 127 pp., wrappers. Yankton, 1870. First edition. $2,500 and up. Also, $950 (A, 1968).

FOSTER, Myles Birket. *A Day in a Child's Life.* Illustrated by Kate Greenaway. Glazed boards and cloth. (London, 1881.) First edition. $150.

FOUNTAIN, Albert J. *Bureau of Immigration of the Territory of New Mexico: Report of Dona Ana County.* 34 pp., wrappers. Santa Fe, 1882. $150–$175.

FOUQUE, F.H.K. de La Motte. *Undine.* Illustrated in color by Arthur Rackham. Vellum with ties. London, 1909. One of 1,000 signed by Rackham. $750–$850. Trade edition: Cloth. $150–$200. New York, 1930. Limited Editions Club. Boxed. $60–$80.

FOUR *Gospels of the Lord Jesus Christ (The).* Decorations by Eric Gill. Half pigskin. Waltham Saint Lawrence, 1931. Golden Cockerel Press. One of 500. In slipcase. $3,000–$3,500. Another issue: One of 12 on vellum. $29,000 and $12,000 (A, 1977).

FOUREGEAUD, Victor H. *The First Californiac.* Illustrated. Blue boards and calf. San Francisco, 1942. Allen Press. First edition. One of 225. $550.

FOURTEENTH *Anniversary of the Society of California Pioneers.* Wrappers. San Francisco. 1864. $100–$125.

FOWLER, Jacob. *The Journal of Jacob Fowler.* Frontispiece. Cloth. New York, 1898. First edition. One of 950. $100.

FOWLES, John. *The Aristos.* Cloth. Boston, (1964). First edition. In dust jacket. $135–$175.

FOWLES, John. *The Collector.* Cloth. London, 1963. First edition. In first dust jacket, without publisher's blurbs. $650–$850. Boston, (1963). Boards. First American edition. In dust jacket. $125–$150. Author's first book.

FOWLES, John. *The Ebony Tower.* Cloth. London, (1974). First edition. In dust jacket. $150–$175. Boston, (1974). First American edition. In dust jacket. $50. Another issue, signed: $200–$250.

FOWLES, John. *The French Lieutenant's Woman.* Cloth. London, (1969). First edition. In dust jacket. $150–$175. Boston, (1969). First American edition. In dust jacket. $50–$75.

FOWLES, John. *The Magus.* Cloth. London, (1966). First edition. In dust jacket. $250–$300. Boston, 1966. First American edition. In dust jacket. $50–$75.

FOX, John, Jr. *A Cumberland Vendetta and Other Stories.* Illustrated. Cloth. New York, 1896. First edition. $40–$50. Author's first book.

FOX, John, Jr. *The Little Shepherd of Kingdom Come.* Illustrated by F.C. Yohn. Smooth red cloth, paper label. New York, 1903. First edition, first issue, with "laugh" for "lap" in line 14, page 61. One of 100 signed by Fox and Yohn. $75–$100. Trade edition: Ribbed red cloth. $25. New York, 1931. Illustrated by N.C. Wyeth. Half vellum. One of 512 signed by Wyeth. $400–$500.

FOX, John, Jr. *The Trail of the Lonesome Pine.* Red cloth. New York, 1908. First edition, first state, with Scribner seal on copyright page. In dust jacket. $100–$150.

FOX, Lady Mary. *Account of an Expedition to the Interior of New Holland.* Contemporary leather. London, 1837. First edition. $300.

FRA *Luca de Pacioli of Borgo San Sepolcro.* Portrait, plates, Boards, vellum spine. New York, 1933. Grolier Club. One of 390. $600–$650.

FRAENKEL, Michael. See *The Need for Anonymity.*

FRAENKEL, Michael. *Bastard Death.* Wrappers. Paris, (1936). First edition. $75–$100.

FRAENKEL, Michael. *Werther's Younger Brother.* Wrappers. New York, (1931). First edition. One of 400. In glassine dust jacket. $100. Author's first book (aside from a pamphlet collaboration).

FRANCE, Its King, Court, and Government. By an American. Cloth. New York, 1840. (By Lewis Cass.) First edition. $50–$75.

FRANCHERE, Gabriel. *Narrative of a Voyage to the Northwest Coast of America, etc.* 3 plates. Cloth. New York, 1854. First edition in English. $250–$300.

FRANCHERE, Gabriel. *Relation d'un Voyage à la Côte du Nord-Ouest de l'Amérique Septentrionale, dans les Annês 1810–1814.* Contemporary calf. Montreal, 1820. First edition. $1,000–$1,500.

FRANCIS, Dick. *Blood Sport.* Cloth. London, (1967). First edition. In dust jacket. $50–$75.

FRANCIS, Grant R. *Old English Drinking Glasses.* 72 plates. Buckram. London, 1926. In dust jacket. $200–$250.

FRANCIS of Assisi, St. *I Fioretti del Glorioso Poverello di Cristo S. Francesco di Assisi.* 54 woodcuts. Vellum. London, 1922. Ashendene Press. One of 240. $1,250. Another issue: One of 12 on vellum. $2,000–$2,500.

FRANCIS of Assisi, St. *Laudes Creaturarum.* London, 1910. Doves Press. One of 250. $250–$300. Another issue: One of 15 on vellum. $1,000 and up.

FRANCIS of Assisi, St. *Un Mazzetto Scelto di Certi Fioretti del Glorioso Poverello di Cristo San Francesco di Assisi insieme col Cantico al sole del Medesimo.* 11 woodcuts. Folio, boards. London, 1904. Ashendene Press. One of 125 on paper. $400–$525. Another issue: Vellum. One of 25 on vellum. $1,200–$1,500.

FRANCIS Parkman. 4 pp., leaflet. (Boston, 1894.) (By Oliver Wendell Holmes.) First edition. (About 50 to 77 printed.) $200–$250.

FRANK Fairleigh; or Scenes from the Life of a Private Pupil. Illustrated by George Cruikshank. 15 parts, blue-green wrappers. London, 1850. (By Frank E. Smedley.) First edition, first issue, with dated title page. $750 and up. Second issue: Cloth. $150.

FRANK, Robert. *The Americans.* Introduction by Jack Kerouac. 83 plates. Oblong, cloth. New York, (1959). First edition. In dust jacket. $400–$500. Also, $300 (A, 1980). (Note: Collecting pressure is on this book because it is both a photographic item *and* a Kerouac item.)

FRANK, Waldo. *The Dark Mother.* Cloth. New York, (1920). First edition. In dust jacket. $75–$100.

FRANKENSTEIN; or The Modern Prometheus. 3 vols., boards, paper labels. London, 1818. (By Mary Wollstonecraft Shelley.) First edition. $8,000–$12,000. Rebound copy, $4,800 in a 1980 catalogue. London, 1831. Cloth. Third edition. With a new preface by the author. $700–$1,000. New York, 1934. Limited Editions Club. $40–$50.

FRANKS, David. *The New-York Directory.* 82 pp., cloth. New York, 1786. First edition. $4,000–$6,000. Also $1,100 (A, 1969). (Note: There is an earlier auction record of $2,500.) New York, 1909. Folding map. Printed wrappers. Reprint. $75–$100.

FRAZER, Sir James George. *Totemism.* Cloth. Edinburgh, 1887. First edition. $75–$100. Author's first book.

FREDERIC, Harold. *The Damnation of Theron Ware.* Dark-green cloth. Chicago, 1896. First edition. $65–$85.

FREDERIC, Harold. *The Deserter and Other Stories.* Cloth. Boston, (1898). First edition. $75–$100.

FREDERIC, Harold. *In the Valley.* 16 plates by Howard Pyle. Cloth. New York, 1890. First edition. $100–$125. London, 1891. Cloth. First English edition. $100.

FREDERIC, Harold. *The Lawton Girl.* Cloth or wrappers. New York, 1890. First American edition. $150.

FREDERIC, Harold. *Marsena and Other Stories of the Wartime.* Cloth. New York, 1894. First edition. $150–$175.

FREDERIC, Harold. *Seth's Brother's Wife.* Tan cloth. New York, 1887. First edition, first issue, with 1886 copyright and no ads. $150–$200. Author's first book.

FREDERICK, J. George (editor). *Artists' and Writers' Chap Book.* Wrappers. (New York), 1933. First edition. $30–$50.

FREDERICK, J.V. *Ben Holladay, the Stagecoach King.* Folding map. Cloth. Glendale, Calif., 1940. First edition. $75–$100.

FREE-and-Easy Songbook (The). Plates. Davy Crockett portrait on title page. Cloth. Philadelphia, 1834. $200–$300.

FREEMAN, Douglas Southall. *R.E. Lee: A Biography.* Illustrated. 4 vols., cloth. New York, 1934–35. First edition. In dust jackets. $250–$300.

FREEMAN, George D. *Midnight and Noonday.* Printed boards and cloth. Caldwell, Kan., 1890. First edition. $150–$200. Also, $125. (A, 1968). Caldwell, 1892. Red cloth. Second edition. $50–$60.

FREEMAN, James W. See *Prose and Poetry of the Live Stock Indsutry.*

FREEMAN, R. Austin. See Ashdown, Clifford.

FREEMAN, R. Austin. *The Cat's Eye.* Pale green cloth. London, (1923). First edition. In dust jacket. $200–$250. New York, 1927. First American edition. In dust jacket. $125–$150.

FREEMAN, R. Austin. *Felo de Se?* Pale blue cloth. London, (1937). First edition. In dust jacket. $200–$250.

FREEMAN, R. Austin. *For the Defence: Dr. Thorndyke.* Gray-blue cloth. London, 1934. First edition . In dust jacket. $200. New York, 1934. Blue cloth. First American edition. In dust jacket. $75.

FREEMAN, R. Austin. *Mr. Polton Explains.* Cloth. London, 1940. First edition. In dust jacket. $200–$250. New York, 1940. Red cloth. First American edition. In dust jacket. $50–$75.

FREEMAN, R. Austin. *The Red Thumb Mark.* Cloth. London, 1907. First edition. In dust jacket. $500–$750.

FREEMAN, R. Austin. *The Singing Bone.* Cloth. London, 1912. First edition. In dust jacket. $400–$500. New York, 1923. Tan cloth. First American edition. In dust jacket. $200–$300.

FREMAUX, Leon J. *New Orleans Characters.* 17 color plates. Folio, cloth and morocco. (New Orleans), 1876. First edition. $400–$600.

FRÉMONT, John Charles. *Geographical Memoir Upon Upper California.* Senate Misc. Doc. No. 148. Folding map (not in all copies). 67 pp., wrappers. Washington, 1848, First edition, with map. $500–$600. Without the map, $150.

FRÉMONT, John Charles. *Narrative of the Exploring Expedition to the Rocky Mountains, in the Year 1842, etc.* Folding map by Rufus B. Sage, 2 plates. Cloth. Syracuse, 1847. (First publication of the famous Sage map.) $750–$1,000.

FRÉMONT, John Charles. *Oregon and California: The Exploring Expedition to the*

Rocky Mountains, Oregon and California. 2 portraits; 2 plates. Cloth. Buffalo, 1849. $75. (One of several reprints of *Report of the Exploring Expedition.*)

FRÉMONT, John Charles. *Report of the Exploring Expedition to the Rocky Mountains in the Year 1842.* Senate edition. 22 plates, 5 maps, one folding. Cloth. Washington, 1845. First edition. $500–$600. House edition, same date. $300–$375.

FRÉMONT, John Charles. *Report on an Exploration of the Country Lying Between the Missouri and the Rocky Mountains, etc.* Senate Doc. 243. 6 plates, folding map. Wrappers. Washington, 1843. First edition. $200–$300.

FRENCH, Capt. W.J. *Wild Jim, the Texas Cowboy and Saddle King.* Portrait. 76 pp., wrappers. Antioch, Ill., 1890. First edition. $400–$600.

FRENCH, William. *Some Recollections of a Western Ranchman.* Gray cloth. London, (1927). First edition. $350–$375. New York, (1928). First American edition. In dust jacket. $250–$300. Lacking jacket, $175.

FREUD, Sigmund. *Totem and Taboo.* Cloth. New York, 1918. First edition in English. $100–$175.

FREYTAS, Father Nicholas de. *The Expedition of Don Diego Dionisio de Penaloza, from Santa Fe to the River Mischipi and Quiviha in 1662.* Edited by John G. Shea. Boards. (New York), 1882. $100–$200.

FRIDGE, Ike. *History of the Chisum War . . . Cowboy Life on the Frontier.* Stiff wrappers. Electra, Tex., (1927). First edition. $400.

FRIEDMAN, Bruce Jay. *Far from the City of Class.* Boards. New York, 1963. First edition. In dust jacket. $50.

FRIEDMAN, Bruce Jay. *Stern.* Cloth. New York, 1962. First edition. In dust jacket. $50–$60. Author's first book.

FRIEDMAN, I.K. *By Bread Alone.* Boards. New York, 1901. First edition. $150–$200.

FRIEDMAN, I.K. *The Lucky Number.* Red cloth. Chicago, 1896. First edition. $50–$75. Author's first book.

FRIEDMAN, I.K. *The Radical.* Cloth. New York, 1907. First edition. In dust jacket. $50–$75.

FRINK, F.W. *A Record of Rice County, Minnesota, in 1868.* 24 pp., wrappers. Faribault, Minn., 1868. First edition. $100–$200. Faribault, 1871. Second edition. $75–$85.

FRINK, Margaret A. *Journal of the Adventures of a Party of California Gold-Seekers.* 2 frontispieces. Cloth. (Oakland, 1897.) First edition. $400–$600.

FROISSART, Sir John. *Chronicles of England, France, Spain, and the Adjoining Countries.* Translated by Thomas Johnes. Illustrations illuminated in gold and colors by H. Noel Humphreys. 2 vols., half red morocco. London, 1852. $300–$400.

FROM Ocean to Ocean in a Winton. Illustrated. 36 pp., wrappers. Cleveland, 1903. Winton Motor Carriage Co. $75.

FROST, A.B. *A Book of Drawings.* Illustrated. Folio, boards. New York, 1904. First edition. $75–$100.

FROST, A.B. *Sports and Games in the Open.* 53 color plates. Folio, pictorial cloth porfolio. New York, 1899. First edition. $250–$350.

FROST, John. *History of the State of California.* Contemporary morocco. Auburn, Calif., 1850. First edition. $150–$200.

FROST, John. *The Mexican War and Its Warriors.* Colored frontispiece, other plates, map. Cloth. New Haven, 1849. First edition. $225.

FROST, Robert. See Robinson, Edwin Arlington, Schreiber, Georges. Also see *Dart-mouth Verse*, 1925; *Poems of Child Labor.*

FROST, Robert. *Away!* Wood engravings by Stefan Martin. Pictorial wrappers. New York, 1958. First edition. One of 185 with Al Edwards imprint. $50–$60.

FROST, Robert. *A Boy's Will.* Bronze, or brown, pebbled cloth, lettered in gilt. London, 1913. First edition, first state, (in 2 variant bindings—the bronze and brown), with all edges untrimmed. $1,000–$1,250. Also, $950 (A, 1972); $700 (A, 1968); inscribed, $1,900 (A, 1977). Special note concerning other later copies: This book offers a classic example of bibliographical confusion—some call it nitpicking—and controversy, which is what makes book collecting a matter of unending fascination for dedicated collectors. The bibliographers are still sorting out the unresolved mysteries of this book in its various forms. Hence any 1913 copy is a "must" for the collector. Following are three additional "states" of the book as defined by authorities on Frost books: Second state, (first issue, second binding), white, or cream, parchment (vellum), stamped in red. Value: $600 and up. Third state, (second issue, third binding), buff (cream) printed wrappers, with horizontal rule at top of the "A" in title. Value: $450 and up. Also, soiled, $150 (A, 1977). Fourth state, (second issue, fourth binding?), wrappers, plain "A." Value: $250 and up. Same issue: One of 135 signed by Frost. $300 and up. Also, $200 (A, 1977). Author's first book. New York, 1915. Cloth. First American edition, first issue, with "aind" for "and" in last line of page 14. In dust jacket. $750–$1,000. Also, $600 (A, 1978).

FROST, Robert. *Collected Poems.* Tan buckram. New York, 1930. Random House. First collected edition. One of 1,000 signed. In dust jacket. $150–$200. Trade issue, later: New York, (1930). Holt. Portrait. Cloth. First edition (so stated). $75–$100. New York, 1939. Title page woodcut. Decorated cloth. In dust jacket. $35–$50. New York, 1949. Cloth. In dust jacket. $35–$50.

FROST, Robert. *Complete Poems.* Cloth. New York, 1949. Holt. First edition. One of 500 signed. In dust jacket. $250–$275. Trade edition: In dust jacket. $50–$75.

FROST, Robert. *The Complete Poems of Robert Frost.* Illustrated. 2 vols., blue-gray cloth. New York, 1950. Limited Editions Club. One of 1,500 signed. Boxed. $200–$350.

FROST, Robert. *A Considerable Speck.* Folio, self-wrappers. No place, (1939). First edition. One of fewer than 100 on Dard Hunter paper, printed by the junior Dard Hunter. $400–$500. Also, $375 (A, 1977).

FROST, Robert. *The Cow's in the Corn.* Decorated boards, spine label. Gaylordsville, N.Y., 1929. Slide Mountain Press. First edition. One of 91 signed. With or without errata slip. $500–$600.

FROST, Robert. *A Further Range.* Tan cloth. New York, (1936). First edition. One of 803 signed. In slipcase. $125–$150. Trade issue, later: Red cloth. First edition. (4,100 printed.) In dust jacket. $35.

FROST, Robert. *The Gold Hesperidee.* 8 pp., wrappers. (Cortland, N.Y., 1935.) Bibliophile Press. First edition, first issue, with "A" on copyright page and with next to last line on page 7 unturned (second issue has the line turned and carried over). $150–$250. Second issue. $100–$125.

FROST, Robert. *Greece.* Self-wrappers. Chicago, (1948). Black Rose Press. First edition. One of 47. In mailing envelope. $300–$350. Also, $250 (A, 1977).

FROST, Robert. *Hard Not to Be King.* Cloth. New York, 1951. First edition. One of 300 signed. In tissue dust jacket. $150–$200.

FROST, Robert. *In the Clearing.* Buckram, New York, (1962). First edition. One of 1,500 signed. Boxed. $75–$125. Trade issue: Cloth. In dust jacket. $20–$25.

FROST, Robert. *The Lone Striker.* Printed wrappers in envelope. (New York, 1933.) First edition. No. 8 in the "Borzoi Chap Books." $75–$100.

FROST, Robert. *The Lovely Shall Be Choosers*. 6 pp., printed brown wrappers. New York, 1929. First edition. One of 475. $35–$50.

FROST, Robert. *A Masque of Mercy*. Half cloth. New York, (1947). First edition. One of 751 signed. Boxed. $75–$100. Trade issue: Blue cloth. In dust jacket. $25–$30.

FROST, Robert. *A Masque of Reason*. Half cloth. New York, (1945). First edition. One of 800 signed. Boxed. $100–$125. Trade issue: Blue cloth. In dust jacket. $25–$30. London, (1949). Cloth. First English edition. In dust jacket. $35.

FROST, Robert. *Mountain Interval*. Blue cloth. New York, (1916). First edition, first issue, with verses 6 and 7, page 88, repeated. In dust jacket. $100–$125. New York, 1921. Bust portrait. Boards. Second edition. In dust jacket. $40–$45.

FROST, Robert. *New Hampshire: A Poem with Notes and Grace Notes*. Woodcuts. Dark-green boards and cloth. New York, 1923. First trade edition. In dust jacket. $50–$75. Another issue: one of 350 signed. In glassine dust jacket. Boxed. $250–$350. London, 1924. Boards. First English edition. $50–$60. Hanover, N.H., 1955. New Dresden Press. Buckram and boards. First separate edition of title poem. One of 750 signed. $100–$125.

FROST, Robert. *North of Boston*. Green buckram. London, (1914). First edition, first state, gold lettering on front cover and spine, blind-stamped rule all around front cover. $1,500–$2,000. Also, $1,400 (A, 1979). Second state, lettered in blind on front. $600–$750. Third state, blue cloth, black lettering (rarest of the bindings). $600–$800. Fourth state, green cloth, blind rule at top and bottom of front cover. $400–$500. Fifth state, leaves 5⅜ by 7¾ inches. $300–$400. Other binding variants: $300–$500 at retail. Also, inscribed copies in all bindings at higher prices than noted here. (Frost signed a great many books!) New York, 1914. Brown boards, cloth back. First American edition, made up of English sheets with a new title page on a stub. In dust jacket. $400–$500. New York, 1915. Linen. Second American edition (first to be printed in America). In dust jacket. $200–$300.

FROST, Robert. *Our Hold on the Planet*. Wrappers. (Christmas token.) (Various places, 1940.) First edition. $35–$40.

FROST, Robert. *Selected Poems*. Green decorated boards and cloth. New York, 1923. First edition, with "March, 1923" on copyright page. In dust jacket. $250–$300. London, (1923). Cloth. First English edition. In dust jacket. $100–$150.

FROST, Robert. *Steeple Bush*. Blue boards and cloth. New York, 1947. First edition. One of 751 signed. Boxed. In tissue dust jacket. $200–$300. Trade issue: Cloth. In dust jacket. $40.

FROST, Robert. *Three Poems*. Wrappers. Hanover, N.H., (1935). First edition. (125 copies printed.) $250–$300.

FROST, Robert. *To a Young Wretch*. Wrappers. (Christmas token.) (Various places, 1937.) First edition. $100–$125.

FROST, Robert. *Robert Frost: Two Letters Written on His Undergraduate Days at Dartmouth College in 1892*. Wrappers, paper label, stapled. Hanover, 1931. First edition. (10 copies printed.) $3,000 and up. Also, loose in wrappers, $2,600 (A, 1977); inscribed, $3,750 (A, 1975).

FROST, Robert. *A Way Out*. Salmon-colored boards, cloth spine. New York, 1929. Harbor Press. First edition. One of 485 signed. In glassine dust jacket. $100–$150.

FROST, Robert. *West-Running Brook*. Green boards and cloth. New York, (1928). First (trade) edition. In dust jacket. $75–$100. Another issue: 4 plates signed by J.J. Lankes. Boards. One of 1,000 signed. Without "First Edition" on copyright page. In glassine jacket. Boxed. $200–$250.

FROST, Robert. *A Witness Tree*. Portrait. Decorated boards and cloth. New York, 1942. First edition. One of 735 signed. Boxed. $125–$150. Trade issue: Blue cloth. In dust jacket. $35. London, (1943). Cloth. First English edition. In dust jacket. $35.

FRUGAL Housewife (The). By the Author of *Hobomok.* Boards. Boston, 1829. (By Lydia Maria Child.) First edition. $150–$200.

FRY, Christopher. *The Boy with a Cart.* Wrappers. London, 1939. First edition. $150. Author's first book.

FRY, Frederick. *Fry's Traveler's Guide, and Descriptive Journal of the Great North Western Territories.* Cloth. Cincinnati, 1865. First edition. $500–$600.

FRY, James B. *Army Sacrifices.* Cloth. New York, 1879. First edition. $100–$150.

FRY, Roger. *Giovanni Bellini.* Illustrated. Boards and cloth. London, 1899. First edition. $75–$100. Author's first book.

FUGITIVE Pieces. 66 pp., green-gray wrappers. No place, (1806). (By George Gordon Noel, Lord Byron.) First edition. Price: In the thousands. All except four copies were destroyed, according to De Ricci. London, 1886. Vellum. Facsimile edition. One of 100. $75–$100. Another issue: One of 7 on Japan paper. $200–$250.

FUGITIVES, An Anthology of Verse. Decorated paper boards, cloth back. New York, (1928). First edition. $100–$125.

FULKERSON, H.S. *Random Recollections of Early Days in Mississippi.* Printed wrappers. Vicksburg, 1885. First edition. $400–$500. Cloth: $250–$300.

FULLER, C.L. *Pocket Map and Descriptive Outline History of the Black Hills of Dakota and Wyoming.* Folding map. 56 pp., stiff wrappers. Rapid City, 1887. First edition. $600–$850.

FULLER, Emeline. *Left by the Indians, or Rapine, Massacre and Cannibalism on the Overland Trail in 1860.* (Cover title.) Portrait. 41 pp., printed wrappers. (Mt. Vernon, Iowa, 1892.) First edition $200–$300. New York, 1936. Facsimile reprint. One of 200. $75.

FULLER, Henry Blake. See Page, Stanton.

FULLER, Henry Blake. *Bertram Cope's Year.* Cloth. Chicago, 1919. First edition. $150–$200.

FULLER, Henry Blake. *The Cliff-Dwellers.* Cloth. New York, 1893. First edition, first issue, with author's name on front cover as "Henry Fuller." $50–$75. (Later, "Henry B. Fuller.")

FULLER, S. Margaret. *Woman in the 19th Century.* Wrappers or cloth. New York, 1845. First edition. $150–$165.

FULLMER, John S. *Assassination of Joseph and Hyrum Smith, the Prophet and the Patriarch of the Church of Jesus Christ of Latter-day Saints.* 40 pp., half leather. Liverpool, 1855. First edition. $500–$750.

FULMORE, Z.T. *The History and Geography of Texas as Told in County Names.* Cloth. (Austin, 1915.) First edition. $100–$200.

FULTON, A.R. *The Red Men of Iowa.* 26 plates. Cloth. Des Moines, 1882. First edition. $100–$200.

FULTON, Robert. *Torpedo War, and Submarine Explosions.* 5 plates. Oblong quarto, cloth. New York, 1810. First edition. $1,500–$2,500.

FUNKHOUSER, W.D. *Wild Life in Kentucky.* Cloth. Frankfort, 1925. $75–$85.

FURBER, George C. *The Twelve Months Volunteer.* Cloth. Cincinnati, 1848. First edition. $150–$200.

G

GADDIS, William. *The Recognitions.* Cloth. New York, (1955). First edition. In dust jacket. $200–$250. Advance copy: Wrappers. $450–$500. Author's first book.

GAG, Wanda. *Millions of Cats.* Boards. New York, 1928. First trade edition. In dust jacket. $100–$125. Another issue. One of 250 signed and with a signed engraving. Boxed. $300.

GAINE, Hugh. *The Journals of Hugh Gaine, Printer.* Edited by Paul Leicester Ford. Plates. 2 vols., boards. New York, 1902. First edition. One of 350. $200–$250. Another issue: Cloth. One of 30 printed on Japan paper. $350–$450.

GAINES, Ernest J. *Catherine Carmier.* Cloth. New York, 1964. First edition. In dust jacket. $100–$125. Author's first book.

GALE, George. *Upper Mississippi.* Frontispiece, maps, plates. Cloth. Chicago, 1867. First edition. $100–$125.

GALLAHER, James. *The Western Sketch-Book.* Plates. Cloth. Boston. 1850 First edition. $150–$200.

GALLATIN, Albert. *Considerations on the Currency and Banking System of the United States.* Wrappers. Philadelphia, 1831. First edition. $125–$150. Cloth: $85–$100.

GALLATIN, Albert. *Letters of Albert Gallatin on the Oregon Question.* Stitched. Washington, 1846. First edition. $75–$100.

GALLATIN, Albert Eugene. *Art and the Great War.* Illustrated. Folio, full morocco. New York, 1919. First edition. One of 100 signed. Boxed. $300–$400. Trade edition: Half cloth. $100.

GALLATIN, Albert Eugene. *Portraits of Whistler.* 40 illustrations. Boards. New York, 1918. First edition. One of 250. Boxed. $150–$200. Trade edition: Half cloth. $100.

GALLICO, Paul. *The Snow Goose.* Illustrated by Peter Scott, including 4 color plates. Morocco. London, 1946. One of 750 signed. $200–$300. Trade edition: In dust jacket. $50–$60.

GALSWORTHY, John. See Sinjohn, John.

GALSWORTHY, John. *The Country House.* Green cloth. London. 1907. First edition, with publisher's windmill stamp in lower right corner of back cover. $75–$85.

GALSWORTHY, John. *The Dark Flower.* Dark-red cloth. London, 1913. First edition, first issue, with 22 pages of ads at end. In dust jacket. $50.

GALSWORTHY, John. *The Forsyte Saga.* Folding genealogical table. Green cloth. London, 1922. First edition, first issue, with genealogical table pulling out to the right. In dust jacket. $150–$200. Another issue: Green limp leather. One of 275 signed. $300–$400.

GALSWORTHY, John. *The Full Moon: A Play in Three Acts.* Green wrappers. London, 1915. First edition, first issue, without the listing of cast on back leaf. $50.

GALSWORTHY, John. *The Island Pharisees.* Green cloth. London, 1904. First edition, first (unpublished) issue, with no mention of this title in publisher's list. $500 and up? No recent auction records, no copies noted in dealer catalogues. Also, $1,375 (A,

1930). First published edition. $35–$50. New York, 1904. Blue cloth. First American edition (750 made from English sheets). $25–$35.

GALSWORTHY, John. *The Man of Property*. Green cloth. London, 1906. First edition, first issue, with broken bar of music on page 200. $150–$175.

GALSWORTHY, John. *A Modern Comedy*. Folding table. Full limp vellum. London, 1929. First edition. One of 1,030 signed. $60–$80. Trade edition: Cloth. In dust jacket. $25.

GALSWORTHY, John. *The Silver Spoon*. Cloth. London, (1926). First edition. One of 265 signed. $60. Trade edition: Cloth. In dust jacket. $25–$30.

GALSWORTHY, John. *Swan Song*. Blue buckram. London, (1928). First edition. One of 525 signed. $50. Trade edition: Cloth. In dust jacket. $25–$35.

GALT, John. See Balwhidder, The Rev. Micah. Also see *The Provost; Ringan Gilhaize; The Steam-Boat.*

GALT, John. *The Bachelor's Wife*. Boards. Edinburgh, 1824. First edition. $300–$350.

GALT, John. *Lawrie Todd*. 3 vols., cloth. London 1830. First edition. $350–$450. New York, 1830. 2 vols. in one, boards. First American edition. $150–$200.

GALTON, Francis. *Finger Prints*. 16 plates. Purple cloth. London, 1892. First edition. $500–$850.

GALTON, Francis. *Hereditary Genius*. Folding table. Cloth. London, 1869. First edition. $350–$500.

GAMEKEEPER at Home (The). Cloth. London, 1878. (By Richard Jefferies.) First edition. $250–$350. London, 1880. $150–$175.

GANCONAGH. *John Sherman and Dhoya*. Gray cloth, lettered in blue; also in yellow wrappers, lettered in black. London, (1891). (By William Butler Yeats.) First edition. Cloth: $600–$750. Wrappers: $750. (Note: The cloth issue is scarcer than the one in wrappers. Most copies offered in recent years have been in poor condition.)

GANNET(T), William, C. *The House Beautiful*. With designs by Frank Lloyd Wright. Folio, half leather. Rivert Forest, Ill., Winter, 1896–97. One of 90 signed by Wright and William Winslow, the publisher (Auvergne Press). $2,500 and up. (Note: Gannett's text first appeared in a pamphlet of 24 pages in Boston in 1895. The original spelled his name correctly.)

GARCES, Francisco. *On the Trail of the Spanish Pioneer*. Translated by Elliott Coues. Illustrated. 2 vols., cloth. New York, 1900. First edition. One of 950. $150–$200.

GARCIA MARQUEZ, Gabriel. *One Hundred Years of Solitude*. Cloth. New York, (1970). First American edition. In dust jacket. $50–$125.

GARCÍA y CUBAS, Antonio. *Atlas Geografico, Estadistico e Histórico de la República Mexicana*. 33 double page maps in color. Folio, boards. Mexico, 1858. One of 300. $750–$1,500.

GARD, Wayne. *Along the Early Trails of the Southwest*. Illustrated. Half leather. Austin. 1969. First edition. One of 250 signed and with an extra set of color plates. $150–$200.

GARD, Wayne. *Sam Bass*. Illustrated. Cloth. Boston, 1936. First edition. In dust jacket. $75–$100.

GARDEN, Alexander. *Anecdotes of the Revolutionary War in America*. First Series. Boards. Charleston, 1822. First edition. $150–$250. Charleston, 1828. Boards. Second Series. First edition. $100–$200. Together, First and Second Series, fine copies: $350.

GARDNER, Alexander. See *Photographic Sketch Book of the War.*

GARDNER, John. *Grendel*. Illustrated. Cloth. New York, 1971. First edition. In dust jacket. $175–$200. (London, 1972.) First English edition. In dust jacket. $50–$60.

GARDNER, John. *Jason and Medea*. New York, 1973. First edition. In dust jacket. $35–$50.

GARDNER, John. *The King's Indian*. Cloth. New York, 1974. First edition. In dust jacket. $30–$40.

GARDNER, John. *Nickel Mountain*. Cloth. New York, 1973. First edition. In dust jacket. $30–$40.

GARDNER, John. *The Resurrection*. Cloth. (New York, 1966.) First edition. In dust jacket. $500–$750. Author's first book.

GARDNER, John. *The Sunlight Dialogues*. Cloth. New York, 1972. First edition. In dust jacket. $30–$40.

GARDNER, John. *The Wreckage of Agathon*. Boards. New York, (1970). First edition. In dust jacket. $75–$100.

GARDNER, Ralph D. *Horatio Alger; or, The American Hero Era*. Illustrated. Cloth. Mendota. Ill., (1964). First edition. In dust jacket. $50–$75.

GARLAND, Hamlin. *The Book of the American Indian*. Colored frontispiece and 34 plates by Frederic Remington. Folio, boards and cloth. New York 1923. First edition. In dust jacket. Boxed. $150–$250. Worn, no jacket or box, $75.

GARLAND, Hamlin. *Cavanagh, Forest Ranger*. Frontispiece. Cloth. New York, 1910. First edition. $50–$60.

GARLAND, Hamlin. *The Light of the Star*. Frontispiece. Cloth. New York, 1904. First edition. $40–$50.

GARLAND, Hamlin. *Main-Travelled Roads*. Gray printed wrappers. Boston, 1891. First edition, first issue with "Arena Library" at top and "First Thousand" at bottom of front cover. $150–$250. Another issue: Blue or gray cloth. $75–$125.

GARLAND, Hamlin. *A Member of the Third House*. Wrappers. Chicago, (1892). First edition. $75–$100. Clothbound issue: $40.

GARLAND, Hamlin. *The Mystery of the Buried Crosses*. Cloth. New York, 1939. First edition. In dust jacket. $75–$85.

GARLAND, Hamlin. *A Pioneer Mother*. Wrappers. Chicago, 1922. First edition. One of 500. $35–$50. Another issue: Boards. One of 25. $85–$100.

GARLAND, Hamlin. *Prairie Songs*. Illustrated. Pictorial cloth. Cambridge, Mass., and Chicago, 1893. First edition. One of 110 de luxe copies. $150–$200. Trade edition: $65–$75.

GARLAND, Hamlin. *A Son of the Middle Border*. Cloth. New York, 1917. First edition. Limited, signed issue. $150. Trade edition: In dust jacket $50–$60. London, (1917). First English edition. $40–$50.

GARLAND, Hamlin. *Under the Wheel: A Modern Play in Six Scenes*. Wrappers. Boston, 1890. First edition. $150. Author's first book.

GARMAN, K.E. *Moving-Picture Circus*. Illustrated. Movable book with 8 specially cut leaves on stiff cardboard. Chicago, 1909. $150–$200.

GARNEAU, Joseph, Jr. *Nebraska: Her Resources, Advantages and Development*. (Cover title.) 24 pp., printed wrappers. Omaha, 1893. First edition. $200–$300.

GARNER, James W. *Reconstruction in Mississippi*. Cloth. New York, 1901. First edition. $150–$200.

GARNETT, David. *The Grasshoppers Come.* Illustrated. Yellow buckram. London, 1931, First edition. One of 200 signed. $75–$100. Trade edition: In dust jacket. $35–$40.

GARNETT, Richard. *The Twilight of the Gods and Other Tales.* Cloth. London, 1888, First edition. $75–$100.

GARRARD, Lewis H. *Wah-To-Yah, and the Taos Trail.* Decorated cloth. Cincinnati, 1850. First edition, first issue, with page 269 misnumbered 26. $600–$800. San Francisco, 1936. Grabhorn Press. Boards. One of 550. $75–$100.

GARRETT, Edmund H. (editor). *Victorian Songs.* Illustrated by Garrett. Vellum, gilt. Boston, 1895. First edition. One of 225. In parchment dust jacket. $100–$125.

GARRETT, Julia Kathryn. *Green Flag Over Texas.* Maps. Cloth. New York, 1939. First edition. In dust jacket. $100–$125.

GARRETT, Pat F. *The Authentic Life of Billy, The Kid.* Frontispiece and 5 plates. 137 pp., pictorial blue wrappers. Santa Fe, 1882. First edition, with ad inside back wrapper, misnumbered pages at the back, and one errata slip. $4,000 or more. (Jack B. Rittenhouse, an Albuquerque bookman, sold a rebound copy [wrappers pasted to boards] for $3,000 in 1980.)

GARVER, Will L. *Brother of the Third Degree.* Cloth. Boston, 1894. First edition. $40–$50.

GARVIE, James. *Abraham Lincoln toni kin, qa Aesop tawoyake kin.* (Life of Abraham Lincoln and Aesop's Fables). 17 pp., printed wrappers. Santee [Indian] Agency, Neb., 1893. $150–$250.

GASCOYNE, David. *Opening Day.* Cloth. London, (1932). First edition. In dust jacket. $250–$350.

GASCOYNE, David. *Poems, 1937–1942.* Color illustrations. Pictorial boards. (London, 1943.) First edition. In dust jacket. $100–$150.

GASKELL, Elizabeth C. See *Cranford; Mary Barton; North and South.*

GASKELL, Elizabeth C. *The Life of Charlotte Brontë.* 2 vols., cloth. London, 1857. First edition. $300–$400.

GASKELL, Elizabeth C. *Sylvia's Lovers.* 3 vols., cloth. London. 1893. First edition. $600–$800.

GASS, Patrick. *Gass's Journal of the Lewis and Clark Expedition.* Edited by James K. Hosmer. Illustrated. Cloth. Chicago, 1904. $50–$60. Another issue: One of 75 on large paper. $125–$150.

GASS, Patrick. *A Journal of the Voyages and Travels of a Corps of Discovery, Under the Command of Capt. Lewis and Capt. Clark, etc.* Boards and leather. Pittsburgh, 1807. First edition. $750–$1,000. London, 1808. First English edition. $400–$750. Philadelphia, 1810. Calf. Second edition (without plates). $300–$350. Philadelphia, 1810. 6 plates added. Calf. Second illustrated edition (actually third edition). $300–$350. Paris, 1810. Map. Wrappers. First French edition. $350–$500. Philadelphia, 1812. 6 plates, folding map. Calf. Fourth edition. $350–$400.

GASS, William H. *In the Heart of the Heart of the Country.* Cloth. New York, (1968). First edition. In dust jacket. $50–$60.

GASS, William H. *Omensetter's Luck.* Blue boards and black cloth. (New York, 1966.) First edition. In dust jacket. $150–$200. London, 1967. Cloth. First English edition. In dust jacket. $100–$125. Author's first book.

GASS, William H. *Willie Masters' Lonesome Wife.* Illustrated. Black cloth. (Evanston, 1968.) First edition. One of 100 (possibly more?) signed. $150. Also, 300 copies, unsigned. $50. Also in wrappers. $15–$20.

GAUGUIN, Paul. *Intimate Journals.* Translated by Van Wyck Brooks. 27 illustrations by Gauguin. Boards. New York, 1921. First edition in English. One of 999. $75–$100.

GAUGUIN, Paul. *Letters to Edouard Vollard and André Fontainas.* 10 woodcuts. Boards and cloth. San Francisco, 1943. Grabhorn Press. One of 250. $150–$200.

GAUTIER, Théophile. *One of Cleopatra's Nights.* Translated by Lafcadio Hearn. Cloth. New York, 1882. First American edition. $200–$300.

GAY, Frederick A. *For Gratuitious Distribution: Sketches of California.* (Cover title.) 16 pp., printed wrappers. (New York, 1848.) First edition. $500–$600.

GEE, Ernest R. *Early American Sporting Books, 1734 to 1846.* Illustrated. Boards. New York, 1928. Derrydale Press. One of 500. $250–$300.

GEM(A): "The City of the Plains." Abilene: The Centre of the "Golden Belt." Woodcuts. 64 pp., printed wrappers. Burlington, Iowa, 1887. First edition $75–$100.

GEM of the Rockies! (The): Manitou Springs. Plates and tables, 23 pp., printed wrappers. Manitou Springs. Colo., (about 1885). First edition. $75–$100.

GENERAL and Statistical Description of Pierce County (Wisconsin). 9 pp., sewed. (Prescott, Wis., 1854.) First edition. $100–$150.

GENERAL Instructions to Deputy Surveyors. Folding diagram. 25 pp., sewed. Little Rock, 1837. First edition. $100–$150.

GENERAL Orders Affecting the Volunteer Force: Adjutant General's Office, 1863. Cloth. Washington, 1864. (Contains Lincoln presidential orders, including Emancipation Proclamation.) $150–$200.

GENERAL Orders Affecting the Volunteer Force: Adjutant General's Office, 1864. Cloth. Washington, 1865. (Contains Lincoln presidential orders.) $150–$200.

GENÊT, Edmond Charles. *Memorial on the Upward Forces of Fluids.* Folding table, 6 plates. Printed brown boards. Albany, 1825. First edition. $1,500–$1,750. Also, $1,100 (A, 1978).

GENIUS of Oblivion (The), and Other Poems. By a Lady of New-Hampshire. Gray boards, paper label on spine. Concord, N.H., 1823. (By Sarah Josepha Hale.) First edition. $200–$300. Author's first book.

GENTHE, Arnold. *As I Remember.* 112 photographic illustrations. Half leather. New York, 1936. First edition. One of 250 signed. $250. Trade edition: Cloth. In dust jacket. $50.

GENTHE, Arnold. *Impressions of Old New Orleans: A Book of Pictures.* Foreword by Grace King. Green boards and cloth. New York, (1926). First edition, with Doran monogram on copyright page. $150–$200.

GEOLOGICAL Survey of Texas: First Annual Report. Austin, 1890. $300. Austin, 1891. Second report. $200. Austin, 1892. Third report. $200.

GEORGE, Henry. *Our Land and Land Policy, National and State.* Folding map in black and red. 48 pp., printed wrappers. San Francisco, 1871. First edition. $300–$350. Also, inscribed, $440 (A, 1979). Author's first book(?).

GEORGE, Henry. *Progress and Poverty.* Green or blue cloth. San Francisco, 1879. "Author's Edition." First edition, first issue, with the slip asking that no reviews be printed. $800–$1,000. Also, $616 (A, 1979); $375 (A, 1980). Second issue, without the slip referring to reviews. $200–$250.

GEORGE, Mason. The Young Backwoodsman. Tan boards, paper label. Boston, 1829. (By Timothy Flint.) First edition. $150–$250.

GEORGE Pierce Baker, A Memorial. Batik boards, paper label. New York 1929. First edition. Large paper copy signed by all the contributors, including Eugene O'Neill. (A few copies only were issued.) In tissue dust jacket. $200–$225.

GEORGIA Scenes, Characters, Incidents, etc., in the First Half Century of the Republic. By a Native Georgian. Brown boards, cloth back, paper labels. Augusta, Ga., 1835. (By Augustus Baldwin Longstreet.) First edition, $1,000–$1,250. Author's first book. New York, 1840. Illustrated. Cloth. Second edition. $300–$400.

GERARD Manley Hopkins. By the Kenyon Critics. Cloth. New York, (1945). First edition. In dust jacket. $75–$85.

GERHARD, Fred. *Illinois As It Is.* Map. Frontispiece, 3 folding maps. Cloth. Chicago, 1857. First edition. $150–$200.

GERNSBACK, Hugo. *Ralph 124C41: A Romance of the Year 2660.* Illustrated. Blue cloth. Boston, 1925. First edition. In dust jacket. $500–$750.

GERSHWIN, George. *George Gershwin's Song-Book.* Illustrated by Alajolov. Portrait, song reproductions. Full blue morocco. New York, 1932. One of 300 signed by Gershwin and Alajolov. $1,000–$1,250. Also, a copy marked "Review," $1,300 (A, 1977). Trade edition: Buckram and suede. $75–$100.

GERSHWIN, George. *Porgy and Bess.* Frontispiece in color. Morocco. New York, 1935. First edition. One of 250 signed by Gershwin, DuBose Heyward, and others. Boxed. $750–$1,000.

GERSTAECKER, Friedrich. *California Gold Mines.* Foreword by Joseph A. Sullivan. Folding map, illustrations. Pictorial boards. Oakland, 1946. One of 500 signed by Sullivan. $75–$100.

GERSTAECKER, Friedrich. *Scenes of Life in California.* San Francisco, 1942. Grabhorn Press. One of 500. $75–$100.

GESNER, Abraham. *A Practical Treatise on Coal, Petroleum, and Other Distilled Oils.* Illustrated. Cloth. New York, 1861. First edition. $350–$400.

GETTING a Wrong Start: A Truthful Autobiography. Terra-cotta cloth. New York, 1915. (By Emerson Hough.) First edition, with "Published March, 1915" on copyright page. $35–$50.

GHIRARDELLI, Ynez. *The Artist H. Daumier.* San Francisco, 1940. Grabhorn Press. One of 250. $100–$125.

GIBBINGS, Robert. *Over the Reefs.* Illustrated by the author. Morocco. London, 1948. First edition. One of 100 signed. $75–$100.

GIBBINGS, Robert. *The Wood Engravings of Robert Gibbings.* Illustrated. Boards. London, (1959). First edition. In acetate dust jacket. $175–$200.

GIBRAN, Kahlil. *Sand and Foam.* Illustrated by the author. Boards. New York, 1926. One of 95 signed. $200–$225.

GIBRAN, Kahlil. *Twenty Drawings.* Illustrated. Boards. New York, 1919. First edition. $150–$200.

GIBSON, Charles Dana. *Americans.* Illustrated. Oblong folio, cloth. New York, 1900. First edition. One of 250 signed. $100–$125.

GIBSON, Charles Dana. *Drawings.* Plates. Oblong folio, boards and cloth. New York, 1897. First edition. $100–$125.

GIBSON, Charles Dana. *Eighty Drawings, Including the Weaker Sex.* Oblong folio, cloth. New York, 1903. First edition. One of 250 signed. $100–$125.

GIBSON, Charles Dana. *The Gibson Book.* Illustrated, 2 vols., oblong folio, boards. New York, 1906. First edition. In dust jacket. $100–$150. New York, 1907. $100–$150.

GIBSON, Charles Dana. *London, As Seen by Gibson.* Illustrated. Oblong folio, cloth. New York, 1897. First edition. $75–$125.

GIBSON, Wilfrid W. *Home: A Book of Poems.* Woodcut. Boards and vellum. London. 1920. Beaumont Press. First edition. One of 35 on vellum, signed. $200–$300. Another issue: One of 260 on paper. $85.

GIDDINGS, Marsh. *First Annual Message to the Legislative Assembly of the Territory of New Mexico.* 54 pp., printed wrappers. Santa Fe, 1871. First edition. $125–$175.

GIFT from Fairly-Land (A). Cloth. New York, (1838). (By James Kirke Paulding.) First edition, first issue. $300–$400. Also, $275 (A, 1977).

GILBERT, Paul T., and Bryson, Charles L. *Chicago and Its Makers.* Illustrated. Buckram. Chicago, 1929. First edition. $100–$150. Another issue: Full morocco. One of 2,000. $400–$500.

GILBERT, W.S. *Comedy and Tragedy.* Wrappers. London, (1884). First edition. $50–$75.

GILBERT, W.S. *The "Bab" Ballads: Much Sound and Little Sense,* Illustrated by the author. Green cloth. London, 1869. First edition, first issue, with Hotten imprint on title page. $200–$225.

GILBERT, W.S. *Iolanthe and Other Operas.* Illustrated by W.R. Flint. Half morocco. London, 1910. First edition. $100–$125.

GILBERT, W.S. *The Mikado.* Illustrated. Cloth. London, 1928. In dust jacket. $100–$125.

GILBERT, W.S. *More "Bab" Ballads.* Green cloth. London, (1873). First edition. $100–$150.

GILBERT, W.S. *A New and Original Extravaganza Entitled Dulcamara; or, The Little Duck and the Great Quack.* Illustration. Orange wrappers. London, 1866. First edition. $500 and up. Author's first published work.

GILBERT, W.S. *Songs of a Savoyard.* Illustrated by the author. Cloth. London, (1890). First edition. $150. London, 1891. $125.

GILBERT, William. *On the Magnet, Magnetick Bodies, etc.* Woodcuts. Folio, limp vellum, silk ties. London, 1900. One of 250. $200–$300.

GILCHRIST, Alexander. *Life of William Blake.* Illustrated. 2 vols., cloth. London, 1863. First edition. $200–$300. London, 1880. Blue cloth. Second edition. $250–$350.

GILDER, Richard Watson. *The New Day.* Pictorial cloth. New York, 1876. First edition. $50. Author's first book.

GILES, William B. *Political Miscellanies.* Calf. (Virginia, 1830.) $65–$85.

GILHAM, William B. *Manual of Instruction for the Volunteers and Militia of the Confederate States.* Folding charts. Cloth. Richmond, 1861. $400–$500.

GILHESPY, F. Brayshaw. *Derby Porcelain.* 77 plates, 13 in color. Buckram. London, 1961. In dust jacket. $35–$50.

GILL, Brendan. *Death in April and Other Poems.* Boards. Windham, 1935. First edition. $100–$125. Author's first book.

GILL, Eric. *Art-Nonsense and Other Essays.* Half calf. London, 1929. First edition. One of 100 signed. $125–$175. Trade edition: Cloth. In dust jacket. $30–$40.

GILL, Eric. *Clothes.* 10 wood engravings by the author. Boards, leather spine. London, 1931. One of 160 signed. $300–$350.

GILL, Eric. *Clothing Without Cloth: An Essay on the Nude.* 4 wood engravings by the author. Cloth. London, 1931. Golden Cockerel Press. One of 500. $250–$275.

GILL, Eric. *An Essay on Typography.* Illustrated. Cloth, (London, 1931.) One of 500 signed. In dust jacket. $150–$250.

GILL, Eric. *From the Jerusalem Diary.* Illustrated. Half cloth. (London), 1953. First edition. One of 300. $80–$100.

GILL, Eric (illustrator). See *The Four Gospels of the Lord Jesus Christ.*

GILLELAND, J.C. *The Ohio and Mississippi Pilot.* 16 maps. Calf, or boards and calf. Pittsburgh, 1820. First edition. $1,500–$2,000.

GILLELEN, F.M.L. *The Oil Regions of Pennsylvania.* 17 maps (one folding), frontispiece, 3 other plates. 67 pp., wrappers. Pittsburgh, (1865?). First edition. $500–$750. possibly more.

GILLETT, James B. *Six Years with the Texas Rangers.* 8 plates. Cloth. Austin, (1921). First edition. $100–$150. New Haven, 1925. Cloth. $25–$30.

GILMOR, Harry. *Four Years in the Saddle.* Cloth. New York, 1866. First American edition. $75–$100.

GINSBERG, Allen. *Ankor Wat.* 10 photographs by Alexandra Lawrence. Cloth. London, (1969). Fulcrum Press. One of 100 signed. $150.

GINSBERG, Allen. *Bixby Canyon Ocean Path Word Breeze.* Illustrated with photographs. New York, 1972. First edition. One of 26 lettered hardcover copies signed. Issued without dust jacket. $125–$135. Ordinary copies, bound in wrappers, $25–$35.

GINSBERG, Allen. *Careless Love.* Wrappers. Madison, Wis., (1978). First edition. One of 280 signed. $50.

GINSBERG, Allen. *Empty Mirror: Early Poems.* Introduction by William Carlos Williams. Decorated wrappers. New York, (1961). Totem Press. First edition. $35.

GINSBERG, Allen. *Howl for Carl Solomon.* First edition. (see next entry.)

GINSBERG, Allen. *Howl and Other Poems.* Introduction by William Carlos Williams. Printed wrappers, San Francisco, (1956). First edition. $250–$300. (Note: *Howl* appeared originally as *Howl for Carl Solomon*, 17 pages mimeographed and stapled at San Francisco State College in 1955. Value: $1,000 and up. Also, an inscribed and corrected copy. $1,400 at auction in October, 1977). San Francisco, 1971. Pictorial cloth. One of 275 signed. $125–$200. Specially bound in morocco by Jennie Sack. $1,600.

GINSBERG, Allen. *The Moments Return.* Illustrated. Half cloth. San Francisco, 1970. First edition. One of 200. Issued without dust jacket. $75–$100. Another issue: Half leather. One of 14 in a special binding. $150.

GINSBERG, Allen. *New Year Blues.* Wrappers. New York, 1972. First edition. One of 100 signed. $75. Another issue: One of 26 lettered and signed. $100.

GINSBERG, Allen. *Planet News: 1961–1967.* Black cloth. San Francisco, 1968. First edition. One of 500 signed. Boxed. $40–$60.

GINSBERG, Allen. *Siesta in Xbalba and Return to the States.* Self-wrappers, stapled. Near Icy Cape, Alaska, July, 1956. First edition. One of about 56 copies mimeographed. $1,500–$2,500.

GINSBERG, Allen. *T.V. Baby Poems.* Boards. (London, 1967). Cape Goliard Press. First edition. One of 100 signed. In dust jacket. $100–$150. Trade edition: Wrappers. $15–$20. New York, 1968. Wrappers. First American edition. $20.

GINSBERG, Allen. *Wales—A Visitation July 29, 1967*. Boards. London, 1968. Cape Goliard Press. First edition. One of 100 signed, with author's recording of poem. In dust jacket. $100–$150. (This actually is the second issue; the first was a publisher giveaway, issued in wrappers. Value: $15–$20.)

GINX'S Baby: His Birth and Other Misfortunes. Cloth. London, 1870. (By John Edward Jenkins.) First edition. $50. Author's first book.

GIRARD, Just. *Adventures of a French Captain, at Present a Planter in Texas*. Boards or cloth. New York, 1878. (By Just Jean Etienne Roy.) $150–$300.

GIRAUD, J.P., Jr. *The Birds of Long Island*. Plate. Cloth. New York, 1844. First edition. $300–$400.

GISSING, George. See *Demos: A Story of English Socialism*.

GISSING, George. *Born in Exile*. 3 vols., slate-gray cloth. London, 1892. First edition. $500–$600.

GISSING, George. *By the Ionian Sea: Notes of a Ramble in Southern Italy*. Illustrated in color and black and white. White cloth. London, 1901. First edition. $175–$200.

GISSING, George. *Charles Dickens: A Critical Study*. Dark-red cloth. London, 1898. First edition. $100–$150.

GISSING, George. *Denzil Quarrier*. Olive cloth. London, 1892. First edition. $150–$200.

GISSING, George. *The Emancipated*. 3 vols., boards and cloth. London, 1890. First edition. $400–$500.

GISSING, George. *Eve's Ransom*. Red cloth. London, 1895. First edition, with 16 pages of ads for Autumn, 1894. $150–$250.

GISSING, George. *The House of Cobwebs and Other Stories*. Blue cloth. London, 1906. First edition. $75–$125.

GISSING, George. *In the Year of Jubilee*. 3 vols., blue cloth. London, 1894. First edition. $400–$500. New York, 1895. Green cloth. First American edition. $50–$75.

GISSING, George. *Isabel Clarendon*. 2 vols., green cloth. London, 1886. First edition. $250–$350.

GISSING, George. *A Life's Morning*. 3 vols., light-blue cloth. London, 1888. First edition. $400–$500.

GISSING, George. *The Nether World*. 3 vols., light-blue or green cloth. London, 1889. First edition. $250–$350.

GISSING, George. *New Grub Street*. 3 vols., dark-green cloth. London, 1891. First edition. $1,250–$1,500.

GISSING, George. *The Odd Women*. 3 vols., blue cloth. London, 1893. First edition. $200–$250.

GISSING, George, *Our Friend the Charlatan*. Illustrated. Cloth. London, 1901. First edition. $100–$125.

GISSING, George. *The Private Papers of Henry Ryecroft*. Green cloth. Westminster, England, 1903. First edition, with three ad leaves. $175. New York, 1903. Cloth. First American edition. $100. Portland, Me., 1921. Boards. One of 25 on Japan vellum. $100–$200. Another issue: One of 700. $35–$50. New York, 1927. Purple cloth. In dust jacket. $75.

GISSING, George, *Thyrza: A Tale*. 3 vols., dark-red cloth. London, 1887. First edition. $400–$500.

GISSING, George. *The Town Traveller*. Light-red cloth. London, 1898. First edition, with ads dated April, 1898. $100–$150.

GISSING, George. *The Unclassed*. 3 vols., blue cloth. London, 1884. First edition. $250–$350.

GISSING, George. *Veranilda: A Romance*. Red cloth. London, 1904. First edition, with 16 pages of ads at back. In dust jacket, $200–$300. Lacking jacket, $75–$100.

GISSING, George. *Will Warburton: A Romance of Real Life*. Red cloth. London, 1905. First edition, with 16 pages of ads at back. $75–$85.

GISSING, George. *Workers in the Dawn*. 3 vols., light-brown cloth. London, 1880. First edition, with black end papers. $2,000–$3,000. Author's first book.

GISSING, George. *A Yorkshire Lass*. Boards, paper label. New York, 1928. First edition. One of 93. In tissue dust jacket. $200–$250.

GIST, Christopher. *Christopher Gist's Journals*. 7 maps. Cloth. Pittsburgh, 1893. First edition. One of 10 on large paper. $400–$500. Another issue: One of 100. $250–$300.

GLASGOW, Ellen. See *The Descendant*.

GLASGOW, Ellen. *The Freeman and Other Poems*. New York, 1902. First edition. $200–$250.

GLASGOW, Ellen. *Phases of an Inferior Planet*. Brown cloth. New York, 1898. First edition, with erratum slip. In dust jacket. $150.

GLASS, E.L.N. *History of the Tenth Cavalry, 1866–1921*. Illustrated. Cloth. Tucson, 1921. First edition, $75–$100.

GLEANINGS from the Inside History of the Bonanzas. 40 pp., printed wrappers. (San Francisco, 1878.) First edition. $125.

GLEESON, William. *History of the Catholic Church in California*. 4 maps and plans, 9 plates. 2 vols., cloth. San Francisco, 1871–72. First edition. $300. San Francisco, 1872. 2 vols. in one. Second edition. $125.

GLEN, Duncan (editor). *Poems Addressed to Hugh MacDiarmid and Presented to Him on His 75th Birthday*. Frontispiece, other illustrations. Boards and leather. (Preston, Lancashire, England, 1967.) One of 50 signed by all the contributors, etc. $150 and up. Another issue: One of 350 signed by editor and illustrator. $100 and up. (Note: MacDiarmid is the pen name of C.M. Grieve.)

GLENN, Allen. *History of Cass County (Missouri)*. Cloth. Topeka, 1917. First edition. $100–$150.

GLISAN, R. *Journal of Army Life*. Folding table, 21 plates. Cloth. San Francisco. 1874. First edition. $150–$200.

GLOVER, Mary Baker. *Science and Health, With Key to the Scriptures*. Black cloth. Boston, 1875. (By Mary Baker Eddy.) First edition, first issue, with errata slip and without index. $1,250–$1,500. Lynn, Mass., 1878. Second edition. $400–$600. Lynn, 1881. 2 vols., cloth. Third edition. $200–$300. Lynn, 1882. 2 vols., cloth. $150–$200. Boston, (1941). One of 1,000. $400–$500.

GODDARD, R.H. *A Method of Reading Extreme Altitudes*. 10 plates. Wrappers. Washington, 1919. First edition. $1,500. Front cover torn, $1,350 (1977 catalogue).

GODWIN, Gail. *The Perfectionists*. Cloth. New York, (1970). First edition. In dust jacket. $35–50. Author's first book.

GODWIN, William. *Deloraine*. 3 vols., boards, London, 1833. First edition. $300–$400.

GODWIN, William. *Essay on Sepulchres.* Engraved frontispiece. Boards, paper label. London, 1809. First edition. $200–$300.

GODWIN, William. *Fleetwood: or, The New Man of Feeling.* 3 vols., boards. London, 1805. First edition. $350–$450.

GODWIN, William. *Life of Geoffrey Chaucer.* Illustrated. 2 vols., calf. London, 1803. First edition. $300–$400.

GODWIN, William. *Mandeville: A Tale of the 17th Century in England.* 3 vols., boards. London, 1817. First edition. $500–$650. Worn, $374 in a 1980 catalogue.

GODWIN, William. *Of Population . . . An Answer to Mr. Malthus' Essay.* Boards. London, 1820. First edition. $750–$1,000.

GOETHE, Johann Wolfgang von. *Faust.* Translated into English rhyme by Robert Talbot. Contemporary calf. London, 1835. First edition of this translation. $100–$150. Lowell, Mass., 1840. Translated by A. Hayward. Cloth. First American edition of this translation. $200–$300. First part only of *Faust (Erster Theil):* (London), 1906. Doves Press. One of 300. $400–$500. This edition, as a set, with the second part of *Faust, Zweiter Theil,* issued by the press in 1910 in 250 copies: $600–$800. London, 1908. 31 color plates by Willy Pogany. Full vellum. One of 250 signed by Pogany. $250–$350. London, (1925). Illustrated by Harry Clarke. Half vellum. In dust jacket. One of 1,000 signed by Clarke. $400–$500.

GOETHE, Johann Wolfgang von. *Torquato Tasso: ein Schauspiel.* Printed in red and black. Vellum. London, 1913. Doves Press. One of 200. $1,200–$1,500. Another issue: One of 22 on vellum. $2,000–$3,000

GOGARTY, Oliver St. John. *Elbow Room.* Boards, linen spine. Dublin, 1939. Cuala Press. One of 450. In glassine dust jacket. $100–$125.

GOGARTY, Oliver St. John. *An Offering of Swans.* Introduction by William Butler Yeats. Boards and cloth, paper label. Dublin, 1923. Cuala Press. First edition. One of 300. In dust jacket. $75–$100.

GOGARTY, Oliver St. John. *Wild Apples.* Preface by William Butler Yeats. Boards and linen. Dublin. 1930. Cuala Press. One of 250. In dust jacket. $85–$100. Another issue: One of 50. $200.

GOLD, Michael. *Jews Without Money.* Cloth. New York, (1930). First edition. In dust jacket. $60–$75.

GOLD, Silver, Lead, and Copper Mines of Arizona. 40 pp., printed wrappers. (Philadelphia, 1867.) First edition. $500.

GOLDING, Louis. *Luigi of Catanzaro.* Wrappers. London, 1926. First edition. One of 100 signed. $175.

GOLDING, W.G. (William). *Poems.* Wrappers. London, 1934. First edition. Author's first book. Catalogued in 1981, with a Golding letter, at $4,000 by Joseph the Provider, booksellers.

GOLDING, William. *Free Fall.* Cloth. London, (1959). First edition. In dust jacket. $100–$125.

GOLDING, William. *Lord of the Flies.* Red cloth. London, (1954). First edition. In dust jacket. $400–$650. Author's first book. New York, (1954). First American edition. In dust jacket. $100–$125.

GOLDING, William. *Pincher Martin.* Cloth. London, (1956). First edition. In dust jacket. $150.

GOLDSBOROUGH, Charles W. *The United States' Naval Chronicle.* Vol. 1. (All published.) Pictorial boards. Washington City, 1824. First edition, with errata slip pasted on last page. $150–$250.

GOLDSCHMIDT, E.P. *The Printed Book of the Renaissance*. 7 plates. Cloth. Cambridge, 1930. One of 750. $150–$200.

GOLDSMITH, Oliver. *Overland in Forty–Nine*. 148 pp., pictorial boards. Detroit, 1896. First edition. $850.

GOLDSMITH, Oliver. *The Vicar of Wakefield*. 12 color illustrations and some in black and white by Arthur Rackham. Parchment. London, (1929). One of 575 signed by the artist. Boxed. $600–$900. London, 1903. Caradoc Press. Vellum. One of 14 on vellum. $1,000 and up. Another issue: One of 360. $150–$250.

GOLL, Claire. *The Diary of a Horse*. 4 illustrations by Chagall. Boards. New York, 1946. One of 320. $65.

GOLL, Yvan. *Jean Sans Terre (Landless John)*. Preface by Allen Tate. Translated by William Carlos Williams and others. Illustrated. Folio, boards. San Francisco, 1944. Grabhorn Press. One of 175. $300–$400.

GOOD, P.P. *The Family Flora and Materia Medica Botanica*. 96 colored plates. 2 vols., cloth. Elizabethtown, N.J., and Cambridge, Mass., (1845–54). $1,000 and up. New York, 1945. 48 colored plates. 2 vols., cloth. $600–$750.

GOOD, P.P. *A Materia Medica Animalia*. 24 color plates. Cloth. Cambridge, Mass., 1853. $150–$175.

GOODMAN, Mitchell. *Light from Under a Bushel*. Wrappers. Madison, 1968. Perishable Press. One of 100. $150–$200.

GOODMAN, Paul. *The Break-Up of Our Camp and Other Stories*. Boards. (Norfolk, 1949.) First edition. In dust jacket. $50–$75.

GOODMAN, Paul. *The Copernican Revolution*. Wrappers. Saugatuck, (1946). First edition. $75.

GOODMAN, Paul. *The Drama of Awareness*. Wrappers. No place, no date (late 1940's). First edition. $150.

GOODMAN, Paul. *The Facts of Life*. Cloth. New York, (1945). First edition. In dust jacket. $50–$75.

GOODMAN, Paul. *Growing Up Absurd*. Cloth. New York, (1960). First edition. In dust jacket. $35–$50.

GOODMAN, Paul. *Red Jacket*. Wrappers. (New York, 1955.) First edition. $50–$75.

GOODMAN, Paul. *The State of Nature*. Cloth. New York, (1946). First edition. In dust jacket. $50–$60.

GOODMAN, Paul. *Stop-light: 5 Dance Poems*. Cloth. Harrington Park, N.J., 1941. First edition. In first dust jacket (red and black without "Vinco" on the spine). $100–$150. In later jacket, $50–$75.

GOODMAN, Paul. *Ten Lyric Poems*. 8 leaves, self–wrappers. (New York, 1934.) First edition. $150–$200. Author's first book.

GOODNIGHT, Charles, III. *The Loving Brand Book*. Illustrated. Leather. Austin, 1965. One of 119. Boxed. $250.

GOODRICH, Samuel G. See Parley, Peter. Also see *The Vagabond*.

GOODSPEED, Charles E. *Angling in America*. Cloth. Boston, 1939. First edition. One of 755 signed. $175–$200.

GOODWIN, H.C. *Pioneer History; or Cortland County and the Border Wars of New York*. 3 portraits. Cloth. New York, 1859. First edition. $75–$100.

GOODWIN, Mrs. L.S. *The Gambler's Fate: A Story of California.* Woodcuts. 50 pp., pictorial wrappers. Boston, 1864. First edition. $80–$100.

GOODYEAR, W.A. *The Coal Mines of the Western Coast of the United States.* Cloth. San Francisco, 1877. First edition. $100–$150.

GOOKIN, Frederick W. *Daniel Gookin, 1612–1687.* 10 plates. Cloth. Chicago, 1912. First edition. One of 202. $85–$125.

GORDON, Alexander. *An Historical and Practical Treatise Upon Elemental Locomotion, by Means of Steam Carriages on Common Roads.* 14 plates. Gray boards. London, 1832. First edition. $200–$350. London, 1834. (Retitled *A Treatise, etc.*) $200–$250.

GORDON, Caroline. *Aleck Maury, Sportsman.* Green cloth. New York, 1934. First edition, first binding. In dust jacket. $200–$250.

GORDON, Caroline. *The Forest of the South.* Cloth. New York, 1945. First edition. In dust jacket. $50–$75.

GORDON, Caroline. *The Garden of Adonis.* Cloth. New York, 1937. First edition, first issue, with "A" on copyright page. In dust jacket. $75–$100.

GORDON, Caroline. *Green Centuries.* Cloth. New York, 1941. First edition. In dust jacket. $50–$75.

GORDON, Caroline. *None Shall Look Back.* Cloth. New York, 1937. First edition. In dust jacket. $75–$100.

GORDON, Caroline. *Penhally.* Cloth. New York, 1931. First edition. In dust jacket. $150–$250. Author's first book.

GORDON, J.E.H. *A Practical Treatise on Electric Lighting.* 23 plates, other illustrations. Cloth. London, 1884. First edition. $200.

GORDON, M.L. *Experiences in the Civil War.* Edited by Donald Gordon. Illustrated. Cloth. Boston, 1922. First edition. $50.

GORDON, Samuel. *Recollections of Old Milestown, Montana.* 19 plates. 42 pp., Miles City, Mont., 1918. First edition. $150.

GOREY, Edward. See: Moore, Merrill; Weary, Ogdred.

GOREY, Edward. *Amphigorey.* Cloth. New York, 1972. First edition. One of 50 signed. Boxed. With original watercolor. $600–$700. Trade edition: In dust jacket. $35–$45.

GOREY, Edward. *The Bug Book.* Wrappers. New York, (1959). First edition. $100–$125. New York, 1960. Boards. In dust jacket. $75–$100.

GOREY, Edward. *The Doubtful Guest.* Illustrated. Boards. Garden City, 1957. First edition. In dust jacket. $125–$150. London, 1958. Boards. In dust jacket. $60–$80.

GOREY, Edward. *The Gilded Bat.* Boards. New York, (1966). First edition. In dust jacket. $40–$60.

GOREY, Edward, *The Iron Tonic.* Decorated wrappers. New York, 1969. Albondocani Press. One of 200 signed. First edition. $150–$175.

GOREY, Edward. *The Listing Attic.* Illustrated. Boards. New York, 1954. First edition. In dust jacket. $125–$150.

GOREY, Edward. *The Object Lesson.* Decorated paper boards. Garden City, 1958. First edition. In dust jacket. $125–$150. (London, 1958.) First English edition. In dust jacket. $75.

GOREY, Edward. *The Sopping Thursday.* Cloth. New York, 1970. One of 26 copies, lettered, signed and in slipcase, with original unpublished drawing. $500–$600. Another issue: Wrappers. One of 300 signed. $35–$50.

GOREY, Edward. *The Unstrung Harp*. Illustrated by the author. Decorated boards. New York, (1953). First edition. In dust jacket. $100–$150. Author's first book.

GOREY, Edward. *The Vinegar Works*. 3 vols., boards, comprising the following titles: *The Gashlycrumb Tinies; The Insect God; The West Wing*. New York, 1963. In decorated slipcase. $75–$125.

GOREY, Edward. *The Willowdale Handcar*. Illustrated. Pictorial wrappers. Indianapolis, (1962). First edition. $50–$60.

GOREY, Edward. *The Wuggly Ump*. Illustrated. Oblong, pictorial boards. Philadelphia, (1963). First edition. In dust jacket. $60–$75.

GORHAM, George C. *The Story of the Attempted Assassination of Justice Field*. Half leather. No place, (about 1893). First edition. $35–$40.

GORIN, Franklin. *The Times of Long Ago*. Cloth. Louisville, 1929. First edition. $35–$50.

GORMAN, Herbert. *James Joyce*. Cloth. New York, 1924. First edition. In dust jacket. $50–$75. (Note: Contains new material by Joyce.)

GORRELL, J.R. *A Trip to Alaska*. 40 pp., printed green wrappers. Newton, Iowa, 1905. First edition. $150–$200.

GOSNELL, Harpur Allen (editor). *Before the Mast in the Clippers*. Composed of the Diaries of Charles A. Abbey. Illustrated. Boards. New York, 1937. Derrydale Press. First edition. One of 950. $150–$200.

GOSSE, Philip H. *Letters from Alabama*. Cloth. London, 1855. First edition. $250–$300. (Incorrectly dated as 1859 by Wright Howes; thanks to collector Harry Strange for correction from his copy.) London, 1895. Cloth. $150–$175.

GOTHEIN, M.L. *A History of Garden Art*. Illustrated, 2 vols., cloth. London or New York, (1928). First edition. In dust jacket. $300–$400.

GOUDY, Frederic W. *A Half Century of Type Design and Typography*. Illustrated, 2 vols., cloth. New York, 1946. First edition. One of 300. $150–$200.

GOUDY, Frederic W. *Typologia: Studies in Type Design and Type-Making*. Illustrated. Half morocco. Berkeley, 1940. First edition. One of 300 signed. Boxed. $150–$250. Trade edition: Cloth. $100–$110.

GOUDY Gaudeamus: In Celebration of the Dinner Given Frederic W. Goudy, etc. Folding title page by Bruce Rogers. Marbled boards and cloth. (New York), 1939. One of 195. $75–$100.

GOUGE, William M. *The Fiscal History of Texas*. Cloth. Philadelphia, 1852. First edition. $150–$200.

GOULD, E.W. *Fifty Years on the Mississippi*. Frontispiece. Pictorial cloth. St. Louis, 1889. First edition. $175–$200.

GOULD, John. *The Birds of Asia*. Edited by R.B. Sharpe. 530 hand-colored lithographed plates. 7 vols., folio, half (or full) morocco. London, 1850–83. $65,000 in a 1981 catalogue. Also, $38,500 (A, 1978). (Compare: $18,000 at auction in 1972; $16,800 in 1968.)

GOULD, John. *The Birds of Australia*. 681 hand-colored lithographed plates. 8 vols., folio morocco (including supplement volume). London, 1840-69. $37,400 (A, 1977). (Compare: $18,750 at auction in 1972; $16,250 in 1971.)

GOULD, John. *The Birds of Great Britain*. 367 hand-colored lithographed plates. 5 vols., half morocco. London, 1862–73. $15,000 (A, 1979); $16,000 (A, 1978).

GOULD, John. *Birds of New Guinea and the Adjacent Papuan Islands.* 320 hand-colored lithographed plates. 5 vols., folio half morocco. London, 1875–88. $37,000 and $35,000 (A, 1979). (Compare: $12,500 at auction in 1970.)

GOULD, Stephen. *The Alamo City Guide.* Illustrated. Pictorial wrappers. (San Antonio), 1882. $950 (in a Texas dealer's 1980 catalogue).

GOULDING, F.R. *Marooner's Island.* Frontispiece. Cloth. Philadelphia, 1869. First edition. $150–$200.

GOULDING, F.R. *Robert and Harold; or, The Young Marooners on the Florida Coast.* Cloth. Philadelphia, 1852. First edition. $200–$300.

GOULDING, F.R. *The Young Marooners on the Florida Coast.* 6 engraved plates. Decorated red cloth. London, 1853. First English edition (of *Robert and Harold; or, The Young Marooners on the Florida Coast*). $200 and up. Philadelphia, 1867. 10 plates. Cloth. New and enlarged edition (of *Robert and Harold*). First printing, with 1866 copyright. $100–$200.

GOVE, Capt. Jesse A. *The Utah Expedition, 1857–58.* 5 plates. Half cloth. Concord, N.H., 1928. First edition. $50–$75. Another issue: One of 50 on large paper. $200–$300.

GOYEN, William. *The House of Breath.* Cloth. New York, (1950). First edition. In dust jacket. $50–$75. Author's first book.

GRABHORN, Edwin. *Figure Prints of Old Japan.* 52 reproductions. Boards. San Francisco, 1959. Grabhorn printing. Book Club of California. One of 400. In dust jacket. $400–$600.

GRABHORN, Edwin. *The Fine Art of Printing.* Stiff wrappers. (San Francisco), 1933. Grabhorn printing. One of 50 for the Roxburghe Club. $150.

GRABHORN, Edwin. *Landscape Prints of Old Japan.* 52 full-color plates. Boards. San Francisco, 1960. Grabhorn printing. Book Club of California. One of 450. $400–$600.

GRABHORN, Jane. *A Commonplace Book for Typophiles.* Boards. New York, 1961. First edition. One of 360. $75–$100.

GRABHORN, Jane Bissell (editor). *A California Gold Rush Miscellany.* Colored plates, folding map. Folio, boards. (San Francisco), 1934. Grabhorn printing. First edition. One of 550. $75–$100.

GRABHORN, Robert. *A Short Account of the Life and Work of Wynkyn de Worde.* San Francisco, 1949. Grabhorn Press. One of 375. $300–$500.

GRACE Darling. 4 pp. (foolscap folded to form pamphlet). Carlisle, England, (1843). (By William Wordsworth.) First edition. $250 and up. (Note: An unauthorized, undated reprint bearing a Newcastle imprint also exists.)

GRACIE, Archibald. *The Truth About Chickamauga.* Plates, folding maps. Cloth. Boston, 1911. First edition. $50.

GRAHAM, G.A. *The Irish Wolfhound.* Cloth. Dursley, Ireland, 1885. First edition. $8,000–$12,000. Also, see Hogan, Edmund, and Graham for reprint edition of 1939.

GRAHAM, J.D. *A Lunar Tidal Wave in Lake Michigan.* 3 plates. Wrappers. Chicago, 1860. First edition. $75–$125.

GRAHAM, Maria. *Journal of a Residence in Chile During the Year 1822 and a Voyage from Chile to Brazil in 1823.* 14 colored plates. Half calf. London, 1824. First edition. $400–$500.

GRAHAM, R.B. Cunninghame. *The District of Menteith.* Illustrated, including an original etching by Sir D. Y. Cameron. Folio, half calf. Stirling [Scotland], 1930. One of 250 signed. In dust jacket. Boxed. $200–$250.

GRAHAM, R.B. Cunninghame. *Notes on the District of Menteith.* Printed gray wrappers. London, 1895. First edition, first issue. $125–$150.

GRAHAM, Tom. *Hike and the Aeroplane.* Colored illustrations by Arthur Hutchins. Decorated cloth. New York, (1912). (By Sinclair Lewis.) First edition, first issue, with "August, 1912" on copyright page. In dust jacket. $750–$1,000. Lacking jacket, $500–$600. Also, $425 (A, 1976); $350 (A, 1975). Sinclair Lewis' first book.

GRAHAM, W.A. *The Custer Myth.* Illustrated. Cloth. Harrisburg, (1953). First edition. In dust jacket. $50–$75.

GRAHAM, W.A. *Major Reno Vindicated.* 30 pp., wrappers. Hollywood, 1935. First edition. $75–$100. Limited issue: Full leather. One of 100 signed. $150–$200.

GRAHAM, W.A. (editor). *The Official Record of a Court of Inquiry Convened . . . By Request of Major Marcus A. Reno to Investigate His Conduct at the Battle of the Little Big Horn, etc.* Multigraphed, 2 vols., folio, cloth. Pacific Palisades, Calif., 1951. One of 125. $350–$500.

GRAHAME, Kenneth. *Dream Days.* Cloth. New York, 1899 (actually 1898). First edition, first issue, with 15 pages of ads at end dated 1898. $75–$125. London and New York, (1902). Illustrated by Maxfield Parrish. $75–$125. London, (1930). Illustrated by Ernest H. Shepard. Boards and vellum. One of 275 signed. Boxed. $400–$450.

GRAHAME, Kenneth. *The Golden Age.* Cloth. London, 1895. First edition. $100–$175. London, 1900 (actually 1899). Illustrated by Maxfield Parrish. Cloth. $100–$125. London, (1928). Illustrated by Ernest H. Shepard. Boards and vellum. One of 275 signed. $150–$200. Trade edition: In dust jacket. $50–$60.

GRAHAME, Kenneth. *Pagan Papers.* Title page designed by Aubrey Beardsley. Cloth. London, 1894. First edition. One of 450. $200–$225. Author's first book.

GRAHAME, Kenneth. *The Wind in the Willows.* Frontispiece by Graham Robertson. Pictorial cloth. London, (1908). First edition. In dust jacket. $1,250–$3,500(!) Also, $3,500 (A, 1977)—a remarkably fine copy. Lacking jacket but relatively fine, $500 and up. New York, 1908. Cloth. First American edition. $150–$200. London, (1931). Illustrated by Ernest H. Shepard. Map. Gray boards and cloth. One of 200 signed. In dust jacket. Boxed. $750–$850. New York, 1940. Limited Editions Club. Edited by A. A. Milne. Illustrated by Arthur Rackham. Boards and cloth. Boxed. $1,000. London, 1951. Illustrated by Rackham. Full white calf. One of 500. Boxed. $600–$850. London, (1964). Illustrated by Rackham. Calf. $300–$400.

GRANT, Blanche C. (editor). *Kit Carson's Own Story.* Plates. 138 pp., wrappers. Taos, 1926. First edition. $75–$85.

GRANT, Maxwell. *The Living Shadow.* Pictorial boards. New York, (1933). (By Walter B. Gibson.) First edition. $100–$125.

GRANT, Robert. *Jack Hall, or The School Days of an American Boy.* Illustrated by F.G. Attwood. Pictorial cloth. Boston, 1888. First edition. $35–$50.

GRANT, U.S. *General Orders, No. 67.* (Announcing the death of Lincoln and the succession of Johnson.) Sewed. Washington, 1868. $100.

GRANT, U.S. *General Orders, No. 74.* 43 pp., sewed. Washington, 1868. $100.

GRANT, U.S. *Message Communicating the Report and Journal of Proceedings of the Commission Appointed to Obtain Concessions from the Sioux Indians.* 90 pp., sewed. Washington, 1876. $100–$125.

GRANT, U.S. *Personal Memoirs.* 2 vols., three-quarters leather. New York, 1885–86. First edition. Large paper issue. $150–$200. Trade edition: Cloth. $20–$30. Half leather, $25–$50.

GRANVILLE, Austyn. *The Fallen Race*. Cloth. Chicago, 1892. First edition. $75–$100.

GRAU, Shirley Ann. *The Black Prince and Other Stories*. Boards. New York, 1955. First edition. In dust jacket. $50–$100. Author's first book.

GRAVES, H.A. *Andrew Jackson Potter, the Noted Parson of the Texan Frontier*. Portrait. Cloth. Nashville, 1881. First edition. $300–$500. Nashville, 1882. Second edition. $150–$300. Nashville, 1883. Third edition. $100–$150. Nashville, 1888. $75–$100.

GRAVES, H.A. (compiler). *Reminiscences and Events of Rev. John Wesley De Vilbiss*. Cloth. Galveston, 1886. First edition. $150–$300.

GRAVES, John. *Goodbye to a River*. Cloth. New York, 1960. First edition. In dust jacket. $35–$50. Author's first book.

GRAVES, Richard S. *Oklahoma Outlaws*. Illustrated. 131 pp., pictorial red wrappers. (Oklahoma City, 1915.) First edition. $50–$75.

GRAVES, Robert. See Riding, Laura (and Graves).

GRAVES, Robert. *Adam's Rib*. Wood engravings by James Metcalf. Brick-red cloth. (London, 1955.) Trianon Press. First edition. One of 250 signed. In dust jacket. Boxed. $200–$250. One of 26 (A to Z). $300–$400. Trade edition: Cloth. In dust jacket. $20.

GRAVES, Robert. *Beyond Giving: Poems*. Wrappers. (London), 1969. First edition. One of 536 signed. $100–$125.

GRAVES, Robert. *But It Still Goes On*. Bright-green cloth. London, (1930). First edition, first state, with reference to "The Child She Bare" on page 157. In dust jacket. $200–$250. Second state, corrected page 157 tipped in. In dust jacket. $100–$125.

GRAVES, Robert. *Colophon to Love Respelt*. Printed wrappers. (London), 1967. First edition. One of 350 signed. In dust jacket. $60–$75.

GRAVES, Robert. *Country Sentiment*. Light-blue boards. London, (1920). First edition. In dust jacket. $150–$200. New York, 1920. First American edition. In dust jacket: $75–$100.

GRAVES, Robert. *The English Ballad*. Cloth. London, 1927. First edition. $75–$125.

GRAVES, Robert. *Fairies and Fusiliers*. Wine-red cloth. London, (1917). First edition. In dust jacket. $250–$350. Second impression: (London, 1919.) Bright-red cloth. $100–$150.

GRAVES, Robert. *The Feather Bed*. Decorated pink boards. Richmond (England), 1923. Hogarth Press. First edition. One of 250 signed. $350–$400.

GRAVES, Robert. *Goliath and David*. Wrappers. (London, 1916.) First edition. (200 copies printed.) $500–$600. Signed copy, $750.

GRAVES, Robert. *Good-bye to All That: An Autobiography*. Illustrated. Salmon-pink cloth. London, (1929). First edition, first state, with poem by Siegfried Sassoon on pages 341–43. In dust jacket. $400–$500. Also $350 (A, 1981). Second state, with Sassoon poem removed and erratum slip at 398–99. In dust jacket. $200–$250. New York. (1930). Red cloth. First American edition. In dust jacket. $150–$200. London, 1957. Cloth. First revised edition. In dust jacket. $50–$65.

GRAVES, Robert. *Impenetrability or the Proper Habit of English*. Light-blue boards. London, 1926. Hogarth Press. First edition. $60–$85.

GRAVES, Robert. *John Kemp's Wager: A Ballad Opera*. White boards. Oxford, 1925. First edition. $75–$100. Another issue: Boards, parchment spine. One of 100 signed. In dust jacket. $200–$300.

GRAVES, Robert. *Lars Porsena, or The Future of Swearing and Improper Language.* Plum-colored boards, paper labels. London, (1927). First edition, with 16 pages of ads. $75. New York, (1927). Blue or olive-green cloth. First American edition. In dust jacket. $75. London, 1972. Buckram. One of 100 signed. In acetate dust jacket. Boxed. $100–$125.

GRAVES, Robert. *Lawrence and the Arabs.* Illustrated. Mustard-colored (orange) cloth. London, (1927). First edition. In dust jacket. $100–$150.

GRAVES, Robert. *Love Respelt.* Illuminated by Aemilia Laracuen. Cloth. London, (1965). First edition. One of 250 signed. In dust jacket. $50–$60. One of 30 out of series copies. $50–$60.

GRAVES, Robert. *Love Respelt Again.* Cloth. Garden City, (1969). First American edition. One of 1,000 signed. In dust jacket. $50–$60.

GRAVES, Robert. *Man Does, Woman Is.* Buff linen, blue cloth spine. London, 1964. First edition. One of 175 signed. In glassine dust jacket. $125–$150. Another issue: One of 26 (A to Z). $200–$225. Trade edition: Cloth. In dust jacket. $10–$20.

GRAVES, Robert. *Mrs. Fisher, or The Future of Humour.* Plum-colored boards, paper labels. London, 1928. First edition. In dust jacket. $100–$150.

GRAVES, Robert. *Mock Beggar Hall.* Gray pictorial boards. London, 1924. Hogarth Press. First edition. $250–$450. (Most copies seen are shabby.)

GRAVES, Robert. *The More Deserving Cases.* Portrait. Red morocco. (Marlborough, England), 1962. Marlborough College Press. First edition. One of 400 signed. $100–$125. Another issue: Blue buckram. One of 350 signed. $100.

GRAVES, Robert. *My Head! My Head!* Decorated red cloth, black spine. London, 1925. First edition. In dust jacket. $250. New York, 1925. Boards. First American edition. In dust jacket. $150–$200.

GRAVES, Robert. *On English Poetry.* Cream-colored boards and cloth, paper label. New York, 1922. First edition, first issue, with misprints "that" for "than that" on page 33 and "have" for "how" on page 145. In dust jacket. $150–$175. (An "earlier" binding in orange boards was catalogued by a Chicago dealer at $450 in 1980.) London, (1922). Bright yellow cloth. First English edition. first issue (with misprints), first binding. In dust jacket. $125–$150. Second state binding, buff boards. $75–$100.

GRAVES, Robert. *Over the Brazier.* Pictorial gray wrappers. London, 1916. Poetry Bookshop. First edition. $600–$750. Also, $350 (A, 1977). Author's first book. London, (1920). Gray boards, blue cloth spine. Second edition. In dust jacket. $200–$300. Lacking jacket, $75–$100.

GRAVES, Robert. *The Pier-Glass.* Portrait. Yellow decorated boards. London, (1921). First edition. (500 printed.) In dust jacket. $200–$300. New York, 1921. Boards. First American edition. In dust jacket. $75–$125.

GRAVES, Robert. *Poems 1953.* Bright-green boards, white cloth spine. London, (1953). First edition. One of 250 signed. In dust jacket. $150. Trade edition: Sea-green cloth. In dust jacket. $75.

GRAVES, Robert. *Poems (1914–1927).* White boards, parchment spine. London, 1927. One of 115 signed. In dust jacket. $500–$600. Also, $350 (A, 1980).

GRAVES, Robert. *Poems (1914–1926).* Slick white cloth with black cobbled design. London, (1927). First edition. In dust jacket. $200–$250.

GRAVES, Robert. *Poems 1929.* Yellow-green cloth. London, 1929. Seizin Press. First edition. One of 225 signed. $150–$250.

GRAVES, Robert. *Poems, 1926–1930.* Maroon cloth, paper labels. London, (1932). First edition. In dust jacket. $100–$125.

GRAVES, Robert. *Poetic Unreason and Other Studies.* Dark-blue cloth, paper label. (London, 1925.) First edition. In dust jacket. $100–$125.

GRAVES, Robert. *The Real David Copperfield.* Blue cloth. London, (1933). First edition. In dust jacket. $100–$125.

GRAVES, Robert. *Seventeen Poems Missing from "Love Respelt."* Wrappers over boards. (London), 1966. First edition. One of 330 signed. $50–$75.

GRAVES, Robert. *The Shout.* Decorated gray boards. London, 1929. First edition. One of 530 signed. In dust jacket. $125–$250.

GRAVES, Robert. *T. E. Lawrence to His Biographer, Robert Graves.* Buff cloth. New York, 1938. First edition. One of 500 signed by Graves (issued with Liddell Hart's book of the same title) with Doubleday imprint. Boxed (with the Liddell Hart book). $250. Also, $150 (A, 1971). London, (1939). Red cloth. First English edition. One of 500 signed by Graves. In dust jacket. Issued boxed as a set with the Liddell Hart book. $250.

GRAVES, Robert. *Ten Poems More.* Boards and green morocco. Paris, 1930. Hours Press. First edition, with misprints on pages 7, 10, and 15. One of 200 signed. In transparent dust jacket. $200–$300.

GRAVES, Robert. *To Whom Else?* Pictorial boards and cloth. Deya, Mallorca, 1931. Seizin Press. First edition. One of 200 signed. $175–$250.

GRAVES, Robert. *Treasure Box.* Light-blue wrappers. (London, 1919.) First edition. One of 200. $500–$650. (Most copies sold are signed.)

GRAVES, Robert. *Welchman's Hose.* Wood engravings by Paul Nash. Decorated boards and cloth. London, 1925. First edition. One of 525. In transparent dust jacket. $225–$300.

GRAVES, Robert. *Whipperginny.* Decorated magenta boards. London, (1923). First edition. In dust jacket. $200–$400. New York, 1923. Boards. First American edition. In dust jacket. $100.

GRAVES, Robert, and Lindsay, Jack (editors). *Loving Mad Tom: Bedlamite Verses of the 16th and 17th Centuries.* Illustrated. Boards and vellum. London, (1927). Fanfrolico Press. First edition. One of 375. $150–$250.

GRAVES, W.W. *Annals of Osage Mission.* Illustrated. Cloth. St. Paul, Kan., 1935. First edition. $100–$200.

GRAY, Asa. *Elements of Botany.* Half leather. New York, 1836. First edition. $500–$600.

GRAY, Asa. *A Manual of the Botany of the Northern United States.* Cloth. Boston, 1848. First edition. $100–$150.

GRAY, David. *The Sporting Works of David Gray.* Illustrated. 3 vols., cloth. New York, 1929. Derrydale Press. First edition. One of 750. Boxed. $150–$175.

GRAY, Henry. *Anatomy, Descriptive and Surgical.* Cloth. London, 1858. First edition. $750–$1,000. Philadelphia, 1859. Illustrated, including color. Calf. $400–$500.

GRAY, John W. *The Life of Joseph Bishop.* Cloth. Nashville, 1858. First edition. $150–$200.

GRAYDON, Alexander. *Memoirs of a Life, Chiefly Passed in Pennsylvania, Within the Last 60 Years.* Cloth. Harrisburg, 1811. First edition. with errata leaf. $150–$175. Edinburgh, 1822. Boards and cloth. First English edition. $100–$125.

GREAT Eastern Gold Mining Co. (The). Map. 7 pp., wrappers. New York, 1880. $150–$200.

GREAT Steam-Duck (The) . . . *An Invention of Aerial Navigation.* By a Member of the LLBB. 32 pp. Louisville, 1841. First edition. $1,500 and up.

GREAT Trans-Continental Railroad Guide. Wrappers. Chicago, 1869. First edition. $200–$250.

GREAT Western Almanac for 1848. Wrappers. Philadelphia, (1847). First edition. $300–$350.

GREAVES, Richard. *Brewster's Millions.* Red cloth. Chicago, 1903. (By George Barr McCutcheon.) First edition. $35–$50.

GRECE, Charles F. *Facts and Observations Respecting Canada, and the United States of America.* Contemporary leather. London, 1819. First edition. $200–$350.

GREELEY, Horace. *An Overland Journey from New York to San Francisco.* Cloth. New York, 1860. First edition. $75–$150.

GREEN, Anna Katharine. *The Circular Study.* Green cloth. New York, 1900. First edition, first binding. $200–$300.

GREEN, Anna Katharine. *Hand and Ring.* Cloth or wrappers. New York, 1883. First edition. $75–$100.

GREEN, Anna Katharine. *The Leavenworth Case: A Lawyer's Story.* Plate. Terra-cotta cloth or wrappers. New York, 1878. First edition. $1,000–$1,250.

GREEN, Ben K. *Back to Back.* Boards. Austin, 1970. First edition. One of 850 signed. Boxed. $65–$125.

GREEN, Ben K. *The Color of Horses.* Illustrated in color. Half cloth and fabrikoid. Flagstaff, Ariz., (1974). First edition. One of 150 signed. Boxed. $200. Trade edition: In dust jacket. $35.

GREEN, Ben K. *The Last Trail Drive Through Downtown Dallas.* Illustrated. Half leather. Flagstaff, (1971). First edition. One of 100 signed and with a Joe Beeler drawing in ink and watercolor. Boxed. $350–$400. Trade edition: Cloth. In dust jacket. $25.

GREEN, Ben K. *The Shield Mares.* Boards. Austin, 1967. First edition. One of 750 signed. Boxed. $225.

GREEN, Ben K. *A Thousand Miles of Mustangin'.* Illustrated. Half cloth. Flagstaff, (1972). First edition. One of 150 signed. Boxed. $150–$175. Trade edition: Cloth. $75.

GREEN, Ben K. *Wild Cow Tales.* Illustrated. Cloth. New York, 1969. First edition. In dust jacket. $35. Another issue: One of 300 signed. $165.

GREEN, Henry. *Back.* Cloth. London, 1950. First edition. In dust jacket. $75- $100.

GREEN, Henry. *Blindness.* Cloth. New York, (1926). First American edition. In dust jacket. $100–$150. Author's first book.

GREEN, Henry. *Concluding.* Cloth. London, 1948. Hogarth Press. First edition. In dust jacket. $75.

GREEN, Henry. *Nothing.* Cloth. London, 1950. First edition. In dust jacket. $75.

GREEN, Jonathan S. *Journal of a Tour on the Northwest Coast of America in the Year 1829.* Edited by Edward Eberstadt. Boards, paper label. New York, 1915. First edition. One of 150. $300–$350. (Note: There were also 10 copies on Japan vellum, and they are of course more valuable.)

GREEN Mountain Boys (The). 2 vols., boards, paper labels. Montpelier, Vt., 1839. (By Daniel Pierce Thompson.) First edition, first issue, with publisher's name misspelled "Waltton" in copyright notice in Vol 2. $500–$750. Also, $550 (A, 1979).

GREEN, Mowbray A. *The Eighteenth Century Architecture of Bath*. Plates and plans. Buckram. Bath, England, 1904. One of 500. $200–$300.

GREEN, Thomas. *The Universal Herbal, or Botanical, Medical and Agricultural Dictionary*. Colored plates. 2 vols., contemporary half calf, gilt paneled spines. Liverpool, (1816–20). First edition. $1,000–$1,200.

GREEN, Thomas J. *Journal of the Texian Expedition Against Mier*. 11 plates, 2 plans. Cloth, New York, 1845. First edition. $350–$500.

GREEN, Thomas M. *The Spanish Conspiracy*. Cloth. Cincinnati, 1891. First edition. $100–$125.

GREENAN, Edith. *Of Una Jeffers*. 5 photographic illustrations. Cloth. Los Angeles, 1939. One of 250. In dust jacket. $150–$200.

GREENAWAY, Kate. See Harte, Bret; Mavor, William; Taylor, Jane and Ann.

GREENAWAY, Kate. *A Apple Pie*. Colored illustrations. Oblong, half cloth. London, (1886). First edition. $150–$200.

GREENAWAY, Kate. *Almanacks*. Illustrated in color by the author. Pictorial boards, wrappers, or cloth. London, (1883–95 and 1897, with no *Almanack* issued in 1896). First editions of these early Greenaway books in fine condition, with dust jackets if so issued, are continuing to rise in price. Complete collections of the *Almanacks* now run into the $3,000–$4,000 range, and the average price for a fine copy is around $200. Very good and acceptable copies can be found for considerably less, however, by patient and careful search. Reprints and twentieth century reproductions are also available at lower prices. This is also the case with Miss Greenaway's other popular illustrated books.

GREENAWAY, Kate. *Kate Greenaway's Alphabet*. Colored illustrations. Pictorial boards. London, (1885?). First edition, first issue. $150–$200.

GREENAWAY, Kate. *Kate Greenaway's Birthday Book for Children*. Verses by Mrs. Sale Barker, 382 illustrations (12 plates in color). Pictorial boards or cloth. London, (1880). First edition. $200–$250. (Sometimes catalogued or listed in the auction records under Mrs. Barker's name.)

GREENAWAY, Kate. *Kate Greenaway's Book of Games*. 24 plates. Pictorial boards. London, (1889). First edition. $200–$250. Signed copy, $350.

GREENAWAY, Kate. *Kate Greenaway Pictures*. Portrait frontispiece, 20 pictures in color. Cloth. London, 1921. In dust jacket. $175–$225.

GREENAWAY, Kate. *Marigold Garden*. Illustrated in color by the author. Pictorial boards and cloth. (London, 1885.) First edition. $200–$250.

GREENAWAY, Kate. *Under the Window: Pictures and Rhymes for Children*. Colored illustrations. Pictorial boards. London, (1878). First edition, first issue, with printer's imprint on back of title page ad with reading "End of Contents" at foot of page 14. In dust jacket. $400. Signed copy, $575.

GREENAWAY, Kate (illustrator). *Dame Wiggins of Lee and Her Seven Wonderful Cats*. Edited by John Ruskin. 22 woodcuts. Gray cloth. London, (1885). First edition with the Greenaway illustrations. $200–$250.

GREENAWAY, Kate (illustrator). *A Day in a Child's Life*. Music by Myles B. Foster. Color illustrations. Pictorial boards in color. London, (1881). First edition. $150–$225.

GREENAWAY, Kate (illustrator). *Language of Flowers*. Colored illustrations. Boards. London, (1884). First edition. $150–$225.

GREENAWAY, Kate (illustrator). *The "Little Folks" Painting Book*. Stories and verses by George Weatherly. Pictorial wrappers. London, (1879). First edition. $150–$250.

GREENAWAY, Kate (illustrator). *Mother Goose or The Old Nursery Rhymes*. Illustrated in color by Kate Greenaway. Various colors of cloth, or wrappers. London, (1881). First edition. Cloth: In dust jacket. $250–$300. Inscribed copies, $400–$500. Wrappers: Approximately the same values if not defective.

GREENAWAY, Kate, and Crane, Walter. *The Quiver of Love*. Colored illustrations. Cloth. (London, 1876.) Marcus Ward & Co. First edition. $400–$500, possibly more if in fine condition.

GREENBURG, Dan W. *Sixty Years: A Brief Review. The Cattle Industry in Wyoming, etc*. Illustrated. 73 pp., pictorial wrappers. Cheyenne, 1932. First edition (so stated). $175–$200.

GREENE, Graham. See Bey, Pilaff.

GREENE, Graham. *Babbling April: Collected Poems*. Boards. Oxford, 1925. First edition. In dust jacket. $500–$750. Also, with review slip, $550 (A, 1977). Lacking jacket, $200–$300. Also, $155 (A, 1976). Author's first book.

GREENE, Graham. *The Bear Fell Free*. Cloth. (London, 1935.) First edition. One of 285 signed. In dust jacket. $250–$300.

GREENE, Graham. *Brighton Rock*. Red cloth. London, (1938). First edition. In dust jacket. $125–$175.

GREENE, Graham. *Confidential Agent*. Cloth. London, 1939. First edition. In dust jacket. $150–$200.

GREENE, Graham. *A Gun for Sale*. Cloth. London, (1936). First edition. In dust jacket. $200–$225.

GREENE, Graham. *The Heart of the Matter*. Cloth. New York, 1948. First American edition. In dust jacket. $75–$125.

GREENE, Graham. *It's a Battlefield*. Black cloth. London, (1934). First edition. In dust jacket. $250–$300. Lacking jacket, $200.

GREENE, Graham. *The Lawless Roads*. Cloth. London, 1939. First edition. In dust jacket with Book Society wraparound band. $1,000–$1,250.

GREENE, Graham. *The Man Within*. Cloth. London, (1929). First edition. In dust jacket. $1,000–$1,250. Also, $1,000 (A, 1981). Garden City, 1929. Green cloth. First American edition. In dust jacket. $150–$175.

GREENE, Graham. *May We Borrow Your Husband?* Decorated boards. London, (1967). First edition. One of 500 signed. In acetate jacket. $150–$175.

GREENE, Graham. *The Name of Action*. Cloth. London, (1930). First edition. In dust jacket. $150–$175.

GREENE, Graham. *Our Man in Havana*. Cloth. London, (1958). First edition. In dust jacket. $125–$150.

GREENE, Graham. *The Power and the Glory*. Cloth. London, 1940. First edition. In dust jacket. $150–$175.

GREENE, Graham. *The Quiet American*. Cloth. London, (1955). First American edition. In dust jacket with wraparound band. $75–$100.

GREENE, Graham. *Rumour at Nightfall*. Red cloth. London, 1931. First edition. In dust jacket. $125–$175.

GREENE, Graham. *Stamboul Train*. Cloth. London, (1932). First edition. In dust jacket. $600–$750.

GREENE, Graham. *The Third Man*. Cloth. London, (1950). First edition. In dust jacket. $200. New York, 1950. Cloth. First American edition. In dust jacket. $50–$75.

GREENE, Max. *The Kanzas Region.* 2 maps. Printed wrappers, or cloth. New York, 1856. First edition. Wrappers: $200. Cloth: $150.

GREENE, Talbot. *American Nights' Entertainment.* Purple cloth. Jonesborough, Tenn., 1860. First edition. $100–$125.

GREENEWALT, Crawford H. *Hummingbirds.* Color plates. Morocco. Garden City, (1960). First edition. One of 500 signed. Boxed. $675–$750. Trade edition: Cloth. In dust jacket. $300–$400.

GREENHOW, Robert. *The Geography of Oregon and California.* Folding map. Wrappers. Boston, 1845. Later edition of his *Memoir.* $300–$400.

GREENHOW, Robert. *The History of Oregon and California.* Map. Calf. Boston, 1844. Enlarged edition of his *Memoir.* $175–$225. Boston, 1845. Wrappers. "Second edition." $200.

GREENHOW, Robert. *Memoir, Historical and Political.* Folding map. Sewed. Washington, 1840. First edition. (Senate Document 174.) $200.

GREER, James K. *Bois d'Arc to Barb'd Wire.* Plates, maps. Pictorial cloth. Dallas, 1936. First edition. In dust jacket. $150–$175.

GREER, James K. *Colonel Jack Hays: Texas Frontier Leader and California Builder.* Illustrated. Cloth. New York, 1952. First edition. In dust jacket. $100–$125.

GREER, James K. (editor). *A Texas Ranger and Frontiersman.* Illustrated. Cloth. Dallas, 1932. First edition. In dust jacket. $100–$125.

GREGG, Alexander. *History of the Old Cheraws.* 4 maps, illustrated. Cloth. New York, 1867. First edition. $50–$75.

GREGG, Asa. *Personal Recollections of the Early Settlement of Wapsinonoc Township and the Murder of Atwood by the Indians.* Tables. Dark purple wrappers. West Liberty, Iowa, (about 1875–1880). First edition. $750–$1,000.

GREGG, Josiah. *Commerce of the Prairies.* 2 maps (one folding), 6 plates. 2 vols., brown pictorial cloth. New York, 1844. First edition, first issue, with only New York in imprint. $1,000–$1,500. Second issue, with imprint "New York and London." $600–$800. (Note: There were also issued in 1844 a small number of first edition copies in black cloth, gilt, with gilt edges, for presentation by the author. Value: $1,500–$2,000.) New York, 1845. 2 vols., cloth. Second edition. $400–$600.

GREGOIRE, H. *An Enquiry Concerning the Intellectual and Moral Faculties, and Literature of Negroes.* Translated by D.B. Warden. Boards. Brooklyn, 1810. First American edition. $350–$500.

GREGORY, Horace. *Chelsea Rooming House.* Cloth. New York, (1930). First edition. In dust jacket. $75–$100. Author's first book.

GREGORY, Isabella Augusta Persse, Lady. *A Book of Saints and Wonders.* Boards and linen. Dundrum, Ireland, 1906. Dun Emer Press. One of 200. $100–$125.

GREGORY, Isabella Augusta Persse, Lady. *Coole.* Boards and linen. Dublin, 1931. Cuala Press. One of 250. In tissue dust jacket. $150–$175.

GREGORY, Isabella Augusta Persse, Lady. *The Kiltartan Poetry Book.* Boards and linen. Dundrum, Ireland, 1918. Cuala Press. One of 400. $100–125.

GREGORY, Isabella Augusta Persse, Lady. *My First Play.* Boards and cloth. London, 1930. First edition. One of 500 signed. In dust jacket. $50–$75. One of 30 presentation copies, signed. $200.

GREGORY, John. *Industrial Resources of Wisconsin.* Cloth. Milwaukee, 1855. First complete edition. $300–$350.

GREGORY, Joseph W. *Gregory's Guide for California Travellers via the Isthmus of Panama.* 46 pp., wrappers. New York, 1850. First edition. $1,500.

GREGORY, Samuel. *History of Mexico; with An Account of the Texan Revolution.* Map (not in all copies). 100 pp., pictorial wrappers. Boston, 1847. First edition. $150–$200. Issue without map: $100–$125.

GREGORY, Thomas Jefferson, and others. *History of Solano and Napa Counties, California.* Illustrated. Maps. Three-quarters leather. Los Angeles, 1912. $100–$125.

GREVILLE, Charles C.F. *The Greville Memoirs.* Edited by Lytton Strachey and Roger Fulford. Frontispieces. 8 vols., buckram. London, 1938. One of 630. $350–$450.

GREVILLE, Fulke, Lord Brooke. *Caelica.* Edited by Una Ellis-Fermor. Boards and leather. Newtown, Wales, 1936. Gregynog Press. One of 225. $400–$500. Another issue: Blue morocco, specially decorated by the Gregynog bindery. $1,000 and up.

GREVILLE, Fulke, Lord Brooke. *The Life of the Renowned Sir Philip Sidney.* Portrait. Limp vellum, silk ties. Bedford Park, Chiswick, England, 1906. One of 11 on vellum. $1,000 and up.

GREY, Zane. *American Anglers in Australia.* Illustrated. Cloth. London, (1937). First English edition. In dust jacket. $250–$300.

GREY, Zane. *Betty Zane.* Illustrated by the author. Cloth. New York, (1903). First edition. $400–$500. Author's first book.

GREY, Zane. *The Day of the Beast.* Cloth. New York, (1922). First edition. In dust jacket. $150. Without jacket, $60.

GREY, Zane. *The Last of the Plainsmen.* Illustrated. Cloth. New York, 1908. First edition. In dust jacket. $250–$350.

GREY, Zane. *The Rainbow Trail.* Cloth. New York, 1915. First edition. In dust jacket. $75–$125.

GREY, Zane. *Riders of the Purple Sage.* Illustrated. Cloth. New York, 1912. First edition, with "Published January 1912" on copyright page. In dust jacket. $200–$300.

GREY, Zane. *Tales of Fishes.* Half morocco. New York, (1919). First edition. $250. Clothbound issue: In dust jacket. $100–$150. (Signed or inscribed copies more, of course.) Other Zane Grey fishing titles in similar format and similarly valued include the following: *Tales of Fishing Virgin Seas.* New York, 1925; *Tales of Fresh-Water Fishing.* New York, 1928; *Tales of Lonely Trails.* New York, (1922); *Tales of Southern Rivers.* New York, (1924); *Tales of Swordfish and Tuna.* New York, 1927; *Tales of Tahitian Waters.* New York, 1931; *Tales of the Angler's El Dorado, New Zealand.* New York, 1926.

GREY, Zane. *Tappan's Burro.* Cloth. New York, (1923). First edition. In dust jacket. $150.

GREYSLAER: A Romance of the Mohawk. 2 vols., cloth, paper labels on spines. New York, 1840. (By Charles Fenno Hoffman.) First edition, with errata slip in first volume. $350–$450.

GRIEVE, C.M. See: Glen, Duncan; MacDiarmid, Hugh; Mc'Diarmid, Hugh.

GRIEVE, Maud. *A Modern Herbal.* 96 plates. 2 vols., cloth. London, (1931). First edition. In dust jackets. $400–$500. New York, 1931. 2 vols., cloth. $400–$500.

GRIFFIN, John H. *The Devil Rides Outside.* Cloth. Fort Worth, 1952. First edition. In dust jacket. $50–$75.

GRIFFITH, George. *A Honeymoon in Space.* Illustrated. Pictorial cloth. London, 1901. First edition. $100–$125.

GRIFFITH, Thomas. *Sketches of the Early History of Maryland.* Frontispiece. Calf. Baltimore, 1821. First edition. $100–$150.

GRIFFITHS, D., Jr. *Two Years' Residence in the New Settlements of Ohio.* Frontispiece. Cloth. London, 1835. First edition. $600–$750.

GRILE, Dod. *Cobwebs: Being the Fables of Zambri, the Parsee.* Illustrated. Heavy pictorial printed wrappers, or boards. (London, about 1884.) "Fun" Office. (By Ambrose Bierce.) Reprint edition of *Cobwebs from an Empty Skull* (see entry following). $75–$100.

GRILE, Dod. *Cobwebs from an Empty Skull.* Illustrated. Blue, brown, or green cloth. London, 1874. (By Ambrose Bierce.) First edition. $250–$300.

GRILE, Dod. *The Fiend's Delight.* Purple-brown cloth. London, (1872). (By Ambrose Bierce.) First edition. $300–$350. Author's first book. New York, 1873. Brown or purple-brown cloth. First American edition, without publisher's ads. $100–$125.

GRILE, Dod. *Nuggets and Dust Panned Out in California.* Yellow pictorial wrappers. London, (1873). (By Ambrose Bierce.) First edition. $125–$150.

GRIMALDI, Joseph. See "Boz."

GRIMM, Jacob L.K. and W.K. *The Fairy Tales of the Brother Grimm.* Translated by Mrs. Edgar Lucas. Illustrated with color plates by Arthur Rackham. Vellum. London, 1909. One of 750 signed by Rackham. $1,000–$1,250. Trade edition: Cloth. $300–$400.

GRIMM, Jacob L.K. and W.K. *Hansel and Gretel and Other Stories.* Illustrated by Kay Nielsen. Boards. London, (about 1925). One of 600 signed by Nielsen. $1,250–$2,000. New York, 1925. Red cloth. First American edition. $550.

GRIMM, Jacob L.K. and W.K. *Little Brother and Little Sister.* Color plates by Arthur Rackham. Cloth. London, (1917). One of 525 signed by Rackham, with an extra plate. $1,250–$1,500. Also, $1,250 (A, 1981). Trade edition: Cloth. $200–$300.

GRIMM, Jacob L.K. and W.K. *Six Fairy Tales.* Illustrated by David Hockney. Folio, calf. London, 1970. Petersburg Press. One of 575 (Edition D), with folder of signed illustrations. $1,500–$2,000.

GRINNELL, George Bird. *American Game-Bird Shooting.* Illustrated. Cloth. New York, (1910). First edition. $75–$100.

GRINNELL, George Bird. *The Cheyenne Indians: Their History and Way of Life.* Illustrated. 2 vols., cloth. New Haven, 1923. First edition. $100–$125.

GRINNELL, George Bird. *The Fighting Cheyennes.* Maps. Cloth. New York, 1915. First edition. In dust jacket. $100–$150.

GRINNELL, George Bird. *The Indians of Today.* Illustrated. Folio, pictorial cloth. Chicago, 1900. First edition. $100–$125. London, (1900). Retitled *The North American Indians, etc.* $100.

GRINNELL, George Bird. *Two Great Scouts and Their Pawnee Battalion.* Map, illustrations. Cloth. Cleveland, 1928. First edition. $65–$75.

GRINNELL, Joseph. *Gold Hunting in Alaska.* Illustrated. Red boards and green cloth. Elgin, Ill., (1901). First edition. $75–$100.

GRINNELL, Joseph, and Storer, Tracy I. *Animal Life in the Yosemite.* Illustrations (some in color). Cloth. Berkeley, 1924. $75–$100.

GRINNELL, Joseph, and others. *The Game Birds of California.* 16 color plates, other illustrations. Cloth. Berkeley, 1918. $75–$100.

GRINNELL, Joseph, and others. *Vertebrate Natural History of a Section of Northern*

California Through the Lassen Peak Region. Folding colored map. Cloth. Berkeley, 1930. $50–$75.

GRISWOLD, David D. *Statistics of Chicago, Ills., Together with a Business Advertiser, and Mercantile Directory for July, 1843.* 24 pp., printed wrappers. (Chicago), 1843. First edition. $800–$1,000. Also, $500 (A, 1967).

GRISWOLD, N.W. *Beauties of California.* 18 color plates. Wrappers. San Francisco, 1883. First edition. $150–$175.

GRISWOLD, Rufus W. *The Republican Court.* Morocco. New York, 1856. First edition. $125–$150.

GRISWOLD, W.M. *A Descriptive List of Novels and Tales Dealing with American Country Life.* 52 pp., stitched, Cambridge, Mass., 1890. First edition. $50–$75.

GRISWOLD, Wayne. *Kansas Her Resources and Developments.* Illustrated. Printed wrappers. Cincinnati, 1871. First edition. $50–$60.

GRONOW, Rees Howell. *The Reminiscences and Recollections of Captain Gronow.* Illustrated. 2 vols., cloth. London, 1889. One of 875. $100–$125.

GROOS, J.J. *Report of the General Land Office.* 21 pp., wrappers. Houston, 1874. $100–$125. Houston, 1876. 27 pp., wrappers. $125–$150.

GROSART, A.B. (editor). *Occasional Issues of Unique and Very Rare Books.* 17 vols., half morocco. London, 1875–81. "Limited to a small number of copies." $1,000 and up.

GROSSMITH, George. *The Diary of a Nobody.* Illustrated by Weedon Grossmith. Light brown cloth. Bristol, England, (1892). First edition. $150–$200.

GROSZ, George. *Ecce Homo.* Illustrated. Boards. New York, 1965. First American edition. In dust jacket. $50–$65.

GROSZ, George. *George Grosz: Twelve Reproductions from His Original Lithographs.* Wrappers. Chicago, 1921. First edition. $100–$150.

GROUPED Thoughts and Scattered Fancies. Wrappers. Richmond, Va., 1845. (By William Gilmore Simms.) First edition. $200–$250.

GROVER, La Fayette (editor). *The Oregon Archives.* Printed yellow wrappers. Salem, 1853 (actually 1854). First edition. $750–$1,000. Also, $400 (A, 1969).

GRYLL Grange. By the Author of *Headlong Hall.* Cloth. London, 1861. (By Thomas Love Peacock.) First edition, with 4 pages of ads at end. $400–$600.

GUÉRIN, Maurice de. *The Centaur.* Translated by George B. Ives. Boards. (Montague, Mass.), 1915. One of 135. Bruce Rogers typography. $400–$500. Rebound in full morocco. Presentation copy, signed by Rogers. $700.

GUIDE, Gazetteer and Directory of Nebraska Railroads. Folding map, 6 plates. 210 pp., wrappers. Omaha, 1872. (By J.M. Wolfe.) First edition. $250–$350.

GUIDE for Emigrants to Minnesota (A). By a Tourist. Map. 16 pp., printed blue wrappers. St. Paul, 1857. First edition. $200–$300.

GUILD, Jo. C. *Old Times in Tennessee.* Green cloth. Nashville, 1878. First edition. $150–$200.

GUINEY, Louise Imogen. *"Monsieur Henri": A Footnote to French History.* Cloth. New York, 1892. First edition. One of 50 signed. $50–$75.

GUINEY, Louise Imogen. *Songs at the Start.* Half morocco. Boston, 1884. First edition. $100–$125. (Also issued in cloth.) Author's first book.

GUNN, Donald. *History of Manitoba from the Earliest Settlement to 1835.* Portrait. Cloth. Ottawa, 1880. First edition. $100–$125.

GUNN, Douglas. *San Diego: Climate, Resources, Topography, Production, etc.* 40 pp., plus 16 pp. of ads, printed wrappers. San Diego, 1886. Fourth edition (first 1886 edition). $400.

GUNN, Otis B. *New Map and Hand-Book of Kansas and the Gold-Mines.* Large map in color, folding into black cloth covers, and accompanied by text pamphlet (*Gunn's Map and Hand-Book, etc.),* bound in salmon-colored printed wrappers. Pittsburgh, 1859. First edition. $3,000–$3,500. Lacking the text pamphlet, $2,000–$2,500.

GUNN, Thom. *The Explorers.* Printed wrappers. Devon, England (1969). First edition. (100 copies issued.) One of 64 plain copies. $100–$110. Also, 20 with a poem in the author's hand, $125; 10 copies with three holograph poems, $150; 6 copies with 19 poems written out, $200.

GUNN, Thom. *A Geography.* Wrappers. Iowa City, 1966. First edition, signed. One of 220 signed. $50–$75.

GUNN, Thom. *Mandrakes.* Illustrated by Leonard Baskin. Half vellum. London, (1973). First edition. One of 150 signed. Boxed. $200.

GUNNISON, John W. *The Mormons; or, Latter-Day Saints, in the Valley of the Great Salt Lake.* Frontispiece. Dark-blue cloth. Philadelphia, 1852. First edition. $100–$150.

GUNSAULUS, Helen C. *The Clarence Buckingham Collection of Japanese Prints: The Primitives.* Plates. Folio, cloth. Chicago, (1955). One of 500. $600–$800.

GUNTER, Archibald Clavering. *Mr. Barnes of New York.* Cloth, or wrappers. New York, 1887. First edition, first issue, with perfect type in copyright notice. Wrappers: $125. Cloth: $75–$100.

GUTHRIE, A.B., Jr. *The Big Sky.* Cloth. New York, 1947. First edition. One of 500 signed. In dust jacket. $50. Trade edition: $25.

GUTHRIE, Ramon. *Trobar Clus.* Blue cloth. Northampton, 1923. First edition. One of 250 signed. In dust jacket. $150–$200. Lacking jacket, $60. Author's first book.

GUY MANNERING; or, The Astrologer. 3 vols., boards. Edinburgh, 1815. (By Sir Walter Scott.) First edition. $300–$400.

GUY Rivers: A Tale of Georgia. 2 vols., cloth, paper labels. New York, 1834. (By William Gilmore Simms.) First edition. $400–$500.

GUYER, I.D. *History of Chicago.* Illustrated. Cloth. Chicago, 1862. First edition. $250–$350.

H

H., H. (translator). *Bathmendi: A Persian Tale.* Translated from the French of Florian. Printed wrappers. Boston, 1867. (Translated by Helen Hunt Jackson.) $150. First publication by the translator.

H., H. *A Century of Dishonor.* Brown cloth. New York, 1881. (By Helen Hunt Jackson.) First edition. $75–$100.

H., H. *Verses.* Cloth. Boston, 1870. (By Helen Hunt Jackson.) First edition. $50–$75. Author's first book.

HABERLY, Loyd. *Almost a Minister: A Romance of the Oregon Hopyards.* Illustrated in color by the author. Patterned paper cover, leather spine. (St. Louis, 1942.) Mound City Press. One of 375. $35–$50.

HABERLY, Loyd. *Anne Boleyn, and Other Poems.* Printed in red and black on handmade paper. Niger morocco. Newtown, Wales, 1934. Gregynog Press. One of 300. $200–$300. Another issue: One of 15 (from the edition) elaborately bound. $1,000–$1,250.

HABERLY, Loyd. *The Antiquary: A Poem.* Morocco. Long Crendon, England, 1933. Seven Acres Press. One of 100 signed. $125–$150.

HABERLY, Loyd. *Artemis: A Forest Tale.* Illustrated in color by Haberly. Full green morocco. (St. Louis, 1942.) Mound City Press. One of 240. $100–$150.

HABERLY, Loyd. *The Boy and the Bird: An Oregon Idyll.* Woodcuts. Full green morocco. Long Crendon, 1932. Seven Acres Press. One of 155 signed. $125–$150.

HABERLY, Loyd. *The City of the Sainted King and Other Poems.* Full orange-red morocco. (Cambridge, Mass.), 1939. One of 200. $100–$125.

HABERLY, Loyd. *The Crowning Years and Other Poems.* Half morocco. Stoney Down, (England), 1937. First edition. (150 copies.) $150–$175.

HABERLY, Loyd. *The Keeper of the Doves.* Morocco. Long Crendon, 1933, Seven Acres Press. One of 100 signed. $125–$150.

HABERLY, Loyd. *Medieval English Paving Tiles.* Half morocco. Oxford, 1937. One of 425. $150–$200.

HABERLY, Loyd. *Poems.* Dark-blue morocco. Long Crendon, 1930. Seven Acres Press. One of 120. $100–$150.

HACKETT, James. *Narrative of the Expedition Which Sailed from England in 1817, to Join the South American Patriots.* Boards. London, 1818. First edition. $400–$450.

HAEBLER, Konrad. *The Early Printers of Spain and Portugal.* Frontispiece and facsimiles. Wrappers. London, 1897 (actually 1896). $150–$200.

HAFEN, LeRoy R. (editor). *The Mountain Men and the Fur Trade of the Far West.* Illustrated. 10 vols., cloth. Glendale, Calif., 1965–72. In plain dust jackets. $350–$475.

HAFEN, LeRoy R. *The Overland Mail, 1849–1869.* Map, 7 plates. Cloth. Cleveland, 1926. First edition. $60–$80.

HAFEN, LeRoy R. *Overland Routes to the Gold Fields.* 7 plates, folding map. Cloth. Glendale, 1942. First edition. $50–$60.

HAFEN, LeRoy R. and Ann W. *The Old Spanish Trail.* Plates and maps. Cloth. Glendale, 1954. First edition. $25–$35.

HAFEN, LeRoy R. and Ann W. (editors). *The Far West and the Rockies, 1820–75.* Illustrated. 15 vols., green cloth. Glendale, 1954–61. $350–$450.

HAFEN, LeRoy R., and Ghent, W. J. *Broken Hand: The Life Story of Thomas Fitzpatrick, Chief of the Mountain Men.* Map, 8 plates. Cloth-backed boards. Denver, 1931. First edition. One of 100 large paper copies, signed. $250–$300. Another issue: Cloth. One of 500. In dust jacket. $100–$150.

HAFEN, LeRoy R., and Young, Francis Marion. *Fort Laramie and the Pageant of the West, 1834–1890.* Illustrated. Cloth. Glendale, 1938. First edition. $50–$60.

HAFEN, Mary Ann. *Recollections of a Handcart Pioneer of 1860.* Plates. Cloth. Denver, 1938. First edition. $35–$50.

HAGGARD, H. Rider. *Allan Quatermain.* Frontispiece, 19 plates. Cloth. London, 1887. First edition, first issue, with "Quartermain" in diagram on page 78. $150–$250. Frayed, rubbed, faded, $55. Another issue: Half brown morocco. One of 112 on large paper. $350–$400. New York, 1887. Wrappers. First American edition. $200.

HAGGARD, H. Rider. *Allan's Wife and Other Tales.* Illustrated. Half leather. London, 1889. First edition, first issue, with Spencer Blackett imprint on spine. One of 100 on large paper. $150–$200. Trade edition: Cloth. $75–$100.

HAGGARD, H. Rider. *Ayesha: The Return of She.* Illustrated. Cloth. London, 1905. First edition. $100–$125. New York, 1905. Red cloth. First American edition. $50.

HAGGARD, H. Rider. *Black Heart and White Heart and Other Stories.* Blue cloth. London, 1900. First edition. $100.

HAGGARD, H. Rider. *Cetywayo and His White Neighbours.* Green cloth. London, 1882. First edition. (750 copies.) $250–$350. Author's first book.

HAGGARD, H. Rider. *Cleopatra.* Illustrated. Half leather. London, 1889. First edition. One of 57 on large paper. $250–$350. Trade edition: Cloth. $75–$100.

HAGGARD, H. Rider. *Colonel Quaritch, V.C.: A Tale of Country Life.* 3 vols., red cloth. London, 1888. First edition. $225.

HAGGARD, H. Rider. *Dawn.* 3 vols., olive-green cloth. London, 1884. First edition. $400–$500. Also, inscribed copy, worn, $1,100 (A, 1975). Author's first novel.

HAGGARD, H. Rider. *Heart of the World.* Illustrated. Dark-blue or black cloth. London, 1896. First edition. $125–$150.

HAGGARD, H. Rider. *Jess.* Red cloth. London, 1887. First edition. $60–$85.

HAGGARD, H. Rider. *King Solomon's Mines.* Folding colored frontispiece, map. Bright-red cloth. London, 1885. First edition, first issue, with the word "Bamamgwato" in line 14, page 10, and "wrod" for "word" in note on page 307. $300–$400.

HAGGARD, H. Rider. *Maiwa's Revenge.* Black cloth. London, 1888. First edition. $75–$100.

HAGGARD, H. Rider. *Mr. Meeson's Will.* Cloth. London, 1888. First edition, first issue, with "Johnson" for "Johnston" in line 1 of page 284. $75–$100.

HAGGARD, H. Rider. *Montezuma's Daughter.* Dark-blue cloth. London, 1893. First edition. $75–$100.

HAGGARD, H. Rider. *Pearl Maiden.* Illustrated. Cloth. London, 1903. First edition. $100–$125.

HAGGARD, H. Rider. *She: A History of Adventure.* Printed wrappers. New York, 1886. First edition. $200–$300. London, 1887. Illustrated. Blue cloth. First English edition, first issue, with "Godness me" in line 38, page 269, etc. $200–$250.

HAGGARD, H. Rider. *Stella Fregelius: A Tale of Three Destinies.* Cloth. New York, 1903. First edition. $125–$150. London, 1904. Dark-blue cloth. First English edition. $125–$150.

HAGGARD, H. Rider. *The Witch's Head.* 3 vols., cloth. London, 1885. First edition. $200–$300.

HAINES, Elijah M. *The American Indian.* Half morocco. Chicago, 1888. First edition. $75–$100.

HAINES, Elijah M. *Historical and Statistical Sketches of Lake County, State of Illinois.* Folding frontispiece. 112 pp., printed wrappers. Waukegan, Ill., 1852. First edition. $250–$300.

HAIR, James T. (publisher). *Gazetteer of Madison County, Illinois.* Cloth. Alton, Ill., 1866. First edition. $100–$125.

HAKES, Harlo. *Landmarks of Steuben County, New York.* Cloth. Syracuse, 1896. First edition. $75–$100.

HAKEWILL, James. *A Picturesque Tour of the Island of Jamaica.* 21 colored aquatint plates. Half leather. London, 1825. First edition. $3,500–$5,000.

HAKEWILL, James. *A Picturesque Tour of Italy.* 63 plates, 36 hand-colored. Folio, half morocco. London, 1820. $500–$750.

HALBERT, Henry S., and Ball, Timothy H. *The Creek War of 1813 and 1814.* Portraits, folding map (not in all copies). Cloth. Chicago, 1895. First edition. $100–$125.

HALE, Edward Everett. See *The Man Without a Country.*

HALE, Edward Everett. *His Level Best and Other Stories.* Cloth. Boston, 1873. First edition. $50–$75.

HALE, Edward Everett. *Kanzas and Nebraska.* Folding map. Cloth. Boston, 1854. First edition. $125–$150.

HALE, Edward Everett. *A Tract for the Day: How to Conquer Texas Before Texas Conquers Us.* 16 pp., self-wrappers. Boston, 1845. First edition. $150–$300, possibly more.

HALE, John. *California as It Is.* Boards. San Francisco, 1954. Grabhorn Press. One of 150. $175–$200.

HALE, Lucretia P. *Last of the Peterkins.* 4 plates. Red cloth. Boston, 1886. First edition. $75–$100.

HALE, Lucretia P. *The Peterkin Papers.* Illustrated by F.G. Attwood. Green cloth. Boston, 1880. First edition. $250.

HALE, Sarah Josepha. See *The Genius of Oblivion.*

HALE, Sarah Josepha. *Northwood: A Tale of New England.* 2 vols., buff boards and rose-colored muslin. Boston, 1827. First edition. $75–$100.

HALE, Sarah Josepha (editor). *The Countries of Europe, and the Manners and Customs of Its Various Nations.* Illustrated. Printed wrappers. New York, (about 1842). First edition. $75–$100.

HALE, Sarah Josepha (editor). *The Good Little Boy's Book.* Printed flexible boards. New York, (about 1848). First edition. $50–$75.

HALE, Sarah Josepha Buell (editor). *Happy Changes; or Pride and Its Consequences.* Printed flexible boards. New York, (about 1842). First edition. $50–$60.

HALE, Will. *Twenty-four Years a Cowboy and Ranchman in Southern Texas and Old Mexico.* 268 pp., stiff purplish-blue wrappers. Hedrick (Headrick), Oklahoma Territory, (1905). (By William Hale Stone.) First edition. $4,000–$5,000. (Note: Only four copies known—two in the Library of Congress, one in the University of Oklahoma Library, and one in private hands.)

HALEY, Alex. *Roots.* Full leather. Garden City, 1976. First edition. One of 500 signed. Boxed. $150. Trade edition: Cloth. In dust jacket. $35.

HALEY, J. Evetts. *Charles Goodnight, Cowman and Plainsman.* Illustrated by Harold Bugbee. Cloth. Boston, 1936. First edition, with dated title page. In dust jacket. $100–$125.

HALEY, J. Evetts. *Charles Schriener, General Merchandise: The Story of a Country Store.* Illustrated by Harold Bugbee. Cloth. Austin, 1944. First edition. $100–$125. Limited edition: $400–$500.

HALEY, J. Evetts. *Fort Concho on the Texas Frontier.* Illustrated by Harold Bugbee. Cloth. San Angelo, 1952. First edition. One of 185 signed. Boxed. $250–$300. Trade edition: Cloth. In dust jacket. $75–$100.

HALEY, J. Evetts. *The Heraldry of the Range.* Illustrated by Harold Bugbee. Cloth. Canyon, Tex., 1949. First edition. In dust jacket. $400–$500.

HALEY, J. Evetts. *Jeff Milton: A Good Man with a Gun.* Illustrated by Harold Bugbee. Cloth. Norman, Okla., 1948. First edition. In dust jacket. $75–$100.

HALEY, J. Evetts. *Life on the Texas Range.* Photographs by Erwin E. Smith. Pictorial cloth. Austin, 1952. First edition. Boxed. $75–$100.

HALEY, J. Evetts. *The XIT Ranch of Texas.* 2 maps, 30 plates. Cloth. Chicago, 1929. First edition. $200–$325. Author's first book.

HALFORD, Frederic M. *Dry Fly Entomology.* Illustrated, including color plates, with 100 artificial flies in sunken mounts. 2 vols., morocco. London, 1897. One of 100 copies, signed. $3,500–$5,000.

HALFORD, Frederic M. *The Dry-Fly Man's Handbook.* Illustrated. Leather and cloth. London, 1913. One of 100 signed. $1,000–$1,500.

HALFORD, Frederic M. *Modern Development of the Dry Fly.* Illustrated, including color plates, with 33 mounted flies in sunken compartments. 2 vols., leather and cloth. London, (1910). One of 75 signed. In slipcase. $3,500–$5,000. New York, (1910) $4,000–$5,000.

HALIBURTON, Thomas Chandler. See *The Clockmaker.*

HALL, Basil. *The Great Polyglot Bibles.* Folio, loose in wrappers. San Francisco, 1966. Book Club of California. One of 400. Boxed. $400–$550.

HALL, Capt. Basil. *Forty Etchings, from Sketches made with the Camera Lucida, in North America, in 1827 and 1828.* Folding map, 20 plates. Printed boards. Edinburgh, 1829. First edition. $500–$600. Edinburgh, 1830. Boards. Fourth edition. $300–$400.

HALL, Capt. Basil. *Travels in North America.* Colored folding map, folding table, 3 vols., half calf. Edinburgh, 1829. First edition. $200–$300. Philadelphia, 1829. Illustrated. 2 vols., boards. First American edition. $100–$150.

HALL, Bert L. *Roundup Years.* Illustrated. Pictorial cloth. (Pierre, S.D., 1954.) First edition. $50–$60.

HALL, Carroll D. (editor). *Donner Miscellany.* Boards. San Francisco, 1947. Book Club of California. (Printed by the Allen Press.) One of 350. $150–$175.

HALL, Donald. *Exiles and Marriages*. Cloth. New York, 1955. First edition. In dust jacket. $50–$60.

HALL, Edward H. *The Great West*. Map. 89 pp., printed wrappers. New York, 1864. First edition. $200–$300. New York, 1865. Map. 198 pp., pictorial wrappers. $450. New York, 1870. Boards. $125–$150. London, 1870. $100–$125.

HALL, Francis. *Travels in Canada and the United States in 1816 and 1817*. Folding map. Boards and calf. London, 1818. First edition. $200–$250. Boston, 1818. Boards. First American edition. $150–$200. London, 1819. Second edition. $150–$200.

HALL, Frederic. *The History of San Jose and Surroundings*. Plates, map. Cloth. San Francisco, 1871. First edition. $125–$150.

HALL, Frederick. *Letters From the East and From the West*. Cloth. Washington, (1840). First edition. $50–$60. Baltimore, 1840. Cloth. $50.

HALL, George Eli. *A Balloon Ascension at Midnight*. Illustrated by Gordon Ross. Boards. San Francisco, 1902. One of 30 on vellum, signed. $125–$150.

HALL, Henry. See *The Tribune Book of Open-Air Sports*.

HALL, J. *Sonora: Travels and Adventures in Sonora*. Cloth. Chicago, 1881. First edition. $1,250 and up.

HALL, James. *The Harpe's Head: A Legend of Kentucky*. Wrappers, or cloth. Philadelphia. 1833. First edition. Wrappers: $150–$200. Cloth: $100–$125.

HALL, James. *Letters from the West*. Boards. London, 1828. First edition. $100–$150.

HALL, James. *Notes on the Western States*. Cloth. Philadelphia, 1838. Later edition of *Statistics of the West*. $50–$60.

HALL, James. *The Romance of Western History*. Frontispiece. Cloth. Cincinnati, 1857. First edition. $50–$60.

HALL, James. *Sketches of History, Life, and Manners in the West*. Vol. 1. (All published.) Brown cloth. Cincinnati, 1834. First edition. $150–$250. Philadelphia, 1835. Frontispiece. 2 vols., cloth. First complete edition. $275.

HALL, James. *Statistics of the West*. Cloth. Cincinnati, 1836. First edition, first printing, purple cloth. $100–$150. Second printing, slate-colored cloth. $75–$100. Cincinnati, 1837. Cloth. $35.

HALL, James (editor). *The Western Souvenir: A Christmas and New Year's Gift for 1839*. Illustrated. Silk. Cincinnati, (1828). First edition. $150–$300.

HALL, James Norman. See Nordhoff, Charles B. (For *Mutiny on the Bounty*.)

HALL, James Norman. *Kitchener's Mob*. Portrait. Cloth. Boston, 1916. First edition. In dust jacket. $50–$75. Author's first book.

HALL, James Norman, and Nordhoff, Charles B. (editors). *The Lafayette Flying Corps*. Illustrated, including colored plates. 2 vols., blue cloth. Boston, 1920. First edition. In dust jackets. $500–$750.

HALL, Manly P. *An Encyclopedic Outline of Masonic, Cabbalistic and Rosicrucian Symbolical Philosophy*. Colored plates, text illustrations. Folio boards and vellum. San Francisco, 1928. John Henry Nash printing. One of 550 signed. Boxed. $550–$600.

HALL, Manly P. *The Secret Teaching of All Ages*. Illustrated. Half morocco. Los Angeles, 1975. "Golden Anniversary Edition" of *An Encyclopedic Outline* (see above entry). One of 550 signed. $200–$300.

HALL, Marguerite Radclyffe. *The Forgotten Island*. Black cloth. London, 1915. First edition. In dust jacket. $100–$150.

HALL, (Marguerite) Radclyffe. *The Master of the House*. Buckram, vellum spine. London, (1932). First edition. One of 172 signed. $125–$200. Trade edition: Cloth. In dust jacket. $75–$100. New York, (1932). First American edition. In dust jacket. $35–$45.

HALL, (Marguerite) Radclyffe. *Miss Ogilvy Finds Herself*. Cloth. London, (1934). First edition. In dust jacket. $50–$75.

HALL, Marguerite Radclyffe. *Poems of the Past and Present*. Green cloth. London, 1910. First edition. In dust jacket. $200–$250.

HALL, Marguerite Radclyffe. *A Sheaf of Verses*. Pink cloth. London, 1908. First edition. $200–$225.

HALL, (Marguerite) Radclyffe. *The Sixth Beatitude*. Half vellum. London, 1936. First edition. One of 125 signed. $175–$200.

HALL, (Marguerite) Radclyffe. *The Well of Loneliness*. Black cloth. London, (1928). First edition, first issue, with "whip" for "whips" on page 50, line 3. In dust jacket. $200–$250. Paris, (1928). Introduction by Havelock Ellis. Black cloth. $200. New York, 1928. Boards and cloth. First American edition. One of 500. In slipcase. $100–$150. New York, 1929. 2 vols., half cloth. One of 225 signed. Boxed. $250–$275.

HALL, Marshall. *New Memoir on the Nervous System*. 5 plates. Boards. London, 1843. First edition. $200–$300.

HALL, Marshall. *Principles of the Theory and Practice of Medicine*. Sheep. Boston, 1839. First American edition. $150–$200. (Note: Contains new material by Oliver Wendell Holmes.)

HALL, Samuel R. *Lectures to Female Teachers on School-Keeping*. Boards. Boston, 1832. First edition. $50–$100.

HALL, Samuel R. *Lectures on School-Keeping*. Boards and cloth. Boston, 1829. First edition. $150–$200.

HALLAS, Richard. *You Play the Black and the Red Comes Up*. Red cloth. New York, 1938. (By Eric Knight.) First edition. In dust jacket. $75–$100.

HALLECK, Fitz-Greene. See Croaker. Also see *Alnwick Castle; Fanny*.

HALLENBECK, Cleve. *The Journal of Fray Marcos de Niza*. Illustrated. Cloth. Dallas, 1949. First edition. In dust jacket. Boxed. $100–$125.

HALLEY, William. *Centennial Year Book of Description of the Contra Costa Under Spanish, Mexican, and American Rule*. Illustrated. Cloth. Oakland, 1876. $75–$150.

HALPER, Albert. *The Chute*. Cloth. New York, 1937. First edition. In dust jacket. $50–$60.

HALSEY, R. T. H. *Pictures of Early New York on Dark Blue Staffordshire Pottery*. 155 illustrations, mostly in color. Cloth. New York, 1899. First edition. One of 286 on handmade paper. $150–$200. Another issue: One of 30 on vellum. $350–$450.

HALSTEAD, Murat. *The Caucuses of 1860*. Cloth. Columbus, Ohio, 1860. First edition. $75–$100.

HAMBLETON, Chalkley J. *A Gold Hunter's Experience*. Green cloth. Chicago, 1898. First edition. $150–$250.

HAMERTON, Philip G. *Etching and Etchers*. Illustrated. Half morocco. London, 1868. First edition. $750–$1,000. London, 1880. Third edition. (With a Whistler etching.) $750.

HAMILTON, Dr. Alexander (1712–56). *Hamilton's Itinerarium*. Map. Half leather. St. Louis, 1907. One of 487. Boxed. $125–$150.

HAMILTON, Gail. *Gala-Days.* Cloth. Boston, 1863. (By Mary Abigail Dodge.) First edition. $75–$100.

HAMILTON, Gail. *A Woman's Wrongs: A Counter-Irritant.* Cloth. Boston, 1868. (By Mary Abigail Dodge.) First edition. $100–$125.

HAMILTON, H. W. *Rural Sketches of Minnesota.* 40 pp., printed wrappers. Milan, Ohio, 1850. First edition. $500 and up. Also, $325 (A, 1974).

HAMILTON, John P. *Travels Through the Interior Provinces of Colombia.* Map, 7 plates. 2 vols., calf. London, 1827. First edition. $350–$500.

HAMILTON, Patrick. *The Resources of Arizona.* 120 pp., gray wrappers. Prescott, 1881. Second edition. $200. San Francisco, 1884. Folding map. Cloth. Third edition. $150–$200. (For first edition, see title entry under "R.")

HAMILTON, W. T. *My Sixty Years on the Plains.* Edited by E. T. Sieber. 8 plates (6 by Charles M. Russell). Cloth. New York, 1905. First edition. $100–$125.

HAMILTON, The Rev. William, and Irvin, the Rev. S. M. *An Ioway Grammar.* Wrappers. (Wolf Creek, Neb.), 1848. Ioway and Sac Mission Press. First edition. $1,000–$1,250.

HAMMER, William J. *Radium, and Other Radio-Active Substances.* Illustrated. Cloth. New York, 1903. First edition. $350–$450.

HAMMETT, Dashiell. *The Dain Curse.* Cloth. New York, 1929. First edition with "dopped in" for "dropped in" in line 19 of page 260. In dust jacket. $1,000 and up. Without jacket, $250–$300.

HAMMETT, Dashiell. *The Glass Key.* Light-green cloth. New York, 1931. First edition. In dust jacket. $1,000. Without jacket, $300–$400.

HAMMETT, Dashiell. *The Maltese Falcon.* Gray cloth. New York, 1930. First edition. In dust jacket. $2,000–$2,500. Also, $2,500 (A, 1981). Without jacket. $500–$750.

HAMMETT, Dashiell. *Red Harvest.* Cloth. New York, 1929. First edition. In dust jacket. $2,000 and up. Without jacket. $400–$500. Author's first book.

HAMMETT, Dashiell. *Secret Agent X-9.* Cloth. Philadelphia, (1934). First edition. In dust jacket. $350–$450.

HAMMETT, Dashiell. *The Thin Man.* Green cloth. New York, 1934. First edition. In first issue (red) dust jacket. $750–$1,000. In second issue (green) dust jacket. $750–$850. Without jacket, $300–$400.

HAMMETT, Dashiell, and Colodny, Robert. *The Battle of the Aleutians.* Illustrated. Oblong, wrappers. (San Francisco, 1944.) First edition. $175–$200.

HAMMOND, John Martin. *Colonial Mansions of Maryland and Delaware.* 65 plates. Cloth. Philadelphia, 1914. First edition. Limited. $100–$125.

HAMMOND, S. H. *Wild Northern Scenes.* 4 plates. Cloth. New York, 1857. First edition. $125.

HANCOCK, R. R. *Hancock's Diary: or, a History of the 2d Tennessee Confederate Cavalry.* 2 plates. Cloth. Nashville, 1887. First edition. $125–$150.

HANDBOOK for Boys. Dark olive khaki cloth, either flexible or hardbound. New York, 1911. First edition of the first official Boy Scouts of America Handbook. $100–$150.

HANDBOOK for Scout Masters: Boy Scouts of America. Cloth. New York, (1914). First edition. In original khaki Scout case. $100–$125. Without the case, $75–$100. (Note: The first *Handbook for Scout Masters.*)

HAND Book of Monterey and Vicinity (The). 152 pp., printed wrappers. Monterey, 1875.
$100–$150.

HAND-BOOK of Ness County, the Banner County of Western Kansas. 36 pp., wrappers.
Chicago, 1887. $175–$225.

HANDLEY Cross: or, Mr. Jorrock's Hunt. 17 color plates and numerous woodcuts by
John Leech. 17 parts in pictorial wrappers. London, 1853–54. (By Robert Smith Surtees.) First illustrated edition. With all the ads and slips and with the words "with the
aid of the illustrious Leech" in the preface. $1,500 and up. (Acceptable but imperfect
sets for less.) London, 1854. Cloth. First illustrated hardbound edition. $400–$750.

HANDLEY Cross; or, The Spa Hunt. 3 vols., boards and cloth. London, 1843. (By Robert
Smith Surtees.) First edition. $200–$300.

HANLEY, James. *Boy*. Cloth. London, 1931. First edition. In dust jacket. $75–$150.

HANLEY, James. *Captain Bottell*. Cloth. London, 1933. First edition. One of 99 signed.
In dust jacket. $150–$175.

HANLEY, James. *Men in Darkness*. Preface by John Cowper Powys. Cloth. London,
(1931). First edition. One of 105 signed. $100.

HANNA, Charles A. *The Wilderness Trail*. Maps and illustrations. 2 vols., cloth. New
York, 1911. First edition. One of 1,000. In dust jackets. Boxed. $150–$200.

HANNOVER, Emil. *Pottery and Porcelain: A Handbook for Collectors*. Illustrated. 3
vols., cloth. London, 1925. First edition. $400–$500.

HANSON, George A. *Old Kent: The Eastern Shore of Maryland*. Cloth. Baltimore,
1876. First edition. $50–$75.

HARBINGER (The): A May-Gift. Cloth, paper spine label. Boston, 1833. First edition.
$100–$150. Worn, $85. (Note: Contains 17 poems by Oliver Wendell Holmes.)

HARDEE, William J. *Rifle and Light Infantry Tactics*. 2 vols., or 2 vols. in one, half
leather. Memphis, 1861. $175–$200. (Other editions in the same year in Richmond
and Philadelphia.)

HARDIN, John Wesley. *The Life of John Wesley Hardin*. Portrait, other illustrations.
144 pp., printed wrappers. Seguin, Tex., 1896. First edition, first issue, with portrait of
Hardin's brother mislabeled "John." $100–$150. Second issue, with the Hardin portrait tipped in. $50–$75.

HARDIN, Mrs. Philomelia Ann Maria Antoinette. *Everybody's Cook and Receipt Book*.
Printed boards. Cleveland, 1842. First edition. $50–$75.

HARDING, George L. *D. B. Updike and the Merrymount Press*. Stiff wrappers. San
Francisco, 1943. Roxburghe Club. One of 150. $125.

HARDING, George L. *Don Augustin V. Zamorano: Statesman, Soldier, Craftsman,
and California's First Printer*. Illustrated. Cloth. Los Angeles, 1934. First edition. In
dust jacket. $150.

HARDWICK, Elizabeth. *The Ghostly Loves*. Cloth. New York, 1945. First edition. In
dust jacket. $75–$100.

HARDY, John. *A Collection of Sacred Hymns, Adapted to the Faith and Views of the
Church of Jesus Christ of Latter Day Saints*. 160 pp. full calf. Boston, 1843. First
edition. $2,000–$3,000.

HARDY, Joseph. *A Picturesque and Descriptive Tour in the Mountains of the High Pyr-
enees*. Map, 24 hand-colored plates. Cloth. London, 1825. First edition. $500–$750.

HARDY, Thomas. See Henniker, Florence. Also see *Desperate Remedies; Under the
Greenwood Tree.*

HARDY, Thomas. *A Changed Man*. Frontispiece and map. Green cloth. London, 1913. First edition. In dust jacket. $100–$275. New York, 1913. Blue cloth. First American edition. $25–$35.

HARDY, Thomas. *A Defence of "Jude the Obscure."* Wrappers. Edinburgh, 1928. First edition. One of 30. $400–$500.

HARDY, Thomas. *Domicilium*. Wrappers. (London, 1916.) First edition. One of 25. $250–$300.

HARDY, Thomas. *The Duke's Reappearance*. Boards. New York, 1927. One of 89. $150.

HARDY, Thomas. *The Dynasts: A Drama of the Napoleonic Wars*. 3 vols., green cloth. London, 1903–06–08. First edition, first issue (of Vol. 1, with date 1903 on title page). In dust jackets. $600–$750. London, 1927. Portrait etching, signed by Francis Dodd, 3 vols., half vellum. One of 525 signed by Hardy. In dust jackets. $600–$800. Lacking jackets, $375.

HARDY, Thomas. *Far from the Madding Crowd*. 12 illustrations by H. Patterson. 2 vols., pictorial green cloth. London, 1874. First English edition, first issue, with "Sacrament" in first line of page 2, Vol. 1. $2,500–$3,000. Also, $2,600 (A, 1977)—a "superb" copy. (Copies in ordinary worn condition bring much lower prices at retail.) New York, 1958. Limited Editions Club. Illustrated. Half leather. Boxed. $35–$50.

HARDY, Thomas. *A Group of Noble Dames*. Light-brown cloth. (London, 1891.) First edition, first issue, with yellow end papers. $75–$125. Second issue, white end papers. $50–$100. New York, 1891. Brown cloth. First American edition. $50–$75.

HARDY, Thomas. *The Hand of Ethelberta*. 11 illustrations by George Du Maurier. 2 vols., terra-cotta cloth. London, 1876. First edition, first issue, with "two or three individuals" instead of "five or six individuals" in caption facing page 146 in Vol. 1. $350–$500. Also, hinges cracked, $200 (A, 1975).

HARDY, Thomas. *Human Shows: Far Phantasies; Songs and Trifles*. Green cloth. London, 1925. First edition. In dust jacket. $60–$100.

HARDY, Thomas. *Jezreel: The Master and the Leaves*. Wrappers. London, 1919. First edition. One of 25 initialed by Florence Emily Hardy. $150.

HARDY, Thomas. *Jude the Obscure*. Map, etching by H. Macbeth-Raeburn. Green cloth. (London, 1896.) First edition, first issue, with Osgood's name on title page and spine. $250–$350. New York, 1896. Cloth. First American edition. In dust jacket. $375 in a 1981 catalogue. New York, 1969. Limited Editions Club. Boxed. $80–$100.

HARDY, Thomas. *A Laodicean; or, The Castle of the De Stancys*. 3 vols., slate-colored cloth. London, 1881. First English edition, first issue, without the word "or" on half title of Vol. 1. $500–$750. Second issue, with the word "or" on half title of Vol. 1. $350–$500.

HARDY, Thomas. *Late Lyrics and Earlier*. Green cloth. London, 1922. First edition. In dust jacket. $100–$125.

HARDY, Thomas. *Life's Little Ironies*. Green cloth. London, (1894). First edition. $150–$200. New York, 1894. Green cloth. First American edition. $100–$125.

HARDY, Thomas. *The Mayor of Casterbridge*. 2 vols., blue cloth. London, 1886. First edition. $300–$400. New York, 1886. Wrappers. First American edition. $100–$150. New York, 1964. Limited Editions Club. Illustrated. Half morocco. Boxed. $50–$60.

HARDY, Thomas. *Moments of Vision and Miscellaneous Verses*. Green cloth. London, 1917. First edition. In dust jacket. $125–$150.

HARDY, Thomas. *No Bell-Ringing*. Wrappers. Dorchester, England, 1925. First edition. One of 25. $150–$200.

HARDY, Thomas. *Notes on "The Dynasts."* Printed wappers. Edinburgh, 1929. First edition. One of 20. $150–$200.

HARDY, Thomas. *Old Mrs. Chundle.* Boards and cloth. New York, 1929. First edition. One of 742. $50–$75.

HARDY, Thomas. *A Pair of Blue Eyes.* 3 vols., green or maroon cloth, yellow end papers. London, 1873. First edition, first issue, with "c" dropped or missing from the word "clouds" in last line on page 5 of Vol. 2. $1,000–$1,500.

HARDY, Thomas. *Poems of the Past and the Present.* White (cream) or dark-green cloth. (London, 1902.) First edition. $300–$400.

HARDY, Thomas. *The Return of the Native.* Frontispiece map. 3 vols., brown cloth. London, 1878. First edition, first binding, with double blind rule on back cover. $2,500–$3,000. Also, $1,900 (A, 1977). New York, 1878. Cream-colored cloth. First American edition. $150–$200. London, 1929. Illustrated by Clare Leighton. Batik boards, vellum spine. One of 500 signed by the artist. Boxed. $100–$125. American issue: Buckram. 1,000 signed. $75–$100.

HARDY, Thomas. *Satires of Circumstance.* Green cloth. London, 1914. First edition. In dust jacket. $175–$300.

HARDY, Thomas. *Selected Poems.* Photogravure portrait on title page. Blue cloth. London, 1916. First edition. $150. London, 1921. Riccardi Press. Woodcut engravings, including title page, by William Nicholson. Vellum. One of 100. In dust jacket. $250–$350. Another issue: Limp vellum with ties. One of 14 on vellum, signed by author and artist. $1,000–$1,250. Another issue: Half cloth. One of 1,025. $75–$125.

HARDY, Thomas. *The Short Stories of Thomas Hardy.* Cloth. London, 1928. First edition. In dust jacket. $75–$125.

HARDY, Thomas. *Song of the Soldiers.* 4 pp., wrappers. Hove, England, 1914. First edition. $50–$75. Another issue: One of 12 privately printed. $250. Hove, 1915. Second printing. $35–$50.

HARDY, Thomas. *Tess of the D'Urbervilles.* 3 vols., brownish-orange cloth with gilt design on cover. (London, 1891.) First edition, first issue, first binding, with "Chapter XXV" for "Chapter XXXV" and with "road" for "load" on page 198, Vol. 3. $3,500–$4,500. Also, $4,500 (A, 1981); $2,000 (A, 1976). (London, 1892.) Second issue, with corrections. $400–$500. New York, 1892. Cloth. First American edition. $75–$100. London, 1926. 41 wood engravings by Vivien Gribble, folding map. Marbled boards, vellum spine. One of 325 signed. In dust jacket. $250–$350.

HARDY, Thomas. *Time's Laughingstocks and Other Verses.* Green cloth. London, 1909. First edition. In dust jacket. $125–$200.

HARDY, Thomas. *The Trumpet-Major.* 3 vols., decorated red cloth. London, 1880. First edition. $1,000–$1,500. New York, 1880. Pictorial cloth. First American edition. $150–$250.

HARDY, Thomas. *Two on a Tower: A Romance.* 3 vols., green cloth. London, 1882. First edition. $250–$300. New York, 1882. Decorated yellow cloth. First American edition. $125–$150.

HARDY, Thomas. *The Well-Beloved.* Etching, map. Ribbed dark-green cloth. London, (1897). First edition, first issue, with Osgood's name on title page and spine. $125–$150.

HARDY, Thomas. *Wessex Poems and Other Verses.* 30 illustrations by the author. Dark green, blue, or white cloth. (London, 1898.) First edition. $125–$150. London, 1908. Illustrated. Cloth. $50–$75.

HARDY, Thomas. *Wessex Tales, Strange, Lively and Commonplace.* 2 vols., green cloth. London, 1888. First edition. $600–$800.

HARDY, Thomas. *Winter Night in Woodland.* 6 pp., wrappers. (London, 1925.) First edition. One of 25. $250–$300.

HARDY, Thomas. *Winter Words in Various Moods and Metres.* Olive-green cloth. London, 1928. First edition. In dust jacket. $75–$100. New York, 1928. Green cloth. First American edition. In dust jacket. $35–$50.

HARDY, Thomas. *The Woodlanders.* 3 vols., smooth dark-green cloth. London, 1887. First edition, first binding, first issue, with ad leaf at end of Vol. 1. $1,250–$1,500. Second binding, pebbled dark-green cloth. $750–$1,000.

HARDY, Thomas. *Yuletide in a Younger World.* Wrappers. New York, 1927. First American edition. One of 27 issued to obtain copyright. $400.

HARE, George H. *Guide to San Jose and Vicinity.* 2 maps. 85 pp., wrappers. San Jose, 1872. First edition. $150–$175.

HARFORD, Henry. *Fan: The Story of a Young Girl's Life.* 3 vols., sage-green cloth. London, 1892. (By W. H. Hudson.) First edition. $1,500–$2,000.

HARGRAVE, Catherine Perry. *A History of Playing Cards.* Illustrated. Cloth. Boston, 1930. First edition. In dust jacket. $250–$350.

HARLAN, Jacob Wright. *California, '46 to '88.* Portrait frontispiece. Cloth. San Francisco, 1888. First edition. $100–$125.

HARLOW, Alvin F. *Old Towpaths.* Illustrated. Cloth. New York, 1926. First edition. $75–$125.

HARLOW, Alvin F. *Old Waybills.* Illustrated. Cloth. New York, 1934. First edition. In dust jacket. $75–$125.

HARLOW, Neal. *The Maps of San Francisco Bay.* Folio, half leather. San Francisco, 1950. Grabhorn Press. One of 375. $500–$600.

HARMAN, S. W. *Hell on the Border.* Portrait, map. Stiff printed green wrappers. Fort Smith, Ark., (1898). First edition. $500–$600. Later: Cloth. $300–$350.

HARMON, Daniel Williams. *A Journal of Voyages and Travels in the Interiour* (sic) *of North America.* Portrait, folding map. Calf. Andover, Mass., 1820. First edition, first issue, with map placed opposite title page and with no errata slip. $600–$750.

HAROLD the Dauntless. Boards. Edinburgh, 1817. (By Sir Walter Scott.) First edition. $250–$350.

HARRIS, Frank. *Elder Conklin and Other Stories.* Cloth. New York, 1894. First edition. $50–$60. Author's first book. London, 1895. Green cloth. First English edition. $35–$50.

HARRIS, Frank. *Joan La Romee: A Drama.* Cloth. London, (about 1926). Fortune Press. First edition. One of 350 signed. In glassine dust jacket. $75–$100.

HARRIS, Frank. *A Mad Love.* 70 pp., printed wrappers. New York, 1920. $35–$50.

HARRIS, Frank. *The Man Shakespeare and His Tragic Life Story.* Boards and vellum. London, 1909. First edition. One of 150 on large paper, signed. $100–$125. Trade edition: Green cloth. $50.

HARRIS, Frank. *Oscar Wilde: His Life and Confessions.* 2 vols., half morocco. New York, 1916. First edition. Japan paper issue. In dust jackets. Boxed. $150–$200.

HARRIS, Frank. *Stories of Jesus the Christ.* Wrappers. New York, 1919. Pearson's 25¢ Library. First edition. $50–$75. (Note: Includes a Shaw contribution.)

HARRIS, George Washington. See Spavery.

HARRIS, Henry. *California's Medical Story*. Half morocco. San Francisco, 1932. Grabhorn Press. One of 200. $75–$100.

HARRIS, Joel Chandler. See Davidson, James Wood.

HARRIS, Joel Chandler. *Daddy Jake the Runaway*. Illustrated. Pictorial cream-colored glazed boards. New York, (1889). First edition. $250–$300. London, 1890 (actually 1889). First English edition. $125–$150.

HARRIS, Joel Chandler. *Free Joe and Other Georgian Sketches*. Pictorial red cloth. New York, 1887. First edition. $150–$200.

HARRIS, Joel Chandler. *Nights with Uncle Remus*. Illustrated. Pictorial gray cloth. Boston, 1883. First edition. $100–$125.

HARRIS, Joel Chandler. *On the Plantation*. Illustrated. Pictorial cloth. New York, 1892. First edition. $75.

HARRIS, Joel Chandler. *Plantation Pageants*. Illustrated. Cloth. Boston, 1899. First edition. $75–$100.

HARRIS, Joel Chandler. *Tales of the Home Folks in Peace and War*. Illustrated. Cloth. Boston, 1898. First edition. In dust jacket. $150–$250.

HARRIS, Joel Chandler. *The Tar-Baby and Other Rhymes of Uncle Remus*. Cloth. New York, 1904. First edition. In dust jacket. $150–$200.

HARRIS, Joel Chandler. *Uncle Remus and Brer Rabbit*. Oblong, pictorial boards. New York, (1906). First edition. $300.

HARRIS, Joel Chandler. *Uncle Remus and His Legends of the Old Plantation*. Olive-green cloth. London, 1881. First English edition of *Uncle Remus: His Songs and His Sayings*. $250–$350.

HARRIS, Joel Chandler. *Uncle Remus: His Songs and His Sayings*. Illustrated by Frederick S. Church and James S. Moser. Pictorial blue cloth. New York, 1881. First edition, first issue, with "presumptive" for "presumptuous" in last line, page 9, and with no mention of this book in ads at back. $500–$600. Author's first book. Second issue, with "presumptuous" in last line, page 9. $300–$400. (For first English edition, see preceding entry.) New York, 1895. Illustrated by A. B. Frost. Vellum. One of 250 signed. $400–$500. Also, $275 (A, 1978). Trade edition: Red buckram. $35–$50. New York, 1920. Edited by Thomas Nelson Page. Illustrated. Pictorial cloth. $75–$125. Mount Vernon, N.Y., (1937). Morocco. One of 50. $100–$125. New York, 1957. Limited Editions Club. Illustrated. Pictorial cloth. Boxed. $100.

HARRIS, Joel Chandler. *Uncle Remus Returns*. Illustrated. Cloth. Boston, 1918. First edition. In dust jacket. $350.

HARRIS, Mark. *Trumpet to the World*. Yellow cloth. New York, (1946). First edition. In dust jacket. $40–$50. Author's first book.

HARRIS, Sarah Hollister. *An Unwritten Chapter of Salt Lake, 1851–1901*. Cloth. New York, 1901. First edition. $200–$250.

HARRIS, Thaddeus Mason. *The Journal of a Tour into the Territory Northwest of the Alleghany Mountains*. 4 maps (3 folding) and a folding plate. Marbled boards, paper spine and paper label. Boston, 1805. First edition. $300–$350.

HARRIS, Thomas Lake. *A Lyric of the Golden Age*. Cloth. New York, 1856. First edition. $75–$125.

HARRIS, Thomas M. *Assassination of Lincoln*. Illustrated. Pictorial cloth. Boston, (1892). First edition. $35–$50.

HARRIS, W. B. *Pioneer Life in California*. 98 pp., pictorial wrappers. Stockton, 1884. First edition. $250.

HARRIS, William Charles. *The Fishes of North America That Are Captured on Hook and Line.* Vol. 1. (All published.) Illustrated. Folio, half leather. New York, 1898. First edition. $200.

HARRIS, William R. *The Catholic Church in Utah.* Map, 25 plates. Cloth. Salt Lake City, (1909). First edition. $50. (Also issued in 2 vols.)

HARRISON, E. J. *The Thrilling, Startling and Wonderful Narrative of Lieutenant Harrison.* Illustration in text. 30 pp., printed buff wrappers. Cincinnati, 1848. First edition. $1,000 and up. (Note: Three copies known.)

HARRISON, Fairfax. *Virginia Land Grants.* Cloth. Richmond, 1925. First edition. $35–$50.

HARRISON, William Henry. *A Discourse on the Aborigines of the Valley of the Ohio.* Folding map. 51 pp., wrappers. Cincinnati, 1838. First edition. $200–$300. Presentation copy with manuscript corrections by Harrison, $3,000 in a 1980 catalogue.

HART, Charles Henry, and Biddle, Edward. *Memoirs of the Life and Works of Jean Antoine Houdon.* 33 full-page plates. Cloth. Philadelphia, 1911. One of 250. $150–$200.

HART, George. *The Violin: Its Famous Makers and Their Imitators.* Illustrated. Cloth. London, 1875. First edition. $135–$200. Boston, 1884. Cloth. $100–$150.

HART, John A., and others. *History of Pioneer Days in Texas and Oklahoma.* 12 plates, 249 pp., cloth. (Guthrie, Okla., 1906.) First edition. $150–$200. Second edition: (Guthrie, 1909?) 271 pp., cloth. $75.

HART, Joseph C. *The Romance of Yachting.* Cloth. New York, 1848. First edition. $150–$175.

HARTE, Bret. See *Oration, Poem, and Speeches; Outcroppings.*

HARTE, Bret. *Condensed Novels and Other Papers.* Illustrated by Frank Bellew. Violet cloth. New York, 1867. First edition. $150–$200. Author's first book.

HARTE, Bret. *Dickens in Camp.* Half cloth. San Francisco, 1922. Grabhorn printing. One of 350. $75–$100.

HARTE, Bret. *"Excelsior."* (Cover title.) 16 pp., oblong, blue wrappers. Five Points, N.Y., (1877). First edition, first issue, with Donaldson imprint. $150. Later issue, without Donaldson imprint: $100 (Also issued in cloth.)

HARTE, Bret. *Gabriel Conroy.* Illustrated. Mauve cloth. Hartford, 1876. First American edition, first binding. $150–$200. London, (1876). 3 vols., cloth. First edition. $150.

HARTE, Bret. *The Heathen Chinee.* 9 lithographed cards in envelope. Chicago, 1870. First separate edition. $125–$200. London, (about 1871). Yellow wrappers. $125.

HARTE, Bret. *The Lost Galleon and Other Tales.* Cloth. San Francisco, 1867. First edition. $300–$350.

HARTE, Bret. *The Luck of Roaring Camp and Other Sketches.* Green or terra-cotta cloth. Boston, 1870. First edition, first issue, without the story "Brown of Calaveras." $400–$500. Second issue: Brown cloth. $200–$300. Boston, 1870. Second edition, with "Brown of Calaveras." $150–$200. San Francisco, 1916. John Henry Nash printing. Half cloth. One of 260. $150–$200. San Francisco, 1948. Grabhorn Press. Folio, half cloth. One of 300. $100–$150.

HARTE, Bret. *Mliss: An Idyl of Red Mountain.* Printed wrappers. New York, (1873). (Pirated edition of the story, which originally appeared in *The Luck of Roaring Camp.* Contains 50 additional chapters by R. G. Densmore.) First edition, first issue, with Harte's name on the title page and front cover. $1,200 (A, 1981). Second issue, with Harte's name removed and with page 34 a cancel leaf. $500–$750. San Francisco, 1948. Grabhorn Press. Half cloth. One of 300. $100–$150.

HARTE, Bret. *The Pliocene Skull.* Illustrated by E. M. Schaeffer. 9 leaves, flexible purple boards and cloth. (Washington, 1871?) First edition, presumed first issue. $150–$250. Presumed second issue: 10 leaves, flexible boards, with drawing of miner on front cover. $75–$100. (Note: Blanck questions this long-accepted sequence but doesn't say why. The first issue has an auction record of $170, set in 1944.) Another issue (?): Green wrappers and cloth. $50 (A, 1981).

HARTE, Bret. *Poems.* Green cloth. Boston, 1871. First edition, first issue, with Fields, Osgood monogram on title page and "S.T.K." for "T.S.K." on page 136. $100–$150.

HARTE, Bret. *The Queen of the Pirate Isle.* 28 color illustrations by Kate Greenaway. Decorated cloth. London, (1886). First edition, first issue, bound in unbleached linen, with green end papers, gilt edges. In pictorial (Greenaway) dust jacket. $400–$500. Boston, 1887 (actually 1886). Illustrated. Cloth. First American edition. $200.

HARTE, Bret. *San Francisco in 1866.* San Francisco, 1951. Grabhorn Press. One of 400. $100–$150.

HARTE, Bret. *The Story of Enriquez.* Boards. San Francisco, 1924. Grabhorn Press. First edition. One of 100. $200–$250.

HARTE, Bret. *Tales of the Argonauts and Other Sketches.* Cloth. Boston, 1875. First edition. $75–$100.

HARTE, Bret. *Tales of the Gold Rush.* Illustrated. Cloth. New York, 1944. Limited Editions Club. First edition. Boxed. $60–$75.

HARTE, Bret. *Tennessee's Partner.* Boards and vellum. San Francisco, 1907. First edition. $50–$75.

HARTE, Bret. *The Wild West.* Hand-colored illustrations. Burlap. Paris, (1930). Harrison of Paris. First edition. One of 36 on vellum. Boxed. $250–$300. Another issue: One of 840. $100–$150.

HARTE, Bret, and Bellows, the Rev. Henry W. *Fourteenth Anniversary of the Society of California Pioneers. Oration: By Rev. Henry W. Bellows. Poem: By Frank Bret Harte, Esq.* Printed wrappers. San Francisco, 1864. First edition. $250–$350.

HARTE, Bret, and Twain, Mark. *Sketches of the Sixties.* Boards and cloth. San Francisco, 1926. First edition. One of 250. In dust jacket. $150–$175. Trade edition: $100.

HARTLEY, L. P. *The Go-Between.* Red cloth. London, (1953). First edition. In dust jacket. $50–$60.

HARTLEY, Marsden. *Twenty-Five Poems.* Wrappers. (Paris, 1923.) First edition. $50–$100.

HARTLEY, Oliver C. *Digest of the Laws of Texas.* Buckram. Philadelphia, 1850. $150–$200.

HARTSHORNE, Albert. *Old English Glasses.* Color frontispiece, plates, numerous drawings. Folio, vellum and cloth. London, 1897. $100–$150.

HARTZENBUSCH, Juan Eugenio. *The Lovers of Teruel.* Translated by Henry Thomas. Morocco. Newtown, Wales, 1938. Gregynog Press. One of 175. $600. Another issue: One of 20 specially bound in morocco by George Fisher. $800–$1,200.

HARVARD Class Day 1910. (Cover title.) Illustrated. 17 leaves, stiff cream wrappers, red cord ties. (Cambridge, Mass.), 1910. $600–$900. Also $600 (A, 1977). (Note: Includes a class ode by T. S. Eliot, his first contribution to a book.)

HARVARD Lyrics. Cloth. Boston, 1899. First edition. (Includes "Vita Mea," the first published work of Wallace Stevens.) $200–$250.

HARVEY, Henry. *History of the Shawnee Indians.* Illustrated. Cloth. Cincinnati, 1855. First edition, first issue, without portrait. $125–$200.

HARVEY, William. *The Anatomical Exercises.* Edited by Geoffrey Keynes. Drawing by Stephen Gooden. Full morocco. London, (1928). Nonesuch Press. One of 1,450. $250–$300.

HASHEESH Eater (The). Blue cloth. New York, 1857. (By Fitz-Hugh Ludlow.) First edition. $200–$250. Author's first book.

HASKELL, Burnette G. *Kaweah, a Co-operative Commonwealth.* 16 pp., wrappers. San Francisco, 1887. First edition. $150.

HASKINS, C. W. *The Argonauts of California.* Cloth. New York, 1890. First edition. $200–$300.

HASTAIN, E. *Township Plats of the Creek Nation.* Full limp morocco. Muskogee, Okla., 1910. $250–$350.

HASTINGS, Frank S. *A Ranchman's Recollections.* Illustrated. Pictorial cloth. Chicago, 1921. First edition. In dust jacket. $100–$125. Lacking jacket, $50.

HASTINGS, Lansford W. *The Emigrant's Guide to Oregon and California.* 152 pp., wrappers, or printed boards. Cincinnati, 1845. First edition. $10,000 and up. Rebound in calf and boards. $6,500. Also, in boards, covers "cracked," $4,000 (A, 1968); rebound in leather, $4,700 (A, 1959); rebound facsimile wrappers, $4,000 (A, 1963).

HASTINGS, Lansford W. *A New History of Oregon and California.* Frontispiece. Half cloth. Cincinnati, 1849. $400–$500.

HASTINGS, Sally. *Poems, on Different Subjects. To Which is Added a Descriptive Account of a Family Tour to the West, in the Year 1800.* Leather. Lancaster, Pa., 1808. First edition. $250–$300.

HASWELL, Anthony (editor). *Memoirs and Adventures of Capt. Matthew Phelps.* Leather. Bennington, Vt., 1802. First edition. $400–$500.

HATFIELD, Edwin F. *History of Elizabeth, New Jersey.* 8 plates. Morocco. New York, 1868. First edition. $125–$150.

HATTERAS, Owen. *Pistols for Two.* Pink wrappers. New York, 1917. (By H. L. Mencken and George Jean Nathan.) First edition. $125–$150.

HAUPT, Herman. *Reminiscences.* Cloth. Milwaukee, 1901. First edition. Limited and signed. $100–$125.

HAVEN, Charles T., and Belden, Frank A. *History of the Colt Revolver.* Illustrated. Cloth. New York, 1940. First edition. Boxed. $150. Another issue: Morocco. Signed. Boxed. $250–$350. New York, (about 1960). Cloth. $35.

HAWBUCK Grange; or, The Sporting Adventures of Thomas Scott, Esq. 8 illustrations by Phiz. Blind-stamped pictorial red cloth. London, 1847. (By Robert Smith Surtees.) First edition, with April ads. $250–$350.

HAWES, Charles Boardman. *The Dark Frigate.* Illustrated by A. L. Ripley. Pictorial cloth. Boston, (1923). First edition. In dust jacket. $50–$60.

HAWES, William Post. *Sporting Scenes and Sundry Sketches.* Edited by Frank Forester. Illustrated. 2 vols., cloth. New York, 1842. First edition. $125–$150.

HAWKER, Peter. *Instructions to Young Sportsmen.* Boards. London, 1814. First edition. $500–$600. London, 1816. Second edition. $250–$350. London, 1824. Third edition. $200–$250. Philadelphia, 1846. Cloth. First American edition. $150–$200.

HAWKER, The Rev. Robert S. *The Cornish Ballads and Other Poems.* Green cloth. London, 1869. First edition. $125.

HAWKER, The Rev. Robert S. *The Quest of the Sangraal: Chant the First.* Cloth. Exeter, England, 1864. First edition. Printed on vellum. $500–$600.

HAWKES, J. C. B., Jr. *Fiasco Hall.* Wrappers. Cambridge, Mass., 1943. (By John Hawkes.) First edition. $500–$750. Author's first book.

HAWKES, John. *The Cannibal.* Gray cloth. (Norfolk, Conn., 1949.) New Directions. First edition, first binding. In dust jacket. $100–$125.

HAWKES, John. *Lunar Landscapes.* Cloth. (New York, 1969.) New Directions. First edition. One of 150 signed. Boxed. $80–$100. Trade edition: In dust jacket. $20.

HAWKES, John. *Second Skin.* Cloth. (New York, 1964.) New Directions. First edition. One of 100 signed. In slipcase. $75–$100. Trade edition: In dust jacket. $35.

HAWKINS, Alfred. *Hawkins's Picture of Quebec; with Historical Recollections.* 14 plates. Boards. Quebec, 1834. First edition. $250–$350.

HAWKS of Hawk-Hollow (The). 2 vols., purple cloth, paper labels. Philadelphia, 1835. (By Robert Montgomery Bird.) First edition. $300–$400.

HAWLEY, A. T. *The Climate, Resources, and Advantages of Humboldt County.* 42 pp., wrappers. Eureka, Calif., 1879. First edition. $450–$500.

HAWLEY, A. T. *The Present Condition, Growth, Progress and Advantages of Los Angeles City and County, Southern California.* Map. 144 pp., printed wrappers. Los Angeles, 1876. First edition. $400–$600.

HAWLEY, R. D. *The Hawley Collection of Violins.* Half cloth. Chicago, 1904. Limited edition. $350–$400.

HAWLEY, W. A. *The Early Days of Santa Barbara.* 5 plates. 105 pp., printed wrappers. New York, 1910. First edition. $100–$150.

HAWLEY, Walter A. *Oriental Rugs: Antique and Modern.* Plates. Half morocco. New York, 1913. $150–$200. New York, 1922. $150. New York, 1937. Cloth. $100–$125.

HAWLEY, Zerah. *A Journal of a Tour Through Connecticut, Massachusetts, New York, etc.* Boards. New Haven, 1822. First edition. $400–$500.

HAWTHORNE, Nathaniel. See *Fanshawe; Peter Parley's Universal History; The Sister Years.*

HAWTHORNE, Nathaniel. *Biographical Stories for Children.* Cloth. Boston, 1842. First edition. $100–$150.

HAWTHORNE, Nathaniel. *The Blithedale Romance.* 2 vols., cloth. London, 1852. First edition. $150–$200. Boston, 1852. Tan cloth. First American edition, with 4 pages of ads at end. $100–$150.

HAWTHORNE, Nathaniel. *The Celestial Rail-Road.* 32 pp., buff wrappers. Boston, 1843. First edition and first separate printing. $1,500 and up. Also, foxed, covers mended, $950 (A, 1974). (Note: No priority established for two publisher imprints— Wilder or Fish—both excessively rare.)

HAWTHORNE, Nathaniel. *Doctor Grimshawe's Secret.* Edited by Julian Hawthorne. Pictorial cloth. Boston, 1883. First edition. $150–$200. Large paper issue, same date but later: One of 250 numbered copies; some signed by the editor. $250–$350.

HAWTHORNE, Nathaniel. *Famous Old People, Being the Second Epoch of Grandfather's Chair.* Cloth, paper label. Boston, 1841. First edition. $200–$250.

HAWTHORNE, Nathaniel. *The Gentle Boy: A Thrice-Told Tale.* Engraved frontispiece. Wrappers. Boston, 1839. First edition. $500–$600.

HAWTHORNE, Nathaniel. *Grandfather's Chair: A History.* Cloth, paper label. Boston, 1841. First edition. $200–$250.

HAWTHORNE, Nathaniel. *The House of the Seven Gables*. Brown cloth. Boston, 1851. First edition, presumed first binding, with roman ampersand in spine imprint and March ads. $600–$750. Worn copy, May ads, $225. New York, 1935. Limited Editions Club. $60–$70.

HAWTHORNE, Nathaniel. *Liberty Tree, with the Last Word of Grandfather's Chair*. Cloth, paper label. Boston, 1841. First edition, first issue, with second line of page 24 ending "in a Con-". $150–$250.

HAWTHORNE, Nathaniel. *Life of Franklin Pierce*. Frontispiece. Printed wrappers, or cloth. Boston, 1852. First edition. $150–$200.

HAWTHORNE, Nathaniel. *Love Letters of Nathaniel Hawthorne*. Portrait. 2 vols., boards and vellum. Chicago, 1907. First edition. One of 67. $300–$400.

HAWTHORNE, Nathaniel. *The Marble Faun; or The Romance of Monte Beni*. 2 vols., brown cloth. Boston, 1860. First American edition, first issue, without "Conclusion" at end. $500–$600. Second issue, with "Conclusion." $200–$300. (For first English edition, which may have preceded the American, see Hawthorne, *Transformation*.)

HAWTHORNE, Nathaniel. *Mosses from an Old Manse*. 2 vols., wrappers, or one volume, cloth. New York, 1846. First edition. Wrappers: $750 and up. One-volume issue: $300–$350.

HAWTHORNE, Nathaniel. *Our Old Home*. Brown cloth. Boston, 1863. First edition, first state, with ad on page 399. $200–$225. London, 1863. 2 vols., cloth. First English edition. $150–$200. (Note: Blanck thinks this was issued simultaneously with the American first.)

HAWTHORNE, Nathaniel. *Passages from the American Note-Books*. 2 vols., green cloth. Boston, 1868. First edition, with spine reading "Ticknor & Co." (Later, "Fields, Osgood & Co.") $200–$250. London, 1870. 2 vols., cloth. First English edition. $100–$125.

HAWTHORNE, Nathaniel. *The Scarlet Letter*. Brown cloth. Boston, 1850. First edition, first issue, with "reduplicate" in line 20 of page 21; "characterss" in line 5 of page 41, and "catechism" in line 29 of page 132. $850–$1,000. Worn copy, $350. Boston, 1850. Cloth. Second edition. $250–$300. New York, 1892. Cloth. Illustrated by F. O. C. Darley. $150. New York, 1904. Morocco. One of 125 on vellum. $500–$650. New York, 1908. Grolier Club. Illustrated. Boards. One of 300. $150–$175. New York, (1915). Illustrated by Hugh Thomson. $125–$150. New York, 1928. Grabhorn Press. Colored woodblocks by Valenti Angelo. Half morocco. One of 980. In dust jacket. $150–$200. New York, 1941. Limited Editions Club. Illustrated by Henry Varnum Poor. Leather. Boxed. $60–$85.

HAWTHORNE, Nathaniel. *The Snow-Image and Other Twice-Told Tales*. Brown cloth. Boston, 1852. First edition. $150–$250. London, 1851. Cloth. First English edition. (Issued simultaneously with American first edition, Blanck suggests. Titled *The Snow-Image, and Other Tales*.) $125–$150.

HAWTHORNE, Nathaniel. *Tanglewood Tales, for Girls and Boys*. Decorated cloth. Boston, 1853. First American edition, first printing, without "George C. Rand" imprint on copyright page. $225–$250. London, 1853. Green cloth. First edition (preceding the American edition by a few days). $150. London, (1918). Illustrated by Edmund Dulac. Half vellum. One of 500 signed by Dulac. $650–$800. Trade edition: Cloth. $80–$125.

HAWTHORNE, Nathaniel. *Transformation*. 3 vols., old rose cloth. London, 1860. First English edition of *The Marble Faun*, which see. $300–$400. (Note: Possibly preceded the American first edition, says Blanck.)

HAWTHORNE, Nathaniel. *True Stories from History and Biography*. Cloth. Boston, 1851. First edition, first issue, with verso of title page imprinted "Cambridge: Printed by Bolles and Houghton." $125–$150.

HAWTHORNE, Nathaniel. *Twice-Told Tales*. Brownish cloth. Boston, 1837. First edition. $1,500 and up. Also, a rubbed copy, $650 (A, 1974); $1,250 (A, 1960)—for a copy "in unusually fine condition . . . lettering on backstrip in brilliant gilt." Retail values for copies in very good condition range up to $750 and more. New York, 1966. Limited Editions Club. Colored illustrations by Valenti Angelo. Blue cloth. Boxed. $40–$50.

HAWTHORNE, Nathaniel. *A Wonder-Book for Girls and Boys.* Frontispiece, 6 plates. Purple or green cloth. Boston, 1852. First edition, first issue, with gilt decorations covering only top third of spine and with no ads. $600–$800. Also, $450 (A, 1976). London, 1852. 8 engravings. Decorated blue cloth. First English edition. $300–$400. London, 1893. Illustrated by Walter Crane. Decorated cloth. $100–$150. Cambridge, Mass., 1893. Crane illustrations. Vellum. One of 250. $400–$500. Ordinary issue, cloth: $100–$150. London, (1922). Illustrated by Arthur Rackham. White buckram. One of 600 signed by the artist. Boxed. $600–$850.

HAWTHORNE, Nathaniel (editor). *Journal of an African Cruiser.* Cloth. New York, 1845. (By Horatio Bridge.) First edition. $150–$250.

HAY, John. *Jim Bludso of the Prairie Bell, and Little Breeches.* Illustrated by S. Eytinge, Jr. 23 pp., printed orange wrappers. Boston, 1871. First edition. $100–$125. Author's first book.

HAY, John. *Letters of John Hay and Extracts from His Diary.* 3 vols., cloth, paper labels. Washington, 1908. First edition. $300–$350.

HAYDEN, Ferdinand V. *Geological and Geographical Atlas of Colorado.* 20 double-page maps, mostly colored. Three-quarters morocco. (Washington), 1877. $200. Washington, 1881. $100–$150.

HAYDEN, Ferdinand V. *Sun Pictures of Rocky Mountain Scenery.* 30 mounted photographs. Half morocco. New York, 1870. First edition. $2,000–$3,000.

HAYDEN, Ferdinand V. *The Yellowstone National Park.* 2 maps. Illustrated in color by Thomas Moran. Folio, half morocco portfolio. Boston, 1876. First edition. $3,000–$4,000.

HAYES, Joseph. *The Desperate Hours.* Cloth. New York, (1954). First edition. In dust jacket. $40–$50.

HAYMOND, Creed. *The Central Pacific Railroad.* 181 pp., wrappers. Washington, (about 1888). First edition. $125–$150.

HAYMOND, Henry. *History of Harrison County, West Virginia.* Cloth. Morgantown, W. Va., (1910). First edition. $100–$125.

HAYWARD, John (compiler). *English Poetry: An Illustrated Catalogue of First and Early Editions Exhibited by the National Book League, 1947.* Facsimiles. Buckram. Cambridge, 1950. One of 550. In dust jacket. $150–$200. Another issue: One of 50. In dust jacket. $350–$400. (An unillustrated version preceded this in 1947. Value: $25–$35.)

HAYWOOD, John. *The Civil and Political History of the State of Tennessee.* Calf. Knoxville, 1823. First edition, with tipped-in copyright slip and inserted printed slip. $500–$600.

HAYWOOD, John. *The Natural and Aboriginal History of Tennessee.* Leather. Nashville, 1823. First edition, with errata leaf. $600–$750.

HAZEL, Harry. *The Flying Artillerist.* 3 full-page woodcuts. 92 pp., wrappers. New York, 1853. (By Justin Jones). First edition. $125–$150.

HAZEL, Harry. *The Flying Yankee, or the Cruise of the Clipper.* Wrappers. New York, (1853). (By Justin Jones.) First edition. $100–$125.

HAZEL, Harry. *Old Put; or, The Days of Seventy-Six.* 104 pp., sewed. New York, (1852). (By Justin Jones.) First edition. $100–$125.

HAZEL, Harry. *The Rebel and the Rover.* Wrappers. Philadelphia, (about 1855). (By Justin Jones.) $100–$125.

HAZEL, Harry. *The West Point Cadet.* Illustrated. 100 pp., printed wrappers. Boston, 1845. (By Justin Jones.) First edition. $125–$150.

HAZEN, Gen. W. B. *A Narrative of Military Service.* Map, illustrations. Cloth. Boston. 1885. $75–$100.

HAZEN, Gen. W. B. *Our Barren Lands.* 53 pp., printed blue wrappers. Cincinnati, 1875. First edition. $400–$500.

HAZEN, Gen. W. B. *Some Corrections of "Life on the Plains."* (Cover title.) 18 pp., wrappers. St. Paul, 1875. First edition. $750–$1,000.

HAZLITT, William. *Characters of Shakespear's Plays.* Boards, paper label. London, 1817. First edition. $150–$250.

HAZLITT, William. *Conversations of James Northcote, Esq., R.A.* Portrait. Boards. paper label. London, 1830. First edition. $150.

HAZLITT. William. *Lectures on the English Poets.* Boards, paper label. London, 1818. First edition, with 4 pages of ads at end dated May 1, 1818. $200–$250.

HAZLITT, William. *Political Essays, with Sketches of Public Characters.* Boards, paper label. London, 1819. First edition. $200–$250.

HEADLEY, John W. *Confederate Operations in Canada and New York.* Portraits. Cloth. New York, 1906. First edition. $85–$100.

HEADLONG Hall. Boards. London, 1816. (By Thomas Love Peacock.) First edition. $500–$600.

HEADSMAN (The). 3 vols., tan boards, or rose-colored cloth. London, 1833. (By James Fenimore Cooper.) First edition. $600–$800. Philadelphia, 1833. 2 vols., blue boards. First American edition. $600–$800.

HEAL, Ambrose. *London Tradesmen's Cards of the 19th Century.* Illustrated. Half vellum. London, 1925. (100 copies printed at the Curwen Press.) $200–$300.

HEAP, Gwinn Harris. *Central Route to the Pacific.* Folding map (not in all copies), 13 tinted plates. Cloth. Philadelphia, 1854. First edition, first issue, with Plate IV lacking a plate or page number, $750. Another issue, without map: $225.

HEARN, Lafcadio. See Bisland, Elizabeth; Gautier, Théophile; Chahta-Ima. Also, see *La Cuisine Créole; Historical Sketch-Book and Guide to New Orleans.*

HEARN, Lafcadio. *Chita: A Memory of Last Island.* Salmon-colored cloth, New York, 1889. First edition. In dust jacket. $150–$250. Lacking jacket, $50–$75.

HEARN, Lafcadio. *Editorials from the Kobe Chronicle.* (Cover title.) Printed white wrappers. (New York, 1913.) First edition. One of 100, with an addenda slip tipped in. $300–$350.

HEARN, Lafcadio. *Gleanings in Buddha-Fields.* Blue cloth. Boston, 1897. First edition. $75–$100.

HEARN, Lafcadio. *Glimpses of Unfamiliar Japan.* Illustrated. 2 vols., black or olive cloth. Boston, 1894. First edition. In dust jackets. $150–$200.

HEARN, Lafcadio. *"Gombo Zhebes"; Little Dictionary of Creole Proverbs.* Gray-blue pictorial cloth. New York, 1885. First edition. $200–$250.

HEARN, Lafcadio. *In Ghostly Japan.* Illustrated. Pictorial blue cloth. Boston, 1899. First edition. $50–$75.

HEARN, Lafcadio. *Insects and Greek Poetry*. Printed blue boards. New York, 1926. First edition. One of 550. In glassine dust jacket. $50–$75.

HEARN, Lafcadio. *Japan: An Attempt at Interpretation*. Colored frontispiece. Tan cloth. New York 1904. First edition. In dust jacket. $75–$100. Lacking jacket, $35–$50.

HEARN, Lafcadio. *Japanese Fairy Tales*. 5 vols., wrappers. Tokyo, (1898–1903). First editions. *(The Boy Who Drew Cats, The Goblin Spider, The Old Woman Who Lost Her Dumpling, The Fountain of Youth, Chin Chin Kobakama.)* $500–$750 for complete sets. (Note: Blanck calls the bibliographical problems connected with these beautiful little woodblock books "insoluble." However, they have frequently been at auction in various forms, including large paper and crepe paper states.)

HEARN, Lafcadio. *The Japanese Letters of Lafcadio Hearn*. Edited by Elizabeth Bisland. Green cloth. Boston, 1910. First edition. One of 200 large paper copies. $100–$125.

HEARN, Lafcadio. *A Japanese Miscellany*. Illustrated. Pictorial green cloth. Boston, 1901. First edition. (Copies with or without "October, 1901" on copyright page are acceptable first editions, Blanck seems to suggest.) In dust jacket, $200–$250. Without dust jacket, $100–$125.

HEARN, Lafcadio. *Kokoro*. Green cloth. Boston, 1896. First edition. $50–$75.

HEARN, Lafcadio. *Kotto*. Illustrated. Pictorial olive cloth. New York, 1902. First edition, presumed first state, with background of title page upside down, artist's monogram in upper right corner. In dust jacket. $200–$250. Without jacket, $100–$125.

HEARN, Lafcadio. *Kwaidan*. Illustrated. Pictorial cloth. Boston, 1904. First edition. In dust jacket. $150–$200. Without jacket, $100. New York, 1932. Limited Editions Club. Color plates. Printed silk binding. In silk wraparound case. $100–$135.

HEARN, Lafcadio. *Leaves from the Diary of an Impressionist*. Facsimile of a Hearn poem. Blue boards. Boston, 1911. First edition. One of 575. In dust jacket. $125–$150.

HEARN, Lafcadio. *Lectures on Tennyson*. Cloth. Tokyo, (1941). First edition. One of 500. In dust jacket. $200–$250.

HEARN, Lafcadio. *Occidental Gleanings*. 2 vols., cloth. New York, 1925. First edition. In dust jacket. $100.

HEARN, Lafcadio. *The Romance of the Milky Way*. Cloth. Boston, 1905. First edition. In dust jacket. $75–$85.

HEARN, Lafcadio. *Shadowings*. Illustrated. Pictorial blue cloth. Boston, 1900. First edition. In blue and silver dust jacket. $150–$200. Without jacket, $75.

HEARN, Lafcadio. *Some Chinese Ghosts*. Pictorial rose-colored cloth. Boston, 1887. First edition. $150–$200. (Also in red and other colors of cloth.)

HEARN, Lafcadio. *Some New Letters and Writings*. Cloth. Tokyo, 1925. First edition. In dust jacket. $150–$200.

HEARN, Lafcadio. *Stray Leaves from Strange Literature*. Blue cloth. Boston, 1884. First edition, first issue, with JR. O. & CO. imprint on spine. $150–$250. Author's first book.

HEARN, Lafcadio. *Two Years in the French West Indies*. Illustrated. Decorated olive cloth. New York, 1890. First edition. $75–$100.

HEARN, Lafcadio. *Youma*. Frontispiece. Cloth, paper labels. New York, 1890. First edition, first binding, white calico with blue design. $100–$125.

HEART of the West (The): An American Story. By an Illinoian. Brown cloth. Chicago, 1871. First edition. $100–$125. (Note: The author's identity remains a mystery.)

HEART, Capt. Jonathan. *Journal*. Edited by C. W. Butterfield, 94 pp., tan printed wrappers. Albany, N.Y., 1885. First edition. One of 150. $250.

HEARTMAN, Charles F. *The New-England Primer*. Facsimiles. Boards. New York, 1915. First edition. One of 265. $100–$150. New York, 1934. Cloth. One of 300. $75–$85.

HEARTMAN, Charles F., and Canny, James R. *A Bibliography of the First Printings of Edgar Allan Poe*. Cloth. Hattiesburg, Miss., 1940. First edition. $100–$125.

HEARTMAN, Charles F., and Rede, Kenneth. *A Bibliographical Checklist of the First Editions of Edgar Allan Poe*. 3 vols., boards. Metuchen. N.J., 1932. Limited to 240, 202, and 100. $100–$150.

HEBARD, Grace R. *Sacajawea*. Plates and maps. Cloth. Glendale, Calif., 1933. First edition. One of 750. $75–$100.

HEBARD, Grace R. *Washakie*. 7 maps, 16 plates. Cloth. Cleveland, 1930. First edition. $75–$85.

HEBARD, Grace R., and Brininstool, E. A. *The Bozeman Trail*. Plates, 2 folding maps. 2 vols., cloth. Cleveland, 1922. First edition. $125–$150. Glendale, Calif., 1960. 2 vols. in one, cloth. $40–$60.

HEBISON, W. C. *Early Days in Texas and Rains County*. 50 pp., wrappers. Emory, Tex., 1917. First edition. $200–$250.

HECHT, Anthony. *Aesopic: Twenty-Four Couplets*. Thomas Bewick illustrations. Boards. Northampton, (1968). Gehenna Press. One of 50 signed by Leonard Baskin, with an extra set of plates. $250–$300.

HECHT, Anthony. *The Seven Deadly Sins*. Illustrated by Leonard Baskin. Oblong, stiff wrappers. Northampton, 1958. First edition. One of 300 signed by author and artist. $250–$300.

HECHT, Anthony. *A Summoning of Stones*. Cloth. New York, (1954). First edition. In dust jacket. $75–$100. Author's first book.

HECHT. Ben. *The Bewitched Tailor*. Drawing by George Grosz. 8 pp., printed wrappers. New York, 1941. First edition. One of 875 signed by author and artist. $75–$100.

HECHT, Ben. *A Book of Miracles*. Cloth. New York, 1939. First edition. In dust jacket. $50–$60.

HECHT, Ben. *A Child of the Century*. Boards and cloth. Chicago, 1954. First edition. In dust jacket. $40–$60.

HECHT, Ben. *Christmas Eve: A Morality Play*. Vellum. (New York), 1928. First edition. One of 111 signed. $100–$125.

HECHT, Ben. *Fantazius Mallare*. Illustrated by Wallace Smith. Cloth. Chicago, 1922. First edition. One of 2,000. In dust jacket. $75–$125.

HECHT, Ben. *A Jew in Love*. Cloth. New York, (1931). First edition. One of 150 signed. Boxed. $100–$135. Trade edition: First issue, with exactly 34 lines on page 306, as in the signed edition. In dust jacket. $50–$60. Later issue, 32 lines: $25.

HECHT, Ben. *The Kingdom of Evil*. Illustrated. Black cloth. Chicago, 1924. One of 2,000. In dust jacket. $50–$75.

HECHT, Ben. *A Thousand and One Afternoons in Chicago*. Illustrated. Boards. Chicago, (1922). First edition. In dust jacket. $75–$100.

HECHT, Ben, and Bodenheim, Maxwell. *Cutie, a Warm Mama*. Orange cloth or orange boards and cloth. Chicago, 1924. (By Ben Hecht alone.) First edition. One of 200 (probably a spurious limitation). In dust jacket. $50–$65.

HECHT, Ben, and Fowler, Gene. *The Great Magoo.* Illustrated. Cloth. New York, (1933). First edition. In dust jacket. $75–$100.

HECHT, Ben, and MacArthur, Charles. *The Front Page.* Cloth. New York, 1928. First edition. In dust jacket. $75–$100.

HECKENDORN & Wilson. *Miners and Business Men's Directory.* (For Tuolumne, Calif.) 104 pp., printed wrappers. Columbia, Calif., 1856. First edition. $1,500–$2,500.

HECKEWELDER, John. *An Account of the History, Manners, and Customs of the Indian Nations.* Calf. Philadelphia, 1818. First edition. $100–$150. Philadelphia, 1819. Second edition. $75–$85.

HECKEWELDER, John. *A Narrative of the Mission of the United Brethren Among the Delaware and Mohegan Indians.* Portrait and errata slip. Boards. Philadelphia, 1820. First edition. $150–$250. Cleveland, 1907. 3 maps, 5 plates. Three-quarters leather. One of 160 on large paper. $150–$175.

HEGAN, Alice Caldwell. *Mrs. Wiggs of the Cabbage Patch.* Olive-green cloth. New York, 1901. First edition, first issue, with gold sky on cover. $50–$60.

HEIDENMAUER (The); or The Benedictines. By the Author of "The Pilot." 3 vols., green or tan boards. London, 1832. (By James Fenimore Cooper.) First edition. $400–$500. Philadelphia, 1832. 2 vols., gray-blue boards. First American edition. $500–$600.

HEINLEIN, Robert A. *Assignment in Eternity.* Brick red cloth. Reading, Pa., (1953). First edition, first binding, with Heinlein's name on spine in letters 3 millimeters high. In dust jacket. $75–$85. Another issue: One of 500 signed. In dust jacket. $150.

HEINLEIN, Robert A. *Beyond This Horizon.* Cloth. Reading, Pa., 1948. First edition. In dust jacket. $75–100. Another issue: One of 500 signed. $150.

HEINLEIN, Robert A. *The Discovery of the Future.* (Cover title.) Wrappers. (Los Angeles, 1941.) First edition. (200 copies.) $300 (A spirit-duplicated copy of a speech to the World Science Fiction Convention.)

HEINLEIN, Robert A. *Double Star.* Boards. Garden City, 1956. First edition. In dust jacket. $75–$100.

HEINLEIN, Robert A. *The Green Hills of Earth.* Boards. Chicago, (1951). First edition. In dust jacket. $175. Also, one of 300 signed on title page, $250–$300.

HEINLEIN, Robert A. *The Man Who Sold the Moon.* Boards. Chicago, (1950). First edition. In dust jacket. $150–$175. (Issued later in cloth.)

HEINLEIN, Robert A. *Revolt in 2100.* Boards. Chicago, (1953). First edition. In dust jacket. $150–$200.

HEINLEIN, Robert A. *Rocket Ship Galileo.* Pictorial cloth. New York, (1947). First edition. In dust jacket. $300–$350. Author's first book.

HEINLEIN, Robert A. *The Rolling Stones.* Cloth. New York, (1952). First edition. In dust jacket. $125–$150.

HEINLEIN, Robert A. *Starman Jones.* Cloth. New York, (1953). First edition. In dust jacket. $125–$150.

HEINLEIN, Robert A. *Starship Troopers.* Cloth. New York, (1959). First edition. In dust jacket. $300–$350.

HEINLEIN, Robert A. *Stranger in a Strange Land.* Cloth. New York, (1961). First edition. In dust jacket. $150–$175.

HEINLEIN, Robert A. *Time for the Stars.* Cloth. New York, (1956). First edition. In dust jacket. $125–$150.

HEINS, Hardy Henry. *A Golden Anniversary Bibliography of Edgar Rice Burroughs.* Cloth. West Kingston, R.I., 1964. Complete edition, revised. $300.

HELFORTH, John. *Nights.* Printed wrappers. (Dijon, France, 1955.) (By Hilda Doolittle.) One of 100. $200–$250.

HELLER, Elinor, and Magee, David. *Bibliography of the Grabhorn Press, 1915–1940.* Illustrated. Full leather. San Francisco, 1940. One of 210 specially bound. $2,500. Trade edition: Boards. $400–$500. Also, see Dorothy and David Magee entry for a related work.

HELLER, Joseph. *Catch-22.* Cloth. New York, 1961. First edition. In dust jacket. $300–$400. London, 1962. First English edition. In dust jacket. $175–$200. Author's first book.

HELLER, Joseph. *Something Happened.* Cloth. New York, 1974. First edition. One of 350 signed. Boxed. $150–$200. Trade edition: Cloth. In dust jacket. $35.

HELM, Mary S. *Scraps of Early Texas History.* Cloth. Austin, 1884. First edition. $350–$425.

HELPER, Hinton R. *The Land of Gold.* Cloth. Baltimore, 1855. First edition. $100–$125.

HEMANS, Felicia. *The League of the Alps, The Siege of Valencia, The Vespers of Palermo, and Other Poems.* Boards, paper label. Boston, 1826. First edition. $50–$60.

HEMANS, Felicia. *Poems.* Boards. Liverpool, 1808. First edition. $100–$150.

HEMINGWAY, Ernest. See Bahr, Jerome; Cohn, Louis Henry; Dashiell, Alfred; Faulkner, William, *Salmagundi*; North, Joseph; Paul, Elliot; Schreiber, Georges. Also see *Kiki's Memoirs; Somebody Had to Do Something; Tabula; Senior Tabula.*

HEMINGWAY, Ernest. *Across the River and into the Trees.* Cloth. New York, 1950. First American edition, first issue, with "A" on copyright page. In dust jacket. $50–$60. (Note: First dust jacket lettered yellow; later, orange.) London, (1950). Green cloth. First edition (preceding the American first by 3 days). In dust jacket. $60–$75.

HEMINGWAY, Ernest. *Death in the Afternoon.* Frontispiece and photographs. Black cloth. New York, 1932. First edition, first issue, with "A" on copyright page. In dust jacket. $300–$350. London, (1932). Illustrated. Orange cloth. First English edition. In dust jacket. $200.

HEMINGWAY, Ernest. *A Farewell to Arms.* Black cloth, gold paper labels, New York, 1929. First edition, first state, without the notice that "none of the characters in this book is a living person." In dust jacket. $500–$600. Second state. In dust jacket. $350–$500. Another issue: Light blue-green boards, vellum spine and corners, black leather label. One of 510 signed. In glassine dust jacket. Boxed. $1,250–$2,000. London, (1929). Cloth. First English edition. In dust jacket. $250–$300. Another issue: Advance copy in wrappers. $400–$500.

HEMINGWAY, Ernest. *Fiesta.* Blue cloth. London, (1927). First English edition of *The Sun Also Rises.* In dust jacket. $500–$650.

HEMINGWAY, Ernest. *The Fifth Column and the First Forty-nine Stories.* Red cloth. New York, 1938. First edition, first printing, with "A" on copyright page. In dust jacket. $225–$250. (Also, 30 advance dummy copies for salesmen, with title page *The First 48.* A copy in a temporary dust jacket brought $1,600 at auction in October, 1977.)

HEMINGWAY, Ernest. *For Whom The Bell Tolls.* Beige cloth. New York, 1940. First edition, first printing, with "A" on copyright page. In first state dust jacket without photographer's name ("Arnold") under author's picture. $250–$300. (There were also 15 presentation copies in advance of publication, all presumably signed by Hemingway. Value: $1,500 and up? Additionally there were 30 dummy copies for salesmen, with 6 pages of text, in advance of publication. A copy sold for $2,000 at auction in October, 1977.) New York, 1942. Limited Editions Club. Cloth. Boxed. $175–$200. Another issue: One of 15 out-of-series presentation copies. $300–$500.

HEMINGWAY, Ernest. *God Rest You Merry Gentlemen.* Red cloth. New York, 1933. First edition. One of 300. In glassine dust jacket. $400–$600.

HEMINGWAY, Ernest. *Green Hills of Africa.* Light green cloth, New York, 1935. First edition, first issue, with "A" on copyright page. In dust jacket. Without fading of spine cloth (usually encountered), $400–$500. In dust jacket but with faded spine. $150–$200. London, 1935. Cloth. First English edition. In dust jacket. $100–$150.

HEMINGWAY, Ernest. *In Our Time.* Frontispiece portrait by Henry Strater. Decorated tan boards. Paris, 1924. Three Mountains Press. First edition. One of 170. $3,500. Also, $2,750 (A, 1977). New York, 1925. Black cloth. First American edition. In dust jacket. $1,000. Also, $750 (A, 1979). London, 1926. Cloth. First English edition. In dust jacket. $500–$600. New York, 1930. Introduction by Edmund Wilson. Cloth. In dust jacket. $100–$150.

HEMINGWAY, Ernest. *Introduction to Kiki of Montparnasse.* (Cover title.) 8 pp., printed white self-wrappers. New York, 1929. First edition. One of 25 for copyright, published by Edward W. Titus. $1,000 (A, 1977).

HEMINGWAY, Ernest. *Men Without Women.* Black cloth, gold labels, New York, 1927. First edition, first state, weighing 15 or 15½ ounces. In dust jacket. $450–$650. Later state, 14½ ounces, in later jacket. $75.

HEMINGWAY, Ernest. *A Moveable Feast.* Illustrated. Cloth. New York, (1964). First edition. In dust jacket. $50–$75. London, (1964). Boards. First English edition. In dust jacket. $30–$40.

HEMINGWAY, Ernest. *The Old Man and the Sea.* Folio, wrappers. *Life* magazine printing of the novel. First edition. Vol. 33, No. 9. Sept. 1, 1952. $10–$15. Uncorrected advance galley proofs of this printing. $500–$650. New York, 1952. Black buckram. First edition, presentation issue (preceding trade edition). One of 30. In tissue dust jacket, $1,300 (A, 1977). Trade edition: Blue cloth. In first issue dust jacket with no mention of the Nobel Prize. $150–$300. London, (1952). Cloth. First English edition. In dust jacket. $50–$75. New York, (1960). Illustrated by C. F. Tunnicliffe and R. Sheppard. Cloth. First illustrated edition. In dust jacket. $75–$100.

HEMINGWAY, Ernest. *The Spanish Earth.* Illustrated. Pictorial tan cloth. Cleveland, 1938. First edition, first issue, with pictorial end papers showing a large FAI banner. One of 50 or 100 copies of a limited edition of 1,000. In glassine dust jacket. $750–$1,000 Second issue, plain end papers: $200–$250.

HEMINGWAY, Ernest. *The Sun Also Rises.* Black cloth, gold labels. New York, 1926. First edition, first state, with "stoppped" for "stopped" on page 181, line 26. In dust jacket. $1,750–$2,000. Also $1,600 (A, 1979). See *Fiesta* for first English edition.

HEMINGWAY, Ernest. *Three Stories & Ten Poems.* Gray–blue wrappers. (Paris, 1923.) Contact Publishing Co. First edition. One of 300. $4,000–$4,250. Also, $4,000 (A, 1979). Author's first book.

HEMINGWAY, Ernest. *To Have and Have Not.* Black cloth. New York, 1937. First edition, first issue, with "A" on copyright page. In dust jacket. $300–$400. London, 1937. Blue cloth. First English edition. In dust jacket. $150–$200.

HEMINGWAY, Ernest. *Today Is Friday.* (Caption title; no title page.) 8 pp., white wrappers (with Jean Cocteau drawing). (Englewood, N.J., 1926.) First edition. One of 300. In printed envelope. $650–$850.

HEMINGWAY, Ernest. *The Torrents of Spring.* Dark green cloth. New York, 1926. First edition. In dust jacket. $600–$900. Paris, 1932 (actually 1931). White wrappers.

In glassine dust jacket. $400–$500. London, (1933). First English edition. In dust jacket. $300–$400. Advance copy: Wrappers. Repaired, $350. (A, 1977).

HEMINGWAY, Ernest. *Two Christmas Tales*. Blue wrappers. (Berkeley), 1959. Hart Press. One of 150. $500. Also, $275 (A, 1979).

HEMINGWAY, Ernest. *Winner Take Nothing*. Black cloth, gold paper labels. New York, 1933. First edition, with "A" on copyright page. In dust jacket. $250–$350. Lacking jacket, $75–$100. (There were also 30 dummy copies for salesmen, title page reading *Stories [Title to Be Determined]*. A copy sold at auction in October, 1977, for $1,800.)

HEMINGWAY, Ernest (editor). *Men at War: The Best War Stories of All Time*. Black cloth. New York, (1942). First edition. In dust jacket. $150–$200.

HENDERSON, Robert W. *Early American Sport: A Chronological Check-List*. Cloth. New York, 1937. Grolier Club. $100–$125.

HENKLE, Moses. *Gospel of Nicodemus, the Believing Jew*. 40 pp., sewed. Columbus, Ohio, 1826. First edition. $75–$100.

HENKLE, Moses. *Last Wills and Testaments of Thirteen Patriarchs, and Gospel of Nicodemus, the Believing Jew*. 67 pp., sewed. Urbana, Ohio, 1827. $75–$100.

HENLEY, William Ernest. *A Book of Verses*. Stiff printed wrappers. London, 1888. First edition. $150–$175. Worn copy, $85.

HENLEY, William Ernest. *Hawthorn and Lavender with Other Verses*. Boards. London, 1901. One of 20. $175–$200.

HENLEY, William Ernest. *London Types*. 12 colored illustrations by William Nicholson. Vellum, London, 1898. First edition. $300–$400. Another issue: Cloth. $150-$200.

HENLEY, William Ernest. *Small Letters*. Frontispiece. Wrappers. (London), 1933. First edition. One of 60. $100–$125.

HENLEY, William Ernest. *A Song of Speed*. Printed wrappers, or cloth. London, 1903. First edition. $75–$100.

HENLEY, William Ernest (editor). *Lyra Heroica: A Book of Verse for Boys*. Boards. London, 1892. One of 100 on large paper. $125–$150.

HENNEPIN, Father Louis. *A Description of Louisiana*. Translated by John G. Shea. Cloth. New York, 1880. One of 250. $150.

HENNIKER, Florence. *In Scarlet and Grey: Stories of Soldiers and Others*. Pictorial title page. Red cloth. London, 1896. First edition. $100. (Note: Contains "The Spectre of the Real," by Thomas Hardy and Florence Henniker.)

HENRIETTA Temple: A Love Story. 3 vols., cloth. London, 1837. (By Benjamin Disraeli.) First edition. $400–$600.

HENRY, Alexander (the younger), and Thompson, David. See: Coues, Elliott (editor).

HENRY, Alexander. *Travels and Adventures in Canada and the Indian Territories*. Boards. New York, 1809. First edition, first issue, without the portrait by Maverick, $500–$600. Second issue, with portrait: $900. Boston, 1901. Cloth. One of 700. $150.

HENRY, Edward Richard. *Classification and Use of Fingerprints*. 11 plates, 3 folding. Cloth. London. 1900. First edition. $250–$350.

HENRY, John Joseph. *An Accurate and Interesting Account of the Hardships and Sufferings of That Band of Heroes, Who Traversed the Wilderness in the Campaign Against Quebec in 1775*. Boards, or leather. Lancaster, Pa., 1812. First edition. $300–$400.

HENRY, John Joseph. *Campaign Against Quebec*. Sheep. Watertown, N.Y., 1844. Revised edition of *An Accurate and Interesting Account, etc.* $100–$150.

HENRY, O. *Cabbages and Kings*. Pictorial black cloth. New York, 1904. (By William Sidney Porter.) First edition, first issue, with "McClure, Phillips & Co." on spine. In dust jacket. $500–$600. Lacking jacket, $150 and up. Author's first book.

HENRY, O. *The Four Million*. Red cloth. New York, 1906. (By William Sidney Porter.) First edition. $100–$125.

HENRY, O. *The Gentle Grafter*. Illustrated. Red cloth. New York, 1908. (By William Sidney Porter.) First edition. $35–$50.

HENRY, O. *The Gift of the Magi*. Illustrated by Stephen Gooden. Half morocco. London, (1939). (By William Sidney Porter.) First edition. One of 105 signed. $150–$175. Another issue: Boards. In dust jacket. $50–$65.

HENRY, O. *Heart of the West*. Pictorial brown cloth. New York, 1907. (By William Sidney Porter.) First edition. In dust jacket. $200–$300. Lacking jacket, $75–$100.

HENRY, O. *The Hiding of Black Bill*. Pictorial wrappers. New York, (about 1913?). (By William Sidney Porter.) First edition. $50–$100.

HENRY, O. *Let Me Feel Your Pulse*. Illustrated. Cloth. New York, 1910. (By William Sidney Porter.) First edition, with October copyright notice. $30–$35.

HENRY, O. *O. Henry Encore: Stories and Illustrations*. Edited by Mary Harrell. Leatherette. Dallas, (1936). (By William Sidney Porter.) First edition. (One of 5 issued for copyright purposes?) $250 and up.

HENRY, O. *Roads of Destiny*. Red cloth. New York, 1909. (By William Sidney Porter.) First edition, first state, with "h" missing in line 6 on page 9. In dust jacket. $200–$250. Lacking jacket, $40–$50.

HENRY, O. *Rolling Stones*. Illustrated. Cloth. Garden City, 1912. (By William Sidney Porter.) First edition. $35–$50.

HENRO, O. *Sixes and Sevens*. Red cloth. Garden City, 1911. (By William Sidney Porter.) First edition. $35–$50.

HENRY, O. *The Trimmed Lamp*. Frontispiece by Alice Barber Stephens. Red cloth. New York, 1907. (By William Sidney Porter.) First edition, with "Published April, 1907" on copyright page. In dust jacket. $100–$150. Lacking jacket, $30–$50.

HENRY, O. *The Voice of the City*. Red cloth. New York, 1908. (By William Sidney Porter.) First edition, first binding, with McClure imprint on spine. In dust jacket. $250–$300. New York, 1935. Limited Editions Club. Buckram. Boxed. $175–$225.

HENRY, O. *Waifs and Strays: 12 Stories*. Cloth. Garden City, 1917. (By William Sidney Porter.) First edition. One of 200. $75–$100.

HENRY, O. *Whirligigs*. Red cloth. New York, 1910. (By William Sidney Porter.) First edition, with "Published September, 1910" on copyright page. In dust jacket. $100–$150. Lacking jacket, $35.

HENRY, Samuel J. *Foxhunting Is Different*. Illustrated. Pictorial cloth. New York, (1938). Derrydale Press. First edition. One of 950. $100–$150.

HENTY, G. A. Note: The popular juvenile novels of this English author are in most cases expensive in English first editions but are widely available at modest prices (mostly under $50) in their American first and reprint versions.

HENTY, G. A. *All But Lost*. 3 vols., cloth. London, 1869. First edition. $1,000–$1,500.

HENTY, G. A. *In the Heart of the Rockies*. Illustrated. Pictorial green cloth. New York, 1894. First edition. $40–$60.

HENTY, G. A. *A March on London*. 8 plates. Cloth. London, 1898 (actually 1897). First edition. $200–$300.

HENTY, G. A. *The March to Coomassie*. Cloth. London, 1874. First edition. $350–$500.

HENTY, G. A. *The Queen's Cup*. 3 vols., cloth. London, 1897. First edition, first issue, with ads dated Nov., 1896. $1,000 and up. Also, $850 (A, 1972).

HENTY, G. A. *St. Bartholomew's Eve*. Cloth. London, 1894 (actually 1893). First English edition. $150–$250.

HENTY, G. A. *Search for a Secret*. 3 vols., cloth. London, 1867. First edition. $1,500–$2,000. Also, $1,625 (A, 1972).

HENTY, G. A. *The Tiger of Mysore*. Map, 12 plates. Cloth. London, 1896 (actually 1895). First edition. $200–$250. New York, 1895. Blue cloth. First American edition. $50.

HENTY, G. A., and others. *Brains and Bravery*. 8 plates by Arthur Rackham. Cloth. London, 1903. First edition. $200–$300.

HENTY, G. A., and others. *Camps and Quarters*. Original printed wrappers. New York, 1889. First edition. $1,000 and up. Also, $950 (A, 1972).

HERBERT, Edward, Lord. *The Autobiography of Edward, Lord Herbert of Cherbury*. Wood engravings by H. W. Bray. Folio, buckram. Newtown, Wales, 1928. Gregynog Press. One of 300. $300–$420. Another issue: One of 25 specially bound in morocco. $1,250–$1,500.

HERBERT, Frank. *Dune*. Blue cloth. Philadelphia, (1965). First edition. In dust jacket. $400–$500.

HERBERT, George. *The Temple*. Portrait frontispiece. Cloth. London, 1927. Nonesuch Press. $75–$100.

HERBERT, George. *Poems*. Illustrated. Marbled boards and cloth. Newtown, 1923. Gregynog Press. One of 300. $250–$300. Another issue: One of 43 specially bound in morocco. $1,000–$1,250.

HERBERT, H. W. See Herbert, W. H.

HERBERT, Henry William. See Forester, Frank; Forrester, Frank; Hawes, William Post; Herbert, W. H. Also see *The Brothers; Cromwell*.

HERBERT, Henry William. *Marmaduke Wyvil*. Drab boards, paper label. London, 1843. First edition. $400–$600. New York, (1843). Printed wrappers. First American edition. $400–$500.

HERBERT, Henry William. *The Quorndon Hounds*. Frontispiece, 3 plates. Cloth. Philadelphia, 1852. First edition. $500–$750.

HERBERT, Henry William. *Ruth Whalley; or, The Fair Puritan*. Printed wrappers (dated 1845 on front). Boston, (1844). First edition. $750–$1,000. Boston, 1845. (Cover title.) Pinkish tan wrappers. Second edition, first state of wrappers, with author's name as "Wm. Henry" instead of "Henry William." $1,000 and up.

HERBERT, Henry William. *The Village Inn*. Wrappers. New York, 1843. First edition. $400–$600.

HERBERT, J. A. *Illuminated Manuscripts*. Color frontispiece, 50 other plates. Cloth. London, 1911. First edition. $75–$125.

HERBERT, Sir William. *Croftus, sive de Hibernia Liber*. Printed from a manuscript at Powis Castle. 2 genealogical tables. Half morocco. London, 1887. Roxburghe Club. $200–$250. Another issue: Printed on vellum. $400–$450.

HERBERT, W. H. *Ringwood the Rover: A Tale of Florida*. Printed wrappers. Philadelphia, 1843. (By Henry William Herbert.) First edition. $500–$750. Second edition, with "H. W. Herbert" as author. $400–$500.

HERBST, Josephine. *Nothing Is Sacred*. Cloth. New York, 1928. First edition. In dust jacket with wraparound band. $100. Author's first book.

HERFORD, Oliver. *An Alphabet of Celebrities*. Illustrated. Cloth. Boston, 1899. First edition. $65–$85.

HERGESHEIMER, Joseph. *Balisand*. Boards and cloth. New York, 1924. First edition. One of 175 signed. Boxed. $50–$60. Trade edition: Cloth. In dust jacket. $15.

HERGESHEIMER, Joseph. *Berlin*. Boards. New York, 1932. First edition. One of 125 signed. Boxed. $100–$125.

HERGESHEIMER, Joseph. *The Bright Shawl*. Boards and vellum. New York, 1922. First edition, with "Published, October, 1922" on copyright page. One of 225 signed. $50–$60.

HERGESHEIMER, Joseph. *Cytherea*. Red buckram. New York, 1922. First edition. One of 275 signed. In dust jacket. $75. Presentation copies: 100 in boards. $35.

HERGESHEIMER, Joseph. *The Happy End*. Buckram. New York, 1919. First edition. One of 60 large paper copies, signed. In dust jacket. $75–$100.

HERGESHEIMER, Joseph. *Java Head*. Cloth. New York, 1919. First edition. One of 100. $50–$60.

HERGESHEIMER, Joseph. *The Lay Anthony*. Cloth. New York, 1914. First edition. In dust jacket. $100–$150. Author's first book.

HERGESHEIMER, Joseph. *The Limestone Tree*. Buckram. New York, 1931. First edition. One of 225 signed. In dust jacket. Boxed. $40–$60.

HERGESHEIMER, Joseph. *The Party Dress*. Limp orange vellum. New York, 1930. First edition. One of 60 on Japan vellum, signed. $100–$150. Another issue: Boards. One of 225 signed. In dust jacket. $40–$50.

HERGESHEIMER, Joseph. *The Presbyterian Child*. Half morocco. New York, 1923. First edition. One of 950 signed. $40–$65. London, 1924. Boards. One of 190 signed. In dust jacket. $50–$60.

HERGESHEIMER, Joseph. *Swords and Roses*. Cloth. New York, 1929. First edition. One of 225 signed. In dust jacket. $50–$60. Trade edition: Gray cloth. In dust jacket. $20.

HERGESHEIMER, Joseph. *The Three Black Pennys*. Brown cloth. New York, 1917. First edition, first issue, with medallion on half title about 2 inches from bottom of page. In dust jacket. $50–$60. New York, 1930. Illustrated. Vellum. One of 170 signed. Boxed. $75–$100.

HERGESHEIMER, Joseph. *Tropical Winter*. Cloth. New York, 1933. First edition. One of 210 signed. In dust jacket. Boxed. $50–$60. Trade edition: Black cloth. In dust jacket. $20.

HERGESHEIMER, Joseph. *Wild Oranges*. Orange boards and cloth. New York, 1918. One of 85. In dust jacket. $75–$100.

HERLIHY, James Leo. *Midnight Cowboy*. Cloth. New York, (1945). First edition. In dust jacket. $50.

HERMAN, William. *The Dance of Death: Author's Copy*. Brown or green cloth. (San Francisco, 1877.) (By Ambrose Bierce and Thomas A. Harcourt.) First edition. $500. San Francisco, 1877. Red or blue cloth. Second edition, with dated title page. $100–$150.

HERNDON, William H., and Weik, Jesse W. *Herndon's Lincoln: The True Story of a Great Life*. 63 plates. 3 vols., blue cloth. Chicago, (1889). First edition. $200–$350. Chicago, 1890. 3 vols., cloth. Second edition. $75–$100.

HERODOTUS. See *The History of Herodotus*.

HERRICK, Robert. *One Hundred and Eleven Poems*. Illustrated by W. Russell Flint. Sheepskin. London, 1955. Golden Cockerel Press. One of 105 copies issued with 8 extra plates signed by Flint. In slipcase, $1,000–$1,200. Another issue: Cloth, parchment spine. One of 450. Boxed. $200–$300.

HERRICK, Robert. *Poems*. Woodcut title page. Vellum. (London, 1895.) Kelmscott Press. One of 250. $1,000–$1,250. Another issue: One of 8 on vellum. $4,000–$5,000.

HERRICK, Robert. *Selections from the Poetry of Robert Herrick*. Illustrated. Cloth. Boston, 1882. First edition. $75–$100.

HERRING, John Frederick. *Portraits of the Winning Horses of the Great St. Leger Stakes*. 10 colored plates. Large folio, leather-backed boards. Doncaster, England, (1824). First edition, first state, with Sheardown & Son imprint on all plates. $5,000 and up. Another edition: (London, 1929.) 15 colored plates. Large folio, leather-backed boards. With a colored proof of "Tarrarre" plate. $5,000 and up.

HERTZ, John. *Racing Memoirs*. Mounted photographic plates, some in color. Half morocco. Chicago, 1954. $150.

HESSE, Herman. *Steppenwolf*. Red cloth. London, (1929). First English edition. In dust jacket. $200–$300.

HEWITSON, William. *Illustrations of New Species of Exotic Butterflies*. 300 plates. 5 vols., half morocco. London, (1856)-76. $2,000 and up.

HEWITT, Edward R. *Secrets of the Salmon*. Half cloth. New York, 1922. First edition. One of 780. $200–$250.

HEWITT, Graily. *Lettering for Students and Craftsmen*. Illustrated. White buckram. London, 1930. One of 380 signed. $300–$350.

HEWITT, Graily. *The Pen & Type-Design*. Illustrated. Full red morocco. London, 1928. First Edition Club. One of 250. $200–$275. Another issue: Boards and cloth. $75–$100.

HEWITT, Randall H. *Across the Plains and Over the Divide*. Folding map, portrait, 58 plates. Pictorial cloth. New York, (1906). First edition. $100–$150.

HEWITT, Randall H. *Notes By the Way: Memoranda of a Journey Across the Plains, from Dundee, Ill., to Olympia, W. T. May 7 to November 3, 1862*. 58 pp., printed wrappers. Olympia, Wash., 1863. First edition. $3,000 and up.

HEWLETT, Maurice. *A Masque of Dead Florentines*. Illustrated. Oblong, tan buckram. London, 1895. First edition. $75–$85.

HEWLETT, Maurice. *Quattrocentisteria*. Illuminated by Valenti Angelo. Folio, half vellum. New York, 1927. One of 175. $75–$85.

HEWLETT, Maurice. *The Song of the Plow*. Frontispiece. Boards. London, (1916). First edition. One of 100 signed. In dust jacket. Boxed. $100–$150.

HEYWARD, Du Bose. *Brass Ankle*. Cloth. New York, (1931). First edition. One of 100 signed. Boxed. $50–$60. Later printing: Trade edition. In dust jacket. $15–$20.

HEYWARD, Du Bose. *The Half Pint Flask*. Boards and cloth. New York, 1929. First edition. One of 175 signed. In dust jacket. $40–$65.

HEYWARD, Du Bose. *Porgy*. Black cloth. New York, (1925). First edition, first issue, with gold-stamped binding and publisher's monogram on copyright page. In dust jacket. $40–$50. (For *Porgy & Bess*, the musical, see Gershwin, George.)

HEYWARD, Du Bose. *Skylines and Horizons.* Cloth. New York, 1924. First edition. In dust jacket. $75–$100. Author's first book.

HIGBEE, Elias, and Thompson, R. B. *The Petition of the Latter-Day Saints.* 13 pp., sewed. Washington, 1840. First edition. $100–$200.

HIGGINBOTHAM, Harlow Niles. *The Making of a Merchant and Other Papers.* Cloth. Wausau, Wis., (1900). Philosopher Press. First edition. One of 100. $75–$100.

HIGGINS, F. R. *Arable Holdings: Poems.* Boards and linen. Dublin, 1933. Cuala Press. One of 300. In tissue dust jacket. $75–$85.

HIGGINS, Godfrey. *Anacalypsis, an Attempt to Draw Aside the Veil of the Saitic Isis.* 6 engraved plates. 2 vols., cloth. London, 1836. First edition, with errata slip. $100–$150.

HIGGINSON, Thomas Wentworth. *The Birthday in Fairy-land: A Story for Children.* Printed wrappers. Boston, 1850. First edition $50–$75.

HILDEBRAND, Samuel S. *Autobiography.* Illustrated. Cloth. Jefferson City, Mo., 1870. First edition. $75–$100.

HILDRETH, Richard. *The History of Banks.* Boards. Boston, 1837. First edition. $100–$175.

HILDRETH, Samuel P. *Biographical and Historical Memoirs of the Early Pioneer Settlers of Ohio.* 6 plates. Cloth. Cincinnati, 1852. First edition. $100–$125.

HILDRETH, Samuel P. *Genealogical and Biographical Sketches of the Hildreth Family.* Cloth. Marietta, Ohio, 1840. $150–$200.

HILDRETH, Samuel P. *Memoirs of the Early Pioneer Settlers of Ohio.* Leather. Cincinnati, 1854. Later reprint of *Biographical and Historical Memoirs.* $75–$100.

HILDRETH, Samuel P. *Pioneer History.* Folding map, 8 plates. Half leather. Cincinnati, 1848. First edition. $150–$200.

HILL, W. H.; A. F.; and A. E. *Antonio Stradivari, His Life and Work.* Illustrated. Morocco. London, 1902. First edition. One of 100. $800–$1,200. Another issue: Half vellum. $600–$800. London, 1909. Second edition. $150–$200.

HILL, W. H.; A. F.; and A. E. *The Violin-Makers of the Guarnieri Family.* Plates. Half vellum. London, 1931. One of 200. $800–$1,000.

HILLARD, Elias B. *The Last Men of the Revolution.* 12 plates, 6 colored; facsimiles (in some copies). Half morocco. Hartford, 1864. First edition. $500–$750.

HILLS, Chester. *The Builder's Guide.* 70 plates. 2 vols. in one, folio, boards. Hartford, 1834. First edition. $400–$500. Hartford, 1846. 50 plates. $300–$400.

HILLS, Sir John. *Points of a Racehorse.* Illustrated. Folio, cloth. London, 1903. $150–$200.

HILLS, John Waller. *A History of Fly-Fishing for Trout.* Half cloth. London, 1921. One of 50 signed. $500–$650.

HILLS, John Waller. *A Summer on the Test.* 12 plates by N. Wilkinson. Cloth. London, (1924). One of 300 signed. $350. Another issue: One of 25, with plates signed by the artist. $1,200–$1,500.

HILLYER, Robert. *Sonnets and Other Lyrics.* Boards. Cambridge, Mass., 1917. First edition. In dust jacket. $35–$50. Author's first book.

HILTON, A. *Oklahoma and Indian Territory Along the Frisco.* Illustrated, 2 folding maps. 91 pp., wrappers. St. Louis, 1905. $100–$200.

HILTON, James. *Good-bye, Mr. Chips.* Cloth. Boston, 1934. First edition. In dust jacket. $75–$100.

HILTON, James. *Random Harvest.* Cloth. Boston, 1941. First edition. In dust jacket. $100.

HIMES, Chester B. *If He Hollers Let Him Go.* Cloth. New York, 1947. First edition. In dust jacket. $125–$150. Author's first book.

HIMES, Chester. *Pinktoes.* Wrappers. Paris, (1961). Olympia Press. First edition. $75–$125.

HIMES, Chester. *The Third Generation.* Cloth. New York, (1954). First edition. In dust jacket. $50–$75.

HIMSELF. See *Sheppard Lee.*

HIND, Henry Youle. *Narrative of the Canadian Red River Exploring Expedition of 1857, etc.* Plates (some colored), folding maps, charts. 2 vols., brown cloth. London, 1860. $1,000–$1,250.

HIND, Henry Youle. *North-West Territory.* Folding maps and plans. Cloth. Toronto, 1859. First edition. $300–$400.

HIND, Henry Youle. *A Sketch of an Overland Route to British Columbia.* Folding map. Dark-green flexible cloth, paper label on front cover. Toronto, 1862. First edition, with errata slip. $1,000 and up.

HINKLE, James F. *Early Days of a Cowboy on the Pecos.* Illustrated. 35 pp., pictorial wrappers. Roswell, N.M., 1937. First edition. $400–$500.

HINMAN, Wilbur F. *The Story of the Sherman Brigade.* Morocco. (Alliance, Ohio), 1897. $35–$50.

HINTON, Richard J. *The Hand-Book of Arizona.* 4 maps, 16 plates. Cloth. San Francisco, 1878. First edition. $100–$125.

HINTS Towards Forming the Character of a Young Princess. 2 vols., boards. London, 1805. (By Hannah More.) First edition. $150–$200.

HIPKINS, A. J., and Gibb, William. *Musical Instruments: Historic, Rare, and Unique.* 50 color plates. Half leather. London, 1888. One of 1,040. $500–$600.

HIRSHBERG, Dr. L. K. *What You Ought to Know About Your Baby.* Cloth. New York, 1910. First edition. In dust jacket. $400–$500. (Note: Written in collaboration with H. L. Mencken.)

HISTORIA Cristiana de la California. Boards and calf. Mexico, 1864. (By El Domingo.) $400.

HISTORICAL and Descriptive Review of the Industries of Tacoma, 1887. 108 pp., unbound. Los Angeles, 1887. $100–$150.

HISTORICAL and Descriptive Review of the Industries of Walla Walla. 112 pp., wrappers. No place, 1891. $150–$175.

HISTORICAL and Scientific Sketches of Michigan. Cloth. Detroit, 1834. First edition. $200–$250.

HISTORICAL Sketch Book and Guide to New Orleans and Environs. Plates, folding map. Pictorial wrappers. New York, 1885. (By Lafcadio Hearn and others.) First edition, first issue, with spelling "Bizoin" (instead of "Bisoin") at head of title page. $400–$500.

HISTORICAL War Map (The). Folding maps, plus maps in text. 56 pp., printed boards. Indianapolis, 1862. Asher & Co. $300–$400.

HISTORY OF Alameda County, California. Portraits. Cloth. Oakland, 1883. (By J. P. Munro-Fraser.) First edition. $200–$350.

HISTORY of Amador County, California. Full leather. Oakland, 1881. First edition. $150–$300.

HISTORY of the Arkansas Valley, Colorado. Illustrated. Half leather. Chicago, 1881. $125–$150.

HISTORY of Beasts and Birds. 25 woodcuts. 30 pp., miniature book. 3⅞ × 2½ inches. Orange wrappers. Cooperstown, N.Y., 1838. $75–$100.

HISTORY of the Bible. Illustrated. 256 pp., miniature book, 2 × 1⁵⁄₁₆ inches. Sheep, gilt spine. Sandy Hill, N.Y., 1925. $100–$125.

HISTORY of the Bible. Woodcuts. 192 pp., miniature book, 2⅙ × 1¾ inches. Calf. Bridgeport, Conn., 1831. $100–$125.

HISTORY of Black Hawk County, Iowa. Illustrated. Half leather. Chicago, 1868. $125–$150.

HISTORY of the Brooklyn and Long Island Fair, Feb. 22, 1864. Leather. Brooklyn, 1864. $75–$100.

HISTORY of the City of Denver, Arapahoe County, and Colorado. Illustrated. Half morocco. Chicago, 1880. First edition. $250–$300.

HISTORY of the Counties of Woodbury and Plymouth, Iowa. Half leather. Chicago, 1890–91. $100–$150.

HISTORY of Crawford and Richland Counties, Wisconsin. Cloth. Springfield, Ill., 1884. (By C. W. Butterfield and George A. Ogle.) First edition. $100–125.

HISTORY of Dearborn and Ohio Counties, Indiana, from Their Earliest Settlement, etc. Cloth. Chicago, 1885. First edition. $100–$150.

HISTORY of the Detection and Trial of John A. Murel, the Great Western Land Pirate. Wrappers. (Lexington, Ky., 1835.) (By Augustus Q. J. Walton.) First edition. $1,000. (For second edition, see title under Walton's name.)

HISTORY of Floyd County, Iowa. Half leather. Chicago, 1882. $100–$125.

HISTORY of Franklin, Jefferson, Washington, Crawford and Gasconade Counties, Missouri. Illustrated. Half leather. Chicago, 1888. $100–$150.

HISTORY of Franklin and Pickaway Counties, Ohio. Illustrated. Half leather. No place, 1880. $100–$125.

HISTORY of Godefrey of Boloyne (The). Vellum with ties. London, 1893. Kelmscott Press. One of 300. $750–$1,000. Another issue: One of 6 on vellum. $2,500–$3,500.

HISTORY of the Great Lakes. Plates, 5 double-page maps. 2 vols., cloth. Chicago, 1899. (Edited by John B. Mansfield.) First edition. $100–$125.

HISTORY of Henry Esmond (The). 3 vols., brown cloth, paper labels. London, 1852. (By William Makepeace Thackeray.) First edition, with 16 pages of ads dated September. $350–$450.

HISTORY of Herodotus of Halicarnassus (The). Translation of G. Rawlinson, revised by A. W. Lawrence. 9 wood engravings, maps. Vellum and cloth. London, 1935. Nonesuch Press. In dust jacket. $400–$500.

HISTORY of Idaho Territory. 2 maps, 69 plates, 2 facsimiles. Half morocco. San Francisco, 1884. First edition. $250–$350.

HISTORY of the Indian Wars with the First White Settlers of the United States (A). Leather. Montpelier, Vt., 1812. (By Daniel C. Sanders.) First edition. $500–$600. Rochester, 1828. Boards. Second edition. (Chapter 27 omitted.) $100–$150.

HISTORY of Jasper County, Missouri. Illustrated. Half leather. Des Moines, 1883. $100–$125.

HISTORY of Jo Daviess County, Illinois. Illustrated. Half leather. Chicago, 1878. $100–$125.

HISTORY of Johnny Quae Genus (The). 24 colored plates by Thomas Rowlandson. 8 parts, wrappers. London, 1822. (By William Combe.) First edition. $1,000–$1,500. London, 1822. Boards. First book edition. $1,000 and up.

HISTORY of the Late War in the Western Country. Boards or leather. Lexington, Ky., 1816. (By Robert B. McAfee.) First edition, with the "extra" printed leaf (of Gen. Winchester's criticism) at end. $400–$550. Bowling Green, Ohio, (1919). Cloth. One of 300. $100–$150.

HISTORY of Lawrence County, Pennsylvania. Half morocco. Philadelphia, 1877. First edition. $125–$150.

HISTORY of Los Angeles County, California. Colored folding map, 113 lithographs. Morocco and cloth. Oakland, 1880. First edition. $450–$550.

HISTORY of Madeira (A). 27 colored plates. Boards or cloth. London, 1821. (By William Combe.) First edition. $800–$1,000.

HISTORY of Marin County, California. Frontispiece, 35 portraits. Full sheep. San Francisco, 1880. (By J. P. Munro-Fraser.) First edition. $350–$450.

HISTORY of Mendocino County, California. Portraits. Sheep. San Francisco, 1880. $300–$400.

HISTORY of Mercer County, Pennsylvania. Half morocco. Philadelphia, 1877. First edition. $100–$125.

HISTORY of Milam, Williamson, Bastrop, Travis, Lee and Burleson Counties, Texas. Half leather. Chicago, 1893. $300–$450.

HISTORY of Montana, 1739–1885. Folding map, plates. Half morocco. Chicago, 1885. (Edited by Michael A. Leeson.) First edition. $300–$350.

HISTORY of Napa and Lake Counties, California. Illustrated. Full sheep. San Francisco, 1881. First edition. $300–$400.

HISTORY of Nevada. 116 plates. Half morocco. Oakland, 1881. (Edited by Myron Angel.) First edition. $500–$600.

HISTORY of Nevada County, California. Illustrated. Oblong folio, cloth, leather spine. Oakland, 1880. (By Frank L. Wells.) First edition. $400–$600.

HISTORY of Ontario County, New York. Half leather. Philadelphia, 1876. $100–$125.

HISTORY of Pike County, Illinois. Half leather. Chicago, 1880. $125–$150.

HISTORY of Pike County, Missouri. Half leather. Des Moines, 1883. $150–$175.

HISTORY of the Regulators of Northern Indiana. 67 pp., printed yellow wrappers. Indianapolis, 1859. First edition. $600–$800.

HISTORY of Sangamon County, Ilinois. Illustrated. Half leather. Chicago, 1881. $100–$125.

HISTORY of San Joaquin County, California. Illustrated. Oblong folio, leather. Oakland, 1879. (By Frank T. Gilbert.) First edition. $400–$550.

HISTORY of San Luis Obispo County, California. Portraits and scenes. Half leather. Oakland, 1883. (By Myron Angel.) First edition. $350–$450.

HISTORY of Santa Barbara and Ventura Counties, California. Half leather. Oakland, 1883. (By Jesse D. Mason.) $150–$200.

HISTORY of a Six Weeks' Tour Through a Part of France, Switzerland, Germany, and Holland. Boards, green cloth spine, paper label. London, 1817. (By Percy Bysshe Shelley.) First edition. $1,000–$1,250, possibly more.

HISTORY of Sonoma County, California. Illustrated. Three-quarters leather. San Francisco, 1880. First edition. $150–$200.

HISTORY of the Steam-Boat Case (A), Lately Discussed by Counsel Before the Legislature of New Jersey. 48 pp., unbound. Trenton, N.J., 1815. $175–$225.

HISTORY of Texas (A), or The Emigrant's Guide to the New Republic, by a Resident Emigrant. Frontispiece (colored in some copies). Cloth. New York, 1844. (Edited by A. B. Lawrence and C. J. Stille.) Third edition of *Texas in 1840.* With color plate. $400–$500. With plate not colored, $300–$400. (For first edition, see title entry *Texas in 1840.*)

HISTORY of Tioga County, Pennsylvania. Cloth. No place, 1897. $100–$125.

HISTORY of Wabasha County, Minnesota. Compiled by Franklyn Curtiss-Wedge and others. Cloth. Winona, Minn., 1920. $50–$75.

HISTORY of Walworth County, Wisconsin. Illustrated. Half leather. Chicago, 1882. $100–$125.

HISTORY of Waukesha County, Wisconsin. Illustrated. Half leather. Chicago, 1880. $100–$125.

HISTORY of Wayne County, New York. Illustrated. Half leather. Philadelphia, 1877. $75–$100.

HITTELL, John S. *The Commerce and Industries of the Pacific Coast of North America.* Folding colored map, plates. Cloth. San Francisco, 1882. First edition. $125–$150.

HITTELL, John S. *A History of the City of San Francisco.* Cloth. San Francisco, 1878. First edition. $125–$150.

HITTELL, John S. *The Resources of Vallejo.* Folding map. Printed wrappers. (Vallejo, Calif., 1869.) First edition. $300–$400.

HITTELL, John S. *Yosemite: Its Wonders and Its Beauties.* 20 mounted photographic views by "Helios." Green cloth. San Francisco, 1868. First edition. $1,250–$1,500. (Note: The plates are by the pioneer photographer Eadweard Muybridge, and the book is much sought for by collectors in both the Americana and photographic fields.)

HITTELL, Theodore H. (editor). *Adventures of James Capen Adams, Mountaineer and Grizzly Bear Hunter, of California.* 12 wood engravings. Cloth. San Francisco, 1860. First edition. $200–$250. Boston, 1860. 12 plates. Cloth. $150.

HOAG, Jonathan E. *The Poetical Works of Jonathan E. Hoag.* Preface by H. P. Lovecraft. Cloth. New York, 1923. First edition. $450 in a 1980 catalogue. (Contains 6 Lovecraft poems.)

HOARE, Sarah. *Poems on Conchology and Botany.* 5 hand-colored plates. Cloth, paper label. London, 1831. First edition. $75–$100.

HOBBS, G. A. *Bilbo, Brewer, and Bribery in Mississippi Politics.* Cloth. (Memphis), 1917. First edition. $50.

HOBBS, James. *Wild Life in the Far West.* 20 plates, colored frontispiece. Cloth. Hartford, 1872. First edition. $250–$300. Hartford, 1873. Second edition. $80–$100. Hartford, 1874. $50. Hartford, 1875. $35.

HOBHOUSE, J. C. (compiler). *Imitations and Translations from the Ancient and Modern Classics.* Pink boards. London, 1809. First edition. $300–$400. (Note: Contains nine new poems by Lord Byron.)

HOBOMOK, a Tale of Early Times. Boards. Boston, 1824. (By Lydia Maria Child.) First edition. $250–$350. Author's first book.

HOBSON, G. D. *English Binding Before 1500.* 55 plates, other illustrations. Folio, buckram. Cambridge, 1929. First edition. One of 500. In dust jacket. $250–$300.

HOBSON, G. D. *Maioli, Canevari and Others.* 6 plates in color, 58 in black and white. Brown morocco. London, 1926. First edition. One of 25. $800–$1,000, or more. Another issue: Cloth. $250–$300. Boston, 1926. Cloth. First American edition. $250–$300.

HOBSON, G. D. *Thirty Bindings.* 30 plates (some in color). Folio, cloth. London, 1926. First Edition Club. One of 600. $200–$300.

HOBSON, R. L. *A Catalogue of Chinese Pottery and Porcelain in the Collection of Sir Percival David.* 180 plates, mostly in color. Folio, linen. London, 1934. First edition. In portfolio box. $1,500–$2,000. Another issue: Silk boards. One of 30 on vellum, signed by Hobson. Boxed. $4,000–$5,000, or more.

HOBSON, R. L. *Chinese Art.* 100 color plates. Cloth. London, 1927. First edition. $150–$200. New York, 1927. First American edition. $150–$200.

HODGE, Frederick W. *Handbook of American Indians North of Mexico.* Map. 2 vols., cloth. Washington, 1907–10. First edition. $100–$150. Washington, 1912. 2 vols. $75–$100. New York, 1959. $35–$50.

HODGE, Gene Meany. *The Kachinas Are Coming.* 18 color plates. Cloth. Los Angeles, 1936. First edition. $150–$200. Flagstaff, Ariz., 1967. Half buckram. In dust jacket. $50–$75.

HODGE, Hiram C. *Arizona As It Is.* Frontispiece, map. Cloth. New York, 1877. First edition. $150–$200.

HODGES, M. C. *The Mestico; or, The War-path and Its Incidents.* 204 pp., printed wrappers. New York, 1850. First edition, with author identified on cover as "W. C. Hodges." $200–$250, possibly more.

HODGSON, Adam. *Letters from North America.* Map, plate. 2 vols., boards. London, 1824. First English edition of *Remarks During a Journey, etc.* With 2 errata slips. $400–$500.

HODGSON, Adam. *Remarks During a Journey Through North America in the Years 1819–21.* Leather. New York, 1823. First (pirated) edition. $300–$400.

HODGSON, J. E. *The History of Aeronautics in Great Britain.* Colored frontispiece, 150 plates, some colored. Buckram. Oxford, 1924. First edition. One of 1,000. $400–$500.

HODGSON, Joseph. *The Alabama Manual and Statistical Register for 1869.* Printed boards. Montgomery, 1869. First edition. $150–$200.

HODGSON, Joseph. *The Cradle of the Confederacy.* Cloth. Mobile, 1876. First edition. $150–$200.

HODGSON, Ralph. *The Last Blackbird and Other Lines.* Cloth. London, 1907. First edition, first issue, edges uncut. $50–$75.

HODGSON, William Hope. *The Boats of the 'Glen Carrig.'* Cloth, London, 1907. First edition. $200–$250.

HODGSON, William Hope. *Captain Gault*. Cloth. New York, 1918. First American edition. In dust jacket. $250–$350.

HODGSON, William Hope. *The House on the Borderland and Other Novels*. Cloth. Sauk City, Wis., 1946. First American edition. In dust jacket. $275–$325.

HODGSON, Mrs. Willoughby. *Old English China*. 16 colored plates and 64 illustrations from photographs. Cloth. London, 1913. First edition. $100–$150.

HOFER, A. F. *Grape Growing*. 32 pp., wrappers. McGregor, Iowa, 1878. First edition. $150.

HOFFMAN, Charles Fenno. See *Greyslaer; A Winter in the West*.

HOFFMAN, Charles Fenno. *The Pioneers of New York* 55 pp., printed tan wrappers. New York, 1848. First edition, with seal on front cover 1⅜ inches wide. $150–$200.

HOFFMAN, Charles Fenno. *Wild Scenes in the Forest and Prairie*. 2 vols., boards, paper label on spine. London, 1839. First edition. $150–$200. New York, 1843. 2 vols., boards. First American edition. $150–$200.

HOGAN, Edmund. *The Irish Wolfdog*. Illustrated. Blue cloth. Dublin, 1897. First edition. $5,000 and up. (Most copies were destroyed by fire.)

HOGAN, Edmund, and Graham, Capt. (G. A.). *The Irish Wolfdog and The Irish Wolfhound*. Illustrated. Blue cloth. Dublin, 1939. $200–$300. (Reprints of the earlier Hogan and Graham works.)

HOGG, Robert, and Bull, H. G. (editors). *The Herefordshire Pomona, Containing Original Figures and Descriptions of the Most Esteemed Kinds of Apples and Pears*. 77 colored plates, 3 plain plates. 2 vols., wrappers or leather. London, 1876–85. First edition. $2,000 and up.

HOLBROOK, John Edwards. *Ichthyology of South Carolina*. Vol. 1 (all published). 28 colored plates. Three-quarters morocco. Charleston, 1855–(57). First edition. $12,000 in a 1981 catalogue. Charleston, 1860. Second edition. $5,000–$10,000.

HOLDEN, W. C. *Alkali Trails*. Maps, illustrations. Cloth. Dallas, (1930). First edition. $100–$125.

HOLDEN, W. C. *Rollie Burns; or, An Account of the Ranching Industry on the South Plains*. Maps, illustrations. Pictorial cloth. Dallas, (1932). First edition, first binding, tan cloth. $125–$150. Second binding, green cloth, without frontispiece. $100–$125.

HOLDEN, W. C. *The Spur Ranch*. Cloth. Boston, (1934). First edition. $150–$200.

HOLDER, Charles F. *All About Pasadena and Its Vicinity*. Wrappers. Boston, 1889. First edition. $100.

HOLDER, Charles F. *The Channel Islands of California*. Cloth. Chicago, 1910. First edition. $75–$100. Second edition, same date. $50.

HOLKHAM Bible-Picture Book (The). Facsimile of the fourteenth-century manuscript. Folio, half morocco, or vellum. London, 1954. (Edited by W. O. Hassall.) $150–$200. Another issue: One of 100 in full morocco, signed. $250–$350.

HOLLEY, Mary Austin. *Texas: Observations, Historical, Geographical and Descriptive*. Folding map. Cloth. Baltimore, 1833. First edition. $1,250–$1,750, possibly more. Lexington, Ky., 1836. Map in color. Gray cloth. Second edition (but an essentially different and re-written book, the first having been designed to encourage emigration, the second to encourage U.S. recognition). $750–$1,000.

HOLLIDAY, George H. *On the Plains in '65*. Illustrated. 97 pp., printed wrappers. No place, 1883. First edition. $600–$750.

HOLLINGSWORTH, John McHenry. *Journal*. Frontispiece in color. Half buckram. San Francisco, 1923. First edition. One of 300. $150–$175.

HOLLISTER, Ovando J. *History of the First Regiment of Colorado Volunteers.* 178 pp., printed wrappers. Denver, 1863. First edition. $2,000–$2,500. (See *The March of the First.*)

HOLLISTER, Ovando J. *The Silver Mines of Colorado.* 87 pp., printed wrappers. Central City, 1867. First edition. $500–$600. Also, $350 (A, 1968). Springfield, Mass., 1867. Cloth. Enlarged edition (retitled *The Mines of Colorado).* $75–$100.

HOLLISTER, Uriah S. *The Navajo and His Blanket.* 10 color plates, other illustrations. Cloth. Denver, 1903. First edition. $150–$200.

HOLMES, John Clellon. *Go.* Cloth. New York, 1952. First edition, first issue, with "A" on copyright page. In dust jacket. $500–$600. Also, $350 (A, 1980). Author's first book.

HOLMES, Mary J. *Cousin Maude, and Rosamond.* Cloth. New York, 1860. First edition. $50–$60.

HOLMES, Mary J. *Tempest and Sunshine; or, Life in Kentucky.* Gray cloth. New York, 1854. First edition. $50–$75.

HOLMES, Oliver Wendell. See Hall, Marshall. Also see *The Autocrat of the Breakfast-Table; Francis Parkman; The Harbinger; The Poet at the Breakfast-Table; Songs of the Class of MDCCCXXIX*

HOLMES, Oliver Wendell. *Astraea: The Balance of Illusions. A Poem.* Yellow boards. Boston, 1850. First edition, first printing, with ampersand in printer's imprint on copyright page set above the line. $150–$200. (Also issued in rough reddish-brown cloth.)

HOLMES, Oliver Wendell. *The Benefactors of the Medical School of Harvard University.* Tan wrappers. Boston, 1850. First edition. $75–$125.

HOLMES, Oliver Wendell. *Border Lines of Knowledge in Some Provinces of Medical Science.* Cloth. Boston, 1862. First edition, with Ticknor & Co. imprint on spine. $150–$200.

HOLMES, Oliver Wendell. *The Claims of Dentistry.* Tan wrappers. Boston, 1872. First edition. $150–$200.

HOLMES, Oliver Wendell. *The Contagiousness of Puerperal Fever.* (Caption title.) 28 pp., printed buff wrappers. (Boston, 1843 or 1844?) First edition. $1,000 and up.

HOLMES, Oliver Wendell. *Currents and Counter-Currents in Medical Science: An Address . . . Before the Massachusetts Medical Society.* Printed salmon-colored wrappers. Boston, 1860. First edition. $300–$400.

HOLMES, Oliver Wendell. *Currents and Counter-Currents in Medical Science. With Other Address and Essays.* Cloth. Boston, 1861. First edition, first issue, with triple-ruled blind-stamped frame enclosing "T & F" initials on cover. $150–$200.

HOLMES, Oliver Wendell. *Elsie Venner: A Romance of Destiny.* 2 vols., brown cloth. Boston, 1861. First edition, "probable" first printing, with ads dated January, 1861. $150–$250.

HOLMES, Oliver Wendell. *Homoeopathy, and Its Kindred Delusions.* Tan boards, paper label. Boston, 1842. First edition. $300–$350.

HOLMES, Oliver Wendell. *Humorous Poems.* Portrait frontispiece. Printed wrappers, or cloth. Boston, 1865. First edition. Wrappers: $150–$175. Cloth: $100–$125.

HOLMES, Oliver Wendell. *John Lothrop Motley: A Memoir.* Portrait. Cloth. Boston, 1879. First American edition. $50–$60. Another issue: Beveled cloth, gilt top. One of 516 on large paper. $100–$150. (Note: An English copyright edition, dated London, 1878, bound in brown cloth, preceded the American edition.)

HOLMES, Oliver Wendell. *Mechanism in Thought and Morals*. Cloth. Boston, 1871. First edition. $100–$125.

HOLMES, Oliver Wendell. *A Mortal Antipathy*. Green cloth. Boston, 1885. First edition, first issue, with *Elsie Venner* listed at $1.50 in ad opposite title page. $75–$100.

HOLMES, Oliver Wendell. *Oration Delivered Before the City Authorities of Boston, on the Fourth of July, 1863*. Printed salmon-colored wrappers. Boston, 1863. First edition. $100–$150. Another issue. "Private Copy": Boston, 1863. Leather or cloth. One of about 12. Inscribed by Holmes. $400–$500.

HOLMES, Oliver Wendell. *Over the Teacups*. Olive-green cloth. Boston, 1891 (actually 1890). First edition, first state, with no price for this book on ad leaf facing title page. $150–$200.

HOLMES, Oliver Wendell. *Poems*. Decorated cloth, paper label. Boston, 1836. First edition, with Boston imprint only. $150–$250. Author's first book. Later 1836 issue: Boston and New York imprint. $100–$150. Boston, 1849. Boards, or cloth. "New and Enlarged Edition." $50–$75.

HOLMES, Oliver Wendell. *The Position and Prospects of the Medical Student*. Printed tan wrappers. Boston, 1844. First edition. $300–$350.

HOLMES, Oliver Wendell. *The Professor at the Breakfast-Table*. Cloth. Boston, 1860. First edition. $100–$125. Another issue: Beveled cloth, edges gilt. Large paper, $150–$200. London, 1860. Cloth. First English edition. $75–$100.

HOLMES, Oliver Wendell. *Puerperal Fever, as a Private Pestilence*. Wrappers or cloth. Boston, 1855. First edition (under this title). In wrappers: $2,500–$3,500. (No copies in cloth noted in recent years.)

HOLMES, Oliver Wendell. *Teaching from the Chair and at the Bedside*. Printed gray wrappers. Boston, 1867. First edition. $200–$300.

HOLMES, Oliver Wendell. *Valedictory Address . . . Harvard University, March 10th, 1858*. Wrappers. Boston, 1858. First edition. $150–$200.

HOLMES, Justice Oliver Wendell. *The Common Law*. Cloth or leather. Boston, 1881. First edition. $500–$600. Author's first book.

HOLMES, Roberta E. *The Southern Mines of California*. Plates and maps. Boards. San Francisco, 1930. Grabhorn Press. One of 250. $150–$175.

HOLY BIBLE. Folio, red cloth. Cleveland, 1949. One of 975 designed by Bruce Rogers. $300–$400. Another issue: One of 20 with a decorative headpiece for each book. $600–$800. A few copies in leather: $1,000.

HOME As Found. By the Author of *Homeward Bound*. 2 vols., cloth, or boards and cloth, with paper spine labels. Philadelphia, 1838. (By James Fenimore Cooper.) First edition, first printing, with a note in Vol. 1 about the paper used in the book. $600–$800.

HOMER. *The Homeric Hymn to Aphrodite*. Translated by F. L. Lucas. 10 wood engravings. Full red morocco. London, 1948. Golden Cockerel Press. One of 100 (from an edition of 750) specially bound, signed by Lucas. Boxed. $400–$600. Another issue: Half morocco. One of 650. $150–$200.

HOMER. *The Odyssey of Homer*. Translated by T. E. Shaw (T. E. Lawrence, of Arabia). With 25 large rondels in gold and black. Small folio, black morocco. (London), 1932. First edition. One of 530 designed by Bruce Rogers. Boxed. $1,000–$1,250. Binding scuffed, $900. Note: A few copies were signed by Lawrence, "T. E. Shaw," and Rogers and bring $2,000–$3,000. Also, $1,500 (A, 1976). New York, 1932. Morocco (11 copies); calf (about 23 copies). First American edition (for copyright purposes). A copy in morocco was sold at a New York auction in October, 1977, for $1,200. Boston, 1929. Translated by George H. Palmer. Illustrated by N. C. Wyeth. Cloth. $100–$125. Another issue: One of 550 signed. With an extra set of color plates. $300–$400.

HOMES in Texas on the Line of the International and Great Northern Railroad. 79 pp., wrappers. Chicago, 1879. (By N. W. Hunter.) First edition. $250–$350.

HONIG, Louis O. *The Pathfinder of the West: James Bridger.* Illustrated. Leatherette. Kansas City, 1951. Limited, signed edition. $50–$75.

HONIG, Louis O. *Westport, Gateway to the Early West.* Illustrated. Cloth. North Kansas City, 1950. One of 525 signed. $50–$75.

HOOD, Thomas. *Humorous Poems.* Illustrated. Cloth. London, 1893. First edition. One of 250 on large paper. $125–$150.

HOOD, Thomas. *Miss Kilmansegg and Her Precious Leg: A Golden Legend.* Illustrated. Boards. (Camden, 1904.) Essex House Press. One of 200. $150–$200.

HOOKER, W. A. *The Horn Silver Mine: Report.* (Cover title.) 5 tinted views, colored map. 32 pp., wrappers. New York, 1879. $150–$175.

HOOPER, Johnson J. *Dog and Gun: A Few Loose Chapters on Shooting.* 105 pp., printed wrappers (woodcut on front). New York, 1856. First edition, published by A. O. Moore, with dated title page. $200–$250.

HOOVER, Herbert C. *Fishing for Fun.* Illustrated. Cloth. New York, (1963). First edition. One of 200 signed. Boxed. $100.

HOOVER, Herbert C. *A Remedy for Disappearing Game Fish.* Woodcuts. Marbled boards and cloth. New York, 1930. First edition. One of 990. Boxed. $100–$125.

HOOVER, Herbert C., and Hoover, Lou Henry (translators). *De Re Metallica.* From the Latin of Georgius Agricola. Illustrated. Parchment boards. London, 1912. First English edition. $400–$500. Signed by Hoover, and sometimes by Mrs. Hoover, $500–$750.

HOPE, Anthony. *The Dolly Dialogues.* 4 plates by Arthur Rackham. Tan wrappers. London, 1894. (By A. H. Hawkins.) First edition, first issue, with "Dolly" as running headband on left-hand pages. $400–$500. Another issue: Blue cloth. $150–$200.

HOPE, Anthony. *The Prisoner of Zenda.* Dark-red cloth. London, (1894). (By A. H. Hawkins.) First edition, first issue, with list of 17 (not 18) titles on page 311. $200–$250.

HOPKINS, Gerard Manley. *Poems.* Edited by Robert Bridges. 2 portraits, 2 double-page facsimiles. Blue-gray boards and linen. London, (1918). First edition. In dust jacket. $500–$750. Lacking jacket, $295 and $225.

HOPKINS, Gerard Manley. *Selected Poems.* London, 1954. Nonesuch Press. One of 1,100. $75–$100.

HOPKINS, Gerard T. *A Mission to the Indians, from the Indian Committee of Baltimore Yearly Meeting, to Fort Wayne in 1804.* Edited by Martha E. Tyson, 198 pp., wrappers. Philadelphia, 1862. First edition. $200–$300.

HOPKINS, Harry C. *History of San Diego: Its Pueblo Lands and Water.* Cloth. San Diego, (1929). $60–$80.

HOPKINS, T. M. *Reminiscences of Col. John Ketcham, of Monroe County, Indiana, by His Pastor, Rev. T. M. Hopkins.* 22 pp., printed wrappers. Bloomington, Ind., 1866. First edition. $300–$350.

HOPPE, E. O. (photographer). See King, Richard.

HOPWOOD, Avery. See Rinehart, Mary Roberts.

HORBLIT, Harrison D. *One Hundred Books Famous in Science.* New York, 1964. Grolier Club. One of 1,000. $250–$350.

HORGAN, Paul. *Great River: The Rio Grande in American History.* Illustrated, including color plates. 2 vols., tan cloth. New York, 1954. First edition. One of 1,000 signed. Boxed. $150–$250. Trade edition: 2 vols., black cloth. Boxed. $35.

HORN, Hosea B. *Horn's Overland Guide.* Folding map. Cloth. New York, 1852. First edition, first issue, 78 pp. $400–$500. Second issue, same date, 83 pp., cloth. $250–$300. New York, (1853). Map (different from that in original edition). Cloth. $200–$250.

HORN, Stanley F. *Invisible Empire.* Illustrated. Cloth. Boston, 1948. First edition. In dust jacket. $50–$75.

HORN, Tom. *Life of Tom Horn, Government Scout and Interpreter.* 13 illustrations. Cloth. Denver, (1904). First edition. $50–$75. Another issue: Printed wrappers ("less scarce," says Ramon F. Adams). $35–$50.

HORNEM, Horace, Esq. *Waltz: An Apostrophic Hymn.* 27 pp., wrappers. London, 1813. (By George Gordon Noel, Lord Byron.) First edition. $7,500 and up. Also, $5,250 (A, 1977). Rebound in full morocco, $4,000. Also, unbound, uncut, some repairs to margins and corners, $3,920 (A, 1965)—the Louis H. Silver copy; rebound in half calf, $1,176 (A, 1960).

HORNUNG, E. W. *Mr. Justice Raffles.* Blue cloth. London, 1909. First edition. $75–$100.

HORSE-SHOE Robinson. 2 vols., purple cloth, paper labels on spines. Philadelphia, 1835. (By John Pendleton Kennedy.) First edition. $400–$500.

HOSACK, David. *Essays on Various Subjects of Medical Science.* 3 vols., half leather. New York, 1824–30. First edition. $300–$400.

HOSHOUR, Samuel Klinefelter. See Altisonant, Lorenzo.

HOSMER, Hezekiah L. *Early History of the Maumee Valley.* 70 pp., printed wrappers. Toledo, Ohio, 1858. First edition. $400–$450. Also, with lower wrapper only, $200 (A, 1978).

HOSMER, Hezekiah L. *Montana: An Address . . . Before the Travellers' Club, New York City, January, 1866.* (Cover title.) 23 pp., printed wrappers. New York, 1866. First edition. $350–$375.

HOSMER, Hezekiah L. *Report of the Committee on Foreign Correspondence of the Grand Lodge of Montana, at Its Seventh Annual Communication.* 55 pp., wrappers. Helena, 1872. $400–$500.

HOSMER, John Allen. *A Trip to the States, by the Way of the Yellowstone and Missouri.* Cloth, or tan printed boards. Virginia City, Mont., 1867. First edition. $3,000–$4,000. Also, last leaf torn away, $800 (A, 1968)—the Streeter copy, in cloth. (Note: The Graff copy at the Newberry Library is in boards).

HOUDINI, Harry. *A Magician Among the Spirits.* Illustrated. Cloth. New York, 1924. (By Ehrich Weiss.) First edition. $150.

HOUDINI, Harry. *The Right Way to Do Wrong: An Exposé of Successful Criminals.* Wrappers. Boston, 1906. (By Ehrich Weiss.) First edition. $100–$150. Author's first book.

HOUGH, Emerson. See *Getting a Wrong Start.*

HOUGH, Emerson. *The Covered Wagon.* Frontispiece. Cloth. New York, 1922. First edition, first issue, with "(1)" below last line of text. In dust jacket. $100–$125. Lacking jacket, $50–$60.

HOUGH, Emerson. *The King of Gee Whiz.* Illustrated. Pictorial cloth. Indianapolis, (1906). First edition, first issue, with last word on page 26 "Banjo." In dust jacket. $125–$150.

HOUGH, Emerson. *The Mississippi Bubble.* Cloth. Indianapolis, (1902). First edition, first issue, with "April" on copyright page and "Hough" on spine (not "Emerson Hough"). In dust jacket. $150–$200. Without jacket, $50–$60.

HOUGH, Emerson. *The Singing Mouse Stories*. Cloth. New York, 1895. First edition. $100–$125. Author's first book.

HOUGH, Emerson. *The Story of the Cowboy*. Illustrated. Decorated cloth. New York, 1897. First edition. $75.

HOUGH, Emerson. *The Story of the Outlaw*. Illustrated. Boards. New York, 1907. First edition, first state, with printer's rule at top of page v. $50–$60.

HOUGH, Emerson. *The Way to the West*. Cloth. Indianapolis, (1903). First edition. $60–$75.

HOUGH, Franklin B. *History of Jefferson County, New York*. Half leather. Albany, 1854. First edition. $100–$150.

HOUGH, Franklin B. *A History of Lewis County . . . New York*. Illustrated. Half leather. Albany, 1860. First edition. $75–$125.

HOUGH, Franklin B. *History of St. Lawrence and Franklin Counties, New York*. Illustrated. Half leather. Albany, 1853. $100–$150.

HOUGH, Franklin B. *Washingtonia*. Plates, folding map. 2 vols., half morocco. Roxbury, Mass., 1865. First edition. One of 91. $75–$100. Another issue: Wrappers. One of 200 on large papger. $75–$125. Also, $70 (A, 1976).

HOUGHTON, Jacob. *The Mineral Region of Lake Superior*. 2 maps on one folding sheet. Cloth. Buffalo, 1846. First edition. $100–$125.

HOUGHTON, W. *British Fresh-Water Fishes*. Illustrated. 2 vols., pictorial cloth. London, (1879). First edition. $750–$1,000.

HOUSE, Homer D. *Wild Flowers of New York*. Illustrated in color. 2 vols., cloth. Albany, 1918. First edition. $75–$100. Albany, 1923. 2 vols., cloth. $50–$75.

HOUSEHOLD, Geoffrey. *Rogue Male*. Cloth. London, 1939. First edition. In dust jacket. $125–$150.

HOUSMAN, A. E. *Fragment of a Greek Tragedy*. Printed wrappers. Cambridge, 1921. First edition. $75–$100.

HOUSMAN, A. E. *Last Poems*. Dark-blue buckram. London, 1922. First edition, first issue, with comma and semicolon missing after "love" and "rain," respectively, on page 52. In dust jacket. $75–$100.

HOUSMAN, A. E. *More Poems*. Portrait. Morocco and cloth. London, (1936). First edition. One of 379. In dust jacket. $75–$100. Another issue: Cloth. First trade edition. In dust jacket. $50. New York, 1936. Cloth. First American edition. $40–$50.

HOUSMAN, A. E. *A Shropshire Lad*. Gray-blue boards, vellum spine, paper label, London, 1896. First edition, first state, with the word "Shropshire" on the label exactly 33 millimeters wide. $800–$1,000. Also, covers faded and worn, $425 (A, 1977). Second state, with 37 millimeter measure, $600–$750. New York, 1897. Boards, vellum spine. First American edition. $800–$1,000. (Note: The entire first edition was 500 copies, 350 for England and 150 for America, with a substitute New York title page.) Philadelphia, (1902). Henry Altemus, publisher. First edition to be printed in America. $250–$350. London, 1914. Vellum. One of 12 on vellum. $1,000 or more. New York, (1935). Heritage Press. Illustrated by Edward A. Wilson. Calf. Boxed. $75. London, 1929. One of 325. $150–$175.

HOUSMAN, Laurence. *False Premises*. Boards. Oxford, 1922. First edition. One of 150 signed. $100–$150.

HOUSMAN, Laurence. *A Farm in Fairyland*. Illustrated. Cloth. London, 1894. First edition. $150–$200. Author's first book.

HOUSMAN, Laurence. *Followers of St. Francis.* Cloth. London, 1923. First edition. In dust jacket. $75–$100.

HOUSMAN, Laurence. *Green Arras.* Illustrated. Green cloth. London, 1896. First edition, with 1896 ads and errata slip. $100–$200.

HOUSMAN, Laurence. *Mendicant Rhymes.* Boards and vellum. London, 1906. Essex House Press. One of 300. $200.

HOUSMAN, Laurence. *Stories from the Arabian Nights.* Mounted color plates by Edmund Dulac. Cloth. London, (1907). $100–$125. Another issue: Vellum with silk ties. One of 350 signed. $300–$350.

HOUSTON, Sam. *Speech of Sam Houston Exposing the Malfeasance and Corruption of John Charles Watrous, Judge of the Federal Court of Texas, and His Confederates.* Frontispiece. New York, 1860. $150–$250.

HOUSTOUN, Mrs. Matilda C. *Texas and the Gulf of Mexico.* 10 plates. 2 vols., cloth. London, 1844. First edition. $400–$500. Philadelphia, 1845. Frontispiece of Santa Anna. Wrappers. First American edition. $200–$300.

HOVEY, Richard. *Poems.* Printed wrappers, or cloth. Washington, 1880. First edition. Wrappers: $200–$300. Cloth: $150. Author's first book.

HOW the Buffalo Lost His Crown. Illustrated by Charles M. Russell. 44 pp., oblong, brown cloth. (New York, 1894.) (By John H. Beacom.) First edition. $1,000 and up. Another issue: Half decorated calf. Presentation copy signed by Beacon. $1,250–$1,500.

HOW to Win in Wall Street. By a Successful Operator. Cloth. New York, 1881. (By Joaquin Miller.) First edition. $50–$75.

HOW, George E., and Howe, Jane P. *English and Scottish Silver Spoons.* Photographs. 3 vols., cloth. London, 1952–57. First edition. One of 550. In dust jackets. $400–$500.

HOWARD, B. B. *The Charter and Ordinances of the City of Galena.* Half calf. Galena, Ill., 1853. $150–$250.

HOWARD, Benjamin C. *A Report of the Decisions of the Supreme Court . . . in the Case of Dred Scott vs. John F. A. Sandford.* Wrappers. New York, 1857. First edition. $100–$150. (The Dred Scott Decision.)

HOWARD, H. R. See *The Life and Adventures of Joseph T. Hare.*

HOWARD, H. R. (editor). *The History of Virgil A. Stewart, and His Adventures in Capturing and Exposing the "Great Western Land Pirate" (John A. Murrell) and His Gang.* Cloth. New York, 1836. First edition. $200–$250. Howard's first book. New York, 1837. Illustrated. Cloth. $75.

HOWARD, James Q. *The Life of Abraham Lincoln.* 102 pp., wrappers. Columbus, Ohio, 1860. First edition, first issue, buff paper covers, 8 unnumbered pages of ads. $500–$600.

HOWARD, Jas. H. W. *Bond and Free.* Frontispiece portrait. Cloth. Harrisburg, 1886. First edition, first issue, with portrait opposite title page. $200–$250.

HOWARD, McHenry. *Recollections of a Maryland Confederate Soldier.* Folding map, plates. Cloth. Baltimore, 1914. First edition. $200–$250.

HOWARD, Oliver Otis. *Account of Gen. Howard's Mission to the Apaches and Navajos.* 12 pp., wrappers. No place, no date. $100–$150.

HOWARD, Oliver Otis. *My Life and Experiences Among Our Hostile Indians.* Illustrated. Cloth. Hartford, (1907). First edition. $100–$150.

HOWARD, Oliver Otis. *Nez Perce Joseph.* 2 portraits and 2 maps. Cloth. Boston, 1881. First edition. $150–$200.

HOWARD, Robert E. *Always Comes Evening*. Cloth. Sauk City, Wis., 1957. First edition. In dust jacket. $300–$350.

HOWARD, Robert E. *The Coming of Conan*. Cloth. New York, (1953). First edition. In dust jacket. $125.

HOWARD, Robert E. *Conan the Barbarian*. Cloth. New York, (1954). First edition. In dust jacket. $150.

HOWARD, Robert E. *Conan the Conqueror*. Cloth. New York, (1950). First edition. In dust jacket. $150–$200.

HOWARD, Robert E. *The Dark Man and Others*. Cloth. Sauk City, 1963. First edition. In dust jacket. $200–$225.

HOWARD, Robert E. *Etchings in Ivory*. Wrappers. Pasadena, Tex., 1968. First edition. (268 copies.) $200–$250.

HOWARD, Robert E. *A Gent from Bear Creek*. Cloth. London, (1937). First edition, with "First printed . . . 1937" on copyright page. $1,000–$1,500. Author's first book. West Kingston, R.I., 1965. Cloth. First American edition. $85–$100.

HOWARD, Robert E. *King Conan*. Cloth. New York, (1953). First edition. In dust jacket. $125.

HOWARD, Robert E. *The Pride of Bear Creek*. Cloth. West Kingston, 1966. First edition. In dust jacket. $85–$100.

HOWARD, Robert E. *Skull-Face and Others*. Cloth. Sauk City, 1946. First edition. In dust jacket. $350–$450.

HOWARD, Robert E. *The Sword of Conan*. Cloth. New York, (1952). First edition. In dust jacket. $150.

HOWARD, William. *Narrative of a Journey to the Summit of Mont Blanc*. Boards. Baltimore, 1821. First edition. $125–$150.

HOWBERT, Irving. *The Indians of the Pike's Peak Region*. 4 plates. Cloth. New York, 1914. First edition. $50–$75.

HOWBERT, Irving. *Memories of a Lifetime in the Pike's Peak Region*. Frontispiece. Cloth. New York, 1925. Enlarged edition of preceding title. $35–$50.

HOWE, E. D. *History of Mormonism*. Frontispiece. Cloth. Painesville, Ohio, 1840. Second edition of *Mormonism Unvailed* [sic]. $350–$400.

HOWE, E. D. *Mormonism Unvailed* [sic]. Frontispiece. Cloth. Painesville, 1834. First edition. $1,500–$2,000.

HOWE, E. W. *The Story of a Country Town*. Illustrated by W.L. Wells. Decorated cloth. Atchison, Kan., 1883. First edition, first issue, with "D. Caldwell, Manufacturer, Atchison, Kan." rubber-stamped inside front cover and no lettering at foot of spine. $100–$150. Author's first book.

HOWE, Henry. *Historical Collections of the Great West*. 2 vols. in one, cloth. Cincinnati, 1851. First edition. $75–$100. Cincinnati, 1852. $50–$75. (Also bound in leather and half leather; numerous other later editions.)

HOWE, Henry. *Historical Collections of Ohio*. Map, woodcuts. Cloth. Cincinnati, 1847. First edition. $100–$125. Cincinnati, 1848. $100–$125. Cincinnati, 1875. $75–$100. Columbus, 1889. 3 vols. in 2, cloth. $60. (Also bound in leather and half leather; numerous other editions.)

HOWE, Henry. *Historical Collections of Virginia*. Map, illustrations, engraved title page. Cloth. Charleston, S.C., 1845. First edition. $125–$150. (Also bound in leather and half leather; numerous other later editions.)

HOWE, John. *Howe's Almanac for the Year of Our Lord, 1804.* Wrappers. Greenwich, Mass., (1803). $100–$150.

HOWE, John. *A Journal Kept by Mr. John Howe, While He Was Employed as a British Spy, During the Revolutionary War.* 44 pp., wrappers. Concord, N.H., 1827. First edition. $500–$750.

HOWE, Julia Ward. See *Passion-Flowers.*

HOWE, Julia Ward. *Later Lyrics.* Green or purple cloth. Boston, 1866. First edition. $75–$100. (Contains first book appearance of "Battle Hymn of the Republic.").

HOWE, Mark A. De Wolfe. *Rari Nantes: Being Verses and a Song.* Wrappers. Boston, 1893. First edition. One of 80. $100–$125. Author's first book.

HOWE, Octavius T. *The Argonauts of '49.* Illustrated. Half cloth. Cambridge, Mass., 1923. First edition. In dust jacket. $100.

HOWE, Octavius T., and Matthews, Frederick C. *American Clipper Ships, 1833–58.* 114 plates. 2 vols.: Vol. 1, marbled boards; Vol. 2, cloth. Salem, 1926–27. First edition. $200–$250.

HOWELLS, William Dean. See *Poems of Two Friends.*

HOWELLS, William Dean. *A Boy's Town.* Frontispiece and 22 plates. Cloth. New York, 1890. First edition, first state, without illustration on page 44. $75–$100.

HOWELLS, William Dean. *A Hazard of New Fortunes.* Illustrated. Wrappers. New York, 1890. First edition, first state. $600–$800. (Cloth copies were later.)

HOWELLS, William Dean. *Italian Journeys.* Illustrated by Joseph Pennell. Cloth. Boston, 1901. In dust jacket. Boxed. $100. Another issue: Boards. One of 300 on large paper. $75. Trade edition: Cloth. $15.

HOWELLS, William Dean. *The Mother and The Father.* Illustrated. Cloth. New York, 1909. First edition. $150–$175.

HOWELLS, William Dean. *My Mark Twain.* Illustrated. Sage-colored cloth. New York, 1910. First edition. $75–$85.

HOWELLS, William Dean. *Niagara Revisited.* Colored illustrations, colored title page. 12 pp., decorated buff boards. Chicago, (about 1884). First edition, with or without 16 pages of ads at end. $150–$175.

HOWELLS, William Dean. *Poems.* Cloth. Boston, 1873. First edition. $150–$200.

HOWELLS, William Dean. *The Rise of Silas Lapham.* Blue or brown cloth. Boston, 1885. First edition, first issue, with "Mr. Howell's Latest Works" in boxed ad facing title page and with unbroken type in the word "sojourner" at bottom of page 176. $125–$175. New York, 1961. Limited Editions Club. Illustrated. Buckram. Boxed. $35.

HOWELLS, William Dean. *Suburban Sketches.* Illustrated by A. Hoppin. Cloth. Boston, 1871. First edition. No records noted for a copy in original cloth. Value? A rebound copy in boards and cloth was offered in a 1979 catalogue at $1,200. Boston, 1872. Revised and enlarged edition. $50–$60. Author's first book of fiction.

HOWELLS, William Dean. *The Undiscovered Country.* Cloth. Boston, 1880. First edition. $75–$100.

HOWELLS, William Dean. *Venetian Life.* 18 aquatints. 2 vols., vellum. Cambridge, Mass., 1892. One of 250 on vellum. $100–$125. Cambridge, 1907. 2 vols., boards. One of 550 signed. $100–$125.

HOWELLS, William Dean, and Hayes, J. L. *Lives and Speeches of Abraham Lincoln and Hannibal Hamlin.* 96 pp., printed buff wrappers. Columbus, Ohio, 1860. First edition, first issue, with pages 95–96 blank. $1,000 and up (?). Excessively rare: Blanck locates one copy, rebound; Howes locates two copies in libraries; we know of another privately held. Second issue, engraving of Republican Wigwam, Chicago, on page 96. $1,000 and up. Also, spine chipped, hinges cracked. $800 (A, 1974). Howes does not mention this issue; Blanck locates two imperfect copies. Another issue: Wigwam on page 95. Howes locates five. Second edition, same date. 2 portraits. 74 pp., cloth. First issue, without period after "o" in imprint. $100 and up. Later issues, same date, with period. $50 and up.

HOWELLS, William Dean; Twain, Mark; and others. *The Niagara Book*. Cloth, or printed wrappers. Buffalo, 1893. First edition, first printing, with no ads at end, page 226 blank, and copyright notice in 3 lines. $250. Second printing: $50–$75.

HOWISON, John. *Sketches of Upper Canada*. Edinburgh, 1821. First edition. $200–$250. Edinburgh, 1822. Second edition. $125–$150. Edinburgh, 1825. Third edition. $100–$125.

HOWITT, Samuel. *The British Sportsman*. 72 plates. Oblong, half morocco. London, no date (but with plates dated 1798–1800). First edition (?). $2,000 and up. London, 1812. Frontispiece, 71 plates. Morocco. (Often listed in records as the first edition.) $2,000 in a London catalogue, 1980. Also, $2,300 (A, 1980).

HOWLAND, S. A. *Steamboat Disasters and Railroad Accidents in the United States*. Illustrated. Sheep. Worcester, Mass., 1840. First edition. $150–$200.

HOWLEY, James P. *The Beothucks or Red Indians of Newfoundland*. Plates. Cloth. Cambridge, Mass., 1915. First edition. $250–$350.

HRDLICKA, Ales. *The Anthropology of Florida*. Cloth. DeLand, 1922. First edition. $125–$150.

HUBBARD, Elbert. *A Message to Garcia*. Suede. East Aurora, N.Y., 1899. First edition. One of 1,000. $50 and up. (Note: The limitation is listed variously as 1,000, 925, 28, which indicates special issues not traced in my researches.)

HUBBARD, Gurdon Saltonstall. *Incidents in the Life of Gurdon Saltonstall Hubbard*. Edited by Henry E. Hamilton. Frontispiece. Cloth. (Chicago), 1888. First edition. $150–$200.

HUBBARD, John Niles. *Sketches of Border Adventures, in the Life and Times of Maj. Moses Van Campen*. Leather. Dansville, N.Y., 1841. First edition. $250–$300. Bath, N.Y., 1841. Leather. $150–$200.

HUBBARD, L. Ron. *Dianetics*. Cloth. New York, (1950). First edition. In dust jacket. $150–$350.

HUBBARD, L. Ron. *Final Blackout*. Cloth. Providence, (1948). First edition. $125.

HUBBARD, L. Ron. *Slaves of Sleep*. Cloth. Chicago, 1948. First edition. In dust jacket. $100–$150.

HUBBARD, Robert. *Historical Sketches of Roswell Franklin and Family*. Half leather. Dansville, N.Y., 1839. First edition. $325. Also, $175 (A, 1974).

HUDSON, Derek. *Arthur Rackham: His Life and Work*. Color plates. Cloth. London, 1960. First edition. In dust jacket. $100–$150. New York, (1960). First American edition. In dust jacket. $100–$150.

HUDSON River Portfolio. See Wall, W. G.

HUDSON, Stephen. *Celeste and Other Sketches*. Wood engravings. Decorated cloth. (London), 1930. (By Sydney Schiff.) First edition. One of 50 on Japan vellum, signed, with an extra set of engravings. Boxed. $300–$350.

HUDSON, W. H. See Harford, Henry; Sclater, P. L., and Hudson, W. H. Also see *A Crystal Age*.

HUDSON, W. H. *Birds in a Village.* Chocolate-colored buckram. London, 1893. First edition. $100–$150.

HUDSON, W. H. *Birds in London.* Illustrated. Cloth. London, 1898. First edition. $100–$150.

HUDSON, W. H. *British Birds.* 8 color plates. Green cloth. London, 1895. First edition. $150–$200.

HUDSON, W. H. *El Ombu.* Light-green cloth, or wrappers. London, 1902. First edition. Cloth: $100–$125. Wrappers: $150–$175.

HUDSON, W. H. *Far Away and Long Ago.* Dark-green cloth. London, 1918. First edition. In dust jacket. $150–$175. London, 1931. Illustrated. Vellum. One of 110. $150–$250. New York, 1943. Limited Editions Club. Illustrated. Half leather. Boxed. $125–$150.

HUDSON, W. H. *Green Mansions.* Light-green cloth. London, 1904. First edition, first issue, without publisher's design on back cover. $300–$400. Second issue. $250–$350. London, 1926. Illustrated. One of 165. $200–$250. New York, 1935. Limited Editions Club. Illustrated. Boards. Boxed. $65–$75. New York, 1944. Frontispiece and 9 color plates. Boards and cloth. Boxed. $100–$150.

HUDSON, W. H. *Idle Days in Patagonia.* Illustrated. Crimson buckram. London, 1893. First edition, with 2 ad leaves at end and "Chapman & Hall" on cover. One of 1,750. $125–$175.

HUDSON, W. H. *A Little Boy Lost.* Illustrated. Dull yellow buckram. London, 1905. First edition. $125–$150. New York, 1920. Illustrated by Dorothy Lathrop. $75.

HUDSON, W. H. *Lost British Birds.* Illustrated. 32 pp., light-green wrappers. (London, 1894.) First edition. $100–$150. (Note: Reprints are dated 1894 on the cover.)

HUDSON, W. H. *The Naturalist in La Plata.* Illustrated. Dark-green cloth. London, 1892. First edition, with ads dated February, 1892, at end. $100–$150.

HUDSON, W. H. *The Purple Land That England Lost.* 2 vols., light-blue cloth. London, 1885. First edition, first issue, with October ads in second volume. $1,250–$1,500. Later issue: Purple cloth. $500–$750. Author's first book. Second edition: Retitled *The Purple Land.* Boards. London, 1929. $100–$150.

HUEFFER, Ford Madox. See Conrad, Joseph, and Hueffer, Ford Madox. Also see Ford, Ford Madox (for books published after 1919, when he changed his name).

HUEFFER, Ford H. Madox. *The Brown Owl.* Boards and cloth. London, 1892 (actually 1891). (By Ford Madox Ford.) First edition. $350–$400. Author's first book.

HUEFFER, Ford Madox. *Between St. Dennis and St. George.* Cloth. London, 1915. (By Ford Madox Ford.) First edition. $50–$75.

HUEFFER, Ford Madox. *The Feather.* Frontispiece. Boards. London, 1892. (By Ford Madox Ford.) First edition. $200–$300.

HUEFFER, Ford Madox. *The Fifth Queen.* Cloth. London, 1906. (By Ford Madox Ford.) First edition. $75–$100.

HUEFFER, Ford Madox. *From Inland and Other Poems.* Wrappers. London, 1907. (By Ford Madox Ford.) First edition. $100–$150.

HUEFFER, Ford Madox. *On Heaven and Other Poems.* Cloth. London, (1918). (By Ford Madox Ford.) First edition. $75.

HUEFFER, Ford Madox. *The Queen Who Flew.* Illustrated. Vellum. London, 1894. (By Ford Madox Ford.) First edition. One of 25 signed. $200–$300. Trade issue: Decorated cloth. $50–$75.

HUEFFER, Ford Madox. *Songs from London.* Wrappers. London, 1910. (By Ford Madox Ford.) First edition. $150–$200.

HUGHES, John T. *California: Its History, Population, Climate, Soil, Productions, and Harbors.* 105 pp., printed wrappers. Cincinnati, 1848. First edition. $200–$250.

HUGHES, John T. *Doniphan's Expedition. Containing an Account of the Conquest of New Mexico.* Frontispiece. 144 pp., printed wrappers. Cincinnati, 1847. First edition, first issue, lacking words "cheap edition" on the covers. $2,500–$3,500. Cincinnati, 1848. Wrappers. Second edition. $100–$200. Cincinnati, 1848. Cloth. Third edition. With map. $300–$350. Cincinnati, no date. Fourth edition. $75–$100. Topeka, 1907. $35.

HUGHES, Langston. *Dear Lovely Death.* Boards. Amenia, N.Y., 1931. First edition. One of 100 signed. $500–$600.

HUGHES, Langston. *Fine Clothes to the Jew.* Boards and cloth. New York, 1927. First edition. In dust jacket. $100–$125. Lacking jacket, $50.

HUGHES, Langston. *I Wonder as I Wander.* Cloth. New York, (1956). First edition, with Rinehart insignia on copyright page. In dust jacket. $50.

HUGHES, Langston. *The Panther and the Lash.* Cloth. New York, 1967. First edition. In dust jacket. $35–$50.

HUGHES, Langston. *Scottsboro Limited: Four Poems and a Play in Verse.* Illustrated with 4 lithographs by Prentiss Taylor. Boards. New York, 1932. First edition. One of 30 signed. $350–$450. Ordinary trade issue: $75–$150.

HUGHES, Langston. *Shakespeare in Harlem.* Illustrated. Cloth. New York, 1942. First edition. In dust jacket. $75.

HUGHES, Langston. *The Weary Blues.* Boards, New York, 1926. First edition. In dust jacket. $200–$250. Author's first book.

HUGHES, Richard. *Gipsy-Night and Other Poems.* Portrait. Boards. London, (1922). Golden Cockerel Press. First edition. One of 750. $125–$150. Chicago, 1922. Portrait. Boards and cloth. One of 63 signed, with a special proof of portrait. $150–$200.

HUGHES, Richard. *A High Wind in Jamaica.* Boards and cloth. London, 1929. First complete English edition. One of 150 signed. $150–$200. Trade edition: Green cloth. In dust jacket. $50–$75. (Note: The first edition was published in New York as *The Innocent Voyage.)*

HUGHES, Richard. *The Innocent Voyage.* Decorated blue boards and blue linen. New York, 1929. First edition. In dust jacket. $75–$125. New York, 1944. Limited Editions Club. Leather. Boxed. $75. (Published in England as *A High Wind in Jamaica.)*

HUGHES, Richard. *The Sisters' Tragedy.* Wrappers. Oxford, 1922. First edition. $100–$125. Author's first book.

HUGHES, Richard. *The Spider's Palace.* Illustrated. Boards and cloth. London, 1931. One of 110 signed. In dust jacket. $100–$150.

HUGHES, Richard B. *Pioneer Years in the Black Hills.* Edited by Agnes Wright Spring. Illustrated. Cloth. Glendale, Calif., 1957. First edition. $50–$60.

HUGHES, Ted. (Note: This poet's habit of inscribing books and providing manuscript copies of poems to be sold with his books makes an accurate record of his book values extremely difficult. The entries that follow are therefore tentative and conditional.)

HUGHES, Ted. *Animal Poems.* Wrappers. London, (1967). First edition. One of 100 signed. $500–$600.

HUGHES, Ted. *The Burning of the Brothel.* Woodcuts in color. Printed wrappers. (London, 1966.) Turret Books. First edition. One of 300. $50–$75. One of 75 (of the edition of 300) signed by Hughes. $100–$150.

HUGHES, Ted. *Crow.* Cloth. London, 1970. First edition. In dust jacket. $50–$60. With a signed poem in author's hand, $150–$200. London, (1973). 12 drawings by Leonard Baskin. Cloth. One of 400 signed. Boxed. $125–$175.

HUGHES, Ted. *Crow Wakes.* Cloth. Essex, 1971. First edition. One of 200. $75–$100.

HUGHES, Ted. *Eat Crow.* Illustrated by Leonard Baskin. Black leather. London, 1971. One of 150 signed. Boxed. $125–$175.

HUGHES, Ted. *Eclipse.* Wrappers. Knotting, 1976. First edition. One of 50 signed. $125.

HUGHES, Ted. *A Few Crows.* Illustrated. Imitation leather. Exeter, 1970. First edition. One of 150. $100–$150.

HUGHES, Ted. *The Hawk in the Rain.* Cloth. London, (1957). First edition. In dust jacket. $150–$250. New York, 1957. Cloth. First American edition. In dust jacket. $75–$125. Author's first book.

HUGHES, Ted. *Lupercal.* Cloth. London, (1960). First edition. In dust jacket. $200.

HUGHES, Ted. *Prometheus on His Crag.* Illustrated. Purple morocco. London, 1973. One of 160 signed, with a signed Leonard Baskin drawing. Boxed. $150–$175.

HUGHES, Ted. *Recklings.* Cloth. London, (1966). Turret Books. One of 150 signed. In dust jacket. $150–$200.

HUGHES, Ted. *Spring Summer Autumn Winter.* Boards. London, 1973. First edition. One of 140 signed. In glassine jacket. Boxed. $200.

HUGHES, Thomas. See *Tom Brown at Oxford; Tom Brown's School Days.*

HUGO, Victor. *Les Miserables.* 3 vols., cloth. London, 1862. First edition in English. $350–$450.

HUGO, Victor. *Toilers of the Sea.* 3 vols., pebbled green cloth. London, 1866. First edition in English. $350–$450. New York, 1960. Limited Editions Club. $100.

HUIE, William Bradford. *The Revolt of Mamie Stover.* Cloth. New York, (1951). First edition. In dust jacket. $50–$75.

HULANISKI, F. J. (editor). *History of Contra Costa County, California.* Illustrated. Half morocco. Berkeley, 1917. First edition. $150–$200.

HULTON, Paul, and Quinn, David Beers. *The American Drawings of John White, 1577–1590.* Frontispiece, 160 plates, 76 in color. 2 vols., folio, red buckram. London, 1964. First edition. $750–$1,000.

HUMANITAS (pseudonym). *Hints for the Consideration of the Friends of Slavery.* 32 pp., half leather. Lexington, Ky., 1805. First edition. $2,000.

HUMFREVILLE, J. Lee. *Twenty Years Among Our Savage Indians.* 250 engravings. Cloth. Hartford, 1897. First edition. $125–$150.

HUMOURIST (The). 40 colored etchings, including vignette title pages by George Cruikshank. 4 vols., pink boards. London, 1819–20. (By George Cruikshank.) First edition, first issue, without "Vol. 1" on title page and with all plates dated 1819. $750–$1,000, or more. Second issue, dated 1819–22: 4 vols., boards. $750–$1,000, or more. London, 1892. 4 vols., half morocco. One of 70 on large paper. $1,000 and up.

HUMPHREY, William. *The Last Husband and Other Stories.* Cloth. New York, 1953. First edition. In dust jacket. $75–$100. Author's first book.

HUMPHREYS, Arthur L. *Old Decorative Maps and Charts.* Illustrated. Buckram. London, 1926. One of 1,500. In dust jacket. $200–$250. Another issue: Half vellum. De luxe edition. One of 100 with separate mounted plates. $300–$400.

HUMPHREYS, Henry Noel. *The Illuminated Books of the Middle Ages.* 39 colored plates, one plain plate. Folio, half calf. London, 1844–49. First edition. $750–$1,000.

HUMPHRIES, Sydney. *Oriental Carpets, Runners and Rugs.* Illustrated. Folio, cloth. London, 1910. $200–$300.

HUNEKER, James. *Mezzotints in Modern Music.* Cloth. New York, 1899. First edition. $75–$100. Author's first book.

HUNEKER, James. *Painted Veils.* Blue boards, vellum spine. New York, (1920). First edition, on watermarked paper. One of 120 signed. $75–$125. New York, 1929. 12 color plates by Majeska. One of 1,250. $75–$100.

HUNT, George M. *Early Days Upon the Plains of Texas.* Portrait. Cloth. Lubbock, (1919). First edition. $200–$300.

HUNT, J. *An Adventure on a Frozen Lake: A Tale of the Canadian Rebellion of 1837–8.* 46 pp., wrappers. Cincinnati, 1853. $250–$350.

HUNT. J. H. L. *Juvenilia; or, A Collection of Poems.* Frontispiece. Boards, paper label. London, 1801. First edition. $500–$600. Leigh Hunt's first book.

HUNT, James H. *A History of the Mormon War.* Cloth. St. Louis, 1844. First edition. $150–$250.

HUNT, James H. *Mormonism: Embracing the Origin, Rise and Progress of the Sect.* Cloth. St. Louis, 1844. Expanded edition of the foregoing title. With errata leaf. $300–$350.

HUNT, John. *Gazetteer of the Border and Southern States.* Folding map in color. Cloth. Pittsburgh, 1863. First edition. $100–$150.

HUNT, Leigh. See Hunt, J. H. L. Also, see *Christianism; The Feast of the Poets; Sir Ralph Esher.*

HUNT, Leigh. *The Autobiography of Leigh Hunt.* Portraits. 3 vols., cloth. London, 1850. First edition. $250–$350.

HUNT, Leigh. *Captain Sword and Captain Pen: A Poem.* Illustrated. Cloth. London, 1835. First edition. $150–$175.

HUNT, Leigh. *The Correspondence of Leigh Hunt.* Edited by His Eldest Son. Portrait. 2 vols., tan cloth. London, 1862. First edition. $150–$200.

HUNT, Leigh. *The Descent of Liberty: A Mask.* London, 1815. First edition. $200–$250.

HUNT, Leigh. *Foliage; or Poems Original and Translated.* Blue boards, label. London, 1818. First edition. $150–$200.

HUNT, Leigh. *Imagination and Fancy.* Cloth. London, 1844. First edition. $100–$150.

HUNT, Leigh. *A Jar of Honey from Mount Hybla.* Engraved title page. Illustrated. Glazed boards. London, 1848. First edition, first binding. $250–$300. (Later issue is plain cloth.)

HUNT, Leigh. *Lord Byron and Some of His Contemporaries.* Illustrated. Boards and cloth. London, 1828. First edition. $150–$200. Second edition, same date. $100–$150.

HUNT, Leigh. *Men, Women and Books.* Portrait. 2 vols., orange cloth. London, 1847. First edition. $150–$200. New York, 1847. 2 vols., cloth. First American edition. $100–$125.

HUNT, Leigh. *The Palfrey.* 6 woodcuts. Cloth. London, 1842. First edition. $400–$500.

HUNT, Leigh. *The Poetical Works of Leigh Hunt.* Pink boards, printed label. London, 1832. First edition. $100–$125.

HUNT, Leigh. *Stories from the Italian Poets.* 2 vols., dark-blue cloth. London, 1846. First edition, with December ads. $150–$200. Rebound set, $55.

HUNT, Leigh. *The Story of Rimini: A Poem.* Boards, white paper back-label. London, 1816. First edition, with half title. $150–$225.

HUNT, Leigh. *Ultra-Crepidarius: A Satire on William Gifford.* Wrappers. London, 1823. First edition. $300–$400.

HUNT, Lynn Bogue. *An Artist's Game Bag.* 4 color plates, other illustrations. Full leatherette. New York, 1936. Derrydale Press. First edition, limited. $250–$350. Trade issue: Cloth. $75–$100.

HUNT, Richard S., and Randel, Jesse F. *Guide to the Republic of Texas.* Folding map. 63 pp., cloth. New York, 1839. First edition. $750–$1,000.

HUNT, Richard S., and Randel, Jesse F. *A New Guide to Texas.* Folding map, 62 pp., cloth. New York, 1845. Second edition of preceding title. $600–$850. New York, 1846 (*sic*). With map dated 1848. $350.

HUNT, Rev. T. Dwight. *Address Delivered Before the New England Society of San Francisco, at the American Theatre.* 20 pp., sewed. San Francisco, 1853. $150.

HUNT, T. Dwight. *The Past and Present of the Sandwich Islands.* Cloth. San Francisco, 1853. First edition. $250–$350.

HUNTER, Alexander. *Johnny Reb and Billy Yank.* Illustrated. Cloth. New York, 1905. First edition. $50–$60.

HUNTER, Dard. *Chinese Ceremonial Paper.* Photographs and paper specimens. Boards and morocco. Chillicothe, Ohio, 1937. First edition. One of 125 signed. Boxed. $2,000–$4,000. Also, $4,200 (A, 1976).

HUNTER, Dard. *The Literature of Papermaking, 1390–1800.* Illustrated. Folio, folding sheets in half canvas folder. (Chillicothe, 1925.) One of 190 signed. $1,500–$2,000.

HUNTER, Dard. *Massachusetts Institute of Technology: Dard Hunter Paper Museum.* Frontispiece photograph. Printed wrappers with woodcut on front. (Cambridge, Mass., 1939.) $250.

HUNTER, Dard. *My Life with Paper.* 58 illustrations, including specimens. Cloth. New York, 1958. First edition. In dust jacket. $100–$125.

HUNTER, Dard. *Old Papermaking.* Illustrated. Folio, boards. Chillicothe, 1923. One of 200 signed. $1,500–$2,000. Also, $1,600 (A, 1979).

HUNTER, Dard. *Old Papermaking in China and Japan.* 31 paper specimens. 11 wood engravings in color, other illustrations and photographs. Folio, linen portfolio. Chillicothe, 1932. One of 200 signed. $3,000–$3,500.

HUNTER, Dard. *Papermaking: The History and Technique of An Ancient Craft.* Illustrated, including folding map. New York, 1943. First edition. In dust jacket. $100–$125.

HUNTER, Dard. *Papermaking by Hand in America.* Frontispiece in color, facsimiles tipped in. Boards and linen. Also morocco. (Chillicothe, 1950.) Mountain House Press. First edition. One of 210 signed. Boxed. $4,000–$6,000. Also, $2,500 (A, 1979); $2,900 (A, 1978).

HUNTER, Dard. *Papermaking by Hand in India.* 27 paper specimens, 85 photographs. India print cloth and calf. New York, 1939. One of 375 signed. In slipcase. $1,500–$2,000. Also, $1,600 (A, 1976).

HUNTER, Dard. *Paper-Making in the Classroom.* 46 plates. Cloth. Peoria, (1931). $200–$300.

HUNTER, Dard. *Papermaking in Indo-China.* Reproductions. Decorated boards and morocco. (Chillicothe), 1947. Mountain House Press. One of 182 on handmade paper. $1,600–$2,000.

HUNTER, Dard. *A Papermaking Pilgrimage to Japan, Korea and China.* Photographs and paper specimens. Boards and morocco. New York, 1936. First edition. One of 370 signed. Boxed. $3,000–$3,500. Also, $2,000 (A, 1976).

HUNTER, Dard. *Papermaking Through Eighteen Centuries.* Illustrated. Buckram. New York, 1930. First edition. In dust jacket. $250–$500. Also, $400 (A, 1976).

HUNTER, Dard. *Primitive Papermaking.* Illustrated. Folding sheets in buckram portfolio, with ties. Chillicothe, 1937. First edition. One of 200. $2,500–$3,000. Also, $2,000 (A, 1978).

HUNTER, Dard, and others. *Five on Paper.* Illustrated. Morocco. North Hills, Pa., 1963. Bird & Bull Press. One of 169. $350–$500.

HUNTER, Dard, Jr. *A Specimen of Type.* Specimens and illustrations. 12 pp., folio, gray-blue wrappers, paper label. Cambridge, Mass., 1940. One of 100 signed. $250–$375.

HUNTER, George. *Reminiscences of an Old Timer.* 16 plates. Pictorial cloth. San Francisco, 1887. First edition. $125–$150. Battle Creek, 1888. Cloth. Third edition. $85–$100.

HUNTER, J. Marvin (compiler). *The Trail Drivers of Texas.* Illustrated. 2 vols., pictorial cloth. (San Antonio, 1920–23.) First edition. $150–$250. Limited, signed issue: One of 100. $400–$600. Second edition: 2 vols., cloth. (San Antonio, 1924.) $100. Nashville, 1925. 2 vols. in one, cloth. In dust jacket. $175. New York, 1963. 2 vols., half morocco. Boxed. $185–$200.

HUNTER, J. Marvin, and Rose, Noah H. *The Album of Gun-Fighters.* Illustrated. Pictorial cloth. (Bandera, Tex., 1951.) First edition. In dust jacket. $75–$100. Limited edition, with signed slip. $185–$200.

HUNTER, John D. *Manners and Customs of Several Indian Tribes Located West of the Mississippi.* Plain boards, paper label. Philadelphia, 1823. First edition. $175–$200.

HUNTER, John D. *Memoirs of a Captivity Among the Indians of North America.* Boards. London, 1823. First English edition of *Manners and Customs* (see preceding entry). $200–$225. London, 1824. Boards. Third edition. $250–$300.

HUNTER, William S., Jr. *Hunter's Ottawa Scenery.* 14 plates. Folio, cloth. Ottawa, 1855. First edition. $500–$750.

HUNTER, William S., Jr. *Hunter's Panoramic Guide from Niagara Falls to Quebec.* Engraved title, folding panoramic chart. Pictorial cloth. Boston, 1857. First edition. $150–$200. Montreal, 1860. $100–$125.

HUNTERS of Kentucky (The). 100 pp., wrappers. New York, 1847. (By Benjamin Bilson.) First edition. $150–$200. (Piracy of James O. Pattie's *Personal Narrative.*)

HUNTINGTON, D. B. *Vocabulary of the Utah and Sho-Sho-Ne, or Snake Dialect, with Indian Legends and Traditions.* 32 pp., stitched. Salt Lake City, 1872. $125–$150.

HURST, Samuel H. *Journal-History of the 73d Ohio Volunteer Infantry.* Cloth. Chillicothe, Ohio, 1866. First edition. $100–$125.

HURSTON, Zora Neale. *Mules and Men.* Illustrated by Miguel Covarrubias. Cloth. Philadelphia, 1935. First edition. In dust jacket. $75–$100.

HURSTON, Zora Neale. *Seraph on the Suwanee.* Wrappers. New York, 1948. First edition. Publisher's advance copy with blurb on front wrapper. $150. Regular trade editon: In jacket. $50–$75.

HURSTON, Zora Neale. *Tell My Horse*. Cloth. Philadelphia, (1938). First edition. In dust jacket. $50–$60.

HUSTON, John. *Frankie and Johnny*. Illustrated by Miguel Covarrubias. Cloth. New York, 1930. First edition. In dust jacket. $50–$75.

HUTCHINGS, James M. *Scenes of Wonder and Curiosity in California*. Illustrated. Decorated cloth. San Francisco, (1860). First edition. $100–$125. San Francisco, 1861. Second edition (or issue). $75–$100. New York, 1870. Green cloth. $50–$75. New York, 1872. Cloth. $75–$100. London, 1865. First English edition. $75–$100.

HUXLEY, Aldous. See *Jonah*.

HUXLEY, Aldous. *After Many a Summer*. Cloth. London, 1939. First edition. In dust jacket. $100–$125.

HUXLEY, Aldous. *Along the Road*. Cloth. London, 1925. First trade edition. In dust jacket. $100. New York, (1925). Boards. First American edition, limited issue. One of 250 signed. In dust jacket. Boxed. $195.

HUXLEY, Aldous. *Antic Hay*. Yellow cloth, yellow stained top. London, 1923. First edition. In dust jacket. $75–$100.

HUXLEY, Aldous. *Apennine*. Boards and cloth, paper label. Gaylordsville, N.Y., 1930. First edition. One of 91 signed. In slipcase. $250–$350.

HUXLEY, Aldous. *Arabia Infelix and Other Poems*. Boards and cloth. New York, 1929. Fountain Press. First edition. One of 692 signed. $100–$150.

HUXLEY, Aldous. *Beyond the Mexique Bay*. Illustrated. Boards and cloth. London, 1934. First edition. One of 210 signed. $150–$200. Trade edition: Orange cloth. In dust jacket. $75–$100.

HUXLEY, Aldous. *Brave New World*. Buckram, leather label. London, 1932. First edition. One of 324 signed. $750–$1,000. Trade edition: Blue cloth. In dust jacket. $350–$400. Garden City, 1932. First American edition. One of 250 signed. $175–$300. New York, 1974. Limited Editions Club. Boxed. $50–$60.

HUXLEY, Aldous. *Brief Candles*. Black cloth. New York, 1930. Fountain Press. First American edition. One of 842 signed. $125–$150. Trade edition: Cloth. In dust jacket. $50–$75. London, 1930. Red cloth. First edition. In dust jacket. $50–$75.

HUXLEY, Aldous. *The Burning Wheel*. Woodcut decorations. Yellow wrappers, paper label. Oxford, 1916. First edition. $750–$1,000. Author's first book.

HUXLEY, Aldous. *The Cicadas and Other Poems*. Boards and cloth. London, 1931. One of 160 signed. In dust jacket. $100–$135. Trade edition: Brown cloth. In dust jacket. $75–$100.

HUXLEY, Aldous. *Crome Yellow*. Yellow cloth, top stained green. London, 1921. First edition. In dust jacket. $100–$125.

HUXLEY, Aldous. *The Defeat of Youth and Other Poems*. Without title page. Decorated stiff wrappers. (Oxford, 1918.) First edition. Limited edition. In tissue dust jacket. $100–$175.

HUXLEY, Aldous. *Do What You Will*. Half cloth. London, 1929. First edition. One of 260 signed. In glassine jacket. $150–$200. Trade edition: Tan cloth. In dust jacket. $75–$100. New York, 1929. Cloth. First American edition. In dust jacket. $75.

HUXLEY, Aldous. *Ends and Means*. Half cloth. London, 1937. First edition. One of 160 signed. $175–$225. Trade edition: Cloth. In dust jacket. $50–$60.

HUXLEY, Aldous. *Essays New and Old*. Boards and buckram. London, 1926. Florence Press. First edition. One of 650 signed. In dust jacket. $125–$175.

HUXLEY, Aldous. *Eyeless in Gaza*. Decorated boards and brown buckram. London, 1936. One of 200 signed. $250–$350. Trade edition: Tan cloth. In dust jacket. $125–$150.

HUXLEY, Aldous. *Holy Face and Other Essays*. Colored illustrations. Buckram. London, 1929. First edition. One of 300. Boxed. $150–$200.

HUXLEY, Aldous. *Leda*. Half cloth. London, 1920. First edition. One of 160 signed. $200–$250. Trade edition: Red cloth, with top stained red. In dust jacket. $50–$75. Garden City, 1929. Cloth. One of 361 signed. Boxed. $150–$250.

HUXLEY, Aldous. *Little Mexican and Other Stories*. Red cloth, top stained red. London, 1924. First edition. In dust jacket. $75–$125.

HUXLEY, Aldous. *Mortal Coils*. Blue cloth, top stained blue. London, 1922. First edition. In dust jacket. $100–$200.

HUXLEY, Aldous. *The Most Agreeable Vice*. Small self-wrappers. Los Angeles, 1938. First edition. One of 500. $75–$100.

HUXLEY, Aldous. *Music at Night and Other Essays*. Boards and buckram. New York, 1931. Fountain Press. First edition. One of 842 signed. $150–$175. Trade edition: Cloth. In dust jacket. $50. London, 1931. Cloth. First English trade edition. In dust jacket. $75–$100.

HUXLEY, Aldous. *The Olive Tree and Other Essays*. Green buckram. London, 1936. First edition. One of 160 signed. $150–$200.

HUXLEY, Aldous. *On the Margin*. Blue-green cloth, top stained blue. London, 1923. First edition, with page vi numbered v in error. In dust jacket. $125–$150.

HUXLEY, Aldous. *Point Counter Point*. Green buckram. London, 1928. First edition. One of 256 signed. $300–$400. Shaken copy, with hinges cracked, $185. Trade edition: Orange cloth. In dust jacket. $200.

HUXLEY, Aldous. *Prisons*. Piranesi plates. Wrappers and cloth-backed board folder. (Paris), 1949. Trianon Press. One of 212 signed. $400–$450.

HUXLEY, Aldous. *Proper Studies*. Boards and cloth. London, 1927. First edition. One of 250 signed. $100–$125. New York, 1928. Cloth. First American edition. In dust jacket. $75.

HUXLEY, Aldous. *Selected Poems*. Decorated boards. Oxford, 1925. First edition. $125–$150.

HUXLEY, Aldous. *Texts and Pretexts*. Decorated boards and buckram. London, 1932. First edition. One of 214 signed. In tissue dust jacket. $150–$200.

HUXLEY, Aldous. *Vulgarity in Literature*. Boards and buckram. London, 1930. First edition. One of 260 signed. $100–$150. (A few copies were bound in leather: $200–$250.) Trade edition: Decorated boards. In dust jacket. $50–$75.

HUXLEY, Aldous. *Wheels*. Decorated boards and cloth. Oxford, 1917. First edition. $75–$100.

HUXLEY, Aldous. *Words and Their Meanings*. Cloth. Los Angeles, (1940). First edition. One of 100 signed. In dust jacket. $200–$225.

HUXLEY, Aldous. *The World of Light*. Boards and buckram. London, 1931. First edition. One of 160 signed. In glassine jacket. $150–$200.

HUXLEY, Aldous (editor). *An Encyclopedia of Pacifism*. Wrappers. London, (1937). First edition. $150–$200.

HUXLEY, Aldous, and Gilbert, Stuart. *Joyce the Artificer.* Wrappers. (London), 1952. First edition. One of 90. $250–$350.

HUXLEY, T. H. *Evidence as to Man's Place in Nature.* Illustrated. Cloth. London, 1863. First edition. $250–$350.

HYDE, Douglas (translator). *The Love Songs of Connacht.* Boards and linen. Dundrum, Ireland, 1904. Dun Emer Press. One of 300. $75–$100.

HYDE, George E. *The Early Blackfeet and Their Neighbors.* 45 pp., wrappers. Denver, 1933. One of 75. $100–$125.

HYDE, George E. *The Pawnee Indians.* 2 vols., printed wrappers. Denver, 1934. One of 100. First edition. $100–$125.

HYDE, George E. *Red Cloud's Folk.* Cloth. Norman, Okla., 1937. First edition. In dust jacket. $50–$75.

HYDE, George E. *Rangers and Regulars.* 47 pp., wrappers. Denver, 1933. One of 50. $85–$125.

HYDE, S. C. *Historical Sketch of Lyon County, Iowa.* Map. 40 pp., wrappers. Le Mars, Iowa, 1872. First edition. $85–$100.

HYMNS and Prayers for Use at the Marriage of Michael Hornby and Nicolette Ward at St. Margaret's Church. 16 pp., blue wrappers. Westminster (London), 1928. Ashendene Press. $100–$125.

HYMNS for Infant Minds. Wrappers. Boston, 1814. (By Ann and Jane Taylor.) $40–$50.

HYNE, C. J. Cutcliffe. *Honour of Thieves: A Novel.* Cloth. London, 1895. First edition. $50–$65.

HYNE, C. J. Cutliffe. *The Lost Continent.* Cloth. London, 1900. First edition. $100.

HYPERION: A Romance. By the author of "Outre-Mer." 2 vols., tan boards, paper labels, white end papers. New York, 1839. (By Henry Wadsworth Longfellow.) First edition, first binding. $500–$750. Also, brown end papers (later), $350 (A, 1975).

I

IBÁÑEZ, Vicente Blasco. *The Four Horsemen of the Apocalypse*. Cloth. New York, 1918. First American edition. In dust jacket. $150. Without jacket, $75.

IBSEN, Henrik. *Peer Gynt: A Dramatic Poem*. Illustrated in color by Arthur Rackham. Full white vellum. London, (1936). One of 460 signed by Rackham. Boxed. $750–$1,000. Trade edition: Cloth. In dust jacket. $150–$200. Philadelphia, (1936). Cloth. First American trade edition. $150–$200. New York, 1955. Limited Editions Club. Illustrated. Pictorial boards. Boxed. $50–$60.

IDAHO: A Guide in Word and Picture. Illustrated. Pictorial cloth. Caldwell, 1937. First edition. In dust jacket. $150–$175. Second printing: $75–$100. (Edited by Vardis Fisher.)

IDE, Simeon. *The Conquest of California: A Biography of William B. Ide*. Illustrations, map. Boards and cloth. Oakland, 1944. Grabhorn Press. One of 500. In dust jacket. $50–$75.

IDE, William Brown. *A Biographical Sketch of the Life of William B. Ide . . . And . . . Account of the Virtual Conquest of California, etc.* Half leather and cloth. (Claremont, N.H., 1880.) (By Simeon Ide.) First edition. $750–$1,000. (80 copies issued.) Another edition: Printed wrappers. (Claremont, 1885?) $500–$600, possibly more.

IDE, William Brown. *Who Conquered California?* Printed boards and cloth. Claremont, N.H., (1880? 1885?) (By Simeon Ide.) First edition. $250–$350.

IDEAL Husband (An). By the Author of *Lady Windermere's Fan*. Lavender cloth. London, 1899. (By Oscar Wilde.) First edition. Large paper issue: One of 100. $800–$1,000. Signed by Wilde, $1,400 (A, 1981). Signed issue: Vellum. One of 12 on vellum. $2,000–$2,500. Trade issue: One of 1,000. Light brownish-red linen. $200–$300.

IDLE Man (The). 6 parts, wrappers. New York, 1821–22. (Edited by Richard Henry Dana. Sr.) $150–$200. (Note: Contains new poems by William Cullen Bryant.)

IDLENESS and Industry Exemplified, in the History of James Preston and Ivy Lawrence. Boards and calf. Philadelphia, 1803. (By Maria Edgeworth.) First American edition. $150–$175.

I KUNSTITUSHUN i Micha i nan vlhpisa Chickasha, Okla i nan apesa yvt apesa tokmak oke. ("Chickasaw People, Their Constitution and Their Law 1857–59. 1867–68. 1870–72.") Translated from English to Chickasaw by Allen Wright. Cloth. Chickasha. Okla., 1872. First edition. $400–$500.

ILLINOIS Central Railroad Company (The), Offers Over 2,000,000 Acres, etc. 64 pp., sewed. New York, 1856. (By John Wilson.) First edition. $125–$150.

ILLINOIS in 1837; A Sketch. Folding colored map. Boards and cloth. Philadelphia, 1837. (By S. Augustus Mitchell?) First edition, first issue, with "animals" misspelled "animalas" on title page. $125–$150. Second issue, error corrected. $100–$125. Philadelphia, 1838. (Title changed to *Illinois in 1837 & 8*). $100.

ILLUSTRATED Album of Biography of Pope and Stevens Counties, Minnesota. Half leather. Chicago, 1888. $150–$200.

ILLUSTRATED Atlas and History of Yolo County, California (The). 50 plates, map in color. Atlas folio, cloth. San Francisco, 1879. First edition. $350.

ILLUSTRATED Historical Atlas of the State of Indiana. Half leather. Chicago, 1876. $250–$300.

ILLUSTRATED History of Los Angeles County (An). Illustrated. Full morocco. Chicago, 1889. First edition. $250–$300.

ILLUSTRATED History of San Joaquin County (An). Full leather. Chicago, 1890. $200–$250.

IMAGINARY Conversations of Literary Men and Statesmen. 2 vols., boards, paper labels. London, 1824. (By Walter Savage Landor.) First edition. $150–$200. (Note: Three other volumes of the *Conversations* subquently appeared.) New York, 1936. Limited Editions Club. Linen. Boxed. $75–$125.

IMAGIST Anthology (The). Edited by Ford Madox Ford and Glenn Hughes. Cloth. New York, (1930). First edition. One of 1,000. In dust jacket. $150–$200. London, 1930. Yellow cloth. First English edition. $100–$125.

IMPARTIAL Appeal (An) to the Reason, Interest, and Patriotism of the People of Illinois, on the Injurious Effects of Slave Labour. 16 pp., disbound. (Philadelphia?), 1824. (By Morris Birkbeck.) $2,000 and up. Also, $1,700 (A, 1967). (Note: Only four copies known.)

IMPARTIAL Inquirer (The). 96 pp., stitched, or in leather binding. Boston, 1811. (By John Lowell.) First edition. $50–$75.

IMPORTANCE of Being Earnest (The). By the Author of *Lady Windermere's Fan.* Reddish-brown linen. London, 1899. (By Oscar Wilde.) First edition. $150–$200. Another issue: One of 100 on large paper, signed. $1,000–$1,250. Also, $800 (A, 1977). Another issue: Vellum. One of 12 on Japan paper, signed. $2,000 and up. Also, copy No. 2, inscribed by Wilde to Edward Strongman, $2,950 in a 1974 catalogue. New York, 1956. 2 vols., decorated boards. Limited edition. Boxed. $125–$200.

IN a Good Cause: A Collection of Stories, Poems, and Illustrations. Decorated vellum boards. London, 1885. First edition. $50–$60. (Note: Contains first appearance of an Oscar Wilde poem, "Le Jardin des Tuileries.")

INCHIQUIN, The Jesuit's Letters, During a Late Residence in the U. S. A. Leather. New York. 1810. (By Charles J. Ingersoll.) First edition. $35–$50.

INCIDENTAL Numbers. Boards, London, 1912. (By Elinor Wylie.) First edition. One of 65. $3,500–$5,000. Also, $1,300 (A, 1976); $3,750 (A, 1974). Author's first book.

INCIDENTS of Border Life. 5 plates. Half calf. Chambersburg, Pa., 1839. (By Joseph Pritts.) First edition, first issue, with only 491 pages. $75–$100. Second issue, 6 plates. 507 pages. $50–$75. Lancaster, Pa., 1841. $35–$50.

INDEX. 20 pp., red wrappers. London, 1915. (By Norman Douglas.) First edition. One of 100. $75–$100. (Note: The index is to nine Capri monographs by Douglas.)

INDEX to "In Memoriam" (An). Dark-brown or purple cloth. London, 1862. (By Charles L. Dodgson.) First edition, first issue, without ads. $300–$400.

INDIAN Council in the Valley of the Walla-Walla, 1855 (The). 32 pp., pale blue printed wrappers. San Francisco, 1855. (By Lawrence Kip.) First edition. $750–$1,000. Eugene, Ore., 1897. $50–$60.

INDIAN Missions (The), in the United States of America, etc. 34 pp., plain blue wrappers. Philadelphia, 1841. First edition. $1,500 and up. Also, $1,100 (A, 1967). (This Jesuit report includes two letters of Pierre Jean De Smet.)

INDIAN Summer. Stitched paper wrappers. (Madison, Wis., 1912.) (By William Ellery Leonard.) First edition. $35–$50.

INDIANS (The): Or Narratives of Massacres and Depredations, etc. By a Descendant of the Huguenots. 79 pp., calf. Rondout, N.Y., 1846. (By Johannes H. Bevier.) First edition. $100.

INDUSTRIAL Prodigy of the New Southwest (The). Illustrated. 157 pp., wrappers. Muskogee, Indian Territory, (about 1902). $75–$100.

INFIDEL (The); or The Fall of Mexico. 2 vols., purple cloth, paper labels. Philadelphia, 1835. (By Robert Montgomery Bird.) First edition. $600–$750. Also, $275 (A, 1979).

INGE, William. *Picnic.* Cloth. New York, (1953). First edition. In dust jacket. $50–$75.

INGELOW, Jean. *The High Tide.* Wrappers. Boston, 1864. First edition. $50–$60.

INGERSOLL, Ernest. *An Island in the Air.* Cloth. New York, 1905. First edition. In dust jacket. $40–$60.

INGERSOLL, Luther A. *Century Annals of San Bernardino County.* (1769 to 1904). Portraits and views. Full morocco. Los Angeles, 1904. First edition. $100–$150.

INGERSOLL, Robert G. *The Gods and Other Lectures.* Cloth. Peoria, 1874. First edition, first binding, lettered title on spine. $50–$75.

INGERSOLL, Robert G. *An Oration Delivered . . . at Rouse's Hall, Poeria, Ill., at the Unveiling of a Statue of Humboldt, September 14th, 1869.* Wrappers. Peoria, 1869. First edition. $100–$150. Author's first published work.

INGOLDSBY, Thomas. *The Ingoldsby Legends, or Mirth and Marvels.* Etchings by George Cruikshank and John Leech. 3 vols., brown cloth. London, 1840–42–47. (By Richard Harris Barham.) First edition. with misprint "topot" on page 350 of Vol. 3 and blank page 236 in Vol. 1. $400–$600. London, 1898. Illustrated by Arthur Rackham. Green cloth. $150–$200. London, 1907. Illustrated by Rackham. White vellum. One of 560 signed by Rackham. $750–$1,000. Ordinary issue: Cloth. $200–$300. New York, 1907. American issue. One of 50. $1,000–$1,250. Also, $800 (A, 1981).

INGRAHAM, Joseph Holt. See *The South-West.*

INGRAHAM, Joseph Holt. *Pierce Fenning, or, The Lugger's Chase.* Illustrated. 95 pp., stitched. Boston, 1846. First edition. $200–$300.

INGRAHAM, Joseph Holt (editor). *The Prince of the House of David.* Illustrated. Cloth. New York, 1855. First edition. $300–$350.

INHERITANCE (The). 3 vols., boards. Edinburgh, 1824. (By Susan Edmonstone Ferrier.) First edition, with half titles. $250–$350.

IN MEMORIAM. Dark-purple cloth. London, 1850. (By Alfred, Lord Tennyson.) First edition, first issue, with "baseness" for "bareness" in line 3, page 198. $300–$400. London, 1900. Vale Press. Cloth. One of 330. $100–$150. London, 1914. Riccardi Press. Vellum with silk ties. One of 12 on vellum. $2,000 and up. London, 1933. Nonesuch Press. Limp vellum. $250–$300. Another issue: Boards. One of 2,000. $50–$75.

IN PRINCIPIO. (The first chapter of Genesis.) Full morocco, by the Doves Bindery. London, (1911). Doves Press. One of 200. $250–$350. Another issue: One of 12 on vellum. $1,000–$1,250.

INMAN, Col. Henry. *The Old Santa Fe Trail.* Frontispiece, 8 plates by Frederic Remington, folding map. Cloth. New York, 1897. First edition. $150–$200.

INMAN, Col. Henry. *Stories of the Old Santa Fe Trail.* Pictorial cloth. Kansas City, 1881. First edition. $125–$150. Author's first book.

INMAN, Col. Henry (editor). *Buffalo Jones' 40 Years of Adventure.* 43 plates. Pictorial cloth. Topeka, 1899. First edition. $175–$200.

INMAN, Col. Henry, and Cody, William F. *The Great Salt Lake Trail.* Map, 8 plates. Pictorial buckram. New York, 1898. First edition, first binding, blue (later brown). $175–$200.

INSTRUCTION for Heavy Artillery . . . for the Use of the Army of the United States.
39 plates, tables, charts. Cloth. Charleston, 1862. $350–$400.

IRENE the Missionary. Green or brown cloth. Boston, 1879. (By John W. DeForest.)
First edition. $50–$60.

IRON, Ralph. *The Story of an African Farm.* 2 vols., cloth. London, 1883. (By Olive
Schreiner.) First edition. $600–$800. Uganda (New York), 1961. Limited Editions
Club. Illustrated by Paul Hogarth. Cloth. Boxed. $50–$60.

IRVING, John. *Setting Free the Bears.* Cloth. New York, (1968). First edition. In dust
jacket. $150–$200.

IRVING, John. *The World According to Garp.* Boards and cloth. New York, (1978).
First edition. In dust jacket. $40–$50.

IRVING, John Treat, Jr. *The Hawk Chief: A Tale of the Indian Country.* 2 vols., cloth.
Philadelphia, 1837. First edition. $300–$400.

IRVING, John Treat, Jr. *The Hunters of the Prairie, or the Hawk Chief.* 2 vols., boards
and cloth. London, 1837. First English edition of *The Hawk Chief.* $150–$250.

IRVING, John Treat, Jr. *Indian Sketches, Taken During an Expedition to the Pawnee
Tribes.* 2 vols., boards, or cloth. Philadelphia, 1835. First edition. $250–$350. London,
1835. 2 vols., boards. First English edition. $100–$150.

IRVING, Washington. See Agapida, Fray Antonio; Crayon, Geoffrey; Depons, Francois;
Knickerbocker, Diedrich; Langstaff, Launcelot; Oldstyle, Jonathan. Also see *Abbots-
ford; Biography of James Lawrence; Legends of the Conquest of Spain; A Tour on the
Prairies.*

IRVING, Washington. *Adventures of Captain Bonneville.* 3 vols., boards, paper label.
London, 1837. First edition. $300–$500. (For first American edition, see *The Rocky
Mountains.*)

IRVING, Washington. *The Angler.* Boards. Portland, Me., 1931. First separate edition.
One of 150 privately printed for A. S. W. Rosenbach. $100–$150.

IRVING, Washington. *Astoria, or Anecdotes of an Enterprise Beyond the Rocky Mountains.* Folding map. 2 vols., blue cloth. Philadelphia, 1836. First edition, first state,
with copyright notice on back of first title page and garbled footnote on page 239 of
Vol. 2. $1,000–$1,500. Second state, $500–$800. London, 1836. 3 vols., gray boards,
paper spine labels. First English edition. $750–$1,000.

IRVING, Washington. *Biography and Poetical Remains of the Late Margeret Miller
Davidson.* Black cloth. Philadelphia, 1841. First edition. $150–$200.

IRVING, Washington. *Chronicles of Wolfert's Roost.* Tan cloth. Edinburgh (London),
1855. First edition, first issue, with *Constable's Miscellany* listed as "In the
Press . . . Volume V" (later reading, "Volume VII"). $400–$500. (For first American edition, see Irving, *Wolfert's Roost.*)

IRVING, Washington. *A History of the Life and Voyages of Christopher Columbus.* 2
folding maps, 4 vols., boards, paper labels. London, 1828. First edition. (Blanck thinks
all copies issued by Murray under this date are acceptable first editions regardless of
variations.) $500–$750. New York, 1828. Folding map. 3 vols., boards, paper labels.
First American edition. $300–$500.

IRVING, Washington. *The Legend of Sleepy Hollow.* Designs by Will Bradley. Pictorial
boards. New York, (1897). $100–$150. London, (1928). Cloth. Illustrated by Arthur
Rackham. $200–$250. Another issue: One of 375 signed by Rackham. $800–
$1,200.

IRVING, Washington. *The Life of George Washington.* 5 vols., cloth. New York, 1855–
59. First edition, with dates as follows: Vols. 1 and 2, 1855; 3, 1856; 4, 1857, and 5,
1859. $200–$300. Another issue: Large paper edition (Vol. 2 dated 1856). One of 110

copies. $400–$500. (Note: See Blanck's detailed description for the complicated publishing history of this book.)

IRVING, Washington. *The Rocky Mountains.* "Digested from the Journal of Captain B. L. E. Bonneville . . . by Washington Irving." 2 folding maps. 2 vols., blue cloth, printed labels. Philadelphia, 1837. First American edition, first issue, with no ads and 2 blank fly leaves at each end. $300–$500. (For first edition, see Irving, *Adventures of Captain Bonneville.)*

IRVING, Washington. *Voyages and Discoveries of the Companions of Columbus.* Cloth. London, 1831. First edition. $200–$300. Philadelphia, 1831. Boards and cloth, paper label. First American edition. $200–$300.

IRVING, Washington. *Wolfert's Roost and Other Papers.* Frontispiece. Slate-green cloth. New York, 1855. First American edition, first issue, with frontispiece and vignette title page on a stub. $200–$250. (For first edition, see Irving, *Chronicles of Wolfert's Roost.)*

ISELIN, Isaac. *Journal of a Trading Voyage Around the World, 1805–1808.* (New York, about 1897.) First edition. (100 copies printed.) $350–$400.

ISHERWOOD, Christopher. See Auden, W. H., and Isherwood, Christopher; Baudelaire, Charles.

ISHERWOOD, Christopher. *All the Conspirators,* Cloth. London, 1928. First edition. In dust jacket. $200–$250. Author's first novel.

ISHERWOOD, Christopher. *The Berlin Stories: The Last of Mr. Norris, Goodbye to Berlin.* Cloth. (Norfolk, Conn.), 1945. New Directions. First edition. In dust jacket. $100–$150.

ISHERWOOD, Christopher. *Goodbye to Berlin.* Cloth. London, 1939. Hogarth Press. First edition. In dust jacket. $150–$200.

ISHERWOOD, Christopher. *Lions and Shadows: An Education in the Twenties.* Portrait frontispiece. Cloth. London, 1938. First edition, first issue. In dust jacket. $150. Norfolk, (1947). New Directions. Blue cloth. First American edition. In dust jacket. $50.

ISHERWOOD, Christopher. *The Memorial: Portrait of a Family.* Cloth. London, 1932. Hogarth Press. First edition. In dust jacket. $125–$175. Norfolk, (about 1946). New Directions. Cloth. First American edition. In dust jacket. $25–$35.

ISHERWOOD, Christopher. *Mr. Norris Changes Trains.* Cloth. London, 1935. Hogarth Press. In dust jacket. $150–$200.

ISHERWOOD, Christopher. *Prater Violet,* Gray cloth. New York, (1945). First edition. In dust jacket. $100–$125. London, (1946). First English edition. In dust jacket. $75–$100.

ISHERWOOD, Christopher. *Sally Bowles.* Cloth. London, 1937. First edition. In dust jacket. $100–$135.

ISHERWOOD, Christopher. *The World in the Evening.* Cloth. London, (1954). First edition. In dust jacket. $75–$100. New York, (1954). Cloth. First American edition. In dust jacket. $50–$60

IVANHOE: A Romance. 3 vols., boards, Edinburgh, 1820. (By Sir Walter Scott.) First edition. $1,500–$2,000. New York. 1951. Limited Editions Club. Illustrated. 2 vols., pictorial cloth. Boxed. $40–$50.

IVES, Joseph C. *Report Upon the Colorado River of the West.* 4 folding maps, 32 plates. Cloth. Washington, 1861. First edition. Senate issue. $200–$250.

IVINS, Virginia W. *Pen Pictures of Early Western Days.* Plates. Cloth. (Keokuk, Iowa), 1905. First edition: $100–$125. Second edition: (Keokuk), 1908. $65.

J

JACKSON, A. P., and Cole, E. C. *Oklahoma! Politically and Topographically Described.* Map (not in all copies). Pictorial wrappers in color. Kansas City, (1885). First edition. $500–$550.

JACKSON, A. W. *Barbariana: or Scenery, Climate, Soils and Social Conditions of Santa Barbara City and County.* 48 pp., printed wrappers. San Francisco, 1888. $100.

JACKSON, Andrew. *Message from the President of the United States, in Compliance with a Resolution of the Senate Concerning the Fur Trade and Inland Trade to Mexico.* 86 pp., unbound. (Washington, 1832.) Senate Doc. 90. First edition. $250–$350.

JACKSON, Andrew. *To the Citizens of Pennsylvania.* 12 pp., wrappers. (Washington, 1834.) $50–$75.

JACKSON, Charles James. *An Illustrated History of English Plate, Ecclesiastical and Secular.* Colored frontispiece. 76 photogravure plates, $1,500 other illustrations. 2 vols., half morocco. London, 1911. First edition. $300–$400.

JACKSON, Mrs. F. Nevill. *Toys of Other Days.* 9 color plates, 273 plain illustrations. Full vellum. London, 1908. One of 50. $300–$350. Another issue: Morocco. One of 150. $200. Ordinary issue: Cloth. $75–$100.

JACKSON, George. *Sixty Years in Texas.* Plates. Cloth. (Dallas, 1908.) First edition, first issue, with 322 pages. $150–$175.

JACKSON, Helen Hunt. See H. H. Also see *Mercy Philbrick's Choice.*

JACKSON, Helen Hunt. *The Procession of Flowers in Colorado.* Illustrated. Cloth. Boston, 1886. First edition. One of 100. $150–$200.

JACKSON, Helen Hunt. *Ramona.* Decorated cloth. Boston, 1884. First edition. $300–$400. Los Angeles, 1959. Limited Editions Club. Introduction by J. Frank Dobie. Cloth. Boxed. $85–$100.

JACKSON, Holbrook. *The Anatomy of Bibliomania.* 2 vols., cloth. London, 1930. Soncino Press. First edition. One of 1,000. $250–$350. Another issue: Morocco. One of 48 signed. $400–$500. New York, 1931. 2 vols., cloth. First American edition. $100–$150. New York, 1950. Cloth. In dust jacket. $30.

JACKSON, Holbrook. *The Fear of Books.* Full black morocco. London, 1932. First edition. One of 40 (of an edition of 2,048), signed. $400–$500. Trade edition: Buckram (2,008 copies). $60–$75.

JACKSON, John. *The Practical Fly-Fisher.* 10 hand-colored plates. Cloth. London, 1854. First edition. $500–$750.

JACKSON, Shirley. *The Lottery.* Cloth. New York, 1949. First edition. In dust jacket. $85–$125.

JACKSON, Shirley. *The Road Through the Wall.* Boards. New York, (1948). First edition. In dust jacket. $125–$150. Author's first book.

JACOB, J. G. *The Life and Times of Patrick Gass.* 4 plates. Cloth. Wellsburg, Va., 1859. First edition. $300–$400.

JACOBS, Thomas Jefferson. *Scenes, Incidents and Adventures in the Pacific Ocean.* Folding plate, numerous other illustrations. Cloth. New York, 1884. First edition. $500.

JACOBS, W. W. *Many Cargoes.* Cloth. London, 1896. First edition. $100–$125. Author's first book.

JAEGER, Benedict and Preston, H. C. *The Life of North American Insects.* Cloth. Providence, 1854. First edition. $50–$75.

JAMES, Edwin (editor). *Account of an Expedition from Pittsburg to the Rocky Mountains.* 2 maps, 8 plates. 3 vols. (including atlas), boards and leather, paper labels. Philadelphia, 1822–23. First edition. $1,200–$1,500. London, 1823. 3 vols., boards. First English edition. $1,000–$1,250.

JAMES, Edwin (editor). *A Narrative of the Captivity and Adventures of John Tanner.* Frontispiece portrait. Tan boards, purple cloth, paper label. New York, 1830. First edition. $600–$750.

JAMES, Frank. *The Only True History of the Life of Frank James. Written by Himself.* (Cover title.) Illustrated. 134 pp., wrappers. (Pine Bluff, Ark., 1926.) First edition. $75–$100. (Note: Ramon F. Adams calls this a "brazen" and "worthless" fake.)

JAMES, Fred. *The Klondike Goldfields and How to Get There.* Map. 68 pp., tan wrappers. London, 1897. First edition. $400–$500.

JAMES, Henry. See Besant, Walter.

JAMES, Henry. *The Ambassadors.* Red cloth. London, 1903. First edition. $125–$150. New York, 1903. Gray-blue boards. First American edition, first issue, with "Published November, 1903" on copyright page. In blue linen dust jacket. $250–$300. New York, 1963. Limited Editions Club. Illustrated. Boards. Boxed. $50–$60.

JAMES, Henry. *The American.* Cloth. Boston, 1877. First edition, first binding, with Osgood imprint on spine. $125–$150.

JAMES, Henry. *The American Scene.* Maroon buckram. London, 1907. First English edition. $75–$100. New York, 1907. Blue cloth. First American edition. $75–$100.

JAMES, Henry. *The Aspern Papers: Louisa Pallant: The Modern Warning.* 2 vols., blue cloth. London, 1888. First edition. $100–$125. (New York): London, 1888. First American edition. $75–$100.

JAMES, Henry. *The Awkward Age.* Brown cloth. New York 1899. First edition, first issue, with sans-serif "p" in spine imprint. $100. London, 1899. Light-blue cloth. First English edition (possibly simultaneous with the New York edition). $150–$175.

JAMES, Henry. *The Beast in the Jungle.* Illustrated. Boards. Kentfield, Calif., 1963. Allen Press. One of 130. $400–$600.

JAMES, Henry. *The Better Sort.* Rose-colored cloth. New York, 1903. First edition, with "Published, February, 1903" on copyright page. $100–$125. London, 1903. Red cloth. First English edition (simultaneous with the American first). $125–$150.

JAMES, Henry. *The Bostonians.* 3 vols., blue cloth. London, 1886. First edition. $500–$750. London, 1886. First one-volume edition. $100–$125. New York, 1886. Red cloth. First American edition. $50–$75.

JAMES, Henry. *A Bundle of Letters.* Stiff printed wrappers. Boston, (1880). First edition, Blanck's state A, with comma after "Jr." on front cover. $75–$100.

JAMES, Henry. *Confidence.* 2 vols., cloth. London, 1880. First edition. $100–$150. Boston, 1880. Brick-colored cloth (one volume). First American edition, first issue, with Houghton, Osgood imprint on spine. $300–$350.

JAMES, Henry. *Daisy Miller: A Comedy.* Wrappers. (London), 1882. First edition. (18 privately printed copies.) $792 (A, 1979). Boston, 1883. Cloth. First published edition. $400.

JAMES, Henry. *Daisy Miller: A Study*. Printed tan or gray wrappers, or green cloth. New York, 1879. First edition. Wrappers: $100–$150. Cloth: $100–$125. New York, 1969. Limited Editions Club. Boxed. $40–$50.

JAMES, Henry. *Daisy Miller and An International Episode*. Vellum. New York, 1892. First edition. One of 250. $150–$175. Trade edition: Cloth. $75.

JAMES, Henry. *The Diary of a Man of Fifty, and A Bundle of Letters*. Tan wrappers, or green cloth. New York, 1880. First edition. Wrappers: $75. Cloth: $35–$50.

JAMES, Henry. *Embarrassments*. Blue cloth. London, 1896. First published edition, first issue, with 4 irises on front of binding. $75–$100. New York, 1896. Maroon cloth. First American edition. $50–$75.

JAMES, Henry. *English Hours*. Illustrated by Joseph Pennell. Gray cloth. London, 1905. First edition. $100–$150. Second binding, half buckram. $75. Boston, 1905. Cloth, or half morocco. First American trade edition. $35. Another issue: Boards. One of 421 on large paper. $150–$200.

JAMES, Henry. *Essays in London and Elsewhere*. Salmon-colored cloth. London, 1893. First edition. $75–$100. New York, 1893. Blue cloth. First American edition. $40–$50.

JAMES, Henry. *The Europeans: A Sketch*. 2 vols., blue cloth. London, 1878 First edition. $250–$300. Boston, 1879. Cloth (in one volume). First American edition. $75–$125.

JAMES, Henry. *The Golden Bowl*. 2 vols., tan cloth. New York, 1904. First edition, with "Published, November, 1904" on copyright page. $75–$100.

JAMES, Henry. *An International Episode*. Gray wrappers, or flexible green cloth. New York, 1879. First edition, first state, with "blue" for "beth" in the first line of page 45. Wrappers: $175–$250. Cloth: $100–$125.

JAMES, Henry. *Italian Hours*. Plates (some colored). Green buckram. London, 1909. First edition. In dust jacket. $250–$350. Boston, 1909. Terra-cotta cloth. First American edition, with "Published November 1909" on copyright page. In dust jacket. Boxed. $150–$250. Second impression: $100.

JAMES, Henry. *The Ivory Tower*. Edited by Percy Lubbock. Portrait. Blue cloth. London, (1917). First edition. $60–$75. New York, 1917. Greenish-brown cloth. First American edition, with "Published October, 1917" on copyright page. In dust jacket. $250.

JAMES, Henry. *The Letters of Henry James*. Edited by Percy Lubbock. 2 portrait frontispieces and facsimile, 2 vols., blue cloth. London, 1920. First edition. In dust jackets. $75–$100. New York, 1920, 2 vols., greenish-black cloth. First American edition. In dust jackets. $75–$100. Lacking jackets, $25–$35.

JAMES, Henry. *Letters of Henry James to Walter Berry*. Printed vellum wrappers. Paris, 1928. Black Sun Press. First edition. One of 16 on Japan vellum, each with an original letter. $400 and up. Another issue: One of 100 on Van Gelder paper. $200–$300.

JAMES, Henry. *A Little Tour in France*. Light brown cloth. Boston, 1885 (actually 1884). First edition, first binding. $100–$125. Cambridge (Mass.), 1900. Illustrated by Joseph Pennell. Boards and cloth. One of 250 large paper copies. $100. Trade edition: (With Boston imprint, not Cambridge.) Cloth. $25. London, 1900. Half vellum. One of 150 on vellum. $150–$200.

JAMES, Henry. *The Madonna of the Future and Other Tales*. 2 vols., blue cloth. London, 1879. First edition. $300–$350.

JAMES, Henry. *"A Most Unholy Trade."* Printed wrapper over flexible boards. (Cambridge, Mass.), 1923. Scarab Press. First edition. One of 100. In tissue dust jacket. $100–$150.

JAMES, Henry. *Notes of a Son and Brother*. Frontispiece. 5 plates. Greenish-brown cloth. New York, 1914. First edition. In dust jacket. $200–$300. London, 1914. Cloth. First English edition. In dust jacket. $200–$250.

JAMES, Henry. *Notes and Reviews*. Half leather and cloth. Cambridge, Mass., 1921. First edition. One of 30 on vellum. $150–$175. Trade edition: $50–$60.

JAMES, Henry. *The Other House*. 2 vols., blue cloth. London, 1896. First English edition $100–$150. New York, 1896. Red cloth (one volume). First American edition (published simultaneously with the London edition?). $100.

JAMES, Henry. *The Outcry*. Cloth. London, (1911). First edition. In dust jacket. $100–$150. New York, 1911. Greenish-brown cloth. First American edition, with "Published September, 1911" on copyright page. In dust jacket. $100.

JAMES, Henry. *A Passionate Pilgrim, and Other Tales*. Cloth. Boston, 1875. First edition, first binding, with "J. R. Osgood & Co." on spine. $800–$1,000. Author's first book.

JAMES, Henry. *The Portrait of a Lady*. 3 vols., blue or dark green cloth. London, 1881. First edition. $750. Boston, 1882. Cloth. First American edition. $175–$200. New York, 1967. Limited Editions Club. Colored plates. Marbled boards and cloth. Boxed. $50–$60.

JAMES, Henry. *Portraits of Places*. Blue-green cloth. London, 1883. First edition, first binding, with "m" in Macmillan larger than other letters. $100–$150. Boston, 1884. Cloth. First American edition. $35–$50.

JAMES, Henry. *The Princess Casamassima*. 3 vols., blue cloth. London, 1886. First edition. $600–$800. London [*sic*], 1886. Blue-green cloth (in one volume). First American edition. $125–$150. London, 1887. First British one-volume edition (same as the preceding but with 1887 title page). $75–$100.

JAMES, Henry. *The Private Life*. Blue cloth. London, 1893. First edition. $150–$200.

JAMES, Henry. *The Real Thing and Other Tales*. Gray-blue cloth. New York, 1893. First edition, first issue, with 1892 copyright. $150–$200. London, 1893. Wrappers. First English edition, with 1893 copyright. $350.

JAMES, Henry. *Refugees in Chelsea*. Boards. Chelsea, (1920). First edition. Ashendene Press. (50 copies on paper.) $1,500–$2,000. Another issue: One of 6 on vellum. $4,000–$5,000.

JAMES, Henry. *The Reverberator*. 2 vols., cloth. London, 1888. First edition. $200–$250. London, 1888. Blue cloth. First American edition. $100.

JAMES, Henry. *Roderick Hudson*. Cloth. Boston, 1876. First edition, first binding, with Osgood imprint on spine. $175–$225. Later binding: Houghton Mifflin imprint on spine. $50–$75. Author's first novel.

JAMES, Henry. *The Sense of the Past*. Edited by Percy Lubbock. Portrait. Blue cloth. London, (1917). First edition. In dust jacket. $150–$295. New York, 1917. Greenish-brown cloth. First American edition, with "Published October, 1917" on copyright page. In dust jacket. $50–$75.

JAMES, Henry. *The Siege of London*. Cloth. Boston, 1883. First edition, with Osgood imprint on spine. $75–$100.

JAMES, Henry. *A Small Boy and Others*. Greenish-brown cloth. New York, 1913. First edition, first issue, with 11-line publisher's ad. In dust jacket. $100–$150. London, 1913. Blue cloth. First English edition (possibly simultaneous with New York edition). In dust jacket. $100–$150.

JAMES, Henry. *The Soft Side*. Maroon buckram. New York, 1900. First edition. $100–$150. London, 1900. Red cloth. First English edition (possibly simultaneous with the New York first). $100–$150.

JAMES, Henry. *The Spoils of Poynton*. Blue cloth. London, 1897. First (?) edition. $150–$200. Boston, 1897. Cloth. First American edition. (Blanck thinks this may have been simultaneous with the English first.) $150–$200.

JAMES, Henry. *Stories Revived*. 3 vols., cloth. London, 1885. First edition, first binding, blue cloth. $300–$400.

JAMES, Henry. *Transatlantic Sketches*. Brown cloth. Boston, 1875. First edition, first binding, with Osgood imprint on spine. $300–$400.

JAMES, Henry. *The Turn of the Screw*. Illustrated. Half morocco. London, 1940. Hand and Flower Press. One of 200. $150–$200. New York, 1949. Limited Editions Club. Illustrated. Buckram. Boxed. $60–$80.

JAMES, Henry. *Views and Reviews*. Vellum, leather spine. Boston, 1908. First edition. One of 160. $150. Trade edition: Olive cloth. $100.

JAMES, Henry. *Washington Square*. Dark olive-green cloth. New York, 1881 (actually 1880). First edition. $75–$200. New York, 1971. Limited Editions Club. Boxed. $30–$40.

JAMES, HENRY. *Washington Square: The Pension Beaurepas: A Bundle of Letters*. 2 vols., cloth. London, 1881. First edition. $125–$175.

JAMES, Henry. *Watch and Ward*. Cloth. Boston, 1878. First edition, first printing, with blank leaf after page 219. $100–$150.

JAMES, Henry. *What Maisie Knew*. Blue cloth. London, 1898 (actually 1897). First edition. $75–$125. Another issue: London, 1897 (actually 1898). Colonial issue. $75–$125. Chicago, (1897). Slate-colored cloth. First American edition. $75–$125.

JAMES, Henry. *The Wheel of Time*. Decorated gray-green cloth. New York, 1893. First edition. $50–$100.

JAMES, Henry. *William Wetmore Story and His Friends*. Frontispiece. 2 vols., green cloth. Edinburgh, 1903. First British edition. $75–$100. Boston, 1903, 2 vols., green cloth. First American edition (issued simultaneously with the Edinburgh edition). $75–$100.

JAMES, Henry. *The Wings of the Dove*. 2 vols., red cloth. New York, 1902. First edition, with "Published, August 1902" on copyright page. $100–$125. London, 1902. First English edition. $100–$125.

JAMES, Jason W. *Memorable Events in the Life of Capt. Jason W. James*. Frontispiece. Cloth, No place, (about 1911). First edition. $285.

JAMES, Jason W. *Memories and Viewpoints*. Cloth. Roswell, N.M., 1928. First edition, $225.

JAMES, Jesse, Jr. *Jesse James, My Father*. 4 portraits. White printed wrappers. Kansas City, Mo., 1899. (Ghostwritten by A. B. Macdonald?) First edition. $150–$200. Cleveland, (1906). Reprint edition. $35.

JAMES, M. R. *Ghost Stories of An Antiquary*. Cloth. London, 1904. First edition. In dust jacket. $500–$600.

JAMES, Philip. *Children's Books of Yesterday*. Edited by G. Geoffrey Holme. Cloth. London, 1933. First edition. In dust jacket. $100–$150.

JAMES, Thomas. *Three Years Among the Indians and Mexicans*. 130 pp., plain wrappers. Waterloo, Ill., 1846. First edition. $6,000–$8,000. Also waterstained and re-backed, $4,100 (A, 1963). St. Louis, 1916. 12 plates. Half cloth. Second edition. One of 365. $100–$150.

JAMES, W. S. *Cow-boy Life in Texas*. 34 plates. Pictorial wrappers. Chicago, (1893). First edition. $250. Chicago, (1898). 27 plates. Cloth. $50–$75.

JAMES, Will. *All in the Day's Riding.* Cloth. New York, 1933. First edition. In dust jacket. $75–$100.

JAMES, Will. *Cowboys North and South.* Illustrated by the author. Pictorial buckram. New York, 1924. First edition. In dust jacket. $125–$140. Author's first book.

JAMES, Will. *Lone Cowboy: My Life Story.* Illustrated. Cloth, leather label. New York. 1930. First edition. One of 250 with an original drawing. $600–$750. Trade edition: Green cloth. In dust jacket. $75–$100.

JAMES, Will. *Smoky the Cowhorse.* Illustrated by the author. Cloth. New York, 1926. First edition. In dust jacket. $125–$150. Without jacket, $50–$75.

JAMES, William. *The Principles of Psychology.* 2 vols., cloth. New York, 1890. First edition. $150–$200. London, (1890). Cloth. First English edition. $75–$100.

JAMES, William F., and McMurry, George H. *History of San Jose, California.* Cloth. San Jose, 1933. First edition. $60–$80.

JAMESON, Anna Brownell. *The Beauties of the Court of King Charles II.* 21 hand-colored engraved portraits on India paper. Calf. London, 1833. $150–$250.

JANSON, Charles William. *The Stranger in America.* Engraved title page, plan of Philadelphia, 9 (sometimes 10) aquatint plates. Boards and calf. London, 1807. First edition. $600–$800. (A copy with 10 plates hand-colored, $928 in a 1978 British catalogue.) Philadelphia, 1807. Boards and calf. First American edition. $400–$500.

JANVIER, Thomas A. *The Aztec Treasure-House.* Illustrated by Frederic Remington. Decorated cloth. New York, 1890. First edition. $150–$200.

JARRELL, Randall. *Blood for a Stranger.* Cloth. New York, (1942). First edition. In dust jacket. $250–$350. Author's first book.

JARRELL, Randall. *Little Friend, Little Friend.* Cloth. New York, 1945. First edition. In dust jacket. $175–$200.

JARRELL, Randall. *Losses.* Cloth. New York, (1948). First edition. In dust jacket. $125–$150.

JARRELL, Randall. *Pictures from an Institution.* Cloth. New York, 1954. First edition. In dust jacket. $50. Advance copy in wrappers. $150.

JARRELL, Randall. *Selected Poems.* Cloth. New York, 1955. First edition. In dust jacket. $50.

JARRELL, Randall. *The Seven-League Crutches.* Cloth. New York, (1951). First edition. In dust jacket. $125–$150.

JEFFERIES, Richard. See *The Gamekeeper at Home.*

JEFFERIES, Richard. *Amaryllis at the Fair.* Cloth. London, 1887. First edition. $125–$150.

JEFFERIES, Richard. *Bevis: The Story of a Boy.* 3 vols., green cloth. London, 1882. First edition. $400–$450.

JEFFERIES, Richard. *Greene Ferne Farm.* Green cloth. London, 1880. First edition. $150–$200.

JEFFERIES, Richard. *Hodge and His Masters.* 2 vols., cloth. London, 1880. First edition. $175–$250.

JEFFRIES, Richard. *Jack Brass, Emperor of England.* 12 pp., tan wrappers. London, 1873. First edition. $400–$600.

JEFFERIES, Richard. *The Open Air.* Printed cloth. London, 1885. First edition. $250–$300.

JEFFERIES, Richard. *Restless Human Hearts*. 3 vols., cloth. London, 1875. First edition. $200–$400.

JEFFERIES, Richard. *Wood Magic: A Fable*. 2 vols., cloth. London, 1881. First edition. $350–$450.

JEFFERS, Robinson. See Powell, Lawrence Clark; Sterling, George; *Continent's End*.

JEFFERS, Robinson. *The Alpine Christ and Other Poems*. Commentary by William Everson. Boards. (Aramos, Calif.), 1973. First edition. One of 250 signed by Everson. $75–$100.

JEFFERS, Robinson. *Apology for Bad Dreams*. 16 pp., wrappers. Paris, 1930. First edition. One of 30 designed by Ward Ritchie. $750–$1,000.

JEFFERS, Robinson. *An Artist*. Frontispiece. Introduction by Benjamin De Casseres. 16 pp., wrappers. (Austin, 1928.) First edition. One of 96 (actually 196). $150–$250. (Printed by John S. Mayfield; most copies destroyed or damaged by fire.)

JEFFERS, Robinson. *Be Angry at the Sun*. Marbled boards and cloth. New York, (1941). First edition. One of 100 signed. In glassine dust jacket. Boxed. $500–$600. Trade edition: Cloth. In dust jacket. $35–$50.

JEFFERS, Robinson. *The Beaks of Eagles*. Folio, 3 leaves, printed yellow wrappers. San Francisco, 1936. Grabhorn Press. First edition. $300–$350.

JEFFERS, Robinson. *Californians*. Blue cloth. New York, 1916. First edition. In dust jacket. $300–$400. Lacking jacket, $150–$200. "Advance Copy, For Review Only" (perforation so stamped on title page). In dust jacket. $350–$500. Lacking jacket, $150. Author's first commercially published book. No place, 1971. Boards and cloth. Introduction by William Everson. One of 50 (of an edition of 500) signed by Everson. $75–$100. Ordinary copies: $35.

JEFFERS, Robinson. *Cawdor and Other Poems*. Buckram. New York, 1928. First edition. One of 375 on large paper, signed. In dust jacket. Boxed. $150–$250. Trade edition: Boards and cloth. In dust jacket. $40–$50. London, 1929. Hogarth Press. Boards. First English edition. $150–$250.

JEFFERS, Robinson. *Dear Judas and Other Poems*. Boards and cloth. New York, 1929. First edition (preceding the limited edition). In dust jacket. $50–$75. Limited edition, same date: Boards, vellum spine. One of 375 signed. In glassine dust jacket. Boxed $200–$250. From the same issue: One of 25 lettered copies. $350–$400. London, 1930. Hogarth Press. Boards. First English edition. $150–$250.

JEFFERS, Robinson. *De Rerum Virtute*. Decorated boards, linen spine, leather label. (San Francisco, 1953.) Grabhorn Press. First edition. One of 30. In plain purple dust jacket. $650–$850.

JEFFERS, Robinson. *Descent to the Dead*. Boards and vellum. New York, (1931). First edition. One of 500 (actually 550) signed. Boxed. $400–$500. (No trade editions issued).

JEFFERS, Robinson. *The Double Axe and Other Poems*. Blue cloth. New York, 1948. First edition. In dust jacket. $35–$50. Also, a few copies (?) with an inserted leaf before title page, signed by Jeffers. $265 in a 1978 catalogue.

JEFFERS, Robinson. *Flagons and Apples*. (By John Robinson Jeffers.) Cinnamon boards, linen spine, paper label. Los Angeles, 1912. First edition. (500 copies.) $600–$800. Author's first book.

JEFFERS, Robinson. *Give Your Heart to the Hawks*. Marbled boards and calf. New York, 1933. First edition. One of 200 signed. $300–$400. Trade edition: Brown cloth. In dust jacket. $50–$75.

JEFFERS, Robinson. *Hope Is Not for the Wise*. Folio, 4 pp., printed wrappers. (San Mateo), 1937. Quercus Press. First edition. One of 24. $600–$800.

JEFFERS, Robinson. *The House-Dog's Grave—Haig's Grave*. Morocco. (San Mateo, 1939.) Quercus Press. One of 30. $500–$700.

JEFFERS, Robinson. *Hungerfield*. Foreword by Frederick Mortimer Clapp. 19 pp., boards, linen spine, morocco label. (San Francisco), 1952. Grabhorn Press. First edition. One of 30. $850–$1,000. New York, (1954). Boards and cloth. First trade edition. In dust jacket. $50–$65.

JEFFERS, Robinson. *The Loving Shepherdess*. 9 etchings by Jean Kellogg. Boards. New York, 1956. First edition. One of 115. Boxed. $400–$450. With an extra suite of plates, $1,000.

JEFFERS, Robinson. *Medea*. Boards and cloth. New York, (1946). First edition, first issue, with word "least" omitted on page 99. In dust jacket. $75–$100. Second issue, corrected. In dust jacket. $30–$40.

JEFFERS, Robinson. *Natural Music*. Folio, leaflet. (San Francisco), 1947. Quercus Press. First edition. 25 special copies, inscribed by Jeffers. $500–$750. 750 ordinary copies: $40–$50.

JEFFERS, Robinson. *The Ocean's Tribute*. 4 pp., folio broadside. San Francisco, 1958. Grabhorn Press. First edition. $85–$100.

JEFFERS, Robinson. *A Poem*. Single sheet, French-folded. (San Mateo), 1937. Quercus Press. First edition. One of 10. $900–$1,200.

JEFFERS, Robinson. *Poems*. Photographic portrait by Ansel Adams. Buckram, paper label. San Francisco, 1928. Book Club of California. First edition. One of 310. Boxed. With Adams' signature. $750–$1,000. Without Adams' signature. $450–$600. Also 10 "printer's copies" in half red morocco, signed. $1,000–$1,500.

JEFFERS, Robinson. *Poetry, Gongorism and a Thousand Years*. 12 pp., decorated boards. (Los Angeles), 1949. Ward Ritchie Press. First edition. One of 200. $300–$400.

JEFFERS, Robinson. *Return: An Unpublished Poem*. 4 pp., wrappers over flexible boards. San Francisco, 1934. Grabhorn Press. One of 250. $150. Another issue: One of 3 on vellum. $1,500–$2,000.

JEFFERS, Robinson. *Roan Stallion, Tamar, and Other Poems*. Purple boards, black cloth spine. New York, 1925. First edition. In dust jacket. $100–$150. Another (later) issue, same date: Marbled boards. Author's Presentation Edition. One of 12. $450–$650. New York, 1926. Second edition (or printing). $35–$45. London, 1928. Hogarth Press. Boards. First English edition. $75–$125. New York, 1935. First Modern Library Edition. Flexible cloth. In dust jacket. $40–$60. (Note: Contains a new introduction by Jeffers).

JEFFERS, Robinson. *Rock and Hawk*. Wrappers. No place, 1934. First edition. One of 20(?)(probably more). $500–$750. (Printed by Frederic Prokosch.)

JEFFERS, Robinson. *Solstice and Other Poems*. Patterned boards and buckram. New York, 1935. Grabhorn printing. One of 320 signed. In gray dust jacket. $175–$300. Trade edition: New York, (1935). Green cloth. In dust jacket. $35–$50.

JEFFERS, Robinson. *Stars*. 8 pp., black boards, white paper label. (Pasadena), 1930. Flame Press. One of 72, with errata leaf. (All except 6 copies were destroyed because of a typographical error.) $1,500–$2,000. Also, $1,000 (A, 1977); $1,500 (A, 1973). Second edition, same date. Printed blue wrappers. One of 110. $200–$400.

JEFFERS, Robinson. *Such Counsels You Gave to Me*. Illustrated by Fritz Eichenberg. Patterned boards and morocco. New York, (1937). Spiral Press. First edition. One of 300 signed. In dust jacket. Boxed. $200–$300. Trade edition: Cloth. In dust jacket. $50–$75.

JEFFERS, Robinson. *Tamar and Other Poems*. Cloth. New York, (1924). First edition. (500 copies.) In plain tan dust jacket. $400–$600.

JEFFERS, Robinson. *Themes in My Poems*. Woodcuts by Mallette Dean. 46 pp., decorated boards, cloth spine, label. San Francisco, 1956. Book Club of California. First edition. One of 350. In plain brown dust jacket. $150–$175.

JEFFERS, Robinson. *Thurso's Landing and Other Poems*. Buckram. New York, (1932). First edition. One of 200 signed. In cellophane dust jacket. Boxed. $250–$300. Also, one of 15 out of series copies. $275–$375. (A, 1979). Trade edition: Boards and cloth. In dust jacket. $50–$75.

JEFFERS, Robinson. *Two Consolations*. 6 leaves, rose or gray boards. (San Mateo), 1940. Quercus Press. First edition. One of 250. $100–$150.

JEFFERS, Robinson. *The Women at Point Sur*. Boards and cloth. New York, 1927. First edition (preceding the limited edition). In dust jacket. $50–$75. Limited edition: New York, (1927). Silver on black boards and vellum. One of 265 signed. In glassine dust jacket. Boxed. $150–$200.

JEFFERS, Una. *Visits to Ireland: Travel Diaries of Una Jeffers*. Foreword by Robinson Jeffers. Boards and cloth. Los Angeles, 1954. Ward Ritchie Press. First edition. One of 300. Boxed. $75–$125.

JEFFERSON, H. E. *Oklahoma: The Beautiful Land*. 202 pp., printed wrappers. Chicago, 1889. First edition. $500 and up.

JEFFERSON, Thomas. *An Appendix to the Notes on Virginia Relative to the Murder of Logan's Family*. 58 pp., sewed. Philadelphia, 1800. First edition. $150–$200.

JEFFERSON, Thomas. *A Manual of Parliamentary Practice for the Use of the Senate of the United States*. Calf. Washington, 1801. First edition. $200–$300.

JEFFERSON, Thomas. *Message from the President of the United States, Communicating Discoveries Made in Exploring the Missouri, Red River, and Washita by Capts. Lewis and Clark, Dr. Sibley, and Mr. Dunbar, etc.* 2 folding tables, map (in some copies). 171 pp., unbound. Washington, 1806. "Printed by Order of the Senate." First edition. With map. $5,000–$6,000. Without map, up to $3,000, possibly more.

JEFFERSON, Thomas. *Notes on the State of Virginia*. Leather. Baltimore, 1800. $150–$300. Boston, 1801. Folding map. Leather. $150–$300. (Note: There are numerous 19th-century editions; ones with the map are more valuable. For the first, anonymous publication, Paris, 1782 (actually 1785), and other 18th-century editions, see the book auction records.)

JEFFREY, J. K. See *The Territory of Wyoming*.

JENKINS, John H. *Cracker Barrel Chronicles: A Bibliography of Texas Town and Country Histories*. Full tan leather. Austin, 1965. First edition. One of 15 signed. Boxed. $150.

JENKS, Ira C. *Trial of David F. Mayberry, for the Murder of Andrew Alger*. (Cover title.) 48 pp., wrappers. Janesville, Wis., 1855. First edition. $250–$300.

JENKS, J. W. P. (*With the Compliments of J. W. P. Jenks:*) *Hunting in Florida in 1874*. (Cover title; caption title for text is *Hunting in Florida*.) Folding map of Everglades. 70 pp., printed buff wrappers. (Providence, R.I., 1884?). First (?) edition. $500–$600.

JENNINGS, A. *Through the Shadows with O. Henry*. Illustrated. Pictorial cloth. New York, (1921). First edition. In dust jacket. $50–$75.

JENNINGS, N. A. *A Texas Ranger*. Tan pictorial cloth. New York, 1899. First edition. $250–$350.

JEREMIAH. See *The Lamentations of Jeremiah*.

JEROME, Chauncey. *History of the American Clock Business for the Past 60 Years*. Printed wrappers. New Haven, 1860. First edition. $150–$200.

JEROME, Jerome K. *Three Men in a Boat*. Illustrated. Light blue cloth. Bristol, England, 1889. First edition, first issue, with title page reading as follows: "Bristol/J. W. Arrowsmith, Quay Street/London/Simpkin, Marshall & Co., 4 Stationer's Hall Court/(rule) 1889/All rights reserved/." $100–$125. New York, 1890. Cloth. First American edition. $50–$60.

JEROME, Jerome K. *Told After Supper*. Illustrated. Pictorial red cloth. London, 1891. First edition. $100.

JERROLD, Douglas. *A Man Made of Money*. 12 plates by John Leech. 6 parts, pictorial wrappers, and cloth. London, 1849. First edition. In parts: $400–$500. Cloth: $250–$350.

JESSE James: The Life and Daring Adventures of This Bold Highwayman and Bank Robber. Pictorial wrappers. Philadelphia, (about 1882). (Anonymous.) First edition. $75–$125.

JEWETT, Sarah Orne. *Betty Leicester*. Decorated cloth. Boston, 1890. First edition, early state, with this book last in ad opposite title page. $50–$75.

JEWETT, Sarah Orne. *Betty Leicester's English Christmas*. Cloth. Boston, 1894. First edition. $200.

JEWETT, Sarah Orne. *The Country of the Pointed Firs*. Cloth. Boston, 1896. First edition. $125–$175.

JEWETT, Sarah Orne. *Deephaven*. Cloth. Boston, 1877. First edition, first issue, with the reading "was" in line 16, page 65. (Later reading, "so.") $75–$100. Author's first book.

JEWITT, Charles. *Temperance Toy*. Hand-colored engravings. 16 pp., printed wrappers. Boston, 1840. $50–$75.

JEWITT, John R. *A Journal, Kept at Nootka Sound*. 48 pp., gray wrappers. Boston, 1807. First edition. $4,850 in a 1981 catalogue. Also, $3,600 (A, 1979).

JEWITT, John R. *Narrative of the Sufferings and Adventures of John R. Jewitt*. Edited by Richard Alsop. 2 plates. Calf. Middletown, 1815. First edition, first issue, with Loomis & Richards imprint. $1,000–$1,250. Second issue, Seth Richards imprint: $800–$1,000. New York, (about 1815). Boards. $650.

JOAQUIN (The Claude Duval of California); or The Marauder of the Mines. 160 pp., pictorial wrappers. New York, (1865—actually later, in the 1870's). (By Henry L. Williams.) First edition. $175–$250. New York, 1888. Decorated cloth. Second edition. $100–$125.

JOCKNICK, Sidney. *Early Days on the Western Slope of Colorado*. 25 plates. Cloth. Denver, 1913. First edition. $150–$200.

JOHL, Janet. *More About Dolls*. Illustrated. Cloth. New York, 1946. First edition. In dust jacket. $100–$110.

JOHL, Janet. *Still More About Dolls*. Illustrated. Cloth. New York, 1950. First edition. In dust jacket. $75–$125.

JOHL, Janet. *Your Dolls and Mine*. Illustrated. Cloth. New York, 1952. First edition. In dust jacket. $75–$100.

JOHN Bull in America; or, The New Munchausen. Boards, or cloth. New York, 1825. (By James Kirke Paulding.) First edition. $150–$250.

JOHN Halifax, Gentleman. 3 vols., brown cloth. London, 1856. (By Dinah M. Craik.) First edition, first issue, with 3 pages of ads at end of Vol. 1, one page at end of Vol. 2, and 2 pages at end of Vol. 3. $600–$800.

JOHN Marr and Other Sailors. 103 pp., printed yellow wrappers. New York, 1888. (By

Herman Melville.) First edition. One of 25. $1,000 and up. Also, $850 (A, 1948)—
"Believed to be Melville's copy,with some corrections in his hand." Princeton, 1922.
Half cloth. One of 175. $60–$100.

JOHN, W. D. *Swansea Porcelain.* 20 color illustrations, others in black and white. Buckram. London, 1958. First edition. $250–$300.

JOHN Woodvil: A Tragedy. Plain pink or blue boards. London, 1802. (By Charles
Lamb.) First edition. $500–$650.

JOHNSON, Benj. F. (of Boone). *"The Old Swimmin'-Hole" and 'Leven More Poems.*
Wrappers. Indinapolis, 1883. (By James Whitcomb Riley.) First edition. $200–$300.
(Note: There exists a 1909 facsimile, which lacks the "W" in "William" on page 41.
Value: about $10.)

JOHNSON, Crisfield (compiler). *The History of Cuyahoga County, Ohio.* Double column pages. Half morocco. Cleveland, 1879. First edition. $85–$125.

JOHNSON, Don Carlos. *A Brief History of Springville, Utah.* Illustrated. Wrappers.
Springville, 1900. First edition, with errata slip. $200–$250.

JOHNSON, Edwin F. *Railroad to the Pacific, Northern Route.* 3 maps, 8 plates. Boards
and calf. New York, 1854. Second (actually first) edition. $300–$350.

JOHNSON, Frank M. *Forest, Lake and River.* Portrait, colored frontispiece. 2 vols.,
bound in suede. Boston, 1902. One of 350. $250–$300.

JOHNSON, Harrison. *Johnson's History of Nebraska.* Frontispiece, other illustrations;
folding map in color. Blue cloth. Omaha, 1880. First edition. $125–$150.

JOHNSON, Henry L. *Gutenberg and the Book of Books.* Illustrated. Folio, buckram.
New York, 1932. One of 750. In slipcase. $125–$150.

JOHNSON, James Weldon. *Along This Way.* Cloth. New York, 1933. First edition. In
dust jacket. $75–$85.

JOHNSON, James Weldon. *Fifty Years and Other Poems.* Half cloth. Boston, (1917).
First edition. One of 110 on Japan vellum, signed. $200–$250.

JOHNSON, James Weldon. *God's Trombones.* Illustrated. Cloth. New York, 1927. First
edition. In dust jacket. $100–$125.

JOHNSON, James Weldon. *Saint Peter Relates an Incident of the Resurrection Day.*
Folio, black boards, gilt. New York, 1940. One of 200 signed. Boxed. $150–$250.

JOHNSON, James Weldon (editor). *The Second Book of Negro Spirituals.* Cloth. New
York, 1926. First edition. $75–$100.

JOHNSON, Josephine. *Now in November.* Cloth. New York, 1934. First edition. In dust
jacket. $50. Author's first book.

JOHNSON, Lionel. *The Art of Thomas Hardy.* Portrait. Boards. London, 1894. First
edition. One of 150. $250–$300. Ordinary issue: Cloth. $75–$85.

JOHNSON, Lionel. *Poems.* Boards. London, 1895. First edition. One of 750. $125. An-
other issue: One of 25 signed. $250–$300.

JOHNSON, Lionel. *Twenty One Poems.* Selected by William Butler Yeats. Boards and
linen. Dundrum, Ireland, 1904. Dun Emer Press. One of 220. $150–$175.

JOHNSON, Overton, and Winter, William H. *Route Across the Rocky Mountains, etc.*
Cloth-backed boards. Lafayette, Ind., 1846. First edition. $1,500–$2,000. Also, soiled
copy, $1,000 (A, 1978).

JOHNSON, Owen. *The Tennessee Shad.* 8 plates by F. R. Gruger. Pictorial cloth. New
York, 1911. First edition. In dust jacket. $175–$250. Lacking jacket, $75–$100.

JOHNSON, Owen. *The Varmint.* Cloth. New York, 1910. First edition. $75–$100. Boston, 1930. Illustrated. Morocco. Limited edition. $75–$85.

JOHNSON, Rossiter. *Phaeton Rogers: A Novel of Boy Life.* Illustrated. Decorated cloth. New York, 1881. First edition. $150–$200.

JOHNSON, Rossiter (editor). *A History of the World's Columbian Expedition.* 4 vols., cloth. New York, 1897–98. First edition. $100–$150.

JOHNSON, Samuel. *A Diary of a Journey into North Wales.* Edited by R. Duppa. Plates. Boards. London, 1816. First edition. $150–$200.

JOHNSON, Samuel. *A Journey to the Western Islands of Scotland.* Half calf, marbled boards. Baltimore, 1810. First American edition. $100–$150.

JOHNSON, Samuel. *London: A Poem, and the Vanity of Human Wishes.* Introduction by T. S. Eliot. Boards. London, 1930. First edition. One of 150 signed by Eliot. $600–$675.

JOHNSON, Sid S. *Some Biographies of Old Settlers.* (Vol. 1—all published.) Cloth. Tyler, Tex., 1900. First edition. $150–$250.

JOHNSON, Sidney S. *Texans Who Wore the Gray.* Illustrated. Cloth. Tyler, (about 1907). First edition. $350–$400.

JOHNSON, Mrs. Susannah. *A Narrative of the Captivity of Mrs. Johnson.* Boards and sheep. Windsor, Vt., 1807. Second edition. $250–$300.

JOHNSON, Theodore T. *Sights in the Gold Region, and Scenes by the Way.* Cloth. New York, 1849. First edition. $185–$225. New York, 1850. Folding map, 7 plates (2 colored). Cloth. Second edition. $200–$300.

JOHNSTON, Carrier Polk, and McGlumphy, W. H. S. *History of Clinton and Caldwell Counties, Missouri.* Half leather. Topeka, 1923. $75–$125.

JOHNSTON, Charles. *A Narrative of the Incidents Attending the Capture, Detention, and Ransom of, etc.* Boards. New York, 1827. First edition. $200–$225. Also, $125 (A, 1975).

JOHNSTON, Lieut. Col. J. E., and others. *Reports of the Secretary of War, with Reconnaisances of Routes from San Antonio to El Paso, etc.* 2 folding maps, 72 plates. Cloth. Washington, 1850. First edition. $200–$350.

JOHNSTON, Mary. *To Have and to Hold.* Illustrated by Howard Pyle and others. Red buckram, paper label. Boston, 1900. First edition. One of 250. $125–$150. Trade edition: Cloth. $25–$35.

JOHNSTON, William G. *Experiences of a Forty-niner.* Portrait, 13 plates. Cloth. Pittsburgh, 1892. First edition. (With later, separately issued, folding map and an extra portrait.) $450–$500.

JOHONNOT, Jackson. *The Remarkable Adventures of Jackson Johonnot.* 24 pp., stitched, Greenfield, Mass., 1816. First edition. $125–$150.

JOINVILLE, John, Lord of. *The History of Saint Louis, King Louis of France.* Illustrated. Dark maroon morocco. Newtown, Wales, 1937. Gregynog Press. One of 200. In slipcase. $1,000–$1,500.

JOLAS, Eugene. See *Transition Stories.*

JOLAS, Eugene. *I Have Seen Monsters and Angels.* Wrappers. Paris: Transition Press, (1938). First edition. $50.

JOLAS, Eugene. *Secession in Astropolis.* Wrappers. Paris, 1929. Black Sun Press. One of 100. In slipcase. $80–$125.

JOLAS, Maria (editor). *A James Joyce Yearbook*. Wrappers. Paris, 1949. Transition Press. First edition. In glassine jacket. $75–$100. (Note: Contains a section, "Ad Writer," attributed to Joyce.)

JONAH: Christmas, 1917. Wrappers. Oxford, 1917. Holywell Press. (By Aldous Huxley.) First edition. One of 50. (Most were inscribed for presentation.) $1,500. Also, an inscribed copy, $1,400 (A, 1977).

JONES, A. D. *Illinois and the West*. Folding map. Cloth. Boston, 1838. First edition. $100–$150.

JONES, Anson B. *Memoranda and Official Correspondence Relating to the Republic of Texas, Its History and Annexation*. Portrait. Cloth. New York, 1859. First edition. $150–$200. Chicago, (1966). Map, facsimile letter. Leather. One of 150. Boxed. $75.

JONES, Charles Colcock. *Religious Instruction of the Negroes in the United States*. Cloth. Savannah, 1842. First edition. $150–$200.

JONES, Charles C., Jr. *Antiquities of the Southern Indians*. 30 plates. Cloth. New York, 1873. First edition. $200–$225.

JONES, Charles C., Jr. *Biographical Sketches of the Delegates from Georgia to the Continental Congress*. Cloth. Boston, 1891. $50.

JONES, Charles C., Jr. *The Dead Towns of Georgia*. Maps. Cloth. Savannah, 1878. First edition. $100.

JONES, Charles C., Jr. *Historical Sketch of the Chatham Artillery*. 3 maps. Half leather. Albany, 1867. First edition. $125.

JONES, Charles C., Jr. *The History of Georgia*. 19 maps and plates. 2 vols., cloth. Boston, 1883. First edition. $150–$250.

JONES, Charles C., Jr. *The History of Savannah, Georgia*. 21 portraits. Half leather. Syracuse, 1890. First edition. $150–$225.

JONES, Charles C., Jr. *The Siege of Savannah in December, 1864*. 184 pp., wrappers. Albany, 1874. First edition. $75–$125. Another issue: One of 10 on large paper. $250–$300.

JONES, Charles C., Jr. (editor). *The Siege of Savannah in 1779*. Map, index (not in all copies). Wrappers. Albany, 1874. First edition. One of 100. With the index: $100–$125. Without index: $75–$100.

JONES, Charles Jess (Buffalo). See Inman, Col. Henry.

JONES, D. W. *Forty Years Among the Indians*. Cloth. Salt Lake City, 1890. First edition, with portrait (not in all copies). $75.

JONES, David. *A Journal of Two Visits Made to Some Nations of Indians on the West Side of the River Ohio, in the Years 1772 and 1773*. Wrappers. New York, 1865. Second edition. One of 200. $100–$150. One of 50 on large paper. $200–$250. (Note: A first edition of David Jones' journal, Burlington, N.J., 1774, brought $5,250 at auction on May 4, 1966.)

JONES, David (Michael). *The Anathemata*. Cloth. London, (1952). First edition. In dust jacket. $75.

JONES, David (Michael). *In Parenthesis*. Illustrated by the author. Cloth. London, 1937. First edition. In dust jacket. $75–$100. Author's first book. London, (1961). Introduction by T. S. Eliot. Blue cloth. One of 70 signed by Jones and Eliot. In plastic dust jacket. $800–$1,000. Trade edition: In jacket. $25. New York, (1962). Tan cloth. First American edition. In dust jacket. $20.

JONES, David (Michael). *The Tribune's Visitation*. Cloth. (London, 1969.) First edition. One of 150 signed. $75–$125.

JONES, E. Alfred. *The Old Silver of American Churches.* 145 plates. Folio, buckram. Letchworth, England, 1913. One of 506. $300–$400. Another issue: One of 6 on hand-made paper. $1,430 (A, 1978).

JONES, E. Alfred. *Old Silver of Europe and America.* 96 plates, Cloth. London, 1928. First edition. $75–$100.

JONES, Gwyn. *The Green Island.* Woodcuts by John Petts. Green and gray morocco. London, 1946. Golden Cockerel Press. One of 100. $175–$200. Ordinary issue: One of 400. $40–$60.

JONES, Herschel V. *Adventures in Americana.* 300 plates. 2 vols., black cloth. New York, 1928. First edition. One of 200. $300.

JONES, James. *From Here to Eternity.* Black cloth. New York, 1951. First edition, with "A" on copyright page. Presentation edition, signed. In dust jacket. $150–$250. Trade edition: Cloth. In dust jacket. $100–$150. Author's first book.

JONES, James. *The Thin Red Line.* Cloth. New York, (1962). First edition, first issue, with "A" on copyright page. In dust jacket. $50.

JONES, Jonathan H. *A Condensed History of the Apache and Comanche Indian Tribes.* Illustrated. Cloth. San Antonio, 1899. First edition. $400–$600. (Note: Better known by its cover title, *Indianology.*)

JONES, J. Wesley (written by John Ross Dix). *Amusing and Thrilling Adventures of a California Artist, while Daguerreotyping a Continent, etc.* Illustrated, including 4 woodcuts in text. 92 pp., pictorial wrappers. Boston, 1854. (By George Spencer Phillips.) First edition. $2,500–$3,000.

JONES, Justin. See Hazel, Harry.

JONES, LeRoi. *Cuba Libre.* (Cover title.) Wrappers. New York, (1961). First edition. $150–$200. Author's first book.

JONES, Owen. *The Grammar of Ornament.* 100 colored lithographs, engraved title page (illuminated), woodcuts. Large folio, half morocco. London, 1856. First edition. $2,500–$3,250. London, (1856). 112 color plates. Cloth, smaller format. $600. London, 1868. 112 plates. Cloth. $300–$350. London, 1910. Cloth. $500.

JONES, Adj. Gen. R. *General Orders, No. 16, Reporting General Court Martial Convened at Fort Kearney, Oregon Route, for Offense Committed There.* 11 pp., sewed. Washington, 1851. $100–$150.

JONES, Samuel. *Pittsburgh in the Year Eighteen-Hundred and Twenty-six.* Frontispiece. Boards. Pittsburgh, 1826. First edition. $1,000 and up.

JONES, T. Gwynn. *Detholiad o' Ganiadau: Collected Poems of T. Gwynn Jones.* Wood engravings by R. A. Maynard. Buckram. Newtown, Wales, 1926. Gregynog Press. One of 474. $150–$200. Another issue: Blue morocco. One of 26 specially bound. $1,500–$2,000.

JONES, Thomas A. *J. Wilkes Booth.* Illustrated. Cloth. Chicago, 1893. First edition. $50–$75.

JONES, William Carey. *Land Titles in California.* 55 pp., wrappers. San Francisco, 1852. First edition. $600–$800.

JONG, Erica. *Fruits and Vegetables, Poems.* Cloth. New York, (1971). First edition. In dust jacket. $50–$75. Author's first book.

JONSON, Ben. *A Croppe of Kisses: Selected Lyrics.* Edited by John Wallis. Folio, morocco and buckram. London, 1937. Golden Cockerel Press. One of 250. $150–$200. Another issue: One of 50 specially bound in morocco. $300–$400.

JONSON, Ben. *The Masque of Queenes.* Illustrated by Inigo Jones. Folio, red vellum. London, 1930. One of 350. Boxed. $75–$100.

JONSON, Ben. *Songs: A Selection*. Colored frontispiece. Boards. London, 1906. Eragny Press. One of 175. $350–$450. Another issue: One of 10 on vellum. $1,000–$1,250.

JONSON, Ben. *Volpone: or The Foxe*. Illustrated by Aubrey Beardsley. Decorated cloth. New York, 1898. One of 1,000. $150–$200. Another issue: Vellum. One of 100 on vellum. $350–$450. New York, 1952. Limited Editions Club. Illustrated. Cloth. Boxed. $80–$100.

JORDAN, Thomas, and Pryor, J. P. *The Campaigns of Lieut.-Gen. N. B. Forrest*. 6 maps, 6 plates. Cloth. New Orleans, 1868. First edition. $100–$125.

JORROCK'S Jaunts and Jollities. 12 illustrations by Phiz. Decorated cloth. London, 1838. (By Robert Smith Surtees.) First edition. $500–$750. Philadelphia, 1838. 2 vols., half cloth. First American edition. $400–$500. London, 1843. 15 color plates by Henry Alken. Green cloth. Second edition, first state, with 8 pages of ads and printer's imprint at end. $750–$1,000. Second edition, late state, with ads announcing a new edition of *The Life of John Mytton*. $600–$775. London, 1869. 16 colored Alken plates. Cloth. Third edition. $400–$450. New York, 1932. Limited Editions Club. Boxed. $40–$50.

JOURNAL Historique de l'Établissement des Français à la Louisiane. Three-quarters morocco. Nouvelle-Orléans, 1831. (By Bernard de la Harpe). First edition. $350–$400.

JOURNAL of the Convention to Form a Constitution for the State of Wisconsin: Begun and Held at Madison on the 5th Day of October, 1846. Boards and calf. Madison, 1847. First edition. $150–$200.

JOURNAL of an Excursion Made by the Corps of Cadets. etc., Under Capt. Patridge. Marbled wrappers. Concord, N. H., 1822. $75–$100.

JOURNAL of the Expedition of Dragoons Under the Command of Col. Henry Dodge to the Rocky Mountains During the Summer of 1835. 2 folding maps. Wrappers, or cloth. (Washington, 1836.) (By Lt. G. P. Kingsbury.) First edition. Wrappers: $250–$350. Cloth: $150–$175.

JOURNAL of the Hartford Union Mining and Trading Company. 88 pp., wrappers. On board the Henry Lee, 1849. (By George G. Webster, or John Linville Hall, who printed it?) First edition. $3,000 and up. Second edition (with title revised to *Around the Horn in '49: Journal, etc.*): (Wethersfield, Conn., or Hartford, 1898.) Cloth. $100–$200. San Francisco, 1928. Book Club of California. Half cloth. One of 250 printed by the Grabhorns. $75–$100.

JOURNAL of the Proceedings of a Convention of Physicians, of Ohio, Held in Columbus, Jan. 5, 1835. Daniel Drake, Chairman. 30 pp., wrappers. Cincinnati, 1835. (Main report by Drake.) $150–$175.

JOURNAL of the Senate of South Carolina, Being the Session of 1863. 190 pp., unbound. Columbia, 1863. $40–$60.

JOURNAL of Sentimental Travels in the Southern Provinces of France. 18 colored plates by Thomas Rowlandson. Boards, morocco, or cloth (remainder). London, 1821. (By William Combe.) First edition. $750–$1,000. Also, $528 and $500 (A, 1979).

JOURNAL of a Tour Around Hawaii, the Largest of the Sandwich Islands. 3 plates, folding map. Boards and cloth. Boston, 1825. (By William Ellis.) First edition. $600–$800.

JOURNAL of a Tour from Boston to Savannah, etc. (A). Cloth. Cambridge, Mass., 1849. (By Daniel Nason.) First edition. $200–$300.

JOUTEL, Henri. *A Journal of the Last Voyage Perform'd by Monsr. de la Sale, to the Gulph of Mexico*. Folding map in pocket. Boards. Chicago, 1896. Caxton Club. One of 206. Boxed. $150–$250. Also, $160 (A, 1975). Another issue: One of 3. $300–$400.

JOYCE, James. See Gorman, Herbert; Jolas, Maria; Skeffington, F. J. C., and Joyce, James A. Also see *Des Imagistes; The Dublin Book of Irish Verse; The Venture*.

JOYCE, James. *Anna Livia Plurabelle*. Edited by Padraic Colum. Cloth. New York, 1928. First edition. One of 850 signed. $1,000–$1,200. Also, $550 (A, 1980). One of 50 on green paper (from the 850-copy edition). $1,250 and up. Also, $700 (A, 1977). London, (1930). Wrappers. First English edition. $50–$75.

JOYCE, James. *Chamber Music*. Cloth (in three or more variant bindings). London, (1907). First edition. $2,000–$2,250. Also, "exceptionally fine," $1,900 (A, 1977). Boston, (1918). Cloth. First (unauthorized) American edition. $250–$400. New York, 1918. Cloth. First American edition. In dust jacket. $1,000.

JOYCE, James, *Collected Poems*. Frontispiece portrait. Decorated boards. New York, 1936. Black Sun Press. First edition. One of 750. In glassine dust jacket. $400–$600. Another issue: One of 50 on vellum, signed. In tissue dust jacket. Boxed. $1,500–$2,000. Another issue: One of 3 lettered and signed copies, $6,000. New York, 1937. Cloth. First trade edition. In dust jacket. $100–$125.

JOYCE, James. *Dubliners*. Red cloth. London, 1914. First edition. In dust jacket. $1,500–$2,500. Also, $1,400 (A, 1977). Without jacket, $950. New York, 1916. Cloth. First American edition (from the English sheets). In dust jacket. $250–$300. New York, 1917. First edition from American sheets. In dust jacket. $250–$300. London, 1922. Egoist Press. In dust jacket. $200.

JOYCE, James. *Exiles*. Green boards and cloth. London, 1918. First edition. $300–$400. Also, presentation copy, signed, $1,300 (A, 1977). New York, 1918. Boards and buckram. First American edition. In dust jacket. $250–$300. Lacking jacket, $100. New York, 1951. Half cloth. One of 1,900. In dust jacket. $100–$125.

JOYCE, James. *Finnegans Wake*. Buckram. London, 1939. First edition. One of 425 on large paper, signed. Boxed. Also, $1,500–$2,250. Also, $1,300 (A, 1978). London, (1939). Cloth. First trade edition. In dust jacket. $400–$500. New York, 1939. Black cloth. First American edition. In dust jacket. $200–$250. Without jacket, $100.

JOYCE, James. *Gas from a Burner*. Long folio broadside. Flushing (Trieste), 1912. Signed by Sylvia Beach, $5,500 (A, 1977). Later edition: Dublin, 1922. $728 (A, 1966).

JOYCE, James. *Haveth Childers Everywhere: Fragment from Work in Progress*. Stiff printed wrappers. Paris, 1930. First edition. One of 500 on Vidalon paper. In glassine dust jacket. Boxed. $500–$600. Worn, $300. Also 75 "Writer's Copies." $500–$750. Another issue: One of 100 on Japanese vellum, signed. Boxed. $750–$1,000. Another issue: One of 10 on vellum, signed. In glassine dust jacket. Boxed. $2,000–$3,000.

JOYCE, James. *The Holy Office*. Broadside. (Pola, Austria-Hungary, 1904 or 1905?) First edition. $2,500–$3,000 and up. Also, $2,100 (A, 1977). (Fewer than 100 printed. So far as can be established, the author's first separately published work.)

JOYCE, James. *Ibsen's New Drama*. Foolscap, boards, paper label. London, (1930). First edition. One of 49. $1,250–$1,500. Also, $1,100 (A, 1977).

JOYCE, James. *James Clarence Mangan*. Foolscap, boards, paper label. London, (1930). First edition. One of 40. $1,500 and up. Also, $1,000 (A, 1977). Also, another issue: This title, bound with *Ibsen's New Drama*, "Press Copy" in colophon. Boxed. $2,500–$3,000.

JOYCE, James. *The Joyce Book*. Blue silk. London, (1933). First edition. One of 500 in printed envelope. $1,500 and up. Also, $1,100 (A, 1977).

JOYCE, James. *The Mime of Mick, Nick, and the Maggies*. Designs in color by Lucia Joyce. Stiff white wrappers. Boxed. The Hague, Netherlands, 1934. First edition. One of 1,029. Boxed. $250–$300. One of 29 copies from the edition signed by Joyce and his daughter. $3,500 and up. Also, $3,250 (A, 1977).

JOYCE, James. *Pomes Penyeach*. Boards. Paris, 1927. First edition, with errata slip. $150–$200. Another issue: One of 13 on handmade paper. $500 and up. Paris, 1932. Oblong folio sheets on Japan paper, illuminated by Lucia Joyce. Green silk folder. One of 25 signed. $3,000 and up. Also, $2,600 (A, 1977). Paris and London, 1932. First English edition. $200–$300. London, (1933.) First edition printed in England. $200–$300.

JOYCE, James. *A Portrait of the Artist as a Young Man.* Blue cloth. New York, 1916. First edition. In dust jacket. $1,500–$4,000. (The latter price, for a "spectacular copy," is from a 1981 catalogue of Joseph the Provider, bookseller.) London, (1917). Green cloth. First English edition (from American sheets). In dust jacket. $150–$250. London, 1918. First English edition printed in England. In dust jacket. $150–$200. London, 1924. Revised edition. In dust jacket. $75–$100. New York, 1968. Limited Editions Club. $150–$175.

JOYCE, James. *Stephen Hero.* Cloth. London, 1944. First edition. In dust jacket. $100–$150. New York, (1944). Green boards and cloth. First American edition. In dust jacket. $40–$60.

JOYCE, James. *Storiella as She Is Syung.* Flexible orange vellum. (London, 1937.) Corvinus Press. One of 176. Boxed. $1,350–$1,850. Also, $950 (A, 1980); $1,200 (A, 1979). One of 25 (of the 176) signed by Joyce. Boxed. $2,000 and up. Also, $2,000 (A, 1977).

JOYCE, James. *Tales Told of Shem and Shaun: Three Fragments from Work in Progress.* Portrait by Brancusi. Wrappers. Paris, 1929. Black Sun Press. First edition. One of 500 on Van Gelder paper. In glassine dust jacket. Boxed. $450–$500. Another issue: One of 100 on vellum, signed (plus 50 not-for-sale copies). Boxed. $1,250–$1,500. Also, $1,000 and $900 (A, 1977). London, (1932). Boards. First English edition (retitled *Two Tales of Shem and Shaun*). In dust jacket. $75–$85.

JOYCE, James. *Two Essays.* See Skeffington.

JOYCE, James. *Ulysses.* Printed blue wrappers. Paris, 1922. First edition. One of 100 on Dutch handmade paper, signed. $13,500–$20,000. Also, $10,000 (A, 1977). Another issue: One of 150 on Verge d'Arches paper. $5,000–$6,000. Also, worn and torn, $2,600 (A, 1977). Another issue: One of 740 on handmade paper. $4,000–$5,000. (Various later printings of the Paris edition appeared through the 1920's.) London, 1922. Egoist Press. Wrappers. First English edition (printed in France), with errata slip and 4-page leaflet of press notices. One of 2,000. $1,000–$1,250. London, 1923. Full red morocco (with limitation notice of 500 in gold on covers). Second English edition (printed in France). One of "at least three" surviving confiscation by British customs agents. $4,000 (A, 1977)— Jonathan Goodwin's copy. Paris, 1927. Blue wrappers. First American edition, unauthorized Samuel Roth piracy. $300–$400. Paris, 1929. Wrappers. First French translation (as *Ulysse*). One of 10 on Van Gelder paper. $2,000 and up. Also, $1,600 (A, 1968). Another issue: One of 25 on Holland paper. $1,500. Another issue: One of 875 on Alfa paper. $750. Hamburg, (1932). Odyssey Press. 2 vols., printed wrappers. First Odyssey Press edition. (One of 25 signed?) $1,750 and up. Also, $1,500 (A, 1968). Ordinary copies: $300–$500. (New York, 1934.) First authorized American edition. Cream-colored cloth. In dust jacket. $150–$175. New York, 1935. Limited Editions Club. Illustrated by Henri Matisse. Pictorial buckram. One of 250 signed by Joyce and Matisse. $2,500–$3,000. Also, $1,900 (A, 1977). Another issue: One of 1,250 signed only by Matisse. $800–$1,000. (Six signed proofs of the Matisse etchings for this book were issued in an edition of 150 in canvas portfolios. A set sold in October, 1977, in New York for $3,250.) London, 1936. Green buckram. First English edition to be printed in England. One of 900. In dust jacket. $500–$600. Another issue: Vellum. One of 100 signed. Boxed. $2,750–$3,000.

JUDD, A. N. *Campaigning Against the Sioux.* Plate, other illustrations. 45 pp., pictorial wrappers. (Watsonville, Calif., 1906.) First edition. $750 and up. Watsonville, 1909. Wrappers. Second edition. $300–$400.

JUDD, Cyril. *Outpost Mars.* Cloth. New York, (1952). (By C. M. Kornbluth and Judith Merrill.) First edition. In dust jacket. $40–$50.

JUDD, Silas. *A Sketch of the Life and Voyages of Capt. Alvah Judd Dewey.* Boards and cloth. Chittenango, N.Y., 1838. First edition. $350–$450.

JUDGES and Criminals: Shadows of the Past. 100 pp. San Francisco, 1858. (By Dr. Henry M. Gray?) First edition. $750–$1,000. (Note: Only 2 copies known, according to Wright Howes.)

JUSTICE and Expediency; or Slavery Considered with a View to Its Rightful and Effectual Remedy, Abolition. Stitched without covers. Haverhill, Mass. 1833. (By John Greenleaf Whittier.) First edition. $450–$500.

JUSTICE, Donald. *The Summer Anniversaries.* Cloth. Middleton, (1960). First edition. In dust jacket. $40–$50. Author's first book.

JUVENILE Lyre. Boards and leather. Boston, 1936. (By Lowell Mason and E. Ives, Jr.) $150–$200.

K

KA Euanelio a Mataio. (Together with *Marako and Ioane.*) Gospels of Matthew, Mark and John in Hawaiian. 3 vols., sewed. Rochester, N.Y., 1828–29. $350–$400.

KABOTIE, Red. *Designs from the Ancient Mimbrenos, with Hopi Interpretation.* Illustrated, including color. Half cloth. San Francisco, 1949. Grabhorn Press. One of 250. $200–$300.

KAFKA, Franz. *America.* Translated by Edwin and Willa Muir. Cloth. London, (1938). First English edition. In dust jacket. $250–$300.

KAFKA, Franz. *The Great Wall of China and Other Pieces.* Translated by Edwin and Willa Muir. Cloth. London, 1933. First edition in English. In dust jacket. $125.

KAIN, Saul. *The Daffodil Murderer.* Yellow (orange) wrappers printed in red. (London), 1913. (By Siegfried Sassoon.) First edition. $150–$200. Presentation copy, signed, $500; soiled copy, $295 (British catalogue, 1977).

KANE, Elisha Kent. *Arctic Explorations.* Plates, 2 folding maps. 2 vols., pictorial cloth. Philadelphia, 1856. First edition. $150–$200.

KANE, Elizabeth D. See *Twelve Mormon Homes Visited, etc.*

KANE, Paul. *Wanderings of an Artist Among the Indians of North America.* Folding map, 8 colored plates, woodcuts. Cloth. London, 1859. First edition. $1,250.

KANE, Thomas Leiper. *The Mormons.* 84 pp., printed wrappers. Philadelphia, 1850. First edition. $250–$300. Second edition, same date. 92 pp., wrappers. $100.

KANE, Thomas Leiper. *The Private Papers of . . . A Friend of the Mormons.* Portrait. Boards and cloth. San Francisco, 1937. Grabhorn Press. $75–$85.

KANT, Immanuel. *Critick of Pure Reason.* Green cloth, paper label. London, 1838. First edition in English. $750 and up. Spine repaired, $500.

KANTOR, MacKinlay. *Andersonville.* Cloth. Cleveland, (1955). First edition. In dust jacket. $25. Limited, signed edition. Boxed. $50–$60.

KANTOR, MacKinlay. *Diversey.* Cloth. New York, 1928. First edition. In dust jacket. $50–$75. Author's first book.

KANTOR, MacKinlay. *Spirit Lake.* Cloth. Cleveland, (1961). First edition. In dust jacket. $25.

KATHERINE Walton; or, The Rebel of Dorchester. Cloth. Philadelphia, 1851. (By William Gilmore Simms.) First edition. $350–$450.

KAVANAGH, Patrick. *The Great Hunger.* Boards and linen. Dublin, 1942. Cuala Press. One of 250. In dust jacket. $150–$200.

KAYE-SMITH, Sheila. *Little England.* Cloth. London, (1918). First edition. In dust jacket. $35–$50.

KAYE-SMITH, Sheila. *The Tramping Methodist.* Cloth. London, 1908. First edition. In dust jacket. $100–$150. Author's first book.

KAZANTZAKIS, Nikos. *Christopher Columbus.* 22 folded sheets in gold wrappers. Kentfield, Calif., 1972. Allen Press. First edition. One of 140. Boxed. $400–$500.

KEATING, William H. (compiler). *Narrative of an Expedition to the Source of St. Peter's River, Lake Winnepeek, etc.* Folding map, 15 plates. 2 vols., boards. Philadelphia, 1824. First edition. $300–$350. London, 1825. Maps, plates, tables. 2 vols., boards. First English edition. $200–$250.

KEATS, John. *Endymion: A Poetic Romance.* Drab buff boards, printed paper label on spine. London, 1818. First edition, first issue, with one line of errata (not 5) and 2 (not 5) ad leaves at end. $5,000 and up. Second issue, with 5-line errata. $4,500 (A, 1981). New York, 1902. Elston Press. Blue cloth. $175–$225. London, (1947). Golden Cockerel Press. Wood engravings. Buckram and vellum. One of 400. $350–$550. Another issue: Vellum. One of 100 specially bound. $650–$850.

KEATS, John. *The Eve of St. Agnes.* Title page design by Frank Lloyd Wright. Cloth. (River Forest, Ill.), 1896. Auvergne Press. One of 65. $1,000–$1,250. London, 1900. Essex House. Boards. One of 125 on vellum. $300–$400.

KEATS, John. *John Keats' Unpublished Poem to His Sister Fanny, 1818.* Facsimile. Vellum-backed cloth. Boston, 1909. Bibliophile Society. First edition. One of 489 on vellum. $100–$125.

KEATS, John. *Lamia, Isabella, The Eve of St. Agnes, and Other Poems.* Boards, paper label; or calf. London, 1820. First edition, with half title and 8 pages of ads at end. $7,500 and up. Waltham Saint Lawrence, England, 1928. Golden Cockerel Press. Woodcuts by Robert Gibbings. Sharkskin and cloth. One of 500. $250–$300. Another issue: One of 15 on vellum. In sharkskin binding by Sangorski & Sutcliffe. $1,500–$1,750.

KEATS, John. *Letters of John Keats to Fanny Brawne, Written in the Years 1819 and 1820.* Edited by Harry Buxton Forman. Etched frontispiece and facsimile. Cloth. London, 1878. First edition. One of 50. $250–$300. Ordinary issue: $65.

KEATS, John. *Life, Letters, and Literary Remains of John Keats.* Edited by Richard Monckton Milnes. Engraved portrait and facsimile. 2 vols., cloth. London, 1848. First edition. $250–$300. New York, 1848. Blue cloth. First American edition. $75.

KEATS, John. *Odes, Sonnets and Lyrics.* Portrait frontispiece. Wrappers. Oxford, 1895. Daniel Press. One of 250. $300–$400.

KEATS, John. *Poems.* Woodcut vignette of Spenser on title page. Boards, paper label on spine. London, 1817. First edition. $10,000 and up. Also, some leaves loose, $4,320 (A, 1965); rebound in morocco, $2,000 (A, 1974); rebound in calf, lacking blank leaf, half title loose, $1,540 (A, 1965). (A copy in boards, inscribed by the poet, was sold at auction in New York in November, 1975, for $15,000.) London, 1894. Kelmscott Press. Vellum. One of 300. $1,000–$1,250. Another issue: One of 7 on vellum. $5,000–$6,000. London, 1898. Vale Press. 2 vols., cloth. One of 210. $600–$750. London, 1914. Doves Press. (As *Selected Poems.*) Edited by T. J. Cobden-Sanderson. Vellum. One of 200. $500–$700. Some copies in morocco by the Doves Bindery. $1,000 and up. Another issue: One of 12 on vellum, $17,000 (A, 1978). London, 1915. Florence Press. 2 vols., limp vellum with ties. One of 250. $100. New York, 1966. Limited Editions Club. Boards and leather. Boxed. $100.

KEATS, John. *Poetical Works.* Printed in double columns within ruled borders. Yellow wrappers. London, 1840. First complete collected edition. $500–$750.

KEATS, John. *Three Essays.* Stiff wrappers. London, (1889). Chiswick Press. First edition. One of 50. Boxed. $150–$200.

KEDDIE, James, Jr. *The Second Cab.* 95 pp., wrappers. Boston, 1947. First edition. One of 300. $75–$85.

KEEP Cool. 2 vols., boards. Baltimore, 1817. (By John Neal.) First edition. $200–$250. Author's first book.

KEES, Weldon. *Collected Poems*. Boards and leather. Iowa City, 1960. Stone Wall Press. First edition. One of 200. $150–$175.

KEES, Weldon. *The Last Man*. Boards and cloth. San Francisco, 1943. First edition. One of 300. (Published without dust jacket.) $100–$125.

KEITH, G. M. *A Voyage to South America and the Cape of Good Hope*. Boards. London, 1819. First edition, first issue, printed by Phillips. $1,500. London, 1819. Revised edition, printed by Vogel. With list of subscribers. $1,500.

KELEHER, William A. *The Fabulous Frontier*. 11 plates. Cloth. Santa Fe, (1945). First edition. One of 500. In dust jacket. $100–$125. Without jacket, $75.

KELEHER, William A. *The Maxwell Land Grant*. Illustrated. Pictorial cloth. Santa Fe, (1942). First edition. In dust jacket. $175–$200.

KELL, Joseph. *One Hand Clapping*. Cloth. London, (1961). (By Anthony Burgess.) First edition. In dust jacket. $75–$125.

KELLER, David H. *The Devil and the Doctor*. Cloth. New York, (1940). First edition. In dust jacket. $50–$60.

KELLER, David H. *The Sign of the Burning Hart*. Cloth. No place, (1948). First American edition. In dust jacket. $200.

KELLER, George. *A Trip Across the Plains*. 58 pp., printed wrappers. (Masillon, Ohio, 1851.) First edition. $4,500. Also, $2,500 (A, 1968).

KELLEY, Edith Summers. *Weeds*. Cloth. New York, (1923). First edition. In dust jacket. $75–$100. Author's first book.

KELLEY, Hall J. *General Circular to All Persons of Good Character Who Wish to Emigrate to the Oregon Territory*. 28 pp., printed wrappers. Charlestown, Mass., 1831. First edition. $600.

KELLEY, Hall J. *A Geographical Sketch of That Part of North America Called Oregon*. Folding map. 80 pp., printed wrappers. Boston, 1830. First edition. $1,250 and up.

KELLEY, Hall J. *History of Colonization of the Oregon Territory*. 12 pp., sewed. Worcester, Mass., 1850. First edition. $1,000 and up.

KELLEY, Hall J. *A History of the Settlement of Oregon and the Interior of Upper California*. 128 pp., printed wrappers. Springfield, Mass., 1868. First edition. $5,000 and up.

KELLEY, Hall J. *A Narrative of Events and Difficulties in the Colonization of Oregon and the Settlement of California*. 92 pp., printed wrappers. Boston, 1852. First edition. $2,000.

KELLEY, Joseph (Bunco). *Thirteen Years in the Oregon Penitentiary*. Illustrated. 142 pp., stiff wrappers. Portland, 1908. First edition. $50–$75.

KELLEY, William Melvin. *A Different Drummer*. Cloth. Garden City, 1962. First edition. In dust jacket. $50–$75. Author's first book.

KELLOGG, H. S. *Life of Mrs. Fmily J. Harwood*. Illustrated. Decorated cloth. Albuquerque, 1903. First edition. $125. (Note: Yes, "Fmily" is what it says.)

KELLOGG, Jay C. *The Broncho Buster Busted and Other Messages*. Wrappers. (Tacoma, 1932.) First edition. $200.

KELLY, Charles. *Old Greenwood: The Story of Caleb Greenwood, Trapper, Pathfinder and Early Pioneer of the West*. Illustrated. Cloth. Salt Lake City, 1936. First edition. One of 350. In dust jacket. $150–$175.

KELLY, Charles. *The Outlaw Trail: A History of Butch Cassidy and His Wild Bunch*.

Illustrated. Pictorial cloth (leatherette). Salt Lake City, 1938. First edition. One of 1,000. In dust jacket. $125. New York, 1959. Pictorial cloth. In dust jacket. $25.

KELLY, Charles. *Salt Desert Trails.* Illustrated. Cloth (leatherette). Salt Lake City, 1930. First edition. $65–$85.

KELLY, Charles (editor). See Lee, John D.

KELLY, Charles, and Birney, Hoffman. *Holy Murder.* Illustrated. Cloth. New York, (1934). First edition. In dust jacket. $35–$50.

KELLY, Charles, and Howe, Maurice L. *Miles Goodyear, First Citizen of Utah.* Illustrated. Cloth. Salt Lake City, 1937. First edition. One of 350. In dust jacket. $75–$85.

KELLY, George Fox. *Land Frauds of California.* 36 pp., wrappers. (Santa Clara?), 1864. First edition. $500 and up.

KELLY, L. V. *The Range Men: The Story of the Ranchers and Indians of Alberta.* Illustrated. Pictorial cloth. Toronto, 1913. First edition. $300–$350.

KELLY, Robert. *Armed Descent.* Wrappers. (New York, 1961.) Hawk's Well Press. First edition. $80–$100. Author's first book.

KELLY, Robert. *Her Body Against Time.* Cloth, or wrappers. Mexico City, 1963. First edition. Cloth (about 50 copies). $75–$85. Wrappers: $20–$25.

KELLY, Robert. *Sonnets.* Illustrated in color by the author. Boards, paper labels. Los Angeles, 1968. First edition. One of 65 signed with an original drawing and/or a holograph poem. $50–$100.

KELLY, Robert. *Weeks.* Printed wrappers. Mexico City, 1966. First edition. $100. (Suppressed by the author because of errors.)

KELLY, William. *An Excursion to California over the Prairie, Rocky Mountains, and Great Sierra Nevada.* 2 vols., cloth. London, 1851. First edition. $400–$500.

KEMPTON-Wace Letters (The). Green decorated cloth. New York, 1903. (By Jack London and Anna Strunsky.) First edition. $100–$150. Reprint edition, same date: Authors named on title page. $75–$100.

KENDAL and Windermere Railway. Two Letters Reprinted from the Morning Post. Sewed. London, (1844). (By William Wordsworth.) First edition, with Whittaker imprint. $300–$500. Kendal, England, (1845). 24 pp., single sheet folded. Revised edition, with Branthwaite imprint. $200–$225.

KENDALL, George Wilkins. *Narrative of the Texan Santa Fe Expedition.* 5 plates, folding map. 2 vols., cloth. New York, 1844. First edition. $400–$600. London, 1844. Map, 5 plates. 2 vols., cloth. First English edition. $400–$450. New York, 1856. 2 vols., cloth. Seventh edition, with two extra chapters and part of Falconer's diary. $750–$1,250. (Note: A classic example of a book which is more valuable in a later edition than in the first edition.)

KENDALL, George Wilkins. *The War Between the United States and Mexico.* Map, 12 colored plates by Carl Nebel. Folio, cloth. New York, 1841. First edition. $1,500–$2,500.

KENDERDINE, T. S. *A California Tramp and Later Footprints.* 39 views. Pictorial cloth. Newtown, Pa., 1888. First edition. $200–$300.

KENILWORTH. 3 vols., boards. Edinburgh, 1821. (By Sir Walter Scott.) First edition. $750–$1,000.

KENNEDY, Edward G. *The Etched Work of Whistler.* 6 vols. (Text vol. and half cloth plate folders.) New York, 1910. First edition. Grolier Club. One of 402. $1,500–$2,000.

KENNEDY, John F. *Inaugural Address.* Portrait. Vellum. Los Angeles, 1965. One of 1,000. $150.

KENNEDY, John F. *Profiles in Courage.* Illustrated. Cloth. New York, (1956). First edition. In dust jacket. $100–$150. (Signed and/or inscribed copies bring considerably more.) New York, 1961. Cloth. "Inaugural Edition." In dust jacket. Signed by the President, $300 (A, 1976).

KENNEDY, John F. *Why England Slept.* Cloth. New York, 1940. First edition. In dust jacket. $500. Also, $400 (A, 1981). London, (1940). Red cloth. First English edition, with ads dated 1940. In dust jacket. $300–$350.

KENNEDY, John F. (editor). *As We Remember Joe.* Portrait frontispiece, photographs. Red cloth. (Cambridge, Mass., 1945.) First edition. $1,000–$1,600. (Signed and/or inscribed copies bring considerably more.)

KENNEDY, John Pendleton. See Secondthoughts, Solomon. Also see *Horse-Shoe Robinson; Rob of the Bowl; Swallow Barn.*

KENNEDY, John Pendleton. *Memoirs of the Life of William Wirt.* Frontispiece. 2 vols., black cloth. Philadelphia, 1849. First edition. $150-$200.

KENNEDY, Margaret. *The Constant Nymph.* Cloth. London, 1924. First edition, first issue, with ads on verso of half title. In dust jacket. $40–$50.

KENNEDY, Margaret. *The Ladies of Lyndon.* Cloth. London, (1923). First edition. In dust jacket. $50.

KENNEDY, Pendleton. See *The Blackwater Chronicle.*

KENNEDY, William. *Texas: Its Geography, Natural History, and Topography.* 118 pp., wrappers. New York, 1844. First edition. $200–$250. (Reprint in part of *Texas: The Rise, Progress, etc.)*

KENNEDY, William. *Texas: The Rise, Progress and Prospects of the Republic of Texas.* Maps, charts. 2 vols., cloth. London, 1841. First edition. $500–$600. Another issue: 2 vols. in one, cloth. $400–$500. Second edition, same date: $300–$400. Fort Worth, 1925. Maps. Cloth. $35.

KENNER, Hugh. *Paradox in Chesterton.* Cloth. London, 1948. First edition. In dust jacket. $100–$150.

KENT, Henry W. (compiler). *Bibliographical Notes on One Hundred Books Famous in English Literature.* Half vellum. New York, 1903. Grolier Club. One of 305. $250–$300. (Issued as a supplement to the Grolier Club title of 1902, *One Hundred Books Famous in English Literature,* which was also limited to 305 copies. This title contains an introduction by George E. Woodberry and is usually available in the $100–$150 price range. Together, the two books are currently valued in the $450–$500 range.)

KENT, Rockwell. *A Birthday Book.* Illustrated by the author. Pictorial cloth (silk). New York, 1931. First edition. One of 1,850, signed. $100–$150.

KENT, Rockwell. *The Bookplates and Marks of Rockwell Kent.* 85 plates. Decorated cloth. New York, 1929. First edition. One of 1,250 signed. In dust jacket. $125–$150.

KENT, Rockwell. *Forty Drawings . . . to Illustrate the Works of William Shakespeare.* Portfolio of drawings. (Garden City, 1936.) First edition. One of 1,000. Boxed. $200–$250.

KENT, Rockwell. *Greenland Journal.* Illustrated. Cloth. New York, (1962). First edition. With a set of 6 lithographs, one signed. Boxed. $125–$150.

KENT, Rockwell. *How I Make a Wood Cut.* Illustrated. Cloth. Pasadena, 1934. First edition. One of 1,000. $50–$75.

KENT, Rockwell. *It's Me O Lord*. Illustrated. Cloth. New York, (1955). In dust jacket. $60–$75.

KENT, Rockwell. *Later Bookplates & Marks of Rockwell Kent*. Illustrated. Cloth. New York, 1937. First edition. One of 1,250 signed. In dust jacket. $100–$125.

KENT, Rockwell. *N. by E.* Illustrated. Pictorial silvered blue buckram. New York, 1930. First edition. One of 900 signed. Boxed. $150–$200. Another issue: Linen, with an extra page, for presentation. One of 100. Boxed. $250–$350. Trade edition: Cloth. In dust jacket. $30–$50.

KENT, Rockwell. *Northern Christmas*. Illustrated. Pictorial boards. New York, (1941). First edition. $50–$65.

KENT, Rockwell. *Rockwellkentiana*. Illustrated. Cloth. First edition. In dust jacket. $50–$75.

KENT, Rockwell. *Salamina*. Illustrated. Blue cloth. New York, 1935. First edition (so stated). In dust jacket. $100.

KENT, Rockwell. *Voyaging Southward from the Strait of Magellan*. Tan buckram. New York, 1924. First edition. In dust jacket. $100–$125. Another issue: Blue boards. One of 110 signed, with an extra signed woodcut. $200–$250.

KENT, Rockwell. *Wilderness: A Journal of Quiet Adventure in Alaska*. 69 illustrations. Gray linen. New York, 1920. First edition, first binding. In dust jacket. $125–$150. Second binding, tan pictorial boards. $100. Author's first book.

KENT, Rockwell (editor). *World-Famous Paintings*. 100 color plates. Brown cloth. New York, (1939). First edition, first binding, with color print of "The Laughing Cavalier" on front cover. $50.

KENTUCKIAN in New-York (The). By a Virginian. 2 vols., cloth. New York, 1834. (By W. A. Caruthers.) First edition. $250–$350.

KENYON, Frederic G. *Ancient Books and Modern Discoveries*. Half vellum. Chicago, 1927. Caxton Club. First edition. One of 350. In dust jacket. Boxed. $350–$500.

KENYON, William Asbury. *Miscellaneous Poems*. Cloth. Chicago, 1845. First edition. $300–$400.

KER, Henry. *Travels Through the Western Interior of the United States*. Half leather. Elizabethtown, N.J., 1816. First edition. $400–$500.

KERCHEVAL, Samuel. *A History of the Valley of Virginia*. Leather. Winchester, Va., 1833. First edition. $600–$750. Woodstock, Va., 1850. Third edition. $75–$100.

KEROUAC, Jack. *Big Sur*. Boards. New York, (1962). First edition. In dust jacket. $50–$75.

KEROUAC, Jack. *The Dharma Bums*. Cloth. New York, 1958. First edition. In dust jacket. $100–$135. London, (1959). Cloth. First English edition. In dust jacket. $50–$75.

KEROUAC, Jack. *Doctor Sax*. Beige cloth, brown spine. New York, (1959). First edition. One of 26 signed. $600–$950. Trade edition: Cloth. In dust jacket. $125–$150. Wrappers: $25.

KEROUAC, Jack. *Excerpts from Visions of Cody*. Boards and cloth. (New York, 1959 or 1960.) New Directions. First edition. One of 750 copies signed. In acetate jacket. $350–$450.

KEROUAC, Jack. *Mexico City Blues*. Boards and cloth. New York, (1959). First edition. One of 26 signed. $750. Trade edition: Cloth. $100–$125. Wrappers: $25.

KEROUAC, Jack. *On the Road*. Cloth. New York, 1957. First edition. In dust jacket.

$250–$350. Another copy, with extra white promotional dust jacket, $750 in a 1978 catalogue; $1,500 in 1980.

KEROUAC, Jack. *The Subterraneans*. Boards and cloth. New York, (1958). First edition. One of 100. $400–$500. Trade edition: Cloth. In dust jacket. $50.

KEROUAC, John (Jack). *The Town and the City*. Cloth. New York, (1950). First edition. In dust jacket. $200-$250. Advance review copy in wrappers: $600-$750. Author's first book.

KEROUAC, Jack. *Visions of Cody*. Introduction by Allen Ginsberg. Cloth. New York, (1972). First edition. In dust jacket. $35.

KEROUAC, Jack. *Visions of Gerard*. Illustrated. Cloth. New York, (1963). First edition. In dust jacket. $50–$75.

KERR, Hugh. *A Poetical Description of Texas, etc.* Cloth. New York, 1838. First edition. $600–$1,000.

KESEY, Ken. *One Flew Over the Cuckoo's Nest*. Cloth. New York, (1962). First edition. In dust jacket. $250–$300. London, (1962—actually 1963). Cloth. First English edition. In dust jacket. $75–$100.

KETTELL, Russell Hawes. *The Pine Furniture of Early New England*. 229 full-page reproductions and 55 working drawings. Linen. Garden City, 1929. First edition, limited. $75–$100.

KETTELL, Samuel. *Specimens of American Poetry, with Critical and Biographical Notices*. 3 vols., boards, paper labels. Boston, 1829. First edition. $200–$300.

KEWEN, Edward John Cage. *Oration and Poem Before the Society of California Pioneers*. Wrappers. San Francisco, 1854. First edition. $50–$60.

KEYES, Daniel. *Flowers for Algernon*. Cloth. New York, (1966). First edition. In dust jacket. $40–$50.

KEYNES, John Maynard. *The Economic Consequences of the Peace*. Cloth. London, 1919. First edition. In dust jacket. $500–$600.

KEYNES, John Maynard. *The General Theory of Employment, Interest, and Money*. Cloth. London, 1936. First edition. In dust jacket. $250–$350. New York, 1936. Cloth. First American edition. In dust jacket. $200.

KHERDIAN, David. *Homage to Adana*. Cloth. Mt. Horeb, Wis., (1970). First edition. One of 120. $85–$100.

KHERDIAN, David. *On the Death of My Father and Other Poems*. Introduction by William Saroyan. Cloth. Fresno, (1970). First edition. One of 26 signed by the poet and Saroyan. In dust jacket. $75–$100.

KIDD, J. H. *Personal Recollections of a Cavalryman with Custer's Michigan Cavalry Brigade in the Civil War*. Cloth. Ionia, Mich., 1908. First edition. $100–$175.

KIDDER, A.V. *An Introduction to the Study of Southwestern Archaeology*. 50 plates. Cloth. New Haven, 1924. First edition. $50–$60.

KIKI'S Memoirs. Translated by Samuel Putnam. Introduction by Ernest Hemingway. Illustrated. Wrappers. Paris, 1930. First edition, with glassine wrapper and imprinted band around book. $150–$200.

KILBOURN, John. *Columbian Geography*. Leather. Chillicothe, Ohio, 1815. First edition. $200–$300.

KILBOURN, John. *The Ohio Gazeteer, or Topographical Dictionary*. Boards, or calf. Columbus, 1816. First edition. $200–$300.

KILBOURNE, E. W. *Strictures on Dr. I. Galland's Pamphlet, Entitled "Villainy Ex-*

posed, with Some Account of His Transactions in Lands of the Sac and Fox Reservation, etc., in Lee County, Iowa. 24 pp., sewed. Fort Madison, Iowa, 1850. First edition. $200–$250.

KILBOURNE, Payne K. *History and Antiquities of the Name and Family of Kilbourne.* 3 plates. Cloth. New Haven, 1856. First edition. $40–$50.

KILMER, Joyce. *The Circus and Other Essays.* Boards. New York, 1916. First edition. In dust jacket. $75–$100.

KILMER, Joyce. *Summer of Love.* Cloth, gilt top. New York, 1911. First edition, first issue, with the Baker & Taylor imprint at foot of spine (later Doubleday, Page & Co.). In dust jacket. $150–$200. Author's first book. Another (preliminary) issue: Trial binding of unlettered red cloth. $200–$300.

KILMER, Joyce. *Trees and Other Poems.* Boards, paper labels. New York, (1914). First edition, first state, without "Printed in U.S.A." on copyright page. In dust jacket. $300–$400. Without jacket, $100.

KIMBALL, Fiske. *The Creation of the Rococo.* 274 illustrations. Buckram and boards. Philadelphia, 1943. In dust jacket. $75–$100.

KIMBALL, Fiske. *The Domestic Architecture of the American Colonies and of the Early Republic.* Illustrated. Cloth. New York, 1922. First edition. In dust jacket. $100.

KIMBALL, Fiske. *Mr. Samuel McIntire, Carver, the Architect of Salem.* Illustrated. Cloth. Portland, Me., 1940. One of 675. In dust jacket. $150–$200.

KIMBALL, Fiske. *Thomas Jefferson, Architect.* Illustrated. Cloth. Boston, 1916. First edition. One of 350. In dust jacket. $200–$300.

KIMBALL, Heber C. *The Journal of Heber C. Kimball.* Edited by R. B. Thompson. 60 pp., printed wrappers. Nauvoo, Ill., 1840. First edition. $1,000–$1,250.

KING and Queen of Hearts (The). 15 plain or colored illustrations. Printed wrappers. London, 1805. (By Charles Lamb.) First edition, early (earliest?) printing, undated cover, name of "Hodgkins" misspelled on cover. $3,000 or more. Various cover dates have been noted on copies at auction—1805 (2 copies), presumed second issue; 1806, 1808, 1809, etc. A copy with an 1805 title page but with cover dated 1806 brought $1,600 at auction in 1981.

KING, Alexander. *Gospel of the Goat.* 30 plates. Folio, boards and morocco. Chicago, 1928. One of 100. $100–$125.

KING, C. W. *Antique Gems and Rings.* Illustrated. 2 vols., cloth. London, 1872. First edition. $125–$150.

KING, C. W. *Handbook of Engraved Gems.* Illustrated. Cloth. London, 1866. First edition. $100–$125.

KING. C. W. *The Natural History of Gems or Decorative Stones.* Illustrated. Cloth. London, 1867. First edition. $200–$250.

KING, Charles. *Campaigning with Crook.* 9 plates. Cloth. New York, 1890. First edition. $35–$50.

KING, Charles. *The Fifth Cavalry in the Sioux War to 1876: Campaigning with Crook.* 134 pp., printed wrappers. Milwaukee, 1880. First edition. $250–$300.

KING, Frank M. *Longhorn Trail Drivers.* Illustrated. Cloth. (Los Angeles, 1940.) First edition. One of 400 signed. $100–$125.

KING, Frank M. *Wranglin' the Past.* Portrait. Leatherette. (Los Angeles, 1935.) First edition. One of 300 signed. $100–$125.

KING, Jeff, and Campbell, Joseph. *Where the Two Came To Their Father: A Navaho*

War Ceremonial. 18 silk screen prints. 2 vols., quarto, wrappers, in large cloth portfolio. New York, (1943). First edition. $500.

KING, Richard. *Narrative of a Journey to the Shores of the Arctic Ocean, in 1833, 1834, and 1835.* Plates, maps. 2 vols., boards. London, 1836. First edition. $400–$450.

KING, Richard, and Hoppe, E. O. *The Book of Fair Women.* Text by King, photographs by Hoppe. Cloth. London, 1922. First edition. In dust jacket. $200–$300.

KING, W. Ross. *The Sportsman and Naturalist in Canada.* 6 color plates, other illustrations. Cloth. London, 1866. First edition. $200–$250.

KING, William. *Chelsea Porcelain.* 171 illustrations (7 colored). Buckram. London, 1922. $125–$150. Another issue: Pigskin. One of 75 signed. $200. Another issue: One of 13 on vellum. $400–$500.

KINGLAKE, A. W. *Eothen, or Traces of Travel Brought Home from the East.* Frontispiece in color, colored plate. Boards and cloth. London, 1844. First edition. $200–$250.

KINGMAN, John. *Letters, Written by John Kingman, While on a Tour to Illinois and Wisconsin, in the Summer of 1838.* 48pp., printed wrappers. Hingham, Mass., 1842. First edition. $800–$1,000.

KINGSLEY, Charles. *At Last: A Christmas in the West Indies.* Illustrated. 2 vols., cloth. London, 1871. First edition. $150–$175.

KINGSLEY, Charles. *The Heroes; or, Greek Fairy Tales for My Children.* 8 illustrations by the author. Pink decorated cloth. Cambridge, 1856 (actually 1855). First edition. $200–$250. London, 1912. Riccardi Press. Illustrated by W. Russell Flint. Vellum. One of 500. In dust jacket. $400–$500. Another issue: One of 12 on vellum, with a duplicate set of plates. $1,000 and up.

KINGSLEY, Charles. *The Water-Babies.* Illustrated. Cloth. London, 1863. First edition, first issue, with "L'Envoi" leaf. $400–$500. Without the leaf, $200–$300. London, 1909. 42 colored plates by Warwick Goble. Vellum. One of 260. $200–$250.

KINGSLEY, Charles. *Westward Ho!* 3 vols., blue cloth. Cambridge, 1855. First edition, with 16 pages of ads at end of Vol. 3 dated February, 1855. $750–$1,000. Later issue, worn, $250. Boston, 1855. Cloth. First American edition. $150–$200. New York, 1947. Limited Editions Club. Illustrated. 2 vols., boards. Boxed. $60–$80.

KINGSLEY, Henry. *Austin Elliot.* 2 vols., blue cloth. London, 1863. First edition, with 2 ad leaves in Vol. 1 and 16 pages of ads in Vol. 2. $100–$200.

KINGSLEY, Henry. *The Recollections of Geoffrey Hamlyn.* 3 vols., blue cloth. Cambridge. 1859. First edition. $400–$500. Author's first book. Boston, 1849. Cloth. First American edition. $30–$40.

KINGSLEY, Henry. *Valentin: A French Boy's Story of Sedan.* 2 vols., brick-red rough cloth. London, 1872. First edition. $75–$100.

KINNELL, Galway. *Black Light.* Boards. Boston, 1966. First edition. In dust jacket. $50.

KINNELL, Galway. *What a Kingdom It Was.* Boards. Boston, 1960. First edition. In dust jacket. $75–$100. Author's first book.

KINNELL, Galway (translator). *Bitter Victory.* By René Hardy. Cloth. Garden City, 1956. First edition. In dust jacket. $40–$65. Kinnell's first book appearance.

KINO, Eusebio F. *Historical Memoir of Primeria Alta.* Edited by Herbert Eugene Bolton. 7 maps, plates. 2 vols., cloth. Cleveland, 1919. One of 750. In dust jackets. $150–$200. Berkeley, 1948. Illustrated. 2 vols. in one, cloth. $60.

KINSELLA, Thomas. *Another September.* Cloth. Dublin, 1958. First edition. In dust jacket. $75.

KINZIE, Mrs. Juliette A. See *Narrative of the Massacre at Chicago.*

KINZIE, Mrs. Juliette A. *Wau-Bun, the "Early Day" in the North-West*, 6 plates. Pictorial cloth. New York, 1856. First edition. $100–$150. London, 1856. First English edition. $50–$65. Chicago, 1901. Caxton Club. Illustrated. Cloth. $50–$75.

KIP, Lawrence. See *The Indian Council in the Valley of the Walla Walla.*

KIP, Lawrence. *Army Life on the Pacific.* Cloth. New York, 1859. First edition. $350.

KIPLING, Rudyard. See *Echoes; Quartette.*

KIPLING, Rudyard. *An Almanac of Twelve Sports.* 12 color plates by William Nicholson. Pictorial boards. London, 1898. First edition. $150.

KIPLING, Rudyard. *Barrack-Room Ballads and Other Verses.* Red cloth. London, 1892. First English edition. $75–$100. Another issue: One of 225 on large paper. $200–$250. Another issue: Half vellum and buckram. One of 30 on vellum. $400–$450. (For first American edition, see Kipling, *Departmental Ditties*.)

KIPLING, Rudyard. *The Benefactors.* Boards and cloth. New York, 1930. First edition. One of 91 copies. Pirated edition. $100–$125.

KIPLING, Rudyard. *"Captains Courageous": A Story of the Grand Banks.* 22 illustrations. Blue cloth, gilt edges. London, 1897. First English edition. In gray dust jacket printed in blue. $500–$800. (Note: A few copies were issued in paper covers in 1896 for copyright purposes.)

KIPLING, Rudyard. *The City of Dreadful Night and Other Places.* Gray-green pictorial wrappers. Allahabad, 1891. No. 14 of Wheeler's Indian Library. First published (and second Indian) edition. $600–$800. Spine chipped, front hinge starting, $500. Also, $400 (A, 1973). Allahabad and London, (1891). Wrappers. First English edition. $300–$400.

KIPLING, Rudyard. *The City of Dreadful Night and Other Sketches.* Sewed, without cover. Allahabad, India, 1890. First (suppressed) edition. $5,000 and up. Also, in contemporary brown cloth. $2,200 (A, 1942). (Note: The only known copy.)

KIPLING, Rudyard. *Collected Verse.* Red cloth. New York, 1907. First edition, first issue, without index. $35. New York, 1910. Color illustrations. Half vellum. First illustrated edition. One of 125 signed. $500–$750. London, 1912. Limp vellum. One of 100 signed. $500–$750. Another issue: One of 500. $75–$100.

KIPLING, Rudyard. *The Courting of Dinah Shadd.* Blue wrappers. New York, 1890. First authorized edition. No. 680 in Harper's Franklin Square Library. $100–$150. (Note: The pirated Hurst clothbound edition, New York, 1890, is considered the genuine first edition. A copy brought $210 at auction in 1930.)

KIPLING, Rudyard. *Departmental Ditties and Other Verses.* Pictorial tan wrappers. Lahore, India, 1886. First edition. (Issued in the form of a government envelope.) $750–$1,000. Also, $600 (A, 1981). Calcutta, India, 1886. Printed boards. Second edition. $400–$600. New York, (1890). Red cloth. First American edition, first issue, with "Lovell" at foot of spine. $350–$400. (Note: This also constitutes the first American edition of *Barrack-Room Ballads*.) London, 1897. Illustrated. Vellum and cloth. First English (and first illustrated) edition. One of 150 on large paper. $350–$500.

KIPLING, Rudyard. *The Feet of the Young Men.* Illustrated with photographs. Brown boards and vellum. Garden City, 1920. First edition. One of 377 signed by the author. $200–$300.

KIPLING, Rudyard. *The Female of the Species.* Oblong, boards. Garden City, 1912. First edition. $25–$35. (Note: There also exists an earlier broadside printing, New York, about 1911. A copy brought $200 at auction in 1981.)

KIPLING, Rudyard. *The Five Nations.* Limp vellum. London, 1903. First edition. One of 30 on vellum. $250. Another issue: Boards. One of 200 large paper copies. $125–$150. Trade edition: Cloth. $35.

KIPLING, Rudyard. *In Black and White*. Gray-green pictorial wrappers. Allahabad, (1888). First edition. No. 3 of the Indian Railway Library. $400–$500. Allahabad and London, (1890). Gray-green wrappers. First English edition. $200–$225.

KIPLING, Rudyard. *The Jungle Book* [and] *The Second Jungle Book*. Illustrated. 2 vols., blue pictorial cloth. London, 1894–95. First editions. In dust jackets. $600–$700. New York, 1968. Limited Editions Club. (*The Jungle Books*.) $50–$75.

KIPLING, Rudyard. *Just So Stories for Little Children*. Illustrated by the author. Decorated red cloth. London, 1902. First edition. In dust jacket. $500–$600. Lacking jacket, $150–$200. Advance copy in torn wrappers: $1,600 (A, 1981).

KIPLING, Rudyard. *Kim*. Illustrated by J. K. Kipling. Green cloth. New York, 1901. First edition, first issue, with rhymed chapter headings for Chapters 8 and 13 only. In dust jacket. $400–$500. London, 1901. Red cloth. First English edition. In dust jacket. $400–$500. (Note: There also exists a single proof copy of the English first, dated 1900 on title page. It brought $800 at auction in 1942.) Lausanne, 1930. Illustrated by F. M. Schmied. Text in French. 2 vols., sheets in board folders. $750. New York, 1962. Limited Editions Club. Cloth. Boxed. $40–$50.

KIPLING, Rudyard. *Letters of Marque*. Red and blue cloth. Allahabad, 1891. First (suppressed) edition. $800–$1,000. London, 1891. Gray-green pictorial wrappers. First English edition, with "Vol. I" notation. (One of about 6 known copies.) $1,000 (A, 1981).

KIPLING, Rudyard. *The Light That Failed*. Blue cloth. London, 1891. First English edition. $150–$200. (Note: A few paperbound copies dated 1890 were issued for copyright purposes.)

KIPLING, Rudyard. *On Dry-Cow Fishing as a Fine Art*. Vignette. Decorated boards. Cleveland, 1926. Rowfant Club. First edition. One of 176. Boxed. $250–$275.

KIPLING, Rudyard. *The Phantom 'Rickshaw and Other Tales*. Gray-green pictorial wrappers. Allahabad, (1889). No. 5 of the Indian Railway Library. First edition, first binding, with apostrophe before the word "Rickshaw" on front cover. $1,000–$1,250. Second issue, without apostrophe. $750–$850. London, (1890). First English edition. $300–$400.

KIPLING, Rudyard. *Plain Tales from the Hills*. Olive-green pictorial cloth. Calcutta, 1888. First edition, first issue, plain blank covers without design and with December, 1887, ads. $1,500. Also, $1,100 (A, 1981). Ordinary copies, with landscape design on front cover, $400 and up.

KIPLING, Rudyard. *Poems, 1886–1929*. 3 vols., red morocco. London, 1929. First edition. One of 525 signed. In dust jackets. $400–$500. Garden City, 1930. 3 vols., vellum boards. One of 537 signed. $400–$500.

KIPLING, Rudyard. *Puck of Pook's Hill*. Red cloth. London, 1906. First edition. $200. New York, 1906. 4 color plates by Arthur Rackham. Pictorial cloth. First illustrated edition. $150–$200. (I have owned two variant bindings of this edition, the differences—in height and design—not mentioned by Kipling or Rackham bibliographers. Either binding appears to be an acceptable first edition.)

KIPLING, Rudyard. *Schoolboy Lyrics*. Brown printed or plain white wrappers. Lahore, 1881. First edition, first issue, plain white wrappers. $5,000–$10,000. Also, $4,300 (A, 1975).

KIPLING, Rudyard. *Sea and Sussex from Rudyard Kipling's Verse*. 24 color plates by Donald Maxwell. Boards and vellum. London, 1926. One of 500 signed. In dust jacket. Boxed. $350–$400. Garden City, 1926. One of 150 signed. $400–$500.

KIPLING, Rudyard. *The Smith Administration*. Wrappers, or cloth. Allahabad, 1891. First edition. $10,000 (A, 1975). (Only 6 copies survived Kipling's suppression of this unauthorized edition.)

KIPLING, Rudyard. *Soldier Tales*. Illustrated. Blue cloth. London, 1896. First edition. In dust jacket. $250–$350. Without jacket, $50–$125.

KIPLING, Rudyard. *Soldiers Three.* Pictorial wrappers, Allahabad, 1888. First edition, first state, without cross-hatching on barrack doors on the cover. $600–$800. Second issue, with the cross-hatching. $400–$600.

KIPLING, Rudyard. *A Song of the English.* Illustrated by W. Heath Robinson. Full white vellum. London, (1909). First edition. One of 500 signed by the artist. Boxed. $400–$700. New York, 1909. Color plates. Cloth. $100–$125.

KIPLING, Rudyard. *Songs of the Sea.* Vellum and boards. London, 1927. First edition. One of 500 large paper copies, signed. In dust jacket. $150–$200.

KIPLING, Rudyard. *Stalky and Co.* Cloth. London, 1899. First edition. $150–$200.

KIPLING, Rudyard. *The Story of the Gadsbys.* Gray-green pictorial wrappers. Allahabad, (1888). No. 2 of the Indian Railway Library. First edition. $350–$400.

KIPLING, Rudyard. *Under the Deodars.* Wrappers. Allahabad, (1888). No. 4 of the Indian Railway Library. First edition, first state of wrappers, without shading around "No. 4" and "One Rupee." $500–$750. Later, with shading on wrappers. $400–$500. London, (1890). Wrappers. First English edition. $350–$400.

KIPLING, Rudyard. *Verse: Inclusive Edition, 1885–1918.* 3 vols., vellum. London, 1919. First edition. One of 100 signed. $400–$500. Trade issue: Red cloth. $150–$200. Garden City, 1919. Boards. One of 250 signed. $350–$400.

KIPLING, Rudyard. *Wee Willie Winkie and Other Child Stories.* Gray-green pictorial wrappers. Allahabad, (1888). No. 6 of the Indian Railway Library. First edition, first issue, with periods after "A" and "H" on cover. $750–$1,000. Rebound, original covers mounted, $300.

KIPLING, Rudyard. *White Horses.* Lilac-colored printed wrappers. London, 1897. First edition (a Thomas J. Wise forgery). $400–$500.

KIPLING, Rudyard. *The White Man's Burden.* Lilac-colored printed wrappers. London, 1899. First English edition (a Thomas J. Wise forgery). $500–$600. (Note: There also exists a true first edition, for copyright, issue in 10 copies, gray wrappers, in New York in 1899. A copy inscribed by Kipling sold for $500 in 1942.)

KIPLING, Rudyard. *With the Night Mail.* Color plates. Cloth. New York, 1909. First edition. $200–$225.

KIPLING, Rudyard. *With Number Three, Surgical & Medical, and New Poems.* Printed wrappers. Santiago de Chile, 1900. First edition. $200–$275. Also, $90 (A, 1981). (Livingston says most of the 400 copies were pulped, a report that has been questioned by other bibliographers.)

KIZER, Carolyn. *The Ungrateful Garden.* Cloth. Bloomington, (1961). First edition. In dust jacket. $60–$75. Author's first book.

KLONDYKE Mines and the Golden Valley of the Yukon (The). 24 pp., self-wrappers. No place, 1897. $100–$150.

KLOSTERHEIM: or the Masque. By the English Opium Eater. Boards, paper label. Edinburgh, 1832. (By Thomas De Quincey.) First edition. $500–$600. Worn and shaken, $180.

KNEEDLER, H. S. *The Coast Country of Texas.* 76 pp., wrappers. Cincinnati, 1896. First edition. $150–$200.

KNEEDLER, H. S. *Through Storyland to Sunset Seas.* Wrappers. Cincinnati, 1896. First edition. $200.

KNICKERBOCKER, Diedrich. *A History of New York, from the Beginning of the World to the End of the Dutch Dynasty.* Engraved plate. 2 vols., blue boards. New York, 1809. (By Washington Irving.) First edition, first state, with 268 pp. in Vol. 1. $1,000 and up. London, 1839. Illustrated by George Cruikshank. $100–$150. New York, 1867. 2 vols., full morocco. Author's revised edition. $200–$300. New York,

1900. Illustrated by Maxfield Parrish. Boards and cloth. $150–$200. Other Parrish editions in 1903 and 1915, comparably priced.

KNIGHT, Dr. (John), and Slover, John. *Indian Atrocities.* 96 pp., plain yellow boards, cloth spine. Nashville, 1843. First edition. $2,000 and up. Also, $1,500 (A, 1967). Cincinnati, 1867. Printed wrappers. One of 500. $100–$125.

KNIGHT, Sarah K., and Buckingham, The Rev. Mr. (Thomas). *The Journals of Madam Knight and Rev. Mr. Buckingham.* Boards. New York, 1825. First edition. $75–$100.

KNISH, Anne. See Morgan, Emanuel, and Knish, Anne.

KNOBLOCK, Byron W. *Bannerstones of the North American Indian.* Frontispiece in color, 270 plates. Half leather. La Grange, Ill., 1939. First edition. One of 50 signed. $175.

KNOWLES, John. *A Separate Peace.* Cloth. London, (1959). First edition. $100–$150. Author's first book.

KNOX, Dudley W. *Naval Sketches of the War in California.* 28 colored drawings by William H. Meyers. Introduction by Franklin D. Roosevelt. Boards, white leather spine. New York, 1939. Grabhorn printing. One of 1,000. $150–$250.

KOCH, Frederick H. (editor). *Carolina Folk-Plays, Second Series.* Cloth. New York, 1924. First edition, with dated title page. In dust jacket. $200–$250. (Note: Contains "The Return of Buck Gavin," Thomas Wolfe's first appearance in a book.)

KOHL, J. G. *Kitchi-Gami: Wanderings Round Lake Superior.* Illustrated. Half calf. London, 1860. First edition in English. $300–$350.

KONINGSMARKE, the Long Finne: A Story of the New World. 2 vols., boards. New York, 1823. (By James Kirke Paulding.) First edition. $200–$300.

KOOP, Albert J. *Early Chinese Bronzes.* 110 plates (3 colored). Cloth. London, 1924. $150–$250. Another issue: Calf. One of 40 on China paper, signed. $350–$400. New York, 1924. Cloth. First American edition. In dust jacket. $150–$250.

KOOPS, Matthias. *Historical Account of the Substances Which Have Been Used to Describe Events . . . from the Earliest Date to the Invention of Paper.* Printed on paper made of straw alone. Morocco. London, 1800. First edition. $400–$600. London, 1801. Boards and cloth. Second edition. $350–$400.

KORAN (The). Sheep. Springfield, Mass., 1806. First American edition. (Printed for Isaiah Thomas.) $300–$400.

KOREN, Elizabeth. *Fra Pioneertiden.* Illustrated. Cloth. Decorah, Iowa, 1914. First edition. $125–$135.

KOSEWITZ, W. F. von. *Eccentric Tales, from the German.* 20 hand-colored etched plates by George Cruikshank from sketches by Alfred Crowquill. Half cloth. London, 1827. First edition. $750–$1,000. Also issued in 5 parts, wrappers: $1,400 (A, 1978).

KOSINSKI, Jerzy. See Novak, Joseph.

KOSINSKI, Jerzy. *The Art of the Self: Essays a Propos 'Steps.'* Wrappers. New York, 1968. First edition. $50.

KOSINSKI, Jerzy. *Notes of the Author on 'The Painted Bird.'* Wrappers. New York, 1965. First edition. $50–$75.

KOSINSKI, Jerzy. *The Painted Bird.* Cloth. Boston, (1965). First edition. In dust jacket. $250–$300. London, 1966. First English edition. In dust jacket. $75.

KOSINSKI, Jerzy. *Steps*. Boards. New York, (1968). First edition. In dust jacket. $75–$85.

KOTZEBUE, Otto Von. *A New Voyage Round the World, 1823–26*. 3 maps and 2 plates. 2 vols., boards, paper labels. London, 1830. First edition in English. $3,000–$4,000.

KOTZEBUE, Otto Von. *A Voyage of Discovery, Into the South Sea and Beering's Straits*. Colored plates, engraved folding charts. 3 vols., brown boards, paper labels. London, 1821. First edition in English. $2,000–$2,500.

KRAKEL, Dean F. *The Saga of Tom Horn*. Illustrated. Cloth. (Laramie, 1954.) First edition (suppressed). In dust jacket. $150. Second edition, with text on pages 13 and 54 revised. $100–$125.

KRAKEL, Dean F. *South Platte Country*. Illustrated. Pictorial wrappers. Laramie, 1954. First edition. $60–$75.

KREYMBORG, Alfred. *Love, Life, and Other Studies*. Boards. New York, (1908). First edition. One of 500. $100–$125.

KREYMBORG, Alfred. *Selected Poems, 1912–1944*. Cloth. New York, 1945. First edition. One of 250 signed. Boxed. $50–$60.

KREYMBORG, Alfred (editor). *Others for 1919: An Anthology of the New Verse*. Boards. New York, 1917. First edition. In dust jacket. $125–$150.

KROEBER, Alfred L. *Handbook of the Indians of California*. Folding map, 10 other maps, 73 plates on 38 sheets. Cloth. Washington, 1925. First edition. $150–$200.

KRUSENSTERN, A. J. von. *Voyage Round the World in the Years 1803, 1804, 1805, and 1806*. 2 color plates, folding map. 2 vols., calf. London, 1813. First edition in English. $3,000–$4,000.

KUNITZ, Stanley J. *Intellectual Things*. Cloth. Garden City, 1930. First edition. In dust jacket. $75–$100. Author's first book.

KUNZ, George Frederick. *The Curious Lore of Precious Stones*. 86 illustrations (6 in color). Pictorial cloth. Philadelphia, (1913). First edition. $200–$250.

KUNZ, George Frederick. *Gems and Precious Stones of North America*. 8 colored plates, other illustrations. Cloth. New York, 1890. First edition, with errata slip. $150–$200.

KUNZ, George Frederick. *Ivory and the Elephant in Art, in Archaeology, and in Science*. Illustrated. Cloth. Garden City, 1916. First edition. $200–$250.

KUNZ, George Frederick. *The Magic of Jewels and Charms*. Illustrated, including color. Pictorial cloth. Philadelphia, (1915). $100–$125.

KUNZ, George Frederick. *Rings for the Finger*. Illustrated. Red cloth. Philadelphia, 1917. First edition. $125–$150.

KUNZ, George Frederick, and Stevenson, Charles Hugh. *The Book of the Pearl*. Illustrated, including color plates. Pale-blue cloth. New York, 1908. First edition. $150–$200. London, 1908. White buckram. First English edition. $150–$200.

KUTTNER, Henry, and Moore, C. L. *No Boundaries*. Cloth. New York, (1955). First edition. In dust jacket. $50–$60.

KUYKENDALL, Ivan Lee. *Ghost Riders of the Mogollon*. Boards. San Antonio, (1954). First edition. In dust jacket. $300. (Suppressed.)

KUYKENDALL, Judge W. L. *Frontier Days*. Portrait. Cloth. (Denver?), 1917. First edition. In dust jacket. $75–$100.

L

L., E. V. *Sparks from a Flint: Odd Rhymes for Odd Times.* Cloth. London, 1890. (By E. V. Lucas?) First edition. $50–$75. Lucas' first book?

LA BREE, Ben (editor). *The Confederate Soldier in the Civil War, 1861–1865.* Illustrated. Folio, cloth. Louisville, 1895. First edition. $200–$300.

LADIES Almanack . . . Written and Illustrated by a Lady of Fashion. Pictorial wrappers. Paris, 1928. (By Djuna Barnes.) First edition. One of 1,000. Issued with glassine wraparound. $175–$250. Another issue: Vellum. One of 40 with hand-colored plates. $1,000 and up. Also, $850 (A, 1977).

LADY Audley's Secret. 3 vols., blue cloth. London, 1862. (By Mary E. Braddon.) First edition. $3,000–$4,000.

LAFITTE: The Pirate of the Gulf. 2 vols., cloth. New York, 1836. (By Joseph Holt Ingraham.) First edition. $250–$300.

LA FONTAINE, Jean de. *The Fables of Jean de la Fontaine.* Translated into English verse by Edward Marsh. 26 engravings on copper by Stephen Gooden. 2 vols., vellum. London, 1931. One of 525 signed by the translator and artist. $350–$450.

LA FRENTZ, F. W. *Cowboy Stuff.* Illustrated by Henry Ziegler. Boards. New York, 1927. First edition, first issue, with 49 plates. One of 500. $500–$600.

LA GUERRA de Tejas sin Máscara. 20 pp., stitched. Mexico, 1845. $300–$400.

LAKESIDE Classics. Cloth, Chicago, 1903–1981. 78 vols., green, black, red, and blue cloth, complete set. $2,000–$3,000. Individual volumes range from $10 to $15 to $100 and more for certain scarce titles, among them William Penn's *Fruits of Solitude* and the series *Memorable American Speeches.*

LAMB, Charles. See An Eye Witness. Also see *The Adventures of Ulysses; Beauty and the Beast; Elia; John Woodvil; The King and Queen of Hearts; The Last Essays of Elia; Mr. H.; Mrs. Leicester's School; The New Year's Feast on His Coming of Age; Poetry for Children.*

LAMB, Charles. *Album Verses, with a Few Others.* Cloth-backed boards, paper label. London, 1830. First edition. $750–$1,000. Also, $480 (A, 1981).

LAMB, Charles. *The Child Angel, a Dream.* Printed in red and black. Vellum. London, 1910. One of 12 on vellum. $400–$600.

LAMB, Charles. *Elia and the Last Essays of Elia.* Woodcut portrait. 2 vols., buckram. Newtown, Wales, 1929. Gregynog Press. One of 285. In slipcase. $350–$450. Another issue: One of 25 specially bound in morocco. $800–$1,000. (For first editions of the *Elia* books, see title entries.)

LAMB, Charles. *The Letters of Charles Lamb, to Which Are Added Those of His Sister Mary Lamb.* Edited by E.V. Lucas. 3 vols., cloth. (London, 1935.) First edition. In dust jackets. $150–$200.

LAMB, Charles. *A Masque of Days.* Illustrated by Walter Crane. Half cloth. London, 1901. In dust jacket. $100–$150.

LAMB, Charles. *Specimens of English Dramatic Poets, Who Lived About the Time of*

Shakespeare: with Notes. Gray boards. London, 1808. First edition. $250–$350. London, 1813. $150.

LAMB, Charles. *Tales from Shakespeare.* 20 plates by William Mulready. 2 vols., boards. London, 1807. First edition, first issue, with imprint on back of page 235. $2,000–$3,000. (Auction values for rebound copies have ranged in recent years to $700 and more.) Second issue, back of page 235 blank. $2,000 and up. London, 1909. Arthur Rackham color plates. Buckram with ties. One of 750 large paper copies, signed by Rackham. $700–$875. Another issue: Ordinary copies, in cloth: $150–$200. (Note: Mary Lamb collaborated in writing this book.)

LAMB, Charles. *The Works of Charles Lamb.* 2 vols., cloth-backed boards, paper labels. London, 1818. First edition, first issue, with ads at end dated "June, 1818." $600–$750. London, 1903. Edited by William Macdonald. 12 vols. $400–$500. London, 1903–05. (*Works* of Charles and Mary Lamb.) 7 vols. $300–$400.

LAMBOURNE, Alfred. *An Old Sketch-Book Dedicated to the Memory of My Father.* 18 plates. 53 pp., plates. 78 pp., atlas folio, half morocco and tan cloth. Boston, (1892). First edition. $350–$450.

LAMBOURNE, Alfred. *The Old Journey: Reminiscences of Pioneer Days.* 18 plates. 53 pp., yellow and buff cloth. (Salt Lake City, 1897.) "Jubilee Edition" (of *An Old Sketchbook*). $50–$60.

LAMBOURNE, Alfred. *Scenic Utah: Pen and Pencil.* 20 plates. White cloth, black leather spine. New York, 1891. First edition. $50–$75.

LÂME PÉNITENTE, ou Le Nouveau Pensez-y-Bien; Considération sur les Vérités Eternelles, etc. Unbound, uncut. Detroit, 1809. (Barthelemi Baudrand, editor.) $1,500 and up. Also, $1,100 (A, 1967). In calf binding, uncut, $750 (1956 catalogue); no other copies noted.

LAMENTATIONS of Jeremiah (The). Folio, morocco. Newtown, Wales, 1933. Gregynog Press. One of 250. $600–$700.

LAMON, Ward H. *The Life of Abraham Lincoln.* Plates and facsimiles. Green or rust-colored cloth. Boston, 1872. First edition. $125–$150.

L'AMOUR, Louis. *Smoke From This Altar.* Cloth. Oklahoma City, (1939). First edition. In dust jacket. $100–$150. Author's first book.

LAMSON, David R. *Two Years' Experience Among the Shakers.* Illustrated. Cloth. West Boylston, Mass., 1848. First edition. $100–$150.

LANCASTER, Joseph. *The British System of Education.* 5 plates, frontispiece. Cloth. Georgetown, 1812. First edition. $50–$75.

LANCASTER, Robert A., Jr. *Historic Virginia Homes and Churches.* Illustrated. Cloth. Philadelphia, 1915. First edition. $75–$100. Philadelphia, 1917. $50–$65.

LANDOR, Walter Savage. See *Count Julian: A Tragedy; The Dun Cow; Idyllia Nova Quinque; Imaginary Conversations; Pericles and Aspasia; Poems from the Arabic and Persian; Poetry by the Author of Gebir; Popery, British and Foreign; Simonidea.*

LANDOR, Walter Savage. *Andrea of Hungary, and Giovanna of Naples.* Boards, paper label; or purple cloth. London, 1839. First edition. $100.

LANDOR, Walter Savage. *Dry Sticks, Fagoted.* Dark-green cloth. Edinburgh, 1858. First edition. $75–$100.

LANDOR, Walter Savage. *Epicurus, Leontion, and Ternissa.* Woodcut border, initial, and ornaments. Pigskin. London, 1896. Vale Press. One of 210. $150–$200.

LANDOR, Walter Savage. *Gebir, Count Julian, and Other Poems.* Boards, cloth spine, label. London, 1831. First edition. $150–$200.

LANDOR, Walter Savage. *Heroic Idyls, with Additional Poems.* Cloth. London, 1863. First edition. $60–$75.

LANDOR, Walter Savage. *The Last Fruit off an Old Tree.* Purple cloth. London, 1853. First edition, with 8 pages of ads. $100.

LANDOR, Walter Savage. *A Modern Greek Idyl.* Green printed wrappers. London, 1917. First edition. One of 30. $150.

LANDOR, Walter Savage. *A Poet's Dream.* Wrappers. Edinburgh, 1928. One of 35, with a manuscript note in Thomas J. Wise's hand. $75–$100.

LANDOR, Walter Savage. *To Elizabeth Barrett Browning and Other Verses.* Green printed wrappers. London, 1917. First edition. One of 30. $150–$200.

LANE, Lydia Spencer. *I Married a Soldier.* Cloth. Philadelphia, 1893. First edition. $75–$85.

LANE, Walter P. *Adventures and Recollections of Gen. Walter P. Lane.* Portrait. 114 pp., wrappers. Marshall, Tex., 1887. First edition. $800–$1,200.

LANG, Andrew. *Ballads and Lyrics of Old France, with Other Poems.* White cloth. London, 1872. First edition. $100–$125. Author's first book.

LANG, Andrew. *The Blue Fairy Book.* Illustrated. Boards. London, 1889. First edition. One of 113. $250–$275. Trade edition: $75–$100. New York, (about 1897). McLoughlin. Pictorial boards. $75–$100.

LANG, Andrew. *The Blue Poetry Book.* Illustrated. Boards. London, 1891. First edition. One of 150. $250–$300. Trade edition: Blue cloth. $100.

LANG, Andrew. *The Gold of Fairnilee.* Illustrated. Cloth. Bristol, England, (1888). First edition. $75–$100. New York, 1888. First American edition. $35–$50.

LANG, Andrew. *The Green Fairy Book.* Illustrated. Boards. London, 1892. First edition. One of 150. $250–$300. Trade edition: Green cloth. $75–$100.

LANG, Andrew. *Old French Title Pages.* Boards. San Francisco, 1924. Grabhorn printing. One of 260. $100–$150.

LANG, Andrew. *The Olive Fairy Book.* Illustrated. Decorated cloth. London, 1907. First trade edition. $75–$100. New York, 1907. Cloth. First American edition. $75–$100.

LANG, Andrew. *Prince Charles Edward.* Illustrated. Half morocco. London, 1900. First edition. One of 350. $200–$225. Another issue: Morocco, extra. $300–$350.

LANG, Andrew. *The Princess Nobody.* Illustrated. Half cloth. London, (1884). First edition. $350–$400.

LANG, Andrew. *The Red Fairy Book.* Illustrated. Gray and white boards. London, 1890. First edition. One of 113 on large paper. $200–$250.

LANG, Andrew. *The Red True Story Book.* Red cloth. London, 1895. First edition. $75–$100.

LANG, Andrew. *The True Story Book.* Illustrated. Boards. London, 1893. First edition. One of 150. $150–$250. Trade edition: Cloth. $75.

LANG, Andrew. *XXII Ballades in Blue China.* Full vellum. London, 1880. First edition. $200–$250. Another copy, morocco. $300–$350.

LANG, Andrew (translator). *The Miracles of Madame Saint Katherine of Fierbois.* Red vellum. Chicago: Way & Williams, 1897. First American edition. One of 50 on vellum. $250.

LANG, H. O. (editor). *History of the Willamette Valley.* 6 plates, facsimile, errata leaf. Calf. Portland, Ore., 1885. First edition. $75–$100.

LANG, William W. *A Paper on the Resources and Capabilities of Texas.* 19 pp., wrappers. (New York), 1881. First edition. $100–$150. Second edition, same date, 31 pp. $75.

LANGFORD, Nathaniel Pitt. *Vigilante Days and Ways.* 15 plates. 2 vols., pictorial cloth. Boston, 1890. First edition. $150–$250.

LANGLEY, Henry G. *The San Francisco Directory for the Year 1858.* Boards. San Francisco, 1858. $350–$500.

LANGSDORFF, George H. von. *Narrative of the Rezanov Voyage to Nueva California, 1806.* Map, plates. Half cloth. San Francisco, 1927. One of 260. $125–$175.

LANGSDORFF, George H. von. *Voyages and Travels in Various Parts of the World During 1803–7.* Maps and plates. 2 vols. boards, or cloth. London, 1813–14. First English edition. $2,500–$3,500. Carlisle, Pa., 1817. Folding plate. 2 vols. in one, sheepskin. First American edition (abridged). $1,000–$1,250.

LANGSTAFF, Launcelot, and others. *Salmagundi; or, The Whim-Whams and Opinions of Launcelot Langstaff, Esq., and Others.* 2 vols., wrappers, or 20 parts, wrappers. New York, 1807–08. (By Washington Irving, William Irving, and James Kirke Paulding.) First edition. $15,000 and up. Also, a set in mixed states and with defects, $11,000 (A, 1971). Most items offered are mixed sets of the parts bound in one or two volumes. Examples: 20 parts (two of them first issue), bound in 2 vols., boards, $1,700 (A, 1974), and 20 parts (16 of them first issue), bound in 2 vols., calf, $2,000 (A, 1963). Most sets sell at much lower prices. No sets noted for sale in recent years. An extremely complicated work, existing in numerous states and difficult to identify. See Blanck, *A Bibliography of American Literature.*

LANGSTON, Mrs. George. *History of Eastland County, Texas.* Illustrated. Cloth. Dallas, 1904. First edition. $175–$300.

LANGWORTHY, Franklin. *Scenery of the Plains, Mountains and Mines.* Cloth. Ogdensburgh, N.Y., 1855. First edition. $400–$500.

LANGWORTHY, Lucius H. *Dubuque: Its History, Mines, Indian Legends.* 82 pp., printed green wrappers. Dubuque, Iowa, (1855). First edition. $200–$300.

LANIER, Sidney. *The Boy's Mabinogion.* Illustrated by Alfred Fredericks. Decorated cloth. New York, 1881. First edition. $150–$200.

LANIER, Sidney. *Florida: Its Scenery, Climate, and History.* Illustrated. Cloth. Philadelphia, 1876. First edition, with dated title page. $200–$225.

LANIER, Sidney. *Letters: Sidney Lanier to Col. John G. James.* Illustrated. Printed wrappers over boards. Austin, 1942. One of 165. In glassine dust jacket. Boxed. $350.

LANIER, Sidney. *Tiger-Lilies.* Cloth. New York, 1867. First edition, first state, with title page on a stub. $100–$150. Second state, title page an integral leaf. $200–$250. Author's first book.

LANMAN, Charles. *Adventures in the Wilds of the United States and British American Provinces.* Illustrated. 2 vols., cloth. Philadelphia, 1856. First American edition. $600–$750.

LANMAN, Charles. *Adventures of an Angler in Canada.* Frontispiece. Half leather. London, 1848. First edition. $400–$500.

LANMAN, Charles. *Haw-Ho-Noo, or Records of a Tourist.* Cloth. Philadelphia, 1850. First edition. $300–$400.

LANMAN, Charles. *A Summer in the Wilderness.* Cloth. New York, 1847. First edition. $300–$400.

LANMAN, Charles. *A Tour to the River Saguenay.* Wrappers. Philadelphia, 1848. First edition. $250–$350.

LANMAN, James H. *History of Michigan.* Folding map. Cloth. New York, 1839. First edition. $200.

LANTHORN Book (The). Half brown leather and green cloth. New York, (1898). (By Stephen Crane and others.) First edition. One of 125 signed by Crane and the other contributors. $1,000–$1,250.

LAPHAM, I. A. *A Geographical and Topographical Description of Wisconsin.* Folding map (with 1844 copyright). Cloth. Milwaukee, 1844. First edition. $400–$500. (Note: First bound book printed in Wisconsin.)

LAPHAM, I. A. *Wisconsin.* Colored map (dated 1845). Cloth. Milwaukee, 1946. Second edition (of *A Geographical and Topographical Description of Wisconsin*). $150–$200.

LARA, A Tale. Jacqueline, a Tale. Drab broads, paper label. London, 1814. (By George Gordon Noel, Lord Byron, and Samuel Rogers.) First edition, with 4 pages of ads. $600–$750.

LARAMIE, Hahn's Peak and Pacific Railway System: The Direct Gateway to Southern Wyoming, Northern Colorado, and Eastern Utah. 110 illustrations. Oblong folio, wrappers. No place, no date (about 1910). $200–$300.

LARCOM, Lucy. *Childhood Songs.* Illustrated. Cloth or leather. Boston, 1875. First edition. $50–$100.

LARCOM, Lucy. *Similitudes.* Cloth. Boston, 1854. First edition. $75–$100. Author's first book.

LARDNER, Ring W. *Bib Ballads.* Illustrated by Fontaine Fox. Decorated brown cloth. Chicago, (1915). First edition. Boxed. $150–$400. Worn copy, $95. Author's first book (500 printed).

LARDNER, Ring W. *The Big Town.* Illustrated. Green cloth. Indianapolis, (1921). First edition. In dust jacket. $100–$150.

LARDNER, Ring W. *Gullible's Travels.* Indianapolis, (1917). First edition. In dust jacket. $250–$350.

LARDNER, Ring W. *How to Write Short Stories (with Samples).* Green cloth. New York, 1924. First edition, first issue, with Scribner seal on copyright page. In dust jacket. $125–$200.

LARDNER, Ring. *Lose with a Smile.* Cloth. New York, 1933. First edition, with Scribner seal. In dust jacket. $75–$125.

LARDNER, Ring W. *The Love Nest and Other Stories.* Green cloth. New York, 1925. First edition, with Scribner seal. In dust jacket. $200–$250.

LARDNER, Ring W. *My 4 Weeks in France.* Cloth. Indianapolis, (1918). First edition. In dust jacket. $150–$200.

LARDNER, Ring W. *Regular Fellows I Have Met.* Green flexible suede. Chicago, 1919. First edition. $350–$500.

LARDNER, Ring W. *Round Up.* Green cloth. New York, 1929. First edition, with Scribner seal. In dust jacket. $150–$175. Without jacket, $50–$75.

LARDNER, Ring W. *Stop Me If You've Heard This One.* Boards. New York, 1929. First edition. $100–$150.

LARDNER, Ring. *The Story of a Wonder Man.* Illustrated. Dark green cloth. New York, 1927. First edition, with Scribner seal. In dust jacket. $200–$250.

LARDNER, Ring W. *Treat 'Em Rough: Letters from Jack the Kaiser Killer.* Illustrated. Green boards, paper labels. Indianapolis, (1918). First edition, first printing, without the poem "To R. W. L." on page 6. In dust jacket. $200–$250. Second printing, with the poem. In dust jacket. $150–$200.

LARDNER, Ring W. *What of It?* Green cloth. New York, 1925. First edition, first issue, with pages 191, 201, 200. In dust jacket. $100–$150. Second issue, pages 191 to 201 corrected by cancel leaf. In jacket. $75–$100.

LARDNER, Ring W. *You Know Me Al.* Brown cloth. New York, (1916). First edition. In dust jacket. $200–$300.

LARDNER, Ring W., Jr. *The Young Immigrunts.* Portraits by Gaar Williams. Pictorial boards. Indianapolis, (1920). First edition. In dust jacket. $200–$250.

LARDNER, Ring W., and Kaufman, George S. *June Moon.* Mauve cloth. New York, 1930. First edition, with "A", and Scribner seal on copyright page. In dust jacket. $100–$150.

LARIMER, Mrs. Sarah L. *The Capture and Escape; or, Life Among the Sioux.* 5 plates. Cloth. Philadelphia, 1870. First edition. $100–$150. Philadelphia, 1871. $75.

LARIMER, William. *Reminiscences of Gen. William Larimer and of His Son William H. H. Larimer.* Plates, portraits, folding chart. Morocco. Lancaster, Pa., 1918. First edition, $400–$500.

LARKIN, Philip. *Jill.* Cloth. London, (1946). First edition. In dust jacket. $400–$500.

LARKIN, Philip. *The North Ship.* Cloth. London, (1945). First edition. In dust jacket. $400–$500. Author's first book.

LARKIN, Thomas O., and others. *California in 1846.* Half cloth. San Francisco, 1935. Grabhorn Press. One of 550. $100–$150.

LAROQUE, François A. *Journal of François A. Laroque from the Assiniboine to the Yellowstone, 1805.* 82 pp., printed wrappers. Ottawa, 1910. First edition. $200–$250.

LARPENTEUR, Charles. *Forty Years a Fur Trader of the Upper Mississippi.* 12 illustrations, 6 maps. 2 vols., blue cloth. New York, 1898. First edition. $100–$125.

LA SALLE, Charles E. *Colonel Crocket, the Texas Trailer.* 84 pp., pictorial wrappers. New York, no date (1871). $100–$150.

LA SALLE, Nicolas de. *Relation of the Discovery of the Mississippi River.* French and English texts. Boards and vellum. Chicago, 1898. Caxton Club. First edition in English. One of 269. $250–$300.

LA SALLE, René Robert Cavelier. *Relation of the Discoveries and Voyages of Cavelier de La Salle.* English and French texts. Half vellum. Chicago, 1901. Caxton Club. One of 227. $300–$400.

LA SHELLE, Kirke. *Poker Rubaiyat.* 12 full-page woodcuts in color by Frank Holme. Colored wrappers. (Phoenix, 1903.) Bandar-Log Press. One of 254. $250–$350.

LAST Days of Pompeii (The). 3 vols., boards. London, 1834. (By Edward Bulwer-Lytton.) First edition, with errata slips in each volume. $500–$600. New York, 1834. 2 vols., muslin. First American edition. $200–$225. New York, 1956. Limited Editions Club. Illustrated. Cloth. Boxed. $100–$175.

LAST Essays of Elia (The). Boards, paper label. London, 1833. (By Charles Lamb.) First English edition (second edition of the Second Series of Elia essays, the first edition having been published in Philadelphia 5 years before; see *Elia* entry). $750–$1,000.

LAST Man (The). 3 vols., boards. London, 1826. (By Mary Wollstonecraft Shelley.) First edition, with ad leaf at end of Vol. 1. $1,000 and up.

LAST of the Mohicans (The). By the Author of "The Pioneers." 2 vols., tan boards, paper labels. Philadelphia, 1826. (By James Fenimore Cooper.) First edition, first issue, with page 89 misnumbered 93 in first volume. $5,000–$7,500. London, 1826, 3 vols., boards. First English edition. $2,000 and up. New York, 1932. Limited Editions Club. Illustrated. Half buckram. Boxed. $50–$75.

LATHAM, H. *Trans-Missouri Stock Raising.* Map. 88 pp., wrappers. Omaha, 1871. First edition. $5,000 and up. Denver, 1962. Illustrated. Pictorial cloth. One of 999. In dust jacket. $10.

LATOUR, A. Lacarrière. *Historical Memoir of the War in West Florida and Louisiana in 1814–15.* With an atlas. 2 vols., boards. Philadelphia, 1816. First edition. $1,500–$2,000.

LATROBE, Charles Joseph. *The Rambler in Mexico.* Folding map. Half calf. London, 1836. First edition. $250.

LAUFER, Berthold. *Paper and Printing in Ancient China.* Chicago, 1931. Caxton Club. One of 250. $150–$175.

LAUGHTON, L. D. Carr. *Old Ship Figure-Heads and Sterns.* 8 colored plates, 48 in monochrome. With 2 portfolios of plates, one a duplicate set of the colored plates and an unpublished plate, matted, the other a series of 8 engraved plates, matted, similar, and apparently unpublished. Three-quarters pigskin. London, 1925. One of 100. $750–$1,000. Ordinary issue: Cloth. In dust jacket. $500–$600.

LA VERDAD Desnuda sobre la Guerra de Tejas, O sea contestación al Folleto Titulado; La Guerra de Tejas sin Mascara. 43 pp., sewed. Mexico, 1845. $300–$450.

LAW, John. *Address Delivered before the Vincennes Historical and Antiquarian Society.* Folding map. 48 pp., wrappers. Louisville, 1839. First edition. $100–$150. Also, $80 (A, 1967).

LAW, John. *Colonial History of Vincennes.* Cloth. Vincennes, Ind., 1858. $75–$100.

LAW of Descent and Distribution Governing Lands of the Creek Nation, as Held by C. W. Raymond, Judge of the U.S. Court for the Indian Territory. 14 pp., printed wrappers. No place, 1903. Democrat Printing Co. $200–$300.

LAWRENCE, Ada, and Gelder, Stuart. *Young Lorenzo: Early Life of D. H. Lawrence.* Illustrated. Vellum. Florence, (1932). First edition. One of 740 (or 750). In dust jacket. $100–$125.

LAWRENCE, D. H. See Davison, Lawrence H.; Verga, Giovanni.

LAWRENCE, D. H. *Amores: Poems.* Cloth. London, (1916). First edition, first issue, with 16 pages of ads at end. $400–$550.

LAWRENCE, D. H. *Apocalypse.* Photographic frontispiece. Boards, leather label. Florence, Italy, 1931. First edition. One of 750. In dust jacket. $150–$200. London, (1932). Frontispiece. Cloth. First English edition. In dust jacket. $50–$75.

LAWRENCE, D. H. *Assorted Articles.* Red cloth. London, 1930. First edition. In dust jacket. $75–$125. New York, 1930. Cloth. First American edition. In dust jacket. $75–$125.

LAWRENCE, D. H. *Bay: A Book of Poems.* Hand-colored illustrations. Decorated boards. (Westminster, 1919.) Beaumont Press. First edition. One of 30 on Japan vellum, signed. $1,250–$1,500. (Note: There were also 3 extra copies of this issue for presentation. Value: $1,500 and up.) Another issue: One of 50 on cartridge paper, with hand-colored illustrations. (About 25 destroyed.) $750–$1,000. Another issue: One of 120 on handmade paper. $500–$600.

LAWRENCE, D. H. *Birds, Beasts and Flowers.* Pink buckram, paper label. New York, 1923. First edition. In dust jacket. $400–$650. London, 1923. Boards and cloth. First English edition. In dust jacket. $60–$80. London, 1930. Cresset Press. 12 engravings. Vellum-backed boards. First illustrated edition. $200–$250. Another issue: Cloth-backed boards. $85–$125. Another issue: Full pigskin. One of 30, with an extra suite of plates. Boxed. $500–$600.

LAWRENCE, D. H. *Collected Poems*. 2 vols., boards, parchment spines. London, 1928. One of 100 signed. In dust jackets. $1,000–$1,250. Trade edition: 2 vols., brown cloth. In jackets $125–$175. New York, (1929). 2 vols., brown cloth. First American edition. Boxed. $50–$80.

LAWRENCE, D. H. *David: A Play*. Tan cloth. London, (1926). First edition. One of 500. In dust jacket. $200–$250. New York, 1926. Boards. First American edition. In dust jacket. $75–$125.

LAWRENCE, D. H. *England, My England and Other Stories*. Blue-gray cloth. New York, 1922. First edition. In dust jacket. $150–$250. London, 1924. Brown cloth. First English edition. In dust jacket. $100–$150.

LAWRENCE, D. H. *The Escaped Cock*. Color frontispiece by Lawrence. White wrappers. Paris, 1929. Black Sun Press. First edition. One of 450 on Van Gelder paper. In glassine dust jacket. Boxed. $150–$300. Another issue: One of 50 on vellum, signed. $750–$1,000. Also, $650 (A, 1977). (Note: Published later in England as *The Man Who Died*.)

LAWRENCE, D. H. *Etruscan Places*. 20 plates. Cloth. London, 1932. First edition. In dust jacket. $125–$200.

LAWRENCE, D. H. *Fantasia of the Unconscious*. Blue ribbed cloth. New York, 1922. First edition. In dust jacket. $200–$250. London, 1923. First English edition. In dust jacket. $150–$200.

LAWRENCE, D. H. *Fire and Other Poems*. Introduction by Robinson Jeffers. Linen. (San Francisco), 1940. Grabhorn Press. First edition. One of 300. In plain tan dust jacket. $300–$400.

LAWRENCE, D. H. *Glad Ghosts*. Wrappers. London, 1926. First edition. One of 500. $100–$125.

LAWRENCE, D. H. *Kangaroo*. Brown cloth. London, (1923). First edition. In dust jacket. $50–$75. New York, 1923. Blue cloth. First American edition. In dust jacket. $40–$60. Paris, (1933). Wrappers. One of 67. $75.

LAWRENCE, D. H. *Lady Chatterley's Lover*. Mulberry boards, paper spine label. (Florence, Italy), 1928. First edition. One of 1,000 signed. In plain dust jacket. $1,000–$1,250. Paris, (1950). Color plates, text drawings. Loose leaves in wrappers. One of 100 on vellum. Boxed. $500–$750.

LAWRENCE, D. H. *The Ladybird, etc.* Brown cloth. London, (1923). First edition (of a book published later in America as *The Captain's Doll*). In dust jacket. $150–$200.

LAWRENCE, D. H. *Last Poems*. Edited by Richard Aldington and G. Orioli. Frontispiece in color. Boards, paper label. Florence, 1932. First edition. One of 750. In dust jacket. Boxed. $300–$350. London, 1933. Boards and cloth. First English edition. In dust jacket. $75–$125. New York, 1933. Blue-green cloth. First American edition. In dust jacket. $75–$125.

LAWRENCE, D. H. *The Letters of D. H. Lawrence*. Edited by Aldous Huxley. Plates. Vellum. London, (1932). First edition. One of 525. In slipcase. $150–$225. Trade issue: Cloth. In dust jacket. $35–$50. Second edition. Same date. Cloth. In dust jacket. $25–$30.

LAWRENCE, D. H. *Look! We Have Come Through!* Bright-red cloth. London, 1917. First edition. In dust jacket. $200–$300. New York, 1919. Cloth. First American edition. In dust jacket. $150–$200.

LAWRENCE, D. H. *The Lost Girl*. Brown cloth. London, (1920). First edition, first issue, with pages 256 and 268 not tipped in and with page 268 reading "whether she noticed anything in the bedrooms, in the beds." In dust jacket. $350–$500. Second issue, pages 256 and 268 tipped in. In dust jacket. $150–$250. New York, 1921. Cloth. First American edition. In dust jacket. $100–$125.

LAWRENCE, D. H. *Love Among the Haystacks*. Cloth. London, 1930. Nonesuch Press. One of 1,600. In dust jacket. $100–$135.

LAWRENCE, D. H. *Love Poems and Others*. Dark-blue cloth. London, 1913. First edition, first binding, smooth blue buckram. In dust jacket. $400–$500.

LAWRENCE, D. H. *The Lovely Lady*. Cloth. London, 1933. First edition. In dust jacket. $75–$125.

LAWRENCE, D. H. *The Man Who Died*. Buckram. London, 1931. First English edition (of a book first published in Paris, 1929, as *The Escaped Cock*). $125–$150.

LAWRENCE, D. H. *Mornings in Mexico*. Cloth. London, 1927. First edition. In dust jacket. $250–$300. New York, 1927. Cloth. In dust jacket. $200–$250.

LAWRENCE, D. H. *My Skirmish with Jolly Roger*. Boards. New York, 1929. First edition. One of 600. In tissue dust jacket. $75–$150.

LAWRENCE, D. H. *Nettles*. Boards or cloth. London, 1930. First edition. $85–$100.

LAWRENCE, D. H. *New Poems*. Gray wrappers. London, 1918. First edition. $200–$250. New York, 1920. Boards, paper labels. First American edition. $80–$100.

LAWRENCE, D. H. *An Original Poem*. With a note by Catherine Carswell. Printed wrappers. (England), 1934. First edition. (150 printed.) $200–$250. Another issue (?): Signed by Carswell. $300.

LAWRENCE, D. H. *The Paintings of D. H. Lawrence*. 26 colored plates. Folio, half morocco and green cloth. London, (1929). Mandrake Press. First edition. One of 500. $800–$1,000. Another issue: One of 10 on Japan paper. $2,000–$3,000.

LAWRENCE, D. H. *Pansies*. Boards and cloth. London, (1929). First edition. In dust jacket. $100–$150. Limited issue: Boards. One of 250 signed. In dust jacket. $400–$500. Another (later) edition, same place and date: White wrappers. "Definitive and Complete Edition." Portrait frontispiece. One of 500 signed. In glassine dust jacket. Boxed. $400–$450. Another issue: Limp leather. One of 50. $800–$1,000. Another issue: Pink wrappers. (Not signed.) $100–$150. New York, 1929. First American edition. In dust jacket. $75–$100.

LAWRENCE, D. H. *The Plumed Serpent*. Brown cloth. London, (1926). First edition. In dust jacket. $125. New York, 1926. Cloth. In dust jacket. $125.

LAWRENCE, D. H. *A Prelude*. Cloth, leather spine. Surrey, England, 1949. Merle Press. First edition. One of 100. $100–$125.

LAWRENCE, D. H. *The Prussian Officer and Other Stories*. Blue cloth. London, (1914). First edition, first variant, with 20 pages of ads at back. In dust jacket. $1,000. Without jacket, $350–$500. Second issue, with 16 pages of ads. In dust jacket. $750. New York, 1914. Cloth. In dust jacket. $75–$85.

LAWRENCE, D. H. *Psychoanalysis and the Unconscious*. Gray boards. New York, 1921. First edition. In dust jacket. $200–$275. London, 1923. First English edition. In jacket. $150–$200.

LAWRENCE, D. H. *The Rainbow*. Blue-green cloth. London, (1915). First edition, with ads dated "Autumn, 1914." In dust jacket. $2,500–$2,750. Variant issue: Red cloth. Colonial Library Edition. In dust jacket. $2,000. Also, $2,200 (A, 1977). New York, 1916. Cloth. First American edition. In dust jacket. $150–$200. Stockholm, 1942. Printed yellow wrappers. Pirated edition. $40–$60.

LAWRENCE, D. H. *Rawdon's Roof*. Decorated boards. London, 1928. First edition. One of 530 signed. In dust jacket. $250–$300.

LAWRENCE, D. H. *Reflections on the Death of a Porcupine and Other Essays.* Marbled boards, canvas spine. Philadelphia, 1925. Centaur Press. First edition. One of 925. Boxed. $175–$200.

LAWRENCE, D. H. *St. Mawr.* (With "The Princess.") Brown cloth. London, (1925). First edition. In dust jacket. $100–$150. New York, 1925. Cloth. First separate edition (without "The Princess"). In dust jacket. $75–$100.

LAWRENCE. D. H. *Sea and Sardinia.* 8 colored plates. Boards and cloth. New York, 1921. First edition. In dust jacket. $200–$250. London, 1923. Cloth. First English edition. In dust jacket. $150–$200.

LAWRENCE, D. H. *Sons and Lovers.* Dark-blue cloth. London, (1913). First edition, first issue, without date on title page. In dust jacket. $1,000, possibly more. Second state, with dated title page tipped in. In dust jacket. $750–$1,000. Also, $650 (A, 1977). New York, 1913. Purple cloth. First American edition. In dust jacket. $200–$275.

LAWRENCE, D. H. *Studies in Classic American Literature.* Blue cloth. New York, 1923. First edition. In dust jacket. $300–$400.

LAWRENCE, D. H. *Sun.* Marbled wrappers. London, 1926. First edition. One of 100. $750–$850. Paris, 1928. Black Sun Press. Wrappers. First unexpurgated edition. One of 150. In dust jacket. Boxed. $600–$800. Another issue: One of 15 on vellum. In glassine dust jacket. Boxed. $1,500 and up. London, 1928. Boards and cloth. In dust jacket. $100–$150.

LAWRENCE, D. H. *Tortoises.* Pictorial boards. New York, 1921. First edition. In dust jacket. $200–$250.

LAWRENCE, D. H. *Touch and Go.* Flexible orange boards, paper labels. London, 1920. First edition. In dust jacket. $150–$200. New York, 1920. Orange boards. First American edition. In dust jacket. $75–$125.

LAWRENCE, D. H. *The Trespasser.* Dark-blue cloth. London, 1912. First edition, with 20 pages of ads at end. $350–$500. New York, 1912. Cloth. First American edition. $200–$250.

LAWRENCE, D. H. *Twilight in Italy.* Blue cloth. London, (1916). First edition. In dust jacket. $400–$500.

LAWRENCE, D. H. *The Virgin and the Gipsy.* White boards, paper label. Florence, 1930. First edition. One of 810. In dust jacket. Boxed. $300–$350. London, (1930). Cloth. First English edition. In dust jacket. $75–$125.

LAWRENCE, D. H. *The White Peacock.* Blue cloth. New York, 1911. First edition, first issue, with integral title page and 1910 copyright date. $6,000–$8,500, possibly more. Also, $3,250 (A, 1972). Second issue, with a tipped-in title page and 1911 copyright date. $1,500–$2,500. Also, $1,100 (A, 1977). London, 1911. Dark blue-green cloth. First English edition, first issue, with publisher's windmill device on back cover and with pages 227–228 and 229–230 not tipped in. $750–$1,000. With leaves tipped in, $600. Author's first book.

LAWRENCE, D. H. *The Widowing of Mrs. Holroyd.* Red cloth. New York, 1914. First edition. In dust jacket. $350–$400. London, 1914. Cloth. First English edition. In dust jacket. $200–$300.

LAWRENCE, D. H. *The Woman Who Rode Away.* Brown cloth. London, (1928). First edition. In dust jacket. $200–$250.

LAWRENCE, D. H. *Women in Love.* Dark blue cloth. New York, 1920. First edition. (1,250 copies.) One of about 18 to 25 signed by Lawrence. In dust jacket. $2,500–$3,000. Unsigned copies, $150–$200. New York, 1920 (actually 1922). Brown boards. First English edition, limited. One of 50 signed. (Copies from the American sheets, issued for the British trade.) $2,000–$2,500. London, (1921). Brown cloth. First English trade edition. In dust jacket. $100–$125.

LAWRENCE, D. H. (translator). *The Story of Dr. Manente.* By A. F. Grazzini. Frontispiece, 2 plates. Parchment boards. Florence, (1929). First edition. One of 200 signed by Lawrence. In tissue jacket. $500–$650. Another issue: One of 1,000. In dust jacket. $75–$100.

LAWRENCE, Frieda. *"Not I, But the Wind."* Boards and cloth. Santa Fe, N.M., 1934. First edition. One of 1,000 signed. In dust jacket. $125–$150. London, 1935. Cloth. First English edition. In dust jacket. $50–$75.

LAWRENCE of Arabia. (Two essays: "The Artist in War and Letters," by B. H. Liddell Hart, and "Himself," by Ronald Storrs.) Boards, and cloth. (London, 1936.) Corvinus Press. First edition. One of 25 on Barcham Green "Boswell" paper (of an edition of 128, signed). $400 and up. Another issue: One of 70. $288 (A, 1972). Another: One of 12 on hand-made paper, printed for Storrs. $384 (A, 1973).

LAWRENCE, Richard Hoe (compiler). *History of the Society of Iconophiles of the City of New York.* Reproductions of 119 plates. Boards and morocco. New York, 1930. First edition. One of 186. $75–$100.

LAWRENCE, T. E. See Graves, Robert; Homer; Shaw, T. E. Also see *The Seven Pillars of Wisdom.*

LAWRENCE, T. E. *Crusader Castles.* Portraits and facsimiles, 2 maps in envelope. 2 vols., half red morocco. London, 1936. Golden Cockerel Press. First edition. One of 1,000. $750–$1,000.

LAWRENCE, T. E. *The Diary of T. E. Lawrence.* Illustrated. Boards and morocco. London, 1937. Corvinus Press. First edition. One of 203. $1,000–$1,250. Another issue: Morocco. One of 30 on Canute paper. Boxed. $2,000 and up. Another: Limp vellum. One of 40 on Medway paper. Boxed. $1,500–$2,000.

LAWRENCE, T. E. *Eight Letters.* Edited by H. Granville-Barker. Wrappers. London, 1939. First edition. One of 50. $1,000–$1,500.

LAWRENCE, T. E. *An Essay on Flecker.* Buckram. London, 1937. Corvinus Press. First edition. One of 30. $1,500 and up. New York, 1937. Printed wrappers. First American edition. One of about 50 for copyright purposes. $1,400 (A, 1977).

LAWRENCE, T. E. *Letter to His Mother.* Plates. Boards. London, 1936. Corvinus Press. First edition. One of 24. $1,500 and up.

LAWRENCE, T. E. *Letters.* Edited by David Garnett. Maps and plates. Buckram. London, 1938. First edition. In dust jacket. $75–$110.

LAWRENCE, T. E. *Letters from T. E. Shaw to Bruce Rogers* [and] *More Letters to Bruce Rogers.* 2 vols., limp buckram. No place, 1933–36. First editions. Limited to 200 and 300, respectively. $1,250–$1,500.

LAWRENCE, T. E. *Men in Print.* Half morocco. (London, 1940.) Golden Cockerel Press. First edition. One of 500. $350–$400. Another issue: Morocco. One of 30 specially bound with supplement. Boxed. $1,000–$1,500.

LAWRENCE, T. E. *Minorities.* Edited by J. M. Wilson. Preface by C. Day-Lewis. Frontispiece portrait. Half calf, leather label. London, 1971. One of 125 signed by Day-Lewis. In glassine dust jacket. $200–$250.

LAWRENCE, T. E. *The Mint: A Day-book of the R.A.F. Depot Between August and December, 1922.* Leather and blue cloth. London, (1955). First published edition. One of 2,000. Boxed. $150–$200. Trade edition: Cloth. In dust jacket. $50–$75.

LAWRENCE, T. E. *Revolt in the Desert.* Frontispiece, map, and portraits. Buckram. London, 1927. First edition. In dust jacket. $75–$100. Another issue: Half morocco. One of 315 on large paper. $250–$350. New York, 1927. Illustrated. Cloth. First American edition. In dust jacket. $25. Another issue: Buckram. One of 250. $150–$200.

LAWRENCE, T. E. *Secret Despatches from Arabia.* Portrait frontispiece. Morocco and cloth. London, (1939). Golden Cockerel Press. First edition. One of 1,000. $400–$600. Another issue: White pigskin. One of 30 with part of the manuscript of *The Seven Pillars of Wisdom.* $1,500–$2,000.

LAWRENCE, T. E. *Seven Pillars of Wisdom.* 66 plates, other illustrations, 4 folding maps. Full leather. (London), 1926. First edition, inscribed "Complete" and signed "T.E.S." (for T. E. Shaw, Lawrence's adopted name). $6,000–$7,500. Ordinary edition: One of 500. $750–$1,000. (For first American copyright edition, one of only two copies, with no author named, see title entry.) London, (1935). Buckram and leather. First published edition. One of 750. In dust jacket. Boxed. $300–$500. Trade edition: Buckram. In dust jacket. $75–$85. Garden City, 1935. Buckram and leather. First published American edition. Limited. In dust jacket. Boxed. $300–$350. Trade edition: Cloth. In dust jacket. $35–$50.

LAWRENCE, T. E. *Shaw-Ede: T. E. Lawrence's Letters to H. S. Ede.* 7 pp. of facsimiles. Morocco. London, 1942. Golden Cockerel Press. One of 500. $400–$500. Another issue: One of 30 specially bound. $1,500 and up.

LAWRENCE, W. J. *The Elizabethan Playhouse and Other Studies.* 30 plates. 2 vols., boards and cloth. Stratford-on-Avon, England, 1912–13. Shakespeare Head Press. One of 760. $100–$150.

LAWS and Decrees of the State of Coahuila and Texas, in Spanish and English. Calf. Houston, 1839. $500–$750.

LAWS and Regulations of Union District, Clear Creek County, C.T. 19 pp., printed wrappers. Central, C.T. (Colorado Territory), 1864. $600–$750. Also, $350 (A, 1968).

LAWS for the Better Government of California. 68 pp. San Francisco, 1848. Only two copies known of this first English book printed in California. $5,000 or more (?).

LAWS of the Cherokee Nation. Half leather. Tahlequah, Indian Territory, 1852. English language edition. $1,350 in a 1981 catalogue.

LAWS of the Choctaw Nation, Made and Enacted by the General Council from 1886 to 1890. (In English and Choctaw.) Cloth. Atoka, Indian Territory, 1890. One of 250. $200–$400.

LAWS OF Gregory District, February 18 & 20, 1860. (Cover title.) 12 pp., printed wrappers. Denver, 1860. $1,000–$1,250. Also, $600 (A, 1968).

LAWS of the Territory of Kansas, Passed at the 2d Session of the General Legislative Assembly. Cloth. Lecompton, (1857). $125–$150.

LAWS of the Territory of Louisiana (The). Sheep. St. Louis, 1808 (actually 1809). $10,000 and up. Also, $8,000 (A, 1967).

LAWS of the Territory of New Mexico. 71 pp., wrappers. Santa Fe, N.M., 1862. $250–$300.

LAWS of the Town of San Francisco (The). 8 pp., wrappers. San Francisco, 1847. First edition. $1,000 and up. Also, an imperfect copy (lacking pages 5-8) in board binder, $1,000 (A, 1968).

LAWS Relating to Internal Improvement in the State of Michigan. 16 pp., sewed. Detroit, 1837. $75–$100.

LAWYERS and Legislators, or Notes on the American Mining Companies. Half calf. London, 1825. (By Benjamin Disraeli.) First edition. $150 and up.

LAY, William, and Hussey, Cyrus M. *A Narrative of the Mutiny on Board the Ship Globe of Nantucket.* Calf. New-London, Conn., 1828. First edition. $600–$800.

LAYARD, Georges. *George Cruikshank's Portraits of Himself.* Illustrated. Vellum and cloth. London, 1897. First edition. One of 250 large paper copies signed by Layard. $150–$200.

LAYNE, J. Gregg. *Annals of Los Angeles*. Plates. Cloth. San Francisco, 1935. First edition. $50–$75.

LAZARUS, Emma. *Poems and Translations*. Cloth. New York, 1867. First edition. $100 and up. Author's first book.

LAZARUS, Emma. *Songs of a Semite*. Cloth. New York, 1882. First edition. $100–$150.

LEA, Albert M. *Notes on the Wisconsin Territory*. Folding map. 53 pp., printed boards. Philadelphia, 1836. First edition. $750–$1,000.

LEA, Homer. *The Vermilion Pencil*. Cloth. New York, 1908. First edition. In dust jacket. $50.

LEA, Pryor. *An Outline of the Central Transit, in a Series of Six Letters to Hon. John Hemphill*. 32 pp., printed wrappers. Galveston, 1859. First edition. $75–$150.

LEA, Tom. *Calendar of the Twelve Travelers Through the Pass of the North*. Illustrated. Folio, cloth. El Paso, Tex., 1946. Carl Hertzog printing. First edition. One of 365 signed. In dust jacket. $500–$750.

LEA, Tom. *The King Ranch*. Illustrated by the author. 2 vols., buckram. Boston, (1957). First edition. Boxed. $125–$150. Another issue: Limited "Private Edition," printed on paper watermarked with running "W" brand. 2 vols., decorated crash linen. Boxed. $500–$800.

LEA, Tom. *Peleliu Landing*. Illustrated. Green cloth. El Paso, 1945. Carl Hertzog printing. One of 500 signed. In glassine dust jacket. $850–$1,000.

LEA, Tom. *Randado*. Illustrated. Stiff wrappers. (El Paso, 1941.) Carl Hertzog printing. First edition. One of 100 signed. $500–$1,000.

LEACH, A. J. *Early Day Stories: The Overland Trail, etc.* 7 plates. Brown cloth. (Norfolk, Neb., 1916.) First edition. In dust jacket. $50–$75.

LEACOCK, Stephen. *Canada: The Foundations of Its Future*. 31 full-page illustrations. Cloth. Montreal, 1941. First edition. Boxed. $125–$150. Also issued in morocco.

LEACOCK, Stephen. *Literary Lapses: A Book of Sketches*. Half linen, green boards, spine label. Montreal, 1910. First edition. In dust jacket. $100–$125. Author's first book of humor (preceded by a 1906 political work).

LEACOCK, Stephen. *Nonsense Novels*. Cloth. London, 1911. First edition. In dust jacket. $75–$100. New York, 1911. Cloth. First American edition. In dust jacket. $100–$125. Montreal, 1911. Green cloth. First Canadian edition. In dust jacket. $150. London, 1921. Illustrated by John Kettlewell, including 8 color plates. Cloth. First illustrated edition. In dust jacket. $75–$100.

LEACOCK, Stephen. *Sunshine Sketches of a Little Town*. Colored frontispiece. Cloth. London, 1912. First edition. In dust jacket. $100–$125.

LEADBEATER, Mary. *Cottage Dialogues Among the Irish Peasantry*. Edited by Maria Edgeworth. Illustrated. 2 vols., boards, paper labels. London, 1811, and Dublin, 1813. First editions. $200–$300.

LEADVILLE Chronicle Annual. 40 pp., wrappers. Leadville, Colo., 1881. $150–$200.

LEADVILLE, Colorado: The Most Wonderful Mining Camp in the World. 44 pp., printed wrappers. Colorado Springs, 1879. (By John L. Loomis.) $300–$350.

LEAF, Munro. *The Story of Ferdinand*. Illustrated by Robert Lawson. Pink decorated boards, cloth spine. New York, 1936. First edition. In dust jacket. $400–$600.

LEAF, Munro. *Wee Gillis*. Illustrated by Robert Lawson. Burlap, paper labels. New York, 1938. First edition. One of 525 signed. Boxed. $175–$300. Trade edition: Boards. In dust jacket. $65.

LEAR, Edward. See Derry, Derry down.

LEAR, Edward. *A Book of Nonsense.* Illustrated. Oblong, stiff wrappers. London, 1855. Second (and enlarged) edition. $1,500–$2,000. (For first edition, see entry under Lear's pen name Derry down Derry.)

LEAR, Edward. *Calico Pie.* Illustrated by the author. Glazed boards. London, no date. First edition. $150–$250.

LEAR, Edward. *Illustrated Excursions in Italy.* Map, 30 plates. 2 vols., folio, cloth. London, 1846. First edition. $1,000 and up.

LEAR, Edward. *Illustrations of the Family Psittacidae, or Parrots.* 42 hand-colored plates. Folio, half morocco. London, 1830–32. First edition. $10,000–$12,000.

LEAR, Edward. *Journal of a Landscape Painter in Corsica.* Illustrated. Cloth. London, 1870. First edition. $500–$600.

LEAR, Edward. *Journals of a Landscape Painter in Albania.* Map. Illustrated in color. Cloth. London, 1851. First edition. $500–$750.

LEAR, Edward. *Journals of a Landscape Painter in Southern Calabria.* 2 maps. Illustrated. Cloth. London, 1852. First edition. $500–$600.

LEAR, Edward. *Laughable Lyrics.* Illustrated. Cloth. London, 1877. First edition. $200–$300.

LEAR, Edward. *More Nonsense, Pictures, Rhymes, Botany, etc.* Illustrated. Boards and linen. London, 1872 (actually 1874). First edition. $350–$400.

LEAR, Edward. *A Nonsense Birthday Book.* Pictorial cloth. London, (after 1872). First edition. $150–$200.

LEAR, Edward. *Nonsense Songs, Stories, Botany, and Alphabets.* Illustrated. Boards and cloth. London, 1871. First edition. $250–$350. Boston, 1871. Illustrated. Boards. First American edition. $250–$300.

LEAR, Edward. *Views in Rome and Its Environs.* Illustrated (plates in sepia). Folio, half morocco. London, 1841. First edition. $1,000–$1,250. Plates hand-colored. $1,500 and up.

LEAR, Edward. *Views in the Seven Ionian Islands.* Illustrated. Folio, cloth. London, 1863. First edition. $2,500– $3,000.

LEATHER Stocking and Silk. Cloth. New York, 1854. (By John Esten Cooke.) First edition. $250–$300. Author's first book.

LEAVES from Margaret Smith's Journal. Cloth, or wrappers. Boston, 1849. (By John Greenleaf Whittier.) First edition. Wrappers: $100–$125. Cloth: $75–$100.

LEAVES of Grass. Portrait frontispiece on plain paper. Dark-green cloth, gilt- and blind-stamped, marbled end papers. Brooklyn, 1855. (By Walt Whitman.) First edition, first issue, without ads or reviews; first binding, gilt lettering and borders on both covers. $10,000–$15,000. Prices at auction for good to fine first-issue copies ranged up to $9,000 through the 1970s and into 1981. Recent auction examples: Binding tightened, spine repaired, $5,000 (1981); spine torn, title page foxed, $6,500 (1980); some pages spotted and browned, $7,000 (1980). Worn copies have been available occasionally at retail prices ranging from a few thousand dollars up to $7,500. Second issue, plain yellow end papers, no gold on back cover. $2,400 (A, 1978). Third issue, same as second but with ads or press notices bound in. $2,000. Brooklyn, 1856. Cloth. Second edition, with ad leaf of Fowler & Wells, the publisher, at back of the book. $2,000 and up. Worn, $1,500. Boston, "Year '85 of the States" (1860–61). Third edition, first issue, with "George C. Rand & Avery" on copyright page, portrait on tinted paper, orange-colored (or brick-red) cloth. $300. Second issue, same date, has portrait on white paper. Same value. Third issue (first pirated issue), without the Rand & Avery notice. $100 and up. New York, 1867. Half morocco or cloth. Fourth edition, with "Ed'n 1867" stamped on back in gold. (Several variant issues, for which see Wells and

Goldsmith, *A Concise Bibliography of the Works of Whitman.*) $200 and up. Washington, 1871. Wrappers, or half morocco. Fifth edition. $1,000 and up. Later in 1871: *Leaves of Grass, Passage to India.* Green wrappers. $50–$100. Camden, 1876. Half cream-colored calf and marbled boards. Sixth edition. "Author's edition," signed. $1,000–$1,200. (For variants, see Wells and Goldsmith, cited above.) Boston, 1881–82. Yellow cloth. Seventh edition, first issue (very rare), with "Third edition" on title page (suppressed). $750–$1,000. Second issue, without "Third Edition" on title page. $150 and up. London, 1881. (Reissue of the suppressed Boston sheets.) $145. Camden, 1882. Dark-green cloth. "Author's Edition," signed. $600 and up. Philadelphia, 1882. Yellow cloth. "First Philadelphia edition," with Whitman's name on cover. $200 and up. Philadelphia, 1884. Yellow cloth. Seventh edition, later issue, with McKay imprint. $200 and up. Philadelphia, 1889. Limp black morocco. One of 300 signed. 70th Birthday Edition. $500 and up. Philadelphia, 1891–92. First issue, brown wrappers. $1,000 and up. Later issue: Dark-green cloth or gray wrappers. $500 and up. Portland, Me., 1919. Mosher Press. Cloth. One of 400. $100 and up. There were also several other issues of this edition: Boards (250 copies). $100 and up; (100 copies), $150 and up; (50 copies on vellum), $200–$300. New York, 1930. Grabhorn printing. 37 woodcuts. Leather-backed mahogany boards. One of 400. $1,250–$1,500. New York, 1942. Limited Editions Club. Edward Weston photographs. 2 vols., boards. $750–$1,000. Worn, $400 in a 1981 catalogue. Mount Vernon, N.Y., (1943). Peter Pauper Press. Half morocco. One of 1,100. $200–$300.

LEAVES of Grass Imprints: American and European Criticisms of "Leaves of Grass." 64 pp., printed brown wrappers. Boston, 1860. First edition. $500–$600.

LEBRIJA, Joaquin, and Berrera, Ignacio. *Análisis e Impugnacion del Proyectô de le Sobre Arbitrios para la Guerra de Tejas.* 31 pp., sewed. Mexico, 1841. $200–$400.

LECKENBY, Charles H. (compiler). *The Tread of Pioneers.* Illustrated. Cloth. Steamboat Springs, Colo., (1945). First edition. $75–$100.

LE CARRE, John. *The Spy Who Came in from the Cold.* Boards. London, 1963. First edition. In dust jacket. $125–$200.

LE CONTE, Joseph. *A Journal of Ramblings Through the High Sierras of California.* 9 mounted photos. Blue cloth. San Francisco, 1875. First edition. $1,500–$2,000.

LE DUC, W. G. *Minnesota Year Book and Traveller's Guide for 1851.* Folding map. Boards, leather spine. St. Paul, (1851). First year of issue. $200–$250. Other issues: For 1852, with frontispiece plate. $100. For 1853, folding map. $50–$100.

LEDYARD, John. See *The Adventures of a Yankee.*

LEE, Andrew. *The Indifferent Children.* Cloth. New York, (1947). (By Louis Auchincloss.) First edition. In dust jacket. $75–$100. Author's first book.

LEE, Fred J. *Casey Jones: Epic of the American Railroad.* Cloth. Kingsport, Tenn., (1939). First edition. In dust jacket. $35.

LEE, Harper. *To Kill a Mockingbird.* Wrappers. Philadelphia, (1960). First edition. Advance reading copy. $175–$200. Trade edition: Boards. In dust jacket. $100–$125. London, (1960). Cloth. First English edition. In dust jacket. $50–$75.

LEE, Maj. Henry, Jr. *The Campaign of 1781 in the Carolinas.* Calf. Philadelphia, 1824. First edition. $175–$250.

LEE, John D. *J. D. Lee's Bekjendelse.* 36 pp., wrappers. Salt Lake City, 1877. $100–$125.

LEE, John D. *The Journals of John D. Lee, 1846–47 and 1859.* Edited by Charles Kelly. Cloth. Salt Lake City, 1938. First edition. One of 250. In dust jacket. $75–$100.

LEE, L. P. (editor). *History of the Spirit Lake Massacre!* (Cover title.) Illustrated. 48 pp., pictorial wrappers. New Britain, Conn., 1857. First edition. $75–$100.

LEE, Nelson. *Three Years Among the Camanches.* 2 plates (including portrait title page). Wrappers, or cloth. Albany, N.Y., 1859. First edition. $1,750, possibly more.

LEE, Susan P. *Memoirs of William Nelson Pendleton*. Portrait. Cloth. Philadelphia, 1893. First edition. $75–$100.

LEE, William, *Junkie*. (and) Helbrant, Maurice, *Narcotic Agent*. Back-to-back in pictorial wrappers. New York, (1953). Ace Books. First edition. $75–$125. (*Junkie* is by William Burroughs. Burroughs' first book.)

LEE Trial (The)! An Exposé of the Mountain Meadows Massacre. 64 pp., printed wrappers. Salt Lake City, 1875. First edition. $850–$1,000.

LEECH, John. *Follies of the Year*. 21 hand-colored plates. Oblong, leather-backed cloth. London, (1864). First collected edition. $250–$400. London, (about 1865). $150–$200.

LEECH, John. *Hunting: Incidents of the Noble Science*. 13 color plates. Oblong, half cloth portfolio. London, 1865. First edition. $1,000 and up. Also, $800 (A, 1977).

LEECH, John. *Mr. Briggs and His Doings: Fishing*. 12 color plates. Oblong, wrappers. London, (1860). First edition. $1,000–$1,200.

LEECH, John. *Portraits of Children of the Nobility*. Illustrated. Cloth. London, 1841. First edition. $400–$600.

LEECH, John. *The Rising Generation*. 12 color plates. Folio, boards and morocco. London, 1848. First edition. $750–$1,000.

LEEPER, David Rohrer. *The Argonauts of Forty-nine*. Illustrated. Cloth. South Bend, 1894. First edition. $75–$100.

LEESE, Jacob P. *Historical Outline of Lower California*. 46 pp., printed wrappers. New York, 1865. First edition. $150–$175.

LE FANU, Joseph Sheridan. See *The Fortunes of Colonel Torlogh O'Brien*.

LE FANU, Joseph Sheridan. *All in the Dark*. 2 vols., cloth. London, 1866. First edition. $250–$350.

LE FANU, Joseph Sheridan. *Checkmate*. 3 vols., cloth. London, 1871. First edition. $350–$450.

LE FANU, Joseph Sheridan. *Chronicles of Golden Friars*. 3 vols., cloth. London, 1871. First edition. $300–$400.

LE FANU, Joseph Sheridan. *The Evil Guest*. Illustrated. Green cloth. London, (1895). First edition, with March ads. $400.

LE FANU, Joseph Sheridan. *Ghost Stories and Tales of Mystery*. Illustrated by "Phiz." Cloth. Dublin, 1851. First edition. $500–$600.

LE FANU, Joseph Sheridan. *Green Tea and Other Ghost Stories*. Cloth. Sauk City, Wis., 1945. First edition. In dust jacket. $125–$150.

LE FANU, Joseph Sheridan. *Guy Deverell*. 3 vols., cloth. London, 1865. First edition. $600–$750.

LE FANU, Joseph Sheridan. *Haunted Lives*. 3 vols., cloth. London, 1868. First edition. $500–$600.

LE FANU, Joseph Sheridan. *The House by the Churchyard*. 3 vols., cloth. London, 1863. First edition. $400–$650. Second edition, same date. 3 vols., in one, cloth. $150–$200.

LE FANU, Joseph Sheridan. *In a Glass Darkly*. 3 vols., cloth. London, 1872. First edition. $400–$500.

LE FANU, Joseph Sheridan. *Madame Crowl's Ghost and Other Tales of Mystery*. Cloth. London, 1923. First edition. In dust jacket. $250.

LE FANU, Joseph Sheridan. *The Purcell Papers*. 3 vols., blue-black cloth. London, 1880. First edition. $300–$450.

LE FANU, Joseph Sheridan. *The Rose and the Key*. 3 vols., cloth. London, 1871. First edition. $250–$350.

LE FANU, Joseph Sheridan. *Wylder's Hand*. 3 vols., cloth. London, 1864. First edition. $350–$500.

LE FANU, Joseph Sheridan. *The Wyvern Mystery*. 3 vols., cloth. London, 1869. First edition, $400–$500.

LEFÈVRE, Raoul. *The Recuyell of the Historyes of Troye*. Translated by William Caxton. Edited by H. Halliday Sparling. Woodcut title, borders, and initials. 3 vols in two, folio, limp vellum with ties. London, 1892. Kelmscott Press. One of 300. $1,000–$1,250. Another issue: One of 5 on vellum. $4,000–$5,000.

LE GALLIENNE, Richard. *The Book-Bills of Narcissus*. Wrappers. Derby, England, 1891. First edition. One of 50 on large paper. $75–$100. Ordinary issue: $40–$60.

LE GALLIENNE, Richard. *English Poems*. Boards. London, 1892. First edition. $35. Another issue: One of 150 on large paper, signed. $150.

LE GALLIENNE, Richard. *Limited Editions: A Prose Fancy*. Wrappers. London, 1893. One of 100 signed. Boxed. $75–$125. Trade edition: $45.

LE GALLIENNE, Richard. *My Ladies' Sonnets*. Boards. (Liverpool), 1887. First edition. One of 250 signed. $100–$200. Ordinary issue: $35–$50. Author's first book.

LE GALLIENNE, Richard. *The Quest of the Golden Girl*. Green cloth. Cambridge, 1896. First edition. $50–$75.

LE GALLIENNE, Richard. *Robert Louis Stevenson: An Elegy and Other Poems, Mostly Personal*. Cloth. London, 1895. First edition. One of 500. $50–$75. Another issue: One of 75 on large paper. $50–$75. Boston, 1895. Boards. One of 500. $50–$75.

LE GALLIENNE, Richard. *The Romance of Perfume*. Illustrated by Georges Barbier. Boards. London, 1928. First edition. $150–$200.

LEGENDS of the Conquest of Spain. By the Author of "The Sketch-Book." Green cloth, paper label. Philadelphia, 1835. (By Washington Irving.) First edition. $350 and up. (No recent sales noted.)

LEGGET, Mortimer Dormer. *A Dream of a Modest Prophet*. Green cloth. Philadelphia, 1890. First edition. $50–$75.

LEGION Book (The). Edited by H. Cotton Minchin. Stephen Gooden copperplate of "Mounted Soldier" (self-portrait) on title page, numerous other illustrations, including 9 color plates. Full white pigskin, gilt- and blind-stamped. London, 1929. One of 100 signed by authors and artists, by Edward, Prince of Wales, and by 5 prime ministers. (Gift book published for the Prince of Wales.) $400–$500.

LEGLER, Henry E. *Of Much Love and Some Knowledge of Books*. Chicago, (1912). Caxton Club. One of 354. $100–$125.

LE GUIN, Ursula. *From Elfland to Poughkeepsie*. Wrappers. Portland, 1973. First edition. One of 100 signed. $85–$125.

LE GUIN, Ursula. *The Left Hand of Darkness*. Cloth. New York, (1969). First edition. In dust jacket. $125–$150.

LE GUIN, Ursula. *A Wizard of Earthsea*. Cloth. Berkeley, (1968). First edition. In dust jacket. $100–$150.

LEHMANN, John. *A Garden Revisited and Other Poems*. Cloth. London, 1931. Hogarth Press. First edition. In dust jacket. $60–$75.

LEIBER, Fritz, Jr. *Night's Black Agents*. Cloth. Sauk City, 1947. Arkham House. First edition. In dust jacket. $85–$100. Author's first book.

LEIGH, William R. *The Western Pony*. 6 color plates, with an extra signed plate laid in. Cloth. New York, (1933). First edition. (100 copies.) In dust jacket. $400–$600. Also, $230 (A, 1974).

LEINSTER, Murray. *Sidewise in Time*. Cloth. Chicago, 1950. (By Will F. Jenkins.) First edition. In dust jacket. $85–$125.

LELAND, Charles Godfrey. *Meister Karl's Sketch-Book*. Cloth. Philadelphia, 1855. First edition. $50–$75. Author's first book.

LELAND, Charles Godfrey. *The Union Pacific Railway*. 95 pp., printed wrappers. Philadelphia, 1867. First edition. $75–$125.

LEONARD, H. L. W. *Oregon Territory*. 88 pp., printed blue or buff wrappers. Cleveland, 1846. First edition. $2,500–$3,000. Also, $1,300 (A, 1969). (Note: Only 3 copies known.)

LEONARD, Irving (translator). *The Mercurio Volante of Dan Carlos De Siguenza y Gongora*. Boards. Los Angeles, 1932. One of 665. In dust jacket. $75–$100.

LEONARD, William Ellery. See *Indian Summer*.

LEONARD, William Ellery. *Aesop and Hyssop*. Decorated gray cloth. Chicago, 1912. First edition. $40–$50.

LEONARD, William Ellery. *Glory of the Morning*. Brown printed wrappers. Madison, Wis., 1912. First edition. $50–$100.

LEONARD, William Ellery. *The Lynching Bee and Other Poems*. Green cloth. New York, 1920. First edition. In dust jacket. $40–$50.

LEONARD, William Ellery. *A Son of Earth: Collected Poems*. Portrait frontispiece. Cream boards, paper label. New York, 1928. First edition. One of 35 lettered copies, signed. $50–$100.

LEONARD, William Ellery. *Two Lives*. Cloth. New York, 1925. First published edition. One of 150 signed. $50–$75.

LEONARD, William Ellery (translator). *The Tale of Beowulf*. Illustrated by Rockwell Kent. Folio, cloth. New York, 1932. First edition. One of 950. $150–$250.

LEONARD, Zenas. *Narrative of the Adventures of Zenas Leonard*. 87 pp., wrappers. Clearfield, Pa., 1839. First edition. $10,000–$12,000. Also, rebound in three-quarters leather and marbled boards, $6,250 (A, 1968); in morocco, tears in 5 leaves repaired, $5,500 (A, 1966); in half morocco, title page repaired, $5,000 (A, 1964). Cleveland, 1904. Illustrated. Cloth. One of 520. $100–$125.

LEROUX, Gaston. *The Phantom of the Opera*. Illustrated in color. Cloth. Indianapolis, 1911. First edition. $125.

LEROUX DE LINCY, A. J. V. *Researches Concerning Jean Grolier, His Life and His Library*. Color plates. Full leather. New York, 1907. Grolier Club. One of 300. $300–$400.

LESLIE, Shane. *The Cantab*. Cloth. London, 1925. First edition. In dust jacket. $75–$100. (Suppressed.)

LES ORNEMENS de la Mémoire, ou les Traits Brillans des Poètes François les Plus Célèbres. Boards. Detroit, 1811. (By Pons Augustin Alletz.) First edition, first issue, with "k" instead of "x" in name of printer, A. Coxshaw. $500–$600.

LESSING, Doris. *African Stories*. Cloth. London, (1964). First edition. In dust jacket. $75–$100.

LESSING, Doris. *Briefing for a Descent Into Hell.* Cloth. London, (1971). First edition. In dust jacket. $50–$60.

LESSING, Doris. *The Golden Notebook.* Cloth. London, (1962). First edition. In dust jacket. $100–$135.

LESSING, Doris. *The Grass is Singing.* Cloth. London, (1950). First edition. In dust jacket with Book Society's wraparound band. $275–$350. Also, $180 (A, 1980). Author's first book.

LESSING, Doris. *The Habit of Being.* Cloth. London, 1957. First edition. In dust jacket. $50–$75.

LESSING, Doris. *Martha Quest.* Cloth. London, (1952). First edition. In dust jacket. $75–$125.

LESTER, C. Edwards. *Sam Houston and His Republic.* Portrait (not in all copies), maps. Half calf. New York, 1846. First edition. $300–$400.

LESTER, John C., and Wilson, D. L. *Ku Klux Klan: Its Origin, Growth and Disbandment.* 117 pp., wrappers. Nashville, 1884. First edition. $150–$200.

LETTER from the Secretary of State, Accompanying Certain Laws of the Northwestern and Indian Territories of the United States, etc. 53 pp., sewed. (Washington), 1802. $125–$150.

LETTER of Amerigo Vespucci (The), Describing His Four Voyages to the New World. Hand-colored map and illustrations by Valenti Angelo. Vellum. San Francisco, 1926. Grabhorn Press. One of 250. Boxed. $150–$250. Also, $150 (A, 1973).

LETTER of J.C. Frémont to the Editor of the National Intelligencer, Communicating some General Results of a Recent Winter Expedition Across the Rocky Mountains, etc. 7 pp., binder's cloth. (Washington, 1854.) $100–$200.

LETTERS from the South. 2 vols., printed boards, New York, 1817. (By James Kirke Paulding.) First edition. $100–$150.

LETTERS of Edward, Prince of Wales, 1304–1305. Edited by Hilda Johnstone. Frontispiece. Half leather. London, 1931. Roxburghe Club. $75–$125.

LETTERS of Runnymede (The). Cloth. London, 1836. (By Benjamin Disraeli.) First edition. $250–$350. Worn, bumped, $95.

LETTS, J. M. See *California Illustrated; A Pictorial View of California.*

LEVER, Charles. See Lorrequer, Harry. Also see *The Confessions of Harry Lorrequer.*

LEVER, Charles. *Davenport Dunn.* Illustrated by H. K. Browne ("Phiz"). 20 parts in 21, wrappers. London, 1857–59. First edition. $300–$350.

LEVER, Charles. *The Knight of Gwynne: A Tale of the Time of the Union.* Frontispiece, title page and 38 plates by "Phiz." 20 parts in 19, wrappers. London, 1846–47. $150–$250.

LEVER, Charles. *Luttrell of Arran.* Illustrated. 16 parts in 15, pictorial wrappers. London, 1863–65. First edition. $200–$300.

LEVER, Charles. *The O'Donoghue: A Tale of Ireland.* 13 parts in 11, wrappers. Dublin, 1845. First edition. $300–$500. Dublin, 1845. Red cloth. First book edition, first binding. $150–$200.

LEVER, Charles. *One of Them.* Illustrated by "Phiz." 15 parts in 14, pictorial wrappers. London, 1861. First edition. $300–$500.

LEVER, Charles. *Roland Cashel.* 20 parts in 19, wrappers. London, 1848–49. First edition. $300–$500. London, 1850. Cloth. First book edition. $150–$250.

LEVER, Charles. *Sir Brook Fossbrooke*. 3 vols., blue cloth. Edinburgh, 1866. First edition, first binding, with publisher's imprint on spine. $400–$500. Rebound in leather, $195.

LEVERTOFF (LEVERTOV), Denise. *The Double Image*. Cloth. London, 1946. Cresset Press. First edition. In dust jacket. $200–$250. Author's first book. Also, $140 (A, 1980).

LEVERTOV, Denise. *The Cold Spring and Other Poems*. Boards. (New York), 1968 (actually 1969). New Directions. First edition. One of 100 signed. In dust jacket. Another issue: One of 8 lettered and signed. Each issue: $125.

LEVERTOV, Denise. *Here and Now*. Wrappers. San Francisco, (1956). First edition. $75.

LEVERTOV, Denise. *In the Night: A Story*. Wrappers. New York, 1968. Albondocani Press. One of 150 signed. $35–$50.

LEVERTOV, Denise. *Life in the Forest*. Cloth. (New York, 1978.) First edition. One of 150 signed. Boxed. $75.

LEVERTOV, Denise. *Overland to the Islands*. Decorated wrappers. Highlands, N.C., 1958. First edition. One of 450. In dust jacket. $40–$50. Another issue: One of 50 signed. $75–$100.

LEVERTOV, Denise. *Three Poems*. Stiff wrappers. Mt. Horeb, Wis., 1968. Perishable Press. One of 250. In dust jacket. $75–$125.

LEVERTOV, Denise. *With Eyes at the Back of our Heads*. Cloth. (New York, 1959.) New Directions. First edition. In dust jacket. $75–$100.

LEVINE, Philip. *The Names of the Lost: Poems*. Cloth. (Iowa City), 1976. First edition. One of 200 signed. $50–$60.

LEVINE, Philip. *On the Edge*. Boards. Iowa City, (1963). Stone Wall Press. First edition. One of 225 signed. $100–$125. Author's first book.

LEVY, Daniel. *Les Français en Californie*. 373 pp., wrappers. San Francisco, 1884. First edition. $150–$200. San Francisco, 1885. Second edition. $100–$125.

LEVY, Julien. *Surrealism*. 64 illustrations. Pictorial boards. New York, 1936. Black Sun Press. First edition. In dust jacket. $125–$150.

LEWIS, Alfred Henry. *The Apaches of New York*. Frontispiece and 10 plates. Red cloth. New York, (1912). First edition. In dust jacket. $40–$50.

LEWIS, Alfred Henry. *The Black Lion Inn*. Frontispiece and 15 plates by Frederic Remington and others. Tan cloth. New York, 1903. First edition, with "Published, May, 1903" on copyright page. In dust jacket. $100–$150. Lacking jacket, $35–$50.

LEWIS, Alfred Henry. *Richard Croker*. Frontispiece and 15 plates. Green cloth. New York, 1901. First edition, first issue, with transposed lines in last paragraph of page 26. $40–$50.

LEWIS, Alfred Henry. *Wolfville*. Frontispiece and 11 plates by Frederic Remington. Cloth. New York, (1897). First edition, first issue, with "Moore" in perfect type in line 18, page 19. $150–$200. (Later printings so identified.) Author's first book.

LEWIS, Alfred Henry. *Wolfville Days*. Frontispiece by Frederic Remington. Red cloth. New York, (1902). First edition. $100–$150.

LEWIS, Elisha J. *The American Sportsman*. Illustrated. Cloth. Philadelphia, 1855. $75–$100. Philadelphia, 1857. $50–$60.

LEWIS, Elisha J. *Hints to Sportsmen*. Cloth. Philadelphia, 1851. First edition. $75–$100.

LEWIS, H. *Das Illustrirte Mississippithal.* Engraved title page, frontispiece, 78 other color plates (one folding.) Boards. Düsseldorf, Germany, (1854–1857). First edition, first issue, with no date on the title page. $13,500 in 1981 catalogue of John Howell: Books, San Francisco.

LEWIS, J. O. *The Aboriginal Port Folio.* 72 colored portraits. 3 advertisements leaves (constituting, with title leaf, all the text). 10 parts, wrappers. Philadelphia, 1836 (actually 1835). First edition. $15,000–$20,000. (A cash sale for $15,000 took place at the 1976 New York International Rare Book Fair.) Incomplete sets are infrequently offered, as, for example, a set of 53 of the plates catalogued late in 1977 by one dealer at $4,500. Howes says that "ordinary" copies have 72 plates, while some have 77 and a few 80. Bound set: Philadelphia, 1835–36. 72 plates. Folio, cloth. Title page missing, some plates torn, rebacked, $4,000 (A, 1978).

LEWIS, John Frederick. *Sketches of Spain and Spanish Character.* Lithograph title page and 25 tinted plates. Folio, half morocco. London, (1836). First edition. $800–$1,000.

LEWIS, Matthew Gregory. See *Tales of Terror.*

LEWIS, Matthew Gregory. *The Isle of Devils.* Marbled boards and gray cloth. London, 1912. Second edition. One of 20 on large paper. $50–$75.

LEWIS, Matthew Gregory. *Journal of a West India Proprietor in the Island of Jamaica.* Cloth. London, 1834. First edition. $200–$250.

LEWIS, Matthew Gregory. *The Life and Correspondence of Matthew Gregory Lewis.* Illustrated. 2 vols., boards. London, 1839. First edition. $250–$300.

LEWIS, Matthew Gregory. *Poems.* Boards, paper label. London, 1812. First edition. $300–$400.

LEWIS, Matthew Gregory. *Romantic Tales.* 4 vols., boards. London, 1808. First edition. $350–$500.

LEWIS, Matthew Gregory. *Tales of Wonder.* 2 vols., boards. London, 1801. First edition. $400–$500. Another issue: 2 vols. on large paper. $500–$600. Dublin, 1801. 2 vols., boards. $300–$400.

LEWIS, Meriwether, and Clark, William. *History of the Expedition Under the Command of Captains Lewis and Clark, etc.* Prepared for the Press by Paul Allen (actually by Nicholas Biddle). Folding map and 5 charts. 2 vols., printed boards. Philadelphia, 1814. First edition. $10,000 (A, 1973)—a badly worn copy; $35,000 (A, 1967)—the exceptionally fine Thomas Winthrop Streeter copy. Previously the highest auction price recorded for this book was $5,200 (1963), earlier prices having ranged from $1,000 to $3,500 (1966) for copies in original binding. Copies rebound in leather: $4,000–$5,000, possibly more. London, 1814. First English edition. (See Lewis and Clark entry under *Travels to the Source of the Missouri River.*) New York, 1842. Folding map. 2 vols., calf. Abridged edition. $200 and up. New York, 1893. Edited by E. Coues. Map. 4 vols., boards and cloth. $300–$400. Chicago, 1902. Edited by James K. Hosmer. 2 vols., cloth. $50–$75. Chicago, 1905. Edited by Hosmer. Cloth. $50–$75.

LEWIS, Meriwether, and Clark, William. *Original Journals of the Lewis and Clark Expedition, 1804–1806.* Edited by Reuben Gold Thwaites. 8 vols., cloth, including atlas of maps and plates. New York, 1904–05. First edition. One of 790. $1,000–$1,250. Another issue: 7 vols. in 14, plus atlas, boards. One of 50 sets on Japan paper. $5,500 (A, 1977). Another issue: One of 200 sets on Van Gelder paper. $800 (A, 1977). New York, 1959–60. 8 vols., cloth. Facsimile of 1904–05 edition. $150–$200. Another issue: One of 15. $500–$600. New York, 1962. 2 vols. Limited Editions Club. $100–$120.

LEWIS, Meriwether, and Clark, William. *Travels to the Source of the Missouri River and Across the American Continent to the Pacific Ocean.* Edited by Thomas Rees. Folding map and 5 charts. Boards and calf. London, 1814. First English edition of *History of the Expedition, etc.* $2,500–$3,000. London, 1815. 6 maps. 3 vols., boards and calf. Second English edition. $300–$450.

LEWIS, Oscar. *Hearn and His Biographers*. Facsimiles. Boards and cloth in portfolio. San Francisco, 1930. Westgate Press (Grabhorn printing). First edition. One of 350. $175–$225.

LEWIS, Oscar. *The Origin of the Celebrated Jumping Frog of Calaveras County*. Decorated by Valenti Angelo. Boards. San Francisco, 1931. Grabhorn Press. One of 250. $100–$150.

LEWIS, Sinclair. See Graham, Tom.

LEWIS, Sinclair. *Arrowsmith*. Blue boards and buckram. New York, (1925). First edition. One of 500 signed. In glassine dust jacket. Boxed. $300–$350. First trade edition with "second printing" on copyright page. Cloth. In dust jacket. $50–$60.

LEWIS, Sinclair. *Babbitt*. Blue cloth. New York, (1922). First edition, first state, with "Purdy" for "Lyte" in line 4, page 49. In dust jacket. $125–$150. London, no date. Purple cloth. First English edition. In dust jacket. $125–$150.

LEWIS, Sinclair. *Cheap and Contented Labor*. Illustrated. 32 pp., pictorial blue wrappers. (New York), 1929. First edition, first state, without quotation marks in front of "Dodsworth" on title page. $100. Later, error corrected. $75.

LEWIS, Sinclair. *Dodsworth*. Cloth. New York, (1929). First edition, with "Published, March, 1929" on copyright page. In dust jacket. $100–$125.

LEWIS, Sinclair. *Elmer Gantry*. Blue cloth. New York, (1927). First edition, first binding with "G" on spine resembling "C" (reading "Elmer Cantry"). In dust jacket. $125–$175. Later binding, corrected. $75–$100.

LEWIS, Sinclair. *Free Air*. Decorated blue cloth. New York, 1919. First edition. In dust jacket. $125–$175.

LEWIS, Sinclair. *The Innocents*. Cloth. New York, (1917). First edition, with "F-R" on copyright page. In dust jacket. $500–$600.

LEWIS, Sinclair. *The Job*. Green cloth. New York, (1917). First edition, with "B-R" on copyright page. In dust jacket. $300–$500.

LEWIS, Sinclair. *Keep Out of the Kitchen*. Printed boards. (New York, 1929.) First edition. (Advertising promotion piece for the story in *Cosmopolitan* magazine.) $650 (A, 1977). Another copy, signed by Lewis, $450 in a 1979 catalogue.

LEWIS, Sinclair. *Kingsblood Royal*. Reddish-brown buckram. New York, (1947). First edition. One of 1,050 signed. Boxed. $100–$150. Trade edition: Cloth. $25.

LEWIS, Sinclair. *Launcelot*. 4 pp., decorated wrappers. (Cambridge, 1932.) First edition in book form. One of 100. $250–$300. (First published in *The Yale Literary Review*.)

LEWIS, Sinclair. *Main Street*. Dark blue cloth. New York, 1920. First edition, first issue, with perfect folio on page 54. In dust jacket. $400–$500. New York, 1937. Limited Editions Club. Grant Wood illustrations. Cloth. Boxed. $100–$125.

LEWIS, Sinclair. *The Man Who Knew Coolidge*. Blue cloth. New York, (1928). First edition. In dust jacket. $100–$150.

LEWIS, Sinclair. *Our Mr. Wrenn*. Cloth. New York, 1914. First edition, with "M-N" on copyright page. In dust jacket. $400–$450. Author's second book and the first under his own name. (For actual first book, see entry under Graham, Tom.)

LEWIS, Sinclair. *The Trail of the Hawk*. Blue cloth. New York, (1915). First edition, with "H-P" on copyright page. In dust jacket. $400–$500. Advance copy: Red cloth wrappers, printed spine label. $700 (A, 1977).

LEWIS, W. S., and Phillips, P. C. (editors). *The Journal of John Work*. Map. Illustrations. Cloth. Cleveland, 1923. First edition. $100–$135.

LEWIS, Wyndham. *The Apes of God*. Illustrated by the author. Light tan cloth. London, 1930. First edition. One of 750 signed. In dust jacket. $300–$400. London, (1931). Cloth. First trade edition. In dust jacket. $100–$125. New York, 1932. Gray cloth. First American edition. In dust jacket. $50–$60. London, (1955). Beige cloth (first binding). 25th Anniversary Edition. One of 1,000 signed. $200.

LEWIS, Wyndham. *The Art of Being Ruled*. Cloth. London, 1926. First edition. In dust jacket. $200–$250.

LEWIS, Wyndham. *Blasting and Bombardiering: Autobiography 1914–1926*. Illustrated. Cloth. London, 1937. First edition. In dust jacket. $150–$175.

LEWIS, Wyndham. *The Caliph's Design*. Boards. London, 1919. The Egoist, Ltd. First edition. $450–$600.

LEWIS, Wyndham. *The Childermass: Section I*. (All published.) Yellow buckram. London, 1928. First edition. One of 225 signed. In dust jacket. $300–$350. Trade edition: Cloth. In dust jacket. $75–$100. New York, 1928. Cloth. First American edition. In dust jacket. $40–$60.

LEWIS, Wyndham. *Count Your Dead: They Are Alive!* Yellow cloth. London, (1937). First edition. In dust jacket. $250–$300.

LEWIS, Wyndham. *The Diabolical Principle and the Dithyrambic Spectator*. Gold-stamped cloth. London, 1931. First edition, first binding. In dust jacket. $200–$250.

LEWIS, Wyndham. *Doom of Youth*. Cloth. London, 1932. First English edition (withdrawn). In dust jacket. $300–$400. New York, 1932. First edition. In dust jacket. $200–$250.

LEWIS, Wyndham. *The Enemy*. Nos. 1–3. (All published.) Illustrated. Pictorial wrappers. London, 1927–29. $350–$450.

LEWIS, Wyndham. *Enemy Pamphlets: No. 1*. Wrappers. London, (1930). $150.

LEWIS, Wyndham. *The Enemy of the Stars*. Illustrated by the author. Pictorial boards and cloth. London, 1932. First edition, first binding, with lettering down instead of up on spine. In dust jacket. $150–$250.

LEWIS, Wyndham. *Hitler*. Cloth. London, 1931. First edition. $250–$350.

LEWIS, Wyndham. *The Ideal Giant*. Boards and cloth. London, (1917). First edition. (About 200.) $350–$450. Author's first written work, a collection of stories.

LEWIS, Wyndham. *Left Wings Over Europe, or, How to Make a War About Nothing*. Cloth. London, (1936). First edition. In dust jacket. $150–$200.

LEWIS, Wyndham. *The Red Priest*. Red cloth. London, (1956). First edition. In dust jacket. $65.

LEWIS, Wyndham. *Tarr*. Cloth. London, 1918. The Egoist, Ltd. Orange-brown cloth. First English edition. In dust jacket. $350–$450. New York, 1918. Cloth. First edition. In dust jacket. $275–$375.

LEWIS, Wyndham. *Thirty Personalities and A Self-Portrait*. 31 plates, loose in buckram and board portfolio. London, (1932). First edition. One of 200 signed. $400–$500.

LEWIS, Wyndham. *Time and Western Man*. Red cloth. London, 1927. First edition. In dust jacket. $250–$350.

LEWIS, Wyndham. *Timon/Athens/Timon/Shakespeare/Timon* (upside down). (Cover title.) 16 illustrations for Shakespeare's "Timon of Athens," without a title page. (London, 1913.) Limited edition, plates laid loose in a folder. $1,500–$2,500. Author's first book (if it can be called a book).

LEWIS, Wyndham. *The Wild Body: A Soldier of Humour and Other Stories*. Decorated boards, cloth spine. London, 1927. First edition. One of 79 signed. In dust jacket.

$400–$600. Trade edition: Orange or red cloth. In cream-colored dust jacket. $125–$175.

LEWIS, Wyndham (editor). *The Tyro*. Nos. 1 and 2. (All published.) Illustrated. Wrappers. London, (1921–22). $300–$400.

LEY y Reglamento Aprobado de la Junta Directiva y Económica del Fondo Piadoso de Californias. 20 pp., calf. Mexico, 1833. $250 and up.

LHOMOND, M. *Elements of French Grammar*. Cloth, paper label. Portland (Brunswick), Me., 1830. (Translated anonymously by Henry Wadsworth Longfellow; Longfellow's first book.) First edition. The only copy noted for sale in many years was a repaired copy, rebound in morocco, sold at auction in 1960 for $200.

LHOMOND, M. *French Exercises*. Purple cloth, paper label. Portland (Brunswick), Me., 1830. (Translated anonymously by Henry Wadsworth Longfellow.) First edition. Rebound in morocco, $100 (A, 1960). (Note: Johnson says that this book and Lhomond's *Elements of French Grammar* were bound as one volume later in 1830 and that the combined book edition of 1831 was "the first book to bear Longfellow's name on the title page.")

LIBER Amoris: or, The New Pygmalion. Pink boards, green cloth spine, paper label on side. London, 1823. (By William Hazlitt.) First edition. $250–$350. London, 1894. Illustrated. Buckram. One of 500. $100–$125.

LIBER Scriptorum: The First Book of the Authors Club. Full morocco. New York, 1893. First edition. One of 251 signed by contributors. $650–$850. *Liber Scriptorum: The Second Book, etc*. New York, 1921. Morocco. One of 251. $150–$200.

LIEBLING, A. J. *Back Where I Came From*. Orange-tan cloth. New York, (1938). First edition. In dust jacket. $200–$250. Author's first book.

LIEBLING, A. J. *Chicago: The Second City*. Illustrated by Steinberg. Pictorial boards. New York, 1952. First edition. In dust jacket. $40–$50.

LIEBLING, A. J. *Mink and Red Herring*. Cloth. Garden City, 1949. First edition. In dust jacket. $50–$75.

LIEBLING, A. J. *The Telephone Booth Indian*. Gray cloth. Garden City, 1942. First edition. In dust jacket. $75–$100.

LIFE Among the Indians. Woodcut plates, 80 pp., colored pictorial wrappers. (New Haven, about 1870.) (By Healy & Bigelow.) Kickapoo Indian medicine promotion pamphlet. $100 and up. (Also, see *Life and Scenes, etc*.)

LIFE and Adventures of Broncho John: His Second Trip up the Trail, by Himself. (Cover title.) Illustrated. 32 pp., pictorial wrappers. (Valparaiso, Ind., 1908.) (By John H. Sullivan.) $125–$150.

LIFE and Adventures of Calamity Jane. By Herself. Portrait. 8 pp., wrappers. Livingston, Mont., (1896). First edition. $300–$400.

LIFE and Adventures of Charles Anderson Chester, the Notorious Leader of the Philadelphia "Killers." Wrappers. Philadelphia, 1850. First edition. $75–$100.

LIFE and Adventures (The) of Joseph T. Hare, the Bold Robber and Highwayman. 16 engravings. Pictorial wrappers. New York, 1847. (By H. R. Howard.) First edition. $100–$150.

LIFE and Adventures of Robert Voorhis, the Hermit of Massachusetts. Portrait. Wrappers. Providence, 1829. First edition, first issue, with "Voorhis" in the title. $275–$350. Later: *Life and Adventures of Robert*. $75–$100.

LIFE, and Most Surprising Adventures of Robinson Crusoe of York, Mariner, etc. (The). Boards. Philadelphia, 1803. (By Daniel Defoe.) $150–$200. London, 1824. Illustrated by George Cruikshank. Calf. $240. (Also, see Defoe entries.)

LIFE and Scenes Among the Kickapoo Indians: Their Manners, Habits and Customs. Portrait, other illustrations. 175 pp., printed wrappers. New Haven, (1839). $100–$125. (Also see *Life Among the Indians.*)

LIFE and Travels of Josiah Mooso (The). Portrait. Cloth. Winfield, Kan., 1888. First edition. $300–$350.

LIFE and Writings of Maj. Jack Downing of Downingville (The), Away Down East in the State of Maine. Boards. Boston, 1833. (By Seba Smith.) First edition. $150–$200.

LIFE for a Life (A). By the Author of "John Halifax, Gentleman," etc. 3 vols., cloth. London, 1859. (By Dinah Maria Mulock.) First edition. $350–$450. Worn and faded, $75.

LIFE in California, etc. By an American. 9 plates. Cloth. New York, 1846. (By Alfred Robinson.) First edition. $300–$400. San Francisco, 1897. Cloth. $75–$100. San Francisco, 1925. Cloth. One of 250. $75–$100.

LIFE in a Man-of-War, etc. By a Fore-Top-Man. Brown cloth. Philadelphia, 1841. (By Henry J. Mercier.) First edition. $100–$150. Boston, 1927. Boards. One of 785. $40–$50.

LIFE in the New World; or Sketches of American Society. Cloth. New York, (1844). (By Karl Postl.) First edition. $100–$125.

LIFE of Col. Edwards. 8 engravings. 31 pp., folded sheets, uncut and unsewed. No place, no date (1842). First edition (?). $1,500. (Adventures of a Texas swindler, catalogued in 1980 as one of two known copies.)

LIFE of Joaquin Murieta the Brigand Chief of California (The). 7 full-page plates. Pictorial wrappers (dated 1861). San Francisco, 1859. (By John R. Ridge.) Second ("spurious") edition. $2,500–$3,000. Also, $1,400 (A, 1968).

LIFE of Major-General Harrison (The). Portrait, plates. Printed boards. Philadelphia, 1840. First edition. $75–$100.

LIFE of MA-KA-TAI-ME-SHE-KIA-KIAK or Black Hawk. Tan boards and cloth. Cincinnati, 1833. (J. B. Patterson, editor.) First edition. $400–$500. Boston, 1834. Pale-green boards. $200–$250. Oquawka, Ill., 1882. Cloth. $75–$100.

LIFE of Saint David (The). Edited by Ernest Rhys. Colored wood engravings. Morocco or vellum. Newtown, Wales, 1927. Gregynog Press. One of 150. $1,000–$1,500. Another issue: One of 25 specially bound by George Fisher. $2,500–$3,000.

LIFE of Stonewall Jackson (The). By a Virginian. Printed wrappers. Richmond, 1863. (By John Esten Cooke.) First edition, with Ayres & Wade imprint. $150–$250.

LIFE, Speeches and Public Services of Abram [sic] Lincoln, Together with a Sketch of the Life of Hannibal Hamlin (The). Portrait. 117 pp., pictorial wrappers. New York, 1860. Wigwam Edition. $150 and up.

LIGHTHALL, William D. (editor). *Songs of the Great Dominion.* Cloth. London, 1889. (By Bliss Carman.) First edition. $50–$60.

LILY and the Totem (The); or, the Huguenots in Florida. Cloth. New York, 1850. (By William Gilmore Simms.) First edition. $100–$150.

LIN, Frank. *What Dreams May Come.* Cloth, or wrappers. Chicago, (1888). (By Gertrude Atherton.) First edition. Wrappers: $300–$400. Cloth: $125–$150. (For first English edition, see author listing.) Author's first book.

LINCOLN, Abraham. *The Life and Public Services of General Zachary Taylor.* Marbled boards. Boston, 1922. First edition. One of 435. $150–$250.

LINCOLN, Abraham, and Douglas, Stephen A. *Political Debates.* Brown rippled, or tan, cloth. Columbus, Ohio, 1860. First edition, first issue, with no ads, no rule on copyright page, and with a "2" at foot of page 17. $200-$300. (Note: Second and later editions of this work differ in various minor details, the principal distinguishing point being the "2" at page 13, instead of 17. For a detailed discussion, see Ernest J. Wessen's pamphlet, *Debates of Lincoln and Douglas: A Bibliographical Discussion.* New York, 1946.)

LINCOLN, Abraham, and Everett, Edward. *The Gettysburg Solemnities: Dedication of the National Cemetery at Gettysburg, Pennsylvania, November 19, 1863, etc.* (Cover title.) 16 pp., printed pamphlet. Washington, (1863). First known printing in pamphlet form of the Gettysburg Address. $15,000 (A, 1967). Also, see Everett, Edward.

LINCOLN, Mrs. D. A. *Frozen Dainties.* 32 pp., wrappers. Nashua, N. H., 1889. First edition. $200-$250.

LINCOLN, Mrs. D. A. *Mrs. Lincoln's Boston Cook Book.* Marbled boards, cloth spine and corners. Boston, 1884. First edition. $1,000-$1,250.

LINCOLN, Joe. *Cape Cod Ballads and Other Verse.* Drawings by E. W. Kemble. Decorated yellow cloth. Trenton, N.J., 1902. (By Joseph C. Lincoln.) First edition. $150-$200. Author's first book.

LINCOLN, Joseph C. *Cape Cod Yesterdays.* 12 mounted plates. Cloth. Boston, 1935. Large paper Chatham edition. One of 1,075 signed. $100-$135.

LINCOLN, Joseph C. *Cap'n Eri.* Cloth. New York, 1904. First edition. $75-$85.

LINDBERGH, Charles A. *The Spirit of St. Louis.* Cloth. New York, 1953. First edition. Limited and signed "Presentation Edition." In dust jacket. $225-$250. Trade edition: In dust jacket. $25-$35.

LINDBERGH, Charles A. *"We": The Famous Flier's Own Story of His Life and His Trans-Atlantic Flight.* Illustrated. Half vellum. New York, 1927. Author's autograph edition. One of 1,000 signed. Boxed. $500-$600. Also, $425 and $250 (A, 1979). Trade edition: Blue cloth. In dust jacket. $50-$75.

LINDLEY, John. *Pomologia Britannica; or Figures and Descriptions of the Most Important Varieties of Fruit Cultivated in Great Britain.* 152 colored plates. 3 vols., half brown morocco. London, 1841. First edition. $2,500-$3,500.

LINDLEY, John. *Rosarum Monographia: or, a Botanical History of Roses.* One plain and 18 colored plates. Boards. London, 1820. First edition. $1,500-$2,000. London, 1830. Second edition. $1,200-$1,500.

LINDSAY, David. *Devil's Tor.* Black cloth. London, (1932). First edition, first binding. In dust jacket. $300-$400.

LINDSAY, Jack. See Graves, Robert, and Lindsay, Jack.

LINDSAY, Jack. *Storm at Sea.* Illustrated. Half morocco. London, 1935. One of 250 signed. $200-$250.

LINDSAY, Norman. *Etchings.* Cloth. London, 1927. One of 129. $350-$450. Another issue: Buckram, vellum spine. One of 31 signed, with a signed etching by Lindsay. $1,000-$1,500. Also, $990 (A, 1979).

LINDSAY, Norman. *A Homage to Sappho.* Illustrated by Jack Lindsay. Vellum. London. 1928. Fanfrolico Press. One of 70 signed. $1,500 and up. Also, $1,320 (A, 1979).

LINDSAY, Vachel. *Adventures While Preaching the Gospel of Beauty.* Cloth. New York, 1914. First edition. In dust jacket. $150-$200.

LINDSAY, Vachel. *The Candle in the Cabin.* Cloth. New York, 1926. First edition. In dust jacket. $85.

LINDSAY, Vachel. *Collected Poems.* Half cloth. New York, 1923. First edition. One of

400 signed. $125–$175. Trade edition: Cloth. In dust jacket. $30–$50. New York, 1925. Illustrated by Lindsay. Pictorial boards. First illustrated edition. One of 350 signed. Boxed. $75–$100. Trade edition: Blue cloth. In dust jacket. $40–$50.

LINDSAY, Vachel. *The Congo and Other Poems*. Pictorial cloth. New York, 1914. First edition. In dust jacket. $75–$125.

LINDSAY, Vachel. *General William Booth Enters into Heaven and Other Poems*. Red cloth. New York, 1913. First edition. In dust jacket. $200–$250. Author's first book.

LINDSAY, Vachel. *The Golden Book of Springfield*. Boards. New York, 1920. First edition. In dust jacket. $100–$125.

LINDSAY, Vachel. *The Golden Whales of California, and Other Rhymes in the American Language*. Reddish-brown decorated cloth. New York, 1920. First edition. In dust jacket. $50–$75.

LINDSAY, Vachel. *A Handy Guide for Beggars*. Cloth. New York, 1916. First edition. In dust jacket. $40–$60.

LINDSAY, Vachel. *In Praise of Johnny Appleseed*. Illustrated by John R. Neill. No place, no date (about 1921). First edition. $100.

LINDSAY, Vachel. *A Memorial of Lincoln Called The Heroes of Time*. 12 pp., stitched wrappers. (Springfield, Ill.), 1910. First edition. $200–$300.

LINDSAY, Vachel. *Proclamation of the Gospel of Beauty*. Broadside. (Springfield, 1912.) First edition. $200–$300.

LINDSAY, Vachel. *Rhymes To Be Traded For Bread*. 12 pp., self-wrappers. (Springfield, 1912.) First edition. $400–$600.

LINDSAY, Vachel. *The Soul of the City Receives the Gift of the Holy Spirit*. Illustrated by the author. Wrappers. (Springfield, 1913.) First edition. $200–$350.

LINDSAY, Vachel. *The Tramp's Excuse and Other Poems*. (Cover title.) Decorations by the author. Printed wrappers with cord tie. (Springfield, 1909.) First edition. $1,000–$1,200. (Note: Both Merle Johnson and the auction records incorrectly—and persistently—list the place of publication as Springfield, Ohio. It is Springfield, Ill.)

LINDSAY, Vachel. *The Wedding of the Rose and the Lotus*. Illustrated stiff printed leaflet poem. 3 pp. (Springfield, 1912.) First edition. $300–$400.

LINDSAY, William S. *History of Merchant Shipping and Ancient Commerce*. 3 maps, 3 plates, numerous other illustrations. 4 vols., cloth. London, 1874–76. $250–$350.

LINDSEY, Charles. *The Prairies of the Western States*. 100 pp., wrappers. Toronto, 1860. First edition. $200–$250.

LINDSLEY, John Berrien. *The Military Annals of Tennessee*. 2 plates. Cloth. Nashville, 1886. First edition. $100–$150.

LINES on Leaving the Bedford St. Schoolhouse. 4 pp., plain wrappers. (Boston, 1880.) (By George Santayana.) First edition. $600–$800. Author's first published work.

LINFORTH, James (editor). *Route from Liverpool to Great Salt Valley*. Folding map and 30 full-page plates. 120 pp., plus "Notice to Subscribers." 15 paperbound parts. Liverpool, July, 1854, to September, 1855. $5,000 and up. Liverpool, 1855. Boards. First edition in book form. With map partly colored by hand. $800–$1,000.

LINGUAL Exercises for Advanced Vocabularians. By the Author of "Recreations." Cloth. Cambridge, 1925. (By Siegfried Sassoon.) First edition. One of 90. $300–$400.

LINKLATER, Eric. *Position at Noon*. Beige buckram. London, (1958). First edition. One of 250 signed. In dust jacket. $100–$125.

LINN, John Blair (1777–1804). *Valerian: A Narrative Poem.* Portrait and silhouette. Boards. Philadelphia, 1805. First edition. $100 and up. (Note: Contains Charles Brockden Brown's sketch of Linn, his brother-in-law.)

LINN, John Blair (1831–1899). *Annals of Buffalo Valley, Pennsylvania.* Illustrated. Cloth. Harrisburg, 1877. First edition. $50–$75.

LINN, John J. *Reminiscences of Fifty Years in Texas.* Illustrated. Cloth. New York, 1883. First edition, with errata slip. $200–$225.

LINSLEY, Daniel C. *Morgan Horses.* Illustrated. Cloth. New York, 1857. First edition. $85–$125. New York, 1860. Cloth. $35–$50.

LINTON, William James. *The Masters of Wood-Engraving.* 196 plates (165 mounted), colored frontispiece. Cloth. London, 1889. First edition. One of 600 signed. $300–$500. New Haven, 1889. First American edition. One of 500. $200–$250. Another issue: One of 100 signed. $300–$500.

LIONEL Lincoln: or, The Leaguer of Boston. By the Author of *The Pioneers.* 2 vols., drab boards, paper labels. New York, 1825–1824. (By James Fenimore Cooper.) First edition. (Vol. 2 is dated 1824.) $500–$600. Also, $200 (A, 1978).

LIPSCOMB, George. *The History and Antiquities of the County of Buckingham.* Numerous maps, plates and woodcuts. 4 vols., half leather. London, 1847. First edition. $500–$600. Another issue: Large paper. $750 and up.

LITCH, Josiah. *The Probability of the Second Coming of Christ About A.D. 1843.* Cloth. Boston, 1838. First edition. $100.

LITTELL, William. *Festoons of Fancy.* Mottled calf. Louisville, Ky., 1814. First edition. $2,000 (A, 1967).

LITTELL, William. *Principles of Law & Equity, etc.* 101 pp., plus errata page, half leather. (Frankfort, Ky.?), 1808. First edition, with errata slip. $100 and up.

LITTLE, James A. *From Kirtland to Salt Lake City.* Illustrated. Cloth. Salt Lake City, 1890. First edition. $75–$100.

LITTLE, James A. *Jacob Hamblin: A Narrative of Personal Experiences as a Frontiersman, Missionary to the Indians, and Explorer.* Cloth. Salt Lake City, 1881. First edition. $50–$60.

LITTLE, James A. *What I Saw on the Old Santa Fe Trail.* Frontispiece. 127 pp., printed wrappers. Plainfield, Ind., (1904). First edition. $100–$150.

LITTLE Lucy: or, The Careless Child Reformed. 33 pp., printed wrappers. Cambridge, Mass., 1820. First edition. $65.

LITTLEHEART, Oleta. *The Lure of the Indian Country.* Moccasin-skin binding. Sulphur, Okla., 1908. First edition. Signed presentation copy, $40.

LIVING Issue (A). 37 pp., wrappers. (Suppressed portion of Dodge's *Our Wild Indians.*) Washington, 1882. (By Richard Irving Dodge.) $250–$300.

LIVINGSTON, Luther S. *Franklin and His Press at Passy.* Illustrated. Boards and cloth. New York, 1914. Grolier Club. First edition. One of 300. $200–$250.

LIZARS, John. *A System of Anatomical Plates of the Body, with Descriptions and Observations.* Text volume, plus folio atlas of 101 colored plates. Leather. Edinburgh, (1822–26). First edition. $800–$1,000.

LLEWELLYN, Richard. *How Green Was My Valley.* Yellow buckram, leather label. London, (1939). First edition. One of 200 signed. In slipcase. $100–$125. Trade edition. Cloth. In dust jacket. $35.

LLEWELLYN, Richard. *None But the Lonely Heart.* Cloth. London, 1943. First edition. One of 250 signed. $100–$125. Trade edition: In dust jacket. $35.

LLOYD, James T. *Steamboat Directory, and Disasters on the Western Waters.* Cloth. Cincinnati, 1856. First edition, first issue, with 326 pp. $100–$125. (Second issue has 331 pp.; valued a little less by purists.)

LOCKRIDGE, Ross, Jr. *Raintree County.* Cloth. Boston, 1948. First edition. In dust jacket. $75. Author's first (and only) book.

LOCKWOOD, Frank C. *The Apache Indians.* Illustrated. Cloth. New York, 1938. First edition. In dust jacket. $75–$100.

LOCKWOOD, Frank C. *Arizona Characters.* Illustrated. Pictorial cloth. Los Angeles, 1928. First edition. In dust jacket. $100–$110.

LOCKWOOD, Frank C. *Pioneer Days in Arizona.* Illustrated. Cloth. New York, 1932. First edition. In dust jacket. $75–$85.

LOCKWOOD, Luke Vincent. *The Pendleton Collection.* 102 full-page plates. Morocco. Providence, 1904. One of 160 on Japan vellum, signed. $400–$500, or more.

LOFTING, Hugh. *Doctor Dolittle's Post Office.* Cloth. New York, (1923). First edition. In dust jacket. $75–$100. London, (1924). Cloth. First English edition. In dust jacket. $75–$100.

LOFTING, Hugh. *The Story of Doctor Dolittle.* Illustrated by the author. Decorated orange-colored cloth, pictorial paper label. New York, 1920. First American edition. In dust jacket. $200–$250. Without jacket, $75–$100.

LOGUE, Christopher. *The Girls.* Half leather. London, 1969. One of 26, signed. $85.

LOGUE, Christopher. *A Song for Kathleen.* Self-wrappers. London, 1958. First edition. One of 100. $100.

LOMAX, John A. *Cowboy Songs.* Facsimile of a Theodore Roosevelt letter. Pictorial cloth. New York, 1910. First edition. In dust jacket. $85–$100.

LONDON, Charmian. *The Book of Jack London.* Illustrated. 2 vols., blue cloth. London, 1921. First edition. In dust jackets. $100–$135. New York, 1921. 2 vols., cloth. First American edition. In dust jackets. $75–$100.

LONDON, Jack. See *The Kempton-Wace Letters.*

LONDON, Jack. *The Abysmal Brute.* Frontispiece. Olive-green cloth, stamped in yellow and dark green. New York, 1913. First edition, first binding, first issue, with "Published, May, 1913" on copyright page. In dust jacket. $300–$400. Lacking jacket, $125–$150. Toronto, 1913. First Canadian edition. In dust jacket. $300–$400.

LONDON, Jack. *The Acorn Planter.* Red cloth. New York, 1916. First edition. In dust jacket. $800 and up. Lacking jacket, $150–$200. London, 1916. First English edition. In dust jacket. $800.

LONDON, Jack. *Adventure.* Dark-blue or red pictorial cloth. New York, 1911. First edition. In dust jacket. $400–$500. Lacking jacket, $100–$125. (Note: Red cloth is said to be scarcer and may be worth a premium.)

LONDON, Jack. *Before Adam.* Illustrated by Charles Livingston Bull. Tan pictorial buckram. New York, 1907. First edition. In dust jacket. $750–$950. Without jacket, $75–$100.

LONDON, Jack. *Burning Daylight.* Frontispiece. Blue and yellow pictorial cloth. New York, 1910. First edition, first printing, with blank leaf after ads. In dust jacket. $250–$350. Without jacket, $50–$75.

LONDON, Jack. *The Call of the Wild.* Illustrated by Philip R. Goodwin and Charles Livingston Bull. Green pictorial cloth. New York, 1903. First edition, first issue, with vertically ribbed cloth. In dust jacket. $1,000 and up. Also, $600 (A, 1981). London, 1903. Decorated blue cloth. First English edition. In dust jacket. $200–$300. New York, 1960. Limited Editions Club. Cloth. Boxed. $80–$100.

LONDON, Jack. *Children of the Frost*. Illustrated by Raphael M. Bray. Green pictorial cloth. New York, 1902. First edition. In dust jacket. $350–$450. Without jacket, $175–$200.

LONDON, Jack. *The Cruise of the Dazzler*. Frontispiece. Cream-colored cloth. New York, 1902. First edition, first issue, with "Published October, 1902" on copyright page. In dust jacket. $1,000 and up. Without jacket, $750.

LONDON, Jack. *The Cruise of the Snark*. Frontispiece in color. Blue cloth, colored print on front cover. New York, 1911. First edition. In dust jacket. $300–$350. Without jacket, $100–$125.

LONDON, Jack. *A Daughter of the Snows*. Illustrated in color by F. C. Yohn. Red pictorial cloth. Philadelphia, 1902. First edition. In dust jacket. $350–$450. Without jacket, $125–$150. London, 1904. Red cloth. First English edition. In dust jacket. $250. Lacking jacket, $100.

LONDON, Jack. *The Dream of Debs*. Pictorial wrappers. Chicago, (1909). First edition, first issue, with ad for Gustavus Myers book on back cover. $125–$150. Second (?) issue, ad headed "Books by Jack London" on back. $75. Later, back cover headed "Study Socialism." $50.

LONDON, Jack. *Dutch Courage and Other Stories*. Portrait frontispiece of London. Cloth. New York, 1922. First edition. In dust jacket. $950. Without jacket, $400–$500.

LONDON, Jack. *The Faith of Men and Other Stories*. Cloth. New York, 1904. First edition. In dust jacket. $300–$350. Lacking jacket, $100–$125.

LONDON, Jack. *The God of His Fathers and Other Stories*. Dark-blue decorated cloth. New York, 1901. First edition. In dust jacket. $350–$400. Lacking jacket, $125–$150.

LONDON, Jack. *Hearts of Three*. Cloth. New York, 1920. First American edition. In dust jacket. $300–$350. Without jacket, $100–$125.

LONDON, Jack. *The House of Pride*. Pictorial light-green cloth. New York, 1912. First edition. In dust jacket. $250–$350. Lacking jacket, $75–$100.

LONDON, Jack. *The Human Drift*. Frontispiece portrait of London. Reddish-brown cloth. New York, 1917. First edition. In dust jacket. $600–$750. Without jacket, $250.

LONDON, Jack. *The Iron Heel*. Blue pictorial cloth. New York, 1908. First edition. In dust jacket. $350–$450. Lacking jacket, $100–$135. Another issue: New York, (1908). Wilshire imprint. In dust jacket. $150–$250. Lacking jacket, $75–$125.

LONDON, Jack. *The Jacket*. Cloth. London, (1915). First edition, with "Published 1915" on back of title page. In dust jacket. $250–$350. (See *The Star Rover* for first American edition.)

LONDON, Jack. *John Barleycorn*. Illustrated by H. I. Dunn. Dark-green (black) cloth. New York, 1913. First edition, first printing, with one blank leaf following page 343. In dust jacket. $650. Lacking jacket, $100–$125.

LONDON, Jack. *The Little Lady of the Big House*. Frontispiece in color. Blue decorated cloth. New York, 1916. First edition. In dust jacket. $300–$350. Lacking jacket, $110.

LONDON, Jack. *Lost Face*. Frontispiece. Blue cloth. New York, 1910. First edition. In dust jacket. $400–$500. Without jacket, $75–$100.

LONDON, Jack. *Love of Life*. Cloth. New York, 1907. First edition. In dust jacket. $250–$350. Lacking jacket, $100–125.

LONDON, Jack. *Martin Eden*. Frontispiece. Dark-blue cloth. New York, 1909. First published edition. In dust jacket. $750–$1,100. Without jacket, $150–$175.

LONDON, Jack. *Michael, Brother of Jerry.* Red cloth. New York, 1917. First edition. In dust jacket. $300–$350. Lacking jacket, $75–$125.

LONDON, Jack. *The Mutiny of the Elsinore.* Cloth. New York, 1914. First edition. In dust jacket. $200–$250. Lacking jacket, $75–$85.

LONDON, Jack. *On the Makaloa Mat.* Decorated light-blue cloth. New York, 1919. First edition. In dust jacket. $200–$250. Lacking jacket, $50–$75.

LONDON, Jack. *The People of the Abyss.* Illustrated from photographs. Cloth. New York, 1903. First edition. $250.

LONDON, Jack. *Revolution.* Printed wrappers. Chicago, (1909). First edition. $150 and up. (Note: This pamphlet occurs in two states: Blanck's A-state, with ad "A Socialist Success," and B-state, with ad "Pocket Library of Socialism." Priority uncertain.)

LONDON, Jack. *Revolution and Other Essays.* Dark-blue or light-tan cloth. New York, 1910. First edition. In dust jacket. $250–$350. Lacking jacket, $75–$125.

LONDON, Jack. *The Road.* Frontispiece. Gray cloth. New York, 1907. First edition. In dust jacket. $300–$350. Lacking jacket, $100–$125.

LONDON, Jack. *The Scarlet Plague.* Cloth. New York, 1915. First published edition. In dust jacket. $300–$350. Lacking jacket, $75–$125.

LONDON, Jack. *Scorn of Women.* Cloth. New York, 1906. First edition. In dust jacket. $1,000 and up. Lacking jacket, $600.

LONDON, Jack. *The Sea-Wolf.* Illustrated by W. J. Aylward. Blue cloth. New York, 1904. First edition, first issue, with spine lettered in gold. In dust jacket. $350–$400. Lacking jacket, $75–$125. Later, spine lettered in white. In dust jacket. $250–$300. New York, 1961. Limited Editions Club. Cloth. Boxed. $50–$65. (Note: Some London collectors now question the long-accepted first issue claim for gold lettering originally made by the bibliographer Merle Johnson.)

LONDON, Jack. *Smoke Bellew.* Illustrated by P. J. Monahan. Blue-gray pictorial cloth. New York, 1912. First edition. In dust jacket. $200–$250. Lacking jacket, $50–$75.

LONDON, Jack. *The Son of the Sun.* Illustrated by A. O. Fischer. Light-blue pictorial cloth. Garden City, 1912. First edition. In dust jacket. $100–$150. Lacking jacket, $50–$100.

LONDON, Jack. *The Son of the Wolf.* Frontispiece. Slate-colored cloth, stamped in silver, or green cloth. Boston, 1900. First edition, first printing, with flyleaf at back; favored first binding in slate-colored cloth. In dust jacket. $1,250 and up. Lacking jacket, $300–$600. Author's first book. (Note: Hensley C. Woodbridge, John London, and George H. Tweney, in *Jack London: A Bibliography*, Georgetown, Calif., 1966, question the long-accepted slate-colored binding as the first. They also note two states of that binding and conclude that either of these as well as two varying green bindings must be considered as firsts; in other words, they say a collector must own all four to be sure he has a correct first edition. A fine bit of hairsplitting for the avid collector to chew over. See Blanck for further comments.)

LONDON, Jack. *The Star Rover.* Frontispiece in color. Blue cloth. New York, 1915. First American edition. In dust jacket. $1,000–$1,350. (For first edition, see *The Jacket.*)

LONDON, Jack. *The Strength of the Strong.* Pictorial wrappers. Chicago, (1911). First edition, first issue, with Kinzie Street address in ads. $100–$150. Second issue, with Ohio Street in ads. $50–$75.

LONDON, Jack. *The Strength of the Strong and Other Pieces.* Frontispiece. Light-blue decorated cloth. New York, 1914. First edition. In dust jacket. $200–$250. Lacking jacket, $75–$85.

LONDON, Jack. *Tales of the Fish Patrol.* Illustrated by George Varian. Decorated cloth.

New York, 1905. First edition. In dust jacket. $350–$450. Lacking jacket, $75–$125.

LONDON, Jack. *War of the Classes.* Dark-red cloth. New York, 1905. First edition. In dust jacket. $300–$450. Lacking jacket, $100–$125.

LONDON, Jack. *When God Laughs and Other Stories.* Illustrated. Dark olive-green pictorial cloth. New York, 1911. First edition. In dust jacket. $300–$400. Without jacket, $75–$125.

LONDON, Jack. *White Fang.* Illustrated, including colored frontispiece. Gray cloth. New York, 1906. First edition, first issue, without tipped-in title page and with no plates missing (they often are). In dust jacket. $400–$500. Without jacket, $50–$75. London, (1907). Dark-gray pictorial cloth. First English edition. $50–$75. New York, 1973. Limited Editions Club. $50–$60.

LONDON, Jack. *Wonder of Woman: A "Smoke Bellew" Story.* Printed wrappers. New York, (1912). First edition. $250–$300.

LONE Star Guide Descriptive of Countries on the Line of the International and Great Northern Railroad of Texas (The). Folding map and table, plates. 32 pp., wrappers. St. Louis (about 1877). (By H. M. Hoxie.) $150–$300.

LONG, Frank Belknap. *The Hounds of Tindalos.* Black cloth. Sauk City, 1946. First edition. In dust jacket. $75–$100.

LONG, Frank Belknap, Jr. *A Man from Genoa and Other Poems.* Cloth. Athol, Mass., 1926. First edition. $150–$175. Signed copy, $250. Author's first book.

LONG, Huey P. *My First Days in the White House.* Illustrated. Boards. Harrisburg, 1935. First edition. In dust jacket. $50–$75.

LONG Island Atlas. Cloth. New York, 1873. Published by Beers, Comstock & Cline. $300–$350.

LONG, Stephen H. *Voyage in a Six-Oared Skiff to the Falls of St. Anthony in 1817.* Map. Cloth. Philadelphia, 1860. First edition. $250–$350. Rebound in half leather, $100.

LONGFELLOW, Henry Wadsworth. See M. Lhomond's *Elements of French Grammar* (Longfellow's first book) and *French Exercises.* Also see *Hyperion; Manuel de Proverbes Dramatiques; Novelas Españolas; Outre-Mer.*

LONGFELLOW, Henry W. *Ballads and Other Poems.* Boards, paper label. Cambridge, Mass., 1842. First edition, first issue, with small "t" in "teacher" in last line of page 88 and with quotation marks at end of line 1, page 34. $250–$350.

LONGFELLOW, Henry W. *The Belfry of Bruges and Other Poems.* White wrappers. Cambridge, 1846. First edition, first state, with date 1845 on front cover and 1846 on title page. $250–$300. (Note: There were also some copies issued in boards.)

LONGFELLOW, Henry Wadsworth. *The Courtship of Miles Standish.* 135 pp., drab printed wrappers, imprinted "Author's Protected Edition," London, 1858. First edition, first printing. $400–$500. Later, cloth, 227 pp. Second printing, $350. Boston, 1858. Brown cloth. First American edition, first printing, with "treacherous" for "ruddy" in third line of page 124. $250–$300. Another issue: Purple "gift" binding. $250–$350.

LONGFELLOW, Henry Wadsworth. *Evangeline: A Tale of Acadie.* Brown or yellow boards, paper label, Boston, 1847. First edition, first printing, with line 1, page 61, reading "Long . . ." (for "Lo . . ."). $400–$500. "Lo" issue: $150–$250.

LONGFELLOW, Henry Wadsworth. *The Golden Legend.* Cloth. Boston, 1851. First edition, $300–$400. London, 1851. Cloth. First English edition. $75–$100. London, 1854. Illustrated. Cloth. $75–$100.

LONGFELLOW, Henry Wadsworth. *Poems on Slavery.* 31 pp., printed yellow wrappers. Cambridge, 1842. First edition. $350–$500. Also $280 (A, 1981).

LONGFELLOW, Henry Wadsworth. *The Seaside and the Fireside.* Cloth or boards. Boston, 1850. First edition. $100–$150. Another (later) issue: Large paper. $75–$100.

LONGFELLOW, Henry Wadsworth. *The Song of Hiawatha.* Green cloth or printed tan wrappers. London, 1855. First edition, with March ads. $500–$600. (No copies noted recently in wrappers.) Boston, 1855. Brown cloth. First American edition, first printing, with November ads and "dove" for "dived" in line 7 of page 96. $300–$400. Also, $200 (A, 1980). Another issue: Blue, green, or red "gift" bindings. $250–$350. Boston, 1856. Blue cloth. Large paper edition. $75–$100. Boston, 1891. Illustrated by Frederic Remington. Vellum. One of 250. $400–$500. Another issue: Cloth or suede. Unnumbered. No recent prices noted.

LONGFELLOW, Henry Wadsworth. *Syllabus de la Grammaire Italienne.* Cloth. Boston, 1832. First edition, first state, with "la traite" for "le traite" in line 13 of advertisement and rule under "Bowdoin College" on title page. $200–$300.

LONGFELLOW, Henry Wadsworth. *Tales of a Wayside Inn.* Cloth. Boston, 1863. First edition, first state of ads on page 11, with "Nearly ready" for this book, which is not priced. $150–$200.

LONGFELLOW, Henry Wadsworth. *"There Was a Little Girl."* Boards. New York, (1883). First edition. $75–$100. (Note: Blanck and others have questioned Longfellow's authorship of this nursery poem.)

LONGFELLOW, Henry Wadsworth. *Voices of the Night.* Tan or drab boards, paper label. Cambridge, 1839. First edition, first state, with line 10 on page 78 reading "His, Hector's arm" instead of "The arm of Hector." $400–$500. (Note: Fewer than 10 copies known, according to the late David A. Randall, curator of the Lilly Library at Indiana University.) Second state. $100–$150. Author's first book of poetry.

LONGFELLOW, Henry Wadsworth (translator). *Coplas de Don Jorge Manrique.* Cloth, paper spine label. Boston, 1833. First edition. $200–$225.

LONGSTREET, Augustus Baldwin. See *Georgia Scenes, Characters, Incidents, etc.*

LONGSTREET, James. *From Manassas to Appomattox.* 44 maps and plates, 2 leaves of facsimiles. Cloth. Philadelphia, 1896. First edition. $75–$100.

LOOMIS, Chester A. *A Journey on Horseback Through the Great West, in 1825.* 27 pp., printed wrappers. Bath, N.Y., (1820's). First edition. $200–$250.

LOOS, Anita. *"Gentlemen Prefer Blondes."* Illustrated. Cloth. New York, 1925. First edition, first issue, with "Divine" for "Devine" on contents page. In dust jacket. $75–$100.

LORANT, Stefan (editor). *The New World: The First Pictures of America.* Illustrated. Cloth. New York, (1946). In dust jacket. Boxed. $75–$100.

LORIMER, George Horace. *Letters from a Self-Made Merchant to His Son.* 36 pp., wrappers. Philadelphia, 1901. First edition. $100–$150. Boston, 1902. Cloth. First (complete) edition. $50–$75.

LORREQUER, Harry (pseudonym for Charles Lever). See *The Confessions of Harry Lorrequer.*

LORREQUER, Harry. *Charles O'Malley, the Irish Dragoon.* Illustrated by H. K. Browne ("Phiz"). 22 parts in 21, printed pink pictorial wrappers. Dublin, 1841. (By Charles Lever.) First edition. $600–$800. Dublin, 1841. 2 vols., boards. First edition in book form. $150–$200. London, 1897. 16 plates by Arthur Rackham. Cloth. $150–$200.

LOTHROP, Amy. *Dollars and Cents.* 2 vols., purple cloth. New York, 1852. (By Anna Bartlett Warner.) First edition. $75–$100.

LOTHROP, Harriet M. S. See Sidney, Margaret.

LOUDON, Archibald. *A Selection of Some of the Most Interesting Narratives, of Outrages, Committed by the Indians, in Their Wars, with the White People.* 2 vols., leather. Carlisle, Pa., 1808–11. First edition, $2,000–$2,500. Also, worn and defective, $1,200 (A, 1979); $1,500 (A, 1967).

LOUDON, Mrs. Jane. *British Wild Flowers.* 60 hand-colored plates. Cloth. London, 1846. First edition. $1,000–$1,250. Rebound copies, a little less. London, (1849). Second edition. $600–$800. (A number of later editions—1849, 1855, 1859, etc.—are all worth about as much as the original.)

LOUDON, Mrs. Jane. *The Ladies' Flower Garden of Ornamental Annuals.* 48 colored plates. Cloth. London, 1840. First edition. $1,250–$1,500. Rebound, a little less. (Note: Editions following in 1842, 1844, and 1849 are about as valuable as the original.) Mrs. Loudon also produced three other books in this series: *Ornamental Bulbous Plants.* London, 1841. 58 colored plates. Cloth. $1,250 and up. *Ornamental Greenhouse Plants.* London, 1848. 75 colored plates. Cloth. $1,000 and up. *Ornamental Perennials.* 96 colored plates. 2 vols., cloth. London, 1843–44. $1,750 and up. As with Mrs. Loudon's wild flower book, the later editions of this color plate series sometimes bring almost as much as the originals.

LOUGHBOROUGH, John. *The Pacific Telegraph and Railway.* 2 folding maps. 80 pp., unbound. St. Louis, 1849. First edition, $600.

LOUGHEED, Victor. *Vehicles of the Air.* Illustrated. Cloth. Chicago, (1909). First edition. $50–$100.

LOVE, Nat. *The Life and Adventures of Nat Love.* Plates. Pictorial cloth. Los Angeles, 1907. First edition. $150–$200.

LOVE, Robertus. *The Rise and Fall of Jesse James.* Frontispiece. Cloth. New York, 1926. First edition. $35–$50.

LOVECRAFT, H. P. *Beyond the Wall of Sleep.* Cloth. Sauk City, Wis., 1943. First edition. One of 1,217. In dust jacket. $500–$750.

LOVECRAFT, H. P. *The Case of Charles Dexter Ward.* Cloth. London, 1951. First edition. In dust jacket. $125–$175.

LOVECRAFT, H. P. *The Cats of Ulthar.* 16 pp., wrappers. Cassia, Fla., 1935. First edition. One of 2,035. In dust jacket. $150.

LOVECRAFT, H. P. *Collected Poems.* Illustrated. Black cloth. Sauk City, 1963. First edition. In dust jacket. $75–$125.

LOVECRAFT, H. P. *The Haunter of the Dark.* Introduction by August Derleth. Cloth. London, 1951. First edition. In dust jacket. $150–$175. Without jacket, $75.

LOVECRAFT, H. P. *Marginalia.* Illustrated. Black cloth. Sauk City, 1944. First edition. One of 2,035. In dust jacket. $175–$225.

LOVECRAFT, H. P. *The Outsider and Others.* Cloth. Sauk City, 1939. First edition. One of 1,268. In dust jacket. $750–$1,000. (Note: This is the first book published by August Derleth's Arkham House.)

LOVECRAFT, H. P. *The Shadow Over Innsmouth.* Illustrated. Cloth. Everett, Pa., 1936. First edition, with errata sheet. In dust jacket. $1,500–$2,000. Author's first published book. (Earliest copies—about 10—were issued without errata sheet. The dust jackets [two types: one printed in yellow and one with an illustration in green] were a later addition, according to Lloyd Currey, specialist in fantasy literature. We have noted one copy in the "green" dust jacket listed at $3,500, but there is apparently no priority for the "green" over the yellow jacket.)

LOVECRAFT, H. P. *The Shunned House.* 59 pp., unbound, folded signatures. Athol, Mass., 1928. First edition, first issue. $1,250–$1,500. (As late as the 1960's these were still available from August Derleth, the publisher of Lovecraft's principal fantasy books, at $17.50.) Later copies, bound in wrappers by R.H. Barlow, a Lovecraft associate. One of 10. $1,000 and up. Special Arkham House issue by Derleth: One of about 100, trimmed and bound in black cloth about 1961. Issued without dust jacket, $850–$1,000. (A copy, crudely bound in boards and canvas, was in the Jonathan Goodwin sale, Part 2, in 1977 but was withdrawn. Author's first book (about 250 copies).

LOVECRAFT, H. P. *Something About Cats and Other Pieces*. Edited by August Derleth. Cloth. Sauk City, 1949. First edition. One of 2,995. In dust jacket. $125–$150.

LOVECRAFT, H. P. *Supernatural Horror in Literature*. Black or (later?) red cloth. New York, 1945. First edition. Black cloth: (Issued without dust jacket.) $50–$75. Red cloth: (Without jacket.) $35–$75.

LOVECRAFT, H. P., and Derleth, August. *The Lurker at the Threshold*. Cloth. Sauk City, 1945. First edition. One of 3,041. In dust jacket. $75–$125.

LOVECRAFT, H. P., and others. *The Shuttered Room and Other Pieces*. Illustrated. Black cloth. Sauk City, 1959. First edition. One of 2,500. In dust jacket. $75–$125.

LOVECRAFT, H. P., and Derleth, August. *The Survivor and Others*. Cloth. Sauk City, 1957. First edition. In dust jacket. $100–$125.

LOVEDAY, John. *Diary of a Tour in 1732 Through Parts of England, Wales, Ireland and Scotland*. Half morocco. London, 1890. Roxburghe Club. $150–$200.

LOVER, Samuel. *Handy Andy: A Tale of Irish Life*. Illustrated by the author. 12 parts, printed wrappers. London, January-December, 1842. First edition. $400–$500. London, 1842. Green cloth. First edition in book form. $200–$300.

LOVING Ballad of Lord Bateman (The). Preface by Charles Dickens. Illustrated by George Cruikshank. Green cloth. London, 1839. (By William Makepeace Thackeray, though sometimes ascribed to Dickens, or to both Thackeray—for the ballad—and Dickens, or to Cruikshank.) First edition, first issue, with the word "wine" in fifth stanza. $500–$750.

LOWE, C. Bruce. *Breeding Racehorses by the Figure System*. Edited by William Allison. Illustrated. Cloth. London, 1895. First edition. $100–$150.

LOWELL, Amy. See *Dream Drops; Some Imagist Poets*.

LOWELL, Amy. *A Dome of Many-Colored Glass*. Boards, cloth spine, paper labels. Boston, 1912. First edition. In dust jackets. $75–$150. Author's first book aside from *Dream Drops*.

LOWELL, Amy. *The Madonna of Carthagena*. Wrappers. No place, 1927. First edition. One of 50. $100–$150.

LOWELL, Amy. *What's O'Clock*. Gray-blue boards and cloth. Boston, 1925. First edition. In dust jacket. $50–$75.

LOWELL, James Russell. See Wilbur, Homer. Also see *Class Poem; A Fable for Critics*.

LOWELL, James Russell. *Among My Books*. Cloth. Boston, 1870. First edition. $35–$50.

LOWELL, James Russell. *Among My Books: Second Series*. Cloth. Boston, 1876. First edition, first state, with 1875 copyright date and "Belles-Letters" on title page. $50–$60.

LOWELL, James Russell. *Conversations on Some of the Old Poets*. Wrappers. Cambridge, Mass., 1845. First edition. $200–$250. (Also issued in cloth and in boards.)

LOWELL, James Russell. *Four Poems*. Boards. Hingham, 1906. First edition. One of 50. $200–$250.

LOWELL, James Russell. *Heartsease and Rue.* Boards and cloth. Boston, 1888. First edition. $100–$125.

LOWELL, James Russell. *Ode Recited at the Commemoration of the Living and Dead Soldiers of Harvard University, July 21, 1865.* Gray boards, paper label. Cambridge, 1865. First edition. One of 50. $1,000–$1,250. Inscribed and initialed by Lowell, $1,750 in a 1981 catalogue.

LOWELL, James Russell. *On Democracy.* 15 pp., wrappers. Birmingham, England, (1884). First edition, first state, privately printed and without price at top of first leaf. $100–$150. Second state (first published edition), with price. $50–$75.

LOWELL, James Russell. *Poems.* Boards, paper label. Cambridge, 1844. First edition. $50–$75.

LOWELL, James Russell. *Poems.* 2 vols., boards or cloth. Boston, 1849. First edition. $75–$100.

LOWELL, James Russell. *Poems: Second Series.* Boards or cloth. Cambridge, 1848. First edition. $75–$100.

LOWELL, James Russell. *The President's Policy.* Wrappers. (Philadelphia, 1864.) First edition, first state, with "crises" spelled "crisises" in first line of text. $100–$150.

LOWELL, James Russell. *Under the Willows and Other Poems.* Cloth. Boston, 1869. First edition, first issue, with errata slip at page 286 and first word in line 7 of page 224 reading "Thy." $75–$150.

LOWELL, James Russell. *The Vision of Sir Launfal.* Printed glazed yellow boards. Cambridge, 1848. First edition. $150–$200.

LOWELL, James Russell. *A Year's Life.* Boards, paper label. Boston, 1841. First edition, with errata slip. $150–$200. Author's first book (preceded by *Class Poem* pamphlet).

LOWELL, Maria. *Poems.* 68 pp., half leather. Cambridge, Mass., 1855. First edition. $250–$350. Cambridge, 1907. Boards. One of 330. Boxed. $50.

LOWELL, Robert. *For the Union Dead.* Green cloth. New York, (1964). First edition, first printing (so stated). In dust jacket. $25–$35. London, 1965. First English edition. In dust jacket. $20–$30.

LOWELL, Robert. *4 by Robert Lowell.* Illustrated by Robert Scott. Decorated wrappers, stitched. (Cambridge, Mass., 1969.) One of 126 copies, signed by Lowell. (Four broadsides, one for each poem.) $350–$400.

LOWELL, Robert. *Hawthorne.* Illustrated. Wrappers. (Columbus, Ohio, 1964.) First edition. One of 150 signed. $350.

LOWELL, Robert. *Land of Unlikeness.* Printed boards. Cummington, Mass., 1944. First edition. One of 250. In tissue jacket, $2,500–$3,000. Another issue: One of 26 signed. $3,000–$4,000. Author's first book.

LOWELL, Robert. *Life Studies.* Cloth. London, (1959). First edition. In dust jacket. $100–$150. New York, 1959. First American edition. In dust jacket. $100–$150.

LOWELL, Robert. *Lord Weary's Castle.* Black cloth. New York, (1946). First edition. In dust jacket. $250–$350.

LOWELL, Robert. *The Mills of the Kavanaughs.* Cloth. New York, (1951). First edition. In dust jacket. $175–$250.

LOWELL, Robert. *Poems, 1938–1949.* Cloth. London, (1950). First edition. In dust jacket. $200–$250.

LOWELL, Robert (translator). *The Voyage and Other Versions of Poems by Baudelaire.*

Illustrated by Sidney Nolan. Folio, blue and purple beveled cloth. London, (1968). First edition. One of 210 signed by Lowell and the illustrator. Boxed. $250–$350.

LOWES, John Livingston. *The Road to Xanadu*. Cloth. Boston, 1927. First edition. One of 300. Boxed. $125–$150.

LOWMAN, Al (compiler). *This Bitterly Beautiful Land: A Texas Commonplace Book*. Woodcuts. Folio, cloth. (Austin, 1972.) First edition. One of 275 signed. $400–$600.

LOWNDES, Mrs. Belloc. *The Lodger*. Cloth. London, (1913). First edition. $200.

LOWRY, Malcolm. *Dark as the Grave Wherein My Friend is Laid*. Cloth. (New York, 1969.) First edition. In dust jacket. $50.

LOWRY, Malcolm. *Hear Us O Lord from Heaven Thy Dwelling Place*. Cloth. Philadelphia, (1961). First edition. In dust jacket. $75–$100.

LOWRY, Malcolm. *Lunar Caustic*. (In French.) Wrappers. Paris, (1963). First edition. $75–$100. London, (1968). Cloth or wrappers. First edition in English. Cloth: In first issue ("Cape Editions") jacket. $75.

LOWRY, Malcolm. *Ultramarine*. Cloth. London, (1933). First edition. In dust jacket. $2,000–$2,250. Lacking jacket, soiled, $1,750 in a 1981 catalogue. Philadelphia, (1962). Cloth. First American edition. In dust jacket. $75–$100. Toronto, (1963). Cloth. First Canadian edition. In dust jacket. $75. Author's first book.

LOWRY, Malcolm. *Under the Volcano*. Gray cloth. New York, (1947). First edition, first binding. In dust jacket. $500–$700. Also, $400 (A, 1979). London, (1947). Cloth. First English edition. In dust jacket. $500.

LOWRY, Robert. *Casualty*. Cloth. (New York, 1946.) First edition. In dust jacket. $50.

LOWRY, Robert. *Hutton Street*. Illustrated. Pictorial wrappers. Cincinnati, 1940. First edition. $50–$100. Author's first book.

LOWRY, Robert. *The Journey Out*. Boards. (Bari, Italy, 1945.) First edition, signed. $75–$100.

LOWRY, Walter. *Tumult at Dusk*. Folding map. Parchment boards. San Francisco, 1963. Grabhorn Press. One of 100. In plastic slipcase. $150–$175.

LOY, Mina. *Lunar Baedeker*. Printed wrappers. (Paris, 1923.) First edition. $125–$150.

LOY, Mina. *Lunar Baedeker & Time Tables*. Cloth. Highlands, N.C., 1958. First edition. Jargon 23. One of 50 signed "author's copies." In acetate dust jacket. $150. (Note: Contains an introduction by William Carlos Williams and others.)

LUBBOCK, Basil. *Adventures by Sea from the Art of Old Time*. 115 plates, including 22 in color. Buckram. London, 1925. First edition. One of 1,750. $200–$300.

LUBBOCK, Basil. *The Last of the Windjammers*. Illustrated. 2 vols., cloth. Boston, 1927. First edition. In dust jacket. $150–$200.

LUBBOCK, Basil, and Spurling, John. *Sail: The Romance of the Clipper Ship*. 78 full-page color plates. 3 vols., cloth. London, 1927–30–36. First edition. One of 1,000. In dust jackets. $1,250–$1,500, or more.

LUBBOCK, F. R. *In Memoriam: Jefferson Davis*. 59 pp., half morocco. Austin, 1891. First edition. $200–$250. Presentation copy, signed, $550.

LUCAS, E. V. See L., E. V.

LUCAS, E. V. *The Book of Shops*. Illustrated in color. Oblong folio, boards and cloth. London, (1899). $50–$75.

LUCAS, E. V. *Playtime and Company*. Illustrated by Ernest H. Shepard. Vellum. London, (1925). One of 15 on vellum, signed by author and artist. $400–$600. Another issue: Boards and cloth. One of 100 signed. In dust jacket. $200–$250.

LUCAS, Thomas J. *Camp Life and Sport in South Africa*. Illustrated. Cloth. London, 1878. $200–$300.

LUCAS, Thomas J. *Pen and Pencil Reminiscences of a Campaign in South Africa*. 21 colored plates. London, (1861). $250–$350.

LUCAS, Victoria. *The Bell Jar*. Cloth. London, (1963). (By Sylvia Plath.) First edition. In dust jacket. $400–$550. New York, 1971. Illustrated. Boards. First American edition. In dust jacket. $50–$75.

LUCE, Edward S. *Keoghe, Comanche and Custer*. Illustrated. Cloth. (St. Louis), 1939. Limited, signed edition. In dust jacket. $300–$350.

LUDLOW, Fitz-Hugh. See *The Hasheesh Eater*.

LUDLOW, N. M. *Dramatic Life as I Found It*. Cloth. St. Louis, 1880. First edition. $75–$100.

LUHAN, Mabel Dodge. *Lorenzo in Taos*. Illustrated. Cloth. New York, 1932. First edition. In dust jacket. $50–$75.

LUHAN, Mabel Dodge. *Taos and Its Artists*. Illustrated. Red cloth. New York, 1947. First edition. In dust jacket. $150–$200.

LUKE Darrell, The Chicago Newsboy. Cloth. Chicago, 1865. First edition. $100–$150.

LUKE, L. D. *Adventures and Travels in the New Wonder Land of Yellowstone Park*. Cloth. Utica, 1886. $75–$100.

LUMPKIN, Wilson. *The Removal of the Cherokee Indians from Georgia*. 2 portraits. 2 vols., cloth. Wormsloe, Ga., 1907. First edition. One of 500. $75–$100.

LUTTIG, John C. *Journal of a Fur-Trading Expedition on the Upper Missouri*. Folding map, 4 plates. Boards and cloth. St. Louis, 1920. First edition. One of 365. $150–$200.

LYELL, Charles. *Principles of Geology*. Maps and plates. 3 vols., leather. London, 1930–32–33. First edition. $750–$1,000.

LYELL, Charles. *Travels in North America*. Map, 6 plates. 2 vols., cloth. London, 1845. First edition. $350–$400.

LYELL, James P. R. *Early Book Illustration in Spain*. Colored frontispiece, 247 other illustrations. Cloth. London, 1926. One of 500. $150–$200.

LYMAN, Albert. *Journal of a Voyage to California, and Life in the Gold Diggings*. Illustrated. Pictorial wrappers, or cloth. Hartford, 1852. First edition. Wrappers: $1,000–$1,500. Cloth: $750–$1,000.

LYMAN, George D. *John Marsh, Pioneer*. Illustrated. Cloth. New York, 1930. First edition. One of 150 signed. $150.

LYMINGTON, Lord. *Spring Song of Iscariot*. Wrappers. Paris, 1929. Black Sun Press. One of 125 on Van Gelder paper. $100–$125. Another issue: One of 25 on Japan paper. $250.

LYNCH, Bohun. *The Prize Ring*. Illustrated. Boards. London, 1925. First edition. One of 750. $100–$150.

LYON, G. F. *The Private Journal of Capt. G. F. Lyon, of H.M. Hecla*. Calf. London, 1824. First edition. $200–$300. Boston, 1824. First American edition. $150–$200.

LYRE, Pinchbeck. *Poems*. Boards. (London, 1931.) (By Siegfried Sassoon.) First edition. In glassine dust jacket. $75–$100.

LYRICAL Ballads with Other Poems. 2 vols., drab boards. London, 1800. (By William Wordsworth and Samuel Taylor Coleridge.) Second edition (so designated on the first volume alone). $1,500–$2,500. London, 1802. 2 vols., boards. Third edition. $200–$400, possibly more. London, 1805. 2 vols., boards. Fourth edition. $200 and up. (Note: The first edition, first issue, 1798, with a Bristol—instead of London—imprint on the title page, is an extremely rare book, of which no complete copy in original pink boards has appeared in many years. A second issue copy with London imprint, was sold at auction for $2,200 in New York City on February 6, 1981.)

LYTLE, Andrew. *Bedford Forrest and His Critter Company*. Illustrated. Pictorial black cloth, paper labels. New York, 1931. First edition, large paper issue by Minton, Balch. In dust jacket. $150–$175. Ordinary issue (smaller format) by Putnam: New York, (1931). In jacket. $50–$75. Author's first book.

LYTLE, Andrew. *The Long Night*. Cloth. Indianapolis, (1936). First edition. In dust jacket. $50–$75.

LYTLE, Andrew. *A Name For Evil*. Cloth. Indianapolis, (1947). First edition. In dust jacket. $50–$60.

LYTTON, Lord (Edward Bulwer). See Bulwer-Lytton, Edward.

M

MABINOGION (The): A New Translation from the White Book of Rhydderch and the Red Book of Hergest. By Gwyn Jones and Thomas Jones. Woodcut title page and other illustrations by Dorothea Braby. Folio, half morocco. London, 1948. Golden Cockerel Press. One of 475. $750–$1,250. Another issue: One of 75 specially bound. $1,500 and up.

McADAM, R. W. *Chickasaws and Choctaws.* Comprising the Treaties of 1855 and 1866. 67 pp., wrappers. Ardmore, Okla., 1891. First edition. $300–$350.

McAFEE, Robert B. See *History of the Late War in the Western Country.*

McALMON, Robert. *Being Geniuses Together.* Blue cloth. London, (1938). First edition. In dust jacket. $800–$1,000. Also, $500 (A, 1977).

McALMON, Robert. *A Companion Volume.* Gray wrappers. (Paris, 1923.) Contact Editions. First edition. $350–$400.

McALMON, Robert. *Distinguished Air (Grim Fairy Tales).* Vellum. Paris, 1925. Contact Editions. First edition. One of 103 on paper. $500–$600. Also, $400 (A, 1977). Another issue: One of 12 on vellum. $750 and up. Phoenix Book Shop of New York City offered a signed copy at $1,350 in 1979.

McALMON, Robert. *Explorations.* Cloth. London, 1921. Egoist Press. First edition. $400–$500. Author's first book.

McALMON, Robert. *A Hasty Bunch.* Wrappers. (Paris, 1922.) Contact Editions. First edition. $400–$500. Also, $375 (A, 1977).

McALMON, Robert. *North America, Continent of Conjecture.* Wrappers. (Paris, 1929.) Contact Editions. First edition. One of 310. In glassine dust jacket. $300–$400.

McALMON, Robert. *Not Alone Lost.* Cloth. Norfolk, Conn., (1937). New Directions. In dust jacket. $150.

McALMON, Robert. *Post-Adolescence.* Wrappers. (Paris, 1923.) Contact Editions. First edition. In glassine dust jacket. $350–$450.

McALMON, Robert. *The Portrait of a Generation.* Stiff wrappers. Paris, (1926). Contact Editions. First edition. One of 200. $350–$400. Another issue: Vellum. One of 10 signed. $600, or more. Also, $475 (A, 1977).

McALMON, Robert. *Village: As It Happened Through a Fifteen Year Period.* Wrappers. (Paris, 1924.) Contact Editions. First edition. $350–$450.

MACARIA: or, Altars of Sacrifice. 183 pp., wrappers. Richmond, 1864. (By Augusta Jane Evans Wilson.) First edition. $350–$500.

MacARTHUR, Douglas. *Military Demolitions.* Illustrated. Printed wrappers. (Fort Leavenworth, Kan., 1909.) First edition. $125–$150.

MACARTHUR, James. *New South Wales: Its Present State and Future Prospects.* Colored map. Cloth. London, 1837. (Written by Edward Edwards from Macarthur's notes.) $300–$400.

MACAULAY, Rose. *Catchwords and Claptrap.* Printed boards. London, 1926. Hogarth Press. First edition. $75–$100.

MACAULAY, Rose. *63 Days: The Story of the Warsaw Rising.* Stiff wrappers. (London), 1945. First edition. $75–$100.

MACAULAY, Thomas Babington. *Evening: A Poem.* Wrappers. Cambridge, 1821. First edition. $150–$250.

MACAULAY, Thomas Babington. *Lays of Ancient Rome.* Brown cloth. London, 1842. First edition. $150–$200.

MACAULAY, Thomas Babington. *Pompeii.* Blue wrappers. (Cambridge, 1819.) First edition. $300–$400. Author's first book.

MacBETH, George. *A Form of Words.* Cloth. Oxford, 1954. First edition. One of 150. $135. Author's first book.

MacCABE, Julius P. Bolivar. *Directory of the City of Detroit.* Printed boards. Detroit, 1837. First edition. $750–$1,000.

MacCABE, Julius P. Bolivar. *Directory of the City of Milwaukee.* Full leather. Milwaukee, 1847. First edition. $400–$500.

MacCABE, Julius P. Bolivar. *A Directory of Cleveland and the Cities of Ohio for the Years 1837–1838.* Printed boards. Cleveland, 1837. First edition. $800–$1,000.

McCAIN, Charles W. *History of the S.S. "Beaver."* Illustrated. Blue cloth. Vancouver, 1894. First edition. $100–$125.

McCALL, Ansel J. *Pick and Pan: Trip to the Diggings in 1849.* 46 pp., printed wrappers. Bath, N.Y., 1889. First edition. $650.

McCALL, George A. *Letters from the Frontiers.* Cloth. Philadelphia, 1868. First edition. $250–$350.

McCALL, Hugh. *The History of Georgia.* 2 vols., boards. Savannah, 1811–16. First edition. $400–$500.

McCALLA, William L. *Adventures in Texas.* Black cloth. Philadelphia, 1841. First edition. $500–$750.

McCARTHY, Mary. *The Company She Keeps.* Cloth. (New York), 1942. First edition. In dust jacket. $50–$75. Author's first book.

McCARTHY, Mary. *The Oasis.* Cloth. New York, (1949). First edition. In dust jacket. $35–$50.

McCARTHY, Mary. *Venice Observed.* Illustrated. Cloth. Paris–New York, (1956). First edition. $50–$75.

McCAULEY, J. E. *A Stove-Up Cowboy's Story.* Illustrated by Tom Lea. Cloth. Dallas, 1943. First edition. One of 700. In dust jacket. $375.

McCLELLAN, Henry B. *The Life and Campaigns of Maj. Gen. J. E. B. Stuart.* Portrait, 7 maps. Cloth. Boston, 1885. First edition. $80–$100.

McCLELLAND, Nancy. *Duncan Phyfe.* Illustrated. Cloth. New York, (1939). First edition. One of 350 signed. Boxed. $125–$175.

McCLELLAND, Nancy. *Historic Wallpapers.* Illustrated, including color plates. Half cloth. Philadelphia, 1924. First edition, limited. $150–$250. Ordinary issue: $100–$150.

McCLINTOCK, John S. *Pioneer Days in the Black Hills.* Edited by Edward Senn. Illustrated. Cloth. Deadwood, (1939). First edition. $100–$125.

McCLINTOCK, Walter. *Old Indian Trails.* 28 plates, including 4 in color. Pictorial cloth. Boston, 1923. First edition. $50–$75. London, 1923. First English edition. $50–$75.

McCLINTOCK, Walter. *The Old North Trail*. Folding map, 9 color plates. Cloth. London, 1910. First edition. $75–$125.

M'CLUNG, John A. *Sketches of Western Adventure*. Boards, linen spine. Maysville, Ky., 1832. First edition. $750–$1,000. Philadelphia, 1832. Second edition. $400–$600.

McCLURE, J. B. *Edison and His Inventions*. Illustrated. Cloth. Chicago, 1879. First edition, first state, with no reviews of his book in the ads and with "With copious illustrations" in one line on title page. $100–$125. (Note: Contains Joel Chandler Harris' "Uncle Remus and the Phonograph.")

McCLURE, Michael. *The Beard*. Folio, pictorial wrappers. (Berkeley, 1965.) First edition. One of 330. $50–$75. (San Francisco), 1967. Coyote Press. Wrappers. $10. Another issue: One of 40 signed. $30–$40.

McCLURE, Michael. *The Cherub*. Full leather. Los Angeles, 1970. Black Sparrow Press. One of 26 signed, with a drawing by the author. $75–$100. Another issue: Boards. One of 250 signed. $25–$35.

McCLURE, Michael. *Dark Brown*. Boards and leather, San Francisco, 1971. One of 25 on Japan paper, signed. $75–$100. Another issue: Wrappers. $15–$20.

McCLURE, Michael. *Ghost Tantras*. Cloth. San Francisco, (1964). First edition. One of 20 signed. $50. Another issue: Wrappers. $15–$20.

McCLURE, Michael. *Hail Thee Who Play*. Printed yellow boards and cloth. Los Angeles, 1968. Black Sparrow Press. First edition. One of 75 signed, with a drawing by the author. In dust jacket. $50–$75. Another issue: Printed wrappers. One of 250 signed. $30–$35.

McCLURE, Michael. *Love Lion Book*. Wrappers. San Francisco, 1966. First edition. $10. Later: Boards. One of 40 signed. $75–$90.

McCLURE, Michael. *Muscled Apple Swift*. Decorated wrappers. (Topango, Calif., 1968.) First edition. One of 63 signed. $75–$85. Ordinary issue (87 copies): $20–$30.

McCLURE, Michael. *Passage*. Wrappers. Big Sur, Calif., 1956. Jargon 20. First edition. One of 200. $250–$350. Author's first book.

McCLURE, Michael. *Poisoned Wheat*. Red cloth. San Francisco, 1965. First edition. One of 24 signed. In dust jacket. $100. Ordinary issue: Wrappers. $15–$20.

McCLURE, Michael. *The Sermons of Jean Harlow & The Curses of Billy the Kid*. Wrappers. San Francisco, 1968. First edition. $25. Later (about 1970), boards. One of 50 signed. $50–$75.

McCLURE, S. S. *My Autobiography*. Red cloth. New York, (1914). (Ghost-written by Willa Cather.) First edition, first issue, with "May, 1914" on copyright page. $150–$200.

McCOLLUM, William. *California As I Saw It*. 72 pp., wrappers. Buffalo, 1850. First edition. $7,500.

McCONKEY, Mrs. Harriet E. (Bishop). *Dakota War Whoop; or, Indian Massacres and War in Minnesota*. 6 portraits. Cloth. St. Paul, 1863. First edition. $300–$400.

McCONNELL, H. H. *Five Years a Cavalryman*. Text on pink paper. Cloth. Jacksboro, Tex., 1889. First edition. $150–$200.

McCONNELL, Joseph Carroll. *The West Texas Frontier*. Cloth. Jacksboro, 1933. First edition, $100–$150.

McCONNELL, W. J. *Early History of Idaho*. 2 plates. Cloth. Caldwell, 1913. First edition. In dust jacket. $75–$100.

McCOOK, Henry C. *American Spiders and Their Spinningwork*. Portrait, 35 hand-colored plates. 3 vols., cloth. London, 1889–93. First edition. "Author's Edition." One of 250. $500–$750. Philadelphia, 1889–93. 3 vols., cloth. First American edition. One of 750. $400–$500.

McCORKLE, John, and Barton, O. S. *Three Years with Quantrell*. 11 plates. Maroon wrappers. Armstrong, Mo., (1914). First edition. $200–$300.

McCORMICK, Richard C. *Arizona: Its Resources and Prospects*. Folding map. 22 pp., buff printed wrappers. New York, 1865. First edition. $100–$150.

McCORMICK, S. J. *Almanac for the Year 1864; Containing Useful Information Relative to the Population, Progress and Resources of Oregon, Washington and Idaho*. 56 pp., wrappers. Portland, (1863). $200 and up.

McCOY, Horace. *No Pockets in a Shroud*. Tan cloth. London, (1937). First edition. In dust jacket. $75–$100.

McCOY, Horace. *They Shoot Horses, Don't They?* Tan cloth. New York, 1935. First edition. In dust jacket. $75–$100. London, 1935. Cloth. In dust jacket. $50–$60. Author's first book.

McCOY, Isaac. *History of Baptist Indian Missions*. Cloth. Washington, 1840. First edition. $250–$350.

McCOY, Isaac. *Remarks on the Practicability of Indian Reform*. 47 pp., wrappers. Boston, 1827. First edition. $300–$400. Half leather. $350. New York, 1829. Half leather. Second edition. $200.

McCOY, Isaac. *Remove Indians Westward*. (Caption title.) 48 pp., sewed. (Washington), 1829. First edition. $100–$150.

McCOY, Joseph G. *Historic Sketches of the Cattle Trade of the West and Southwest*. Portraits and plates. Pictorial cloth. Kansas City, 1874. First edition. $750–$1,250.

McCRACKEN, Harold. *The American Cowboy*. Illustrated, including color plates. Cloth. Garden City, 1973. First edition. One of 300 signed. Boxed. $150. Trade edition: In dust jacket. $35.

McCRACKEN, Harold. *The Charles M. Russell Book*. Illustrated, including color plates. Leather. Garden City, 1957. First edition. One of 250 signed. Boxed. $600–$750. Trade edition: Buckram. In dust jacket. $35–$50. Another issue (?): "Special Edition" in leather. $150.

McCRACKEN, Harold. *The Frank Tenney Johnson Book*. Illustrated, including color plates, by Johnson. Garden City, 1974. First edition. One of 350 signed, with an extra color plate. Boxed. $300–$350.

McCRACKEN, Harold. *The Frederic Remington Book*. Illustrated. Leather. Garden City, 1966. First edition. One of 500 signed. Boxed. $350–$425.

McCRACKEN, Harold. *Frederic Remington's Own West*. Illustrated. Calf. New York, 1960. First edition. One of 167 signed. Boxed. $300–$400.

McCRACKEN, Harold. *George Catlin and the Old Frontier*. Illustrated, including colored plates. Decorated leather. New York, 1959. One of 250, with extra color plate tipped in at front. Boxed. $200–$350. Trade edition: Cloth. In dust jacket. $25–$35.

McCULLERS, Carson. *The Ballad of the Sad Cafe*. Cloth. Boston, 1951. First edition. In dust jacket. $75–$125.

McCULLERS, Carson. *The Heart Is a Lonely Hunter*. Cloth. Boston, 1940. First edition. In dust jacket. $225–$300. Author's first book.

McCULLERS, Carson. *The Member of the Wedding*. Cloth. Boston, 1946. First edition. In dust jacket. $75–$125.

McCULLERS, Carson. *Reflections in a Golden Eye*. Cloth. (Boston), 1941. First edition. In dust jacket. $150–$225.

McCUTCHEON, George Barr. See Greaves, Richard.

McCUTCHEON, George Barr. *Brood House: A Play in Four Acts*. Boards. New York, 1910. First edition. One of 75. $75–$85.

McCUTCHEON, George Barr. *A Fool and His Money*. Cloth. New York, 1913. First edition. One of 50 signed. In dust jacket. $75–$85.

McCUTCHEON, George Barr. *Graustark*. Pictorial cloth. Chicago, 1901. First edition, first issue, with "Noble" instead of "Lorry" in line 6 of page 150. $50–$75. Author's first book.

McCUTCHEON, George Barr. *Kindling and Ashes*. Boards. New York, 1926. First edition. One of 25 signed. $75–$100. Trade edition: Cloth. In dust jacket. $20–$30.

McCUTCHEON, George Barr. *One Score and Ten*. Boards. New York, 1919. First edition. One of 30 signed. $75–$100.

McCUTCHEON, George Barr. *The Prince of Graustark*. Color illustrations by A. I. Keller. Boards. New York, 1914. One of 40 signed. $150–$250. Trade edition: Cloth. In dust jacket. $50–$75.

McCUTCHEON, George Barr. *Viola Gwyn*. Boards and parchment. New York, 1922. First edition. One of 50 signed. $75–$125.

McCUTCHEON, John T. *Bird Center*. Illustrated. Pictorial boards and cloth. Chicago, 1904. First edition. $40–$60.

McDANIELD, H. F., and Taylor, N. A. *The Coming Empire: or, 2,000 miles in Texas on Horseback*. Cloth. New York, (1877). First edition. $100–$150.

MacDIARMID, Hugh. See Duval, K. D.; Glen, Duncan; Grieve, C. M. (Note: The following listings under MacDiarmid's name include books with title pages reading "M'Diarmid" and "Mc'Diarmid.")

MacDIARMID, Hugh. *Cunninghame Graham: A Centenary Study*. Cloth. Glasgow, (1952). (By C. M. Grieve.) First edition. In dust jacket. $35–$50.

MacDIARMID, Hugh. *Direadh I, II, III*. Boards and leather. Frenich, Foss, England, 1974. (By C. M. Grieve.) First edition. One of 200 signed. Boxed. $150–$250.

MacDIARMID, Hugh. *A Drunk Man Looks at the Thistle*. Cloth. Edinburgh, 1926. (By C. M. Grieve.) First edition. In dust jacket. $250–$300.

MacDIARMID, Hugh. *The Fire of the Spirit*. Blue wrappers. Glasgow, 1965. (By C. M. Grieve.) One of 50 signed. $90–$100. Another issue: Wrappers. One of 350. $25.

MacDIARMID, Hugh. *First Hymn to Lenin and Other Poems*. Portrait frontispiece. Half black morocco and boards. London, (1931). (By C. M. Grieve.) Unicorn Press. First edition. One of 50 signed. $250–$350. Another issue: Red and black buckram. One of 450. Boxed. $150.

MacDIARMID, Hugh. *The Kind of Poetry I Want*. Boards and vellum. Edinburgh, 1961. (By C. M. Grieve.) First edition. One of 300 signed. Boxed. $200–$250. Another issue: One of 500. Boxed. $60–$75.

MacDIARMID, Hugh. *O Wha's Been Here Afore Me, Lass*. 4 pp., folded. No place, 1931. Blue Moon Press. (By C. M. Grieve.) First edition. One of 100 signed. $90–$100.

MacDIARMID, Hugh. *Penny Wheep*. Blue cloth. (Edinburgh), 1926. (By C. M. Grieve.) First edition. In dust jacket. $100–$125. Second binding: Boards. $85–$100.

MacDIARMID, Hugh. *Poetry Like the Hawthorn. From In Memoriam James Joyce.* Stiff yellow wrappers. Hemel Hempstead, England, 1962. (By C. M. Grieve.) First edition. One of 25 signed (from an issue of 150). $50–$75. Unsigned, $25–$35.

MacDIARMID, Hugh. *Sangschaw.* Cloth. (Edinburgh), 1925. (By C. M. Grieve.) First edition. In dust jacket. $250–$350. Poet's first book of verse.

MacDIARMID, Hugh. *Scots Unbound and Other Poems.* Frontispiece. Cloth. Stirling, Scotland, 1932. (By C. M. Grieve.) First edition. One of 350 signed. $100–$125.

MacDIARMID, Hugh. *Second Hymn to Lenin.* Wrappers. Thakeham, (1932). (By C. M. Grieve.) First edition. One of 100. $250–$300. London, 1935. Cloth. In dust jacket. $125–$150.

MacDIARMID, Hugh. *Stony Limits and Other Poems.* Cloth. London, 1934. (By C. M. Grieve.) First edition. In dust jacket. $125–$175.

MacDIARMID, Hugh. *Sydney Goodsir Smith.* Buckram, leather label. Edinburgh, 1963. (By C. M. Grieve.) First edition. One of 35 specially bound and signed by the author. $125–$150. Another issue: Wrappers. One of 100. $60–$80.

MacDIARMID, Hugh. *To Circumjack Cencrastus, or the Curly Snake.* Wrappers, or cloth. Edinburgh, 1930. (By C. M. Grieve.) First edition. Wrappers: $75–$100. Cloth. In dust jacket. $75–$100. Another issue: Blue morocco extra. Binding signed by Arthur Currie. $250 and up.

MacDIARMID, Hugh. *The Uncanny Scot.* Edited by Kenneth Buthlay. Buckram. (London, 1968.) (By C. M. Grieve.) First edition. One of 40 signed by Grieve. In dust jacket. $100–$125.

MacDIARMID, Hugh. *When the Rat-Race Is Over.* Gray wrappers. London, 1962. (By C. M. Grieve.) First edition. One of 40 signed. $75–$100.

MacDIARMID, Hugh. *Whuchulls: A Poem.* Wrappers. London, 1966. (By C. M. Grieve.) One of 100. $50–$75.

MacDIARMID, Hugh (editor). *The Voice of Scotland.* Vol. XIX, No. 3. Loose leaves, printed one side only, in cloth case. (Edinburgh, 1961.) (C. M. Grieve, editor.) Proof copies of an unpublished issue of this Scottish quarterly. (Only a few copies were run off for the editor.) $200 and up.

MacDONAGH, Donagh. *Veterans and Other Poems.* Boards and linen. Dublin, 1941. Cuala Press. First edition. One of 270. In dust jacket. $50–$60.

MACDONALD, John Ross. *The Drowning Pool.* Cloth. New York, 1950. (By Kenneth Millar.) First edition. In dust jacket. $125–$150.

MACDONALD, Ross. *The Chill.* Cloth. New York, 1964. (By Kenneth Millar.) First edition. In dust jacket. $125.

MACDONALD, Ross. *The Galton Case.* Cloth. New York, 1959. (By Kenneth Millar.) First edition. In dust jacket. $125–$135.

MacDONALD, George. *At the Back of the North Wind.* Illustrated by Arthur Hughes. Cloth. London, 1871. First edition. $500–$600. New York, 1871. Cloth. First American edition. $200–$250.

MacDONALD, George. *Dealings with the Fairies.* Illustrated by Arthur Hughes. Cloth. London, 1867. First edition. $350–$450.

MacDONALD, George. *Malcolm.* 3 vols., cloth. London, 1875. First edition. $300–$400.

MacDONALD, George. *Phantastes.* Cloth. London, 1858. First edition, with 16 pages of ads at end. $175–$250. London, 1912. Cloth. $50–$75.

MacDONALD, George. *The Princess and the Goblin*. Illustrated by Arthur Hughes. Cloth. London, 1897. First edition. $350–$400.

MacDONALD, George. *Within and Without: A Dramatic Poem*. Cloth. London, 1855. First edition. $200–$300. Author's first book.

MacDONALD, James. *Food from the Far West*. Decorated cloth. London, 1878. First edition. $200–$250. New York, (1878). Cloth. First American edition. $250.

MacDONALD, James, and Sinclair, James. *History of Hereford Cattle*. Illustrated. Cloth. London, 1886. First edition. $100–$150.

McDONALD, Archibald. *Peace River: A Canoe Voyage from Hudson's Bay to Pacific, by the Late George Simpson . . . in 1828*. Edited by Malcolm McLeod. Folding map. 119 pp., printed wrappers. Ottawa, 1872. First edition, with errata. $450–$500.

McDONALD, Frank V. (editor). *Notes Preparatory to a Biography of Richard Hayes McDonald*. Vol. 1. (All published.) Illustrated. Brown cloth. Cambridge, Mass., 1881. First edition. One of 150. $300–$400. Also, $225 (A, 1973).

McDONALD, John. *Biographical Sketches of Gen. Nathaniel Massie, Gen. Duncan McArthur, Capt. William Wells, and Gen. Simon Kenton*. Calf. Cincinnati, 1838. First edition. $150–$200.

M'DONELL, Alexander. *A Narrative of Transactions in the Red River Country*. Folding map. Boards. London, 1819. First edition. $1,250–$1,500.

MACDOUGALL, William. *The Red River Rebellion*. 68 pp., wrappers. Toronto, 1870. First edition. $100–$150.

McEACHRAN, D. *Notes of a Trip to Bow River North-West Territories*. Cloth (not original). Montreal, 1881. First edition. $150–$175.

McELROY, Joseph. *A Smuggler's Bible*. Cloth. New York, (1966). First edition. In dust jacket. $100–$125. Also, uncorrected proof, in wappers. $225. London, (1968). First English edition. In dust jacket. $50–$75.

MacFALL, Haldane. *Aubrey Beardsley: The Clown, the Harlequin, the Pierrot of His Age*. Illustrated. Cloth. New York, 1927. First edition. $100–$125.

MacFALL, Haldane. *Aubrey Beardsley, the Man and His Work*. Portrait and 10 plates. Half cloth. London, 1928. First edition. In dust jacket. $125–$150. Another issue: Cloth. One of 100 on handmade paper, with 6 extra illustrations. $200–$225.

MacFALL, Haldane. *The Book of Lovat*. Half cloth. London, 1923. First edition. One of 150 signed. In dust jacket. $150–$175. Ordinary issue: In dust jacket. $50–$75.

MacFALL, Haldane. *The Splendid Wayfaring*. Cloth. London, 1913. First edition. In dust jacket. $100–$150.

MacFALL, Haldane. *The Wooings of Jezebel Pettyfer*. Pictorial cloth. London, 1898. First edition, first issue, with portrait of Jezebel on front cover. $150–$200. (Most copies destroyed by fire.) Author's first book.

McFEE, William. *Aliens*. Cloth. London, 1914. First edition, first state, with ads dated 1915. In dust jacket. $40–$60. New York, 1916. Cloth. First American edition. In dust jacket. $25.

McFEE, William. *Casuals of the Sea*. Frontispiece in color. Cloth. London, 1916. First edition. In dust jacket. $125–$150. Also, $75 (A, 1975).

McFEE, William. *The Harbourmaster*. Boards and cloth. Garden City, 1931. First edition. One of 377 signed. Boxed. $40–$60. Garden City, 1932. Cloth. First trade edition. In dust jacket. $25.

McFEE, William. *Iron Men and Wooden Ships*. Woodcuts by Edward A. Wilson. Folio, boards. New York, 1924. First edition. One of 200 signed. Boxed. $75–$100.

McFEE, William. *Letters from an Ocean Tramp.* Colored frontispiece. Blue cloth. London, 1908. First edition, first state, with "Cassell & Co." at foot of spine. $150–$175. Author's first book.

McFEE, William. *The Reflections of Marsyas.* Boards. Gaylordsville, N.Y., 1933. Slide Mountain Press. One of 300 signed. In glassine dust jacket. $40–$50.

McFEE, William. *A Six-Hour Shift.* Boards, vellum spine. Garden City, 1920. First edition. One of 377 signed. In dust jacket. $40–$60.

McGAW, James F. *Philip Seymour, or, Pioneer Life in Richland County, Ohio.* 2 plates. Cloth. Mansfield, Ohio, 1858. First edition. $200–$250.

McGEE, I., and Maria. *The Mormon Endowment: A Secret Drama, or Conspiracy in the Nauvoo Temple in 1846.* Illustrated. 24 pp., pictorial wrappers. Syracuse, 1847. First edition. $3,250. (One of two known copies.)

McGEE, Joseph H. *Story of the Grand River Country, 1821–1905.* Portrait. Brown printed wrappers. (Gallatin, Mo., 1909.) First edition. $100–$150.

McGLASHAN, C. F. *History of the Donner Party: A Tragedy of the Sierras.* Cloth. Truckee, Calif., (1879). First edition. $600–$800. San Francisco, 1880. Illustrated. Cloth. Second edition. $300–$350.

McGOWAN, Edward. *Narrative of Edward McGowan.* Illustrated. Pictorial wrappers. San Francisco, 1857. First edition. $600–$800. San Francisco, 1917. (As *Narrative of Ned McGowan.*) Boards. One of 200. In dust jacket. $100.

McGREEVY, Thomas. *Poems.* Cloth. London, 1934. First edition. In dust jacket. $35–$50.

McGUANE, Thomas. *The Sporting Club.* Cloth. New York, (1968). First edition. In dust jacket. $75–$100.

MACHEN, Arthur. See Siluriensis, Leolinus.

MACHEN, Arthur. *Bridles and Spurs.* Green boards and cloth. Cleveland, 1951. Grabhorn printing for the Rowfant Club. One of 178. Boxed. $110–$125.

MACHEN, Arthur. *The Canning Wonder.* Boards and vellum. London, 1925. One of 130 signed. In dust jacket. $125–$150. Trade edition: Cloth. In dust jacket. $50–$60.

MACHEN, Arthur. *The Chronicle of Clemendy.* Frontispiece. Half vellum. Carbonnek, Wales, 1888. First edition. One of 250. Boxed. $100–$125. Carbonnek, 1923. (Printed in U.S.A.) Blue boards, parchment spine. One of 1,050 signed. In dust jacket. $50–$75.

MACHEN, Arthur. *The Cosy Room and Other Stories.* Pink cloth. London, (1936). First edition. In dust jacket. $100.

MACHEN, Arthur. *Dog and Duck.* Illustrated. Batik boards and cloth. London, 1924. First edition. One of 150 (of an edition of 900) signed. In dust jacket. $150.

MACHEN, Arthur. *Dreads and Drolls.* Boards, parchment spine. London, 1926. First edition. One of 100 signed. In dust jacket. $100–$125.

MACHEN, Arthur. *Far Off Things.* Boards. London, (1922). First edition. One of 100 signed. In dust jacket. $125–$150. Trade edition, later: Green cloth. In dust jacket. $35–$50.

MACHEN, Arthur. *The Great God Pan and the Inmost Light.* Pictorial blue cloth. London, 1894. First edition. $125–$150.

MACHEN, Arthur. *The Green Round.* Cloth. London, (1933). First edition. In dust jacket. $75–$100. Sauk City, 1968. Black cloth. First American edition. In dust jacket. $25–$35.

MACHEN, Arthur. *The Hill of Dreams*. Frontispiece. Dark-red buckram. London, 1907. First edition, with "E. Grant Richards" at bottom of spine. In dust jacket. $100. London, (1922). Cloth. One of 150 signed. In dust jacket. $175–$200.

MACHEN, Arthur. *The House of Souls*. Frontispiece. Pictorial light-gray buckram. London, 1906. First edition. In dust jacket. $100–$125. Without jacket, $50–$60.

MACHEN, Arthur. *Notes and Queries*. Green buckram, paper label. London, 1926. First edition. One of 265 signed. In dust jacket. $75–$100. Trade edition: Cloth. In dust jacket. $30–$35.

MACHEN, Arthur. *Ornaments in Jade*. Cloth. New York, 1924. First edition. One of 1,000 signed. In dust jacket. Boxed. $75–$85.

MACHEN, Arthur. *The Shining Pyramid*. Edited by Vincent Starrett. Illustrated. Black cloth. Chicago, 1923. One of 875. In dust jacket. $75–$100. London, 1925. Blue cloth. First English edition. One of 250 signed. In dust jacket. $100–$125. Trade edition: Cloth. In dust jacket. $25–$35.

MACHEN, Arthur. *Strange Roads. With the Gods in Spring*. Cloth. London, 1923. First edition. In glassine jacket. $35. London, 1924. Half vellum. One of 300 signed. $100.

MACHEN, Arthur. *Things Near and Far*. Boards. London, (1923). First edition. One of 100 signed. $75–$100. Trade edition: Cloth. $25.

MACHEN, Arthur. *The Three Impostors*. Blue cloth. London, 1895. First edition. $100–$125.

McILVAINE, William, Jr. *Sketches of Scenery and Notes of Personal Adventure, in California and Mexico*. 16 plates, including engraved title page. Purplish cloth. Philadelphia, 1850. First edition. $1,500–$1,750. San Francisco, 1951. Grabhorn printing. Folio, half cloth. One of 400. $125–$150.

McINTIRE, Jim. *Early Days in Texas: A Trip to Hell and Heaven*. 16 plates, pictorial cloth. Kansas City, Mo., (1902). First edition. $200–$400.

MACK, Effie. *Nevada: A History of the State*. Map, facsimiles. Glendale, Calif., 1936. First edition. One of 250 signed. $75–$100.

MACK, Solomon. *A Narraitive [sic] of the Life of Solomon Mack*. 48 pp., wrappers. Windsor, Vt., (1811?). First edition. $500–$750. Also, lacking back cover, $500 (A, 1979).

MACKAIL, J. W. *The Life of William Morris*. 22 illustrations. 2 vols., cloth. London, 1899. First edition. $50–$75. Also, rebound in morocco by Douglas Cockerell, $375 (A, 1975). London, 1901. Half morocco. $50–$60.

MACKAIL, J. W. *William Morris: An Address*. Vellum. London, 1901. Doves Press. First edition. One of 300. $200–$350. Another issue: Morocco. Specially bound by the Doves Bindery. Boxed. $1,000–$1,500. One of 15 on vellum. $750–$1,000. London, 1902. Boards, vellum spine. $100 and up. London, 1905. Boards. $55.

MACKAY, Charles. *Memoirs of Extraordinary Popular Delusions and the Madness of Crowds*. 5 portraits. 3 vols., gray cloth. London, 1841. First edition. $200–$300.

MACKAY, Charles. *The Mormons: Their Progress and Present Condition*. 10 parts, wrappers. London, 1851. First edition. $300–$350. London, 1851. Cloth. First book edition. $50–$65.

MACKAY, Malcolm S. *Cow-Range and Hunting Trail*. 38 illustrations. Cloth. New York, 1925. First edition. In dust jacket. $200–$250.

McKAY, Claude. *Banjo*. Decorated boards and cloth. New York, 1929. First edition. In dust jacket. $100–$125.

McKAY, Claude. *Gingertown.* Cloth. New York, 1932. First edition. In dust jacket. $100–$125.

McKAY, Claude. *Harlem Shadows: The Poems of Claude McKay.* Boards and cloth, paper label. New York, (1922). First edition. In dust jacket. $200–$250.

McKAY, Claude. *A Long Way from Home.* Green cloth. New York, (1937). First edition. In dust jacket. $85.

McKAY, Claude. *Songs of Jamaica.* Wrappers over boards. Kingston, 1912. First edition. $600–$800. Author's first book.

McKAY, Claude. *Spring in New Hampshire and Other Poems.* Wrappers. London, 1920. First edition. $250–$300.

McKAY, Richard C. *Some Famous Sailing Ships.* 10 color plates, 48 illustrations. Boards and cloth. New York, 1928. One of 250. $150–$200. New York, (1934). One of 200 signed. Boxed. $150–$200.

McKAY, Richard C. *South Street: A Maritime History of New York.* 48 illustrations. Two-tone cloth. New York, (1934). One of 200 signed. Boxed. $150.

McKAY, Robert H. *Little Pills.* 3 plates. Khaki cloth. Pittsburg, Kan., 1918. First edition. $75–$100.

McKAY, William, and Roberts, W. *John Hoppner, R.A.* Illustrated. Cloth. London, 1909. $100–$125. London, 1909–14. 2 vols., buckram (including supplement). $150–$175.

MacKAYE, Percy. *Johnny Crimson: A Legend of Hollis Hall.* Cover design by Eric Pape. Wrappers. Boston, 1895. First edition. $75–$100. Author's first book.

MacKAYE, Percy. *The Mystery of Hamlet, King of Denmark.* Folio, cloth. New York, 1950. First edition. One of 357. $150–$200.

McKEE, James Cooper. *Narrative of the Surrender of a Command of U.S. Forces at Fort Fillmore, N.M., in July A.D. 1861.* (Cover title.) 30 pp., printed self-wrappers. New York, 1881. Second edition. $200–$250. (The rare first edition appeared in Prescott, Arizona Territory, in 1878. Estimated value: $1,000 and up.)

McKEE, Dr. W. H. *The Territory of New Mexico and Its Resources.* Map. 12 pp., printed wrappers. New York, 1866. First edition. $2,000–$2,500.

MACKENNA, F. Severne. *Worcester Porcelain.* Frontispiece in color, 80 plates. Buckram. Leigh-on-Sea, 1950. One of 500 signed. In dust jacket. $150–$175.

McKENNEY, Thomas L. *Sketches of a Tour to the Lakes.* 29 full-page engravings, some in color. Boards, paper label. Baltimore, 1827. First edition. $300–$400.

McKENNEY, Thomas L., and Hall, James. *History of the Indian Tribes of North America.* Map, 120 colored plates and list of subscribers. 3 vols., folio, cloth, or half leather. Philadelphia, 1836–38–44. First edition. $12,000–$20,000. (Less, of course, for defective or much worn sets.) Another issue: 20 parts, wrappers. (Very rare.) Catalogued at $30,000 in 1981 by John Howell–Books, San Francisco. (In 1974 the price had been $19,500.) (Further notes: The first publisher of the folio 3-volume edition of this great color plate work was Biddle of Philadelphia, who followed up with a revised, or second folio, edition in 1837. In 1838 F. W. Greenough of Philadelphia issued still another folio version dated 1838–42–44, reprinted later by still another Philadelphia house, D. Rice & J. G. Clark. Each of these early editions is still prized for the quality of the Indian portraits. Prices have ranged in recent years from $5,000 to $10,000 at auction, while retail prices have been even higher. Even broken, or incomplete, sets bring very high prices because the plates have been widely used for decoration and are sold individually for varying high prices, depending on the subject and the condition of the plates and their coloring. Mixed sets from the several editions are frequently offered also. Thus the price range is wide for any set, complete, incomplete, or mixed that may come to market. See the book auction records for further information.) A modern version, in small quarto format: Edinburgh, 1933–34. 3 vols., blue cloth. In dust jackets. Boxed. $300–$400.

MACKENZIE, Alexander. *Voyages from Montreal, on the River St. Lawrence, Through the Continent of North America.* Frontispiece, 3 folding maps. Boards and cloth. London, 1801. First edition. $2,000–$2,500. London, 1802. 2 vols., boards. Second edition. $750–$1,000 or more. New York, 1802. Folding map. Boards. First American edition. $600–$800. Philadelphia, 1802. 2 vols., boards. $500–$750. (Note: Imperfect copies of all these editions, rebound and with defects of various kinds, appear frequently at auction and in the catalogues of dealers and, as usual, are acceptable substitutes for all but the most demanding collectors.)

MACKENZIE, Compton. *Extraordinary Women.* Cloth. London, 1928. First edition. One of 100 signed. In dust jacket. $125–$150.

MACKENZIE, Compton. *Poems.* Gray wrappers. Oxford, 1907. First edition. $100–$125.

MACKENZIE, James. *Angina Pectoris.* Illustrated. Cloth. London, (1923). First edition. $150–$200.

McKIM, Randolph H. *A Soldier's Recollections: Leaves from the Diary of a Young Confederate.* Cloth. New York, 1911. First edition. $60–$80.

McKNIGHT, Charles. *Old Fort Duquesne: or, Captain Jack, the Scout.* Cloth. Pittsburgh, 1873. First edition. $50–$75.

McKNIGHT, George S. *California 49er: Travels from Perrysburg to California.* (Cover title.) 27 pp., printed red wrappers. Perrysburg, Ohio, 1903. First edition. $150–$200.

McKUEN, Rod. *And Autumn Came.* Cloth. New York, (1954). First edition. In dust jacket. $75–$100. Author's first book.

McLAUGHLIN, James. *My Friend the Indian.* Illustrated. Cloth. Boston, 1910. First edition. $35–$50.

McLEOD, Donald. *A Brief Review of the Settlement of Upper Canada.* Cloth, paper label. Cleveland, 1841. First edition. $750–$850.

McLEOD, Donald. *History of Wiskonsan, from Its First Discovery to the Present Period.* 4 plates, folding map. Cloth. Buffalo, 1846. First edition. $250–$300. (Note: Wright Howes says some copies have plates and no map and others map and no plates.)

MacLEISH, Archibald. See *Class Poem,* 1915.

MacLEISH, Archibald. *American Letters for Gerald Murphy.* Half leather and cloth. Arroyo Grande, 1935. First edition. One of 150. $200. Another, covers dusty. $75.

MacLEISH, Archibald. *Conquistador.* Folding map. Cloth. Boston, 1932. First edition. In dust jacket. $50–$65. London, 1933. First English edition. In dust jacket. $50.

MacLEISH, Archibald. *Einstein.* Printed wrappers. Paris, 1929. Black Sun Press. First edition. One of 100 on Van Gelder paper. Boxed. $150–$200. One of 50 on vellum, signed. Boxed. $350–$450.

MacLEISH, Archibald. *The Happy Marriage and Other Poems.* Boards, paper label. Boston, 1924. First edition. In dust jacket. $50–$75.

MacLEISH, Archibald. *Land of the Free.* Illustrated with photographs. Linen. New York, (1938). First edition. In dust jacket. $100–$125.

MacLEISH, Archibald. *New Found Land.* Wrappers. Paris, 1930. Black Sun Press. First edition. One of 100 numbered copies (of an edition of 135). Boxed. $75–$100. One of 35 on vellum, signed. Boxed. $125–$150. One of 10 of the vellum copies initialed by Harry Crosby. $200–$250. Boston, 1930. (Printed in Paris.) Blue boards. First American edition. Boxed. $75.

MacLEISH, Archibald. *Nobodaddy*. Black cloth. Cambridge, Mass., 1926. First edition. One of 700. $50–$100. Another issue: One of 50 on large paper. $125–$150.

MacLEISH, Archibald. *The Pot of Earth*. Gold decorated boards. Cambridge, 1925. First edition. One of 100 on handmade paper. In dust jacket. Boxed. $75–$100. Boston, 1925. Boards. Trade edition. In dust jacket. $25–$30.

MacLEISH, Archibald. *Public Speech; Poems*. Full calf. New York, (1936). First edition. One of 275 signed. In glassine dust jacket. Boxed. $50–$75.

MacLEISH, Archibald. *Songs for a Summer Day*. Wrappers. (New Haven), 1913. First edition. $150–$250. Author's first book.

MacLEISH, Archibald. *Streets in the Moon*. Decorated boards and cloth. Boston, 1926. First edition. One of 60 on handmade paper, signed. Boxed. $125–$135. Another issue: One of 540. $30–$35.

MacLEISH, Archibald. *Tower of Ivory*. Boards, paper labels. New Haven, 1917. First edition. In dust jacket. $300–$400. Also, $275 (A, 1977). Author's first hardbound book.

McLUHAN, Herbert Marshall. *The Mechanical Bride*. Cloth. New York, (1951). First edition. In dust jacket. $40–$50. Author's first book.

McMASTER, S. W. *Sixty Years on the Upper Mississippi*. 300 pp., flexible wrappers. Rock Island, Ill., 1893 (printer's foreword dated Galena, Ill., 1895). First edition. $175–$200.

McMURTRIE, Douglas C. *The Beginnings of Printing in Chicago*. Half cloth. Chicago, 1931. One of 160. $75–$125.

McMURTRIE, Douglas C. *The Beginnings of Printing in Utah*. Half cloth. Chicago, 1931. One of 160. $75–$125.

McMURTRIE, Douglas C. *Bibliography of Chicago Imprints, 1835–50*. Buckram. Chicago, 1944. One of 200. $100–$125.

McMURTRIE, Douglas C. *Early Printing in Michigan*. Cloth. Chicago, 1931. One of 250. $150–$175.

McMURTRIE, Douglas C. *Early Printing in New Orleans, 1764–1810*. Illustrated. Half cloth. New Orleans, 1929. One of 410. $125.

McMURTRIE, Douglas C. *Early Printing in Tennessee*. Cloth. Chicago, 1933. One of 900. $125.

McMURTRIE, Douglas C. *Early Printing in Wisconsin*. Cloth. Seattle, 1931. First edition. One of 300. $125–$150.

McMURTRIE, Douglas C. *Early Printing in Wyoming*. Cloth. Hattiesburg, Miss., 1943. $100.

McMURTRIE, Douglas C. *Eighteenth Century North Carolina Imprints, 1749–1800*. Fascimiles. Cloth. Chapel Hill, 1938. One of 200. In dust jacket. $75–$100.

McMURTRIE, Douglas C. *The First Printers of Chicago*. Half cloth. Chicago, 1927. One of 650. $35. Another issue: One of 250. $75.

McMURTRIE, Douglas C. *The Golden Book*. Illustrated. Half morocco. Chicago, 1927. First edition. One of 220 signed. $75–$125. Trade edition: Cloth. In dust jacket. $50–$60.

McMURTRIE, Douglas C. *A History of Printing in the United States*. Vol. II. (All published.) Cloth. New York, 1936. First edition. $150–$175. (Covers Middle and South Atlantic states.)

McMURTRIE, Douglas C. *Jotham Meeker: Pioneer Printer of Kansas.* Portrait and facsimiles. Cloth. Chicago, 1930. One of 650. $75–$100.

McMURTRIE, Douglas C. *Pioneer Printing in Texas.* Wrappers. Austin, 1932. One of 200. $75–$100.

McMURTRIE, Douglas C., and Allen, Albert H. *Early Printing in Colorado.* Cloth. Denver, 1935. First edition. $75–$100.

McMURTRIE, Douglas C., and Eames, Wilberforce. *New York Printing.* 78 illustrations. Cloth. Chicago, 1928. $75–$100.

McMURTRIE, Henry. *Sketches of Louisville and Its Environs.* Map and table. Boards. Louisville, 1819. First edition. $200–$250.

McMURTRY, Larry. See Ray, Ophelia.

McMURTRY, Larry. *Horseman, Pass By.* Boards and cloth. New York, (1961). First edition. In dust jacket. $275–$350. Author's first book.

McMURTRY, Larry. *In a Narrow Grave.* Cloth. Austin, 1968. Encino Press. First edition, first issue, with "skyscrappers" for "skyscrapers," page 105, and other errors. (Suppressed.) In dust jacket. $275–$350. Second issue, errors corrected: In dust jacket. $75–$150. Limited issue: Half leather. One of 250 signed. Boxed. $250–$300.

McMURTRY, Larry. *It's Always We Rambled: An Essay on Rodeo.* Boards. New York, 1974. First edition. One of 300 signed. (Issued without dust jacket.) $85–$100.

McMURTRY, Larry. *The Last Picture Show.* Tan cloth. New York, 1966. First edition. In dust jacket. $100–$125.

McMURTRY, Larry. *Leaving Cheyenne.* Cloth. New York, (1963). First edition. In dust jacket. $175–$225.

MacNEICE, Louis. *Autumn Journal.* Cloth. London, 1939. First edition. In dust jacket. $100–$125.

MacNEICE, Louis, *Blind Fireworks.* Cloth. London, 1929. First edition. In dust jacket. $350–$450. Author's first book.

MacNEICE, Louis. *The Earth Compels.* Cloth. London, 1939. First edition. In dust jacket. $75.

MacNEICE, Louis. *I Crossed the Minch.* Illustrated. Cloth. London, (1938). First edition. In dust jacket. $100–$150.

MacNEICE, Louis. *The Last Ditch.* Boards, linen spine, paper label. Dublin, 1940. Cuala Press. First edition. One of 450. In tissue dust jacket. $150–$250.

MacNEICE, Louis. *Poems.* Cloth. London, 1935. First edition. In dust jacket. $100–$125.

MacNEICE, Louis. *Poems.* Cloth. New York, (1937). First edition. (Same title as the 1935 book but not the same content.) In dust jacket. $75–$100.

MacNEICE, Louis. *Springboard.* Cloth. London, 1944. First edition. In dust jacket. $40–$60. New York, (1945). First American edition. In dust jacket. $35–$45.

McNEIL, Samuel. *McNeils [sic] Travels in 1849, to, Through and from the Gold Regions.* 40 pp., plain wrappers. Columbus, Ohio, 1850. First edition. $5,000 and up. Also, $3,500 (A, 1968)—the Thomas W. Streeter copy, one of only 5 known.

MacNUTT, Francis A. *Bartholomew de Las Casas, His Life, Apostolate, and Writings.* Portrait. 2 vols., half cloth. Cleveland, 1909. First edition. In dust jackets. $75–$150.

MACOMB, David B. *Answer to Enquiries Relative to Middle Florida.* 5 unnumbered leaves. Tallahassee, 1827. First edition. $1,000–$1,500.

MACON, T. J. *Reminiscences of the 1st Company of Richmond Howitzers.* Cloth. Richmond, (about 1909). First edition. $100–$125.

McPHEE, John. *A Sense of Where You Are.* Cloth. New York, (1965). First edition. In dust jacket. $75–$85. Author's first book.

MACQUOID, Percy. *The History of English Furniture.* Illustrated, including color plates. 4 vols., buckram. London, 1904–08. First edition. $750–$875.

MACQUOID, Percy, and Edwards, Ralph. *The Dictionary of English Furniture.* 43 color plates, about 3,000 other illustrations. 3 vols., folio, buckram. London, 1924–27. First edition. $600–$800. London, 1954. 3 vols., folio, buckram. $600–$800.

McSHEEHY, H. J. *A Hunt in the Rockies.* Frontispiece and photographs. 135 pp., printed red wrappers. Logansport, Ind., 1893. First edition. $300–$400, possibly more.

McWHORTER, Lucullus V. *The Border Settlers of Northwestern Virginia from 1768 to 1795.* Cloth. Hamilton, Ohio, 1915. First edition. $75–$85.

McWILLIAMS, John. *Recollections.* Portrait. Cloth. Princeton, (about 1919). First edition. $100–$125.

MACY, John (editor). *American Writers on American Literature.* Cloth. New York, 1931. First edition. In dust jacket. $75–$100.

MADARIAGA, Salvador de. *Don Quixote: An Introductory Essay in Psychology.* Boards and linen. Newtown, Wales, 1934. Gregynog Press. One of 250. $200–$300.

MADDEN, Frederic W. *Coins of the Jews.* Illustrated. Folio, half leather. London, 1881. First edition. $150–$175. London, 1903. Second edition. $100.

MADDEN, R. R. *The Island of Cuba.* Boards. London, 1849. First edition. $150–$200.

MADISON, James. *Message from the President of the United States, Recommending an Immediate Declaration of War Against Great Britain.* 12 pp., sewed. Washington, 1812. $200–$300.

MAGEE, David. *The Hundredth Book: A Bibliography of . . . The Book Club of California.* 18 reproductions, many in color. Folio, half cloth. San Francisco, 1958. Grabhorn printing. One of 400. In dust jacket. $200–$300.

MAGEE, Dorothy, and Magee, David. *Bibliography of the Grabhorn Press, 1940–1956.* Illustrated. Folio, half morocco. San Francisco, 1957. One of 225. $650–$850. (See Heller entry for related work.)

MAGNA Carta and Other Charters of English Liberties. Tan pigskin. (London, 1938.) Guyon House Press. One of 250. $150–$200.

MAGOFFIN, Susan Shelby. *Down the Santa Fe Trail and into Mexico.* Edited by Stella M. Drumm. Map, plates. Cloth. New Haven, 1926. First edition. In dust jacket. $125–$150.

MAGOUN, F. Alexander. *The Frigate Constitution and Other Historic Ships.* Illustrated, including 16 folding plates. Buckram. Salem, 1928. One of 97 large paper copies. $300–$425. Ordinary issue: $75–$85.

MAGRUDER, Allan B. *Political, Commercial and Moral Reflections, on the Late Cession of Louisiana, to the United States.* Boards. Lexington, Ky., 1803. First edition. $3,000–$3,500.

MAGUIRE, H. N. *The Coming Empire: A Complete and Reliable Treatise on the Black*

Hills, Yellowstone and Big Horn Regions. 7 plates, folding map. Cloth. Sioux City, Iowa, 1878. First edition. $300–$400.

MAGUIRE, H. N. *The Lakeside Library: The People's Edition of the Black Hills and American Wonderland.* (Caption title.) Illustrations and map. 36 pp., stitched. Chicago, 1877. First edition. $300 and up. Also, $150 (A, 1968).

MAHAN, A. T. *The Influence of Sea Power upon History.* Illustrated. Cloth. Boston, 1890. First edition. $275–$600. London, (1892?). 557 pp., cloth. First English edition. $200.

MAHAN, A. T. *The Navy in the Civil War.* Illustrated. Cloth. New York, 1883. First edition. $100–$150. Author's first book.

MAID Marian. Boards. London, 1822. (By Thomas Love Peacock.) First edition. $500–$600.

MAILER, Norman. *Barbary Shore.* Black boards. New York, (1951). First edition, with circled "R" on copyright page. In dust jacket. $50–$75.

MAILER, Norman. *Deaths for the Ladies and Other Disasters.* Printed wrappers. New York, (1962). First edition. $75–$100. Another issue: Cloth. In dust jacket. $125–$150.

MAILER, Norman. *Gargoyle, Guignol, False Closet.* 4 pp., leaflet. Dublin, 1964. First edition. One of 100. $100–$150.

MAILER, Norman. *Marilyn.* Illustrated. Cloth. (New York, 1973.) First edition. Limited and signed. Boxed. $100–$125.

MAILER, Norman. *The Naked and the Dead.* Black boards. New York, (1948). First edition, with circled "R" on copyright page. In dust jacket. $250–$325. Author's first book. (Note: A hefty book bound in notoriously cheap fashion—paper over boards—thus rare in fine condition immediately after publication.) London, (1949). Full wine-colored morocco. First English edition. One of 240 bound for the Collector's Book Club. $250–$300. Another issue: One of 13. $400–$500.

MAILLARD, N. Doran. *The History of the Republic of Texas, from the Discovery of the Country to the Present Time.* Folding map. Dark-blue cloth. London, 1842. First edition. $350–$600.

MAJOR, Charles. See Caskoden, Edwin.

MAJOR Jones's Courtship; or Adventures of a Christmas Eve. 61 pp., wrappers. Savannah, Ga., 1850. (By William Tappan Thompson.) First edition. $75–$150.

MAJOR Jones's Sketches of Travel, Comprising the Scenes, Incidents, and Adventures in His Tour from Georgia to Canada. Illustrated by F. O. C. Darley. Philadelphia, 1848. (By William Tappan Thompson.) First edition. $200–$250.

MAJORS, Alexander. *Seventy Years on the Frontier.* Frontispiece and plates. Blue pictorial cloth, or wrappers. Chicago, 1893. First edition. Cloth: $85–$100. Wrappers: $125–$150.

MALAMUD, Bernard. *The Natural.* Red, blue, or gray cloth. New York, (1952). First edition. In dust jacket. $125–$150. Author's first book. (Note: Red cloth has been called the first binding, a point disputed by a gray cloth copy seen with a review slip pasted in.)

MALAMUD, Bernard. *The Tenants.* Orange cloth. New York, (1971). First edition, first binding. One of 250 signed. In dust jacket. $100–$150. Trade edition: In dust jacket. $25. London, (1972). Cloth. First English edition. In dust jacket. $25.

MALET, Capt. H. E. *Annals of the Road.* 10 colored plates, woodcuts. Cloth. London, 1876. First edition. $100–$150.

MALKIN, B. H. *A Father's Memoirs of His Child.* Folding map, 3 plates. Boards. London, 1806. First edition. $125–$175.

MALORY, Sir Thomas. *Le Morte D'Arthur.* Illustrated by Aubrey Beardsley. 12 parts, printed wrappers. London, (1893–94). One of 300 on Dutch handmade paper. $1,500–$2,000. Another issue: 3 vols., pictorial cloth. One of 300. $1,500–$2,000. Another issue: 2 vols., cloth. One of 1,500. $600–$800. Another: Full vellum. $750. London, 1909. Cloth. Second Beardsley edition. $400–$500. London, 1910–11. Riccardi Press. Illustrated in color by W. Russell Flint. 4 vols., limp vellum or boards. One of 500. In dust jackets. Boxed. $500–$800. Also, one of 12 on vellum in a Riviere binding. $6,500 (A, 1978). London, 1913. Ashendene Press. Illustrated by Charles and Margaret Gere. Folio, full cowhide. One of 145 (colophon errs; the issue was 147). Boxed. $2,000–$2,500. Another issue: One of 8 on vellum. $4,000–$5,000. London, 1917. Illustrated by Arthur Rackham. Vellum. One of 500 signed by Rackham. $850–$1,250. Also, with an original watercolor by Rackham, $6,200 (A, 1981). New York, 1917. Full leather. American Rackham edition. One of 250. Boxed. $1,000–$1,250. London or New York, 1917. Clothbound Rackham issues: $300–$500. London, 1927. Illustrated by Beardsley. Half vellum. One of 1,600. $350–$400. London, (1929). Illustrated by Flint. Morocco. $500–$750. London, 1933. Shakespeare Head Press. Illustrated. 2 vols., morocco. One of 370. $500–$600. New York, 1936. Limited Editions Club. Illustrated by Robert Gibbings. 2 vols., boards. Boxed. $200–$300.

MALRAUX, André. *The Metamorphosis of the Gods.* Illustrated. Red morocco. Garden City, 1960. First American edition. One of 50 signed. Boxed. $200–$300. Trade edition: Cloth. In dust jacket. $30–$40.

MALRAUX, André. *The Psychology of Art.* Illustrated. 3 vols., cloth. (New York, 1949–50.) First American edition. In dust jacket. $200–$250.

MALRAUX, André. *The Voices of Silence.* Illustrated. Cloth. Garden City, 1953. First American edition. In dust jacket. Boxed. $60–$85. Another issue: Full leather. One of 160 signed. Boxed. $350–$400.

MALRAUX, André. *The Walnut Trees of Altenburg.* Translated by A. W. Fielding. Cloth. London, 1952. First English edition. In dust jacket. $80–$100.

MALTHUS, Thomas Robert. *Definitions in Political Economy.* Boards. London, 1827. First edition. $300–$350.

MALTHUS, Thomas Robert. *An Essay on the Principle of Population.* Boards. London, 1803. Second edition. $200–$250. (Note: The anonymous first edition, London, 1798, boards, sells for $3,000 and up if in fine condition.) Washington, 1809. 2 vols., contemporary calf. First American edition. $500.

MALTHUS, Thomas Robert. *An Inquiry into the Nature and Progress of Rent.* Boards. London, 1815. First edition. $350–$400.

MALTHUS, Thomas Robert. *Principles of Political Economy.* Boards. London, 1820. First edition. $1,000–$1,500. Boston, 1821. Boards. First American edition. $200–$300.

MAN Without a Country (The). 23 pp., terra-cotta wrappers. Boston, 1865. (By Edward Everett Hale.) First edition, first issue, without the publisher's printed yellow "Announcement" slip tipped in. $400–$500. Also, $300 (A, 1981). Second issue, with the "Announcement" slip tipped in. $250–$350. New York, 1902. Vellum. "Birthday Edition." One of 80 on Japan paper. $100–$125. New York, 1936. Limited Editions Club. Boxed. $25–$35.

MANGAM, William D. *The Clarks of Montana.* Illustrated, including folding facsimile. Stiff brown wrappers. (New York: Silver Bow Press), 1939. First edition. $300. Second edition (rewritten and retitled *The Clarks: An American Phenomenon*): New York, 1941. Blue cloth. In dust jacket. $250. Without jacket, $200.

MANIFIESTO al Mundo, La Justicia y la Necesidad de la Independencia de la Nueva España. 19 pp., sewed. Puebla, Mexico, 1821. (By Manuel de la Barcena.) First edition. $600–$750.

MANLY, William Lewis. *Death Valley in '49*. 4 plates. Cloth. San Jose, 1894. First edition. $100–$135.

MANN, Thomas. *The Beloved Returns*. Boards. New York, 1940. First American edition. One of 395 signed. In dust jacket. Boxed. $150–$250. Advance copy in wrappers: $175.

MANN, Thomas. *Buddenbrooks, Verfall einer Familie*. 2 vols., half morocco. Berlin, 1901. First edition. $200–$300. Author's first book. London, 1924. Translated by H. T. Lowe-Porter. 2 vols., cloth. First edition in English. In dust jacket. $150.

MANN, Thomas. *Doctor Faustus*. Green cloth. New York, 1948. First edition in English. In dust jacket. $150–$200.

MANN, Thomas. *Joseph and his Brothers*. 4 vols., cloth. London, 1934–35–(38). First edition in English. In dust jackets. $300–$350.

MANN, Thomas. *The Magic Mountain*. 2 vols., half vellum. New York, 1927. One of 200 signed. $300–$400. New York, 1962. Limited Editions Club. Illustrated. Half cloth. Boxed. $75–$85.

MANN, Thomas. *Nocturnes*. Lithographs by Lynd Ward. Pictorial cloth. New York, 1934. One of 1,000 signed. Boxed. $150–$200.

MANN, Thomas. *A Sketch of My Life*. White buckram. Paris, (1930). First edition. One of 695 on Van Gelder paper. $150–$200. Another issue: One of 75 on vellum. $300–$325.

MANN, Thomas. *Sleep, Sweet Sleep*. Boards. (New York), 1934. First edition. In glassine dust jacket. $100.

MANSFIELD, Edward D. *Exposition of the Natural Position of Mackinaw City, and the Climate, Soil, and Commercial Elements of the Surrounding Country*. 2 maps. 47 pp., printed wrappers. Cincinnati, 1857. First edition. $150–$200.

MANSFIELD, Katherine. *The Aloe*. Buckram. London, 1930. First edition. One of 750. In dust jacket. $100–$135. New York, 1930. Boards. First American edition. One of 975. In dust jacket. Boxed. $50–$75.

MANSFIELD, Katherine. *Bliss and Other Stories*. Brick-red cloth. London, (1920). First edition, with page 13 numbered 3. In white dust jacket with author's portrait. $150–$200. New York, 1921. Cloth, paper label. First American edition. In dust jacket. $50–$60.

MANSFIELD, Katherine. *The Doves' Nest and Other Stories*. Blue-gray cloth, blue spine lettering. London, (1923). First edition, first issue, with verso of title page blank. One of 25. In dust jacket. $300–$400. Second issue, with "First published June, 1923" on back of title page. In dust jacket. $100–$125.

MANSFIELD, Katherine. *The Garden Party and Other Stories*. Light-blue cloth, lettered in blue. London, (1922). First edition, first issue, with "sposition" for "position" in last line on page 103. In strawberry-colored dust jacket. One of 25. $500–$650. Later binding state, orange (ocher) lettering. In dust jacket. $150–$200. London, (1939). Verona Press. 16 color lithographs by Marie Laurencin. Decorated cloth. One of 1,170. In dust jacket. Boxed. $300–$400. Another issue: Full morocco. One of 30. Boxed. $700–$800.

MANSFIELD, Katherine. *In a German Pension*. Green cloth. London, (1911). First edition. In orange (ocher) dust jacket. $400–$500. Author's first book.

MANSFIELD, Katherine. *The Journal of Katherine Mansfield*. Edited by J. Middleton Murry. Cloth. London, 1927. First edition. In dust jacket. $75–$100.

MANSFIELD, Katherine. *The Little Girl and Other Stories*. Cloth. New York, 1924. First American edition (of *Something Childish and Other Stories*). In dust jacket. $75–$100.

MANSFIELD, Katherine. *Poems*. Brown boards, red leather spine label. London, (1923). First edition. In cream-colored dust jacket. $150–$175.

MANSFIELD, Katherine. *Prelude*. Blue pictorial wrappers. Richmond, England, (1918). Hogarth Press. First edition, with or without design on covers by J. D. Fergusson. $200–$250. Another issue: Blue boards and linen. One of 300. $300–$350.

MANSFIELD, Katherine. *Something Childish and Other Stories*. Gray buckram. London, (1924). First edition, first issue, without "First published 1924" on verso of title page. In dust jacket. $250–$275. Second issue. In dust jacket. $150–$200.

MANSFIELD, Katherine. *To Stanislaw Wyspianski*. Printed wrappers. London, 1938. One of 100 printed for Bertram Rota. $100–$125.

MANSFIELD Park: A Novel. By the Author of *Sense and Sensibility* and *Pride and Prejudice*. 3 vols., blue boards, white paper labels. London, 1814. (By Jane Austen.) First edition, with Vols. 1 and 3 bearing Sidney imprint on back of half titles and Vol. 2 the Roworth imprint. $5,000–$7,500. Also, $4,250 (A, 1974). London, 1816. 3 vols., cloth. $500 and up.

MANUAL of Military Surgery. Prepared for the Use of the Confederate States Army. 30 lithograph plates. Cloth-backed wrappers. Richmond, 1863. (By John J. Chisholm.) First illustrated edition (?). $850. Earlier editions: Richmond, 1861. $300 (A, 1978). Richmond, 1862. $130 (A, 1979); $250 (A, 1978).

MANUEL de Proverbes Dramatiques. 288 pp., cloth, printed spine label. Portland (Brunswick), Me., 1830. First edition. No record in modern times. First edition, second issue, with last page misnumbered 188. (Edited anonymously by Henry Wadsworth Longfellow.) Rebound in morocco, $80 (A, 1960). (Note: Blanck's *BAL* also describes a preliminary issue of the same edition with only 156 pages.)

MARCH of the First (The). (First Regiment of Colorado Volunteers.) 36 pp., stitched, plus 4 pp. of ads. Denver, 1863. First edition. $3,500. Also, $2,000 (A, 1968). (See Hollister, Ovando J.)

MARCLIFFE, Theophilus. *The Looking Glass: A True History of the Early Years of an Artist*. Boards. London, 1805. (By William Godwin.) First edition. $1,000–$1,200.

MARCUS Aurelius Antonius. *The Thoughts of the Emperor Marcus Aurelius*. Translated by George Long. Wrappers. London, 1897. Ashendene Press. One of 30. $3,000 and up. London, 1909. Illustrated by W. Russell Flint. Limp vellum with ties. One of 17 on vellum. $2,000–$3,000. Another issue: Vellum or half cloth. One of 500. $250–$350.

MARCY, Randolph B. *Exploration of the Red River of Louisiana*. (Senate Exec. Doc. 54.) 65 plates. 2 maps. 2 vols., brown cloth and green cloth (atlas case). Washington, 1853. First edition, $100–$150. Washington, 1854. Second edition, printed by Tucker. $100. Washington, 1854. House version, printed by Nicholson. $100.

MARCY, Randolph B. *The Prairie Traveler: A Hand-Book for Overland Expeditions*. Map, frontispiece. 10 plates. Cloth. New York, 1859. First edition. $350–$400. London, 1863. Edited by R. F. Burton. Map. Half morocco. First English edition. $400.

MARDERSTEIG, Hans. *Pastonchi: A Specimen of a New Letter for Use on the "Monotype."* Illustrated with plates and booklet inserts. Marbled boards and vellum. (London, 1928.) One of 200 on Fabriano paper, printed by Mardersteig. $150–$200.

MARIGNY, Bernard. *Réflexions sur la Campagne du Gen. Jackson en Louisiane en 1814–15*. 51 pp., wrappers. Nouvelle-Orléans. 1848. First edition. $200–$300.

MARK Twain's Sketches. See Twain, Mark.

MARKET Harborough; or, How Mr. Sawyer Went to the Shires. Cloth. London, 1861. (By George John Whyte-Melville.) First edition. $350–$450.

MARKHAM, Edwin. *The Man with the Hoe*. 4 pp., printed wrappers. San Francisco, 1899. First book edition. $150 and up. (Earlier, Jan. 15, 1899: Special supplement to

San Francisco Sunday *Examiner*, containing first separate printing of the poem, 44 pp. $200 and up.) New York, 1899. Green cloth. Second edition, first issue, with "fruitless" for "milkless" in line 5, page 35. $50–$75.

MARKHAM, Edwin. *New Poems: Eighty Songs at Eighty*. Portrait. Boards and leather. Garden City, 1932. First edition (so stated). One of 100 signed. Boxed. $75–$100. Trade edition: Cloth. In dust jacket. $25.

MARKLAND, Abraham. *Pteryplegia: The Art of Shooting–Flying*. Hand-colored plates by Robert Ball. Boards. New York, 1931. Derrydale Press. One of 200 signed by the artist. $400–$500. Another issue: Black and white plates. One of 300. $100–$150.

MARKS, B. *Small Scale Farming in Central California*. 48 pp., printed wrappers. San Francisco, 1888. $100–$125.

MARKS, M. R. *The Advantages and Resources of Orange County, Florida*. 2 maps. 16 pp., wrappers. Orlando, Fla., (1879). $100–$125.

MARLOWE, Christopher. *Edward the Second*. Hand-colored illustrations. Folio, vellum. London, 1929. Aquila Press. One of 40. $300–$350. Another issue: One of 500. $100–$125.

MARLOWE, Christopher. *The Famous Tragedy of the Rich Jew of Malta*. Engravings by Eric Ravilious. Cloth. London, 1933. Golden Hours Press. One of 250. $150–$200.

MARLOWE, Christopher, and Chapman, George. *Hero and Leander*. Illustrated. Vellum. London, 1894. Vale Press. One of 220. $400–$500. London, 1933. Golden Hours Press. Illustrated by Lettice Sanford. Cloth. One of 206, not all of which were bound. $175–$225.

MARQUAND, John P. See Clark, Charles E.

MARQUAND, John P. *The Late George Apley*. Green cloth. Boston, 1937. First edition, first issue, with "Pretty Pearl" in first line of page 19. In dust jacket. $75–$100.

MARQUAND, John P. *Ming Yellow*. Cloth. Boston, 1935. First edition. In dust jacket. $75–$125.

MARQUAND, John P. *Point of No Return*. Cloth. Boston, 1949. First edition. One of 600 signed. In dust jacket. $75–$125. Trade edition: In dust jacket. $35.

MARQUAND, John P. *The Unspeakable Gentleman*. Cloth. New York, 1922. First edition, with Scribner seal on copyright page. In dust jacket. $100–$125. Another issue: Boards and cloth. Limited, signed, for booksellers. $150–$200. Author's first novel.

MARQUIS, Don. *Archy and Mehitabel*. Black cloth. Garden City, 1927. First edition, first printing. In dust jacket. $100–$125.

MARQUIS, Don. *Danny's Own Story*. Illustrated by E. W. Kemble. Green cloth. Garden City, 1912. First edition. In dust jacket. $100. Author's first book.

MARQUIS, Don. *Dreams and Dust*. Cloth. New York, (1915). First edition. In dust jacket. $35–$50.

MARQUIS, Don. *How Hank Signed the Pledge in a Cistern*. Wrappers. New York, (about 1912). First edition. $40–$60.

MARQUIS, Don. *The Old Soak, and Hail and Farewell*. Boards and cloth. Garden City, 1921. First edition. In dust jacket. $50–$60.

MARQUIS, Thomas B. *A Warrior Who Fought Custer*. Illustrated. Cloth. Minneapolis, 1931. First edition, first binding, with "Midwest" on spine. In dust jacket. $75–$100.

MARRANT, John. *A Narrative of the Life of John Marrant*. 48 pp., wrappers. Halifax, 1812. (Edited by William Aldridge.) $100–$125. (Note: One of innumerable nineteenth-century reprints of a book first published in London in 1785. Howes calls it "one of the earliest written by an American Negro.")

MARRIAGE: A Novel. 3 vols., boards. Edinburgh, 1818. (By Susan Edmonstone Ferrier.) First edition. $1,000–$1,250.

MARRIOTT, William. *A Collection of English Miracle-Plays or Mysteries.* Boards, paper labels. Basel, Switzerland, 1838. First edition. $50–$100.

MARRYAT, Frank. *Mountains and Molehills.* 18 woodcuts, 8 color plates. Salmon-colored cloth. London, 1855. (By Francis S. Marryat.) First edition. $500–$600. Also, $475 (A, 1979). New York, 1855. Frontispiece. Pictorial cloth. First American edition. $150–$200.

MARRYAT, Frederick. See *Mr. Midshipman Easy; Olla Podrida; Percival Keene; Snarleyyow.*

MARRYAT, Frederick. *A Diary in America.* 6 vols., (Parts I and II, each 3 vols.), boards. London, 1839. First edition. $300–$400. Philadelphia, 1839–40. 3 vols., half cloth (2 vols., 1839, and 2d Series, 1 vol., 1840). First American edition. $200–$250.

MARRYAT, Frederick. *Jacob Faithful.* 3 vols., half cloth. London, 1834. First edition. $150–$250.

MARRYAT, Frederick. *The Little Savage.* Illustrated. 2 vols., green cloth. London, 1848–49. First edition. $200–$350.

MARRYAT, Frederick. *Masterman Ready.* Illustrated. 3 vols., cloth. London, 1841–42–42. First edition. $400–$600. Also, a presentation set, signed, $1,300 in a 1980 catalogue.

MARRYAT, Frederick. *The Mission.* Map, frontispiece. 2 vols., cloth. London, 1845. First edition, with 32 pages of ads in Vol. 1. $250–$350.

MARRYAT, Frederick. *Narrative of the Travels and Adventures of Monsieur Violet, in California, Sonora and Western Texas.* Map. 3 vols., cloth. London, 1843. First edition. $400–$600. Second edition: London, 1843. 3 vols., cloth. With map. Retitled: *The Travels and Romantic Adventures of Monsieur Violet, etc.* $400–$600.

MARRYAT, Frederick. *Poor Jack.* Illustrated. 12 parts, pictorial wrappers. London, 1840. First edition. $400–$500. London, 1840. Pictorial cloth. First book edition. $150–$200.

MARRYAT, Frederick. *The Privateer's Man.* 2 vols., cloth. London, 1846. First edition, with many ads in first volume. $250–$350.

MARRYAT, Frederick. *The Settlers in Canada.* 2 frontispieces. 2 vols., cloth. London, 1844. First edition. $150–$200.

MARRYAT, Frederick. *Stories of the Sea.* Cloth. New York, 1836. First American edition. $75–$100.

MARSH, James B. *Four Years in the Rockies.* Portrait. Cloth. New Castle, Pa., 1884. First edition. $350–$450.

MARSH, John. *Hannah Hawkins, the Reformed Drunkard's Daughter.* Cloth. New York, 1844. First edition. $75–$100.

MARSH, W. Lockwood. *Aeronautical Prints and Drawings.* Illustrated, including color plates. Cloth. London, 1924. First edition. In dust jacket. $250–$350. Another issue: Pigskin. One of 100. $400–$500.

MARSHALL, Humphrey. *The History of Kentucky.* Calf. Frankfort, 1812. First edition. $1,000–$1,250. Frankfort, 1824. 2 vols., sheepskin. Second edition. $400–$500.

MARSHALL, John. *Opinion of the Supreme Court, etc. in the Case of Samuel Worces-*

ter Versus the State of Georgia. 39 pp., sewed. Washington, 1832. First edition. $250–$300. Second edition, same date. 20 pp., half calf. $100–$150.

MARSHALL, L. G. *The Arabian Art of Taming and Training Wild and Vicious Horses.* 36 pp., wrappers. (Circleville, Ohio), 1857. $150–$200.

MARSHALL, Paule. *Brown Girl, Brownstones.* Cloth. New York, 1959. First edition. In dust jacket. $75–$100. Author's first book.

MARSHALL, William I. *Acquisition of Oregon, and the Long Suppressed Evidence About Marcus Whitman.* Portrait. 2 vols., green cloth. (Seattle), 1905. First edition. $150–$250. Portland, 1911. 2 vols., cloth. $100–$125.

MARTIAL Achievements of Great Britain and Her Allies from 1799 to 1815 (The). 52 colored plates. Half morocco. London, (1814–15). $2,000–$3,000. London, (about 1835). 51 color plates. Morocco. $950 (A, 1981).

MARTIN, Aaron. *An Attempt to Show the Inconsistency of Slave-Holding, with the Religion of the Gospel.* 16 pp., stitched. Lexington, Ky., 1807. First edition. $2,000–$2,500. Also, $1,200 (A, 1967).

MARTIN Faber, the Story of a Criminal. 2 vols., cloth. New York, 1838. (By William Gilmore Simms.) First edition. $300–$450.

MARTIN, Fredrik R. *The Miniature Painting and Painters of Persia, India and Turkey from the 8th to the 18th Century.* 271 collotype plates, 48 text illustrations, 5 plates in gold and colors by W. Griggs. 2 vols., folio, buckram. London, 1912. $2,000–$3,000.

MARTINEAU, Harriet. *Feats on the Fjord.* Illustrated by Arthur Rackham. Cloth. London, 1899. First edition. $100–$150. London, (1911). Plates in color. Cloth. $100–$150.

MARTINEAU, Harriet. *How to Observe Morals and Manners.* Cloth, London, 1848. First edition. $100–$150.

MARTINEAU, Harriet. *Retrospect of Western Travel.* 3 vols., cloth. London, 1838. First edition. $350–$400. New York, 1838. 2 vols., half linen. First American edition. $200–$300.

MARTINEAU, Harriet. *Society in America.* 3 vols., cloth. London, 1837. First edition. $500–$600. New York, 1837. 2 vols., cloth. $200–$300.

MARTÍNEZ CARO, Ramón. *Verdadera Idea de la Primera Campaña de Tejas y Sucesos Ocurridos despues de la acción de San Jacinto.* Printed wrappers. Mexico, 1837. First edition. $1,000–$1,500. Rebound in leather, $1,250.

MARVEL, Ik. *Dream Life.* Cloth. New York, 1851. (By Donald G. Mitchell.) First edition, first state, with stereotyper's slug on copyright page. $35–$50.

MARVEL, Ik. *Fresh Gleanings.* 2 vols., printed wrappers, or one vol., cloth. New York, 1847. (By Donald G. Mitchell.) First edition. Wrappers: $100–$150. Cloth: $40–$50.

MARVEL, Ik. *Looking Back at Boyhood.* 21 pp., wrappers. (Norwich, Conn.), June, 1906. (By Donald G. Mitchell.) First edition. $75–$100.

MARVEL, Ik. *The Reveries of a Bachelor.* Dark-blue cloth, or leather. New York, 1850. (By Donald G. Mitchell.) First edition, first printing, with last word, "sleep," on page 29 in perfect type. $75–$100. Another issue: Presentation binding. One of 8 inscribed. $200–$250.

MARVIN, Frederic R. *Yukon Overland: The Gold-Digger's Handbook.* Folding map, 18 plates. Printed orange wrappers. Cincinnati, 1898. First edition. $150–$200.

MARVY, Louis (and Thackeray, William Makepeace). *Sketches After English Land-*

scape Painters. With Short Notices by W. M. Thackeray, 20 color plates. Folio, cloth. London, (1850). First edition. $250–$350.

MARX, Groucho. *Beds.* Cloth. New York, 1930. First edition. In dust jacket. $50–$60.

MARX, Karl. *Capital.* 2 vols., red cloth. London, 1887. First edition in English (of the first volume of Marx's major work). $1,250–$1,500. New York, 1889. Yellow cloth. First American edition. $500–$600.

MARY BARTON; A Tale of Manchester Life. 2 vols., mulberry cloth. London, 1848. (By Elizabeth C. Gaskell.) First edition. $1,000–$1,250. Author's first book.

MASEFIELD, John. *Ballads.* Printed wrappers. London, 1903. First edition. No. 13 of "The Vigo Cabinet Series." $65–$85.

MASEFIELD, John. *The Bird of Dawning.* 4 color plates. Buckram. London, 1933. First illustrated edition. One of 300 signed. Boxed. $40–$50.

MASEFIELD, John. *Collected Poems.* Portrait. Cream-colored cloth, leather label. London, 1923. First edition. One of 530 signed. Boxed. $50–$60.

MASEFIELD, John. *The Coming of Christ.* Boards and vellum. London, 1928. First edition. One of 275 signed. In dust jacket. $75–$100

MASEFIELD, John. *The Hawbucks.* Boards, vellum spine. London, 1929. First edition. One of 275 signed. $50–$60. Trade edition: Cloth. In dust jacket. $35.

MASEFIELD, John. *John M. Synge: A Few Personal Recollections.* Boards and linen. Dundrum, Ireland, 1915. Cuala Press. First edition. One of 350. $75–$125. Signed by W. B. Yeats on colophon page, $165.

MASEFIELD, John. *Salt Water Ballads.* Blue buckram. London, 1902. First edition, first issue, with Grant Richards imprint on title page. One of 500. $450–$600. Author's first book.

MASEFIELD, John. *Some Memories of W. B. Yeats.* Boards and linen. Dublin, 1940. Cuala Press. First edition. One of 370. In tissue dust jacket. $150–$200.

MASEFIELD, John. *Sonnets and Poems.* Blue cloth, paper labels. Lollingdon, England, 1916. First edition. In dust jacket. $65–$75.

MASEFIELD, John. *South and East.* Color plates. Vellum. London, 1929. One of 260 signed. Boxed. $50–$75.

MASEFIELD, John. *The Trial of Jesus.* Boards. London, 1925. First edition. One of 525 signed. In dust jacket. Boxed. $75–$100.

MASEFIELD, John. *The Wanderer of Liverpool.* Colored frontispiece, 4 diagrams (3 folding), other plates. Black cloth. London, 1930. First edition. One of 525 signed. Boxed. $75–$100. New York, 1930. Illustrated. Boards and cloth. One of 350 signed. Boxed. $50–$75.

MASON, A. E. W. *At the Villa Rose.* Light blue cloth. London, 1910. First edition, first binding. $150–$200.

MASON, Emily V. (editor). *The Southern Poems of the War.* Cloth. Baltimore, 1867. First edition. $100–$150.

MASON, The Rev. George. *Ode on the Loss of the Steamship Pacific.* 4 pp., printed wrappers. Nanaimo, B.C., 1875. $125–$150.

MASON, Richard Lee. *Narrative of Richard Lee Mason in the Pioneer West.* Half leather. New York, (1915). First edition. One of 160. $100–$150. Another issue: One of 10 on vellum. $200–$250.

MASON, Z. H. *A General Description of Orange County, Florida.* Map. 56 pp., wrappers. Orlando, (1881). First edition. $250–$300.

MASON, Otis T. *Indian Basketry.* Illustrated, including color plates. 2 vols., pictorial buckram. New York, 1904. First edition. $300–$400.

MASQUE of Poets (A). Black or red cloth. Boston, 1878. First edition. With Emily Dickinson's poem "Success," her only book appearance in her lifetime. (The black cloth "No Name" and "Red Line" red cloth issues were simultaneous. Red copies are scarcer.) $300–$500.

MASSIE, J. Cam. *A Treatise on the Eclectic Southern Practice of Medicine.* Sheepskin. Philadelphia, 1854. First edition. $150–$200.

MASSON, L. F. R. *Les Bourgeois de la Compagnie du Nord-Ouest.* Folding map. 2 vols., green and orange wrappers. Quebec, 1889–90. First edition. $300–$350.

MASTERMAN, Walter S. *The Flying Beast.* Cloth. New York, (1932). First American edition. In dust jacket. $35–$45.

MASTERS, Edgar Lee. See Ford, Webster; Wallace, Dexter.

MASTERS, Edgar Lee. *Along the Illinois.* Cloth. Prairie City, Ill., 1942. First edition. $35–$50.

MASTERS, Edgar Lee. *A Book of Verses.* Gray boards. Chicago, 1898. First edition. $175–$250. Author's first book.

MASTERS, Edgar Lee. *Gettysburg, Manila, Acoma.* Cloth. New York, 1930. First edition. One of 375 signed. In dust jacket. Boxed. $75–$100.

MASTERS, Edgar Lee. *Godbey: A Dramatic Poem.* Boards and cloth. New York, 1931. First edition. One of 347 signed. Boxed. $60–$75.

MASTERS, Edgar Lee. *The Golden Fleece of California.* Woodcut illustrations. Cloth. Weston, Vt., (1936). First edition. One of 550 signed. In glassine dust jacket. Boxed. $75–$85. New York, (1936). Cloth. First trade edition. In dust jacket. $25.

MASTERS, Edgar Lee. *Illinois Poems.* Cloth. Prairie City, Ill., 1941. First edition. In dust jacket. $150–$200.

MASTERS, Edgar, Lee. *The Leaves of the Tree.* Printed wrappers. Chicago, 1909. First edition. $75–$100.

MASTERS, Edgar Lee. *Lee: A Dramatic Poem.* Cloth. New York, 1926. First edition. One of 250 signed. $50–$75. Trade edition: Cloth. In dust jacket. $25–$30.

MASTERS, Edgar Lee. *Lincoln: The Man.* Illustrated. Half vellum and cloth. New York, 1931. First edition. One of 150 signed. In glassine dust jacket. $100–$125.

MASTERS, Edgar Lee. *Maximilian.* Wrappers with paper labels, or boards. Boston, 1902. First edition. Wrappers: $200. Boards: $75–$85.

MASTERS, Edgar Lee. *The New Spoon River.* Vellum and boards. New York, 1924. First edition. One of 360 signed. $85–$110.

MASTERS, Edgar Lee. *The New Star Chamber and Other Essays.* Boards. Chicago, 1904. First edition. $85–$125.

MASTERS, Edgar Lee. *The Serpent in the Wilderness.* Boards and cloth. New York, (1933). First edition. One of 400 signed. In glassine dust jacket. Boxed. $75–$85. One of 84 copies (of the same issue), with a page of the manuscript inserted. $200–$250.

MASTERS, Edgar Lee. *Spoon River Anthology.* Blue cloth. New York, 1915. First edition, first issue, measuring exactly ⅞ inches across top. In dust jacket. $500–$600. Lacking jacket, $250–$300. New York, 1942. Limited Editions Club. Illustrated. Buckram. Boxed. $80–$100.

MATHER, E. Powys. *Procreant Hymn.* Engravings by Eric Gill. Buckram. Waltham St. Lawrence, England, 1916. Golden Cockerel Press. One of 200. $300–$600.

MATHERS, John, and A Solid Gentleman. *The History of Mr. John Decastro.* 4 vols., boards. London, 1815. (By George Colman the Younger.) First edition. $300–$400.

MATHESON, Richard. *Born of Man and Woman.* Cloth. Philadelphia, 1954. First edition. In dust jacket. $40–$50. Author's first book.

MATHESON, Richard. *A Stir of Echoes.* Cloth. Philadelphia, (1958). First edition. In dust jacket. $35.

MATHEWS, A. E. *Canyon City, Colorado, and Its Surroundings.* Map. 5 plates. Cloth. New York, 1870. First edition. $3,000–$3,500.

MATHEWS, A. E. *Pencil Sketches of Colorado.* 23 plates in color. Cloth. (New York), 1866. First edition. $4,000–$5,000. Facsimile reprint: (Denver, 1961.) Oblong folio, cloth. $50–$75.

MATHEWS, A. E. *Pencil Sketches of Montana.* 31 plates (4 folding). Cloth. New York, 1868. First edition. $3,000–$3,500.

MATHEWS, Alfred E. *Gems of Rocky Mountain Scenery.* 20 plates. Cloth. New York, 1869. First edition. $1,500–$1,750.

MATHEWS, Alfred E. *Interesting Narrative; Being a Journal of the Flight of Alfred E. Mathews, of Stark Co., Ohio, from the State of Texas, etc.* 34 pp., sewed. (New Philadelphia, Ohio), 1861. First edition. $1,000–$1,250.

MATHEWS, Edward J. *Crossing the Plains . . . in '59.* Cloth. No place, (1930?). First edition. $150 and up.

MATHEWS, Mrs. M. M. *Ten Years in Nevada.* Illustrated. Leather, or cloth. Buffalo, N.Y., 1880. First edition. $200–$250.

MATSELL, George W. *Vocabulum; or, the Rogue's Lexicon.* Cloth. New York, (1859). First edition. $50–$75.

MATSON, N. *French and Indians of the Illinois River.* Frontispiece (an original signed photograph). Green cloth. Princeton, Ill., 1874. First edition. $175.

MATSON, N. *Memories of Shaubena.* Illustrated. Cloth. Chicago, 1878. First edition. $100.

MATSON, N. *Reminiscences of Bureau County.* Cloth. Princeton, Ill., 1872. First edition. $75–$100.

MATTHEWS, Sallie Reynolds. *Interwoven, a Pioneer Chronicle.* Portrait. Orange suede. Houston, 1936. First edition. First binding. $400–$500. El Paso, 1958. Cloth. In dust jacket. $225.

MATTHIESSEN, Peter. *At Play in the Fields of the Lord.* Cloth. New York, (1965). First edition. In dust jacket. $30–$40. Also, advance copy in wrappers. $75–$85.

MATTHIESSEN, Peter. *Race Rock.* Cloth. New York, (1954). First edition. In dust jacket. $50–$75. Author's first book.

MATURIN, Charles Robert. See *Melmoth the Wanderer.*

MATURIN, Charles Robert. *Women; Or, Pour et Contre: A Tale.* 3 vols., boards. Edinburgh, 1818. First edition. $750–$1,000.

MAUGHAM, W. Somerset. *Ah King: Six Stories.* Blue cloth. London, (1933). First edition. In dust jacket. $50. Another issue: Buckram. One of 175 signed. Boxed. $250–$300. Garden City, 1933. Black cloth. First American edition. In dust jacket. $50.

MAUGHAM, W. Somerset. *Ashenden, or The British Agent*. Blue-gray cloth. London, 1928. First edition. In dust jacket. $150–$175.

MAUGHAM, W. Somerset. *The Bishop's Apron*. Cloth. London, 1906. First edition. $100–$150.

MAUGHAM, W. Somerset. *The Book-Bag*. Portrait frontispiece. Half cloth and blue and white boards. Florence, Italy, 1932. First edition. One of 725 signed. In dust jacket. $200–$250.

MAUGHAM, W. Somerset. *Cakes and Ale*. Blue cloth. London, (1930). First edition, first issue, with "won" instead of "won't" in line 14 of page 147. In dust jacket. $65–$75. Second issue, corrected. In dust jacket. $50. Garden City, 1930. First American edition. In dust jacket. $50–$60. London, (1954). Decorations by Graham Sutherland. Boards and leather. One of 1,000 signed. Boxed. $300–$350.

MAUGHAM, W. Somerset. *The Casuarina Tree*. Cloth. London, 1926. First edition. In dust jacket. $150.

MAUGHAM, W. Somerset. *The Constant Wife*. Blue cloth. New York, 1926. First edition. In dust jacket. $75–$125. London, 1927. Black cloth. First English edition. In dust jacket. $75–$125.

MAUGHAM, W. Somerset. *Cosmopolitans: Very Short Stories*. Blue cloth. London, (1936). First edition. In dust jacket. $50–$75. Another issue: Red buckram. One of 175 signed. $200–$250.

MAUGHAM, W. Somerset. *Don Fernando*. Cloth. London, 1935. First edition. In dust jacket. $75–$85. Another issue: Buckram. One of 175 signed. Boxed. $150–$175. Garden City, 1935. Black cloth. First American edition. In dust jacket. $40–$50.

MAUGHAM, W. Somerset. *The Explorer*. Cloth. London, 1908 (actually 1907). First edition. $125. New York, 1909. Illustrated. Cloth. First American and first illustrated edition. $75–$125.

MAUGHAM, W. Somerset. *The Gentleman in the Parlour*. Cloth. London, (1930). First edition. In dust jacket. $75–$100.

MAUGHAM, W. Somerset. *The Hero*. Red cloth. London, 1901. First edition. $150.

MAUGHAM, W. Somerset. *The Judgment Seat*. Frontispiece by Ulrica Hyde. Cloth. London, 1934. Centaur Press. First edition. One of 150 signed. In dust jacket. $150–$225.

MAUGHAM, W. Somerset. *The Land of the Blessed Virgin*. Boards. London, 1905. First edition. $225–$300.

MAUGHAM, W. Somerset. *The Letter: A Play in Three Acts*. Cloth. London, (1927). First edition. $150–$175. (Also issued in wrappers.)

MAUGHAM, W. Somerset. *Liza of Lambeth*. Decorated green cloth. London, 1897. First edition. $750–$1,000. Author's first book. London, 1947. Vellum and boards. Jubilee Edition. One of 1,000 signed. In dust jacket. $150–$175.

MAUGHAM, W. Somerset. *The Magician*. Cloth. London, 1908. First edition. $100–$150. New York, 1909. First American edition. $100–$135.

MAUGHAM, W. Somerset. *The Making of a Saint*. Illustrated. Pictorial cloth. Boston, 1898. First edition, first issue, with "In Press" under this title in ads. $200–$250.

MAUGHAM, W. Somerset. *A Man of Honour*. Printed wrappers. London, 1903. Chapman & Hall. First edition. $750 and up. (Only 150 printed.)

MAUGHAM, W. Somerset. *The Merry-Go-Round*. Blue cloth. London, 1904. First edition. $150–$175.

MAUGHAM, W. Somerset. *Mrs. Craddock*. Cloth. London, 1902. First edition. $150–$200.

MAUGHAM, W. Somerset. *The Moon and Sixpence*. Sage-green cloth. London, (1919). First edition, first issue, with 4 pages of ads, including a list of 6 (not 7) novels by Eden Phillpotts. In dust jacket. $150. New York, (1919). Tan cloth. First American edition, first state, with "Maughan" for "Maugham" on front cover and spine. In dust jacket. $150.

MAUGHAM, W. Somerset. *My South Sea Island*. Wrappers. Chicago, 1936. First edition, first issue, with "Sommerset" on title page. $500–$600. Also, $300 (A, 1980). Second issue, error corrected. One of 50. $300–$350.

MAUGHAM, W. Somerset. *The Narrow Corner*. Cloth. London, (1932). First edition. In dust jacket. $75–$100.

MAUGHAM, W. Somerset. *Of Human Bondage*. Green cloth. New York, (1915). First edition, first issue, with Doran imprint and misprint in line 4 of page 257. In dust jacket. $750–$1,000. London, (1915). Blue cloth. First English edition, first state, with ads at end. In dust jacket. $500–$600. Garden City, 1936. Illustrated by Schwabe. Buckram. First illustrated edition. One of 751 signed. In dust jacket. Boxed. $175–$250. New York, 1938. Limited Editions Club. Edited by Theodore Dreiser. Illustrated by John Sloan. 2 vols., cloth. Boxed. $350–$450.

MAUGHAM, W. Somerset. *Of Human Bondage; With A Digression on the Art of Fiction*. Printed boards. (Washington), 1946. One of 500 signed. $100–$150.

MAUGHAM, W. Somerset. *The Painted Veil*. Cloth. New York, (1925). First edition. In dust jacket. $35. Another issue: Boards. One of 250 signed. In dust jacket. $250–$300. London, (1925). Blue cloth. First English edition, first issue, with "Hong-Kong" (not "Tching-Yen" in line 15, page 16, etc. $400–$500.

MAUGHAM, W. Somerset. *The Razor's Edge*. Buckram. Garden City, 1944. First edition. One of 750 signed. Boxed. $200–$300.

MAUGHAM, W. Somerset. *The Sacred Flame*. Black cloth, paper labels. New York, 1928. First edition, first issue, measuring 6¾ × 5¹/₁₆ inches. In dust jacket. $125–$150. London, 1928 (actually 1929). First English edition (American sheets with new title page). In dust jacket. $100–$125.

MAUGHAM, W. Somerset. *Strictly Personal*. Buckram. Garden City, 1941. First edition. One of 515 signed. Boxed. $175–$225. Trade edition: In dust jacket. $50.

MAUGHAM, W. Somerset. *The Summing Up*. Black cloth. London, (1938). First edition. In dust jacket. $40–$50. Garden City, 1938. Black cloth. First American edition. In dust jacket. $40. New York, 1954. Buckram. One of 391 signed. Boxed. $200–$250.

MAUGHAM, W. Somerset. *The Unconquered*. Cloth. New York, 1944. One of 300 signed. In dust jacket. $125–$150.

MAUGHAM, W. Somerset. *The Unknown*. Boards. London, 1920. First edition. $125–$150.

MAUGHAM, W. Somerset. *The Vagrant Mood: Six Essays*. Boards and calf. London, (1952). First edition. One of 500 signed. In glassine dust jacket. Boxed. $175–$200. Garden City, 1953. Black cloth. First American edition. In dust jacket. $25.

MAUGHAM, W. Somerset. *A Writer's Notebook*. Blue buckram, vellum spine. London, (1949). First edition. One of 1,000 signed. Boxed. $150–$175. Trade edition: In first issue dust jacket listing "Maughamiana." $50. Garden City, 1949. Cloth. First American edition. One of 1,000 signed. Boxed. $150–$175. Trade edition: Cloth. In dust jacket. $40.

MAULDIN, Bill. *Mud, Mules and Mountains*. Introduction by Ernie Pyle. 48 pp., wrappers. (Italy), 1944. First edition. $75–$100.

MAULDIN, William Henry (Bill). *Star Spangled Banter*. Pictorial wrappers. San Antonio, 1941. First edition. $75–$100. The cartoonist's first book.

MAURELLE, Don Antonio. *Abstract of a Narrative of an Interesting Voyage from Manilla to San Blas, etc.* Calf. Boston, 1801. $300–$350.

MAUROIS, André. *Ariel: A Shelley Romance*. Wrappers. (London), 1935. Penguin Books. First edition of the first Penguin paperback. In dust jacket. $150–$200. Also $95 and $132 (A, 1978).

MAURY, M. F. *The Physical Geography of the Sea*. 12 plates. Cloth. New York, 1855. First edition. $450–$550.

MAVERICK, Samuel Augustus. *Notes on the Storming of Bexar in the Close of 1835*. Edited by F. C. Chabot. Illustrated. Cloth. San Antonio, 1942. One of 100 signed by Chabot. $200–$300.

MAVOR, William. *The English Spelling-Book*. Illustrated by Kate Greenaway. Pictorial boards. London, 1885 (actually 1884). First Greenaway edition. $125–$150.

MAW, Henry Lister. *Journal of a Passage from the Pacific to the Atlantic*. Folding map. Boards. London, 1829. First edition. $250–$350.

MAWE, John. *Travels in the Interior of Brazil*. Map, 8 plates. Boards. London, 1812. First edition. $600–$800. London, 1821. Map, 5 color plates. Boards. Second edition. $350–$450. Philadelphia, 1816. Illustrated. Boards. $300–$400.

MAXIMILIAN , Prince of Wied. *Travels in Brazil*. 9 plates. Half leather. London, 1820. First English edition. $400–$500.

MAXIMILIAN, Prince of Wied. *Travels in the Interior of North America*. Translated by H. E. Lloyd. Folding map, 81 colored vignettes and plates. 2 vols., half morocco (text plus atlas folio volume). London, 1843–44. First edition. $20,000–$25,000. Also, $25,000 (A, 1979). (The atlas volume alone, valued for the plates, is actually worth $10,000 to $15,000, possibly more.)

MAXWELL, William Audley. *Crossing the Plains: Days of '57*. Illustrated. Brown pictorial wrappers. (San Francisco, 1915.) First edition. $50–$75.

MAY, Robert L. *Rudolph the Red-Nosed Reindeer*. Illustrated in color by Denver Gillen. Pictorial orange wrappers. (Chicago), 1939. First edition. $300 (Christmas give-away for Montgomery Ward.) Later edition: Evanston, no date. Miniature book bound in full leather for the Schori Press. Limited and signed by May and Ward Schori. $100–$150.

MAY, Sophie. *Dottie Dimple*. 3 woodcut plates by N. Brown. Decorated brown cloth. Boston, 1865. (By Rebecca S. Clarke.) First edition. $100–$125.

MAY, Sophie. *Little Prudy*. Cloth. Boston, 1865. (By Rebecca S. Clarke.) First edition. $75–$100.

MAYER, Alfred M. (editor). *Sport with Gun and Rod in American Woods and Waters*. Illustrated. 2 vols., half leather. Edinburgh, 1884. First edition. $300–$350.

MAYER, Luigi. *Views in the Ottoman Dominions*. 71 colored plates. 3 vols., folio, boards or 2 vols., boards. London, 1810. $2,000–$3,000, and possibly more. (Other Luigi Mayer color plate books have enjoyed high favor in the recent inflationary rise of illustrated works. They include *Views in Palestine*, London, 1804; *Views in Egypt*, London, 1801; and *Views in the Ottoman Empire*, London, 1803.)

MAYHEW, Augustus. *Paved with Gold, or The Romance and Reality of London Streets*. Illustrated by Hablot K. Browne. 13 parts, wrappers. London, (1857–58). First edition. $400–$600. London, 1858. Cloth. First book edition. $150–$200.

MAYHEW, Experience. *Indian Narratives*. Frontispiece. Half leather and boards. Boston, (1829). First American edition. $150–$200.

MAYHEW, Henry. *London Characters.* Illustrated. Cloth. London, 1874. First edition. $150–$250.

MAYHEW, Henry. *London Labour and the London Poor.* 4 vols., cloth. London, 1861–62. $400–$500.

MAYNARD, Charles J. *Atlas of Plates from the Directory to the Birds of Eastern North America.* Wrappers. West Newton, Mass., 1905. $200–$250.

MAYNARD, Charles J. *The Birds of Eastern North America.* Wrappers. Newtonville, Mass., 1881. $200–$250. Newtonville, 1896. Cloth. $150–$200.

MAYNARD, Charles J. *The Butterflies of New England.* 8 hand-colored lithographs. Half morocco. Boston, 1886. First edition. $200–$250.

MAYNARD, Charles J. *The Eggs of North American Birds.* 9 parts, wrappers. Boston, (1890). $200–$250.

MAYNARD, G. W. *Report on the Property of the Alice Gold and Silver Mining Co., Butte.* Maps, plates. 28 pp., wrappers. New York, 1882. $100–$150.

MAYO, Robert. *Political Sketches of Eight Years in Washington.* Cloth. Baltimore, 1839. First edition. $150–$200.

MEAD, Peter B. *An Elementary Treatise on American Grape Culture and Wine Making.* Cloth. (New York), 1867. First edition. $75.

MEADE, Gen. G. G. *Report of the Ashburn Murder.* 130 pp., printed wrappers. (Atlanta, about 1868.) With errata slip and leaf of explanation from Meade. $100.

MEANS, James. *Manflight.* 29 pp., printed wrappers. Boston, 1891. First edition. $75–$100.

MEANS, James. *The Problem of Manflight.* Diagrams. 20 pp., pictorial wrappers. Boston, 1894. $75–$125.

MEEKE, Mrs. (Mary). *The Veiled Protectress; or, the Mysterious Mother.* 5 vols., contemporary half calf. London, 1819. First edition. $250.

MEEKER, Ezra. *Washington Territory West of the Cascade Mountains.* 52 pp., printed wrappers. Olympia, Wash., 1870. First edition. $750–$1,000.

MEIKLE, James. *Famous Clyde Yachts, 1880–87.* 31 colored aquatints, mounted as drawings, with tissue guards. Atlas folio, cloth. Glasgow, 1888. $300–$400.

MEINE, Franklin J. (editor). *The Crockett Almanacs.* Gray cloth. Chicago: Caxton Club, 1955. First edition. $75–$100.

MEINHOLD, William. *Sidonia the Sorceress.* Translated by Lady Wilde. Illustrated. Limp vellum with ties. London, 1893. Kelmscott Press. One of 300. $500–$750. Another issue: One of 10 on vellum. $3,000–$4,000.

MELINCOURT. By the Author of *Headlong Hall.* 3 vols., boards. London, 1817. (By Thomas Love Peacock.) First edition. $400–$500.

MELINE, James F. *Two Thousand Miles on Horseback.* Map. Cloth. New York, 1867. First edition. $100–$150.

MELISH, John. *A Geographical Description of the United States.* 3 maps. Boards. Philadelphia, 1815. First edition. $300. Philadelphia, 1816. 5 maps. Boards. Second edition. $100–$150. Philadelphia, 1818. 4 maps. Boards. Third edition. $200–$250. Philadelphia, 1822. 12 maps. Boards. $150.

MELISH, John. *A Military and Topographical Atlas of the United States.* 8 maps and plans, 5 folding. Half leather. Philadelphia, 1813. First edition. $1,000–$1,250. Philadelphia, 1815. 12 maps and plans, 9 folding and colored in outline. Half leather. $1,000–$1,500.

MELLICHAMPE: A Legend of the Santee. 2 vols., cloth, paper labels. New York, 1836. (By William Gilmore Simms.) First edition. $400–$500.

MELLICK, Andrew D. *The Story of an Old Farm.* Frontispiece. Cloth. Somerville, N.J., 1889. First edition. $100–$125.

MELMOTH the Wanderer. 4 vols., boards and cloth. Edinburgh, 1820. (By Charles Robert Maturin.) First edition, first binding (cloth is later). $750–$1,000. Edinburgh, 1821. 4 vols., boards. Second edition. $400–$500.

MELTZER, David. *The Dark Continent.* Brown cloth. (Berkeley), 1967. First edition. One of 31 signed. (Issued without dust jacket.) $50–$75.

MELTZER, David. *Luna.* Pictorial boards. Los Angeles, 1970. One of 200 signed. $35–$50.

MELTZER, David. *The Process.* Cloth. Berkeley, 1965. First edition. One of 25 signed. In dust jacket. $50–$75.

MELTZER, David. *Ragas.* Pictorial wrappers. (San Francisco, 1959.) First edition. $75.

MELTZER, David. *Round the Poem Box.* Leather. Los Angeles, 1969. One of 26 signed, with an original illustration by the author. $35. Another issue: One of 125 signed. $40–$50.

MELTZER, David. *Yesod.* Cloth. London, (1969). One of 100 signed. In glassine dust jacket. $50–$60. Trade edition: Cloth. In dust jacket. $20.

MELTZER, David, and Schenker, Donald. *Poems.* Glazed white wrappers, taped spine (as issued). (San Francisco, 1957.) First edition. One of 470. $50–$75. Another issue: Hardbound. One of 30 signed. $100–$125. First book for both poets.

MELVILLE, Herman. See *John Marr and Other Sailors; Timoleon.*

MELVILLE, Herman. *The Apple Tree and Other Sketches.* Boards. Princeton, 1922. First edition. One of 175 on handmade paper. In slipcase. $150–$200. Trade edition: Cloth. $35.

MELVILLE, Herman. *Battle-Pieces and Aspects of the War.* Blue, green, or salmon-colored cloth. New York, 1866. First edition, first issue, with "hundred" misspelled "hnndred" in copyright notice. $800–$1,000. (There was no English edition.)

MELVILLE, Herman. *Benito Cereno.* Illustrated in color by E. McKnight Kauffer. Folio, buckram. London, 1926. Nonesuch Press. One of 1,650. $150–$175. (Note: See entry following under *Billy Budd.*)

MELVILLE, Herman. *Billy Budd and Other Prose Pieces.* Edited by Raymond W. Weaver. Cloth. London, 1924. First edition. One of 750. (Issued as part of the *Works.*) In dust jacket. $100–$150.

MELVILLE, Herman. *Billy Budd [and] Benito Cereno.* Illustrated. White sailcloth. New York, 1965. Limited Editions Club. Boxed. $75–$100.

MELVILLE, Herman. *Clarel: A Poem and Pilgrimage in the Holy Land.* 2 vols., brick-red or green cloth, chocolate end papers. New York, 1876. First edition. $1,000 and up. Also, $600 (A, 1981).

MELVILLE, Herman. *The Confidence-Man.* Green or purple-brown cloth. New York, 1857. First edition, without half title. $1,000–$1,200. London, 1857. Yellow-brown cloth. First English edition, first issue, without "Roberts" in publisher's name below ads on recto of front free end paper. $800–$1,000. Variant (later?) issue: $800 (A, 1981).

MELVILLE, Herman. *The Encantadas (Las Encantadas).* Edited by Victor W. Von Hagen. Colored woodcuts by Mallette Dean. Pictorial boards and cloth. Burlingame, Calif., 1940. Grabhorn printing. One of 550. $125–$150.

MELVILLE, Herman. *Israel Potter*. Purple-brown or green cloth, yellow end papers. New York, 1855. First edition, without half title; first state, with perfect type in first line of page 113. $500–$600. Second state, imperfect type on page 113. $200–$250. London, 1855. Cloth. First English edition. $200–$250.

MELVILLE, Herman. *A Journal up the Straits, October 11, 1856–May, 1857*. Edited by Raymond W. Weaver. Portrait frontispiece. Marbled cloth. New York, 1935. First edition. One of 650. In dust jacket. $150–$200.

MELVILLE, Herman. *Mardi: and A Voyage Thither*. 3 vols., pale-green cloth, white end papers with blue designs. London, 1849. First edition, without half title in Vol. 1. $300–$400. New York, 1849. 2 vols., dark purple-brown or green muslin, or wrappers. First American edition with 8 pages of ads at end of Vol. 2. Cloth: $600–$750. Wrappers: $600–$750.

MELVILLE, Herman. *Moby-Dick; or, The Whale*. Slate-blue, black, brown, or scarlet cloth, orange or marbled end papers. New York, 1851. First American edition, with publisher's name blind-stamped at center of sides, 6 blank leaves at front and back. $7,500–$10,000. Also, at auction in varying condition, all less than fine: $2,200 (1981); $3,600 (1978); $2,800 (1977); $5,000 (1976); $4,250 (1974). (For first edition, see *The Whale*, following.) Chicago, 1930. Lakeside Press. Illustrated by Rockwell Kent, 3 vols., silver-decorated cloth. One of 1,000. In aluminum slipcase. $1,000–$1,250. Also, $1,000 (A, 1980). New York, 1943. Limited Editions Club. Illustrated by Boardman Robinson. 2 vols., full morocco. Boxed. $150–$200. San Francisco, 1979. Illustrated by Barry Moser. Full morocco. One of 250. Boxed. $1,500–$2,000.

MELVILLE, Herman. *Narrative of a Four Months' Residence Among the Natives of a Valley of the Marquesas Islands; or, A Peep at Polynesian Life*. Map. 2 parts, wrappers, or cloth (two parts bound as one). London, 1846. First edition (of the book published later that year in New York as *Typee*), first issue, with the reading "Pomarea" on page 19, line 1. Wrappers: $4,000–$5,000. Red cloth: First book edition. $3,000–$5,000. Also, $1,000 (A, 1978); $2,000 (A, 1974). Author's first book. Second issue: "Pomare." $2,000. London, 1847. Cloth. $200–$300.

MELVILLE, Herman. *Omoo: A Narrative of Adventures in the South Seas*. Map. 2 parts printed gray or brown wrappers, or cloth (in one volume). London, 1847. First edition. Wrappers: $5,000–$10,000. Red cloth: First book edition. $1,500–$2,000. (No recent price data on copies in original binding.) New York, 1847. Frontispiece map, one illustration. 2 parts, cream-white wrappers, or pictorial cloth (one volume). First American edition. Wrappers: $5,000 and up. Also, stained and worn, $2,250 (A, 1974). Cloth: First book edition. $1,500–$2,000, or more. Also, $450 (A, 1979); spine torn, $650 (A, 1976). New York, 1961. Limited Editions Club. Illustrated. White linen. Boxed. $50–$75.

MELVILLE, Herman. *The Piazza Tales*. Pale-blue cloth. New York, 1856. First edition, first issue, with yellow end papers. $1,200–$1,500. Also, $600 (A, 1978). London, 1856. Rose cloth. First English edition. (An unrecorded issue.) $2,500 (A, 1981). Other copies, blue binding. $500 and up.

MELVILLE, Herman. *Pierre; or, The Ambiguities*. Gray cloth, or wrappers. New York, 1852. First edition, cloth, with 4 blank pages at front and back, no half title, gray-green end papers. $1,000 and up for either cloth or wrappers. London, 1852. Blue embossed cloth, yellow end papers. First English edition. $500 and up.

MELVILLE, Herman. *Poems*. Cloth. London, 1924. First edition. (Issued as part of the *Works*.) In dust jacket. $150–$175.

MELVILLE, Herman. *Redburn: His First Voyage*. 2 vols., dark blue cloth, white end papers with the blue pattern. London, 1849. First edition. $1,500–$2,500. Also, $1,300 (A, 1981); $1,200 (A, 1974). New York, 1849. Purple-brown muslin, or wrappers. First American edition, first issue, with October ads. $750 and up.

MELVILLE, Herman. *The Refugee*. Cloth. Philadelphia, (1865). First edition. $75. (Pirated edition of *Israel Potter*.)

MELVILLE, Herman. *Some Personal Letters*. Edited by Meade Minnigerode. Portrait, 2 facsimiles. Half linen. New York, 1922. First edition. In dust jacket. $75–$100.

MELVILLE, Herman. *Typee: A Peep at Polynesian Life.* Map frontispiece. 2 parts, thick fawn-colored printed wrappers. New York, 1846. First American edition (of *Narrative of a Four Months' Residence Among the Natives of a Valley of the Marquesas*). $5,000–$10,000. Another issue: Cloth (blue or brown), in one volume. First American book edition, with 4 pages of ads. $1,500–$2,000. (No recent price data on copies in original binding.) Author's first book. New York, 1847. Cloth. Revised edition, with 8 pages of ads. $250–$350. Also, $110 (A, 1978). New York, 1935. Limited Editions Club. Illustrated. Printed boards. Boxed. $60–$80.

MELVILLE, Herman. *The Whale.* 3 vols., bright-blue and cream-colored cloth, pale-yellow end papers. London, 1851. First edition (of the book published later that year in New York as *Moby-Dick*). $20,000 or more. Also, $17,000 (A, 1974). Another copy, worn and soiled, $8,500 (in a 1977 catalogue).

MELVILLE, Herman. *White-Jacket: or, the World in a Man-of-War.* 2 vols., light-blue cloth, yellow end papers. London, 1850. First edition. $600–$750. New York, 1850. 2 parts, yellow wrappers, or one vol., purple-brown or blue-gray cloth, with 6 pages of ads. First American edition. Wrappers: $10,000. Also, $7,500 (A, 1976). Cloth (one volume); $1,500–$2,000. Also, worn, $350 (A, 1974). London, 1853. 2 vols. in one, cloth. First English one-volume edition. $500 and up.

MELVILLE, Herman. *The Works of Herman Melville.* 16 vols., cloth. London, 1922–(24). ("Standard Edition.") First edition. One of 750. In dust jackets. $1,500–$1,750. (Also issued in full or half leather.)

MEMOIRS of a Fox-Hunting Man. Blue cloth. London, (1928). (By Siegfried Sassoon.) First edition, first issue, with round trimmed fore-edges. In dust jacket. $50–$75. Another issue: Cloth. One of 260 signed. $300–$400. London, (1929). Illustrated by William Nicholson. Vellum. One of 300 signed. In dust jacket. Boxed. $300–$400.

MEMOIRS of an Infantry Officer. Blue cloth. London, (1930). (By Siegfried Sassoon.) First edition, first issue, with untrimmed edges. In dust jacket. $50–$65. Another issue: Blue cloth. One of 750 signed. $200–$250. London, 1931. Illustrated by Barnett Freedman. Parchment (or vellum) boards. One of 320 signed. In dust jacket. Boxed. $200–$225. Trade edition: Cloth. In dust jacket. $50–$75.

MEMOIRS of the Life of the Late John Mytton, Esq. 12 plates in color by John Alken. Cloth. London, 1835. (By C. J. Apperley.) First edition. $1,250–$1,500. London, 1837. 18 plates. Cloth. Second edition. $750–$1,000. London, 1851. 18 plates. Cloth. Third edition. $600–$700.

MEMORANDA: Democratic Vistas. Light-green wrappers. Washington, 1871. (By Walt Whitman.) First edition, first printing. $500–$600. (For later printing, Whitman identified as author on title page, see Whitman entry under this title.)

MEMORIA sobre las Proporciones Naturales de las Provincias Internas Occidentales, Causas de que Han Provenido sus Atrasos, etc. 62 pp., sewed. Mexico, 1822. $850–$1,000.

MEMORIAL and Biographical History of Johnson and Hill Counties, Texas. Illustrated. Leather. Chicago, 1892. First edition. $300–$350.

MEMORIAL and Biographical History of McLennan, Falls, Bell and Coryell Counties, Texas. Half leather. Chicago, 1893. $350–$500.

MEMORIAL to the Legislature of New York (A), Upon the Effects of the Passage of the Grade of the Western States Through the Welland and Oswego Canals. 24 pp., sewed. Rochester, 1845. $75–$100.

MEMORIAL to the President and Congress for the Admission of Wyoming Territory to the Union. 75 pp., wrappers. Cheyenne, 1889. $125–$150.

MENCKEN, H. L. See Hatteras, Owen; Hirshberg, Dr. L. K.

MENCKEN, H. L. *The American Language.* Black cloth. New York, 1919. First edition. One of 1,500. In dust jacket. $50–$75. Another issue: One of 25 signed. In dust jacket, $750–$850.

MENCKEN, H. L. *The Artist*. Boards. Boston, 1912. First edition. In dust jacket. $75–$100.

MENCKEN H. L. *Damn! A Book of Calumny*. Cloth. New York, 1918. First edition. In dust jacket. $100–$135.

MENCKEN, H. L. *George Bernard Shaw: His Plays*. Cloth. Boston, 1905. First edition. In dust jacket. $75–$100.

MENCKEN, H. L. *In Defense of Women*. Cloth. New York, 1918. First edition, first issue, with publisher's name misspelled "Ppilip." In dust jacket. $200–$250. Second issue, with name corrected. In dust jacket. $150–$200.

MENCKEN, H. L. *The Literary Capital of the United States*. Wrappers. Chicago, 1920. First edition. $100–$125.

MENCKEN, H. L. *A Little Book in C Major*. Cloth. New York, 1916. First edition. In dust jacket. $125–$150.

MENCKEN, H. L. *Menckeniana: A Schimpflexikon*. Vellum. New York, 1928. First edition. One of 80 signed. Boxed. $250–$300. Another issue: Red boards and cloth. One of 230 signed. Boxed. $150–$200. Trade edition: Cloth. In dust jacket. $40–$50.

MENCKEN, H. L. *Notes on Democracy*. Cloth. New York, (1926). First edition. In dust jacket. $30–$35. Another issue: One of 200 signed. $100–$125. Another issue: Vellum. One of 35 on vellum, signed. $500–$600.

MENCKEN, H. L. *The Philosophy of Friedrich Nietzsche*. Red cloth. Boston, 1908. First edition, first state, with "Friedrich" omitted on spine. $100–$150.

MENCKEN, H. L. *Prejudices: First Series*. Cloth. New York, (1919). First edition. In dust jacket. $50–$60. Another issue: One of 50 signed. Boxed. $200–$225.

MENCKEN H. L. *Prejudices: Second Series*. Cloth. New York, (1920). First edition. In dust jacket. $50–$60. Another issue: One of a few large paper copies, signed. $300 and up.

MENCKEN, H. L. *Prejudices: Third Series*. Cloth. New York, (1922). First edition. In dust jacket. $50–$60. Another issue: one of 110 signed. Boxed. $125–$150.

MENCKEN, H. L. *Prejudices: Fourth Series*. Cloth. New York, (1924). First edition. In dust jacket. $50–$60. Another issue: One of 200 signed. Boxed. $125–$150.

MENCKEN, H. L. *Prejudices: Fifth Series*. Cloth. New York, (1926). First edition. In dust jacket. $50–$60. Another issue: One of 200 signed. Boxed. $125–$150.

MENCKEN, H. L. *Prejudices: Sixth Series*. Cloth. New York, (1927). First edition. In dust jacket. $50–$60. Another issue: One of 50 on vellum, signed. $250–$300. Another issue: One of 140 on rag paper, signed. $150–$175.

MENCKEN, H. L. *A Treatise on the Gods*. Cloth. New York, 1930. First edition. In dust jacket. $75–$125. Another issue: Vellum. One of 375 signed. $175–$225.

MENCKEN, H. L. *Ventures into Verse*. Illustrated. Boards, paper label, or brown wrappers. Baltimore, 1903. First edition. Wrappers: $1,000–$2,000, possibly more. Also, inscribed by Mencken, $900 (A, 1969). Boards: $1,000 and up. Also, a presentation copy inscribed by Mencken, $3,250 (A, 1977). (About 100 copies believed printed in all; 45 noted are in boards, and presumably the rest were in wrappers.) Author's first book. Baltimore, (1960). Second edition (facsimile of the first edition). One of 250. $30–$40.

MENCKEN, H. L. (editor). *The Gist of Nietzsche*. Cloth. Boston, 1910. First edition. In dust jacket. $125–$150.

MENCKEN, H. L., and Nathan, George Jean. *Heliogabalus: A Buffoonery in 3 Acts*. Black cloth. New York, 1920. First edition. One of 2,000. In dust jacket. $50–$60.

Another issue: Vellum. One of 60 signed by the authors. $250–$350. Another issue: Wrappers. $35.

MENCKEN, H. L.; Nathan, George Jean; and Wright, Willard Huntington. *Europe After 8:15.* 7 plates by Thomas Hart Benton. Decorated yellow cloth. New York, 1914. First edition, first binding, with blue stamping. In dust jacket. $150–$175.

MERA, H. P. *The Rain Bird: A Study in Pueblo Design.* Illustrated by Tom Lea. Wrappers. Santa Fe, 1937. First edition. In dust jacket. $150.

MERCEDES of Castile: Or, the Voyage to Cathay. By the Author of *The Bravo.* 2 vols., cloth, paper labels. Philadelphia, 1840. (By James Fenimore Cooper.) First edition. $400–$450.

MERCER, A. S. *The Banditti of the Plains.* Illustrated. Map. Cloth. (Cheyenne, 1894.) First edition. $2,000–$3,000, or more. Sheridan, Wyo., 1930. Wrappers. $75. San Francisco, 1935. Grabhorn Press. Illustrated. Half cloth. One of 1,000. $60–$75.

MERCER, A. S. *Washington Territory: The Great North-West.* 38 pp., printed wrappers. Utica, 1865. First edition. $800–$1,000.

MERCY Philbrick's Choice. Black cloth. Boston, 1876. (By Helen Hunt Jackson.) First edition. $75–$85.

MEREDITH, George. See D., B., and M., W. G. entry.

MEREDITH, George. *The Amazing Marriage.* 2 vols., green cloth. Westminster (London), 1895. First edition. $100–$150.

MEREDITH, George. *Beauchamp's Career.* 3 vols., green cloth. London, 1876. First edition. $300–$400.

MEREDITH, George. *Diana of the Crossways.* 3 vols., cloth. London, 1885. First complete book edition. $350–$450.

MEREDITH, George. *The Egoist.* 3 vols., cloth. London, 1879. First edition. $750–$1,000. Also, $700 (A, 1978).

MEREDITH, George. *Emilia in England.* 3 vols., purple cloth. London, 1864. First edition. $500–$600.

MEREDITH, George. *Farina.* Cloth. London, 1857. First edition. $300–$400.

MEREDITH, George. *Lord Ormont and His Aminta.* 3 vols., cloth. London, 1894. First edition. $150–$200.

MEREDITH, George. *Modern Love and Poems of the English Roadside.* Green cloth. London, 1862. First edition. $250–$300. Portland, Me., 1891. Heavy printed wrappers. First American edition. In dust jacket. $100–$125.

MEREDITH, George. *One of Our Conquerors.* 3 vols., blue cloth. London, 1891. First edition. $100–$125.

MEREDITH, George. *The Ordeal of Richard Feverel.* 3 vols., brown cloth. London, 1859. First edition. $300–$400.

MEREDITH, George. *Poems.* Green cloth. London, (1851). First edition. With half title and with errata slip at end. $350. Author's first book.

MEREDITH, George. *Rhoda Fleming: A Story.* 3 vols., cloth. London, 1865. First edition. $500–$750. Rebound in full leather, $350.

MEREDITH, George. *The Shaving of Shagpat.* Brown cloth. London, 1856. First edition. $200–$250. New York, 1955. Limited Editions Club. Illustrated. Boards and leather. Boxed. $35–$45.

MEREDITH, George. *The Tale of Chloe. The House on the Beach. The Case of General*

Ople and Lady Camper. Boards and parchment. London, 1894. One of 250. $175–$250. Trade edition: Cloth. $75.

MEREDITH, George. *Vittoria.* 3 vols., purple or maroon cloth. London, 1867. First edition. $200–$300.

MEREDITH, William. *Love Letter from an Impossible Land.* Boards. New Haven, 1944. First edition. In dust jacket. $85–$125. Author's first book.

MERRICK, George B. *Old Times on the Upper Mississippi.* Illustrated. Blue cloth. Cleveland, 1909. First edition. $50–$75.

MERRICK, Leonard. *Conrad in Quest of His Youth: An Extravagance of Temperament.* Cloth. London, 1903. First edition. $60–$75.

MERRILL, James. *The Black Swan and Other Poems.* Wrappers. Athens, 1946. First edition. One of 100. $250–$350.

MERRILL, James. *The Country of a Thousand Years of Peace.* Cloth. New York, 1959. First edition. In dust jacket. $50–$60.

MERRILL, James. *First Poems.* Cloth. New York, 1951. First edition. One of 990. In dust jacket. $100–$125. Author's first commercially published book.

MERRILL, James. *Jim's Book: A Collection of Poems and Short Stories.* (By James Ingram Merrill.) Maroon buckram and gray boards. New York, 1942. First edition. In glassine dust jacket. $1,000–$1,500.

MERRILL, James. *Short Stories.* Wrappers. Pawlet, Vt., 1954. Banyan Press. First edition. One of 210 signed. $300–$400.

MERRILL, James. *Violent Pastoral.* Wrappers. (Cambridge, Mass., 1965.) First edition. One of 100 signed. $60–$85.

MERRIMAN, Henry Seton. *From One Generation to Another.* 2 vols., pea-green cloth. London, 1892. (By Hugh Stowell Scott.) First edition. $300–$325.

MERRITT, Abraham. *Burn Witch Burn.* Cloth. New York, (1933). First edition. In dust jacket. $135–$150.

MERRITT, Abraham. *Creep, Shadow!* Cloth. Garden City, 1934. First edition. In dust jacket. $50–$75.

MERRITT, Abraham. *Dwellers in the Mirage.* Cloth. New York, (1932). First edition. In dust jacket. $250–$350.

MERRITT, Abraham. *The Face in the Abyss.* New York, (1931). First edition. In dust jacket. $75–$100.

MERRITT, Abraham. *The Moon Pool.* Cloth. New York, 1919. First edition, first printing, without ad on page (434). In dust jacket. $150–$200. Author's first book. (Also issued in wrappers.)

MERRITT, Abraham. *The Ship of Ishtar.* Red-brown cloth, stamped in yellow. New York, 1926. First edition, first binding. In dust jacket. $175–$200.

MERRY-MOUNT; a Romance of the Massachusetts Colony. 2 vols., cloth. Boston, 1849. (By John Lothrop Motley.) First edition. $75–$100. Second edition, same date. $50. (Also issued as 2 vols. in one, cloth.)

MERRY Tales of the Three Wise Men of Gotham (The). Boards and cloth. New York, 1826. (By James Kirke Paulding.) First edition. $75–$100.

MERTON, Thomas. *Original Child Bomb.* Cloth. (New York, 1961.) New Directions. One of 500, signed. $100–$125. Trade edition: Boards. $25.

MERTON, Thomas. *The Seven-Storey Mountain.* Cloth. New York, (1948). First edition. In dust jacket. $50–$75.

MERTON, Thomas. *Thirty Poems.* Tan boards. Norfolk, (1944). First edition. In dust jacket. $50–$75. Wrappers: $40. Author's first book.

MERTON, Thomas. *The Tower of Babel.* Woodcut illustrations. Folio, boards and vellum. (Norfolk), 1957. New Directions. First edition. One of 250 signed. Boxed. $400–$450.

MERTON, Thomas. *The Waters of Siloe.* Illustrated. Cloth. New York, (1949). First edition. In dust jacket. $35–$50.

MERTON, Thomas. *What Are These Wounds?* Cloth. Milwaukee, 1950. First edition. In dust jacket. $50–$65.

MERWIN, W. S. *The Dancing Bears.* Blue boards. New Haven, 1954. First edition. In dust jacket. $75–$100.

MERWIN, W. S. *A Mask for Janus.* Foreword by W. H. Auden. Blue boards. New Haven, 1952. First edition. In dust jacket. $100–$135. Author's first book.

MERWIN, W. S. *Three Poems.* Oblong, stiff wrappers. New York, 1968. One of 100 signed. $75–$125. (There were also 26 lettered copies.)

MERYMAN, Richard. *Andrew Wyeth.* Color plates. Oblong, two-tone buckram. Boston, 1968. First trade edition, first printing. In dust jacket. $400–$500. (Note: There was also a De Luxe Edition, suede and buckram, 300 signed copies, published at $2,500. It was still being offered at that price in 1980. A fairly good example of manufactured rarity, and a sobering lesson for those who get too serious about "books as investments.")

MESSAGE of the President . . . to Both Houses of Congress . . . First Session of the 18th Congress. 8 leaves. Washington: Giles & Seaton, 1823. (By James Monroe.) First printing. Senate issue (simultaneous with House issue). $1,000–$1,250. (The Monroe Doctrine.)

METCALF, Samuel L. *A Collection of Some of the Most Interesting Narratives of Indian Warfare in the West.* Portrait. Leather. Lexington, 1821. First edition. $600–$750.

METCALFE, John. *The Feasting Dead.* Black cloth. Sauk City, Wis., 1954. First edition. In dust jacket. $65–$75.

MEXICAN Treacheries and Cruelties. Illustrated. 32 pp., pictorial wrappers. Boston, 1847. First edition. (By Lieut. G. N. Allen.) $75–$100. Boston, 1848. Second edition, $100–$150.

MEXICO and the United States: An American View of the Mexican Question. By a Citizen of California. 33 pp., printed wrappers. San Francisco, 1866. $100–$150.

MEXICO in 1842 . . . to Which is Added, An Account of Texas and Yucatan, and of the Santa Fe Expedition. Folding map. Cloth. New York, 1842. (By George F. Folsom or Charles J. Folsom?) First edition. $300–$500.

MEXICO, su Evolución Social. L. Justus Sierra, editor. 3 vols., folio, leather. Mexico, 1900–02. $300–$400.

MEYER, George. *Autobiography of George Meyer: Across the Plains with an Ox Team in 1849.* 2 portraits. Printed tan wrappers. Shenandoah, Iowa, 1908. First edition. $150–$200.

MEYERS, William H. *Journal of a Cruise to California and the Sandwich Islands.* Frontispiece, 10 color plates. Folio, half leather. San Francisco, 1955. Grabhorn Press. One of 400 for the Book Club of California. In dust jacket. $250–$350.

MEYERS, William H. *Naval Sketches of the War in California, 1846–1847.* Descriptive text by Dudley Know. Introduction by Franklin D. Roosevelt. Folio, half white leather. San Francisco, 1939. Grabhorn Press. One of 1,000. $150–$200.

MEYERS, William H. *Sketches of California and Hawaii*. Folio, cloth, paper label. (San Francisco), 1970. Book Club of California. One of 450. $150–$175.

MEYNELL, Alice. *Essays*. Boards. London, 1914. First edition. One of 250 on orange paper. $75–$100. Trade edition: Blue buckram. $20–$30.

MEYNELL, Alice. *Other Poems*. White wrappers. (London, 1896.) One of 50 printed for Christmas cards. $150.

MEYNELL, Alice. *Poems*. Brown cloth. London, 1893. First edition (under this title). One of 50 signed. $150–$175. (For actual first edition, see Thompson, A. C., *Preludes*.) London, 1913. Portrait. Blue boards and cloth. One of 250 signed. $50–$60. Trade edition: Blue buckram. $40–$50.

MEYNELL, Alice. *The Rhythm of Life and Other Essays*. Cloth. London, 1893. First edition. One of 50 signed. $100–$125. Trade edition: $50.

MEYNELL, Alice. *Ten Poems, 1913–1915*. Limp vellum. Westminister (London), 1915. First edition. One of 50. $200–$250.

MEYNELL, Francis. *Typography*. Illustrated, including color. Buckram. London, 1923. Pelican Press. $150–$175.

MEYRICK, Samuel R. *A Critical Inquiry into Antient Armour as It Existed in Europe, but Particularly in England from the Norman Conquest to the Reign of Charles II*. Illustrated, including hand-colored plates. 3 vols., folio, half morocco. London, 1824. First edition. $750–$1,000. London, 1842. 3 vols., half leather. Second edition. $750–$1,000.

MEYRICK, Samuel R., and Skelton, J. *Engraved Illustrations of Antient Arms and Armour, from the Collection of Llewelyn Meyrick*. 2 frontispieces, 2 engraved titles, 2 vignettes and 151 engraved plates. 2 vols., half morocco. London, 1830. $300–$500.

MICHAEL Bonham: or, the Fall of Bexar. By a Southron. Wrappers. Richmond, 1852. (By William Gilmore Simms.) First edition. $300–$400.

MICHAUX, F. A. *Travels to the Westward of the Allegany Mountains*. Translated by B. Lambert. Folding map. Boards. London, 1805. (Printed by Mawman.) First English edition. $500–$600. London, 1805. (Printed by Crosby.) Boards. Second English edition. $300–$400. London, 1805. (Printed by Phillips.) Another translation. Third English edition. $200–$300.

MICHENER, James A. *Centennial*. Blue cloth. New York. (1974). First edition. One of 500 signed. In slipcase. $175.

MIDDLETON, Christopher. *Poems*. Cloth. London, (1944). First edition. In dust jacket. $50–$75. Author's first book.

MIGHTY Magician (The). (Half title only): Bound with *Such Stuff as Dreams Are Made Of*. (Half title only.) The two plays apparently to have been published as *Two Dramas of Calderon* (but no title page known to exist). 132 pp., gray wrappers, with imprint at end: "John Childs & Son." Bungay, (1865). (By Edward Fitz Gerald.) First edition. $500–$750.

MIKESELL, Thomas (editor). *The History of Fulton County, Ohio*. Leather. Madison, Wis., 1905. First edition. $100–$135.

MILES, Gen. Nelson A. *Personal Recollections and Observations*. Illustrated by Frederic Remington and others. Pictorial cloth, leather, or half leather. Chicago, 1896. First edition, first issue, with caption under frontispiece reading "General Miles." $200–$250. Second issue, with rank under portrait as "Maj. Gen." $125–$150. Chicago, 1897. Second edition. With an added plate at end. $75–$125.

MILES, William. *Journal of the Sufferings and Hardships of Capt. Parker H. French's*

Overland Expedition to California. 24 pp., printed wrappers. Chambersburg, Pa., 1851. First edition. $3,500–$3,750.

MILITARY Commanders and Designating Flags of the United States Army, 1861–1865. (Cover title.) Plates. Half leather. Philadelphia, 1887. $250 and up.

MILL, John Stuart. *Autobiography.* Green cloth. London, 1873. First edition, first issue, without errata. $125–$150.

MILL, John Stuart. *On Liberty.* Cloth. London, 1859. First edition. $250–$350.

MILL, John Stuart. *Principles of Political Economy.* 2 vols., cloth. London, 1848. First edition. $850–$1,200. London, 1849. 2 vols., cloth. Second edition. $400–$450. London, 1865. 2 vols., cloth. Sixth edition. $200.

MILL, John Stuart. *The Subjection of Women.* Cloth. London, 1869. First edition. $600–$800.

MILLAR, Kenneth. See John Ross Macdonald and Ross Macdonald, pseudonyms.

MILLAR, Kenneth. *Blue City.* Cloth. New York, 1947. First edition. In dust jacket. $125–$175.

MILLAR, Kenneth. *The Dark Tunnel.* Cloth. New York, 1944. First edition. In dust jacket. $200–$250. Author's first book.

MILLAY, Edna St. Vincent. See Boyd, Nancy; Earle, Ferdinand.

MILLAY, Edna St. Vincent. *The Ballad of the Harp-Weaver.* Illustrated. Pictorial red wrappers. New York, 1922. First edition. One of 500. $150–$200. Another issue: One of 5 on Japan vellum. $750–$850.

MILLAY, Edna St. Vincent. *The Buck in the Snow and Other Poems.* Boards and cloth. New York, 1928. First edition (so stated). In dust jacket. $35. Another issue: Full blue limp leather. $50–$60. Another issue: One of 479 signed. In glassine dust jacket. Boxed. $150–$175. Another issue: Boards and vellum. One of 36 on vellum, signed. In glassine dust jacket. Boxed. $300–$500. London, 1928. First English edition. In dust jacket. $35–$50.

MILLAY, Edna St. Vincent. *Conversation at Midnight.* Blue boards and cloth. New York, 1937. First edition. In dust jacket. $35. Another issue: Full blue limp leather. Boxed. $50–$75. Another issue: Boards and cloth. One of 579 signed. In glassine dust jacket. Boxed. $100–$150. Another issue: One of 36 on vellum, signed. In glassine dust jacket. Boxed. $400–$600.

MILLAY, Edna St. Vincent. *Fatal Interview: Sonnets.* Boards and cloth. New York, 1931. First edition, first issue, with top edges stained yellow. In dust jacket. $30–$50. Another issue: One of 479 signed. In glassine dust jacket. Boxed. $75–$100. Another issue: One of 36 on vellum, signed. In glassine dust jacket. Boxed. $500. Another issue: One of 6 exhibition copies, bound in marbled boards and cloth. $1,000 and up.

MILLAY, Edna St. Vincent. *A Few Figs from Thistles.* Wrappers, New York, 1920. First edition. $175–$200.

MILLAY, Edna St. Vincent. *The Harp-Weaver and Other Poems.* Cloth. New York, 1923. First edition. In dust jacket. $75–$100.

MILLAY, Edna St. Vincent. *Huntsman, What Quarry?* Boards and cloth. New York, 1939. First edition. In dust jacket. $35. Another issue: Full blue limp leather. Boxed. $50–$60. Another issue: Boards and cloth. One of 551 signed. In glassine dust jacket. Boxed. $125. Another issue: Boards and vellum. One of 36 on vellum. In glassine dust jacket. Boxed. $300–$350. '

MILLAY, Edna St. Vincent. *Invocation to the Muses.* Sewed wrappers. New York, 1941. First edition. One of 60. $200–$250.

MILLAY, Edna St. Vincent. *The King's Henchman.* Boards and cloth. New York, 1927.

First edition. In dust jacket. $50–$60. Another issue: One of 158 signed. In glassine dust jacket. Boxed. $150–$200. Another issue: One of 31 on vellum, signed. $300–$375. Another issue: "Artist's Edition." One of 500 signed. $150–$175.

MILLAY, Edna St. Vincent. *The Lamp and the Bell*. Printed green wrappers. New York, 1921. First edition. $100–$150.

MILLAY, Edna St. Vincent. *Poems*. Cloth. London, 1923. First edition. In dust jacket. $150.

MILLAY, Edna St. Vincent. *Poems Selected for Young People*. Boards and cloth. New York, 1929. First edition. One of 1,050 signed. Boxed. $75–$85.

MILLAY, Edna St. Vincent. *The Princess Marries the Page*. Decorations by J. Paget Fredericks. Full blue leather. New York, 1932. First edition. Boxed. $50–$60. Another issue: Boards and cloth. In dust jacket. $35.

MILLAY, Edna St. Vincent. *Renascence: (A Poem)*. Plain wrappers, sewed. New York, 1924. First separate edition. (Printed by Frederic and Bertha Goudy.) Limited. $200.

MILLAY, Edna St. Vincent. *Renascence and Other Poems*. Black cloth. New York, 1917. First edition, first issue, on Glaslan watermarked paper. In dust jacket. $500–$600. Another issue: White vellum paper boards. One of 15 (actually 17) on Japan vellum, signed. $5,500 (A, 1977). Author's first book.

MILLAY, Edna St. Vincent. *Second April*. Black cloth. New York, 1921. First edition, first state, on Glaslan watermarked paper. In dust jacket. $200–$250.

MILLAY, Edna St. Vincent. *Wine from These Grapes*. Boards and cloth, or leather. New York, 1934. First edition. In dust jacket. $40–$50. (Note: Also issued as part of a 2-vol. set with *Epitaph for the Race of Man*. One of 299 sets on paper, Vol. 1 of each set signed. $100–$150.) Another issue: One of 36 on vellum, signed. $400–$500.

MILLER, Andrew. *New States and Territories*. Folding map table. 32 pp., boards. (Keene, N.H., 1818.) First edition. $1,500–$2,000. Another edition: (Keene), 1819. Illustrated, folding map table. 96 pp., boards. Second edition. $1,500.

MILLER, Arthur. *After the Fall*. Light-brown buckram. New York, (1964). First edition. One of 999 signed. (500 for private distribution.) In acetate jacket. Boxed. $125–$150. Trade edition: Boards and cloth. In dust jacket. $40–$50.

MILLER, Arthur. *All My Sons*. Cloth. New York, (1947). First edition. In dust jacket. $50–$75.

MILLER, Arthur. *Death of a Salesman*. Pictorial orange cloth. New York, 1949. First edition. In dust jacket. $75–$100. London, 1949. First English edition. In dust jacket. $35–$50.

MILLER, Arthur. *Situation Normal*. Yellow cloth. New York, (1944). First edition. In dust jacket. $100–$125. Author's first book.

MILLER, Benjamin S. *Ranch Life in Southern Kansas and the Indian Territory*. Frontispiece. 163 pp., printed wrappers. New York, 1896. First edition. $350–$400. Rebound in cloth, $300.

MILLER, E. *The History of Page County, from the Earliest Settlement in 1843 to 1876, etc.* Folding map. Limp black cloth. Clarinda, Iowa, 1876. First edition. $75–$100.

MILLER, Francis Trevelyan. *The World in the Air*. 1,200 illustrations, 2 vols., boards. New York, 1930. First edition. One of 500 signed. $250.

MILLER, Henry. *Account of a Tour of the California Missions, 1856*. Pencil drawings by Miller. 59 pp., boards. San Francisco, 1952. Grabhorn Press. One of 375. Boxed. $125–$165.

MILLER, Henry (novelist). See Flapdoodle, Phineas.

MILLER Henry. *The Air-Conditioned Nightmare.* Beige (probable first binding) or gray cloth. (New York, 1945.) New Directions. First edition. In dust jacket. $75.

MILLER, Henry. *Aller Retour New York.* Wrappers. Paris, (1935). First edition. One of 150 signed. $1,000. Also, $550 (A, 1980); $792 (A, 1979). (New York), 1945. Cloth. First American edition. One of 500. (Issued without dust jacket.) $40–$50.

MILLER, Henry. *Black Spring.* Pictorial wrappers. Paris, (1936). Obelisk Press. First edition, with yellow paper censorship band, "Cannot be bought in England and U.S.A." $500–$850. Paris, (1938). Wrappers. Second edition. $150. New York, (1963). Boards and cloth. First American edition. In dust jacket. $25.

MILLER, Henry. *The Books in My Life.* Cloth. (Norfolk, Conn., 1952.) (Printed in Ireland.) First edition. In dust jacket. $100–$125.

MILLER, Henry. *The Colossus of Maroussi.* Boards and cloth. San Francisco, (1941). Colt Press. First edition. One of 100 signed. (Issued without dust jacket.) $500–$650. Another issue: Cloth, paper label. $75–$125.

MILLER, Henry. *The Cosmological Eye.* Tan cloth, with brown lettering and photograph of an eye inset on cover. Norfolk, (1939). New Directions. First edition. In first state dust jacket (spine lettered in white). $200–$225. London, (1945). First English edition. In dust jacket. $50.

MILLER, Henry. *Hamlet.* Vol. 1 and 2 (the second with Michael Fraenkel). 2 vols., wrappers. (Santurce, Puerto Rico, 1939) and New York, (1941). First edition. $300–$400. (A combined edition with the title *The Michael Fraenkel-Henry Miller Correspondence Called Hamlet* was published in wrappers in London in 1962. Value: $100–$125.)

MILLER, Henry. *Into the Night Life.* Illustrated by Bezalel Schatz. Folio, cloth (Berkeley, 1947.) First edition. One of 800 signed by the author and the artist. Boxed. $700–$800. (Most of the edition was destroyed.)

MILLER, Henry. *Maurizius Forever.* Colored drawings by Miller. Green boards. San Francisco, 1946. Colt Press. First edition. One of 500. Printed at the Grabhorn Press. In plain brown dust jacket. $150.

MILLER, Henry. *Max and the White Phagocytes.* Thick tan wrappers. Paris, (1938). Obelisk Press. First edition. $500–$600. Second edition, same date. $350.

MILLER, Henry. *Money and How It Gets That Way.* Wrappers. Paris, (1938). Booster Broadside No. 1. $250–$350. Also a presentation copy, signed, $225 (A, 1980).

MILLER, Henry. *Murder the Murderer.* Printed wrappers. (Big Sur, Calif., 1944.) First edition. $50–$75.

MILLER, Henry. *Nexus.* Wrappers. Paris, (1960). Obelisk Press. First edition (?). $100–$125. ("Generally accepted as the true first edition," according to Robert A. Wilson, New York specialist dealer in modern literature.)

MILLER, Henry. *Order and Chaos Chez Hans Reichel.* Introduction by Lawrence Durrell. Leather-backed cloth. (Tucson, 1966.) First edition. "Green Oasis edition." One of 11 signed. In dust jacket. Boxed. $250–$350. Another issue: "Crimson Oasis edition." One of 26 signed. In jacket and box. $200–$250. Another issue: "Blue Oasis edition." One of 99 signed. In dust jacket. Boxed. $125–$150. Another issue: "Cork Edition." One of 1,399. Boxed. $85–$100.

MILLER, Henry. *Plexus.* 2 vols., wrappers. Paris, (1953). First English language (and first authorized) edition. $200–$250.

MILLER, Henry. *Quiet Days in Clichy.* Photographs by Brassai. Printed wrappers. Paris, 1956. Olympia Press. First edition. $225–$300.

MILLER, Henry. *Reflections on the Death of Mishima.* Pictorial boards. Santa Barbara, 1972. First edition. One of 200 signed. $35–50.

MILLER, Henry. *Remember to Remember*. Cloth. (New York, 1947.) New Directions. First edition. In dust jacket. $75.

MILLER, Henry. *Scenario (A Film with Sound)*. Double-page frontispiece by Abraham Rattner. Wrappers, unbound. Paris, 1937. One of 200 signed. $750–$1,000.

MILLER, Henry. *Semblance of a Devoted Past*. Illustrated by Miller. Stiff wrappers. Berkeley, 1944. First edition. One of 1,150 (actually 1,650). $75.

MILLER, Henry. *Sexus*. 2 vols., cloth. Paris, 1948. First edition. $150–$175.

MILLER, Henry. *The Smile at the Foot of the Ladder*. Pictorial boards and cloth. New York, (1948). First edition. In dust jacket. $125–$150. (San Francisco), 1955. Greenwood Press. Printed wrappers. One of 500. In glassine dust jacket. $50–$60.

MILLER, Henry. *The Time of the Assassins: A Study of Rimbaud*. Half cloth and cut-out boards. New York, (1956). First edition. In acetate dust jacket. $75.

MILLER, Henry. *Tropic of Cancer*. Preface by Anaïs Nin. Decorated wrappers. Paris, (1934). Obelisk Press. First edition, with "First published September 1934" on copyright page and with wraparound band. $5,000–$7,500. "Lightly used and lightly chipped," $3,500 in a 1981 catalogue. Also, $4,100 (A, 1980). Author's first book. Paris, 1935. Plain wrappers. Second printing. In dust jacket. $500. New York, 1940. Cloth. First (printed) American edition. $75–$100. New York, (1961). Grove Press. Introduction by Karl Shapiro. Preface by Anaïs Nin. Patterned boards and cloth. One of 100 signed. First authorized American edition. (Issued without dust jacket.) $200–$375. Trade edition: Boards. In dust jacket. $35–$50. Later in 1961, cloth, in jacket. $25.

MILLER, Henry. *Tropic of Capricorn*. Decorated wrappers. Paris, (1939). Obelisk Press. First edition, with price on spine and with errata slip. $650–$750.

MILLER, Henry. *Watercolors, Drawings and His Essay "The Angel Is My Watermark!"* Illustrated. Small folio, cloth. London, 1962. First edition. With each of the 12 reproductions signed by Miller. $200–$250. New York, (1962). First American edition. In glassine dust jacket. $100–$125.

MILLER, Henry. *What Are You Going to Do About Alf?* Printed wrappers. Paris, 1935. First edition. $800–$1,000. Paris, (1938). Wrappers. Second edition. $100–$125. Berkeley, (1944). Printed self-wrappers. One of 738. First American edition. $25–$30. (London, 1971.) First English edition. One of 100 signed. In dust jacket. $125. Unsigned copies (250). $50.

MILLER, Henry. *The Wisdom of the Heart*. Brown cloth, with labels on spine and front cover. (New York, 1941.) New Directions. First edition, first binding. One of 1,500. In dust jacket. $100–$125. London, (1947). First English edition. In dust jacket. $50.

MILLER, Henry. *The World of Sex*. Blue cloth. (Chicago, 1940.) One of 250. In dust jacket. $250–$300. Later: Blue cloth. (New York, 1940.) "One of 1,000." $75.

MILLER, Henry; Hiler, Hilaire; and Saroyan, William. *Why Abstract?* Cloth. (New York, 1945.) New Directions. First edition. In dust jacket. $100. London, (1948). Falcon Press. Cloth. First English edition. In dust jacket. $100.

MILLER, Cincinnatus H. *Joaquin, et al*. Portland, Ore., 1869. (By Joaquin Miller.) First edition. $200–$250.

MILLER, Joaquin. See Miller, Cincinnatus H. Also see *How to Win in Wall Street; Specimens*.

MILLER, Joaquin. *'49, The Gold-Seeker of the Sierras*. Printed wrappers. New York, 1884. First edition. $75–$100. (Also issued in cloth, and in boards and cloth.)

MILLER, Joaquin. *An Illustrated History of Montana*. Illustrated. 2 vols., morocco. Chicago, 1894. First edition. $150–$175.

MILLER, Joaquin. *Life Amongst the Modocs: Unwritten History*. Cloth. London, 1873. First edition. $150–$175.

MILLER, Joaquin. *Memorie and Rime*. Printed tan wrappers. New York, 1884. First edition. $75. Another issue: Cloth. $50–$60.

MILLER, Joaquin. *Overland in a Covered Wagon*. Edited by Sidney A. Firman. Illustrated. Cloth. New York, 1930. First edition, first printing, with "(1)" below last line of text. In dust jacket. $35–$50.

MILLER, Joaquin. *Pacific Poems*. Green cloth, gilt. London, 1871. First edition. ("Suppressed by the author and extremely scarce."—DeRicci.) $1,000 and up. Also, rubbed, $475 (A, 1971).

MILLER, Joaquin. *A Royal Highway of the World*. Illustrated. Cloth. Portland, 1932. First edition. One of 245. $50–$60.

MILLER, Joaquin. *Songs of the Mexican Seas*. Cloth. Boston, 1877. First edition. $50–$60.

MILLER, Joaquin. *Songs of the Sierras*. Cloth. London, 1871. First edition. $75–$85. Boston, 1871. Cloth. First published American edition, first binding, with "R.B." at foot of spine. $75–$100.

MILLER, Joaquin. *Songs of the Sun-Lands*. Green cloth. London, 1873. First edition. $100–$125. Another issue: Large paper. $150.

MILLER, Joaquin. *Unwritten History: Life Among the Modocs*. Cloth. Hartford, 1874. First American edition (of *Life Amongst the Modocs*). $100–$150.

MILLER, John F. *A Refutation of the Slander and Falsehoods Contained in a Pamphlet Entitled Sally Miller, etc.* 70 pp., wrappers. New Orleans, 1845. $150–$200.

MILLER, Lewis B. *A Crooked Trail*. Wrappers, cloth spine. Pittsburgh, (1908). First edition. $150.

MILLER, Lewis. B. *Saddles and Lariats*. Illustrated. Pictorial cloth. Boston, 1912. First edition. $100–$125.

MILLER, Patrick. *The Green Ship*. 8 wood engravings by Eric Gill, with an extra set of the plates on Japan vellum. Full morocco. London, 1936. Golden Cockerel Press. One of 62. $500–$600. Another issue: Half morocco and boards. One of 134. $200–$300.

MILLER, Patrick. *Woman in Detail*. 5 illustrations by Mark Severin, with a duplicate set of the 5 plates and with 3 additional ones in a pocket at the end. Half morocco and boards. London, 1947. Golden Cockerel Press. One of 100 signed. $200–$300. Another issue: One of 430. $50–$75.

MILLER, T. L. *History of Hereford Cattle*. Illustrated. Pictorial cloth. Chillicothe, Mo., 1902. First edition. $100–$125.

MILLER, Thomas. *Common Wayside Flowers*. Illustrated by Birket Foster. Decorated brown cloth. London, 1860. First edition. $85.

MILLER, William. *Evidence from Scripture and History of the Second Coming of Christ, About the Year 1843*. Boards. Troy, N.Y. 1838. First edition. $150–$175.

MILLS, Anson. *Big Horn Expedition*. Folding map. 15 pp., tan printed wrappers. No place, no date (1874?). First edition. $500–$600. Also, $250 (A, 1968).

MILLS, Robert. *Atlas of the State of South Carolina*. 29 double-page maps, colored by hand. Folio, half leather. Baltimore, (about 1826). First edition. (Issued to accompany Mills' *Statistics:* see item following.) $750–$1,000.

MILLS, Robert. *Statistics of South Carolina*. Map (not in all copies). Boards. Charleston, 1826. First edition. $100–$150.

MILLS, Samuel J., and Smith, Daniel. *Report of a Missionary Tour . . . West of the Alleghany Mountains.* Wrappers. Andover, 1815. First edition. $300–$400.

MILLS, William W. *Forty Years at El Paso, 1858–1898.* Frontispiece. Cloth. (Chicago, 1901.) (Printed at El Paso, Tex.) First edition. $200–$225. El Paso, 1962. Mesquite Edition. $200.

MILMINE, Georgine. *The Life of Mary Baker G. Eddy and the History of Christian Science.* Edited by Willa S. Cather. Illustrated. Cloth. New York, 1909. (Largely written by Miss Cather.) First edition. $150–$200. London, 1909. Cloth. First English edition. $50–$75.

MILNE, A. A., See Grahame, Kenneth; Shepard, Ernest H.

MILNE, A. A. *By Way of Introduction.* Cloth. London, (1929). First edition. In dust jacket. $40–$50. New York, (1929). Decorated boards and cloth. First American edition. One of 166 on vellum, signed. Boxed. $150–$200. Trade edition: Boards and cloth. In dust jacket. $40–$50.

MILNE, A. A. *The Christopher Robin Story Book.* Illustrated by Ernest H. Shepard. Pictorial cloth. London, (1926). First edition. In dust jacket. $75. New York, (1929). Pictorial boards and cloth. One of 350 signed. $350–$400.

MILNE, A. A. *A Gallery of Children.* 12 full-page illustrations in color by Saida. Folio, white buckram. London, 1925. First edition. One of 500 signed. $700–$800.

MILNE, A. A. *The House at Pooh Corner.* Decorations by Ernest H. Shepard. Boards and buckram. London, (1928). First edition. One of 350, signed. In dust jacket. $450–$550. Another issue: Vellum. One of 20 on Japan paper, signed. $1,000–$1,250. Trade edition: Pink cloth. In dust jacket. $250–$300. New York, (1928). Illustrated. Cloth. First American edition. One of 250 signed. $300–$375. Trade edition: Cloth. In dust jacket. $150–$200.

MILNE, A. A. *Lovers in London.* Cloth. London, 1905. First edition. $125–$150. Author's first book.

MILNE, A. A. *Michael and Mary: A Play.* Green cloth. London, 1930. First edition. One of 260 signed. $100–$150.

MILNE, A. A. *Now We Are Six.* Illustrated by Ernest H. Shepard. Boards and cloth. London, (1927). First edition. One of 200 signed. In dust jacket. $550–$600. Another issue: Vellum. One of 20 on Japan paper, signed. $800–$1,000. Trade edition: Pictorial maroon cloth. In dust jacket. $250–$300.

MILNE, A. A. *The Red House Mystery.* Cloth. London, (1922). First edition. In dust jacket. $350–$500.

MILNE, A. A. *The Secret and Other Stories.* Cloth. New York, 1929. Fountain Press. First edition. One of 742 signed. In glassine dust jacket. $75–$100.

MILNE, A. A. *Those Were the Days.* Decorated buckram. London, (1929). First edition. One of 250 signed. In dust jacket. $135–$175. Trade edition: Cloth. In dust jacket. $50–$60.

MILNE, A. A. *Toad of Toad Hall: A Play from Kenneth Grahame's Book "The Wind in the Willows."* Board and buckram. London, (1929). First edition. One of 200 signed by Milne and Grahame. In dust jacket. $400–$450. Trade edition: Cloth. In dust jacket. $100–$110.

MILNE, A. A. *When I Was Very Young.* Illustrated by Ernest H. Shepard. Cloth. New York, 1930. Fountain Press. First edition. One of 842 signed. Boxed. $200–$250.

MILNE, A. A. *When We Were Very Young.* Illustrated by Ernest H. Shepard. Boards and cloth. London, (1924). First edition. One of 100 signed. In dust jacket. $600–$650. Trade edition, first issue: Pictorial blue cloth, plain end papers, page ix not numbered. In dust jacket. $300. Later copies, $150–$200. New York, (1924). Pictorial boards and cloth. First American edition. One of 100 signed. In dust jacket. $500–$600.

MILNE, A. A. *Winnie-the-Pooh.* Illustrated by Ernest H. Shepard. Boards and buckram. London, (1926). First edition. One of 350 signed. In dust jacket. $500–$600. Another issue: Vellum. One of 20 on vellum, signed. $900–$1,000. Trade edition. Pictorial green cloth. In dust jacket. $300–$350. New York, (1926). Pictorial boards and cloth. First American edition. One of 200 signed. In dust jacket. $500–$800.

MILTON, John. *Areopagitica.* Blue boards. (London, 1903.) Eragny Press. First issue of this edition. One of 40 saved from a fire (out of an edition of 226 copies). $1,000–$1,250. London, 1907. Doves Press. Limp vellum. One of 300. $500–$600. Another issue: One of 25 on vellum. $3,000–$4,000.

MILTON, John. *Comus.* Vellum. London, 1902. Essex House Press. One of 150 on vellum. $300. London, (1921). Illustrated in color by Arthur Rackham. Parchment. One of 550 signed by Rackham. $750–$1,000. Trade edition: Cloth. $200–$300. Newtown, Wales, 1931. Gregynog Press. Illustrated by Blair Hughes-Stanton. Boards and buckram. One of 250. $300–$350. Another issue: Morocco. One of 25 specially bound by George Fisher. $600–$750. London, 1937. Nonesuch Press. Illustrated. Boards. Boxed. $100–$150. New York, 1954. Limited Editions Club. Illustrated by Edmund Dulac. Boards. Boxed. $400–$600.

MILTON, John. *Four Poems: L'Allegro, Il Penseroso, Arcades, Lycidas.* Wood engravings by Blair Hughes-Stanton. Red morocco. Newtown, 1933. Gregynog Press. One of 250 on Japan vellum. $600. Another issue: One of 14 specially bound by George Fisher. $1,000 and up.

MILTON, John. *Hymn on the Morning of Christ's Nativity.* Woodcut by Noel Brooke. 16 pp., folio, blue wrappers. (London), 1928. Ashendene Press. One of "about 220 copies." $800–$1,000.

MILTON, John. *Paradise Lost.* Woodcuts by Mary Groom. Half pigskin. London, 1937. Golden Cockerel Press. One of 200. $1,200–$1,600.

MILTON, John. *Paradise Lost* [and] *Paradise Regain'd.* Printed in red and black. 2 vols., vellum. London, 1902–05. Doves Press. One of 300. $1,000–$1,500. Another issue: 2 vols., vellum. One of 25 on vellum. Each vol., $4,000–$6,000. Another issue: 2 vols. One of 3 on vellum with initials in gold. $48,400 (A, 1978).

MILTON, John. *Paradise Lost* [and] *Paradise Regained.* Illustrated by D. Galanis. 2 vols., folio, pigskin. London, 1931. Cresset Press. One of 195. Boxed. $400–$500. Another issue: 2 vols., sharkskin. One of 10 on vellum. Boxed. $2,500 and up.

MILTON, John. *Poems in English.* 53 plates by William Blake. 2 vols., half vellum and brown boards. London, 1926. Nonesuch Press. One of 1,450 on Van Gelder paper. $300–$350. Another issue: 2 vols. in one, vellum. One of 90 on India paper. $800–$1,000.

MILTON, John. *Samson Agonistes.* Marbled boards. Italy, 1931. One of 103 printed by Victor Hammer (his first book). Harrow Weald, 1931. Raven Press. One of 275. $125–$150.

MINNESOTA Guide (The). 94 pp., wrappers. St. Paul, 1869. (By J. F. Williams.) First edition. $100–$150.

MIRIAM Coffin, or, The Whale Fisherman: A Tale. 2 vols., cloth. New York, 1834. (By Joseph C. Hart.) First edition. $200–$250.

MIROURE of Man's Salvacionne (The): a Fifteenth Century Translation into English of the "Speculum Salvationis." With a facsimile page. Half morocco. London, 1888. $200–$250.

MIRRLEES, Hope. *Paris: A Poem.* Wrappers, paper label. Richmond, England, 1919. Hogarth Press. First edition. $100.

MIRROR of Olden Time Border Life. 13 plates (17 in some). Leather. Abingdon, Va., 1849. (By Joseph Pritts.) First edition. $150–$200.

MISCELLANIES. By the Author of *Letters on the Eastern States*. Boards. Boston, 1821. (By William Tudor.) First edition. $75–$100.

MISFORTUNES of Elphin (The). Boards. London, 1829. (By Thomas Love Peacock.) First edition. $500–$600. Newtown, Wales, 1928. Gregynog Press. Woodcuts. Buckram-backed cloth. One of 250. $200–$300. Another issue: Morocco. One of 25 bound by George Fisher. $1,500–$2,000.

MR. DOOLEY in Peace and in War. Green cloth. Boston, 1898. (By Finley Peter Dunne.) First edition. $50–$75. Author's first book.

MR. FACEY Romford's Hounds. 24 color plates by John Leech and "Phiz" (H. K. Browne). 12 parts, pictorial wrappers. London, 1864–65. (By Robert Smith Surtees.) First edition, with first state wrappers of Part I reading "Mr. Facey Romford's Hounds" (second state and all subsequent parts read "Mr. Romford's Hounds"). $800–$1,250. London, 1865. Pictorial cloth. First book edition. $200–$300.

MR. H., or Beware a Bad Name. 36 pp., sewed. Philadelphia, 1813. (By Charles Lamb.) First edition. $1,500–$2,500.

MR. MIDSHIPMAN Easy. 3 vols., boards and cloth. London, 1836. (By Frederick Marryat.) First edition. $300–$400. London, 1858. Cloth. $75–$100.

MR. SPONGE'S Sporting Tour. 13 color plates and 84 woodcuts by John Leech. 13 parts in 12, pictorial wrappers. London, 1852–53. (By Robert Smith Surtees.) First edition, first issue, with the dedication to Lord Elcho (second issue reading "Earl Elcho"). $600–$800. Second issue. $500–$600. London, 1853. Pictorial cloth. First edition, first issue, in book form. $150–$300.

MRS. LEICESTER'S School: or, The History of Several Young Ladies, Related by Themselves. Frontispiece by J. Hopwood. Boards. London, 1809. (By Charles and Mary Lamb.) First edition, first issue, with only one ad on last leaf. $1,500–$2,000.

MITCHEL, Martin. *History of the County of Fond du Lac, Wisconsin*. 96 pp., printed yellow wrappers. Fond du Lac, 1854. First edition. $300–$400.

MITCHELL, Donald G. See Marvel, Ik.

MITCHELL, Donald G. *The Dignity of Learning: A Valedictory Oration*. Printed wrappers. New Haven, 1841. First edition. $75–$100.

MITCHELL, G. R. *The Pacific Gold Company of Gilpin County, Colorado*. 19 pp., wrappers. Boston, 1866. $125–$150.

MITCHELL, Isaac. *The Asylum; or, Alonzo and Melissa*. Frontispiece. 2 vols., calf. Poughkeepsie, 1811. First edition. $250 and up. Author's first (and only) book. (Note: Many later editions appeared with Daniel Jackson, Jr., as the author.)

MITCHELL, John D. *Lost Mines of the Great Southwest*. Cloth. (Phoenix, 1933.) First edition. $75–$100.

MITCHELL, Joseph. *The Missionary Pioneer*. Tan boards. New York, 1827. First edition. $300–$350.

MITCHELL, Margaret. *Gone with the Wind*. Gray cloth. New York, 1936. First edition, first issue, with "Published May, 1936" on copyright page and no note of other printings. In first issue dust jacket, with *Gone with the Wind* listed in the second column of Macmillan book list on back panel. $600–$800. In second issue jacket, with the novel listed at top of list in first column: $500 or more. Without jacket, $200. (Note: Typographical errors in the first printing persisted through the eighth printing, according to Richard B. Harwell, the Georgia bookman and librarian.)

MITCHELL, S. Augustus. See *Illinois in 1837*.

MITCHELL, S. Augustus (publisher). *Accompaniment to Mitchell's New Map of Texas, Oregon and California, with the Regions Adjoining*. 46 pp., text and large colored map, folding into leather covers. Philadelphia, 1846. First edition. $500–$600.

MITCHELL, S. Augustus (publisher). *Description of Oregon and California, Embracing An Account of the Gold Regions.* Folding map in color. Gold-stamped cloth. Philadelphia, 1849. First edition. $600–$800.

MITCHELL, S. Augustus. *Traveller's Guide Through the United States.* Folding map. 74 pp., leather. Philadelphia. (1836). First text edition under this title. $300–$400. Philadelphia, 1839. Half leather. $250. New York, 1851. $100–$175.

MITCHELL, S. Weir. See S., E. W., and M., S. W. Also see *The Wonderful Stories of Fuz-Buz the Fly.*

MITCHELL, S. Weir. *Hugh Wynne, Free Quaker.* Illustrated by Howard Pyle. 2 vols., gray or light brown cloth. New York, 1897. First edition, first issue, with last word on page 54, Vol. 1, being "in" and line 16 on page 260, Vol. 2, reading "before us." $150–$200. Later issue, text corrected: 2 vols., gray boards, white cloth spines, paper labels. One of 60 large paper copies, signed, with separate plates by Howard Pyle laid in. $450. (Note: A few copies of the first edition, first issue, exist with an 1869 title page—not published. One of these was sold at auction in the 1972–73 season for $1,400.)

MITCHELL, S. Weir. *Mr. Kris Kringle.* Boards and cloth. Philadelphia, 1893. First edition. $50–$75.

MITCHELL, S. Weir. *Researches upon the Venom of the Rattlesnake.* Folio, wrappers. Washington, 1861. $100–$150.

MITCHELL, S. Weir, and others. *Gunshot Wounds and Other Injuries of Nerves.* Wrappers. Philadelphia, 1864. $200–$225.

MITCHELL, W. H. *Geographical and Statistical History of the County of Olmstead.* 121 pp., printed wrappers. Rochester, Minn., (1866). First edition. $100–$125.

MITCHELL, W. H. *Geographical and Statistical Sketch of the Past and Present of Goodhue County.* 191 pp., wrappers. Minneapolis, 1869. First edition. $100–$125.

MITFORD, John. *The Adventures of Johnny Newcome in the Navy.* Color plates. Half calf. London, 1819. Second edition. $300–$400. London, 1823. Third edition. $325. (See Alfred Burton entry for first edition.)

MITFORD, Mary Russell. *Our Village.* Boards. London, 1824. First edition. $400–$450. London, 1893. Illustrated by Hugh Thompson. Cloth. One of 470. $125. London, 1910. Thompson illustrations. Half leather. $100–$125.

MITFORD, Mary Russell. *Poems.* Boards. London, 1810. First edition, with leaf of "Alterations." $300–$400. Author's first book.

MIVART, St. George. *Dogs, Jackals, Wolves, and Foxes.* Illustrated, including 45 color plates. Cloth. London, 1890. First edition. $500–$700.

MIVART, St. George. *A Monograph of the Lories, or Brush-Tongued Parrots.* 61 colored plates and 4 colored maps. Cloth. London, 1896. First edition. $4,500.

MODERN Griselda (The). Blue-gray boards. London, 1805. (By Maria Edgeworth.) First edition. $400–$600.

MOELLHAUSEN, Baldwin. *Diary of a Journey from the Mississippi to the Coasts of the Pacific with a United States Government Expedition.* Translated by Mrs. Percy Sinnett. Illustrations, including color plates. Folding map. 2 vols., cloth. London, 1858. First edition in English. $1,000–$1,500.

MOFFETTE, Joseph F. *The Territories of Kansas and Nebraska.* 2 folding maps. Cloth. New York, 1855. First edition. $1,000–$1,250. New York, 1856. Second edition. $500.

MOKLER, A. J. *History of Natrona County, Wyoming.* Illustrated. Buckram. Chicago, 1923. First edition. $150–$175.

MOLL Pitcher, a Poem. Blue printed wrappers. Boston, 1832. (By John Greenleaf Whittier.) First edition. (Note: No copy in original wrappers has been noted at sale for many years. Estimated retail value: $1,500–$2,500. Rebound copies, $500 and up.) Philadelphia, 1840. (*Moll Pitcher, and the Minstrel Girl: Poems.*) Wrappers. $200–$300.

MOMADAY, N. Scott. *House Made of Dawn.* Cloth. New York, (1968). First edition. In dust jacket. $75.

MONASTERY (The). 3 vols., boards, paper spines and labels. Edinburgh, 1820. (By Sir Walter Scott.) First edition. $400–$500.

MONETTE, John W. *History of the Discovery and Settlement of the Valley of the Mississippi.* 3 maps, 4 plans, 2 plates. Cloth. New York, 1846. First edition. $250–$350.

MONIKINS (The): A Tale. By the Author of "The Spy." 3 vols., drab tan boards. London, 1835. (By James Fenimore Cooper.) First edition. $400–$600. Philadelphia, 1835. 2 vols., boards. First American edition. $400–$600.

MONKS, William. *History of Southern Missouri and Northern Arkansas.* Cloth. West Plains, Mo., 1907. First edition. $100–$125.

MONODY on the Death of the Right Honorable R. B. Sheridan. 12 pp., wrappers. London, 1816. (By George Gordon Noel, Lord Byron.) First edition, first issue, with first line on page 11 beginning "To weep," etc. $1,000 and up. (Very rare; no copies in original wrappers for sale in many years.) Second issue, line 1 on page 11 beginning "To mourn." $300–$500. (Rebound and disbound copies of both issues are occasionally offered at more modest prices.)

MONROE Doctrine (The). See *Message of the President* . . . (1823).

MONROE, Harriet. *The Columbian Ode.* Pictorial wrappers. Chicago, 1893. First (Souvenir) edition. In original envelope. $80–$100.

MONROE, Harriet. *Valeria and Other Poems.* Vellum and cloth. Chicago, 1891. First edition. $100–$125. Author's first book. Chicago, 1892. Cloth. First published edition. $75.

MONROE, James. *The Memoir of James Monroe, Esq., Relating to His Unsettled Claims Upon the People and Government of the U.S.* 60 pp., sewed. Charlottesville, Va., 1828. $150–$175.

MONROE'S Embassy, or the Conduct of the Government, in Relation to Our Claims to the Navigation of the Missisippi [sic]. 57 pp., wrappers. Philadelphia, 1803. (By Charles Brockden Brown.) $300–$350. (Note: Signed at the end with the pseudonym Poplicola.)

MONT Saint Michel and Chartres. Blue cloth, leather label on spine. Washington, 1904. (By Henry Adams.) First edition. Privately printed. $1,000 and up. Washington, 1912. Second (first revised and enlarged) edition. (500 copies.) $1,000. Boston, 1913. Half brown cloth and tan boards. First published edition. $50–$75. New York, 1957. Limited Editions Club. Cloth and leather. Boxed. $40–$60.

MONTAGUE, C. E. *A Hind Let Loose.* Cloth. London, (1910). First edition. In dust jacket. $100–$150. Author's first book.

MONTAGUE, C. E. *A Writer's Notes on His Trade.* Introduction by H. M. Tomlinson. Woodcut portrait. Buckram and boards. London, 1930. First edition. One of 700 signed by Tomlinson. $75. Trade edition: Cloth. In dust jacket. $25–$35.

MONTAIGNE, Michel de. *Essays.* Translated by John Florio. 3 vols., folio, half cloth. Boston, 1902–03–04. One of 265 designed by Bruce Rogers. In dust jackets and folding cases. $750–$1,250. London, 1931. Nonesuch Press. 2 vols., full morocco. Boxed. $200–$250.

MONTANA, Its Climate, Industries and Resources. Illustrated. 74 pp., wrappers. Helena, Mont., 1884. First edition. $150–$200.

MONTANA Territory, History and Business Directory 1879. Map. 5 plates. Printed boards and leather. Helena, (1879). (By F.W. Warner.) First edition. $300–$600.

MONTGOMERY, Cora. *Eagle Pass; or, Life on the Border.* Stiff wrappers. New York, 1852. (By Mrs. William L. Cazneau.) First edition. $100–$150.

MONTULE, Eduard. *A Voyage to North America, and the West Indies, in 1821.* Folding and full-page plates. Printed wrappers. London, 1821. First edition in English. $300–$400. Rebound in cloth, $175.

MOODY, William Vaughn. *The Masque of Judgment.* Cloth. Boston, 1900. First edition. $100. Another issue: Boards. One of 150. $150–$200. Author's first book.

MOODY, William Vaughn. *Poems.* Boards. Boston, 1901. First edition. One of 150 on large paper. $75–$100.

MOORCOCK, Michael. *The Stealer of Souls.* Orange boards. London, 1963. First edition. In dust jacket. $75–$100. (Later binding is green.)

MOORCOCK, Michael. *Stormbringer.* Cloth. London, (1965). First edition. In dust jacket. $50–$60.

MOORE, Sir Alan Hilary. *Sailing Ships of War, 1800–1860.* 90 full-page plates, 12 in color. Cloth. London, 1926. One of 1,500. $200–$300. Another issue: Half leather. One of 100. $400–$500.

MOORE, Brian. *The Lonely Passion of Judith Hearn.* Cloth. London, 1955. First edition. In dust jacket. $60–$75. Boston, (1955). Boards. First American edition. In dust jacket. $35–$45.

MOORE, C. L. *Northwest of Earth.* Cloth. New York, (1954). First edition. In dust jacket. $50–$60.

MOORE, C. L. *Shambleau and Others.* Cloth. New York, (1953). First edition. In dust jacket. $75.

MOORE, Clement C. See *A New Translation, etc.; The New York Book of Poetry; Observations upon Certain Passages in Mr. Jefferson's "Notes on Virginia."*

MOORE, Clement C. *Christmas Carol. The Visit of Saint Nicholas.* Broadside; text printed in blue. Philadelphia, (1842). $35–$50.

MOORE, Clement C. *The Night Before Christmas.* Color plates by W. W. Denslow. Pictorial boards. New York, 1902. $100–$150. Philadelphia, (1931). 4 color plates and text drawings by Arthur Rackham. Cloth. In dust jacket. $250–$350. London, (1931). Wrappers. In dust jacket. $300–$400. London or Philadelphia, (1931). Vellum. One of 550. Boxed. $750–$1,000.

MOORE, Clement C. *Poems.* Brown boards. New York, 1844. First edition. $250–$300.

MOORE, Clement C. *A Visit from St. Nicholas.* Illustrated by F. O. C. Darley. Pictorial wrappers. New York, 1862. $75–$100.

MOORE, Edward. *We Moderns: Enigmas and Guesses.* Cloth. London, (1918). (By Edwin Muir.) First edition. In dust jacket. $100–$150. Muir's first book.

MOORE, Edward A. *The Story of a Cannoneer Under Stonewall Jackson.* Cloth. New York, 1907. First edition. $100–$150.

MOORE, George. *The Brook Kerith.* Half brown cloth, marbled sides. Edinburgh, 1916. First edition. $50–$75. Another issue: Parchment and boards. One of 250 signed. $100–$125. London, 1929. Illustrated by Stephen Gooden. Vellum. One of 375 signed by Moore and Gooden. $200–$300. New York, 1929. Illustrated by Gooden. Half vellum. One of 500. $125–$175.

MOORE, George. *Flowers of Passion.* Black cloth. London, 1878. First edition, with 1877 copyright and errata slip. $300–$400.

MOORE, George. *Literature at Nurse, or, Circulating Morals.* Self-wrappers, sewed. London, 1885. First edition. $400–$500.

MOORE, George. *Memoirs of My Dead Life.* Blue-gray cloth. London, 1906. First edition. $75–$100. New York, 1920. Boards and parchment. One of 1,500 (not signed). In dust jacket. $25. London, 1921. Colored frontispiece and decorated title page. Boards and parchment. One of 1,030 signed. $35–$45.

MOORE, George. *A Modern Lover.* 3 vols., blue cloth. London, 1883. First edition. $400–$500.

MOORE, George. *A Mummer's Wife.* Cloth. London, 1885. First edition. $150–$200.

MOORE, George. *Pagan Poems.* Blue cloth. London, 1881. First edition. $400–$500. (Note: Moore removed the title page from most copies and complete copies are rare.)

MOORE, George. *Peronnik the Fool.* Boards. New York, 1926. Bruce Rogers printing. $75–$85. Chapelle-Reanville, France, 1928. Hours Press. Cloth. Revised edition. One of 200 signed. $150. London, 1933. Engravings by Stephen Gooden. Full vellum. One of 525 signed by author and artist. $100–$150.

MOORE, George. *A Story-Teller's Holiday.* Half vellum. London, 1918. First edition. One of 1,000 signed. In dust jacket. $35–$50. New York, 1918. Cloth. First American edition. One of 1,250 signed. $25. New York, 1928. 2 vols., cloth. One of 1,250 signed. In dust jacket. Boxed. $25–$35.

MOORE, George. *Ulick and Soracha.* Engraved plate by Stephen Gooden. Buckram. London, 1926. Nonesuch Press. One of 1,250 on vellum, signed. In dust jacket. $50–$80.

MOORE, H. Judge. *Scott's Campaign in Mexico.* Cloth. Charleston, 1849. First edition. $250–$350.

MOORE, Henry. *Heads, Figures and Ideas.* Illustrated. Boards and cloth. London, 1958. First edition. In dust jacket. $150–$225. Another issue: One of 150 with a signed Moore lithograph in color. $500–$600.

MOORE, Julia A. *The Sentimental Song Book.* 54 pp., wrappers. Grand Rapids, 1876. First edition. $100 and up.

MOORE, Marianne. *The Absentee: A Comedy in Four Acts.* Blue cloth. New York, 1962. First edition. One of 326 signed. In tissue dust jacket. $125–$150.

MOORE, Marianne. *Collected Poems.* Cloth. London, (1951). First edition, with or without errata slip. In dust jacket. $50–$60.

MOORE, Marianne. *Complete Poems.* Half buckram. New York, (1967). First edition, with or without errata slip. In dust jacket. $50–$60.

MOORE, Marianne. *Eight Poems.* 10 hand-colored drawings. Half cloth. New York, (1963). First edition. One of 195 signed. Boxed. $400–$500. Also, a copy with addendum slip and "With the Author's Compliments" slip, $500 (A, 1977).

MOORE, Marianne. *Marriage: Manikin No. 3.* 16 pp., light-blue pictorial wrappers. New York, (1923). First edition, with 4-page leaflet by Glenway Wescott laid in, as issued. $450–$550.

MOORE, Marianne. *Nevertheless.* Cloth. New York, (1944). First edition, first printing. In dust jacket. $60–$75.

MOORE, Marianne. *Observations*. Cloth-backed boards, paper label. New York, 1924. First edition. In dust jacket. $300–$400.

MOORE, Marianne. *The Pangolin and Other Verse*. Drawings by George Plank. Decorated boards, paper label. (London), 1936. First edition. One of 120. $500–$600. Also, $425 (A, 1977).

MOORE, Marianne. *Poems*. Decorated wrappers, paper label. London, 1921. Egoist Press. First edition. $300. Author's first book.

MOORE, Marianne. *Predilections*. Cloth. New York, 1955. First edition. In dust jacket. $50–$60.

MOORE, Marianne. *Selected Poems*. Introduction by T. S. Eliot. Green or turquoise cloth. New York, 1935. First edition. In first issue dust jacket with $2 price. $75–$100. London, (1935). Red cloth (purple later). First English edition. In dust jacket. $50–$75.

MOORE, Marianne. *Silence*. Wrappers, paper label. Cambridge, Mass., 1965. First edition. One of 25. $200.

MOORE, Marianne. *Tipoo's Tiger*. Printed wrappers. New York, 1967. First edition. One of 126 signed, and with correction in line 24 in author's hand. $100–$150.

MOORE, Marianne. *What Are Years*. Cloth. New York, 1941. First edition, first printing. In dust jacket. $75–$85.

MOORE, Marianne (translator). *The Fables of La Fontaine*. Cloth. New York, 1954. One of 400 signed. In glassine jacket. Boxed. $150–$200. Trade edition: In dust jacket. $30–$40. New York, (1965). Cloth. Revised edition. In dust jacket. $25.

MOORE, Marianne, and Wallace, David. *Letters from and to the Ford Motor Company*. Half cloth. New York, 1958. First edition. One of 550. Boxed. $100–$125.

MOORE, Marinda B. (Mrs. M. B.) *The Dixie Primer, for the Little Folks*. Wrappers. Raleigh, 1863. Third edition. $70 (A, 1976).

MOORE, Marinda B. (Mrs. M. B.) *The Dixie Speller*. Boards, Raleigh, 1864. $300–$400.

MOORE, Marinda B. (Mrs. M. B.) *The Geographical Reader, for the Dixie Children*. 48 pp., boards. Raleigh, 1863. First edition. $400–$500.

MOORE, Marinda B. (Mrs. M. B.) *Primary Geography*. 6 colored double-spread maps. Cloth. Raleigh, 1864. Second edition. $325 (A, 1978).

MOORE, Merrill. *Case Record from a Sonnetorium*. Cartoons by Edward St. John Gorey. Cloth. New York, (1951). First edition. In dust jacket. $50–$75.

MOORE, S. S., and Jones, T. W. *The Traveller's Directory*. 38 maps on 22 leaves. 52 pp., contemporary calf. Philadelphia, 1802. First edition. $500–$750. Philadelphia, 1804. $500–$600.

MOORE, Thomas. *The Epicurean: A Tale*. Boards, paper label. London, 1827. First edition. $100–$150.

MOORE, Thomas. *Fables for the Holy Alliance*. Boards. London, 1823. First edition. $150.

MOORE, Thomas. *Irish Melodies*. Boards. Dublin, 1820. First edition. $100–$125. London, 1821. Boards. First authorized edition. $150–$200. London, 1846. Half morocco. $75–$100.

MOORE, Thomas. *Lalla Rookh, an Oriental Romance*. Boards. London, 1817. First edition. $300–$400.

MOORE, Thomas. *The Loves of the Angels: A Poem.* Boards. London, 1823. First edition. $200–$250.

MOORE, Thomas. *Lyrics and Satires.* Selected by Sean O'Faolain. 5 designs by Hilda Roberts. Boards and cloth. Dublin, 1929. Cuala Press. One of 130. In dust jacket. $100–$125.

MOORE, Thomas. *Paradise and the Peri.* Illuminated borders. Folio, leather, or cloth. (London, about 1860.) First edition. $75–$100.

MOORE, Thomas (translator). *The Odes of Anacreon.* Morocco. London, 1800. First edition. $75–$100.

MOORE, T. Sturge. *A Brief Account of the Origin of the Eragny Press* Illustrated. Boards. London, 1903. Eragny Press. One of 235. $600–$800. Another issue: One of 6 on vellum. $4,000 or more.

MOORE, T. Sturge. *The Little School: A Posy of Rhymes.* Woodcuts. Boards. London, 1905. Eragny Press. One of 185. In dust jacket. $400–$500. Another issue: Morocco. One of 10 on vellum. $1,000–$1,250.

MOORE, T. Sturge. *The Vinedresser and Other Poems.* Cloth. London, 1899. Unicorn Press. First edition. $100–$150. Author's first published book.

MORE, Hannah. See *Hints Towards Forming the Character of a Young Princess.*

MORE, Hannah. *Sacred Dramas, Chiefly Intended for Young Persons.* Calf. Boston, 1801. First American edition. $75–$100.

MORE Hints on Etiquette. Illustrated. Cloth. London, 1838. (By George Cruikshank or Charles Dickens?) First edition. $150–$250.

MORE, Sir Thomas. *Utopia.* Woodcut borders and initials, printed in black and red. Vellum with ties. London, 1893. Kelmscott Press. $800–$1,200. Another issue: One of 6 on vellum. $5,000–$6,000. (London, 1906.) Ashendene Press. Boards and linen. One of 100. $1,500–$2,000. Another issue: Morocco. One of 20 on vellum. $4,000–$5,000. Waltham Saint Lawrence, England, 1929. Golden Cockerel Press. Decorations by Eric Gill. Buckram. $200–$300. New York, 1934. Limited Editions Club. Woodcuts by Bruce Rogers. Vellum and boards. Boxed. $100–$125.

MORECAMP, Arthur. *The Live Boys; or, Charlie and Nasho in Texas.* Pictorial cloth. Boston, (1878). (By Thomas Pilgrim.) First edition. $100–$150. Pilgrim's first book.

MOREHEAD, James T. *Address in Commemoration of the First Settlement of Kentucky.* Printed wrappers. Frankfort, 1840. First edition. $100–$150.

MORFI, Juan Agustin. *History of Texas, 1673–1779.* Map, 4 plates. 2 vols., boards and cloth. Albuquerque, 1935. First edition. One of 500. $150–$300. New York, 1967. Facsimile edition. $50–$60.

MORGAN, Charles. *The Gunroom.* Cloth. London, 1919. First edition. $60–$80. Author's first novel.

MORGAN, Charles. *Sparkenbroke.* Morocco. London, 1936. First edition. One of 210 signed. $175–$200. Trade edition: Green cloth. In dust jacket. $40.

MORGAN, Dale L. See Ashley, William H.

MORGAN, Dale L. *Jedediah Smith and the Opening of the West.* 20 plates. Cloth. Indianapolis, (1953). First edition. In dust jacket. $50–$75.

MORGAN, Dale L., and Wheat, Carl I. *Jedediah Smith and His Maps of the American West.* 7 folding maps. Cloth. San Francisco, 1954. First edition. One of 530. $500–$750.

MORGAN, Dick T. *Morgan's Manual of the U. S. Homestead and Townsite Laws*. Buff printed wrappers. Guthrie, Okla., 1893. First edition. $150–$300.

MORGAN, Emanuel. *Pins for Wings*. Illustrated by William Saphier. Boards. (New York, 1920.) (By Witter Bynner.) First edition. $100–$125.

MORGAN, Emanuel, and Knish, Anne. *Spectra: A Book of Poetic Experiments*. Boards. New York, 1916. (By Witter Bynner [Morgan] and Arthur Davison Ficke [Knish].) First edition. (Issued without dust jacket.) $100–$125.

MORGAN, Jane. *Tales for Fifteen*. Printed tan boards. New York, 1823. (By James Fenimore Cooper.) First edition. Extremely rare; no sales noted in any records consulted. Value: $1,000 and up?

MORGAN, John Hill, and Fielding, Mantle. *The Life Portraits of Washington and Their Replicas*. Illustrated. Folio, cloth. Philadelphia, (1931). First edition. One of 1,000. $75–$125. Another issue: Full morocco. Limited, signed by the authors. In dust jacket. Boxed. $200–$300.

MORGAN, Lewis H. *The American Beaver and His Works*. Map, 23 plates. Cloth. Philadelphia, 1868. First edition. $100.

MORGAN, Lewis H. *Ancient Society*. Cloth. New York, 1877. First edition. $100–$150.

MORGAN, Lewis H. *The Indian Journals of Lewis Henry Morgan*. Illustrated, including color plates and maps. Oblong, cloth. Ann Arbor, Mich., (1959). In dust jacket. $50–$75.

MORGAN, Lewis H. *The League of the Ho-De'-No-Sau-Nee, or Iroquois*. 21 plates, map, table. Cloth. Rochester, 1851. First edition. $75–$100. Another issue: Maps and plates colored by hand. $200–$300. New York, 1922. Edited by H. H. M. Lloyd. 2 vols. in one, cloth. $50–$75.

MORGAN, Martha M. (editor). *A Trip Across the Plains in the Year 1849*. 31 pp., printed wrappers. San Francisco, 1864. First edition. $5,000–$6,000.

MORGAN, Thomas J. *A Glance at Texas*. 16 pp., three-quarters morocco. Columbus, 1844. First edition. $1,500.

MORIER, James. See *Ayesha*.

MORISON, Stanley. *The Art of the Printer*. Illustrated. Cloth. London, 1925. In dust jacket. $100–$125.

MORISON, Stanley. *English Liturgical Books*. Green buckram. (Cambridge, 1942.) First edition. One of 21 bound (from an edition of 50). $150–$200. (Suppressed and never actually published in this form.)

MORISON, Stanley. *The English Newspaper*. Illustrated. Folio, cloth. Cambridge, 1932. First edition. In dust jacket. $250–$350.

MORISON, Stanley. *Four Centuries of Fine Printing*. Illustrated with 625 facsimiles. Folio, cloth. London, (1924). One of 390. $400–$500. Another issue: Morocco. One of 13 signed. $750–$1,000. London, (1949). 272 facsimile title pages. Calf. Second edition, revised. One of 200. $300–$400.

MORISON, Stanley. *Fra Luca de Pacioli of Borgo S. Sepolcro*. Boards, vellum spine. New York, 1933. First edition. One of 390. $500–$600. Another issue: One of 7 on large paper. $600–$750.

MORISON, Stanley. *Modern Fine Printing*. Facsimiles. Folio, cloth. London, 1925. First edition. One of 650 in English. $350–$500.

MORISON, Stanley. *On Type Faces*. Illustrated. Folio, half cloth. London, 1923. First edition. One of 750. In dust jacket. $150–$200.

MORISON, Stanley (editor). *A Newly Discovered Treatise on Classic Letter Design.* Facsimile reproduction. Vellum and boards. Paris, 1927. First edition. One of 350. Boxed. $350–$500.

MORLEY, C. D. *The Eighth Sin.* Printed pale blue-gray wrappers. Oxford, 1912. (By Christopher Morley.) First edition. One of 250. $600–$800. Also: $400 (A, 1981); presentation copy, inscribed, $600 (A, 1977). Author's first book.

MORLEY, Christopher. *Blythe Mountain Vermont.* Cloth. Brattleboro, (1931). First edition. One of 500. $50–$75.

MORLEY, Christopher. *The Haunted Bookshop.* Cloth. New York, 1919. First edition, first state, with page number at bottom of page 76 and perfect "Burroughs" above it. In dust jacket. $150–$200.

MORLEY, Christopher. *Old Loopy: A Love Letter for Chicago.* Illustrated. Cloth. Chicago, 1935. First edition. $50–$60.

MORLEY, Christopher. *The Palette Knife.* Illustrated in color. Pictorial cloth. Chelsea, N.Y., 1929. First edition. One of 450 signed. $100–$150.

MORLEY, Christopher. *Parnassus on Wheels.* Gray boards, tan cloth spine. Garden City, N.Y., 1917. First edition, first state, with space between the "Y" and "e" in "Years" in line 8, page 4. In dust jacket. $400–$500. Lacking jacket, $200–$250.

MORLEY, Christopher. *Paumanok.* Boards. Garden City, 1926. First edition. One of 107 signed. In dust jacket. $125–$150.

MORLEY, Christopher. *Songs for a Little House.* Boards. New York, (1917). First edition, first state, with quotation from Southwell facing title page. In dust jacket. $125–$150.

MORLEY, Christopher. *Where the Blue Begins.* Pictorial cream and blue marbled boards, blue cloth spine. Garden City, 1922. First edition. In dust jacket. $75–$100. London, (1925). Illustrated by Arthur Rackham, including 4 color plates. Half black cloth and white boards. First De Luxe illustrated edition. One of 175 signed by Rackham. Boxed. $1,250–$1,500. London and New York, (1925). Rackham illustrations. Half black cloth and green and blue boards. First American De Luxe edition. One of 100 signed by Morley and Rackham. In tissue dust jacket. Boxed. $2,000–$2,500. London, (1925). Rackham illustrations. Blue cloth. First Rackham trade edition. In dust jacket. $200–$250.

MORPHIS, J. M. *History of Texas.* Plates, folding map in color. Cloth. New York, 1874. First edition. $150–$200.

MORRELL, Benjamin. *Narrative of Four Voyages to the South Seas. North and South Pacific Ocean.* Portrait. Boards and cloth. New York, 1832. First edition. $400.

MORRELL, Z. N. *Flowers and Fruits from the Wilderness; or 36 Years in Texas.* Cloth. Boston, 1872. First edition. $100–$200.

MORRIS, Eastin. *The Tennessee Gazetteer.* Printed boards, leather spine. Nashville, 1834. First edition, $1,000–$1,250.

MORRIS, May. *Decorative Needlework.* Boards. London, 1893. First edition. One of 125 copies. $300.

MORRIS, William. *Child Christopher and Goldilind the Fair.* Woodcuts. 2 vols., decorated boards and cloth. London, 1895. Kelmscott Press. One of 600. $400–$500. Another issue: One of 12 on vellum. $1,500–$2,000.

MORRIS, William. *The Defence of Guenevere, and Other Poems.* Printed in black and red. Woodcut borders. Vellum with ties. London, 1892. Kelmscott Press. One of 300. $600–$1,000. Another issue: One of 10 on vellum. $4,000–$5,000.

MORRIS, William. *A Dream of John Ball and A King's Lesson.* Woodcut borders and designs by Morris and E. Burne-Jones. Vellum with ties. London, 1892. Kelmscott Press. One of 300. $400–$600. Another issue: One of 11 on vellum. $4,000–$5,000.

MORRIS, William. *The Earthly Paradise.* Woodcut title. 8 vols., vellum with ties. London, 1896–97. Kelmscott Press. One of 225. $1,000–$1,500. Another issue: One of 6 on vellum. $5,000–$6,000.

MORRIS, William. *Gothic Architecture.* Blue boards. (London, 1893.) Kelmscott Press. One of 45 on vellum (of an edition of 1,545). $1,000–$1,250. Ordinary copies, first issue, with "Eyk" for "Eyck" on page 45: $350. Later, $175–$200.

MORRIS, William. *Guenevere.* 8 plates. Half cloth. London, 1930. Fanfrolico Press. One of 450. $150–$200.

MORRIS, William. *In Praise of My Lady.* Half leather. New York, 1928. Aries Press. One of 31. $150.

MORRIS, William. *The Life and Death of Jason: A Poem.* Woodcut frontispiece, other decorations by E. Burne-Jones. Vellum with ties. London, 1895. Kelmscott Press. One of 200. $1,000–$1,250. Another issue: One of 6 on vellum: $4,000–$6,000.

MORRIS, William. *Love Is Enough.* Woodcut borders and 2 illustrations by E. Burne-Jones. Vellum with ties. London, 1897. Kelmscott Press. One of 300. $1,000–$1,500. Another issue: One of 8 on vellum. $4,000–$5,000.

MORRIS, William. *News from Nowhere.* Woodcut frontispiece, borders, and initials. Vellum with ties. London, 1892. Kelmscott Press. One of 300. $800–$1,200. Another issue: One of 10 on vellum. $4,000–$5,000.

MORRIS, William. *Note by William Morris on His Aims in Founding the Kelmscott Press.* Woodcuts. Boards and cloth. London, 1898. Kelmscott Press. With errata slip. One of 525. $750–$850. (Note: The last book printed at the Kelmscott Press.)

MORRIS, William. *Poems by the Way.* Vellum. London, 1891. Kelmscott Press. One of 300 on paper. $600–$800. Another issue: One of 13 on vellum. $6,500.

MORRIS, William. *Printing: An Essay.* Boards. Park Ridge, Ill., 1903. First edition. Limited. $200–$300.

MORRIS, William. *The Roots of the Mountains.* Decorated cloth. London, 1890 (actually 1899). One of 250. First edition. $150–$200.

MORRIS, William. *Sir Galahad: A Christmas Mystery.* Leather. London, 1858. First edition. $75–$100. (A Thomas J. Wise forgery.) New Rochelle, N.Y., 1902. Elston Press. Half vellum. One of 80. $150–$200. (Chicago, 1904.) Blue Sky Press. Gray paper over blue cloth boards. One of 500 designed by Thomas Wood Stevens. $75–$100. Another issue: One of 25 on vellum. $150–$200.

MORRIS, William. *The Story of the Glittering Plain.* Woodcut title and borders. Illustrations by Walter Crane. Vellum with ties. London, 1891. Kelmscott Press. One of 200. Boxed. $1,000–$1,500. London, 1894. Vellum. One of 250. Boxed. $1,000–$1,500. Another issue: One of 7 on vellum. $5,000–$6,000.

MORRIS, William. *The Story of Gunnlaug the Worm-tongue and Raven the Skald.* (All copies have spaces where initial capital letters were to have been printed at the beginning of each chapter.) Boards and cloth. London, 1891. Chiswick Press. One of 75. $175–$225.

MORRIS, William. *The Sundering Flood.* Woodcuts. Boards and cloth, London, 1897. Kelmscott Press. One of 300. $400–$600. (A copy on vellum was sold for $9,500 at the 1979 International Antiquarian Book Fair at San Francisco.)

MORRIS, William. *Under an Elm-Tree.* Wrappers (?). Aberdeen, 1891. First edition. $75–$100. (Note: H. Buxton Forman forged wrappers for this pamphlet.)

MORRIS, William. *The Water of the Wondrous Isles.* Woodcut borders and initials.

Vellum with ties. London, 1897. Kelmscott Press. One of 250. $800–$1,200. Another issue: One of 6 on vellum: $5,000–$6,000.

MORRIS, William. *The Well at the World's End*. 4 woodcuts and initial letters by E. Burne-Jones. Vellum with ties. London, 1896. Kelmscott Press. One of 350. $1,000–$1,500. Another issue: One of 8 on vellum. $4,000–$5,000.

MORRIS, William. *The Wood Beyond the World*. Woodcut frontispiece, other illustrations. Vellum with ties. London, 1894. Kelmscott Press. First edition. One of 350. $750–$1,000. Another issue: One of 8 on vellum. $4,000–$5,000.

MORRIS, William (translator). *Of the Friendship of Amis and Amile*. Woodcut title and borders. Full red morocco. London, 1894. Kelmscott Press. One of 500. $300–$400. Another issue: One of 15 on vellum. $2,000–$2,500.

MORRIS, William (translator). *The Tale of the Emperor Coustans and of Over the Sea*. 2 woodcut titles and borders. Boards and linen. (London, 1894.) Kelmscott Press. One of 525. $400–$600. Another issue: One of 20 on vellum. $2,000–$3,000.

MORRIS, William, and Wyatt, A. J. (translators). *The Tale of Beowulf*. Woodcut title and borders. Vellum with ties. London, 1895. Kelmscott Press. One of 300. $750–$1,000. Another issue: One of 8 on vellum. $4,000–$5,000.

MORRIS, Wright. *The Deep Sleep*. Cloth. New York, 1953. First edition. In dust jacket. $50–$75.

MORRIS, Wright. *The Field of Vision*. Cloth. New York, (1956). First edition. In first state (blue and black) dust jacket. $50–$75. London, (1957). Cloth. In dust jacket. $35.

MORRIS, Wright. *God's Country and My People*. Cloth. New York, (1958). First edition. In first state dust jacket with price "$7.95" (later changed to $10). $75–$85.

MORRIS, Wright. *The Home Place*. Illustrated. Cloth. New York, 1948. First edition. In dust jacket. $125–$150.

MORRIS, Wright. *The Inhabitants*. Illustrated with author's photographs. Cloth. New York, 1946. First edition. In dust jacket. $125–$150.

MORRIS, Wright. *Man and Boy*. Cloth. New York, 1951. First edition. In dust jacket. $50–$65.

MORRIS, Wright. *The Man Who Was There*. Cloth. New York, 1945. First edition. In dust jacket. $75–$85.

MORRIS, Wright. *My Uncle Dudley*. Cloth, paper label. New York, (1942). First edition. In dust jacket. $100–$110.

MORRIS, Wright. *The World in the Attic*. Cloth. New York, 1949. First edition. In dust jacket. $75–$125.

MORRISON, Arthur. *The Dorrington Deed-Box*. Illustrated. Red cloth. London, (1896). First edition. $200–$250.

MORRISON, Arthur. *Tales of Mean Streets*. Green cloth. London, 1894. First edition, with October ads. $150. Author's first book.

MORRISON, James. *Journal*. Illustrated by Robert Gibbings. Buckram. (London), 1935. Golden Cockerel Press. One of 125. $300–$400.

MORRISON, Toni. *The Bluest Eye*. Cloth. New York, (1970). First edition. $50–$75. Author's first book.

MORRISON, Toni. *Sula*. Cloth. New York, 1974. First edition. In dust jacket. $50–$75.

MORROW, William C. *Blood-Money*. Cloth. San Francisco, 1882. First edition. $225.

MORSE, A. Reynolds. *Dali: A Study of His Life and Work*. Illustrated. Oblong folio, cloth. Greenwich, Conn., (1958). First American edition. In acetate dust jacket. $75–$100.

MORSE, Jedidiah. *A Report to the Secretary of War . . . on Indian Affairs*. Colored folding map. Boards. New Haven, 1822. First edition, with errata leaf. $300–$350.

MORSE, John F., and Colville, Samuel. *Illustrated Historical Sketches of California*. No. 1 (all published). Frontispiece. Pictorial wrappers. Sacramento, 1854. First edition. $600–$800.

MOSKOWITZ, Sam. *The Immortal Storm: A History of Science-Fiction Fandom*. Spiral-bound wrappers. Atlanta, 1951. First edition. One of 150. $150–$200.

MOSS, Howard. *The Toy Fair*. Cloth. New York, 1954. First edition. In dust jacket. $60–$75.

MOSS, Howard. *The Wound and the Weather*. Cloth. New York, (1946). First edition. In dust jacket. $50–$75. Author's first book.

MOTLEY, Willard. *Knock on Any Door*. Gray cloth. New York, (1947). First edition, first issue, with '(1)' in last line on page 504. In dust jacket. $50–$60. Author's first book.

MOTT, Mrs. Mentor. *The Stones of Palestine*. 12 mounted photographs by Francis Bedford. Cloth. London, 1865. First edition. $400–$600.

MOULTRIE, William. *Memoirs of the American Revolution*. 2 vols., calf. New York, 1802. First edition. $1,000–$1,500.

MOWRY, Sylvester. *Memoir of the Proposed Territory of Arizona*. Map (not in all copies). 30 pp., printed wrappers. Washington, 1857. First edition. $2,000–$2,500.

MUIR, Edwin. See Moore, Edward.

MUIR, Edwin. *Chorus of the Newly Dead*. Wrappers, paper label. Richmond, England, 1926. Hogarth Press. First edition. $75–$100.

MUIR, Edwin. *First Poems*. Boards, printed label. London, 1925. First edition. $75–$100.

MUIR, Edwin. *Latitudes*. Cloth. New York, 1924. First edition. In dust jacket. $50–$75. London, 1926. Cloth. First English edition. In dust jacket. $50.

MUIR, Edwin. *Six Poems*. Half cloth. Warlingham, England, 1932. Samson Press. First edition. One of 110. $150–$200.

MUIR, John. *The Mountains of California*. Illustrated. Tan cloth. New York, 1894. First edition, first issue, with folio 1 on first text page. In dust jacket. $250–$350. Author's first book.

MUIR, John (editor). *Picturesque California*. 130 full-page plates, other illustrations. 2 vols., folio, calf. San Francisco, (1888). $750–$1,000.

MUIR, Percy H. *English Children's Books, 1600–1900*. Illustrated, including color plates. Cloth. London, 1954. First edition. In dust jacket. $100. New York, 1954. Illustrated. Blue cloth. First American edition. In dust jacket. $75–$100.

MUIR, Percy H. *Points, 1874–1930*. Illustrated. Parchment and boards. London, 1931. First edition. One of 500. $125–$150.

MUIR, Percy H. *Points, 1866–1934*. Illustrated. Parchment and boards. London, 1931. First edition. One of 750. $125–$150.

MULFORD, Clarence E. *Bar-20*. Illustrated by N. C. Wyeth and F. E. Schoonover. Pictorial cloth. New York, 1907. First edition, first issue, with the reading "Blazing Star" in the list of illustrations. In dust jacket. $150–$185. Author's first book.

MULFORD, Clarence E. *Bar-20 Days*. Illustrated by Maynard Dixon. Brown cloth. Chicago, 1911. First edition. In dust jacket. $125–$150.

MULLAN, John. *Miners' and Travelers' Guide to Oregon, etc.* Folding colored map. Cloth. New York, 1865. First edition. $350–$500.

MULLAN, John. *Report on the Construction of a Military Road from Fort Walla-Walla to Fort Benton*. 4 folding maps, 110 plates, 8 colored. Cloth. Washington, 1863. First edition. $250–$300.

MULLET, J. C. *A Five Years' Whaling Voyage*. 68 pp. Cleveland, 1859. First edition. $400–$500.

MULOCK, Dinah Maria (Mrs. Craik). See *The Adventures of a Brownie; The Fairy Book; John Halifax, Gentlemen; A Life for a Life; The Ogilvies*.

MUMEY, Nolie. *Bloody Trails Along the Rio Grande*. Portrait, map. Cloth. Denver, 1938. Limited edition. In dust jacket. $35–$50.

MUMEY, Nolie. *Calamity Jane*. Folding map, illustrations, 2 pamphlets in envelope at end. Boards, pictorial label. Denver, 1950. One of 200 signed. $150–$225.

MUMEY, Nolie. *Creede: History of a Colorado Mining Town*. Illustrated. Half cloth. Denver, 1949. One of 500 signed. $50–$75.

MUMEY, Nolie. *History of the Early Settlements of Denver*. Map, 2 folding plates. Boards and vellum. Glendale, Calif., 1942. First edition. One of 500 signed. $50–$75.

MUMEY, Nolie. *James Pierson Beckwourth*. Folding map. Boards. Denver, 1957. First edition. One of 500. $50–$75.

MUMEY, Nolie. *John Williams Gunnison*. Colored portrait, plates, folding map. Boards. Denver, 1955. First edition. One of 500 signed. $75–$100.

MUMEY, Nolie. *The Life of Jim Baker*. Frontispieces, other illustrations, map. Boards. Denver, 1931. First edition. One of 250 signed. $200–$250.

MUMEY, Nolie. *March of the First Dragoons to the Rocky Mountains in 1835*. Errata slip, plates, folding map. Boards. Denver, 1957. First edition. One of 350 signed. $50–$75.

MUMEY, Nolie. *Old Forts and Trading Posts of the West*. Vol 1. (All published.) Cloth. Denver, 1956. First edition. One of 500. $50–$75.

MUMEY, Nolie. *Pioneer Denver, Including Scenes of Central City, Colorado City, and Nevada City*. Folding plate, other illustrations. Boards. Denver, 1948. First edition. One of 240 signed. $75–$100.

MUMEY, Nolie. *Poker Alice*. Illustrated, including folding map. Pictorial wrappers. Denver, 1951. First edition. One of 500. First issue: Map with New Mexico labeled as Nevada. In tissue dust jacket. $50–$75. Later, map corrected; $40–$60.

MUMEY, Nolie. *A Study of Rare Books*. Illustrated. Half cloth and boards. Denver, 1930. First edition. One of 1,000 signed. $175–$250.

MUMEY, Nolie. *The Teton Mountains*. Boards. Denver, 1947. First edition. One of 700. $50–$75.

MUMEY, Nolie (editor). *Edward Dunsha Steele: A Diary of His Journey from Lodi, Wisc., Across the Plains to Boulder, Colo., in 1859*. Half cloth. Boulder, 1960. One of 500. $50–$75.

MUNDY, Talbot. *The Ivory Trail*. Cloth. Indianapolis, (1919). First edition. In dust jacket. $100–$150.

MUNDY, Talbot. *Queen Cleopatra*. Cloth. Indianapolis, (1929). First edition. One of 265 signed. $100.

MUNDY, Talbot. *Rung Ho!* Cloth. New York, 1914. First edition. In dust jacket. $125–$175. Author's first book.

MUNDY, Talbot. *Tros of Samothrace*. Cloth. New York, 1934. First edition. In dust jacket. $150–$200.

MUMFORD, Lewis. *The Story of Utopias*. Cloth. New York, (1922). First edition. In dust jacket. $75–$100. Author's first book.

MUNRO, H. H. See Saki.

MUNRO, Robert. *A Description of the Genessee Country, in the State of New-York*. Map. 16 pp., boards. New York, 1804. (By Charles Williamson.) First edition. $375–$450.

MUNROE, Kirk. *The Fur-Seal's Tooth*. Illustrated by W. A. Rogers. Pictorial cloth. New York, 1894. First edition. $35–$50.

MUNROE, Kirk. *Wakulla: A Story of Adventure in Florida*. Illustrated. Cloth. New York, 1886. First edition. $35–$50. Author's first book.

MUNSON, Gorham. *Waldo Frank: A Study*. Original photographic frontispiece portrait by Alfred Stieglitz. Boards. New York, (1923). First edition. One of 500. In dust jacket. $500–$600.

MUNTHE, Axel. *The Story of San Michele*. Cloth. London, (1929). First edition. With printed slip about distribution of profits. Boxed. $50–$65.

MURDER by Deputy U. S. Marshal E. M. Thornton of E. M. Dalton Waylaid and Assassinated in Cold Blood. 16 pp., wrappers. Salt Lake, 1886. $100–$200.

MURDOCH, Iris. *Sartre: Romantic Rationalist*. Cloth. London, 1953. First edition. In dust jacket. $75–$100. Author's first book.

MURRAY, Charles A. *Travels in North America*. 2 plates. 2 vols., cloth. London, 1839. First edition. $300–$500. New York, 1839. 2 vols., cloth. First American edition. $300–$500.

MURRAY, Keith A. *The Modocs and Their War*. Unbound. Norman, Okla., (1959). First edition. Advance copies which escaped warehouse fire, $75–$125. Second printing, bound in cloth, same date. In dust jacket. $40.

MURRAY, Lois L. *Incidents of Frontier Life*. 2 portraits. Cloth. Goshen, Ind., 1880. First edition. $150.

MY Darling's A. B. C. Accordion sheet of 26 leaves with colored alphabet. Orange boards. Philadelphia, (about 1835–40). $300.

MYERS, Frank. *Soldiering in Dakota*. Wrappers. Huron, S. D., 1888. First edition. $600–$750. Pierre, S. D., 1936. Wrappers. $35–$50.

MYERS, J. C. *Sketches on a Tour Through the Northern and Eastern States*. Contemporary sheepskin. Harrisonburg, Va., 1849. First edition. $150–$200.

MYRICK, Herbert. *Cache la Poudre: The Romance of a Tenderfoot in the Days of Custer*. Illustrated. Cloth. New York, 1904. First edition. $85–$100. Another issue: Buckskin. One of 500 signed. $150–$200.

MYSTERIES and Miseries of San Francisco (The). By a Californian. Cloth. New York, (1853). First edition. Rebound in morocco and marbled boards, internally waterstained, $750. (Note: This is the Thomas W. Streeter copy, purchased for $175 in 1959 from my friend the late Paul Schopflin, and sold at auction in 1968 for $425. Mr. Streeter notes, "No other copy seems to be recorded," but Wright's *American Fiction, 1850–1875* lists a copy in the Library of Congress. Author unknown.)

MYSTERIES of a Convent. By a Noted Methodist Preacher. 112 pp., wrappers. Philadelphia, (1854). First edition. $75–$100.

MYSTERIES of Mormonism (The): A Full Exposure of Its Secret Practices and Hidden Crimes. By an Apostle's Wife. Wrappers. New York, 1882. $300–$400.

MYSTERIOUS Marksman (The): or The Outlaws of New York. Wrappers. Cincinnati, (about 1855). (By Emerson Bennett.) First edition. $300–$500.

N

NABOKOFF, Vladimir. *Laughter in the Dark*. Cloth. Indianapolis, (1938). (By Vladimir Nabokov.) First American edition. In the dust jacket. $225–$300. Author's first book to be issued in the United States. (Published in England as *Camera Obscura*.)

NABOKOFF–SIRIN, Vladimir. *Camera Obscura*. Translated by Winifred Roy. Cloth. London, (1936). (By Vladimir Nabokov.) First edition. (Issued without dust jacket.) $1,000–$1,500. First novel by the author to be published in English. (See *Laughter in the Dark*, above.)

NABOKOFF–SIRIN, Vladimir. *Despair*. Cloth. London, (1937). (By Vladimir Nabokov.) First edition. In dust jacket. $200–$250.

NABOKOV, Vladimir. *Bend Sinister*. Cloth. New York, 1947. First edition. In dust jacket. $125–$150. London, (1947). Boards. First English edition. In dust jacket. $100.

NABOKOV, Vladimir. *Conclusive Evidence: A Memoir*. Cloth. New York, (1951). First edition. In dust jacket. $200–$225.

NABOKOV, Vladimir. *The Eye*. Cloth. New York, 1965. First edition in English. In dust jacket. $75–$85. London, (1966). Boards. First English edition. In dust jacket. $50.

NABOKOV, Vladimir. *Invitation to a Beheading*. Boards. New York, (1959). First American edition. In dust jacket. $40–$60.

NABOKOV, Vladimir. *Lolita*. 2 vols., wrappers. Paris, (1955). Olympia Press. First edition, first issue, with the price of 900 francs on back covers. $500–$750. Paris, (1958). Second printing. $100. New York, (1955). Boards. First American edition. In dust jacket. $100–$125. London, (1959). Boards. First English edition. In dust jacket. $75–$100.

NABOKOV, Vladimir. *Nikolai Gogol*. Tan cloth. Norfolk, Conn., (1944). First edition. In dust jacket. $75–$85.

NABOKOV, Vladimir. *Nine Stories*. Printed blue wrappers. (New York, 1947.) First edition. $100–$150. Another issue: One of a few in stamped cloth. $750–$1,000.

NABOKOV, Vladimir. *Pale Fire*. Black cloth. New York, (1962). First edition, first impression. In dust jacket with "First Impression" imprint. $100–$125. London, (1962). First English edition. In dust jacket. $50–$75.

NABOKOV, Vladimir. *Poems*. Drawings by Robin Jacques. Cloth. Garden City, 1959. First edition. In dust jacket. $100–$125. London, (1961). Light-blue pebbled boards. First English edition. In dust jacket. $50–$75.

NABOKOV, Vladimir. *The Real Life of Sebastian Knight*. Rough cloth, paper labels. Norfolk, Conn., (1941). New Directions. First edition, first issue (with binding as described). In dust jacket. $300–$450. London, (1945). Cloth. First English edition. In dust jacket. $50.

NABOKOV, Vladimir. *Speak, Memory*. Cloth. London, 1951. First English edition. In dust jacket. $150–$175.

NABOKOV, Vladimir. *The Waltz Invention*. Cloth. (New York), 1966. Phaedra. First edition in English. In first (pink) dust jacket. $100. In second (blue) jacket. $65–$75.

NABOKOV, Vladimir (translator). *Three Russian Poets: Selections from Pushkin, Lermontov, and Tyutchev.* Stiff wrappers. Norfolk, (1944). New Directions. First edition. $125. London, 1947. Cloth. In dust jacket. $50. (Retitled *Pushkin, Lermontov, and Tyutchev: Poems.*)

NANSEN, Fridtjof. *Farthest North.* 127 maps and plates, 2 vols., pictorial cloth. London, 1897. First edition in English. $100–$125.

NAPTON, William B. *Over the Santa Fe Trail, 1857.* Illustrated. 99 pp., pictorial wrappers. Kansas City, 1905. First edition. $150–$200.

NARRATIVE and Report of the Causes and Circumstances of the Deplorable Conflagration at Richmond. Sheepskin and oak boards. (Richmond, Va?), 1812. First edition. $100–$200.

NARRATIVE of the Adventures and Sufferings of Capt. Daniel D. Heustis (A). Frontispiece, 168 pp., printed wrappers. Boston, 1847. First edition. $1,000–$1,250.

NARRATIVE of Arthur Gordon Pym (The). Blue or gray cloth, paper label on spine. New York, 1838. (By Edgar Allan Poe.) First edition. $1,250–$1,500. Also $950 (A, 1980). London, 1838. Cloth. First English edition. $750–$1,000. New York, 1930. Limited Editions Club. Boards. Boxed. $40–$50.

NARRATIVE of the Captivity and Providential Escape of Mrs. Jane Lewis. (Cover title.) Woodcut plate. 24pp., cloth. (New York), 1833. (By William P. Edwards ?) First edition. $300. New York, 1834. Wrappers. $150.

NARRATIVE of the Captivity and Sufferings of Ebenezer Fletcher of New-Ipswich (A). 22 pp., stitched. Windsor, Vt., 1813. Second edition. $300. New-Ipswich, N.H., 1827. Fourth edition (so stated; it is actually the third edition). $150 and up. New-Ipswich, (about 1828). $75. (Note: There are only 3 known copies of the first edition, published in Amherst in 1798.)

NARRATIVE of the Captivity and Sufferings of Mrs. Hannah Lewis. 24 pp., including folding woodcut plate. Boston, 1817. (By William P. Edwards.) First edition. $400–$500. Second edition, same date: $160 (A, 1980). Another edition: (Identical main title except "Harriet" for "Hannah"): Boston, 1821. Half morocco. $100 (A, 1971).

NARRATIVE of the Capture and Burning of Fort Massachusetts. Boards. Albany, 1870. (By the Rev. John Norton.) One of 100. $75–$100. (Note: The first edition, Boston, 1748, is very rare.)

NARRATIVE of the Capture and Providential Escape of Misses Frances and Almira Hall, etc. Plate. 24 pp., printed wrappers. (St. Louis?), 1832. (By William P. Edwards?) First edition. $850–$1,000. Later: 26 pp., (1833). Second edition. $875.

NARRATIVE of Dr. Livingston's Discoveries in Central Africa, from 1849 to 1856. Folding woodcut map. Illustrated boards. London, 1857. First edition, with David Livingstone's name spelled "Livingston." $100 and up.

NARRATIVE of the Extraordinary Life of John Conrad Shafford. Frontispiece, 25 pp., wrappers. New York, 1840. First edition. $250 and up. New York, 1841. $110 (A, 1976).

NARRATIVE of the Facts and Circumstances Relating to the Kidnapping and Presumed Murder of William Morgan (A). 36 pp., stitched. Batavia, N.Y., 1827. First edition. $250.

NARRATIVE of the Life and Adventures of Matthew Bunn. 55 pp., sewed. Batavia, 1828. Seventh edition. $35.

NARRATIVE of the Massacre at Chicago, August 15, 1812, and of Some Preceding Events. Frontispiece map. 34 pp., printed wrappers. Chicago, 1844. (By Mrs. Juliette A. Kinzie.) First edition. $2,500–$3,000. Also, $2,500 (A, 1980).

NARRATIVE of Occurrences (A), in the Indian Countries of North America. Stiff printed wrappers. London, 1807. (By Samuel Hull Wilcocke?) $750–$1,000.

NARRATIVE of Some of the Adventures, Dangers, and Sufferings of a Revolutionary Soldier (A). Cloth. Hallowell, Me., 1830. (By James Sullivan Martin?) First edition. $100–$125.

NARRATIVE of the Sufferings and Adventures of Capt. Charles H. Barnard (A). Folding map, 6 plates. Boards. New York, 1829. First edition. $250–$300.

NARRATIVE of the Sufferings of Massy Harbison. 66 pp., leather. Pittsburgh, 1825. First edition. $400–$600. Pittsburgh, 1828. 98 pp., boards and linen. Second edition. $325. Beaver, Pa., 1836. Half cloth. Fourth edition. $75–$100.

NARRATIVE of the Suppression by Col. Burr (A), of the "History of the Administration of John Adams." Stitched. New York, 1802. (By James Cheetham.) First edition. $200–$300.

NARRATIVE of the Tragical Death of Mr. Darius Barber and His Seven Children (A). Frontispiece. 24 pp., wrappers. Boston, (about 1818). First edition. Very rare; Howes says "4 perfect copies known." $750–$1,000.

NASBY, Petroleum V. *The Nasby Papers.* 64 pp., printed wrappers, Indianapolis, 1864. (By David Ross Locke.) First edition, first binding, with "Indianaolis" on front cover. $125–$150. Author's first book.

NASH, Ogden. *Hard Lines.* Illustrated by O. Soglow. Tan cloth. New York, 1931. First edition. In dust jacket. $100–$125.

NASH, Ogden. *Scrooge Rides Again.* Decorated wrappers. (Berkeley), 1960. First edition. (150 copies.) $50–$60.

NATHAN, George Jean. See Hatteras, Owen; Mencken, H. L., and Nathan, George Jean.

NATHAN, Robert. *The Concert.* Cloth. New York, 1940. First edition. One of 250 signed. $75–$125.

NATHAN, Robert. *Peter Kindred.* Cloth. New York, 1919. First edition. In dust jacket. $50–$75. Author's first book.

NATIONAL Elgin Watch Company's Illustrated Almanac for 1875 (The). Printed wrappers. Chicago, (1874). First edition. $150–$200. (Note: Includes "My Rococo Watch," by Louisa May Alcott.)

NATURE. Cloth. Boston, 1836. (By Ralph Waldo Emerson.) First edition, first state, with page 94 misnumbered 92. $750–$1,000. Emerson's first published book. New York, 1929. Boards. One of 250. In dust jacket. $300–$400.

NAUTICAL Reminiscences. By the Author of *A Mariner's Sketches.* Boards and cloth. Providence, 1832. (By Nathaniel Ames.) First edition. $100.

NAVAL Achievements of Great Britain and Her Allies from 1793 to 1817 (The). 55 hand-colored plates. Half morocco. London, (1817). $6,500–$7,500.

NAVAL Monument (The). 25 plates. Errata slip. Calf. Boston, 1816. (By Abel Bowen.) First edition. $250–$350.

NAVIGATOR (The). Boards or wrappers. Pittsburgh, 1804. (By Zadok Cramer.) Fourth edition (of *The Ohio and Mississippi Navigator,* which see) and first edition with this title. The two copies known are in institutional libraries. Pittsburgh, 1806. 14 charts. 94 pp., plain wrappers. Fifth edition. $2,000–$2,500. Some later editions and relative values: Pittsburgh, 1808. $750–$1,000. Pittsburgh, 1811. $500–$600. Pittsburgh, 1814. $400–$500.

NEAGOE, Peter (editor). *Americans Abroad.* Illustrated. Yellow cloth, tan cloth spine. The Hague, Netherlands, 1932. First edition. In dust jacket. $300–$400. (Note: This anthology contains Henry Miller's first book appearance, as well as new material by William Carlos Williams and others.)

NEAL, John. See Adams, Will. Also, see *Authorship: A Tale; Brother Jonathan; Keep Cool; Seventy-Six.*

NEAL, John. *The Moose-Hunter; or, Life in the Maine Woods.* Wrappers. New York, (1864). First edition, first issue, with No. 73 announced on the inside of the front cover. $300–$400.

NEAL, John. *Rachel Dyer: A North American Story.* Boards and cloth. Portland, Me., 1828. First edition. $300–$400.

NEAL, Joseph Clay. *Peter Ploddy, and Other Oddities.* Boards. Philadelphia, 1844. First edition. $35–$50.

NECESSITY of a Ship-Canal Between the East and West (The). 45 pp., printed wrappers. Chicago, 1863. (By J. W. Foster.) First edition. $125–$150.

NEED for Anonymity (The). Wrappers. Paris, (1930). (By Michael Fraenkel and Walter Loewenfels.) First edition. $150–$200. Fraenkel's first book.

NEESE, George M. *Three Years in the Confederate Horse Artillery.* Cloth. New York, 1911. First edition. $75–$100.

NEIHARDT, John G. *Black Elk Speaks.* Illustrated, including color plates. Decorated cloth. New York, 1932. First edition. In dust jacket. $50–$75.

NEIHARDT, John G. *A Bundle of Myrrh.* Limp leather. (New York), MCMIII (1903). First edition. One of 5. $500–$600. New York, 1907. Boards and cloth. Revised edition. $75.

NEIHARDT, John G. *Collected Poems.* 2 vols., cloth. New York, 1926. First edition. One of 250 signed. In dust jackets. $75–$125.

NEIHARDT, John G. *The Divine Enchantment: A Mystical Poem.* Cloth. New York, 1900. First edition. $250. Author's first book.

NEIHARDT, John G. *The Lonesome Trail.* Frontispiece. Pictorial cloth. New York, 1907. First edition. $50.

NEIHARDT, John G. *The Song of Hugh Glass.* Cloth. New York, 1915. First edition. In dust jacket. $60–$75.

NEIHARDT, John G. *The Song of the Indian Wars.* Cloth. New York, 1925. First edition. One of 500 signed. In dust jacket. $100–$125. Trade edition: Cloth. In dust jacket. $30–$40.

NEIHARDT, John G. *The Song of Three Friends.* Cloth. New York, 1919. First edition. In dust jacket. $50–$60.

NEIHARDT, John G. *The Splendid Wayfaring.* Cloth. New York, 1920. First edition. In dust jacket. $75–$85.

NEIL, John B. *Biennial Message of the Governor of Idaho to the 11th Session of the Legislature of Idaho Territory.* 19 pp., wrappers. Boise City, Idaho, 1880. $125–$150.

NEMEROV, Howard. *The Homecoming Game.* Cloth. New York, 1957. First edition. In dust jacket. $40–$50.

NEMEROV, Howard. *The Image and the Law.* Black cloth. (New York, 1947.) First edition. In dust jacket. $100–$125. Author's first book.

NEMEROV, Howard. *The Painter Dreaming in the Scholar's House.* Oblong, stiff wrappers. New York, 1968. One of 126 signed. In dust jacket. $50–$60.

NEMEROV, Howard. *Stories, Fables, and Other Diversions.* Half vellum. Boston, 1971. First edition. One of 100 signed. $75.

NERUDA, Pablo. *Bestiary/Bestiario.* Woodcuts by Antonio Frasconi. Folio, boards and cloth. New York, (1965). First edition. One of 300 signed, with a signed frontispiece woodcut. Boxed. $200–$250.

NERUDA, Pablo. *Heights of Macchu Picchu.* Boards. London, (1966). First English edition. In dust jacket. $50–$65.

NERUDA, Pablo. *We Are Many.* Translated by Alastair Reid. Boards. London, (1967). First edition in English. One of 100 signed. In dust jacket. $150–$200.

NESBIT, Edith. *Ballads and Lyrics of Socialism, 1883–1908.* Cloth. London, 1908. First edition. $100.

NESBIT, Edith. *The Magic World.* Illustrated. Cloth. London, 1912. First edition. $65–$75.

NESBIT, Edith. *The Railway Children.* 20 plates. Cloth. London, (1906). First edition, $100–$125.

NESBIT, Edith. *The Story of the Treasure Seekers.* 17 plates. Cloth. London, 1899. First edition. $150–$175.

NESBIT, Edith. *Wet Magic.* Cloth. London, (1913). First edition. $75–$85.

NETTLE, George. *A Practical Guide for Emigrants to North America.* Folding map in color. Printed yellow wrappers. London, 1850. First edition. $200–$250.

NEVILL, Ralph. *British Military Prints.* Plates, including color. London, 1909. First edition. $100–$150.

NEVILL, Ralph. *Old English Sporting Books.* Plates, including color. Buckram. London, 1924. First edition. One of 1,500. $150–$200.

NEVILL, Ralph. *Old English Sporting Prints and Their History.* 103-full-page plates, 47 in color. Buckram. London, 1923. First edition. One of 1,500. $150–$200.

NEVINSON, Henry W. *The Plea of Pan.* Vellum. London, 1901. First edition. $75–$100.

NEW BEDFORD and Fairhaven Signals. Boards. New Bedford, Mass., 1834. $150–$200.

NEW Country: Prose and Poetry. Edited by Michael Roberts. Cloth. London, 1933. Hogarth Press. First edition. $50–$60. (Note: Contains first appearance of three W. H. Auden poems.)

NEW Empire (The): Oregon, Washington, Idaho. Folding map. Wrappers. Portland, Ore., 1888. First edition. $75–$100.

NEW ENGLAND Primer (The). While this perennially popular publication flowered in the earlier years of the new American nation, scores of publishing houses continued to bring out various versions through the earlier part of the nineteenth century. Some collectible and representative imprints beginning with 1800, which is the starting point for this *Handbook:* Hartford (John Babcock), 1800, value range for copies in good condition: $150–$200; Walpole, N.H., (Nichols), 1806, $100–$125; Greenfield, Mass., (Denio & Phelps), 1810, $150–$200; Walpole, (Isaiah Thomas), 1814, $75; Philadelphia, (John Bioren), 1816, $150–$200; Newark, N.J., (William Tuttle), 1817, $150–$250; Trenton, N.J., (George Sherman), 1817, $250–$300; Albany, (G. J. Loomis), 1818, $75–$100; Hartford, (George Goodwin), 1820, $100–$150; Brattleboro, Vt., (Holbrook & Fessenden), 1825, $100–$150; and Chillicothe, Ohio, (Carruthers), about 1826, $200–$250.

NEW Guide of the Conversation in Portuguese and English (The). Introduction by Mark Twain. Unbound sheets. Boston, 1883. First edition. $300. In cloth: $125. (Note: Blanck does not list this but records a London paperback of 1884 by this title.)

NEW Poets. Spiral-bound stiff wrappers. Prairie City, Ill., 1941. Press of James A. Decker. First edition. $50–$75.

NEW Ritual for "Sam" (A): Written by One Connected with the Cincinnati Times, and Dedicated to "Sam's" Numerous Friends. Wrappers. Cincinnati, 1855. First edition. $50–$75.

NEW SPAIN and the Anglo-American West: Contributions Presented to Herbert E. Bolton. Portrait. 2 vols., cloth. (Los Angeles, 1932.) First edition. One of 500. Boxed. $150–$200.

NEW TESTAMENT of Our Lord and Saviour Jesus Christ. Translated into the Choctaw Language. Leather. New York, 1848. First edition. $400–$500. Also, $190 (A, 1979). New York, 1854. Cloth. Second edition. $75–$100.

NEW Texas Spelling Book (The). Pictorial boards. Houston, 1863. (By E. H. Cushing.) $1,000–$1,500.

NEW Topographical Atlas of St. Lawrence County, New York. Colored maps and plans. Cloth. Philadelphia, 1865. First edition. $300–$350.

NEW Translation with Notes (A), of the Third Satire of Juvenal. Marbled boards and cloth. New York, 1806. (By Clement C. Moore and John Duer.) First edition, with "Additional Errata" leaf. $100. Moore's first book appearance.

NEW Year's Feast on His Coming of Age (The). Hand-colored woodcuts. Stiff wrappers. London, 1824. (By Charles Lamb.) First edition. $750–$1,000.

NEW YORK Book of Poetry (The). Engraved half title. Cloth. New York, 1837. (Edited anonymously by Charles Fenno Hoffman.) First edition. $250–$350. Also, $160 (A, 1979). (Note: Contains first book appearance of Clement C. Moore's "A Visit from St. Nicholas.")

NEW YORK and Oro-Fino Gold and Silver Mining Co. of Idaho. 31 pp., wrappers. New York, 1865. First edition. $125–$150.

NEW YORK Primer (The). Woodcuts. 33 pp., blue pictorial wrappers. New York, 1818. $125–$150.

NEW ZEALAND, Graphic and Descriptive. Edited by W. T. L. Travers. Map, 25 colored lithographic views, 19 other views on 6 plates, woodcuts in text. Folio, half cloth. London, 1877. $750–$1,000.

NEWBERRY, Clare Turlay. *Marshmallow.* Illustrated. Pictorial boards. New York, (1942). First edition, with duplicate illustration tipped in for framing. In dust jacket. $50.

NEWBERRY, J. S. *Report on the Properties of the Ramshorn Consolidated Silver Mining Company at Bay Horse, Idaho.* 16 pp., wrappers. New York, (1881). $125–$150.

NEWELL, Rev. Chester. *History of the Revolution in Texas.* Folding map. Cloth. New York, 1838. First edition. $400–$600.

NEWELL, Peter. See *Topsys & Turveys.*

NEWELL, Peter. *The Hole Book.* Illustrated in color by the author. Stapled blue cloth, pictorial cover label. New York, (1908). First edition, with "Published October 1908" below copyright notice. In dust jacket. $250. Lacking jacket, $75.

NEWELL, Peter. *Pictures and Rhymes.* 50 plates. Boards. New York, 1899. First edition. $50–$75.

NEWELL, Peter. *The Rocket Book.* 22 colored plates. Cloth. New York, (1912). First edition. $75–$100.

NEWELL, Peter. *A Shadow Show.* 36 color plates. Pictorial boards. New York, 1896. First edition. $75–$100.

NEWHALL, J. B. *The British Emigrants' "Hand Book."* (Cover title.) 99 pp., printed yellow wrappers. London, 1844. First edition. $750–$850.

NEWHALL, John B. *Sketches of Iowa.* Map in color. Cloth. New York, 1841. First edition. $350–$500.

NEWMAN, John Henry, Cardinal. See *The Dream of Gerontius; Verses on Various Occasions.*

NEWMAN, John Henry, Cardinal. *Apologia Pro Vita Sua.* 8 parts, printed wrappers. London, 1864. First edition. $1,250–$1,500. London, 1864. Cloth. First book edition. $500–$600.

NEWMAN, John Henry, Cardinal. *Discourses Addressed to Mixed Congregations.* Cloth. London, 1849. First edition. $75–$85.

NEWMAN, John Henry, Cardinal. *Lectures.* Cloth. London, 1837. First edition. $75.

NEWMAN, John Henry, Cardinal. *Lectures on Justification.* Cloth, paper label. London, 1838. First edition. $75–$100.

NEWMAN, John Henry, Cardinal, and others (editors). *Lyra Apostolica.* Purple cloth. Derby, England, 1836. First edition. $250.

NEWMARK, Harris. *Sixty Years in Southern California. 1853–1913.* 33 plates. Cloth. New York, 1916. First edition. $50–$75. Boston, 1930. Edited by M. H. and M. R. Newmark. 43 plates. Cloth. $40–$50.

NEWTON, A. Edward. *The Amenities of Book Collecting and Kindred Affections.* Illustrated. Half cloth. Boston, 1918. First edition, with erratum slip and without index. In dust jacket. $100–$125. Author's first book.

NEWTON, A. Edward. *Derby Day and Other Adventures.* Illustrated. Cloth. Boston, 1934. First edition. In dust jacket. $15–$20. Another issue: Half cloth. One of 1,129 signed. Boxed. $85.

NEWTON, A. Edward. *Doctor Johnson: A Play.* Illustrated. Boards. Boston, 1923. First edition. In dust jacket. $25. Another issue: One of 585 signed. Boxed. $75–$125.

NEWTON, A. Edward. *End Papers.* Illustrated. Cloth. Boston, 1933. First edition. In dust jacket. $25. Another issue: Boards and cloth. One of 1,351 signed. Boxed. $50–$75.

NEWTON, A. Edward. *The Format of the English Novel.* Illustrated, including colored frontispiece. Cloth. Cleveland, 1928. First edition. One of 289. Boxed. $75–$100.

NEWTON, A. Edward. *The Greatest Book in the World.* Boards. Boston, (1925). First edition. In dust jacket. $25. Another issue: One of 470 signed. $75–$100.

NEWTON, A. Edward. *A Magnificent Farce and Other Diversions of a Book Collector.* Illustrated. Boards. Boston, (1921). First edition. In dust jacket. $25. Another issue: One of 265 signed. Boxed. $75–$100.

NEWTON, A. Edward. *Newton on Blackstone.* Cloth. Philadelphia, 1937. First edition. One of 2,000 signed. In dust jacket. $40–$50.

NEWTON, A. Edward. *On Books and Business.* Boards. (New York), 1930. First edition. One of 325 signed. $50–$75.

NEWTON, A. Edward. *Rare Books, etc.* (Sale catalogue.) Illustrated. 3 vols., printed gray boards. New York, 1941. In dust jackets. $100–$125.

NEWTON, A. Edward. *This Book Collecting Game.* Illustrated. Half cloth. Boston,

1928. First edition. In dust jacket. $25. Another issue: One of 990 signed. $100–$125.

NEWTON, A. Edward. *A Tourist in Spite of Himself.* Cloth. Boston, 1930. First edition. In dust jacket. $25. Another issue: One of 525 signed. $50–$60.

NEWTON, J. H. (Editor). *History of the Pan-handle . . . West Virginia.* Maps and plates. Cloth. Wheeling, W. Va., 1879. First edition. $100–$150.

NEWTON, J. H. (editor). *History of . . . Venango County, Pennsylvania.* 47 plates. Half leather. Columbus, Ohio, 1879. $150–$200.

NEWTON, James. *A Complete Herbal.* 176 copper plates. Boards. London, 1802. $150. London, 1805. $250–$300.

NICHOLS, Beach. *Atlas of Schuyler County, New York.* 21 maps in color, 31 leaves. Cloth. Philadelphia, 1874. $300–$350.

NICHOLS, John. *The Sterile Cuckoo.* Cloth. New York, 1965. First edition. In dust jacket. $40–$50. Author's first book.

NICHOLSON, William. *Clever Bill.* Illustrated by the author. Pictorial boards. (New York, about 1926 or 1927.) First American edition. $125.

NICK of the Woods, or The Jibbenainosay. 2 vols., purple cloth, paper label, Philadelphia, 1837. (By Robert Montgomery Bird.) First edition. $500–$600.

NICOLLETT, Joseph Nicolas. *Report Intended to Illustrate a Map of the Hydrographical Basin of the Upper Missouri River.* Senate Doc. 237, 26th Congress, 2d session. Folding map, 170 pp., wrappers. or cloth. Washington, 1843. First edition. $300–$375. Washington, 1845. House Doc. 52. Smaller map. Sewed. $100–$150.

NICOLSON, Majorie Hope. *Voyages to the Moon.* Cloth. New York, 1948. First edition. In dust jacket. $75–$85.

NIELSEN, Kay (illustrator). *East of the Sun and West of the Moon.* (By Peter Christen Asbjornsen and Jorgen I. Moe.) 25 color plates. Cloth. London, (1914). First edition. $800–$1,000. Another issue: Vellum. One of 500 signed. $2,500–$3,000. Also, $1,700 (A, 1980).

NIGGER of the "Narcissus" (The). Preface. (Caption title only.) 7 pp., wire-stitched sheets. (Hythe, England, 1902.) (By Joseph Conrad.) First edition. One of 100. Privately printed for Conrad, who had suppressed this preface in the first edition of his 1898 novel. (About 40 copies were accidentally destroyed.) $1,700 (A, 1977).

NIGHTINGALE, Florence. *Notes on Nursing.* Flexible cloth. London, (1859). First edition. $300–$450. Later, ads dated 1860: $120–$250. New York, 1860. First American edition. $100–$150.

NIGHTMARE Abbey. Blue boards, paper spine, paper label. London, 1818. (By Thomas Love Peacock.) First edition. $500–$600.

NILE Notes of a Howadji. Cloth, or tan printed wrappers. New York, 1851. (By George William Curtis.) First edition. Wrappers: $200–$300. Cloth: $75–$100. Author's first book.

NIMMO, Joseph, Jr. *Range and Ranch Cattle Traffic.* (Caption title.) 4 folding maps, 200 pp., wrappers. (Washington, 1884.) First edition. $1,500–$2,000. (Most copies offered have been bound or are in protective slipcases.)

NIMROD. *The Life of a Sportsman.* 36 colored plates by Alken. Cloth. London, 1842. (By C.J. Apperley.) First edition, first issue, in blue cloth. $1,500 and up. Second issue, red cloth. $1,000 and up. London, 1901. 2 vols., boards. One of 60 large paper copies. $300. Ordinary copies: $100–$150.

NIMROD. *Remarks on the Condition of Hunters, the Choice of Horses, and their Man-*

agement. Half calf, leather label. London, 1831. (By C. J. Apperley.) First collected edition. $300–$400.

NIMROD'S Hunting Tours. 18 hand-colored plates. Grained calf. London, 1903. (By C. J. Apperley.) One of 500. $350–$450.

NIN, Anaïs. *Children of the Albatross.* Cloth. New York, 1947. First edition. In dust jacket. $75–$85.

NIN, Anaïs. *D. H. Lawrence: An Unprofessional Study.* Facsimiles. Black cloth. Paris, 1932. First edition. One of 550. In dust jacket. $200–$250. Author's first book.

NIN, Anaïs. *The House of Incest.* Covered wrappers. Paris, (1936). First edition. One of 249 signed. $400–$450. (New York, 1947.) Gemor Press. Illustrated by Ian Hugo. Pictorial orange cloth. First American edition. $75. One of 50 signed. $150.

NIN, Anaïs. *Ladders to Fire.* Cloth. New York, 1946. First edition. In dust jacket. $75.

NIN, Anaïs. *This Hunger.* 5 hand-colored woodcuts by Ian Hugo. Decorated boards. (New York, 1945.) Gemor Press. First edition. One of 50 signed. $250–$300. Trade edition: One of 1,000. $100.

NIN, Anaïs. *Under a Glass Bell and Other Stories.* Cloth. New York, (1944). First edition. (300 copies.) In dust jacket. $100.

NIN, Anaïs. *Unpublished Selections from the Diary of Anaïs Nin.* Wrappers. Athens, Ohio, (1968). First edition. One of 140 signed. $300–$350.

NIN, Anaïs. *Winter of Artifice.* Wrappers. Paris, (1939). Obelisk Press. First edition. $100–$150. (New York, 1942.) Copper engravings by Ian Hugo. Pictorial boards. First American edition. (500 printed.) $125–$150.

NINA Balatka. 2 vols., cloth. Edinburgh, 1867. (By Anthony Trollope.) First edition, first issue, with ad leaf inset in Vol. 1. $400–$600.

NINETY-FIRST Psalm (The). 4 leaves. Wood engravings. (London, 1944.) Golden Cockerel Press. Boxed. $100–$150. Another issue: One of 50 specially bound. $300–$400.

NOEL, Theophilus. *Autobiography and Reminiscences of Theophilus Noel.* Illustrated. Red cloth. Chicago, 1904. First edition. $100–$125.

NONESUCH Century (The): An Appraisal, a Personal Note and a Bibliography of the First Hundred Books Issued by the Press, 1923–1934. Illustrated. Buckram. London, 1936. One of 750. In dust jacket. $500–$750.

NORDEN, Charles. *Panic Spring.* Cloth. New York, (1937). (By Lawrence Durrell.) First edition. In dust jacket. $300–$400.

NORDHOFF, Charles. *California for Health, Pleasure and Residence.* Illustrated, map. Cloth. New York, 1872. First edition. $100.

NORDHOFF, Charles B. See Hall, James Norman (for *The Lafayette Flying Corps).*

NORDHOFF, Charles B., and Hall, James Norman. *Mutiny on the Bounty.* Cloth. Boston, 1932. First edition, first issue, with plain end papers. In jacket. $50–$75. New York, 1947. Limited Editions Club. Boxed. $40–$50.

NORMAN, Don Cleveland. *The 500th Anniversary Pictorial Census of the Gutenberg Bible.* Illustrated. Full leatherette. Chicago, 1961. First edition. One of 985. In slipcase. $400–$500.

NORMYX. *Unprofessional Tales.* Pictorial white cloth. London, 1901. (By Norman Douglas and Elsa Fitzgibbon.) First edition. One of 750. $300–$350. Norman Douglas' first book, written in collaboration with his wife.

NORRIS, Frank. *Blix.* Tan pictorial cloth. New York, 1899. First edition. $50–$60.

NORRIS, Frank. *A Deal in Wheat and Other Stories of the New and Old West.* Illustrated by Frederic Remington and others. Red cloth. New York, 1903. First edition. $75–$100.

NORRIS, Frank. *A Man's Woman.* Red cloth. New York, 1900. First edition. $50–$60.

NORRIS, Frank. *McTeague: A Story of San Francisco.* Red cloth. New York, 1899. First edition, first issue, with "moment" as last word on page 106. $300–$500. San Francisco, 1941. Colt Press. Illustrated. Buckram and boards. One of 500. $100–$150.

NORRIS, Frank. *Moran of the Lady Letty.* Green cloth. New York, 1898. First edition. $75–$125.

NORRIS, Frank. *The Octopus.* Red cloth. New York, 1901. First edition, first issue, with "J. J. Little" device on copyright page. $100–$200.

NORRIS, Frank. *The Pit.* Red cloth. New York, 1903. First edition. $40–$60. Another issue: Gray boards, paper label. Presentation edition. $100.

NORRIS, Frank. *The Responsibilities of the Novelist and Other Literary Essays.* Green cloth. New York, 1903. First edition, first state, with untrimmed edges. $75.

NORRIS, Frank. *Yvernelle: A Legend of Feudal France.* Illustrations, some in color. Cloth, or leather. Philadelphia, 1892 (actually 1891). First edition. $850–$1,250. Author's first book.

NORRIS, J. W. *A Business Advertiser and General Directory of the City of Chicago for the Year 1845–6.* Folding plate. 156 pp., wrappers. Chicago, 1845. First edition. $1,500–$2,000.

NORRIS, J. W. *General Directory and Business Advertiser of the City of Chicago for the Year 1844.* 116 pp., printed wrappers. Chicago, 1844. First edition, first printing. $1,000–$1,500. Another issue: cloth, with binder's slip bound in. $1,000–$1,500. (Note: This is the first Chicago city directory.)

NORRIS, Thomas Wayne (book collection). *A Descriptive and Priced Catalogue . . . of California and the Far West.* Illustrated. Boards and cloth. Oakland, 1948. $100–$150.

NORTH and South. 2 vols., cloth. London, 1855. (By Elizabeth C. Gaskell.) First edition. $800–$1,000.

NORTH, Andrew. *Plague Ship.* Cloth. New York, (1956). (By Alice Mary Norton, whose main pseudonym is Andre Norton.) First edition. In dust jacket. $50–$75.

NORTH, Joseph. *Men in the Ranks: The Story of 12 Americans in Spain.* Foreword by Ernest Hemingway. Wrappers. New York, 1939. First edition. $75–$100.

NORTH, Thomas. *Five Years in Texas; or, What You Did Not Hear During the War.* Cloth. Cincinnati, 1870. First edition. $100–$125.

NORTHANGER Abbey; and Persuasion. By the Author of *Pride and Prejudice, etc.* 4 vols., blue-gray or pink boards and linen, white paper labels. London, 1818. (By Jane Austen.) First edition. $3,000–$4,000. Also, $2,200 (A, 1981).

NORTHERN Route to Idaho (The). Large folding map, 8 pp. of text. Cloth. St. Paul, (1864). (By D. D. Merrill.) $1,250–$2,000.

NORTHERN Traveller (The). 16 maps and 4 plates. Boards. New York, 1825. (By Theodore Dwight, Jr.) First edition. $150–$250. New York, 1826. Second edition. $100–$150.

NORTON, Andre. *Star Man's Son, 2250 A.D.* Cloth. New York, (1952). (By Alice Mary Norton.) First edition. In dust jacket. $50–$60.

NORTON, Harry J. *Wonder-Land Illustrated; or, Horseback Rides Through the Yellowstone National Park.* Map, 18 plates. Pictorial wrappers. Virginia City, Mont., (1873). First edition. $100–$125.

NOTES on California and the Placers. 2 plates (not in all copies). 128 pp., printed wrappers. New York, 1850. (By James Delavan.) First edition. $1,500–$2,000, possibly more.

NOTORIOUS Outlaw (The), Jessie James. 13 pp., pictorial wrappers. New York, (1883?). First (?) edition. $500 in a 1981 catalogue.

NOTT, Manford A. *Across the Plains in '54.* 232 pp., wrappers. (San Francisco, about 1915.) "Second" (actually first) edition. $150–$200.

NOTT, Stanley Charles. *Chinese Jade Throughout the Ages.* 39 color illustrations, 182 in black and white. Cloth. London, 1936. In dust jacket. $100–$125.

NOVAK, Joseph. *The Future Is Ours, Comrade.* Cloth. Garden City, 1960. (By Jerzy Kosinski.) First edition. In dust jacket. $185–$225. Kosinski's first book.

NOVAK, Joseph. *No Third Path.* Cloth. Garden City, 1962. (By Jerzy Kosinski.) First edition. In dust jacket. $60.

NOVELAS Espanolas. Marbled boards. Portland, Me., 1830. First edition. (Edited anonymously by Henry Wadsworth Longfellow.) $100 and up.

NOWLIN, William. *The Bark Covered House.* 6 plates. Cloth. Detroit, 1876. First edition. $1,500–$1,750.

NOYES, Al J. *In the Land of Chinook: or, The Story of Blaine County.* 24 plates. Cloth. Helena, (1917). First edition. $100–$150.

NOYES, Alva J. *The Story of Ajax: Life in the Big Horn Basin.* Frontispiece, 12 plates. Cloth. Helena, 1914. First edition. $100–$150.

NUTT, Frederic. *The Complete Confectioner.* Frontispiece. Leather. New York, 1807. $300.

NUTTALL, Thomas. *The Genera of North American Plants.* 2 vols., boards. Philadelphia, 1818. First edition. $350–$500.

NUTTALL, Thomas. *Journal of Travels into the Arkansa Territory, During the Year 1819.* Folding map, 5 plates. Boards. Philadelphia, 1821. First edition. $750–$1,000.

NUTTALL, Zelia. *The Book of the Life of the Ancient Mexicans.* Part I. 90 pp. of color plates. Oblong, leather. Berkeley, 1903. $80–$100.

NUTTING, Wallace. *The Clock Book.* Cloth. Framingham, Mass., 1924. First edition. In dust jacket. $50–$75. Garden City, 1935. Cloth. In dust jacket. $25.

NYE-STARR, Kate. *A Self-Sustaining Woman; or, The Experience of Seventy-Two Years.* Portrait. Red cloth. Chicago, 1888. First edition. $2,500–$3,000. Also, $1,600 (A, 1976).

O

OAK Openings (The); or, The Bee-Hunter. By the Author of *The Pioneers.* 2 vols., printed tan wrappers. New York, 1848. (By James Fenimore Cooper.) First American edition. $400–$600.

OAKWOOD, Oliver. *Village Tales, or Recollections of By-past Times.* Cloth. Trenton, N.J., 1827. (By Stacy Gardner Potts.) First edition. $50–$75.

OATES, Joyce Carol. *By the North Gate.* Cloth. New York, (1963). First edition. In dust jacket. $125–$150. Author's first book.

OATES, Joyce Carol. *Cupid and Psyche.* Wrappers, paper label. New York, 1970. First edition. One of 200 signed. $75–$100.

OATES, Joyce Carol. *A Garden of Earthly Delights.* Cloth. New York, (1967). First edition. In dust jacket. $100–$125.

OATES, Joyce Carol. *Them.* Cloth. New York, 1969. First edition. In dust jacket. $50–$75.

OATES, Joyce Carol. *Upon the Sweeping Flood and Other Stories.* Cloth. New York, (1966). First edition. In dust jacket. $100. London, (1973). First English edition. In dust jacket. $40–$50.

OATES, Joyce Carol. *With Shuddering Fall.* Cloth. New York, (1964). First edition. In dust jacket. $100–$125. London, (1964). First English edition. In dust jacket. $50–$60.

OATES, Joyce Carol. *Women In Love and Other Poems.* Decorated wrappers. New York, 1968. First edition. One of 150 signed. $75–$100.

O'BEIRNE, H. F. *Leaders and Leading Men of the Indian Territory. Vol. 1, History of the Choctaws and Chickasaws.* (All published.) 7 plates. Cloth. Chicago, 1891. First edition. $300.

O'BETJEMAN, Deirdre. *Some Immortal Hours: A Rhapsody of the Celtic Twilight.* 7 leaves, folio. London, 1962. (By John Betjeman.) One of 12 (of a total issue of 20) copies of a facsimile printing of the author's holograph manuscript, hand-colored and signed by Betjeman. $500–$600.

O'BRIEN, Fitz-James. *Poems and Stories.* Cloth. Boston, 1881. First edition. $150. Author's first (and only) book (posthumous).

O'BRIEN, Fitz-James. *What Was It?* Drawings by Leonard Baskin. Wrappers. New York, 1974. One of 200 signed by Baskin. $75–$100.

O'BRIEN, Flann. *At Swim-Two-Birds.* Cloth. London, (1939). First edition. In dust jacket. $1,000–$1,200. New York, 1939. Cloth. First American edition. In dust jacket. $150–$175. Author's first book.

O'BRIEN, Tim. *Going After Cacciato.* Cloth. New York, (1978). First edition. In dust jacket. $25–$50.

O'BRIEN, Tim. *If I Die in a Combat Zone.* Cloth. (New York, 1973.) First edition. In dust jacket. $250–$350. Author's first book.

O'BRIEN, Tim. *Northern Lights*. Cloth. New York, (1975). First edition. In dust jacket. $35–$75.

O'BRYAN, William. *A Narrative of Travels in the United States . . . and Advice to Emigrants and Travellers Going to That Interesting Country*. Portrait. Dark-blue cloth. London, 1836. First edition. $300–$400.

OBSERVATIONS on the Wisconsin Territory. Folding map. Cloth. Philadelphia, 1835. (By William Rudolph Smith.) First edition. $450–$600.

OBSERVATIONS upon Certain Passages in Mr. Jefferson's "Notes on Virginia." 32 pp., plain blue-gray wrappers. New York, 1804. (By Clement C. Moore?) First edition. $100. If Moore wrote this, it is his first publication.

O'CASEY, Sean. *Drums Under the Window*. Cloth. London, 1945. First edition. In dust jacket. $50–$60.

O'CASEY, Sean. *The Plough and the Stars*. Portrait. Boards and cloth. London, 1926. First edition. In dust jacket. $75–$100. New York, 1926. Cloth. First American edition. In dust jacket. $65.

O'CASEY, Sean. *Rose and Crown*. Cloth. London, 1952. First edition. In dust jacket. $50–$60.

O'CASEY, Sean. *The Saint and Mary Kate*. Cloth. London, 1932. First edition. In dust jacket. $200–$225.

O'CASEY, Sean. *The Silver Tassie*. Portrait. Boards and cloth. London, 1928. First edition. $50–$75.

O'CASEY, Sean. *Two Plays*. Cloth. London, 1926. First edition. In dust jacket. $75–$100.

O'CASEY, Sean. *Windfalls*. Cloth. London, 1934. First edition. In dust jacket. $75.

O CATHASAIGH, P. *The Story of the Irish Citizen Army*. Gray wrappers. Dublin, 1919. (By Sean O'Casey.) First edition. $100–$150. Author's first book.

O'CONNOR, Flannery. *A Good Man Is Hard to Find*. Cloth. New York, (1955). First edition. In dust jacket. $185–$225.

O'CONNOR, Flannery. *The Violent Bear it Away*. Cloth. New York, (1960). First edition. In dust jacket. $100–$150.

O'CONNOR, Flannery. *Wise Blood*. Cloth. New York, (1952). First edition. In dust jacket. $250–$275. Author's first book.

O'CONNOR, Frank. *A Lament for Art O'Leary*. Boards. Dublin, 1940. Cuala Press. First edition. One of 130. In dust jacket. $500–$750.

O'CONNOR, Frank. *Lords and Commons*. Boards and linen. Dublin, 1938. Cuala Press. First edition. One of 250. In dust jacket. $125–$175.

O'CONNOR, Frank. *A Picture Book*. Illustrated by Elizabeth Rivers. Boards, linen spine. Dublin, 1943. Cuala Press. First edition. One of 480. In dust jacket. $125–$175.

O'CONNOR, Frank. *Three Old Brothers and Other Poems*. Boards. London, (1936). First edition. In dust jacket. $100–$125.

O'CONNOR, Frank. *Three Tales*. Boards, linen spine. Dublin, 1941. Cuala Press. One of 250. In dust jacket. $150–$175.

O'CONNOR, Frank. *The Wild Bird's Nest*. Boards and cloth. Dublin, 1932. Cuala Press. One of 250. $150–$175.

OCULUS. *The Home of the Badgers*. 36 pp., tan printed wrappers. Milwaukie [sic],

1845. (By Josiah B. Grinnell.) First edition. $1,500–$2,000. (For second edition, see *Sketches of the West*.)

ODE Performed in the Senate-House, Cambridge, on the Sixth of July, MDCCCXLVII at the First Commencement After the Installation of His Royal Highness the Prince Albert, Chancellor of the University. 8 pp., printed wrappers. Cambridge, 1847. (By William Wordsworth.) First edition. $1,000 or more.

ODE to Napoleon Buonaparte. 16 pp., wrappers. London, 1814. (By George Gordon Noel, Lord Byron.) First edition. $1,000–$2,000. Also, $850 (A, 1977).

ODES. Gray wrappers. (London, 1868.) (By Coventry Patmore.) First edition. $300–$400.

ODETS, Clifford. *Golden Boy*. Brown cloth. New York, (1937). First edition. In dust jacket. $75.

ODETS, Clifford. *Three Plays*. Brown cloth. New York, (1935). First edition. In dust jacket. $50–$60.

OEHLER, Andrew. *The Life, Adventures, and Unparalleled Sufferings of Andrew Oehler*. Leather. (Trenton, N.J.), 1811. First edition. $150–$250.

O'FAOLAIN, Sean. *The Born Genius*. Green buckram. Detroit, 1936. One of 250 signed. Boxed. $100–$135.

O'FAOLAIN, Sean. *Midsummer Night Madness/& Other Stories*. Preface by Edward Garnett. Green cloth. London, (1932). First edition. In dust jacket. $200–$225. Author's first book.

O'FAOLAIN, Sean. *A Nest of Simple Folk*. Green cloth. London, (1933). First edition. In dust jacket. $100–$125.

O'FAOLAIN, Sean. *There's a Birdie in the Cage*. Green cloth. London, 1935. First separate edition. One of 285 signed. In dust jacket. $75–$125.

OFFICIAL Historical Atlas of Alameda County. Folding maps, full-page views. Atlas folio, half leather. Oakland, 1878. First edition. $300–$350.

OFFICIAL State Brand Book of Colorado (The). Illustrated. Cloth. Denver, 1894. $200–$250.

OFFUTT, Denton. *The Educated Horse*. Illustrated. Cloth. Washington, 1854. $50.

O'FLAHERTY, Liam. *The Assassin*. Cloth. London, (1928). First edition. One of 150 signed. $135–$200.

O'FLAHERTY, Liam. *The Black Soul*. Black cloth, paper label. London, (1924). First edition. In dust jacket. $100–$110.

O'FLAHERTY, Liam. *The Child of God*. Wrappers. London, 1926. First edition. One of 100 signed. $100–$150. Another issue: One of 25 signed. $150–$325.

O'FLAHERTY, Liam. *Civil War*. Wrappers. London, 1925. First edition. One of 100 signed. $200–$225.

O'FLAHERTY, Liam. *Darkness: A Tragedy*. Portrait. Wrappers. London, 1926. First edition. One of 100 signed. $150–$200.

O'FLAHERTY, Liam. *The Ecstasy of Angus*. Green cloth. London, 1931. Chiswick Press. First edition. One of 365 signed. $150–$200.

O'FLAHERTY, Liam. *The Fairy Goose*. Boards. New York, 1927. One of 1,190 signed. $50–$75.

O'FLAHERTY, Liam. *The Hollywood Cemetery*. Cloth. London, 1935. First edition. In dust jacket. $100–$150.

O'FLAHERTY, Liam. *The Informer*. Cloth. London, (1925). First edition. In dust jacket. $300–$400.

O'FLAHERTY, Liam. *The Puritan*. Orange cloth. London, 1932. First edition. In dust jacket. $150–$175.

O'FLAHERTY, Liam. *Red Barbara and Other Stories*. Half cloth. New York, 1928. First edition. One of 600 signed. $80–$100.

O'FLAHERTY, Liam. *Return of the Brute*. Cloth. London, 1929. First edition. In dust jacket. $75. New York, 1930. Cloth. First American edition. In dust jacket. $55.

O'FLAHERTY, Liam. *Thy Neighbor's Wife*. Black cloth. London, (1923). First edition. In dust jacket. $125–$175. Author's first book.

OGDEN, George W. *Letters from the West*. Boards. New Bedford, Mass., 1823. First edition. $600–$750.

OGILVIES (The). 3 vols., cloth. London, 1849. (By Dinah Maria Mulock.) First edition. $400–$500. Author's first novel.

O'HARA, Frank. *A City Winter and Other Poems*. Illustrated by Larry Rivers. Decorated wrappers. New York, 1951. First edition. One of 130. $350–$450. Another issue: Boards and cloth. One of 20 with an original drawing by Rivers. $1,350. (Same price in two different 1981 catalogues.)

O'HARA, Frank. *The Collected Poems of Frank O'Hara*. Cloth. New York, 1971. First edition. In suppressed dust jacket with a photograph of Larry Rivers' drawing of a nude O'Hara. $100–$150. In later jacket, $25–$35.

O'HARA, Frank. *In Memory of My Feelings*. Illustrated. Folio, printed sheets in folder and slipcase. New York, (1967). One of 2,500. $100–$150.

O'HARA, Frank. *Meditations in an Emergency*. Cloth. New York, (1957). One of 15, signed by the poet, each numbered and containing as frontispiece (loose) an original drawing by Grace Hartigan. In slipcase. $250–$300. Ordinary edition: $20–$25.

O'HARA, Frank. *Odes*. Silk-screen prints by Michael Goldberg. Folio, boards. New York, (1960). First edition. One of 225 signed by author and artist. In acetate dust jacket. $350.

O'HARA, John. *And Other Stories*. Green cloth. New York, (1968). First edition. One of 300 signed. Boxed. $40–$50. Trade edition: Cloth. In dust jacket. $15.

O'HARA, John. *Appointment in Samarra*. Pictorial wrappers. New York, (1934). "Presentation Edition" (so imprinted on end paper), laid into dust jacket of published book. $500–$1,000. First trade edition: Black cloth. Errata slip laid in. In dust jacket. $350–$400. Also, $250 (A, 1977). Author's first book.

O'HARA, John. *Butterfield 8*. Black cloth. New York, (1935). First edition. In dust jacket. $125–$150.

O'HARA, John. *The Doctor's Son*. Black cloth. New York, (1935). First edition. In dust jacket. $50–$75.

O'HARA, John. *Hope of Heaven*. Cloth. New York, (1938). First edition. In dust jacket. $75–$100.

O'HARA, John. *The Instrument*. Brown cloth. New York, (1967). First edition. One of 300 signed. Boxed. $60–$75. Trade edition: Cloth. In dust jacket. $15.

O'HARA, John. *The Lockwood Concern*. Blue cloth. New York, (1965). First edition. One of 300 signed. Boxed. $60–$75. Trade edition: Cloth. In dust jacket. $15.

O'HARA, John. *Pal Joey*. Black cloth. New York, (1940). First edition. In dust jacket. $65–$85. Advance copy: Wrappers. $125.

O'HARA, John. *Ten North Frederick*. Cloth. New York, (1955). First edition. In dust jacket. $35.

OLD *Fashioned Mother Goose'* [sic] *Melodies (The)*. Pictures in color. Cloth. (New York), 1879. First edition. $75–$100. (Note: Contains "There was a Little Girl," probably by Henry Wadsworth Longfellow.)

OLD, R. O. *Colorado: United States, of America. Its History, Geography, and Mining*. 64 pp., printed tan wrappers. London, 1869. First edition. $500–$600.

OLDER, (Mr. and Mrs.) Fremont. *The Life of George Hearst, California Pioneer*. Illustrated. Vellum. San Francisco, 1933. John Henry Nash printing. First edition. $400–$500.

OLDHAM, Williamson S., and White, George W. *Digest of the General Statute Laws of the State of Texas*. Cloth. Austin, 1859. $150–$250.

OLDSTYLE, Jonathan. *Letters of Jonathan Oldstyle, Gent*. By the Author of *The Sketch-Book*. Brown wrappers. New York, 1824. (By Washington Irving.) First edition. $300–$400.

OLIPHANT, Laurence. *Minnesota and the Far West*. Folding map and 7 plates. Half leather. Edinburgh, 1855. First edition. $150–$200.

OLIVER, Frederick S. See *Phylos the Tibetan*.

OLIVER, John W. (publisher). *Guide to the New Gold Region of Western Kansas and Nebraska*. Folding map. 32 pp., printed wrappers. New York, 1859. First edition. $5,000–$6,000.

OLLA Podrida. 3 vols., boards and cloth, or cloth. London, 1840. (By Frederick Marryat.) First edition. $250–$350. London, 1849. Cloth. $75–$100.

OLLIVANT, Alfred. *Bob: Son of Battle*. Green decorated cloth. New York, 1898. First edition. $75–$100.

OLMSTED, Frederick Law. *A Journey Through Texas*. Folding map. Cloth. New York, 1857. First edition. $150–$200.

OLSEN, Tillie. *Tell Me a Riddle*. Cloth. Philadelphia, 1961. First edition. In dust jacket. $75–$100. London, (1964). Cloth. First English edition. In dust jacket. $50–$75. Author's first book.

OLSON, Charles. *Call Me Ishmael*. Yellow cloth. New York, (1947.) First edition. In dust jacket. $150–$175. Author's first book. New York, (1958). Boards. One of 100. $100–$125.

OLSON, Charles. *Human Universe and Other Essays*. Edited by Donald Allen. Woodcut by Robert LaVigne, photography by Kenneth Irby. Decorated boards, vellum spine. San Francisco, 1965. First edition. One of 250. In plain dust jacket. $100–$125.

OLSON, Charles. *In Cold Hell, In Thicket*. Wrappers. (Dorchester, Mass., 1953.) First edition. $100–$125.

OLSON, Charles. *Letter for Melville 1951*. Wrappers. (Black Mountain, N.C., 1951.) First edition. $400–$450. (About 50 printed.)

OLSON, Charles. *The Maximus Poems*. Boards. New York, 1960. First complete edition. One of 26 lettered and signed. $200. Another issue: One of 75. $100. (Issued without dust jacket.) Trade edition: Wrappers. $10–$15.(First printing has $1.95 on back cover.)

OLSON, Charles. *Mayan Letters*. Printed wrappers. (Mallorca), 1953 (actually 1954). Divers Press. First edition. One of 600. $100–$150.

OLSON, Charles. *O'Ryan 12345678910*. Linen, vellum spine. (San Francisco, 1965.) First edition. One of 26 signed. $175–$250. Trade edition: Wrappers. $10.

OLSON, Charles. *Stocking Cap: A Story.* Printed white wrappers, tied. San Francisco, 1966. Grabhorn printing. First edition. One of 100. $75–$125. Ordinary copies: Green wrappers. $15–$25.

OLSON, Charles. *'West.'* Boards. London, 1966. First edition. One of 25 signed. In dust jacket. $175–$250. Trade edition: Wrappers. $15.

OLSON, Charles. *Y & X.* Illustrated by Corrado Cagli. Printed wrappers. (Washington), 1948. Black Sun Press. First edition. One of 100. Boxed. $100–$125. Another issue: One of 400 in envelope. $40–$50.

OMAR Khayyam. See *The Rose Garden of Omar Khayyam; Rubaiyat of Omar Khayyam.*

ON English Prose Fiction as Rational Amusement. (Caption title.) 44 pp., sewed. (London, late in 1869?) (By Anthony Trollope.) First edition. $750–$1,000.

ON the Plains; or, The Race for Life. 62 pp., pictorial yellow wrappers. New York, (1863). (By Edward S. Ellis.) $300–$400.

ON the "White Pass" Pay-Roll. By the President of the White Pass & Yukon Route. 15 plates. Dark-blue cloth. Chicago, 1908. (By S. H. Graves.) First edition. $300–$350.

ONDERDONK, James L. *Idaho: Facts and Statistics.* Wrappers. San Francisco, 1885. First edition. $150–$300.

ONE and Twenty: Duke Narrative and Verse, 1924–1945. First edition. In dust jacket. $100. (Contains two short stories by William Styron, his first book appearance.)

ONE Hundred Books Famous in English Literature. See Kent, Henry W.

ONE Hundred Influential American Books Printed Before 1900. Illustrated. Boards and cloth. New York, 1947. Grolier Club. First edition. One of 600. $150–$200.

O'NEILL, Eugene. See Sanborn, Ralph; Shay, Frank. Also see *George Pierce Baker, a Memorial.*

O'NEILL, Eugene. *Ah, Wilderness!* Blue cloth. New York, 1933. First edition. In dust jacket. $25. Another (later) issue: Blue calf. One of 325 signed. Boxed. $200–$250.

O'NEILL, Eugene. *All God's Chillun Got Wings, and Welded.* Buff boards and cloth. New York, (1924). First edition. In dust jacket. $85–$100.

O'NEILL, Eugene. *Anna Christie.* Yellow boards, or wrappers. London, (1923). First separate edition. Boards: In dust jacket. $100. Wrappers: $100. New York, 1930. 12 illustrations by Alexander King. Purple and red boards, black cloth spine. First illustrated (and first American) edition. One of 775. In dust jacket. Boxed. $200–$225. Another issue: One of 12 in morocco, signed and with an original lithograph. $650 (A, 1978).

O'NEILL, Eugene. *Before Breakfast.* Light blue-green wrappers. New York, 1916. First separate edition. $150–$200. (Second book appearance; for the first appearance see entry following under *Provincetown Plays: Third Series.*)

O'NEILL, Eugene. *Beyond the Horizon.* Brown boards and cloth. New York, (1920). First edition, probable first state, with capital letters on front cover 9/16 inch high. In dust jacket. $125. Second issue. In dust jacket. $100.

O'NEILL, Eugene. *Days Without End.* Blue cloth. New York, (1934). First edition. In dust jacket. $50–$75. Another (later) issue: Morocco. One of 325 signed. $200.

O'NEILL, Eugene. *Desire Under the Elms.* Pictorial black cloth. New York, 1925. First separate edition. In dust jacket. $75–$100.

O'NEILL, Eugene. *Dynamo.* Green cloth. New York, 1929. First edition. In dust jacket. $35. Another (later) issue: Purple vellum. One of 775 signed. Boxed. $150–$200.

O'NEILL, Eugene. *The Emperor Jones: Diff'rent: The Straw.* Buff boards and cloth. New York, (1921). First edition, first issue, with plain (not mottled) boards. In dust jacket. $150. Cincinnati, (1921). White wrappers. $150. New York, 1928. 8 illustrations in color by Alexander King. Boards and cloth. One of 775 signed. In dust jacket. Boxed. $200–$250.

O'NEILL, Eugene. *Gold.* Blue-green boards and cloth. New York, (1921). First edition (with 1920 copyright). In dust jacket. $175.

O'NEILL, Eugene. *The Great God Brown: The Fountain: The Moon of the Caribbees and Other Plays.* Green cloth. New York, 1926. First edition. In dust jacket. $75–$100. London, (1926). (*The Great God Brown.*) Bright-blue cloth. First English edition. In dust jacket. $50–$75.

O'NEILL, Eugene. *The Hairy Ape: Anna Christie: The First Man.* Buff boards and cloth. New York, (1922). First edition. In dust jacket. $100. London, (1923). (*The Hairy Ape and Other Plays.*) Bright-blue cloth. First English edition. In dust jacket. $75. New York, (1929). 9 illustrations in color by Alexander King. Boards. First separate and illustrated edition. One of 775 signed. In dust jacket. Boxed. O'NEILL, Eugene. *The Iceman Cometh.* Blue cloth. New York, (1946). First edition. In dust jacket. $75.

O'NEILL, Eugene. *Lazarus Laughed.* Green cloth. New York, 1927. First edition. In dust jacket. $50. Another (later) issue: Vellum and boards. One of 775 signed. In dust jacket. Boxed. $200–$225.

O'NEILL, Eugene. *Long Day's Journey into Night.* Black and gray cloth. New Haven, 1956. First edition. In dust jacket. $60–$75.

O'NEILL, Eugene. *Marco Millions.* Green cloth. New York, 1927. First edition. In dust jacket. $50. Another (later) issue: Vellum and boards. One of 450 signed. Boxed. $175.

O'NEILL, Eugene. *The Moon of the Caribbees and Six Other Plays of the Sea.* Brown boards and cloth. New York, 1919. First edition, first state, ⅞ inch thick. In dust jacket. $125. Second state, 1³/₁₆ inches thick, $75. London, (1923). Bright-blue cloth. First English edition. In dust jacket. $50–$75.

O'NEILL, Eugene. *Mourning Becomes Electra.* Cloth. New York, 1931. First edition. (Issued simultaneously with Theatre Guild edition.) In dust jacket. $75–$100. Another (later) issue: Japan vellum. One of 550 signed. Boxed. $200–$250. Also, an advance copy, 3 vols., tan wrappers, $300 (A, 1977). London, (1932). Blue cloth. First English edition. In dust jacket. $50–$75.

O'NEILL, Eugene. *Strange Interlude.* Green cloth. New York, 1928. First edition. In dust jacket. $75–$100. Another (later) issue: Vellum. One of 775 signed. Boxed. $300–$350. London, (1928). Blue cloth. First English edition. In dust jacket. $50–$60.

O'NEILL, Eugene. *Thirst and Other One Act Plays.* Dark gray boards, tan cloth spine, paper labels. Boston, (1914). First edition. In dust jacket. $750–$850. Also, inscribed by the author, $800 (A, 1977). Author's first book.

O'NEILL, Eugene, and others. *The Provincetown Plays: First Series.* Printed light-blue wrappers. New York, 1916. First edition. $150–$175. (Note: Contains first book appearance of O'Neill's *Bound East for Cardiff.*)

O'NEILL, Eugene, and others. *The Provincetown Plays: Third Series.* Orange wrappers. New York, 1916. First edition. In green dust jacket. $125–$200. (Note: Contains first book appearance of O'Neill's *Before Breakfast;* see separate title entry.)

ONIONS, Oliver. *Good Boy Seldom.* Cloth. London, (1911). First edition. In dust jacket. $75–$100.

ONKEN, Otto. See Wells, William, and Onken, Otto.

ONLY Authentic Life of Abraham Lincoln, Alias "Old Abe," a Son of the West. (Cover title.) Illustrated. 16 pp., printed yellow wrappers. (New York, 1864.) $400–$500.

ONTWA, The Son of the Forest: A Poem. Boards. New York, 1832. (By Henry Whiting.) First edition. $1,000. Also, rebacked, $600 (A, 1977).

OPPEN, George. *Discreet Series.* Preface by Ezra Pound. Cloth. New York, 1934. First edition. In dust jacket. $125–$150.

OPPENHEIMER, Joel. *Acts.* Printed wrappers. Driftless, Wis., (1976). Perishable Press. One of 112 signed. In dust jacket. $60–$75.

OPTIC, Oliver. *The Boat Club; or, The Bunkers of Rippleton.* Frontispiece, 3 plates. Slate-purple pictorial cloth. Boston, 1855. (By William Taylor Adams.) First edition. $200–$250. Another issue: Pictorial presentation binding. $300–$400. First Oliver Optic book.

ORATION, Poem, and Speeches . . . June 5th, 1867. Printed wrappers. San Francisco, 1867. $200 and up. (Note: Includes a poem by Bret Harte.)

ORBELIANI, Sulkhan-Saba. *The Book of Wisdom and Lies.* Translated by Oliver Waldrop. Woodcut title and borders. Vellum with ties. London, 1894. Kelmscott Press. One of 250. $500–$750.

ORCUTT, William Dana. *The Book in Italy.* Plates, including color. Folio, boards. New York, 1928. One of 750. In dust jacket. $150–$200. Trade edition: Cloth. In dust jacket. $25. London, 1928. Half vellum. One of 750. In dust jacket. $150–$200.

ORCUTT, William Dana. *In Quest of the Perfect Book.* Plates, including color. Half vellum. Boston, 1926. First edition. One of 365. In dust jacket. $125–$150. Trade edition: Cloth. In dust jacket. $25.

ORCUTT, William Dana. *The Kingdom of Books.* Plates, including color. Half vellum. Boston, 1927. One of 475 signed. Boxed. $100–$125. Trade edition: Cloth. In dust jacket. $25.

ORCUTT, William Dana. *The Magic of the Book.* Illustrated. Half vellum. New York, 1930. First edition. One of 375 signed. In dust jacket. $100–$125. Trade edition: Cloth. In dust jacket. $25.

ORDINARY Evening in New Haven, (An). Wrappers. New Haven, 1949. First edition. Transactions of the Connecticut Academy of Arts and Sciences. $100–$150. (Contains an 11-page poem by Wallace Stevens written to mark a Sesquicentennial celebration.)

ORDNANCE Manual for the Use of the Officers of the Confederate States of America. 33 plates. Cloth. Charleston, 1863. $500–$750.

OREGON: Agricultural, Stock Raising, Mineral Resources, Climate, etc. (Published by U.P.R.R.) 68 pp., wrappers. Council Bluffs, Iowa, 1888. $175–$225.

O'REILLY, Bernard. *Greenland, the Adjacent Seas, and the North-West Passage.* 3 folding maps, 18 plates. Half cloth. London, 1818. First edition. $600–$700.

O'REILLY, Harrington. *Fifty Years on the Trail.* Illustrated by Paul Frenzeny. Pictorial cloth. London, 1889. First edition. $150–$200. London, 1890. Wrappers. Second edition. $100–$150. New York, 1889. Cloth. First American edition. $100–$125.

ORIGIN and Traditional History of the Wyandotts. Cloth. Toronto, 1870. (By Peter D. Clarke.) First edition. $75–$100.

ORIGO, Iris. *Allegra.* Cloth. London, 1935. Hogarth Press. First edition. In dust jacket with wraparound band. $75–$100.

ORIOLI, G. *Adventures of a Bookseller.* Pictorial orange wrappers folded over blue paper. Florence, Italy, (1937). First edition. One of 2 on blue paper, signed. $250 and up. Another issue: One of 300 signed. $150.

ORME, Edward. *Collection of British Field Sports.* Colored title page and 20 colored plates after Howitt. Oblong folio, half morocco. London, 1807–08. First edition. $37,400 (A, 1979). Guildford, England, 1955. 29 color plates. Facsimile. Folio, full crimson morocco. One of 20 with an original plate included. $1,500 and up. Ordinary issue: Half morocco. $400–$600.

ORR, George. *The Possession of Louisana by the French.* 44 pp., boards. London, 1803. First edition. $150–$200.

ORR, N. M. (compiler). *The City of Stockton.* 64 pp., printed wrappers. Stockton, Calif., 1874. First edition. $150–$175.

ORR and Ruggles. *San Joaquin County.* Map, plates. 130 pp., wrappers. Stockton, 1887. First edition. $150–$200.

ORTEGA, Luis. *California Hackamore (La Jáquima).* 109 photographs, 29 sketches by Al Napoletano. Pictorial leather. (Sacramento, 1948.) First edition. ORTON, Richard H. *Records of California Men in the War of the Rebellion, 1861–1867.* Cloth. Sacramento, 1890. First edition. $75–$100.

ORVIS, Charles F., and Cheny, A. Nelson (compilers). *Fishing with the Fly.* 15 color plates. Cloth. Manchester, Vt., 1883. First edition. $250–$350.

ORWELL, George. *Animal Farm: A Fairy Story.* Dark green cloth. London, 1945. (By Eric Arthur Blair.) First edition. In presumed first dust jacket (with blue advertisement on verso). $400–$500. In presumed later jacket (red ad). $400–$450. New York, (1946). Cloth. First American edition. In dust jacket. $150–$200. Advance proof copy in wrappers: $400.

ORWELL, George. *Burmese Days.* Cloth. New York, 1934. (By Eric Arthur Blair.) First edition. In dust jacket. $500–$750. London, 1935. Cloth. First English edition. In dust jacket. $250–$300. Author's first novel.

ORWELL, George. *A Clergyman's Daughter.* Cloth. London, 1935. (By Eric Arthur Blair.) First edition. In dust jacket. $400–$450.

ORWELL, George. *Down and Out in Paris and London.* Cloth. London, 1933. (By Eric Arthur Blair.) First edition. In dust jacket. $600–$800. New York, 1933. Cloth. First American edition. In dust jacket. $400–$450. Author's first book.

ORWELL, George. *Homage to Catalonia.* Cloth. London, 1938. (By Eric Arthur Blair.) First edition. In dust jacket. $500–$600. Also, $396 (A, 1980). New York, 1952. Cloth. First American edition. In dust jacket. $20–$30.

ORWELL, George. *Keep the Aspidistra Flying.* Cloth. London, 1936. (By Eric Arthur Blair.) First edition. In dust jacket. $300–$500.

ORWELL, George. *The Lion and the Unicorn.* Cloth. New York, 1941. (By Eric Arthur Blair.) First edition. In dust jacket. $100–$150. London, (1941). Cloth. First English edition. In dust jacket. $100–$150.

ORWELL, George. *Nineteen Eighty-four.* Green cloth. London, 1949. (By Eric Arthur Blair.) First edition. In dust jacket. $350–$450. New York, 1949. Gray cloth. First American edition. In red (first issue) dust jacket. $150–$200. Advance copy in wrappers: $450.

ORWELL, George. *Politics & the English Language.* Printed wrappers. (Evansville), 1947. (By Eric Arthur Blair.) First edition. $150–$200.

ORWELL, George. *The Road to Wigan Pier.* Foreword by Victor Gollancz. Illustrated. Limp orange cloth wrappers. London, 1937. (By Eric Arthur Blair.) First edition, wrappers lettered "Left Book Club Edition." $100–$125. Trade Edition: Cloth. $50.

ORWELL, George. *Shooting an Elephant and Other Essays.* Cloth. London, 1950. (By Eric Arthur Blair.) First edition. In dust jacket. $150–$250.

OSBORNE, Eric. *Victorian Detective Fiction.* Introduction by John Carter. Cloth. London, 1966. First edition. One of 500 signed by Carter and by Dorothy Glover and Graham Greene, whose collection is catalogued in the book. In dust jacket. $250–$350.

OSBORNE, John. *Inadmissible Evidence.* Cloth. London, (1965). First edition. In dust jacket. $50–$75.

OSBORNE, John. *Look Back in Anger.* Cloth. London, 1957. First edition. In dust jacket. $75. His first play.

OSBORNE, John. *Luther.* Cloth. London, (1961). First edition. In dust jacket. $35–$50.

OSBORNE, John, and Creighton, Anthony. *Epitaph for George Dillon.* Cloth. London, (1958). First edition. In dust jacket. $50–$60.

OSCEOLA; or, Fact and Fiction: A Tale of the Seminole War. By a Southerner. Illustrated. Cloth. New York, 1838. (By James Birchett Ransom.) First edition. $250–$300.

OSGOOD, Ernest Staples. *The Day of the Cattleman.* 14 plates and maps. Cloth. Minneapolis, 1929. First edition. In dust jacket. $125–$200.

OSGOOD, Frances S. *The Poetry of Flowers and Flowers of Poetry.* Half leather. New York, 1851. $75–$100.

O'SHAUGHNESSY, Arthur W. E. *An Epic of Women and Other Poems.* Pictorial title page, 2 plates. Purple cloth. London, 1870. First edition. $100–$150.

O'SHAUGHNESSY, Arthur W. E. *Music and Moonlight.* Cloth. London, 1874. First edition. $75–$100.

O'SHAUGHNESSY, Arthur W. E. *Songs of a Worker.* Cloth London, 1881. First edition. $75–$100.

OSLER, Sir William. *An Alabama Student and Other Biographical Essays.* Cloth. Oxford, England, 1908. First edition. $150–$175. New York, 1908. Cloth. First American edition. $100–$125. New York, 1909. Second edition. $50.

OSLER, Sir William. *Aphasia and Associated Speech Problems.* Illustrated. Cloth. New York, 1920. $75.

OSLER, Sir William. *The Cerebral Palsies of Children.* Cloth. Philadelphia, 1889. First edition. $100–$150.

OSLER, Sir William. *The Evolution of Modern Medicine.* Cloth. New Haven, 1921. First edition. $250–$350.

OSLER, Sir William. *Incunabula Medica: A Study of the Earliest Printed Medical Books, 1467–1480.* Illustrated. Boards and cloth. London, 1923. First edition. $400–$500.

OSLER, Sir William. *Lectures on the Diagnosis of Abdominal Tumors.* Cloth, or wrappers. New York, 1894. $75–$100. New York, 1895. Wrappers. $50. London, 1898. Cloth. $50.

OSLER, Sir William. *On Chorea and Choreiform Affections.* Cloth. Philadelphia, 1894. First edition. $200–$300.

OSLER, Sir William. *The Principles and Practice of Medicine.* Cloth. New York, 1892. First edition. $300–$400. Edinburgh, 1894. Cloth. First English edition. $300–$500.

OSLER, Sir William. *Science and Immortality.* Cloth. Boston, 1904. First edition. $50–$75.

OSLER, Sir William. *Students' Notes.* Half cloth. Montreal, 1882. First edition. $100.

OSLER, Sir William (editor). *Bibliotheca Osleriana: A Catalogue of Books Illustrating the History of Medicine and Science.* Cloth. Oxford, 1929. First edition. $400–$500.

O'SULLIVAN, Vincent. *The Houses of Sin.* Parchment. London, 1897. First edition. One of 400. $200.

OTERO, Miguel Antonio. *The Real Billy the Kid.* Illustrated. Cloth. New York, 1936. First edition. In dust jacket. $50–$75.

OTIS, James. *Jenny Wren's Boarding-House.* Illustrated. Pictorial brown or blue cloth. Boston, (1893). (By James Otis Kaler.) First edition. $50–$75.

OTIS, James. *Toby Tyler or Ten Weeks with a Circus.* Illustrated by W. A. Rogers. Light brown, green, or orange cloth. New York, 1881. (By James Otis Kaler.) First edition. $150–$200.

OUIDA. *Syrlin.* 3 vols., cloth. London, 1980. (By Marie Louise de la Ramée.) First edition. $300–$400.

OUIDA. *A Tale of a Toad.* Decorated cloth and morocco. London, 1939. Corvinus Press. (By Marie Louise de la Ramée.) One of 24. $250–$300.

OUIDA. *Under Two Flags.* 3 vols., cloth. London, 1867. (By Marie Louise de la Ramée.) First edition. $300–$400.

OUTCROPPINGS: Being Selections of California Verse. Cloth. San Francisco, 1866. First edition, probable first issue, with "Staining" spelled "Sraining" on page 70 and with no ornament on page 102. $150–$200. (Note: Edited anonymously by Bret Harte.)

OUTRE-MER: A Pilgrimage Beyond the Sea. Nos. I and II. Marbled wrappers and blue wrappers or boards. Boston, 1833 and 1834. (By Henry Wadsworth Longfellow.) First editions. $1,000 and up. Also, No. I in wrappers, No. II in boards, $600 (A, 1981). (Note: A complicated title bibliographically; for example, there are at least three wrapper variants on No. I, while No. II may be in either wrappers or boards of various colors. For a full discussion, see BAL.) Also issued clothbound as 2 vols. in one. $200 and up.

OVID. *The Amores of P. Ovidius Naso.* Translated by E. Powys Mathers. 5 engravings on copper by T. E. Laboureur. Half morocco. Waltham Saint Lawrence, England, 1932. Golden Cockerel Press. One of 350. $150–$250.

OWEN, John Pickard. *The Fair Haven.* By the Late John Pickard Owen. Edited by William Bickersteth Owen. Green cloth. London, 1873. (By Samuel Butler, of *Erewhon.*) First edition. $50–$75.

OWEN, Richard E., and Cox, E. T. *Report on the Mines of New Mexico.* (Cover title.) 59 pp., printed wrappers. Washington, 1865. First edition. $500–600.

OWEN, Robert. See Campbell, Alexander.

OWEN, Robert. *A New View of Society.* 4 parts in one, boards. London, 1813–14. First edition. $500–$600. London, 1816. Boards. Second edition. $150–$200.

OWEN, Robert Dale. *A Brief Practical Treatise on the Construction and Management of Plank Roads.* Plate. Cloth. New Albany, Ind., 1850. First edition. $125–$150.

OWEN, Wilfred. *Poems.* Cloth, paper label. London, 1920. First edition. In dust jacket. $300–$450. Author's first book. London, 1931. First complete edition. In dust jacket. $75.

OWEN, Wilfred. *Thirteen Poems.* Drawings by Ben Shahn and Leonard Baskin. Folio, half morocco. Northampton, Mass., 1956. Gehenna Press. One of 400 signed by Baskin. $250–$400. Another issue: One of 35 specially bound and with a proof of portrait signed by both artists. $500–$600.

OWENS, Rochelle. *Not Be Essence That Cannot Be.* Stiff printed wrappers. New York, (1961). First edition. $30–$40. Author's first book.

OZICK, Cynthia. *Trust.* Cloth. New York, (1966). First edition. In dust jacket. $75–$100. London, (1966). Cloth. First English edition. In dust jacket. $60–$65.

P

P., E. *Hugh Selwyn Mauberley.* Brown cloth. (London), 1920. (By Ezra Pound.) Ovid Press. First edition. One of 165 from an edition of 200. $1,500–$2,000. Also $1,300 (A, 1977). Another issue: Cloth. One of 20 signed. $2,000–$2,500. Also, soiled, $1,430 (A, 1979). Another issue: Parchment boards. One of 15 on vellum. $3,000.

PACKARD, Wellman, and Larison, G. *Early Emigration to California.* 2 portraits, 23 pp., printed wrappers. Bloomington, Ill., 1928. First edition. One of 30. $400–$500.

PAGAN Anthology. (The). Boards, paper label. New York, (1918). First edition. $300–$400. (Contains two poems by Hart Crane, constituting his first book appearance.)

PAGE, Stanton. *The Chevalier of Pensieri-Vani.* Cloth, or wrappers. Boston, (1890). (By Henry Blake Fuller.) First edition. Wrappers: $200–$250. Cloth: $100–$150. Author's first book.

PAGE, Thomas Nelson. *In Old Virginia.* Pictorial cloth. New York, 1887. First edition, first issue, with no advertisement for "Free Joe" on last page. $50–$75.

PAGE, Thomas Nelson. *Two Little Confederates.* Illustrated. Blue cloth. New York, 1888. First edition, first printing, with 10 ad pages at back. $75–$100.

PAINE, Albert Bigelow. *Captain Bill McDonald, Texas Ranger.* Illustrated. Cloth. New York, 1909. First edition. $100–$125. Another issue: Morocco. $150–$200.

PAINE, Albert Bigelow. *Thomas Nast: His Period and His Pictures.* Illustrated. Cloth. New York, 1904. First edition. $75–$125.

PALEY, Grace. *The Little Disturbances of Man.* Cloth. Garden City, 1959. First edition. In dust jacket. $65–$85. London, 1960. Cloth. First English edition. In dust jacket. $50–$75. Author's first book.

PALGRAVE, Francis Turner. *The Golden Treasury of the Best Songs and Lyrical Poems of the English Language.* Cloth. Cambridge, 1861. First edition. $200–$300.

PALINURUS. *The Unquiet Grave: A Word Cycle.* Frontispiece and 3 collotype plates. Gray wrappers. London, 1944. (By Cyril Connolly.) Curwen Press. First edition. One of 1,000. $250–$300.

PALLADINO, Lawrence B. *Indian and White in the Northwest.* Illustrated. Cloth, or half leather. Baltimore, 1894. First edition. $150–$250.

PALLAS, P. S. *Travels Through the Southern Provinces of the Russian Empire.* Maps and plates. 2 vols., boards, paper labels. London, 1802–03. First English edition. $1,250–$1,500.

PALMER, H. E. *The Powder River Indian Expedition, 1865.* 59 pp., printed gray wrappers. Omaha, 1887. First edition. $300–$350.

PALMER, Harry. *Base Ball: The National Game of the Americans.* 69 pp., wrappers. Chicago, 1888. $100 and up.

PALMER, Joel. *Journal of Travels over the Rocky Mountains, to the Mouth of the Columbia River, etc.* Brown printed wrappers. Cincinnati, 1847. First edition, first issue, with date 1847 on paper cover not overprinted or changed, and with errata slip tipped in. $2,000. Rebound in half leather, $1,500. Cincinnati, 1852. Half leather. Second edition. $500–$750.

PALMER, William J. *Report of Surveys Across the Continent.* 3 maps and profile, 20 photographic plates. Wrappers. Philadelphia, 1869. First edition. $750–$1,000. Later issue, cloth: $550.

PAPWORTH, John B. *Hints on Ornamental Gardening.* 28 hand-colored plates, sepia plate, woodcut plans. Boards. London, 1823. First edition. $1,250.

PAPWORTH, John B. *Rural Residences.* 27 full-page hand-colored aquatint plates. Boards. London, 1818. First edition. $1,250–$1,500.

PAPWORTH, John B. *Select Views of London.* 76 colored aquatint plates, 5 folding. Boards. London, 1816. First book edition. $3,000–$3,500.

PAREDES Y ARRILLAGA, Mariano. *Ultimas Communicaciones Entre el Gobierno Mexicano y el Enviada Estraordinario y Ministro Plenipotenciario Nombrado por el de los Estados Unidos.* 22 pp., wrappers. Mexico, 1846. $500.

PARKER, A. A. *A Trip to the West and Texas.* 2 plates. Cloth. Concord, N.H., 1835. First edition. $400–$500. Concord, 1836. Colored folding map and 3 plates. Cloth. Second edition. $400–$500. (Note: Howes reports 2 plates in the first edition, but my own copy came with 3. Howes says not all copies of the second edition included the map; in such cases the value should be around $300 or less.)

PARKER, Aaron. *Forgotten Tragedies of Indian Warfare in Idaho.* 10 pp., double-column, wrappers. Grangeville, Idaho, 1925. $100–$125.

PARKER, Dorothy. *After Such Pleasures.* Buckram, New York, 1933. First edition. One of 250 signed. Boxed. $75–$100. Trade edition: Tan cloth. In dust jacket. $25.

PARKER, Dorothy. *Death and Taxes.* Half cloth. New York, 1931. First edition. One of 250 signed. Boxed. $100–$125. Trade edition (second printing): In jacket. $20–$25.

PARKER, Dorothy. *Laments for the Living.* Cloth. New York, 1930. First edition. In dust jacket. $75–$100. Paris, 1932. Black Sun Press. Printed wrappers. $100–$110.

PARKER, Dorothy. *Men I'm Not Married To.* Boards. Garden City, 1922. First edition. (Bound in, inverted and with separate title, *Women I'm Not Married To,* by Franklin P. Adams.) In dust jacket. $75–$85. Author's first book.

PARKER, Dorothy. *Not So Deep as a Well.* Illustrated by Valenti Angelo. Half buckram. New York, 1936. First edition. One of 485 signed. $75–$100. Trade edition: Cloth. In dust jacket. $25–$30.

PARKER, Dorothy. *Sunset Gun.* Boards and cloth. New York, 1928. First edition. One of 275 signed. Boxed. $100–$150. Trade edition: Boards. In dust jacket. $40–$50.

PARKER, Frank J. (editor). *Washington Territory! The Present and Prospective Future of the Upper Columbia Country.* 17 pp., printed wrappers. Walla Walla, Wash., 1881. First edition. $400–$500.

PARKER, Henry W. *How Oregon Was Saved to the U.S.* 10 pp., wrappers. New York, 1901. $35–$50.

PARKER, J. M. *An Aged Wanderer: A Life Sketch of . . . A Cowboy on the Western Plains in Early Days.* 32 pp., wrappers. San Angelo, Tex., no date. First edition. $400–$500.

PARKER, John R. *The United States Telegraph Vocabulary.* 3 plates, one in color. Pictorial boards. Boston, 1832. First edition. $150–$175.

PARKER, Samuel. *Journal of an Exploring Tour Beyond the Rocky Mountains.* Folding map, plate. Cloth. Ithaca, 1838. First edition. $500–$600.

PARKER, Solomon. *Parker's American Citizen's Sure Guide.* Boards. Sag Harbor, N.Y., 1808. First edition. $150–$175.

PARKER, W. B. *Notes Taken During the Expedition Commanded by Capt. R. B. Marcy.* Cloth. Philadelphia, 1856. First edition. $400–$500.

PARKER & Huyett. *The Illustrated Miners' Hand-Book and Guide to Pike's Peak.* 6 plates, 2 folding maps. Cloth. St. Louis, 1859. (By Nathan H. Parker and D. H. Huyett.) First edition. $5,000–$6,000.

PARKMAN, Francis. *The California and Oregon Trail.* 2 vols., printed wrappers, or one volume in cloth. New York, 1849. First edition. Wrappers: $12,500—the Thomas W. Streeter copy, catalogued in Fall, 1981, by the Jenkins Company. Others, $5,000 and up. Clothbound, with frontispiece and engraved title page: $1,500–$2,000. Second issue, with page 7 numbered 8. $1,500 and up. Rebound in morocco, $450 in a recent catalogue. (See the Streeter sale catalogue for a note on the inconclusive bibliographical data on this book.)

PARKMAN, Francis. *History of the Conspiracy of Pontiac and the War of the North American Tribes.* 4 maps. Gray cloth. Boston, 1851. First edition. $125–$150.

PARKMAN, Francis. *The Old Regime in Canada.* Cloth. Boston, 1874. First edition. One of 75 on large paper. $150.

PARKMAN, Francis. *The Oregon Trail.* Illustrated by Frederic Remington. Leather, or pictorial tan cloth. Boston, 1892. First edition. Leather: $400–$500. Cloth: $350–$400. Boston, 1925. Illustrated by Remington and N. C. Wyeth. Half cloth. One of 875. $250–$350. New York, 1943. Limited Editions Club. $80–$100.

PARLEY, Peter. *Peter Parley's Universal History, on the Basis of Geography.* 2 vols., cloth. Boston, 1837. (By Nathaniel Hawthorne.) First edition. $1,000–$1,500.

PARLEY, Peter. *The Tales of Peter Parley About America.* 32 (30?) engravings. Blue boards, red leather spine. Boston, 1827. (By Samuel G. Goodrich.) First edition. $3,000–$4,000. Also, badly worn, $2,750 (A, 1974). Author's first book.

PARMLY, Levi Spear. *A Practical Guide to the Management of the Teeth.* Boards. Philadelphia, 1819. First edition. $175–$200.

PARNELL, Thomas. *Poems.* Selected by Lennox Robinson. Boards and linen. Dublin, 1927. Cuala Press. One of 200. In dust jacket. $75–$125.

PARRY, William Edward. *Journal of a Second Voyage for the Discovery of a North-West Passage.* 39 plates, maps and charts. Cloth. London, 1824. First edition. $500–$600.

PARRY, William Edward. *Journal of a Voyage for the Discovery of a North-West Passage . . . in the Years, 1819–20.* 20 plates and maps. Boards. London, 1821. First edition, with errata slip. $500–$750.

PARSONS, George Frederic. *The Life and Adventures of James W. Marshall.* Portrait frontispiece. Cloth. Sacramento, 1870. First edition. $150–$200. San Francisco, 1935. Grabhorn Press. Boards. $75–$100.

PARTISAN (The): A Tale of the Revolution. 2 vols., cloth, paper labels, New York, 1835. (By William Gilmore Simms.) First edition. $400–$500.

PASADENA as It Is Today from a Business Standpoint. (Cover title.) 32 pp., printed wrappers. (Pasadena, 1886.) $150–$200.

PASADENA, California, Illustrated. Plates. 45 pp., pictorial wrappers. Pasadena, 1886. $100–$125.

PASADENA, Los Angeles County, Southern California. 36 pp., wrappers. Los Angeles, 1898, $100–$125.

PASQUIN, Peter. *A Day's Journal of a Sponge.* 6 hand-colored plates. Wrappers. London, 1824 (By M. Egerton.) $475–$550.

PASSION-Flowers. Cloth. Boston, 1854. (By Julia Ward Howe.) First edition. $200–$250. Author's first book.

PASTERNAK, Boris. *Doctor Zhivago.* Cloth. London, 1958. First edition in English. In dust jacket $50–$75.

PASTERNAK, Boris. *Selected Poems.* Cloth. London, 1946. First edition. In dust jacket. $50–$60.

PATCHEN, Kenneth. A Cautionary Note: We have yet to find a reliable bibliographical guide to this author's bewildering variety of hand-painted books. The listings that follow, some from catalogue and auction sources, are tentative only. For further help, consult a specialist poetry dealer.

PATCHEN, Kenneth. *Before the Brave.* Red cloth. New York, (1936). First edition. In dust jacket. $300–$500.

PATCHEN, Kenneth. *Cloth of the Tempest.* Cloth. New York, (1943). First edition. In dust jacket. $150–$200.

PATCHEN, Kenneth. *The Dark Kingdom.* Wrappers, painted by the author. New York, (1942). First edition. One of 75 signed. Boxed. $300–$350. Trade edition: Cloth. In dust jacket. $20–$25.

PATCHEN, Kenneth. *Fables and Other Little Tales.* Boards and cloth, paper labels. Karlsruhe, Germany, 1953. First edition. One of 50 with covers hand-painted by Patchen, signed. $125–$200. Ordinary issue: Wrappers. One of 450. $50–$75.

PATCHEN, Kenneth. *The Famous Boating Party.* Boards and cloth. (New York, 1954.) First edition. One of 50 with covers hand-painted by Patchen and with limitation in Patchen's hand, signed. $200–$600. Ordinary copies: In dust jacket. $50–$100.

PATCHEN, Kenneth. *First Will and Testament.* Red buckram. Norfolk, (1939). First edition. In dust jacket. $250. (800 printed.) New York, (1948). Second edition. One of 126 signed. In dust jacket. $200.

PATCHEN, Kenneth. *Glory Never Guesses.* Silk-screened poems on Japanese papers, some leaves hand-colored by Patchen, in portfolio wrappers. (Palo Alto, 1955.) First edition. One of 200. $200–$300.

PATCHEN, Kenneth. *Hurrah for Anything.* Illustrated. Boards. Highlands, N.C., 1957. First edition. One of 100. $300–$375.

PATCHEN, Kenneth. *The Journal of Albion Moonlight.* Boards and cloth. (Mount Vernon, N.Y., 1941.) First edition. One of 50 signed. Boxed. $250. Second issue: One of 295. In dust jacket. $150.

PATCHEN, Kenneth. *Memoirs of a Shy Pornographer.* Black cloth. New York, 1945. First edition. In dust jacket. $75–$100. London, (1948). First English edition. In dust jacket. $75.

PATCHEN, Kenneth. *The Moment.* Hand-painted and -lettered by the author. Woven boards, vellum spine. No place, (1955). First edition. One of 47. $100–$150. Another edition: (Alhambra, Calif., 1960.) Folio, vellum and cloth. One of 42 signed. $300–$750.

PATCHEN, Kenneth. *Orchards, Thrones and Caravans.* Boards. San Francisco, (1952). First edition. "Vellum edition." One of 170 signed. $300. Another issue: Boards. One of 90. "Engraver's edition," with cover engraving by David Ruff, signed by Patchen and Ruff. $300–$400.

PATCHEN, Kenneth. *Panels for the Walls of Heaven.* Hand-painted boards. (Berkeley), 1946. First edition. (750 copies.) Issued in several hand-painted cover designs. $150–$250. Also, 150 signed copies: $500–$750.

PATCHEN, Kenneth. *Poem-Scapes.* Hand-painted boards. Highlands, 1958. First edition. One of 75 signed. $100–$150. Another (?) issue: One of 42 signed, and including a hand-written poem. $75–$150. Trade edition: Stiff wrappers. $7.50–$10.

PATCHEN, Kenneth. *Red Wine and Yellow Hair.* Boards and cloth. New York, (1949). First edition. One of 108 with covers hand-painted by author and with limitation notice in Patchen's hand, signed. $300–$650. Trade edition: Cloth. In dust jacket. $35–$50.

PATCHEN, Kenneth. *See You in the Morning.* Cloth. New York, (1947). First edition. In dust jacket. $100–$125.

PATCHEN, Kenneth. *Sleepers Awake.* Red cloth. (New York, 1946.) First (black paper) edition. One of 148 signed. $100–$125. Another issue: White cloth, with original decoration on cover by the author. One of 75 signed. In dust jacket. $200–$250. Trade edition: Cloth. In dust jacket. $75–$100.

PATCHEN, Kenneth. *A Surprise for the Bagpipe Players.* Silk-screened poems on Japanese papers, some leaves hand-colored by Patchen, in portfolio wrappers. (Palo Alto, 1956.) First edition. One of 200. $200–$300.

PATCHEN, Kenneth. *To Say If You Love Someone.* Cloth. Prairie City, Ill., (1930). Press of James A. Decker. First edition. In dust jacket. $150–$200. Author's first book.

PATER, Walter. *Appreciations, with An Essay on Style.* Cloth. London, 1889. First edition. $50–$75.

PATER, Walter. *Essays from "The Guardian."* Boards. London, 1896. Chiswick Press. First edition. One of 100. $75–$125.

PATER, Walter. *An Imaginary Portrait.* Wrappers. London, 1894. Daniel Press. One of 250. $75–$100.

PATER, Walter. *Imaginary Portraits.* Cloth. London, 1887. First edition. $100–$125.

PATER, Walter. *Marius the Epicurean.* 2 vols., cloth. London, 1885. First edition. $75–$85. Portland, Me., 1900. 2 vols., half morocco. One of 450. $300. London, 1913. 2 vols., vellum. One of 12 on vellum. $1,000–$1,250. London, 1929. Illustrated by Thomas Mackenzie. 2 vols., half vellum. One of 325 signed by Mackenzie. $200–$225.

PATER, Walter. *Plato and Platonism: A Series of Lectures.* Cloth. New York, 1893. First American edition. One of 100. $125–$150.

PATER, Walter. *The Renaissance: Studies in Art and Poetry.* Illustrated. Limp wrappers. Portland, 1902. One of 35 on vellum. $250–$300.

PATER, Walter. *Sebastian Van Storck.* 8 colored plates. Cloth. London, 1927. One of 1,050. $200–$300.

PATER, Walter. *Studies in the History of the Renaissance.* Dark-green cloth. London, 1873. First edition. $125. Author's first book.

PATHFINDER (*The*); or, *The Inland Sea.* By the Author of *The Pioneers.* 3 vols., boards and cloth, paper labels. London, 1840. (By James Fenimore Cooper.) First edition. $400–$600. Philadelphia, 1840. 2 vols., green or purple cloth, paper labels. First American edition, first issue, without copyright notice in Vol. 1 and with printer's imprint at about center of page 2. $500–$600. Also, $150 (A, 1977). New York, 1965. Limited Editions Club. Buckram. Boxed. $40–$60.

PATMORE, Coventry. See *The Angel in the House; Odes.*

PATMORE, Coventry. *Faithful For Ever.* Cloth. London, 1860. First edition. $150–$200.

PATMORE, Coventry. *Poems.* Cloth. London, 1844. First edition. $100–$150. Author's first book.

PATMORE, Henry John. *Poems.* Vellum. Oxford, 1884. Daniel Press. One of 125. $200–$250.

PATON, Alan. *Cry, the Beloved Country.* Cloth. London, 1948. First edition. $50–$75. New York, 1948. Cloth. First American edition. In dust jacket. $50.

PATTERSON, A. W. *History of the Backwoods; or, The Region of the Ohio.* Folding map. Cloth. Pittsburgh, 1843. First edition. $400–$500.

PATTERSON, Joseph Medill. *A Little Brother of the Rich.* Cloth. Chicago, 1908. First edition. In dust jacket. $100–$125. Without jacket, $45.

PATTERSON, Lawson B. *Twelve Years in the Mines of California.* Cloth. Cambridge, Mass., 1862. First edition. $150–$200.

PATTERSON, Samuel. *Narrative of the Adventures and Sufferings of Samuel Patterson.* Contemporary leather. Palmer, Mass., 1817. First edition (?). $500–$600. Also, $180 (A, 1976, 1977, and 1979); catalogued in 1981 by a Rhode Island dealer at $45. (Ghostwritten by Ezekiel Terry. Wright Howes cites an 1817 Rhode Island printing as the first edition, and lists the Palmer edition as a "second issue," but other authorities question this.)

PATTIE, James O. *The Personal Narrative of James O. Pattie, of Kentucky.* Edited by Timothy Flint. 5 plates. Mottled calf. Cincinnati, 1831. First edition, first issue, published by John H. Wood. $8,500–$10,000, possibly more. Cincinnati, 1833. Second issue (reissue of the 1831 sheets with new title page). $1,200–$1,500.

PATTON, The Rev. W. W., and Isham, R. N. *U.S. Sanitary Commission, No. 38: Report on the Condition of Camps and Hospitals at Cairo . . . Paducah and St. Louis.* 12 pp., stitched. Chicago, 1861. First edition. $100–$150.

PAUL, Elliot, and Allen, Jay. *All the Brave.* Illustrated by Luis Quintinalla. Preface by Ernest Hemingway. Pictorial wrappers. New York, (1939). First edition. $75.

PAUL, William. *The Rose Garden.* 15 color plates. Cloth. London, 1848. First edition. $400–$500.

PAULDING, Hiram. *Journal of a Cruise of the United States Schooner Dolphin.* Folding map. Green cloth. New York, 1831. First edition. $1,000–$1,250.

PAULDING, James Kirke. See Langstaff, Launcelot. Also see *A Christmas Gift from Fairy-Land; Chronicles of the City of Gotham; The Dutchman's Fireside; A Gift from Fairy-Land; John Bull in America; Koningsmarke; Letters from the South; The Merry Tales of the Three Wise Men of Gotham; A Sketch of Old England; Westward Ho!*

PAULDING, James Kirke. *The Backwoodsman: A Poem.* Boards. Philadelphia, 1818. First edition. $150–$200.

PAULDING, James Kirke. *Slavery in the United States.* Cloth. New York, 1836. First edition. $75–$100.

PAULINE: A Fragment of a Confession. Gray or brown boards, paper label. London, 1833. (By Robert Browning.) First edition. $16,000 (A, 1929—the Jerome Kern copy). Author's first book. London, 1886. Edited by Thomas J. Wise. Boards. One of 400. $150–$200. Another issue: One of 25 on large paper. $350–$400.

PAULISON, C. M. K. *Arizona: The Wonderful Country.* 31 pp., printed wrappers, Tucson, 1881. First edition. $2,500–$3,000.

PAYNE, John Howard. *Clari; or, The Maid of Milan; An Opera, in Three Acts.* Stitched, old paper wrappers. London, 1823. First edition. $500 and up. (Note: This work contains on page 8 the first printing of Payne's "Home! Sweet Home!")

PAYNE, John Howard. *Indian Justice: A Cherokee Murder Trial at Tahlequah in 1840.* Edited by Grant Foreman. Illustrated. Cloth. Oklahoma City, 1934. First edition. $150.

PAYNE, John Howard, and Bishop, Henry R. *Home! Sweet Home! Sung by Miss M. Tree, in Clari.* 4 pp., folio, sheet music. London, (1823). First separate edition. $300 and up.

PEACOCK, Francis. *Sketches Relative to the History and Theory, but More Especially to the Practice of Dancing.* Boards. Aberdeen, Scotland, 1805. First edition. $350–$400.

PEACOCK, Thomas Love. See *Crotchet Castle; Gryll Grange; Headlong Hall; Maid Marian; Melincourt; The Misfortunes of Elphin; Nightmare Abbey; Rhododaphne.*

PEACOCK, Thomas Love. *The Genius of the Thames.* Boards. London, 1810. First edition. $350–$450.

PEACOCK, Thomas Love. *Palmyra and Other Poems.* Frontispiece. Boards. London, 1806. First edition. $500–$750.

PEACOCK, Thomas Love. *The Philosophy of Melancholy; A Poem in Four Parts.* Boards. London, 1912. First edition. $400–$500.

PEAKE, Mervyn. *Captain Slaughterboard Drops Anchor.* Illustrated. 48 pp., boards and cloth. (London, 1939.) First edition. In dust jacket. $150–$200. London, 1945. Color illustrations. Second edition. In dust jacket. $150–$200.

PEAKE, Mervyn. *Drawings.* Cloth. London, 1949. First edition. $100–$125.

PEAKE, Mervyn. *Gormenghast.* Cloth. London, 1950. First edition. In dust jacket. $200.

PEAKE, Mervyn. *Titus Groan.* Cloth. (London), 1946. First edition. In dust jacket. $200–$250.

PEARSE, James. *A Narrative of the Life of James Pearse.* Boards and leather. Rutland, Vt., 1825. First edition. $200–$250.

PEARSON, Edmund L. *The Voyage of the Hoppergrass.* Illustrated by Thomas Fogarty. Pictorial cloth. New York, 1913. First edition. In dust jacket. $50–$75.

PEARSON, Jonathan, and others. *The History of the Schenectady Patent.* 28 maps and plates. Albany, 1883. Second edition. One of 300. $50–$75. Another issue. One of 50 on large paper. $100–$125.

PEATTIE, Donald Culross. *An Almanac for Moderns.* Lynd Ward illustrations. Cloth. New York, (1935). First edition. In dust jacket. $50–$75. New York, 1938. Limited Editions Club. $50–$60.

PEATTIE, Donald Culross. *Audubon's America.* Color plates and other illustrations. Cloth. Boston, 1940. First edition. In dust jacket. $20–$25. Another issue: Limited edition, with an extra set of color plates. $75–$100.

PEATTIE, Donald Culross. *A Book of Hours.* Decorations by Lynd Ward. Buckram. New York, 1937. First edition. One of 550 signed. Boxed. $75–$125. Trade edition: Cloth. In dust jacket. $30.

PEATTIE, Elia W. *How Jacques Came into the Forest of Arden.* Illustrated. Boards. Chicago, (1901). Blue Sky Press. One of 25 on vellum. $100–$110. Another issue: Tan morocco. One of 3. Boxed. $150–$200.

PECK, George Wilbur. *Peck's Bad Boy and His Pa.* Wrappers, or cloth. Chicago, 1883. First edition, first issue, with the text ending on page 196, the last word in perfect type, and with the printer's rules on the copyright page ⅞ inch apart. Wrappers: $300–$400. Cloth: $200–$250.

PECK, John M. *A Discourse in Reference to the Decease of the Late Governor of Illinois, Ninian Edwards.* 20 pp., printed wrappers. Rock Spring, Ill., 1834. First edition. $1,000–$1,250.

PECK, John M. *A Gazetteer of Illinois.* Cloth. Jacksonville, Ill., 1834. First edition. $200–$300. Philadelphia, 1837. Cloth, paper label. Second edition. $150–$200.

PECK, John M. *A Guide for Emigrants, Containing Sketches of Illinois, Missouri, and the Adjacent Parts.* Map in color. Cloth. Boston, 1831. First edition. $200–$250. Enlarged edition: Boston, 1836. (Retitled *A New Guide for Emigrants to the West.*) $200–$250.

PEEK, Peter V. *Inklings of Adventure in the Campaigns of the Florida Indian War.* (Cover title.) 72 pp., double columns, printed yellow wrappers. Schenectady, 1846. First edition. $4,500–$5,000. Schenectady, 1860. Pictorial wrappers. $350. (Note: Catalogued by a New York dealer in the 1950's as, "so far as we can trace, the only known copy." The same dealer had sold the first edition copy noted above in 1936.)

PEESLAKE, Gaffer. *Bromo Bombastes: A Fragment from a Laconic Drama.* Black boards, paper label. London, 1933. Caduceus Press. (By Lawrence Durrell.) First edition. One of 100. $2,000 and up. Also, binding marked, $1,600 (A, 1977).

PEET, Frederick T. *Civil War Letters and Documents of Frederick T. Peet.* Boards. Newport, R.I., 1915. First edition. One of 50. $75–$125.

PEET, Frederick T. *Personal Experiences in the Civil War.* Boards. New York, 1905. First edition. One of 50. $75–$125.

PEIRCE, A. C. *A Man from Corpus Christi.* Cloth. New York, 1894. First edition. $200–$275.

PELAYO: A Story of the Goth. 2 vols., cloth, paper labels. New York, 1838. (By William Gilmore Simms.) First edition. $300–$400.

PELHAM. 3 vols., boards. London, 1828. (By Edward Bulwer-Lytton.) First edition, with ad leaf in Vol. 3. $600–$750. New York, 1829. 2 vols., boards. First American edition. $200–$250.

PEN Knife Sketches; Or, Chips of the Old Block. 24 full-page illustrations. Wrappers. Sacramento, 1853. (By Alonzo Delano.) First edition. $500–$600. Second edition, same year: $300–$400. (For a modern reprint, see entry under author's name.)

PENDENNIS, Arthur (editor). *The Newcomes.* Illustrated by Richard Doyle. 24 parts in 23, yellow wrappers. London, 1853–55. (By William Makepeace Thackeray.) First edition. $1,000 and up for fine copies with all major bibliographical points. $500 and up for copies in mixed state, repaired, etc. London, 1854–55. 2 vols., cloth. First book edition. $300–$400. (Note: As with most 19th-century publications in paperbound parts, *The Newcomes* is a complicated problem for collectors and requires the use of a bibliography to determine its degree of bibliographical correctness. Any set in good condition should be carefully examined for proper evaluation.)

PENDLETON, Nathaniel Green. *Military Posts—Council Bluffs to the Pacific Ocean.* (Caption title.) Folding map. Sewed. (Washington, 1843.) $75–$100.

PENN, William (pseudonym). *Essays on the Present Crisis in the Present Condition of the . . . Indians.* Stitched. Boston, 1829. (By Jeremiah Evarts.) First edition. $50–$75. Philadelphia, 1830. Stitched. $35–$40.

PENNELL, Elizabeth R., and Pennell, Joseph. *The Glory of New York.* 24 color reproductions. Folio, cloth. New York, 1926. First edition. One of 350. In dust jacket. Boxed. $150–$200.

PENNELL, Elizabeth R., and Pennell, Joseph. *Our Philadelphia.* Boards. Philadelphia, 1914. First edition. One of 289 signed. With 10 extra lithographs. $200–$350. Trade edition: Cloth. $75–$100.

PENNELL, Joseph. *The Adventures of an Illustrator.* Illustrated. Half leather. Boston, 1925. Limited edition, signed. $100–$150. Trade edition: Cloth. $50–$60.

PENROSE, Charles W. *"Mormon" Doctrine, Plain and Simple.* Cloth. Salt Lake City, 1882. First edition. $75–$100.

PENTLAND Rising (The). Green wrappers. Edinburgh, 1866. (By Robert Louis Stevenson.) First edition. $1,500–$2,000. Also, soiled, $1,300 (A, 1980). Stevenson's first book.

"PEOPLE'S Reville" (The): Souvenir Hill City, Graham County, Kansas. (Cover title.) 112 pp., wrappers. Topeka, 1906. $50–$60.

PEPPER, Capt. George W. *Personal Recollections of Sherman's Campaigns in Georgia and the Carolinas*. Cloth. Zanesville, Ohio, 1866. First edition. $150–$200.

PEPYS, Samuel. *Memoirs . . . Comprising His Diary from 1659 to 1669*. Edited by Richard, Lord Braybrooke. Portraits, views and facsimiles. 2 vols., boards, paper labels. London, 1825. First edition. $2,000–$2,500, possibly more. Also, foxed, hinges cracked, $950 (A, 1976). Another issue: One of 12 on thick paper, stamped "Presentation Copy." $550 (A, 1974)—in contemporary morocco. London, 1828. 5 vols., boards. Second (and first octavo) edition. $300–$350. New York, 1942. Limited Editions Club. Illustrated. 10 vols., pictorial boards and buckram. $125–$150. (Note: There have been numerous other editions of the Pepys diary, most of them multivolume versions. See the British and American book auction records for detailed listings.)

PERCEVAL, Dean. *A Thousand Miles in a Canoe*. Printed wrappers. Bushnell, Ill., 1880. First edition. $1,250–$1,500.

PERCIVAL Keene. 3 vols., boards. London, 1842. (By Frederick Marryat.) First edition. $200–$300.

PERCY, Stephen. *Robin Hood and His Merry Foresters*. 8 full-page hand-colored illustrations. Cloth. New York, 1855. (By Joseph Cundall.) $100–$125.

PERCY, Walker. *The Last Gentleman*. Cloth. New York, (1966). First edition. $75–$85.

PERCY, Walker. *Love in the Ruins*. Cloth. New York, (1971). First edition. In dust jacket. $50–$60.

PERCY, Walker. *The Moviegoer*. Cloth. New York, 1961. First edition. In dust jacket. $250–$400. London, 1963. First English edition. In dust jacket. $75–$100. Author's first book.

PERELMAN, S. J. *Dawn Ginsbergh's Revenge*. Apple-green "plush" binding. (Second issue had silver cloth.) New York, (1929). First edition. In dust jacket. $200–$250. Second binding. In dust jacket. $150–$200. Author's first book.

PEREZ DE LUXAN, Diego. *Expedition into New Mexico Made by Antonio de Espejo, 1582–1583*. Translated by George Peter Hammond and Agapito Rey. Half vellum. Los Angeles, 1929. One of 500 copies. $200–$250.

PERICLES and Aspasia. 2 vols., drab boards, blue-green cloth, paper labels. London, 1836. (By Walter Savage Landor.) First edition. $250–$350. Philadelphia, 1839. 2 vols., cloth. First American edition. $150–$200.

PERKINS, Charles Elliott. *The Pinto Horse*. Illustrated by Edward Borein. Pictorial boards. Santa Barbara, 1927. First edition. In dust jacket. $150–$250.

PERKINS, Frederick B. *The Central Park Photographed*. Mounted frontispiece and 52 mounted photographs. Morocco. New York, 1864. $1,800 (A, 1980).

PERKINS, Frederick B. *Scrope; or, The Lost Library*. Red cloth. Boston, 1874. First edition. $200.

PERKINS, Lucy Fitch. *The Dutch Twins*. Illustrated by the author. Pictorial olive cloth. Boston, 1911. First edition, first issue, with blank end papers. $100–$150. Second issue: Green cloth, pictorial end papers. $50–$75.

PERLES, Alfred. *Reunion in Big Sur*. Wrappers. London, 1959. First edition. One of 25 signed. $75. Ordinary copies: $20.

PERRY, Oliver Hazard. *Hunting Expeditions of Oliver Hazard Perry*. 3 plates. Cloth. Cleveland, 1899. First edition. One of 100. $750–$1,000.

PERSE, St. J. *Anabasis*. French and English texts. Translated by T. S. Eliot. Blue-green cloth. London, 1930. (By Alexis St. Leger Leger.) First edition in English. In white dust jacket. $35–$50. Another issue: Green cloth. One of 350 signed by Eliot. In cellophane dust jacket. Boxed. $500–$650. Second trade issue: London, 1930 (actually 1937). Green cloth. In green dust jacket. $35–$50. New York, (1938). Black cloth. First American edition (second edition, revised). In dust jacket. $35–$50.

PERSE, St. John. *Rains (Pluies)*. Translated by Denis Devlin. Wrappers. Sewanee, Tenn., 1945. (By Alexis St. Leger Leger.) First edition in English. One of 75 signed. $125.

PERSONAL Reminiscences of a Maryland Soldier. Cloth. Baltimore, 1898. (By G. W. Booth.) First edition. $150.

PETER Parley's Universal History. Maps and engravings. 2 vols., black cloth. Boston, 1837. (Compiled by Nathaniel Hawthorne and his sister Elizabeth.) First edition, with "Great Tree" design in gilt on covers. $1,000–$1,500.

PETER Pilgrim; or a Rambler's Recollections. 2 vols., green or purple muslin, paper labels. Philadelphia, 1838. (By Robert Montgomery Bird.) First edition. $350–$450.

PETERS, DeWitt C. *Kit Carson's Life*. Illustrated. Cloth. Hartford, 1874. $125. Hartford, 1875. Cloth. $75–$100. London, (about 1875). Cloth. $75–$100. (Note: This is an enlarged version of the title following.)

PETERS, DeWitt C. *The Life and Adventures of Kit Carson, the Nestor of the Rocky Mountains*. 10 plates. Cloth. New York, 1858. First edition. $150–$200. New York, 1859. Cloth. $100–$125.

PETERS, Fred J. *Railroad, Indian and Pioneer Prints by N. Currier and Currier and Ives. Clipper Ship Prints. Sporting Prints*. Illustrated. 3 vols., cloth. New York, 1930. Limited edition. Boxed. $150–$200.

PETERS, Harry T. *America on Stone: A Chronicle of American Lithography*. 154 plates, 18 in color. Cloth. Garden City, 1931. First edition. One of 751. Boxed. $800–$1,200. Also, $550 and $600 (A, 1980).

PETERS, Harry T. *California on Stone*. 112 plates. Cloth. Garden City, 1935. First edition. One of 501. In dust jacket. Boxed. $800–$1,000. Also, $450 (A, 1980).

PETERS, Harry T. *Currier and Ives, Printmakers to the American People*. 300 reproductions (including color). 2 vols., cloth. Garden City, 1929–31. First edition. One of 510. In dust jackets. $800–$1,000. Garden City, 1942. Cloth. Special edition in one volume. In dust jacket. $50–$60.

PETERSEN, Carl. *Each in Its Ordered Place: A Faulkner Collector's Notebook*. Green morocco-grained cloth. Ann Arbor, (1975). First edition, first printing. (1,000 copies.) In dust jacket. $100–$150. Second printing (falsely identified on copyright page as "first printing"). Orange cloth, sepia end papers (instead of green as in true first printing); text on different paper from first printing, and with better clarity in illustrations. (400 printed.) Issued without dust jacket. $75–$100.

PETERSEN, William J. *Steamboating on the Upper Mississippi*. Decorated cloth. Iowa City, 1937. First edition. $60–$80.

PETITION of the Latter-Day Saints, Commonly Known as Mormons (The). (Caption title.) 13 pp., sewed. Washington, 1840. (By Elias Higbee, Robert B. Thompson, and others.) $100–$125.

PETTER, Rodolphe. *English-Cheyenne Dictionary*. Folio, full black calf. Kettle Falls, Wash., 1913–15. First edition. One of 100. $200–$225.

PHAIR, Charles. *Atlantic Salmon Fishing*. Edited by Richard C. Hunt. Illustrated. Folio, cloth. New York, (1937). Derrydale Press. One of 950. In dust jacket. $300–$400.

Another issue: 2 vols., half morocco. One of 40 signed, with portfolio of mounted flies. $7,500–$10,000.

PHELPS'S Traveller's Guide Through the United States. Folding map. Leather. New York, 1838. (By Humphrey Phelps.) First edition. $500–$750. New York, 1847. Third edition. $650. New York, 1852. $300 (A, 1978).

PHELPS, Noah A. *A History of the Copper Mines and Newgate Prison, at Granby, Conn.* 34 pp., wrappers. Hartford, 1845. $100–$150.

PHELPS, William D. See Webfoot (pseudonym).

PHILBY, H. St. J. B. *A Pilgrim in Arabia.* Portrait. Buckram, leather spine. London, 1943. Golden Cockerel Press. One of 350. $500–$600.

PHILIP Dru, Administrator. Cloth. New York, 1919. (By Col. E. M. House.) First edition. In dust jacket. $125–$150.

PHILLIPS, D. L. *Letters from California.* Cloth. Springfield, Ill., 1877. First edition. $125–$150.

PHILLIPS, Philip A. S. *Paul de Lamerie, Citizen and Goldsmith of London.* Illustrated. Folio, cloth. London, 1935. One of 250. $500–$600.

PHILLIPS, Sir Richard. *Modern London.* Folding frontispiece, folding map, 31 colored plates of "Cries of London" with gray borders. Half calf. London, 1804. $1,500–$2,000.

PHILLPOTTS, Eden. *Children of the Mist.* Frontispiece. Blue cloth. London, 1898. First edition, first printing with the "8" present on page 48. $100–$125.

PHILLPOTTS, Eden. *A Dish of Apples.* Illustrations, including color, by Arthur Rackham. White cloth. London, (1921). One of 500, signed. $800–$1,000. Another issue: One of 55 on Batchelor's Kelmscott paper. $1,500–$1,750. Trade edition: Cloth. $200–$250.

PHILLPOTTS, Eden. *The Girl and the Faun.* Illustrated by Frank Brangwyn. Half vellum. London, 1916. One of 350 signed. $300–$400. Trade edition: Cloth. In dust jacket. $125–$150.

PHILLPOTTS, Eden. *My Adventure in the Flying Scotsman.* Colored cloth. London, 1888. First edition, first issue. $200. Author's first book.

PHOTOGRAPHIC Sketch Book of the War. 100 gold-toned albumen prints, with leaf of text for each. 2 vols., oblong folio, morocco. Washington, (1865–66). (By Alexander Gardner.) First edition. $15,000–$20,000. Also, $13,000 (A, 1979).

PHYLOS the Tibetan. *An Earth Dweller's Return.* Illustrated. Cloth. Milwaukee, 1940. (By Frederick S. Oliver.) First edition. $50–$75.

PICKETT, Albert James. *History of Alabama, and Incidentally of Georgia and Mississippi.* Map, 3 plans, 8 plates. 2 vols., cloth. Charleston, 1851. First edition. $200–$300. Second edition, same place and date. $125–$200.

PICKETT, Albert James. *Invasion of the Territory of Alabama, by 1,000 Spaniards, Under Ferdinand de Soto, in 1540.* 41 pp., wrappers. Montgomery, 1849. First edition. $300–$350.

PICKTHALL, Marmaduke. *Said the Fisherman.* Cloth. London, 1903. First edition. $150. Author's first book.

PICTORIAL View of California (A). By a Returned Californian. 48 plates. Cloth. New York, 1853. (By J. M. Letts.) Later edition of *California Illustrated.* $400–$600.

PIGAFETTA, Antonio. *Magellan's Voyage Around the World.* Portrait, maps, facsimiles. 3 vols., cloth. Cleveland, 1906. One of 350. $150–$200. New Haven, 1969. 2 vols., folio, cloth. $200–$225.

PIGMAN, Walter Griffith. *Journal*. Edited by Ulla Staley Fawkes. Boards. Mexico, Mo., 1942. First edition. One of 200. $50–$75.

PIGS Is Pigs. Decorated oyster-white wrappers. Chicago, 1905. Railways Appliances Company. (By Ellis Parker Butler.) First edition. $400–$450. (Note: Author's name appears only on decoration at first text page.).

PIKE, Albert. *Prose Sketches and Poems, Written in the Western Country*. Brown cloth, leather label. Boston, 1834. First edition. $1,000–$1,500.

PIKE, Corp. (James). *The Scout and Ranger*. Portrait, 24 plates. Black cloth. Cincinnati, 1865. First edition, first issue, with errata leaf and uncorrected errors. $600–$800. Second issue, without errata leaf. $400–$500.

PIKE County Puzzle, Vol. 1, No. 1. 4 pp. (Burlesque of country newspaper.) Camp Interlaken, Pa., 1894. (By Stephen Crane.) $150 and up.

PIKE, Z. M. *An Account of Expeditions to the Sources of the Mississippi*. Portrait, 4 maps, 2 charts, 3 tables. 2 vols., boards. Philadelphia, 1810. First edition. $1,500–$1,750. Another issue: Maps in separate cloth atlas-folder. $2,500–$3,500.

PIKE, Z. M. *An Account of a Voyage up the Mississippi River*. Map. 68 pp., stitched, plain wrappers. (Washington, 1807?) (By Nicholas King from Pike's notes?) First edition. $1,500–$2,000. Also, $1,100 (A, 1967).

PIKE, Z. M. *Exploratory Travels Through the Western Territories of North America*. 2 maps. Boards. London, 1811. First English edition (of *An Account of Expeditions to the Sources of the Mississippi*). $1,500–$2,000. Also, rebound in modern cloth, $880 (A, 1980).

PILCHER, Joshua. *Report on the Fur Trade and Inland Trade to Mexico*. Cloth. Washington, 1832. First edition. $150–$200.

PILGRIM, Thomas. See Morecamp, Arthur.

PILOT (The): A Tale of the Sea. By the Author of *The Pioneers*. 2 vols., blue boards, paper labels. New York, 1823. (By James Fenimore Cooper.) First edition. $400–$600. London, 1824. 3 vols., boards. First English edition. $300–$500. New York, 1968. Limited Editions Club. $35–$45.

PILOT Knob. Mendota. Map, portrait, and plates. 23 pp., pictorial wrappers. (St. Paul, 1887.) (By Gen. H. H. Sibley.) First edition. $100–$125.

PINDAR. *Odes of Victory*. Translated by C. J. Billson. 90 wood engravings by John Farleigh. 2 vols., limp vellum with ties, lettered in gold on front covers and spines. Stratford, England, 1928. Shakespeare Head Press. 2 vols., folio boards. One of 250. $150–$200. Stratford, 1930. Vellum. One of 7 on vellum. Boxed. $1,500–$2,250.

PINKERTON, A. F. *Jim Cummins: or, The Great Adams Express Robbery*. Illustrated. Pictorial cloth. Chicago, 1887. First edition. $75–$125.

PINKERTON, Allan. *The Detective and the Somnambulist*. Frontispiece. Cloth. Chicago, 1875. First edition, first state, with no mention of this book in ads. $75–$100.

PINKERTON, Allan. *The Expressman and the Detective*. Cloth. Chicago, 1874. First edition. $65–$85.

PINKERTON, Allan. *The Spy of the Rebellion*. Illustrated. Cloth. New York, 1883. First edition. $50–$60.

PINKERTON, Allan. *Tests on Passenger Conductors*. 35 pp., wrappers. Chicago, 1867. First edition. $150–$250. Author's first book.

PINKERTON, Allan. *Thirty Years a Detective*. Illustrated. Cloth. Hartford, 1884. $75.

PINKERTON, William A. *Train Robberies, Train Robbers, and "Hold-up" Men*. Illustrated. Wrappers. Chicago, 1907. First edition. $75–$100. (Note: Adams, in *Six-Guns and Saddle Leather*, lists an undated edition without locating place of publication.)

PINTER, Harold. *The Birthday Party: A Play in Three Acts.* Pictorial wrappers. London, (1959). First edition. $125.

PINTER, Harold. *The Birthday Party and Other Plays.* Cloth. London, (1960). First edition. In dust jacket. $50–$75.

PINTER, Harold. *The Caretaker.* Wrappers. London, (1960). First edition. $150.

PINTER, Harold. *Five Screen Plays.* Cloth. London, 1971. One of 150 signed. In glassine jacket. $75.

PINTER, Harold. *The Homecoming.* Cloth. London, (1965). First edition. In dust jacket. $50–$75. London, 1968. Illustrated. One of 200 signed. Boxed. $250–$400.

PINTER, Harold. *Monologue.* Full leather. London, (1973). First edition. One of 100 signed. Boxed. $100.

PINTER, Harold. *No Man's Land.* Cloth. London, (1975). First edition. One of 150 signed. In acetate jacket. $75–$85.

PINTER, Harold. *Old Times.* Cloth. London, 1971. One of 150 signed. In acetate jacket. $75–$100.

PINTER, Harold. *Poems.* Half red morocco. London, 1968. First edition. One of 200 signed. $75–$85. London, (1971). Half leather. Second edition. One of 100 signed. In acetate dust jacket. $75.

PIONEERING on the Plains. Journey to Mexico in 1848. The Overland Trip to California. (Cover title.) Illustrated. 119 pp., wrappers. (Kaukauna, Wis., 1924.) (By Alexander W. McCoy and others.) First edition. $150–$250.

PIONEERS (The); or, The Sources of the Susquehanna: A Descriptive Tale. By the Author of *Precaution.* 2 vols., tan boards, paper labels. New York, 1823. (By James Fenimore Cooper.) First edition, first issue, with E. B. Clayton imprint in Vol. 1 and with folio 329 at left side of page in Vol. 2. $500–$600. Second issue. $400–$500. London, 1823. 3 vols., boards. First English edition. $300–$400.

PIPER, Watty. *The Little Engine That Could.* Illustrated in color by Lois Lenski. New York, (1930). First edition. $75.

PITMAN, Benn (reporter). *The Assassination of President Lincoln and the Trial of the Conspirators.* Illustrated. Cloth. Cincinnati, 1865. First edition. $75–$100.

PITMAN, Benn (reporter). *The Trials for Treason at Indianapolis.* Illustrated. Cloth. Cincinnati, 1865. First edition. $75–$100.

PITTSBURGH Business Directory. Cloth, paper label. Pittsburgh, 1837. (By Isaac Harris.) With errata leaf. $125–$150.

"PLAIN OR Ringlets?" 13 colored plates. Other illustrations by John Leech. 13 parts in 12, wrappers. London, 1859–60. (By Robert Smith Surtees.) First edition. $500–$650. London, 1860. Pictorial cloth. First book edition. $150–$200.

PLAIN Speaker (The): Opinions on Books, Men, and Things. 2 vols., boards, paper labels. London, 1826. (By William Hazlitt.) First collected edition. $200–$300.

PLATH, Sylvia. See Lucas, Victoria. Also, see *A Winter Ship.*

PLATH, Sylvia. *Ariel.* Cloth. London, (1965). First edition. In dust jacket. $200–$250. New York, (1966). Cloth. First American edition. In dust jacket. $50–$75.

PLATH, Sylvia. *The Colossus.* Cloth. London, (1960). First edition. In dust jacket. $150–$175. Author's first book (aside from the leaflet *A Winter Ship*). New York, 1962. Cloth. First American edition. In dust jacket. $100–$125.

PLATH, Sylvia. *Crystal Gazer and Other Poems.* Vellum, leather, or half buckram. London, 1971. Rainbow Press. One of 400. Boxed. $100–$150.

PLATH, Sylvia. *Fiesta Melons.* Introduction by Ted Hughes. Cloth. Exeter, 1971. First edition. One of 150. In dust jacket. $100. Note: 75 signed by Hughes. $250–$300.

PLATH, Sylvia. *Lyonnesse.* Vellum, leather, or half leather. London, 1971. Rainbow Press. First edition. One of 300. Boxed. $150. Another issue: One of 100 with special manuscript reproductions on end papers. Boxed. $250–$300.

PLATH, Sylvia. *Million Dollar Month.* Stiff wrappers. (Frensham, England, 1971.) First edition. One of 150. $75–$100.

PLATH, Sylvia. *Pursuit.* Drawings and an etching by Leonard Baskin. Morocco. (London),1973. Rainbow Press. One of 100 with signed frontispiece by Baskin. Boxed. $250–$325.

PLATH, Sylvia. *Three Women: A Monologue for Three Voices.* Illustrated. White cloth. (London), 1968. First edition. One of 180 (?) numbered copies. $125–$150. Another issue: Boards and leather. One of 5 on handmade paper. $500–$750.

PLATH, Sylvia. *Uncollected Poems.* Facsimile. Wrappers. (London, 1965.) Turret Books. First edition. One of 150. $200–$250.

PLATH, Sylvia. *Wreath for a Bridal.* Stiff wrappers. (Frensham, 1970.) First edition. One of 100. In tissue dust jacket. $150–$200.

PLATO. *The Phaedo of Plato.* Translated by William Jowett. Title and initials in red Buckram. Waltham Saint Lawrence, England, 1930. Golden Cockerel Press. With letter laid in calling attention to error of translator's name as William instead of Benjamin. $150–$250.

PLATT, P. L., and Slater, N. *The Travelers' Guide Across the Plains, upon the Overland Route to California.* Folding map. 64 pp., printed yellow wrappers. Chicago, 1852. First edition. $7,500–$10,000. San Francisco, 1963. Edited by Dale Morgan. Illustrated. Black boards, orange cloth spine. Second edition. In acetate dust jacket. $50.

PLEASANTS, J. Hall, and Sill, Howard. *Maryland Silversmiths, 1715–1830.* Illustrated. Half cloth. Baltimore, 1930. One of 300. $250–$350.

PLEASANTS, W. J. *Twice Across the Plains, 1849–1856.* 10 plates, 2 portraits. Pictorial green cloth. San Francisco, 1906. First edition. $400–$600.

PLIMPTON, Florus B. *The Lost Child.* (Cover title.) 79 pp., wrappers. Cleveland, 1852. First edition. $200–$300.

PLOMER, William. *Address Given at the Memorial Service for Ian Fleming.* Black cloth, paper label. (London), 1962. First edition. In dust jacket. $50–$75.

PLOMER, William. *The Case Is Altered.* Cloth. London, 1932. Hogarth Press. First edition. In dust jacket. $100–$125.

PLOMER, William. *The Fivefold Screen.* Black cloth. London, 1932. First edition. One of 450 signed. In dust jacket. $100–$125.

PLOMER, William. *Notes for Poems.* Cloth. London, 1927 (actually 1928). Hogarth Press. First edition. In tissue jacket. $125.

PLOMER, William. *Sado.* Orange cloth. London, 1931. First edition. In dust jacket. $50–$60.

PLOMER, William. *Selected Poems.* Cloth. London, (1940). First edition. In dust jacket. $75–$100.

PLOMER, William. *Turbott Wolfe.* Cloth. London, 1925. First edition. $100–$125.

PLUMBE, John, Jr. *Sketches of Iowa and Wisconsin.* Folding map on thin paper. 103 pp., printed wrappers. St. Louis, 1839. First edition. $2,250–$2,500.

POE, Edgar Allan. See *The Narrative of Arthur Gordon Pym; Tamerlane and Other Poems.*

POE, Edgar Allan. *Al Aaraaf, Tamerlane, and Minor Poems.* Blue or reddish-tan boards, ivory paper spine. Baltimore, 1829. First edition. (Some copies misdated 1820 on title page; a few also stitched, without covers.) $50,000 and up. Also, stitched, without covers, $40,000 (A, 1974); boards, $1,600 (A, 1954); $1,100 and $1,250 (A, 1947); stitched, $2,000 (A, 1954) and same copy, $3,100 (A, 1939); "first edition, early issue, bound with 5 others, half roan on marbled boards of circa 1840," $10,000 (A, 1968).

POE, Edgar Allan. *The Bells and Other Poems.* 28 color plates by Edmund Dulac. Folio, decorated vellum with silk ties. London, (about 1912). One of 750 large paper copies, signed by Dulac. $600–$800. Another issue: Cloth. $150–$200.

POE, Edgar Allan. *The Conchologist's First Book.* Illustrated. Printed pictorial boards, leather spine. Philadelphia, 1839. First edition, first state, with snail plates in color. $500–$600. Plates uncolored, $400. Philadelphia, 1840. Boards. Second edition. $200–$250.

POE, Edgar Allan. *Edgar Allan Poe Letters Till Now Unpublished.* Illustrated. Boards. Philadelphia, 1925. First edition. One of 1,500. $75–$100.

POE, Edgar Allan. *Eureka: A Prose Poem.* Black cloth. New York, 1848. First edition, with 12 or 16 pages of ads at end. $400–$500. New York, (about 1928). Facsimile edition of a copy with Poe's own handwritten revisions. One of 50. $75–$100.

POE, Edgar Allan. *The Fall of the House of Usher.* Illustrated by Alastair. Printed wrappers. Paris, 1928. Black Sun Press. One of 300. $250–$350. Maastricht, Holland, 1930. Illustrated. Cloth. $200–$300.

POE, Edgar Allan. *Histoires Extraordinaires.* Par Edgar Poe. Translated by Charles Baudelaire. Wrappers. Paris, 1856. First edition in French of Poe's *Tales.* $1,000–$1,500. Paris, 1857. (As *Nouvelles Histoires Extraordinaires.*) Wrappers. $500–$750. Paris, 1927–28. Etchings. 4 vols., morocco. One of 10 on Hollande paper. (No recent prices noted.)

POE, Edgar Allan. *Histoires Grotesques et Sérieuses.* Translated by Charles Baudelaire. Half leather. Paris, 1865. (No recent prices noted.)

POE, Edgar Allan. *The Journal of Julius Rodman.* Colored illustrations. Half cloth and boards. San Francisco, 1947. Grabhorn printing. One of 500. $50–$75.

POE, Edgar Allan. *La Chute de la Maison Usher.* Translated by Charles Baudelaire. Illustrated. Three-quarters morocco. Paris, 1922. One of 72 on Japan paper. (No recent prices noted.)

POE, Edgar Allan. *Mesmerism: "In Articulo Mortis."* 16 pp., stitched, without covers. London, 1846. First edition. $750–$1,000. Also, $450 (A, 1981).

POE, Edgar Allan. *Murders in the Rue Morgue.* Facsimile of Drexel Institute manuscript. 2 water colors. Folio, half morocco. Philadelphia, (1895). $100–$150. Antibes, (1958). Allen Press. Boards. One of 150. $150–$175. Also see Poe, *The Prose Romances.*

POE, Edgar Allan. *Poems.* Pale-green cloth. New York, 1831. Second edition (so identified on title page, but actually the first edition). $10,000–$15,000. Also, stained, binding detached, $6,250 (A, 1966). London, 1881. Cloth. One of 50 on large paper. $150–$200. Brussels, 188. (sic.—actually 1888). Translated by Mallarmé. Illustrated by Manet. Wrappers. $750–$1,000. Brussels, 1897. Wrappers. One of 500. $200 and up. London, 1900. Illustrated by W. Heath Robinson. $150–$250. New York, 1943. Limited Editions Club. Boxed. $40–$50.

POE, Edgar Allan. *The Prose Romances of Edgar A. Poe, etc. Uniform Serial Edi-*

tion . . . No. 1. Containing the Murders in the Rue Morgue, and The Man That Was Used Up. 40 pp., wrappers. Philadelphia, 1843. First edition. $25,000–$50,000. Also, in facsimile wrappers, $20,000 (A, 1974); in (original?) wrappers, stained and torn, $20,000 (A, 1973). Also, see Poe, *Murders in the Rue Morgue.*

POE, Edgar Allan. *The Raven and Other Poems.* Printed wrappers, or cloth. New York, 1845. First edition, first issue, with "T. B. Smith, Stereotyper" on copyright page. $24,000 (A, 1981). London, 1846. Cloth. First English edition with new title page tipped in over sheets of the American first. $1,000–$1,500. New York, 1884. Edited by E. C. Stedman. 26 plates by Gustave Doré. Folio, pictorial cloth. $400–$500. New York, 1906. Illustrated by Galen J. Perrett. Morocco. One of 26. $500–$600. San Francisco, 1907. Illustrated by Perrett. Half leather. In dust jacket. $250–$300.

POE, Edgar Allan. *The Raven and Other Poems. (&) Tales.* 2 vols in one, dark blue cloth. New York, 1845. First edition of each work in the one-volume format; first issue of *The Raven* (see preceding entry) and third issue of *Tales* (see entry following), without stereotyper's slug. $3,000–$4,000.

POE, Edgar Allan. *Some Letters of Edgar Allan Poe to E. H. N. Patterson of Oquawka, Illinois.* Edited by Eugene Field. Folio, cloth. Chicago, 1898. Caxton Club. One of 186. Boxed. $300–$500.Worn copy, $225. (Note: Poe reportedly sent about five copies of his *Murders in the Rue Morgue* to this rural Illinois friend. They have never been found.)

POE, Edgar Allan. *Tales.* Printed buff wrappers, or cloth. New York, 1845. First edition, first state, with T. B. Smith and H. Ludwig slugs on copyright page, 12 pp. of ads at back. $15,000 and up. Also, rebound in morocco, $10,000 in a 1980 catalogue.

POE, Edgar Allan. *Tales of the Grotesque and Arabesque.* 2 vols., purplish cloth, paper labels. Philadelphia, 1840. First edition, first issue, with page 213 in Vol. 2 wrongly numbered 231. $10,000–$15,000. Second issue, page 213 correctly numbered. $5,000–$10,000. Another issue: 2 vols. in one. Page 213 correctly numbered, 4 pages of ads bound in at end. $10,000–$15,000. Also, in contemporary leather, $5,000 (A, 1967). Chicago, 1930. Lakeside Press. Full morocco. One of 1,000. $150–$200.

POE, Edgar Allan. *Tales of Mystery and Imagination.* Illustrated by Harry Clarke. Pictorial vellum. London, 1919. One of 170 signed by Clarke. $1,000–$1,500. London, (1935). Illustrated by Arthur Rackham. Full pictorial vellum. One of 460 signed by Rackham. $1,500–$2,000. Also, $1,500 (A, 1981). London, (1935). Cloth. First trade edition. In dust jacket. $500–$600. Also, $450 (A, 1981). New York, 1941. Limited Editions Club. $50–$60.

POEMS. Wrappers. (London, 1906.) Chiswick Press. (By Siegfried Sassoon.) First edition. $500 and up. Also, inscribed, $2,743 (A, 1975). Author's first book. London, (1911). Wrappers. One of 35 signed. $500–$750.

POEMS and Ballads of Young Ireland. White cloth. Dublin, 1888. First edition. $250–$300. (Note: Contains four contributions by William Butler Yeats.)

POEMS By Two Brothers. Drab boards, paper label. London, (1827). (By Alfred, Charles and Frederick Tennyson.) First edition. $1,250–$1,500. Also, rubbed, $770 (A, 1977); spine split, $1,000 (A, 1974). Alfred Tennyson's first book. London, 1893. Cloth. One of 300. $200–$250.

POEMS Chiefly in the Scottish Dialect. By a Native of Scotland. Contemporary calf. Washington, Pa., 1801. (By David Bruce.) First edition. $400–500. (Note: Contains original material also by H. H. Brackenridge.)

POEMS from the Arabic and Persian. Sewed. Warwick, England, 1800. (By Walter Savage Landor.) First edition, first issue, with "Rivington" in imprint and 10 leaves only. $200–$250. Second issue, without "Rivington" in imprint, 12 leaves. $150–$200.

POEMS of Child Labor. Wrappers. New York, 1924. First edition. $75–$100. (Note: Published by the National Child Labor Committee; includes a poem by Robert Frost.)

POEMS of Two Friends. Brown cloth. Columbus, Ohio, 1860. (By William Dean Howells and John J. Piatt.) First edition. $500–$750. Howells' first book.

POEMS on Various Occasions. Gray-green boards, pink label lettered "Poems." Newark, (England), 1807. (By George Gordon Noel, Lord Byron.) First edition. $1,000 and up.

POET at the Breakfast-Table (The). Cloth. Boston, 1872. (By Oliver Wendell Holmes.) First edition, first state, with "Talle" for "Table" in the running head on page 9. $100–$150.

POETRY by the Author of "Gebir." 111 pp., sewed. Warwick, England, (1800). (By Walter Savage Landor.) First edition, with pages 65–111, later suppressed, intact. $500 and up. London, 1802. Blue wrappers. First published edition, first issue, with Sharpe's imprint stamped by hand on page 64, where the text ends. $200 and up.

POETRY for Children, Entirely Original. Illustrated. 2 vols., green boards, red leather spines. London, 1809. (By Charles and Mary Lamb.) First edition. $10,000 or more (?). (Note: A very rare book, with auction records of $2,200 in 1900 and $3,300 in 1920, and $375 in 1941. A defective copy with title leaf in Vol. 2 from another copy brought $620 at auction in 1976, but no fine copies have appeared for sale in many years.) Boston, 1812. Boards. First American edition. $500–$600.

POET'S PACK (The), Of George Washington High School. By Members of The Poetry Club and the Poetry Class, 1927–1931. Cloth. New York, 1932. Contains first four book-published poems by Delmore Schwartz. First edition. $50–$75.

POLK, James K. *Message of the President of the United States in Relation to the Indian Difficulties in Oregon . . . March 29, 1848.* (Caption title.) (Washington, 1848.) $50–$75.

POLLARD, Alfred W. *An Essay on Colophons.* Folio, half vellum. Chicago, 1905. Caxton Club. One of 252. Boxed. $150–$200.

POLLARD, Alfred W. *Fine Books.* 40 plates. Cloth. London, 1912. First edition. In dust jacket. $75–$100. New York, 1912. Plates. Cloth. First American edition. In dust jacket. $100–$125.

POLLARD, Alfred W. *Last Words on the History of the Title-Page.* Colored frontispiece and facsimiles. Folio, buckram. London, 1891. One of 260. $100–$125.

POLLARD, Alfred W. *Records of the English Bible.* Cloth. London, 1911. First edition. $100–$125.

POLLARD, Alfred W. *Shakespeare Folios and Quartos.* Illustrated. Boards. London, 1909. First edition. $150–$175.

POLLARD, Alfred W., and others. *Cobden-Sanderson and the Doves Press.* Folio, vellum. San Francisco, 1929. John Henry Nash printing. First edition. One of 27. $1,500.

POLLARD, Edward A. *The First Year of the War.* 374 pp., printed wrappers. Richmond, 1862. First edition. $150–$200.

POLLARD, Edward A. *The Lost Cause.* Folding map in color. New York, 1867. First edition. $50–$75.

POLLARD, Edward A. *Observations in the North.* 142 pp., wrappers. Richmond, 1865. First edition. $400–$500.

POLLARD, Edward A. *The Seven Days' Battles in Front of Richmond.* 45 pp., printed wrappers. Richmond, 1862. First edition. $400–$500.

POLLARD, Edward A. *The Southern Spy.* 103 pp., wrappers. Richmond, 1861. First edition. $400–$500.

POLLARD, Hugh B. C. *A History of Firearms.* Illustrated. Cloth. London, 1926. $150–$200. London, 1930. $150. London, 1933. $150.

POLLARD, Hugh B. C., and Barclay-Smith, Phyllis. *British and American Game-Birds.* Illustrated. Half leather. New York, 1939. Derrydale Press. First edition. One of 125. $400–$500. London, 1945. Half leather. $200–$250.

POLLEY, J. B. *Hood's Texas Brigade.* 25 plates. Cloth. New York, 1910. First edition. $350–$450.

POLLEY, J. B. *A Soldier's Letters to Charming Nellie.* 16 plates. Cloth. New York, 1908. First edition. $200–$250.

POLLOCK, J. M. *The Unvarnished West: Ranching As I Found It.* Illustrated. Pictorial cloth. London, (1911). First edition. $300–$350.

POLONIUS: A Collection of Wise Saws and Modern Instances. Green cloth. London, 1852. (By Edward Fitz Gerald.) First edition. $100–$150.

POOLE, Ernest. *The Harbor.* New York, 1915. First edition. In dust jacket. $35–$50.

POOLE, Ernest. *Katharine Breshovsky: For Russia's Freedom.* Pictorial wrappers. Chicago, 1905. First edition. $75–$100. Author's first book.

POOR, M. C. *Denver, South Park and Pacific.* Illustrated, with map in pocket. Cloth. Denver, 1949. First edition. One of 1,000 signed. In dust jacket. $350–$400.

POOR Sarah. 18 pp., sewed. (Park Hill, Indian Territory, Oklahoma), 1943. Park Hill Mission Press. $100 and up. (Note: Originally this story of "a pious Indian woman" was a publication of the American Tract Society of New York.)

POORE, Ben Perley. *A Descriptive Catalogue of the Government Publications of the United States.* Cloth. Washington, 1885. $100–$125. New York, 1962. 2 vols., cloth. $100–$125.

POPE, Alexander. *The Rape of the Lock.* Illustrated by Aubrey Beardsley. Cloth. London, 1896. $400–$500.

POPE, Saxton. *Hunting with the Bow and Arrow.* Illustrated. Boards and cloth. (San Francisco, 1923.) First edition. $75–$100.

POPERY, British and Foreign. Printed wrappers. London, 1851. (By Walter Savage Landor.) First edition. $150.

PORCHER, Francis P. *Resources of the Southern Fields and Forests, Medical, Economical, and Agricultural, Being Also a Medical Botany of the Confederate States.* Half leather. Charleston, 1863. First edition. $750–$1,000.

PORTALIS, Baron Roger (editor). *Researches Concerning Jean Grolier, His Life and His Library.* Illustrated. Three-quarters morocco. New York, 1907. Grolier Club. One of 300. Boxed. $200–$250.

PORTER, Edwin H. *The Fall River Tragedy.* Plates. Cloth. Fall River, Mass., 1893. First edition. $250–$300.

PORTER, Eleanor H. *Pollyanna.* Illustrated. Pink silk cloth. Boston, 1913. First edition. $300–$400. London, 1913. Blue cloth, pictorial cover label. First English edition. $50–$75.

PORTER, Gene Stratton. *Birds of the Bible.* Illustrated. Pictorial cloth. Cincinnati, (1909). First edition. $100–$135.

PORTER, Gene Stratton. *Friends in Feathers.* Pictorial cloth. Garden City, 1917. First edition. $75–$85.

PORTER, Gene Stratton. *The Keeper of the Bees.* Pictorial cloth. Garden City, 1925. First edition. In dust jacket. $75–$100.

PORTER, Gene Stratton. *Laddie: A True-Blue Story.* 4 color plates. Cloth. New York, 1913. First edition. In dust jacket. $100–$150.

PORTER, Gene Stratton. *The Song of the Cardinal.* Illustrated by the author's camera studies. Buckram. Indianapolis, (1903). First edition. $150–$200. Author's first book.

PORTER, Jane. *The Scottish Chiefs: A Romance.* 5 vols., boards. London, 1810. First edition with errata leaf at end of Vol. 1. $600–$800.

PORTER, Katherine Anne. See F., M. T.

PORTER, Katherine Anne. *A Christmas Story.* Illustrated by Ben Shahn. Oblong cloth. New York, (1967). One of 500 signed by both author and artist. Boxed. $75–$85.

PORTER, Katherine Anne. *The Collected Essays and Occasional Writings of Katherine Anne Porter.* Frontispiece portrait in color. Half leather. New York, (1970). First edition. One of 250 signed. $75–$100.

PORTER, Katherine Anne. *Flowering Judas.* Boards and cloth. New York, (1930). First edition. One of 600. In glassine dust jacket. $200–$250. New York, (1935). Cloth. First augmented edition, first printing. In dust jacket. $40–$60.

PORTER, Katherine Anne. *French Song Book.* Blue boards and cloth. (Paris), 1933. First edition. One of 595 signed. In dust jacket. $300. Another issue: One of 15 on Spanish paper, signed. $400–$500.

PORTER, Katherine Anne. *Hacienda.* Cloth. (New York, 1934.) First edition. One of 895. With errata slip. Boxed. $150–$225. (Most copies signed.)

PORTER, Katherine Anne. *The Leaning Tower and Other Stories.* Cloth. New York, (1944). First edition. In dust jacket. $50–$60.

PORTER, Katherine Anne. *Noon Wine.* Decorated boards, paper label. Detroit, 1937. First edition. One of 250 signed. Boxed. $150–$250.

PORTER, Katherine Anne. *Outline of Mexican Popular Arts and Crafts.* Cloth. (Los Angeles), 1922. First edition. $500–$600.

PORTER, Katherine Anne. *Pale Horse, Pale Rider.* Light-blue cloth. New York, (1939). First edition, first printing. In dust jacket. $50–$75.

PORTER, Katherine Anne. *Selected Short Stories.* Wrappers. (New York, 1945.) Armed Services Edition. $35–$50.

PORTER, Katherine Anne (translator). *The Itching Parrot.* By José Joaquín Fernández de Lizardi. Cloth. Garden City, 1942. First edition. In dust jacket. $50.

PORTER, Lavinia Honeyman. *By Ox Team to California.* Portrait. Cloth. Oakland, 1910. First edition. One of 50. $450–$600.

PORTER, William Sidney (Or, later, Sydney). See Henry, O.

PORTRAIT and Biographical Album of Henry County, Iowa. Three-quarters leather. Chicago, 1888. $125–$150.

PORTRAIT and Biographical Album of Jo Daviess County, Illinois. Three-quarters leather. Chicago, 1889. $125–$150.

PORTRAIT and Biographical Album of Otoe and Cass Counties, Nebraska. Three-quarters leather. Chicago, 1889. $150–$175.

PORTRAIT and Biographical Album of Will County, Illinois. Three-quarters leather. Chicago, 1890. $100–$125.

PORTRAIT and Biographical Record of Denver and Vicinity. Leather. Chicago, 1898. $350.

PORTRAIT and Biographical Record of Dickinson, Saline, McPherson and Marion Counties, Kansas. Three-quarters leather. Chicago, 1893. $150–$175.

PORTRAIT and Biographical Record of Sheboygan County, Wisconsin. Three-quarters leather. Chicago, 1894. $100–$125.

POSEY, Alex. *The Poems of Alex Posey, Creek Indian Poet.* Arranged by Mrs. Minnie Posey. Cloth. Topeka, 1910. First edition. $35–$50.

POSNER, David. *Love as Image.* Wrappers. London, 1952. First edition. One of 150. $75–$100.

POSNER, David. *A Rake's Progress.* 17 plates. Half cloth. London, (1967). First edition, with errata leaf. $150–$200.

POSNER, David. *S'un Casto Amor.* Wrappers. Oxford, 1953. First edition. One of 30. $150.

POST, Melville Davisson. *The Corrector of Destinies.* Cloth. New York, (1908). First edition. In dust jacket. $500–$600. Lacking jacket, $300.

POST, Melville Davisson. *Uncle Abner.* Blue cloth. New York, 1918. First edition. $400–$500. (More with a dust jacket, which we've never seen.)

POSTON, Charles D. *Apache Land.* Portrait and views. Cloth. San Francisco, 1878. First edition. $125–$175.

POSTON, Charles D. *Speech of the Hon. Charles D. Poston, of Arizona, on Indian Affairs.* 20 pp., printed wrappers. New York, 1865. $750–$850.

POSTSCRIPT to the Statement Respecting the Earl of Selkirk's Settlement Upon the Red River, in North America. (Caption title.) 28 pp. (195–222), plain wrappers. (Montreal, 1818.) (By John Halkett.) $500–$750. Also, $450 (A, 1969).

POTT, J. S. *A Plain Statement of Fact, etc.* (Claims of Florida inhabitants against British forces.) 16 pp., half morocco. London, 1838. $200–$250.

POTTER, Beatrix. *Ginger and Pickles.* Illustrated by the author. Pictorial boards. London, 1909. First edition. $125–$150. New York, 1909. Boards. First American edition. $75–$100.

POTTER, Beatrix. *Peter Rabbit's Almanac for 1929.* 13 color plates. Tan boards. New York, 1928. First American edition. $150–$175.

POTTER, Beatrix. *The Pie and the Patty-Pan.* Illustrated in color by the author. Pictorial cloth. London, 1905. First edition. $200. New York, 1905. Illustrated. Boards. $75–$100.

POTTER, Beatrix. *The Roly-Poly Pudding.* Illustrated in color by the author. Cloth. London, (1908). First edition. $150–$250.

POTTER, Beatrix. *The Story of a Fierce Bad Rabbit.* Illustrated by the author. Panoramic wallet-style cloth binding. London, 1906. First edition. $250–300.

POTTER, Beatrix. *The Story of Miss Moppet.* Illustrated by the author. Panoramic wallet-style cloth. London, 1906. First edition. $250–$300.

POTTER, Beatrix. *The Tailor of Gloucester.* Frontispiece, 15 color illustrations by the author. Pink boards, rounded spine. (London, 1902.) First trade edition, with misprints on pages 26 and 34. $500 and up. Also, $420 (A, 1977). Another edition, privately printed: (London, 1902.) Limited to 500. $900 and up.

POTTER, Beatrix. *The Tale of Benjamin Bunny.* Illustrated in color by the author. Cloth. London, 1904. First edition. $150–$250.

POTTER, Beatrix. *The Tale of the Flopsy Bunnies.* Illustrated in color by the author. Boards. London, 1909. First edition. $150–$200.

POTTER, Beatrix. *The Tale of Jemima Puddle-Duck.* Color plates. Cloth. London, 1908. First edition. $250–$300.

POTTER, Beatrix. *The Tale of Little Pig Robinson.* 6 color plates. Boards. Philadelphia, (1930). First American edition. $175.

POTTER, Beatrix. *The Tale of Mrs. Tiggy-Winkle.* Frontispiece and 26 colored illustrations by the author. Boards. London, 1905. First edition. $150–$200.

POTTER, Beatrix. *The Tale of Mrs. Tittlemouse.* Color plates. Boards. London, 1910. First edition. $150–$200.

POTTER, Beatrix. *The Tale of Peter Rabbit.* Colored frontispiece, 41 illustrations in black and white by the author. Boards, flat spine. London, (1901). First edition; with copyright undated (privately printed). One of 250. $2,000 and up. Also, $1,840 (A, 1977). (London), 1902. Boards, rounded spine. First edition, second issue (also privately printed). One of 200. $1,250 and up. London, 1902. First published edition (trade edition). $300–$400. Also, $200 (A, 1977).

POTTER, Beatrix. *The Tale of Pigling Bland.* Illustrated in color by the author. Boards. London, 1913. First edition. $150–$200.

POTTER, Beatrix. *The Tale of Timmy Tiptoes.* Illustrated. Boards. London, 1911. First edition. $200–$250.

POTTER, Beatrix. *Wag-by-Wall.* Illustrated. Cloth. London, 1944. One of 100. In dust jacket. $350–$500.

PORTER, Jack. *Cattle Trails of the Old West.* Illustrated, folding map. Wrappers. Clayton, N. M., (1935). First edition. $100–$125. Clayton, (1939). Enlarged edition. $50–$75.

POTTER, Jack. *Lead Steer and Other Tales.* Illustrated. Pictorial wrappers. Clayton, N.M., 1939. First edition. $100–$125.

POTTER, Theodore Edgar. *Autobiography.* Portraits. Cloth. (Concord, N.H., 1913.) First edition. $125–$150.

POTTLE, Frederick A. *Boswell and the Girl from Botany Bay.* Boards and cloth. New York, 1937. One of 500. In dust jacket. $35–$50

POTTLE, Frederick A. *The Literary Career of James Boswell.* Cloth. Oxford, 1929. First edition. In dust jacket. $50–$60.

POUND, Ezra. See P., E.; Bosschere, Jean de; Cavalcanti, Guido; Fenollosa, Ernest; Thornton, Richard. Also, see *The Book of the Poets' Club; The Catholic Anthology; Des Imagistes.*

POUND, Ezra. *A Lume Spento.* Green wrappers. (Venice), 1908. First edition. $7,500–$10,000. Also, an inscribed and corrected presentation copy, $18,000 (A, 1977). Author's first book. Milan, (1958). Stiff gray wrappers. One of 2,000. In dust jacket. $50. (New York, 1965.) First American edition. $35.

POUND, Ezra. *ABC of Reading.* Red cloth. London, 1934. First edition. In dust jacket. $200–$300. New Haven, 1934. Green cloth. First American edition. In dust jacket. $150–$175.

POUND, Ezra. *Antheil and the Treatise on Harmony.* Red wrappers. Paris, 1924. Three Mountains Press. First edition. One of 40 on Arches paper. $500–$600. Also, $375 (A, 1977). Ordinary issue: One of 560. $250–$300. Chicago, 1927. Brown cloth. First American edition. In dust jacket. $50–$75.

POUND, Ezra. *Antologia.* Wrappers. Rome, 1956. One of 100. $150–$200.

POUND, Ezra. *Canto CX.* Frontispiece drawing of Pound. Wrappers. (Cambridge, 1965.) First edition. One of 80. $100–$150.

POUND, Ezra. *Cantos LII-LXXI.* Black cloth. London, (1940). First edition. In dust jacket. $100–$150. Norfolk, (1940). Black cloth. First American edition. One of 500 with envelope and pamphlet, *Notes on Ezra Pound's Cantos, Structure and Rhetoric.* $75–$100. Another issue: One of 500 without the envelope. $50–$60.

POUND, Ezra. *Canzoni.* Gray cloth. London, 1911. First edition, first binding. $200–$300.

POUND, Ezra, *Canzoni & Ripostes.* Brown boards, London, 1913. (First edition sheets of *Canzoni and Ripostes* bound with new title page and half title.) $100–$150.

POUND, Ezra. *Carta da Visita.* Decorated wrappers. (Rome), 1942. First edition. $100–$150.

POUND, Ezra. *Diptych Rome-London,* Folio, boards. (Norfolk, 1957—actually 1958.) New Directions. One of 125 signed. Boxed. $600–$750. (London, 1957, i.e. 1958). Faber & Faber. One of 50 signed. $400–$500. Milan, (1957, i.e. 1958). One of 25 signed. $400–$500. (These books were issued simultaneously as part of a total edition of 200 produced at the Officina Bodoni in Verona, Italy.)

POUND, Ezra. *A Draft of the Cantos 17-27.* Initials by Gladys Hynes. Folio, red vellum boards. London, 1928. First edition. One of 70 on Roma paper. $1,000–$1,500. Also, $950 (A, 1977). (There were also 4 copies on vellum signed by the author and the artist, 5 on Japan paper, signed by Pound, 15 on Whatman paper. The 15 on Whatman paper were bound in green vellum, the others being variously bound or unbound, according to the Pound bibliographer Donald M. Gallup.)

POUND, Ezra. *A Draft of XVI Cantos.* Three-quarters white vellum and boards (later in red vellum). Paris, 1925. First edition. One of 70 on Roma paper (of an edition of 90). $2,750–$3,250. Another issue: One of 15 on Whatman paper. $3,000 and up. (A few copies were in folded, gathered, unbound sheets. There were also 5 copies on Japan paper, signed by Pound. One was offered in a 1980 catalogue at $7,500.)

POUND, Ezra. *A Draft of XXX Cantos.* Beige linen. Paris, 1930. Hours Press. One of 200. $1,000–$1,500. Also, $1,200 (A, 1980). Another issue: Red-orange leather. One of 10 on Texas Mountain paper, signed. $2,750 (A, 1977). (Note: There were also 2 on vellum for Pound.) New York, (1933). Black cloth. First American edition. In dust jacket. $200–$300. London, (1933). Black cloth. First English edition. In dust jacket. $150–$200.

POUND, Ezra. *Drafts and Fragments of Cantos CX-CXVII.* Folio, red cloth, paper labels; New York, (1968). New Directions and Stone Wall Press. First edition. With errata slip. One of 310 signed. Boxed. $300–$400. Also, $275 (A, 1980); $300 (A, 1977). New York, 1968. Cloth. Trade edition. In dust jacket. $25. London, (1970). Cloth. $25.

POUND, Ezra. *Exultations.* Maroon boards. London, 1909. First edition. $200–$250. Also, $200 (A, 1977).

POUND, Ezra. *The Fifth Decad of Cantos.* Black cloth. London, (1937). First edition. In dust jacket. $175–$200. New York, (1937). Black cloth. First American edition. In dust jacket. $50–$75.

POUND, Ezra. *Gaudier-Brzeska: A Memoir.* Illustrated. Gray-green cloth. London, 1916. First edition. $150–$200. American issue: Olive green cloth. $100–$150. London, (1939). Green cloth. $100–$125. Milan, (1957). Wrappers. First state, with "Episten" uncorrected. $50–$75.

POUND, Ezra. *Homage to Sextus Propertius.* Blue boards. London, (1934). First separate edition. In dust jacket. $150–$200.

POUND, Ezra. *How to Read.* Red cloth, stamped in silver. London, (1931). First edition, first binding. In dust jacket. $125–$150. Paris, (1932). Wrappers. $200–$225.

POUND, Ezra. *Imaginary Letters.* Stiff printed white wrappers. Paris, 1930. Black Sun Press. First edition. One of 300. In glassine dust jacket. Boxed. $200–$250. Another issue: One of 50 on vellum, signed. Boxed. $500–$750. (There were also 25 copies not for sale.)

POUND, Ezra. *Indiscretions; or, Une Revue de Deux Mondes.* Gray boards and yellow cloth. Paris, 1923. Three Mountains Press. First edition. (300 printed.) $1,000.

POUND, Ezra. *Instigations.* Blue cloth. New York, (1920). First edition. In dust jacket. $150–$200.

POUND, Ezra. *Lustra.* Frontispiece portrait. Tan cloth. (London, 1916.) First edition. One of 200. $750–$850. London, 1916. Tan cloth. Second impression, with altered text. $100–$125. New York, 1917. Blue cloth. First American edition. One of 60. In dust jacket. $500–$600. Second impression: Yellow boards. In dust jacket. $400.

POUND, Ezra. *Make it New: Essays.* Green cloth. London, (1934). First edition. In dust jacket. $200–$250. New Haven, 1935. Tan cloth. First American edition. In dust jacket. $100–$150.

POUND, Ezra. *Pavannes and Divisions.* Frontispiece. Dark-blue cloth. New York, 1918. First edition, first binding. In dust jacket. $150. Later binding, gray cloth, same date. In dust jacket. $80–$100.

POUND, Ezra. *Personae.* Drab boards, London, 1909. First edition, first issue (with binding as described). $300–$400. New York, 1926. Dark blue cloth. First American edition. In dust jacket. $350.

POUND, Ezra. *Personae and Exultations.* Boards, London, 1913. First (combined) edition. In glassine dust jacket. $100–$150.

POUND, Ezra. *The Pisan Cantos.* Black cloth. (New York, 1948.) First edition. In dust jacket. $150–$200. London, (1949). Black cloth. First English edition. In dust jacket. $50.

POUND, Ezra. *Poems 1918–1921, Including Three Portraits and Four Cantos.* Boards and vellum. New York, (1921). First edition. In dust jacket. $250–$300.

POUND, Ezra. *Polite Essays.* Red cloth. London, (1937). First edition. In dust jacket. $100–$150. Norfolk, no date. First American edition. In dust jacket. $125.

POUND, Ezra. *Provenca: Poems Selected from "Personae," "Exultations" and "Canzoniere."* Tan boards, Boston, (1910). First edition, first issue, with boards stamped in dark brown instead of green. In dust jacket. $300–$350. Without jacket, $145.

POUND, Ezra. *Quia Pauper Amavi.* Boards and cloth, paper label. London, (1919). Egoist, Ltd. First edition. One of 110 on handmade paper, signed. (Issued without dust jacket.) $1,000–$1,250. First trade edition: $200–$300.

POUND, Ezra. *A Quinzaine for This Yule.* Wrappers. (London, 1908.) First edition, first issue, with "Weston St. Llewmy" for "Weston St. Llewmys" in line 6 on page 21. $750–$1,000. Second issue, corrected. $500–$750. Also, $308 (A, 1966).

POUND, Ezra. *Redondillas, or Something of That Sort.* Blue boards, linen spine, label. (New York, 1967.) New Directions. Grabhorn-Hoyem printing. One of 110 signed. In dust jacket. $400–$500.

POUND, Ezra. *Ripostes.* Streaky gray cloth. London, 1912. First edition. $150–$200. London, 1915. Wrappers. Fourth issue. (400 copies). $100–$125.

POUND, Ezra. *Section: Rock-Drill.* Gray boards. Milan, 1955. First edition. One of 500. $100–$125. (New York, 1956.) Black cloth. First American edition. In dust jacket. $35. London, (1957). Black cloth. First English edition. In dust jacket. $35.

POUND, Ezra. *Selected Poems.* Introduction by T. S. Eliot. Gray boards. London, (1928). First edition. One of 100 signed. $800–$1,000. Also, $500 (A, 1977). Trade edition: Green cloth. In dust jacket. $85–$100.

POUND, Ezra. *The Spirit of Romance.* Olive-brown cloth. London, (1910). First edition, first binding. In dust jacket. $125–$175. Norfolk, (1953). New Directions. Cloth. In dust jacket. $30–$50.

POUND, Ezra. *Thrones*. Tan boards. Milan, 1959. First edition. One of 300. In glassine dust jacket. $75–$125. London, (1960). Red cloth. First English edition. In dust jacket. $40–$50. (Norfolk, 1959.) New Directions. Black cloth. First American edition. In dust jacket. $25.

POUND, Ezra. *Umbra*. Gray boards and cloth. London, 1920. First edition. In dust jacket. $300–$375. Worn, lacking jacket, $150 and $200. Another issue: Boards, parchment. One of 100 signed. $750–$1,000. Also, $800 (A, 1976).

POUND, Ezra (editor). *Active Anthology*. Red-brown cloth. London, (1933). First edition. In dust jacket. $175–$200.

POUND, Ezra (translator). *Cathay*. Printed wrappers. London, 1915. First edition. $450–$550.

POUND, Ezra (translator). *Confucius: The Unwobbling Pivot and The Great Digest*. Wrappers. (Norfolk), 1947. New Directions. First edition, without Chinese text. $50–$75. (Norfolk, 1951.) Black cloth. New edition, with Chinese text and with title altered to read *Confucius: The Great Digest and The Unwobbling Pivot*. In dust jacket. $50–$75.

POUND, Ezra (translator). *The Sonnets and Ballate of Guido Cavalcanti*. Boards, vellum paper spine. Boston, (1912). First edition. In dust jacket. $200–$250. Lacking jacket, $125. London, 1912. Gray cloth. First English edition. $100–$150.

POUND, Ezra (translator). *Ta Hio: The Great Learning*. Translated from Confucius' works. Wrappers. Seattle, 1928. First edition. $65–$75. Norfolk, (1936, i.e. 1938). Wrappers. $50.

POWELL, Anthony. *Afternoon Men*. Cloth. London, 1931. First edition. In dust jacket. $200–$250. Author's first novel.

POWELL, Anthony. *Caledonia: A Fragment*. Boards and cloth. London, (1934). First edition. In dust jacket. $150–$175.

POWELL, Anthony. *From a View to a Death*. Cloth. London, 1933. First edition. In dust jacket. $125–$150.

POWELL, Anthony. *Venusberg*. Cloth. London, 1932. First edition. In dust jacket. $150–$200.

POWELL, C. Frank. *Life of Gen. Zachary Taylor*. 96 pp., wrappers. New York, 1846. First edition. $100–$125.

POWELL, H. M. T. *The Santa Fe Trail to California, 1849–1852*. Edited by Douglas S. Watson. Maps and other illustrations. Half morocco. San Francisco, (1931). Grabhorn Press. One of 300. $1,250–$1,500. Also, $700 (A, 1977); inscribed by E. Grabhorn, $1,050 (A, 1980).

POWELL, J. W. *Canyons of the Colorado*. Illustrated, including 10 folding plates. Cloth. Meadville, Pa., 1895. First edition. $1,000–$1,250. (About 100 copies printed.)

POWELL, Lawrence Clark. *The Alchemy of Books*. Decorated boards. Los Angeles, (1954). Ward Ritchie Press. First edition. $50–$75.

POWELL, Lawrence Clark. *Robinson Jeffers, the Man and His Work*. Foreword by Robinson Jeffers. Decorations by Rockwell Kent. Cloth, paper label. Los Angeles, 1934. First edition. One of 750. In dust jacket. $50–$75.

POWELL, Willis J. *Tachyhippodamia, or, Art of Quieting Wild Horses in a Few Hours*. Cloth. New Orleans, 1838. First edition. $750–$1,000.

POWER, Tyrone. *Impressions of America*. 2 plates. 2 vols., boards and linen. London,

1936. First edition. $250–$350. Philadelphia, 1836. 2 vols., cloth. First American edition. $150–$200.

POWERS, J. F. *Prince of Darkness and Other Stories.* Cloth. New York, 1947. First edition. In dust jacket. $100. Author's first book.

POWERS, Stephen. *Afoot and Alone: A Walk from Sea to Sea by the Southern Route.* 12 plates. Cloth. Hartford, 1872. First edition. $100–$200.

POWYS, John Cowper. *Autobiography.* Portrait frontispiece. Brown cloth. London, (1934). First edition. In dust jacket. $75.

POWYS, John Cowper. *Ballads and Other Poems.* Boards. London, 1893. First edition. $80–$100. Author's first book.

POWYS, John Cowper. *Ducdame.* Cloth. London, 1925. First English edition. In dust jacket. $100–$125.

POWYS, John Cowper. *A Glastonbury Romance.* Boards and calf. New York, 1932. First edition. One of 204 signed. $400.

POWYS, John Cowper. *In Defense of Sensuality.* Cloth. New York, 1930. First edition. In dust jacket. $75–$100. London, 1930. First English edition. $75.

POWYS, John Cowper. *Lucifer, a Poem.* Half morocco. London, 1956. First edition. One of 560 signed. $150–$175.

POWYS, John Cowper. *Odes and Other Poems.* Cloth. London, 1896. First edition. $350–$400.

POWYS, John Cowper. *Owen Glendower: An Historical Novel.* 2 vols., cloth. New York, 1940. First edition. Boxed. $100–$110.

POWYS, John Cowper. *The Owl, the Duck and—Miss Rowe! Miss Rowe!* Boards, Chicago, 1930. Black Archer Press. First edition. One of 250 signed. Boxed. $200–$225.

POWYS, John Cowper. *Poems.* Boards. London, 1899. First edition. $175–$250.

POWYS, John Cowper. *Psychoanalysis and Morality.* Half vellum. San Francisco, 1923. Grabhorn printing. One of 500 signed. $75–$100.

POWYS, John Cowper. *Rodmoor: A Romance.* Cloth. New York, 1916. First edition. $150–$200.

POWYS, John Cowper. *Wolf Solent.* 2 vols., cloth. New York, 1929. First edition. In dust jacket. $75–$100. London, (1929). First English edition. $75.

POWYS, John Cowper, and Powys, Llewellyn. *Confessions of Two Brothers.* Cloth. Rochester, 1916. First edition. In dust jacket. $200–$250.

POWYS, Llewellyn. *A Baker's Dozen.* Illustrated. Cloth. Herrin, Ill., (1939). First edition. One of 493 signed. Boxed. $75.

POWYS, Llewellyn. *The Book of Days.* 12 etchings. Half green morocco. London, 1937. Golden Cockerel Press. One of 55 signed, with an extra set of plates. $450–$500. Ordinary copies (245 of 300): $250–$300.

POWYS, Llewellyn. *Glory of Life.* Woodcuts by Robert Gibbings. Vellum and cloth. (London, 1934.) Golden Cockerel Press. One of 275. $400–$500. Another issue: One of 2 on vellum. $2,500.

POWYS, Llewellyn. *The Twelve Months.* Illustrated by Robert Gibbings. Morocco. Oxford, 1936. First edition. One of 100 signed. $300–$325.

POWYS, T. F. *Fables.* 4 drawings by Gilbert Spencer. Buckram. London, 1929. One of 750 signed. $75. New York, (1929). Cloth. In dust jacket. $25.

POWYS, T. F. *Goat Green, or The Better Gift*. Illustrated. Half morocco. London, 1937. Golden Cockerel Press. One of 150 signed. $150–$175. Another issue: Wrappers. $300.

POWYS, T. F. *An Interpretation of Genesis*. Boards. London, 1929. First edition. One of 490 signed. In dust jacket. Boxed. $100–$125. New York, 1929. White boards. First American edition. One of 260 signed. In glassine dust jacket. Boxed. $100–$125.

POWYS, T. F. *The Key of the Field*. Woodcut frontispiece. Buckram. London, 1930. First edition. One of 550 signed. In dust jacket. $50–$75.

POWYS, T. F. *Mr. Weston's Good Wine*. Illustrated. Cloth. London, 1927. One of 660 signed. In dust jacket. $100–$125.

POWYS, T. F. *Soliloquies of a Hermit*. Boards and cloth. London, 1918. First English edition (of *The Soliloquy of a Hermit*). In dust jacket. $100–$125.

POWYS, T. F. *The Soliloquy of a Hermit*. Cloth. New York, 1916. First edition. In dust jacket. $125–$175. Author's first book.

POWYS, T. F. *Two Stories*. Illustrated with wood engravings. Half leather. Hastings, England, 1967. First edition. One of 25 signed by the illustrator Reynolds Stone. In slipcase. $200–$250. Another issue: One of 525. $50.

POWYS, T. F. *Uncle Dottery*. Illustrated by Eric Gill. Half vellum and green linen. Bristol, England, 1930. First edition. One of 300 signed. In dust jacket. $100–$125. Same issue: One of 50, with an extra set of engravings. $200–$250.

POWYS, T. F. *When Thou Wast Naked*. London, 1931. Golden Cockerel Press. One of 500 signed. $200.

PRACTICAL Guide for Emigrants to North America (A). Folding map in color. 57 pp., printed wrappers. London, 1850. (By George Nettle.) First edition. $150–$175.

PRAIRIE (The): A Tale, By the Author of *The Spy*. 3 vols., boards and cloth, paper labels. London, 1827. (By James Fenimore Cooper.) First edition. $1,000–$1,250. Philadelphia, 1827. 2 vols., boards, paper labels. First American edition, with copyright notices corrected by slip pasted in. $1,500–$2,000. Paris, 1827. 2 vols., half leather. $750–$1,000. New York, 1940. Limited Editions Club. $40–$45.

PRAIRIEDOM: Rambles and Scrambles in Texas. By A. Suthron. Map. Cloth. New York, 1845. (By Frederick Benjamin Page.) First edition. $500–$1,000. New York, 1846. Second edition. $250–$350.

PRATT, Parley P. *Late Persecution of the Church of Jesus Christ, of Latter Day Saints*. Cloth. New York, 1840. $300–$500.

PRECAUTION: A Novel. 2 vols., boards, or leather. New York, 1820. (By James Fenimore Cooper.) First edition, with errata leaf. $7,500—$10,000 Also, with spines chipped and "Vol. II broken," $2,250 (A, 1976). Cooper's first book.

PRÉCIS Touchant la Colonie du Lord Selkirk, sur La Rivière Rouge, sa Destruction en 1815 et 1816, et le Massacre du Gouverneur Semple et de Son Parti. Boards, Montreal, 1818. (By John Halkett.) First edition. $300–$350.

PRESCOTT, George Bartlett. *The Speaking Telephone*. Illustrated. Cloth, New York, 1878. First edition. $75.

PRESCOTT, William H. *The History of the Conquest of Mexico*. Maps, other illustrations. 3 vols., cloth. New York, 1843. First edition, $200–$300.

PRESCOTT, William H. *The History of the Conquest of Peru*. Illustrated. 2 vols., cloth. New York, 1847. First American edition, first issue, with no period after "integrity," line 20, page 467. Vol. II. $200–$300. Later, $150–$200. Mexico, 1957. Limited Editions Club. Leather. Boxed. $80–$125.

PRESIDENT Lincoln Campaign Songster (The). 72 pp., printed wrappers. New York, (1864). First edition. $100–$150.

PRICE, George F. *Across the Continent with the 5th Cavalry*. 4 portraits. Pictorial cloth. New York, 1883. First edition. $250–$300.

PRICE, R. K. *Astbury, Whieldon, and Ralph Wood Figures, and Toby Jugs*. 68 plates, including 18 in color. Half buckram. London, 1922. One of 500. In dust jacket. $400–$500.

PRICE, Reynolds. *Late Warning*. Wrappers, paper label. New York, 1968. First edition. One of 176 signed. $75–$100.

PRICE, Reynolds. *A Long and Happy Life*. Cloth. New York, 1962. First edition. In first dust jacket, with names in pale green on the back. $100–$175. London, 1962. First English edition. In dust jacket. $50–$60. Author's first book.

PRICE, Reynolds. *The Names and Faces of Heroes*. Cloth. New York, 1963. First edition. In dust jacket. $50–$75.

PRICHARD, James C. *A Treatise on Diseases of the Nervous System*. Part I (all published). Half leather. London, 1822. First edition. $600–$750.

PRICHARD, James C. *A Treatise on Insanity*. Leather. London, 1835. First edition. $750–$850. Philadelphia, 1837. $150–$175.

PRIDE and Prejudice. By the Author of *Sense and Sensibility*. 3 vols., blue boards, paper labels. London, 1813. (By Jane Austen.) First edition, with November ads and with ruled lines in half title of Vol. 3 1⅖ inches (1 inch in second edition). $5,000–$20,000. Also, $4,000 (A, 1974). Rebound in leather, $2,500 in a recent catalogue. London, 1813. Second edition, $1,500 and up. New York, 1940. Limited Editions Club. $80–$100.

PRIEST, Josiah. *Stories of the Revolution*. Folding plate. 32 pp., half calf. Albany, 1836. $150–$200.

PRIEST, Josiah. *A True Narrative of the Capture of David Ogden*. (Cover title.) Woodcut. Self-wrappers. Lansingburgh, 1840. First edition. $200–$300.

PRIESTLEY, J. B. *Angel Pavement*. Cloth. London, 1930. First edition. One of 1,025 signed. $100–$125.

PRIESTLEY, J. B. *Brief Diversions*. Boards and cloth. Cambridge, 1922. First collected edition. In dust jacket. $125.

PRIESTLEY, J. B. *The Chapman of Rhymes*. Wrappers. London, 1918. First edition. $400–$600. Also, $350 (A, 1977). Author's first book.

PRIESTLEY, J. B. *Faraway*. Morocco. London, (1932). First edition. In dust jacket. $150–$200.

PRIESTLEY, J. B. *The Town Major of Miraucourt*. Vellum. London, 1930. First edition. One of 525 signed. $150.

PRIMAVERA: Poems by Four Authors. Wrappers. Oxford, 1890. First edition. $100. (Note: Contains poems by Stephen Phillips, Laurence Binyon, and others.)

PRINCE Dorus; or, Flattery Put Out of Countenance. Colored plate. Stiff blue or yellow wrappers. London, 1811. (By Charles Lamb.) First edition. $1,000 and up. Also, "broken," $300 (A, 1980). London, 1818. Yellow-brown wrappers. $400 and up. London, 1889. 9 hand-colored illustrations. Half vellum. $100 and up.

PRINCE, William Robert, and Prince, William. *A Treatise on the Vine*. Boards. New York, 1830. First edition. $400.

PRITCHETT, R. T. *Historical and Ethnographical Smokiana*. Illustrated in color. London, 1890. First edition. $200–$250.

PRITCHETT, V. S. *Marching Spain.* Cloth. London, (1928). First edition. In dust jacket. $250. Author's first book.

PRITTS, Joseph. *Mirror of Olden Time Border Life.* 13 plates (17 in a few copies). Cloth. Abingdon, Va., 1849. $100–$150.

PROCEEDINGS of Congress, in 1796, on the Admission of Tennessee as a State, into the Union. 15 pp., sewed. Detroit, 1835. $150–$200.

PROCEEDINGS of a Convention to Consider the Opening of the Indian Territory, Held at Kansas City, Mo., Feb, 8, 1888. 80 pp., wrappers. Kansas City, 1888. $200–$300.

PROCEEDINGS of the First Annual Session of the Territorial Grange of Montana. Diamond City, 1875. $300–$400.

PROCEEDINGS of a General Meeting Held at Chester Courthouse, July 5th, 1831. 16 pp., sewed. Columbia, S.C., 1832. $100–$150.

PROCEEDINGS of the Harbor and River Convention. Held in Chicago, July 5th, 1847. 79 pp., wrappers. Chicago, 1847. First edition. $350.

PROCEEDINGS of a Meeting, and Report of a Committee of Citizens in Relation to Steamboat Disasters in the Western Lakes. 22 pp., sewed. Cleveland, 1850. $100–$125.

PROCEEDINGS of the National Ship Canal Convention. Wrappers. Chicago, 1863. First edition. $150–$200.

PROCEEDINGS of the Republican National Convention, Held at Chicago, May 16, 17 and 18, 1860. 153 pp., wrappers. Albany, 1860. $300–$350. Another edition: Chicago, 1860. 44 pp., sewed. $150–$200.

PROCEEDINGS of the St. Louis Chamber of Commerce, in Relation to the Improvement of the Navigation of the Mississippi River. 44 pp., sewed. St. Louis, 1842. $100–$125.

PROCEEDINGS of Sundry Citizens of Baltimore, Convened for the Purpose of Devising the Most Efficient Means of Improving the Intercourse Between That City and the Western States. 38 pp., sewed. Baltimore, 1827. $200–$300.

PROCTOR, Thomas H. *The Banker's Dream.* Pictorial wrappers. Vineland, N.J., 1895. First edition. $50.

PROGRESSIVE Men of Southern Idaho. Frontispiece by Charles M. Russell, other illustrations. Leather. Chicago, 1904. First edition. $300–$350.

PROKOSCH, Frederic. *Age of Thunder.* Cloth. New York, (1945). First edition. One of 30 signed, sheet of original ms. bound in. $100–$125.

PROKOSCH, Frederic. *Death at Sea: Poems.* Cloth. New York, 1940. First edition. One of 55 signed, sheet of original ms. bound in. Boxed. $100–$150.

PROKOSCH, Frederic. *Three Songs—Three Images.* 2 vols., wrappers. New Haven, 1932. One of 10 large paper copies. $200–$300.

PROMETHEUS Bound. Translated from the Greek of Aeschylus. And *Miscellaneous Poems by the Translator.* Dark-blue cloth, paper label on spine. London, 1833. (By Elizabeth Barrett Browning.) First edition. $100–$150.

PROPERT, W. A. *The Russian Ballet in Western Europe, 1909–1920.* Illustrated, including color plates. Boards and cloth. London, 1921. First edition. One of 500. $500–$600. (Note: There were 150 copies issued for America.)

PROSCH, J. W. *McCarver and Tacoma.* 2 plates. Cloth. Seattle, (1906). First edition. $75–$100.

PROSE and Poetry of the Live Stock Industry of the United States. Vol. 1. (All published.) Leather. Denver and Kansas City, (1905). (Edited by James W. Freeman). First edition. $5,000–$7,500. New York, 1959. Half leather. Boxed. $150–$175.

PROSPECTUS of Hope Gold Company. (Gold dirt lode in Gilpin County, Colorado.) 25 pp., wrappers. New York, 1864. $125–$150.

PROSPECTUS of the Deadwood Gulch Hydraulic Mining Co. of Deadwood Gulch, Lawrence County, Black Hills, of the Territory of Dakota. Folding map, 12 pp. wrappers. Deadwood, 1882. $150–$200.

PROSPECTUS of the Leadville & Ten Mile Narrow Gauge Railway Company of Leadville, Col. (Cover title.) 20 pp., printed wrappers. Leadville, 1880. $250–$300.

PROSPERO and Caliban. *The Weird of the Wanderer.* Dark blue cloth. London, 1912. (By Baron Corvo [Frederick William Rolfe] and Charles Harry Pirie-Gordon.) First edition. In dust jacket. $400–$500.

PROTEUS. *Sonnets and Songs.* Cloth. London, 1875. (By Wilfrid Scawen Blunt.) First edition. $300–$350. Author's first book.

PROUST, Marcel. *47 Unpublished Letters from Marcel Proust to Walter Berry.* White wrappers. Paris, 1930. Black Sun Press. One of 200 on Arches paper. Boxed. $200–$250. (Note: There was also another issue of 15, including an original autograph letter, but in most cases the original letter has been removed by autograph collectors.)

PROVOST (The). Boards, marbled spine, paper label. Edinburgh, 1822. (By John Galt.) First edition. $300–$400.

PSALMAU Dafydd. Decorated paper covers, morocco spine. (Newtown, Wales, 1929.) Gregynog Press. One of 200. $400. (Note: The Psalms of David in Welsh.)

PUGET SOUND Business Directory and Guide to Washington Territory, 1872, 3 colored plates of ads. Boards and leather. Olympia, (1872). First edition. $600 and up.

PUGET SOUND Directory, 1887. Illustrated. Boards. No place, 1887. (R. L. Polk.) Worn copy, $400.

PULITZER, Ralph. See Burke, John.

PURDY, James. *Don't Call Me by My Right Name and Other Stories.* Blue-gray printed wrappers. New York, 1956. First edition. $75–$100. Author's first book.

PURDY, James. *An Oyster Is a Wealthy Beast.* Oblong boards. (San Francisco, 1967.) First edition. One of 50 signed, with an original drawing. $250–$300. Also, 200 signed copies in wrappers. $50–$60.

PURDY, James. *63: Dream Palace.* Printed wrappers. New York, 1956. First edition. $75–$100.

PURVIANCE, Levi. *The Biography of David Purviance.* Cloth. Dayton, 1848. First edition. $50–$60.

PUSHKIN, Alexander. *The Golden Cockerel.* Illustrated by Edmund Dulac. Cloth. New York, (1949). Limited Editions Club. Boxed. $125–$175.

PUSS in Boots. Illustrated in color. 10 pp., pictorial boards. New York, (1880's). McLoughlin book with overlays on center spread. $75–$100.

PUT'S Golden Songster. 64 pp., wrappers. San Francisco, (1858). (By John A. Stone.) First edition, $100–$125.

PUZO, Mario. *The Dark Arena.* Cloth. New York, (1955). First edition. In dust jacket. $35–$50. Author's first book.

PUZO, Mario. *The Godfather.* Boards. New York, (1969). First edition. In dust jacket. $50.

PYLE, Howard. *The Garden Behind the Moon.* Illustrated by the author. Cloth. New York, 1895. First edition. $100–$125.

PYLE, Howard. *Howard Pyle's Book of the American Spirit.* Edited by Merle Johnson and Francis J. O'Dowd. Illustrated, including color plates, by Pyle. Boards and cloth. New York, 1923. First edition, with "B-X" on copyright page. In dust jacket. $150–$200. Another issue: One of 50 signed by the editors. In dust jacket. $300–$350. Also, one of 6 signed copies, with an original Pyle drawing for the book. $650–$750.

PYLE, Howard. *Howard Pyle's Book of Pirates.* Edited by Merle Johnson. Illustrated, including color plates, by Pyle. Boards and cloth. New York, 1921. First edition, with "K–V" at foot of copyright page. In dust jacket. $150–$175. Another issue: One of 50 on vellum, signed by Johnson. In dust jacket. Boxed. $400–$500.

PYLE, Howard. *Men of Iron.* New York, 1892. Illustrated by Pyle. Cloth. First edition, first issue (1¹/₁₆ inches across top of covers). $125–$150. Second issue. $50–$75.

PYLE, Howard. *The Merry Adventures of Robin Hood.* Illustrated, including color plates, by Pyle. Full leather. New York, 1883. First edition. $300–$400. London, 1883. Cloth. First English edition. $75. Author's first book. New York, 1933. Illustrated by N. C. Wyeth and with 2 drawings by Andrew Wyeth. Cloth. Brandywine Edition. In dust jacket. $300–$350.

PYLE, Howard. *A Modern Aladdin.* Illustrated by Pyle. Cloth. New York, 1892. First edition. $125.

PYLE, Howard. *Otto of the Silver Hand.* Illustrated by the author. Half calf and cloth. New York, 1888. First edition. $350–$500. London, 1888. Pictorial cloth. First English edition. $150.

PYLE, Howard. *Pepper and Salt.* Illustrated by the author. Pictorial buckram. New York, 1886. First edition. $200–$225.

PYLE, Howard. *The Price of Blood.* Colored illustrations by Pyle. Pictorial boards and cloth. Boston, 1899. First edition, first binding, with unlettered spine. $150. Second binding, spine lettered. $150.

PYLE, Howard. *Rejected of Men.* Illustrated by Pyle. Cloth. New York, 1903. First edition, with "Published June, 1903" on copyright page. In dust jacket. $150.

PYLE, Howard. *The Ruby of Kishmoor.* Illustrated. Cloth. New York, 1908. First edition. In dust jacket. $75–$100.

PYLE, Howard. *The Story of the Champions of the Round Table.* Cloth. New York, 1905. First edition. In dust jacket. $135–$150.

PYLE, Howard. *The Story of the Grail and the Passing of Arthur.* Illustrated by the author. Cloth. New York, 1910. First edition. In dust jacket. $100–$150.

PYLE, Howard. *The Story of King Arthur and His Knights.* Illustrated by Pyle. Cloth. New York, 1903. First edition. In dust jacket. $135–$150.

PYLE, Howard. *The Story of Sir Launcelot and His Companions.* Illustrated by Pyle. Cloth. New York, 1907. First edition. In dust jacket. $150–$165.

PYLE, Howard. *The Wonder Clock.* Illustrated by Pyle. Half leather. New York, 1888. First edition. $300–$400.

PYLE, Howard. *Yankee Doodle.* Illustrated by Pyle. Pictorial boards. New York, 1881. First edition. $300–$400. First book illustrated by Pyle.

PYNCHON, Thomas. *The Crying of Lot 49.* Cloth. Philadelphia, (1966). First edition. In dust jacket. $100–$135. London, 1967. Cloth. In dust jacket. $50–$75.

PYNCHON, Thomas. *Gravity's Rainbow*. Cloth. New York, (1973). First edition. In dust jacket. $100–$125. Wrappers (issued simultaneously): $35–$40.

PYNCHON, Thomas. *V*. Cloth. Philadelphia, (1963). First edition. In dust jacket. $300–$350. Author's first book. Advance copy in wrappers: $750–$850. London, 1963. Cloth. First English edition. $150.

PYNE, W. H. *The Costume of Great Britain*. 60 hand-colored plates. Morocco. London, 1804 (actually after 1817). $2,250–$2,500.

PYNE, W. H. *The History of the Royal Residences of Windsor Castle, St. James's Palace, Carlton House, Kensington Palace, Hampton Court, Buckingham House, and Frogmore*. 100 colored engravings. 3 vols., morocco, gilt. London, 1819. First edition, first issue, with pre-publication watermarks. $4,000–$5,000. Another issue: Large paper. $5,000 and up.

PYRNELLE, Louise-Clarke. *Diddie, Dumps, and Tot, or Plantation Child-Life*. Pictorial cloth. New York, 1882. First edition. $300–$400.

Q

QUAKER Partisans (The). Cloth. Philadelphia, 1869. (By William Gilmore Simms?) First edition. $200–$250.

QUARTETTE. By Four Anglo-Indian Writers. Wrappers. Lahore, India, 1885. (By Rudyard Kipling and his sister, mother, and father.) First edition. $2,000 or more. Also, some defects, $1,100 (A, 1974).

QUEEN, Ellery. *The Chinese Orange Mystery*. Cloth. New York, 1934. (By Frederic Dannay and Manfred B. Lee.) First edition. In dust jacket. $100–$125.

QUEEN, Ellery. *The Devil to Pay*. Cloth. New York, 1938. (By Frederic Dannay and Manfred B. Lee.) First edition. In dust jacket. $100–$125.

QUEEN, Ellery. *The Dutch Shoe Mystery*. Cloth. New York, 1931. (By Frederic Dannay and Manfred B. Lee.) First edition. In dust jacket. $85–$100.

QUEEN, Ellery. *The Egyptian Cross Mystery*. Cloth. New York, 1932. (By Frederic Dannay and Manfred B. Lee.) First edition. In dust jacket. $100.

QUEEN, Ellery. *The Spanish Cape Mystery*. Cloth. New York, 1935. (By Frederic Dannay and Manfred B. Lee.) First edition. In dust jacket. $75–$100.

QUEEN, Ellery (editor). *The Misadventures of Sherlock Holmes*. Frontispiece by F. D. Steele. Cloth. Boston, 1944. (Edited by Frederic Dannay and Manfred B. Lee.) First edition. In dust jacket. $250–$300.

QUEENY, Edgar M. *Cheechako*. Illustrated. Cloth. New York, 1941. First edition. One of 1,200. $75–$100.

QUEENY, Edgar M. *Prairie Wings: Pen and Camera Flight Studies*. Illustrated. Cloth. New York, 1946. In dust jacket. $400–$500. Another issue: Morocco. One of 225 signed. $1,250. Philadelphia, 1947. Cloth. Second edition. In dust jacket. $250–$300.

QUENTIN Durward. 3 vols., boards and cloth, paper labels. Edinburgh, 1823. (By Sir Walter Scott.) First edition. $800–$1,000. Also, badly worn, $200.

QUICKFALL. *Western Life, and How I Became a Bronco Buster*. Portrait. 96 pp., pictorial wrappers. London, (1890). (By Bob Grantham?) First edition. $500–$600.

QUILLER-COUCH, Sir Arthur. See Rackham, Arthur, *Book of Pictures*.

QUILLER-COUCH, Sir Arthur. *In Powder and Crinoline*. Illustrated by Kay Nielsen, including 24 color plates. Boards, buckram spine. London, (about 1913). $450–$600. Another issue: Vellum. One of 500 signed. $1,500–$2,000.

QUILLER-COUCH, Sir Arthur. *The Sleeping Beauty and Other Fairy Tales*. 30 colored plates by Edmund Dulac. Cloth. London, (about 1910). In dust jacket. $300–$400. Another issue: Morocco. One of 1,000. $600–$800.

QUILLER-COUCH, Sir Arthur. *The Twelve Dancing Princesses and Other Fairy Tales*. Illustrated by Kay Nielsen. Pictorial cloth. New York, (about 1920). $300–$350.

QUINN, Seabury. *Roads*. Black cloth. Illustrated. Sauk City, Wis., 1948. Arkham House. In dust jacket. $50.

QUIZ. *The Grand Master, or Adventures of Qui Hi in Hindostan: A Hudibrastic Poem in Eight Cantos.* Folding frontispiece, 26 plates by Thomas Rowlandson. Boards. London, 1816. (An imitation of William Combe but not by him.) First edition, with errata slip and leaf containing pages 31–32. $800–$1,000. Also, $362 (A, 1980).

R

R., J. *Poems*. Cloth. (London), 1850. (By John Ruskin.) First edition. $750–$1,000.

RACKHAM, Arthur. *The Arthur Rackham Fairy Book*. Illustrated, including color. Full vellum. London, (1933). One of 460 signed. Boxed. $750–$1,000.

RACKHAM, Arthur. *Arthur Rackham's Book of Pictures*. Edited by Sir Arthur Quiller-Couch. Illustrated, including color. Cloth. London, 1913. First edition. In dust jacket. $600–$800. Another issue: One of 1,030 signed by Rackham. In dust jacket. $750–$1,000. Another: One of 30, inscribed and with an original drawing. $1,500–$2,000. New York, (1914). Cloth. American edition. In dust jacket. $600–$800. London, (1927). Cloth. In dust jacket. $200–$300.

RACKHAM, Bernard. *The Ancient Glass of Canterbury Cathedral*. 21 plates in color and 80 in monochrome. Buckram. London, 1949. $200–$250.

RACKHAM, Bernard, and Read, Herbert. *English Pottery*. Cloth. London, 1924. First edition. In dust jacket. $125–$150. Another issue: Pigskin. One of 75 signed. $250–$300.

RADER, J. L. *South of Forty*. Cloth. Norman, Okla., 1947. First edition. $75–$100.

RADIGUET, Raymond. *The Count's Ball*. Cloth. New York, (1929). First edition in English. In dust jacket. $100–$150.

RADIGUET, Raymond. *The Devil in the Flesh*. Cloth. New York, 1932. First American edition. In dust jacket. $125.

RAFINESQUE, C. S. *Circular Address on Botany and Zoology*. 36 pp., sewed. Philadelphia, 1816. $175–$225.

RAFINESQUE, C. S. *A Life of Travels and Researches in North America and South Europe*, 148 pp., wrappers. Philadelphia, 1836. First edition. $400–$500.

RAFINESQUE, C. D. *Medical Flora*. 100 plates, printed in green. 2 vols., boards. Philadelphia, 1828–30. First edition. $1,250–$1,500.

RAHT, Carlysle Graham. *The Romance of Davis Mountains and Big Bend Country*. Map, 13 plates. Cloth. El Paso, (1919). First edition. In dust jacket. $75–$85.

RAILROAD to San Francisco. (Caption title.) No place, no date (1849). (By P. P. F. DeGrand.) $125–$150.

RAINE, Kathleen. *Six Dreams and Other Poems*. Illustrated. Boards. London, 1968. First edition. One of 100 signed. $50–$60.

RAINE, Kathleen. *Stone and Flower*. Illustrated. Cloth. London, (1943). First edition. In dust jacket. $75. Author's first book.

RAINE, William MacLeod. *Cattle Brands: A Sketch of Bygone Days in the Cow-Country*. 8 pp., wrappers. Boston, (1920). First edition. $100–$125.

RAINE, William MacLeod. *A Daughter of Raasay*. Illustrated. Cloth. New York, (1902). First edition. In dust jacket. $150–$200. Lacking jacket, $75–$100. Author's first book.

RAINES, C. W. *A Bibliography of Texas.* Cloth. Austin, Tex., 1896. First edition. $100–$200. Facsimile reprint: Houston, 1955. Cloth. One of 500. Boxed. $25.

RAKOSI, Carl. *Two Poems.* Pictorial wrappers. New York, (1932). First edition. $100–$150.

RALFE, J. *The Naval Chronology of Great Britain.* 60 colored plates. 3 vols., half morocco. London, 1820. First edition. $4,000–$5,000. Also, $3,200 (A, 1980).

RALPH, Julian. *On Canada's Frontier.* Illustrated. Cloth. New York, 1892. First edition. $100–$125.

RAMAL, Walter. *Songs of Childhood.* Frontispiece. Decorated blue cloth and vellum. London, 1902. (By Walter De La Mare.) First edition. In dust jacket. $600–$750. De La Mare's first book.

RAMIREZ, D. José F. *Memorias, Negociaciones y Documentos, etc.* Boards, or wrappers. Mexico City, 1853. $150–$200.

RAMSAY, David. *The History of South Carolina.* 2 folding maps. 2 vols., half leather. Charleston, 1809. First edition. $500–$600.

RAMSDELL, Charles W. *Reconstruction in Texas.* 324 pp., wrappers. New York, 1910. First edition. Wrappers: $100–$150. Cloth. $60–$75.

RAMSEY, Alexander. *Message of Governor Ramsey.* (On the Sioux uprising.) Wrappers. St. Paul, 1862. First edition. $150–$250.

RAMSEY, J. G. M. *The Annals of Tennessee.* Folding map and plan. Leather, or cloth. Charleston, 1853. First edition. $250–$350. Philadelphia, 1853. Cloth. Second edition. $250.

RANCK, George W. *History of Lexington, Kentucky.* Illustrated. Cloth. Cincinnati, 1872. First edition. $75–$100.

RAND, Ayn. *Atlas Shrugged.* Cloth. New York, 1957. First edition. In dust jacket. $100–$125.

RAND, Ayn. *The Fountainhead.* Cloth. Indianapolis, (1943). First edition. In dust jacket. $150–$175.

RAND, Ayn. *The Night of January 16th.* Cloth. New York, (1968). First edition. In dust jacket. $25–$35.

RAND, Ayn. *We the Living.* Blue cloth. London, (1936). First edition. $500–$750.

RANDALL, Thomas E. *History of the Chippewa Valley.* Cloth. Eau Claire, Wis., 1875. First edition. $75–$100.

RANKIN, M. Wilson. *Remniscences of Frontier Days.* Frontispiece. Boards. Denver, (1938). First edition. $100–$125.

RANKIN, Melinda. *Texas in 1850.* Cloth. Boston, 1850. First edition. $300–$350. Rebound in leather, $225.

RANSOM, John Crowe. See *Armageddon, etc.*

RANSOM, John Crowe. *Chills and Fever.* Batik boards, cloth spine, paper label. New York, 1924. First edition. In dust jacket. $150–$250.

RANSOM, John Crowe. *Grace After Meat.* Boards, paper label. London, 1924. First edition. One of 400. (Issued without dust jacket.) $350–$400.

RANSOM, John Crowe. *Poems About God.* Brown boards, paper label. New York, 1919. First edition. $350–$475. Author's first book.

RANSOM, John Crowe. *Selected Poems*. Cloth. New York, 1945. First edition. In dust jacket. $75–$100.

RANSOM, John Crowe. *Two Gentlemen in Bonds*. Decorated boards, cloth spine, paper label. New York, 1927. First edition. In dust jacket. $200–$250.

RANSOM, John Crowe. *The World's Body*. Cloth. New York, 1938. First edition. In dust jacket. $75–$100.

RANSOM, Will. *Private Presses and Their Books*. Illustrated. Cloth. New York, 1929. First edition. One of 1,200. In dust jacket. $200–$250.

RANSOME, Arthur. *Oscar Wilde: A Critical Study*. Cloth. London, 1912. First edition. $50–$75.

RAREY, J. S. *The Modern Art of Taming Wild Horses*. Wrappers. Columbus, Ohio, 1856. First edition. $400–$600. Austin, 1856. 62 pp., wrappers. Third edition, revised and corrected. $100 and up.

RATHBONE, Frederick. *Old Wedgwood*. Illustrated, including color plates. Half morocco. London, 1898. First edition. One of 200. $750–$1,000.

RAVENSNEST: or, The Redskins. 3 vols., boards, green or blue cloth spine. London, 1846. (By James Fenimore Cooper.) First English edition of *The Redskins*. $600–$800.

RAWLINGS, Marjorie Kinnan. *The Yearling*. Decorations by Edward Shenton. Cloth. New York, 1938. First edition, with Scribner's "A" on copyright page. In dust jacket. $75–$100. New York, 1939. Illustrated. Cloth. One of 770. In dust jacket. Boxed. $200–$250.

RAWSTORNE, Lawrence. *Gamonia: or the Art of Preserving Game*. 15 hand-colored plates. Green morocco. London, 1837. First edition, with errata slip at end. $2,000–$2,500. Also, $1,500 (A, 1980); $1,000 (A, 1981).

RAY, Ophelia. *Daughter of the Tejas*. Cloth. New York, (1965). (By Larry McMurtry, as ghost-writer.) In gray (probable first) dust jacket. $85–$100. In white jacket. $65–$75.

RAYMOND, Dora Neill. *Captain Lee Hall of Texas*. Map, illustrations. Cloth. Norman, Okla., 1940. First edition. In dust jacket. $35–$50.

READ, C. Rudston. *What I Heard, Saw and Did at the Australian Gold Fields*. Large folding map, tinted lithograph plates. Cloth. London, 1853. First edition. $175–$250.

READ, Herbert. See Rackham, Bernard.

READ, Herbert. *Eclogues*. Illustrated. Boards and cloth. London, 1919. Beaumont Press. One of 50. $75–$85.

READ, Herbert. *English Stained Glass*. Colored frontispiece, 70 full-page plates. Cloth. London, 1926. First edition. $100–$125.

READ, Herbert. *The Green Child*. Cloth. London, (1935). First edition. In dust jacket. $100–$150.

READ, Herbert. *Mutations of the Phoenix*. Half cloth. London, 1923. First edition. $75–$100.

READ, Herbert. *Staffordshire Pottery Figures*. Plates (6 colored). Cloth. London, 1929. First edition. In dust jacket. $100–$125.

READ, Herbert, and others. *Surrealism*. Plates. Cloth. London, 1936. First edition. $150.

READ, Opie. *An American in New York.* Pictorial red cloth. Chicago, 1905. Autographed edition. $50.

READ, Opie. *An Arkansas Planter.* Illustrated by W. W. Denslow and Ike Morgan. Pictorial green cloth. Chicago, (1896). First edition. $50–$60.

READ, Opie. *Bolanyo.* Illustrated. Tan cloth (cover designed by Maxfield Parrish). Chicago, 1897. First edition. $150–$200.

READ, Thomas Buchanan. *A Summer Story: Sheridan's Ride and Other Poems.* Cloth. Philadelphia, 1865. First edition. $50.

READE, Charles. *The Cloister and the Hearth.* 4 vols., cloth. London, 1861. First edition, first issue, without ads and with words transposed on page 372 of Vol. 2. $1,250–$1,500. New York, 1861. Cloth. First American edition. $200–$250. Worn, spines faded, $115. New York, 1932. Limited Editions Club. Cloth. In dust jacket. Boxed. $35–$40.

READE, Charles. *The Course of True Love Never Did Run Smooth.* Pink boards. London, 1857. First edition, first binding. $150–$250.

READE, Charles. *"It Is Never Too Late to Mend."* 3 vols., cloth. London, 1856. First edition. $500–$600. Worn and soiled, $285.

READINGS in Crabbe's "Tales of the Hall." Red or green cloth. Guildford, England, 1879. (By Edward Fitz Gerald.) First edition. $75–$100.

REAGAN, John H. *Memoirs, with Special Reference to Secession and the Civil War.* 4 plates. Cloth. New York, 1906. $175–$200.

REAL Life in Ireland. 19 hand-colored aquatints. Boards. London, 1821. First edition. $750–$1,000. (An imitation of Pierce Egan.)

REAL Life in London. By an Amateur. 32 colored plates by Alken, Rowlandson, etc. 21 parts in wrappers. London, 1821–22. (Imitation of Pierce Egan.) First edition. $2,500–$3,500. London, 1821–22. 32 colored plates. 2 vols., boards. First book edition. (Often with 2 extra plates.) $1,500 and up. Another issue: Morocco. Printed on large paper. $2,000 and up.

RECIO, Jesus T. *Tomochie! Episodios de la Companía de Chihuahua, 1893.* Boards and leather. Rio Grande City, Tex., 1894. $300–$500.

RÉCIT des Événements qui ont eu Lieu sur le Territoire des Sauvages. Boards. Montreal, 1818. (By Simon McGillivray.) $250–$300.

RECREATIONS. Boards, parchment spine. (London, 1923.) (By Siegfried Sassoon.) First edition. One of 75. Inscribed, $500. Another issue: One of 6 on large paper. Inscribed, $750.

RED Rover (The): A Tale. By the Author of *The Pilot.* 3 vols., wrappers (?). Paris, 1827. (By James Fenimore Cooper.) First edition. (No copy noted.) London, 1827. 3 vols., boards (?). First English edition. (No copy in original boards noted.) Half calf. $800–$1,000. Philadelphia, 1828. 2 vols., blue-gray boards, paper labels. First American edition. (Vol. 2 dated 1827.) $500 and up.

REDMOND, Pat. H. *History of Quincy (Ill.) and Its Men of Mark.* Cloth. Quincy, 1869. $100–$150.

REDPATH, James, and Hinton, Richard J. *Hand-book to Kansas Territory and the Rocky Mountains' Gold Region.* 3 maps in color on 2 large folding sheets. Cloth. New York, 1859. First edition. $450–$500.

REDSKINS (The). By the Author of *The Pathfinder.* 2 vols., printed brown wrappers. New York, 1846. (By James Fenimore Cooper.) First edition. $1,000–$1,250. (For first English edition, see *Ravensnest.*)

REED, Andrew, and Matheson, James. *A Narrative of the Visit to the American Churches by the Deputation from the Congregational Union of England and Wales.* 4 plates, folding map. 2 vols., leather. London, 1835. First edition. $250–$300.

REED, Ishmael. *The Free-Lance Pallbearers.* Cloth. Garden City, 1967. First edition. In dust jacket. $50–$65. Author's first book.

REED, J. W. *Map of and Guide to the Kansas Gold Region.* Map. 24 pp., printed wrappers. New York, 1859. First edition. $3,000–$3,500.

REED, John. *The Day in Bohemia.* Printed wrappers. New York, 1913. First edition. One of 500. Boxed. $200–$225.

REED, John. *Insurgent Mexico.* Cloth. New York, 1914. First edition. In dust jacket. $75–$100.

REED, John. *Sangar: To Lincoln Steffens.* Boards. Riverside, Conn., 1913. First separate edition. Limited. Boxed. $100–$150. Author's first book.

REED, John. *Tamburlaine and Other Verses.* Boards. Riverside, Conn., 1917. First edition. One of 450 (of an edition of 500). $125–$150. Another issue: One of 50 on handmade paper. In tissue dust jacket. $250–$350. Trade edition: In dust jacket. $60.

REED, John. *Ten Days That Shook the World.* Illustrated. Cloth. New York, 1919. First edition. In dust jacket. $150–$175. Lacking jacket, $75–$100.

REED, Nathaniel. *The Life of Texas Jack.* Illustrated. Pictorial wrappers. (Tulsa, 1936.) First edition. $750.

REED, S. G. *A History of the Texas Railroads.* Blue cloth. Houston, (1941). Limited, signed edition. $150–$300.

REED, Silas. *Report of . . . Surveyor General of Wyoming Territory, for the Year 1871.* Tables. 46 pp., wrappers. Washington, 1871. First edition. $250–$300.

REED, Talbot Baines. *A History of the Old English Letter Foundries.* Illustrated. Half leather. London, 1887. First edition. $175–$200. London, (1952). Cloth. In dust jacket. $75–$100.

REED, Wallace P. *History of Atlanta, Georgia.* 46 portraits. 2 parts in one, cloth. Syracuse, 1889. First edition. $75–$100.

REED, William. *Life on the Border, Sixty Years Ago.* 120 pp., wrappers. Fall River, Mass., 1882. First edition. $50–$75.

REES, William. *Description of the City of Keokuk.* 24 pp., printed self-wrappers. Keokuk, Iowa, 1854. First edition. $225–$250. Keokuk, 1855. 22 pp., with wrapper title. Second edition. $100–$135.

REES, William. *The Mississippi Bridge Cities: Davenport, Rock Island and Moline.* Woodcut frontispiece. 32 pp., sewed. (Rock Island, Ill.), 1854. First edition. $150–$200.

REESE, Lizette Woodworth. *A Branch of May: Poems.* Gray cloth. Baltimore, 1887. First edition. $250–$275. Author's first book. Portland, Me., 1920. Mosher Press. Boards. One of 450. Boxed. $75.

REESE, Lizette Woodworth. *A Handful of Lavender.* Decorated cloth and parchment. Boston, 1891. First edition. $50–$75.

REESE, Lizette Woodworth. *White April and Other Poems.* Cloth. New York, (about 1930). First edition. In dust jacket. $50–$75.

REGULATIONS and List of Premiums of the Jerauld County Agricultural and Industrial Society for the First Fair to Be Held at Wessington Springs, D.T. 16 pp., wrappers. Wessington Springs, Dakota Territory, 1884. $125–$150.

REGULATIONS for the Uniform and Dress of the Army of the United States. 25 chromolithographs. 13 pp., cloth. Philadelphia, 1851. $500 and up.

REICHEL, Anton. *The Chiaroscurists of the XVI–XVII–XVIII Centuries.* 111 full-color reproductions. Folio, boards. Cambridge, no date. $400–$500.

REID, A. J. *The Resources and Manufacturing Capacity of the Lower Fox River Valley.* Folding map and panorama, plates. 56 pp., wrappers. Appleton, Wis., 1874. First edition. $75–$100.

REID, Forrest. *Apostate.* Cloth. London, (1926). First edition. One of 50 signed. $75–$100.

REID, Forrest. *Illustrators of the Sixties.* Illustrated. Buckram. London, 1928. First edition. In dust jacket. $250–$300.

REID, J. M. *Sketches and Anecdotes of the Old Settlers and New Comers.* 187 pp., wrappers. Keokuk, Iowa, 1876. First edition. $300–$350.

REID, John C. *Reid's Tramp, or A Journal of the Incidents of Ten Months Travel Through Texas, New Mexico, Arizona, Sonora, and California.* Cloth. Selma, Ala., 1858. First edition. $7,500–$9,500. Also, spine faded, $4,000 (A, 1980).

REID, Mayne. *The Headless Horseman.* 20 plates. 2 vols., cloth. London, (1886). (By Thomas M. Reid.) First book edition. $400–$500.

REID, Mayne. *No Quarter!* 3 vols., cloth. London, 1888. First edition. (By Thomas M. Reid.) $350–$400.

REID, Mayne. *Osceola the Seminole.* Cloth. New York, (1858). (By Thomas M. Reid.) First American edition. $300–$400.

REID, Mayne. *The Quadroon; or, A Lover's Adventures in Louisiana.* 3 vols., orange or gray cloth. London, 1856. (By Thomas M. Reid.) First edition. $500–$600.

REID, Mayne. *The White Chief: A Legend of Northern Mexico.* 3 vols., cloth. London, 1855. (By Thomas M. Reid.) First edition. $400–$500.

REID, Mayne. *The Wild Huntress.* 3 vols., cloth. London, 1861. (By Thomas M. Reid.) First edition. $400–$500.

REID, Mayne. *The Wood-Rangers.* 3 vols., cloth. London, 1860. (By Thomas M. Reid.) First edition. $400–$500.

REID, Samuel C., Jr. *The Scouting Expeditions of McCulloch's Texas Rangers.* 12 plates and plan. Cloth. Philadelphia, 1847. First edition. $300–$350. Philadelphia, 1848. Cloth. $500–$750.

REID, Thomas M. See Reid, Mayne.

REIGN of Terror in Kanzas (The). 34 pp., wrappers. Boston, 1856. (By Charles W. Briggs.) First edition. $600–$750.

RELIEF Business Directory, Names and New Locations in San Francisco, Oakland, Berkeley and Alameda of 4,000 San Francisco Firms and Business Men. 64 pp., wrappers. Berkeley, May, 1906. $200–$300. (Issued after the great earthquake and fire of 1906.)

REMARKS Addressed to the Citizens of Illinois, on the Proposed Introduction of Slavery. 14 pp., disbound. (Vandalia?, 1824?) (By Morris Birkbeck.) $3,000–$3,500.

REMARQUE, Erich Maria. *All Quiet on the Western Front.* Buckram. London, (1929). First edition in English. In dust jacket. $100–$150. Boston, 1929. Gray cloth. First American edition. In dust jacket. $75. (Note: The first edition in German, *Im Westen Nichts Neues*, Berlin, 1929, wrappers, is worth roughly $100–$150 if in fine condition.) New York, 1969. Limited Editions Club. Cloth. Boxed. $60–$75.

ERICH MARIA REMARQUE

REMARQUE, Erich Maria. *The Road Back*. Illustrated. Cloth. London, (1931). First edition in English. In dust jacket. $65–$100. Boston, 1931. Cloth, First American edition. In dust jacket. $75. Advance copy in wrappers: $100–$125.

REMINGTON, Frederic. *Crooked Trails*. 49 plates. Pictorial tan cloth. New York, 1898. First edition. In dust jacket. $200–$250.

REMINGTON, Frederic. *Done in the Open*. Introduction by Owen Wister. Illustrations by Remington. 90 pp., folio, cream-colored pictorial boards. New York, 1902. First edition, first issue, with Russell imprint and with "Frederick" instead of "Frederic" on front cover. $400–$500. Another issue: Suede leather. One of 250 signed. $1,000 and up. Later issue: New York, 1902. Collier imprint. Half cloth. $200–$250. New York, 1903. Half cloth. $75–$100.

REMINGTON, Frederic. *Drawings*. 61 plates. Oblong folio, pictorial boards and cloth. New York, 1897. First edition. Boxed. $400–$500. Another issue: Suede leather. One of 250 signed. $1,500. New York, 1898. Cloth. $400–$500.

REMINGTON, Frederic. *Frederic Remington's Own West*. Edited by Harold McCracken. Colored frontispiece, other illustrations. Cowhide. New York, (1960). First edition. One of 167 signed by McCracken. Boxed. $400–$500. Trade edition: Cloth. In dust jacket. $40–$50.

REMINGTON, Frederic. *Frontier Sketches*. Illustrated by the author. Oblong, pictorial boards. Chicago, (1898). First edition. $300–$400.

REMINGTON, Frederic. *John Ermine of the Yellowstone*. Illustrated by the author. Brown cloth. New York, 1902. First edition. $75–$100. (Note: First edition copies, as well as reprints, misspell the author's name "Reminington" on the spine.)

REMINGTON, Frederic. *Men with the Bark On*. Illustrated by the author. Pictorial orange-tan cloth. New York, 1900. First edition, first issue, 7/8 inch thick (later 1 1/8 inches). $125–$185.

REMINGTON, Frederic. *Pony Tracks*. Illustrated by the author. Brown decorated cloth, or leather. New York, 1895. First edition. $300–$350. Leather: $400–$500. Author's first book.

REMINGTON, Frederic. *A Rogers Ranger in the French and Indian War*. Printed wrappers. (New York), 1897. First edition. $100–$125.

REMINGTON, Frederic. *Sundown Leflare*. Illustrated by the author. Brown pictorial cloth. New York, 1899. First edition. $75–$85.

REMINGTON, Frederic. *The Way of an Indian*. Illustrated by the author. Cloth. New York, 1906. First edition, first issue, February, crimson cloth, yellow lettering with "Fox, Duffield & Company" on spine and page 9 so numbered. $500–$650. Also, $450 (A, 1977).

REMINISCENCES of a Campaign in Mexico. Map, frontispiece. Cloth. Nashville, 1849. (By John B. Robertson.) First edition. $250.

REMSBURG, John E., and Remsburg, George J. *Charley Reynolds, Soldier, Hunter, Scout and Guide*. Portrait. Cloth. Kansas City, 1931. First book edition. One of 175. $150.

REMY, Jules, and Brenchley, Julius L. *A Journey to Great Salt Lake City*. Map, 10 plates. 2 vols., cloth. London, 1861. First edition in English. $500–$600. (The first edition, *Voyage au pays des Mormons*, Paris, 1860, was issued in both cloth and wrappers and is valued in the $750–$1,000 range.)

RENFROW, W. C. *Oklahoma and the Cherokee Strip*. Folding map. 16 pp., wrappers. Chicago, 1893. $75–$100.

RENNER, Frederic G. *Charles M. Russell: Paintings, Drawings, and Sculpture in the Amon G. Carter Collection. A Descriptive Catalogue*. Illustrated, including color.
</body>

Decorated cloth. Austin, (1966). First edition. One of 250 signed, and with an extra color plate and a portfolio of color plates laid in. Boxed. $250–$300.

REPLY to the Essay on Population, by the Rev. T. R. Malthus (A). Leather-backed gray boards. London, 1807. (By William Hazlitt.) First edition. $1,000–$1,500. Also, $1,300 (A, 1980)—A. Edward Newton's copy, which brought $80 at auction of the Newton books in 1941.

RÉPONSE a une Addresse de la Chambre des Communes, en date du 23 Avril 1869, Demandant un Rapport Indiquant le Progrès qui ont été faits dans L'Ouverture d'une Communication entre Fort William el l'Établissement de la Rivière Rouge . . . Par Ordre Hector L. Langevin, Secrétaire d'État. 88 pp., half morocco. Ottawa, 1869. $250–$300.

REPORT from a Select Committee of the House of Representatives, on the Overland Emigration Route from Minnesota to British Oregon. Printed wrappers, marbled spine. St. Paul, Minn., 1858. $600–$750.

REPORT From the Select Committee on the Hudson's Bay Company. 3 elephant folio colored folding maps by Arrowsmith. Half morocco. London, 1857. First edition. $400–$500. (Note: There was also an advance issue in wrappers, 2 parts, same date, catalogued in the 1950's by a New York dealer at $250. Estimated current value: $500 and up.)

REPORT of a Committee Appointed by the Trustees of the Town of Milwaukee, Relative to the Commerce of That Town and the Navigation of Lake Michigan. 12 pp., sewed. Milwaukee, 1842. (By I. A. Lapham and F. Randall.) $350–$400.

REPORT of the Board of Canal Commissioners, to the General Assembly of Ohio. Sewed. Columbus, Ohio, 1824. $150–$200.

REPORT of the Board of Directors of Internal Improvements of the State of Massachusetts, on the Practicability and Expediency of a Rail-Road from Boston to the Hudson River, and from Boston to Providence. 6 folding plans. Boston, 1829. $100–$150.

REPORT of the Board of Internal Improvements for the State of Kentucky, and Reports of the Engineers. 47 pp., sewed. (Frankfort, Ky., 1836.) $100–$125.

REPORT of the Canal Commissioners, to the General Assembly of Ohio. 54 pp., stitched. Columbus, 1825. $45. Another issue: 66 pp., sewed. $75–$100.

REPORT of the Commissioner of Public Buildings, with the Documents Accompanying the Same. 36 pp., stitched. (Madison, Wis., 1842.) (By John Smith.) $60–$100.

REPORT of the Committee to Whom Was Referred, on the 26th Ultimo, the Consideration of the Expediency of Accepting from the State of Connecticut, a Cession of Jurisdiction of the Territory West of Pennsylvania, Commonly Called the Western Reserve of Connecticut. 31 pp., calf. (Philadelphia), 1800. $125–$150.

REPORT of the General Assembly upon the Subject of the Proceedings of the Bank of the U.S., Against the Officers of State. 37 pp., sewed. Columbus, Ohio, 1820. $100–$125.

REPORT of the Proceedings Connected with the Disputes Between the Earl of Selkirk and the North-West Company. Half leather. London, 1819. (Samuel Hull Wilcocke, editor.) $650–$750. Montreal, 1819. Calf. $650–$750.

REPORT of the Secretary of the Interior, Communicating . . . the Report of J. Ross Browne, on the Late Indian War in Oregon and Washington Territories. 66 pp., stitched. Washington, 1858. First edition. $100–$150.

REPORT of the Trial of Frederick P. Hill, etc. 60 pp., wrappers. Chicago, 1864. (Allan Pinkerton, editor.) First edition. $125–$150.

REPORT on the Committee of the Society of Arts. Engraved folding plate and 5 engraved full-page reproductions. Boards. London, 1819. $50–$60.

REPORT on the Governor's Message, Relating to the "Political Situation," "Polygamy," and "Governmental Action." 13 pp., wrappers. Salt Lake, 1882. $125–$150.

REPORT on the Subject of a Communication between Canandaigua Lake and the Erie Canal, Made at a Meeting of the Citizens. 23 pp., sewed. Canandaigua, N.Y., 1821. $75–$100.

REPORT Relative to the Excitements, on the Part of British Subjects, of the Indians to Commit Hostility Against the U.S., and the Late Campaign on the Wabash. 43 pp., sewed. Washington City, 1812. $75–$100.

REPORTS and Resolutions of the General Assembly of the State of South Carolina. Gathered, not sewed, but punched for stitching. Columbia, 1863. $75–$100.

REPORTS of the Committee of Investigation Sent in 1873, by the Mexican Government, to the Frontier of Texas. 3 folding maps. Boards and leather. New York, 1875. $200–$300.

REPORTS of Territorial Officers of the Territory of Colorado. Wrappers. Central City, 1871. $100–$125.

REPPLIER, Agnes. *Books and Men.* Boards and cloth. Boston, 1882. First edition. $50–$75. Author's first book.

REPTON, Humphry. *Observations on the Theory and Practice of Landscape Gardening.* Portrait frontispiece and 27 plates, 10 in full color. Contemporary leather. London, 1803. First edition. $4,000–$5,000. London, 1805. $3,000–$4,000.

RESIGNATION: An American Novel by a Lady. 2 vols., marbled boards and calf. Boston, 1825. (By Sarah Ann Evans.) First edition, with errata leaf in Vol. 1. $200–$250.

RESOURCES and Development of the Territory of Washington. Folding map. 72 pp., sewed. Seattle, 1886. $100–$150.

RESOURCES of Arizona (The). 71 pp., wrappers. (Florence, Ariz., 1881.) (By Patrick Hamilton.) First edition. $350. (For later editions, see author entry.)

REVERE, Joseph W. *A Tour of Duty in California.* 6 plates, folding map. Cloth. New York, 1849. First edition. $400–$500.

REVIEW of the Opinion of the Supreme Court in the Case of Cohen vs. Virginia, etc. 78 pp., stitched. Steubenville, Ohio, 1821. (By Charles Hammond.) $150–$175.

REXROTH, Kenneth. *The Art of Worldly Wisdom.* Green boards and cloth. Prairie City, Ill., 1949. First edition. Signed by the author. Errata slip laid in. $175. Sausalito, Calif., (1953). Boards. Second edition. In dust jacket. $125.

REXROTH, Kenneth. *In What Hour.* Blue cloth. New York, 1940. First edition. In dust jacket. $100–$125. Author's first book.

REXROTH, Kenneth. *The Signature of All Things.* Boards. (New York, 1950.) First edition. In dust jacket. $50–$75.

REYNARDSON, C. T. S. Birch. *'Down the Road' or Reminiscences of a Gentleman Coachman.* Colored lithographs. Cloth. London, 1875. First edition. $175–$250. Second edition, same date. $125–$150.

REYNOLDS, H. D. (editor). *Wells Cathedral.* Frontispiece, 4 plans (one folding), a folding table, 8 plates and text illustrations. Folio, morocco. London, (1881). $75–$100.

REYNOLDS, J. N. *Voyage of the United States Frigate Potomac.* Illustrated. Half leather. New York, 1835. First edition. $250–$350.

REYNOLDS, John. *My Own Times.* Portrait. Cloth. Illinois (Belleville), 1855. First edition. $400–$500. Also, rebacked, stained, $225 (A, 1980).

REYNOLDS, John. *The Pioneer History of Illinois*. Cloth. Belleville, 1852. First edition. $300–$400. Also, foxed, faded, $200 (A, 1980).

REYNOLDS, John. *Sketches of the Country on the Northern Route from Belleville, Ill., to the City of New York, and Back by the Ohio Valley*. Black cloth. Belleville, 1854. First edition. $600–$750.

REZNIKOFF, Charles. *Five Groups of Verse*. Cloth. New York, (1927). First edition. One of 375. In dust jacket. $50–$75.

REZNIKOFF, Charles. *Going To and Fro and Walking Up and Down*. Cloth. New York, (1941). First edition. In dust jacket. $50.

REZNIKOFF, Charles. *Jerusalem the Golden*. Cloth. New York, (1934). First edition. In dust jacket. $75–$125.

REZNIKOFF, Charles. *Nine Plays*. Cloth. New York, (1927). First edition. One of 400. In dust jacket. $50–$75.

REZNIKOFF, Charles. *Rhythms*. Wrappers. Brooklyn, (1918). First edition. $750–$850. Author's first book.

REZNIKOFF, Charles. *Testimony*. Cloth. New York, (1934). First edition. In dust jacket. $100–$125.

RHODES, Eugene Manlove. *The Best Novels and Stories of Eugene Manlove Rhodes*. Cloth. Boston, 1949. First edition. In dust jacket. $40–$50.

RHODES, Eugene Manlove. *Beyond the Desert*. Cloth. Boston, 1934. First edition, with dated title page. In dust jacket. $50–$75.

RHODES, Eugene Manlove. *Bransford in Arcadia*. Cloth. New York, 1914. First edition. In dust jacket. $35–$50.

RHODES, Eugene Manlove. *The Desire of the Moth*. Cloth. New York, 1916. First edition. In dust jacket. $150–$175.

RHODES, Eugene Manlove. *Good Men and True*. Cloth. New York, 1910. First edition. In dust jacket. $100–$125. Author's first book.

RHODES, Eugene Manlove. *The Little World Waddies*. Illustrated. Cloth. Chico, Calif., (1946). First edition. In dust jacket. $150. (El Paso), 1946. Illustrated by Harold Bugbee. Cloth. $135.

RHODES, Eugene Manlove. *Once in the Saddle and Paso Por Aqui*. Cloth. Boston, 1927. First edition. In dust jacket. $40–$50.

RHODES, Eugene Manlove. *The Proud Sheriff*. Cloth. Boston, 1935. First edition. In dust jacket. $50–$60.

RHODES, Eugene Manlove. *Say Now Shibboleth*. Boards and cloth. Chicago, 1921. Book Fellows. First edition. One of 400. In tissue dust jacket. $100–$135.

RHODES, Eugene Manlove. *Stepsons of Light*. Cloth. Boston, (1921). First edition. In dust jacket. $40–$50.

RHODES, Eugene Manlove. *The Trusty Knaves*. Cloth. Boston, 1933. First edition. In dust jacket. $40–$50.

RHODES, Eugene Manlove. *West Is West*. Frontispiece. Cloth. New York, 1917. First edition. In dust jacket. $50–$60.

RHODODAPHNE: or The Thessalian Spell: A Poem. Blue boards. London, 1818. (By Thomas Love Peacock.) First edition. $400–$500.

RICARDO, David. *On the Principles of Political Economy, and Taxation*. Contemporary calf. London, 1817. First edition. $5,000 and up. Also, $4,750 (A, 1977).

RICE County: Its Resources. 20 pp., wrappers. Faribault, Minn., 1869. $150–$200.

RICH, Adrienne Cecile. *Ariadne: A Play in Three Acts and Poems.* 59 pp., blue wrappers. (Baltimore), 1939. First edition. In tissue dust jacket. $1,750 in a 1978 catalogue. (Note: The poet's first published work—juvenilia.)

RICH, Adrienne Cecile. *A Change of World.* Foreword by W. H. Auden. Boards. New Haven, 1951. First edition. In dust jacket. $75–$100. Author's first book as an adult.

RICH, Adrienne Cecile. *The Diamond Cutters and Other Poems.* Cloth. New York, (1955). First edition. In dust jacket. $75–$100.

RICHARD Hurdis; or, the Avenger of Blood. 2 vols., cloth, paper labels. Philadelphia, 1838. (By William Gilmore Simms.) First edition. $350–$400.

RICHARDS, Laura E. *Captain January.* Gray boards, white cloth spine. Boston, 1891. First edition, first state, with typography and presswork note at foot of copyright page. $125–$135.

RICHARDS, Laura E. *Five Mice in a Mouse-Trap.* Cloth. Boston, 1881. First edition. $150–$175.

RICHARDS, Thomas Addison. *American Scenery Illustrated.* Morocco. New York, (1854). First edition. $250–$350.

RICHARDS, Thomas Addison. *Georgia Illustrated.* Plates. 44 pp., leather. Penfield, Ga., 1842. First edition. $300–$400.

RICHARDS, Thomas Addison. *The Romance of American Landscape.* 16 engravings. Morocco. New York, (1854). First edition. $250–$300.

RICHARDSON, Dorothy. *Dawn's Left Hand.* Cloth. London, (1931). First edition. In dust jacket. $100–$125.

RICHARDSON, Dorothy. *Interim.* Cloth. London, (1919). First edition. In dust jacket. $75–$100.

RICHARDSON, Dorothy. *Pointed Roofs.* Cloth. London, 1915. First edition. $40–$60. New York, 1919. Cloth. In dust jacket. $50. Author's first book.

RICHARDSON, Maj. John. *Eight Years in Canada.* Portrait. Cloth. Montreal, 1847. First edition. $500–$600. Also, lacking portrait, $200 (A, 1980).

RICHARDSON, Rupert N. *The Comanche Barrier to South Plains Settlement.* Illustrated. Cloth. Glendale, Calif., 1933. $100–$150.

RICHARDSON, Rupert N., and Rister, C. C. *The Greater Southwest.* Cloth. Glendale, 1934. First edition. $50–$75.

RICHARDSON, William H. *The Journal of William H. Richardson: A Private Soldier in Col. Doniphan's Command.* 84 pp., wrappers. Baltimore, 1847. First edition. $4,000–$5,000, possibly more. Baltimore, 1848. Illustrated. Half leather. Second edition. $1,000. New York, 1848. Third edition. $750.

RICHEY, James H. *A Trip Across the Plains in 1854.* 8 pp., wrappers. (Richey, Calif., 1908.) First edition. $75–$100.

RICHMOND, C. W., and Vallette, H. F. *A History of Du Page County, Illinois.* Cloth. Chicago, 1857. First edition. $150–$200.

RICHMOND During the War; Four Years of Personal Observation. Cloth. New York, 1867. (By Sally A. Brock.) First edition. $100–$125.

RICHTER, Conrad. *Brothers of No Kin and Other Stories.* Red cloth. New York, (about 1924). First edition. In white (first) dust jacket. $250–$350. In later (orange) jacket. $200–$300. Author's first book.

RICHTOFEN, Walter, Baron Von. *Cattle-Raising on the Plains of North America.* Cloth. New York, 1885. First edition. $400–$475.

RIDGE, John R. See Yellow Bird. Also see *The Life of Joaquin Murieta.*

RIDGE, John R. *Joaquin Murieta, the Brigand Chief of California.* Color plates, folding reward poster facsimile. Boards. San Francisco, 1932. Grabhorn printing. One of 400. $75–$85.

RIDGE, John R. *The Life and Adventures of Joaquin Murieta the Celebrated California Bandit.* Printed wrappers. San Francisco, (1874). Third (?) edition. $375 (A, 1968). (Note: This edition included a reprinting, with separate title page, of Eugene T. Sawyer's biography of another bandit, Tiburcio Vasquez, and is listed by Wright Howes as a reprint of the third edition, which he records as published in 1871. For first edition, see Yellow Bird. Also, see Sawyer, Eugene T.)

RIDGE, John R. *Poems.* Original photographs as frontispiece. Cloth. San Francisco, 1868. First edition. $100.

RIDGE, Lola. *Firehead.* Half morocco. New York, 1929. First edition. One of 30 signed. $50–$75. Trade edition: In dust jacket. $20.

RIDING, Laura. *Americans.* Boards and cloth. No place, 1934. Primavera Press. First edition. One of 200. $200–$250.

RIDING, Laura. *The Close Chaplet.* Boards, paper label. New York, (1926). First edition. $400–$500. Author's first book.

RIDING, Laura. *Collected Poems.* Cloth. New York, 1938. First American edition. In dust jacket. $110–$225.

RIDING, Laura. *Experts are Puzzled.* Cloth. London, (1930). First edition. In dust jacket. $200–$250.

RIDING, Laura. *Four Unposted Letters to Catherine.* Boards and leather. Paris, (1930). Hours Press. First edition. One of 200 signed. In glassine dust jacket. $250–$300.

RIDING, Laura. *Laura and Francesca.* Decorated blue boards and cloth. Deya, Majorca, 1931. Seizin Press. First edition. One of 200 signed. In glassine dust jacket. $300–$375.

RIDING, Laura. *The Life of the Dead.* Illustrated by John Aldridge. Stiff wrappers. London, (1933). First edition. One of 200 signed. $250–$300.

RIDING, Laura. *Lives of Wives.* Green cloth. London, (1939). First edition. In dust jacket. $150–$200.

RIDING, Laura. *Love as Love, Death as Death.* Tan or gray cloth. London, 1928. Seizin Press (its first book). First edition. One of 175 signed. In tissue jacket. $250–$350.

RIDING, Laura. *Progress of Stories.* Cloth. London, (1935). First edition. In dust jacket. $135–$150.

RIDING, Laura. *The Second Leaf.* Wrappers (actually a broadside folded to make 4 leaves). Deya, 1935. Seizin Press. First edition. Limited (fewer than 100). $275–$475.

RIDING, Laura. *Though Gently.* Decorated boards and cloth. Deya, 1930. Seizin Press. First edition. One of 200 signed. In glassine dust jacket. $250–$300.

RIDING, Laura. *A Trojan Ending.* Cloth. London, (1937). First edition. In dust jacket. $350. New York, (1937). First American edition. In dust jacket. $100–$150.

RIDING, Laura. *Twenty Poems Less.* Half leather and boards. Paris, 1930. Hours Press. First edition. One of 200 signed. In glassine dust jacket. $300–$350.

RIDING, Laura. *Voltaire*. Wrappers. London, 1927. Hogarth Press. First edition. $300–$350.

RIDING, Laura, and Graves, Robert. *A Pamphlet Against Anthologies*. Cloth. Garden City, 1928. First American edition. In dust jacket. $75–$150. London, 1928. Cloth. First edition. In dust jacket. $50–$75.

RIDING, Laura, and Graves, Robert. *A Survey of Modernist Poetry*. Boards and cloth. London, 1927. First edition. One of 1,000. In dust jacket. $125–$275.

RIDINGS, Sam P. *The Chisholm Trail*. Folding map, frontispiece, and text illustrations. Cloth. Guthrie, Okla., (1936). First edition. In dust jacket. $75–$100.

RIDLER, Anne (editor). *The Little Book of Modern Verse*. Preface by T. S. Eliot. Cloth. London, 1941. First edition. In dust jacket. $75–$100.

RIENZI, The Last of the Tribunes. 3 vols., boards. London, 1835. (By Edward Bulwer-Lytton.) First edition, with errata slips for Vols. 2 and 3 tipped into Vol. 2. $600–$800.

RILEY, James Whitcomb. See Johnson, Benj. F. (of Boone).

RILEY, James Whitcomb. *Character Sketches, The Boss Girl, A Christmas Story, and Other Sketches*. Cloth, or printed wrappers. Indianapolis, 1886. First edition, first printing, with copyright notice in the name of Riley and an exclamation point after "sir" in line 5 of page 9. Cloth: $75–$100. Wrappers: $75–$100.

RILEY, James Whitcomb. *The Flying Islands of the Night*. Illustrated. Cloth. Indianapolis, 1892. First edition. In vellum dust jacket. $150–$200. Another issue (actually issued in 1891): White flexible boards. In dust jacket. $200–$250.

RILEY, James Whitcomb. *Rhymes of Childhood*. Cloth. Indianapolis, 1891. First edition, first state, with child's head illustrated on front cover. $50–$85.

RILKE, Rainer Maria. *Primal Sound and Other Prose Pieces*. Illustrated. Boards. Cummington, Mass., 1943. First edition. One of 175. $350–$450.

RILKE, Rainer Maria. *The Sonnets to Orpheus*. Illustrated by Kurt Roesch. Boards. New York, (1944). One of 45 with the engravings signed. In dust jacket. $1,650.

RIMBAUD, Arthur. See Schwartz, Delmore.

RINEHART, Mary Roberts. *The Man in Lower Ten*. Illustrated by Howard Chandler Christy. Cloth. Indianapolis, (1909). First edition. In dust jacket. $50–$75.

RINEHART, Mary Roberts, and Hopwood, Avery. *The Bat: A Novel from the Play by Mary Roberts Rinehart and Avery Hopwood*. Cloth. New York, (1926). First edition. In dust jacket. $50–$60. (Note: Believed to have been written by Stephen Vincent Benét.)

RINGAN Gilhaize. 3 vols., boards. Edinburgh, 1823. (By John Galt.) First edition. $350–$500.

RINGWALT, John Luther (editor). *American Encyclopedia of Printing*. Cloth. Philadelphia, 1871. First edition. $250–$300.

RIPLEY, R. S. *The War with Mexico*. 14 plans. Cloth. New York, 1849. First edition. $200–$300. London, 1850. Half morocco. First English edition. $500.

RISTER, Carl Coke. *The Southwestern Frontier, 1865–1881*. Maps. Cloth. Cleveland, 1928. First edition. $150–$175.

RITTENHOUSE, Jack D. *American Horse-Drawn Vehicles*. Illustrated. Cloth. Los Angeles, 1948. First edition. In dust jacket. $125.

RIVER Dove (The); with Some Quiet Thoughts on the Happy Practice of Angling. 14

engravings. Half leather. (London?, about 1845.) (By John L. Anderdon.) One of 25 privately printed. $250–$300.

RIVERS, Elizabeth. *Stranger in Aran.* Illustrations (4 in color) by author. Boards, linen spine. Dublin, 1946. Cuala Press. One of 280. In dust jacket. $125–$175.

RIVES, Reginald. *The Coaching Club, Its History, Records, and Activities.* Illustrated. Cloth. New York, 1935. Derrydale Press. One of 300. $750.

ROB of the Bowl. 2 vols., cloth, paper labels on spines. Philadelphia, 1838. (By John Pendleton Kennedy.) First edition. $300–$400.

ROB ROY. 3 vols., boards, paper labels. Edinburgh, 1818. (By Sir Walter Scott.) First edition. $500–$750.

ROBB, John S. See *Streaks of Squatter Life, etc.*

ROBB, John S. *Kaam, or Daylight.* Pictorial wrappers. Boston, 1847. First edition. $300–$400. Also, $200 (A, 1968).

ROBBINS, Aurelia. *A True and Authentic Account of the Indian War, etc.* 28 pp., wrappers. New York, 1836. $150–$200.

ROBBINS, Tom. *Another Roadside Attraction.* Cloth. Garden City, 1971. First edition. In dust jacket. $150–$200. Author's first book.

ROBBINS, Tom. *Even Cowgirls Get the Blues.* Cloth. Boston, 1976. First edition. In dust jacket. $85–$125.

ROBERTS, Mrs. D. W. *A Woman's Reminiscences of Six Years in Camp with the Texas Rangers.* Illustrated. 64 pp., wrappers. Austin, (1928). First edition. $50–$75.

ROBERTS, Elizabeth Madox. *Black Is My Truelove's Hair.* Boards, green buckram spine. New York, 1938. First edition. One of 175 signed. Boxed. $40–$50.

ROBERTS, Elizabeth Madox. *A Buried Treasure.* Green buckram. New York, 1931. First edition. One of 200 signed. Boxed. $40–$60.

ROBERTS, Elizabeth Madox. *The Great Meadow.* Green buckram. New York, 1930. First edition. One of 295 large paper copies, signed. Boxed. $40–$60.

ROBERTS, Elizabeth Madox. *In the Great Steep's Garden.* (Cover title.) Wrappers. (Colorado Springs, 1915.) First edition. $65–$75. Author's first book.

ROBERTS, Elizabeth Madox. *Under the Tree.* Boards. New York, 1922. First edition. In dust jacket. $50–$75.

ROBERTS, Kenneth. *Arundel.* Dark-blue cloth. Garden City, 1930. First edition. In dust jacket. $50–$75.

ROBERTS, Kenneth. *Europe's Morning After.* Decorated cloth. New York, (about 1921). First edition, first issue, with "B-V" on copyright page. In dust jacket. $200–$250. Author's first book.

ROBERTS, Kenneth. *Lydia Bailey.* Cloth. Garden City, 1947. First edition. Gray buckram. One of 1,050 signed, with a page of the ms., with corrections in Roberts' hand, laid in. In dust jacket. Boxed. $75–$100. Trade edition: Cloth. In dust jacket. $25.

ROBERTS, Kenneth. *Northwest Passage.* Dark-green cloth. Garden City, 1937. First edition. In dust jacket. $25–$35. Another issue: 2 vols., cloth. One of 1,050 signed. In dust jackets. Boxed. $150–$300.

ROBERTS, Kenneth. *Oliver Wiswell.* Cloth. New York, 1940. First edition. 2 vols., cloth. One of 1,050 signed. Boxed. $125–$200. Trade edition: Cloth. $25.

ROBERTS, Kenneth. *Rabble in Arms.* Cloth. Garden City, 1933. First edition. In dust jacket. $75–$100.

ROBERTS, Kenneth. *Sun Hunting*. Illustrated. Blue-green cloth. Indianapolis, (1922). First edition. In dust jacket. $75–$100.

ROBERTS, Kenneth. *Trending into Maine*. Illustrated by N. C. Wyeth. Tan buckram. Boston, 1938. First edition, with "Published June 1938" on copyright page. In dust jacket. $25. Another issue: Cloth. One of 1,075 signed. Boxed. $200–$300. With an extra set of the Wyeth plates in envelope. $350–$425.

ROBERTS, Kenneth. *Why Europe Leaves Home*. Cloth. (Indianapolis, 1922.) First edition. $60–$75.

ROBERTS, Oran M. *A Description of Texas*. 8 colored plates, 5 double-page maps. Cloth. St. Louis, 1881. First edition. $200–$250.

ROBERTS, W. H. *Northwestern Washington*. Folding map. 52 pp., wrappers. Port Townsend, Wash., 1880. First edition. $400–$500.

ROBERTSON, John W. *Francis Drake and Other Early Explorers Along the Pacific Coast*. 28 maps. Illustrations by Valenti Angelo. Vellum and boards. San Francisco, 1927. Grabhorn Press. One of 1,000. $200–$250.

ROBERTSON, Wyndham, Jr. *Oregon, Our Right and Title*. Folding map. Boards and cloth, or printed wrappers. Washington, 1846. First edition. Either binding: $1,000–$1,500.

ROBIDOUX, Mrs. Orral M. *Memorial to the Robidoux Brothers*. Map. 16 plates. Cloth. Kansas City, 1924. First edition. $80–$100.

ROBINSON, Charles Edson. *A Concise History of the United Society of Believers Called Shakers*. Illustrated. Boards and calf. East Canterbury, N.H., (1893). $150–$175.

ROBINSON, Charles. N. *Old Naval Prints, Their Artists and Engravers*. Illustrated, including 24 plates in color. Cloth. London, 1924. In dust jacket. $200–$225.

ROBINSON Crusoe. See Defoe, Daniel. Also, see *The Family Robinson Crusoe*.

ROBINSON, Edwin Arlington. *Amaranth*. Cloth. New York, 1934. First edition. Large paper issue, one of 226, signed. $60–$80. Trade edition: Green cloth. In dust jacket. $25.

ROBINSON, Edwin Arlington. *Captain Craig: A Book of Poems*. Cloth, paper label. Boston, 1902. First edition, first issue, with "Published October, 1902" on copyright page. One of 125 untrimmed. $100–$150.

ROBINSON, Edwin Arlington. *Cavender's House*. Boards. New York, 1929. First edition. One of 500 signed. In slipcase. $50–$60. Trade edition: Cloth. In dust jacket. $25.

ROBINSON, Edwin Arlington. *The Children of the Night*. Muslin. Boston, 1897. First edition. One of 50 on Japan vellum. $1,250–$1,500. Also, $1,100 (A, 1974). Another issue: Cloth. One of 500 on Batchworth laid paper. $300–$350.

ROBINSON, Edwin Arlington. *Dionysus in Doubt*. Cloth-backed boards. New York, 1925. First edition. One of 350 large paper copies, signed. Boxed. $50–$60. Trade edition: Cloth. First issue, with gray (instead of white) labels. In dust jacket. $25.

ROBINSON, Edwin Arlington. *Fortunatus*. Boards, paper label. Reno, 1928. Grabhorn printing. First edition. One of 171 signed. $150–$250. One of 12 on brown paper, signed, for presentation. $500-$750.

ROBINSON, Edwin Arlington. *The Glory of the Nightingales*. Cloth. New York, 1930. First edition. One of 500 signed. Boxed. $50–$60. Trade edition: Green cloth. In dust jacket. $30.

ROBINSON, Edwin Arlington. *King Jasper*. Introduction by Robert Frost. Cloth. New

York, 1935. First edition. One of 250 large paper copies. $65–$85. Trade edition: Cloth. In dust jacket. $30.

ROBINSON, Edwin Arlington. *The Man Who Died Twice.* Boards and cloth. New York, 1924. First edition. One of 500 signed. Boxed. $50–$65. Trade edition: Red cloth. In dust jacket. $25.

ROBINSON, Edwin Arlington. *Matthias at the Door.* Green cloth. New York, 1931. First edition, first state, with no punctuation at end of fifth line from bottom of page 97. One of 500 signed. Boxed $50–$65. Trade edition: Cloth. In dust jacket. $20.

ROBINSON, Edwin Arlington. *Modred: A Fragment.* Boards and cloth. New York, 1929. First edition. One of 250 signed. In slipcase. $75–$100.

ROBINSON, Edwin Arlington. *Nicodemus.* Cloth. New York, 1932. First edition. One of 235 large paper copies, signed. Boxed. $60–$80. Trade edition: In dust jacket. $20.

ROBINSON, Edwin Arlington. *Sonnets 1889–1927.* Boards and cloth. New York, 1928. First edition. One of 561. $40–$50. Another issue: One of 9 on green paper. $175–$250.

ROBINSON, Edwin Arlington. *Three Poems.* Cloth. Cambridge, Mass., 1928. First (pirated) edition. One of 15 copies. $150.

ROBINSON, Edwin Arlington. *The Torrent and the Night Before.* Blue wrappers. (Gardiner, Me.), 1896. First edition. $1,000–$1,250. Also, inscribed by Robinson, $1,400 (A, 1977); $1,900 (A, 1974). Author's first book. New York, 1928. One of 110 signed. $200–$250.

ROBINSON, Edwin Arlington. *Tristram.* Half cloth. New York, 1927. First edition, first state, with "rocks" for "rooks," line 2 on page 86. One of 350 large paper copies, signed. Boxed. $75–$100. Trade and Literary Guild editions: Cloth. In dust jacket. $25. (Note: The Guild issue, preceding the trade, has "rooks," not "rocks.")

ROBINSON, Jacob. *Sketches of the Great West.* 71 pp., wrappers. Portsmouth, N.H., 1848. First edition. $4,500–$5,000.

ROBINSON, John, and Dow, George F. *The Sailing Ships of New England, 1607–1907.* 3 vols., cloth. Series I, II, and III. Salem, 1922–24–28. $400.

ROBINSON, Lennox (editor). *A Little Anthology of Modern Irish Verse.* Blue boards, linen back, paper label. Dublin, 1928. Cuala Press. First edition. One of 300. In plain dust jacket. $125–$150.

ROBINSON, Rowland Evans. See *Forest and Stream Fables.*

ROBINSON, Rowland Evans. *Uncle 'Lisha's Shop.* Cloth. New York, 1887. First edition. $35–$50. Author's first book.

ROBINSON, W. Heath. *Bill the Minder.* Illustrated by the author, including 16 color plates. Vellum. London, 1912. One of 380 signed. $1,000–$1,800.

ROBINSON, William Davis. *Memoirs of the Mexican Revolution.* Boards. Philadelphia, 1820. First edition. $300–$350. London, 1821. 2 vols., half linen. $300–$350.

ROBSON, John S. *How a One Legged Rebel Lives, or a History of the 52nd Virginia Regiment.* Wrappers. Richmond, 1876. $100.

ROCHESTER, John Wilmot, Earl of. *Collected Works.* Edited by John Hayward. Boards and buckram. London, 1926. Nonesuch Press. $100–$125. Another issue: Boards and vellum. One of 75. $200.

ROCK, Marion Tuttle. *Illustrated History of Oklahoma.* 90 plates. Cloth. Topeka, 1890. First edition. $450–$500.

ROCKY Mountain Directory and Colorado Gazettier for 1871. Illustrated. Cloth. Denver, (1870). $250.

RODD, Rennell. *Rose Leaf and Apple Leaf.* Introduction by Oscar Wilde. Vellum. Philadelphia, 1882. First edition. De luxe issue. $200–$300. London, 1904. Wrappers. One of 200. $100–$135. Portland, Me., 1906. Mosher Press. Green morocco. One of 5 on vellum. $750.

RODENBOUGH, Theodore F. *From Everglade to Canon with the Second Dragoons.* Illustrated. Cloth. New York, 1875. First edition. $450–$500.

RODENBOUGH, Theodore F. *Uncle Sam's Medal of Honor.* Cloth. New York, (1886). First edition. $50–$75.

RODITI, Edouard. *Prison Within Prison.* Wrappers. Prairie City, Ill., (1941). First edition. $150–$200.

RODKER, John. *Poems.* Wrappers. London, (1915). First edition. $125. Author's first book.

RODRIGUEZ DE SAN MIQUEL, Juan. *Documentos Relativos al Piadoso Fondo de Misiones para Conversión y Civilización de las Numerosas Tribus Barbaras de la Antigua y Nueva California.* 60 pp., calf. Mexico, 1845. First edition. $350–$450. Another edition, same date, 28 pages added. Wrappers. $300–$400.

RODRIGUEZ DE SAN MIQUEL, Juan. *Segundo Cuaderno de Interesantes Documentos Relativos a los Bienes del Fondo Piadoso de Misiones, para Conversión y Civilización de las Tribus Barbaras de las Californias.* 32 pp., wrappers. Mexico, 1845. $400–$600.

ROE, Azel Stevens. *James Montjoy: or I've Been Thinking.* 2 parts, wrappers. New York, 1850. First edition. $50–$75.

ROE, Edward Payson. *Barriers Burned Away.* Cloth. New York, 1872. First edition. $75–$100.

ROETHKE, Theodore. See *Ten Poets.*

ROETHKE, Theodore. *Collected Poems.* Cloth. Garden City, 1966. First edition. In dust jacket. $75.

ROETHKE, Theodore. *The Lost Son and Other Poems.* Cloth. Garden City, 1948. First edition. In dust jacket. $150. London, (1948). Cloth. First English edition. In dust jacket. $75.

ROETHKE, Theodore. *Open House.* Cloth. New York, 1941. First edition. One of 1,000. In dust jacket. $350–$400. Author's first book.

ROETHKE, Theodore. *Praise to the End!* Cloth. Garden City, 1951. First edition. In dust jacket. $100–$125.

ROETHKE, Theodore. *Sequence, Sometimes Metaphysical.* Illustrated. Boards. Iowa City, (1963). First edition. One of 330. Boxed. $250–$325. Another issue: One of 60 signed. $500–$650.

ROETHKE, Theodore. *The Waking: Poems 1933–1953.* Cloth. Garden City, 1953. In dust jacket. $100–$150.

ROETHKE, Theodore. *Words for the Wind.* Cloth. London, 1957. First edition. In dust jacket. $150–$175. Garden City, 1958. Cloth. First American edition. In dust jacket. $100–$125.

ROGERS, A. N. *Communication Relative to the Location of the U.P.R.R. Across the Rocky Mountains Through Colorado Territory.* Wrappers. Central City, Colo., 1867. $450–$500.

ROGERS, Robert. *Journals of Maj. Robert Rogers.* Edited by Franklin B. Hough. Map. Cloth. Albany, 1883. $250–$275.

ROGERS, Samuel. See *Lara, A Tale; Jacqueline, a Tale.*

ROGERS, Samuel. *Human Life: A Poem*. Boards. London, 1819. First edition, first issue, with Bensley misprint on page 4 and 100. $300–$400.

ROGET, Peter Mark. *Thesaurus of English Words*. Cloth. Boston, 1854. First American edition. $150.

ROHMER, Sax. *Seven Sins*. Cloth. London, 1944. First edition. In dust jacket. $75–$100.

ROLFE, Frederick William. See Corvo, Baron; Corvo, Frederick Baron; Prospero and Caliban.

ROLFE, Frederick William. *Don Renato*. Edited by Cecil Woolf. Illustrated. Cloth. London, 1963. One of 300. Boxed. $125. (The original 1909 edition is very rare.)

ROLFE, Fr. *Don Tarquinio*. Violet cloth. London, 1905. First edition, first binding. $400–$500. Later, red cloth: $400.

ROLFE, Fr. *Hadrian the Seventh*. Cloth. London, 1904. First edition, first issue, purple cloth; title and drawing stamped in white. $450. Second issue, title and drawing blind-stamped. $300–$350.

ROLLINS, Philip Ashton. *Jinglebob*. Illustrated in color by N. C. Wyeth. Cloth. New York, 1930. First edition. In dust jacket. $100–$125.

ROLLINSON, John K. *History of the Migration of Oregon-Raised Herds to Mid-Western Markets: Wyoming Cattle Trails*. Plates, maps, colored frontispiece by Frederic Remington. Cloth. Caldwell, Idaho, 1948. First edition. One of 1,000 signed. $100–$125.

ROLLINSON, John K. *Hoofprints of a Cowboy and a U.S. Ranger*. Cloth. Caldwell, 1941. First edition. In dust jacket. $75–$85.

ROLLO Learning to Talk. Woodcut illustrations. Decorated cloth. Philadelphia, 1841. (By Jacob Abbott.) New edition (of *The Little Scholar Learning to Talk,* 1835). $75.

ROLPH, J. Alexander. *Dylan Thomas: A Bibliography*. Illustrated. Cloth. London, (1956). First edition. In dust jacket. $50–$75.

ROMANCE of Indian History: or, Thrilling Incidents in the Early Settlement of America. 24 pp., wrappers. New York, (185-?). (By Adam Poe.) $100.

ROOSEVELT, Eleanor. *This I Remember*. Frontispiece and plates. Buckram. New York, (1949). First edition. One of 1,000 on large paper, signed. Boxed. $75–$125. Trade edition: Cloth. In dust jacket. $25.

ROOSEVELT, Eleanor. *This is My Story*. Buckram. New York, 1937. First edition. One of 258 signed. $150–$200.

ROOSEVELT, Franklin D. *The Democratic Book, 1936*. Illustrated. Folio, wrappers. (Philadelphia), 1936. Limited edition, signed by F. D. R. $275. Another copy, signed by Eleanor Roosevelt, $175 (A, 1978).

ROOSEVELT, Franklin D. *The Happy Warrior: Alfred E. Smith*. 40 pp., black cloth. orange label. Boston, 1928. First edition. In dust jacket. $100.

ROOSEVELT, Franklin D. *Looking Forward*. Cloth. New York, (1933). First edition. In dust jacket. $50–$75.

ROOSEVELT, Franklin D. *Whither Bound?* Cloth. Boston, 1926. First edition. In dust jacket. $100–$150. Author's first book.

ROOSEVELT, Theodore. *Big Game Hunting in the Rockies and on the Great Plains*. 55 etchings. Signed frontispiece. Full tan buckram. New York, 1899. First edition. One of 1,000 signed. $400–$500.

ROOSEVELT, Theodore. *Hunting Trips of a Ranchman.* 20 plates. Buckram. New York, 1885. First edition. Limited Medora Edition of 500. $350–$500. New York, 1886. Cloth. First trade edition. $100–$150. London, 1886. Illustrated. Cloth. First English (and second) edition. $125–$150.

ROOSEVELT, Theodore. *Letter . . . Accepting the Republican Nomination for President of the United States.* 32 pp., self-wrappers. (New York), 1902. First edition. $100–$150.

ROOSEVELT, Theodore. *List of Birds Seen in the White House Grounds.* 4 pp., leaflet. (Washington), 1908. First edition. $150–$200.

ROOSEVELT, Theodore. *Naval War of 1812.* Cloth. New York, 1882. First edition. $100–$150. (Note: Second edition so indicated on title page.)

ROOSEVELT, Theodore. *Outdoor Pastimes of an American Hunter.* 49 plates. Half calf and boards. New York, 1905. First edition. One of 260 signed. In dust jacket. $350.

ROOSEVELT, Theodore. *Ranch Life and the Hunting Trail.* Illustrated by Frederic Remington. All edges gilt, light-colored, coarse weave, tan buckram, cover design in green and gold. New York, (1888). First edition. In dust jacket. $350–$500.

ROOSEVELT, Theodore. *The Rough Riders.* Cloth. New York, 1899. First edition. $150–$200.

ROOSEVELT, Theodore. *Some American Game.* Wrappers. New York, 1897. First edition. $200–$300.

ROOSEVELT, Theodore. *Theodore Roosevelt: An Autobiography.* Illustrated. Cloth. New York, 1913. First edition. In dust jacket. $100–$150.

ROOSEVELT, Theodore. *The Wilderness Hunter.* Tan or brown cloth. New York, (1893). First edition, with chapter headings in brown. $75. Another issue: Buckram. One of 200 signed. $300–$400.

ROOSEVELT, Theodore. *The Winning of the West.* 4 vols., cloth. New York, 1889–96. First edition. (Vol. 1: 1889; Vol. 2: 1889; Vol. 3: 1894; Vol. 4: 1896.) First edition, first issue, with "diame-" as last word on page 160 and "ter" as first word on page 161. $400–$500. New York, 1900. Illustrated. 4 vols. $75–$100. Another issue: Half morocco. One of 200 with a page of ms. $1,000–$1,500.

ROOSEVELT, Theodore, and Minot, H. D. *The Summer Birds of the Adirondacks.* 4 pp., leaflet. (New York, 1877.) First edition. $400–$500. Roosevelt's first published separate work.

ROOT, Frank A., and Connelley, William E. *The Overland Stage to California.* Illustrated. Map. Pictorial cloth. Topeka, 1901. First edition. $125–$200.

ROOT, Riley. *Journal of Travels from St. Josephs* (sic) *to Oregon, etc.* 143 pp., printed wrappers and cloth spine. Galesburg, Ill., 1850. First edition. $4,500–$5,000.

ROOT, Riley. *Musical Philosophy.* 20 pp., wrappers, Galesburg, Ill., 1866. First edition. $75–$125.

ROS, Amanda. *Irene Iddesleigh.* Cloth. Belfast, 1897. First edition with slip of "Printer's Errors." $100–$150. (A novel often called the foremost example in the English language of bad writing.)

ROSE. Victor M. *Ross' Texas Brigade.* Illustrated. Louisville, 1881. First edition. $850–$1,000.

ROSE Garden of Omar Khayyam (The). Miniature book, magnifying glass, proof sheet and text "A Thimbleful of Books," contained in a case. Worcester, Mass., 1932. $150.

ROSEN, Peter. *Pa-Ha-Sa-Pah, or The Black Hills of South Dakota.* 27 plates. Pictorial cloth. St. Louis, 1895. First edition. $175–$200.

ROSENBACH, A. S. W. *Early American Children's Books*. Edited by A. Edward Newton. Hand-colored plates. Full blue morocco. Portland, Me., 1933. One of 88 signed. Boxed. $500–$650. Another issue: Half morocco. One of 585 signed. Boxed $300–$450.

ROSENBERG, Isaac. *Poems*. Portrait. Cloth. London, 1922. First edition. In dust jacket. $100–$135.

ROSENTHAL, Leonard. *The Kingdom of the Pearl*. Illustrated in color by Edmund Dulac. Boards and vellum. New York or London, (1920). One of 100 signed by Dulac. In dust jacket. $800–$1,000. Another issue: Boards and cloth. In dust jacket. One of 675. In dust jacket. $400–$500.

ROSS, Alexander. *Adventures of the First Settlers on the Oregon or Columbia River*. Frontispiece (in some copies), folding map. Cloth. London, 1849. First edition. $1,000–$1,500.

ROSS, Alexander. *The Fur Hunters of the Far West*. Map, 2 plates. 2 vols., cloth. London, 1855. First edition. $500–$750.

ROSS, Alexander. *The Red River Settlement*. Frontispiece. Cloth. London, 1856. First edition. $250–$350.

ROSS, Harvey L. *The Early Pioneers and Pioneer Events of the State of Illinois*. Portrait. Cloth. Chicago, 1898. First edition. $75–$100.

ROSS, John. *Narrative of a Second Voyage in Search of a North-West Passage*. Charts, folding map, plans, 25 plates (9 in color). Cloth. London, 1835. $500–$750. (Also issued in 2 volumes.)

ROSS, John. *A Voyage of Discovery . . . for the Purpose of Exploring Baffin's Bay*. Folding maps, tables, plates (15 in color). Half calf. London, 1819. First edition. $1,250–$2,000.

ROSS, Mrs. William P. *The Life and Times of Honorable William P. Ross*. Portrait. Cloth. Fort Smith, 1893. First edition. $100–$200.

ROSSETTI, Christina. *Goblin Market*. Cloth. Frontispiece by William Morris. Cloth. First edition. $300–$350. London, (1933). Illustrated by Arthur Rackham, including 4 color plates. Pictorial wrappers. First Rackham edition. In dust jacket. $100–$175. Another issue: First De Luxe Rackham edition. Limp vellum. One of 410 signed by Rackham. In slipcase. $750–$1,000. Philadelphia, (1933). First American Rackham trade edition. Red cloth. In dust jacket. $200–$300.

ROSETTI, Christina. *Poems*. Chosen by Walter de la Mare. Wood-engraving portrait by R. A. Maynard. Printed on Japanese vellum. Red morocco, by the Gregynog bindery. Newtown, Wales, 1930. Gregynog Press. One of 25 specially bound. Boxed. $1,000–$1,250. Ordinary issue: Boards and calf. One of 300. $350–$400.

ROSSETTI, Christina. *The Prince's Progress and Other Poems*. Cloth. London, 1866. First edition. $225.

ROSSETTI, Christina. *Speaking Likenesses*. Illustrated. Blue cloth. London, 1874. First edition, first binding. $150–$200.

ROSSETTI, Christina. *Verses*. Boards. Hammersmith (London), 1906. Eragny Press. One of 175 on paper. $400. Another issue: One of 10 on vellum. $1,000–$1,500.

ROSSETTI, Dante Gabriel. *Ballads and Narrative Poems*. Woodcut title and initials. Limp vellum with ties. London, 1893. Kelmscott Press. One of 310. $1,000–$1,250. Another issue: One of 6 on vellum. $5,000–$6,000.

ROSSETTI, Dante Gabriel. *Ballads and Sonnets*. Boards. London, 1881. First edition. One of 25 on large paper. $300–$350. Ordinary issue: Blue cloth. $100–$175.

ROSSETTI, Dante Gabriel. *The Blessed Damozel*. Illustrated by Kenyon Cox. Folio, cloth. New York, 1886. First edition. Large paper, printed in sepia. $250–$300. London, 1898. Vale Press. Oblong, boards. One of 310. $250. Another issue: Cloth. One of 65 on vellum. $500. London, 1903. Illustrated by James Guthrie. Vellum. One of 5 on vellum. $1,500–$2,000. (Park Ridge, Ill., 1903.) Village Press. Parchment. One of 110 printed by Frederick Goudy. $200.

ROSSETTI, Dante Gabriel. *Hand and Soul.* Wrappers. London, 1869. First separate edition. $300–$400. London, 1895. Kelmscott Press (for Way & Williams, Chicago). Woodcut title and borders. Vellum. One of 525 (300 for America and 225 for England). $1,250–$1,500. Another issue: One of 21 on vellum (10 for England and 11 for America). $3,000–$4,000. London, 1899. Vale Press. Morocco. One of 210. In dust jacket. $600.

ROSSETTI, Dante Gabriel. *Poems.* Printed wrappers. (London, 1869.) First edition privately printed. $1,000 and up. London, 1870. Cloth. First published edition. $300. Another issue: Half vellum. One of 25 on Whatman paper. $400–$500. London, 1904. Plates, 2 vols., half morocco. $150. Another issue: 2 vols., vellum. One of 30. $300–$400. New York, 1903. Edited by Elizabeth L. Cary. Illustrated. 2 vols., blue cloth. $60. Another issue: 2 vols., leather. One of 500. $150.

ROSSETTI, Dante Gabriel. *Sonnets and Lyrical Poems.* Woodcut title and borders by William Morris. Printed in black and red. Vellum with ties. London, 1894. Kelmscott Press. One of 310. $400–$600. Another issue: One of 6 on vellum. $2,500–$3,500.

ROSSI, Mario M. *Pilgrimage in the West.* Boards and linen. Dublin, 1933. Cuala Press. One of 300. $75–$125.

ROTH, Henry. *Call It Sleep.* Cloth. New York, 1934. First edition. In dust jacket. $1,000 or more. Also, $850 (A, 1978).

ROTH, Philip. *Goodbye, Columbus.* Black cloth. Boston, 1959. First edition. In dust jacket. $150–$200. Author's first book.

ROTHENSTEIN, William. *Men and Memories: Recollections* . . . *1872–1900.* 2 vols., black cloth. London, (1931). First edition. $50–$75.

ROTHERT, Otto A. *The Outlaws of Cave-in-Rock.* 10 maps and plans. Cloth. Cleveland, 1927. First edition. In dust jacket. $75–$100.

ROYALL, Anne. See *Sketches of History, Life, and Manners, in the United States.*

ROYALL, Anne. *The Tennessean.* Boards. New Haven, 1827. First edition. $500–$600.

ROYIDIS, Emmanuel. *Pope Joan.* Translated by Lawrence Durrell. Cloth. London, (1954). First edition. In dust jacket. $50–$75.

RUBAIYAT Of Omar Khayyam, The Astronomer-Poet of Persia. Translated into English verse. Brown wrappers. London, 1859. (Translated by Edward Fitz Gerald.) First edition (250 printed.) $10,000–$15,000. Also, spine chipped, soiled, $7,500 (A, 1981); $10,500 (A, 1976). Madras, India, 1862. Limp green cloth. One of 50 reprinted from the London first edition with a note by M. Garcin de Tassy. $1,000 and up. London, 1868. Wrappers. Second English edition. $2,000–$3,000. Also, $1,100 (A, 1981). London, 1872. Half leather and dark red cloth. Third English edition. $250–$300. London, 1879. Frontispiece. Half cloth. Fourth English edition. $300–$400. London, 1896. Ashendene Press. Gray wrappers. One of 50. $1,500–$2,000. Boston, 1898. Cloth. First American edition. $200–$400. London, 1909. Illustrated by Edmund Dulac. Vellum. One of 750 signed by Dulac. Boxed. $750–$1,000. Cloth bound: $300–$350. London, 1913. Riccardi Press. Vellum. One of 12 on vellum. $1,000 and up. London, 1920. Illustrated by Blanche McManus. Vellum. One of 21 on vellum. $600–$1,000. London, 1938. Golden Cockerel Press. Illustrated. Vellum. One of 270. $300–$600. Another issue: Morocco. One of 30 with extra engravings. $1,000 or more. New York, 1940. Heritage Press. Color plates by Arthur Szyk. Pictorial padded calf and marbled boards. $150–$300. (There have been innumerable other editions, in English as well as in many other languages, since 1859. See the book auction records.)

RUBEK, Sennoia. *The Burden of the South, in Verse.* Frontispiece. Printed wrappers. New York, (about 1864). (By John Burke.) First edition. $50–$75.

RUDD, Dan A., and Bond, Theo. *From Slavery to Wealth: The Life of Scott Bond.* Illustrated. Cloth. Madison, Ark., 1917. First edition. $75–$100.

RUDO Ensayo. See Smith, Buckingham.

RUKEYSER, Muriel. *Elegies.* Boards. No place, (1949). First edition. One of 300 signed. In slipcase. $60–$75.

RUKEYSER, Muriel. *The Green Wave.* Cloth. New York, 1948. First edition. In dust jacket. $40–$50.

RUKEYSER, Muriel. *Theory of Flight.* Cloth. New Haven, 1935. First edition. In dust jacket. $100–$125.

RULES and Orders of the House of Representatives of the Territory of Washington, 1864–5. 32 pp., wrappers. Olympia, Washington Territory, 1864. $100–$200, possibly more.

RULES and Regulations of the Utah and Northern Railway, for the Government of Employees. Calf. Salt Lake City, 1879. $100–$200.

RULES for the Government of the Council of Wisconsin Territory. 10 pp., plain wrappers. Madison, Wis., 1843. $50–$60. Madison, 1845. 11 pp., plain wrappers, $100–$125.

RULES for the Government of the House of Representatives of Wisconsin Territory. 10 pp., plain wrappers, Madison, 1845. $100–$125.

RULES, Regulations, and By-Laws of the Board of Commissioners to Manage the Yosemite Valley and Mariposa Big Tree Grove. 23 pp., wrappers. Sacramento, 1885. $150–$200.

RUNYON, Damon. *The Tents of Trouble.* Flexible cloth. New York, (about 1911). First edition. $125–$150. Author's first book.

RUPP, I. Daniel. *History of the Counties of Berks and Lebanon.* 3 plates. Sheep. Lancaster, Pa., 1844. First edition. $75–$100.

RUPP, I. Daniel. *History of Lancaster County, Pennsylvania.* Illustrated. Sheep. Lancaster, 1844. First edition. $100–$125.

RUPPANEER, Antoine. *Hypodermic Injections in the Treatment of Neuralgia, Gout, and Other Diseases.* Cloth. Boston, 1865. First edition. $500–$750.

RUSK, Fern H. *George Caleb Bingham.* Illustrated. Cloth. Jefferson City, Mo., 1917. One of 500. $250–$300.

RUSKIN, John. See R., J. Also see Greenaway, Kate (illustrator), *Dame Wiggins of Lee.*

RUSKIN, John. *The Elements of Drawing.* Cloth. London, 1857. First edition. $100–$125.

RUSKIN, John. *The King of the Golden River.* Illustrated by Richard Doyle. Boards. London, 1851. First edition. $300–$400. New York, 1930. Illustrated. Black calf. One of 50, each with a holograph letter, signed by Ruskin, tipped in. Boxed. $250–$300. London, (1932). Illustrated by Arthur Rackham. Vellum. One of 570 signed by Rackham. Boxed. $500–$750. Trade issue: Cloth. $125–$200.

RUSKIN, John. *The Harbours of England.* 12 mezzotint plates by J. M. W. Turner. Folio, decorated blue cloth. London, 1856. First edition. $750–$1,000.

RUSKIN, John. *Lectures on Landscape.* 25 plates. Folio, cloth. Orpington, 1897. First edition. $400–$500.

RUSKIN, John. *The Nature of Gothic: A Chapter of the Stones of Venice.* Preface by

William Morris. Illustrated. Vellum with ties. London, 1892. Kelmscott Press. One of 500. $600–$700.

RUSKIN, John. *The Political Economy of Art*. Cloth. London, 1857. First edition. $400–$500. Also, in a special Doves Press binding, $1,200 (A, 1979).

RUSKIN, John. *Praeterita: Outlines of Scenes and Thoughts Perhaps Worthy of Memory in My Life Past*. Engraved plate. 3 vols., in 28 original parts, printed wrappers. Sunnyside, Orpington, Kent, 1885–1889. First editions. One of 600 large paper copies. $250–$500.

RUSKIN, John. *The Seven Lamps of Architecture*. 14 plates. Cloth. London, 1849. First edition. $150–$200.

RUSKIN, John. *The Stones of Venice*. Illustrated, 3 vols., cloth. London, 1851–53. First edition. $400–$500.

RUSKIN, John. *Unto This Last: Four Essays on the First Principles of Political Economy*. Cloth. London, 1862. First edition. $250–$300. London, 1907. Doves Press. Vellum. One of 300. $400–$500. Another issue: One of 12 on vellum $2,500–$3,000.

RUSSELL, Alex J. *The Red River Country, Hudson's Bay and North-west Territories, etc..* Folding map. Wrappers. Ottawa, 1869. First edition. $150–$200. Montreal, 1879. Folding map, 8 folding plates. Wrappers. Third edition. $150–$200.

RUSSELL, Bertrand. *German Social Democracy*. Cloth. London, 1896. First edition. $1,000–$1,500. Author's first book.

RUSSELL, Charles M. (illustrator). See *How the Buffalo Lost His Crown*.

RUSSELL, Charles M. *Back-trailing on the Old Frontiers*. 16 full-page drawings by the author. 56 pp., pictorial wrappers. Great Falls, Mont., 1922. First edition. $250–$300.

RUSSELL, Charles M. *Good Medicine*. Introduction by Will Rogers, Illustrated by the author. Cloth. New York, 1930. First edition. In dust jacket. $150–$250. Another issue: (With title page dated 1929). Half buckram. One of 134 on large paper. $800–$1,000. From the same issue: Blue buckram. One of 59 copies for presentation. $2,000–$3,000.

RUSSELL, Charles M. *More Rawhides*. Illustrated by the author. 60 pp., pictorial wrappers. Great Falls, 1925. First edition. $175–$250.

RUSSELL, Charles M. *Pen and Ink Drawings*. 2 vols., oblong boards and cloth. Pasadena, (1946). First edition. $150–$200.

RUSSELL, Charles M. *Pen Sketches*. 12 plates. Oblong, leatherette. Great Falls, (1898). First edition. $1,000–$1,500.

RUSSELL, Charles M. *Rawhide Rawlins Stories*. Illustrated by the author. Pictorial wrappers. Great Falls, 1921. First edition. $200. Another issue: Full limp leather. Presentation copy. $600.

RUSSELL, Charles M. *Trails Plowed Under*. Cloth. New York, 1927. First edition. In dust jacket. $150–$175.

RUSSELL, George W. See E., A.

RUSSELL, Morris C. *Western Sketches. Trail Echoes. Straws of Humor*. (Cover title.) Portrait. Wrappers, cord ties. Lake City, Minn., 1904. First edition, signed by the author. $250–$300.

RUSSELL, Osborne. *Journal of a Trapper, or Nine Years in the Rocky Mountains*. Blue cloth. (Boise, 1914.) First edition. (100 printed.) $400–$500. Boise, (1921). Cloth. Second edition. (100 copies.) $300. (Portland), 1955. Champoeg Press. One of 750. $75.

RUSSELL, Peter (editor). *A Collection of Essays . . . To Be Presented to Ezra Pound on His 65th Birthday.* Portrait frontispiece. Tan cloth. London, (1950). First edition. In dust jacket. $100–$150.

RUSSELL, W. Clark. *The Tale of the Ten.* 3 vols., cloth. London, 1896. First edition. $400–$500.

RUSSELL, W. Clark. *The Wreck of the "Grosvenor."* 3 vols., cloth. London, 1877. First edition. $800–$1,000.

RUST, Margaret. *The Queen of the Fishes.* 16 woodcuts, 4 colored, by Lucien Pissarro. Vellum. Epping, England, 1894. Eragny Press. One of 150 on vellum. $1,000–$1,250. Also, $600 (A, 1977). (Note: The first book produced by this press.)

RUTH Whalley; or, The Fair Puritan. (Cover title.) 72 pp., pink wrappers. Boston, 1845. (By Henry William Herbert.) $500–$600. (Note: In some copies the author is listed as "William Henry Herbert." There is also said to be an 1844 edition.)

RUTHERFORD, Ernest. *Radio-Activity.* Illustration. Cloth. Cambridge, 1904. First edition. $350–$400.

RUTTENBER, E. M. *History of the County of Orange: With a History of the Town and City of Newburgh.* Plates, maps. Newburgh, N.Y., 1875. First edition. $80–$100.

RUXTON, George F. *Life in the Far West.* Cloth. Edinburgh, 1849. First edition. $200–$250. New York, 1849. Cloth. $150–$200.

RYAN, Abram Joseph. *Father Ryan's Poems.* Portrait and one illustration. Cloth. Mobile, 1879. First edition. $150–$200. Author's first book. Large paper edition (retitled *Poems: Patriotic, Religious, Miscellaneous*): Baltimore, 1880. Cloth. $150.

RYAN, William R. *Personal Adventures in Upper and Lower California in 1848–49.* 23 plates. Cloth. London, 1850. First edition. $300–$400.

RYNNING, Thomas H. *Gun Notches.* Cloth. New York, 1931. First edition. In dust jacket. $50.

S

S., E. W., and M., S. W. *The Children's Hour.* Illustrated. Cloth. Philadelphia, 1864. (By Elizabeth W. Sherman and S. Weir Mitchell.) First edition. $250–$300.

S., P. B. *Zastrozzi: A Romance.* Dark blue-gray boards, drab cloth spine, paper label. London, 1810. (By Percy Bysshe Shelley.) First edition. (No record of a copy in original binding for many years. The last rebound copy in the auction sales of the last decade was a shabby one, which brought a little under $300 in 1972. Obviously among the rarer Shelley items, and what a fine copy would be worth in the present market is strictly a guessing game.) London, 1955. Golden Cockerel Press. Plates. Morocco. One of 60 on vellum with duplicate set of 8 plates. Boxed. $200–$350. Another issue: Boards. One of 200. Boxed. $75–$100.

S., S. *Vigils.* Frontispiece by Stephen Gooden. Full morocco. (Bristol), 1934. (By Siegfried Sassoon.) First edition. One of 23 signed by the author and the artist. $750–$1,000. Another issue: One of 272 signed by Sassoon. $200–$300.

S., S. H. *Nine Experiments.* Green wrappers. Hampstead, England, 1928. (By Stephen Spender.) First edition. One of about 18 copies issued. Bad presswork required filling in some letters by hand in ink. In cloth case, with leather label. $2,100. (This copy, catalogued by a New York dealer in 1968, belonged to Spender's sister-in-law. An inscribed copy was offered by a New York dealer in 1973 at $5,000.)

SABIN, Edwin L. *Building the Pacific Railway.* Cloth. Philadelphia, 1919. First edition. In dust jacket. $50–$60.

SABIN, Edwin L. *Kit Carson Days (1809–1868).* Maps, plates. Brown cloth. Chicago, 1914. First edition. $75–$125. Chicago, 1919. Second edition. $50. New York, 1935. 2 vols., cloth. Revised edition. One of 1,000. $50. One of 200 signed. $100–$125.

SABINE and Rio Grande Railroad Co. Memorial of Duff Green, President. 50 pp. Washington, 1860. $75–$150, possibly more.

SACRED Writings of the Apostles and Evangelists of Jesus Christ, etc. (The). New Testament translation by George Campbell, James McKnight, and Philip Doddridge. Preface by Alexander Campbell. Contemporary calf. Buffaloe, Brooke County, Va., 1826. First edition. $200–$300.

SACK and Destruction of the City of Columbia, S.C. Wrappers. Columbia, 1865. (By William Gilmore Simms.) First edition. Up to $500.

SACKVILLE-WEST, Victoria. *All Passion Spent.* Cloth. London, 1931. Hogarth Press. First edition. $150.

SACKVILLE-WEST, Victoria. *The Edwardians.* Half vellum. (London), 1930. First edition. One of 125 signed. (Issued without dust jacket.) $150.

SACKVILLE-WEST, Victoria. *The Garden.* Cloth. London, 1946. First edition. One of 750 signed. In plain white dust jacket. $150–$225.

SACKVILLE-WEST, Victoria. *Heritage.* Cloth. New York, (1919). First American edition. In dust jacket. $125–$150.

SACKVILLE-WEST, Victoria. *Knole and the Sackvilles.* Cloth. London, 1922. First edition. In dust jacket. $150.

SACKVILLE-WEST, Victoria. *Orchard and Vineyard.* Boards. London, 1926. First edition. In dust jacket. $100.

SACKVILLE-WEST, Victoria. *Nursery Rhymes.* Vellum and cloth. London, 1947. First edition. One of 25 signed. $200–$225. Another issue: Blue cloth. One of 225. $80–$100.

SACKVILLE-WEST, Victoria. *Sissinghurst.* Boards, London, 1931. First edition. One of 500 signed. $150.

SACKVILLE-WEST, Victoria. *Twelve Days.* Illustrated. Marbled cloth. London, 1928. First edition. In dust jacket. $75–$125.

SADLEIR, Michael. *Fanny by Gaslight.* Cloth. London, 1940. First edition. In dust jacket. $150.

SADLEIR, Michael. *Forlorn Sunset.* Frontispiece. Purple morocco. London, 1947. First edition. One of 25 signed. $200.

SADLEIR, Michael. *Hyssop.* Cloth. London, (1915). First edition. In dust jacket. $50–$60. Author's first novel.

SADLEIR, Michael. *XIX Century Fiction: A Bibliographical Record.* Illustrated. 2 vols., cloth. London, (1951). First edition. One of 1,025. $350–$400.

SAGE, Rufus B. *Scenes in the Rocky Mountains.* Half calf. Philadelphia, 1847. Second edition. $300–$400. (For first edition, see title entry.)

SAGE, Rufus B. *Wild Scenes in Kansas and Nebraska, the Rocky Mountains, etc.* Half leather. Philadelphia, 1855. Third ("revised") edition (of *Scenes in the Rocky Mountains,* which see under title entry). $100–$125.

SAGRA, Ramón de la. *Historia Económica-Política y Estadística de la Isla de Cuba.* Wrappers. Havana, 1831. First edition. $800–$1,000.

ST. CLAIR, Maj. Gen. (Arthur). *A Narrative of the Manner in Which the Campaign Against the Indians, in the Year 1791, Was Conducted.* Boards. Philadelphia, 1812. First edition, with errata. $350–$450. Half morocco. $175–$250.

ST. IRVYNE; or, The Rosicrucian: A Romance. By a Gentleman of the University of Oxford. Drab boards, green cloth spine. London, 1811. (By Percy Bysshe Shelley.) First edition. $2,000 and up. Also, rebound, two signatures misbound, $418 (A, 1976).

ST. JOHN, James Augustus, and D'Avennes, Emile Prisse. *Oriental Album.* 30 full-page color plates. Elephant folio, half morocco. London, 1848. $2,000–$2,500.

ST. JOHN, John R. *A True Description of the Lake Superior Country.* 2 folding maps. Printed cloth. New York, 1846. First edition. $300–$350.

ST. RONAN'S Well. 3 vols., boards. Edinburgh, 1824. (By Sir Walter Scott.) First edition. $300–$500.

SAINT-EXUPÉRY, Antoine de. *Flight to Arras.* Translated by Bernard Lamotte. Cloth. New York, (1942). First American edition. $100.

SAINT-EXUPÉRY, Antoine de. *The Little Prince.* Translated from the French by Katherine Woods. Illustrated in color by the author. Cloth. New York, (1943). First American edition. One of 525. Signed. In dust jacket. $500 and up. Trade edition: In dust jacket. $100–$125.

SAINT-EXUPÉRY, Antoine de. *Night-Flight.* Translated by Stuart Gilbert. Wrappers, Paris, 1932. In cellophane dust jacket. $150–$200. New York, 1932. Cloth. First American edition. In dust jacket. $150.

SAINT-EXUPÉRY, Antoine de. *Wind, Sand and Stars.* Translated by Lewis Galentiere.

Cloth. New York, (1939). First American edition. One of 500 signed. Boxed. $100–$125.

SAISSY, Jean-Antoine. *An Essay on the Diseases of the Internal Ear.* Frontispiece. Sheep. Baltimore, 1829. First American edition. $200–$250.

SAKI. *Beasts and Super-Beasts.* Cloth. London, 1914 (By H. H. Munro.) First edition. $75–$100.

SAKI. *Reginald.* Red cloth. London, (1904). (By H. H. Munro.) First edition. $75–$100.

SAKI. *The Westminster Alice.* Green wrappers. London, (about 1902). (By H. H. Munro.) First edition. $150–$250.

SALAMAN and Absal: An Allegory. Translated from the Persian of Jami by Edward Fitz Gerald. Frontispiece. Blue cloth. London, 1856. First edition. $150–$200.

SALATHIEL: A Story of the Past, the Present, and the Future. 3 vols., half calf. London, 1828. (By the Rev. George Croly.) First edition. $150.

SALAZAR Ylarregui, José. *Datos de los Trabajos Astronómicos y Topográficos. Dispuestos en Forma de Diario.* 2 folding maps. Blue wrappers. Mexico, 1850. First edition. $600–$850.

SALE, Edith Tunis. *Manors of Virginia in Colonial Times.* 49 plates. Cloth. Philadelphia, 1909. First edition. $125.

SALINGER, J. D. See Barrows, R. M. *The Kit Book for Soldiers, Sailors and Marines.*

SALINGER, J. D. *The Catcher in The Rye.* Black cloth. Boston, 1951. First edition. In presumed first-issue dust jacket without book-club slug. $350–$500. Author's first book.

SALINGER, J. D. *Nine Stories.* Cloth. Boston, (1953). First edition. In dust jacket. $350–$400.

SALINGER, J. D. *Raise High the Roof Beam, Carpenters, and Seymour: An Introduction.* Cloth. Boston, (1959). First edition, first issue, without dedication page. In dust jacket. $200–$225. Second issue, with dedication page tipped in in front of half title. $40–$50. Third issue, with dedication correctly placed. $25.

SALMON, Richard. *Troutflies.* Fly-tying material tipped in. Full maroon leather. New York, 1975. First edition, De Luxe issue. One of 29 signed, with an original drawing by the author. In dust jacket. Boxed. $1,200–$1,500. Another issue: Green cloth. One of 589 signed. Boxed. $500–$650.

SALPOINTE, John B. *A Brief Sketch of the Mission of San Xavier del Bac with a Description of Its Church.* 20 pp., wrappers. San Francisco, 1880. First edition. $150–$175.

SALPOINTE, John B. *Soldiers of the Cross.* Portrait. 45 plates. Cloth. Banning, Calif., 1898. First edition. $400–$500.

SALT Lake City Directory and Business Guide (The). Folding map, folding view. 53–219 pp., as issued, boards. Salt Lake City, 1869. (By Edward L. Sloan.) First edition. $150–$250.

SALTEN, Felix. *Bambi, A Life in the Woods.* Illustrated by Kurt Wiese. Pictorial boards. New York, 1928. First edition. In dust jacket. $75–$100.

SALTER, James. *The Hunters.* Cloth. New York, (1956). First edition. In dust jacket. $35–$45. Author's first novel.

SALTUS, Edgar. *Balzac.* Cloth, paper label. Boston, 1884. First edition. $40–$50. Author's first book.

SALZMANN, C. G. *Gymnastics for Youth*. 9 plates. Boards. London, 1800. First English edition. $250–$300. Philadelphia, 1802. First American edition. Leather. $150.

SAN BERNARDINO County, California, Illustrated Description of. 34 pp., printed wrappers. San Bernardino, 1881. $175–$200.

SAN BERNARDINO County, California. Ingersoll's Century Annals of San Bernardino County, 1769–1904. Full leather. Los Angeles, 1904. $100–$150.

SAN FRANCISCO Bay and California in 1776. Maps and facsimiles. 7 pp., boards. Providence, 1911. (By Pedro Font.) One of 125. $200–$300.

SAN FRANCISCO Board of Engineers: Report upon the City Grades. 27 pp., wrappers. San Francisco, 1854. $150–$175.

SAN FRANCISCO Directory for the Year 1852–53. Frontispiece, double-page map. Half leather. San Francisco, 1852. First edition. $750–$1,000.

SANBORN, Ralph, and Clark, Barrett H. *A Bibliography of the Works of Eugene O'Neill*. Illustrated. Cloth. New York, 1931. First edition. One of 500. $75. (Note: Contains previously unpublished work by O'Neill.)

SANDBURG, Carl. See Sandburg, Charles A.; Wright, Philip Green.

SANDBURG, Carl. *Abraham Lincoln: The Prairie Years*. Illustrated, 2 vols., blue cloth. New York, (1926). First edition. In dust jackets. Boxed. $50–$75. Large paper issue: 2 vols., boards and cloth. First state, with line 9 on page 175 of Vol. 1 reading "ears" instead of "eyes." One of 260 signed. In dust jackets. Boxed. $400–$450. Later, "ears" corrected. $350–$400.

SANDBURG, Carl. *Abraham Lincoln: The War Years*. Illustrated. 4 vols., blue cloth. New York, (1939–41). First edition. In dust jackets. Boxed. $100–$150. Large paper issue: Brown buckram. One of 525 sets on all rag paper, numbered and signed. Boxed. In dust jackets. $350–$450.

SANDBURG, Carl. *Always the Young Strangers*. Cloth. New York, (1953). First edition. $20–$25. Another issue. Cloth. One of 600 on large paper, signed. Boxed. $150–$185.

SANDBURG, Carl. *The American Songbag*. Red cloth. New York, (1927). First edition. In dust jacket. $150–$185.

SANDBURG, Carl. *Bronze Wood*. Frontispiece, 8 pp., orange boards. (San Francisco, 1942.) Grabhorn Press. First edition. One of 195. In dust jacket. $175–$225.

SANDBURG, Carl. *Chicago Poems*. Cloth. New York, 1916. First edition, with ads at back dated "3'16." In dust jacket. $250–$350. The poet's first book, aside from the pamphlet *In Reckless Ecstasy*.

SANDBURG, Carl. *The Chicago Race Riots*. Printed wrappers. New York, 1919. First edition. $150–$250.

SANDBURG, Carl. *Cornhuskers*. Boards, New York, 1918. First edition, first state, with page 3 so numbered at foot of page. In dust jacket. $150–$200.

SANDBURG, Carl. *Early Moon*. Cloth. New York, (1930). First edition, first printing. In dust jacket. $150–$175.

SANDBURG, Carl. *Good Morning, America*. Cloth. New York, 1928. First edition. In dust jacket. $50–$65. Limited issue: Cloth. One of 811 signed. $150–$200. (Note: A few were printed on blue paper.)

SANDBURG, Carl. *Lincoln Collector*. Illustrated. Cloth. New York, (1949). First edition. $25–$35. Large paper issue: Cloth. One of 2,425 signed. Boxed. $100–$125.

SANDBURG, Carl. *A Lincoln and Whitman Miscellany*. Cloth. Chicago, 1938. First edition. One of 250. $150–$200.

SANDBURG, Carl. *Mary Lincoln, Wife and Widow.* Cloth. New York, (1932). First edition, first printing. $25–$30. Large paper issue: One of 260 signed. $150–$250.

SANDBURG, Carl. *M'Liss and Louie.* Wrappers. Los Angeles, 1929. First edition. One of 125. $200–$250.

SANDBURG, Carl. *The People, Yes.* Cloth. New York, (1936). First edition, first printing. In dust jacket. $75. Large paper issue: One of 270 signed. In slipcase $150–$225.

SANDBURG, Carl. *Poems of the Midwest.* Illustrated. Cloth. Cleveland, (1946). One of 950. Boxed. $150.

SANDBURG, Carl. *Potato Face.* Boards and cloth. New York, (1930). First edition. In dust jacket. $100–$150.

SANDBURG, Carl. *Remembrance Rock.* Cloth. New York, (1948). First edition. In dust jacket. $35. Another issue: 2 vols., buckram. One of 1,000 signed. In glassine dust jackets. Boxed. $100–$150.

SANDBURG, Carl. *Rootabaga Pigeons.* Illustrated. Pictorial cloth. New York, (1923). First edition. In dust jacket. $125–$175.

SANDBURG, Carl. *Rootabaga Stories.* Illustrated by Maud and Miska Petersham. Pictorial cloth. New York, (1922). First edition. In dust jacket. $150–$200.

SANDBURG, Carl. *Slabs of the Sunburnt West.* Cloth. New York, (1922). First edition, first issue, with text ending at the foot of page 75. In dust jacket. $150–$200.

SANDBURG, Carl. *Smoke and Steel.* Green boards. New York, 1920. First edition. In dust jacket. $200–$275. Without jacket, spine chipped, $100.

SANDBURG, Carl. *Steichen the Photographer.* Illustrated. Cloth. New York, (1929). First edition. One of 925 signed by author and artist. $800–$850.

SANDBURG, Charles A. *In Reckless Ecstasy.* Wrappers. Galesburg, Ill., 1904. (By Carl Sandburg.) First edition. $2,000 and up. Author's first book.

SANDERS, Alvin Howard. *At the Sign of the Stock Yard Inn.* Illustrated. Half leather. Chicago, 1915. First edition. $50.

SANDERS, Daniel C. *A History of the Indian Wars with the First Settlers of the United States.* Sheep. Montpelier, Vt., 1812. First edition. $500–$600.

SANDERS, Capt. John. *Memoir on the Military Resources of the Valley of the Ohio.* 19 pp., unbound. Pittsburgh, 1845. First edition. $150–$175. Washington, 1845. 24 pp., unbound, $100–$150.

SANDOZ, Mari. *The Battle of the Little Bighorn.* Half morocco. Philadelphia, 1966. First edition. One of 249 signed. $150–$185.Trade edition: Cloth. In dust jacket. $25.

SANDOZ, Mari. *The Beaver Men.* Illustrated. Half leather. New York, (1964). First edition. One of 185 signed. $150–$175. Trade edition: Cloth. In dust jacket. $25.

SANDOZ, Mari. *The Cattlemen.* Illustrated. Cloth. New York, (1958). First edition. In dust jacket. $15–$20. Advance presentation copy, signed. In dust jacket. $100. Another issue: Half cloth. One of 199 signed. Boxed. $150–$200.

SANDOZ, Mari. *Crazy Horse.* Illustrated. Cloth. New York, 1942. First edition. In dust jacket. $60–$75.

SANDOZ, Mari. *Old Jules.* Illustrated. Cloth. Boston, 1935. First edition. In dust jacket. $75. Author's first book.

SANDOZ, Mari. *Old Jules Country.* Folding map. Illustrated by Bryan Forsyth. Half leather. New York, 1965. One of 250 signed and specially bound. $200. Trade edition: Cloth. In dust jacket. $15–$20.

SANDOZ, Maurice. *The Maze*. Illustrated by Salvador Dali. Cloth. Garden City, 1945. First edition. In dust jacket. $75–$125.

SANDOZ, Maurice. *On the Verge*. Illustrated in color by Salvador Dali. Cloth. Garden City, (1959). First edition. In dust jacket. $75–$100.

SANDS, Frank. *A Pastoral Prince: The History and Reminiscences of Joseph Wright Cooper*. Illustrated. Pictorial cloth. Santa Barbara, 1893. First edition. $150–$250.

SANFORD, Nettle. *History of Marshall County, Iowa*. 5 plates. Cloth. Clinton, 1867. $125–$150.

SANSOM, Joseph. *Sketches of Lower Canada, Historical and Descriptive*. Frontispiece view of Quebec. Boards. New York, 1817. First edition. $200–$250.

SANSOM, William. *A Bed of Roses*. Cloth. London, 1954. Hogarth Press. First edition. In dust jacket. With wraparound band. $50–$60.

SANTAYANA, George. See *Lines on Leaving the Bedford St. Schoolhouse*.

SANTAYANA, George. *Lucifer*. Cloth. Chicago, 1899. First edition. $75–$85. Cambridge. Mass., 1924. Black cloth. One of 450. $100–$125.

SANTAYANA, George. *Poems*. Cloth. London, (1922). First edition. One of 100 signed. $175–$200.

SANTAYANA, George. *Sonnets and Other Verses*. Buckram. Cambridge, Mass., 1894. First edition. One of 450. $75–$100. Another issue: Limp vellum. One of 50 on vellum. $250–$335. Author's first book.

SANTEE, Ross. *Cowboy*. Illustrated by the author. Pictorial cloth. New York, 1928. First edition. In dust jacket. $80–$125. Lacking jacket, $50.

SANTEE, Ross. *Men and Horses*. Illustrated. Cloth. New York, (1926). First edition. In dust jacket. $100–$150. Author's first book.

SANTLEBEN, August. *A Texas Pioneer*. Cloth. New York, 1910. First edition. In dust jacket. $250–$350.

SAPPINGTON, John. *The Theory and Treatment of Fevers*. Calf. Arrow Rock, Mo., 1844. $100–$125.

SARA, Col. Delle. *Silver Sam; or, the Mystery of Deadwood City*. 166 pp., wrappers. New York, (1877). $100–$125.

SARGENT, Charles Sprague. *The Silva of North America*. Illustrated. 14 vols., printed boards. Boston, 1890–1902. First edition. In dust jackets. $2,000–$3,000.

SARGENT, George B. *Notes on Iowa*. Map. 74 pp., cloth. New York, 1848. First edition. $750–$1,000.

SAROYAN, William. *A Christmas Psalm*. Rose boards, white cloth spine. San Francisco, (1935). Grabhorn Press. First edition, with greeting card and envelope, as issued, laid in. One of 200 signed. $100–$125.

SAROYAN, William. *Contes*. 8 colored woodcuts. Pictorial wrappers. (Paris, 1953.) One of 100 signed. $150–$200.

SAROYAN, William. *The Daring Young Man on The Flying Trapeze*. Gray cloth, paper label. New York, 1934. First edition. In dust jacket. $100–$150. London, (1935). Cloth. First English edition. In dust jacket. $200. Author's first book.

SAROYAN, William. *The Fiscal Hoboes*. Boards. New York, 1949. First edition. One of 250 signed. $100–$150. (Also issued in wrappers.)

SAROYAN, William. *Fragment*. Folio, wrappers. (San Francisco, 1938.) First edition. One of 150 signed. $150–$200.

SAROYAN, William. *Harlem as Seen by Hirschfeld*. 24 mounted plates, some in color. Folio. Cloth. New York, (1941). First edition. One of 1,000. In slipcase. $400–$550.

SAROYAN, William. *Hilltop Russians in San Francisco*. 30 colored plates by Pauline Vinson. Boards and cloth. San Francisco, 1941. Grabhorn Press. (Issued without dust jacket.) $200–$225.

SAROYAN, William. *My Name is Aram*. Illustrated. Cloth. New York, (1940). First edition. In dust jacket. $50–$75.

SAROYAN, William. *A Native American*. Illustrated. Cloth. San Francisco, 1938. First edition. One of 450 signed. (Issued without dust jacket.) $150–$175.

SAROYAN, William. *Saroyan's Fables*. Illustrated by Warren Chappell. (New York), 1941. First edition. One of 1,000 signed. Boxed. $75–$100.

SAROYAN, William. *A Special Announcement*. Cloth. New York, 1940. First edition. One of 250 signed. In tissue dust wrapper. $150–$200.

SAROYAN, William. *Those Who Write Them and Those Who Collect Them*. Printed wrappers. Chicago, 1936. Black Archer Press. One of 50. $100–$125. (Note: There are variant colored wrappers; no priority.)

SAROYAN, William. *Three Times Three*. Cloth. Los Angeles, (1936). First edition. One of 250 signed. In dust jacket. $75–$100.

SARTON, May. *Encounter in April*. Cloth. Boston, 1938. First edition. In dust jacket. $125–$150. Author's first book.

SARTON, May. *Shadow of a Man*. Cloth. New York, (1950). First edition. In dust jacket. $50–$60.

SARTOR Resartus. (Reprinted from *Fraser's Magazine*.) Various bindings; wrappers, calf, morocco, etc. (London), 1834. (By Thomas Carlyle.) First edition. One of about 48, 50, or 58 (bibliographers differ) privately printed for the author's friends. In full morocco, $1,500–$2,000. Also, $950 (A, 1980); in original wrappers, inscribed, $2,200 (A, 1978). London, 1838. Boards and calf. First published English edition. $200–$250. London, 1907. Doves Press. Vellum. One of 300. $400–$600. Another issue: One of 15 on vellum. $2,000–$3,000.

SASSOON, Siegfried. See Kain, Saul; Lyre, Pinchbeck; S., S. Also see *Lingual Exercises for Advanced Vocabularians; Memoirs of a Fox-Hunting Man; Memoirs of an Infantry Officer; Poems; Recreations*.

SASSOON, Siegfried. *An Adjustment*. Frontispiece. Wrappers. Royston, England, 1955. First edition. One of 150 initialed by the author. Boxed. $100–$125.

SASSOON, Siegfried. *Counter-Attack and Other Poems*. Wrappers. London, 1918. First edition. $75–$100. New York, (1918). First American edition. In dust jacket. $25–$35.

SASSOON, Siegfried. *Emblems of Experience*. Wrappers. Cambridge, 1951. First edition. One of 75 signed. $175.

SASSOON, Siegfried. *The Heart's Journey*. Boards and parchment. New York, 1927. First edition. One of 500, signed. In dust jacket. $200–$300. Another issue: One of 9 on green paper. In dust jacket. $300–$350. London, 1938. Blue cloth. First English trade edition. In dust jacket. $50–$75.

SASSOON, Siegfried. *Nativity*. Wrappers. New York, 1927. First American edition. One of 27 to obtain copyright. $320 (A, 1981); $325 (A, 1977).

SASSOON, Siegfried. *The Old Huntsman and Other Poems*. Boards. London, 1917. First edition, with errata slip. In dust jacket. $125–$175.

SASSOON, Siegfried. *The Path to Peace*. Boards and vellum. Worcester, 1960. One of 500. $200–$250. Another issue: One of 20 gilded by Margaret Adams. $500–$650.

SASSOON, Siegfried. *Picture Show*. Boards. (Cambridge), 1919. First edition. One of 200. In plain dust jacket. $300–$350. Presentation copy inscribed to Edith Sitwell, $600 (in a 1977 English catalogue).

SASSOON, Siegfried. *The Redeemer*. Unnumbered leaves, unbound. Cambridge, 1916. One of about 250. $200–$300.

SASSOON, Siegfried. *Satirical Poems*. Cloth. London, 1926. First edition. In dust jacket. $250–$300.

SASSOON, Siegfried. *Sherston's Progress*. Buckram. London, 1936. First edition. One of 300 signed. $150–$200. Garden City, 1936. Cloth. First American edition. In dust jacket. $75.

SASSOON, Siegfried. *Something About Myself*. Wrappers. Worcester, 1966. First edition. One of 250. $150–$200.

SASSOON, Siegfried. *The Tasking*. Boards and cloth. London, 1964. First edition. One of 100 signed. $300–$400.

SASSOON, Siegfried. *To the Red Rose*. Green boards. London, 1931. First edition. One of 400 signed. $75–$100.

SASSOON, Siegfried. *War Poems*. Red cloth. London, 1919. First edition. In dust jacket. $100–$150.

SATANSTOE; or, The Littlepage Manuscripts. By the Author of *Miles Wallingford*. 2 vols., printed yellow wrappers. New York, 1845. (By James Fenimore Cooper.) First American edition. $1,000–$1,500. London, 1845. 3 vols., boards, paper label. First edition. $600–$800. (Note: Cooper's name appeared on the title page of this edition.)

SATTERLEE, M. P. *A Detailed Account of the Massacre by the Dakota Indians of Minnesota in 1862*. Wrappers. Minneapolis, 1923. $150–$200.

SAUER, Martin. *An Account of a Geographical and Astronomical Expedition to the Northern Parts of Russia*. Folding map, 14 plates. Boards and calf. London, 1802. First edition. $1,000–$1,500.

SAUNDERS, James E. *Early Settlers of Alabama*. Part I. (All published). Cloth. New Orleans, 1899. First edition. $150–$250.

SAUNDERS, Louise. *The Knave of Hearts*. Illustrated in color by Maxfield Parrish. Pictorial cloth. New York, 1925. First edition. In plain buff dust jacket. $800–$1,000. (Note: We have seen one mint copy in a special box, as distributed by A. L. Burt of Chicago. Scribner was the publisher. The spiral-bound Racine, Wis., issue, a later reprint, is sometimes offered as a "first" edition at prices up to $500 or more.)

SAUNDERS, Marshall. *Beautiful Joe: An Autobiography*. Mottled olive cloth. Philadelphia, 1894. First edition, first issue, with American Baptist Publication Society imprint. $125–$150.

SAUVAN, Jean-Baptiste-Balthazar. *Picturesque Tour of the Seine, from Paris to the Sea*. Map, colored vignette title and tailpiece, 24 colored aquatint plates. Half morocco. London, 1821. First edition. $3,000–$4,000. Another issue: One of 50 on large paper. $5,000, or more.

SAVAGE, Timothy. *The Amazonian Republic, Recently Discovered in the Interior of Peru*. Boards, paper label. New York, 1842. First edition. $250–$350.

SAVAGE, William. *Practical Hints on Decorative Printing*. Illustrated with colored woodcuts. Boards, paper label. London, 1822. First edition. One of 227. $2,500.

SAVONAROLA, Hieronymus. *Epistola de Contemptu Mundi*. Illustrated. Red morocco. London, 1894. Kelmscott Press. One of 150. $800–$1,000. Another issue: One of 6 on vellum. $2,500–$3,000.

SAVOY (The): An Illustrated Quarterly. Illustrations by Aubrey Beardsley. 8 parts. (All published.) Decorated boards and wrappers. London, 1896. $1,000–$1,250.

SAWYER, C. J., and Darton, F. J. Harvey. *English Books, 1475–1900: A Signpost for Collectors*. Illustrated. 2 vols., buckram. London, 1927. $250–$300.

SAWYER, Eugene T. *The Life and Career of Tiburcio Vasquez*. Printed wrappers. (San Jose, 1875.) First edition. $300–$400. Oakland, 1944. Grabhorn Press. Boards and cloth. One of 500. $50–$60. (See Ridge, John R., for another edition.)

SAWYER, Lorenzo. *Way Sketches*. Illustrated. Cloth. New York, 1926. One of 385. $75–$125. Large paper issue: Boards, parchment spine. One of 35. In glassine dust jacket. $135–$150.

SAWYER, Ruth. *Roller Skates*. Illustrated by Valenti Angelo. Pictorial cloth. New York, 1936. First edition. $50–$60.

SAXON, Lyle. *Lafitte the Pirate*. Colored frontispiece. Cloth. New York, (1930). First edition. In dust jacket. $50–$60.

SAXTON, Charles. *The Oregonian; or History of the Oregon Territory*. 48 pp., printed wrappers. Oregon City, 1846. First edition. $1,500.

SAYERS, Dorothy L. *Creed or Chaos*. Wrappers. London, (1940). First edition. $40.

SAYERS, Dorothy L. *Gaudy Night*. Cloth. London, 1935. First edition. In dust jacket. $100–$125.

SAYERS, Dorothy L. *Lord, I Thank Thee*. Wrappers. Stamford, Conn., 1942. Overbrook Press. First edition. One of 100. $125–$150.

SAYERS, Dorothy L. *Op. 1*. Wrappers. Oxford, 1916. First edition. $350–$400.

SAYERS, Dorothy L. *The Other Six Deadly Sins*. Wrappers. London, (1943). First edition. $25–$30.

SAYERS, Dorothy L., and Byrne, M. St. Clare. *Busman's Honeymoon: A Detective Comedy*. Cloth. London, 1937. First edition. In dust jacket. $250.

SCAMMON, Charles M. *The Marine Mammals of the North-Western Coast of North America, etc.* 27 plates. Cloth. San Francisco, 1874. First edition. $600–$750.

SCENES in the Rocky Mountains, Oregon, California, New Mexico, Texas and Grand Prairies. By a New Englander. Folding map. Printed wrappers, or cloth. Philadelphia, 1846. (By Rufus B. Sage.) First edition. Either binding: $750–$1,000. (Note: For later editions, see Sage, Rufus B.)

SCHAEFFER, L. M. *Sketches of Travels in South America, Mexico and California*. Cloth. New York, 1860. First edition. $150–$225.

SCHALDACH, William J. *Carl Rungius, Big Game Painter*. Cloth. West Hartford, Vt., (1945). First edition. One of 160. $750.

SCHALDACH, William J. (artist). *Fish by Schaldach*. 60 full-page plates, 8 in color. Pictorial parchment. Philadelphia, 1937. One of 157 signed. $1,500–$1,750. Another issue: One of 1,560. $300–$350.

SCHARF, John Thomas. *History of the Confederate States Navy*. 42 plates. Boards. New York, 1887. First edition. $125–$150. Albany, 1894. Cloth. Second edition. $75–$125.

SCHARF, John Thomas. *History of Delaware*. Illustrated. 2 vols., half morocco. Philadelphia, 1888. First edition. $150–$200.

SCHARF, John Thomas. *History of Maryland.* Folding charts and maps. Illustrated. 3 vols., half leather. Baltimore, 1879. First edition. $200.

SCHARF, John Thomas. *History of Westchester County, New York.* Illustrated, 2 vols., cloth. Philadelphia, 1886. First edition. $300–$350.

SCHARF, John Thomas. *History of Western Maryland.* Map, 109 plates, table. 2 vols., cloth. Philadelphia, 1882. First edition. $150–$200.

SCHARMANN, H. B. *Overland Journey to California.* Portrait. Cloth. (New York, 1918.) First edition in English. $150–$200.

SCHATZ, A. H. *Opening a Cow Country.* Plates, maps. Wrappers. Ann Arbor, 1939. First edition. $100–$150.

SCHLEY, Frank. *American Partridge and Pheasant Shooting.* Illustrated. Cloth. Frederick, Md., 1877. First edition. $150–$200.

SCHMIDT, Gustavus. *The Civil Law of Spain and Mexico.* Cloth. New Orleans, 1851. First edition. $350–$450.

SCHMITZ, Joseph M. *Texan Statecraft, 1836–1845.* Cloth. San Antonio, 1941. One of 200. $35–$50.

SCHOBERL, Frederick. *Picturesque Tour from Geneva to Milan by Way of the Simplon.* Map, 36 color plates. Cloth, or boards. London, 1820. First edition. $2,000–$3,000. (This was a $200–$250 book at retail a decade ago—a striking example of the recent sharp rise in value for color plate books.)

SCHOEPF, Johann David. *Travels in the Confederation.* Translated and edited by Alfred J. Morrison. Portrait, 2 facsimiles. 2 vols., cloth. Philadelphia, 1911. First American edition (and first in English). $125–$150.

SCHOMBURGK, Robert H. *The History of Barbados.* Map, 8 plates. Half calf. London, 1848. First edition. $400–$500.

SCHOOLCRAFT, Henry R. *An Address Delivered Before the Was-ah Ho-de-no-son-ne, or New Confederacy of the Iroquois.* 48 pp., sewed. Rochester, 1846. First edition. $150–$175.

SCHOOLCRAFT, Henry R. *Algic Researches.* 2 vols., cloth. New York, 1839. First edition. $300–$400.

SCHOOLCRAFT, Henry R. *A Discourse Delivered on the Anniversary of the Historical Society of Michigan.* 44 pp., wrappers. Detroit, 1830. First edition. $150–$250.

SCHOOLCRAFT, Henry R. *Historical and Statistical Information Respecting the . . . Indian Tribes, etc.* Numerous maps, plates, and tables. 6 vols., cloth. Philadelphia, 1851–57. First edition. $2,000–$2,500. (For reprint, see Schoolcraft, *Information Respecting the History, etc.*)

SCHOOLCRAFT, Henry R. *The Indian Tribes of the United States.* Edited by Francis S. Drake. 100 plates. 2 vols., buckram. Philadelphia, 1884. First edition. $200–$250. London, 1885. 2 vols., cloth. $200–$250. (A condensation from Schoolcraft.)

SCHOOLCRAFT, Henry R. *Information Respecting the History, Condition, and Prospects of the Indian Tribes of the United States.* Illustrated. 6 vols., cloth. Philadelphia, 1853–57. Reprint of *Historical and Statistical Information.* $1,500–$2,000.

SCHOOLCRAFT, Henry R. *Inquiries Respecting the History . . . of the Indian Tribes of the United States.* (Caption title.) Printed wrappers. (Washington, about 1847–50). $500–$600.

SCHOOLCRAFT, Henry R. *Journal of a Tour into the Interior of Missouri and Arkansaw.* Folding map. Leather. London, 1821. First edition. $250–$300.

SCHOOLCRAFT, Henry R. *The Myth of Hiawatha, and Other Oral Legends.* Cloth. Philadelphia, 1856. First edition. $100–$150.

SCHOOLCRAFT, Henry R. *Narrative of an Expedition Through the Upper Mississippi to Itasca Lake.* 5 maps. Cloth, paper label. New York, 1834. First edition. $200–$300.

SCHOOLCRAFT, Henry R. *Narrative Journal of Travels Through the Northwestern Regions of the U.S., etc.* Engraved title page, folding map, 7 plates. Boards. Albany, 1821. First edition, with errata slip. $200–$250.

SCHOOLCRAFT, Henry R. *Notes on the Iroquois.* Cloth. Albany, 1847. $250–$350.

SCHOOLCRAFT, Henry R. *Personal Memoirs of a Residence of 30 Years with the Indian Tribes.* Portrait (not in all copies). Cloth. Philadelphia, 1851. First edition. $150–$200.

SCHOOLCRAFT, Henry R. *Travels in the Central Portions of the Mississippi Valley.* 5 maps and plates. Boards. New York, 1825. First edition. $200–$250.

SCHOOLCRAFT, Henry R. *A View of the Lead Mines of Missouri.* 3 plates. Boards. New York, 1819. First edition. $150–$200.

SCHOOLCRAFT, Henry R., and Allen, James. *Expedition to North-West Indians.* (Caption title.) Map. 68 pp., modern wrappers. (Washington, 1834.) $200–$250.

SCHRANTZ, Ward L. *Jasper County, Missouri, in the Civil War.* Frontispiece, 9 plates. Cloth. Carthage, Mo., 1923. $60–$75.

SCHREINER, Olive. See Iron, Ralph.

SCHREYVOGEL, Charles. *My Bunkie and Other Pictures of Western Frontier Life.* 36 plates. Oblong pictorial boards. New York, 1909. First edition. Boxed. $1,000–$1,250.

SCHULTZ, Christian. *Travels on an Inland Voyage, etc.* Portrait, 2 (sometimes 3) plates, 4 (sometimes 5) maps. 2 vols., leather. New York, 1810. First edition. $400–$600.

SCHUYLER, James. *Salute.* Original silk screen prints by Grace Hartigan. Folio, boards. New York, (1960). First edition. One of 200 signed. In glassine dust jacket. $250–$300. Author's first book.

SCHWARTZ, Delmore. See *The Poet's Pack.*

SCHWARTZ, Delmore. *Genesis: Book One.* Boards. (New York, 1943.) New Directions. First edition. In dust jacket. $100–$135.

SCHWARTZ, Delmore. *In Dreams Begin Responsibilities.* Cloth. Norfolk, Conn. (1938). First edition. In dust jacket. $225. Author's first book.

SCHWARTZ, Delmore. *Shenandoah.* Wrappers, or boards. Norfolk, (1941). First edition. Boards. $100–$125. Wrappers: $100–$150.

SCHWARTZ, Delmore. *The World Is a Wedding.* Cloth. (Norfolk, 1948.) First edition. In dust jacket. $85.

SCHWATKA, Frederick. *Four Summers in Alaska.* Illustrated. Cloth. St. Louis, 1892. First edition. $100–$125.

SCHWAB, John Christopher. *The Confederate States of America, 1861–1865.* Cloth. New York, 1901. First edition. $75–$100.

SCHWERDT, C. F. G. R. *Hunting, Hawking, Shooting.* 382 plates, including many in color. 4 vols., folio, full or half morocco. London, 1928–37. One of 300 signed. $3,000–$3,500.

SCHWETTMAN, Martin W. *Santa Rita, the University of Texas Oil Discovery.* 43 pp., wrappers. (Austin?), 1943. First edition. $50–$100.

SCLATER, P. L., and Hudson, W. H. *Argentine Ornithology*. 20 hand-colored plates. 2 vols., blue-gray boards. London, 1888–89. First edition. One of 200 signed. $2,500–$3,000.

SCOLLARD, Clinton. *Poems*. Boards. Boston, 1914. First edition. One of 100 signed. $50.

SCORESBY, William, Jr. *Journal of a Voyage to the Northern Whale-Fishery*. 8 maps and plates. Boards, paper label. Edinburgh, 1823. First edition. $500–$750.

SCOT, Reginald. *The Discoverie of Witchcraft*. Edited by Montague Summers. Cloth, or morocco and buckram. (London), 1930. One of 1,275. In dust jacket. $150–$200. (Reprint of the 1584 first edition.)

SCOTT, Evelyn. *On William Faulkner's "The Sound and the Fury."* Wrappers, printed cover label. New York, 1929. First edition. $75–$85.

SCOTT, James L. *A Journal of a Missionary Tour Through Pennsylvania*. Decorated cloth. Providence, 1843. First edition. $400–$500.

SCOTT, John. *The Indiana Gazetteer*. 143 pp., leather. Centreville, Ind., 1826. First edition. $500–$750.

SCOTT, John. *Partisan Life with Col. John S. Mosby*. Illustrated. Cloth. New York, 1867. First edition. $65–$75. London, 1867. First English edition. $50–$60.

SCOTT, Michael. See *Tom Cringle's Log*.

SCOTT, Peter. *Morning Flight*. 16 color plates. Cloth. London, 1935. First edition. One of 750 signed. In dust jacket. $500–$600.

SCOTT, Peter. *Wild Chorus*. Illustrated by the author, including mounted color plates. Blue cloth. London, (1938). First edition. One of 1,250 signed. In dust jacket. Boxed. $500–$600.

SCOTT, R. F. *Scott's Last Expedition*. Illustrated, including folding maps and color plates. 2 vols., cloth. London, 1913. First edition. $125–$150.

SCOTT, Sir Walter. See Clutterbuck, Captain. Also see *The Abbot; Anne of Geierstein; The Antiquary; The Fortunes of Nigel; Guy Mannering; Harold the Dauntless; Ivanhoe; Kenilworth; The Monastery; Quentin Durward; Rob Roy; Saint Ronan's Well; Waverley; Woodstock*.

SCOTT, Sir Walter. *The Field of Waterloo*. Brown wrappers. Edinburgh, 1815. First edition. $200–$250.

SCOTT, Sir Walter. *Halidon Hill: A Dramatic Sketch, from Scottish History*. 109 pp., drab wrappers. Edinburgh, 1822. First edition. $200–$300.

SCOTT, Sir Walter. *The Lady of the Lake*. Portrait. Boards. London, 1810. First edition. $400–$500. Large paper issue: $500–$750.

SCOTT, Sir Walter. *The Lay of the Last Minstrel*. Boards, paper label. Edinburgh, 1805. First edition. $400–$600. (Indianapolis, 1910.) Illustrated by Howard Chandler Christy. Decorated green cloth. In dust jacket. Boxed. $125.

SCOTT, Sir Walter. *Marmion*. Boards. London, 1808. First edition. $300–$400.

SCOTT, Winfield. *Memoirs of Lieut. Gen. Scott*. Portraits. 2 vols., cloth. New York, 1864. First edition. $35–$50.

SCRIPPS, J. L. *The Undeveloped Northern Portion of the American Continent*. 20 pp., printed wrappers. Chicago, 1856. First edition. $300–$350. Another, half morocco, $300.

SCROPE, William. *The Art of Deer-Stalking*. 12 plates. Wrappers. London, 1838. First edition. $400–$500. Rebound in half leather, $300.

SCROPE, William. *Days and Nights of Salmon Fishing in the Tweed.* 13 plates. Wrappers. London, 1843. First edition. $600–$800.

SEALSFIELD, Charles. *The Cabin Book; or, Sketches of Life in Texas.* 3 parts, printed wrappers. New York, 1844. (By Karl Postl.) First American edition. $600–$800. London, 1852. Cloth. First English edition. $250–$300. (Note: This book appeared first in the German language in 1841. Howes lists the first edition as published in Zurich; Thomas W. Streeter located an 1841 Leipzig edition. Value: $2,000?)

SEAVER, Edwin. *The Company.* Cloth. New York, 1930. First edition. In dust jacket. $40–$50.

SEAVER, James E. *A Narrative of the Life of Mrs. Mary Jemison, Who Was Taken by the Indians in the Year 1755, etc.* Boards. Canandaigua, N.Y., 1824. First edition. $1,000–$1,200.

SECONDTHOUGHTS, Solomon. *Quodlibet.* Cloth. Philadelphia, 1840. (By John Pendleton Kennedy.) First edition. $150–$200.

SEDGWICK, Catharine M. *The Linwoods; or "Sixty Years Since" in America.* 2 vols., cloth, paper labels. New York, 1835. First edition. $100–$125.

SEDGWICK, John. *Correspondence of John Sedgwick.* 2 vols., cloth. (New York), 1902–03. First edition. One of 300. $50–$75.

SEEGER, Alan. *Poems.* Dark-brown cloth. New York, 1916. First edition. In dust jacket. $100. Author's first book.

SEELIGSON, Mrs. Leila. *A History of Indianola.* 16 pp., wrappers. Cuero, Tex., (1930–31). $75.

SELBY, Julian A. *Memorabilia and Anecdotal Reminiscences of Columbia, S.C.* Portrait. Cloth. Columbia, 1905. First edition. $50–$75.

SELECT Views in Sicily. 36 full-page colored aquatint plates. Folio, half leather. London, 1825. (By Achille Etienne de la Salle Gigault.) $2,500–$3,000.

SELIGMANN, Herbert J. *Lawrence: An American Interpretation.* Cloth. New York, 1924. First edition. In dust jacket. $75. Also, in wrappers, $75.

SELKIRK, (Thomas Douglas), Earl of. *A Sketch of the British Fur Trade in North America.* Boards. London, 1816. First edition. $1,500.

SELTZER, Charles Alden. *The Council of Three.* Cloth. New York, 1900. First edition. $50–$60. Author's first book.

SENIOR Tabula. Printed wrappers. Oak Park, Ill., June, 1917. (Includes "Class Prophecy," by Ernest Hemingway.) $500–$750. Also, $500 (A, 1977).

SENSE and Sensibility. By a Lady. 3 vols., blue or pink boards, paper labels. London, 1811. (By Jane Austen.) First edition, with ruled lines of half title in Vol. 1 measuring ⅘ inch (1½ inches in second edition). $15,000–$20,000. Also, bindings defective, $13,000 (A, 1981).

SEREDY, Kate. *The White Stag.* Lithographs by the author. Cloth. New York, 1937. First edition. In dust jacket. $50–$75.

SERVICE, Robert W. *Rhymes of a Red Cross Man.* Cloth. Toronto, 1916. First edition. $75–$125. New York, 1916. Pictorial red cloth. First American edition. $50–$75.

SERVICE, Robert W. *Rhymes of a Rolling Stone.* Cloth. Toronto, 1912. First edition. $50.

SERVISS, Garrett P. *A Columbus of Space.* Illustrated. Cloth. New York, 1911. First edition. $125–$150.

SERVISS, Garrett P. *The Moon Metal.* Cloth. New York, 1900. First edition. $200–$250.

SETON, Ernest Thompson. *Animal Heroes.* Illustrated. Cloth. New York, 1905. First edition. $100–$150.

SETON, Ernest Thompson. *Life Histories of Northern Animals.* Illustrated. 2 vols., cloth. New York, 1909. First edition. Boxed. $250–$300. London, 1910. 2 vols., cloth. $200–$250.

SETON, Ernest Thompson. *Studies in the Art Anatomy of Animals.* Illustrated. Cloth. London, 1896. First edition. $150–$200.

SETON, Ernest Thompson. *Wild Animals I Have Known.* 20 drawings by author. Pictorial cloth. New York, 1898. First edition, first issue, without the words "The Angel whispered don't go" in the last paragraph on page 265. One of 260. $250–$300. Trade issue: $150–$175. London, (1898). Cloth. First English edition. $100–$150. New York, 1900. Illustrated. One of 1,000 signed. $150–$175. London, 1901. Cloth. First English edition. $75.

SETON-THOMPSON, Ernest. *The Birch-Bark Roll of the Woodcraft Indians.* Illustrated. 71 pp., birchbark wrappers. New York, 1906. First separate edition. $100–$125.

SETON-THOMPSON, Ernest. *Boy Scouts of America: A Handbook of Woodcraft, Scouting, and Life-craft.* Pictorial wrappers. New York, 1910. First edition, "probably earlier state," with printer's slug on copyright page. $125–$150.

SEUSS, Dr. *And to Think I Saw It on Mulberry Street.* Illustrated in color by the author. Pictorial boards. New York, 1937. (By Theodore Geisel.) First edition. In dust jacket. $150–$175. Author's first nonsense book for children.

SEUSS, Dr. *The Seven Lady Godivas.* Color illustrations. Pictorial cloth. New York, (1939). (By Theodore Geisel.) First edition. In dust jacket. $50–$75.

SEVEN and Nine Years Among the Camanches and Apaches. Plates. Cloth. Jersey City, 1873. (By Edwin Eastman.) First edition. $75–$100.

SEVEN Little Sisters Who Live on the Round Ball That Floats in the Air (The). Illustrated. Decorated cloth. Boston, 1861. (By Jane Andrews.) First edition. $100–$125.

SEVEN Pillars of Wisdom (The). Specimen sheets. Half red buckram, vellum spine. New York, 1926. (By T. E. Lawrence.) First American (copyright) edition, with author's name accidentally omitted from title page. One of 24 (stated 22), of which 10 were offered for sale at $10,000 each. $2,500–$3,500. Another issue: Out of series. One of 2 specially bound in three-quarters blue buckram for George H. Doran, the publisher, as presentation copies. $5,000 or more. (For first edition, see entry under Lawrence.)

SEVENTY-SIX . . . (A Novel). 2 vols., boards. Baltimore, 1823. (By John Neal.) First edition. $200–$250.

SEWALL, Rufus King. *Sketches of St. Augustine.* 6 plates, 69 pp., cloth. New York, 1848. First edition. $100–$200. Pages 39 and 40 removed, as with most copies, $60–$80.

SEWARD, W. H. *Communication upon the Subject of an Intercontinental Telegraph, etc.* Folding map. 52 pp., wrappers. Washington, 1864. First edition. $500–$600.

SEWELL, Anna. *Black Beauty.* Blue, red, or brown cloth. London, (1877). First edition. $600–$750. Boston, (1890). Orange printed wrappers, or buff boards. First American edition. Wrappers: $475. Boards: $150–$200. London, 1915. Illustrated in color by Lucy Kemp-Welch. Cloth. One of 600 signed. $250–$300.

SEXTON, Anne. *All My Pretty Ones.* Cloth. Boards and cloth. Boston, 1962. First edition. In dust jacket. $50–$60.

SEXTON, Anne. *The Book of Folly*. Boards and cloth. Boston, 1972. First edition. One of 500 signed. In tissue dust jacket. Boxed. $50.

SEXTON, Anne. *To Bedlam and Part Way Back*. Boards and cloth. Boston, 1960. First edition. In dust jacket. $125–$175. Author's first book.

SEYD, Ernest. *California and Its Resources*. 2 plates (some tinted), 2 folding maps. Cloth. London, 1858. First edition. $500–$600.

SEYMOUR, E. S. *Emigrant's Guide to the Gold Mines of Upper California*. Folding map. 104 pp., wrappers. Chicago, 1849. First edition. $2,000–$2,500.

SEYMOUR, E. S. *Sketches of Minnesota*. Printed wrappers, or cloth. New York, 1850. First edition. Wrappers: $300–$400. Cloth: $285.

SEYMOUR, Ralph Fletcher. *Some Went This Way*. Illustrated. Cloth. Chicago, 1945. First edition. In dust jacket. $35.

SEYMOUR, Silas. *A Reminiscence of the Union Pacific Railroad*. Plates. Printed wrappers. Quebec, 1873. First edition. $300–$400.

SEYMOUR, W. D. *The Isthmian Routes*. 27 pp., sewed. New York, 1863. First edition. $150–$200.

SEYMOUR. William N. *Madison Directory and Business Advertiser*. Map. Leather. Madison, Wis., 1855. First edition. $175–$225.

SHACKLETON, E. H. *The Heart of the Antarctic*. Illustrated, including color plates and folding maps. 3 vols., cloth. London, 1909. First edition. $300–$400. Limited issue: 3 vols., signed by all in the Shore party. One of 300. $1,500–$2,000. Philadelphia, 1909. 2 vols., cloth. $100.

SHAFFER, Ellen. *The Garden of Health*. Illustrated. Folio, boards and linen. (San Francisco, 1957.) Book Club of California. One of 300, with a leaf from the 1499 *Hortus Sanitatis*. In dust jacket. $200–$250.

SHAFFER, Ellen. *The Nuremberg Chronicle . . . A Monograph*. Illustrated. 61 pp., pictorial cloth. Los Angeles, 1950. Plantin Press. One of 300, with an original leaf from the *Chronicle* (1497). $300–$400.

SHAHN, Ben (illustrator). *The Alphabet of Creation*. Signed frontispiece, other illustrations. Cloth. New York, (1954). First edition. One of 50 signed. Boxed. $1,500.

SHAKESPEARE Rare Print Collection. Edited by Seymour Eaton. 146 plates. 12 parts, in portfolio. (New York), 1900. Connoisseur Edition. $50–$85.

SHAKESPEARE, William. *Antony and Cleopatra*. Printed in red and black. Vellum. London, 1912. Doves Press. One of 200. $500–$700. Another issue: Specially bound by the Doves Bindery. $1,500–$2,000. Another: One of 15 on vellum. $6,400 (A, 1978). San Francisco, 1960. Grabhorn Press. Illustrated in color by Mary Grabhorn. Folio, parchment. One of 185. $250–$300.

SHAKESPEARE, William. *As You Like It*. Illustrated in color by Hugh Thomson. Morocco. London, (1909). $100–$125. Another issue: Vellum with ties. One of 500 signed by Thomson. $400–$600.

SHAKESPEARE, William. *Comedies, Histories and Tragedies*. Introduction by Sidney Lee. Facsimile from the 1st Folio edition. Folio, cloth. Oxford, 1901 (1902). One of 1,000 signed. Boxed. $350–$400.

SHAKESPEARE, William. *Coriolanus*. Vellum. London, 1914. Doves Press. One of 200. $600–$800. Another issue: One of 15 on vellum, specially bound in morocco by the Doves Bindery. $4,000–$6,000. Also, $4,000 (A, 1978).

SHAKESPEARE, William. *Hamlet, Prince of Denmark*. Vellum or white pigskin. London, 1909. Doves Press. Printed in red and black. One of 250. $750–$1,000. Another issue: One of 15 on vellum: $4,500 (A, 1980). Weimar, Germany, 1930. Cranach Press.

Illustrated by Edward Gordon Craig. Boards. One of 300. $3,000–$4,000. New York, (1933). Limited Editions Club. $100–$150.

SHAKESPEARE, William. *Julius Caesar*. Vellum. London, 1913. Doves Press. One of 200. $750–$1,000. Another issue: One of 15 on vellum. $1,500–$2,500. Another, elaborately bound, $4,000 (A, 1978). San Francisco, 1954. Grabhorn Press. Illustrated by Mary Grabhorn. Folio, half leather. One of 180. $275–$350.

SHAKESPEARE, William. *King Lear*. Edited by G. K. Chesterton. 10 plates. Cloth. San Francisco, (1930). $200–$300. San Francisco, 1959. Grabhorn Press. Illustrated in color by Mary Grabhorn. Cloth. One of 180. $350–$400. London, 1963. 16 plates by Oskar Kokoschka. Folio, unsewn sheets, in box. One of 275 signed. $800–$1,200. Another issue: Pigskin. With an added signed lithograph. $1,500–$1,750.

SHAKESPEARE, William. *Macbeth*. Illustrations in color by Mary Grabhorn. Boards, leather spine. (San Francisco, 1952.) Grabhorn Press. One of 180. Boxed. $350–$450.

SHAKESPEARE, William. *The Merry Wives of Windsor*. Illustrated by Hugh Thomson. Pictorial vellum, silk ties. London, 1910. One of 350 signed by the artist. $300–$400.

SHAKESPEARE, William. *A Midsummer Night's Dream*. Illustrated by Arthur Rackham. Full white vellum with ties. London, 1908. One of 1,000 signed by Rackham. $800–$1,200. Trade edition: Gold-stamped cloth. $350–$400. San Francisco, 1955. Grabhorn Press. Illustrated in color by Mary Grabhorn. Parchment. One of 180. Boxed. $350–$450.

SHAKESPEARE. William. *Othello*. Portraits in color by Mary Grabhorn. Boards, leather spine. San Francisco, 1956. Grabhorn Press. One of 185. $250–$300.

SHAKESPEARE, William. *The Poems of William Shakespeare*. Edited by F. S. Ellis. Limp vellum with ties. London, 1893. Kelmscott Press. One of 500. $1,000–$1,250. Another issue: One of 10 on vellum. $3,000–$4,000. New York, 1941. Limited Editions Club. 2 vols., pictorial boards. $125–$150.

SHAKESPEARE, William. *Poems and Sonnets*. Morocco. London, 1960. Golden Cockerel Press. One of 100. $750. Another issue: Buckram. One of 470. $200.

SHAKESPEARE, William. *The Rape of Lucrece*. Printed in red and black. Text from the first edition. Vellum. London, 1915. Doves Press. One of 175. $500–$600. Another issue: One of 10 on Vellum, bound in morocco by the Doves Bindery and specially initialed, $6,600 (A, 1978).

SHAKESPEARE, William. *Sonnets*. Vellum. London, 1909. Doves Press. One of 250. $800–$1,000. Another issue: One of 15 on vellum. $2,500–$3,000.

SHAKESPEARE, William. *The Tempest*. 40 color plates by Edmund Dulac. Vellum with ties. London, 1908. One of 500 signed by Dulac. $600–$850. Another issue: cloth. $200–$250. Montagnola, Italy, 1923 (actually 1924). Green parchment. One of 230. $1,200–$1,500. Another issue: One of 6 on vellum. $4,000–$5,000. London, (1926). Vellum. 21 color plates by Rackham. One of 520 signed by Rackham. In dust jacket. $1,000–$1,200. Trade issue: Cloth. In dust jacket. $500–$750. San Francisco, 1951. Grabhorn Press. Illustrated by Mary Grabhorn. Half cloth. One of 160. $300–$400.

SHAKESPEARE, William. *Twelfth Night*. 29 engravings. Folio. morocco and boards. Waltham Saint Lawrence, 1932. Golden Cockerel Press. One of 275. $400–$500.

SHAKESPEARE, William. *Venus and Adonis*. Vellum. London, 1912. Doves Press. One of 200. $850–$1,000. Another issue: One of 15 on vellum, specially bound by the Doves Bindery. $8,400 (A, 1978).

SHAPIRO, Karl. *Poems*. Cloth. Baltimore, 1935. First edition. One of 200 signed. $700–$800. Author's first book.

SHAPIRO, Karl. *Trial of a Poet*. Cloth. New York, (1947). One of 250 signed. In tissue dust jacket. Boxed. $50–$65. Trade edition: In dust jacket. $15–$20.

SHAPIRO, Karl. *V-Letter and Other Poems.* Tan cloth. New York, (1944). First edition. In dust jacket. $50–$60.

SHARAN, James. *The Adventures of James Sharan.* Leather. Baltimore, 1808. First edition. $100–$175.

SHARP, Mrs. Abbie (Gardner). *History of the Spirit Lake Massacre.* Illustrated. Cloth. Des Moines, 1885. First complete edition. $50–$75. (Sometimes catalogued under "Abigail Gardiner" or "Mrs. Abbie Gardner-Sharp.")

SHATTUCK, Lemuel. *A History of the Town of Concord.* Folding map. Half leather. Boston, 1835. First edition. $75–$100.

SHAW, Edward. *Civil Architecture.* 95 engravings. Calf. Boston, 1831. First edition. $100–$150. Boston, 1832. 97 plates. Second edition. $50–$75. Boston, 1836. 100 plates. Sheep. Fourth edition. $50–$100.

SHAW, Edward. *The Modern Architect.* 65 plates. Cloth. Boston, 1855. First edition. $200–$300.

SHAW, Edward. *Rural Architecture.* 52 plates. Calf. Boston, 1843. First edition. $50–$75.

SHAW, George Bernard. See Harris, Frank. Also see *This Is the Preachment on Going to Church.*

SHAW, George Bernard. *Androcles and the Lion.* Printed wrappers. London, 1913. First edition, with title page reading: "Rough Proof—Unpublished." One of 50 privately printed. $400–$500. Also, $350 (A, 1977). London, 1916. Cloth. (With *Overruled* and *Pygmalion* added to title.) In dust jacket. $50–$75.

SHAW, George Bernard. *Back to Methuselah: A Metabiological Pentateuch.* Light gray-green cloth. London, 1921. First edition. In dust jacket. $75–$100. New York, 1939. Limited Editions Club. Cloth. $50–$75.

SHAW, George Bernard. *Cashel Byron's Profession.* Printed blue wrappers. (London), 1886. First edition. $500–$600. Chicago, 1901. Pictorial cloth. First American edition. $150–$200.

SHAW, George Bernard. *A Discarded Defence of Roger Casement.* Wrappers. London, 1922. First edition. One of 25. $200–$300.

SHAW, George Bernard. *The Doctor's Dilemma, Getting Married, and The Shewing Up of Blanco Posnet.* Cloth. London, 1911. First edition. In dust jacket. $75–$100.

SHAW, George Bernard. *Heartbreak House, Great Catherine, and Playlets of the War.* Cloth. London, 1919. First edition. In dust jacket. $40–$50.

SHAW, George Bernard. *How to Settle the Irish Question.* Blue printed wrappers. Dublin, (1917). First edition. $50–$60. Second issue: Green wrappers. $40–$50.

SHAW, George Bernard. *The Intelligent Woman's Guide to Socialism and Capitalism.* Green cloth. London, 1928. First edition. In dust jacket. $85–$100. New York, 1928. Cloth. First American edition. In dust jacket. $75–$100.

SHAW, George Bernard. *John Bull's Other Island and Major Barbara.* Green cloth. London, 1907. First edition, first issue, with Archibald Constable & Co. imprint on title page. $50. New York, 1907. Green cloth. First American edition. $35.

SHAW, George Bernard. *Love Among the Artists.* Green cloth. Chicago, 1900. First authorized edition. $75–$85.

SHAW, George Bernard. *Man and Superman.* Green cloth. Westminster (London), 1903. First edition. $75–$100. New York, 1962. Limited Editions Club. Illustrated. Pictorial cloth. Boxed. $75–$85.

SHAW, George Bernard. *Mrs. Warren's Profession: A Play in Four Acts.* Cloth. London, 1902. First edition. $75–$100.

SHAW, George Bernard. *Nine Answers.* Green boards. No place, (1923). First edition. One of 62 privately printed by Jerome Kern. $325.

SHAW, George Bernard. *Passion, Poison and Petrifaction.* Printed wrappers. New York (1907). First edition. $150.

SHAW, George Bernard. *The Perfect Wagnerite.* Blue and tan cloth. London, 1898. First edition. $100–$150.

SHAW, George Bernard. *Plays: Pleasant and Unpleasant.* Portrait. 2 vols., green cloth. London, 1898. First edition. $75–$100. Chicago, 1898. 2 vols., cloth. First American edition. $75.

SHAW, George Bernard. *Pygmalion: A Romance in Five Acts.* Printed wrappers. London, 1913. First edition, first issue, with title page reading: "Rough Proof, Unpublished." $600-$800. (London), 1914. Wrappers. Second edition. $300–$350.

SHAW, George Bernard. *Saint Joan: A Chronicle Play.* Blue-gray wrappers. London, 1923. First edition, first issue, with title page reading "Rough Proof, Unpublished." $400–$600. Inscribed copy, $850. London, 1924. Cloth. First published edition. In dust jacket. $75–$100. London, (1924). Illustrated by Charles Ricketts. Folio, boards and cloth. First illustrated edition. One of 750. In dust jacket. $300–$350.

SHAW, George Bernard. *Shaw Gives Himself Away: An Autobiographical Miscellany.* Frontispiece woodcut portrait. Dark-green morocco, inlaid with red leather. Newtown, Wales, 1939. Gregynog Press. One of 300. $600–$800.

SHAW, George, Bernard. *The Shewing Up of Blanco Posnet.* 36 pp., printed wrappers. New York, 1909. First (copyright) edition. One of 25. $250–$350.

SHAW, George Bernard. *An Unsocial Socialist.* Scarlet cloth. London, 1887. First edition, first state, with title of Shaw's first novel incorrectly given on title page and with publisher's name spelled wrong on spine. $200–$250. Second state, with novel's title corrected and with publisher's name on spine stamped over. $150–$200.

SHAW, George Bernard. *War Issues for Irishmen: An Open Letter to Col. Arthur Lynch from Bernard Shaw.* Gray wrappers. Dublin, 1918. First edition. $400–$600. (Suppressed.)

SHAW, Henry. *The Decorative Arts, Ecclesiastical and Civil, of the Middle Ages.* 41 engravings, 18 in color. Half leather. London, 1851. First edition. $400–$600.

SHAW, Henry. *Dresses and Decorations of the Middle Ages.* Hand-colored plates and other illustrations. 2 vols., folio, boards. London, 1843. First edition. $500–$650.

SHAW, Henry. *Examples of Ornamental Metal Work.* 50 plates. Boards. London, 1836. First edition. $150–$250.

SHAW, Irwin. *Bury the Dead.* Cloth. New York, (1936). First edition. In dust jacket. $75. Author's first book.

SHAW, Irwin. *Sailor Off the Bremen.* Cloth. New York, 1939. First edition. In dust jacket. $50–$60.

SHAW, Joshua. *United States Directory for the Use of Travellers and Merchants, etc.* Leather. Philadelphia, (1822). First edition. $350–$500.

SHAW, R. C. *Across the Plains in Forty-nine.* Portrait. Cloth. Farmland, Ind., 1896. First edition. $125–$150.

SHAW, T. E. (adopted name). See Homer; Lawrence, T. E.

SHAY, Frank (editor). *Contemporary One-Act Plays of 1921.* Green cloth. Cincinnati,

(1922). First edition. In dust jacket. $50–$75. (Note: Includes Eugene O'Neill's *The Dreamy Kid*—first book appearance of the play.)

SHAY, Frank (editor). *Iron Men and Wooden Ships.* Introduction by William McFee. Illustrated by Edward A. Wilson. Cloth. Garden City, 1924. First edition. One of 200 with a lithograph signed by Wilson. $200–$250.

SHEA, John Gilmary. *Early Voyages Up and Down the Mississippi.* Boards. Albany, N.Y., 1861. First edition. $60–$75. Large paper issue: $150. Albany, (1902). Boards. Facsimile reprint. $75.

SHEA, John Gilmary. *A History of the Catholic Church Within . . . the United States.* Illustrated. 4 vols., cloth. New York, 1886–92. First edition. $100–$150.

SHELDON, Charles M. *In His Steps: "What Would Jesus Do?"* Brown and white printed wrappers. Chicago, 1897. First edition. $250–$500. (One of the best-selling novels of American publishing history; rare in original wrappers.)

SHELLEY, Mary W. See *Falkner; The Fortunes of Perkin Warbeck; Frankenstein; Valperga; The Last Man.*

SHELLEY, Percy Bysshe. See *S., P. B.* Also see *History of a Six Weeks' Tour, etc.; St. Irvyne; Epipsychidion.*

SHELLEY, Percy Bysshe. *Adonais: An Elegy on the Death of John Keats.* 25 pp., blue ornamental wrappers. Pisa, Italy, 1821. First edition. $10,000–$15,000. Also, $10,560 (A, 1979). Rebound copies, $5,000–$10,000. Cambridge (London), 1829. Green wrappers. Second (first English) edition. $1,000 and up. Also, "stitched, as issued," $638 (A, 1980).

SHELLEY, Percy Bysshe. *Alastor: or, The Spirit of Solitude: and Other Poems.* Boards, paper label on spine. London, 1816. First edition. $2,000 and up. Also, rebound in calf. $850 (A, 1979).

SHELLEY, Percy Bysshe. *The Cenci.* Wrappers, or boards. (Leghorn), Italy, 1819. First edition. (250 copies.) $3,000–$4,000. Also, one of "a few" copies on thin paper, in original wrappers. $1,900 (A, 1977). (Most copies are on heavier paper.) London, 1821. Wrappers. First English edition. $400–$600. New Rochelle, 1903. Elston Press. Boards. $200.

SHELLEY, Percy Bysshe. *The Complete Works of Percy Bysshe Shelley.* 10 vols., cloth, vellum spines. London, 1926–27. One of 780. Boxed. $350.

SHELLEY, Percy Bysshe. *Hellas: A Lyrical Drama.* Stiff drab wrappers. London, 1822. First edition. $1,000 and up.

SHELLEY, Percy Bysshe. *Laon and Cythna.* Boards. London, 1818. First edition, first issue, with four-line quotation from Pindar on half title. $4,000 and up. Second issue, same date, without Pindar lines. Boards. $3,000 and up.

SHELLEY, Percy Bysshe. *Letters from Percy Bysshe Shelley to J. H. Leigh Hunt.* Edited by Thomas J. Wise. 2 vols., cloth. London, 1894. First edition. (30 copies.) $750–$1,000.

SHELLEY, Percy Bysshe. *Letters of Percy Bysshe Shelley.* With an Introductory Essay by Robert Browning. Dark-red cloth. London, 1852. First edition. $200–$250. (Suppressed as forgeries.)

SHELLEY, Percy Bysshe. *The Masque of Anarchy: A Poem.* Preface by Leigh Hunt. Gray-blue boards. London, 1832. First edition, with white spine label lettered vertically "Shelley's Masque." $500–$600.

SHELLEY, Percy Bysshe. *Miscellaneous Poems.* Boards. London, 1826. First edition. $400–$600.

SHELLEY, Percy Bysshe. *Poems. (Poetical Works.)* 3 vols., vellum. (Hammersmith, 1894–95). Kelmscott Press. (250 copies.) $1,500–$2,250. Another issue: One of 6 on vellum. $6,000–$8000. (London, 1901–02.) Vale Press. Decorations by Charles Ricketts. 3 vols., white buckram. $300–$400. London, 1914. Doves Press. Limp vellum. One of 200. $400–$600. Another issue: One of 12 on vellum. $1,900 (A, 1978). New York, 1971. Limited Editions Club. $50–$65.

SHELLEY, Percy Bysshe. *Posthumous Poems.* Boards, paper label on spine. London, (1824). First edition, first issue, without errata leaf. $600–$800.

SHELLEY, Percy Bysshe. *Prometheus Unbound.* Blue-gray boards, paper label. London, 1820. First edition, first issue, with "Miscellaneous" misprinted "Misellaneous" in table of contents. $2,000–$2,500. Also, $1,000 (A, 1977). Second issue, with misprint corrected. $1,500–$2,000. London, 1904. Essex House Press. Morocco. One of 20 on vellum. Boxed. $1,000 and up. Another issue: Limp vellum. One of 200 on paper. $200–$300.

SHELLEY, Percy Bysshe. *Queen Mab: A Philosophical Poem.* Boards. London, 1813. First (privately printed) edition. $10,000 and up. Shelley removed the title, dedication, and imprint from many copies. An unmutilated copy, with hinges split, was sold at auction for $6,000 in June, 1976. London, 1821. Boards. Second (first published) edition. $600–$800.

SHELLEY, Percy Bysshe. *The Revolt of Islam.* Blue boards, white paper label on spine. London, 1817 (actually 1818). First edition, first issue, incorrectly dated on title page. $2,500–$3,500. London, 1818. Second issue, correctly dated. $1,000–$2,000.

SHELLEY, Percy Bysshe. *Rosalind and Helen.* Drab wrappers. London, 1819. First edition, with 2 ad leaves at end. $500–$750.

SHELLEY-ROLLS, Sir John C. E. *Yachts of the Royal Yacht Squadron, 1815–1932.* Buckram. London, 1933. First edition. $100–$150.

SHEPARD, A. K. *The Land of the Aztecs.* Cloth. Albany, 1859. First edition. $100–$150.

SHEPARD, Ernest H. *Fun and Fantasy.* Introduction by A. A. Milne. 7 color plates. Cloth. London, (1927). First edition. One of 150 signed. $135–$175. Trade edition: Boards. $50–$60.

SHEPARD, Odell. *A Lonely Flute.* Boards. Boston, 1917. First edition. In dust jacket. $30–$50. Author's first book.

SHEPPARD Lee. Written by Himself. 2 vols., floral cloth. New York, 1836. (By Robert Montgomery Bird.) First edition. $400–$500.

SHEPPERD, Tad. *Pack & Paddock.* Illustrated. Boards. New York, (1938). Derrydale Press. First edition. One of 950. $150–$200.

SHERIDAN, Philip H. *Outline Descriptions of the Posts in the Military Division of the Missouri, etc.* Maps, including a folding map. Cloth. Chicago, 1872. First edition. $150–$200.

SHERIDAN, Richard Brinsley. *The School for Scandal.* Illustrated. Quarto, vellum with ties. Oxford, 1930. One of 7 on vellum. $2,500–$2,750.

SHERMAN, Elizabeth Ware. See S., E. W., and M., S. W.

SHERWELL, Samuel. *Old Recollections of an Old Boy.* Portrait. Cloth. New York, 1923. First edition. $75–$100.

SHERWOOD, J. Ely. *California: Her Wealth and Resources.* 40 pp., wrappers. New York, 1848. First edition. $1,200.

SHIEL, M. P. *Children of the Wind.* Cloth. London, 1923. First edition. In dust jacket. $150–$250.

SHIEL, M. P. *The Last Miracle.* Pictorial black cloth. London, 1906. First edition. $100–$125.

SHIEL, M. P. *Prince Zaleski.* Decorated purple cloth. London, 1895. First edition, with two ad catalogues at back. $300–$400.

SHIEL, M. P. *The Purple Cloud.* Cloth. London, 1929. First edition. One of 105 signed. $300–$400.

SHIEL, M. P. *Shapes in the Fire.* Cloth. London, 1896. First edition. $250–$300.

SHIELDS, G. O. *The Battle of the Big Hole.* 8 plates. Cloth. New York, 1889. First edition. $75–$100.

SHIELDS, G. O. *Cruising in the Cascades.* Illustrated. Cloth. Chicago, 1889. First edition. $100.

SHILLIBEER, Lieut. J. *A Narrative of the Briton's Voyage to Pitcairn's Island.* 16 etchings (not 18 as title erroneously states). Contemporary boards. Taunton, 1817. First edition, with errata leaf and instructions to the binder. $500–$750. London, 1817. 11 plates. Boards. Second edition. $400–$500. London, 1818. 12 plates. Half calf. Third edition. $300–$400.

SHINN, Charles Howard. *Graphic Description of Pacific Coast Outlaws.* (Caption title.) Portrait. 32 pp., wrappers. (San Francisco, about 1890–95.) First edition. $350–$500.

SHINN, Charles Howard. *Mining Camps.* Cloth. New York, 1885. First edition. $150.

SHINN, Charles Howard. *Pacific Rural Handbook.* Cloth. San Francisco, 1879. First edition. $100–$125.

SHIPLEY, Conway. *Sketches in the Pacific.* 26 tinted plates. Folio, cloth. London, 1851. First edition. $5,000.

SHIPMAN, Mrs. O. L. *Taming the Big Bend.* Folding map, 4 plates. Cloth. (Marfa, Tex., 1926.) First edition. $250.

SHOBER, G. A. *A Choice Drop of Honey from the Rock Christ, or a Short Word of Advice to All Saints and Sinners.* 30 pp., wrappers. New Market, Va., 1811. $150–$250.

SHOEMAKER, James. *Directory of the City of Mankato, and Blue Earth County.* Printed boards. Mankato, Minn., 1888. $125–$150.

SHORT History of Gen. R. E. Lee (A). 15 pp., pictorial wrappers, miniature. New York, 1888. $50–$75.

SHORT History of T. J. Jackson (A). 15 pp., pictorial wrappers, miniature. New York, 1888. $50–$75.

SHOWMAN'S Series III (The): Theatre Picture Book. Pop-up book with colored folding scenes. Pictorial boards. New York, (about 1885). $150–$200.

SHUTE, Henry A. *The Real Diary of a Real Boy.* Cloth. Boston, 1902. First edition. $100–$150.

SIDNEY, Margaret. *Five Little Peppers and How They Grew.* Green, blue, or brown pictorial cloth. Boston, (1880). (By Harriet M. S. Lothrop.) First edition, first state, with 1880 copyright and with caption on page 231 reading "said Polly." $200–$300.

SIDNEY, Sir Philip. *The Defence of Poesie and Certain Sonnets.* Engraved portrait. Limp vellum, with ties. Bedford Park, Chiswick, 1906. Caradoc Press. Vellum. One of 14 (of an edition of 364) printed in red and black on vellum. $400–$600. Ordinary issue: Boards. One of 350. $100–$150.

SIEBERT, Wilbur Henry. *Loyalists in East Florida.* 6 maps and plates. 2 vols., buckram. DeLand, Fla., 1929. First edition. One of 355. $175–$200.

SIEGE of Corinth (The). Drab wrappers. London, 1816. (By George Gordon Noel, Lord Byron.) First edition. $400–$500.

SILL, Edward Rowland. *The Venus of Milo and Other Poems*. Printed cream wrappers. Berkeley, 1883. First edition, with copyright stamp on title page. $50–$75.

SILLIMAN, Benjamin. *A Description of the Recently Discovered Petroleum Region in California*. (Cover title.) Printed wrappers. New York, 1864. First edition. $750–$1,000.

SILLIMAN, Benjamin. *Report upon the Oil Property of the Philadelphia and California Petroleum Co.* 2 maps. 36 pp., wrappers. Philadelphia, 1865. First edition. $300–$400, possibly more.

SILLITOE, Alan. *The Loneliness of the Long Distance Runner*. Cloth. London, (1959). First edition. In dust jacket with wraparound band. $100–$125.

SILURIENSIS, Leolinus. *The Anatomy of Tobacco*. White parchment boards. London, (1884). (By Arthur Machen.) First edition. $150–$175. Author's first book (aside from the anonymous privately printed pamphlet *Eleusinia*, Hereford, Wales, 1881, of which only one copy is known).

SILVER Mines of Virginia and Austin, Nevada. 19 pp., wrappers. Boston, 1865. $300–$350.

SIMAK, Clifford D. *City*. Boards. (Hicksville, or New York, 1952.) First edition. $100.

SIMAK, Clifford D. *The Creator*. Wrappers. (Los Angeles, 1946.) First edition. $50. Author's first book.

SIMMONS, Albert Dixon. *Wing Shots: A Series of Camera Studies of . . . Birds . . . on the Wing*. Cloth. New York, (1936). Derrydale Press. First edition. In dust jacket. $150–$200.

SIMMS, Jeptha R. *The American Spy, or Freedom's Early Sacrifice*. 63 pp., wrappers. Albany, 1846. First edition. $100–$150.

SIMMS, Jeptha R. *History of Schoharie County*. Plates. Cloth. Albany, 1845. First edition. $85–$150.

SIMMS, Jeptha R. *Trappers of New York*. 4 plates. Cloth. Albany, 1850. First edition. $200–$225. Albany, 1860. Red buckram. $100–$125.

SIMMS, William Gilmore. See *Atalantis; Beauchampe; Border Beagles; Carl Werner; The Damsel of Darien; Grouped Thoughts and Scattered Fancies; Guy Rivers; The Lily and the Totem; Martin Faber; Mellichampe; Michael Bonham; The Partisan; Pelayo; Richard Hurdis; Sack and Destruction of Columbia, S.C.; The Wigwam and the Cabin; The Yemassee*.

SIMMS, William Gilmore. *Areytos; or, Songs of the South*. Wrappers. Charleston, 1846. First edition. $300–$400.

SIMMS, William Gilmore. *The Cassique of Accabee*. Wrappers. Charleston, 1849. First edition. $300–$400.

SIMMS, William Gilmore. *Egeria; or, Voices of Thought and Counsel for the Woods and Wayside*. Cloth. Philadelphia, 1853. First edition. $100–$150.

SIMMS, William Gilmore. *Father Abbot, or, The Home Tourist*. Wrappers. Charleston, 1849. First edition. $250–$300.

SIMMS, William Gilmore. *The Forayers; or, The Raid of the Dog-Days*. Cloth. New York, 1855. First edition. $200–$300.

SIMMS, William Gilmore. *Helen Halsey; or, The Swamp State of Conelachita*. Wrappers. New York, 1845. First edition. $300–$400.

SIMMS, William Gilmore. *The History of South Carolina*. Cloth. Charleston, 1840. First edition. $150–$200.

SIMMS, William Gilmore. *The Life of Chevalier Bayard*. Frontispiece, other illustrations. Cloth. New York, 1847. First edition. $100–$125.

SIMMS, William Gilmore. *The Life of Francis Marion*. Cloth. New York, 1844. First edition. $75–$100.

SIMMS, William Gilmore. *Lyrical and Other Poems*. Cloth. Charleston, 1827. First edition. $300–$500. Author's first book.

SIMMS, William Gilmore. *Marie De Berniere*. Cloth. Philadelphia, 1853. First edition. $200–$300.

SIMMS, William Gilmore. *Norman Maurice; or, The Man of the People*. Wrappers. Richmond, Va., 1851. First edition. $300–$350.

SIMMS, William Gilmore. *Poems: Descriptive, Dramatic, Legendary and Contemplative*. 2 vols., cloth. New York, 1853. First edition. $250–$300. Charleston, 1853. 2 vols., cloth. $175–$200.

SIMMS, William Gilmore. *Southward Ho! A Spell of Sunshine*. Cloth. New York, 1854. First edition. $250–$300.

SIMMS, William Gilmore. *The Spartanburg Female College Oration*. Wrappers. Spartanburg, S.C., 1855. First edition. $150–$200.

SIMMS, William Gilmore (editor). *War Poetry of the South*. Cloth. New York, 1866. First edition. $75–$100.

SIMONIDEA. Blue boards. Bath, England, (1806). (By Walter Savage Landor.) First edition. $300–$400.

SIMPLE Truths in Verse, for the Amusement and Instruction of Children, at an Early Age. Illustrated. Boards. Baltimore, (about 1820). (By Mary Belson Elliot.) First American edition. $50–$60.

SIMPSON, Elizabeth M. *Bluegrass Houses and Their Traditions*. Illustrated. Cloth. Lexington, 1932. First edition. In dust jacket. $50–$75.

SIMPSON, George. *Journal of Occurrences in the Athabasca Department, etc.* Edited by E. E. Rich. Cloth. Toronto, 1938. One of 550. $150–$200.

SIMPSON, George. *Narrative of a Journey Round the World, During the Years 1841 and 1842*. Portrait, folding map. 2 vols., cloth. London, 1847. First edition. $400–$500. Philadelphia, 1847. 2 vols. in one, cloth. First American edition. $250–$300.

SIMPSON, Harold B. *Gaines Mill to Appomattox*. Illustrated. Full leather. Waco, Tex., 1963. First edition. One of 50 signed. $150.

SIMPSON, Henry I. *The Emigrant's Guide to the Gold Mines*. Folding map. 30 pp., wrappers. New York, 1848. First edition. $3,000–$3,500. Also, covers frayed, $950 (A, 1977).

SIMPSON, Gen. James H. *Coronado's March in Search of the Seven Cities of Cibola*. Map. 34 pp., wrappers. Washington, 1884. $100–$125.

SIMPSON, Capt. James H. *Report of Explorations Across the Great Basin of the Territory of Utah, etc.* Folding map, plates, errata leaf. Cloth. Washington, 1876. First edition. $100–$135.

SIMPSON, James H. *Journal of a Military Reconnaissance, from Santa Fe, N.M., to the Navajo Country*. Folding map, 72 plates, including color. Cloth. Philadelphia, 1852. First separate printing. $400–$600.

SIMPSON, James H. *Report from the Secretary of War . . . and Map of the Route from Fort Smith, Ark., to Santa Fe, N.M.* (Caption title.) 4 folding maps. Stitched. (Washington, 1850.) First edition. Senate issue. $100–$150. House issue: One folding map. 2 plates. $100–$150.

SIMPSON, James H. *Report of the Secretary of War . . . and Map of Wagon Roads in Utah.* (Caption title.) Large folding map. (Washington, 1859.) First edition. $150–$200.

SIMPSON, Louis. *The Arrivistes: Poems, 1940–1949.* Wrappers. New York, (1949). First edition. $150. Author's first book.

SIMPSON, Thomas. *Narrative of the Discoveries on the Northwest Coast of America.* 2 maps. Cloth. London, 1843. First edition. $400–$500.

SINCLAIR, Upton. *A Home Colony. A Prospectus.* 23 pp., wrappers. New York, (1906). First edition. $40–$50.

SINCLAIR, Upton. *The Jungle.* Green cloth. New York, 1906. First edition, first issue, with Doubleday imprint and with the "1" in date on copyright page in perfect type. $85–$100. Variant first edition (issued simultaneously): New York, 1906. Jungle Publishing Co. First state, with unbroken type on copyright page and with "Sustainers' Edition" note tipped in. $85–$100.

SINCLAIR, Upton. *King Midas.* Cloth. New York, 1901. First edition. $50.

SINCLAIR, Upton. *Oil!* Printed wrappers. Long Beach, (1927). First edition. $35–$50.

SINCLAIR, Upton. *Samuel the Seeker.* Cloth. No place, (1910). First edition. In dust jacket. $75–$100.

SINCLAIR, Upton. *Singing Jailbirds.* Wrappers. Pasadena, (1924). First edition. $35–$50.

SINCLAIR, Upton. *Springtime and Harvest.* Red cloth. New York, 1910. First edition. $200–$250.

SINGLETON, Arthur. *Letters from the South and West.* Stiff wrappers, or boards. Boston, 1824. (By Henry Cogswell Knight.) First edition. $200–$250.

SINISTRARI, Ludovico. *Demoniality.* Translated into English by Montague Summers. Vellum. London, 1927. First edition. One of 90 (of an edition of 1,290) on handmade paper, signed by Summers. $225.

SINJOHN, John. *From the Four Winds.* Olive-green cloth. London, 1897. (By John Galsworthy.) First edition. One of 500. $750–$1,000. Author's first book.

SINJOHN, John. *Jocelyn.* Cloth. London, 1898. (By John Galsworthy.) First edition, first issue, with "you" for "my" on page 257, third line from bottom. $300–$400.

SINJOHN, John. *A Man of Devon.* Blue cloth. Edinburgh and London, 1901. (By John Galsworthy.) First edition, with ads dated "4/01." $300–$400.

SINJOHN, John. *Villa Rubein.* Cherry-red cloth. London, 1900. (By John Galsworthy.) First edition. $300–$400.

SIRINGO, Charles A. *A Cowboy Detective.* Illustrated. Pictorial cloth. Chicago, 1912. First edition, first issue, published by Conkey. $200. Another binding: Special first issue presentation copies, in pebble-grained leather (unrecorded in bibliographies), inscribed by Siringo. $400–$500. Second issue, same date. 2 vols., wrappers. $150. Another edition: New York, 1912. Pictorial wrappers. $225.

SIRINGO, Charles A. *History of "Billy the Kid."* 142 pp., stiff pictorial wrappers. (Santa Fe, 1920.) First edition. $750.

SIRINGO, Charles A. *A Lone Star Cowboy.* Illustrated. Pictorial cloth. Santa Fe, 1919. First edition. $100–$125.

SIRINGO, Charles A. *Riata and Spurs*. 16 plates. Pictorial cloth. Boston, 1927. First edition, first issue, with "1927" on title page. In dust jacket. $300–$350. Lacking jacket, $150–$200. Boston (1927). Pictorial cloth. Second issue, with many changes. Lacking jacket, $50.

SIRINGO, Charles A. *The Song Companion of a Lone Star Cowboy*. Pictorial wrappers. Santa Fe, (1919). First edition. $400.

SIRINGO, Charles A. *A Texas Cowboy, or, Fifteen Years on the Hurricane Deck of a Spanish Pony*. Illustrated, including chromolithographic frontispiece in color. Wrappers, or black pictorial cloth. Chicago, 1885. First edition. Wrappers: $5,000 and up. Cloth: $4,000–$5,000. Chicago, 1886. Siringo & Dobson. 8 plates, 347 pp. Second edition. $750. Another issue, same collation, same place and date: Rand McNally,wrappers. $400–$750.New York, (1886). Wrappers. $200–$300. New York, (1950). Illustrated by Tom Lea. Cloth. In dust jacket. $50.

SIR *Ralph Esher; or, Adventures of a Gentleman of the Court of Charles II*. 3 vols., boards. London, 1832. (By Leigh Hunt.) First edition. $400–$500. Also, $200 (A, 1979).

SISTER *Years (The); Being the Carrier's Address, to the Patrons of the Salem Gazette, for the First of January, 1839*. (Cover title.) 8 pp., printed self-wrappers. Salem, Mass., 1839. (By Nathaniel Hawthorne.) First edition. $500 and up.

SITGREAVES, Lorenzo. *Report of an Expedition down the Zuni and Colorado Rivers*. 79 plates, some tinted; folding map. Cloth. Washington, 1853. First edition. $350–$450. Washington, 1854. Cloth. $350.

SITWELL, Edith. *Alexander Pope*. Illustrated. Yellow buckram. London, (1930). First edition. One of 220 signed. In dust jacket. Boxed. $175–$225.

SITWELL, Edith. *Collected Poems*. Cloth. London, 1930. One of 320 signed. In dust jacket. $100–$150. Trade edition: Cloth. In dust jacket. $50–$100.

SITWELL, Edith. *Facade*. Colored frontispiece. Boards. London, 1920. First edition. One of 150 signed. $150–$250. London, 1922. Boards. Second edition. $150–$200.

SITWELL, Edith. *Five Poems*. Cloth. London, 1928. First edition. One of 275 signed. $75–$100.

SITWELL, Edith. *In Spring*. 3 wood engravings by Edward Carrick. Green boards, yellow label. London, 1931. First (special) edition. (15 copies signed by author and artist and one stanza in author's handwriting.) In tissue dust jacket. $100–$125. Another issue: One of 350 signed. $35–$50.

SITWELL, Edith. *Jane Barston, 1719–1746*. Yellow boards. London, 1931. One of 250 signed. $100–$125.

SITWELL, Edith. *The Mother and Other Poems*. Wrappers. Oxford, 1915. First edition. $250–$375. Author's first book. (500 copies issued.).

SITWELL, Edith. *The Pleasures of Poetry*. First, Second, and Third Series. 3 vols., cloth. London, 1930–31–32. First editions. In dust jackets. $200–$250.

SITWELL, Edith. *Popular Song*. Boards. London, 1928. First edition. One of 500 signed. $75–$125.

SITWELL, Edith. *Street Songs*. Cloth. London, 1942. First edition. In dust jacket. $50–$60.

SITWELL, Edith. *The Wooden Pegasus*. Boards and cloth. Oxford, 1920. First edition. In dust jacket. $50–$60.

SITWELL, Edith, and Sitwell, Osbert. *Twentieth Century Harlequinade*. Cloth. Oxford, 1916. First edition. One of 500. $50–$75.

SITWELL, Osbert. *At the House of Mrs. Kinfoot.* Wrappers. London, 1921. First edition. One of 101 signed. $150.

SITWELL, Osbert. *Before the Bombardment.* Cloth. London, 1926. First edition. In dust jacket. $50–$75.

SITWELL, Osbert. *The Collected Satires and Poems of Osbert Sitwell.* Portrait frontispiece. Cloth. (London), 1931. First edition. Limited and signed. $50–$75.

SITWELL, Osbert. *England Reclaimed.* Buckram. London, 1927. First edition. One of 165 signed. In dust jacket. $100–$150.

SITWELL, Osbert. *Miss Mew.* Half linen and boards. (London), 1929. First edition. One of 101 signed. $75–$100.

SITWELL, Osbert. *Who Killed Cock-Robin?* Boards. London, 1921. First edition. In dust jacket. $75–$125.

SITWELL, Osbert. *The Winstonburg Line: 3 Satires.* Pictorial wrappers. London, 1919. First edition. $125–$150. Author's first book.

SITWELL, Sacheverell. *The Cyder Feast and Other Poems.* Yellow buckram. (London), 1927. One of 165 signed. $150–$200.

SITWELL, Sacheverell. *Doctor Donne and Gargantua.* Wrappers. London, 1921. First edition. One of 101 signed. $300–$375. London, 1930. Boards. One of 200 signed. $75–$100. London, 1923. (Same title, but *second canto.*) One of 35. $650–$700.

SITWELL, Sacheverell. *The People's Palace.* Frontispiece. Wrappers. Oxford, 1918. First edition. (400 copies.) $175–$200.

SITWELL, Sacheverell. *Two Poems, Ten Songs.* Decorated boards. London, 1929. First edition. One of 275 signed. $125–$150.

SITWELL, Sacheverell, and Lambert, Constant. *The Rio Grande.* Boards. London, 1929. First edition. One of 75 signed. $250–$350. Unsigned (but numbered), $200.

SITWELL, Sacheverell; Blunt, Wilfred; and Synge, Patrick M. *Great Flower Books, 1700–1900.* 36 plates, 20 in color. Folio, half morocco. London, 1956. First edition. One of 295 signed by the authors. Boxed. $1,250–$1,750. Another issue: Half cloth. One of 1,750. In dust jacket. $750–$850.

SITWELL, Sacheverell; Buchanan, Handasyde; and Fisher, James. *Fine Bird Books, 1700–1900.* 38 plates in color, 36 in black and white. Folio, half morocco. London, 1953. One of 295 signed by the three authors. $1,250–$1,750. Another issue: Buckram and boards. One of 2,000. In dust jacket. $750–$850.

SIX to One; A Nantucket Idyl. Tan or gray cloth. New York, 1878. (By Edward Bellamy.) First edition, first state, cloth. $200–$300. Later state, printed wrappers: $150–$200. Author's first book.

SIXTY Years of the Life of Jeremy Levis. 2 vols., boards, cloth spines, paper labels. New York, 1831. (By Laughton Osborn.) First edition. $75–$100.

SKEFFINGTON, F. J. C., and Joyce, James A. *Two Essays.* 4 leaves, pink printed wrappers. Dublin, (1901). First edition. Joyce's first published book, containing his essay "The Day of the Rabblement." $4,000 in a 1981 catalogue; $3,000 in a 1980 catalogue.

SKELTON, John. *The Tunning of Elynour Rummynge.* Illustrated by Leonard Baskin. Boards. Worcester, Mass., 1953. Gehenna Press. One of 118. $500–$600.

SKETCH of the Geographical Rout [sic] *of a Great Railway . . . Between the Atlantic States and the Great Valley of the Mississippi.* Folding map. 16 pp., wrappers. New York, 1829. (By William C. Redfield.) First edition. $300–$400. New York, 1830. Second edition. Rebound in cloth. $100 (A, 1979).

SKETCH of the History of South Carolina, etc. (A). Cloth. Charleston, 1856. (By William James Rivers.) First edition. $75–$125.

SKETCH of Old England (A). By a New England Man. 2 vols., printed boards. New York, 1822. (By James Kirke Paulding.) First edition. $200–$300.

SKETCH of St. Anthony and Minneapolis. Frontispiece, 4 plates, map. 32 pp., wrappers. St. Anthony, 1857. First edition. With errata slip. $400–$500.

SKETCH of the Seminole War, and Sketches During the Campaign. Leather. Charleston, 1836. First edition. $200–$300.

SKETCHES by "Boz." Illustrated by George Cruikshank. 3 vols. (First Series, 1836, 2 vols., dark-green cloth; Second Series, 1837, pink cloth.) London, 1836–37. (By Charles Dickens.) First edition. $5,000 and up. Also, First Series, 2 vols., $1,900 (A, 1978). Author's first book. London, 1837–39. 20 parts, pictorial pink wrappers. $5,000–$10,000. Also, some plates stained, $5,000 (A, 1976). (Complete sets with all ads and wrappers in the first state are rare. Imperfect sets are available at much lower prices than are quoted here.)

SKETCHES by a Traveller. Calf. Boston, 1830. (By Silas P. Holbrook.) First edition. $125–$150.

SKETCHES of History, Life and Manners in the United States. By a Traveller. Woodcut frontispiece view. Boards. New Haven, 1826. (By Anne Royall.) First edition. $400–$500.

SKETCHES of the History of Ogle County, Ill. 88 pp., wrappers. Polo, Ill., 1859. (By Henry R. Boss.) First edition. $125–$150.

SKETCHES of Mission Life Among the Indians of Oregon. Frontispiece and 4 plates. Cloth. New York, 1854. (By H. K. W. Perkins? or Z. A. Mudge?) First edition. $250.

SKETCHES of Springfield. By a Citizen. 49 pp., plus 21 pp. of ads, wrappers. Springfield, Ohio, (1852). $100–$150.

SKETCHES of the West, or the Home of the Badgers. Folding map. 48 pp., wrappers. Milwaukee, 1847. (By Josiah B. Grinnell.) Second edition (of *The Home of the Badgers,* which see under Grinnell's pseudonym, Oculus). $350–$400.

SKINNER, B. F. *Walden Two.* Cloth. New York, 1948. First edition. In dust jacket. $50–$60.

SKINNER, J. S. *The Dog and the Sportsman.* Illustrated, including engraved title page. New York, 1845. First edition. $200–$250.

SLAUGHTER, Mrs. Linda W. *The New Northwest.* 24 pp., wrappers. Bismarck, 1874. First edition. $1,500–$2,000, possibly more.

SLOAN, Edward L. (editor). *Salt Lake City: Gazetteer and Directory.* Cloth. Salt Lake City, 1874. $200–$300.

SLOAN, Robert. W. *Utah Gazetteer and Directory of Logan, Ogden, Provo and Salt Lake Cities.* Cloth. Salt Lake City, 1884. $200–$300.

SLOCUM, Joshua. *Sailing Alone Around the World.* Cloth. New York, 1900. First edition. $125.

SLOCUM, Joshua. *Voyage of the Destroyer from New York to Brazil.* 47 pp., wrappers. Boston, 1894. First edition. $100–$125.

SMART, Stephen F. *Leadville, Ten Mile . . . And All Other Noted Colorado Mining Camps.* 2 folding maps, 56 pp., printed wrappers. Kansas City, 1879. First edition. $400–$600. (For a similar work, see Willis Sweet entry.)

SMEDLEY, Frank E. See *Frank Fairleigh.*

SMEDLEY, William. *Across the Plains in '62*. Map and portrait. 56 pp., boards. (Denver, 1916.) First edition. $100–$125.

SMITH, Alexander. *Dreamthorp*. Green cloth. London, 1863. First edition. $75–$125. Boston, 1864. Cloth. First American edition. $75–$100.

SMITH, Alexander. *Poems*. Cloth. London, 1853. First edition, with inserted ads dated November, 1852. $75–$85. Author's first book.

SMITH, Alice R. H., and Smith, D. E. H. *The Dwelling Houses of Charleston*. Illustrated. Cloth. Philadelphia, 1917. First edition. $75–$125.

SMITH, Arthur D. Howden. *Porto Bello Gold*. Cloth. New York, (1924). First edition. In dust jacket. $50–$60.

SMITH, Ashbel. *Reminiscences of the Texas Republic*. Cloth. Galveston, 1876. First edition. One of 100. $250–$300.

SMITH, Buckingham (translator). *The Discovery of Florida*. Decorations by Mallette Dean. Folio, gold boards and cloth. (San Francisco, 1946.) Grabhorn printing for the Book Club of California. One of 280. $200–$400. (For an earlier printing, see next entry.)

SMITH, Buckingham (translator). *Narratives of the Career of Hernando de Soto in the Conquest of Florida*. Folding map. Boards. New York, 1866. One of 75. $500–$600.

SMITH, Buckingham (translator). *Rudo Ensayo, Tentativa de una Provencional Descripción Geographica de la Provincia de Sonora*. 208 pp., printed gray wrappers. San Agustin (St. Augustine, Fla.), 1863. (By Juan Nentuig?) First edition. One of 10 large paper copies. $750–$1,000. Regular issue: One of 160. $500–$650. (Note: Actually printed in Albany, N.Y.)

SMITH, Charles H. *The History of Fuller's Ohio Brigade, 1861–1865*. Illustrated. Cloth. Cleveland, 1909. $50–$75.

SMITH, Charles Hamilton. *Orders of Knighthood*. Title and 74 watercolor drawings of knights, some with manuscript captions beneath. Folio, half red morocco. London, (about 1830). $1,500–$2,000.

SMITH, Charles Hamilton. *Selections of the Ancient Costume of Great Britain & Ireland*. 60 full-page color plates. Boards. London, 1814. $1,500–$1,750. London, 1815. Half morocco. $1,000–$1,250.

SMITH, Clark Ashton. *The Abominations of Yondo*. Cloth. Sauk City, 1960. First edition. In dust jacket. $65–$75.

SMITH, Clark Ashton. *The Dark Chateau and Other Poems*. Cloth. Sauk City, 1951. First edition. In dust jacket. $250–$275.

SMITH, Clark Ashton. *The Double Shadow and Other Fantasies*. (Cover title.) 30 pp., wrappers. (Auburn, Calif., 1933.) First edition. $150–$175. Presentation copy, signed, with author's corrections. $250.

SMITH, Clark Ashton. *Genius Loci and Other Tales*. Cloth. Sauk City, 1948. First edition. In dust jacket. $75–$85.

SMITH, Clark Ashton. *Lost Worlds*. Cloth. Sauk City, 1944. First edition. In dust jacket. $125–$150.

SMITH, Clark Ashton. *Odes and Sonnets*. Preface by George Sterling. Decorations by Florence Lundborg. Blue boards, tan cloth spine, paper label. San Francisco, 1918. First edition. One of 300. $150–$180.

SMITH, Clark Ashton. *Out of Space and Time*. Cloth. Sauk City, 1942. First edition. In dust jacket. $200–$250.

SMITH, Clark Ashton. *Poems in Prose.* Illustrated. Cloth. Sauk City, 1964. First edition. In dust jacket. $85–$100.

SMITH, Clark Ashton. *Spells and Philtres.* Cloth. Sauk City, 1958. First edition. In dust jacket. $300–$325.

SMITH, Clark Ashton. *The Star-Treader and Other Poems.* Buff pictorial boards. San Francisco, 1912. First edition. In dust jacket. $125–$150. Author's first collection of verse.

SMITH, Edward E. *The History of Civilization.* Illustrated. 6 vols., half leather. Reading, Pa., 1953–1955. Fantasy Press. One of 75 sets, 60 inscribed individually to original subscription buyers, the others autographed. In acetate dust jackets and cardboard box. $2,000. (Note: Although these are Fantasy Press reprints they are prized by some fantasy-science fiction collectors. The six titles are: *Triplanetary,* Reading, 1948; *First Lensman,* 1950; *Galactic Patrol,* 1950; *Gray Lensman,* 1951; *Second Stage Lensman,* 1953; and *Children of the Lens,* 1954.)

SMITH, Emma (editor). *A Collection of Sacred Hymns for the Church of the Latter Day Saints.* Marbled boards and cloth. Kirtland, Ohio, 1835. First edition. $4,000–$5,000. Also, $2,000 (A, 1968).

SMITH, F. Hopkinson. *American Illustrators.* Folio, 5 parts, printed wrappers in printed board folder. New York, 1892. First edition. One of 1,000. $100–$125.

SMITH, F. Hopkinson. *Colonel Carter of Cartersville.* Cloth. Boston, 1891. First edition, first issue, with no mention of the book in ads. $100–$125.

SMITH, F. Hopkinson. *Venice of Today.* 21 colored plates, 12 plain plates. Half morocco. New York, 1896. First book edition. $75–$100. Another issue: One of 118 on handmade paper. $300–$400. New York, 1902. Half morocco. $150–$200. (Note: This title first appeared in 20 paperbound parts in 1895. I have noted no copies for sale in modern times.)

SMITH, Frank Meriweather (editor). *San Francisco Vigilance Committee of '56.* 83 pp., wrappers. San Francisco, 1883. First edition. $150–$250. Rebound in cloth, $100–$150.

SMITH, Harry B. *First Nights and First Editions.* Cloth. Boston, 1931. First edition. One of 260 signed. In dust jacket. $60–$75.

SMITH, Harry B. *A Sentimental Library.* Half vellum. (New York), 1914. First edition. In dust jacket. $250–$300.

SMITH, J. Calvin. *A New Guide for Travelers Through the United States.* Folding map in color. Cloth, or leather. New York, 1846. $150–$200. New York, 1848. $100–$125.

SMITH, J. Calvin. *The Western Tourist and Emigrant's Guide.* Colored folding map. Cloth, or leather. New York, 1839. First edition. $150–$200. New York, 1845. $50–$75.

SMITH, James E. *A Famous Battery and Its Campaigns, 1861–64.* Cloth. Washington, 1892. First edition. $100.

SMITH, James F. *The Cherokee Land Lottery, etc.* Contemporary calf. New York, 1838. First edition. $250–$300.

SMITH, Jodie (editor). *History of the Chisum War.* Illustrated. Stiff pictorial wrappers. (Electra, Tex., 1927.) (By Ike Fridge.) First edition. $100–$150.

SMITH, John Thomas. *Antiquities of Westminster.* Illustrated, including color plates. 2 vols., half leather. London, 1807–(09). First edition. $600–$750. Also, $400 (A, 1977).

SMITH, John Thomas. *Cries of London, Exhibiting Several of the Itinerant Traders of Ancient and Modern Times.* Portrait and 30 hand-colored etchings. Half leather and cloth. London, 1839. First edition. $300–$400. Another issue: Large paper. $500–$600.

SMITH, Johnston. *Maggie: A Girl of the Streets.* Yellow printed wrappers. (New York, 1893.) (By Stephen Crane.) First edition. $5,000–$6,000. Also, $3,500 and $3,000 (A, 1973). (For the second edition, see the entry under Crane, Stephen.).

SMITH, Joseph, Jr. See *A Book of Commandments.*

SMITH, Joseph, Jr. *The Book of Mormon.* Leather. Palmyra, N.Y., 1830. First edition, first issue, with two-page preface and testimonial leaf at end and without index. $5,000. Author's first book. Second issue, without testimonials, etc. $4,000–$5,000. Kirtland, Ohio, 1837. Second edition. $1,000–$1,500. Nauvoo, Ill., 1840. Third edition. $600–$800. Liverpool, 1841. Leather. First English edition. $1,000 and up.

SMITH, Joseph, Jr., and others (editors). *Doctrine and Covenants of the Church of the Latter Day Saints.* Leather. Kirtland, 1835. First edition. $3,000–$4,000.

SMITH, Kate Douglas. *The Story of Patsy. A Reminiscence.* 27 pp., wrappers. San Francisco, 1883. (By Kate Douglas Wiggin.) First edition. $400–$500. Also, $350 (A, 1977). Author's first separate publication.

SMITH, Lillian. *Killers of the Dream.* Cloth. New York, 1949. First edition. In dust jacket. $40–$50.

SMITH, Logan Pearsall. *Trivia.* Cloth. London, 1902. First edition. One of 300. In tissue dust jacket. $110–$250. Garden City, 1917. Half leather. One of 100. $125.

SMITH, Logan Pearsall. *Unforgotten Years.* Cloth. London, 1938. First edition. In dust jacket. $30–$50.

SMITH, Logan Pearsall. *The Youth of Parnassus and Other Stories.* Blue cloth. London, 1895. First edition, first issue. $100. Author's first book.

SMITH, Michael. *A Geographical View, of the Province of Upper Canada, and Promiscuous Remarks upon the Government, etc.* 107 pp., wrappers. Hartford, 1813. First edition. $350–$450.

SMITH, Moses. *History of the Adventures and Sufferings of Moses Smith.* 2 plates. Boards. Brooklyn, N.Y., 1812. First edition. $100–$125. Albany, 1814. 2 plates. Calf. $75–$100.

SMITH, Nathan. *A Practical Essay on Typhous Fever.* Half calf. New York, 1824. First edition. $300–$350.

SMITH, Patti. *Kodak.* Wrappers. (Philadelphia, 1972.) First edition. One of 100 signed. $75–$100.

SMITH, Mrs. Sarah. *A Journal Kept by Mrs. Sarah Foote Smith While Journeying with Her People from Wellington, Ohio, to Footeville, Town of Nepeuskun, Winnebago County, Wis., April 15 to May 10, 1846.* Boards, paper label. (Kilbourn, Ohio, 1905.) $250.

SMITH, Thorne. *Biltmore Oswald: The Diary of a Hapless Recruit.* Pictorial boards. New York, (1918). First edition. In dust jacket. $75–$125. Author's first book.

SMITH, Thorne. *Topper: An Improbable Adventure.* Red cloth. New York, 1926. First edition. In dust jacket. $125–$150.

SMITH, W. L. G. *Life at the South; or, Uncle Tom's Cabin As It Is.* Cloth. Buffalo, 1852. First edition. $100–$125.

SMITH, Wallace. *Garden of the Sun: A History of the San Joaquin Valley, 1772–1939.* Cloth. Los Angeles, (1939). First edition. $75.

SMITH, William H. *History of Canada.* Folding table. 2 vols., boards, paper labels.

Quebec, 1815 (actually 1826). First edition. $500–$750. Later edition: (Quebec, 1827). 2 vols., half morocco, $400–$500.

SMITH, William Jay. *Poems*. Cloth. New York, 1947. First edition. In dust jacket. $75. Author's first book.

SMITHWICK, Noah. *The Evolution of a State*. 5 plates. Cloth. Austin, (1900). First edition. $75–$125, possibly more. Another issue: One of 10 signed. $1,000 and up.

SMYTH, Henry de Wolf. *A General Account of . . . Methods of Using Atomic Energy for Military Purposes*. Wrappers. Washington, 1945. First (official) edition. $800–$1,200. London, 1945. (*Atomic Energy: A General Account*.) Wrappers. First English edition. $300–$400.

SMYTHE, Henry. *Historical Sketch of Parker County and Weatherford, Texas*. Cloth. St. Louis, 1877. First edition. $650.

SNARLEYYOW, or The Dog Fiend. 3 vols., boards. London, 1837. (By Frederick Marryat.) First edition. $350–$400. Philadelphia, 1837. 2 vols., cloth. First American edition. (Published with by-line "F. Marryat.") $150–$200.

SNELLING, William J. See Bell, Solomon; also, see *Tales of the Northwest*.

SNELLING, William J. *The Polar Regions of the Western Continent Explored*. Contemporary calf. Boston, 1831. First edition. $175–$200.

SNODGRASS, W. D. *Heart's Needle*. Cloth. New York, 1959. First edition. One of 1,500. In dust jacket. $125–$175. (Hessle, England, 1960.) Cloth. First English edition. In dust jacket. $50–$60.

SNOW, C.P. *Death Under Sail*. Cloth. London, (1932). First edition. In dust jacket. $50–$60.

SNOW, C.P. *The New Men*. Cloth. London, 1954. First edition. In dust jacket. $25–$35.

SNYDER, Gary. *The Back Country*. Cloth. London, (1967). First edition. One of 100 signed. In dust jacket. $85–$100. Trade edition: In dust jacket. $40.

SNYDER, Gary. *The Blue Sky*. Oblong, wrappers. New York, 1969. First edition. One of 126 signed. $100–$125.

SNYDER, Gary. *The Fudo Trilogy*. Illustrated. Boards and cloth. Berkeley, 1973. First edition. One of 108 signed. In glassine jacket. $125–$150.

SNYDER, Gary. *Myths and Texts*. Illustrated. Decorated wrappers. New York, (1960). First edition. $75.

SNYDER, Gary. *A Range of Poems*. Cloth. London, 1966. First edition. In dust jacket. $50. Another issue: 50 numbered copies. $75–$85. Another issue: 50 numbered and signed. $150.

SNYDER, Gary. *Regarding Wave*. Cloth. Iowa City, (1969). First edition. One of 280 signed. (Issued without dust jacket.) $75–$100.

SNYDER, Gary. *Riprap*. Japanese-style blue and white wrappers. (Ashland, Mass.), 1959. Origin Press. First edition. $350–$450. Author's first book.

SNYDER, Gary. *Six Sections from Mountains and Rivers Without End*. Wrappers. (San Francisco), 1965. First edition. $35. London, (1967). Fulcrum Press. Green cloth. First English edition. One of 100 signed. In dust jacket. $50–$75. Trade edition: $20.

SNYDER, Gary. *Three Worlds, Three Realms, Six Roads*. Illustrated. Wrappers. Marlboro, Vt., (1966). First edition. One of 200. $100–$135.

SNYDER, Gary (translator). *The Wooden Fish: Basic Sutras & Gathas of Rinzai Zen*.

Prepared by Kanetsuki Gutesu and Gary Snyder. Wrappers. (Kyoto, Japan), 1961. First edition, with errata slip laid in. $400–$450.

SOLDIER'S Story of the War (A). 9 plates (some copies without plates). Cloth. New Orleans, 1874. (By Napier Bartlett.) First edition, with plates. $100–$150.

SOMBRERO (The). Quarter-Centennial Number. Yearbook of the Class of 1895. University of Nebraska. White and red cloth. Lincoln, Neb., (1894). First edition. $500–$750. 'Also, $400 (A, 1977). (Note: Contains Willa Cather's and Dorothy Canfield's prize story "The Fear That Walks by Noonday." See this title in Cather listing for reprint edition.)

SOME Antiquarian Notes. 56 pp., red wrappers. Naples, 1907. (By Norman Douglas.) First edition. One of 250. $200–$250.

SOMEBODY Had to Do Something. Wrappers. Los Angeles, 1939. First edition. $150. (Contains tributes to James P. Lardner, killed in the Spanish Civil War, including material by Ernest Hemingway and Ring Lardner, Jr.)

SOME Imagist Poets. Printed wrappers. Boston, 1915. (Edited by Amy Lowell.) First edition. $75–$100. London, 1915. Pink printed wrappers. First English edition. $75–$100. Other annual numbers: Boston, 1916. Boards. First edition. $50–$75. Boston, 1917. Boards. First edition. In dust jacket. $50.

SONG of Roland (The). Translated by Isabel Butler. 7 hand-colored illustrations by Bruce Rogers. Boards, vellum spine. (Cambridge, Mass., 1906.) One of 220. First edition. $600–$650.

SONGS of the Class of MDCCCXXIX. Cream-yellow wrappers. Boston, 1854. First edition. (Contains 3 poems by Oliver Wendell Holmes.) About 6 copies are known to exist; none has appeared for sale in many years. Boston, 1859. Second edition, with 8 Holmes poems. $50–$75.

SONN, Albert H. *Early American Wrought Iron*. Illustrated. 3 vols., cloth. New York, 1928. First edition. In dust jackets. $500–$600.

SONTAG, Susan. *The Benefactor*. Black cloth. New York, (1963). First edition. In dust jacket. $50. Author's first book.

SOULE, Frank; Gihon, Frank; and Nisbet, James. *The Annals of San Francisco*. 6 plates, 2 maps. Leather. New York, 1855. First edition. $300–$400. Palo Alto, 1966. Facsimile reprint. Cloth. $75. Another issue: Morocco. One of 60. $150.

SOUTH Carolina Jockey Club (The). Cloth. Charleston, 1857. (By John B. Irving.) First edition. $150–$200.

SOUTHERN Business Directory and General Commercial Advertiser (The). Vol. 1. (All published.) Illustrated. Charleston, 1854. $125–$150.

SOUTHERN Business Guide, 1881–82. Illustrated. Cloth. New York, 1882. $100–$125.

SOUTHERN History of the War. Illustrated. Cloth. New York, 1863. First edition. $200–$275.

SOUTHERN Primer (The). Illustrated. Wrappers. Richmond, 1860. $150–$175.

SOUTHEY, Robert. *All for Love; and The Pilgrim to Compostella*. Cloth, paper label. London, 1829. First edition. $150–$200.

SOUTHSPRING Ranch (The). Illustrated. 28 pp., wrappers. Colorado Springs, (1902?). First edition. $250.

SOUTH-WEST (The). By a Yankee. 2 vols., cloth, paper labels. New York, 1835. (By Joseph Holt Ingraham.) First edition. $400–$500. Author's first book.

SOWELL, A. J. *Early Settlers and Indian Fighters of Southwest Texas.* 12 plates. Cloth. Austin, 1900. First edition. $250–$385.

SOWELL, A. J. *Rangers and Pioneers of Texas.* Illustrated. Pictorial cloth. San Antonio. 1884. First edition. $500–$750.

SPALDING, C. C. *Annals of the City of Kansas.* 7 plates. Cloth. Kansas City, 1858. First edition, $1,000–$1,250.

SPARGO, John. *Anthony Haswell: Printer, Patriot, Balladist.* 35 facsimiles. Half morocco. Rutland, Vt., 1925. First edition. One of 300. $150.

SPARGO, John. *The Potters and Potteries of Bennington.* Boards. Boston, 1926. First edition. One of 800. $75–$100.

SPARK, Muriel. *Not to Disturb.* Illustrated. Boards and cloth. London, 1971. One of 500 signed, with an original etching by Michael Ayrton. In glassine dust jacket. $100–$125.

SPARK, Muriel. *The Prime of Miss Jean Brodie.* Cloth. London, 1961. First edition. In dust jacket. $85–$100.

SPARROW, Walter Shaw. *A Book of Sporting Painters.* 138 illustrations, some in color. Buckram. London, (1931). First edition. $150–$175. Another issue: One of 125 with 2 extra plates. $200–$300.

SPARROW, Walter Shaw. *British Sporting Artists, from Barlow to Herring.* 27 color plates, other illustrations. Cloth. London, (1922). First edition. $200–$225. Limited issue: Buckram. One of 95 signed. $300–$350.

SPAVERY (compiler). *The Harp of a Thousand Strings: or, Laughter for a Lifetime.* Illustrated. Cloth. New York, (1858). (By George Washington Harris.) First edition, first printing, with frontispiece in black and gray and with imprints of Craighead and Jenkins on copyright page. $400–$600. (The pen name Spavery in this case was used for Harris' pseudonym "Samuel Putnam Avery." The engravings are attributed on the title page to "S.P. Avery." The book contains a reprint, unsigned, of an early English magazine prose piece by Lewis Carroll. The reprinting—the first of any of Carroll's work anywhere—was unauthorized.)

SPEARS, John R. *Illustrated Sketches of Death Valley and Other Borax Deserts of the Pacific Coast.* Printed wrappers or cloth. Chicago, 1892. First edition. $150–$200.

SPECIMENS. 54 pp., pink wrappers, stitched. (Canyon City, Ore. 1868.) (By Joaquin Miller—preface signed "C. H. Miller.") First edition. $3,000–$3,500. Also, an inscribed copy, $1,900 (A, 1976). Author's first book—rigorously suppressed by him.

SPECIMENS: A Stevens-Nelson Paper Catalogue. (Specimen sheets of fine papers, with text.) Half goatskin and boards. (New York, about 1950–53.) Boxed. $275–$400.

SPEED, Thomas. *The Wilderness Road.* Map. Cloth. Louisville, 1886. First edition. $75–$100.

SPEER, Emory. *The Banks County Ku-Klux.* 60 pp., wrappers. Atlanta, 1883. First edition. $150–$175.

SPENCER, Elizabeth. *Fire in the Morning.* Red cloth. New York, 1948. First edition. In dust jacket. $125. Author's first novel.

SPENCER, Mrs. George E. *Calamity Jane: A Story of the Black Hills.* Frontispiece. Wrappers. New York, (about 1887). (By William L. Spencer.) First edition. $250.

SPENCER, Herbert. *Education: Intellectual, Moral, and Physical.* Cloth. New York, 1861. First edition. In slipcase. $40–$50.

SPENCER, Herbert. *The Principles of Biology.* 2 vols., cloth. London, 1864–67. First edition. $300–$400.

SPENCER, Herbert. *Social Statics*. Cloth. London, 1851. First edition. $50–$75. Author's first book.

SPENCER, J. W. *Reminiscences of Pioneer Life in the Mississippi Valley*. Portrait. Cloth. Davenport, Iowa, 1872. First edition. $100–$150.

SPENCER, O. M. *Indian Captivity: A True Narrative of the Capture of, etc.* Gray wrappers. Washington, Pa., 1835. First edition (?). $500–$600. New York, 1835. $500–$600. New York, 1836. Third edition. $75–$100.

SPENDER, Stephen. See S., S. H.

SPENDER, Stephen. *The Burning Cactus*. Cloth. London, 1936. First edition, first issue, with first and final leaves blank. In dust jacket. $40–$50.

SPENDER, Stephen. *Poems*. Black cloth. London, (1933). First edition. In dust jacket. $100–$150. New York, 1934. Blue cloth. $60–$75.

SPENDER, Stephen. *Returning to Vienna 1947*. Wrappers. (London, 1947.) Banyan Press. One of 500 signed. $60–$75.

SPENDER, Stephen. *Ruins and Visions: Poems*. Blue-green cloth. London, (1942). First edition. In dust jacket. $100–$125. New York, (1942). Red cloth. First American edition. In dust jacket. $50.

SPENDER, Stephen. *Twenty Poems*. Wrappers. Oxford, (1930). First edition. One of 135. $500–$650. Signed copies (75 of the 135). $750–$1,000.

SPENDER, Stephen. *Vienna*. Cloth. London, 1934. First edition. In dust jacket. $85–$125.

SPENSER, Edmund. *The Faerie Queene*. Folio, half leather and vellum. Chelsea (London), 1923. Ashendene Press. One of 180. $1,500–$2,000. Another issue: One of 10 on vellum. $2,500–$3,000.

SPENSER, Edmund. *Minor Poems*. London, 1925. Ashendene Press. One of 200 on paper. $1,500–$2,000. Another issue: One of 15 on vellum. $2,500–$3,000.

SPENSER, Edmund. *The Shepheardes Calender*. 12 woodcuts. Boards and linen. London, 1896. Kelmscott Press. One of 225. $850–$1,000. Another issue: One of 6 on vellum, specially bound. $6,000–$8,000. London, 1930. Cresset Press. Boards, vellum spine. One of 350. In dust jacket. Boxed. $325–$350.

SPEYER, Leonora. *Holy Night: A Yuletide Masque*. Designs by Eric Gill. Stiff blue decorated wrappers. New York, 1919. One of 500. $75–$100. Author's first book.

SPICER, Jack. *After Lorca*. Wrappers. (San Francisco, 1957.) First edition. One of 500. $150. Author's first book.

SPICER, Jack. *Lament for the Makers*. Wrappers. (Oakland, 1962.) First edition. One of 100. $275–$325.

SPIELMANN, M. H., and Layard, G. S. *Kate Greenaway*. 53 colored plates, other illustrations. White cloth. London, 1905. One of 500 with an original pencil sketch by Kate Greenaway inserted. $1,000–$1,250. Trade edition: Purple cloth. $250–$300.

SPILLANE, Mickey. *I, the Jury*. Cloth. New York, 1947. First edition. In dust jacket. $80–$125. Author's first book.

SPILMAN, The Rev. T. E. *Semi-Centenarians of Butler Gover Township, Montgomery County (Illinois)*. Boards and cloth. (Butler), 1878. First edition. $100–$125.

SPIRIT of the Age (The). Boards, paper label. London, 1825. (By William Hazlitt.) First edition. $75–$100.

SPORTS of Childhood (The). 18 pp., wrappers. Northampton, Mass., (about 1830–40).

First edition(?). $50–$75. (Henderson, in *Early American Sport*, also lists a New Haven edition of about 1839.)

SPORTSMAN'S Portfolio of American Field Sports (The). 20 full-page wood engravings, title page vignette, illustration at end. Oblong wrappers. Boston, 1855. First edition. $2,500–$3,500.

SPOTTS, David L. *Campaigning with Custer*. Map, 13 plates. Cloth. Los Angeles, 1928. First edition. One of 800 (Howes says all but about 300 burned). $150–$200.

SPRAGUE, John T. *The Origin, Progress, and Conclusion of the Florida War*. Folding map, 8 plates. Cloth. New York, 1848. First edition. $150–$175.

SPRAGUE, John T. *The Treachery in Texas*. 35 pp., wrappers. New York, 1862. First edition. $75.

SPRING: Infancy,—The Spring of Life. 8 woodcuts. 16 pp., pictorial wrappers. New York, (about 1815–20). (Children's toybook published by Samuel S. Wood.) $100–$150.

SPRING, Agnes Wright. *The Cheyenne and Black Hills Stage and Express Routes*. Map, 17 plates. Cloth. Glendale, Calif., 1949. First edition. $60–$80.

SPRING, Agnes Wright. *Seventy Years: A Panoramic History of the Wyoming Stock Growers Association*. Illustrated. Stiff pictorial wrappers. (Cheyenne), 1942. First edition. $75–$100.

SPRUNT, James. *Chronicles of the Cape Fear River*. Half leather. Raleigh, 1914. First edition. $60–$75.

SPY (The): A Tale of the Neutral Ground. By the Author of *Precaution*. 2 vols., boards, paper labels, New York, 1821. (By James Fenimore Cooper.) First edition. $10,000–$13,500. (Note. There are said to be only three known sets in original boards.) New York, 1963. Limited Editions Club. Cloth. $40–$50.

SPYRI, Johannes. *Heidi*. Translated by Louise Brooks. Cloth. Boston, 1885. First American edition. $150–$175.

SQUIER, E. G., and Davis, E. H. *Ancient Monuments of the Mississippi Valley*. Map, 48 plates. Folio, cloth. Washington, 1848. First edition. $75–$100. New York, 1848. Second issue. $75–$100.

SQUIRE, J. C. *The Muse Absent*. Wrappers. New York, 1929. First edition. One of 750 signed, in envelope. $100–$125.

SQUIRE, Watson C. *Resources and Development of Washington Territory*. Folding map. 72 pp., wrappers. Seattle, 1886. First edition. $75–$100.

STAFFORD, Jean. *Boston Adventure*. Cloth. New York, (1944). First edition. In dust jacket. $50. Author's first book.

STAFFORD, William E. *Down in My Heart*. Green cloth. Elgin, Ill., (1947). First edition. In dust jacket. $75–$100. Author's first book.

STAFFORD, William E. *Eleven Untitled Poems*. Wrappers. Mt. Horeb, Wis., 1968. First edition. One of 250. In dust jacket. $75–$100.

STAFFORD, William E. *Traveling Through the Dark*. Cloth. New York, (1962). First edition, with National Book Award sticker on cover. In dust jacket. $75.

STAFFORD, William E. *Weather*. Wrappers. Mt. Horeb, Wis., (1969). First edition. One of 207. In dust jacket. $75–$100.

STANARD, Mary Newton. *Colonial Virginia*. 93 plates. Cloth. Philadelphia, 1917. First edition. Limited. $85.

STANLEY, David S. *Diary of a March from Fort Smith, Ark., to San Diego, Calif., Made in 1853.* 37 pp., multigraphed. No place, no date. In cloth case. $150–$175.

STANLEY, F. *The Grant That Maxwell Bought.* Map, 15 plates. Cloth. (Denver, 1952.) (By Father Stanley Crocchiola.) First edition. One of 250 signed. $300–$350.

STANLEY, F. *The Las Vegas Story.* Illustrated. Cloth. (Denver, 1951.) (By Father Stanley Crocchiola.) First edition. $50–$75.

STANLEY, F. *One Half Miles from Heaven, or, The Cimmaron Story.* 155 pp., wrappers, Denver, 1949. (By Father Stanley Crocchiola.) First edition. $60–$75.

STANSBERY, Lon R. *The Passing of 3D Ranch.* Illustrated. Cloth. (Tulsa, about 1930.) First edition. $200–$300.

STANSBURY, P. *A Pedestrian Tour of 2,300 Miles, in North America, etc.* 9 plates. Boards, New York, 1822. First edition. $150–$175.

STANTON, Schuyler. *Daughters of Destiny.* Red cloth. Chicago, (1906). (By L. Frank Baum.) First edition. $150–$200.

STAPLEDON, Olaf. *Darkness and the Light.* Cloth. London, (1942). First edition. In dust jacket. $150–$200.

STAPLEDON, Olaf. *Latter-Day Psalms.* Cloth. Liverpool, 1914. First edition. In dust jacket. $200–$250.

STAPLEDON, Olaf. *Star Maker.* Cloth. London, (1937). First edition. In dust jacket. $150–$250.

STAPP, William P. *The Prisoners of Perote.* Wrappers, or cloth. Philadelphia, 1845. First edition. Wrappers: $500–$750. Cloth: $500–$650.

STAR City of the West (The): Pueblo and Its Advantages. 24 pp., folded. Pueblo, Colo., 1889. $125–$150.

STARBUCK, Alexander. *History of the American Whale Fishery, etc.* 6 plates. Cloth. Waltham, Mass., 1878. First edition. $250–$300. New York, 1964. 2 vols., half leather. Boxed. One of 50. $200–$300. Trade edition: 2 vols., cloth. Boxed. $35–$50.

STARKEY, James. *Reminiscences of Indian Depredations.* 25 pp., wrappers. St. Paul, 1891. First edition. $150–$175.

STARR, Julian. *The Disagreeable Woman.* Green cloth. New York, 1895. (By Horatio Alger, Jr.) First edition. $600–$800.

STARRETT, Vincent. *All About Mother Goose.* Boards. (Glen Rock, Pa.), 1930. First edition. One of 275. In glassine jacket. $150–$200.

STARRETT, Vincent. *Ambrose Bierce: A Bibliography.* Portrait. Boards. Philadelphia, 1929. First edition. One of 45 large paper copies, signed. In tissue jacket. $150.

STARRETT, Vincent. *Arthur Machen: A Novelist of Ecstasy and Sin.* Boards and cloth. Chicago, 1918. First edition. One of 250. $250–$300. Author's first book.

STARRETT, Vincent. *Books Alive.* Cloth. New York, 1940. First edition. In dust jacket. $50.

STARRETT, Vincent. *Et Cetera: A Collector's Scrap-Book.* Half cloth. Chicago, 1924. First edition. One of 625. $50–$75.

STARRETT, Vincent. *Flame and Dust.* Half cloth. Chicago, 1924. First edition. One of 450. In dust jacket. $75–$85.

STARRETT, Vincent. *Penny Wise and Book Foolish.* Cloth. New York, 1929. First edition, with wrong "t" on page 107. In dust jacket. $50–$75. Another issue: One of 300 signed. Boxed. $150.

STARRETT, Vincent. *Persons from Porlock*. Wrappers. Chicago, 1933. First edition. One of 300 signed. $125. Revised edition, with *and Other Interruptions* added to the title: Chicago, 1938. Boards. One of 399 signed. In dust jacket. $75–$100.

STARRETT, Vincent. *The Private Life of Sherlock Holmes*. Illustrated. Cloth. New York, 1933. First edition. In dust jacket. $150.

STARRETT. Vincent. *Stephen Crane: A Bibliography*. Half cloth. Philadelphia, 1923. First edition. One of 300. In dust jacket. $75–$100.

STARRETT, Vincent. *221B: Studies in Sherlock Holmes*. Cloth. New York, 1940. First edition. In dust jacket. $200.

STARRETT, Vincent. *The Unique Hamlet*. Boards. Chicago, 1920. First edition. One of 250. $1,000 (A, 1981).

STARRETT, Vincent (editor). *In Praise of Stevenson*. Boards and cloth. Chicago, 1919. First edition. One of 300. $75–$100.

STATE of Indiana Delineated (The). Boards, leather spine. New York, 1838. First edition. (Published by J. H. Colton to accompany his separately published map, which is inserted in some copies.) With the map, $750 and up. Without the map, $500.

STATEMENT Respecting the Earl of Selkirk's Settlement of Kildonan, upon the Red River, in North America. Folding map. 125 pp., boards. London, (about 1817). (By John Halkett.) First edition. $400–$500. London, 1817. Second (enlarged) edition. 194 pp., boards. With title altered to *Statement Respecting the Earl of Selkirk's Settlement upon the Red River, in North America*. $350–$400.

STEAD, William T. *If Christ Came to Chicago*. Pictorial wrappers. Chicago, 1894. First edition. $75–$150.

STEAM-BOAT (The). Boards, marbled cloth spine. Edinburgh, 1822. (By John Galt.) First edition. $400–$500.

STEARNS, Samuel. *The American Herbal or Materia Medica*. Calf. Walpole, N.H., 1801. First edition. $600–$750.

STEDMAN, Edmund C. *Poems, Lyrical and Idyllic*. Cloth. New York, 1860. First edition. $75–$100. Author's first book.

STEDMAN, Edmund C. *Songs and Ballads*. Morocco. New York, 1884. First edition. One of 100 on Japan paper. Boxed. $100–$150.

STEDMAN, John G. *Narrative of a Five Years' Expedition Against the Revolted Negroes of Surinam in Guiana on the Wild Coast of America*. 80 full-page colored engravings, map. 2 vols., marbled boards and calf. London, 1813. Third edition. $750–$1,000.

STEEDMAN, Charles J. *Bucking the Sagebrush*. 3 portraits, folding map, 9 Charles M. Russell plates. Pictorial cloth. New York, 1904. First edition. $200–$250.

STEEL, Flora A. (editor). *English Fairy Tales*. 16 color plates by Arthur Rackham. Vellum. London, 1918. One of 500 signed by Rackham. $800–$1,200. Trade edition: Cloth. $200–$300. New York, 1918. Half cloth. $200–$300.

STEELE, James W. *The Klondike*. Illustrated, 2 maps. 80 pp., pictorial gray wrappers. Chicago, 1897. First edition. $150–$200.

STEELE, James W. *The Sons of the Border*. Cloth. Topeka, 1873. First edition. $80–$100.

STEELE, John. *Across the Plains in 1850*. 7 plates. Cloth. Chicago, 1930. Caxton Club. First edition. $75–$100.

STEELE, John. *In Camp and Cabin: Mining Life and Adventure, in California, etc.* 81 pp., printed wrappers. Lodi, Wis., 1901. First edition. $250–$300.

STEELE, R. J., and others (compilers). *Directory of the County of Placer.* Boards and calf. San Francisco, 1861. $600–$750.

STEELE, Zadock. *The Indian Captive.* Calf. Montpelier, Vt., 1818. First edition. $300–$400.

STEFANSSON, Vilhjalmur. *Ultima Thule: Further Mysteries of the Arctic.* Maps, illustrated. Cloth. New York, 1940. First edition. One of 100 signed. $75–$100.

STEFFENS, Lincoln. *John Reed Under the Kremlin.* Introduction by Clarence Darrow. Wrappers. Chicago, 1922. First edition. One of 235. $150–$200.

STEFFENS, Lincoln. *The Shame of the Cities.* Cloth. New York, 1904. First edition. $75–$100. Author's first book.

STEGNER, Wallace. *The Big Rock Candy Mountain.* Cloth. New York, 1943. First edition. In dust jacket. $50–$75.

STEIN, Gertrude. See Cerwin, Herbert; Toklas, Alice B.

STEIN, Gertrude. *Absolutely Bob Brown, or, Bobbed Brown.* Wrappers. Pawlet, Vt., 1955. Banyan Press. First edition. One of 52. In plain white envelope. $200–$250.

STEIN, Gertrude. *An Acquaintance with Description.* Oyster-white linen. London, 1929. Seizin Press. First edition. One of 225 signed. In glassine dust jacket. $300–$400.

STEIN, Gertrude. *Before the Flowers of Friendship Faded Friendship Faded.* Wrappers. Paris, (1931). First edition. One of 118 signed (of an edition of 120). In glassine dust jacket. $600–$800. Also, $500 (A, 1977).

STEIN, Gertrude. *Blood on the Dining Room Floor.* Half buckram and boards. (Pawlet, Vt., 1948.) Banyan Press. One of 626. In glassine dust jacket. Boxed. $200–$350.

STEIN, Gertrude. *A Book Concluding with As a Wife Has a Cow: A Love Story.* 4 lithographs (one in color) by Juan Gris. Wrappers. Paris, (1926). One of 102 signed. In glassine dust jacket. $2,500–$3,500. Another issue: One of 10 on Japan vellum, signed. $5,500 (A, 1977).

STEIN, Gertrude. *Chicago Inscriptions.* Stiff wrappers, stapled. (Chicago), 1934. First edition. $300–$400.

STEIN, Gertrude. *Composition As Explanation.* Green boards. London, 1926. Hogarth Press. First edition. $125–$150.

STEIN, Gertrude. *Dix Portraits.* Translated by G. Hugnet and Virgil Thomson. Illustrated by Picasso and others. Decorated wrappers. Paris, (1930). First edition. One of 10 on Japan vellum, signed, and with an autograph page of text by Miss Stein. In glassine jacket. $1,500 (A, 1977). Other issues: One of 25 on Holland paper, signed by author and translators. In glassine dust jacket. $400–$750. One of 65 on Velin d'Arches paper, signed. In dust jacket. $350–$400. Trade copies: One of 402 on Alfa paper without illustrations. In printed dust jacket plus glassine jacket. $75–$100.

STEIN, Gertrude. *An Elucidation.* (Cover title.) Wrappers. (Paris), 1927. First edition. $100–$165. (Issued as a supplement to *Transition* magazine after having been printed there with errors.)

STEIN, Gertrude. *The Geographical History of America or The Relation of Human Nature to the Human Mind.* Black and white cloth. (New York, 1936.) First edition. In dust jacket. $300–$400.

STEIN, Gertrude. *Geography and Plays.* Foreword by Sherwood Anderson. Cloth and boards. Boston, (1922). First edition, first binding, with lettering on front cover. In dust jacket. $350–$500. Second binding, cover unlettered. $100–$150.

STEIN, Gertrude. *Have They Attacked Mary. He Giggled.* Woodcut. Printed red wrappers. (West Chester, Pa., 1917.) First edition. One of 200. $500–$600. Also, $500 (A, 1977).

STEIN, Gertrude. *How to Write.* Boards, paper labels on spine. Paris, (1931). First edition. One of 1,000. (Issued without dust jacket.) $125–$150.

STEIN, Gertrude. *Lectures in America.* Frontispiece. Beige cloth. New York, (1935). First edition. In dust jacket. $250–$350.

STEIN, Gertrude. *Lucy Church Amiably.* Boards. Paris, 1930. First edition. In plain brown paper dust jacket. $225–$250.

STEIN, Gertrude. *The Making of Americans.* Wrappers. (Dijon, 1925.) First edition. One of 500. $750–$900. Another issue: One of 5 on vellum, with a letter by Miss Stein inserted. $10,000–$15,000. Also, $5,600 (A, 1975). New York, 1926. Cloth. First American edition. $750–$1,000. Also, $450 (A, 1977); $500 (A, 1975).

STEIN, Gertrude. *Matisse Picasso and Gertrude Stein, with Two Shorter Stories.* Wrappers, Paris, (1933). First edition. In glassine dust jacket. Boxed. $300–$450. (Note: The box is dated 1932; the colophon is 1933.)

STEIN, Gertrude. *Morceaux Choisis de la Fabrication des Américains.* Portrait frontispiece by Christian Bérard. Wrappers. Paris, (1929). First edition. One of 85 on Verge paper, signed by author and illustrator. In glassine jacket. $400–$550. Another issue: One of 400 (without frontispiece or signature). $175–$250. Another issue: One of 5 on Japan vellum, with a manuscript page by Miss Stein. Signed by artist and author. $3,000–$4,000. Another issue: One of 5 on Van Gelder paper, signed. $1,500.

STEIN, Gertrude. *Narration: Four Lectures.* Introduction by Thornton Wilder. Blue, black and gilt cloth. Chicago, (1935). First edition. One of 120 signed by Stein and Wilder. Boxed. $500–$600. Ordinary edition (unsigned): Orange cloth. In orange dust jacket. $125–$150.

STEIN, Gertrude. *Operas and Plays.* Wrappers. Paris, (1932). First edition. Boxed. $400–$450.

STEIN, Gertrude. *Picasso.* Illustrated. Pictorial wrappers. Paris, 1938. First edition. $200–$250. London, (1938). Rose-colored cloth. First English edition. In dust jacket. $50–$75. (New York), 1939. Cloth. In dust jacket. $75.

STEIN, Gertrude. *Portrait of Mabel Dodge at the Villa Curonia.* Stitched wrappers. (Florence, 1912.) First edition, with imprint at foot of last page. $1,500–$2,000.

STEIN, Gertrude. *Portraits and Prayers.* Pictorial cloth. New York, (1934). First edition. In cellophane dust jacket. $150–$200.

STEIN, Gertrude. *Tender Buttons. Objects. Food. Rooms.* Boards, paper label. New York, 1914. First edition. (Issued without dust jacket.) $300–$350.

STEIN, Gertrude. *Things as They Are: A Novel in 3 Parts.* Cloth. Pawlet, Vt., 1950. First edition. One of 516. (Issued without dust jacket.) $100–$150. Another issue: One of 26 lettered copies. $500–$600.

STEIN, Gertrude. *Three Lives.* Blue cloth. New York, 1909. First edition. (1,000 printed; issued without dust jacket.) $1,000–$1,250. Also $600 (A, 1980). Author's first book. New York and London, 1915. First English edition. $750–$1,000. Also $500 (A, 1977). (300 issued from American sheets, with new title page.) London, 1920. First English trade edition. $250–$300.

STEIN, Gertrude. *Useful Knowledge.* Cloth. New York, (1928). First edition. In dust jacket. $150–$200. London, (1928). First English edition. In dust jacket. $150–$250.

STEIN, Gertrude. *A Village Are You Ready Yet Not Yet.* Illustrated by Elie Lascaux. Wrappers. Paris, (1928). First edition. One of 102 signed. In glassine dust jacket. $400–$500. Another issue: One of 10 on Japan vellum signed. $950 (A, 1977).

STEIN, Gertrude. *What Are Masterpieces?* Portrait frontispiece. Blue cloth. (Los Angeles, 1940.) First edition. In dust jacket. $125–$150. Another issue: One of more than 50 signed. In dust jacket. $500–$600.

STEIN, Gertrude. *The World Is Round*. Illustrated by Clement Hurd. Boards. New York, (1939). First edition. One of 350 signed. Boxed. $300–$400. Trade edition: Blue boards. In dust jacket. $50–$85. London, (1939). First English edition. Red cloth. In dust jacket. $60–$75.

STEINBECK, John. See Cerwin, Herbert. Also see *El Gabilan*.

STEINBECK, John. *Bombs Away*. Illustrated. Blue cloth. New York, 1942. First edition. In dust jacket. $50–$100.

STEINBECK, John. *Burning Bright*. Gray cloth. New York, 1950. First edition. In dust jacket. $50–$85. London, (1951). Blue cloth. First English edition. In dust jacket. $40–$75.

STEINBECK, John. *Cannery Row*. Buff cloth. New York, 1945. First edition, first binding. In dust jacket. $100–$150. Second binding, yellow cloth: $100. Advance copy: Blue wrappers. $500–$600. London, (1945). Cloth. First English edition. $150–$200.

STEINBECK, John. *Cup of Gold: A Life of Henry Morgan, Buccaneer, with Occasional Reference to History*. Yellow cloth. New York, 1929. First edition, first issue, top edges stained and "First Published August, 1929" on copyright page. In dust jacket. $2,500–$3,500. New York, (1936). Red cloth. First edition, second issue, with "Covici Friede" on spine. In dust jacket. $400–$500. New York, (1936). Blue cloth. Second edition. In dust jacket. $100. London, (1937). Blue cloth. First English edition. In dust jacket. $1,000–$1,500. Author's first book.

STEINBECK, John. *East of Eden*. Green buckram. New York, 1952. First edition. One of 1,500 signed. In glassine dust jacket. Boxed. $300–$350. Trade edition: Green cloth. In dust jacket. $100–$150.

STEINBECK, John. *The First Watch*. Wrappers. (New York), 1947. Grabhorn printing. First edition. One of 60 in mailing envelope. $1,500–$2,000. Also, $1,100 (A, 1977).

STEINBECK, John. *The Forgotten Village*. Coarse buckram. New York, 1941. First edition, first issue, with "First Published in May 1941" on copyright page. In dust jacket. $75–$100.

STEINBECK, John. *The Grapes of Wrath*. Pictorial beige cloth. New York, (1939). First edition, with yellow top edges, "First Published in April 1939" on copyright page, and with first edition notice on front flap of dust jacket. In dust jacket. $400–$450. Also, a set of uncorrected galley proofs, $1,700 (A, 1977); also a salesman's clothbound dummy copy, $3,500 in a catalogue of the John Valentine collection in 1980 and $1,100 (A, 1977). London, (1939). Blue cloth. First English edition. In dust jacket. $150. New York, 1940. Limited Editions Club. 2 vols. Boxed. $200–$250.

STEINBECK, John. *How Edith McGillcuddy Met RLS*. Boards and cloth, paper labels. Cleveland, 1943. Rowfant Club. (Grabhorn printing.) First edition. One of 152. $1,500–$2,000. Worn copy, $1,650 in a 1980 catalogue.

STEINBECK, John. *In Dubious Battle*. Yellow cloth. New York, (1936). First edition. In dust jacket. $200–$300. Another issue: Beige cloth. One of 99 signed. Boxed. $2,000–$2,750.

STEINBECK, John. *John Steinbeck Replies*. 4-page leaflet, unbound. (First page is a letter to Steinbeck by L.M. Birkhead, pages 2 and 3 are his reply.) (New York, 1940.) $175. (See *A Letter by John Steinbeck. . . .*)

STEINBECK, John. *John Steinbeck's Foreword to "Between Pacific Tides."* Blue wrappers. (Stanford), 1948. First edition. One of 10. $4,500.

STEINBECK, John. *A Letter by John Steinbeck to the Friends of Democracy*. (Cover title.) Boards, paper label. Stamford, Conn., 1940. First edition with title. (A reprint of *John Steinbeck Replies*.) One of 350 by the Overbrook Press. In dust jacket. $200–$300.

STEINBECK, John. *A Letter from John Steinbeck.* Orange wrappers. (New York), 1964. First edition. One of 150. $300–$500.

STEINBECK, John. *The Log from the Sea of Cortez.* Red cloth. New York, 1951. Revised edition of *Sea of Cortez,* with a new 67-page chapter, "About Ed Ricketts." In dust jacket. $100–$150. London, (1958). Blue cloth. First English edition. In dust jacket. $150–$200.

STEINBECK, John. *The Long Valley.* Rust-colored cloth. New York, 1938. First edition. In dust jacket. $125–$175.

STEINBECK, John. *The Moon is Down.* Blue cloth, top edges blue. New York, 1942. First edition, first issue, without printer's name on copyright page and with large period between "talk" and "this" in line 11 on page\12. In dust jacket. $100–$125. Second issue: Red or blue cloth, the period removed. $30–$60. Advance copy: Sewed, in wrappers. $400. London, (1942). Brown or rust cloth. First English edition. In dust jacket. $50–$75.

STEINBECK, John. *Nothing So Monstrous: A Story.* Donald McKay drawings. Decorated boards. (New York), 1936. First edition. One of 370. In tissue dust jacket. $500–$750, possibly more.

STEINBECK, John. *Of Mice and Men.* Tan cloth. New York, (1937). First edition, first state, with "and only moved because the heavy hands were pendula" at page 9, second and third lines from bottom of page. In dust jacket. $150–$300. Second state, the two lines corrected. $75–$100. London, (1937). Blue cloth. First English edition. In dust jacket. $150–$300. Play version: New York, (1937). Beige cloth. In dust jacket. $350–$500.

STEINBECK, John. *The Pastures of Heaven.* Green cloth. New York, 1932. First edition, first issue, with Brewer, Warren & Putnam imprint on title page and spine. In dust jacket. $1,000–$1,250. Second issue, Robert O. Ballou imprint on spine. In dust jacket. With a 4-page Ballou brochure, *The Neatest Trick of the Year.* $500–$750. Another copy, no brochure. $250–$300. (Note: There was a third issue dated 1932 on title page with a Ballou imprint on title page and spine. The fourth issue, in 1935, undated, has Ballou title and spine imprints.) New York, (1945). Wrappers. Armed Services Edition. $25.

STEINBECK, John. *The Pearl.* Brown cloth. New York, 1947. First edition. In first state dust jacket, with photo of Steinbeck looking to his left (instead of right). $100–$125. In second jacket, $50–$75. London, (1948). Blue cloth. First English edition. In dust jacket. $50.

STEINBECK, John. *Positano.* English text. Pictorial wrappers. Salerno, Italy, (1954). First edition, first issue. $200–$300.

STEINBECK, John. *The Red Pony.* Flexible decorated beige cloth. New York, 1937. First edition. One of 699 signed. Boxed. $500–$750. Another issue: One of 26 lettered copies. $1,000–$1,250, possibly more.

STEINBECK, John. *A Russian Journal.* Cloth. New York, 1948. First edition. In dust jacket. $75–$125.

STEINBECK, John. *Saint Katy the Virgin.* Printed boards, cloth spine. (New York, 1936.) First edition. One of 199 signed. (Issued as a Christmas greeting by Covici-Friede with greeting slip inserted.) In glassine dust jacket. $1,000–$1,500.

STEINBECK, John. *Sweet Thursday.* Beige cloth. New York, 1954. First edition. $50–$75. Advance review copy in wrappers: $100–$150. London, (1954). Green cloth. First English edition. In dust jacket. $35.

STEINBECK, John. *"Their Blood is Strong."* Pictorial wrappers. San Francisco, 1938. First edition. $300–$450. Second printing (so stated): $75–$90.

STEINBECK, John. *To a God Unknown.* Green cloth. New York, (1933). First edition, first issue, with Robert O. Ballou imprint. In dust jacket. $750–$850. Second issue, Covici-Friede imprint. In dust jacket. $300–$425.

STEINBECK, John. *Tortilla Flat*. Illustrated. Tan cloth. New York, (1935). First edition. In dust jacket. $400–$750. Advance copy: One of about 500 in wrappers. $650–$950. London, (1935). Blue cloth. First English edition. In dust jacket. $400–$650. New York, (1947). Illustrated. Cloth. First illustrated edition. In dust jacket. $100–$175.

STEINBECK, John. *Vanderbilt Clinic*. Illustrated. Wrappers. (New York, 1947.) First edition. $150–$250.

STEINBECK, John. *The Wayward Bus*. Dark red-orange cloth. New York, 1947. First edition, first binding. In dust jacket. $75–$125. London, (1947). Red cloth. First English edition, first binding. In dust jacket. $35–$50.

STEINBECK, John. *The Winter of Our Discontent*. Bright blue cloth. New York, 1961. First edition, with "First Published in 1961" on copyright page. In dust jacket. $50–$75. Another issue: Dark blue buckram. One of 500. In dust jacket and acetate wrapper with "Limited Edition" stamped in red. $150–$225. London, (1961). Purple cloth. First English edition. In dust jacket. $35.

STEINBECK, John, and Ricketts, Edward F. *Sea of Cortez*. Illustrated, including maps. Green cloth. New York, 1941. First published edition. In dust jacket. $200–$250. (Note: There was an earlier issue in brown wrappers without the scientific matter included. Value: $2,500.)

STENDHAL. *Red and Black*. Translated by E. P. Robins. Frontispiece. 2 vols., red cloth. London, 1898. (By Marie Henri Beyle.) First edition in English. One of 200. $800–$1,000.

STEPHENS, Alexander H. *A Constitutional View of the Late War Between the States*. Map, plates, 2 vols., cloth. Philadelphia, 1868–70. First edition. $50–$75.

STEPHENS, Alexander H. *Speech in January, 1861, Before the Georgia State Convention*. 12 pp., wrappers. Baltimore, 1864. $50–$75.

STEPHENS, Mrs. Ann S. *Malaeska: The Indian Wife of the White Hunter*. Printed orange wrappers. New York, (1860). First edition, first issue, with covers $6^5/8 \times 4^1/2$ inches, and without woodcut on cover. $300–$500.

STEPHENS, Ann Sophia. *High Life in New York*. Wrappers. (New York, 1843.) First edition. $150. Author's first separate book.

STEPHENS, Ann Sophia (editor). *The Portland Sketch Book*. Cloth. Portland, Me., 1836. First edition. $75–$100. Author's first book appearance.

STEPHENS, James. See Esse, James.

STEPHENS, James. *The Charwoman's Daughter*. Cloth. London, 1912. First edition. In dust jacket. $40–$50.

STEPHENS, James. *Collected Poems*. Boards and vellum. London, 1926. One of 500 large paper copies, signed. In dust jacket. $150–$175.

STEPHENS, James. *The Crock of Gold*. Green cloth. London, 1912. First edition. In dust jacket. $400–$750. London, 1926. Illustrated. Half vellum. One of 525 signed. In dust jacket. $275–$450. New York, 1942. Limited Editions Club. Cloth. $50–$60.

STEPHENS, James. *Etched in Moonlight*. Light-blue cloth. London, 1928. First edition. In dust jacket. $40–$75. New York, 1928. Half cloth. First American edition. One of 750 signed. In dust jacket. Boxed. $100–$110.

STEPHENS, James. *Green Branches*. Wrappers. Dublin, 1916. First edition. One of 500 signed. $80–$125. New York, 1916. Half vellum. First American edition. One of 500. In dust jacket. $75–$100.

STEPHENS, James. *The Insurrection in Dublin*. Cloth. London, 1916. First edition. $80–$100.

STEPHENS, James. *Insurrections*. Brown boards. Dublin, 1909. First edition. In dust jacket. $100–$135.

STEPHENS, James. *Irish Fairy Tales*. Illustrated by Arthur Rackham. Vellum and boards. London, 1920. First edition. One of 520 signed by Rackham. $750–$1,000. Trade issue: Cloth. $300–$400.

STEPHENS, James. *Julia Elizabeth*. Decorated boards. New York, 1929. First edition. One of 861 signed. $60–$75.

STEPHENS, James. *Little Things*. Boards and cloth. Freelands, (1924). First edition. One of 25 signed. $100–$150. Another issue: Printed wrappers. One of 200 signed. $65–$85.

STEPHENS, James. *Optimist*. Illustrated. Boards and cloth. Gaylordsville, N.Y. 1929. First edition. One of 89 signed. $150–$175.

STEPHENS, James. *A Poetry Recital*. Boards. London, 1925. First edition. In dust jacket. $50–$60.

STEPHENS, John L. *Incidents of Travel in Central America, Chiapas and Yucatan*. Folding map, other maps and plans, 66 plates, other illustrations. 2 vols., cloth. New York, 1841. First edition. $600–$750. First edition. $150–$200.

STEPHENS, Lorenzo Dow. *Life Sketches of a Jayhawker of '49*. 6 plates. 68 pp., printed wrappers. (San Jose), 1916. First edition. $100–$150.

STERLING, George. *The Caged Eagle and Other Poems*. Cloth. San Francisco, 1916. First edition, first issue, with "to" for "too" in line 5, page 34. $75–$100.

STERLING, George. *Ode on the Opening of the Panama-Pacific International Exposition*. Boards and cloth. San Francisco, 1915. First edition. One of 525. $50–$60.

STERLING, George. *The Testimony of the Suns and Other Poems*. Black cloth. San Francisco, 1903. First edition. $100–$125. Author's first book. San Francisco, 1927. John Henry Nash printing. Folio, boards. One of 300. (Facsimile of title poem with comments by Ambrose Bierce.) $75–$100.

STERLING, George. *To a Girl Dancing*. Printed boards. (San Francisco, 1921.) Grabhorn Press. First edition. One of 120. $200–$225.

STERLING, George. *Truth*. Blue paper boards, cloth spine, two paper labels. Chicago, 1923. First edition. One of 285 signed. $60–$75.

STERLING, George; Taggard, Genevieve; and Rorty, James. *Continent's End: An Anthology of Contemporary California Poets*. Boards, pigskin spine. San Francisco, 1925. Book Club of California. First edition. One of 600. In half morocco slipcase. $100.

STERNE, Laurence. *A Sentimental Journey Through France and Italy*. Illustrated by Polia Chentoff. Wrappers. Paris, 1929. Black Sun Press. One of 335 on Arches paper. In tissue jacket. Boxed. $100.

STERNE, Laurence. *The Life and Opinions of Tristram Shandy*. Illustrated. 3 vols., cloth. Waltham St. Lawrence, 1929. Golden Cockerel Press. One of 500. $175–$375.

STEVENS, C. A. *Berdan's United States Sharpshooters in the Army of the Potomac*. Illustrated. Cloth. St. Paul, 1892. $150–$175.

STEVENS, George W. *Adventures, American Anecdotes, Biographical, Historical and Descriptive*. Cloth, printed label. Dansville, 1845. First edition. $75–$100.

STEVENS, Isaac I. *Campaigns of the Rio Grande and of Mexico*. 108 pp., wrappers. New York, 1851. First edition. $350–$450.

STEVENS, Isaac I. *A Circular Letter to Emigrants Desirous of Locating in Washington Territory*. 21 pp., sewed. Washington, 1858. First edition. $250–$350.

STEVENS, Wallace. See *Harvard Lyrics; An Ordinary Evening in New Haven; Verses from the Harvard Advocate*.

STEVENS, Wallace. *The Auroras of Autumn*. Blue cloth. New York, 1950. First edition. In dust jacket. $100–$135.

STEVENS, Wallace. *The Collected Poems of Wallace Stevens*. Brown cloth. New York, 1954. First collected edition. One of 2,500. In dust jacket. $125–$150.

STEVENS, Wallace. *Esthetique du Mal*. Illustrated by Wightman Williams. Half leather. (Cummington, Mass.), 1945. Cummington Press. First edition. One of 40 signed by author and artist. In glassine dust jacket. $850–$1,000. Ordinary copies (300), unsigned: $200–$250.

STEVENS, Wallace. *Harmonium*. Checkered boards; later, striped boards. New York, 1923. First edition, first binding. In dust jacket. Either binding: $600–$800. Also, inscribed but lacking jacket, $350 (A, 1977). Third binding: Blue cloth. In dust jacket. $200–$300, possibly more. Author's first book. New York, 1931. Boards. In dust jacket. $250–$300.

STEVENS, Wallace. *Ideas of Order*. Ivory wrappers. New York, 1935. First edition. One of 165 signed. In glassine dust jacket. Boxed. $1,000–$1,500. New York, 1936. Striped cloth. First edition (so called on verso of title page but actually the second, a trade issue a year after the first edition), first binding (later in plain boards). In dust jacket. $200–$250.

STEVENS, Wallace. *The Man with the Blue Guitar & Other Poems*. Cloth. New York, 1937. First edition. In first issue dust jacket, with "conjunctioning" on front flap. $500–$1,000. Also, $900 (A, 1980). New York, 1952. Cloth. In dust jacket. $100.

STEVENS, Wallace. *The Necessary Angel*. Green cloth. New York, 1951. First edition. In dust jacket. $100–$150.

STEVENS, Wallace. *Notes Toward a Supreme Fiction*. Cloth. Cummington, Mass., 1942. First edition. One of 193. In acetate dust jacket. $400–$450. Another issue: One of 80 signed. $1,000–$1,500. Also, $1,100 (A, 1977). Cummington, (1943). Boards. Second edition. One of 330. In plain paper jacket. $200.

STEVENS, Wallace. *Opus Posthumous*. Cloth. New York, 1957. First edition. In dust jacket. $100–$125. London, (1959). Cloth. First English edition. In dust jacket. $50–$75.

STEVENS, Wallace. *Owl's Clover*. Wrappers. New York, (1936). First edition. One of 105 signed. $2,500–$3,000. Also, $3,250 (A, 1976); advance copy signed by the publisher, $1,700 (A, 1977).

STEVENS, Wallace. *Parts of a World*. Boards. New York, 1942. First edition. In dust jacket. $150–$200.

STEVENS, Wallace. *A Primitive Like an Orb*. Illustrated by Kurt Seligmann. Olive-green wrappers. New York, 1948. First edition. One of 500. $150–$200.

STEVENS, Wallace. *Raoul Dufy: A Note*. 4 pp., wrappers. (New York, 1953.) First edition. One of 200. $400–$750.

STEVENS, Wallace. *Selected Poems*. Black boards. London, (1952). Fortune Press. First edition. In white dust jacket. $200–$250. (Suppressed because it was unauthorized.) London, (1953). Faber & Faber. Purple cloth. First authorized edition. In dust jacket. $200–$250.

STEVENS, Wallace. *Three Academic Pieces*. Boards. (Cummington), 1947. First edition. One of 102 signed (of an edition of 246). $800–$900. Also, spine faded. $550 (A, 1977). Unsigned copy, $400 (A, 1980).

STEVENS, Wallace. *Transport to Summer*. Green boards and cloth. New York, 1947. First edition. In dust jacket. $300–$350.

STEVENS, Wallace. *Two or Three Ideas*. Printed self-wrappers. Amherst, 1951. First edition. $300.

STEVENS, Walter B. *Through Texas: A Series of Interesting Letters*. Illustrated. Wrappers. (St. Louis), 1892. First edition. $100–$125.

STEVENS, William. See *The Unjust Judge*.

STEVENS & Conover. *Branch County Directory and Historical Record*. Cloth. Ann Arbor, 1871. $100–$125.

STEVENSON, B. F. *Letters from the Army*. Cloth. Cincinnati, 1864. $50–$60.

STEVENSON, R. Randolph, M. D. *The Southern Side: or, Andersonville Prison*. Cloth. Baltimore, 1876. $100–$125.

STEVENSON, Robert Louis. See *The Pentland Rising*.

STEVENSON, Robert Louis. *Across the Plains*. Cream-colored cloth. London, 1892. First edition. One of 100 on large paper. $150. (Hillsborough, Calif., 1950.) Allen Press. Illustrated. Boards. One of 200. $200–$250.

STEVENSON, Robert Louis. *Ballads*. Portraits. Blue cloth. London, 1890. First English edition. $80–$125. Another issue: White cloth. One of 100 on large paper. $200–$250.

STEVENSON, Robert Louis. *The Black Arrow*. Red cloth. London, 1888. First English edition. $85–$125. New York, 1916. Illustrated by N. C. Wyeth. Cloth. In dust jacket. $250–$300.

STEVENSON, Robert Louis. *Catriona, A Sequel to "Kidnapped."* Blue cloth. London, 1893. First English book edition. $75–$100.

STEVENSON, Robert Louis. *A Child's Garden of Verses*. Blue cloth. London, 1885. First edition. $500–$750. Also, $500 (A, 1981). London, 1896. Illustrated by Charles Robinson. Cloth. First illustrated edition. One of 150 large paper copies. $300–$400. Also, $202 (A, 1979). Trade issue: $100–$125. New York, 1944. Limited Editions Club. $60–$80.

STEVENSON, Robert Louis. *Familiar Studies of Men and Books*. Pictorial green cloth. London, 1882. First edition. $100–$125.

STEVENSON, Robert Louis. *Father Damien*. Wrappers, stapled. Sydney, Australia, 1890. First edition. One of 25. $1,250–$1,500. Edinburgh, 1890. Unbound sheets in board portfolio. One of 30 on vellum. $150–$200. Also, $65 (A, 1976). London, 1890. Wrappers. First published edition. $150–$200. Oxford, 1901. Printed wrappers. One of 299 on vellum. $200–$250. Portland, Me., 1905. Vellum. One of 4 on vellum. $250–$350. San Francisco, 1930. John Henry Nash printing. 2 vols., half vellum. $100.

STEVENSON, Robert Louis. *The Graver & the Pen, or Scenes from Nature with Appropriate Verses*. Woodcuts. Gray wrappers. Edinburgh, (1882). First edition. $750–$1,000.

STEVENSON, Robert Louis. *An Inland Voyage*. Frontispiece by Walter Crane. Blue cloth. London, 1878. First edition. $400–$500. Author's first novel. Stamford, Conn., 1938. Overbrook Press. 25 plates by Jean Hugo. Half calf. One of 150. $100–$150.

STEVENSON, Robert Louis. *Island Nights' Entertainments*. Illustrated. Cloth. New York, 1893. First edition. $225–$250. London, 1893. Cloth. First English edition, first issue, with price correction in ink in list of Stevenson's works. $150–$250.

STEVENSON, Robert Louis. *Kidnapped*. Folding frontispiece map. Cloth. (London), 1886. First edition. (Issued in various colors of cloth—blue, red, brown, and green—with blue as first.) Blue cloth, first issue, with the reading "business" in line 11 of page

40, etc. $600–$750. Second issue, in bright red cloth, with the reading "pleasure" on line 11 of page 40, etc. $250–$350. New York, 1913. Illustrated by N. C. Wyeth. Cloth. In dust jacket. $250–$300. New York, 1938. Limited Editions Club. Cloth. $40–$50.

STEVENSON, Robert Louis. *The Master of Ballantrae.* Red cloth. London, 1889. First edition. $100–$150. (There was also a "trial" edition of only 10 copies published in London in wrappers in 1888, according to De Ricci. A copy was sold at auction for $615 at Sotheby's in 1915.) New York, 1965. Limited Editions Club. Boxed. $50–$60.

STEVENSON, Robert Louis. *Memoirs of Himself.* Boards. Philadelphia, 1912. First edition. One of 45 on Whatman paper. $150–$200.

STEVENSON, Robert Louis. *The Merry Men and Other Tales and Fables.* Decorated blue cloth. London, 1887. First edition, with 32 pages of ads at end dated September, 1886. $100–$125.

STEVENSON, Robert Louis. *New Arabian Nights.* 2 vols., green cloth. London, 1882. First edition, first issue, with yellow end papers in Vol. 1. $500–$600.

STEVENSON, Robert Louis. *On the Thermal Influence of Forests.* Blue wrappers. Edinburgh: Neill and Co., 1873 (1895?). First edition. $250–$350. (A Thomas J. Wise forgery.)

STEVENSON, Robert Louis. *The Silverado Squatters.* Decorated green cloth. London, 1883. First edition, first issue, with 32-page catalogue dated 1883 at back. $300–$400. There was also a 10-copy trial issue of Chapter 1, 14 pages, green wrappers, London, (1883), published for copyright: $725 (A, 1952); inscribed copy, $2,400 (A, 1946). San Francisco, 1952. Grabhorn Press. Boards and cloth. One of 900. In original plain wrapper. $100–$150.

STEVENSON, Robert Louis. *The South Seas: A Record of Three Cruises.* Cloth. London, 1890. First edition. One of about 20 or 22 copies privately printed for copyright purposes. $1,000–$2,000.

STEVENSON, Robert Louis. *The Story of a Lie.* Folded sheets. London, 1882. First edition. (Withdrawn before publication.) $300 and up. Also, $225 (A, 1978). (A Thomas J. Wise forgery.)

STEVENSON, Robert Louis. *The Strange Case of Dr. Jekyll and Mr. Hyde.* Printed wrappers, or pink cloth. London, 1886. First English edition, first issue, in wrappers, with the date on front cover altered in ink from 1885 to 1886. $600–$800. Cloth: $350–$450. New York, 1886. Wrappers, or cloth. First edition. Wrappers: $400–$750. Cloth: $500–$750. New York, 1952. Limited Editions Club. Marbled boards. Boxed. $40–$50.

STEVENSON, Robert Louis. *The Suicide Club.* Illustrated. Wrappers over boards. New York, (1941). First edition. One of 86 (of 100), signed by the artist Karl Schrag and issued with an extra set of the 18 etchings. Boxed. $150.

STEVENSON, Robert Louis. *Thomas Stevenson: Civil Engineer.* Wrappers. (London), 1887. First edition. $200. (A Thomas J. Wise forgery.)

STEVENSON, Robert Louis. *Three Letters from Robert Louis Stevenson.* Boards. London, 1902. Essex House Press. First edition. One of 60. $250–$300.

STEVENSON, Robert Louis. *Ticonderoga.* Vellum boards. Edinburgh, 1887. First edition. One of 50. $400–$500. (A Thomas J. Wise forgery.)

STEVENSON, Robert Louis. *Travels with a Donkey in the Cevennes.* Frontispiece by Walter Crane. Green cloth. London, 1879. First edition. $400–$500. New York, 1957. Limited Editions Club. $40–$50.

STEVENSON, Robert Louis. *Treasure Island.* Green, gray, blue or rust-colored cloth. London, 1883. First edition, early issue, with ads dated July, 1883. $1,000–$1,250. Boston, 1884. Frontispiece map, illustrated. Pictorial cloth. First American (and first illustrated) edition. $750. London, 1885. Illustrated. Red cloth. First English illustrated edition. $400–$500. (Note: The McCutcheon sale catalogue, New York, 1926, No. 563, erroneously calls this the first illustrated edition.) London, 1927. Illustrated by Edmund Dulac. Vellum. One of 50 signed. $750–$1,000. Also, $550 (A, 1979). Trade edition: Cloth. $200–$300. New York, (1927). Dulac illustrations. Cloth. First American trade edition. In dust jacket. $100–$125. Philadelphia, 1930. Illustrated by Lyle Justis. Tan cloth. First printing. In dust jacket and slipcase. $100–$125. New York, 1941. Limited Editions Club. Cloth. $75–$100. Extra lithograph bound in, $125. London, 1949. Illustrated by Mervyn Peake. In dust jacket. $250–$300.

STEVENSON, Robert Louis. *Underwoods.* Green cloth. London, 1887. First edition, with July ads at back. $75–$100. Large paper issue: White buckram. One of 50. In dust jacket. $250–$325.

STEVENSON, Robert Louis. *Vailima Letters.* 2 vols., green buckram. Chicago, 1895. First edition. $50–$75. Large paper issue: One of 100. $100–$150. London, 1895. Terra-cotta cloth. First English edition. $40–$60. Large paper issue: Cloth. One of 125. $125–$150.

STEVENSON, Robert Louis. *Virginibus Puerisque and Other Papers.* Orange cloth, beveled edges. London, 1881. First edition, with ads dated "8.80." $225–$300. New York, 1893. Etched portrait by G. Mercier. Blue-green boards, paper label. One of 212. $75–$100. London, 1910. Florence Press. Illustrated by Norman Wilkinson. Vellum. One of 12 on vellum. $750–$1,000. Another issue: One of 250. $50–$75.

STEVENSON, Robert Louis. *The Weir of Hermiston.* Blue buckram. London, 1896. First edition, with March ads. $75–$100.

STEVENSON, Robert Louis, and Henley, William Ernest. *Macaire: A Melodramatic Farce in Three Acts.* Printed wrappers. Edinburgh, 1885. First edition. $200–$250. Chicago, 1895. Separately printed sheets from The Chap Book. American copyright edition. $100–$150. Later, book edition: Green buckram. $25–$35.

STEVENSON, Robert Louis, and Osbourne, Lloyd. *The Ebb Tide.* Cloth. Chicago, 1894. First edition. $50–$75. London, 1894. Pictorial cloth. First English edition, first issue, with 20 pages of ads at back. $75–$125.

STEVENSON, Robert Louis, and Osbourne, Lloyd. *The Wrecker.* Illustrated. Blue cloth. London, 1892. First edition. $75–$100.

STEVENSON, Robert Louis, and Van De Grift, Fanny. *More New Arabian Nights. The Dynamiter.* Cloth, or green pictorial wrappers. London, 1885. First edition. Either binding: $200–$300.

STEWART, Sir William Drummond. See *Altowan.*

STEWART, William F. *Last of the Filibusters.* 85 pp., pictorial wrappers. Sacramento, 1857. First edition. $650–$750.

STIFF, Edward. *The Texan Emigrant.* Folding map in color. Cloth. Cincinnati, 1840. First edition. $500–$750.

STILL, James. *Hounds on the Mountain.* Cloth. New York, 1937. First edition. One of 700. In dust jacket. $50–$60.

STILL, James. *River of Earth.* Cloth. New York, 1940. First edition. In dust jacket. $50–$60.

STILLMAN, Jacob D. B. B. *The Horse in Motion, as Shown by Instantaneous Photography.* 107 plates, 9 in color, by Eadweard Muybridge. Cloth. Boston, 1882. First edition. $600–$750. Also, $350 (A, 1980). London, 1882. Cloth. $350–$400.

STILLMAN, Samuel. *Select Sermons on Doctrinal and Practical Subjects.* Illustrated. Calf. Boston, 1808. $50–$75.

STILLWELL, Margaret Bingham. *Gutenberg and the Catholicon of 1460.* Folio, cloth.

New York, 1936. With an original leaf of the Catholicon printed by Gutenberg in 1460. In slipcase. $2,500–$3,000. Also, $2,250 (A, 1980).

STIPP, G. W. (compiler). *The Western Miscellany.* Calf. Xenia, Ohio, 1827. First edition. $3,500–$4,000. Also, $1,700 (A, 1967).

STIRLING, James. *Letters from the Slave States.* Map. Cloth. London, 1857. First edition. $200–$250.

STOBO, Maj. Robert. *Memoirs of Maj. Robert Stobo.* 78 pp., boards. London, 1800. First edition. $250–$350. Pittsburgh, 1854. Folding frontispiece, map. Cloth. First American edition. $200–$250.

STOCKTON, Frank R. *The Casting Away of Mrs. Lecks and Mrs. Aleshine.* Cloth, or wrappers. New York, (1886). First edition, first issue, with signatures (divisions of paper) at pages 9, 25, 49, 57, 73, 81, 97, 105, 121, and 125. Wrappers, first state, with ads for *Century* and *St. Nicholas* magazines: $150–$175. Cloth, first state, half inch across top of covers: $100–$125.

STOCKTON, Frank R. *The Floating Prince and Other Fairy Tales.* Cloth. New York, 1881. First edition. $150–$200.

STOCKTON, Frank R. *The Great War Syndicate.* Printed wrappers. New York, 1889. First edition, published by Collier. $50–$75.

STOCKTON, Frank R. *The Lady, or the Tiger? and Other Stories.* Pictorial gray and brown cloth. New York, 1884. First edition. $125–$150.

STOCKTON, Frank R. *Rudder Grange.* Pictorial red or green cloth. New York, 1879. First edition, first issue, with 18 chapters and no ads or reviews of this title. $75–$100.

STOCKTON, Frank R. *A Storyteller's Pack.* Illustrated. Green cloth. New York, 1897. First edition. $50–$60.

STOCKTON, Frank R. *Tales Out of School.* Illustrated. Pictorial cloth. New York, 1876. First edition. $75–$100.

STOCKTON, Frank R. *Ting-a-Ling.* Illustrated. Pictorial purple cloth. New York, 1870. First edition. $250–$400. Author's first book.

STOCKTON, Frank R. *What Might Have Been Expected.* Pictorial cloth. New York, 1874. First edition. $75–$85.

STODDARD, Maj. Amos. *Sketches, Historical and Descriptive of Louisiana.* Boards. Philadelphia, 1812. First edition. $200–$250.

STODDARD, Herbert L. *The Bob-White Quail.* Illustrated. Cloth. New York, 1931. First edition. One of 260 signed, and with an original drawing signed by Frank W. Benson. $400–$600.

STODDARD, Richard Henry. *Abraham Lincoln: An Horation Ode.* Wrappers. New York, (1865). First edition. $50–$60.

STODDARD, William O. *Little Smoke: A Tale of the Sioux.* Illustrated by Frederick S. Dellenbaugh. Pictorial cloth. New York, 1891. First edition. $100–$125.

STOKER, Bram. *Dracula.* Yellow cloth. Westminister (London), 1897. First edition, first issue, without ads. $900–$1,200. Second issue, with ads at back. $500–$600. New York, 1899. Pictorial cloth. First American edition. $350. New York, 1965. Limited Editions Club. Boxed. $60–$80.

STOKER, Bram. *The Lady of the Shroud.* Cloth. London, 1909. First edition. $100–$150.

STOKER, Bram. *Under the Sunset.* Illustrated. Vellum. London, 1882. First edition. $250. Author's first book.

STOKES, I. N. Phelps. *The Iconography of Manhattan Island.* Many plates, some in color. 6 vols., half vellum. New York, 1915–28. First edition. One of 360. In dust jackets. Boxed. $3,000–$3,500. Another issue: One of 42 on Japan vellum. $5,000 and up.

STOKES, I. N. Phelps, and Haskell, Daniel C. *American Historical Prints: Early Views of American Cities.* Illustrated. Cloth. New York, 1932. $350–$450. New York, 1933. Cloth. $300–$350.

STONE, Charles P. *Notes on the State of Sonora.* 28 pp., printed wrappers. Washington, 1861. First edition. $300–$350.

STONE, Grace Zaring. See Vance, Ethel.

STONE, Robert. *Dog Soldiers.* Cloth. Boston, 1974. First edition. In dust jacket. $50–$60.

STONE, Robert. *A Hall of Mirrors.* Cloth. Boston, 1967. First edition. In dust jacket. $75–$100. Author's first book.

STOPPARD, Tom. *Lord Malquist and Mr. Moon.* Cloth. London, (1966). First edition. In dust jacket. $150. New York, 1968. Boards. First American edition. In dust jacket. $75–$100. Author's first book.

STOREY, David. *This Sporting Life.* Boards. (London, 1960.) First edition. In dust jacket. $75–$100. Author's first book.

STORIES from the Harvard Advocate. Half morocco. Cambridge, Mass., 1896. First edition. $40–$50.

STORY of Cripple Creek (A), the Greatest Gold Mining Camp on Earth. Folding map, 28 pp., wrappers. (Denver, 1896.) First edition. $100–$125.

STORY of Louis Riel, Rebel Chief (The). Illustrated. Cloth. Toronto, 1885. (By J. E. Collins.) First edition. $100–$125.

STORY of the Three Bears (The). Illustrated by Harrison Weir and John Absolon. 12 leaves, yellow hand-colored wrappers. New York, (about 1870). $40–$60.

STOTZ, Charles Morse. *The Early Architecture of Western Pennsylvania.* Cloth. Pittsburgh, 1936. First edition. $50–$75.

STOUT, Rex. *Fer-de-Lance.* Cloth. New York, 1934. First edition. In dust jacket. $400–$500. (First of the Nero Wolfe detective novels.)

STOUT, Rex. *How Like a God.* Purple cloth. New York, 1929. First edition. In dust jacket. $175–$250. Author's first book.

STOUT, Rex. *The League of Frightened Men.* Black cloth. New York, (1935). Black cloth. New York, (1935). First edition. In dust jacket. $300–$400.

STOUT, Tom. *Montana, Its Story and Biography.* Illustrated. 3 vols., cloth. Chicago, 1921. First edition. $250–$350.

STOWE, Harriet Beecher. See Beecher, Harriet Elizabeth.

STOWE, Harriet Beecher. *Dred: A Tale of the Great Dismal Swamp.* 2 vols., black cloth. Boston, 1856. First edition. $250–$350.

STOWE, Harriet Beecher. *A Key to Uncle Tom's Cabin.* Cloth, or wrappers. Boston, 1853. First edition. Wrappers: $150–$200. Cloth: $75–$125. London, (1853?). Green cloth. $75.

STOWE, Harriet Beecher. *Uncle Sam's Emancipation.* Cloth. Philadelphia, 1853. First edition. $50–$75.

STOWE, Harriet Beecher. *Uncle Tom's Cabin.* Title vignette, 6 plates. 2 vols., pictorial wrappers, or 2 vols., cloth. Boston, 1852. First edition, first printing, first issue, wrappers, with slug of Hobart and Robbins on copyright page. $5,000 and up. (The Paul Hyde Bonner copy, with the spines gauzed, brought $1,025 at auction in 1934. No comparably fine copy in wrappers seems to have been offered since.) First printing, second issue (cloth) binding, $3,000 and up. Also, "Gift" binding of gilt-decorated brown cloth, $4,500 in a 1975 catalogue. For price ranges on numerous other copies— defective, rebound, and in various "gift" bindings—see the current auction records in *American Book-Prices Current*. Examples: Worn and shaken, $600 (1981); repaired, $1,700 (1980). London, 1852. Cassell imprint. Illustrated by George Cruikshank. 13 parts, pictorial wrappers. First English edition. $200–$300. London, 1852. Cloth. First English book edition, with Cassell imprint. $150–$250. London, 1852, 40 plates. Cloth. C. H. Clarke, publisher. $75–$100. New York, 1938. Limited Editions Club. Marbled boards and leather. $60–$85. (Note: The English listings here are tentative and controversial. So far as we can determine there is still no clear-cut determination among bibliographers as to which of the more than 50 London editions of 1852 is the true first English edition.)

STRACHEY, Lytton. *Books and Characters*. Portrait. Green cloth. London, 1922. First edition. In dust jacket. $35–$50.

STRACHEY, Lytton. *Elizabeth and Essex*. Half cloth. New York, 1928. One of 1,060 signed. $100–$125.

STRACHEY, Lytton. *Portraits in Miniature*. Half cloth. London, 1931. First edition. Limited and signed issue. $125–$150. Trade issue: Buckram. In dust jacket. $30–$40.

STRAHORN, Mrs. Carrie A. *15,000 Miles by Stage*. Numerous illustrations, including 4 in color by Charles M. Russell. Cloth. New York, 1911. First edition. $200–$300. New York, 1915. Second edition. $150.

STRAHORN, Robert E. *The Hand-book of Wyoming, and Guide to the Black Hills and Big Horn Regions*. 14 plates. 272 pp., printed wrappers. Cheyenne, 1877. First edition. $300–$500. Also, in cloth: $200.

STRAHORN, Robert E. *Montana and Yellowstone National Park*. 191 pp., flexible cloth wrappers, plus 14 pp. ads. Kansas City, 1881. First edition. $200–$225.

STRAHORN, Robert E. *The Resources of Montana Territory*. Map. Cloth. Helena, 1879. First edition. $250.

STRAHORN, Robert E. *To the Rockies and Beyond*. Folding map. Wrappers. Omaha, 1878. First edition. $300–$350. Also in cloth: $225. Omaha, 1879. Illustrated. Cloth. Second edition. $150–$250.

STRAND, Mark. *Sleeping With One Eye Open*. Cloth. Iowa City, 1963. Stone Wall Press. First edition. One of 225. In acetate dust jacket. $75. Author's first book.

STRANG, James J. *The Book of the Law of the Lord*. 80 pp., cloth. (Kansas City, 1927.) $150–$200. (For earlier editions, see title entry.)

STRANG, William. *The Earth Fiend*. Etchings by the author. Buckram. London, 1892. First edition. One of 150 signed. $350.

STRANGE, Edward F. *The Colour-Prints of Hiroshige*. 16 colored, 36 plain plates. Buckram. London, 1925. In dust jacket. $300–$350. Another issue: Vellum. One of 250. $500.

STRANGER in Lowell (The). Wrappers. Boston, 1845. (By John Greenleaf Whittier.) First edition. $200.

STRANGER'S Guide to St. Louis, or What to See and How to See It. Folding map. Cloth. St. Louis, 1867. First edition. $150–$200.

STRATTON, R. B. *Captivity of the Oatman Girls, etc*. Woodcut portrait and map. 231 pp., printed wrappers. San Francisco, 1857. Second edition of *Life Among the Indians*

(entry following). $500–$750. Chicago, 1857. (Reprint.) $500–$750. New York, 1858.
3 plates. Cloth. Third edition, enlarged. $250–$300.

STRATTON, R. B. *Life Among the Indians*. Illustrated. 183 pp., wrappers. San Francisco, 1857. First edition. $2,500–$3,000. San Francisco, 1935. Grabhorn Press. Plates. Half cloth. One of 550. $75–$100. (See preceding entry.)

STRAUSS, David Friedrich. *The Life of Jesus*. 3 vols., blue-green cloth. London, 1846. (Translated by George Eliot [Mary Ann Evans].) First edition in English. $1,000–$1,500. Worn copy, $730 in a 1981 catalogue. George Eliot's first book.

STREAKS of Squatter Life, and Far-West Scenes. Illustrated by F. O. C. Darley. Half calf. Philadelphia, 1847. (By John S. Robb.) First edition. $150–$250.

STREETER, Floyd Benjamin. *Prairie Trails and Cow Towns*. 12 plates. Cloth. Boston, (1936). First edition. In dust jacket. $200–$225.

STREETER, Thomas W. See *Americana—Beginnings*.

STREETER, Thomas W. *Bibliography of Texas*. 5 vols. (Part I, 2 vols; Part II, one vol.; Part III, 2 vols.), cloth. Cambridge, Mass., 1955–56–60. First edition. One of 600. In dust jackets. $600–$750. Parts I and II, 3 vols., $300–$350. Part III, 2 vols. $200–$250.

STREETER, Thomas W. (sale). *The Celebrated Collection of Americana Formed by the Late Thomas Winthrop Streeter*. 8 vols., blue boards (including index), or blue cloth. New York, 1966–69. $750–$1,000. (An indispensable reference. The copies in boards, while first, are less desirable than cloth because the cheap bindings deteriorate rapidly.)

STREETT, William B. *Gentlemen Up*. Illustrated, including color. Green cloth. New York, 1930. Derrydale Press. First edition. One of 850. In dust jacket. $100–$125. Another issue: Half morocco. One of 75 signed with a signed etching. $1,250–$1,500.

STRIBLING, T. S. *The Cruise of the Dry Dock*. 4 color illustrations. Green cloth. Chicago, (1917). First edition. In dust jacket. $150–$175. Author's first book.

STRICKLAND, William. *Reports on Canals, Railways, Roads, and Other Subjects*. Plates. Oblong, boards and leather. Philadelphia, 1826. First edition. $500–$600. Also, $400 (A, 1977).

STRICTURES on a Voyage to South America, as Indicated by the "Secretary of the (Late) Mission" to La Plata, etc. By a Friend of Truth and Sound Policy. 108 pp., printed wrappers. Baltimore, 1820. (By H. M. Brackenridge.) $125–$150.

STRONG, L. A. G. *The Jealous Ghost*. Cloth. London, 1930. First edition. One of 75 signed. In dust jacket. $75–$100.

STRONG, Gen. W. E. *A Trip to the Yellowstone National Park in July, August, and September, 1875*. 2 folding maps, 7 signed photos, 7 plates. Half morocco. Washington, 1876. First edition. $600–$750. (Note: In some copies there are fewer than 7 signatures of the participants in this hunting trip.)

STUART, Granville. *Forty Years on the Frontier*. 15 plates. 2 vols., cloth. Cleveland, 1925. First edition. $175–$200.

STUART, Jesse. *Beyond Dark Hills*. Cloth. New York, 1938. First edition. In dust jacket. $100–$125. New York, (1972). Pictorial cloth. One of 950 signed. Boxed. $60.

STUART, Jesse. *Foretaste of Glory*. Cloth. New York, 1946. First edition. In dust jacket. $75–$100.

STUART, Jesse. *Harvest of Youth*. 80 pp. Howe, Okla., (1930). First edition. $1,000 and up. Author's first book.

STUART, Jesse. *Man with a Bull-Tongue Plow.* Beige cloth. (New York, 1934.) First edition. In dust jacket. $250–$350.

STUART, Jesse. *Taps for Private Tussie.* Cloth. New York, 1943. First edition (so stated). In dust jacket. $75–$125. New York, (1943). Books, Inc., edition. Illustrated by Thomas Hart Benton. In dust jacket. $35–$50.

STUART, Jesse. *Trees of Heaven.* Cloth. New York, 1940. First edition. In dust jacket. $100–$150.

STUART, Joseph A. *My Roving Life.* Illustrated. 2 vols., boards and cloth. Auburn, Calif., 1895. First edition. $1,000-$1,250.

STUART, Robert. *The Discovery of the Oregon Trail.* Edited by Philip Ashton Rollins. Cloth. New York, 1935. First edition. $35–$50.

STUDER, Jacob H. *The Birds of North America.* 119 color plates. Folio, morocco. New York, 1888. $1,000–$1,250. New York, 1903. Half leather. $400. Another copy, worn, $130 (A, 1980). (Note: This series of color plate books began with the publication of a first edition in Columbus, Ohio, in 1878, and there have been many reprinted editions. A decade ago they were relatively inexpensive, selling for as little as $35 at retail, but the current interest in color plate books has driven them up dramatically.)

STURGEON, Theodore. *More Than Human.* Boards. New York, (1953). First edition. In dust jacket. $200–$250. (Also issued in wrappers.)

STURGEON, Theodore. *Without Sorcery.* Illustrated. Cloth. Philadelphia, (1948). First edition. In dust jacket. $100. Another issue: Buckram. One of about 92 signed. Boxed. $300. Author's first book.

STURGIS, Thomas. *Common Sense View of the Sioux War.* 52 pp., wrappers. Cheyenne, 1877. First edition. $150–$200.

STYRON, William. *The Confessions of Nat Turner.* Cloth. New York, (1967). First edition. One of 500 signed. Boxed. $75–$85. Trade edition: In dust jacket. $25.

STYRON, William. *Lie Down in Darkness.* Brown cloth. Indianapolis, (1951). First edition. In dust jacket. $150–$200. Author's first book.

STYRON, William. *Set This House on Fire.* Cloth. New York, (1960). First edition. In first dust jacket (lettered in red). $75. London, (1961). Cloth. First English edition. In dust jacket. $40–$50.

STYRON, William. *This Quiet Dust.* (Cover title.) Printed blue wrappers. (New York, 1967.) First edition. $300.

SUÁREZ Y Navarrō, Juan. *Defensa que el Licenciado José G.P. Garay Hizo ante el Juez Primero de lo Civil, Don Gayetano Ibarra, etc.* 64 pp., sewed. Mexico, 1849. $300–$350.

SUGDEN, Alan V. *A History of English Wallpaper, 1509–1914.* 70 color plates and 190 half-tone illustrations. Folio, blue buckram. New York or London, (1925). First edition. In dust jacket. Boxed. $500–$600.

SULLIVAN, Frank. *The Life and Times of Martha Heppelthwaite.* Yellow cloth. New York, 1926. First edition. In dust jacket. $65–$85. Author's first book.

SULLIVAN, Louis H. *A System of Architectural Ornament.* Illustrated. Folio, half cloth. New York, 1924. First edition. One of 1,000. $300–$400.

SULLIVAN, Maurice S. *The Travels of Jedediah Smith.* Map, 12 plates. Pictorial cloth. Santa Ana, Calif., 1934. First edition. $150–$200.

SULLIVAN, W. John L. *Twelve Years in the Saddle for Law and Order on the Frontiers of Texas.* 13 plates. Cloth. Austin, 1909. First edition. $100–$200.

SULZBERGER, Cyrus. *The Resistentialists.* Boards. New York, (1962). First edition.

In dust jacket. $400–$500. (Suppressed because of the author's unauthorized use of three Ernest Hemingway letters.)

SUMMARY View (A) of the Millenial Church (Commonly Called Shakers). Calf. Albany, 1823. (By Calvin Green and Seth Y. Wells.) First edition. $100–$150.

SUMMERFIELD, Charles. *The Rangers and Regulators of the Tanaha*. Frontispiece, plates. Cloth. New York, (1956). (By Alfred W. Arrington.) First edition. $65–$85.

SUMMERS, Montague. See Scot, Reginald; Sinistrari, Ludovico.

SUNDERLAND, LaRoy. *Mormonism Exposed and Refuted*. 54 pp., printed wrappers. New York, 1838. First edition. $1,500–$2,000.

SUPERNATURALISM of New England (The). Printed wrappers. New York, 1847. (By John Greenleaf Whittier—his name on cover but not on title page.) First edition. $200–$250.

SURTEES, Robert Smith. See *"Ask Mamma"; The Analysis of the Hunting Field; Handley Cross; Hawbuck Grange; Mr. Facey Romford's Hounds; Mr. Sponge's Sporting Tour; Jorrocks' Jaunts and Jollities; "Plain or Ringlets?"*

SUTHERLAND, Thomas A. *Howard's Campaign Against the Nez Perce Indians*. 48 pp., wrappers. Portland, Ore., 1878. First edition. $750–$1,000.

SUTRO, Adolph. *The Mineral Resources of the United States*. Folding map, plates. Cloth. Baltimore, 1868. First edition. $100–$125.

SUTRO, Adolph. *The Sutro Tunnel and Railway to the Comstock Lode in Nevada*. 2 folding maps. 37 pp., printed wrappers. London, 1873. $100–$125.

SUTTER, Johann August. *Diary of Johann August Sutter*. Edited by Douglas S. Watson. 3 colored plates, 3 facsimiles. Boards. San Francisco, 1932. First edition. One of 500. $75–$100.

SUTTER, Johann August. *New Helvetia Diary*. 2 color plates, facsimile, map. Half cloth. San Francisco, 1939. Grabhorn Press. One of 950. $100–$150.

SUTTON, J. J. *History of the 2nd Regiment, West Virginia Cavalry Volunteers*. Cloth. Portsmouth, Ohio, 1892. $100–$125.

SWADOS, Harvey. *Out Went the Candle*. Cloth. New York, 1955. First edition. In dust jacket. $50–$60. Author's first book.

SWALLOW Barn, or A Sojourn in the Old Dominion. 2 vols., half cloth and boards, paper labels. Philadelphia, 1832. (By John Pendleton Kennedy.) First edition. $300–$400. Author's first book.

SWAMP Outlaws (The), or The Lowery Bandits of North Carolina. 84 pp., wrappers. New York, (1872). $125–$150.

SWAN, Alonzo M. *Canton: Its Pioneers and History*. Cloth. Canton, Ill., 1871. First edition. $75–$100.

SWAN, Alonzo M. *Life, Trial, Conviction, Confession and Execution of John Osborn, the Murderer of Mrs. Adelia Mathews, etc.* 85 pp., wrappers. Peoria, 1872. First edition. $100. Peoria, 1873. 95 pp., wrappers. Second edition. (Name of the murderer changed to John Marion Osborne.) $50 and up.

SWAN, James G. *The Northwest Coast*. Folding map, plates. Cloth. New York, 1857. First edition. $100–$125.

SWASEY, William F. *The Early Days and Men of California*. Portrait, 2 plates. Calf. Oakland, (1891). First edition. $150–$300.

SWEET, Willis. *The Carbonate Camps, Leadville and Ten-Mile, of Colorado*. Maps and plates. 83 pp., pictorial wrappers. Kansas City, 1879. First edition. $250–$350. (For a similar work, see Stephen F. Smart entry.)

SWIFT, Jonathan. *Gulliver's Travels*. 13 color plates by Arthur Rackham. Cloth. London, 1909. One of 750 signed by Rackham. $750–$1,000. Trade edition: (Only 12 color plates.) Cloth. In dust jacket. $200–$250. New York, 1929. Limited Editions Club. $100–$135. London, 1930. Cresset Press. 12 colored engravings by Rex Whistler. 2 vols., morocco and boards. One of 195. In slipcase. $2,500–$3,000.

SWINBURNE, Algernon Charles. Note: So many of the books and pamphlets once attributed to Swinburne have turned out to be forgeries by Thomas J. Wise that the listing of them here would constitute a bibliographical nightmare for both compiler and reader. For this reason, I have listed here only a few of the better known items of Swinburniana.

SWINBURNE, Algernon Charles. *Astrophel and Other Poems*. Cloth. London, 1894. First edition, first issue, with February ads. $200–$250.

SWINBURNE, Algernon Charles. *Atalanta in Calydon: A Tragedy*. White cloth. London, 1865. First edition, with only 111 pages. $750–$1,000. London, 1894. Kelmscott Press. Woodcut title, initials, etc. Vellum, silk ties. One of 250. $1,000–$1,200. Another issue: One of 8 on vellum. $2,500–$3,000.

SWINBURNE, Algernon Charles. *Chastelard: A Tragedy*. Cloth. London, 1865. First edition, first issue, Moxon imprint and November ads. $150–$200.

SWINBURNE, Algernon Charles. *Erechtheus: A Tragedy*. Cloth. London, 1876. First edition. $100–$135.

SWINBURNE, Algernon Charles. *The Jubilee*. Wrappers. London, 1887. First edition. One of 25 printed on paper. $150–$250.

SWINBURNE, Algernon Charles. *Laus Veneris*. Illustrated. Cloth. London, 1948. Golden Cockerel Press. One of 650. $200–$250. Another issue: One of 100 specially bound. $500–$600.

SWINBURNE, Algernon Charles. *Lucretia Borgia*. Illustrated. Full leather. (London), 1942. Golden Cockerel Press. One of 30 specially bound with manuscript facsimile. $600–$750. Another issue: One of 320. $200–$250.

SWINBURNE, Algernon Charles. *Marino Faliero, A Tragedy*. Green cloth. London, 1885. First edition, with 32 pages of ads. $75.

SWINBURNE, Algernon Charles. *Pasiphae: A Poem*. Illustrated. Buckram. (London 1950.) Golden Cockerel Press. One of 500. $150–$200. Another issue: Vellum. One of 100 specially bound. $350–$450.

SWINBURNE, Algernon Charles. *Poems and Ballads*. Cloth. London, 1866. First edition, first issue, with E. Moxon imprint. $300–$350. Second issue with J. C. Hotten imprint. $150–$250.

SWINBURNE, Algernon Charles. *Poetical Fragments*. Wrappers. London, 1916. One of 25 signed by Clement Shorter. $75–$125.

SWINBURNE, Algernon Charles. *The Queen-Mother. Rosamond. Two Plays*. Slate-gray cloth, white spine label. London, 1860. First edition, first issue, with "A. G. Swinburne" on spine and Pickering imprint on title page. $2,500–$3,000. Author's first book.

SWINBURNE, Algernon Charles. *A Song of Italy*. Bright blue cloth. London, 1867. First edition. $85–$125.

SWINBURNE, Algernon Charles. *Songs Before Sunrise*. Blue-green cloth. London, 1871. First edition. $125–$150. Large paper issue: Morocco. One of 25. $600–$800. London, 1909. Florence Press. Levant morocco extra. One of 12 on vellum. $750–$1,000. Another issue: Vellum. One of 600 on paper. $200–$225.

SWINBURNE, Algernon Charles. *The Springtide of Life: Poems of Childhood*. 9 color plates, numerous text illustrations by Arthur Rackham. Half vellum. London, 1918. One of 765 signed by Rackham. $600–$800. Trade edition: Cloth. In dust jacket. $150–$250.

SWINBURNE, Algernon Charles. *Under the Microscope*. Wrappers. London, 1872. First edition, with suppressed leaf laid in. $750–$1,000.

SWINBURNE, Algernon Charles. *William Blake: A Critical Essay*. 8 plates. Cloth. London, 1868. First edition, first issue, with the word "Zamiel" below woodcut on title page. $400–$500.

SWISHER, James. *How I Know*. Plates. Cloth. Cincinnati, 1880. First edition. $100–$300. Cincinnati, 1881. Second edition. $75–$100.

SWISS Family Robinson (The). 2 vols., boards. New York, 1832. (By Johann David Wyss.) First American edition. $300–$500. New York, 1963. Limited Editions Club. $40–$50. Also see *The Family Robinson Crusoe*.

SYMONDS, John Addington. *Animi Figura*. Cloth. London, 1882. First edition. $100–$150.

SYMONDS, John Addington. *The Escorial: A Prize Poem*. Wrappers. Oxford, 1860. First edition. $300–$350. Author's first book.

SYMONDS, John Addington. *Essays Speculative and Suggestive*. 2 vols., cloth. London, 1890. First edition. $100–$125.

SYMONDS, John Addington. *In the Key of Blue and Other Prose Essays*. Light-blue or cream cloth. London, 1893. First edition, with 15 pages of ads at end. $250–$350. (The blue cloth binding is scarce.) Another issue: Vellum. One of 50 on large paper. $350–$500.

SYMONDS, John Addington. *The Life of Michael Angelo Buonarotti*. 2 vols., cloth. London, 1893. First edition. $300–$400.

SYMONDS, John Addington. *The Renaissance*. Wrappers. Oxford, 1863. First edition. $100–$125.

SYMONDS, John Addington. *Renaissance in Italy*. 7 vols., cloth. London, 1880–86. (First issue copies of *The Age of Despots*, *The Revival of Learning*, and *The Fine Arts* without stars on spines.) $500–$600.

SYMONDS, John Addington. *The Sonnets of Michael Angelo Buonarroti and Tommaso Campanella*. Translated into rhymed English. Dark blue cloth. London, 1878. First edition. $50–$75.

SYMONDS, John Addington. *Wine, Women and Song: Mediaeval Latin Students' Songs*. Cloth. London, 1884. First edition. $40–$50. Another issue: Vellum. One of 50 on large paper. $75–$100.

SYMONDS, John Addington. *Walt Whitman: A Study*. 5 plates. Cloth. London, 1893. First edition. $60–$80.

SYMONDS, Mary, and Preece, Louisa. *Needlework Through the Ages*. 8 color plates, 96 other plates. Half vellum. London, 1928. $350–$400.

SYMONS, A. J. A. *The Quest for Corvo*. Black cloth. London, (1934). First edition. In dust jacket. $100–$125. New York, 1934. Cloth. First American edition. In dust jacket. $75.

SYMONS, Arthur. *Aubrey Beardsley*. Half cloth. London, 1898. First edition. $100–$150. London, 1905. Half vellum. Second edition. One of 150 on large paper. $200–$250. Ordinary issue: Boards. $100–$125.

SYMONS, Arthur. *An Introduction to the Study of Browning*. Green cloth. London, 1886. First edition. $75. Author's first book.

SYMONS, Arthur. *The Loom of Dreams*. Printed wrappers. (London), 1901. First edition. One of 12. $375.

SYMONS, Arthur. *Silhouettes*. London, 1892. Gray boards. First edition. One of 250. $50–$60. Another issue: One of 25 on large paper, signed. $100–$150.

SYMONS, Arthur. *Studies in Strange Souls*. Illustrated. Half leather. London, 1929. First edition. One of 12 on vellum, signed. $250–$275.

SYMONS, Arthur. *A Study of Thomas Hardy*. Photogravures of Hardy by Alvin Langdon Coburn. London, 1927. First edition. One of 100 signed by Symons and Coburn. $650.

SYNGE, John M. *The Aran Islands*. Drawings. Cloth. Dublin, 1906. First edition. In dust jacket. $200–$300. Dublin, 1907. Illustrated by Jack B. Yeats. $150–$200. Another issue: One of 150 on large paper, signed by Synge and Yeats. $600–$750.

SYNGE, John M. *Deirdre of the Sorrows: A Play*. Preface by W. B. Yeats. Boards, linen spine. Dundrum, Ireland, 1910. Cuala Press. First edition. One of 250. $150–$200. New York, 1910. Boards and cloth. One of 50. $750–$1,000. (All except five on vellum and five on handmade paper were reported destroyed by the publisher, John Quinn.)

SYNGE, John M. *A Few Personal Recollections, with Biographical Notes by John Masefield*. Cloth. Dundrum, 1913. Cuala Press. First edition. One of 350. $125–$175.

SYNGE, John M. *In the Shadow of the Glen*. Pale-gray printed wrappers. New York, 1904. First edition. One of 50 published for copyright purposes. $1,000–$2,000. Also, $900 (A, 1977). Author's first book. (For first English edition, see *The Shadow of the Glen*.)

SYNGE, John M. *The Playboy of the Western World*. Portrait. Cloth. Dublin, 1907. First edition. $250–$350. Another issue: White linen. One of 25 on handmade paper. $600–$800.

SYNGE, John M. *Poems and Translations*. Blue boards, tan linen spine, paper label. Dundrum, 1909. Cuala Press. One of 250. $125–$150. New York, 1909. Boards and cloth. One of 50. $350–$450.

SYNGE, John M. *The Shadow of the Glen, Riders to the Sea*. Printed green wrappers. London, 1905. First English edition. $200–$250. (For first edition, see *In the Shadow of the Glen*.) Synge's first commercially published book. Boston, 1911. Half vellum. $50.

SYNGE, John M. *The Tinker's Wedding*. Rust-colored cloth, beige spine. Dublin, 1907. First edition. In dust jacket. $250.

SYNGE, John M. *The Well of the Saints*. Wrappers. London, 1905. First edition, first issue. $250–$300. London, 1905. Boards and cloth. Second issue, with introduction by William Butler Yeats. $150–$200. New York, 1905. One of 50. First American edition. $300–$350.

SYNGE, John M. *The Works of John Millington Synge*. Portraits. 4 vols., cloth. Dublin, 1910. First edition. $250–$300. Boston, 1912. 4 vols., cloth. $200–$250.

SYNTAX, Doctor. *Doctor Syntax in Paris*. 18 colored plates by Williams. Boards. London, 1820. (By William Combe?) First edition. $400–$500.

SYNTAX, Doctor. *The Life of Napoleon: A Hudibrastic Poem in 15 Cantos*. 30 color plates by George Cruikshank. Boards. London, 1815. (By William Combe.) First edition. $1,250–$1,500.

SYNTAX, Doctor. *The Tour of Doctor Syntax Through London*. 19 colored plates. 8 parts, wrappers. London, 1820. (Sometimes attributed to William Combe, but not by him, says De Ricci.) First edition. $1,000 and up. London, 1820. Boards. First book edition. $750–$1,000.

SYNTAX, Doctor. *The Tours* . . .(1st, 2d, and 3d.) (By William Combe.) *The Tour of Doctor Syntax in Search of the Picturesque.* Frontispiece, title page, and 29 colored plates by Thomas Rowlandson. Boards. London, 1812. First edition. *The Tour of Doctor Syntax in Search of Consolation.* 24 colored plates by Rowlandson. Boards. London, 1820. First edition. *The Tour of Doctor Syntax in Search of a Wife.* 24 colored plates by Rowlandson. Boards. London, (1921–22). First edition. Copies in original boards are rare, few having been at public sale since the 1940's. Estimated value today: $5,000 and up. Copies in bindings: $1,000–$2,000 and up. Many later editions and mixed sets at lower prices show the continuing popularity of the series. They include the 3-vol. *Tours of Doctor Syntax.* 80 color plates by Rowlandson. Pink boards, paper labels, uncut. London, 1823. First miniature edition, with printed title issued in Vol. 2 only.

SYRACUSE Poems, 1963–1969. Edited by George P. Elliott. Cloth. Syracuse, (1970). First edition. In dust jacket. $75–$100. (Contains poems by W. D. Snodgrass and others. Some copies signed by contributors: $100–$150.)

SZYK, Arthur (artist). *Ink and Blood: A Book of Drawings.* Text by Struthers Burt. 74 plates. Morocco. New York, 1946. First edition. One of 1,000 signed by Szyk. Boxed. $350–$450.

T

TABB, John Banister. *Lyrics*. Boards. Boston, 1897. First edition. One of 5 on China paper. $300–$350. Other issues: One of 50 on handmade paper. $125–$175. One of 500. $25.

TABB, John Banister. *Poems*. Boards and cloth. Boston, 1894. First edition. One of 50 on handmade paper. $200. Boston, 1895. Cloth. Second edition. One of 500. $25.

TABULA. Vols. XXII, No. 2. Pictorial wrappers. Oak Park, Ill., February, 1916. (High school literary magazine with Ernest Hemingway story "The Judgment of Manitou.") $950 (A, 1978). Vol. XXII, No. 3, April, 1916. (With Hemingway's "A Matter of Color.") $750–$1,000. Also, stained, $750 (A, 1977). Vol. XXIII, No. 3. March, 1917. (With 3 Hemingway poems.) $750–$1,000. Also, spine chipped, $650 (A, 1977). (Other issues of this magazine with Hemingway materials have ranged from $80 up at auction in recent years.)

TACITUS, C. Cornelius. *De Vita et Moribus Julii Agricolae Liber*. Vellum. London, 1900. Doves Press. One of 225. $350–$500. Another issue: One of 5 on vellum. In special morocco binding by the Doves Bindery. $2,420 (A, 1978). First book printed at the Doves Press.

TAFT, Robert. *Artists and Illustrators of the Old West*. Illustrated. Cloth, New York, 1953. First edition. In dust jacket. $50–$60.

TAFT, Robert. *Photography and the American Scene: A Social History, 1839–89*. Cloth. New York, 1938. First edition. In dust jacket. $150–$200. New York, 1942. Cloth. In dust jacket. $50–$75.

TAGGARD, Genevieve. *For Eager Lovers*. Boards, paper labels, New York, 1922. First edition. In dust jacket. $100–$125. Author's first book.

TAGGARD, Genevieve. *The Life and Mind of Emily Dickinson*. Boards. New York, 1930. First edition. One of 200 on large paper, signed. $100–$125. Ordinary copies: $30–$40.

TAGGARD, Genevieve. *Travelling Standing Still*. Boards. New York, 1928. First edition. One of 110 signed. In dust jacket. Boxed. $125–$150.

TAGGARD, Genevieve (editor). *May Days: An Anthology of Masses-Liberator Verse, 1912–1924*. Cloth. New York, 1925. First edition. In dust jacket. $50–$75.

TAGORE, Rabindranath. *The Post Office: A Play*. Preface by William Butler Yeats. Boards and cloth. Dundrum, Ireland, 1914. Cuala Press. One of 400. $100–$125. New York, 1914. Blue cloth. First American edition. $50–$60.

TALBOT, Theodore. *The Journals of Theodore Talbot*. Edited by Charles H. Carey. Cloth. Portland, Me., 1931. First edition. $35–$50.

TALES of the Northwest; or, Sketches of Indian Life and Character. By a Resident from Beyond the Frontier. Boards. Boston, 1830. (By William J. Snelling.) First edition. $350–$400. Author's first book.

TALES of Terror; with an Introductory Dialogue. Engraved half title. Wrappers. London, 1801. (By Matthew G. Lewis.) First edition. $400–$500. London, 1808. Half leather. Second edition. $100–$150.

TALES of Travels West of the Mississippi. Map. Illustrated. Boards and cloth. Boston, 1830. (By William J. Snelling.) First edition. $600–$800. Also, $425 (A, 1977).

TALLACK, William. *Friendly Sketches in America.* Cloth. London, 1861. First edition. $135.

TALLAHASSEE Girl (A). Cloth. Boston, 1882. (By Maurice Thompson.) First edition. $75–$100.

TALLAPOOSA Land, Mining and Manufacturing Co., Haralson County. Map. 32 pp., wrappers. Tallapoosa, Ga., 1887. $100–$125.

TALLENT, Annie D. *The Black Hills; or The Last Hunting Grounds of the Dakotahs.* 50 plates. Cloth, or half leather. St. Louis, 1899. First edition. Either binding: $125–$175.

TAMERLANE and Other Poems. By a Bostonian. Printed wrappers. Boston, 1827. (By Edgar Allan Poe.) First edition. $100,000 and up. Also, a copy described as "the finest known" brought $123,000 at auction in New York in 1974. (Note: Exact facsimiles exist which require careful examination to distinguish from the original.) London, 1884. Vellum. One of 100. $100–$150. San Francisco, 1923. 2 vols., boards (folio plus a smaller facsimile volume). One of 150. $200–$300.

TANNER, Henry S. *A Brief Description of the Canals and Railroads of the United States.* Maps. 31 pp., cloth. Philadelphia, 1834. First edition. $200–$250. Second edition, same place and date. 63 pp., 2 plates, map. $200. New York, 1840. Enlarged edition. (*A Description, etc.*) 3 maps. 2 diagrams, 272 pp. $250–$300. Also, $150 (A, 1978).

TANNER, Henry S. *A New American Atlas.* 16 double-page and 2 large folding maps. Folio, half leather. Philadelphia, 1823. First edition. $3,000–$4,000.

TARASCON, Louis A. *An Address to the Citizens of Philadelphia, on the Great Advantages Which Arise from the Trade of the Western Country, etc.* 13 pp., wrappers. Philadelphia, 1806. First edition. $750–$1,000.

TARASCON, Louis A., and others. *Petition . . . Praying the Opening of a Wagon Road from the River Missouri, North of the River Kansas, to the River Columbia.* 12 pp., sewed. Washington, 1824. $250.

TARBELL, Ida M. *The History of the Standard Oil Company.* Illustrated. 2 vols., cloth. New York, 1904. First edition. $150–$200.

TARCISSUS: The Boy Martyr of Rome, in the Diocletian Persecution, A.D. CCCIII. (By Baron Corvo [Frederick William Rolfe]). 4 leaves, printed gray wrappers. (Saffron Walden, Essex, England, 1880—actually 1881.) First edition. $3,000–$4,000. Also, $1,600 (A, 1980); $1,980 (A, 1979); $1,700 (A, 1977); $2,375 (A, 1971). Author's first book.

TARG, William (editor). *Bibliophile in the Nursery.* Illustrated. Cloth. Cleveland, (1957). First edition. In dust jacket. $75–$85.

TARG, William (editor). *Bouillabaise for Bibliophiles.* Cloth. Cleveland, (1955). First edition. In dust jacket. $35–$50.

TARG, William (editor). *Carrousel for Bibliophiles.* Red cloth. New York, 1947. First edition. In dust jacket. $50.

TARKINGTON, Booth. *Christmas This Year.* Manuscript facsimile and full-page plate. Wrappers. (Los Angeles, 1945.) First edition. One of 52. $40–$50.

TARKINGTON, Booth. *The Gentleman from Indiana.* Pictorial green cloth, top stained green. New York, 1899. First edition, first issue, with "eye" as last word in line 12, page 245; with line 16 reading "so pretty". $150–$200. Author's first published book.

TARKINGTON, Booth. *Lady Hamilton and Her Nelson.* Cloth. New York, 1945. First edition. One of 300 signed. In dust jacket. $50–$75.

TARKINGTON, Booth. *Monsieur Beaucaire.* Illustrated. Red cloth, gilt top. New York, 1900. First edition, first issue, with Gilliss Press seal on page after end of text exactly ½ inch in diameter. $100–$125.

TARKINGTON, Booth. *Penrod.* Illustrated by Gordon Grant. Cloth: first, blue mesh; second, blue ribbed cloth. Garden City, 1914. First edition, first state, with page viii so numbered and with "sence" for "sense" in third line from bottom of page 19. In dust jacket. $1,000–$1,500. Also, $950 (A, 1977).

TARKINGTON, Booth. *Penrod and Sam.* Illustrated by Worth Brehm. Pictorial light-green cloth. Garden City, 1916. First edition, first issue, with perfect type on pages 86, 141, 144, 149, and 210. In dust jacket. $250–$350.

TARKINGTON, Booth. *Penrod Jashber.* Illustrated. Cloth. Garden City, 1929. First edition. In dust jacket. $75–$100.

TARKINGTON, Booth. *Seventeen.* Cloth or leather. New York, (1916). First edition, first issue, with letters "B-Q" beneath copyright notice. In dust jacket. $150–$200.

TARKINGTON, Booth. *The Two Vanrevels.* Cloth. New York, 1902. First edition. In dust jacket. $200–$300. Another issue (later): White boards. One of 500 signed. $100–$125. Another issue: Brown boards (also with first edition notice). One of 500 signed. $75–$100.

TARRANT, Sgt. E. *The Wild Riders of the 1st Kentucky Cavalry.* Cloth. Louisville, (1894). $175–$200.

TATE, Allen. *Christ and the Unicorn.* Wrappers. West Branch, Iowa, 1966. Cummington Press. First edition. One of 125 (actually 100). $75.

TATE, Allen. *The Fathers.* Cloth. New York, 1938. First edition. In dust jacket. $75–$85.

TATE, Allen. *The Hovering Fly and Other Essays.* Illustrated. Boards. (Cummington, Mass.), 1949. First edition. One of 245. $250.

TATE, Allen. *Jefferson Davis, His Rise and Fall.* Cloth, paper labels. New York, 1929. First edition. In dust jacket. $50–$65.

TATE, Allen. *The Mediterranean and Other Poems.* Green wrappers. New York, 1936. First edition. One of 165 on Strathmore all-rag paper, signed. In tissue jacket. Boxed, $400–$500. Another issue: Cloth. Signed but not numbered. $200–$300. Another issue: One of 12 signed. $1,250.

TATE, Allen. *Mr. Pope and Other Poems.* Cloth, paper labels. New York, 1928. First edition. In dust jacket. $200–$300.

TATE, Allen. *On the Limits of Poetry.* Cloth. New York, 1948. First edition. In dust jacket. $50–$75.

TATE, Allen. *Poems, 1928–1931.* Cloth. New York, 1932. First edition. In acetate jacket. $75–$100.

TATE, Allen. *Reason in Madness.* Green cloth. New York, (1941). First edition. In dust jacket. $75.

TATE, Allen. *Stonewall Jackson, the Good Soldier: A Narrative.* Cloth, paper labels. New York, (1928). First edition. In dust jacket. $200–$250. Author's first separate book.

TATE, Allen. *Two Conceits for the Eye to Sing, If Possible.* Wrappers, paper label. (Cummington), 1950. First edition. One of 300. $75.

TATE, Allen. *The Winter Sea: A Book of Poems.* Decorated cloth. (Cummington), 1944. First edition. One of 300. In plain paper dust jacket. $100–$125.

TATE, Allen, and Wills, Ridley. *The Golden Mean and Other Poems*. Wrappers. (Nashville, 1923.) First edition. One of 200 numbered copies. $2,000–$3,000. Tate's first book.

TATE, Allen (translator). *The Vigil of Venus*. Boards. (Cummington, 1943.) First edition. One of 430. In tissue dust jacket. $100–$150.

TATE, James. *Cages*. Wrappers. Iowa City, 1966. First edition. One of 45. $100. Author's first book.

TATE, James. *Hottentot Ossuary*. Cloth. Cambridge, Mass., 1974. First edition. One of 50 signed. In dust jacket. $75.

TATTERSALL, C. E. C. *A History of British Carpets*. 116 plates (55 in color). Buckram. London, (1934). First edition. $150–$250.

TATTERSALL, George. *The Pictorial Gallery of English Race Horses*. 90 plates. Cloth. London, 1850. First edition. $1,000–$1,250.

TAUNTON, Thomas Henry. *Portraits of Celebrated Racehorses*. 463 plates. 4 vols., half morocco. London, 1887–88. First edition. $1,000–$1,250.

TAYLOR, Bayard. *Eldorado, or, Adventures in the Path of Empire, etc.* 8 lithograph views. 2 vols., cloth. New York, 1850. First edition with list of illustrations in Vol. 2 giving Mazatlan at page 8 instead of page 80. $600–$800. Second edition, with Mazatlan reference corrected. $500–$750. London, 1850. 2 vols., cloth. First English edition. $150–$200.

TAYLOR, Bayard. *The Story of Kennett*. Cloth. New York, 1866. First edition. $50–$75.

TAYLOR, Bayard. *Ximena and Other Poems*. Boards. Philadelphia, 1844, First edition. $250–$300. Author's first book.

TAYLOR, F. *A Sketch of the Military Bounty Tract of Illinois*. 12 pp., boards and calf. Philadelphia, 1839. First edition. $175–$200.

TAYLOR, F. W. *The Principles of Scientific Management*. 118 pp., green cloth. New York, 1911. First edition. $750–$1,000. Later, enlarged issue, red cloth. $200–$250.

TAYLOR, James W. *Northwest British America and Its Relations to the State of Minnesota*. Map. Cloth. St. Paul, 1860. First edition. $2,000–$2,500. Also, $1,800 (A, 1976).

TAYLOR, James W. *The Sioux War*. Wrappers. St. Paul, 1862. First edition. $1,000. St. Paul, 1863. Second edition. $500–$750.

TAYLOR, Jane and Ann. *Little Ann and Other Poems*. Illustrated in color by Kate Greenaway. Pictorial boards and cloth. (London, about 1883–84.) Published by Warne. $225–$300.

TAYLOR, John W. *Iowa, the "Great Hunting Ground" of the Indian; and the "Beautiful Land" of the White Man*. 16 pp., printed wrappers. Dubuque, 1860. First edition. $250–$300.

TAYLOR, Joseph Henry. *Beavers—Their Ways and Other Sketches*. 20 plates. Cloth. Washburn, N.D., 1904. First edition. $100–$125.

TAYLOR, Joseph Henry. *Sketches of Frontier and Indian Life*. 12 plates. Half leather and boards. Pottstown, Pa., 1889. First edition. $300–$400.

TAYLOR, Joseph Henry. *Twenty Years on the Trap Line*. 8 plates. 154 pp., boards and calf. Bismarck, N.D., 1891. First edition. $200–$225. Second edition, same place and date. 173 pp., maroon cloth. $100–$150.

TAYLOR, Lee M. *The Texan; A Tale of Texas*. Cloth. (Texas), 1908. With pages 171–174 removed (as in all copies noted). $50–$75.

TAYLOR, Oliver I. *Directory of Wheeling and Ohio County*. 2 plates, including tinted frontispiece. Half leather. Wheeling, W. Va., 1851. First edition. $150–$200.

TAYLOR, Peter. *A Long Fourth and Other Stories*. Cloth. New York, (1948). First edition. In dust jacket. $50–$75. Author's first book.

TAYLOR, Philip Meadows. *Confessions of a Thug*. 3 vols., boards. London, 1839. First edition. $400–$500. Author's first book.

TAYLOR, Thomas U. *Fifty Years on Forty Acres*. Illustrated. Cloth. Austin(?), 1938. First edition. $50–$100.

TAYLOR, Thomas U. *Jesse Chisholm*. Illustrated. Cloth. Bandera, Tex., (1939). First edition. $100–$150.

TAYLOR, Zachary. *Letters of Zachary Taylor from the Battle-Fields of the Mexican War*. Half cloth. Rochester, 1908. One of 300. $75–$100.

TEASDALE, Sara. *Love Songs*. Cloth. New York, 1917. First edition. In dust jacket. $100–$135.

TEASDALE, Sara. *Sonnets to Duse and Other Poems*. Boards, paper labels. Boston, 1907. First edition. $200–$250. Author's first book.

TEASDALE, Sara. *Stars To-Night*. Illustrated by Dorothy P. Lathrop. Cloth. New York, 1930. First edition. One of 150 signed. In dust jacket. $100–$135.

TEHAUNTEPEC Railway: Its Location Features and Advantages Under the LaSere Grant of 1869. Folding map. Cloth. New York, 1869. $100–$125.

TEMPLAR (The). To Which Is Added "Tales of the Passaic." By a Gentleman of New York. Half calf. Hackensack, N.J., 1822. First edition. $150–$250.

TEN Poets. Oblong, decorated wrappers. (Seattle, 1962.) First edition. One of 37 (of an edition of 537) specially bound and signed by the ten poets, including Theodore Roethke. $150–$175.

TEN Thousand a Year. 6 vols., boards, paper labels. Philadelphia, 1840–41. (By Samuel Warren.) First edition, first issue, without volume number on title page of Vol. 1. $800–$1,000. Second issue, with volume number on title page of first volume. $750–$800. Edinburgh, 1841. 3 vols., dark brown or plum-colored cloth. First English edition. $300–$400.

TENNYSON, Alfred, Lord. See *In Memoriam; Poems by Two Brothers*.

TENNYSON, Alfred, Lord. *Carmen Saeculare; An Ode in Honour of the Jubilee of Queen Victoria*. Wrappers. London, 1887 (actually about 1895). $300–$400. (A suspected Thomas J. Wise forgery.)

TENNYSON, Alfred, Lord. *Enoch Arden*. Green cloth. London, 1864. First edition, first issue, with ads dated August, 1864. $200–$250. Boston, 1864. Brown cloth. First American edition. $100–$150.

TENNYSON, Alfred, Lord. *Idylls of the King*. Green cloth. London, 1859. First edition, first issue, with verso of title page a blank. $200–$250. London, 1868. Illustrations after Gustave Doré. Folio, cloth. $150–$200. London, 1875. 20 mounted photographs by Julia Margaret Cameron. Half leather. Inscribed by Cameron. $1,320 (A, 1977). New York, 1952. Limited Editions Club. Illustrated by Lynd Ward. Boxed. $50–$60.

TENNYSON, Alfred, Lord. *Maud, and Other Poems*. Green cloth. London, 1855. First edition, with yellow end papers and 8 pages of ads dated July, 1855, and a last leaf advertising Tennyson's books. $100–$150. (Note: Contains first printing of "The

Charge of the Light Brigade.") London, 1893. Kelmscott Press. One of 500. $500–$750. Another issue: One of 5 on vellum. $3,500–$4,000. London, 1905. Essex House. One of 125 on vellum. $400.

TENNYSON, Alfred, Lord. *Poems*. Boards, white spine label. London, 1833 (actually 1832). First edition. $500–$600. London, 1842. 2 vols., boards. $500–$750. London, 1857. Cloth. First illustrated edition. $300–$400. London, 1889. Illustrated by Lear. Folio, half morocco. One of 100 proof copies on Japan paper, signed by Tennyson. $800–$1,000.

TENNYSON, Alfred, Lord. *Poems, Chiefly Lyrical*. Drab or pink boards, white spine label. London, 1830. First edition, first issue, with page 91 misnumbered 19. $600–$750. Author's first separate book of poems.

TENNYSON, Alfred, Lord. *Poems MDCCCXXX. MDCCCXXXIII*. Printed wrappers. Toronto (London), 1862. Pirated edition. $200–$400.

TENNYSON, Alfred, Lord. *The Sailor Boy*. Cream-colored printed wrappers. London, 1861. First edition. $200–$250. (A Wise forgery.)

TENNYSON, Alfred, Lord. *Seven Poems and Two Translations*. Vellum. London, 1902. Doves Press. One of 325. $300–$400. Another issue: One of 25 on vellum. Boxed. $1,500–$2,000.

TENNYSON, Alfred, Lord. *Tiresias and Other Poems*. Cloth. London, 1885. First edition. $75–$150. Northampton, Mass., (1970). Engraved title page. 5 signed etchings, one in color, by Leonard Baskin. One of 50 signed. Boxed. $600–$750.

TENNYSON, Charles. *Sonnets and Fugitive Pieces*. Boards, or cloth. Cambridge, 1830. First edition. $200–$300.

TENNYSON, Frederick. *Days and Hours*. Cloth. London, 1854. First edition. $100–$125. Author's first book.

TENNYSON, Frederick. *Poems of the Day and Year*. Frontispiece portrait, woodcut title page. Red cloth. London, 1895. First edition. $75–$85.

TERHUNE, Albert Payson. *Caleb Conover, Railroader*. Cloth. New York, 1907. First edition. In dust jacket. $75–$100.

TERHUNE, Albert Payson. *Lad of Sunnybank*. Cloth. New York, 1929. First edition. In dust jacket. $75–$85.

TERRITORY of Wyoming (The); Its History, Soil, Climate, Resources, etc. 84 pp., printed wrappers. Laramie City, Wyoming Territory, 1874. (By J. K. Jeffrey.) First edition. $500–$750.

TEXAS Almanac (The). Wrappers. Galveston, 1857. (First of this series.) $1,000. Other issues: 1859, $750; 1860, $750; 1861, $750; 1867, $350; 1868, $300; 1870, $250.

TEXAS in 1840, or The Emigrant's Guide to the New Republic. Colored frontispiece. Cloth. New York, 1840. (By A. B. Lawrence and C. J. Stille.) First edition. $500–$600.

TEXAS, the Home for the Emigrant from Everywhere. Folding map. 43 pp., printed wrappers. Houston, 1875. (By J. B. Robertson.) First edition. $200–$300. St. Louis, 1876. $100–$150.

THACHER, J. B. *Christopher Columbus*. Plates. 3 vols., half vellum. New York, 1903–04. $300–$350. Another issue: 3 vols. in 6, plus portfolio of facsimiles of published accounts of the voyages of Columbus. $400–$500.

THACHER, James. *Observations on Hydrophobia*. Hand-colored plate. Full leather. Plymouth, Mass., 1812. First edition. $300–$350.

THACKERAY, William Makepeace. See Marvy, Louis; Pendennis, Arthur; Titmarsh,

M. A.; Wagstaff, Theophile. Also see *The Loving Ballad of Lord Bateman; The History of Henry Esmond.*

THACKERAY, William Makepeace. *The Adventures of Philip on His Way Through the World.* 3 vols., brown cloth. London, 1862. First edition. $500.

THACKERAY, William Makepeace. *The Book of Snobs.* Illustrated by the author. Green pictorial wrappers. London, 1848. First edition, first issue, with page 126 misnumbered 124. $150–$200. New York, 1852. Cloth. First American edition. $75–$100.

THACKERAY, William Makepeace. *The English Humourists of the Eighteenth Century.* Blue marbled cloth. London, 1853. First edition, first or second issues. $100–$150. New York, 1853. First American edition. $50–$75.

THACKERAY, William Makepeace. *The Four Georges.* Illustrated. Cloth. New York, 1860. First edition. $150–$200. London, 1861. First English edition, first issue, with November ads and with title page reading "Sketches of Manners, Morals, Court, and Town Life." $125–$175.

THACKERAY, William Makepeace. *The Great Hoggarty Diamond.* Vignette on title page. Buff wrappers. New York, (1848). First edition, first issue, with "82 Cliff Street" on title page (later "306 Pearl Street"). $10,000, or more. Also, $8,000 (A, 1977). London, 1849. (Retitled *The History of Samuel Titmarsh and the Great Hoggarty Diamond.*) Pictorial glazed white wrappers. First English edition. $5,000 and up.

THACKERAY, William Makepeace. *The History of Pendennis.* 46 full-page plates and other illustrations by the author. 24 parts in 23, printed yellow wrappers. London, 1848–50. First edition. $750–$1,000. London, 1849–50. 2 vols., cloth. First book edition. $200–$300. New York, 1850. Illustrated. 2 vols., black cloth. First American edition. $150–$200.

THACKERAY, William Makepeace. *The Orphan of Pimlico, and Other Sketches.* Illustrated by Thackeray. Boards. London, 1876. First edition. $500–$750. (Note: There is much hairsplitting over the various states of the plates.)

THACKERAY, William Makepeace. *Vanity Fair: A Novel Without a Hero.* Illustrated by the author. 20 parts in 19, yellow pictorial wrappers. London, 1847–48. First edition, first issue, with the heading in rustic type on page 1, woodcut of the Marquis of Steyne on page 336 (later omitted), and the reading "Mr. Pitt" on page 453 (later "Sir Pitt"). $7,000 (A, 1981). (As with most nineteenth century books issued in parts, there are complicated bibliographical "points" in identifying issues and states of the edition. Perfect sets, with all "correct" points and required advertisements, are extremely rare, and most sets offered for sale are in one way or other defective or in mixed states. Thus the price range is wide and scarcely predictable.) London, 1848. Cloth. First book edition, first issue, with engraved title page date of 1849. $800–$1,500. New York, 1848. Cloth. First American edition. $400–$500. New York, 1931. Limited Editions Club. 2 vols., boards. Boxed. $80–$100.

THACKERAY, William Makepeace. *The Virginians: A Tale of the Last Century.* 24 parts, printed yellow wrappers. London, 1857–59. First edition. $750–$1,000 and up. (See the note concerning "points" in the *Vanity Fair* entry above.) London, 1858–59. 2 vols., cloth. First book edition. $250–$300.

THAXTER, Celia. *An Island Garden.* Illustrated by Childe Hassam. Cloth. Boston, 1894. First edition. $300–$400. London, 1894. Cloth. First English edition. $100–$150. Boston, 1895. $200.

THAXTER, Celia. *Poems.* Brown cloth. New York, 1872. First edition. $100–$125. Author's first book.

THAYER, William M. *The Pioneer Boy, and How He Became President.* Illustrated. Cloth. Boston, 1863. First edition. $100–$125.

THEOCRITUS. *The Idylls.* Translated by Andrew Lang. 20 color plates after drawings by W. Russell Flint. 2 vols., vellum. London, 1922. One of 500. $500–$600. Another issue: Boards and cloth. One of 500. In dust jackets. $400–$500. London, (1929). Famfrolico Press. (*Complete Poems*.) Translated by Jack Lindsay. Illustrated by Lionel Ellis. $200–$250.

THERION, The Master. *The Book of Thoth*. 8 color plates. 78 other illustrations. Half morocco. (London), 1944. (By Aleister Crowley.) First edition. One of 200 signed. $400–$500.

THEROUX, Paul. *Waldo*. Cloth. Boston, 1967. First edition. In dust jacket. $50–$75. Author's first book.

THIS Is the Preachment on Going to Church. Vellum. East Aurora, N.Y., 1896. (By George Bernard Shaw.) First edition. One of 26 on Japan paper. $150–$200. Another issue: Half cloth. $50. (Note: These are pirated items issued by Elbert Hubbard.)

THISSELL, G. W. *Crossing the Plains in '49*. 11 plates. Cloth. Oakland, 1903. First edition. $125–$175.

THOM, Adam. *A Charge Delivered to the Grand Jury of Assiniboia, 20th February, 1845*. 44 pp., printed wrappers. London, 1848. $150–$300.

THOM, Adam. *The Claims to the Oregon Territory Considered*. Printed self-wrappers. London, 1844. First edition. $175–$200.

THOMAS, D. M. *Two Voices*. Wrappers. London, 1968. First edition. One of 50 signed. In tissue jacket. $250–$300. Trade edition: Issued without jacket. $75–$100.

THOMAS, David. *Travels Through the Western Country in the Summer of 1816*. Folding map. Errata slip. Boards or cloth. Auburn, N.Y., 1819. First edition. $300–$400.

THOMAS, Dylan. *Adventures in the Skin Trade*. Black cloth. London, (1955). First separate edition, first issue, with "First published in Great Britain 1955" on verso of title page. In dust jacket. $125–$150.

THOMAS, Dylan. *Adventures in the Skin Trade and Other Stories*. Gray cloth. (New York or Norfolk, Conn., 1955.) New Directions. First edition. In dust jacket. $100–$125.

THOMAS, Dylan. *Caseg Broadsheet No. 5. From in Memory of Ann Jones*. (Caption title.) One sheet, quarto, printed one side only. Llanllechid (Llandyssul, South Wales), (1942). First edition. One of 500. $250–$350.

THOMAS, Dylan. *A Child's Christmas in Wales*. Pale-gray printed boards. Norfolk, (1954). First (separate) edition. (A Christmas token of New Directions, Thomas' American publisher, 1955.) In dust jacket. $100–$150. (New York, 1969.) Illustrated by Fritz Eichenberg. Oblong folio, half calf and linen. With separate stiff portfolio and 5 wood engravings signed by the artist. One of 100. $350–$400.

THOMAS, Dylan. *Collected Poems 1934–1952*. Portrait. Dark-blue cloth. London, (1952). First English edition, "ordinary" issue, with "First published 1952" on verso of title page. In dust jacket. $150–$250. Proof copy, same place and date, pale-green wrappers printed in black, lacking dedication and without the poem "Paper and Sticks." 65 copies printed. $300–$400. Limited issue, same place and date: Full dark-blue morocco. One of 65 signed. $1,250–$1,500. Also, $850 (A, 1977). London, 1954. Light-brown canvas. Reader's Union edition. In dust jacket. $50. (Later issues are in finer brown cloth.)

THOMAS, Dylan. *The Collected Poems of Dylan Thomas*. Blue cloth. (New York, 1953.) New Directions. First American edition (of *Collected Poems 1934–1952*), first issue, with "daughters" misprinted "daughers" in last line on page 199. In dust jacket. $100–$150. (Note: Some first edition copies, identifiable as indicated, have dust jackets imprinted "second printing," because, as the publishers have stated in a letter to me, "we simply ran out of dust jackets.")

THOMAS, Dylan. *Conversation About Christmas.* Wrappers (6 leaves stapled, including printed covers). (New York), 1954. First separate edition. $100–$125.

THOMAS, Dylan. *Deaths and Entrances.* Orange cloth. London, (1946). First edition, with "First published 1946" on verso of title page. In dust jacket. $125–$250.

THOMAS, Dylan. *The Doctor and the Devils.* Red cloth. London, (1953). First published edition, with "First published 1953" on verso of title page. $50–$60. New Directions imprint: (New York, or Norfolk, 1953.) Red cloth. First American edition, first issue, identical with English edition except for substitution of New Directions imprint for Dent, etc. In dust jacket. $75–$100. Second issue, gray cloth, with "Second printing" on dust jacket. $20–$30. Proof copies (unpublished): London, (1947). First edition, first issue, in cork-colored wrappers, with date on verso of title page (35 printed). $450. Signed and/or inscribed copies, $1,000–$1,500 and up. Also, with revisions in Thomas' hand, $960 (A, 1969). London, (1953). Green wrappers (97 printed). Second issue of the proofs. $300 and up.

THOMAS, Dylan. *18 Poems.* Black cloth. London, (1934). First edition, first issue, with flat spine and lacking leaf between half title and title page. In dust jacket. $600–$850. Same imprint, second issue, with rounded back and with leaf between half title and title (published 1936). In dust jacket. $300–$400. Author's first book. London, (about 1940). Second (?) edition (unrecorded by J. Alexander Rolph, *Dylan Thomas: A Bibliography,* but appearing in two binding variants in the Feinberg sale in 1968). Blue or green boards and cloth. In dust jacket. $75–$100. London, (about 1942). Fortune Press imprint. Red buckram. Rolph's second edition. $75–$100. Later issue, green boards and cloth: In dust jacket. $50–$75.

THOMAS, Dylan. *The Hand.* Colored drawing by Frederic Prokosch as frontispiece. Wrappers. Venice, 1939. One of 3 (of 10) on Arches paper. $1,500–$2,000.

THOMAS, Dylan. *In Country Sleep and Other Poems.* Green boards. (New York or Norfolk, 1952.) New Directions. First edition. With picture of Thomas attached to title page. In dust jacket. $100–$125. Limited edition, same imprint: Buff-gray cloth. One of 100 signed. In dust jacket? Boxed. $750–$1,000.

THOMAS, Dylan. *The Map of Love: Verse and Prose.* Portrait frontispiece by Augustus John. Fine-grained mauve cloth, gilt, top edges purple. London, (1939). First edition, first issue (mauve cloth). In dust jacket. $200–$250. Second issue, plum-colored cloth (published 1947). Third issue, purple cloth (published 1948). Fourth issue, purple cloth, unstained top edges. (The second and third issues were 250 copies each as against 1,000 for the first issue and 500 for the fourth, according to Rolph.)

THOMAS, Dylan. *New Poems.* 32 pp., mauve boards, or mauve wrappers. Norfolk, (1943). First edition. Boards: In dust jacket, $150–$200. Wrappers: $150–$200. (Note: This actually is a second printing, the entire first printing having been destroyed, according to Rolph.)

THOMAS, Dylan. *Portrait of the Artist as a Young Dog.* Cloth. London, (1940). First edition, first issue, with "First published 1940" on verso of title page. In dust jacket. $150–$200. Proof copy, printed wrappers. $300–$400. Also, $225 (A, 1968). Norfolk, (1940). Brick-red cloth. First American edition. In dust jacket. $125–$150. Norfolk, (1950). Yellow cloth. Second printing (so stated). $35. London, 1948. Guild Books. Wrappers. First printing. $25–$35.

THOMAS, Dylan. *A Prospect of the Sea.* Blue cloth. London, (1955). First edition, with "First published July, 1955" on verso of title page. In dust jacket. $65–$75. Proof copy (so imprinted) in wrappers. $100–$150. Second edition, same date. In dust jacket. $25–$35.

THOMAS, Dylan. *Quite Early One Morning: Broadcasts.* Portrait frontispiece. Blue cloth. London, (1954). First edition, first issue, with full stop after "sailors" at end of verse 5 on pages 3 and 11. In dust jacket. $85–$125. New Directions imprint: (New York, 1954). Gray cloth. First American edition, first issue, without note of later impression on dust jacket. $35–$50.

THOMAS, Dylan. *Selected Writings of Dylan Thomas.* Pinkish mauve or green cloth.

(Norfolk, 1946.) First edition, without printing number on front flap of dust jacket. In dust jacket. $75–$100.

THOMAS, Dylan. *Twenty-five Poems*. Gray boards. London, (1936). First edition. One of 730. In dust jacket. $300–$400. Also, proof copy containing only 23 poems, $500 (A, 1976).

THOMAS, Dylan. *Twenty-six Poems*. Decorated boards, canvas spine, paper label. (New York or Norfolk, 1950.) First edition. New Directions. One of 87 signed. Boxed. $1,250—$1,500. There were also 10 copies printed on Japan vellum (2 for Thomas, the rest for New Directions, his American publisher); no copies noted for sale. London, (1950). First English edition, identical (save for Dent imprint) with the American edition, which preceded it by three months. One of 50 signed, for the English market. Boxed. $1,000 and up.

THOMAS, Dylan. *Under Milk Wood*. Light-brown cloth. London, (1954). First edition, with "First published 1954" on verso of title page. In dust jacket. $150–$225. "Advance proof copy," wrappers. $800–$1,000. Also, $400 (A, 1977). New Directions imprint: (New York, 1954.) Mulberry-brown cloth. First American edition. In dust jacket. $75–$100.

THOMAS, Dylan. *The World I Breathe*. Light-brown buckram. Norfolk, (1939). First edition, first issue, with single star on either side of Thomas' name on title page and on spine (later copies having five stars on either side). In dust jacket. $750–$1,000.

THOMAS, Edward. *Chosen Essays*. Wood engravings. Blue morocco. Newtown, Wales, 1926. Gregynog Press. One of 33 thus bound, (from a limited edition of 350.) $600–$750. Another issue: Buckram. One of 317. $250.

THOMAS, Edward. *Selected Poems*. Buckram. Newtown, Wales, 1927. Gregynog Press. One of 275 on vellum. $250–$300.

THOMAS, Henry W. *History of the Doles-Cook Brigade, Army of Northern Virginia*. Cloth. Atlanta, 1903. First edition. $100–$150.

THOMAS, Hugh. *The World's Game*. Cloth. London, 1957. First edition. $50–$60. Author's first book.

THOMAS, Isaiah. *The History of Printing in America*. 2 plates, 3 facsimiles. 2 vols., calf. Worcester, Mass., 1810. First edition. $500–$750. Albany, 1874. 2 vols., cloth. Second edition. $200–$250. Barre, Mass., 1972. Imprint Society. Edited by Marcus A. McCorison. One of 1,950 signed by the editor, with a leaf from the first edition of 1810. $200–$225.

THOMAS, Jerry. *The Bar-Tender's Guide*. Cloth. New York, 1862. First edition. $100–$150.

THOMAS, Joseph B. *Hounds and Hunting Through the Ages*. Cloth. New York, 1928. First edition. Derrydale Press. One of 750. $300–$350. New York, 1929. Second edition. One of 250. $100–$150.

THOMAS, Lowell. *The First World Flight*. Illustrated. Half vellum. Boston, 1925. First edition. One of 575 signed by Thomas and the aviators. $200–$300.

THOMAS, P. J. *Founding of the Missions*. Map, plates. Cloth. San Francisco, 1877. First edition. $150–$200.

THOMAS Wolfe Memorial (The). Illustrated. Decorated wrappers. Asheville, (1949). First edition. $40–$50. (Issued to raise funds for a Thomas Wolfe Memorial Arts Center.)

THOMPSON, A. C. *Preludes*. Illustrated. Green cloth. London, 1875. (By Alice Meynell.) First edition, first issue, with brown end papers. $100. Author's first book (republished later under the name Alice Meynell as *Poems*, which see under her name).

THOMPSON, Capt. B. F. *History of the 112th Regiment of Illinois Volunteer Infantry, 1862–1865.* Cloth. Toulon, Ill., 1885. First edition. $100–$150.

THOMPSON, Daniel Pierce. See *The Adventures of Timothy Peacock, Esquire; The Green Mountain Boys.*

THOMPSON, Daniel Pierce. *May Martin.* Cloth. Montpelier, Vt., 1835. First edition. $400–$600. Also, $280. (A, 1979).

THOMPSON, Daniel Pierce (editor). *The Laws of Vermont, 1824–34, Inclusive.* Calf. Montpelier, 1835. First edition. $300–$400. Author's first book.

THOMPSON, David. *David Thompson's Narrative of His Explorations in Western America: 1784–1812.* Edited by J. B. Tyrell. 23 maps and plates. Cloth. Toronto, 1916. Champlain Society. First edition. One of 550. $600–$750. Also, $240 (A, 1979).

THOMPSON, David. *History of the Late War, Between Great Britain and the U.S.A.* Boards or leather. Niagara, U. C. (Upper Canada), 1832. First edition. $250–$300.

THOMPSON, Edwin P. *History of the First Kentucky Brigade.* 6 plates. Cloth. Cincinnati, 1868. First edition. $175–$200.

THOMPSON, Francis. *Poems.* Decorated boards. London, 1893. First edition. With ads at back dated October. One of 500. $100–$125. Another issue: Vellum. One of 12 signed. $400–$500.

THOMPSON, Francis. *Sister-Songs: An Offering to Two Sisters.* Green, gray, or brown cloth. London, 1895. First edition, with ads at back dated 1895. (First published edition of *Songs Wing-to-Wing.*) $200–$250.

THOMPSON, Francis. *Songs Wing-to-Wing: An Offering to Two Sisters.* (Cover title.) Wrappers. London, (1895). First edition, first issue (of *Sister-Songs*), with no title page and no dedication leaf. $400–$500.

THOMPSON, Hunter S. *Fear and Loathing in Las Vegas.* Illustrated. Cloth. New York, (1971). First edition. In dust jacket. $75.

THOMPSON, Hunter S. *Hell's Angels.* Cloth. New York, (1967). First edition. In dust jacket. $50–$75.

THOMPSON, Kay. *Eloise.* Drawings by Hilary Knight. Boards. New York, 1955. First edition. In dust jacket. $75–$100.

THOMPSON, Maurice. See *A Tallahassee Girl.*

THOMPSON, Maurice. *Alice of Old Vincennes.* Green cloth, pictorial label on front cover. Indianapolis, (1900). First edition, first issue, with running headline in bold-face capital letters and no page of "Acknowledgment" at end of text. In dust jacket. $125–$200. Lacking jacket, $50–$75. Advance publisher's presentation copy, with printed label so stating, blue-gray cloth, pictorial label. In dust jacket. $150–$250.

THOMPSON, Maurice. *Hoosier Mosaics.* Cloth. New York, 1875. First edition. $100–$125. Author's first book.

THOMPSON, Maurice. *The Story of Louisiana.* Cloth. Boston, (1888). First edition. $50–$75.

THOMPSON, Maurice. *The Witchery of Archery.* Cloth. New York, 1878. First edition. $150–$200.

THOMPSON, R. A. *Central Sonoma: A Brief Description of the Township and Town of Santa Rosa, Sonoma County, California.* Printed wrappers. Santa Rosa, Calif., 1884. First edition. $200–$300.

THOMPSON, R. A. *Conquest of California.* Portrait, 3 plates. 33 pp., wrappers. Santa Rosa, 1896. First edition. $85–$100.

THOMPSON, R. A. *Historical and Descriptive Sketch of Sonoma County, California.* Map. Printed wrappers. Philadelphia, 1877. First edition. $150–$250.

THOMPSON, R. A. *The Russian Settlement in California Known as Fort Ross.* 2 plates, other illustrations. 34 pp., wrappers. Santa Rosa, 1896. First edition. $200–$250.

THOMPSON, Ruth Plumly. *The Gnome King of Oz.* Illustrated. Green cloth. Chicago, (1927). First edition. In dust jacket. $400–$500. Also, $300 (A, 1978).

THOMPSON, Ruth Plumly. *Handy Mandy in Oz.* Illustrated. Cloth. Chicago, (1937). First edition. $120 (A, 1978).

THOMPSON, Ruth Plumly. *Pirates in Oz.* Cloth. Chicago, (1931). First edition. In dust jacket. $150 (A, 1978).

THOMPSON, Ruth Plumly. *The Wishing Horse of Oz.* Cloth. Chicago, (1935). First edition. With hinges cracked. $180 (A, 1978).

THOMSON, James [1700–48]. *The Seasons.* Engravings by F. Bartolozzi and P. W. Tomkins. Contemporary calf. London, 1807. $200.

THOMSON, James [1834–82]. *The City of Dreadful Night and Other Poems.* Cloth. London, 1880. First edition. One of 40 on large paper. $350–$400. Ordinary issue: $125. Portland, Me., 1892. Mosher Press. Leather. One of 400. $125–$150.

THOMSON, James [1834–82]. *Vane's Story, Weddah, etc.* Cloth. London, 1881. First edition. $100–$125.

THOREAU, Henry David. *Autumn: From the Journal of Henry D. Thoreau.* Cloth. Boston, 1892. First edition. $150–$200.

THOREAU, Henry David. *Cape Cod.* Purple cloth. Boston, 1865 (actually 1864). First edition, with no pagination on title page and leaf following. $500–$600. Boston, 1896. Colored illustrations by Amelia M. Watson. 2 vols., decorated cloth. $200–$250.

THOREAU, Henry David. *Early Spring in Massachusetts: From the Journal of Henry D. Thoreau.* Boston, 1881. First edition. $100–$150.

THOREAU, Henry David. *Excursions.* Engraved portrait. Green cloth. Boston, 1863. First edition. $500–$600. Also, worn and stained, $100 (A, 1980).

THOREAU, Henry David. *The First and Last Journeys of Thoreau.* Edited by Franklin B. Sanborn. Engraved limitation plate in Vol. 1, engraved portrait of Thoreau in Vol. 2, manuscript facsimiles. 2 vols., brown boards and parchment. Boston, 1905. First edition. One of 10 on vellum. In slipcase. $500–$600. Ordinary copies: One of 479. $50.

THOREAU, Henry David. *Letters to Various Persons.* Cloth. Boston, 1865. First edition. $150–$175.

THOREAU, Henry David. *The Maine Woods.* Green cloth, chocolate end papers. Boston, 1864. First edition, first issue, with one-leaf ad of *Atlantic Monthly* at end reading "The Thirteenth Volume." $400–$500.

THOREAU, Henry David. *Summer: From the Journal of Henry D. Thoreau.* Double-page frontispiece map. Green cloth. Boston, 1884. First edition. $100–$125.

THOREAU, Henry David. *Walden or, Life in the Woods.* Cloth. Boston, 1854. First edition, with "post" for "port" on page 24, "single spruce" for "double spruce" on page 137, and "white spruce" for "black spruce" on page 217. (Tipped-in ads range from April to December; April ads presumably are earliest.) With April ads: $1,500–$2,000. Also (ads not indicated), inscribed copy, $3,700 (A, 1980); April ads, worn, $650 (A, 1980). With May ads: $1,250–$1,500. Later ads, 1854: $500 and up. Boston, 1909. 2 vols., half vellum. One of 483. $400–$600. Chicago, 1930. Lakeside Press. Illustrated. Half buckram. One of 1,000. $150–$200. New York, 1936. Limited Editions Club. Boards. Boxed. $350–$400.

THOREAU, Henry David. *A Week on the Concord and Merrimack Rivers*. Brown cloth, yellow end papers. Boston, 1849. First edition, with 3 lines dropped at bottom of page 396—usually written in with pencil by Thoreau. $2,500–$3,000. Also, binding badly frayed, $1,400 (A, 1977). (Note: The 3 lines are missing in all copies issued.) Author's first book.

THOREAU, Henry David. *Winter: From the Journal of Henry D. Thoreau*. Cloth. Boston, 1888 (actually 1887). First edition. $100–$150.

THOREAU, Henry David. *A Yankee in Canada, with Anti-Slavery and Reform Papers*. Cloth. Boston, 1866. First edition. $500–$600. (Contains "Civil Disobedience.")

THORNTON, Alfred. See *The Adventures of a Post Captain*.

THORNTON, J. Quinn. *Oregon and California in 1848*. Folding map. 2 vols., cloth. New York, 1849. First edition. $350–$400. Rebound in half leather, $350. New York, 1855. 2 vols., cloth. $150–$200.

THORNTON, Richard (editor). *Recognition of Robert Frost: Twenty-Fifth Anniversary*. Cloth. New York, (1937). First edition. In dust jacket. $150. (Includes tributes by Pound and other poets.)

THORNTON, Robert John. *The Temple of Flora*. 25 portraits, 31 hand-colored plates. Half leather. London, 1810. $10,000–$15,000. London, 1812. $3,000–$3,500.

THORP, N. Howard (Jack). *Songs of the Cowboys*. 50 pp., pictorial wrappers. Estancia, N.M., (1908). First edition. $2,000–$2,500.

THOUGHTS on the Destiny of Man. 96 pp., wrappers. (Harmony, Ind.), 1824. (By Father George Rapp.) First edition. $600–$750.

THOUGHTS on the Proposed Annexation of Texas to the United States. 55 pp., wrappers. New York, 1844. (By Theodore Sedgwick.) First edition. $100–$150.

THOUSAND Miles in a Canoe from Denver to Leavenworth (A). Wrappers. Bushnell, Neb., 1880. (By W. A. Spencer.) First edition. $300–$350.

THRALL, The Rev. Homer S. *A Pictorial History of Texas*. Folding map. Leather, or cloth. St. Louis, 1878. First edition. $250–$300. St. Louis, 1879. Cloth. Fourth edition. $150–$200.

THRALL, The Rev. S. C. *The President's Death: A Sermon Delivered at Christ Church*. 12 pp., wrappers. New Orleans, 1865. First edition. $125–$150.

THREE Monographs. 56 pp., light-brown printed wrappers. Naples, Italy, 1906. (By Norman Douglas.) First edition. One of 250. $100–$150.

THUCYDIDES. *The History of the Peloponnesian War*. Translated by Benjamin Jowett. Folio, white pigskin. London, 1930. Ashendene Press. One of 260 printed on paper. $2,000–$2,500. Another issue: One of 20 on vellum. $10,000–$12,000.

THURBER, James. *The Last Flower: A Parable in Pictures*. Oblong, boards. New York, 1939. First edition. In dust jacket. $75–$100.

THURBER, James. *The Owl in the Attic and Other Perplexities*. Illustrated. Introduction by E. B. White. Yellow cloth. New York, 1931. First edition. In dust jacket. $100–$175.

THURBER, James. *The Thirteen Clocks*. Illustrated in color by Marc Simont. Boards and cloth. New York, (1950). First edition, first printing, Simont credit line on title page in black (later red). $100–$150. (Note: The illustrator's first name, Marc, is misspelled "Mark.")

THURBER, James, and White, E. B. *Is Sex Necessary? Or Why You Feel the Way You Do*. Illustrated. Green boards, black cloth spine. New York, 1929. First edition. In dust jacket. $100–$150. Thurber's first book.

THURMAN, Wallace. *The Blacker the Berry: A Novel of Negro Life*. Brown cloth. New York, 1929. First edition. In dust jacket. $100–$150.

THWAITES, Reuben Gold. *Historic Waterways: Six Hundred Miles of Canoeing Down the Rock, Fox, and Wisconsin Rivers*. Cloth. Chicago, 1888. First edition. $150. Author's first book.

TIERNEY, Luke. *History of the Gold Discoveries on the South Platte River*. 27 pp., wrappers. Pacific City, Iowa, 1859. First edition. $15,000–$20,000. Without covers, $12,500 in 1981 catalogue of John Howell—Books, San Francisco.

TILLSON, Christina Holmes. *Reminiscences of Early Life in Illinois by Our Mother*. 4 plates. Cloth. (Amherst, Mass., about 1872.) First edition. $750–$1,000.

TIMLIN, William M. *The Ship That Sailed to Mars*. 48 mounted color plates. Boards. London, 1923. First edition. In dust jacket. $1,000–$1,500. Rebound copy, $1,000. New York, (1923). Boards. In dust jacket. $1,200.

TIMMONS, Wilbert H. *Morelos of Mexico: Priest, Soldier, Statesman*. Illustrated by José Cisneros. Cloth. El Paso, 1963. "Pesos" edition. One of 500 signed. In dust jacket. Boxed. $75–$100.

TIMOLEON. 70 pp., printed buff wrappers. New York, 1891. (By Herman Melville.) Caxton Press. First edition. One of 25. Copies with Melville's signature pasted in, $510 (A, 1944); $375 (A, 1945). (No recent sales noted.)

TIMOTHY Crump's Ward; or, The New Year's Loan and What Came of It. Purple cloth, or wrappers. Boston, 1866. (By Horatio Alger, Jr.) First edition. Published by Loring. Either binding: $2,500–$3,000.

TIPTON, R. B. *Directory of Marshalltown*. Printed boards. Marshalltown, Iowa, 1884. $100–$125.

TITMARSH, M. A. [Michael Angelo] (editor). *Comic Tales and Sketches*. 12 tinted plates. 2 vols., black or brown cloth. London, 1841. (By William Makepeace Thackeray.) First edition. $300–$400.

TITMARSH, M. A. *Doctor Birch and His Young Friends*. 16 color plates by the author. Wrappers. London, 1849. (By William Makepeace Thackeray.) First edition. $200–$300.

TITMARSH, M. A. *The Irish Sketch-Book*. Wood engravings. 2 vols., green cloth. London, 1843. (By William Makepeace Thackeray.) First edition. $600–$800. First book of which Thackeray acknowledged authorship.

TITMARSH, M. A. *Jeames's Diary; or, Sudden Riches*. Woodcuts. Wrappers. New York, 1846. (By William Makepeace Thackeray.) First edition. $2,000 and up. Very rare, with only 3 copies known to bibliographers.

TITMARSH, M. A. *The Kickleburys on the Rhine*. 15 illustrations in color by the author. Wrappers. London, 1851. (By William Makepeace Thackeray.) First edition. $400–$500.

TITMARSH, M. A. *"Our Street."* 16 color plates. Wrappers. London, 1848. (By William Makepeace Thackeray.) First edition. $400–$500. Another issue: Boards, plates uncolored. $200–$300.

TITMARSH, M. A. *The Second Funeral of Napoleon: In Three Letters to Miss Smith, of London, and the Chronicle of the Drum*. Frontispiece, 3 plates, picture of Napoleon on front cover. Wrappers. London, 1841. (By William Makepeace Thackeray.) First edition, first issue, with six lines of shading on the cheek of Napoleon on front cover. $500 and up. (Note: A copy of this rarity was sold in 1914 for $825. The so-called "second issue" apparently is a reprint, done about 1880, according to De Ricci, and with the illustrations lithographed. Its value is nominal.)

TITTSWORTH, W. G. *Outskirt Episodes*. Portrait (tipped to title page). Red cloth. (Avoca, Iowa, 1927.) First edition. In dust jacket. $150–$200.

TODD, Frederick P. *Soldiers of the American Army, 1775–1941.* Frontispiece and 24 hand-colored plates by Fritz Kredel. Folio, morocco. New York, 1941. First edition. One of 24 signed. $500.

TODD, The Rev. John. *The Lost Sister of Wyoming.* Frontispiece. Cloth. Northampton, Mass., 1842. First edition. $50–$75.

TODD, Ruthven. *Over the Mountain.* Cloth. London, 1939. First edition. In dust jacket. $50–$75.

TODHUNTER, John. *A Sicilian Idyll.* Illustrated by Walter Crane. Vellum and boards. London, 1890. One of 50 signed. $100–$150.

TOKLAS, Alice B. *The Autobiography of Alice B. Toklas.* Blue cloth. New York, (1933). (By Gertrude Stein.) First edition, published by Harcourt, Brace. In dust jacket. $250–$350. (Note: Gertrude Stein was not identified on title pages as the author until the paperback editions of the 1950's and 1960's. Also, it should be noted that the Literary Guild edition of 1933, although proclaiming itself a "first edition," is not such.)

TOLKIEN, J. R. R. *The Adventures of Tom Bombadil.* Pictorial boards. London, (1962). First edition. In dust jacket. $60. Boston, 1963. Boards. First American edition. In dust jacket. $50.

TOLKIEN, J. R. R. *The Devil's Coach-Horses.* Wrappers. London, (about 1925). First edition. $125–$150.

TOLKIEN, J. R. R. *The Fellowship of the Ring.* Cloth. London, 1953. First edition. In dust jacket. $850–$1,000. (First volume in the *Lord of the Rings* sequence.) London, (1966). Cloth. Second English edition, revised, first printing. In dust jacket. $50–$75.

TOLKIEN, J. R. R. *Farmer Giles of Ham.* Illustrated, including 2 color plates. Boards. London, 1949. First edition. In dust jacket. $150–$250. Boston, 1950. Cloth. First American edition. In dust jacket. $100–$125.

TOLKIEN, J. R. R. *The Hobbit.* Illustrated by the author. Green cloth. London, (1937). First edition. In dust jacket. $2,000–$2,500. Boston, 1938. Cloth. First American edition. In dust jacket. $250–$350. Toronto, 1976. Wrappers. First Canadian edition. $100.

TOLKIEN, J. R. R. *The Lord of the Rings.* (3 vols., cloth: *The Fellowship of the Ring,* 1953; *The Two Towers,* 1954; *The Return of the King,* 1955.) First editions. $3,000 or more, for a perfect set in dust jackets. Also, $2,500 (A, 1979). (It is almost impossible to assemble a uniformly fine set because of the almost inevitable uneven wear resulting from the spread in publication dates.) Proof copies: One set was sold by Melissa and Mark Hime, California dealers, for $11,000 in 1980. (For individual volumes see title entries.) London, 1960. 3 vols., cloth. Second edition. In dust jackets. $100–$150. Boston, 1967. 3 vols., cloth. With a new Foreword by the author. First American revised edition, first printing. In dust jacket. $200–$250.

TOLKIEN, J. R. R. *A Middle Earth Vocabulary.* Brown wrappers. Oxford, 1922. First edition. $650–$850. Author's first book.

TOLKIEN, J. R. R. *The Return of the King.* Cloth. London, 1955. First edition. In dust jacket. $250–$350. (Third volume in the *Lord of the Rings* sequence.)

TOLKIEN, J. R. R. *The Silmarillion.* Cloth. London, (1977). First edition. In dust jacket. $35–$50. Boston, 1977. Cloth. First American edition, first issue, with perfect text on lines 27–32 of page 229. $35–$50.

TOLKIEN, J. R. R. *The Two Towers.* Cloth. London, 1954. First edition. In dust jacket. $850–$1,000. (Second volume in the *Lord of the Rings* sequence.) London, (1966). Cloth. Second English edition, revised, first printing. In dust jacket. $50–$75.

TOLSTOY, Leo. *Anna Karenina.* Cloth. New York, 1886. First edition in English. New

York, 1933. Limited Editions Club. 2 vols. Boxed. $125–$175. Another issue, 1951: 2 vols. Boxed. $50.

TOLSTOY, Leo. *Resurrection.* Cloth. New York, 1900. First edition in English. $75–$100.

TOLSTOY, Leo. *War and Peace.* Translated from the French by Clara Bell. 6 vols., decorated brown cloth. New York, 1886. First edition in English. $750–$1,000. New York, 1938. Limited Editions Club. 6 vols. $80–$100.

TOLSTOY, Leo. *Where God Is Love Is.* Blue wrappers. London, 1924. Ashendene Press. One of about 200 issued as a Christmas token from St. John and Cicely Hornby. $500 and up.

TOM Brown at Oxford. 3 vols., blue cloth. Cambridge, 1861. (By Thomas Hughes.) First edition. $500–$600. Second edition, same date: $300–$350.

TOM Brown's School Days. By an Old Boy. Blue cloth. Cambridge, 1857. (By Thomas Hughes.) First edition. $1,500–$2,000.

TOM Cringle's Log. 2 vols., cloth. London, 1833. (By Michael Scott.) First edition. $400–$500.

TOME, Philip. *Pioneer Life; or, Thirty Years a Hunter.* Woodcut frontispiece. Cloth. Buffalo, 1854. First edition. $500–$600.

TOMKINSON, G. S. *A Select Bibliography of the Principal Modern Presses . . . in Great Britain and Ireland.* Illustrated. Boards and cloth. London, 1928. First edition. $150–$200.

TOMLINSON, Charles. *Relations and Contraries.* Wrappers. (Aldington, Kent, England, 1951.) First edition, $75. Author's first book.

TOMLINSON, H. M. *All Our Yesterdays.* Boards and cloth. New York, 1930. First edition. One of 350. $75–$100. Trade edition: Black cloth. In dust jacket. $15–$20. London, (1930). Cloth. First English edition. One of 1,025 signed. $50–$60. Trade edition: Cloth. First issue, with error in running head on page 67. In dust jacket. $15–$20.

TOMLINSON, H. M. *Ports of Call.* Cloth. London, 1942. Corvinus Press. One of 30 signed. Boxed. $100–$150.

TOMLINSON, H. M. *The Sea and the Jungle.* Frontispiece. Green cloth. London, (1912). First edition, first issue, with 10 ad leaves at back. In dust jacket. $200–$250. Author's first book. London, or New York, 1930. Illustrated by Clare Leighton. Cloth. One of 515 signed. In dust jacket. $75–$100. Trade edition: Boards and cloth. In dust jacket. $25.

TOMLINSON, H. M. *Thomas Hardy.* Frontispiece by Zhenya Gay, signed. Cloth. New York, 1929. One of 76 signed by the author. $75–$100.

TOMLINSON, H. M. *Under the Red Ensign.* Cloth. London, 1926. First edition. In dust jacket. $50–$75.

TOOMER, Jean. *Essentials.* Black cloth, paper labels. Chicago, 1931. First edition. One of 1,000. In dust jacket. $125–$150.

TOOMER, Jean. *The Flavor of Man.* Wrappers. Philadelphia, (1949). First edition. $100.

TOPOGRAPHICAL Description of the State of Ohio, Indian Territory, and Louisiana (A). 5 plates, errata slip. Calf, or sheep. Boston, 1812. (By Jervis Cutler.) First edition. $500–$600.

TOPONCE, Alexander. *Reminiscences of Alexander Toponce, Pioneer, 1839–1923.* 14 plates. Fabrikoid. (Ogden, Utah, 1923.) First edition. $125–$150.

TOPPING, E. S. *The Chronicles of the Yellowstone.* Folding map. Cloth. St. Paul, 1883. First edition. $100–$125.

TOPSYS & Turveys. 31 leaves with colored illustrations. Oblong folio, pictorial boards. New York, 1893. (By Peter Newell.) First edition. $150–$200. Author's first book.

TORNEL, José Maria (translator). *Diario Histórico del Ultimo Viaje que Hizo M. de La Sale para Descubrir el Desembocadero y Curso del Missicipi.* Boards. New York, 1831. $200–$350.

TORRENCE, Ridgely. *The House of a Hundred Lights.* Gold-decorated boards. Boston. 1900. First edition. $80–$100. Author's first book.

TORY, Geoffroy. *Champ Fleury.* Translated by George B. Ives. Vellum and boards. New York, 1927. Grolier Club. Printed by Bruce Rogers. One of 7 on larger paper (of an edition of 397). $750–$1,000. Regular issue: One of 390. In dust jacket. Boxed $500–$600.

TOUR of Doctor Prosody (The). 20 colored plates by C. Williams and W. Read. Boards. London, 1821. $750–$1,000. (Note: Sometimes attributed to William Combe, but not by him, according to De Ricci.)

TOUR on the Prairies (A). By the author of *The Sketch-Book.* Boards, or cloth. London, 1835. (By Washington Irving.) First edition. $400–$600. Philadelphia, 1835. Blue or green cloth, paper label. First American edition, first state, without "No. 1" on the label. $400–$600. Second state. $300–$400.

TOUR Through Part of Virginia in the Summer of 1808 (A). 31 pp. New York, 1809. (By John E. Caldwell.) First edition. $175–$200.

TOURGEE, Albion W. See *A Fool's Errand.*

TOWER, Col. Reuben. *An Appeal to the People of New York in Favor of the Construction of the Chenango Canal, etc.* 32 pp., sewed. Utica, 1830. First edition. $100–$125.

TOWLER, J(ohn). *The Silver Sunbeam: A Practical and Theoretical Text-Book on Sun-Drawing and Photographic Printing.* Cloth. New York, 1864. First edition. $300–$400. "Second thousand" (second printing), same date, $200–$250. New York, 1870. Seventh edition. $100. New York, 1879. Ninth edition. With mounted original Artotype by Bierstadt. $200.

TOWNSEND, George Alfred. *The Real Life of Abraham Lincoln.* Frontispiece. 15 pp., printed wrappers. New York, 1867. First edition. $100–$150.

TOWNSEND, John K. *Narrative of a Journey Across the Rocky Mountains.* Cloth. Philadelphia, 1839. First edition. $400–$500.

TOWNSHEND, John K. *Sporting Excursions in the Rocky Mountains.* Engraved frontispieces. 2 vols., full leather. London, 1840. First English edition of the preceding item, with the author's name spelled "Townshend" instead of "Townsend". $300–$400.

TOWNSHEND, R. B. *The Tenderfoot in New Mexico.* Illustrated. Cloth. London, (1923). First edition. In dust jacket. $75. New York, 1924. Illustrated. Cloth. First American edition. $65.

TOWNSHIP Maps of the Cherokee Nation. 130 maps. Folio, cloth. Muskogee, Okla., no date. $150–$200.

TRACY, J. L. *Guide to the Great West.* 2 maps. Cloth. St. Louis, 1870. First edition. $150–$175.

TRAGEDY of Count Alarcos (The). Cloth. London, 1839. (By Benjamin Disraeli.) First edition. $300–$350. Also issued in wrappers.

TRAIN, M. *Ray Burton: A Chicago Tale.* Wrappers. Chicago, 1895. First edition. $50–$75.

TRAITS of American Indian Life and Character. By a Fur Trader. 6 plates. Half cloth. San Francisco, 1933. (By Peter Skene Ogden or Duncan Finlayson.) Grabhorn printing (attributing it to Finlayson). One of 500. $100–$125.

TRANSACTIONS of the Chicago Academy of Sciences. Vol. 1, Part 1, and Vol. 1, Part 2. Plates, lithographs, folding map, separate title page for Part 2. Half leather. Chicago, 1867 and 1869. First edition. (All published.) $1,000, or more.

TRANSCRIPT of Record of Proceedings Before the Mexican and American Mixed Claims Commission with Relation to the "Pious Fund of the Californias." Washington, 1902. $60–$75.

TRANSITION Stories. Edited by Eugene Jolas and R. Sage. Pictorial boards and cloth. New York, 1929. First edition. One of 100. In dust jacket. $250–$300.

TRAUBEL, Horace L. (editor). *At the Graveside of Walt Whitman: Harleigh, Camden, New Jersey, March 30th, and Sprigs of Lilac.* 37 pp., printed gray wrappers. (Philadelphia), 1892. First edition. $100–$125.

TRAUBEL, Horace L. (editor). *Camden's Compliment to Walt Whitman.* Frontispiece. Red cloth. Philadelphia, 1889. First edition. $100–$125.

TRAVELS of Capts. Lewis and Clarke (The). Folding map and 5 portraits of Indians. Calf. Philadelphia, 1809. First edition. $350–$450. (Note: A spurious work. For authentic first edition see entry under Lewis' name.)

TRAVELS in Louisiana and the Floridas, in the Year, 1802. Translated from the French by John Davis. Boards, paper label. New York, 1806. (By Berquin-Duvallon.) First edition in English. $750–$1,000.

TRAVEN, B. *The Bridge in the Jungle.* Green cloth. New York, 1938. First American edition. In dust jacket. $75–$100. Another copy, with publisher's prospectus, $125. London, (1940). First English edition. In dust jacket. $50.

TRAVEN, B. *The Death Ship: The Story of an American Sailor.* Cloth. London, 1934. First edition in English. In dust jacket. $150. New York, 1934. Black cloth. First American edition, first printing. In dust jacket. $100–$150. Author's first book.

TRAVEN, B. *The General from the Jungle.* Cloth. London, (1954). First edition in English. In dust jacket. $75–$100.

TRAVEN, B. *The Rebellion of the Hanged.* Cloth. London, (1952). First edition in English. In dust jacket. $75. New York, 1952. First American edition. In dust jacket. $75–$100.

TRAVEN, B. *Der Schatz der Sierra Madre.* Orange-colored pictorial cloth. Berlin, 1927. First edition (of *The Treasure of the Sierra Madre*). $300–$400.

TRAVEN, B. *The Treasure of the Sierra Madre.* Cloth. London, 1934. First edition in English. In dust jacket. $150. New York, 1935. Cloth. First American edition. In dust jacket. $75–$125.

TRAVERS, P. L. *Mary Poppins.* Illustrated by Mary Shepard. Pictorial cloth. (London, 1934.) First edition. In dust jacket. $150. New York, (1934). Pictorial blue cloth. In dust jacket. $75. Author's first book.

TREADWELL, Edward F. *The Cattle King.* 4 plates. Cloth. New York, 1931. First edition. In dust jacket. $50–$75. Boston, 1950. Cloth. In dust jacket. $25.

TREATISE on Tennis (A). By a Member of the Tennis Club. Folding engraved diagram of court. Boards. London, 1822. (By Robert Lukin.) First edition. $250–$350.

TREATY Between the United States and the Chasta and Other Tribes of Indians. Wrappers. (Washington, 1855.) (By Joel Palmer.) $400–$500.

TREATY Between the United States and the Comanche and Kiowa Tribes of Indians . . . Proclaimed May 26, 1866. 8 pp., folio. (Washington, 1866.) $400.

TREATY Between the United States and the Creek and Seminole Tribes of Indians . . . Ratified March 6, 1845. 6 pp., folio. (Washington, 1845.) $400–$500.

TREATY Between the United States and the Kickapoo Indians. 6 pp., sewed. Washington, 1854. $150.

TREATY Between the United States and the Klamath and Moadoc Tribes and Yahooskin Band of Snake Indians . . . Proclaimed Feb. 17, 1870. 8 pp., folio. (Washington, 1870.) $350–$500.

TREATY Between the United States and the Nez Perce Tribe of Indians . . . Proclaimed April 20, 1867. 10 pp., folio. (Washington, 1867.) $400–$450.

TREATY Between the United States and the Senecas, etc. Folio, 20 pp., sewed. Washington, 1868. First edition. $250.

TRELAWNY, Edward John. See *The Adventures of a Younger Son.*

TRENT, William. *Journal of Captain William Trent from Logstown to Pickawillany, A.D. 1752.* Cloth. Cincinnati, 1871. First edition. $50–$75.

TRIAL of Impeachment of Levi Hubbell. Contemporary calf. Madison, Wis., 1853. First edition. $100–$125.

TRIALS of A. Arbuthnot and R. C. Ambrister (The), Charged with Exciting the Seminole Indians to War Against the United States of America. 80 pp., morocco. London, 1819. First edition. $300–$350.

TRIBUNE Book of Open Air Sports (The). Edited by Henry Hall. Illustrated. Pictorial cloth. New York, 1887. First edition. $300–$400. (Note: This is the first book composed by linotype.)

TRIBUNE Tracts No. 6, Life of Abraham Lincoln. 32 pp., sewed. New York, 1860. (By John Locke Scripps.) $250 and up. (Note: This book first appeared in an undated Chicago edition of 1860, 32 pp., under the caption title *Life of Abraham Lincoln.* That edition is rare, worth $1,000 and up.) Detroit, 1900. Leather, with Lincoln photograph on heavy porcelain bound in. $425 (A,1978).

TRIGGS, J. H. *History and Directory of Laramie City, Wyoming Territory.* 91 pp., printed wrappers. Laramie City, 1875. First edition. $750–$1,000.

TRIGGS, J. H. *History of Cheyenne and Northern Wyoming, etc.* Folding map. 144 pp., printed wrappers. Omaha, 1876. First edition. $750–$1,000.

TRIPLETT, Frank. *The Life, Times and Treacherous Death of Jesse James.* Plates. Pictorial cloth. Chicago, 1882. First edition. $200–$250.

TRIPP, C. E. *Ace High: The Frisco Detective.* Introduction by David Magee. Illustrated. Boards and cloth. San Francisco, 1948. Grabhorn Press. One of 500. $50–$60.

TRISTRAM, W. Outram. *Coaching Days and Coaching Ways.* Pictorial cloth. London, 1888. First edition. Large paper issue. $100–$150. Regular issue: $60–$80. London, 1893. One of 250. $100–$125. London, 1924. Illustrated. Leather. $350–$500.

TROLLOPE, Anthony. See *Nina Balatka; On English Prose Fiction as a Rational Amusement.*

TROLLOPE, Anthony. *The American Senator.* 3 vols., pinkish ochre cloth. London, 1877. First edition, first binding. $1,200. Worn, $400.

TROLLOPE, Anthony. *Australia and New Zealand.* 8 colored maps. 2 vols., cloth. London, 1873. First edition, first issue, with dark green end papers. $250–$400.

TROLLOPE, Anthony. *An Autobiography.* Portrait. 2 vols., cloth. Edinburgh, 1883. First edition, first issue, with smooth (not ribbed) red cloth covers. $350–$450.

TROLLOPE, Anthony. *Ayala's Angel.* 3 vols., orange cloth. London, 1881. First edition. $800. Worn, $250.

TROLLOPE, Anthony. *The Barsetshire Novels.* Edited by Michael Sadleir. 14 vols., cloth. London, 1929. Shakespeare Head Press. One of 525 sets. $1,500.

TROLLOPE, Anthony. *Barchester Towers.* 3 vols., cloth. London, 1857. First edition, first binding, brown cloth. $1,000–$1,250. Second binding, tan cloth, with 24 pp. of ads dated October, 1860. $900 (A, 1974). New York, (1859?). 2 vols. in one, purple-brown cloth. First American edition, without printer's imprint on back of title page. $200–$300. New York, 1958. Limited Editions Club. Boxed. $40.

TROLLOPE, Anthony. *The Belton Estate.* 3 vols., scarlet cloth. London, 1866. First edition. $1,000–$1,500. Also, $950 (A, 1974); $650 (A,1970).

TROLLOPE, Anthony. *The Bertrams.* 3 vols., dark gray-purple cloth. London, 1859. First edition. $1,250–$2,000.

TROLLOPE, Anthony. *Can You Forgive Her?* Illustrated. 20 parts, buff wrappers. London, 1864–65. First edition. $750–$1,000. London, 1864–(65). 2 vols., crimson cloth. First book edition. $400–$600.

TROLLOPE, Anthony. *Castle Richmond.* 3 vols., dark purple-gray cloth. London, 1860. First edition, first binding, without line under the author's name on spine, first issue text (as defined in the Michael Sadleir bibliography). $750–$1,000. Also, second issue, with line under author's name on spine and ads in Vol. 3 dated May. $800. New York, 1860. Green cloth. First American edition. $200–$250.

TROLLOPE, Anthony. *The Claverings.* Illustrated. Wrappers (26 chapters only). New York, 1866. First edition. $800–$1,000. Another edition: New York, 1866 (actually 1867). Gray lilac cloth. First complete edition. $500–$750. London, 1867. Illustrated. 2 vols., bright green cloth. First English edition. $750–$850.

TROLLOPE, Anthony. *Doctor Thorne.* 3 vols., gray-purple cloth. London, 1858. First edition. $400–$600. Second edition, same date. $250–$300.

TROLLOPE, Anthony. *The Duke's Children.* 3 vols., blue-green cloth. London, 1880. First edition. $400–$500. New York, 1880. Stitched, as issued. $500–$600.

TROLLOPE, Anthony. *An Editor's Tales.* Pinkish-brown cloth. London, 1870. First edition. $300–$400.

TROLLOPE, Anthony. *The Eustace Diamonds.* Printed wrappers, or cloth. New York, 1872. First edition. Either binding: $750–$1,000. London, 1873. 3 vols., brown cloth, spine title in gold. First English edition, correct binding. $750–$1,000.

TROLLOPE, Anthony. *The Fixed Period.* 2 vols., red cloth. Edinburgh, 1882. First edition. $1,000–$1,250.

TROLLOPE, Anthony. *Framley Parsonage.* Millais illustrations. 3 vols., gray-purple cloth. London, 1861, First edition. $500–$750. (Note: Copies with April ads at end of Vol. 3 preferred.) New York, 1861. Cloth. First American edition. $300–$400.

TROLLOPE, Anthony. *The Golden Lion of Granpere.* Reddish-brown cloth. London, 1872. First edition. $400–$500. New York, 1872. Illustrated. Wrappers. $500–$750.

TROLLOPE, Anthony. *He Knew He Was Right.* Illustrated by Marcus Stone. 32 parts, gray-green wrappers. London, 1868–69. First edition. $750–$1,000. New York, 1869. Illustrated. 2 vols., wrappers. First American edition. $300–$400. London, 1869. Illustrated. 2 vols., green cloth. First English book edition. $400–$500.

TROLLOPE, Anthony. *How the "Mastiffs" Went to Iceland.* Illustrated. Blue cloth. London, 1878. First edition. $450–$600.

TROLLOPE, Anthony. *Hunting Sketches*. Red cloth. London, 1865. First edition, with May ads. $300–$400.

TROLLOPE, Anthony. *John Caldigate*. 3 vols., cloth. London, 1879. First edition, first binding, lilac-gray cloth. $600–$900.

TROLLOPE, Anthony. *The Kellys and the O'Kellys*. 3 vols., boards. London, 1848. First edition. $2,500–$3,000. Also, rebound in half morocco, $950 (A, 1970). New York, 1860. Cloth. First American edition. $700–$800.

TROLLOPE, Anthony. *Kept in the Dark*. Frontispiece by Millais. 3 vols., olive-brown cloth. London, 1882. First edition. $600–$800.

TROLLOPE, Anthony. *La Vendee: An Historical Romance*. 3 vols., boards, or cloth. London, 1850. First edition, first issue, with verso of title pages blank. Either binding: $1,000–$1,500. Also, boards, $750 (A, 1970).

TROLLOPE, Anthony. *Lady Anna*. 2 vols., red-brown cloth. London, 1874. First edition. $600–$800.

TROLLOPE, Anthony. *The Landleaguers*. 3 vols., green cloth. London, 1883. First edition. $350–$500.

TROLLOPE, Anthony. *The Last Chronicle of Barset*. Illustrated. 32 parts, pictorial wrappers. London, 1866–67. First edition. $1,000–$1,500. London, 1867. 32 plates. 2 vols., blue cloth. First book edition. $400–$600. New York, 1867. Illustrated. Cloth. First American edition. $200–$250. Worn, $115. (Note: Both the parts issue and the book issue of the English first edition are complicated books with confusing issue points; see the Michael Sadleir bibliography.)

TROLLOPE, Anthony. *The Life of Cicero*. 2 vols., dark-red cloth. London, 1880. First edition, first issue, with black end papers. $300–$400.

TROLLOPE, Anthony. *London Tradesmen*. Boards and cloth. London, 1927. First edition. One of 530. In glassine dust jacket. $100–$125.

TROLLOPE, Anthony. *Lotta Schmidt and Other Stories*. Maroon cloth. London, 1867. First edition. $450–$650.

TROLLOPE, Anthony. *The Macdermots of Ballycloran*. 3 vols., dark brown cloth. London, 1847. First edition, first issue (with 1847 on title page). $5,000–$10,000. Author's first book. London, 1848. Cloth. Second issue (with 1848 title page). $1,000 and up.

TROLLOPE, Anthony. *Marion Fay*. 3 vols., yellow-ochre cloth. London, 1882. First edition $900–$1,200. New York, 1882. Illustrated. Wrappers. First American edition. $300–$400.

TROLLOPE, Anthony. *Miss Mackenzie*. 2 vols., dark-green cloth. London, 1865. First edition. $400–$500. Rebound in half leather, $250.

TROLLOPE, Anthony. *North America*. 2 vols., pinkish maroon cloth. London, 1862. First edition, with October ads. $400–$500. New York, 1862. Gray cloth. First American (pirated) edition. $200–$300.

TROLLOPE, Anthony. *Orley Farm*. Illustrated by J. E. Millais. 20 parts, buff wrappers. London, 1861–62. First edition. $1,250–$1,500. London, 1862. 2 vols., purple-brown cloth. First book edition. $500–$750. (Note: As with *The Last Chronicle of Barset,* this is an extremely complex book to sort out bibliographically; see Sadleir's bibliography.)

TROLLOPE, Anthony. *Phineas Redux*. 26 illustrations. Cloth. New York, 1874. First American edition. $100–$125.

TROLLOPE, Anthony. *The Prime Minister*. 8 parts, gray wrappers, or brown cloth. London, 1876. First edition. $1,000 and up. London, 1876. 4 vols., red-brown cloth. First book edition. $500–$600.

TROLLOPE, Anthony. *Rachel Ray*. 2 vols., pinkish red cloth. London, 1863. First edition, first issue, with volume numbers on spines in roman (not block) type. $800–$1,200.

TROLLOPE, Anthony. *Ralph the Heir*. Illustrated. 19 parts, buff wrappers. London, 1870–71. First edition. $3,000 (A, 1970). London, 1871. 3 vols., brown cloth. $600–$800. New York, 1871. Illustrated. Cloth. First American (and first illustrated) edition. $250–$350. Worn, $95.

TROLLOPE, Anthony. *Sir Harry Hotspur of Humblethwaite*. Scarlet-orange cloth. London, 1871. First edition. $200–$250. (For issue points, see Sadleir.) New York, 1871. Cherry-red or green cloth. First American edition. $200–$250.

TROLLOPE, Anthony. *The Small House at Allington*. Illustrated by Millais. 2 vols., green cloth. London, 1864. First edition, first issue, with "hobbledehoya" in first line of page 33. $500–$1,000. Worn, $165.

TROLLOPE, Anthony. *South Africa*. Folding map in color. 2 vols., scarlet cloth. London, 1878. First edition. $300–$400.

TROLLOPE, Anthony. *The Struggles of Brown, Jones, and Robinson*. Wrappers. New York, 1862. First edition. $1,000 and up. London, 1870. Illustrated. Brown cloth. First English and first illustrated edition. $350–$500.

TROLLOPE, Anthony. *Tales of All Countries*. (First and Second series.) 2 vols., blue cloth. London, 1861 and 1863. First editions. $600–$800.

TROLLOPE, Anthony. *Thackeray*. Smooth cream cloth, paper label. London, 1879. First edition, first binding. $150–$200.

TROLLOPE, Anthony. *Thompson Hall*. Illustrated. Pictorial boards. London, 1885. First separate edition. $300–$400.

TROLLOPE, Anthony. *The Three Clerks*. 3 vols., boards, blue cloth spine, labels. London, 1858. First edition. $1,000 and up. Also, variant issue: Cloth. $800 (A, 1970). New York, 1860. Plum-colored cloth. First American edition. $200–$300. Worn, $85.

TROLLOPE, Anthony. *Travelling Sketches*. Scarlet cloth. London, 1866. First edition. $300–$400.

TROLLOPE, Anthony. *The Vicar of Bulhampton*. Illustrated. 11 parts, decorated gray-blue wrappers. London, 1869–70. First edition. $750–$1,000. London, 1870. Brown cloth. First book edition. $300–$400.

TROLLOPE, Anthony. *The Warden*. Brown cloth. London, 1855. First edition, first binding, with 24 pages of ads dated September, 1854. $1,000 and up. Inscribed copy, $1,750. New York, 1862. Wrappers. First American edition. $600–$800.

TROLLOPE, Anthony. *The Way We Live Now*. Illustrated. 20 parts, pictorial wrappers. London, 1874–75. First edition. $750–$1,000. London, 1875. 2 vols., green cloth. First book edition. $600–$800.

TROLLOPE, Anthony. *Why Frau Frohmann Raised Her Prices, and Other Stories*. 2 vols., green cloth. London, 1882. First edition. $800–$1,200.

TROLLOPE, Frances. See *Domestic Manners of the Americans*.

TROLLOPE, Frances. *Uncle Walter*. 3 vols., boards and cloth, paper labels. London, 1852. First edition. $250–$350.

TROLLOPE, Frances. *The Vicar of Wrexhill*. 3 vols., boards, paper labels. London, 1837. First edition. $300–$400.

TROLLOPE, T. Adolphus. *A Summer in Brittany*. Edited by Frances Trollope. 14 plates, 2 in color. 2 vols., purple cloth. London, 1840. First edition. $200–$225.

TROWBRIDGE, John Townsend. See Creyton, Paul.

TROWBRIDGE, John Townsend. *Cudjo's Cave*. Pictorial half title. Cloth. Boston, 1864. First edition, first printing, listing the "L'Envoy" as beginning on page 503 (later, page 501). $150–$250.

TROWBRIDGE, John Townsend. *Jack Hazard and His Fortunes*. Cloth. Boston, 1871. First edition. $75–$100.

TROWBRIDGE, John Townsend. *The South: A Tour of Its Battlefields and Ruined Cities*. Cloth. Hartford, 1866. First edition. $75–$100.

TRUETT, Velma Stevens. *On the Hoof in Nevada*. Portraits, other illustrations. Oblong pictorial buckram. Los Angeles, 1950. First edition. $75–$100. Second binding, with "Nevada Publications" on spine, $40–$50.

TRUMAN, Maj. Ben. C. *Life, Adventures and Capture of Tiburcio Vasquez, the Great California Bandit and Murderer*. Frontispiece map. 44 pp., pictorial wrappers. Los Angeles, 1874. First edition. $500–$600. Los Angeles, 1941. Cloth and leather. One of 100. $50–$75.

TRUMAN, Benjamin C. *Occidental Sketches*. Cloth. San Francisco, 1881. First edition. $85–$100.

TRUMAN, Harry S. *Mr. Citizen*. Cloth. (New York, 1960.) First edition. One of 1,000 signed. Boxed. $150–$250. Trade edition: In dust jacket. $75.

TRUMBO, Dalton. *Eclipse*. Cloth. London, (1935). First edition. In dust jacket. $200–$250. Author's first book.

TRUMBO, Dalton. *Johnny Got His Gun*. Yellow cloth. Philadelphia, (1939). First edition. In dust jacket with wraparound band. $75–$125.

TRYPHE. *Clinq Petits Dialogues Grecs*. Wrappers. Paris, 1902. (By Natalie C. Barney.) First edition. $125–$175. Author's first book.

TSA TOKE, Monroe. *The Peyote Ritual*. 15 color plates. Boards and cloth. San Francisco, 1957. Grabhorn Press. One of 325. $300–$375.

TUCKER, Beverley. *The Partisan Leader*. Printed wrappers. Richmond, 1862. Reprint of the anonymous 1836 novel forecasting the Civil War. $350–$400.

TUCKER, E. *History of Randolph County, Indiana*. Half leather and cloth. Chicago, 1882. First edition. $100–$125.

TUCKER, Dr. Joseph C. *To the Golden Goal, and Other Sketches*. Cloth. San Francisco, 1895. First edition. One of 50. $200–$225.

TUER, Andrew W. *History of the Horn-Book*. With 7 facsimile hornbooks in pockets. 2 vols., vellum. London, 1896. First edition. $600–$850. London, 1897. 2 vols., brown buckram. With 3 facsimile hornbooks. $400–$600.

TUER, Andrew W. *Pages and Pictures from Forgotten Children's Books*. Illustrated. Cloth. London, 1898–99. First edition. $100–$150.

TUFTS, James. *A Tract Descriptive of Montana Territory*. Map. 15 pp., folded sheets. New York, 1865. First edition. One of 24 on fine paper. $200–$300. Another issue: Sewed. $300–$400.

TULLIDGE, Edward W. *The History of Salt Lake City and Its Founders*. 33 plates. Half morocco. Salt Lake City, (about 1886). $300–$400. (Note: The first edition, with 3 plates, was published 1883–84, according to Howes.)

TURNBULL, Robert J. See Brutus.

TURNER, Frederick Jackson. *The Significance of the Frontier in American History*. 34 pp., wrappers. Madison, Wis., 1894. First separate edition. $1,500 and up.

TURNER, Mary Honeyman Ten Eyck. *These High Plains.* Portrait and plates. Cloth, pictorial label. Amarillo, 1941. First edition. One of 150. $200–$300.

TURNER, Orsamus. *History of the Pioneer Settlement of Phelps and Gorham's Purchase.* Boards and leather. Rochester, 1851. First edition. $200–$300.

TURNER, T. G. *Gazetteer of the St. Joseph Valley.* Frontispiece and plate. Cloth. Chicago, 1867. First edition. $150.

TURNER, T. G. *Turner's Guide from the Lakes to the Rocky Mountains.* Cloth. Chicago, 1868. First edition. $150–$250.

TURNLEY, Parmenas T. *Reminiscences of Parmenas T. Turnley, from the Cradle to Three-Score and Ten.* 6 plates. Cloth. Chicago, (1892). First edition. $125–$175.

TURRILL, H. B. *Historical Reminiscences of the City of Des Moines.* Double-page frontispiece plate and 7 other plates. 144 pp., printed dark blue wrappers. Des Moines, 1857. First edition. $150–$200.

TUTTLE, C. R. *History of Grand Rapids.* Cloth. Grand Rapids, 1874. First edition. $100–$150.

TUTTLE, J. H. *Wam-dus-ky: A Descriptive Record of a Hunting Trip to North Dakota.* Illustrated. Cloth. Minneapolis, 1893. First edition. $350–$550.

TWAIN. Mark See Harte, Bret, and Twain, Mark. Also see *Date 1601; What Is Man?*

TWAIN, Mark. *Adventures of Huckleberry Finn.* Illustrated. Pictorial red cloth. London, 1884. (By Samuel Langhorne Clemens.) First edition (preceding the American first). $800–$1,000. New York, 1885. Green or blue cloth (green being the most common) and various leathers. First American edition, first issue (as commonly defined, with "was" for "saw" in line 23 on page 57; with "Him and another man" given incorrectly in list of illustrations as being on page 88 and with page 283 on a stub). $1,500–$2,500. Defective copies bring less, of course. (Note: There appears to be no clearcut definition of a "first issue" *Huck* because of the many bibliographical complexities in this famous book, which is still confusing the experts. For this reason "early issue" or "mixed state" *Hucks* which may differ in various minor ways from the so-called "first issue" copies are acceptable as first editions to most collectors. The price for fine copies ranges from the $600–$800 level, for "mixed state" issues, to $1,000 and up for "early issue" firsts.) Prospectuses for this book: Copies noted at $4,750 and $5,750. Montreal, 1885. Red or green cloth. First Canadian edition. Two copies, one at $2,500 and another at $3,250, in a recent catalogue. Both were worn. New York, 1933. Limited Editions Club. Boxed. $75–$150. New York, 1942. Limited Editions Club. Boxed. $100–$175.

TWAIN, Mark. *The Adventures of Tom Sawyer.* Illustrated. Red cloth. London, 1876. (By Samuel Langhorne Clemens.) First edition (preceding the American first). $2,000, or more. Toronto, 1876. Illustrated. Cloth. First Canadian edition (also preceding the American). $750 and up. Hartford, 1876. Illustrated. Blue cloth (or various leathers). First American edition, first issue, printed on calendered paper, with versos of half title and preface blank. $2,000–$5,000. Second issue, lacking the two blank pages: $500 and up. New York, 1939. Limited Editions Club. Boxed. $125–$200.

TWAIN, Mark. *The American Claimant.* Illustrated. Gray-green cloth. New York, 1892. (By Samuel Langhorne Clemens.) First edition. $100–$150. London, 1892. Cloth. First English edition. $75–$100.

TWAIN, Mark. *Be Good, Be Good: A Poem.* (Cover title.) 4 pp., French-folded, printed in green. New York, 1931. (By Samuel Langhorne Clemens.) First edition. $125–$200. Another issue: One of 10 or 12 printed in blue on vellum. $600–$800.

TWAIN, Mark. *The Celebrated Jumping Frog of Calaveras County, And Other Sketches.* Edited by John Paul. Cloth, various colors. New York, 1867. (By Samuel Langhorne Clemens.) First edition, first issue, with perfect "i" in "this" in last line on page 198 and with page of yellow tinted ads preceding title page. $4,000–$5,000. Also, $2,750 (A, 1977). (Note: There is a long-standing controversy concerning the priority pers (title in blue). (London), 1900. (By Samuel Langhorne Clemens.) First edition. $250–$300.

TWAIN, Mark (so designated on binding, but not on title page). *Personal Recollections of Joan of Arc.* Red buckram. New York, 1896. (By Samuel Langhorne Clemens.) First edition, first state, with ads listing third and fourth volumes of *Memoirs of Barras* as "just ready." $150–$175. London, 1896. Red cloth. First English edition, with Twain's name on title page. Issued simultaneously with American edition. $250–$300.

TWAIN, Mark. *The Prince and the Pauper.* Illustrated. Pictorial red cloth. London, 1881. (By Samuel Langhorne Clemens.) First edition, first issue, with ads dated November. $250 and up. Montreal, 1881. Blue cloth or gray-blue wrappers. First (?) edition. (Blanck says, "Probably simultaneous with the London edition.") $550 in cloth, $1,250 in wrappers in a 1980 catalogue. Boston, 1882. Green cloth (or various leathers). First American edition, first issue, with Franklin Press imprint on copyright page. $300 and up. (Note: This complicated book also exists in its American first edition in an issue of "6 or 8" copies—Twain was uncertain when he signed a copy for the New York Public Library—on China paper, with white linen binding. New York, 1964. Limited Editions Club. Boxed. $80–$100.

TWAIN, Mark. *Pudd'nhead Wilson: A Tale.* Illustrated. Red cloth. London, 1894. (By Samuel Langhorne Clemens.) First English edition (of *The Tragedy of Pudd'nhead Wilson,* which see). $150–$175.

TWAIN, Mark. *Pudd'nhead Wilson's Calendar for 1894.* (Cover title.) 16 pp. (3 x 2½ inches), printed yellow wrappers. (Dawson's Landing, Mo., *i.e.,* New York, 1893.) (By Samuel Langhorne Clemens.) First edition. $2,000–$2,500.

TWAIN, Mark. *Punch, Brothers, Punch!* Pictorial wrappers, or cloth. New York, (1878). (By Samuel Langhorne Clemens.) First edition, first issue, with Twain's name in Roman capitals on title page. Wrappers: $250–$350. Cloth: $250–$350.

TWAIN, Mark. *Queen Victoria's Jubilee.* Illustrated. Printed white boards. (New York (?), 1910.) (By Samuel Langhorne Clemens.) First edition. One of 195. $375–$450.

TWAIN, Mark. *Roughing It.* Illustrated. Black cloth (or various leathers). Hartford, 1872. (By Samuel Langhorne Clemens.) First American edition, first issue, with no words missing in lines 20 and 21 of page 242. $300–$400. Kentfield, Calif., 1953. Boards. One of 200. $100–$125.

TWAIN, Mark. *The Stolen White Elephant.* Decorated red cloth. London, 1882. First edition. $150–$200. Boston, 1882. Tan cloth. First American edition. $150–$200.

TWAIN, Mark. *To the Person Sitting in Darkness.* (Cover title.) 16 pp., self-wrappers. (New York, 1901.) (By Samuel Langhorne Clemens.) First edition. $250–$300.

TWAIN, Mark. *Tom Sawyer Abroad, Tom Sawyer, Detective, and Other Stories.* Illustrated by Dan Beard. Red cloth. New York, 1896. (By Samuel Langhorne Clemens.) First edition. $750–$1,000.

TWAIN, Mark. *The Tragedy of Pudd'nhead Wilson.* Illustrated. Brown cloth (or leather). Hartford, 1894. (By Samuel Langhorne Clemens.) First American edition. $250–$400. (For English first edition, see Twain, *Pudd'nhead Wilson.*) New York, 1974. Limited Editions Club. $50.

TWAIN, Mark. *A Tramp Abroad.* Illustrated. Black cloth (or various leathers). Hartford, 1880. (By Samuel Langhorne Clemens.) First edition, first state, with frontispiece entitled "Moses," not "Titian's Moses." $400–$450. London, 1880. 2 vols., red cloth. First English edition. $300–$400. Another issue: In one volume. $200.

TWAIN, Mark. *A True Story.* Illustrated. Green or terra-cotta cloth. Boston, 1877. (By Samuel Langhorne Clemens.) First edition, first binding, with J R O monogram on front cover. $800. (Later issues have monogram H O.)

TWAIN, Mark. *What Is Man?* Blue cloth. London, 1910. (By Samuel Langhorne Clemens.) First English edition. $100–$135. (For first edition, see title entry.)

TWAIN, Mark (editor). *Tom Sawyer Abroad*. By Huck Finn. Illustrated by Dan Beard. Tan cloth. New York, 1894. (By Samuel Langhorne Clemens.) First American edition. $200–$300. London, 1894. Pictorial red cloth. First English edition, first binding. $200–$300.

TWAIN, Mark, and Warner, Charles Dudley. *The Gilded Age*. Illustrated. Black cloth (or various leathers). Hartford, 1873. (By Samuel Langhorne Clemens and Warner.) First edition, first issue, without the tailpiece illustration on page 403. $600–$1,200. (A book of bibliographical complexity. Any copy with an 1873 title page is probably valuable. Consult a specialist bookseller for help if you find one.)

TWEEDIE, William. *The Arabian Horse: His Country and People*. 10 plates, 25 text illustrations, maps and tables. Green decorated cloth. London, 1894. $400–$500. Large paper issue: Half morocco. One of 100. $600–$800.

TWELVE Mormon Homes Visited in Succession on a Journey Through Utah to Arizona. Cloth. Philadelphia, 1874. (By Elizabeth D. Kane.) First edition. $150.

TWENTIETH Century History of Southwest Texas (A). Illustrated. Quarto, morocco. Chicago, 1907. $750.

TWENTY Letters to Joseph Conrad. 12 pamphlets, wrappers. London, 1926. First edition. One of 220 sets. Boxed. $200.

TWENTY Poems. White buckram. London, 1909. First edition. One of 25. $150–$200. (Note: Supposedly contains four poems by George Meredith.)

TWIN Cities Directory and Business Mirror for the Year 1860, Including the Cities of Davenport, Iowa; Rock Island, Ill., and Moline, Ill. Vol. 1. Cloth. Davenport, 1859. (E. Coy & Co., publisher.) $200–$250.

TWINING, Elizabeth. *Illustrations of the Natural Order of Plants, Arranged in Groups*. 160 colored lithograph plates. 2 vols., tall folio, half morocco. London, 1849–55. $6,000 and up.

TWITCHELL, Ralph Emerson. *The Leading Facts of New Mexican History*. Folding maps, color frontispiece, other illustrations. 2 vols., cloth. Cedar Rapids, Iowa, 1911–12. First edition. One of 1,500. $150–$200.

TWITCHELL, Ralph Emerson. *Old Santa Fe*. Illustrated. Cloth. (Santa Fe., 1925.) First edition, limited. $100–$125.

TWITCHELL, Ralph Emerson (editor). *The Spanish Archives of New Mexico*. 42 plates and facsimiles. 2 vols., cloth. (Cedar Rapids), 1914. Torch Press. $200–$250.

TWO Admirals (The): A Tale. By the Author of *The Pilot*. 2 vols., purple muslin, paper labels. Philadelphia, 1842. (By James Fenimore Cooper.) First American edition. $1,000–$1,250. London, 1842. 3 vols., boards and cloth, paper labels. First edition. (Issued under Cooper's name.) $600–$750.

TWO Generals (The). 8 pp., printed on a single sheet, unbound. No place, no date (1868?). (By Edward Fitz Gerald.) First edition. $200 and up.

TWO Rivulets. See Whitman, Walt.

TWO Years Before the Mast. A Personal Narrative of Life at Sea. (Harpers' Family Library No. CVI.) Tan, black, or gray cloth. New York, 1840. (By Richard Henry Dana, Jr.) First edition, first issue, with perfect "i" in the word "in," first line of copyright notice. $3,000–$4,000. Also, $2,250 (A, 1974); inscribed by the author's father, $3,500 (A, 1977). Second issue: $500 and up. London, (1904). Cloth. Illustrated by Arthur Rackham. $300–$350. Chicago, 1930. Lakeside Press. Illustrated by Edward A. Wilson. Pictorial linen. One of 1,000. Boxed. $150–$175. New York, 1936. Grabhorn printing. Illustrated. Boards. One of 1,000. In dust jacket. $150–$200. New York, 1947. Limited Editions Club. Cloth. Boxed. $40–$50.

TYLER, Anne. *If Morning Ever Comes*. Cloth. New York, 1964. First edition. In dust jacket. $50–$150.

TYLER, Anne. *The Tin Can Tree*. Cloth. New York, 1965. First edition. In dust jacket. $40–$75.

TYLER, Daniel. *A Concise History of the Mormon Battalion in the Mexican War*. Full leather. (Salt Lake City), 1881 (actually 1882). First edition. $400–$500. Spine worn, $200.

TYLER, Parker. *The Metaphor in the Jungle and Other Poems*. Portrait by Tchelitchew. Cloth. Prairie City, Ill., 1940. First edition. (250 copies.) $300–$375.

TYLER, Parker (editor). *Modern Things*. Purple and white cloth. New York, (1934). First edition. In dust jacket. $200–$250.

TYNAN, Katherine. *Twenty One Poems*. Selected by W. B. Yeats. Blue boards and linen. Dundrum, Ireland, 1907. Dun Emer Press. One of 200. $300.

TYNAN, Kenneth. *He That Plays the King*. Half leather. London, 1950. First edition. One of 50. $250. Author's first book.

TYNDALE, William (translator). *The Boke off the Revelacion off Sanct Jhon the Devine, Done into Englysshe*. Vellum. London, 1901. Ashendene Press. One of 54. $1,500–$1,750.

TYNDALL, John. *Essays on the Floating-Matter of the Air in Relation to Putrefaction and Infection*. Cloth. London, 1881. First edition. $300–$400.

TYPES of Successful Men in Texas. Red leather. Austin, Tex., 1890. $200–$300.

TYSON, James L., M.D. *Diary of a Physician in California*. 92 pp., printed wrappers. New York, 1850. First edition. $400–$500. Oakland, Calif., 1955. One of 500. $40–$50.

TYSON, Philip T. *Geology and Industrial Resources of California*. Folding maps, charts, tables. Cloth. Baltimore, 1851. $125–$150.

TYSON, Robert A. *History of East St. Louis*. Folding map and folding view of stockyards. 152 pp., wrappers. East St. Louis, 1875. First edition. $300–$350.

U

UDELL, John. *Incidents of Travel to California, Across the Great Plains.* Portrait, errata leaf. Cloth. Jefferson, Ohio, 1856. First edition. $400–$500.

UDELL, John. *Journal of John Udell, Kept During a Trip Across the Plains.* Vignette portrait. 47 pp., wrappers. Jefferson, Ohio, 1868. Second edition. $1,250–$1,500. Los Angeles, 1946. Edited by Lyle H. Wright. Half morocco. One of 35 signed by Wright. $75–$100. Another issue: Cloth. One of 750. $35. (Note: The first edition of Udell's *Journal,* 45 pp., printed wrappers, including cover title, appeared in Suisun City, Calif., in 1859 and is known in only one surviving copy. The following facsimile was published by Yale University.) (New Haven, 1952.) Printed wrappers. One of 200. $50.

ÚLTIMAS Communicaciones entre el Gobierno Mexicano y el Enviado Estraordinario y Ministro Plenipotenciario nombrado por el de los Estados Unidos, sobre la Cuestión de Tejas, etc. 22 pp., printed wrappers. Mexico, 1846. $750–$1,000.

UNCLE Abe's Republican Songster. Wrappers. San Francisco, 1860. $100–$150.

UNDER the Greenwood Tree. 2 vols., green cloth. London, 1872. (By Thomas Hardy.) First edition. $750–$1,000.

UNIFORM and Dress of the Army of the Confederate States. 15 plates by Ernest Crehen. 5 pp., boards, paper label. Richmond, 1861. First edition, first issue, with black-and-white plates. $400–$600. Second issue, same date, with 9 of the 15 plates in color, plus errata slip and tipped-in colored strip illustrating field caps. $1,000–$1,500.

UNITED States Enrollment Laws (The), for Calling Out the National Forces. Wrappers. New York, 1864. $75–$100.

UNITED States "History" as the Yankee Makes and Takes It. By a Confederate Soldier. 99 pp., yellow wrappers. Glen Allen, 1900. (By John Cussons.) $100–$125.

UNJUST Judge (The). By a Member of the Ohio Bar. Cloth. Mansfield, Ohio, 1854. (By William Stevens.) First edition. $75–$100.

UPDIKE, D. B. *Notes on the Merrymount Press and Its Work.* Cloth. Cambridge, Mass., 1934. First edition. One of 500. $100–$135.

UPDIKE, John. *The Angels.* Wrappers. (Pensacola), 1968. First edition. One of 150. In mailing envelope. $400–$500.

UPDIKE, John. *Assorted Prose.* Cloth. New York, 1965. First edition. In dust jacket. $50. Another issue with tipped-in leaf signed by author: In dust jacket. $175. (London, 1965.) Cloth. First English edition. In dust jacket. $25–$35.

UPDIKE, John. *Bath After Sailing.* Wrappers, paper label. (Stevenson, Conn., 1968.) First edition. One of 125 signed. $250–$300.

UPDIKE, John. *The Carpentered Hen and Other Tame Creatures.* Boards and cloth. New York, (1958.) First edition. In first state dust jacket, with "two children" in biographical information. $300–$350. Author's first book.

UPDIKE, John. *Hoping for a Hoopoe.* Cloth. London, 1959. First English edition (of *The Carpentered Hen).* In dust jacket. $40–$50.

UPDIKE, John. *The Indian.* Stapled wrappers. (Marvin, S.D., 1971.) First edition. $35–$40.

UPDIKE, John. *Midpoint and Other Poems.* Cloth. New York, 1969. First edition. One of 350 signed. Boxed. $100. Trade edition: In dust jacket. $25.

UPDIKE, John. *The Music School.* Boards. New York, 1966. First edition, first issue, with transposed lines in the poem on page 46. In dust jacket. $125. Second issue: $15–$20. (London, 1967.) Cloth. First English edition. In dust jacket. $35.

UPDIKE, John. *Of the Farm.* Cloth. New York, 1965. First edition. In dust jacket. $50. Advance proof copy, spiral bound wrappers: $375.

UPDIKE, John. *On Meeting Authors.* Wrappers. Newburyport, 1968. First edition. One of 250. In original envelope. $450.

UPDIKE, John. *Pigeon Feathers.* Cloth. New York, 1962. First edition. In dust jacket. $50. (London, 1962.) Cloth. First English edition. In dust jacket. $45–$50.

UPDIKE, John. *The Poorhouse Fair.* Boards and cloth. New York, 1959. First edition. In dust jacket. $125–$150. Author's first novel.

UPDIKE, John. *Rabbit, Run.* Boards. New York, 1960. First edition. In dust jacket. $125–$150. (London, 1961.) Cloth. First English edition. In dust jacket. $40–$65.

UPDIKE, John. *The Same Door.* Boards. New York, 1959. First edition. In dust jacket. $100–$150. (London, 1962.) First English edition. In dust jacket. $40–$65.

UPDIKE, John. *Six Poems.* Wrappers. (New York), 1973. First edition. One of 100 signed. $200. Another issue: One of 26 lettered and signed. $400–$500.

UPDIKE, John. *Three Texts from Early Ipswich.* Wrappers. Ipswich, Mass., 1968. First edition. One of 50 signed. $200. Another issue: One of 26 lettered and signed. $350–$400. Trade edition (unsigned): $50.

UPFIELD, Arthur W. *The House of Cain.* Cloth. London, (1928). First edition. In dust jacket. $300–$350. Author's first book.

UPHAM, Samuel C. *Notes from Sunland, on the Manatee River, Gulf Coast of South Florida.* Frontispiece. 83 pp., printed wrappers. Braidentown, Fla., 1881. First edition. $150–$200. Second edition (so stated), same date. $100–$125.

UPS and Downs: A Book of Transformation Pictures. Illustrated in color. 16 pp., with pull slides to change pictures (a movable book). Boards. London, (about 1890). $100–$150.

URREA, José. *Diario de las Operaciones Militares de la División que al Mando del Gen. José Urrea Hizo la Campana de Tejas.* Half leather. Victoria, Mexico, 1838. First edition. $3,500–$4,000.

V

VAGABOND (The): A New Story for Children. 16 pp., wrappers. Hartford, 1819. (By Samuel Griswold Goodrich.) First edition. $100–$150.

VAIL, Alfred. *Description of the American Electro-Magnetic Telegraph.* 14 wood engravings. Wrappers. Washington, 1845. First edition. $125–$200.

VAIL, Isaac Newton. *Alaska: Land of the Nugget. Why?* 68 pp., wrappers. Pasadena, 1897. $100–$125.

VAIL, Isaac Newton. *Ophir's Golden Wedge.* 36 pp., wrappers. Pasadena, 1893. $75–$125.

VALENTIA, George, Viscount. *Voyages and Travels to India, Ceylon, the Red Sea, Abyssinia, and Egypt, 1802–6.* 69 engraved views and folding maps. 3 vols., boards. London, 1809. First edition. Large paper issue: $750–$1,000. Ordinary issue: $600–$750.

VALENTINER, Wilhem R. *Rembrandt Paintings in America.* 175 plates. Half morocco. New York, 1931. First edition. In dust jacket. $75–$100. Limited issue: Full morocco. One of 200 signed. $125–$150.

VALÉRY, Paul. *Eupalinos, or The Architect.* Translated by William M. Stewart. Buckram. London, 1932. One of 250 signed. $100–$135.

VALÉRY, Paul. *Introduction to the Method of Leonardo Da Vinci.* Translated by Thomas McGreevey. Boards. London, 1929. One of 50. $100–$125.

VALPERGA: Or, The Life and Adventures of Castruccio, Prince of Lucca. 3 vols., blue-gray boards. London, 1823. (By Mary Wollstonecraft Shelley.) First edition, without half titles. $2,000–$2,500. Also, $1,300 (A, 1977).

VAN BUREN, A. D. *Jottings of a Year's Sojourn in the South.* Cloth. Battle Creek, 1859. First edition. $100–$150.

VANCE, Ethel. *Escape.* Cloth. Boston, 1939. (By Grace Zaring Stone.) First edition. In dust jacket. $50–$75.

VAN CLEVE, Mrs. Charlotte O. C. *"Three Score Years and Ten"; Life-Long Memories of Fort Snelling, Minn., and Other Parts of the West.* Portrait. Cloth. (Minneapolis), 1888. First edition. $75–$100.

VANDERBILT, Harold S. *On the Wind's Highway.* Illustrated. Cloth. New York, 1939. First edition. Boxed. $200–$225.

VANDERBILT, William K. *Taking One's Own Ship Around the World.* 19 color plates. 112 photographs. Half (or full) morocco. New York, 1929. One of 200. Boxed. $150–$250.

VANDERBILT, William K. *To Galapagos on the Ara.* (New York, 1926.) Boards and leather. One of 900. $50–$75. Another issue: New York, 1927. Boards and calf. One of 500. $350–$400.

VANDERBILT, William K. *West Made East with the Loss of a Day.* 7 color plates, 13 charts. Cloth. New York, 1933. One of 800. $50–$75. Another issue: Half morocco. One of 200 on Rives paper. $300–$400.

VAN DE WATER, Frederic F. *Glory Hunter: A Life of Gen. Custer.* 2 maps, 13 plates. Cloth. Indianapolis, (1934). First edition. In dust jacket. $75–$85.

VAN DINE, S. S. *The Benson Murder Case.* Cloth. New York, 1926. (By Willard Huntington Wright.) First edition. In dust jacket. $200–$250. Author's first book.

VAN DOREN, Mark. *Spring Thunder and Other Poems.* Boards. New York, 1924. First edition. $50–$65. Author's first book.

VAN LOON, Hendrik Willem. *The Story of Mankind.* Illustrated by the author. Cloth, pictorial label. (New York), 1921. First edition. In dust jacket. $100–$125.

VAN TRAMP, John C. *Prairie and Rocky Mountain Adventures.* 61 plates. Leather. Columbus, Ohio, 1858. First edition. $125–$150. Columbus, 1867. Leather. $50–$60. Columbus, 1870. Leather. $50–$60.

VAN VECHTEN, Carl. *Firecrackers: A Realistic Novel.* Boards and cloth. New York, 1925. First edition. One of 205 signed. Boxed. $75–$100.

VAN VECHTEN, Carl. *Music After the Great War.* Purple cloth, paper labels. New York, 1915. First edition. In dust jacket. $100–$125. Author's first book.

VAN VECHTEN, Carl. *Nigger Heaven.* Decorated cloth, printed spine label. New York, 1926. First edition. One of 205 signed. Boxed. $100–$125.

VAN VECHTEN, Carl. *Parties.* Lemon-yellow vellum, silver decorations. New York, 1930. One of 250 signed. In dust jacket. $75–$100. Trade edition: Yellow cloth. In dust jacket. $20.

VAN VECHTEN, Carl. *Spider Boy: A Scenario for a Moving Picture.* Half cloth. New York, 1928. First edition. One of 220. Boxed. $100–$150. Another issue: Red vellum. One of 75 on vellum. Boxed. $125–$150.

VAN VECHTEN, Carl. *The Tattooed Countess.* Boards and cloth. New York, 1924. First edition. One of 150 signed. Boxed. $100–$150. Trade edition: Cloth. In dust jacket. $75.

VAN VECHTEN, Carl. *The Tiger in the House.* Half cloth. New York, 1920. First edition. In dust jacket. $50–$75.

VAN VOGT, A. E. *Slan: A Story of the Future.* Cloth. Sauk City, Wis., 1946. Arkham House. First edition. In dust jacket. $150–$200.

VAN VOGT, A. E. *The Weapon Makers.* Cloth. Providence, (1947). First edition. In dust jacket. $75–$100.

VAN ZANDT, Nicholas Biddle. *A Full Description of the Soil, Water, Timber, and Prairies of Each Lot, or Quarter Section of the Military Lands Between the Mississippi and Illinois Rivers.* 127 pp., plus separately issued folding map. Boards and calf. Washington City, 1818. First edition. $3,500–$4,000.

VANZETTI, Bartolomeo. *Background of the Plymouth Trial.* 38 pp., wrappers. Chelsea, Mass., 1927. First edition. $50–$75.

VAUGHAN, Henry. *Poems.* Illustrated. Boards. (Newtown, Wales), 1924. Gregynog Press. One of 500. $150–$250.

VAUGHAN, Dr. John. *A Concise History of the Autumnal Fever, Which Prevailed in the Borough of Wilmington, in the Year 1802.* 32 pp., wrappers. Wilmington, Del., 1803. First edition. $175–$200.

VAUGHN, Robert. *Then and Now, or 36 Years in the Rockies.* Illustrated. Pictorial cloth. Minneapolis, 1900. First edition. $150–$175.

VEBLEN, Thorstein. *The Theory of the Leisure Class.* Green cloth. New York, 1899. First edition. $250–$300.

VEDDER, Elihu. *Doubt and Other Things.* Illustrated by Vedder. Parchment. Boston, 1922. First edition. One of 500. Boxed. $75–$100.

VEGA CARPIO, Lope Félix de (attributed to). *The Star of Seville.* Translated by Henry Thomas. Half morocco. Newtown, Wales, 1935. Gregynog Press. One of 175. $500–$750.

VELASCO, José Francisco. *Sonora: Its Extent, Population, Natural Productions, Indian Tribes, Mines, Mineral Lands, etc.* Translated by William F. Nye. Cloth. San Francisco, 1861. First American edition. $200–$250.

VELIKOVSKY, Immanuel. *Worlds in Collision.* Cloth. New York, 1950. First edition. In dust jacket. $50–$60. Author's first book.

VENABLE, W. H. *Beginnings of Literary Culture in the Ohio Valley.* Cloth. Cincinnati, 1891. First edition. $100–$125.

VENTURE (The): An Annual of Art and Literature. 23 plates. Pictorial cloth. London, 1905 (actually 1904). First edition. ("Two Songs," included here, is James Joyce's first appearance in a clothbound book.) $250–$300.

VERGA, Giovanni. *Little Novels of Sicily.* Translated by D. H. Lawrence. Red cloth, spine label. New York, 1925. First edition, first binding. In dust jacket. $100–$125.

VERGA, Giovanni. *Mastro—Don Gesualdo.* Translated by D. H. Lawrence. Cloth. New York, 1923. First edition. In dust jacket. $100–$125. London, 1925. Cloth. First English edition. In dust jacket. $100–$125.

VERINO, Ugolino. *Vita di Santa Chiara Vergine.* Printed in black and red. 4 facsimile pages. White vellum. London, 1921. Ashendene Press. One of 236. $500–$750. Another issue: Full red vellum. One of 10 on vellum. $2,000–$3,000.

VERNE, Jules. *Five Weeks in a Balloon.* Red cloth. New York, 1869. First American edition. $100–$125. New York, 1873. Blue cloth. $50–$75.

VERNE, Jules. *From the Clouds to the Mountains.* 5 plates. Pictorial reddish cloth. Boston, 1874. First American edition. $100–$125.

VERNE, Jules. *From the Earth to the Moon.* Illustrated. Cloth. London, 1873. First English edition. $250–$300. New York, 1874. Illustrated. Cloth. First American edition. $150–$225.

VERNE, Jules. *The Fur Country; or, Seventy Degrees North Latitude.* 100 full-page illustrations. Pictorial cloth. Boston, 1874. First American edition. 100–$125.

VERNE, Jules. *Mistress Branican.* Illustrated, including 2 maps and 12 colored engravings. Pictorial red cloth. Paris, no date. First edition. $75–$125.

VERNE, Jules. *The Mysterious Island.* Illustrated. Cloth. Chicago, 1876. First American edition. $75–$100.

VERSES. (By Edith Newbold Jones.) Wrappers. Newport, R.I., 1878. First edition. (Edith Wharton's anonymous first book.) $500–$750.

VERSES by Two Undergraduates. Wrappers. (Cambridge, Mass.), 1905. (By Van Wyck Brooks and John Hall Wheelock.) First edition. $75. First book for both authors.

VERSES from the Harvard Advocate. Cloth. Cambridge, 1906. First edition. $100–$125. (Note: Contains five poems by Wallace Stevens.)

VERSES on Various Occasions. Green cloth. London, 1868. (By John Henry, Cardinal Newman.)First edition. $150. Second edition, same date, 368 pp. $100.

VESPUCCI, Amerigo. *Letter of Amerigo Vespucci Describing His Four Voyages to the New World.* Map in color, illustrations by Valenti Angelo. Vellum. San Francisco, 1926. One of 250. Boxed. $200–$250.

VESTAL, Stanley. *Big Foot Wallace*. Illustrated. Cloth. Boston, 1942. (By Walter S. Campbell.) First edition. In dust jacket. $50–$75.

VICENTIO, Ludovico. *The Calligraphic Models of Ludovico degli Arrighi, Surnamed Vicentio*. Edited by Stanley Morrison. 64 pp., facsimile. Montagnola (Paris), 1926. One of 300. $500–$750.

VIDAL, Gore. See Box, Edgar.

VIDAL, Gore. *The City and The Pillar*. Cloth. New York, (1948). First edition. In dust jacket. $65–$75.

VIDAL, Gore. *In a Yellow Wood*. Cloth. New York, 1947. First edition. In dust jacket. $75–$100.

VIDAL, Gore. *The Judgment of Paris*. Cloth. New York, 1952, First edition. In dust jacket. $50–$60.

VIDAL, Gore. *A Search for the King*. Cloth. New York, 1950. First edition. In dust jacket. $50–$60.

VIDAL, Gore. *The Season of Comfort*. Cloth. New York, 1949. First edition. In dust jacket. $75–$100.

VIDAL, Gore. *Williwaw*. Cloth. New York, 1946. First edition. In dust jacket. $100–$125. Author's first book.

VILLA, José Garcia. *Footnote to Youth*. Cloth. New York, 1933. First edition. In dust jacket. $75–$100. Author's first book.

VINDICATION of the Recent and Prevailing Policy of Georgia in Its Internal Affairs, etc. (A). 90 pp., wrappers (?). Athens, Ga., 1827. (By Augustin S. Clayton.) First edition. $250–$300.

VIRGINIA Illustrated. Cloth. New York, 1857. (By David Hunter Strother.) First edition. $100–$150.

VIRGINIA Speller and Reader (The). Boards. Richmond, 1865. $250–$300.

VISCHER, Edward. *Missions of Upper California*. 15 plates. Wrappers. San Francisco, 1872. First edition. $300–$350.

VISCHER, Edward. *Sketches of the Washoe Mining Region*. Cloth portfolio with 29 mounted plates (25 numbered) and 24 pp. of text, wrappers. San Francisco, 1862. First edition. $1,500–$2,000. Also, $1,100 (A, 1968)—the Streeter copy (catalogued "24 pp., 24 plates"). (Note: Another copy was offered in a Boston dealer's catalogue in 1957 as with 25 numbered plates and four other mounted plates at $850. Howes' *U.S.-iana* calls for 26 plates.)

VISIT to Texas (A). Folding map in color, 4 plates. Cloth. New York, 1834. (Attributed to Col. W. W. Morris and Dr. M. [or E.] Fisk[e]?) First edition. $650–$750. New York, 1836. Cloth. Second edition, with plates omitted. $400–$500.

VISSCHER, William Lightfoot. *"Black Mammy": A Song of the Sunny South*. Illustrated. Cloth. Cheyenne, 1885. First edition. $75–$100. Author's first book.

VISSER, H. F. E. *Asiatic Art*. Illustrated, including color frontispiece. Black cloth. New York, (1948). First edition. In dust jacket. $75–$100.

VIVIAN, George. *Scenery of Portugal and Spain*. 35 hand-colored plates. Half morocco. London, 1839. First edition. $2,000–$3,000.

VIVIAN, George. *Spanish Scenery*. Engraved title, 27 other plates. Half morocco. London, 1838. First edition. $2,000–$3,000.

VIVIAN Grey. 5 vols., boards, paper labels. London, 1826. (By Benjamin Disraeli.) First edition. $500–$600. Author's first novel.

VIZETELLY, Henry. *A History of Champagne*. Illustrated. Cloth. London, 1882. First edition. $300–$400.

VOIAGE and Travaile of Sir John Maundeville (The). Illuminated by Valenti Angelo. Full or half morocco. New York, 1928. Grabhorn Press (Random House). One of 150. $2,000–$2,250.

VOICE of Scotland (The). See MacDiarmid, Hugh.

VOLNEY, C. F. *A View of the Soil and Climate of the United States*. 2 folding plates, 2 folding maps. Leather. Philadelphia, 1804. First American edition. $200–$250.

VOLTAIRE, Jean François Marie Arouet de. *Candide*. Translated by Richard Aldington. Illustrated by Rockwell Kent and colored by hand. Cloth, leather spine. New York, 1928. Limited edition. One of 95 signed. Boxed. $400–$600. Ordinary issue (not hand-colored): Buckram. One of 1,470 signed by Kent. $125–$200.

VON HAGEN, Victor W. *The Aztec and Maya Papermakers*. Illustrated, including paper samples. Cloth. New York, 1943. First edition. One of 220 signed. $400–$500.

VON OETTINGEN, B. *Horse Breeding in Theory and Practice*. Cloth. London, 1909. $100–$150.

VONNEGUT, Kurt, Jr. *Canary in a Cat House*. Pictorial wrappers. Greenwich, (1961). First edition. $75–$100.

VONNEGUT, Kurt, Jr. *Cat's Cradle*. Two-toned cloth. New York, (1963). First edition. In dust jacket. $75–$100.

VONNEGUT, Kurt, Jr. *God Bless You, Mr. Rosewater*. Cloth. New York, (1965). First edition. In dust jacket. $100.

VONNEGUT, Kurt, Jr. *Mother Night*. Wrappers. Greenwich, Conn., (1962). Fawcett Publications. First edition. $75. New York, (1966). Boards. First hardbound edition. In dust jacket. $75–$85.

VONNEGUT, Kurt, Jr. *Player Piano*. Boards. New York, 1952. First edition, with the Scribner seal and "A" on copyright page. In dust jacket. $150–$200. Advance copy in wrappers: $500–$600. Author's first book.

VONNEGUT, Kurt, Jr. *The Sirens of Titan*. Pictorial wrappers. (New York, 1959.) First edition. $100. Boston, 1961. Cloth. First hardbound edition. In dust jacket. $100–$125.

VONNEGUT, Kurt, Jr. *Slapstick*. Cloth. New York, (1976). First edition. One of 250 signed. Boxed. $75–$100.

VONNEGUT, Kurt, Jr. *Slaughterhouse-Five*. Cloth. (New York, 1969.) First edition, first printing. In dust jacket. $75–$100.

VONNEGUT, Kurt, Jr. *Welcome to the Monkey House*. Boards. (New York, 1968.) First edition. In dust jacket. $75–$125.

VOORHEES, Luke. *Personal Recollections of Pioneer Life on the Mountains and Plains of the Great West*. Portrait. 75 pp., cloth. Cheyenne, (1920). First edition. $125–$150.

VORAGINE, Jacobus de. *The Golden Legend*. Translated by William Caxton. Edited by H. S. Ellis. Illustrated. 3 vols., boards. London, 1892. Kelmscott Press. One of 500. $1,500–$2,000.

VOSBURGH, W. S. *Cherished Portraits of Thoroughbred Horses from the Collection of William Woodward*. 70 plates. Full morocco. New York, 1929. Derrydale Press. Limited edition on vellum. $2,000–$2,500. Also, $1,500 (A, 1980).

VOYAGE *to Mexico and Havanna (A); Including Some General Observations on the United States.* By an Italian. Half calf. New York, 1841. (By Charles Barinetti). First edition. $225–$250.

VOYNICH, E. L. *The Gadfly.* Red or brown cloth. New York, 1897. First American edition. $50–$60.

W

W., E. B. *The Lady is Cold: Poems by E. B. W.* Boards. New York, 1929. (By E. B. White.) First edition. In dust jacket. $75–$100. Author's first book.

WADSWORTH, Edward. *The Black Country.* Introduction by Arnold Bennett. 20 drawings and signed woodcut frontispiece. Cloth. London, 1920. One of 50 on Japan vellum, with special additional woodcut. $500–$600. Ordinary copies: In dust jacket. $100–$125.

WAGNER, Lieut. Col. A. L., and Kelley, Comm. J. D. *The United States Army and Navy: Their Histories, etc.* 43 colored plates. Oblong folio, leatherette. Akron, Ohio, 1899. First edition. $200–$250.

WAGNER, Henry R. *Bullion to Books.* Illustrated. Cloth. Los Angeles, 1942. First edition. In dust jacket. $100–$150.

WAGNER, Henry R. *The Cartography of the Northwest Coast of America to the Year 1800.* 2 vols., folio, cloth. Berkeley, 1937. First edition. In dust jackets. Boxed. $500–$600.

WAGNER, Henry R. *The Plains and the Rockies.* Boards and cloth. San Francisco, 1920. First edition (suppressed). With 6-page pamphlet of corrections. $300–$400. San Francisco, 1921. Boards. First published edition. $100–$150. San Francisco, 1937. Revised by C. L. Camp. Grabhorn Press. Cloth. Second edition. One of 600. $400–$450. Columbus, Ohio, 1953. Cloth. Third edition. $200–$250. Another issue: Boards. De luxe edition. One of 75. Boxed. $400–$500.

WAGNER, Henry R. *Sir Francis Drake's Voyage Around the World.* Maps, plates. Cloth. San Francisco, 1926. First edition. $200–$225. Another issue: Morocco and cloth, extra-illustrated. One of 100 signed. $200–$250.

WAGNER, Henry R. *Sixty Years of Book Collecting.* Portrait frontispiece. Boards. (Los Angeles), 1952. First edition. One of 200. $150–$250.

WAGNER, Henry R. *Spanish Explorations in the Strait of Juan de Fuca.* Maps, illustrations. Cloth. Santa Ana, Calif., 1933. First edition. One of 425. $200–$250. Another issue: Vellum. One of 25 signed and extra-illustrated. $500–$600.

WAGNER, Henry R. *The Spanish Southwest. 1542–1794.* Half morocco. Berkeley, 1924. First edition. One of 100. $350–$450. Another issue: Vellum. One of 20 signed and extra-illustrated. $500–$600. Albuquerque, 1937. 2 vols., half vellum. $200–$250.

WAGNER, Henry R. *The Spanish Voyages to the Northwest Coast of America.* Maps, plates. Cloth. San Francisco, 1929. First edition. $200–$250. Another issue: Vellum. One of 25 signed and extra-illustrated. $500–$600.

WAGNER, Henry R. (editor). *California Voyages, 1539–1541.* Cloth. San Francisco, 1925. First edition. $75–$125.

WAGNER, Richard. *The Flying Dutchman.* Vellum. London, 1938. Corvinus Press. One of 130. Boxed. $175–$200.

WAGNER, Richard. *The Rhinegold & The Valkyrie.* Translated by Margaret Armour. 34 color plates by Arthur Rackham. Vellum. London, 1910. One of 1,150 signed by the artist. $1,000–$1,250. London, 1910. Cloth. Trade edition. $150–$200. New York,

1910. Cloth. American trade edition. $150–$200. London, (1920). Cloth. $150–$200. London, (1939). Cloth. $100.

WAGNER, Richard. *Siegfried and the Twilight of the Gods.* Translated by Margaret Armour. Illustrated by Arthur Rackham. Pictorial vellum. London, 1911. One of 1,150 signed. In half morocco slipcase. $750–$1,000. London, 1911. Cloth. Trade edition. $150–$200. London, 1924. Cloth. $100–$150.

WAGSTAFF, Theophile. *Flore et Zephyr: Ballet Mythologique.* 9 tinted plates (including cover title) by the author. Wrappers. London, 1836. (By William Makepeace Thackeray.) First edition. $2,000–$2,500. Also, lacking one plate, $792 (A, 1979). Author's first separate publication.

WAIN, John. *Mixed Feelings! Nineteen Poems.* Wrappers. Reading, England, 1951. First edition. One of 120. $150–$200. Author's first book.

WAKEFIELD, John A. *History of the War Between the United States and the Sac and Fox Nations of Indians, etc.* Boards and calf. Jacksonville, Ill., 1834. First edition. $600–$800.

WAKEFIELD, Priscilla. *A Family Tour Through the British Empire.* Contemporary calf, leather label. Philadelphia 1804. First American edition. $100–$125.

WAKOSKI, Diane. *Coins and Coffins.* Printed wrappers. (New York, 1962.) First edition. $100–$125. Author's first printed book.

WAKOSKI, Diane. *The Diamond Merchant.* Gray cloth, paper label. Cambridge, Mass., (1968). First edition. One of 99 signed. In dust jacket. $75–$85.

WAKOSKI, Diane. *Discrepancies and Apparitions.* Cloth. Garden City, 1966. First edition. In dust jacket. $50–$60.

WAKOSKI, Diane. *The Lament of the Lady Bank Dick.* Boards. Cambridge, (1969). First edition. One of 109 signed. In glassine dust jacket. $100.

WAKOSKI, Diane. *The Magellanic Clouds.* Boards. Los Angeles, 1970. Black Sparrow Press. One of 250 signed. In acetate dust jacket. $50–$60. Another issue: Wrappers. $10.

WAKOSKI, Diane. *On Barbara's Shore.* Boards. Los Angeles, 1971. First edition. One of 100 signed. In acetate dust jacket. $75. Another issue: Wrappers. $10.

WAKOSKI, Diane. *Thanking My Mother for Piano Lessons.* Wrappers. Mt. Horeb, Wis., 1969. One of 250. $100–$125.

WALCOTT, Mary Vaux. *North American Wildflowers.* 400 color plates. 5 vols., cloth portfolios. Washington, 1925–29. One of 500 signed. Boxed. $400–$600. Ordinary issue: $200–$300.

WALDROP, Keith. *Songs from the Decline of the West.* Calf. Mt. Horeb, (1970). First edition. One of 120. $60.

WALGAMOTT, Charles S. *Reminiscences of Early Days.* Plates. 2 vols., cloth. (Twin Falls, Idaho, 1926–27.) First edition. $100–$150.

WALGAMOTT, Charles S. *"Six Decades Back."* Cloth. Caldwell, Idaho, 1936. Second edition (or *Reminiscences of Early Days*). $50–$75.

WALKER, Charles D. *Biographical Sketches of the Graduates and Élèves of the Virginia Military Institute Who Fell During the War between the States.* Cloth. Philadelphia, 1875. $100–$150.

WALKER, Judson E. *Campaigns of General Custer in the North-West, and the Final Surrender of Sitting Bull.* Illustrated. Wrappers. New York, 1881. First edition. $250.

WALKER, Tacetta. *Stories of Early Days in Wyoming: Big Horn Basin.* Illustrated. Cloth. Casper, Wyo., (1936). First edition. $35–$50.

WALL, Bernhardt. *Ten Etched Poems: First Series.* Boards, paper label. New York, 1924. First edition. One of 50 signed. $50–$75.

WALL, Oscar G. *Recollections of the Sioux Massacre.* Illustrated. Cloth. Lake City, Minn., 1909. First edition. $125.

WALL, W. G. *Wall's Hudson River Portfolio.* 21 color plates. Oblong atlas folio, boards and calf. New York, (about 1826). First edition. $4,000–$5,000, possibly more. (Note: The last two sales noted at auction were in 1948: copies without title page, $1,700 each.) New York, 1828. Second edition (or state), without title page. $4,000–$5,000, possibly more.

WALLACE, Dexter. *The Blood of the Prophets.* Boards. Chicago, 1905. (By Edgar Lee Masters.) First edition. $75–$100.

WALLACE, Ed. R. *Parson Hanks: 14 Years in the West.* Wrappers. Arlington, Tex., (1906?). First edition. $150–$200.

WALLACE, Edgar. *The Four Just Men.* Frontispiece. Yellow cloth. London, 1905. First edition, first issue, with folding frontispiece plate and "Solution" leaf at end. $100–$150.

WALLACE, Edgar. *The Mission That Failed! A Tale of the Raid and Other Poems.* Wrappers. (Cape Town, 1898.) First edition. $300–$400. Author's first book.

WALLACE, Edgar. *Writ in Barracks.* Cloth. London, 1900. First edition. $50–$75.

WALLACE, Lew. *Ben-Hur: A Tale of the Christ.* Light-blue floral cloth. New York, 1880. First edition, first issue, with dated title page, six-word dedication. $250–$300. (Copies in brown cloth and other colors are considered later issues.) New York, 1960. Limited Editions Club. Boxed. $40–$50.

WALLACE, Lew. *The Fair God.* Cloth. Boston, 1873. First edition, first state on thin paper, bound in beveled boards. $100–$125. Author's first book.

WALTER Kennedy: An American Tale. Boards, leather spine label. London, 1805. (By John Davis.) First edition. $500–$600.

WALTER, William W. *The Sharp Sickle: Text Book of Eschatology.* Cloth. Aurora, Ill., (1938). First edition. Boxed. $50.

WALTERS, L. D. O. (compiler). *The Year's at the Spring: An Anthology of Recent Poetry.* Illustrated by Harry Clarke. Vellum. London or New York, 1920. One of 250 signed by Clarke. $600–$850.

WALTERS, Lorenzo D. *Tombstone's Yesterday.* Illustrated. Cloth. Tucson, 1928. First edition. In dust jacket. $100–$125.

WALTHER, C. F., and Taylor, I. N. *The Resources and Advantages of the State of Nebraska.* (Cover title.) Folding map. 27 pp., wrappers. (Omaha, 1871.) First edition. $175–$200.

WALTON, Izaak (or Isaac), and Cotton, Charles. *The Compleat [or Complete] Angler.* (Note: First published in 1653.) For seventeenth and eighteenth century editions— beyond the arbitrary range of this *Handbook*—see the book auction records. There have been innumerable editions since 1653. Following are a few representative examples since our starting date of 1800: New York, 1847. Edited by George W. Bethune. 2 portraits, 2 plates, other illustrations. 2 parts bound in one vol., light tan cloth, horizontal red stripes. First American edition. Large paper issue, with proof impressions of plates. $1,000–$1,500. Ordinary issue: $750–$1,000. London, 1888. "Lea & Dove Edition." Edited by R. B. Marston. Illustrated, including 54 photogravures. 2 vols., full morocco (large paper issue of 250) or half morocco (ordinary issue of 500). $2,000–$3,000. (The photos are on India paper in the large paper version.) London, 1893. "Tercentenary Edition." Illustrated. 2 vols., half vellum and green cloth. One of 350.

In green cloth jackets. $750–$1,000. London, 1902. "Winchester Edition." Illustrated with etchings by William Strang and D. Y. Cameron. 2 vols., full vellum. One of 150 large paper copies signed by the artists. $500–$750. London, 1927. 16 wood engravings by Eric Fitch Daglish. Half vellum. One of 100 with an extra signed engraving. Boxed. $350–$500. London, (1931). Illustrated by Arthur Rackham. Vellum. One of 775 signed by Rackham. $750–$1,000. Trade edition: Cloth. $250–$300.

WALTON, W. M. *Life and Adventures of Ben Thompson, the Famous Texan.* 15 plates, 229 pp., pictorial wrappers. Austin, 1884. First edition. $1,500–$1,750.

WANDREI, Donald. *Dark Odyssey.* Illustrated. Cloth. St. Paul, (1931). First edition. One of 400 signed. In dust jacket. $125–$150.

WANDREI, Donald. *The Eye and the Finger.* Cloth. (Sauk City, Wis.), 1944. First edition. In dust jacket. $100–$125.

WANDREI, Donald. *Poems for Midnight.* Illustrated. Cloth. Sauk City, 1964. First edition. In dust jacket. $75–$100.

WANDREI, Donald. *The Web of Easter Island.* Cloth. Sauk City, 1948. First edition. In dust jacket. $50.

WAR in Florida (The). By a Late Staff Officer. Folding map. 2 plates. Green cloth. Baltimore, 1836. (By Woodburn Potter.) First edition. $300–$350. Also, rebound in half leather, one map repaired, $70 (A, 1980).

WAR in Texas (The). By a Citizen of the United States. 57 pp., printed wrappers. Philadelphia, 1836. (By Benjamin Lundy.) First edition under this title (but second, enlarged, edition of an earlier Philadelphia pamphlet of the same date, *The Origin and True Causes of the Texas Insurrection*). $350. (Note: *Origin and True Causes* brought $160 at auction in New York in 1980.)

WARD, D. B. *Across the Plains in 1853.* (Cover title.) Portrait. 55 pp., printed wrappers. (Seattle, 1911.) First edition. $150–$200.

WARD, Lynd. *God's Man: A Novel in Woodcuts.* 143 plates, no text. Pictorial boards and cloth. New York, (1929). First edition. In dust jacket. $125–$175. Another issue: One of 409 signed. Boxed. $200–$250.

WARD, Lynd. *Prelude to a Million Years: A Book of Wood Engravings.* Boards. New York, 1933. First edition. One of 920 signed. $200–$250.

WARD, Lynd. *Vertigo: A Novel in Woodcuts.* Pictorial cloth. New York, 1937. First edition. In dust jacket. $150–$175.

WARD, Mary Jane. *The Snake Pit.* Cloth. New York, (1946). First edition. In dust jacket. $50.

WARDER, T. B., and Catlett, J. M. *Battle of Young's Branch, or, Manassas Plain.* 2 folding maps. Wrappers, or half leather. Richmond, 1862. First edition. $500–$750.

WARE, Eugene. *The Indian War of 1864.* Frontispiece. Cloth. Topeka, 1911, First edition. $150–$200.

WARE, Eugene. *The Lyon Campaign in Missouri.* Cloth. Topeka, 1907. First edition. $125.

WARE, Joseph E. *The Emigrants' Guide to California.* Folding map. 56 pp., cloth. St. Louis, (1849). First edition. $2,500–$3,000. The last two copies to sell at auction lacked the map: $1,000 (1948); $500 (1968)—the Streeter copy, offered later at retail for $1,000.

WARNER, Charles Dudley. *Backlog Studies.* Illustrated. Boards. Cambridge, Mass., 1899. One of 250 signed. $75–$100.

WARNER, Charles Dudley. *My Summer in a Garden.* Cloth. Boston, 1871. First edition. $75. Author's first book.

WARNER, Matt, and King, Murray E. *The Last of the Bandit Riders.* Illustrated. Pictorial cloth. Caldwell, Idaho, 1940. First edition. In slipcase. $75–$85.

WARNER, Susan B. See Wetherell, Elizabeth.

WARRE, Henry J. *Sketches in North America and the Oregon Territory.* Map, 20 colored views (on 16 sheets). Large folio, boards. (London, 1848.) First edition. $10,000–$15,000.

WARREN, Edward. *A Doctor's Experiences in Three Continents.* Cloth. Baltimore, 1855. $200–$275.

WARREN, Edward. *An Epitome of Practical Surgery for Field and Hospital.* Boards and cloth. Richmond, 1863. First edition. $500–$600.

WARREN, John. *The Conchologist.* 34 plates, 17 colored. Morocco. Boston, 1843. First edition. $250–$300.

WARREN, John C. *Etherization: With Surgical Remarks.* Cloth. Boston, 1848. First edition. $400–$500.

WARREN, Robert Penn. *All the King's Men.* Cloth. New York, (1946). First edition. In dust jacket. $75–$85.

WARREN, Robert Penn. *Blackberry Winter.* Illustrated. Boards, paper label. (Cummington, Mass.), 1946. First edition. One of 280 on Arches paper, signed. $300–$400.

WARREN, Robert Penn. *Eleven Poems on the Same Theme.* Printed wrappers. Norfolk, Conn., (1942). First edition. $75–$125. Another issue: Boards. $100–$150.

WARREN, Robert Penn. *John Brown: The Making of a Martyr.* Portrait. Cloth. New York, 1929. First edition. In dust jacket. $400–$500. Author's first book.

WARREN, Robert Penn. *Night Rider.* Cloth. Boston, 1939. First edition. In dust jacket. $100–$150. Author's first novel.

WARREN, Robert Penn. *Selected Poems: New and Old, 1923-1966.* Cloth. New York, (1966). First edition. One of 250 signed. In dust jacket. Boxed. $75–$125. Trade edition: In dust jacket. $20.

WARREN, Robert Penn. *Selected Poems: 1923-1943.* Cloth. New York, (1944). First edition. In dust jacket. $135–$150.

WARREN, Robert Penn. *Thirty-six Poems.* Wrappers. New York, 1935. First edition. One of 165 signed. In tissue dust jacket. $200–$425.

WARREN, Samuel. See *Ten Thousand a-Year.*

WASHBURNE, The Rev. Cephas. *Reminiscences of the Indians.* Cloth. Richmond, (1869). First edition. $200–$300.

WASHINGTON, Booker T. *The Future of the American Negro.* Cloth. Boston, 1899. First edition. $200–$250. Author's first book.

WASHINGTON, Booker T. *Up from Slavery: An Autobiography.* Cloth. New York, 1901. First edition. $50–$75. New York, 1970. Limited Editions Club. Boxed. $30–$40.

WASSON, George S. *Sailing Days on the Penobscot.* Boards and cloth. Salem, Mass., 1932. One of 97 on rag paper. $150–$200. Trade edition: Cloth. In dust jacket. $75–$85.

WASSON, R. Gordon. *The Hall Carbine Affair.* Illustrated. Half morocco. Danbury, Conn., 1971. One of 250. Boxed. $125–$200.

WASSON, R. Gordon. *Soma: Divine Mushroom of Immortality.* Illustrated, including color plates. Half morocco. New York, 1968. First edition. One of 680. Boxed. $550.

WASSON, Valentina Pavlona, and Wasson, R. Gordon. *Mushrooms, Russia and History.* Color plates, folding maps and plates. 2 vols. , folio, buckram. New York, (1957). First edition. One of 521. Boxed. $2,000.

WATER Witch (The), or The Skimmer of the Seas. By the Author of *The Pilot.* 3 vols., boards, paper labels. Dresden, 1830. (By James Fenimore Cooper.) First edition. $8,000–$10,000. Also, one spine chipped, $3,750 (A, 1976). London, 1830. 3 vols., brown boards, paper labels. First English edition. $1,000–$1,500. Philadelphia, 1831. Blue or tan boards. First American edition. $600–$800.

WATERLOO, Stanley. *The Seekers.* Red cloth. Chicago, 1900. First edition. $75–$125.

WATERLOO, Stanley. *The Story of Ab.* Illustrated. Cloth. Chicago, 1897. First edition. $125–$150.

WATERLOO, Stanley. *The Wolf's Long Howl.* Pictorial cloth. Chicago, 1899. First edition. $100–$125.

WATERS, Frank. *The Colorado.* Illustrated. Red cloth. New York, (1946). First edition, with Rinehart "R" on copyright page. In dust jacket. $35.

WATERS, Frank. *Leon Gaspard.* Illustrated, including color, by Gaspard. Cloth. Flagstaff, Ariz., 1964. First edition. One of 500 signed. Boxed. $85–$100. Trade edition: In dust jacket. $25.

WATERS, Frank. *Masked Gods: Navaho and Pueblo Ceremonialism.* Illustrated. Cloth. Albuquerque, 1950. First edition. In dust jacket. $75. Another issue: One of 300 signed. $150–$200.

WATERS, Frank. *The Story of Mrs. Virgil Earp.* Cloth. New York, (1960). First edition. In dust jacket. $50.

WATERS, Frank. *The Wild Earth's Nobility.* Cloth. New York, 1935. First edition. In dust jacket. $75–$100. Author's first book.

WATKINS, C. L. *Photographic Views of the Falls and Valley of Yo-Semite.* Map and 52 (or 62?) mounted photographs. Folio, morocco. San Francisco, 1863. First edition. $10,000–$15,000. Also, $8,250 (A, 1978).

WATKINS, C. L. *Photographs of the Columbia River and Oregon.* 51 mounted albumen prints. Elephant folio, morocco with redwood inlay. San Francisco, (about 1873). $100,000 (A, 1979).

WATKINS, C. L. *Photographs of the Pacific Coast.* 49 mounted albumen prints. Elephant folio, morocco with redwood inlay. San Francisco, (about 1873). Lacking spine, $98,000 (A, 1979).

WATKINS, C. L. *Watkins New Series Columbia River Scenery, Oregon.* 40 plates. Oblong, leather. No place, (about 1880). $8,250 (A, 1979).

WATKINS, Lucy. *The History and Adventures of Little James and Mary.* 15 pp., wrappers. Philadelphia, (1810). $100–$125.

WATKINS, Lura W. *Early New England Potters and Their Wares.* Illustrated. Cloth. Cambridge, Mass., 1950. $40–$50.

WATSON, Douglas S. *West Wind: The Life Story of Joseph Reddeford Walker.* Plates, folding map. Boards. Los Angeles, 1934. First edition. One of 100. $300–$400. Trade edition: $150–$200.

WATSON, Douglas S. (editor). *California in the Fifties.* 50 views. Oblong folio, cloth. San Francisco. 1936. One of 850. In dust jacket. $400–$450.

WATSON, Douglas S. (editor). *The Spanish Occupation of California.* Illustrated. Boards and cloth. San Francisco, 1934. Grabhorn Press. One of 550. $100–$150.

WATSON, Frederick. *Hunting Pie.* Illustrated. Boards. New York, (1938). Derrydale Press. First edition. One of 750. $100–$150.

WATSON, William. *The Eloping Angels.* Cloth. London, 1893. First edition. One of 250. $50–$60. Trade edition: Cloth. $25.

WATSON, William. *Epigrams of Art, Life and Nature.* Cloth. Liverpool, 1884. First edition. One of 50. $100–$125.

WATSON, William. *Excursions in Criticism.* Boards. London, 1893. First edition. One of 50. $75–$100. Trade edition: Cloth. $25.

WATSON, William. *The Father of the Forest and Other Poems.* Frontispiece portrait. Cloth. London, 1895. First edition. One of 75. $100–$125. Also, in a special leather binding, $700 (A, 1980).

WATSON, William. *Odes and Other Poems.* Cloth. London, 1894. First edition. One of 75. $100–$125.

WATSON, William. *The Purple East: A Series of Sonnets on England's Desertion of Armenia.* Frontispiece. Cloth. London, 1896. First edition. One of 75. $85–$125.

WATSON, William. *Wordsworth's Grave and Other Poems.* Frontispiece. Boards. London, 1890. First edition. $75–$100.

WATTS, W. J. *Cherokee Citizenship and a Brief History of Internal Affairs in the Cherokee Nation.* (Cover title.) Portrait. Wrappers. Muldrow, Indian Territory (Okla.), 1895. $150–$200.

WATTS, W. W. *Old English Silver.* 307 plates. Cloth. New York, 1924. First American edition. $80–$125. London, 1924. Cloth. First English edition. $125–$150. One of 40 in leather binding. $200–$300.

WAUGH, Alec. *Hot Countries.* Illustrated by Lynd Ward. Pictorial cloth. New York, (1930). First edition. In dust jacket. $50–$75.

WAUGH, Evelyn. *Basil Seal Rides Again.* Cloth. London, 1963. First edition. One of 750 signed. $150–$175. Boston, (1963). Cloth. First American edition. One of 1,000 signed. In dust jacket. $150–$200.

WAUGH, Evelyn. *Black Mischief.* Cloth. London, 1932. First trade edition. In dust jacket, with Book Society wraparound band. $150–$200. Large paper issue: Purple cloth. One of 250 signed. (Issued without dust jacket.) $250–$350.

WAUGH, Evelyn. *Decline and Fall.* Illustrated. Cloth. London, 1928. First edition. In dust jacket. $300–$350. Lacking jacket. $150–$175.

WAUGH, Evelyn. *A Handful of Dust.* Frontispiece. Cloth. London, 1934. First edition. In dust jacket. $100–$125. Another issue: Wrappers. One of 12 signed. $1,500.

WAUGH, Evelyn. *The Holy Places.* Woodcuts by Reynolds Stone. Morocco. London, 1952. First edition. One of 50 signed. In dust jacket. $800–$1,000. New York, 1953. First American edition. One of 950. In dust jacket. $100–$125.

WAUGH, Evelyn. *Labels: A Mediterranean Journal.* Illustrated. Light-blue cloth. London, (1930). First edition. One of 110 signed, specially bound with a leaf of the original manuscript. $600–$750. Trade edition: Cloth. In dust jacket. $150–$175.

WAUGH, Evelyn. *Love Among the Ruins.* Illustrated. Decorated cloth. London, 1953. First edition. One of 350 signed. In glassine dust jacket. $325–$400.

WAUGH, Evelyn. *The Loved One.* Illustrated by Stuart Boyle. Buckram. London, (1948). First edition. One of 250 signed. (Issued without dust jacket.) $200–$300.

Trade issue: In dust jacket. $50. Boston, 1948. Gray cloth. First American edition. In dust jacket. $50–$60.

WAUGH, Evelyn. *P. R. B.: An Essay on the Pre-Raphaelite Brotherhood*. Boards and linen. London, 1926. First edition, with errata slip. $750–$1,000. Also, inscribed, $1,010 (A , 1974).

WAUGH, Evelyn. *Remote People*. London, 1931. First edition. In dust jacket. $250–$350.

WAUGH, Evelyn. *Scoop*. Cloth. London, (1938). First edition. In dust jacket, with Book Society band. $125–$200. (Note: A California bookseller recently catalogued a copy in "first issue" dust jacket, with "aily Bear" at top of jacket instead of a blank space, at $650.)

WAUGH, Evelyn. *They Were Still Dancing*. Cloth. New York, 1932. First American edition (of *Remote People*). In dust jacket. $300.

WAUGH, Evelyn. *Vile Bodies*. Cloth. London, 1930. First edition. In dust jacket. $250–$300. Lacking jacket, $75–$100.

WAUGH, Evelyn. *Waugh in Abyssinia*. Cloth. London, (1936). First edition. In dust jacket. $125–$150.

WAUGH, Evelyn. *Wine in Peace and War*. Illustrations by Rex Whistler. Decorated boards. London, (1947). First edition. In plain dust jacket. $125–$150. Another issue: Leather. One of 100 signed. $300–$400.

WAUGH, Lorenzo. *Autobiography of Lorenzo Waugh*. Illustrated. Cloth. Oakland, 1883. First edition. $85–$100.

WAVERLEY; or, 'Tis Sixty Years Since. 3 vols, boards, paper labels. Edinburgh, 1814. (By Sir Walter Scott.) First edition, first issue, with "our" instead of "your" in first line on page 136 in Vol. II. $3,500–$4,000. Also, $2,250 (A, 1974). Only a few copies known in original boards. One was catalogued by an English dealer early in 1970 at $3,600. Acceptable rebound copies in contemporary leather range in price up to $500 or more at retail.

WAYLAND, John W. *History of Rockingham County*. Plates. Buckram. Dayton, Va., 1912. $125–$150.

WAYLAND, John W. *Historic Homes of Northern Virginia and the Eastern Panhandle of Western Virginia*. Cloth. Staunton, Va., 1937. First edition. $75–$85.

WEARY, Ogdred. *The Beastly Baby*. Illustrated. Wrappers. (New York, 1962.) (By Edward Gorey.) First edition. $200–$300.

WEATHERLY, Frederick Edward. *Magic Pictures: A Book of Changing Scenes*. 16 pp. with pull slides to change pictures (a movable book). Pictorial cloth. London, (about 1890). $200–$250.

WEATHERLY, Frederick Edward. *Pretty Polly: A Novel Book for Children*. 4 double-page 3-dimensional color plates. Half cloth. London, (about 1895). First edition. $250.

WEATHERLY, Frederick Edward. *Punch and Judy and Some of Their Friends*. Illustrated by Patty Townsend. Half cloth. London, (1885). $150–$200.

WEAVER, John V. A. *In American—Poems*. Boards. New York, 1921. First edition. In dust jacket. $75–$85. Author's first book.

WEBB, Mary. *The Chinese Lion*. Decorated boards, red cloth spine, red label on front cover. London, 1937. First edition. One of 350. Boxed. $85–$100.

WEBB, Mary. *The Golden Arrow*. Cloth. London, 1916. First edition. In dust jacket. $350–$400. Author's first book.

WEBB, Mary. *Gone to Earth*. Dark-red cloth. London, (1917). First edition. In dust jacket. $200.

WEBB, Mary. *The House in Dormer Forest*. Green cloth. London, (1920). First edition. In dust jacket. $150–$175.

WEBB, Mary. *Precious Bane*. Green cloth. London, (1924). First edition. In dust jacket. $350–$450. Second edition, same date. Cloth. In dust jacket. $200–$250.

WEBB, Mary. *Seven for a Secret: A Love Story*. Green cloth. London, (1922). First edition. In dust jacket. $150–$200.

WEBB, Mary. *The Spring of Joy: A Little Book of Healing*. Cloth. London, 1917. First edition. In dust jacket. $125–$150. Without jacket, $85.

WEBB, Sidney. *Soviet Communism: A New Civilisation?* Boards. (London, 1935.) First edition. $50–$75.

WEBB, Walter Prescott. *The Great Plains*. Illustrated. Cloth. Boston, (1931). First edition, first issue, with error in heading of Chapter 2. In dust jacket. $100–$150.

WEBB, Walter Prescott. *The Texas Rangers*. Illustrated. Cloth. Boston, 1935. First edition. In dust jacket. $85–$100. Another issue: Half leather. One of 250 signed. Boxed. $400–$550.

WEBBER, C. W. *The Hunter-Naturalist; Romance of Sporting, or Wild Scenes and Wild Hunters*. Engraved title page and 9 colored lithographs, other illustrations. Cloth, leather spine and corners. Philadelphia, (1851). First edition. $500–$600.

WEBBER, C. W. *Old Hicks the Guide*. Cloth. New York, 1848. First edition. $150–$200. Another issue: 2 vols., wrappers. $500–$750.

WEBBER, C. W. *Wild Scenes and Song Birds*. 20 colored plates. Morocco. New York, 1854 (actually 1853). First edition. $250–$300. New York, 1855. Cloth. $150–$200.

WEBER, Carl J. *A Thousand and One Fore-Edge Paintings*. Illustrated. Half cloth. Waterville, Me., 1949. First edition. One of 1,000. In dust jacket. $250.

WEBER, Max. *Cubist Poems*. Cloth. London, 1914. First edition. $150–$250. Author's first book. (Also issued in wrappers.)

"WEBFOOT." *Fore and Aft; Or, Leaves from the Life of an Old Sailor*. Illustrated. Cloth. Boston, 1871. (By William D. Phelps.) First edition. $300–$400.

WEBSTER, George G. See Hall, J. L.

WEBSTER, Jean. *Daddy-Long-Legs*. Illustrated by the author. Decorated cloth. New York, 1912. First edition. In dust jacket. $100–$125. Lacking jacket, $50.

WEBSTER, Noah. See Ford, Paul Leicester (for *Webster Genealogy*).

WEBSTER, Noah. *An American Dictionary of the English Language*. Portrait. 2 vols., light-brown boards, linen spines, paper labels. New York, 1828. First edition. With two-page ad leaf laid in. $3,000–$3,500. Rebacked copy, $2,750.

WEBSTER, Noah. *A Compendious Dictionary of the English Language*. Full leather, leather spine label. Hartford, 1806. First edition. $1,250–$1,500.

WEBSTER, Noah. *A Dictionary of the English Language Compiled for the Use of Common Schools in the United States*. Calf, red morocco label. New Haven, 1807. First edition. $400–$600.

WEIDMAN, Jerome. *I Can Get It for You Wholesale*. Cloth. New York, 1937. First edition. In dust jacket. $50–$60. Author's first book.

WEINBAUM, Stanley G. *Dawn of Flame and Other Stories*. Portrait. Leather. (Milwaukee, 1936.) First edition. $600.

WEIZMANN, Chaim. *Trial and Error*. 2 vols., cloth. New York, (1949). First edition. One of 500 signed. $150–$250. Trade edition: In dust jacket. $25–$35.

WELBY, Adlard. *A Visit to North America*. 14 plates. Leather. London, 1821. First edition. $500–$750.

WELCH, Denton. *Maiden Voyage*. Frontispiece portrait. Cloth. London, 1943. First edition. In dust jacket. $100–$125. Author's first book.

WELCH, Lew. *Courses*. Leather. San Francisco, 1968. First edition. $60.

WELCH, Lew. *Wobbly Rock*. Wrappers. (San Francisco), 1960. First edition. One of 500. $50. Author's first book.

WELLMAN, Paul. *The Callaghan Yesterday and Today*. Illustrated, map. Stiff pictorial wrappers. Encinal, (about 1945). First edition. $175.

WELLS, H. G. *The Adventures of Tommy*. Boards. London, (1929). First edition. In dust jacket. $125–$150.

WELLS, H. G. *Ann Veronica*. Cloth. London, 1909. First edition. In dust jacket. $100–$125. New York, 1909. First American edition. In dust jacket. $75–$100.

WELLS, H. G. *Brynhild*. Cloth. London, 1937. First edition. In dust jacket. $65–$75.

WELLS, H. G. *Certain Personal Matters*. Cloth. London, 1898. First edition. $150–$200.

WELLS, H. G. *The Country of the Blind*. Wood engravings. Orange vellum. London, 1939. Golden Cockerel Press. One of 30 signed. $750–$1,000. Ordinary copies: One of 280. $400–$500.

WELLS, H. G. *The Door in the Wall*. Illustrated with Alvin Langdon Coburn photogravures. Boards. New York, 1911. One of 600. $1,250–$1,500.

WELLS, H. G. *The First Men in the Moon*. Illustrated by Claude Shepperson. Dark-blue cloth. London, 1901. First edition, first issue, gilt lettering on cover. In dust jacket. $950. Without jacket. $200–$300.

WELLS, H. G. *Floor Games*. Illustrated. Pictorial cloth. London, 1911. First edition, first state, pages 8½ inches tall. In dust jacket. $200–$250.

WELLS, H. G. *The Food of the Gods*. Cloth. London, 1904. First edition, first issue, with ads dated "2/7/04." In dust jacket. $350–$400. Lacking dust jacket, $125. New York, 1904. Olive cloth. First American edition. $65–$75.

WELLS, H. G. *Guide to the New World*. Cloth. London, 1941. First edition. In dust jacket. $35–$50.

WELLS, H. G. *The History of Mr. Polly*. Illustrated. Cloth. London, (1910). First edition, first issue, with "Trepanned" on page 8 of ads at back. In dust jacket. $100–$150.

WELLS, H. G. *The Invisible Man*. Red cloth. London, 1897. First edition, first issue, page (1) numbered page 2 in error. $200–$300. New York, 1897. Cloth. First American edition. $75–$125. New York, 1967. Limited Editions Club. Cloth. Boxed. $40.

WELLS, H. G. *The Island of Doctor Moreau*. Brown cloth. London, 1896. First edition, with 32 pp. of ads in back. $250–$350. New York, 1896. Black cloth. First American edition, first binding. $150–$200.

WELLS, H. G. *The Mind at the End of Its Tether*. Cloth. London. (1945). First edition. In dust jacket. $75–$100.

WELLS, H. G. *The Sea Lady*. Cloth. London, 1902. First edition. $100–$125. New York, 1908. Green cloth. First American edition. $75.

WELLS, H. G. *Select Conversations with an Uncle (Now Extinct) and Two Other Reminiscences*. Cloth. London, 1895. First edition. $300–$400. Wells' first literary work.

WELLS, H. G. *The Stolen Bacillus and Other Stories*. Cloth. London, 1895. First edition. $275.

WELLS, H. G. *Tales of Space and Time*. Olive cloth. London, 1900 (actually 1899). First English edition. $300–$400. New York, 1899. Green cloth. First American edition. $200–$300. (Currey says the English edition is first; not all bibliographers agree.)

WELLS, H. G. *Text-Book of Biology*. 2 vols., dark green cloth. London, (1893). First edition, first binding. $500–$750. (Note: Brown cloth is a later binding.) Author's first book.

WELLS, H. G. *Thirty Strange Stories*. Pictorial boards. New York, 1897. First edition. $250–$325.

WELLS, H. G. *The Time Machine*. Gray cloth. London, 1895. First edition, first issue, with ads at back and purple stamping on cloth. $300–$400. Second issue: No ads; cloth lettered in brown. $150–$200. (A simultaneous issue in wrappers, without ads, also is recorded.)

WELLS, H. G. *Tono-Bungay*. Green cloth. London, 1909. First edition. $75–$100.

WELLS, H. G. *Twelve Stories and a Dream*. Cloth. London, 1903. First edition. $100–$150.

WELLS, H. G. *The War in the Air*. 16 plates. Pictorial blue cloth. London, 1908. First edition. In dust jacket. $350–$500. Without jacket, $125. New York, 1908. Illustrated by Eric Pape. First American edition. $125.

WELLS, H. G. *The War of the Worlds*. Gray cloth. London, 1898. First edition. $300–$400.

WELLS, H. G. *When the Sleeper Wakes*. 3 plates. Cloth. London, 1899. First edition. $150–$250. New York, 1899. Green cloth. First American edition. $125–$150.

WELLS, H. G. *The Wonderful Visit*. Red cloth. London, 1895. First edition. $150–$250. New York, 1895. Green cloth. First American edition. $250–$300.

WELLS, H. G. *The World of William Clissold*. 3 vols., cloth. London, 1926. First edition. One of 198 signed. $250–$300.

WELLS, H. G. *The World Set Free*. Green cloth. London. 1914. First edition. In dust jacket. $150.

WELLS, Oliver (editor). *An Anthology of the Younger Poets*. Boards. Philadelphia, 1932. First edition. One of 500. In dust jacket. $75–$100. (Contains 5 poems by William Faulkner.)

WELLS, William, and Onken, Otto. *Western Scenery; or, Land and River, Hill and Dale, in the Mississippi Valley*. Pictorial title page, 19 full-page lithographic views, 52 pp. of text. Boards and calf. Cincinnati, 1851. First edition. $2,500–$5,000.

WELLS, William Charles. *An Essay on Dew*. Boards. London, 1814. First edition. $750–$1,000.

WELLS, Winifred. *The Hesitant Heart*. Lavender boards. New York, 1919. First edition. $50–$75. Author's first book.

WELTY, Eudora. *The Bride of the Innisfallen*. Boards. New York, (1955). First edition. In dust jacket. $30–$40.

WELTY, Eudora. *A Curtain of Green*. Brown cloth. Garden City, 1941. First edition. In dust jacket. $250–$450. Author's first book.

WELTY, Eudora. *Delta Wedding*. Brown cloth. New York, (1946). First edition. In dust jacket. $100–$125. London, 1947. First English edition. In dust jacket. $85.

WELTY, Eudora. *The Golden Apples*. Boards. New York, (1949). First edition. In dust jacket. $150–$200.

WELTY, Eudora. *Losing Battles*. Cloth. New York. (1970). First edition. In dust jacket. $25. Another issue: One of 300 signed. In acetate dust jacket. Boxed. $125–$150.

WELTY, Eudora. *Music from Spain*. Decorated boards, paper spine label. Greenville, Miss., 1948. First edition. One of 775 signed. In opaque dust jacket. $200–$225.

WELTY, Eudora. *The Optimist's Daughter*. Cloth. New York, (1972). First edition. In dust jacket. $35. Limited edition: One of 300 signed. Boxed. $85–$125.

WELTY, Eudora. *A Pageant of Birds*. Wrappers. (New York, 1974.) First edition. One of 300 signed. $75–$100. Another issue: One of 26 signed and lettered. $150–$200.

WELTY, Eudora. *Place in Fiction*. Cloth. New York, 1957. First edition. One of 300 signed. In tissue dust jacket. $150–$200.

WELTY, Eudora. *The Ponder Heart*. Boards. New York, (1954). First edition. In dust jacket. $75–$100.

WELTY, Eudora. *The Robber Bridegroom*. Blue cloth. Garden City, 1942. First edition. In dust jacket. $150–$200.

WELTY, Eudora. *Short Stories*. Boards. New York, (1949). First edition. One of 1,500. In glassine dust jacket. $100–$125.

WELTY, Eudora. *A Sweet Devouring*. Wrappers. New York, 1969. First edition. One of 26 lettered copies, signed. $150–$200. Another issue: One of 150 signed. $75–$100.

WELTY, Eudora. *Three Papers on Fiction*. Wrappers. Northampton, Mass., 1962. First edition. $50–$60.

WELTY, Eudora. *The Wide Net and Other Stories*. Blue cloth. New York, (1943). First edition. In dust jacket. $150–$175.

WENTWORTH, Lady Judith Anne. *The Authentic Arabian Horse and His Descendants*. 26 color plates, numerous other illustrations. Blue cloth. London, (1945). First edition. In dust jacket. $400–$600. London, 1962. Second edition. In dust jacket. $150–$200. New York, 1962. Cloth. In dust jacket. $150–$200.

WENTWORTH, Lady Judith Anne. *Thoroughbred Racing Stock and Its Ancestors*. 21 color plates. Red buckram. London, 1938. First edition. In dust jacket. $400–$500. London, (1960). Second edition. In dust jacket. Boxed. $150–$200.

WEPT of Wish Ton-Wish (The): A Tale. By the Author of *The Pioneers*. 2 vols., boards, paper labels. Philadelphia, 1829. (By James Fenimore Cooper.) First American edition. $2,000–$3,000. (For first edition, see *The Borderers*.)

WERTH, John J. *A Dissertation on the Resources and Policy of California*. 87 pp., cloth. Benicia, 1851. First edition. $1,000–$1,250.

WESCOTT, Glenway. *The Babe's Bed*. Cloth. Paris, 1930. First edition. One of 375 signed. $350–$450. Another issue: One of 18 on parchment. $500–$600.

WESCOTT, Glenway. *The Bitterns: A Book of Twelve Poems*. Black wrappers with printed silver design. Evanston, Ill., (1920). First edition, signed. In cloth folding case. $300–$400. Author's first book.

WESCOTT, Glenway. *A Calendar of Saints for Unbelievers*. Illustrated by Pavel Tchelitchew. Half morocco. Paris, 1932. First edition. One of 40 signed. Boxed. $400–$500. Another issue: Cloth. One of 695. In glassine dust jacket. Boxed. $250–$300.

WESCOTT, Glenway. *Good-bye, Wisconsin.* Boards and cloth. New York, 1928. First edition. One of 250 signed. Boxed. $40–$85. Trade edition: Cloth. In dust jacket. $25.

WESCOTT, Glenway. *The Grandmothers*. Cloth-backed boards. New York, 1927. First edition. One of 250 signed. Boxed. $40–$60. Trade edition: Cloth. In dust jacket. $25.

WESCOTT, Glenway. *Natives of Rock, XX Poems: 1921–1922.* Boards. New York, 1925. First edition. One of 25 on vellum. Boxed. $150–$200. Another issue: One of 550 plain copies. In glassine dust jacket. Boxed. $30–$40.

WEST, Anthony. *On a Dark Night.* Cloth. London, 1951. First edition. In dust jacket, with Book Society wraparound band. $50–$60.

WEST, Goldsmith B. *The Golden Northwest.* Illustrated. Cloth. Chicago, 1878. First edition. $50–$75.

WEST, John C. *A Texan in Search of a Fight.* 189 pp., wrappers. Waco, 1901. First edition. $250–$300. Also issued in cloth.

WEST, Nathanael. *A Cool Million.* Light tan cloth. New York, (1934). First edition, first binding. In dust jacket. $250–$350. Also, "probably an advance issue or trial binding in russet cloth without publisher's name at bottom of spine," $85 (A, 1970). (Note: Green cloth is a later binding.) London, (1954). Cloth. First English edition. In dust jacket. $50–$75.

WEST, Nathanael. *The Day of the Locust.* Cloth, paper label. New York, (1939). First edition. In dust jacket. $500–$600. Without jacket, $175.

WEST, Nathanael. *The Dream Life of Balso Snell.* Printed stiff wrappers. Paris, (1931). Contact Editions. First edition. One of 485. In tissue dust jacket. $800–$1,250. (Note: Fifteen copies were bound in blue and white or dark blue cloth.) Author's first book.

WEST, Nathanael. *Miss Lonelyhearts.* Cloth. New York, (1933). Liveright, publisher. First edition. In dust jacket. $500–$600. New York, (1933). Harcourt, Brace. "New edition." In dust jacket. $200. New York, (1933). Greenberg. (Remainder imprint.) In jacket. $50–$60.

WEST, Rebecca. *Elegy.* Buckram. New York, 1930. One of 250 signed. $60.

WEST, Rebecca. *The Judge.* Cloth. London, (1922). First edition. In dust jacket. $100–$150.

WEST, Rebecca. *The Return of the Soldier.* Cloth. New York, 1918. First edition. In dust jacket. $100–$150. London, (1918). Cloth. First English edition. In jacket. $135.

WESTCOTT, Edward Noyes. *David Harum.* Yellow cloth. New York, 1898. First edition, first state, with perfect "J" in "Julius" in next to last line of page 40. $75–$100. Author's first book. New York, (1900). First illustrated edition. White boards. One of 750. In dust jacket. $50–$75.

WESTERN Agriculturist (The) and Practical Farmer's Guide. Frontispiece, plates. Leather. Cincinnati, 1830. $150–$200.

WESTERN Reserve Register for 1852, (The). Cloth. Hudson, Ohio. 1852. First issue. $100–$150.

WESTON, Edward (photographer). *California and the West.* (By Charis Wilson Weston and Edward Weston.) Illustrated. Cloth. New York, (1940). First edition. In dust jacket. $200–$250.

WESTON, Edward (photographer). *Edward Weston.* 40 plates. Half vellum. New York, 1932. First edition. One of 550 signed by Weston. $600–$750.

WESTON, Edward (photographer). *Fifty Photographs.* (By Weston and others.) Half cloth. New York, (1947). First edition. One of 1,500 initialed by Weston. In dust jacket. $600–$750.

WESTON, Edward (photographer). *My Camera on Point Lobos.* Illustrated. Folio, spiral binding. Yosemite National Park and Boston, 1950. First edition. In dust jacket. $400–$500.

WESTON, Silas. *Four Months in the Mines of California; or, Life in the Mountains.* 24 pp., printed wrappers. Providence, 1854. Second edition (of *Life in the Mountains*). $350–$400. (See below.)

WESTON, Silas. *Life in the Mountains: or Four Months in the Mines of California.* 36 pp., printed wrappers. Providence, 1854. First edition. $300–$400.

WESTROP, M. S. Dudley. *Irish Glass.* 40 plates. Buckram. London, (about 1920–21?). $100–$135.

WESTWARD Ho! 2 vols., cloth. New York, 1832. (By James Kirke Paulding.) First edition. $250–$350.

WETHERBEE, J., Jr. *A Brief Sketch of Colorado Territory and the Gold Mines of That Region.* 24 pp., printed wrappers. Boston, 1863. First edition. $1,750–$2,500.

WETHERELL, Elizabeth. *Queechy.* 2 vols., cloth. New York, 1852. (By Susan B. Warner.) First edition. $150–$250. London, 1852. 2 vols., cloth. First English edition. $150.

WETHERELL, Elizabeth. *The Wide, Wide World.* 2 vols., cloth. New York, 1851. (By Susan B. Warner.) First edition, first issue, brown cloth. $150–$200. Later, blue cloth. $100–$150. London, 1853. 2 vols., red cloth. First English edition. $50–$60.

WETMORE, Alphonso (compiler). *Gazetteer of the State of Missouri.* Frontispiece and folding map. Cloth. St. Louis, 1837. First edition. $400–$500.

WETMORE, Helen Cody. *Last of the Great Scouts: The Life Story of Col. William F. Cody, "Buffalo Bill."* Illustrated. Cloth. (Duluth, 1899.) First edition, with 267 pages. $200–$250. Another issue, 296 pages: One of 500 signed by Cody. $375. Ordinary copies (not signed), $75.

WEYMAN, Stanley J. *A Gentleman of France.* 3 vols., green cloth. London, 1893. First edition. $300–$400.

WEYMAN, Stanley J. *The House of the Wolf.* Decorated gray cloth. London, 1890. First edition. $300–$350. Author's first book.

WEYMAN, Stanley J. *Under the Red Robe.* 2 vols., cloth. London, 1894. First edition. $750–$1,000.

WHALING Directory of the United States in 1869. Colored flags. Cloth. New Bedford, Mass., 1869., $200–$300.

WHARTON, Clarence. *Remember Goliad.* 61 pp., boards. Houston, 1931. One of 100. $75–$125.

WHARTON, Edith. See *Verses.* (By Edith Newbold Jones.)

WHARTON, Edith. *Ethan Frome.* Cloth, top edges gilt. New York, 1911. First edition, first issue, with perfect type in last line of page 135. In dust jacket. $300–$400. New York, 1922. Boards. One of 2,000. $50–$75. (New York), 1939. Limited Editions Club. Cloth. Boxed. $40–$50.

WHARTON, Edith. *Italian Villas and Their Gardens.* Illustrated by Maxfield Parrish and others. Pictorial cloth. New York, 1904. First edition. $125–$150.

WHARTON, Edith. *Quartet: Four Stories.* Boards. Kentfield, Calif., 1975. Allen Press. One of 140. $450.

WHARTON, Edith. *Twelve Poems.* Buckram and boards. London, 1926. Medici Society. First edition. One of 130 signed. In dust jacket. $200–$300.

WHARTON, Edith (editor). *The Book of the Homeless.* Illustrated. Boards. New York, 1916. First American edition. One of 125 on Van Gelder paper. $300. Another issue: One of 50 with portfolio of plates and facsimilies. $400–$450.

WHARTON, J. E. *History of the City of Denver.* Printed pink wrappers. Denver, 1866. First edition. $800–$1,000.

WHAT Is Man? Gray-blue boards, green-black leather label on spine. New York, 1906. (By Samuel Langhorne Clemens.) First edition, first issue, with "thinks about" as last line of page 131. One of 250. In tissue dust jacket. Boxed. $400–$500. Second issue with "thinks about it," $150–$200. (Note: The first English edition, London, 1910, cloth, identifies Twain as author. See Twain, *What Is Man?*)

WHEAT, Carl I. *Books of the Gold Rush.* Illustrated. Pictorial boards and cloth. San Francisco, 1949. Grabhorn Press. First edition. One of 500. $250–$300.

WHEAT, Carl I. *Mapping the Trans-Mississippi West.* Illustrated. 5 vols. in 6 vols., folio, buckram, leatherette spine. San Francisco, 1957–63. Grabhorn Press. First edition. One of 1,000. $850–$1,000.

WHEAT, Carl. I. *The Maps of the California Gold Region, 1848–57.* 26 maps. Folio, cloth. San Francisco. 1942. Grabhorn Press. First edition. One of 300. $1,000 and up. Also, $900 (A, 1980). Another issue: Three-quarters calf. One of 22 with map by Gibbs added. $1,250, possibly more. (No recent prices noted.)

WHEAT, Carl I. *The Pioneer Press of California.* Boards and cloth. Oakland, 1948. First edition. One of 450. $150–$175.

WHEAT, Marvin T. See Cincinnatus.

WHEATLEY, Phillis. *Memoir and Poems of Phillis Wheatley, a Native African and a Slave.* Cloth, red paper label on front cover. Boston, 1834. Reprint of the London edition of 1773. $150–$200.

WHEELER, Edward L. *Deadwood Dick's Doom; or, Calamity Jane's Last Adventure.* 16 pp., self-wrappers. New York, 1881. Beadle's Half-Dime Library. First edition. $50–$75. New York, 1887. Beadle's Pocket Library. Reprint. $25.

WHEELER, Ella. *Drops of Water: Poems.* Purple cloth. New York, 1872. (By Ella Wheeler Wilcox.) First edition. $50. Author's first book.

WHEELER, William. *In Memoriam: Letters of William Wheeler.* Illustrated. Cloth. (Cambridge, Mass.), 1875. First edition. $65–$100.

WHERE Men Only Dare to Go, or, The Story of a Boy Company. By an Ex-Boy. Frontispiece. Cloth. Richmond, 1885. (By Royall W. Figg.) $100–$125.

WHILLDIN, M. A. *Description of Western Texas.* 28 plates, folding map, 120 pp., pictorial wrappers. Galveston, 1876. First edition. $550–$650.

WHISTLER, James McNeill. *The Gentle Art of Making Enemies.* Boards. London, 1890. One of 250 signed. $250–$350.

WHITAKER, Arthur Preston (editor). *Documents Relating to the Commercial Policy of Spain in the Floridas.* 7 maps and plates. Cloth. DeLand, Fla., 1931. First edition. One of 360. $60–$75.

WHITAKER, Fess. *History of Corporal Fess Whitaker.* Illustrated. Cloth. (Louisville, Ky., 1918.) First edition. $50–$75.

WHITE, Diana. *The Descent of Ishtar*. Frontispiece. Boards, paper label. London, 1903. Eragny Press. One of 226. In dust jacket. $380–$425.

WHITE, E. B. See W., E. B. Also, see Thurber, James.

WHITE, E. B. *Charlotte's Web*. Illustrated by Garth Williams. Pictorial cloth. New York, (1952). First edition. In dust jacket. $125–$200.

WHITE, E. B. *Stuart Little*. Illustrated by Garth Williams. Pictorial cloth. New York, (1945). First edition. In dust jacket. $125–$200.

WHITE, The Rev. George. *Statistics of the State of Georgia*. Large hand-colored map. Cloth. Savannah, 1849. First edition, with errata leaf. $175–$225.

WHITE, Gilbert. *The Writings of Gilbert White of Selborne*. Wood engravings by Eric Ravilious. 2 vols., gray buckram. London, 1938. Nonesuch Press. One of 850. Boxed. $600–$800.

WHITE, Joseph M. *A New Collection of the Laws . . . of Great Britain, France and Spain*. 2 vols., cloth. Philadelphia, 1839. $150–$200.

WHITE, Owen P. *The Autobiography of a Durable Sinner*. Cloth. New York, (1942). First edition, first issue, with pages 239-244 intact as part of original binding. In dust jacket. $150–$250. Second issue, with pages 239-244 reset and tipped in. $50.

WHITE, Owen P. *Out of the Desert*. Illustrated. Cloth. El Paso, 1923. First edition. $100–$125.

WHITE, Owen P. *Trigger Fingers*. Cloth. New York, 1926. First edition. In dust jacket. $50–$75.

WHITE, Philo. *Agricultural Statistics of Racine County*. 16 pp., wrappers. Racine, Wis., 1852. Presentation copy from author. $150–$200.

WHITE, Stewart Edward. *Arizona Nights*. 7 color illustrations by N.C. Wyeth. Cloth. New York, 1907. First edition. In dust jacket. $150. Lacking jacket, $60–$75.

WHITE, Stewart Edward. *The Claim Jumpers*. Cloth, printed wrappers, or marbled boards with leather spine. New York, 1901. First edition. Wrappers: $50–$75. Cloth or boards: $30–$50. Author's first book.

WHITE, Stewart Edward. *The Forest*. Illustrated by Thomas Fogarty. Cloth, paper label. New York, 1903. First edition. One of 80 large paper copies signed by the author. $100–$150.

WHITE, T. H. See Aston, James.

WHITE, T. H. *The Elephant and the Kangaroo*. Blue cloth. New York, (1947). First edition. In dust jacket. $50. London, 1948. Green cloth. First English edition. In dust jacket. $50.

WHITE, T. H. *England Have My Bones*. Black cloth. London, 1936. First edition. In dust jacket. $100.

WHITE, T. H. *Farewell Victoria*. Orange cloth, paper labels. New York, 1934. First American edition, first binding. In dust jacket. $100–$125.

WHITE, T. H. *The Green Bay Tree*. Wrappers. (Cambridge, England, 1929.) First edition. $350. Author's first book.

WHITE, T. H. *Loved Helen and Other Poems*. Black cloth. London, (1929). First edition. In dust jacket. $150. Author's first book under his own name.

WHITE, T. H. *Mistress Masham's Repose*. Illustrated. Cloth. New York, (1946). First edition, first issue, brown end papers. In dust jacket. $50–$75.

WHITE, T. H. *The Once and Future King.* Cloth. London, 1958. First edition. In dust jacket. $75–$100.

WHITE, T. H. *The Sword in the Stone.* Black cloth. London, 1938. First edition. In dust jacket. $150–$250.

WHITE, T. H. *The Witch in the Wood.* Gray cloth. London, (1940). First English edition. In dust jacket. $150.

WHITE, William Allen. *The Court of Boyville.* Illustrated by Orson Lowell and Gustav Verbeek. Pictorial buckram. New York, 1899. First edition. $100–$150.

WHITE, William Allen. *The Real Issue.* Buckram. Chicago, 1896. First edition. $50.

WHITE, William Allen, and Paine, Albert Bigelow. *Rhymes by Two Friends.* Illustrated. Blue cloth. Fort Scott, Kan., (1893). First edition. $100–$150. First book for each author.

WHITEHEAD, Charles E. *Wild Sports in the South.* Illustrated. Cloth. New York, 1860. First edition. $125–$150.

WHITEHEAD, Henry S. *Jumbee and Other Uncanny Tales.* Cloth. (Sauk City, Wis.), 1944. First edition. In dust jacket. $100–$125.

WHITELY, Ike. *Rural Life in Texas.* 82 pp., pictorial wrappers. Atlanta, 1891. First edition. $300–$350.

WHITMAN, Walt. See *Leaves of Grass; Leaves of Grass Imprints.*

WHITMAN, Walt. *After All, Not to Create Only.* 11 folio numbered sheets, printed on one side only, stitched. (Washington, 1871.) First edition, first (proof) issue. Very rare in proof state. Estimated value: $500 and up. The last copy at auction, along with a 4-line Whitman poem in author's hand, brought $200 (1951). Boston, 1871. Green, maroon, or brown cloth. First book edition. $250–$300. Another issue: Limp cloth wrappers. $300–$400.

WHITMAN, Walt. *An American Primer.* Illustrated. Edited by Horace Traubel. Boards, vellum spine. Boston, 1904. First edition, first binding. One of 500. $75–$100. Second issue and binding, blue cloth. $50–$75.

WHITMAN, Walt. *As a Strong Bird on Pinions Free, And Other Poems.* Green cloth. Washington, 1872. First edition. $400–$600. (Note: Although "Leaves of Grass" appears in small letters above this title, this is not one of the later editions of the book of the same title.)

WHITMAN, Walt. *Autobiographia, or The Story of a Life.* Gray cloth. New York, 1892. First edition, with Charles L. Webster imprint. $100–$150.

WHITMAN, Walt. *The Book of Heavenly Death.* Compiled from *Leaves of Grass* by Horace Traubel. Portrait. Boards, paper label. Portland, 1905. Mosher Press. One of 50 on Japan vellum. In dust jacket. Boxed. $200–$250. Another issue: One of 500. $75–$100.

WHITMAN, Walt. *Calamus: A Series of Letters, Written During the Years 1868–1880 . . . to a Young Friend (Peter Doyle).* Cloth. Boston, 1897. First edition. $150–$250. Another issue: Boards, cloth back, paper label. One of 35 on large paper. $300–$350.

WHITMAN, Walt. *Complete Poems and Prose, 1855–1888.* Portrait title page, one plate. Half cloth and boards, paper label. (Philadelphia, 1888–89.) First edition. One of 600 signed. $750–$850. Rebound in leather, $450. Inscribed copy, $1,100 (A, 1981).

WHITMAN, Walt. *Criticism: An Essay.* Gray boards, paper label. Newark, 1913. First edition. One of 100. $75–$100.

WHITMAN, Walt. *Democratic Vistas*. See entry under the title *Memoranda: Democratic Vistas*; also, see same title entry under Whitman, following.

WHITMAN, Walt. *Franklin Evans; or The Inebriate*. (By Walter Whitman.) 31 pp., pamphlet without covers. New York, 1842. First edition. Issued as a supplement to the *New World*. $3,000–$4,000. Also, $2,800 (A, 1972). Whitman's first separately published work. (Note: According to Wayne Somers, consignor of this copy, one of two known in this state, the pamphlet exists in two states, of which this copy, with 6½ cents as the price on front, is the second. The first state copies, of which there are also only two known, bore a price of 12½ cents. The last copy in this state was sold at auction in 1945.) Rebound in half morocco, $400 (A, 1980).

WHITMAN, Walt. *The Gathering of the Forces*. Edited by Cleveland Rogers and John Black. 2 vols., boards. New York, 1920. First edition. Limited. In dust jackets. $100–$150.

WHITMAN, Walt. *Good-bye, My Fancy. 2nd Annex to Leaves of Grass*. Phototype portrait. Green or maroon cloth. Philadelphia, 1891. First edition. $300–$400. Large paper issue: $400–$500. Also, $200 (A, 1977). Advance copy, sewn, unopened, signed on title page by Whitman, $900 (A, 1980).

WHITMAN, Walt. *The Half-Breed and Other Stories*. Edited by T.O. Mabbott. Illustrated. Half cloth. New York, 1927. First edition. One of 155. $75–$100. Another issue: One of 30 with illustrations signed in proof by the artist, Allen Lewis. $150–$200.

WHITMAN, Walt. *Lafayette in Brooklyn*. Boards. New York, 1905. First edition. One of 235 numbered copies. $40–$60. Another issue: One of 15 on Japan vellum. $500–$600.

WHITMAN, Walt. *Letters Written by Walt Whitman to His Mother*. Greenish–gray wrappers. New York, 1902. First edition. Only 5 copies printed. $1,000 or more? (No price records noted.)

WHITMAN, Walt. *Memoranda: Democratic Vistas*. Light-green wrappers. Washington, 1871. First edition, later printing (the first did not have Whitman's name on title page but only in copyright notice). $500–$600. (For first printing, see the title entry.)

WHITMAN, Walt. *Memoranda During the War*. 2 portraits. Red-brown cloth, green end papers. Camden, N.J., 1875–76. First edition, first printed page beginning "Remembrance Copy" and with space below for autograph (all copies signed). $600–$800. Another issue, without the portraits and the leaf headed "Remembrance Copy": $350–$450.

WHITMAN, Walt. *New York Dissected: A Sheaf of Recently Discovered Newspaper Articles*. Cloth. New York, 1936. First edition. One of 750. $75.

WHITMAN, Walt. *Notes & Fragments*. Edited by Richard Maurice Bucke. Blue pebbled cloth. (London, Ont., Canada), 1899. First edition. One of 225 signed by Bucke. $100.

WHITMAN, Walt. *November Boughs*. Frontispiece portrait. Maroon or green cloth. Philadelphia, 1888. First edition. $150–$250. Large paper issue: Dark green cloth, or limp red or blue cloth. $300–$400.

WHITMAN, Walt. *Pictures: An Unpublished Poem*. Boards, paper label. New York, 1927. First edition. One of 700. $200–$250.

WHITMAN, Walt. *Poems by Walt Whitman*. Edited by William Michael Rossetti. Frontispiece portrait. Ad leaf pasted in. Cloth, gilt panel on cover. London, 1868. First edition, first issue, without price on spine. $200–$250.

WHITMAN, Walt. *Poems from Leaves of Grass*. 24 colored illustrations by Margaret Cook. Green cloth. London, 1913. First edition, first issue, without gold decorations on cover and spine. In dust jacket. $150–$250.

WHITMAN, Walt. *Rivulets of Prose.* Edited by Carolyn Wells and Alfred F. Goldsmith. Cloth. New York, 1928. First edition. One of 499. $100–$150.

WHITMAN, Walt. *Specimen Days & Collect.* Light-blue wrappers or yellow cloth. Philadelphia. 1882—83. First edition, first issue, with Rees Welsh & Co. imprint. $150–$200. Philadelphia, 1883. Cloth. David McKay imprint. First edition, second issue. $150–$175.

WHITMAN, Walt. *Two Rivulets.* Portrait frontispiece, signed "Walt Whitman." Half calf. Camden, 1876. First edition. $400–$500. Another issue: "Centennial Edition." One of 100. $750–$1,000.

WHITMAN, Walt. *The Uncollected Poetry and Prose of Walt Whitman.* Illustrated. 2 vols., green cloth. Garden City, 1921. First edition. In dust jackets. $75–$100.

WHITMAN, Walt. *Walt Whitman's Diary in Canada.* Edited by W. S. Kennedy. Gray boards and vellum. Boston, 1904. First edition. One of 500. $300–$350.

WHITMAN, Walt. *Walt Whitman's Drum-Taps.* Brown cloth. New York, 1865. First edition, first issue, with only 72 pages. $800–$1,000. New York, 1865–66. Second issue, with 24 more pages and separate title page, "Sequel, etc." $500–$600. Also, $250 (A, 1980).

WHITMAN, Walt. *Walt Whitman's Workshop.* Gray boards and cloth. Cambridge, Mass., 1928. First edition. One of 750. $100–$125.

WHITMAN, Walt. *When Lilacs Last in the Dooryard Bloomed.* Vellum. London, 1900. Essex House Press. One of 125. $300–$350.

WHITMAN, Walt. *The Wound Dresser.* Edited by Richard Maurice Bucke. Red buckram. Boston, 1898. First edition, first printing, with 1897 copyright notice. $75–$100. Large paper issue: One of 60 signed by Bucke. $125–$150.

WHITMER, David. *An Address to All Believers in Christ.* 77 pp., wrappers. Richmond, Mo., 1887. First edition. $125–$150.

WHITNEY, Mrs. A. D. T. See *Faith Gartney's Girlhood.*

WHITNEY, Henry C. *Life on the Circuit with Lincoln.* 67 plates. Cloth. Boston, (1892). First edition. $50–$75.

WHITNEY, J. D. *The Auriferous Gravels of the Sierra Nevada of California.* Folding maps and plates. Cloth. Cambridge, Mass., 1880. First edition. $125–$150.

WHITNEY, J. D. *The Yosemite Book.* 28 photographic plates, 2 maps. Half leather. New York, 1868. First edition. (250 printed.) $3,000–$4,000. Second edition: New York, 1869. (Retitled *The Yosemite Guide-Book.*) Half leather. $500–$600. Also, $225 (A, 1980).

WHITTIER, John Greenleaf. See Dinsmoor, Robert, *Incidental Poems.* Also see *Justice and Expediency; Leaves from Margaret Smith's Journal; Moll Pitcher; The Stranger in Lowell; The Supernaturalism of New England.* (Note: Whittier's numerous publications, with all the complicated [and sometimes confusing] bibliographical points, are exhaustively covered in Thomas F. Currier's *A Bibliography of John Greenleaf Whittier,* Cambridge, Mass., 1937. The list here includes representative scarce and important items.)

WHITTIER, John Greenleaf. *At Sundown.* Pea-green cloth. Cambridge, 1890. First edition. One of 250 with facsimile autograph presentation slip. $100–$125.

WHITTIER, John Greenleaf. *The Captain's Well.* Illustrated by Howard Pyle. 4 pp., leaflet, imitation alligator leather binding. Supplement to New York Ledger, January 11, 1890. First edition. $300–$400.

WHITTIER, John Greenleaf. *The Demon Lady.* 8 pp., wrappers. No place, 1894. One of 25. $150–$200.

WHITTIER, John Greenleaf. *The King's Missive, and Other Poems*. Portrait. Reddish-brown cloth. Boston, 1881. First edition. $50–$75.

WHITTIER, John Greenleaf. *Legends of New England*. Boards and cloth, paper label. Hartford, 1831. First edition, first state, with next to last line on page 98 reading "the go" for "they go." $150–$200. Author's first book.

WHITTIER, John Greenleaf. *Miriam and Other Poems*. Frontispiece. Cloth. Boston, 1871. First edition, first issue, with publisher's monogram on spine. $75–$100.

WHITTIER, John Greenleaf. *Mogg Megone: A Poem*. Slate-colored cloth. Boston, 1836. First edition. $300–$400.

WHITTIER, John Greenleaf. *The Panorama, and Other Poems*. Cloth. Boston, 1856. First edition, without ads. $75–$100.

WHITTIER, John Greenleaf. *Poems*. Leather, or cloth. Philadelphia, 1838. First edition. $150–$200. New York, 1945. Limited Editions Club. Boxed. $30–$35.

WHITTIER, John Greenleaf. *Poems Written During the Progress of the Abolition Question in the United States*. Frontispiece. Cloth. Boston, 1837. First edition, first issue, 96 pp. $150. Second issue, 103 pp. $50–$75.

WHITTIER, John Greenleaf. *A Sabbath Sane*. Printed wrappers. Boston, 1854. First edition. $50–$75.

WHITTIER, John Greenleaf. *Snow-Bound*. Green, blue, or terra-cotta cloth. Boston, 1866. First edition, first issue, with last page of text numbered "52" below printer's slug. $400–$500. New York, 1930. Limited Editions Club. Boards and cloth. Boxed. $30–$40.

WHITTOCK, Nathaniel. *The Decorative Painters' and Glaziers' Guide*. Plates, many colored. Leather. London, 1827. First edition. $300–$400. London, 1828. Second edition. $200–$300. London, 1832. Third edition. $150. London, 1841. Half leather. $250.

WHO'S Who In America. Cloth. Chicago. 1899. First edition. $50–$75.

WHYTE-MELVILLE, George John. See *Market Harborough*.

WHYTE-MELVILLE, George John. *"Bones and I."* Brown cloth. London, 1868. First edition. $250–$300.

WHYTE-MELVILLE, George John. *Digby Grand: An Autobiography*. 2 vols., cloth. London, 1853. First edition. $300–$400. Author's first novel.

WHYTE-MELVILLE, George John. *The Queen's Maries: A Romance of Holyrood*. 2 vols., lilac cloth. London, 1862. First edition. $300–$450.

WHYTE-MELVILLE, George John. *Rosine*. Frontispiece, 7 plates. Cloth. London, 1877. First edition. $200–$350.

WHYTE-MELVILLE, George John. *Sister Louise, or The Story of a Woman's Repentance*. Frontispiece, 7 plates. Cloth. London, 1876. First edition. $300–$400.

WIENER, Norbert. *Cybernetics*. Cloth. New York, (1948). First edition. In dust jacket. $150.

WIENERS, John. *Ace of Pentacles*. Boards. New York, 1964. First edition. One of 75, signed, with manuscript portion tipped in. In glassine dust jacket. $50–$75. Another issue: Leather. One of 12 signed with a poem tipped in. $100–$150. Trade edition: Wrappers. $10.

WIENERS, John. *Youth*. Stiff wrappers. New York, 1970. First edition. One of 126 signed, plus an unknown number of copies not for sale. $35–$50.

WIERZBICKI, F. P. *California as It Is and as It May Be*. 60 pp., glazed lavender wrappers. San Francisco, 1849. First edition, with errata leaf. (The first book written and published in California.) $6,000–$10,000. Also, rebound in half cloth, $3,600 (A, 1973). (Note: The most recent sale of a copy in original wrappers was in 1945, when the C. G. Littell copy brought $475 at auction; it is now in the Everett D. Graff collection at the Newberry Library, Chicago. A Newberry duplicate, rebound in half morocco, with title page bearing part of the author's presentation inscription, brought $3,500 at auction in 1968.) San Francisco, 1849. 76 pp., errata, saffron wrappers. Second edition. $3,000 and up. Also, defective, $1,000 (A, 1971); $2,600 (A, 1968)— the Streeter copy. San Francisco, 1933. Grabhorn Press. Boards and cloth. One of 500. In dust jacket. $125–$150.

WIGGIN, Kate Douglas. See Smith, Kate Douglas.

WIGGIN, Kate Douglas. *Children's Rights: A Book of Nursery Logic*. Cloth. Boston, 1892. First edition. $35.

WIGGIN, Kate Douglas. *Rebecca of Sunnybrook Farm*. Green pictorial cloth. Boston, 1903. First edition, first issue, with publisher's imprint on spine in type only $1/16$ inch high. In dust jacket. $300–$400. Without jacket, $75–$100.

WIGWAM and the Cabin (The). First Series. Wrappers. New York, 1845. (By William Gilmore Simms.) First edition. $500–$750. Later: With the Second Series. 2 vols. in one, cloth. New York, 1845. $400–$500. (Note: The Second Series in wrappers has not appeared for sale in many years.)

WILBARGER, J. W. *Indian Depredations in Texas*. 38 plates (37 listed). Pictorial cloth. Austin, 1889. First edition. $650. Austin, 1890. Second edition. $300–$400. Austin, 1933. Facsimile. Pictorial cloth. $60–$80.

WILBUR, Homer (editor). *Meliboeus-Hipponax. The Biglow Papers*. Cloth, or glazed boards. Cambridge, Mass., 1848. (By James Russell Lowell.) First edition, first issue, with George Nichols only as publisher. $300–$400. Later, Putnam's name added to imprint, $200–$300.

WILBUR, Richard. *The Beautiful Changes and Other Poems*. Cloth. New York, (1947). First edition. In dust jacket. $100–$135. Author's first book.

WILBUR, Richard. *Ceremony and Other Poems*. Cloth. New York, (1950). First edition. In dust jacket. $75–$100.

WILBUR, Richard. *Poems 1943–1956*. Cloth. London, (1957). First edition. In dust jacket. $75–$100.

WILBUR, Richard. *Seed Leaves: Homage to R. F.* Illustrated by Charles E. Wadsworth. Wrappers, paper label. Boston, (1974). First edition. One of 160 signed by poet and artist. In portfolio wrappers. $175–$225.

WILBUR, Richard. *Things of This World*. Cloth. New York, (1956). First edition. In dust jacket. $50–$60.

WILBUR, Richard (compiler). *A Bestiary*. Illustrated by Alexander Calder. Pictorial buckram. New York, (1955). First edition. One of 750 signed. Boxed. $175–$225. Another issue: Folio, half morocco. One of 50 signed by author and artist and with a signed pen-and-ink drawing by Calder. $1,000–$1,250, possibly more.

WILCOX, Ella Wheeler. See Wheeler, Ella.

WILDE, Oscar. See C. 3.3.; Young, Dal. Also see *Children in Prison; An Ideal Husband; The Importance of Being Earnest*.

WILDE, Oscar. *The Birthday of the Infanta*. Illustrated by Alastair. Wrappers. Paris, 1928. Black Sun Press. First edition. One of 9 on vellum with an original drawing. $600 (A, 1977). New York, 1929. Illustrated by Pamela Bianco. Boards. One of 500 signed by the artist. Boxed. $150.

WILDE, Oscar. *De Profundis*. Blue buckram. London, (1905). First English edition, first issue, with ads dated February. $125–$150. Later, ads dated March. $75–$100. Large paper issues: White cloth. One of 200 on handmade paper. $400–$450. One of 50 on Japan vellum. Boxed. $1,000–$1,500. London, (1949). Introduction by Vyvyan Holland. Morocco. One of 200 signed by Holland. $200–$250.

WILDE, Oscar. *The Fisherman and His Soul*. Illustrations and initials in color, illuminated in gold. Boards and silk. (San Francisco, 1939.) Grabhorn Press. One of 200. $150–$200.

WILDE, Oscar. *The Happy Prince and Other Tales*. Illustrated by Walter Crane and Jacomb Hood. Vellum boards. London, 1888. First edition. $400–$450. Another issue: One of 75 signed. $1,500–$2,000. Also, $1,400 (A, 1981). London, 1913. Vellum. Illustrated by Charles Robinson. One of 260. $750–$1,000.

WILDE, Oscar. *A House of Pomegranates*. 4 plates. White cloth, green cloth spine. London, 1891. First edition. $600–$750. London, 1915. Color plates by Jessie M. King. Decorated cloth. $500–$550.

WILDE, Oscar. *Impressions of America*. Stiff wrappers. Sunderland, 1906. First edition. One of 500. $150. Another issue: One of 50 on handmade paper. $300–$400.

WILDE, Oscar. *Intentions*. Moss-green cloth. London, 1891. First edition. $200–$300.

WILDE, Oscar. *Lady Windermere's Fan: A Play About a Good Woman*. Reddish-brown linen. London, 1893. First edition. $300–$400. Large paper issue: One of 50. $1,250–$1,500. Also, $1,000 (A, 1981). New York, 1973. Limited Editions Club. Boxed. $40–$50.

WILDE, Oscar. *Lord Arthur Savile's Crime & Other Stories*. Salmon-colored boards. London, 1891. First edition. $150–$200.

WILDE, Oscar. *Oscariana. Epigrams*. Printed wrappers. (London), 1895. First edition. $100–$150.

WILDE, Oscar. *The Picture of Dorian Gray*. Rough gray beveled boards, vellum spine. London, (1891). First edition, with letter "a" missing from "and" on page 208 in eighth line from the bottom. In buff dust jacket. $2,500–$3,000. Also, $2,200 (A, 1981). Another issue: One of 250 signed. (Error corrected.) $2,000–$3,000. Also, $1,700 (A, 1981). New York, 1957. Limited Editions Club. $100.

WILDE, Oscar. *Poems*. White parchment boards. London, 1881. First edition, first issue, with the word "maid" in line 3, stanza 2, page 136. One of 250. $600–$800. London, 1892. Violet cloth. One of 220 signed. $1,500.

WILDE, Oscar. *Ravenna*. Recited in the Theatre. Oxford, June 26, 1878. 16 pp., printed wrappers. Oxford, 1878. First edition, with Oxford University seal on title page and cover. $600–$650. (The Newdigate Prize Poem.) Author's first book.

WILDE, Oscar. *Salome: Drame en Un Acte*. Purple wrappers. Paris, 1893. First edition. $400–$500. Another issue: One of 50 on Van Gelder paper. $1,000–$1,500. London, 1894. Illustrated by Aubrey Beardsley. Decorated cloth. First English edition. One of 500. $1,000–$1,250. Large paper issue: One of 100 on vellum. $3,800 (A, 1981).London, 1904. Beardsley illustrations. Boards. One of 250. Pirated edition, suppressed. $200–$250. Paris, 1922. Illustrated by Alastair. Pictorial wrappers. In glassine dust jacket. $200–$250. San Francisco, 1927. Grabhorn Press. Illustrated. Boards. One of 195. Boxed. $150. New York, 1938. Limited Editions Club. 2 vols., cloth. Boxed. $80–$100.

WILDE, Oscar. *The Soul of Man*. Light-brown printed wrappers. London, 1895. First edition. One of 50. $750–$1,000.

WILDE, Oscar. *The Soul of Man Under Socialism*. Boards, green linen spine. Boston, 1910. First "authorized" American edition. $75–$125.

WILDE, Oscar. *The Sphinx*. Decorations by Charles Ricketts. Vellum. London, 1894. First edition. One of 250. $1,500–$2,000. Another issue: One of 25 on large paper (issued later, with Boston firm of Copeland and Day added to London imprint). $4,000 (A, 1981). London, 1920. Illustrated by Alastair. Cloth. One of 1,000. $500–$600.

WILDE, Oscar. *Vera; or, The Nihilists.* Gray wrappers. London, 1880. First edition (issued privately). $4,000–$6,000. Very rare, with a $570 auction record, 1920. A presentation copy sold for $375 in the early 1950's and when reoffered in the 1959 auction season brought $650. (New York), 1882. Wrappers. Second edition (first American edition), privately issued. $300–$400. London, 1902. Wrappers. One of 200. $150–$200.

WILDE, Oscar. *A Woman of No Importance.* Cloth. London, 1894. First edition. $200. De luxe edition: Cloth. One of 50 large paper copies. $800–$1,000. Also, $550 (A, 1981).

WILDER, Laura Ingalls. *Farmer Boy.* Illustrated by Helen Sewell. Pictorial cloth. New York, 1933. First edition. In dust jacket. $125–$150.

WILDER, Laura Ingalls. *Little House on the Prairie.* Illustrated by Helen Sewell. Pictorial cloth. New York, 1935. First edition. In dust jacket. $125–$150.

WILDER, Laura Ingalls. *On the Banks of Plum Creek.* Illustrated by Helen Sewell and Mildred Boyle. Pictorial cloth. New York, 1937. First edition. In dust jacket. $125–$150.

WILDER, Thornton. *The Angel That Troubled the Waters.* Blue boards and cloth. New York, 1928. First edition. One of 775 signed. In dust jacket. $200. London, 1928. Blue cloth. First English edition. One of 260 signed. In dust jacket. $50–$75.

WILDER, Thornton. *The Bridge of San Luis Rey.* Tan cloth. London, 1927. First edition (preceding American edition by a few days). In dust jacket. $150–$200. New York, 1927. Cloth. First American edition, "preliminary issue," with title page printed only in black. In dust jacket. $300–$400. Regular trade issue, title page printed in green and black: In dust jacket. $50–$75. New York, 1929. Illustrated by Rockwell Kent. Pictorial cloth, leather label. One of 1,100 signed by Wilder and Kent. Boxed. $200–$225.

WILDER, Thornton. *The Cabala.* Blue figured cloth or tan figured cloth. New York, 1926. First edition, first printing, with "conversation" for "conversion" in line 13, page 196. Blue (only a few copies issued): In dust jacket. $75–$125. Tan: In dust jacket. $75. Author's first book.

WILDER, Thornton. *The Eighth Day.* Blue cloth. New York, (1967). First edition. One of 500 signed. Boxed. $50–$60. Trade edition: In dust jacket. $20.

WILDER, Thornton. *The Ides of March.* Cloth. New York, (1948). First edition. One of 750 signed. In dust jacket. $75. Trade edition: Cloth. In dust jacket. $15.

WILDER, Thornton. *James Joyce, 1882-1941.* Wrappers. (Aurora, N. Y., 1941.) First edition. One of 150. $250–$300.

WILDER, Thornton. *The Long Christmas Dinner and Other Plays in One Act.* Boards, imitation vellum spine. New Haven, 1931. First edition. One of 525 signed. In dust jacket. Boxed. $35–$60. Trade edition: Brick cloth. In dust jacket. $25.

WILDER, Thornton. *The Merchant of Yonkers.* Cloth, paper labels. New York 1939. First edition, with "4-9/ First edition/C-O" on copyright page. In dust jacket. $60–$75.

WILDER, Thornton. *The Woman of Andros.* Cloth. New York, 1930. First edition. In dust jacket. $100–$110. London, 1930. Cloth. First English edition. One of 260 signed. $100–$150. Trade edition: In dust jacekt. $25.

WILKES, Charles. *Narrative of the United States Exploring Expedition, During the Years 1838–42.* Illustrated. 6 vols., cloth, including atlas volume. Philadelphia, 1845. First unofficial edition (after the 1844 set printed for Congress). $1,000–$1,500.

WILKES, Charles. *Synopsis of the Cruise of the United States Exploring Expedition*

During the Years 1838–42. Folding map. 56 pp., wrappers. Washington, 1842. First edition. $500–$600.

WILKES, Charles. *Western America, Including California and Oregon.* 3 folding maps. Printed tan wrappers. Philadelphia, 1849. First edition. $750–$1,000.

WILKES, George. *The History of Oregon, Geographical and Political.* Folding map. 127 pp., printed wrappers. New York, 1845. First edition. $1,500–$2,000.

WILKESON, Samuel. *Wilkeson's Notes on Puget Sound.* 47 pp., wrappers. (New York, 1870?) First edition. $300. Second edition, 44 pages. $300. Abridged edition, 32 pages. $300.

WILKINSON, Gen. James. *Memoirs of My Own Times.* 9 folding tables, 3 folding facsimiles. 4 vols., boards and calf. Philadelphia, 1816. First edition, including atlas of 19 maps and plans. $1,000–$1,250.

WILL, George F. *Notes on the Arikara Indians and Their Ceremonies.* 48 pp., wrappers. Denver, 1934. Old West Series. One of 75. $75–$100.

WILLARD, John Ware. *A History of Simon Willard, Inventor and Clockmaker.* Cloth. (Boston), 1911. One of 500. $400–$500.

WILLCOX, R. N. *Reminiscences of California Life.* Cloth. (Avery, Ohio), 1897. First edition. $200.

WILLETT, William M. (editor). *A Narrative of the Military Actions of Col. Marinus Willet.* Portrait, plan, facsimile letter. Half leather. New York, 1831. First edition. $275.

WILEY, S. H. *An Historical Paper Relating to Santa Cruz, California.* 37 pp., printed wrappers. San Francisco, 1876. First edition. $150–$175.

WILLIAMS, Alpheus F. *The Genesis of the Diamond.* 221 plates, 30 colored. 2 vols., buckram. London, 1932. First edition. $150–$300.

WILLIAMS, Charles. *Poems of Conformity.* Cloth. London, 1917. First edition. In dust jacket. $75–$100. Author's first book.

WILLIAMS, Charles. *War in Heaven.* Cloth. London, 1930. First edition. In dust jacket. $50–$75. Author's first novel.

WILLIAMS, Mrs. Ellen. *Three Years and a Half in the Army.* Cloth. New York, (1885). First edition. $100–$150.

WILLIAMS, G. T. *Receipts and Shipments of Livestock at Union Stock Yards for 1890.* 40 pp., wrappers. Chicago, 1891. $300–$400.

WILLIAMS, Jesse. *A Description of the United States Lands of Iowa.* Folding map in color. Green cloth. New York, 1840. First edition. $600–$800.

WILLIAMS, John A. *The Angry Ones.* Pictorial wrappers. New York, (1960). Ace paperback. First edition. $50–$60. Author's first book.

WILLIAMS, John G. *The Adventures of a Seventeen-Year-Old Lad.* Cloth. Boston. 1894. First edition. $100–$150.

WILLIAMS, John Lee. *The Territory of Florida.* Folding map, portrait, 2 plates. Cloth. New York, 1837. First edition. $250–$300. New York, 1839. Cloth. $75–$100.

WILLIAMS, John Lee. *A View of West Florida.* Folding map. Boards and leather. Philadelphia, 1827. First edition. $150–$200.

WILLIAMS, John R. *Biographical Sketch of the Life of William G. Greene, of Menard County, Ill.* 18 pp., cloth. No place, 1874. $60–$75.

WILLIAMS, Joseph. *Narrative of a Tour from the State of Indiana to the Oregon Ter-*

ritory. 48 pp., plain blue wrappers. Cincinnati, 1843. First edition. $5,000–$7,500. Also, $3,000 (A, 1968)—the Streeter copy, with front wrapper only. New York, 1921. Cloth. One of 250. $50–$60.

WILLIAMS, Margery. *The Velveteen Rabbit or How Toys Become Real.* Illustrated by William Nicholson. Pictorial boards. London, 1922. First edition. $500–$600. Spine ends chipped, name in crayon on half title, $300.

WILLIAMS, O. W. *In Old New Mexico, 1879–1880: Reminiscences of Judge O. W. Williams.* 48 pp., wrappers. No place, no date. $100–$150.

WILLIAMS, R. H. *With the Border Ruffians.* Illustrated. Cloth. New York, 1907. First American edition. $75–$100. London, 1907. First English edition. $50–$60.

WILLIAMS, Tennessee. *American Blues.* Printed wrappers. (New York, 1948.) First edition, first issue, with "85¢" as price and with author's name misspelled on cover. $100–$150. Second issue, name corrected. $50–$75.

WILLIAMS, Tennessee. *Baby Doll.* Cloth. (New York, 1956.) First edition. In dust jacket. $50–$60. London, 1957. Boards. First English edition. In dust jacket. $35–$50.

WILLIAMS, Tennessee. *Battle of Angels.* Printed wrappers (comprising double number, Nos. 1 and 2, of *Pharos*, Spring, 1945). (Murray, Utah, 1945.) First edition. $300–$400. Author's first book.

WILLIAMS, Tennessee. *Cat on a Hot Tin Roof.* Tan cloth. (Norfolk, Conn., 1955.) First edition. In dust jacket. $75–$100.

WILLIAMS, Tennessee. *The Glass Menagerie.* Rust or blue cloth. New York, 1945. First edition, first printing. In dust jacket. $150–$175. London, (1948). First English edition. In dust jacket. $50.

WILLIAMS, Tennessee. *Grand: A Short Story.* Cloth. New York, 1964. First edition. One of 300 signed. In glassine dust jacket. $125–$150. Another issue: One of 26 lettered copies, signed. $175–$200.

WILLIAMS, Tennessee. *Hard Candy: A Book of Stories.* Patterned boards, cloth spine. (Norfolk, 1954.) First edition. Limited edition. Boxed. $65–$85. (Norfolk, 1959.) Boards. In dust jacket. $30.

WILLIAMS, Tennessee. *I Rise in Flames, Cried the Phoenix.* Boards and cloth. Norfolk, (1952). First edition. One of 300 signed (of an edition of 310). Boxed. $300–$350. Another issue: One of 10 on Umbria paper, signed. Boxed. $1,000–$1,500.

WILLIAMS, Tennessee. *In the Winter of Cities: Poems.* White parchment boards, gilt. (Norfolk, 1956.) First edition. One of 100 signed. In slipcase. $350–$400. Trade edition: Patterned boards and cloth. In dust jacket. $35–$50.

WILLIAMS, Tennessee. *The Kingdom of Earth, with Hard Candy.* Cloth. (New York, 1954.) New Directions. One of 100 signed, plus 20 for "presentation." $750–$1,000.

WILLIAMS, Tennessee. *One Arm and Other Stories.* Boards, vellum spine. (Norfolk, 1949.) First edition. One of 50 signed. Boxed. $750–$850. Trade edition: Boards and cloth. Boxed. $75–$100. (Note: Most of the first edition copies bear a tipped-in title leaf with the copyright in Williams' name, but about 20 are said to exist with an integral title leaf with an incorrect copyright credit by New Directions. Value: $300–$375.)

WILLIAMS, Tennessee. *The Roman Spring of Mrs. Stone.* Marbled boards, vellum spine. (Norfolk, 1950.) First edition. One of 500 signed. Boxed. $200–$250. Trade edition: Black cloth. In dust jacket. $30.

WILLIAMS, Tennessee. *The Rose Tattoo.* Rose cloth. (New York or Norfolk, 1951.) First edition, first binding. In dust jacket. $75–$100.

WILLIAMS, Tennessee. *A Streetcar Named Desire.* Pink decorated boards. (Norfolk,

1947.) First edition. In dust jacket. $250–$300. Same place and date: Fifth printing, with text revised. In dust jacket. $50.

WILLIAMS, Tennessee. *Summer and Smoke*. Blue cloth. (Norfolk, 1948.) First edition. In dust jacket. $75–$100.

WILLIAMS, Tennessee. *27 Wagons Full of Cotton and Other One-Act Plays*. Light-gray cloth. (Norfolk, 1946.) First edition. In dust jacket. $100–$135. (Norfolk), 1953. Third edition. Buckram. (First appearance of two plays, *Something Unspoken and Talk to Me Like the Rain*.) In dust jacket. $50.

WILLIAMS, Tennessee. *The Two-Character Play*. Cloth. (New York, 1969.) First edition. One of 350 signed. Boxed. $150–$175.

WILLIAMS, Tennessee, and Windham, Donald. *You Touched Me! A Romantic Comedy*. Green boards. New York, (1947). First edition. In dust jacket. $250–$350. Same: In gray printed wrappers. $250–$350.

WILLIAMS, Thomas J. C. *A History of Washington County* (Maryland). 2 vols., cloth. (Hagerstown), 1906. First edition. $80–$100.

WILLIAMS, William Carlos. See Ginsberg, Allen; Loy, Mina.

WILLIAMS, William Carlos. *Al Que Quiere! A Book of Poems*. Yellow boards. Boston, 1917, First edition. In glassine dust jacket. $400–$450. (Some copies in tan boards, slightly larger, with author's name "Williams" on spine. No priority.)

WILLIAMS, William Carlos. *The Broken Span*. Boards. Norfolk, Conn., (1941). First edition. In dust jacket. $100–$150. Also in wrappers, $65–$85.

WILLIAMS, William Carlos. *The Build-Up*. Boards and cloth. New York, (1952). First edition. In dust jacket. $75–$85.

WILLIAMS, William Carlos. *The Clouds, Aigeltinger, Russia, &c*. Cloth, paper label on spine. (Aurora, N.Y., and Cummington, Mass.), 1948. First edition. One of 310. $150. One of 60 (of the same issue) signed. Boxed. $300–$400.

WILLIAMS, William Carlos. *The Cod Head*. Wrappers, with label. San Francisco, 1932. First edition. One of 125 signed. $400–$600.

WILLIAMS, William Carlos. *The Collected Later Poems*. Buckram. (Norfolk, 1950.) New Directions. First edition. One of 100 signed. Boxed. $350–$400. Trade edition: Cloth. In dust jacket. $40–$60.

WILLIAMS, William Carlos. *Collected Poems, 1921-1931*. Preface by Wallace Stevens. Cloth. New York, 1934. First edition. In dust jacket. $150–$175.

WILLIAMS, William Carlos. *The Complete Collected Poems 1906–1938*. Buckram. Norfolk, (1938). First edition. One of 50 signed. Boxed. $400–$450. Trade edition: Buckram. In dust jacket. $100–$125.

WILLIAMS, William Carlos. *The Desert Music and Other Poems*. Boards and cloth. New York, (1954). First edition. One of 100 signed. In glassine dust jacket. Boxed. $275–$350. Trade edition: Cloth. In dust jacket. $50–$60.

WILLIAMS, William Carlos. *An Early Martyr and Other Poems*. Wrappers. New York, 1935. First edition. One of 145 signed (of an edition of 165). In glassine dust jacket and green slipcase. $450–$550. (20 copies on special paper were issued in a yellow slipcase for presentation. Value: $850–$1,000.)

WILLIAMS, William Carlos. *Go Go. (Manikin No. 2)*. Stiff printed wrappers. (New York, 1923.) First edition. In publisher's envelope. (150 copies printed.) $750–$1,000. Also, $1,000 (A, 1977).

WILLIAMS, William Carlos. *The Great American Novel*. Boards and cloth, paper label. Paris, 1923. Three Mountains Press. First edition. One of 300. $275–$375.

WILLIAMS, William Carlos. *In the American Grain*. Buckram. New York, 1925. First edition. In dust jacket. $150–$200.

WILLIAMS, William Carlos. *In the Money*. Cloth. Norfolk, (1940). First edition. In dust jacket. $75–$85.

WILLIAMS, William Carlos. *The Knife of the Times and Other Stories*. Cloth, paper labels. Ithaca, (1932). First edition. One of 500. In dust jacket. $400–$500. Also, $300 (A, 1977).

WILLIAMS, William Carlos. *Kora in Hell: Improvisations*. Frontispiece. Gray boards. Boston, 1920. First edition. In dust jacket. $200–$250.

WILLIAMS, William Carlos. *Life Along the Passaic River*. White cloth. Norfolk, 1938. First edition. In dust jacket. $75–$100.

WILLIAMS, William Carlos. *A Novelette and Other Prose*. Printed green wrappers. (Toulon, 1932.) First edition. $300–$350. Also, covers faded, $175 (A, 1977).

WILLIAMS, William Carlos. *Paterson*. (Books 1, 2, 3, 4, and 5.) 5 vols., cloth. (New York, 1946–48–49–51–58.) First editions. In dust jackets. $750–$850. Also, $600 (A, 1977). (Books 1–4 were limited to 1,000 copies; Book 5 bears no limitation notice.)

WILLIAMS, William Carlos. *The Pink Church*. Printed wrappers. Columbus, Ohio, 1949. First edition. One of 400. $75–$100. Another state: One of 25 (from the same issue), signed. $250–$300.

WILLIAMS, William Carlos. *Poems*. 22 pp., printed brown wrappers. (Rutherford, N.J.), 1909. First edition, first state, with "of youth himself, all rose-y-clad," in line 5 of first poem. (100 copies printed, of which two are known.) Second state, with "of youth himself all rose-yclad." (100 copies printed, about 12 known.) Either state: $10,000, or more. (An inscribed presentation copy in the second state was sold for $16,000 at the first Jonathan Goodwin auction in New York in March, 1977.)

WILLIAMS, William Carlos. *The Selected Letters*. Boards and cloth. New York, (1957). First edition. One of 75 signed. Boxed. $350–$400.

WILLIAMS, William Carlos. *Sour Grapes*. Boards, paper label. Boston, 1921. First edition. In dust jacket. $300–$350. (Note: Author's name on spine label only.)

WILLIAMS, William Carlos. *Spring and All*. Printed wrappers. (Paris, 1923.) First edition. One of 300. In glassine dust jacket. $350–$450. Also, $300 (A, 1977).

WILLIAMS, William Carlos. *The Tempers*. Boards. London, 1913. First edition. In glassine dust jacket. $750–$1,000. Author's first hardbound book.

WILLIAMS, William Carlos. *A Voyage to Pagany*. Cloth. New York, 1928. First edition. In dust jacket. $200–$250.

WILLIAMS, William Carlos. *The Wedge*. Boards. (Cummington), 1944. First edition. One of 380. In glassine dust jacket. $175–$200.

WILLIAMS, William Carlos. *White Mule*. Buckram. Norfolk, 1937. First edition. In dust jacket. $150–$250.

WILLIAMSON, George C. *The History of Portrait Miniatures*. 107 plates. 2 vols., folio, white cloth. London, 1904. One of 500. $500–$600. One of 50 with hand-colored plates. $800–$1,000.

WILLIAMSON, Henry. *The Beautiful Years*. Blue cloth. London, (1921). First edition. (750 copies.) $150–$200. Author's first book.

WILLIAMSON, Henry. *The Patriot's Progress*. Wood engravings by William Kermode. Half vellum. London, (1930). First edition. One of 350 signed. Boxed. $150–$200.

WILLIAMSON, Henry. *The Star-Born*. Vellum. London, 1933. First edition. One of 70. $400–$600.

WILLIAMSON, Henry. *Tarka the Otter.* Vellum. (London), 1927. First edition. One of 100 signed. $350–$400. Trade edition: Cloth. $100.

WILLIAMSON, Henry. *The Wet Flanders Plain.* Half vellum. London, 1929. First edition. One of 80. $150–$200.

WILLIAMSON, Hugh. *The History of North Carolina.* Folding map. 2 vols., calf. Philadelphia, 1812. First edition. $350–$500.

WILLIAMSON, Jack. *Darker Than You Think.* Green cloth. Reading, Pa., 1948. First edition. One of 500 issued with autographed plate. $100. Without plate, $55.

WILLIAMSON, Jack. *The Humanoids.* Cloth. New York, 1949. First edition. In dust jacket. $50–$60.

WILLIAMSON, James J. *Mosby's Rangers.* Cloth. New York, 1896. First edition. $100–$150. New York, 1909. Cloth. Second edition. $75–$100.

WILLIS, Nathaniel Parker. *American Scenery.* 117 views by W. H. Bartlett. 2 vols., cloth or leather. London, 1840. First edition. $850–$1,000.

WILLIS, Nathaniel Parker. *Pencillings by the Way.* 3 vols., boards. London, 1835. First edition. $350–$400.

WILLIS, Nathaniel Parker. *Sketches.* Glazed boards and cloth, paper label. Boston, 1827. First edition. $150–$250. Author's first book.

WILLIS, William L. *History of Sacramento County.* Illustrated. Three-quarters leather. Los Angeles, 1913. $150–$175.

WILLMOTT, Ellen Ann. *The Genus Rosa.* Colored and plain plates. 25 parts, gray wrappers. London, (1910)–14. Half leather. First edition. $1,500–$2,000. London, 1914. 2 vols., half leather. $2,000–$2,500. Also, $1,540 (A, 1980).

WILLOUGHBY, Edwin Elliott. *The Making of the King James Bible.* 31 pp., folio, boards and cloth. Los Angeles, 1956. Plantin Press. One of 290 with a leaf from a 1611 Bible. $250.

WILLYAMS, Cooper. *A Voyage up the Mediterranean in HMS "Swiftsure."* 42 plates, folding map. Calf. London, 1802. First edition. $1,500–$2,000.

WILSON, Angus. *The Wrong Set and Other Stories.* Cloth. London, 1949. First edition. In dust jacket. $75–$125. Author's first book.

WILSON, Edmund. *Axel's Castle.* Cloth, paper label. New York, 1931. First edition. In dust jacket. $100–$150.

WILSON, Edmund. *The Boys in the Back Room.* Cloth, paper label. San Francisco, 1941. Colt Press. First edition. One of 100 signed. In acetate dust jacket. $400–$500. Trade edition: Boards and cloth, paper label. In dust jacket. $100–$125.

WILSON, Edmund. *I Thought of Daisy.* Cloth. New York, 1929. First edition. In dust jacket. $150–$200.

WILSON, Edmund, *Memoirs of Hecate County.* Green cloth. Garden City, 1946. First edition. In dust jacket. $75–$125.

WILSON, Edmund. *Note Books of Night.* Cloth. San Francisco, 1942. Colt Press. First trade edition. In dust jacket. $125–$150. Another issue: Wrappers. Signed. $500.

WILSON, Edmund. *Poets, Farewell?* Boards. New York, (1929). First edition. In dust jacket. $300–$350.

WILSON, Edmund. *This Room & This Gin & These Sandwiches.* Wrappers. New York, 1937. First edition. $200–$250.

WILSON, Edmund. *To the Finland Station.* Cloth. New York, 1940. First edition. In dust jacket. $225–$250. London, 1941. Cloth. First English edition. In dust jacket. $125.

WILSON, Edmund. *The Triple Thinkers.* Cloth. New York, 1938. First edition. In dust jacket. $150–$200.

WILSON, Edmund, and Bishop, John Peale. *The Undertaker's Garland.* Cloth. New York, 1922. First edition. In dust jacket. $200–$250. Another issue: Boards. One of 50 for "bookseller friends." $350–$500. Wilson's first book.

WILSON, Elijah N. *Among the Shoshones.* 8 plates. Red cloth. Salt Lake City, (about 1910). First (suppressed) edition, with 222 pages. $225–$250. Second edition, same place and date, 247 pages. $50–$75.

WILSON, Harry Leon. *Merton of the Movies.* Cloth. Garden City, 1922. First edition. In dust jacket. $75–$100.

WILSON, Harry Leon. *Ruggles of Red Gap.* Illustrated. Cloth. Garden City, 1915. First edition. In dust jacket. $90–$100.

WILSON, Harry Leon. *Zigzag Tales from the East to the West.* Illustrated by C. Jay Taylor. Cloth. New York, 1894. Decorated wrappers, or cloth. Wrappers: $100–$125. Cloth: $50. Author's first book.

WILSON, John Albert. *History of Los Angeles County, California.* Illustrated. Leather and cloth. Oakland, 1880. First edition. $450–$550.

WILSON, Sir John. *The Royal Philatelic Collection.* Edited by Clarence Winchester. 12 color facsimiles, 48 monochrome plates, other illustrations. Full red morocco. London, 1952. First edition. $150–$300.

WILSON, Obed G. *My Adventures in the Sierras.* Portrait. Cloth. Franklin, Ohio, 1902. First edition. $75–$100.

WILSON, Richard L. *Short Ravelings from a Long Yarn, or Camp and March Sketches of the Santa Fe Trail.* Edited by Benjamin F. Taylor. Illustrated. Printed boards. Chicago, 1847. First edition. $3,600–$4,200. Santa Ana, Calif., 1936. Cloth. $50–$75.

WILSON, Robert. *The Travels of Robert Wilson: Being a Relation of Facts.* Portrait, plates. Mottled calf. London, 1807. $200–$300.

WILSON, Woodrow. *Congressional Government.* Cloth. Boston, 1885. First edition, first issue, with publisher's monogram on spine. $150–$200. Author's first book.

WILSON, Woodrow. *George Washington.* Illustrated. Cloth. New York, 1897. First edition. $100–$125.

WILTSEE, Ernest A. *Gold Rush Steamers (of the Pacific).* Illustrated. Cloth. San Francisco, 1938. Grabhorn Press. One of 500. $100–$150.

WINDELER, B. C. *Elimus.* 12 designs by Dorothy Shakespear. Gray boards. Paris, 1923. Three Mountains Press. First edition. One of 300. $150.

WINDELER, Bernard. *Sailing Ships and Barges of the Western Mediterranean and the Adriatic Seas.* Map. 17 hand-colored copperplate engravings by Edward Wadsworth. Cloth. London, 1926. One of 450. Boxed. $350–$400.

WINDHAM, Donald. *The Hitchhiker.* Printed wrappers. (Florence, 1950.) First edition. One of 250 signed. $75–$100.

WING-and-Wing (The). By the Author of *The Pilot.* 2 vols., printed terra-cotta wrappers. Philadelphia, 1842. (By James Fenimore Cooper.) First American edition (of the novel issued first in London under the title *The Jack O'Lantern* and under Cooper's name; see author entry). $800–$1,200. Later issue, wrappers dated 1843. $600–$800.

WINKLER, A. V. *The Confederate Capital and Hood's Texas Brigade.* Illustrated. Cloth. Austin, 1894. First edition. $200.

WINSHIP, George Parker. *The First American Bible.* Cloth. Boston, 1929. Merrymount Press. One of 157 with a leaf from John Eliot's Indian Bible of 1663. $350–$400.

WINSHIP, George Parker. *William Caxton.* Boards, vellum spine. London, 1909. Doves Press. One of 54 for the Club of Odd Volumes (from an edition of 300). $500–$750. Others, not of this series, $400–$600. Another issue: One of 15 on vellum. $3,200 (A, 1978).

WINSHIP, George Parker (editor). *The Journey of Francisco Vasquez de Coronado, 1540–1542.* Cloth. San Francisco, 1933. One of 550. $150–$175.

WINSOR, Kathleen. *Forever Amber.* Cloth. New York, 1944. First edition. In dust jacket. $50–$75. Author's first book.

WINTER Ship (A). Leaflet. Edinburgh, 1960. (By Sylvia Plath.) First edition. $300–$400. Author's first published work.

WINTER in the West (A). By a New Yorker. 2 vols., cloth. New York, 1835. (By Charles Fenno Hoffman.) First edition. $200–$250. Author's first book.

WINTERS, Yvor. *Before Disaster.* Printed green wrappers. Tryon, N.C., 1934. First edition. $75–$100.

WINTERS, Yvor. *The Immobile Wind.* Wrappers. Evanston, (1921). First edition. $200–$300. Author's first book.

WINTERS, Yvor. *The Magpie's Shadow.* Printed blue wrappers. Chicago, 1922. First edition. $200–$300.

WINTERS, Yvor. *Maule's Curse: Seven Studies in the History of American Obscurantism.* Blue cloth. Norfolk, (1938). First edition. In dust jacket. $50–$75.

WINTERS, Yvor. *The Proof.* Decorated boards. New York, 1930. First edition. In dust jacket. $50–$60.

WINTERS, Yvor. *Three Poems.* Wrappers. (Cummington, Mass.), 1950. First edition. One of 300. $75–$125.

WIRT, Mrs. E. W. *Flora's Dictionary.* 58 hand-colored plates. Morocco. Baltimore, 1837. $500–$600. Baltimore, 1855. Cloth. $400–$500.

WISDOM of Jesus (The), the Son of Sirach. Commonly Called Ecclesiasticus. Orange vellum, silk ties. London, 1932. Ashendene Press. One of 328. $1,500–$2,000. Another issue: Morocco. One of 25 printed on vellum. $5,000 and up.

WISE, George. *Campaigns and Battles of the Army of Northern Virginia.* 2 portraits. Cloth. New York, 1916. First edition. $100–$150.

WISE, John. *A System of Aeronautics.* Illustrated. Cloth or half leather. Philadelphia, 1850. First edition. $600–$800.

WISLIZENUS, Frederick A. *A Journey to the Rocky Mountains in the Year 1839.* Folding map. Boards and cloth. St. Louis, 1912. First edition in English. One of 500. $125–$150.

WISLIZENUS, Frederick A. *Memoir of a Tour to Northern Mexico.* 3 folding maps. Boards. Washington, 1848. First edition. $200–$300.

WISTAR, Caspar. *A System of Anatomy for the Use of Students of Medicine.* 2 vols., boards. Philadelphia, 1811–14. First edition. $300–$350.

WISTAR, Isaac Jones. *Autobiography of Isaac Jones Wistar, 1827–1905.* Folding map, portrait, plates. 2 vols., boards and cloth, leather spine labels. Philadelphia, 1914. First edition. One of 250. $250–$300. Philadelphia, 1937. Illustrated. Buckram. In dust jacket. $40.

WISTER, Owen. *The Virginian.* Illustrated. Yellow pictorial cloth. New York, 1902. First edition. In dust jacket. $250–$350. New York, 1911. Illustrated by Frederic Remington and Charles M. Russell. Boards. One of 100. Boxed. $800–$1,000. New York, 1930. Limited Editions Club. $30–$40.

WITHERS, Alexander S. *Chronicles of Border Warfare.* Leather. Clarksburg, Va., 1831. First edition. $250–$300.

WODEHOUSE, P. G. *Big Money.* Cloth. London, (1931). First edition. In dust jacket. $200.

WODEHOUSE, P. G. *Carry On, Jeeves!* Cloth. New York, (1927). First American edition. In dust jacket. $125.

WODEHOUSE, P. G. *The Pothunters.* Illustrated by R. Noel Pocock. Cloth. London, 1902. First edition. In dust jacket. $1,000–$1,250. Also, $880 (A, 1980). Author's first book.

WODEHOUSE, P. G. *Psmith, Journalist.* Cloth. London, 1915. First edition. $225–$250.

WODEHOUSE, P. G. *Ukridge.* Pictorial cloth. London, 1924. First edition. $175–$200.

WODEHOUSE, P. G. *Uncle Fred in the Springtime.* Cloth. Garden City, 1939. First edition. $75.

WODEHOUSE, P. G. *William Tell Told Again.* Cloth. London, 1904. First edition. $400–$600.

WOIWODE, Larry. *What I'm Going to Do, I Think.* Cloth. New York, (1969). First edition. In dust jacket. $50–$65. Also, unbound advance copy in dust jacket for the book. $100. Author's first book.

WOLF, Edwin, II, and Fleming, John. *Rosenbach: A Biography.* Illustrated. Cloth. Cleveland, (1960). First edition. One of 250 signed. Boxed. $150. Trade edition: In dust jacket. $50–$60.

WOLFE, Humbert. *Cursory Rhymes.* Illustrated by Albert Rutherston. Cloth. London, 1927. One of 500 signed. $125–$150.

WOLFE, Humbert. *The Silver Cat and Other Poems.* Boards. New York, 1928. One of 780. In dust jacket. $125–$150.

WOLFE, Humbert. *The Uncelestial City.* Cloth. London, 1930. First edition. One of 400 signed. In dust jacket. $150.

WOLFE, Thomas. See Dashiell, Alfred; Koch, Frederick H.; Schreiber, Georges. Also see *Thomas Wolfe Memorial (The).*

WOLFE, Thomas. *America.* Wrappers. (San Mateo, Calif., 1942.) Published by the Greenwood Press. First separate edition. One of 150. $100.

WOLFE, Thomas. *The Crisis in Industry.* 14 pp., printed wrappers. Chapel Hill, N.C., 1919. First edition. $400–$500. Author's first separate work.

WOLFE, Thomas. *The Face of a Nation.* Cloth. New York, 1939. First edition. In dust jacket. $40–$60. (Scribner and Literary Guild issues were simultaneous.)

WOLFE, Thomas. *From Death to Morning.* Brown cloth. New York, 1935. First edition, first binding, with code letter "A" on copyright page. In dust jacket. $125–$150. London, (1936). Cloth. First English edition. In dust jacket. $125–$150.

WOLFE, Thomas. *From Of Time and the River America.* Chicago, 1942. $40–$50. (Privately reprinted section from *Of Time and the River*, done by a class in typography. See *America* entry.)

WOLFE, Thomas. *Gentlemen of the Press*. Cloth, paper label. Chicago, (1942). First edition. One of 350. $150–$200.

WOLFE, Thomas. *The Hills Beyond*. Cloth. New York, (1941). First edition. In dust jacket. $75–$100.

WOLFE, Thomas. *Look Homeward, Angel*. Blue cloth, gilt. New York, 1929. First edition, first issue, with seal of Scribner Press on copyright page. In first state dust jacket with Wolfe's picture on back. $500–$750. Author's first novel. London, (1930). Cloth. First English edition. In dust jacket. $300.

WOLFE, Thomas. *Mannerhouse: A Play in a Prologue and Three Acts*. Black cloth. New York, 1948. First edition. One of 500. In dust jacket. Boxed. $100–$125. Trade edition: Cloth. In dust jacket. $35.

WOLFE, Thomas. *A Note on Experts: Dexter Vespasian Joyner*. Cloth. New York, 1939. First edition. One of 300. In glassine dust jacket. $350–$400.

WOLFE, Thomas. *Of Time and the River*. Black cloth. New York, 1935. First edition, with "A" on copyright page. In dust jacket. $100–$150.

WOLFE, Thomas. *The Story of a Novel*. Cloth. New York, 1936. First edition, with "A" on copyright page. In dust jacket. $75–$85.

WOLFE, Thomas. *To Rupert Brooke*. 4 leaves, printed wrappers. (Paris), 1948. One of 100 used as a Christmas greeting. $150–$175.

WOLFE, Thomas. *The Web and The Rock*. Blue cloth. New York, 1939. First edition, first printing. In dust jacket. $150–$200.

WOLFE, Thomas. *You Can't Go Home Again*. Cloth. New York, (1940). First edition, first printing. In dust jacket. $150. London, (1947). First English edition. In dust jacket. $125–$150.

WOMAN'S Daring; As Shown by the Testimony of the Rock. Recorded by an Exultant Woman and a Hugh-millerated Man. 24 pp., unbound (self-wrappers with cover title?). (Annisquam, Mass.?, 1872.) First edition. Last leaf crudely mended, $250. (Note: Contains a contribution by Thomas A. Janvier, his first book appearance.)

WONDERFUL Providence (A), in Many Incidents at Sea. 24 pp., wrappers. Buffalo, 1848. (By Capt. Elijah Holcomb.) First edition. $100–$125.

WONDERFUL Stories of Fuz-Buz the Fly and Mother Grabem the Spider (The). 9 engraved plates. Half morocco. Philadelphia, 1867. (By S. Weir Mitchell.) First edition. One of 170 on large paper. $500–$600. First trade edition: Cloth. $150–$200.

WOOD, Charles Erskine Scott. *Imperialism Versus Democracy*. Wrappers. New York, 1899. First edition. $125. Author's first book.

WOOD, Charles Erskine Scott. *A Masque of Love*. 87 pp., boards. Chicago, 1904. First edition. $75–$125.

WOOD, Mrs. Henry. *East Lynne*. 3 vols., violet cloth. London, 1861. First edition. $1,000–$1,500. Also, in a presentation binding, inscribed, $4,750 (A, 1977).

WOOD, James H. *The War, Stonewall Jackson, His Campaigns and Battles, The Regiment, as I Saw Them*. Cloth. Cumberland, Md., (about 1910). $100–$150.

WOOD, John. *Journal of John Wood*. 76 pp., printed wrappers. Chillicothe, Ohio, 1852. First edition. $3,500–$5,000. Columbus, Ohio, 1871. 112 pp., printed wrappers. Second edition. $400–$600.

WOOD, R. E. *Life and Confessions of James Gilbert Jenkins: the Murderer of 18 Men.* Illustrated. 56 pp., wrappers. Napa City, 1864. First edition. $250–$300.

WOOD, Silas. *A Sketch of the First Settlement of the Several Towns on Long Island.* Half leather. Brooklyn, 1824. First edition. $250.

WOOD, W. D. *Reminiscences of Reconstruction in Texas.* 58 pp., wrappers. (San Marcos, Tex.), 1902. First edition. $100–$200.

WOOD, William. *Zoography, or the Beauties of Nature Displayed.* Aquatint plates by William Daniell. 3 vols., calf. London, 1807. First edition. $500–$750.

WOODMAN, David, Jr. *Guide to Texas Emigrants.* Map, plate. Light-blue cloth. Boston, 1835. First edition. $2,000–$2,500, possibly more.

WOODRUFF, W. E. *With the Light Guns in '61–'65.* Cloth. Little Rock, 1903. First edition. $150–$250.

WOODS, Daniel B. *Sixteen Months at the Gold Diggings.* Cloth. New York, 1851. First edition. $250–$350.

WOODS, John. *Two Years' Residence . . . on the English Prairie, in the Illinois Country.* 2 maps and plan. Boards. London, 1822. First edition. $1,000–$1,250. Another issue: One map instead of 2. Rebound, $750.

WOODSON, W. H. *History of Clay County, Missouri.* Cloth. Topeka, 1920. $60–$80.

WOODSTOCK. 3 vols., boards. Edinburgh, 1826. (By Sir Walter Scott.) First edition. $300–$400.

WOODWARD, John, and Burnett, George. *A Treatise on Heraldry.* 56 plates, many colored, other illustrations. 2 vols., cloth or half morocco. Edinburgh, 1892. $150–$200. Edinburgh, 1896. 66 plates, many colored, etc. 2 vols., half leather. One of 325. $150–$250.

WOODWARD, W. E. *Bunk.* Cloth. New York, 1923. First edition. In dust jacket. $40–$50. Author's first book.

WOODWARD, William. *The Gallant Fox: A Memoir.* Color plates, charts, pedigrees. Red morocco. New York, 1931. Derrydale Press. One of 25 in leather. $9,500 in a 1977 catalogue. (25 copies are said to have been bound in wrappers.)

WOODWORTH, Samuel. *The Champions of Freedom, or The Mysterious Chief.* 2 vols., boards. New York, 1816–18. $100–$150.

WOOLF, Leonard. See Bunin, I.A.

WOOLF, Leonard. *The Hotel.* Cloth. London, 1939. Hogarth Press. First edition. In dust jacket. $125.

WOOLF, Leonard. *Stories of the East.* Buff wrappers. Richmond, England, 1921. Hogarth Press. First edition. $60–$80.

WOOLF, Leonard. *The Village in the Jungle.* Blue cloth. London, 1913. First edition. In dust jacket. $400–$500. London, 1931. Cloth. First Hogarth Press edition. In dust jacket. $50–$75.

WOOLF Virginia. See Cameron, Julia M.

WOOLF, Virginia. *Beau Brummell.* Boards and cloth. New York, 1930. First edition. One of 550 signed. In glassine dust jacket. Boxed. $350–$450.

WOOLF, Virginia. *Between the Acts.* Cloth. London, 1941. Hogarth Press. First edition. In dust jacket. $125–$135. New York, (1941). Cloth. First American edition. In dust jacket. $65.

WOOLF, Virginia. *The Captain's Death Bed.* Blue cloth. New York, 1950. First edition. In dust jacket. $75–$85. London, 1950. First English edition. In dust jacket. $100–$125.

WOOLF, Virginia. *The Common Reader.* White boards and cloth. London, 1925. Hogarth Press. First edition. In dust jacket. $150–$250. London, 1932. Cloth. Second Series (same title). In dust jacket. $150. New York, 1948. Blue cloth. First and Second Series in one volume. First American edition thus. In dust jacket. $75.

WOOLF, Virginia. *The Death of the Moth and Other Essays.* Cloth. London, (1942). First edition. In dust jacket. $150. New York, (1942). Cloth. First American edition. In dust jacket. $50–$75.

WOOLF, Virginia. *Flush: A Biography.* Illustrated by Vanessa Bell. Buff cloth. London, 1933. Hogarth Press. First edition. In dust jacket (imprinted "Large Paper Edition"). $200. Ordinary issue: $50–$60.

WOOLF, Virginia. *Granite and Rainbow.* Blue cloth. London, 1958. First edition. In dust jacket with Book Society wraparound band. $100.

WOOLF, Virginia. *Hours in a Library.* Frontispiece. Boards and cloth. New York, (1957). First edition. In glassine dust jacket. $75.

WOOLF, Virginia. *Jacob's Room.* Yellow cloth. Richmond, 1922. Hogarth Press. First edition. In dust jacket. $175–$275. Also, one of about 40 signed, with subscriber's list, $750–$1,000.

WOOLF, Virginia. *Kew Gardens.* Woodcut by Vanessa Bell. Wrappers. Richmond, 1919. Hogarth Press. First edition, first issue, with correction slip pasted to imprint at end. $1,500. Also, $1,400 (A, 1980). Second issue, "Richard Madley for the Hogarth Press." $750–$1,000. London, (1927). Hogarth Press. Boards. One of 500. In dust jacket. $350–$400.

WOOLF, Virginia. *The Mark on the Wall.* (Cover title—no title page.) White wrappers. Richmond, 1919. "Second edition" (actually first separate edition, having previously appeared in *Two Stories,* published jointly with her husband Leonard Woolf). $750–$1,000. Also, $650 (A, 1979).

WOOLF, Virginia. *Mr. Bennett and Mrs. Brown.* White wrappers. London, 1924. Hogarth Press. First edition. In dust jacket. $100–$150.

WOOLF, Virginia. *Mrs. Dalloway.* Cloth. London, 1925. First edition. In dust jacket. $350–$500. New York, 1925. Orange cloth. First American edition. In dust jacket. $100–$150.

WOOLF, Virginia. *The Moment and Other Essays.* Cloth. London, 1947. Hogarth Press. First edition. In dust jacket. $100–$125. New York, (1948). Cloth. First American edition. In dust jacket. $75.

WOOLF, Virginia. *Monday or Tuesday.* Woodcuts by Vanessa Bell. Decorated boards and cloth. Richmond, 1921. Hogarth Press. First edition. (Issued without dust jacket.) $200–$450.

WOOLF, Virginia. *Night and Day.* Cloth. London, 1919. First edition. In dust jacket. $350–$450.

WOOLF, Virginia. *On Being Ill.* Vellum and cloth. (London), 1930. Hogarth Press. First edition. One of 250 signed. In dust jacket. $650–$800.

WOOLF, Virginia. *Orlando: A Biography.* Brown, or orange, cloth. London, 1928. Hogarth Press. First English edition, first issue, brown cloth. In dust jacket. $150–$250. Second issue: $75–$125. New York, 1928. Plates. Black cloth. First American edition. One of 861 signed. (Issued without dust jacket.) $450–$750. Another issue: Half morocco. One of 11 on green paper. $1,000 and up. Inscribed copy, $4,500.

WOOLF, Virginia. *A Room of One's Own.* Cloth. New York and London, 1929. First edition. One of 492 signed. $450–$600. (Of this edition, 100 were reserved for Great Britain. All copies bore both New York, Fountain Press, and London, Hogarth Press, imprints. I have found no record of a New York dust jacket, although the London copies were provided with pink jackets.)

WOOLF, Virginia. *Street Haunting.* Boards and blue or green morocco. San Francisco, 1930. Grabhorn Press. One of 500 signed. Boxed. $450–$500.

WOOLF, Virginia. *Three Guineas.* 5 plates. Yellow cloth. London, 1938. Hogarth Press. First edition, first binding. In dust jacket. $125–$185.

WOOLF, Virginia. *To the Lighthouse.* Blue cloth. London, 1927. Hogarth Press. First edition. In dust jacket. $300–$350. New York, (1927). Cloth. First American edition. In dust jacket. $300–$350.

WOOLF, Virginia. *The Voyage Out.* Cloth. London, 1915. First edition. In dust jacket. $1,000 and up. New York, 1920. Cloth. First American edition. In dust jacket. $200–$250. London, 1927. Cloth. First Hogarth Press edition. In dust jacket. $50–$100. Author's first book.

WOOLF, Virginia. *The Waves.* Purple cloth. London, 1931. Hogarth Press. First edition. In dust jacket. $275–$450. New York, (1931). Cloth. First American edition. In dust jacket. $200.

WOOLF, Virginia. *A Writer's Diary.* Orange cloth. London, 1953. First edition. In dust jacket. $125. New York, 1954. Pink cloth. First American edition. In dust jacket. $65–$85.

WOOLF, Virginia. *The Years.* Green cloth. London, 1937. Hogarth Press. First edition. In dust jacket. $150–$250.

WOOLF, Virginia, and Woolf, L. S. *Two Stories.* Wrappers or paper-backed cloth. Richmond, 1917. Hogarth Press. First edition. $3,500–$4,000. Signed by Virginia Woolf, $4,500 in a 1979 catalogue. Also, in wrappers, $2,700 (A, 1980). First book of the Hogarth Press.

WOOLLCOTT, Alexander. *Our Lady's Juggler: An Antique Legend as Retold from the Air.* Woodcut title page. 8 pp., tan cloth. (San Mateo), 1937. Quercus Press. One of 30. $150–$200.

WOOLLCOTT, Alexander. *While Rome Burns.* Cloth. New York, 1934. First edition. One of 500 signed. In glassine dust jacket. $50–$75.

WOOLLCOTT, Alexander. *Woollcott's Second Reader.* Vellum. New York, 1937. First edition. Limited and signed. $75.

WOOLWORTH, James M. *Nebraska in 1857.* Colored folding map. Printed cloth. Omaha, 1857. First edition. $400–$600, possibly more.

WOOTEN, Dudley G. (editor). *A Comprehensive History of Texas, 1865 to 1897.* 23 plates. 2 vols., leather. Dallas, 1898. First edition. $300–$400.

WORDSWORTH, William. See *Grace Darling; Kendel and Windermere Railway, etc.; Lyrical Ballads; Ode Performed in the Senate-House.*

WORDSWORTH, William. *A Decade of Years: Poems, 1798-1807.* Printed in red and black. Limp vellum. London, 1911. Doves Press. One of 200. $500–$600. Another issue: One of 12 on vellum. $4,000–$5,000.

WORDSWORTH, William. *The Excursion, Being a Portion of the Recluse, a Poem.* Drab boards. London, 1814. First edition. $600–$750.

WORDSWORTH, William. *A Letter to a Friend of Robert Burns.* Wrappers. London, 1816. First edition. $800–$1,000. Rebound in morocco, repaired, $286 (A, 1980).

WORDSWORTH, William. *Memorials of a Tour on the Continent, 1820.* Boards. London, 1822. First edition. $400–$600.

WORDSWORTH, William. *Ode on the Intimations of Immortality.* Colored frontispiece by Walter Crane. Vellum. London, 1903. Essex House Press. One of 150 on vellum. $400–$600.

WORDSWORTH, William. *Peter Bell, a Tale in Verse.* Frontispiece. 88 pp., drab wrappers, paper label on back. London, 1819. First edition. $800–$1,000. Also, rebacked, worn, $450 (A, 1977).

WORDSWORTH, William. *Poems.* 2 vols., boards, paper labels. London, 1807. First edition, first issue, with period after "Sonnets" on page (103) of Vol. 1 and "fnuction" on page 98 of Vol. 2. $1,250–$1,500. London, 1815. 2 vols., boards, with frontispiece added to each volume. $300–$400. London, (1902). Vale Press. 6 woodcuts. White buckram. One of 310. $150–$250.

WORDSWORTH, William. *The Prelude, or Growth of a Poet's Mind: An Autobiographical Poem.* Dark-red cloth. London, 1850. First edition. $400–$450. London, 1915. Doves Press. Vellum. One of 155. $600–$650. Another issue: One of 10 on vellum. $7,500–$10,000. Also, $6,160 (A, 1978).

WORDSWORTH, William. *The River Duddon: A Series of Sonnets.* Boards and cloth. London, 1820. First edition. $350–$500.

WORDSWORTH, William. *Thanksgiving Ode, January 18, 1816.* Dark-green wrappers. London, 1816. First edition. $400–$500.

WORDSWORTH, William. *The Waggoner: A Poem, to Which Are Added, Sonnets.* Drab wrappers, label. London, 1819. First edition. $400–$500.

WORDSWORTH, William. *The White Doe of Rylstone.* Frontispiece. Drab boards, paper label. London, 1815. First edition. $750–$1,000. Also, worn, $375 (A, 1977).

WORDSWORTH, William. *Yarrow Revisited, and Other Poems.* Drab boards, paper label on spine, or cloth. London, 1835. First edition, with inserted errata slip. Either binding: $400–$500, possibly more.

WORK, John. See Lewis, W. S., and Phillips, P. C.

WOUK, Herman. *The Caine Mutiny.* Cloth. Garden City, 1951. First edition. In dust jacket. $40.

WRIGHT, Austin Tappan. *Islandia.* Beige buckram. New York, (1942). First edition, first issue, with Farrar & Rinehart insignia on copyright page. In dust jacket. With Basil Davenport prospectus pamphlet *An Introduction to Islandia,* $350–$400. Without prospectus, $250–$300. Lacking jacket but with prospectus, $150–$175. Lacking both jacket and pamphlet, $75. Author's first and only book.

WRIGHT, E. W. (editor). *Lewis and Dryden's Marine History of the Pacific Northwest.* Plates. Morocco. Portland, 1895. First edition. $500–$600.

WRIGHT, Frank Lloyd. See Gannet(t), William C., *The House Beautiful.*

WRIGHT, Frank Lloyd. *An Autobiography.* Illustrated. Cloth. New York, 1932. First edition. In dust jacket. $250–$300. New York, (1943). Oblong, cloth. Second edition. In dust jacket. $150.

WRIGHT, Frank Lloyd. *Buildings, Plans and Designs.* 100 plates, loose in half cloth portfolio. New York, (1963). Limited edition. $600–$750.

WRIGHT, Frank Lloyd. *The Disappearing City.* Illustrated. Green cloth, with black map design. New York, (1932). First edition, first binding. In dust jacket. $250. Second binding: Blue cloth, map label on cover. Same value.

WRIGHT, Frank Lloyd. *Drawings for a Living Architecture.* 200 drawings by the author (75 colored). Oblong folio, cloth. New York, 1959. First edition. In dust jacket. $1,000–$1,250.

WRIGHT, Frank Lloyd. *The Future of Architecture.* Illustrated. Cloth. New York, 1953. First edition. In dust jacket. $50–$60.

WRIGHT, Frank Lloyd. *Genius and the Mobocracy.* Illustrated by Louis H. Sullivan. Cloth. New York, (1949). First edition. In dust jacket. $50–$60.

WRIGHT, Frank Lloyd. *The Japanese Print.* Illustrated. Orange wrappers. Chicago, 1912. First edition (suppressed). $1,500–$2,000. (Note: All except about 50 burned by the publisher when Wright protested the binding.) First published edition: Printed boards. One of 35 on vellum. $750–$1,000. Ordinary issue: $100–$150.

WRIGHT, Frank Lloyd. *Modern Architecture.* Boards. Princeton, 1931. First edition. $300.

WRIGHT, Frank Lloyd. *The Natural House.* Illustrated. Cloth. New York, 1954. First edition. In dust jacket. $75–$100.

WRIGHT, Frank Lloyd. *On Architecture.* Edited by Frederick Gutheim. Cloth. New York, 1941. First edition. In dust jacket. $75–$100.

WRIGHT, Frank Lloyd. *Studies and Executed Buildings.* 2 vols., oblong folio, cloth. (Berlin, 1910.) First edition. $2,500–$3,500.

WRIGHT, Harold Bell. *The Shepherd of the Hills.* Illustrated. Cloth. Chicago, 1907. First edition, with "Published, September, 1907" on copyright page. $150–$250. (Burt printings are later.)

WRIGHT, Harold Bell. *That Printer of Udell's: A Story of the Middle West.* Illustrated by John Clitheroe Gilbert. Pictorial cloth. Chicago, 1903. First edition. $75–$100. Author's first book.

WRIGHT, Harold Bell. *The Winning of Barbara Worth.* Red cloth. Chicago, (1911). First edition. In dust jacket. $100–$150.

WRIGHT, Harry. *Harry Wright's Pocket Base Ball Score Book, No. 1.* Cloth, paper label. Boston, 1876. $100–$150.

WRIGHT, Isaac. *Wright's Family Medicine.* Sheepskin. Madisonville, Tenn., 1833. $125.

WRIGHT, James. *The Branch Will Not Break.* Cloth. Middletown, Conn., (1963). First edition. In dust jacket. $25–$30.

WRIGHT, James. *The Green Wall.* Foreword by W. H. Auden. Boards. New Haven, 1957. First edition. In dust jacket. $40–$50. Author's first book.

WRIGHT, John Lloyd. *My Father Who Is on Earth.* Gray cloth. New York, (1946). First edition. In dust jacket. $35–$50.

WRIGHT, Joseph (editor). *The English Dialect Dictionary.* 6 vols., half morocco. London, 1898-1905. First edition. $200–$300. New York, 1962. 6 vols., cloth. Reprint. $150–$200.

WRIGHT, Peter. *A Free Foot-Stool.* Cloth. New York, 1909. First American edition. $250.

WRIGHT, Philip Green. *The Dreamer.* Foreword by Charles A. Sandburg. White boards. Galesburg, Ill., (1906). First edition. $400–$500. (Carl Sandburg's first prose writing—set, printed and bound, but not published, two years before his first book, *In Reckless Ecstasy.*)

WRIGHT, Richard. *How "Bigger" Was Born.* Printed wrappers. (New York, 1940.) First edition. $65–$75.

WRIGHT, Richard. *Native Son.* Dark-blue cloth, stamped in red. New York, 1940. First edition, first binding. In yellow and green (first) dust jacket. $75–$100. Second binding, gray cloth: In grayish (second) dust jacket. $50–$60.

WRIGHT, Richard. *The Outsider.* Cloth. New York, (1953). First edition. In dust jacket. $40–$50.

WRIGHT, Richard. *12 Million Black Voices: A Folk History of the Negro in the United*

States. Photographs selected by Edwin Rosskam. Cloth. New York, 1941. First edition. In dust jacket. $50–$75.

WRIGHT, Richard. *Uncle Tom's Children: Four Novellas.* Red cloth. New York, 1938. First edition. In dust jacket. $125–$150. Author's first book.

WRIGHT, Robert M. *Dodge City, the Cowboy Capital.* Colored frontispiece, 40 plates. Cloth. (Wichita, 1913.) First edition, with 344 pp. $150–$200. Second edition, same place and date, 342 pp., black-and-white portrait. $75–$100.

WRIGHT, S. Fowler. *The World Below.* Cloth. Chicago, (1949). Limited, signed edition. In dust jacket. $35–$50.

WRIGHT, Capt. T. J. *History of the 8th Regiment., Kentucky Volunteer Infantry.* Cloth. St. Joseph, 1880. $150–$250.

WRIGHT, Willard Huntington. See Van Dine, S.S.

WRIGHT, William. See De Quille, Dan.

WRIGHT, William. *The Oil Regions of Pennsylvania.* Cloth. New York, 1865. First edition. $200.

WROTH, Lawrence C. *The Early Cartography of the Pacific.* Folding facsimile maps. Cloth. New York, 1934. First edition. One of 100. $150–$250.

WYANDOTTE; or The Hutted Knoll. 3 vols., boards. London, 1843. (By James Fenimore Cooper.) First edition. $500–$750. Philadelphia, 1843. 2 vols., wrappers. First American edition. $600–$800.

WYATT, M. D. *The Art of Illuminating.* Illustrated. Decorated brown cloth, or morocco. London, 1860. First edition. $250–$350.

WYATT, Sir Thomas. See Wiat, Sir Thomas.

WYETH, Andrew. *Four Seasons.* Preface by Lloyd Goodrich. 12 reproductions. Folio, cloth. New York, (1963). First edition. Boxed. $75. Another issue: One of 500 signed. Boxed. $1,000–$1,250.

WYETH, John A. *Life of Gen. Nathan Bedford Forrest.* 55 plates, maps. Cloth. New York, 1899. First edition. $150–$175.

WYETH, John B. *Oregon; or A Short History of a Long Journey.* 87 pp., printed wrappers. Cambridge, Mass. 1833. First edition, first issue, with half title. $1,500–$2,000. Cleveland, 1906. Cloth. Reprint (with John K. Townsend's *Journey Across the Rockies to the Columbia).* $150.

WYLIE, Elinor. See *Incidental Numbers.*

WYLIE, Elinor. *Angels and Earthly Creatures: A Sequence of Sonnets.* Decorated wrappers. Henley-on-Thames, 1928. First edition. One of 51 numbered copies. About half of this edition were signed, the rest left unsigned at the author's death. In dust jacket, signed. $1,000 and up. Unsigned, $500 and up. Also, $425 (A, 1977). New York, 1929. Portrait. Black cloth. First American edition (and first commercially published). One of 200. Boxed. $150. Trade edition: In dust jacket. $35.

WYLIE, Elinor. *Collected Poems.* Cloth. New York, 1932. First edition. One of 260 on large paper. $100–$125. Trade edition: In dust jacket. $25.

WYLIE, Elinor. *Mr. Hodge & Mr. Hazard.* Blue buckram. New York, 1928. First edition. One of 145 (actually 150) signed. Boxed. $150.

WYLIE, Elinor. *Nets to Catch the Wind.* Cloth. New York, 1921. First edition, first issue, on unwatermarked paper. In dust jacket. $200–$250. (First book under her name.)

WYLIE, Elinor. *The Orphan Angel.* Boards and cloth. New York, 1926. One of 160 on rag paper, signed. Boxed. $150–$200. Another issue: Vellum. One of 30 on vellum, signed. Boxed. $400.

WYLIE, Elinor. *Trivial Breath*. Cloth. New York, 1928. First edition, with "In" for "An" in line 9 of page 13. One of 100 signed. In glassine jacket. $100–$125. Trade edition: Boards. $25.

WYLIE, Elinor. *The Venetian Glass Nephew*. Boards. New York, 1925. First edition, first issue, without publisher's monogram on copyright page. One of 250 signed. $150–$200. Trade edition: Cloth. In dust jacket. $75–$100.

WYNDHAM, John. *The Day of the Triffids*. Cloth. London, (1951). First English edition. In dust jacket. $200–$225.

WYSS, Johann David. See *The Family Robinson Crusoe* and *The Swiss Family Robinson*.

X

XENOPHON. *Cyropaedia: The Institution and Life of Cyrus, the First of That Name, King of Persians.* Translated by Philemon Holland. (Reprint of 1632 edition.) Folio, goatskin. Newtown, Wales, 1936. Gregynog Press. One of 150. $1,000–$1,500. Special issue: One of 15 bound by George Fisher. Morocco. $2,000–$3,000.

Y

YALE Book of Student Verse, 1910–1919 (The). Boards. New Haven, 1919. First edition. $75–$100. (Note: Includes poems by Stephen Vincent Benét, Wilder, MacLeish, and others.)

YATES, Edmund Hodgson. *My Haunts and Their Frequenters.* Illustrated. Wrappers. London, 1854. First edition. $50. Author's first book.

YATES, Richard. *Revolutionary Road.* Boards. Boston, (1961). First edition. In dust jacket. $50. Author's first book.

YE Minutes of Ye CLXXVIIth Meeting of Ye Sette of Odd Volumes. Transcribed by John Todhunter. Printed wrappers. (London, 1896.) One of 154. $300–$400.

YEAR of Scandal: How The Washington Post Covered Watergate and the Agnew Crisis. Compiled by Laura Longley Babb. Illustrated. Quarto, blue cloth. Washington, 1973. First edition. One of 100 for presentation. $850 and up.

YEARY, Mamie. *Reminiscences of the Boys in Gray, 1861–1865.* Cloth. Dallas, 1912. First edition. $125–$250.

YEATS, John Butler. *Early Memories.* Preface by W.B. Yeats. Boards and linen. Dundrum, Ireland, 1923. Cuala Press. One of 500. $125–$150.

YEATS, John Butler. *Further Letters.* Selected by Lennox Robinson. Boards and linen. Dundrum, 1920. Cuala Press. One of 400. $100–$125.

YEATS, John Butler. *La la Noo.* Boards and linen. Dublin, 1943. Cuala Press. One of 250. In dust jacket. $125–$150.

YEATS, John Butler. *Passages from the Letters of John Butler Yeats.* Selected by Ezra Pound. Boards and linen. Dundrum, 1917. Cuala Press. One of 400. $125–$150.

YEATS, William Butler. See Allingham, William; Bax, Clifford; Dunsany, Lord; Ganconagh; Gogarty, Oliver St. John.

YEATS, William Butler. *The Bounty of Sweden.* Boards and linen. Dublin, 1925. Cuala Press. One of 400. In glassine dust jacket. $125–$150.

YEATS, William Butler. *The Cat and the Moon and Certain Poems.* Boards and linen. Dublin, 1924. Cuala Press. First edition. One of 500. $100-$150.

YEATS, William Butler. *Cathleen ni Houlihan.* Vellum, silk ties. London, 1902. Caradoc Press. First edition. One of 8 on Japan vellum. $1,540 (A, 1980). First regular edition: Cream-colored boards, leather spine. (300 copies.) $750.

YEATS, William Butler. *The Celtic Twilight.* Olive-green cloth. London, 1893. First edition, first binding, with publisher's name on back in capital letters. $150–$200. Later binding, capitals and lower case lettering, $100–$150. New York, 1894. Cloth. First American edition. $75–$100.

YEATS, William Butler. *Collected Works.* Portraits. 8 vols., buckram. Stratford-on-Avon, 1908. $1,200.

YEATS, William Butler. *The Countess Kathleen.* Frontispiece. Japan vellum boards. London, 1892. First edition. One of 30 on vellum, signed by the publisher. $750. Another issue: Dark-green boards, parchment spine. One of 500. $200–$250. London, 1919. Wrappers. Revised edition. $75–$100.

YEATS, William Butler. *The Cutting of an Agate.* Green boards. New York, 1912. First edition. In dust jacket. $100–$150. London, 1919. Dark-blue cloth. First English edition. In dust jacket. $100–$125.

YEATS, William Butler. *The Death of Synge, and Other Passages from an Old Diary.* Boards and linen. Dublin, 1928. Cuala Press. First edition. One of 400. In dust jacket. $125–$165.

YEATS, William Butler. *Deirdre.* Gray boards, green cloth spine, paper label. London, 1907. First edition, with printer's imprint on page 48. $100–$125.

YEATS, William Butler. *Discoveries: A Volume of Essays.* Blue boards and linen. Dundrum, 1907. Dun Emer Press. First edition. One of 200. $125–$175.

YEATS, William Butler. *Dramatis Personae.* Boards and linen. Dublin, 1935. Cuala Press. One of 400. In dust jacket. $125–$150. New York, 1936. In dust jacket. $125–$150.

YEATS, William Butler. *Early Poems and Stories.* Boards. New York, 1925. First American edition. One of 250 signed. $300–$350. Trade edition: Cloth. In dust jacket. $125.

YEATS, William Butler. *Eight Poems.* Wrappers. London, (1916). Morland Press. One of 200. $200.

YEATS, William Butler. *Essays.* Cloth. London, 1924. First edition. In dust jacket. $100-$175. New York, 1924. Boards and cloth. One of 250 signed. $400–$550.

YEATS, William Butler. *Essays: 1931 to 1936.* Boards and linen. Dublin, 1937. Cuala Press. One of 300. In dust jacket. $150–$200.

YEATS, William Butler. *Estrangement: Being Some Fifty Thoughts from a Diary Kept by William Butler Yeats.* Boards and linen. Dublin, 1926. Cuala Press. First edition. One of 300. In dust jacket. $150–$175.

YEATS, William Butler. *Four Years.* Boards and linen. Dundrum, 1921. Cuala Press. First edition. One of 400. $150–$175.

YEATS, William Butler. *A Full Moon in March.* Dark-green cloth. London, 1935. First edition. In dust jacket. $150–$200.

YEATS, William Butler. *The Golden Helmet.* Gray boards. New York, 1908. First edition. One of 50. $200–$250.

YEATS, William Butler. *The Green Helmet and Other Poems.* Gray boards and linen. Dundrum, 1910. Cuala Press. One of 400. With erratum slip. $200–$250. New York, 1912. Boards. First American edition. $100–$125.

YEATS, William Butler. *The Hour Glass.* Unbound. London, 1903. First edition. (12 copies issued; without covers.) $2,000 and up. (Among the scarcest of Yeats items. An inscribed copy brought $170 at auction in 1941; no other sales noted.) New York, 1904. Blue cloth. $150–$200. Another issue: Parchment. One of 100 on vellum. $350. (Dublin, 1914.) Cuala Press. Gray wrappers. (50 copies.) $800–$1,250.

YEATS, William Butler. *The Hour Glass, Cathleen ni Houlihan, The Pot of Broth: Being Volume Two of Plays for an Irish Theatre.* Gray boards and green cloth. London, 1904. First English edition. $75–$100.

YEATS, William Butler. *Ideas of Good and Evil.* Green boards and cloth. London, 1903. First edition. $75–$100. Dublin, 1905. Boards and linen. Second edition. $35–$50.

YEATS, William Butler. *If I Were Four-and-Twenty.* Boards and linen. Dublin, 1940. Cuala Press. One of 450. In dust jacket. $150–$175.

YEATS, William Butler. *In the Seven Woods.* Printed in red and black. Linen. Dundrum, 1903. Dun Emer Press. First edition. One of 325. In tissue dust jacket. $200–$275. (First book from the Dun Emer Press.)

YEATS, William Butler. *John Sherman and Dhoya.* See Ganconagh.

YEATS, William Butler. *The King of the Great Clock Tower, Commentaries and Poems.* Boards and linen, paper label. Dublin, 1934. Cuala Press. One of 400. $150–$200.

YEATS, William Butler. *The King's Threshold.* Gray boards. New York, 1904. First edition. One of 100 signed. Boxed. $750–$850.

YEATS, William Butler. *The Land of Heart's Desire.* Wrappers. London, 1894. First edition, first state without the two fleurons after the word "Desire" on front cover. $300–$350. Chicago, 1814 (actually 1894). Boards. First American edition. One of 450. $150. Portland, Me., 1903. Boards. One of 100 on Japan paper. $75. Another issue: One of 10 on vellum, signed by T.B. Mosher as publisher. $850.

YEATS, William Butler. *Last Poems and Plays.* Green cloth. London, 1940. First trade edition (after 500-copy Cuala Press edition of *Last Poems and Two Plays*). In dust jacket. $150–$200. New York, 1940. Cloth. First American edition. In dust jacket. $100–$150.

YEATS, William Butler. *Last Poems and Two Plays.* Boards and linen. Dublin, 1939. Cuala Press. One of 500. In dust jacket. $150–$200.

YEATS, William Butler. *Later Poems.* Light-green cloth. London, 1922. First edition. $125–$175. New York, 1927. Boards. First American edition. One of 250 signed. In glassine jacket. Boxed. $100–$150. Trade issue: Cloth. $15–$20.

YEATS, William Butler. *Michael Robartes and the Dancer.* Printed in red and black. Boards and linen. Dundrum, 1920. Cuala Press. First edition. One of 400. $125–$150.

YEATS, William Butler. *Modern Poetry.* Bright-green wrappers. London, 1936. First edition. One of 1,000. $100–$150. (Scarce despite the limitation; the Yeats bibliographer Allan Wade says hundreds of copies were destroyed by incendiary bombs.)

YEATS, William Butler. *Mosada. A Dramatic Poem.* Brown wrappers. Dublin, 1886. First edition. $5,000 and up. Also, $3,500 (A, 1971); $2,296 (A, 1962); inscribed by Yeats, $3,750 (A, 1963). Author's first book. Dublin, 1943. Cuala Press. Cream-colored parchment wrappers. One of 50. In dust jacket. $800–$1,000 (Note: This poem was first published in the *Dublin University Review,* June, 1886, Vol. 2, No. 6, original decorated wrappers.)

YEATS, William Butler. *New Poems.* Boards and linen. Dublin, 1938. Cuala Press. One of 450. In glassine dust jacket. $175–$225.

YEATS, William Butler. *Nine Poems.* Wrappers. London, 1918. First edition. One of 25. $300–$500.

YEATS, William Butler. *October Blast: Poems.* Boards and linen. Dublin, 1927. Cuala Press. One of 350. In dust jacket. $150–$200.

YEATS, William Butler. *On the Boiler.* Pictorial blue-green wrappers. Dublin, (1939). Cuala Press. Second edition. (Only about 4 copies of the first edition were printed, according to Mrs. Yeats.) $100–$125.

YEATS, William Butler. *A Packet for Ezra Pound.* Boards and linen. Dublin, 1929. Cuala Press. One of 425. In plain dust jacket. $250–$350.

YEATS, William Butler. *Pages from a Diary Written in Nineteen Hundred and Thirty.* Yellow boards and linen. Dublin, 1944. Cuala Press. One of 280. In dust jacket. $150–$200.

YEATS, William Butler. *Per Amica Silentia Lunae.* Dark-blue cloth. London, 1918. First edition, with errata slip. $150.

YEATS, William Butler. *The Player Queen.* Wrappers. London, 1922. First separate edition. $100–$125.

YEATS, William Butler. *Plays and Controversies.* Boards and cloth. New York, 1924. One of 250 signed. Boxed. $100–$150.

YEATS, William Butler. *Plays for an Irish Theatre.* Illustrated. Boards. London, 1911. First edition, first issue, with white end papers. $175–$225.

YEATS, William Butler. *Plays in Prose and Verse.* Cloth. London, 1922. First edition. In dust jacket. $150–$175. New York, 1924. Boards. First American edition. One of 250 signed. In dust jacket. $150–$175.

YEATS, William Butler. *Poems.* Light-brown cloth. London, 1895. First edition. One of 25 printed on vellum, signed by Yeats. $800–$1,000. Trade edition: 750 copies. $200–$300. Second issue: Boston imprint of Copeland & Day added to title page. $150–$200. London, 1899. Dark-blue cloth. Second English edition. $125–$175. London, 1901. Dark-blue cloth. Third English edition. $75–$100. London, 1904. Fourth English edition. $75. Inscribed by Yeats, $325 in a dealer's catalogue and listed as "first edition." London, 1908. Cloth. Fifth English edition. $50–$100. London, 1912. Pictorial blue cloth. Sixth English edition. $75–$100. Dublin, 1935. Blue wrappers. Cuala Press. One of 30. $600–$800. London, 1949. 2 vols., olive-green cloth. Definitive Edition. One of 375 signed. Boxed. $850–$1,000.

YEATS, William Butler. *Poems Written in Discouragement, 1912-1913.* Dark-gray wrappers, stitched with red cord. Dundrum, 1913. Cuala Press. One of 50. $1,500.

YEATS, William Butler. *Responsibilities and Other Poems.* Dark-blue cloth. London, 1916. First edition. $125–$165. New York, 1916. Gray boards and cloth. First American edition. In dust jacket. $60–$80.

YEATS, William Butler. *Responsibilities: Poems and a Play.* Gray boards and linen. Dundrum, 1914. Cuala Press. First edition. One of 400. $125–$175.

YEATS, William Butler. *Reveries over Childhood and Youth.* With a blue board portfolio containing a colored plate and 2 portraits. Gray boards and linen. Dundrum, 1915. Cuala Press. One of 425. $200–$250. New York, 1916. Cloth. First American edition. $50–$75. London, 1916. Dark-blue cloth. First English edition. $50–$75.

YEATS, William Butler. *The Secret Rose.* Illustrated by John Butler Yeats. Dark-blue cloth. London, 1897. First edition, first binding, with "Lawrence & Bullen" on spine. $250–$275.

YEATS, William Butler. *A Selection from the Love Poetry of William Butler Yeats.* Gray boards and linen. Dundrum, 1913. Cuala Press. One of 300. $100–$150.

YEATS, William Butler. *Seven Poems and a Fragment.* Gray boards and linen. Dundrum, 1922. Cuala Press. First edition. One of 500. $150–$200.

YEATS, William Butler. *The Shadowy Waters.* Dark-blue cloth. London, 1900. First edition. $75–$100. New York, 1901. Gray boards. First American edition. $100–$125.

YEATS, William Butler. *The Singing Head and The Lady.* Decorated wrappers. (Bryn Mawr, Pa.), 1934. First edition. One of 2 or 3 signed by Yeats from an edition of 20. $2,000.

YEATS, William Butler. *Stories of Michael Robartes and His Friends.* 2 woodcut illustrations. Boards and linen. Dublin, 1931. First edition. Cuala Press. One of 450. In dust jacket. $125–$175.

YEATS, William Butler. *Stories of Red Hanrahan.* Blue boards and linen. Dundrum, 1904. Dun Emer Press. First edition. One of 500. In dust jacket. $125–$150.

YEATS, William Butler. *Synge and the Ireland of His Time.* Gray boards and linen. Dundrum, 1911. Cuala Press. First edition. One of 350. $150.

YEATS, William Butler. *The Tables of the Law. The Adoration of the Magi.* Portrait frontispiece. Buckram. (London), 1897. First edition. One of 110. $500–$675. London, 1904. Blue wrappers. First unlimited edition. $50–$75. Stratford-on-Avon, 1914. Shakespeare Head Press. Cloth. Second unlimited edition. One of 510. $100–$125.

YEATS, William Butler. *Three Things.* Blue boards. London, 1929. First edition. One of 500 large paper copies, signed. $125–$135. Trade issue (Ariel Poems): Blue wrappers. (Cover title only.) $10–$15.

YEATS, William Butler. *The Tower.* Pictorial cloth. London, 1928. First edition. In dust jacket. $300–$350. New York, 1928. Green cloth. First American edition. In dust jacket. $100–$125.

YEATS, William Butler. *The Trembling of the Veil.* Portrait. Blue boards and parchment. London, 1922. First edition. One of 1,000 signed. In dust jacket. $400–$450.

YEATS, William Butler. *Two Plays for Dancers.* Green boards and linen. (Dundrum), 1919. Cuala Press. First edition. One of 400. $100–$150.

YEATS, William Butler. *The Variorum Edition of the Poems of William Butler Yeats.* Buckram. New York, 1957. First edition. One of 825 signed. Boxed. $350–$400.

YEATS, William Butler. *A Vision.* Blue boards. London, 1925. First edition. One of 600 signed. In dust jacket. $400–$550.

YEATS, William Butler. *The Wanderings of Oisin and Other Poems.* Dark-blue cloth. London, 1889. First edition, first binding. One of 500. $800–$1,000. Author's first regularly published hardbound book.

YEATS, William Butler. *The Wild Swans at Coole, Other Verses, and a Play in Verse.* Dark-blue boards and linen. Dundrum, 1917. Cuala Press. First edition. One of 400. $150–$175. London, 1919. Dark-blue cloth. In dust jacket. $125–$175. New York, 1919. Blue boards. First American edition. In dust jacket. $75–$100.

YEATS, William Butler. *The Wind Among the Reeds.* Dark-blue cloth. London, 1899. First edition, first issue, without correction slip. $150–$200. Second issue, same date, with correction slip. $40–$60.

YEATS, William Butler. *The Winding Stair.* Dark-blue cloth. New York, 1929. Fountain Press. First American edition. One of 642, signed. In dust jacket. $400–$500. (Another New York edition of 1929, unpublished, bears the imprint of Crosby Gaige. Sheets of this edition, signed by Yeats, brought $275 at auction in 1971. A Chicago bookseller listed a set at $2,000 late in 1977.) London, 1933. Olive-green cloth. First English edition (with *And Other Poems* added to title). In dust jacket. $100–$125. New York, 1933. Cloth. First American edition. In dust jacket. $50–$60.

YEATS, William Butler. *Words for Music Perhaps and Other Poems*. Blue boards and linen. Dublin, 1932. Cuala Press. One of 450. In dust jacket. $150–$200.

YEATS, William Butler. *The Words upon the Window Pane: A Play in One Act*. Blue boards and linen. Dublin, 1934. Cuala Press. First edition. One of 350. In dust jacket. $150–$175.

YEATS, William Butler (editor). *Fairy and Folk Tales of the Irish Peasantry*. Cloth. London, 1888. First edition, with errata slip. $200–$250.

YEATS, William Butler (editor). *Irish Fairy Tales*. Cloth. London, 1892. First edition. $250–$300.

YEATS, William Butler, and Johnson, Lionel. *Poetry and Ireland: Essays*. Boards and linen. Dundrum, 1908. Cuala Press. First edition. One of 250. $125–$175.

YELLOW BIRD. The Life and Adventures of Joaquin Murieta. 2 plates. 90 pp., wrappers. San Francisco, 1854. (By John R. Ridge.) First edition. $20,000 and up(?). Howes: "One copy known." $10,000 at auction (1967)—the Streeter copy. (For later editions, see *The Life of Joaquin Murieta;* also see Ridge, John R.)

YELLOW Book (The): An Illustrated Quarterly. 13 vols., printed and pictorial yellow cloth. London, 1894–97. $600–$1,000.

YELLOWPLUSH Correspondence (The). Boards and cloth, paper label. Philadelphia, 1838. (By William Makepeace Thackeray.) First edition, with text starting at page 13, as issued. $300–$350. First publication in book form of any of Thackeray's works.

YEMASSEE (The): A Romance of Carolina. 2 vols., cloth, paper labels. New York, 1835. (By William Gilmore Simms.) First edition, first issue, with copyright notice pasted in Vol. 1. $400–$600.

YOAKUM, Henderson K. *History of Texas*. Folding document, 4 maps, 5 plates. 2 vols., cloth. New York, 1855. First edition. $600–$1,000. New York, 1856. 2 vols., cloth. Second edition. $300–$400. Austin, 1935. 2 vols., cloth. Facsimile edition. $50.

YOUNG, Andrew W. *History of Chautauqua County, New York*. Half morocco. Buffalo, 1875. First edition. $100–$125.

YOUNG, Ansel. *The Western Reserve Almanac for the Year 1844*. 32 pp., wrappers. Cleveland, (1843). $100–$200.

YOUNG, Dal. *Apologia pro Oscar Wilde*. Printed wrappers. London, (1895). First edition. $75–$100.

YOUNG Duke (The). By the author of *Vivian Grey*. 3 vols., boards, paper spines with labels. London, 1831. (By Benjamin Disraeli.) First edition, first issue, with half titles to Vols. 2 and 3 and advertisement leaf at end of Vol. 3. $400–$600.

YOUNG, Harry (Sam). *Hard Knocks: A Life Story of the Vanishing West*. 25 plates. Boards. Portland, 1915. First edition. $100–$125. Chicago, (1915). 18 plates. Cloth. $35–$50.

YOUNG, John R. *Memoirs*. 4 portraits. Cloth. Salt Lake City, 1920. First edition. $100–$125.

YOUNGBLOOD, Charles. L. *Adventures of Chas. L. Youngblood During Ten Years on the Plains*. Portrait. Cloth. Boonville, Ind., 1882. First edition. $200–$250.

Z

ZACCARELLI, John. *Zaccarelli's Pictorial Souvenir Book of the Golden Northland.* Oblong, wrappers. Dawson, (1908). $100–$125

ZAMACOIS, Niceto de. *El Buscador de Oro en California.* 81 pp., wrappers. Mexico, 1855. $100.

ZAMORANO 80 (The): A Selection of Distinguished California Books. Cloth. Los Angeles, 1945. First edition. One of 500. $75–$125.

ZANGWILL, Israel. *Children of the Ghetto.* 3 vols., decorated cloth. London, 1892. First edition. $300–$400.

ZAVALA, Lorenzo de. *Ensayo Historico de las Revoluciones de Mexico, etc.* 2 vols. (Vol. 1, Paris, 1831.) Vol. 2, New York, 1832. First edition. $500–$800.

ZOGBAUM, Rufus F. *Horse, Foot and Dragoons.* Illustrated. Cloth. New York, 1888. First edition. $75–$100.

ZOUCH, Thomas. *The Life of Isaac Walton.* Illustrated. Boards and calf. London, 1823. First edition. $125–$150.

ZUCKER, A. E. *The Chinese Theater.* Plates, 4 original paintings in color on silk, other illustrations. Pictorial cloth. Boston, 1925. First edition. One of 750. $100–$150.

ZUKOFSKY, Louis. See *Columbia Verse: 1897–1924.*

ZUKOFSKY, Louis. *"A" 1—12.* Cloth. (Ashland, Mass.), 1959. First edition. With note by W. C. Williams. One of 200. Errata slip laid in. In glassine dust jacket. $150–$250.

ZUKOFSKY, Louis. *"A"—14.* Cloth. (London, 1967.) One of 250 signed. In dust jacket. $35. Another issue: One of 26 lettered copies, signed. $50–$75.

ZUKOFSKY, Louis. *Barely and Widely.* Oblong, wrappers. New York, 1958. First edition. One of 300 signed. $100–$125.

ZUKOFSKY, Louis. *First Half of "A"—9.* Mimeographed. In manila envelope. New York, (1940). "First Edition, Limited to 55 Autographed Copies." $1,000. Author's first book.

ZUKOFSKY, Louis. *5 Statements For Poetry.* 58 pp., mimeographed, pale blue wrappers, stapled. No place, 1958. First edition. (About 110 produced.) $150–$200.

ZUKOFSKY, Louis. *I Sent Thee Late.* (Cambridge, Mass., 1965.) First edition. One of 20 signed. In original envelope. $200–$250.

ZUKOFSKY, Louis. *Initial.* Wrappers. New York, 1970. First edition. One of 100 signed. $50–$75.

ZUKOFSKY, Louis. *It Was.* Cloth. (Kyoto, Japan, 1961.) First edition. One of 50 signed. $100–$150.

ZUKOFSKY, Louis. *Iyyob.* Oblong, wrappers. London, (1965). Turret Books. One of 100 signed. $100–$125.

ZUKOFSKY, Louis. *Prepositions.* Cloth. London, (1967). First edition. One of 150 signed. In dust jacket. $50–$75.

ZUKOFSKY, Louis. *A Test of Poetry.* Cloth. Brooklyn, 1948. First edition. In dust jacket. $75–$125.

ZUKOFSKY, Louis. *An Unearthing.* Wrappers. (Cambridge, 1965.) First edition. One of 77 signed. $100–$125.

ZUKOFSKY, Louis (editor). *An "Objectivists" Anthology.* Wrappers. (Dijon, France), 1932. First edition. $400–$450. (Contributors include T. S. Eliot, William Carlos Williams.)